The Bodhisattva Path to Unsurpassed Enlightenment

The Tsadra Foundation Series

published by Snow Lion, an imprint of Shambhala Publications

Tsadra Foundation is a U.S.-based nonprofit organization that contributes to the ongoing development of wisdom and compassion in Western minds by advancing the combined study and practice of Tibetan Buddhism.

Taking its inspiration from the nineteenth-century nonsectarian Tibetan scholar and meditation master Jamgön Kongtrül Lodrö Tayé, Tsadra Foundation is named after his hermitage in eastern Tibet, Tsadra Rinchen Drak. The Foundation's various program areas reflect his values of excellence in both scholarship and contemplative practice, and the recognition of their mutual complementarity.

Tsadra Foundation envisions a flourishing community of Western contemplatives and scholar-practitioners who are fully trained in the traditions of Tibetan Buddhism. It is our conviction that, grounded in wisdom and compassion, these individuals will actively enrich the world through their openness and excellence.

This publication is a part of the Tsadra Foundation's Translation Program, which aims to make authentic and authoritative texts from the Tibetan traditions available in English. The Foundation is honored to present the work of its fellows and grantees, individuals of confirmed contemplative and intellectual integrity; however, their views do not necessarily reflect those of the Foundation.

Tsadra Foundation is delighted to collaborate with Shambhala Publications in making these important texts available in the English language.

The Bodhisattva Path to Unsurpassed Enlightenment

A Complete Translation of the Bodhisattvabhūmi

Ārya Asaṅga

TRANSLATED BY
Artemus B. Engle

FOREWORD BY
*His Holiness
the Fourteenth Dalai Lama*

SNOW LION
BOULDER
2016

Snow Lion
An imprint of Shambhala Publications, Inc.
2129 13th Street
Boulder, Colorado 80302
www.shambhala.com

9 8 7 6 5 4 3 2

Printed in the United States of America

Shambhala Publications makes every effort to print on acid-free, recycled paper.

Snow Lion is distributed worldwide by Penguin Random House, Inc., and its subsidiaries.

LIBRARY OF CONGRESS CATALOGING-IN-PUBLICATION DATA
Names: Asaṅga. | Engle, Artemus B., 1948– translator.
Title: The Bodhisattva path to unsurpassed enlightenment: a complete translation of the Bodhisattvabhūmi / Ārya Asaṅga; translated by Artemus B. Engle.
Other titles: Yogācārabhūmi. Bodhisattvabhūmi. English.
Description: First edition. | Boulder: Snow Lion, 2016. | Series: The Tsadra Foundation Series | Includes bibliographical references and index. | Translated from Sanskrit and Tibetan.
Identifiers: LCCN 2015009863 | ISBN 9781559394291 (hardback: alk. paper)
Subjects: LCSH: Yogācāra (Buddhism) | BISAC: RELIGION / Buddhism / Sacred Writings. | RELIGION / Buddhism / Tibetan. | RELIGION / Buddhism / Rituals & Practice.
Classification: LCC BQ3062.E5 E55 2016 | DDC 294.3/85—dc23
LC record available at http://lccn.loc.gov/2015009863

Contents

Foreword by His Holiness the Fourteenth Dalai Lama vii

Abbreviations ix

Translator's Introduction xv

Book I: The Support

1. The Spiritual Lineage 3
2. Generating Enlightenment Mind 21
3. One's Own and Others' Aims 35
4. The Nature of Reality 63
5. Power 105
6. Ripening 141
7. Enlightenment 159
8. The Lineages of the Powers 171
9. Generosity 205
10. Morality 237
11. Patience 313
12. Effort 331
13. Meditative Absorption 343
14. Wisdom 355

15. The Principles for Attracting a Following 365
16. Worship, Service, and the Immeasurables 387
17. The Spiritual Qualities That Are Conducive to Enlightenment 415
18. The Qualities of a Bodhisattva 465

Book II: The Qualities That Accord with the Support

1. The Marks of a Bodhisattva 495
2. Factions 505
3. Superior Attitudes 511
4. The Pleasurable States 517

Book III: The Perfection of the Support

1. Births 583
2. Embracing 587
3. The Stages 595
4. Conduct 601
5. The Marks and the Secondary Signs 607
6. Preeminence 621

The Successive Order of the Topics 665

Outline and Summary Verses 671
Bibliography 693
Index 703

THE DALAI LAMA

Foreword

This book, *The Bodhisattva Path to Unsurpassed Enlightenment* (*Bodhisattvabhūmi*), is a key work of Sanskrit Buddhist literature. It was composed by Ārya Asaṅga (fourth century C.E.), who along with Ārya Nāgārjuna is remembered as one of the trailblazing charioteers of the Mahāyāna tradition.

The Buddha's teachings and subsequent Buddhist literature can be appraised in several different ways. If we consider the three turnings of the wheel of Dharma, the first deals with the Four Noble Truths, the foundation of all Buddhist doctrine. The second comprises the Perfection of Wisdom teachings and the third explains the nature of the mind. A bodhisattva makes him- or herself familiar with all these teachings. The Perfection of Wisdom teachings can be explained in terms of their view, which Nāgārjuna expounded in his writings on the Middle Way (Madhyamaka), or in terms of the stages of the path of training, which Asaṅga expounded in his encyclopedic *Treatise on the Stages of the Practice of Yoga* (*Yogācārabhūmiśāstra*).

The fifteenth volume of this extensive treatise is the work translated here, *The Bodhisattva Path to Unsurpassed Enlightenment* (*Bodhisattvabhūmi*). It deals, as the title suggests, with the stages of the path, the training, and education of a bodhisattva. The text was taught and studied at the great Nalanda University. It not only outlines the practice of meditation and cultivation of the six perfections—generosity, ethics, patience, effort, meditation, and wisdom—but encourages the acquisition of broad knowledge and general education in the pursuit of enlightenment. The focus of that education is the five sciences, which include study of Buddhist and non-Buddhist philosophical views, grammar, logic, medicine, and crafts.

The comprehensive Buddhist traditions brought from India to Tibet followed this approach. This text was among the six principal texts of the Kadampa tradition that, following Atīśa, was founded in the eleventh century C.E. by Dromtonpa. These included the *Garland of Birth Stories*

(*Jātakamālā*), the *Collection of Utterances* (*Udānavarga*), Śāntideva's *Guide to the Bodhisattva's Way of Life* (*Bodhicaryāvatāra*) and *Compendium of Training* (*Śikṣāsamuccaya*), as well as Maitreya's *Ornament of Mahāyāna Sutras* (*Mahāyānasūtrālaṃkāra*).

The author of this text, Ārya Asaṅga, propounded the Yogācāra school of thought, sometimes referred to as the Mind Only school. This text is composed from that point of view. This means there are places where its assertion of which teachings are "definitive" and which are "provisional" differs from what is asserted from Nāgārjuna's Middle Way (Madhyamaka) point of view. Nevertheless, Ārya Asaṅga is widely accepted to have been a third-ground bodhisattva, which means he had a perfect realization of emptiness.

I would like to express my heartfelt appreciation of the skill and effort Artemus Engle has brought to the work of translating this important work into English. These days I regularly encourage followers of the Buddha to be twenty-first-century Buddhists, to make themselves fully acquainted with what kind of person the Buddha was and what he taught. I urge them wherever possible to consult and study the great Indian texts. This translation of Asaṅga's *Bodhisattva Path to Unsurpassed Enlightenment* provides a significant opportunity for readers of English to do just that.

Tenzin Gyatso, the Fourteenth Dalai Lama
October 31, 2015

Abbreviations

Publication and translation details about each work appear in the bibliography, listed under the author and/or title that is given below in parentheses.

AAA	*Abhisamayālaṃkārālokaḥ* (Haribhadra)
AK	*Abhidharmakośakārikā* (Vasubandhu)
AKB	*Abhidharmakośabhāṣyam* (Vasubandhu)
AKV	*Sphuṭārthābhidharmakośavyākhyā* (Yaśomitra)
ANS	*Akṣayamatinirdeśasūtram* (Tibetan title: *Blo gros mi zad pas bstan pa'i mdo*)
ANṬ	*Akṣayamatinirdeśaṭīkā* (Vasubandhu; Tibetan title: *Blo gros mi zad pas bstan pa rgya cher 'grel pa*)
APMK	*Aṣṭasāhasrikāprajñāpāramitāmarmakaumudī* (Abhayākāragupta; Tibetan title: *Shes rab kyi pha rol tu phyin pa brgyad stong pa'i 'grel pa gnad kyi zla ba'i 'od*)
AS	*Abhidharmasamuccayaḥ* (Asaṅga)
ASBh	*Abhidharmasamuccayabhāṣyam* (Jinaputra)
BBh	*Bodhisattvabhūmiḥ* (Asaṅga)
BBhVṛ	*Bodhisattvabhūmivṛttiḥ* (Guṇaprabha; Tibetan title: *Byang chub sems pa'i sa'i 'grel pa*)
BBhVy	*Bodhisattvabhūmivyākhyā* (*Samudramegha; Tibetan title: *Byang chub sems dpa'i sa'i rnam par bshad pa*)
BCA	*Bodhicaryāvatāraḥ* (Śāntideva)
BChKG	*Byang chub sems dpa'i sa'i dka' 'grel* (gTsang nag pa brTson 'grus seng ge)
BChZhL	*Byang chub sems dpa'i tshul khrims kyi rnam bshad byang chub gzhung lam* (Tsong kha pa Blo bzang grags pa)
BHSD	*Buddhist Hybrid Sanskrit Dictionary,* by Franklin Edgerton
BŚPBh	*Bodhisattvaśīlaparivartabhāṣyam* (Guṇaprabha; Tibetan title: *Byang chub sems dpa'i tshul khrims kyi le'u'i bshad pa*)
BŚPṬ	*Bodhisattvaśīlaparivartaṭīkā* (Jinaputra; Tibetan title: *Byang chub sems dpa'i tshul khrims kyi le'u'i rgya cher 'grel pa*)

BSV	*Bodhisattvasaṃvaraviṃśikā* (Candragomī; Tibetan title: *Byang chub sems dpa'i sdom pa nyi shu pa*)
BSVP	*Bodhisattvasaṃvaraviṃśikāpañjikā* (Bodhibhadra; Tibetan title: *Byang chub sems dpa'i sdom pa nyi shu pa'i dka' 'grel*)
D	Nalinakṣa Dutt's Sanskrit edition of the *Bodhisattvabhūmiḥ* (Asaṅga)
DB	*Daśabhūmikasūtram*
DBV	*Daśabhūmivyākhyānam* (Vasubandhu; Tibetan title: *Sa bcu pa'i rnam par bshad pa*)
f., ff.	folio(s)
GB2	*sGra sbyor bam po gnyis pa*
Inner Science	*The Inner Science of Buddhist Practice,* by Artemus B. Engle
Kg.	*bKa' 'gyur* (Tibetan collection of sūtras and tantras)
MMK	*Mūlamadhyamakakārikā* (Nāgārjuna)
MSA	*Mahāyānasūtrālaṃkārakārikā* (Maitreya Nātha)
MSAVṛBh	[*Mahāyāna*] *Sūtrālaṃkāravṛttibhāṣyam* (Sthiramati; Tibetan title: *mDo sde rgyan gyi 'grel bshad*)
MSAVy	[*Mahāyāna*] *Sūtrālaṃkāravyākhyā* (Vasubandhu)
MV	*Madhyāntavibhāgakārikā* (Maitreya Nātha)
MVBh	*Madhyāntavibhāgabhāṣyam* (Vasubandhu)
MVṬ	*Madhyāntavibhāgaṭīkā* (Sthiramati)
MVy	*Mahāvyutpattiḥ* (Tibetan title: *Bye brag tu rtogs pa chen po*)
MW	*A Sanskrit-English Dictionary* by Monier-Williams
PP	*Prasannapadā* (Candrakīrti)
PS	*Pañcaskandhaprakaraṇam* (Vasubandhu; references to page numbers are to those of the English translation in *Inner Science*)
PSV	*Pañcaskandhaprakaraṇavibhāṣyam* (Sthiramati; references to page numbers are to those of the English translation in *Inner Science*)
PTS	*The Pali Text Society's Pali-English Dictionary*
PVPP	*Pañcaviṃśatisāhasrikāprajñāpāramitāsūtram*
RA	*Ratnāvalī* (Nāgārjuna)
S	Sanskrit
ŚBh	*Śrāvakabhūmiḥ* (Asaṅga)
T	Tibetan
TBh	*Triṃśikābhāṣyam* (Sthiramati)
Tg.	*bsTan 'gyur* (Tibetan collection of translations of Indian treatises)
Toh.	Tohoku catalogue numbers from *A Complete Catalogue of the Tibetan Buddhist Canons* (nos.1–4569) and *A Catalogue of the Tohoku University Collection of Tibetan Works on Buddhism* (nos. 5001–7083); see separate listings in last section of bibliography.
v., vv.	verse(s)
VS	*Viniścayasaṃgrahaṇī* (Asaṅga; Tibetan title: *rNam par gtan la dbab pa bsdu ba*)

W	Unrai Wogihara's Sanskrit edition of the *Bodhisattvabhūmiḥ*
YBh	*Yogācārabhūmiḥ* (Asaṅga). Page number references are to the Sanskrit edition of Parts 1–5 only; identified as *The Yogācāra-bhūmi of Ācārya Asaṅga* in the bibliography.
YBhV	*Yogācārabhūmivyākhyā* (authorship attributed to Jinamitra; Tibetan title: *rNal 'byor spyod pa'i sa rnam par bshad pa*)
*	An asterisk at the start of a Sanskrit word indicates that the term is not attested in extant sources but is reconstructed based on its translation into Tibetan.

འདྲེན་པ་མཉམ་མེད་སྟོན་པ་བཅོམ་ལྡན་འདས། །
རྒྱལ་ཚབ་དམ་པ་རྗེ་བཙུན་མི་ཕམ་མགོན། །
རྒྱལ་བས་ལུང་བསྟན་འཕགས་པ་ཐོགས་མེད་ཞབས། །
སངས་རྒྱས་བྱང་སེམས་གསུམ་ལ་གསོལ་བ་འདེབས། །

The Teacher and Blessed One who is the unparalleled leader;
Exalted Ajita, protector and supreme Dharma successor;
Venerable Ārya Asaṅga, prophesied by the Victorious One—
I pray for blessings to these three, the Buddha and two bodhisattvas.

—Je Tsongkapa Losang Drakpa
Opening the Door to the Supreme Path

Translator's Introduction

The great Indian master Asaṅga is universally recognized as one of the most important spiritual figures in the Great Vehicle tradition of the Buddhist faith. He is regarded as the founder of the Yogācāra school that systematized the teachings set forth by Buddha Śākyamuni in the third and final turning of the Dharma Wheel. The foremost canonical scripture associated with the tenets of this school is *The Discourse That Clarifies the Intent.*[1] Asaṅga describes the philosophical view presented in this discourse as revealing the form of reality "that is characterized by the absence of duality,"[2] which he interprets as meaning the reality that transcends the concepts of both being and nonbeing. The former position, which is identified as the one held by the Buddhist realist traditions, considers the Buddha's first turning of the Dharma Wheel as the definitive teaching on spiritual truth. This doctrine is illustrated in such teachings as the Buddha's initial discourse on the four noble truths. By contrast, the latter position of "nonbeing" is identified as the one held by those scholars who based their view on the second turning of the Dharma Wheel. Asaṅga describes them as "certain individuals who have listened to the profound sutras associated with the Great Vehicle [tradition]," but who have "failed to comprehend in a proper manner the meaning that is being taught [in them]."[3] This statement is understood as a reference to the other major philosophical system of the Great Vehicle tradition, that of the Mādhyamika or Middle Way school that was founded approximately two centuries earlier by the illustrious Indian master Nāgārjuna. Thus, Asaṅga saw the new system that he championed as the true interpretation of the

1. S: *Saṃdhinirmocana Sūtra,* T: *dGongs pa nges par 'grel pa'i mdo.*

2. See *BBh,* Book 1, chapter 4, section entitled "The Concepts of Being and Nonbeing" [I.4.2].

3. See note 296 and accompanying text.

Buddha's Middle Way in that it avoids the fundamental errors of these two established Buddhist traditions. The realists are portrayed as committing the error of imputing a type of real essential nature that does not exist and Nāgārjuna's followers as committing the error of denying a form of ultimate reality that does exist.

A prophecy that appears in the canonical text *Mañjuśrī's Fundamental Sacred Precepts* declares in part:

> A *bhikṣu* of that time named [A]saṅga,
> One who is learned in the scriptural teachings on reality,
> Having distinguished repeatedly and in manifold ways
> The sutras of definitive and provisional meaning,
>
> Shall become a practitioner of scriptural exegesis
> Who is intent upon explaining [the nature of] the world.

The same passage concludes:

> After experiencing a prolonged period of ease
> As he is born repeatedly in this long-lasting samsara,
> This great being, in the regular way, shall become
> One who has attained enlightenment.[4]

Little is known about Asaṅga's actual life. It is generally believed that he was born in the fourth century C.E. in the ancient city of Purushapura, the present-day Peshawar in the Federally Administered Tribal Areas of Pakistan. The Chinese pilgrim Xuanzang, who visited India in the seventh century C.E., also reported the existence of a monastic retreat near the sacred city of Ayodhya that was considered to have been the site where Asaṅga previously lived and taught. Tibetan accounts state that Asaṅga worshipped Maitreya, and that after having gained a direct vision of the future buddha, he received instructions directly from that divine being. The Tibetan tradition refers to the texts thus received as the Five Teachings of Maitreya.[5] Three of these works—*The Ornament of the Great Vehicle's Discourses,*[6] *Dif-*

4. *Mañjuśrīmūlakalpaḥ,* Sanskrit edition, p. 482.

5. T: *Byams chos sde lnga.*

6. S: *Mahāyānasūtrālaṃkāraḥ,* T: *Theg pa chen po mdo sde'i rgyan.*

ferentiating the Middle Way from Extremes,[7] and *Differentiating Phenomena from Ultimate Reality*[8]—describe the principal tenets that are upheld by the Yogācāra school. However, according to the Gelukpa tradition of Tibetan Buddhism, the remaining two works—*The Ornament of Realizations*[9] and *The Higher Doctrine of the Great Vehicle*[10]—are aligned more closely with the Middle Way school of Master Nāgārjuna. This would seem problematic given Asaṅga's attitude toward this school as noted above.

The other main body of Indian Yogācāra literature is the collection of works known as the *Stages of Spiritual Practice.*[11] This material, whose authorship, according to the Tibetan tradition, is attributed in its entirety to Asaṅga, is referred to as the Five Sections on the Stages.[12] The first of the five sections, known as *The Main Treatise on the Stages,*[13] represents the central work of the overall corpus. Though the complete *Main Treatise* comprises seventeen stages, it is contained in three separate parts in the Tibetan Tengyur. The first part, which is identified by the title of the entire collection—that is, *The Stages of Spiritual Practice*—actually contains only fifteen of the seventeen stages that make up the *Main Treatise.* This portion is also known by the name *The Treatise of Multiple Stages.*[14] The second part to be found in the Tengyur, entitled *The Stage of a Listener,*[15] represents the thirteenth section of the *Main Treatise.* This text describes the entire path of the Lesser Vehicle tradition, beginning with the spiritual lineage possessed by this type of practitioner and ending with a description of the state of an arhat. The third Tengyur portion, which makes up the fifteenth section of the *Main Treatise,* is the text that is presented here in translation as *The Stage of a Bodhisattva.*[16]

The remaining four works in the Five Sections on the Stages are considered to be supplementary in nature. The first, which is called *A Collection of*

7. S: *Madhyāntavibhāgaḥ,* T: *dBus dang mtha' rnam par 'byed pa.*

8. S: *Dharmadharmatāvibhāgaḥ,* T: *Chos dang chos nyid rnam par 'byed pa.*

9. S: *Abhisamayālaṃkāraḥ,* T: *mNgon par rtogs pa'i rgyan.*

10. T: *Mahāyānottaratantraḥ,* T: *Theg pa chen po rgyud bla ma.*

11. T: *Yogācārabhūmiḥ,* T: *rNal 'byor spyod pa'i sa.*

12. T: *Sa sde lnga.*

13. T: *Sa'i dngos gzhi.*

14. T: *Sa mang po pa.*

15. S: *Śrāvakabhūmiḥ,* T: *Nyan thos kyi sa.* Hereafter abbreviated as *ŚBh.*

16. S: *Bodhisattvabhūmiḥ,* T: *Byang chub sems dpa'i sa.* Hereafter abbreviated as *BBh.*

Determinations,[17] presents discussions of additional topics that pertain to each of the seventeen sections of *The Main Treatise on the Stages* except for the fourteenth, which addresses the vehicle of the solitary realizer, one of the three traditional Buddhist "vehicles" or spiritual path systems.

Following the order of the Tengyur, the next supplementary work is *A Collection on [Canonical] Topics,* which contains subject matter relating to the three "baskets" of canonical scriptures—that is, those of the Sutras, the Vinaya scriptures, and the *Mātṛkā.* In this context, the latter term should be taken to mean the collection of instructions and explanations of terms that make up the Abhidharma doctrine. In fact, the Tengyur version of this treatise only presents the first two sections. The first section, which relates to the Sutra collection, carries the title of the entire work—namely, *A Collection on [Canonical] Topics.* The second section is identified as a separate work under the title *Collection on the Vinaya.*[18] Butön Rinchen Drup attempts to explain the absence of the *Mātṛkā* section in the Tengyur by citing a passage from the *Collection of Determinations* which states: "The *Mātṛkā* collection consists of *The [Treatise in] Seventeen Stages* and the four [supplementary] *Collections.*"[19] However, the presence of a distinct *Mātṛkā* section in the Chinese translation of *The Collection on [Canonical] Topics* suggests that a Sanskrit original of this material did exist but, for whatever reason, was not translated into Tibetan.

The third supplementary work, entitled *A Collection of Canonical Expressions,*[20] contains explanations of a broad range of canonical terms and expressions. They are divided into a section on terminology that relates to "the side of virtue" and a section on terminology that relates to "the side of evil." The fourth and final supplementary work is entitled *A Collection on Exegesis*[21] and addresses a variety of principles that pertain to the aim of explaining the Dharma in an effective manner.

Two somewhat abbreviated works, *The Summary of the Great Vehicle*[22]

17. S: *Viniścayasaṃgrahaṇī,* T: *rNam par gtan la dbab pa bsdu ba.*

18. T: *'Dul ba bsdu ba.*

19. T: *rNam par gtan la dbab bsdu ba,* f. 188b. For this and subsequent citations, full publication data may be found in the bibliography.

20. S: *Paryāyasaṃgrahaṇī,* T: *rNam grangs bsdu ba.*

21. S: **Vyākhyāsaṃgrahaṇī,* T: *rNam par bshad pa bsdu ba.*

22. S: *Mahāyānasaṃgrahaḥ,* T: *Theg pa chen po bsdus pa.*

and *The Compendium of Higher Learning,*[23] complete the principal body of works on Yogācāra doctrine that are attributed to Asaṅga.

The Tengyur also contains a number of additional works of central importance to the Yogācāra school that were authored by Asaṅga's brother, Vasubandhu. These include commentaries to three of the Five Teachings of Maitreya—namely, *The Ornament of the Great Vehicle's Discourses, Differentiating the Middle Way from Extremes,* and *Differentiating Phenomena from Ultimate Reality*—and a commentary to Asaṅga's *Summary of the Great Vehicle.* Vasubandhu also wrote commentaries to a number of influential Great Vehicle sutras, including the *Diamond-Cutter,*[24] *The Teachings of Akṣayamati,*[25] and *The Sutra on the Ten Stages,*[26] as well as a number of brief original works that present Yogācāra doctrine, such as *The Thirty Verses, The Twenty Verses, The Short Treatise on the Five Heaps,* and *The Short Treatise on Karma.* He is also generally recognized as the author of the extremely influential *Treasury of Higher Learning*[27] and its autocommentary, although these latter two texts were not written from the perspective of the Yogācāra school.

Another Indian scholar who wrote important commentaries to Yogācāra literature is Sthiramati. His contributions include detailed subcommentaries on Vasubandhu's commentaries to *The Ornament of the Great Vehicle's Discourses* and *Differentiating the Middle Way from Extremes,* as well as commentaries to two of Vasubandhu's original works, *The Thirty Verses* and *The Short Treatise on the Five Heaps.*

Though this list of titles is by no means exhaustive, it represents a significant portion of the most influential Indian treatises of this philosophical movement. All of these works were also translated into Tibetan and have had a lasting impact on the form of Buddhism that is practiced in Tibet. Just as Nāgārjuna's Sixfold Collection on Correct Reasoning,[28] along with

23. S: *Abhidharmasamuccayaḥ,* T: *Chos mngon pa kun las btus pa.*

24. S: *Vajracchedikā,* T: *rDo rje gcod pa.*

25. S: *Akṣayamatinirdeśaḥ,* T: *Blo gros mi zad pas bstan pa.*

26. S: *Daśabhūmikā,* T: *Sa bcu pa'i mdo.*

27. S: *Abhidharmakośakārikā,* T: *Chos mngon pa'i mdzod kyi tshig le'ur byas pa.*

28. T: *Rigs pa'i tshogs drug.* They are (1) *Root Verses on the Middle Way* (S: *Mūlamadhyamakakārikā,* T: *dBu ma rtsa ba'i tshig le'ur byas pa*); (2) *Sixty Verses on Reasoning* (S: *Yuktiṣaṣṭikā,* T: *Rigs pa drug cu pa*); (3) *Seventy Verses on Emptiness* (S: *Śūnyatāsaptatiḥ,* T: *sTong pa nyid bdun cu pa*); (4) *The Short Treatise on Shattering [Logical Categories]* (S:

Āryadeva's *Four Hundred Verses*[29] represent the seminal works of the Middle Way school, the Five Teachings of Maitreya and Five Sections on the Stages also constitute the literature that underpins the effort to establish and systematize a new way of understanding Buddhist Abhidharma from the perspective of the Great Vehicle tradition. Prior to this time, the dominant Buddhist philosophical tradition in the northern and especially the northwestern reaches of the Indian subcontinent seems to have been that of the Sarvāstivāda school. Clearly, Asaṅga reached a stage in his spiritual development where he disagreed with the realist elements of this philosophical tradition, and, even though the Great Vehicle tradition had been established for some time, there was no comparable body of treatises that provided a comprehensive exposition of a Great Vehicle version of the three recognized Buddhist "vehicles" or path systems. Moreover, as already noted, Asaṅga also was at odds with the philosophical tenets of the Middle Way school, so much so that he even refers to their position as that of a "preeminent nihilist."[30]

Although the availability of a complete English translation of Asaṅga's *Stage of a Bodhisattva* may be seen as contributing to our understanding of the development of Indian Buddhist thought, this was not my main reason for undertaking this effort. I was introduced to Buddhist literature primarily through two distinct bodies of writings: one was the Tibetan literary genre known as Lamrim, or Stages of the Path, and the other was the Indian and Tibetan literature associated with Ācārya Vasubandhu's great Abhidharma treatise, *The Treasury of Higher Learning.* I will have more to say about the connection between these two subjects later.

The Lamrim teachings were introduced into Tibet by the Indian pandit Dīpaṃkara Śrījñāna, who is also known by such epithets as Atīśa and the Great Lord,[31] in the first half of the eleventh century. This system of spiritual practice, which has been preserved in an unbroken lineage of Tibetan lamas down to the present, represents a synthesis of several Great Vehicle

Vaidalyaprakaraṇam, T: *Zhib mo rnam par 'thag pa'i rab tu byed pa*); (5) *Rebuttal of* [*All*] *Controversy* (S: *Vigrahavyāvartanī,* T: *rTsod pa bzlog pa*); and (6) *Establishing* [*the Validity of*] *the Conventional* (S: *Vyavahārasiddhiḥ,* T: *Tha snyad sgrub pa*).

29. S: *Catuḥśatakaśāstrakārikā,* T: *bsTan bcos bzhi brgya pa zhes bya ba'i tshig le'ur byas pa.*

30. See note 298 and accompanying portions of the main text.

31. T: *jo bo rje.*

teaching lineages described as the "merging of three rivers."[32] This expression is a reference to the bodies of literature and instruction associated with the three traditions known as the lineage of extensive activities,[33] the lineage of the profound view,[34] and the lineage of the powerful activities.[35] While all three are identified as originating with Buddha Śākyamuni, the first one—the lineage of extensive activities—proceeds initially to Maitreya, who transmitted it to Asaṅga, and thereafter through a succession of teachers that reaches Atīśa. Both of the latter two lineages were first taught by the Buddha to the bodhisattva Mañjuśrī, who then transmitted them to Nāgārjuna. However, the principal works of the third lineage, the lineage of the powerful activities, are two compositions by the eighth-century Indian master Śāntideva—namely, his *Entry into the Conduct That Leads to Enlightenment*[36] and *The Compendium of Training.*[37]

Native Tibetan sources describe the Lamrim instructions as being made up of two principal subjects, those of view and conduct. With regard to the view held by Atīśa, the following statement is recorded in one of the earliest Tibetan biographies:

> Initially, the Lord held the [philosophical] view of his Guru Ratnākaraśānti—[namely,] that of [the branch of] the Mind Only school [which asserts that] the aspect [of objects perceived by sensory forms of consciousness] is false.[38] However, [Atīśa] later abandoned that [position] and adopted the view of Ācārya Nāgārjuna's system. [To placate his teacher] for having abandoned that [earlier] view, the Lord made a sizable offering to his Guru [Ratnākara]śānti; however, the latter was not satisfied. [Ratnākaraśānti] is said to have declared [to Atīśa], "A disciple must be one who upholds the view [of his master]."[39]

32. T: *chu bo gsum 'dres.*

33. T: *rgya chen spyod brgyud.*

34. T: *zab mo lta brgyud.*

35. T: *rlabs chen spyod brgyud.*

36. S: *Bodhicaryāvatāraḥ,* T: *Byang chub sems dpa'i spyod pa la 'jug pa.*

37. S: *Śikṣāsamuccayaḥ,* T: *bSlab pa kun las btus pa.*

38. T: *sems tsam rnam rdzun pa.*

39. 'Brom ston pa rGyal ba'i 'byung gnas, *Jo bo rin po che rje dpal ldan A ti sha'i rnam thar*

Even though Atīśa eventually adopted the view of the Middle Way school, this does not mean that he regarded those who pursued a different Buddhist philosophical system unfavorably. In fact, among all his one hundred and fifty-seven spiritual teachers, the one he revered most was Lama Serlingpa,[40] who adhered to the philosophical view of the Yogācāra school. Tibetan biographical works report that Atīśa exhibited the following behavior toward this teacher:

> Whenever he recalled Lama Serlingpa or heard his name [mentioned], he would invariably raise his joined palms to the crown of his head and express a verse of praise. When asked why he reacted this way toward [Lama] Serlingpa but not any of his other lamas, it is said that he would reply, "This limited form of altruistic mind[41] that I possess is due to the kindness of Lama Serlingpa," and then join his palms [in respect].[42]

The principal literature associated with each of the three just-mentioned lineages contains comprehensive forms of instruction that address both philosophical view and bodhisattva conduct. However, the instructions that derive from the Indian masters associated with the lineage of extensive activities pertain largely, though not exclusively, to the topic of conduct. There are, however, two notable exceptions, one of which is the topic of meditation—by which I mean the instructions that relate to the practice of quiescence[43] and to the form of insight[44] that represents the worldly path.[45] The teachings on this topic rely heavily on such Yogācāra works as

---

rgyas pa yongs grags (*The Extensive Biography of the Precious Lord, the Glorious Master Atisha*), f. 16a.

40. T: *Bla ma gser gling pa*. His ordination name was Dharmakīrti and he was from the island of Sumatra, which was known as the Isle of Gold (S: *suvarṇadvīpaḥ,* T: *gser gling*).

41. T: *sems bzang po*. Literally, "auspicious," "kindly," or "excellent" mind, in Lamrim usage this expression is understood to be a reference to *bodhicitta,* literally "enlightenment mind," which is the aspiration to attain supreme enlightenment.

42. *rNam thar rgyas pa* (*Extensive Biography*), f. 23b.

43. S: *śamathaḥ,* T: *zhi gnas.*

44. S: *vipaśyanā,* T: *lhag mthong.*

45. S: *laukikamārgaḥ,* T: *'jig rten pa'i lam*. This expression refers to the forms of insight meditation practice that bring attainment of the four meditative absorptions (S: *dhyānam,* T: *bsam gtan*) of the form realm and the four formless states of composure (S: *samāpattiḥ,*

The Stage of a Listener, The Compendium of Higher Learning, The Ornament of the Great Vehicle's Discourses, and *Differentiating the Middle Way from Extremes,* along with the commentaries of Vasubandhu and Sthiramati on the latter two works.

As noted earlier, the body of Yogācāra literature described above represents a Great Vehicle version of Abhidharma doctrine. Although this material is not the main focus of the Lamrim instruction, it does inform a great deal of Tibetan philosophical literature on the nature of the Buddhist path and its ultimate goal as understood from the perspective of the Great Vehicle. Two distinct Indian traditions of Abhidharma doctrine have had a major influence on the development of Tibetan Buddhism. Referred to as the "lower" and "higher" Abhidharma systems, respectively, the former is principally made up of the doctrine found in Vasubandhu's *Treasury of Higher Learning* along with its autocommentary and the latter is identified with the doctrine that is presented in Asaṅga's *Compendium of Higher Learning.* However, the "higher" system of Abhidharma doctrine can be understood more broadly to include the entire body of Yogācāra literature identified above. This literature builds upon the "lower" Abhidharma tradition, which is mainly concerned with the ten root mental afflictions and the methods of effecting their permanent abandonment through attaining the transcendent realization of the insubstantiality of a personal self.[46] The Great Vehicle tradition identifies a second type of obstacle that impedes attainment of the supreme enlightenment of a Buddha. It is known as "the obscurations to that which needs to be known"[47] and the corresponding form of realization that abandons it is the transcendent realization that perceives the insubstantiality of phenomena.[48] This path system also defines ten ārya bodhisattva stages that culminate in supreme enlightenment. While the basic elements of this doctrine are also evident in such earlier works as Nāgārjuna's *Jewel Garland,*[49] the Yogācāra literature describes them in much greater detail and with more precision.

T: *snyoms par 'jug pa*). This subject is addressed extensively in Asaṅga's *ŚBh* and in a more abbreviated form in *The Compendium of Higher Learning.* See also *Inner Science,* pp. 169–178.

46. S: *pudgalanairātmyam,* T: *gang zag gi bdag med.*

47. S: *jñeyāvaraṇam,* T: *shes bya'i sgrib pa.*

48. S: *dharmanairātmyam,* T: *chos kyi bdag med.*

49. S: *Ratnāvalī,* T: *Rin chen phreng ba.*

What is also interesting is that the principal elements of this "higher" Abhidharma system are upheld even by later Indian traditions that did not adhere to the Yogācāra view of ultimate reality, such as the syncretic doctrine described by Tibetan scholars as the Yogācāra-Svatantrika branch of the Middle Way school.[50] Proponents of this doctrine include such Indian masters as Śāntarakṣita and Haribhadra. The latter, in particular, is an important figure in the commentarial tradition associated with the *Ornament of Realizations,* one of the Five Teachings of Maitreya mentioned earlier. This important work is described as an analysis of the path that is taught implicitly in the Perfection of Wisdom literature. As part of their commentarial literature on this treatise, Tibetan scholars of the Gelukpa school have devised elaborate explanations of the path system of the three Buddhist vehicles known by the generic term "formulation of the paths and their stages."[51] These works also draw heavily on such texts as Asaṅga's *Compendium of Higher Learning.*

At a relatively young age the great Tibetan master Je Tsongkapa was recognized as an accomplished scholar of the *Ornament of Realizations.* However, it was not until he had reached his late thirties and had become well versed in a broad range of Buddhist teachings that he received teachings on the Lamrim tradition from two spiritual teachers.[52] This instruction made such a strong impression on him that he wrote the following in a personal letter to one of his closest spiritual teachers, Lama Umapa Pawo Dorje:[53]

> Previously, through maintaining a high regard for the great canonical scriptures as well as the stainless forms of reasoning that seek [to fathom] their intent, I had developed in a substantial way [an understanding of] the stages [of spiritual knowledge] that must be generated in the mind. However, I did not remain satisfied with that [level of understanding]. Motivated by an attitude that was concerned solely with [the furtherance of]

50. T: *rNal 'byor spyod pa'i dbu ma rang rgyud pa.*

51. T: *sa dang lam gyi rnam gzhag.*

52. One was known as Namkha Gyeltsen, the great adept from Hlodrak (T: lHo brag grub chen Nam mkha' rgyal mtshan, 1321–1401), and the other was the scholar-practitioner Khenchen Chökyab Zangpo (T: mKhan chen Chos skyabs bzang po, dates uncertain).

53. T: Bla ma dBu ma pa dpa' bo rdo rje (dates uncertain). This teacher was instrumental in introducing Je Tsongkapa to practices associated with the cult of Mañjuśrī.

the teaching, I prayed continuously for blessings to my tutelary deity [whom I regard as being] inseparable in nature from my guru and, through striving [to carry out] many forms [of spiritual practice that are designed] to accumulate [virtue] and eliminate [obstacles], I now have an understanding [that appreciates the manner in which] the canonical scriptures in general and also the great treatises that explain their intent—not just in the form of selected excerpts but in their entirety—represent [teachings] that can be applied to one's spiritual practice.

[The system of instruction] that enables one to ascertain this point easily is [the one known as] the Stages of the Path to Enlightenment. [This system, which] unerringly establishes the stages of the paths associated with both the Sutra[54] and Mantra [forms of the Great] Vehicle tradition, [was taught] by one who reached the far shore of the ocean-like philosophical systems of both our own [Buddhist schools] and those of other [non-Buddhist traditions], one who knew unerringly [all] the crucial elements of the three trainings that represent the essence of the inner science [of Buddhist practice] and who did not merely accept them but also developed an experiential realization of them—namely, Dīpaṃkara Śrījñāna, a great being who was tutored by many learned spiritual teachers that had also attained [high levels of] realization and who also received blessings from an immeasurable number of exalted tutelary deities. Having recognized the marvelous nature [of this body of instruction], it is one that I use exclusively for teaching disciples the stages of spiritual development.

Since this instruction is seen to teach the totality of [all] the canonical scriptures, the treatises that explain their intent, and the personal instruction [that relates to them] by combining them into one path system, when it is both taught by someone who knows how to teach it and put into practice by someone who knows how to listen to it, it also becomes evident that the totality

54. Literally, the Vehicle of Defining Attributes (T: *mtshan nyid kyi thegpa*), this expression means the Abhidharma doctrine contained in the three Buddhist Sūtrayāna path systems, namely, those of the Listeners' Vehicle, the Solitary Realizers' Vehicle, and the nontantric form of the Great Vehicle.

> of the canonical scriptures and not just some minor form of instruction has been arranged into an orderly system. Therefore, I have not taught a wide variety of other guiding instructions.[55]

It is widely understood that the instructions of the Lamrim teaching system place more emphasis on practice than doctrinal theory and that these practices represent effective techniques for bringing about a series of very specific forms of spiritual realization. However, as Je Tsongkapa's letter suggests, one of the major benefits of this body of teachings is that it has the capacity to instill in the practitioner a genuine appreciation of the true import of the great canonical scriptures and their commentaries. This represents one of the four unique qualities of the Lamrim instruction, which is described as the "greatness that enables all the sacred scriptures to be recognized as personal instruction."[56] That being so, one can infer that if a Buddhist practitioner should find the leisure and opportunity to study the major Indian works of the Great Vehicle tradition, this should serve to deepen and strengthen the forms of spiritual understanding that the Lamrim instruction and practice are designed to generate. This, in fact, is the main reason that I undertook to translate Asaṅga's *Stage of a Bodhisattva*.

In Part One of *The Inner Science of Buddhist Practice* I sought to explain how an understanding of the Buddhist doctrine of the five heaps can enhance one's understanding of three essential forms of spiritual knowledge: (1) the belief that regards the relation between karma and its results correctly, (2) an unerring realization of the insubstantiality of the person, and (3) an unerring realization of the insubstantiality of entities. I believe that a similar kind of benefit can also be achieved through undertaking a careful study and analysis of *The Stage of a Bodhisattva*. In the case of Asaṅga's work, I would maintain that the practitioner will gain a uniquely strong appreciation of the Great Vehicle tradition, not only by learning precise explanations of the individual practices but also by developing a clearer sense of their role in relation to the path as a whole. The following two examples should help to illustrate this point.

In a section from chapter 4 of Book I, Asaṅga describes how a correct understanding of ultimate reality promotes the unique form of bodhisattva

55. Tsong kha pa, *Bla ma dBu ma pa la mdo khams su phul ba* (*Letter Sent to Lama Umapa in Dokham*), pp. 335–336.

56. T: *gsung rab thams cad gdams ngag tu 'char ba'i che ba.*

conduct that is required in the Great Vehicle tradition. Bear in mind that his description does not require one to accept the Yogācāra interpretation of the nature of ultimate truth.

As noted earlier, a realization of the insubstantiality of entities is primarily understood to serve as the antidote for the type of obstacle known as the obscuration to that which needs to be known. This type of obscuration is defined as one that can only be overcome by the unique forms of transcendent realization and spiritual practice that are cultivated in the Great Vehicle tradition. Another fundamental principle of the bodhisattva path is that a practitioner must not prematurely eradicate in its totality the other major type of obstacle, known as the obscuration of the mental afflictions,[57] as this would prevent one from fulfilling the central motivation for seeking supreme enlightenment—that is, to attain the ability to act on behalf of others in the highest way possible. Hence, a bodhisattva must take birth in samsara deliberately and repeatedly for a vast period of time, so that he or she can fully amass the forms of merit and wisdom that are necessary to achieve a buddha's unsurpassed form of enlightenment.

Asaṅga refers to the wisdom that comprehends emptiness as a "great means for [bringing about] the attainment of unsurpassed true and complete enlightenment." Here, in part, is how he explains the significance of this description:

> A bodhisattva who applies him- or herself using conviction about [the meaning of] emptiness during various births as he or she continues to be reborn in samsara in order to ripen sentient beings and also to ripen the qualities of a buddha in him- or herself will understand samsara as it truly is. [That bodhisattva] will also not allow his or her mind to become [overly] upset by [the unsatisfactory nature of] samsara through [having contemplated] the aspects of impermanence, etc. [A bodhisattva who] fails to understand samsara as it truly is will be unable to maintain a mind that is [largely] unaffected by all the mental afflictions of desire, hatred, and ignorance, etc. And [a bodhisattva] who cannot maintain a mind that is largely unaffected [by the mental afflictions] will become a person who wanders [continuously] in samsara with an agitated mind and [a person] who can

57. S: *kleśāvaraṇam*, T: *nyon mongs pa'i sgrib pa*.

> neither ripen the qualities of a buddha [in him- or herself] nor ripen [other] sentient beings. Moreover, if a bodhisattva allows his or her mind to become [overly] upset by [the unsatisfactory nature of] samsara through [having contemplated] the aspects of impermanence, etc., then he or she, having developed such [an attitude], will very quickly bring about [the] complete extinction [of samsaric rebirths]. The bodhisattva who very quickly brings about [the] complete extinction [of his or her samsaric rebirths] will, in that way, also fail to ripen the qualities of a buddha in him- or herself and fail to ripen [other] sentient beings, much less attain unsurpassed true and complete enlightenment.[58]

This passage outlines how a firm conviction regarding the meaning of emptiness enables a bodhisattva to engender a particular form of equanimity that accomplishes two aims. The phrase "understand samsara as it truly is" means that the practitioner comprehends that samsara does not possess a real mode of being. This understanding provides one with a unique ability to avoid developing overt forms of the mental afflictions even while interacting with many different kinds of sentient beings. In the chapter on morality, Asaṅga describes the degree to which a practitioner of the Great Vehicle must gain this ability:

> Thus, [a bodhisattva] must attain a state of self-discipline in which [his or her] mind remains so free of afflictions that, even though not an arhat, he or she can interact with entities that have the potential to cause the outflows to arise in such a manner that the unafflicted state of mind which he or she possesses is even superior to that of an arhat.[59]

The statement that a bodhisattva will "not allow his or her mind to become [overly] upset by [the unsatisfactory nature of] samsara" means that despite being acutely aware of samsara's unsatisfactory nature, the genuine practitioner of the Great Vehicle can resist any inclination to prematurely

58. *BBh,* Book I, chapter 4, in the section entitled "Nondual Wisdom Is a Great Means" [I.4.3].

59. In *BBh,* Book I, chapter 10, see the secondary bodhisattva offense identified as "Regarding Samsara with Complacence" [I.10.2.10.14].

terminate his or her own samsaric existence by destroying all of the mental afflictions and continue to "ripen sentient beings and also ripen the qualities of a buddha in him- or herself." Again, the ability to possess such self-control is greatly enhanced if one has developed a firm understanding of the ultimate nature of reality. This is a key point regarding how the wisdom that comprehends the ultimate nature of reality can contribute to a bodhisattva's practice of the Great Vehicle's form of morality training.

Another example is the presentation that appears in chapter 8, "The Lineages of the Powers." This is the first in a series of ten chapters that address the manner in which bodhisattvas are to train themselves. It is organized around seven topics that represent the elements that are essential to the training of the Great Vehicle tradition: (1) cultivating devotion toward eight objects, (2) seeking to learn the Dharma, (3) teaching the Dharma, (4) developing a form of practice that accords with the Dharma teachings, giving (5) correct instruction and (6) counsel, and (7) practicing the four principles of attracting a following.

All of these subjects can be combined into two categories: (1) learning the Dharma for oneself and (2) teaching it to others. Learning the Dharma includes all five of the major branches of learning: (1) the inner science, (2) the science of logic, (3) the science of grammar, (4) the science of treating disease, and (5) the science of the categories of crafts and occupations. The first of these—the inner science—refers to all twelve divisions of the Buddha's speech and is the most important of the five branches of learning. Asaṅga describes it as having two forms: (1) the form that correctly sets forth causes and results and (2) the form that sets forth the principles that what has been done will not perish and that what has not been done will not yield any fruition. After identifying ten types of causes and five kinds of results, the first of these two forms is presented in three categories: (1) how worldly entities are produced, (2) how the samsaric process of affliction is perpetuated, and (3) the process that liberates one from samsara. All three categories are explained in terms of the language that pertains to the doctrine of the twelve limbs of dependent origination. At the conclusion of this discussion, Asaṅga makes these two observations:

> Having realized in this manner the form of the Buddha's speech that correctly sets forth causes and results, and as a consequence of continually cultivating [the aspect of] his or her [spiritual] lineage that relates to the power of knowledge regarding proper

> conditions and improper conditions, a bodhisattva gradually causes [the spiritual lineage of that power] to be refined and further developed.
>
> [A deed that] was not done by one individual or that was done by another will not yield any ripening for that individual. Moreover, those deeds that [an individual] did perform will not perish even after a hundred kalpas with regard to [their ability to] yield a result. Having realized in this manner, as set forth in the Buddha's speech, that what has not been done will not yield any fruition and what has been done will not perish, a bodhisattva gradually causes the [aspect of his or her] spiritual lineage [that relates to] the power of knowledge regarding [the fact that] one's deeds are one's own to be refined and further developed.[60]

"The power of knowledge regarding proper conditions and improper conditions" and the "power of knowledge regarding [the fact that] one's deeds are one's own" are the first two of a buddha's ten powers, which are explained at length in the final chapter of the work. Thus, Asaṅga identifies the process of learning and continually cultivating one's understanding of the Buddha's teaching as the principal activity that causes the "lineages" of those two powers—that is, the capacities to attain them—to be "refined and further developed."

Later in this same eighth chapter, the proper method of providing spiritual instruction to others is defined in terms of eight aspects. They are that the "individual [who intends to give the instruction] examines and realizes (1) [the nature of] the mind, . . . (2) the faculties, . . . (3) the attitude, . . . and (4) the latent propensities [of the person who is to be instructed], (5) causes [that person] to undertake [any of] a variety of means of practice . . . in whatever manner is appropriate [to that person], . . . [and then] (6) teaches [that person] the Middle Way as the antidote to wrongly grasping at the eternalistic extreme, . . . (7) teaches [that person] the Middle Way as the antidote to wrongly grasping at the nihilistic extreme, . . . [and] (8) causes [that person] to abandon the exaggerated pride [in which he or she mistakenly thinks] that [he or she] has accomplished [or attained] something that has not been

60. *BBh,* Book I, chapter 8, last two paragraphs in section entitled "Five Kinds of Results" [I.8.2.2].

accomplished [or attained]." Asaṅga then identifies a link between each of these aspects and the remaining eight of a buddha's ten powers:

> A bodhisattva who in this very manner either receives instruction from another person or provides it to others gradually causes the spiritual lineages of eight powers to be refined and further developed, [namely,] (1) that of the power of knowledge regarding the absorptions, the liberations, and entering states of one-pointed concentration; (2) that of the power of knowledge regarding superior and inferior faculties; (3) that of the power of knowledge regarding diverse forms of devotion; (4) that of the power of knowledge regarding diverse constituent elements; (5) that of the power of knowledge regarding the paths that lead everywhere; (6) that of the power of knowledge regarding the recollection of former existences; (7) that of the power of knowledge regarding death and rebirth; and (8) that of the power of knowledge regarding termination of the outflows.[61]

These two passages definitively convey the meaning of the title of this chapter, which is that a bodhisattva's continuous effort to pursue spiritual learning for him- or herself combined with the subsequent manner in which he or she undertakes to teach the Dharma to others represent the seeds from which the supreme knowledge of enlightenment in the form of a buddha's ten powers will ultimately arise. In this way, the practitioner gains a unique conceptual understanding of the way in which these two activities contribute to the attainment of the ultimate goal. This type of analysis is typical of the approach that is taken throughout Asaṅga's work.

A Manual for the Entire Bodhisattva Collection of Discourses

I believe it is also reasonable to describe *The Stage of a Bodhisattva* as a work that represents a new development in the history of the Buddhist Abhidharma tradition and one that focuses exclusively and in a unique manner on the doctrine of the Great Vehicle. At the end of this work, Asaṅga describes

61. *BBh,* Book I, chapter 8, last paragraph of the section entitled "Instruction" [I.8.5].

it with a variety of phrases;[62] however, the one that that he uses repeatedly throughout the work is that it is a "manual for the [entire] bodhisattva collection of discourses."[63] The Sanskrit term being translated here as "manual" is *mātṛkā* (T: *ma mo*), an expression that was also used to refer to the early Buddhist tabular compilations of Abhidharma terminology and their defining characteristics.[64] A more precise understanding of what Asaṅga meant by this term can be gained from several of his other writings. The opening topic of the second chapter of part 2 of the *Compendium of Higher Learning*[65] is a description of the twelvefold classification of the Buddha's teachings. Of the twelve categories, the tenth is called "extensive discourses"[66] and the twelfth is referred to as "instructions."[67] In *A Collection on Exegesis* the category of "extensive discourses" is explained as follows:

> Regarding this [topic], the extensive discourses fully present the bodhisattva path—which is to say, the seven stages[68] and the four types of conduct[69]—and fully present the qualities of a buddha—which is to say, the one hundred and forty unique buddha qualities that range from the four forms of complete purity up to the knowledge of all aspects and of what is most excellent—[all of which are] described in *The Stage of a Bodhisattva*. Because these teachings are great in number, highly exalted [in their subject matter], and practiced for three vast periods of time [each consisting] of a countless number [of kalpas], they are called the "extensive discourses."[70]

62. He refers to the work as "a manual for the bodhisattva collection," "a summary of the Great Vehicle," "an explanation of the path that leads to destruction and [the path that] avoids destruction," and "the basis for developing the purity of unobstructed knowledge."

63. S: *bodhisattvasūtrapiṭakamātṛkā*, T: *byang chub sems dpa'i mdo sde'i sde snod kyi ma mo*.

64. Cf. *Encyclopedia of Indian Philosophy*, vol. 7, pp. 84–89.

65. *Abhidharmasamuccaya*, p. 78.

66. S: *vaipulyam*, T: *shin tu rgyas pa'i sde*.

67. S: *upadeśaḥ*, T: *gtan la dbab par bstan pa'i sde*.

68. Cf. *BBh*, Book III, chapter 3.

69. *BBh*, Book III, chapter 4.

70. *rNam par bshad pa bsdu ba*, f. 54b.

A few lines later the same work describes the category of teachings known as "instructions":

> Regarding this [topic], [the division of the Buddha's speech called] "instructions" contains the *mātṛkā* compilations that have been extracted from the [sutra] discourses. Regarding these, all [of the extracts from] the sutra discourses that constitute the definitive meaning[71] [of the Buddha's teaching] are called *mātṛkā* compilations. [Those sutra teachings] in which the defining characteristics of entities are presented, as well as [the instructions] in which the defining characteristics of entities are presented unerringly by those listeners who are abiding in the realization that perceives the nature of things, are [what are contained in] the *mātṛkā* compilations and they are also [what are contained in] the Abhidharma [collection].
>
> Just as an alphabet[72] is the starting point for [learning] treatises on language and secular crafts, the explanations of the defining characteristics of entities should be understood [as the starting point for learning the Buddha's overall teaching]. Just as the written word cannot become evident without an alphabet, likewise [the meanings of] the twelve categories of the sutra teachings will not become evident if [the meanings of] the defining characteristics of entities have not been established and they will become evident when [the meanings of the defining characteristics of entities] have been established. The *mātṛkā* compilations are called the Abhidharma because they present the defining characteristics [of entities] unerringly. [Thus,] the explanations of [all] the remaining [categories of] sutra teachings that are based upon the *mātṛkā* compilations are what make up the category [of Buddhist teachings] that is called "instructions."[73]

These passages clarify the sense in which Asaṅga considered his *Stage of a Bodhisattva* to be a compendium of all the authoritative instructions that

71. S: *nītārtham*, T: *nges pa'i don*.

72. S: *mātṛkā*, T: *yi ge'i phyi mo*. This Sanskrit term can also mean an "alphabet."

73. *rNam par bshad pa bsdu ba*, ff. 54b–55a.

pertain to the Great Vehicle tradition of Buddhism. As such, the work can fairly be described as an Abhidharma guide to all of the vast and profound subjects taught throughout the canonical literature of the Great Vehicle tradition. I translate the term *mātṛkā* here as "manual" because, unlike the early Abhidharma tabulations of terms and their defining characteristics, *The Stage of a Bodhisattva* is a prose literary work that organizes its explanations within the context of a systematic framework. Moreover, its style and scope are unparalleled among all the Indian treatises that were translated and incorporated into the various historical traditions of Tibetan Buddhism.

The Structure of *The Stage of a Bodhisattva*

The logical structure of Asaṅga's treatise is arranged in several layers and requires some attention in order to be fully comprehended. The opening passage indicates that the subject matter, which is made up of the Great Vehicle's path together with its result, will be presented in these ten topics: (1) support, (2) marks, (3) factions, (4) superior attitudes, (5) pleasurable states, (6) births, (7) embracing, (8) stages, (9) conduct, and (10) preeminence. The overall text itself is divided into three major sections, described as (1) the support, (2) the qualities that accord with the support, and (3) the perfection of the support. The most striking point to be noticed at the outset is that the first of the just-mentioned ten topics takes up the entirety of the first of the three main divisions. Referred to as Book I in this translation, it contains eighteen chapters that form slightly less than three-fourths of the whole work. The remaining nine of the above ten topics are addressed in individual chapters of the latter two sections, referred to as Book II and Book III. The four chapters of Book II correspond, in the same order, to the next four of the ten topics. Book III, which contains six chapters, addresses the remaining five topics but also includes a separate chapter, entitled "The Marks and the Secondary Signs," which make up one hundred and twelve of a buddha's one hundred and forty unique qualities. This penultimate chapter is presumably to be understood as forming part of the tenth topic, "preeminence," also the title of the final chapter of the work, which is devoted to the remaining twenty-eight unique qualities of a buddha.

In addition to the chapter titles, a number of summary verses appear at different places throughout the work to indicate how specific topics are further organized around a series of related subtopics. For instance, the summary verses that appear at the beginning of chapters 9 through 15 are identical in that they all make reference to same nine aspects of practice. Each of chapters 9 through 14 is devoted to one of the six perfections of generosity, morality, patience, effort, meditative absorption, and wisdom, while chapter 15 discusses the principles for attracting a following. The significance of the nine aspects of practice listed in these particular summary verses is revealed at the end of chapter 15, where it is explained that the ten forms of eight of the nine aspects of practice collectively bring about a particular element of a buddha's enlightenment. For example, the ten forms of the first category are "all-inclusive" forms of generosity, morality, etc., up to an "all-inclusive" form of sameness of purpose. The perfection of this group of ten "all-inclusive" forms of practice is identified as collectively producing the result that unsurpassed true and complete enlightenment constitutes a state in which a buddha's "body possesses an adamantine nature and a state in which the true Dharma remains in existence for a long time." Similarly, the perfection of the ten forms of the next seven aspects of practice is identified as being the cause for a different element of enlightenment. This type of description, which establishes a causal relation between a particular aspect of practice and the ultimate goal of buddhahood, is an important and recurring theme throughout the work.

The remaining summary verses for the most part simply present a list of the topics that are about to be addressed at that point in the work. While a number of chapters have no summary verses, this is either because the main topics of those chapters have already been referenced in earlier verses, as is the case of chapter 2 and chapters 4 through 7 of Book I, or because the subject matter being addressed is limited in scope and complexity, as is the case with the first five chapters of Book III.

None of the headings that have been included in the English translation appear in the original work. While formatted in a manner that suggests a particular hierarchical system, they do not serve to clarify the logical structure of Asaṅga's treatise that was discussed above and have been added simply to highlight the range of points that are being addressed within the context of a particular topic. An outline containing all the headings and summary verses can be found immediately following the conclusion of the English translation.

Book I, The Support

The term "support"[74] refers to the foundation of the Great Vehicle's path, which Asaṅga explains in relation to three subjects: (1) the bodhisattva's spiritual lineage, (2) the initial development of enlightenment mind, and (3) all the spiritual qualities that are conducive to enlightenment.[75] The bodhisattva's spiritual lineage is a support in that it renders him or her capable of attaining supreme enlightenment. The initial development of enlightenment mind is a support in that it allows a practitioner who has generated this mind to apply him- or herself to the training. The spiritual qualities that are conducive to enlightenment are a support in that they constitute the means by which unsurpassed true and complete enlightenment can be attained.

At the beginning of the third chapter, Asaṅga classifies the spiritual training itself into three categories: (1) that in relation to which bodhisattvas train themselves, (2) the manner in which they train themselves, and (3) the individuals who are the ones that train themselves. The first of these categories is made up of seven topics that form the principal objectives of the practice: (1) one's own aim, (2) others' aims, (3) the meaning of reality, (4) spiritual power, (5) the ripening of beings, (6) the ripening of a buddha's qualities in oneself, and (7) true and complete enlightenment. These topics are addressed in chapters 3 through 7.

The phrase "the manner in which they train themselves" refers to the entire range of the individual forms of practice. This material is described in the next ten chapters and includes (1) the nature of the Dharma teachings that need to be learned for oneself and then subsequently taught to others as well as practiced in a proper manner (chapter 8); (2) the six perfections (chapters 9 through 14); (3) the means of attracting a following (chapter 15); (4) how to worship the Three Jewels, serve a spiritual teacher, and cultivate the four immeasurables (chapter 16); and (5) a group of seventeen spiritual qualities and forms of knowledge that need to be developed (chapter 17). The category of the individuals who are "the ones who train themselves" is addressed in chapter 18, the last chapter of Book I, which describes a range of attributes that genuine bodhisattvas are expected to possess. Among all

74. S: *ādhāraḥ,* T: *gzhi.*

75. S: *bodhipakṣyā dharmāḥ,* T: *byang chub kyi phyogs kyi chos rnams.* Although this expression is often associated with a collection of thirty-seven forms of spiritual practice, its use here is meant in a somewhat broader sense. See *BBh,* Book I, chapter 17.

the well-known and traditional topics of the Great Vehicle doctrine that are discussed in Book I, special mention should be given to the unique presentation of one hundred and ten ways in which to cultivate great compassion that appears in chapter 16.

Book II, The Qualities That Accord with the Support

The purpose of Book II, entitled "The Object of Mental Application That Relates to the Qualities That Accord with the Support," is to describe how the bodhisattva who correctly practices all the forms of training that are explained in Book I will engender the spiritual attributes that enable him or her to progress along the path of the Great Vehicle. Chapter 1, entitled "Marks," describes five characteristics that identify an individual as a genuine bodhisattva: (1) sympathy, (2) agreeable speech, (3) fortitude, (4) openhandedness, and (5) the ability to explain profound meanings and intents.

Chapter 2, entitled "Factions," describes the two lifestyles that bodhisattvas adopt—that of a householder or that of a homeless ascetic. Whichever of these two groups a bodhisattva may belong to, four specific qualities must be developed if he or she hopes to quickly attain enlightenment: (1) the quality of having completed one's spiritual activities well, (2) skillfulness, (3) providing assistance to others, and (4) dedication.

Chapter 3 identifies and describes fifteen types of superior attitude. Chapter 4, the final chapter in Book II and the second longest of the entire work, identifies thirteen "pleasurable states,"[76] twelve of which pertain to bodhisattvas and the last of which refers to a buddha's state of supreme enlightenment. The term "pleasurable state" is synonymous with the more familiar term "stage." Most of this chapter is a summary of the important Great Vehicle discourse known as *The Sutra on the Ten Stages.*[77] However, Asaṅga also includes a discussion of the shortcomings that are met with in the second of the thirteen pleasurable states, called the Pleasurable State of Conduct That Is Based upon Devotion.[78] Because this pleasurable state occurs before one has attained the transcendent realization of a bodhisattva ārya, this presentation is not based upon a corresponding section of *The Sutra on the Ten Stages.*

76. S: *vihāraḥ,* T: *gnas pa.*

77. S: *Daśabhūmikasūtram,* T: *Sa bcu pa'i mdo.*

78. S: *adhimukticaryāvihāraḥ,* T: *mos pas spyod pa'i gnas pa.*

Book III, Perfection of the Support

The third main section of *The Stage of a Bodhisattva,* entitled "The Object of Mental Application That Relates to the Perfection of the Support," addresses advanced stages of a bodhisattva's career and ultimately the attainment of unsurpassed enlightenment. Chapter 1, entitled "Births," describes the manner in which a bodhisattva takes birth intentionally in a variety of forms that allow him or her to act on behalf of sentient beings in a far-reaching manner. These culminate with the "final birth," which is the one in which a bodhisattva attains enlightenment.

Chapter 2, entitled "Embracing," refers to a variety of ways in which a bodhisattva provides assistance to sentient beings. The Sanskrit original of the term that is translated as "embracing"[79] is derived from a verbal root that literally means "to take hold of fully." While this root has a broad range of meanings, in the present context the derivative noun refers to an attitude that cherishes all sentient beings and helps them in a variety of ways.

Chapter 3 describes seven bodhisattva stages and identifies the correspondence between them and the thirteen pleasurable states that were explained in Book II, chapter 4. The seven stages are (1) the stage of the spiritual lineage, (2) the stage of conduct that is based upon devotion, (3) the stage of a pure superior attitude, (4) the stage of practicing conduct, (5) the stage of certainty, (6) the stage of certain conduct, and (7) the stage that is the perfect manner of going. These spiritual levels, which are differentiated on the basis of the ways in which bodhisattvas carry out practices on behalf of others, are also referenced twice in Book I and once in Book II.

Chapter 4 of Book III describes four comprehensive types of bodhisattva conduct: (1) conduct relating to the perfections, (2) conduct that is conducive to enlightenment, (3) conduct relating to supernatural knowledge, and (4) conduct relating to the ripening of sentient beings. These four types of conduct are discussed in the *Discourse in Response to Questions Posed by Ratnacūḍa,* one of the forty-nine discourses that make up the *dKon brtsegs* section of the Tibetan Kangyur.

As noted earlier, chapters 5 and 6, the final two of the work, describe one hundred and forty unique qualities of a buddha. Chapter 5 addresses the first one hundred and twelve, which are (1) the thirty-two marks of a great person and (2) the eighty secondary signs. Chapter 6 presents the

79. S: *parigrahaḥ,* T: *yongs su 'dzin pa.*

remaining twenty-eight qualities: (1) the four forms of complete purity, (2) the ten powers, (3) the four forms of intrepid confidence, (4) three forms of closely placed recollection, (5) three forms of having nothing that needs to be concealed, (5) great compassion, (6) the state of being completely free of confusion, (7) complete destruction of the traces, and (8) knowledge of all aspects and of what is most excellent. Among the latter groups of special qualities, Asaṅga's presentation of the ten powers is one of the most detailed treatments of this subject to be found in any of the Indian treatises that have played a central role in the development of Tibetan Buddhism.

The Correspondence between Asaṅga's Work and *The Ornament of Discourses*

Even a cursory examination of Asaṅga's *Stage of a Bodhisattva* and *The Ornament of the Great Vehicle's Discourses* will reveal that the subject matter and structure of both works is strikingly similar. Only the first two topics of the *Ornament*—that is, (1) establishing the authenticity of the Great Vehicle tradition and (2) the practice of taking refuge—are not addressed explicitly in Asaṅga's work. However, the titles and topics of the next seven chapters are identical in both treatises. With regard to this similarity, the opening verse in chapter 10 of *The Ornament of Discourses,* entitled "Devotion," summarizes the ten topics that have been addressed in the work up to that point:

> (1) Introduction, (2) proof, (3) refuge,
> (4) Lineage, and, likewise, (5) developing the mind,
> (6) One's own and others' aims, (7) the nature of reality,
> (8) Power, (9) ripening, and (10) enlightenment.[80]

Vasubandhu's brief comment on this verse affirms the correspondence between the respective chapters of the *Ornament* and Asaṅga's work:

> This [series of topics] that begins with the introductory verses [and continues] up to the chapter on enlightenment should be understood as corresponding to [the first seven chapters of

80. *MSA,* ch. 10, v. 1. S: *ādiḥ siddhiḥ śaraṇaṃ gotraṃ citte tathaiva cotpādaḥ / svaparārthas tattvārthaḥ prabhāvaparipākabodhiś ca;* T: *Dang po sgrub skyabs rigs dang ni / de bzhin du ni sems bskyed dang / rang gzhan don dang de nyid don / mthu dang yongs smin byang chub bo.*

> *The Stage of a Bodhisattva* that end with] the chapter on enlightenment.[81]

The topics of the next six chapters of the *Ornament,* in the same order, form the subject matter of a single chapter of *The Stage of a Bodhisattva*—that is, chapter 8, which is called "The Lineages of the Powers." These are (1) devotion, (2) seeking the Dharma, (3) teaching the Dharma to others, (4) the form of practice that accords with the Dharma, (5) instruction and counsel, and (6) deeds that are supported by skillful means. I have already commented on the unique way in which Asaṅga identifies the causal relationship that exists between these topics and the ultimate goal of unsurpassed enlightenment.

Chapter 16 of the *Ornament,* entitled "The Perfections," corresponds to Book I, chapters 9 through 15 of the *The Stage of a Bodhisattva.* In addition, chapters 17, 18, and 19 of the *Ornament* have the same titles and main subject matter as the final three chapters in Book I of Asaṅga's work.

Book II of *The Stage of a Bodhisattva,* which consists of four chapters, closely parallels the forty-two verses that comprise the *Ornament*'s twentieth chapter.[82] The first three chapters of Book II address the topics of (1) the marks of a bodhisattva (*MSA,* ch. 21, vv. 1, 2); (2) the two factions of householders and homeless ascetics (*MSA,* ch. 21, vv. 3–5); and (3) superior attitudes (*MSA,* ch. 21, v. 6). The only anomaly is that verses 7 and 8 of this chapter in the *Ornament* form the topics of the first two chapters of Book III of Asaṅga's work—which are entitled "Births" and "Embracing." Verses 9 through 42 address the ten ārya bodhisattva stages, which are also discussed at length in the final chapter of Book II of *The Stage of a Bodhisattva.*

81. *Mahāyānasūtrālaṃkāravyākhyā,* p. 52. S: *eṣa ca bodhyadhikara ādim ārabhya yāvat bodhipaṭalānusāreṇānugantavyaḥ;* T: *byang chub kyi skabs 'di dang po nas bzung ste / ril gyis byang chub kyi le'u yi rjes su 'brang ste / sbyar bar khong du chud par bya'o.*

82. *The Ornament of the Great Vehicle's Discourses* is usually described as being made up of twenty-one chapters. However, the way in which the chapters are identified varies. One view counts the first six verses of the text as a separate chapter of introduction and also regards the final sixty-one verses as constituting a single chapter entitled "Conduct and Preeminence." Another formulation considers the first chapter to be made up of the first six verses along with the next fourteen that comprise the topic of establishing the authenticity of the Great Vehicle. According to that system, the final sixty-one verses are divided into two distinct chapters. The first forty-two of these make up chapter 20, entitled "Conduct," and the final nineteen verses form the last—twenty-first—chapter, entitled "Preeminence."

As just noted, the first two chapters in Book III of *The Stage of a Bodhisattva* correspond to verses 7 and 8 of chapter 20 in the *Ornament.* The seven bodhisattva stages that are described in the third chapter of Book III are not explicitly addressed in the *Ornament.* However, chapter 4 of Book III, which is entitled "Conduct," addresses the four types of conduct that are mentioned in chapter 20, verse 42 of the *Ornament.*

Book III, chapter 5 of *The Stage of a Bodhisattva,* which describes the thirty-two marks and eighty secondary signs of a buddha, corresponds to chapter 21, verse 49 of the *Ornament.* Chapter 6, the final chapter of *The Stage of a Bodhisattva,* and the final chapter of the *Ornament,* are both entitled "Preeminence."[83] The eight categories of a Tathāgata's unique qualities that are discussed in this chapter of Asaṅga's work are all referenced among the verses of homage to the Buddha that appear at the end of *The Ornament of Discourses.*

THE BENEFITS OF COMBINING THE PRACTICE OF THE TWO TREATISES

Asaṅga's *Stage of a Bodhisattva* is not a commentary on *The Ornament of the Great Vehicle's Discourses* in the way that Vasubandhu's *Exposition of the Ornament of Discourses*[84] and Sthiramati's *Annotated Explanation of the Ornament of Discourses*[85] are. It doesn't cite or directly address any of the *Ornament*'s verses as, for example, his *Summary of the Great Vehicle* does. Nevertheless, a comparison of the two works will readily enable one to identify the germ of many of Asaṅga's discussions among the *Ornament*'s verses. Despite this fact, the overall structure of *The Stage of a Bodhisattva* and the manner in which the explanations of each topic are formulated are such that Asaṅga's work can be read and studied on its own. Thus, the two treatises might best be described as companion works, by which I mean that a simultaneous side-by-side reading of them will enhance one's understanding of their common subject matter.

83. S: *pratiṣṭhā,* T: *rab tu gnas pa* or *mthar thug pa.* Asaṅga explains this term in *BBh,* Book III, chapter 6, the section entitled "Buddhahood Is Called a State of Preeminence" [III.6.11.3].

84. S: *Sūtrālaṃkāravyākhyā,* T: *mDo sde'i rgyan gyi bshad pa.* This commentary gives a literal explanation of the root text.

85. S: *Sūtrālaṃkāravṛttibhāṣyam,* T: *mDo sde'i rgyan gyi 'grel bshad.* Sthiramati's work is a detailed commentary to both Vasubandhu's exposition and the root text.

The style and tone of the two works is also quite different. *The Ornament of Discourses* delineates the principles of the Great Vehicle tradition in what might be described as lofty language and typically defines spiritual practices in their most idealized form. For most readers, the verse format also requires further explanation in order for its import to be fully understood. By contrast, *The Stage of a Bodhisattva* is written in a more accessible style that not only defines each element of the practice in straightforward language but also explains how each form of practice fits into the overall process of spiritual development, ranging from the initial stage of generating enlightenment mind up to the final attainment of supreme enlightenment. It should be recalled as well that *The Stage of a Bodhisattva* forms one of the seventeen sections in the Abhidharma work entitled *The Main Treatise on the Stages,* whereas *The Ornament of Discourses* is an independent work.

The Tibetan master Je Tsongkapa notes the great value of studying the two works jointly in his *Brief Account of My Spiritual Life:*[86]

> Following that, by skillfully combining [study of] *The Stage of a Bodhisattva* and the *Ornament of Discourses*
> And properly striving [to reflect jointly on their import],
> I came to recognize all the works of the Dharma Lord Ajita[87]
> And his followers as instructions on spiritual practice.[88]

In his explanation of this verse, Purbuchok Ngawang Jampa[89] notes that even when *The Stage of a Bodhisattva* is studied independently it explains fully and in an excellent manner how a practitioner who possesses the spiritual lineage of the Great Vehicle generates the two types of enlightenment mind, cultivates the six perfections and four means of attracting a following, progressively attains the ten ārya stages of the Great Vehicle path, and ultimately achieves the one hundred and forty unique qualities of a bud-

86. T: *Rang gi rtogs pa brjod pa mdo tsam du bshad pa.* Also known by the popular name *Spiritual Aims Fufilled* (T: *'Dun legs ma*).

87. T: *Mi pham pa.* An epithet of Maitreya.

88. Item no. 58 in the author's *Miscellaneous Works* (T: *bKa' 'bum thor bu*). The verse reads: *De nas byang sa mdo sde'i rgyan gnyis po / legs par sbyar te tshul bzhin rab 'bad pas / mi pham chos rje'i gzhung dang rje 'brang gi / gzhung kun nyams su len pa'i gdams par shar.*

89. T: Phur bu lcog Ngag dbang byams pa (1682–1762). See listing for his commentary in the bibliography.

dha. However, if one studies Asaṅga's work and *The Ornament of Discourses* jointly—with the latter serving as a root text and the former as its commentary—and meditates diligently on their common subject matter using the system of practice presented in Je Tsongkapa's *Great Treatise on the Stages of the Path,*[90] then all the literature of the Yogācāra tradition will come be recognized as personal instruction on how to correctly pursue one's spiritual practice. Such an approach will also help to avoid the fault of developing merely an abstract, intellectual understanding of this great body of literature.

How to Combine the Study and Practice of the Two Treatises

The eighteenth-century Gelukpa master scholar Thüken Losang Chökyi Nyima[91] composed a work entitled *The Sun That Illuminates the Excellent Path of the Great Vehicle*[92] in which he explains how to carry out the combined study and practice of these two treatises. His analysis begins by identifying the structure of each treatise separately and describing how their respective presentations parallel one another, and then characterizes Asaṅga's work as follows:

> Although *The Stage of a Bodhisattva* does not address all of the *Ornament*'s subject matter in exactly the same order and was not written as a word commentary[93] that interprets the actual language [of a particular text], it does supplement the explanations that appear there by delineating [various topics] that are not addressed and expanding on those that are presented in an abbreviated form. It [also] takes individual elements [of the topics that are] described there at great length and presents them in a form that is easily understood. In certain instances where

90. T: *Lam rim chen mo.* This is Je Tsongkapa's most extensive work on the Lamrim instruction.

91. T: Thu'u bkwan Blo bzang chos kyi nyi ma (1737–1802). He is also known as Thüken Dharma Vajra.

92. T: *Theg chen lam bzang gsal ba'i nyi ma*. See listing in bibliography under Thu'u bkwan Blo bzang chos kyi nyi ma.

93. T: *tshig 'grel*. Vasubandhu's *Exposition of the Ornament of Discourses* is in fact this type of commentary.

> the elements of a particular practice are addressed at length in [the *Ornament*], [*The Stage of a Bodhisattva*] describes them from the perspective of the practitioner who undertakes them. Likewise, [topics that are] described at length in [the *Ornament*] as antidotes [for particular obstacles] are presented in [*The Stage of a Bodhisattva*] from the perspective of the opposing qualities that those [antidotes] are meant to abandon, or [topics that are] described in [the *Ornament*] as objects to be abandoned are presented in [*The Stage of a Bodhisattva*] from the perspective of [the qualities that constitute] their antidotes. These and other [similar] characteristics [define *The Stage of a Bodhisattva* as] an unsurpassed form of interpretive commentary[94] [that explains the essential import of a particular work].[95]

Thüken Rinpoche's explanation of how to combine the study and practice of the two works follows the outline of *The Stage of a Bodhisattva,* in that the entire path and its result are included within the ten topics that are discussed in the three main sections of the work: (1) the support, (2) the qualities that accord with the support, and (3) the perfection of the support. However, he begins each topic by describing how it is presented in *The Ornament of Discourses* and then follows this with a formulation of the special characteristics of the explanations found in Asaṅga's work.

As noted earlier, the first of the three types of support is the Great Vehicle's spiritual lineage. Thüken Rinpoche's analysis of this topic can serve to illustrate the methodology that he recommends for all the remaining subjects as well. He begins by pointing out the main differences between the two presentations. In the case of *The Ornament of Discourses,* after presenting the initial summary verse, the text first sets forth an argument in support of the existence of multiple forms of spiritual lineage (verse 2) and then asserts the preeminence of the Great Vehicle's spiritual lineage (verse 3). This is followed by a brief description of its two main forms and a literal interpretation of the term *gotram* (verse 4). By contrast, *The Stage of a Bodhisattva* opens with a detailed and precise description of the essential characteristics of the spiritual lineage, followed by the assertion that the superiority of the Great Vehicle's spiritual lineage stems from the fact that it

94. T: *don 'grel.* Literally, a "meaning commentary."

95. *Theg chen lam bzang gsal ba'i nyi ma,* f. 9b.

alone permits a bodhisattva to eliminate both types of obscuration, not just that of the mental afflictions as with the spiritual lineage of the listener and solitary realizer disciples. Thüken Rinpoche characterizes this latter point as being especially important in that it reveals how the two fundamental categories of bondage in samsara and deliverance from it can be explained in their entirety on the basis of the distinction between an unrefined spiritual lineage and one that has been perfected.

The topic of the signs that indicate the presence of the Great Vehicle's spiritual lineage in an individual is also addressed differently in the two works. While *The Ornament of Discourses* mentions four signs, Asaṅga's work mainly addresses the last one—that an individual can be observed to carry out virtuous activities[96]—and gives a very detailed and extensive description of the range of activities that an individual who possesses this spiritual lineage can be observed to carry out in relation to each of the six perfections of generosity, morality, patience, effort, meditative absorption, and wisdom.

The Ornament of Discourses also identifies four unfavorable qualities that lead someone who possesses the Great Vehicle's spiritual lineage to pursue activities that are antithetical to spiritual development (verse 7). In addition to these same four faults, *The Stage of a Bodhisattva* adds four causes that will prevent a bodhisattva from attaining supreme enlightenment.

Finally, Thüken Rinpoche observes that while *The Stage of a Bodhisattva* does not address the *Ornament*'s two similes for the Great Vehicle's spiritual lineage (verses 9 and 10) or the final verse that describes its exalted nature, their import is included within the various explanations that Asaṅga does present in his work. *The Stage of a Bodhisattva* also does not distinguish between a temporary and permanent absence of spiritual lineage as the *Ornament* (verse 8) does; instead it simply states that "if someone does not possess the [Great Vehicle's] spiritual lineage, he or she will absolutely never, under any circumstances, attain enlightenment." Thüken Rinpoche explains that the main reason for these differences is that the purpose of *The Ornament of Discourses* is to describe the substantive content of all the Buddhist discourses. As such, it addresses the topic of spiritual lineage in a more general way that not only describes all of its various forms but also provides a justification for their differences. However, *The Stage of a Bodhisattva* limits itself to the more specific discussion of those individuals who possess the

96. S: *samācaraḥ śubhasya,* T: *dge ba yang dag par spyad pa.*

invariable form of Great Vehicle's spiritual lineage and presents that subject within the context of the unique forms of instruction that serve to refine and develop it. Thüken Rinpoche concludes his analysis by describing how practitioners who wish to train themselves in relation to this topic should combine the instructions contained in the two works:

> Begin by learning what qualities determine the existence of a spiritual lineage, as well as the various categories of spiritual lineage, as presented in the *Ornament,* followed by the way in which *The Stage of a Bodhisattva* identifies the characteristics that constitute its essential nature and other related points. After that, generate a conviction regarding the Great Vehicle's spiritual lineage by combining together and reflecting jointly on (1) the reasons for its superiority, which are described similarly in both the *Stage* and the *Ornament;* (2) the two similes that are presented in the *Ornament;* and (3) the way in which the lineage brings about [two forms of] purity, and the like, as described in *The Stage of a Bodhisattva.* Reflect with particular care on the manner in which *The Stage of a Bodhisattva* describes the capacity to attain unsurpassed enlightenment as being determined entirely by the presence or absence of the [Great Vehicle's] form of spiritual lineage. As you relate these points to your own mind continuum, if you recognize that you possess the invariable form of this type of spiritual lineage, reflect on that fact joyfully. If you determine that you do not possess its invariable form, since the *Ornament* states that [unfavorable] conditions can cause the variable form [of the Great Vehicle's spiritual lineage] to change [into the spiritual lineage of the Lesser Vehicle], pursue as intensely as possible and in many ways the methods for transforming your spiritual lineage into that of the supreme vehicle and also generate an intense aspiration [to be successful in that aim].
>
> Moreover, it isn't sufficient for you to possess a particular spiritual lineage; you must cause it to be awakened. Both the *Stage* and the *Ornament* describe the same four disadvantages or unfavorable conditions that will prevent it from being awakened. In addition, *The Stage of a Bodhisattva* mentions four [unfavorable causes] that are unique to bodhisattvas. Both works also describe the same four favorable qualities [that promote its awakening].

> After reflecting on these points, carry out an unerring form of practice that rejects [the unfavorable qualities] and develops [the favorable ones]. Having done so, do not rely on uncertain or random signs to determine if your spiritual lineage has been awakened. Instead, examine your mind stream to discover whether or not you possess any of the four signs mentioned in the *Ornament* and especially the signs associated with the six perfections that are described in *The Stage of a Bodhisattva*. Also train yourself skillfully [to develop those qualities], for it is extremely important at the outset to plant the seeds for the entire body of the path that pertains to the Conquerors' sons and daughters as it is taught in the susbsequent portions [of these two works].
>
> This orderly arrangement of the successive practices to carry out in relation to the topic of the spiritual lineage by supplementing whatever [instructions] are not delineated in either the *Stage* or the *Ornament* with the explanations found in the companion work should be used as a model for determining the [proper] methods to employ in combining [the study and practice of] the remaining chapters [of these two works]. Merely comparing what each work has to say about those topics that are clearly delineated in both treatises in essentially the same manner does not in the slightest way represent the genuine purpose for combining [the study and practice of] the *Stage* and the *Ornament*.[97]

Thüken Rinpoche offers similar analyses of the succeeding chapters of both works, in each case highlighting their differences and identifying the supplementary discussions to be found in *The Stage of a Bodhisattva*. In doing so, he provides practitioners with a unique blueprint for how to study these two important works jointly in a way that will enhance their spiritual development.

The Translation

The English translation that follows was prepared using two published versions of the Sanskrit text—the 1936 edition of Professor Unrai Wogihara and the 1978 edition of Dr. Nalinaksha Dutt—along with several versions

97. *Theg chen lam bzang gsal ba'i nyi ma*, f. 12a–12b.

of the Tibetan translation that is contained among the different editions of the Tengyur collection. Broadly speaking, the presentations found in the Sanskrit and Tibetan versions parallel each other closely. Only in a few instances does the Tibetan translation contain a brief passage that is not found in either of the two Sanskrit editions.

The availability of the Sanskrit original proved to be extremely helpful in interpreting a number of somewhat convoluted Tibetan passages as well as others that appear to be erroneous due to corruption. For their part, the Tibetan translations also served to clarify several mistaken readings of the Sanskrit original that appear in the published editions. These anomalies are identified throughout the translation in the notes. Another resource that I relied on heavily is the Tibetan translation of a word commentary[98] to Asaṅga's work written by the Indian scholar *Samudramegha.[99] Tāranātha lists him among a number of important Buddhist figures that lived around the time of King Dharmapāla of Bengal, whose reign lasted from 770–810 C.E. I have cited Samudramegha's explanations extensively in the notes to provide further clarification of Asaṅga's text.

Concerning the translation of the personal pronoun when it refers to the singular form of the Sanskrit noun *bodhisattva*, I would like to note the following. Although the term is typically declined as a masculine noun, in this translation it should be taken to mean, in a gender-neutral sense, "a being who aspires to enlightenment." That is to say, it refers to a model practitioner of the Great Vehicle's path system without specifying a person of either gender. Parenthetically, the term *bodhisattva* can be—and, in fact, is—also declined in the feminine when it refers unambiguously and exclusively to a female person or persons. In conjunction with the term *bodhisattva,* the Sanskrit uses two demonstrative pronouns as the third-person personal pronoun, which are invariably used in the masculine form in both the singular and plural simply to conform to the gender of the noun to which they refer. Again, they can and should be taken in the gender-neutral sense of "that one" where they indicate the singular subject of a statement and "that one's" where they indicate the possessive. Since those particular phrases would be awkward to use in the English translation and because I would like to convey explicitly this gender-neutral sense to the reader, I have decided to render the third-person singular personal pronoun as "he or she" and "his or her,"

98. S: *vyākhyā*, T: *rnam par bshad pa*.

99. Original Sanskrit name uncertain, T: rGya mtsho sprin.

etc., wherever possible. Although these pairs of gender-specific pronouns do not appear together in the original, I have adopted this convention to convey the implicit sense of the text more accurately than if only the singular forms "he" and "his" were used. This can be thought of in the same way as the well-known passage from the *Heart Sutra* which states, "O Śāriputra, whatever son of good family or daughter of good family is desirous of practicing the profound perfection of wisdom . . ." In fact, Asaṅga uses this pair of terms several times in this work.

There are, however, several instances in the treatise where a preferential view of the male gender is expressed. The first occurs in chapter 3, where Asaṅga formulates "eight maturations" that are said to endow a bodhisattva with the ability to pursue the spiritual practice more effectively. The seventh of these attributes is "the quality of being a male." Another example occurs near the end of chapter 8, where the text states that a "woman cannot attain unsurpassed true and complete enlightenment." Immediately following this sentence, the text continues, "Once a bodhisattva has passed beyond the first [period of a] countless number of kalpas he abandons the state of being a woman, and [from then on] until he sits at the seat of enlightenment, he will never again become a woman." Near the end of Book II, chapter 4, the text further notes that "The [first] interval of countless great kalpas is [the period during which] one goes beyond the pleasurable state of conduct that is based upon devotion and attains the pleasurable state of great joy." These latter two statements taken together clearly imply the view that after a bodhisattva has reached the status of an ārya, he will always be reborn as a male. Therefore, because it represents more accurately the author's intent, only the male pronoun is used in the descriptions of the pleasurable states of an ārya that occur in Book II, chapter 4.

I am personally sympathetic to the fact that many female readers will react unfavorably to this dogma. At the same time, I do not believe that it needs to be taken as simply a gratuitous denigration of the female gender. Since this issue has been addressed at length by a number of contemporary scholars, I will not comment upon it further here beyond expressing the sincere hope that all readers will be able to appreciate the singular importance that this work clearly merits in the history of Buddhist literature.

Having no knowledge of Chinese, I was not personally able to consult any of the translations contained in the Chinese scripture collections that pertain to the literature of the Yogācāra tradition. However, I did receive help from two friends—Dr. Patrick Carré, a colleague who is also a fellow with the Tsadra Foundation, and Dr. Shenghai Li of the Harvard Divinity School. Both of these scholars kindly consulted a number of Chinese translations on my behalf to help clarify several difficult passages. I would also like to thank Dr. Péter-Dániel Szántó, a research fellow at Oxford University, who has been very patient in responding to my numerous queries relating to Sanskrit.

This translation would not have been possible without the generous support of the Tsadra Foundation, for which I am deeply grateful. I hope that my efforts will contribute in some measure to the continued study and practice of the Buddha's precious Teachings. I readily accept responsibility for any and all errors I may have committed inadvertently. Finally, I wish to acknowledge the unfailing support that I continue to receive from my dear wife, Bali.

BOOK I

The Support

Obeisance to all the buddhas and bodhisattvas.
Obeisance to Ārya Maitreya.

I

The Spiritual Lineage

Ten topics serve to encompass the bodhisattvas' path of the Great Vehicle, together with its result.

What are the ten?

They are the support, marks, factions, superior attitudes, pleasurable states, births, embracing, the stages, conduct, and preeminence.

Summary verse:

> Support, marks, factions,
> Superior attitudes, pleasurable states,
> Births, embracing, stages,
> Conduct, and, lastly, preeminence.

Support [I.1.1]

What is the support?[100]

In this case, (1) the bodhisattva's own spiritual lineage, (2) the initial act of generating enlightenment mind, and (3) all the spiritual qualities that are conducive to enlightenment[101] are called the "support."

100. S: *ādhāraḥ,* T: *gzhi.* The basic meanings of this noun include "support," "prop," "substratum," and "receptacle." *BBhVy* (f. 3a) gives this interpretation: "It is a support because [other things] are supported by it—that is to say, it is an entity that promotes the attainment [of something]."

101. S: *bodhipakṣyā dharmāḥ,* T: *byang chub kyi phyogs kyi chos rnams.* This expression is often associated with the following collection of thirty-seven forms of spiritual practice: (1) the four closely placed recollections, (2) the four correct forms of abandonment, (3) the four elements of spiritual accomplishment, (4) the five faculties, (5) the five powers, (6) the seven

Why is that?

In this context, through depending upon and relying upon the [Great Vehicle's] spiritual lineage, a bodhisattva becomes fit for and capable of attaining unsurpassed true and complete enlightenment. Therefore, the [Great Vehicle's] spiritual lineage is called a support in that it is a capability.

In this context, through depending upon and relying upon the initial development of enlightenment mind, the bodhisattva applies him- or herself to generosity, and he or she applies him- or herself to morality, patience, effort, meditative absorption, and wisdom. Similarly, one applies oneself to the six perfections, the accumulation of merit, the accumulation of wisdom, and all of the entities that are conducive to enlightenment. Therefore, the initial act of generating enlightenment mind is called a support in that it is a bodhisattva's means of application to the practice.

In this context, through relying upon and depending upon that very means of application to the bodhisattva practice, a bodhisattva will bring to completion unsurpassed true and complete enlightenment. Therefore, the activity of applying oneself to the bodhisattva practice is called a support in that it brings to completion [a bodhisattva's] great enlightenment.

Because a person who does not abide in the [Great Vehicle's] spiritual lineage lacks that spiritual lineage, he or she is not capable of bringing to completion unsurpassed true and complete enlightenment, even though he or she may generate [enlightenment] mind and put forth effort [in relation to the practice]. Conversely, it should be understood that the [Great Vehicle's] spiritual lineage is a support even for a bodhisattva who has not yet developed [enlightenment] mind and who has not yet commenced the bodhisattva practice. But if someone who abides in the [Great Vehicle's] spiritual lineage both fails to generate [enlightenment] mind and fails to undertake the conduct that leads to enlightenment, then despite having the capacity to achieve enlightenment, he or she will not attain enlightenment

---

limbs of enlightenment, and (7) the eight limbs of the āryas' path. However, *BBh,* Book I, chapter 17 addresses a broader range of seventeen topics under this heading, among which these thirty-seven spiritual qualities constitute one. *BBhVy* (f. 3b) describes this expression in the following manner: "The entities that are conducive to enlightenment are all the spiritual qualities subsumed within the perfections of generosity and the rest. They should be understood [literally] as being 'of the side of enlightenment' because they are favorable to the attainment of enlightenment. In the world, that which is favorable to another thing is described as being 'of its side' (S: **tatpakṣya,* T: *de'i phyogs*)."

quickly. [On the other hand,] it should be understood that someone who is the opposite of that[102] will attain [enlightenment] quickly.

Moreover, the spiritual lineage that is called a "support" is also called a "basis,"[103] a "cause," a "foundation,"[104] an "originator,"[105] a "[necessary] antecedent,"[106] and a "source."[107] Just as [these synonyms can be used to refer to] the spiritual lineage, they can also [be used to refer to] the initial act of generating [enlightenment] mind and all the spiritual qualities that are conducive to enlightenment.[108]

The Two Types of Spiritual Lineage [1.1.2]

What is the [Great Vehicle's] spiritual lineage?

In brief, the [Great Vehicle's] spiritual lineage is of two types: that which exists naturally[109] and that which has been developed.[110]

Regarding this [topic], the [Great Vehicle's] spiritual lineage that exists naturally is a quality of bodhisattvas' six [inner] bases.[111] Its [nature] is such

102. That is, he or she not only abides in the Great Vehicle's spiritual lineage but also has both generated enlightenment mind and is actively engaged in the spiritual practice.

103. S: *upastambhaḥ,* T: *rton pa. BBhVy* (f. 5a): "It is a basis because it causes the continuum of the result to remain in existence (T: *'bras bu gnas pa'i rgyun 'byung bar byed pas rgyu nyid kyi phyir rton pa zhes bya'o*)."

104. S: *niśrayaḥ,* T: *rten.* Literally, "an object to lean on." *BBhVy* (f. 5a): "It is a foundation because it continues to exist even after the result has arisen (T: *'bras bu'i dus na yang rjes su 'jug pas rten to*)."

105. S: *upaniṣad,* T: *nyer gnas.* Literally, "that which sits near." *BBhVy* (f. 5a): "It is an originator because it causes something to arise successively (T: *rim gyis 'byung bar byed pas na nyer gnas so*)."

106. S: *pūrvaṃgamaḥ,* T: *sngon du 'gro ba. BBhVy* (f. 5a): "It is a [necessary] antecedent in the sense that it must precede the arising of a result (T: *'bras bu'i sngon du 'gro ba yin pa'i phyir sngon du 'gro ba zhes bya'o*)."

107. S: *nilayaḥ,* T: *gnas. BBhVy* (f. 5a): "It is a source in that [it is a place from which] results come forth (T: *'bras bu nges par 'gro ba'i phyir gnas*)."

108. Both Sanskrit editions have "all bodhisattva conduct" (S: *sarvā bodhisattvacaryā*) instead of "all the spiritual qualities that are conducive to enlightenment" (T: *byang chub kyi phyogs kyi chos thams cad*).

109. S: *prakṛtistham,* T: *rang bzhin gyis gnas pa.*

110. S: *samudānītam,* T: *yang dag par bsgrubs pa.*

111. S: *ṣaḍāyatanāni,* T: *skye mched drug.* Buddhist Abhidharma literature formulates twelve "bases" as the inner and outer conditions for the arising of consciousness. The six inner bases

that it has existed as an unbroken series since beginningless time and it is [a quality that is] obtained through the natural order of things. The form of spiritual lineage that is developed is one that is obtained through the prior cultivation of virtue roots. In the present usage, [the term "spiritual lineage"] is meant to apply to both types. This spiritual lineage,[112] moreover, is also called a "seed,"[113] a "constituent element,"[114] and a "fundamental nature."[115] Additionally, the form [of the spiritual lineage] that has not yet borne fruit[116] is subtle, because of the absence of any fruit. The form that has borne fruit is distinct, by virtue of the presence of that fruit.

Since the bodhisattvas who are endowed with this spiritual lineage surpass all the listeners and solitary realizers, let alone all other sentient beings, it should be known as a quality that is unsurpassed.

Why is that?

In brief, there are two types of purity: the purity [of having removed] the

---

are the faculties of the eye, ear, nose, tongue, body, and mind. The six outer bases are the objects of the six types of consciousness—that is, visible form, sound, smells, tastes, tangible objects, and the entities that are perceived by mind consciousness. *BBhVy* (ff. 5b–6a) gives three explanations for why Asaṅga describes the natural form of the spiritual lineage as a quality of the six inner bases. The first one is that this seed or potential for developing the transcendent virtuous qualities cannot be identified as being either identical with or distinct from conditioned entities. The six inner bases are the particular conditioned entities with which the spiritual lineage is associated. Moreover, since these faculties represent the substantive basis of a sentient being (T: *sems can dang rdzas kyi rtsa bar gyur pa*), this form of the spiritual lineage can also be described as "a quality of a sentient being." The second explanation is that the six faculties are the inner causes for developing any and all forms of virtuous states of mind; hence, the potential for generating those virtuous qualities is identified with them. The third explanation is that when an individual undergoes the transformation that follows the perfection of his or her spiritual development, those very six inner bases represent the substantive entities that will become the name and form (S: *nāmarūpam,* T: *ming dang gzugs*) aspects of that enlightened being.

112. *BBhVy* (f. 6b): "It is a spiritual lineage because it is the source of transcendent qualities."

113. S: *bījam,* T: *sa bon. BBhVy* (f. 6b): "It is a seed because it is a cause that gives rise to those [transcendent qualities]."

114. S: *dhātuḥ,* T: *khams. BBhVy* (f. 6b): "It is a constituent element because it brings forth results that are in agreement with it."

115. S: *prakṛtiḥ,* T: *rang bzhin. BBhVy* (f. 6b): "It is a fundamental nature because it is not something that has been artificially created."

116. *BBhVy* (f. 6b): "'The form [of the spiritual lineage] that has not yet borne fruit' means the form that has not [produced] a result that can be perceived. Moreover, it should be understood that 'result' here means either a sign of the spiritual lineage or a sign of being a bodhisattva."

obscurations of the mental afflictions[117] and the purity [of having removed] the obscurations to that which needs to be known.[118] Regarding these, the spiritual lineage that is possessed by listeners and solitary realizers brings a purity that is gained through the removal of the obscurations of the mental afflictions, but not [a purity that is gained] through the removal of the obscurations to that which needs to be known. However, the spiritual lineage of the bodhisattvas brings them a purity that is gained through the removal of both the obscurations of the mental afflictions and the obscurations to that which needs to be known. Therefore, [that spiritual lineage] is the most outstanding of all, and thus it is said to be "unsurpassed."

The Superiority of Bodhisattvas [1.1.3]

In addition, there are four ways in which the bodhisattvas should be known as superior to the listeners and the solitary realizers.

What are the four?

[The bodhisattvas' superiority] is one that is due to their [superior] faculties, their [superior] pursuit, their [superior] skill, and their [superior] result. Regarding this [point], the [bodhisattvas'] superiority that is due to their [superior] faculties is the following. A bodhisattva is naturally one who possesses sharp faculties, whereas a solitary realizer possesses middling faculties, and a listener possesses [relatively] weak faculties.

Regarding this [point], the [bodhisattvas'] superiority that is due to their [superior] pursuit is the following. Listeners and solitary realizers are dedicated [only] to pursuing what is beneficial to themselves. Bodhisattvas are dedicated not only to pursuing what is beneficial to themselves, but also to pursuing what is beneficial to others, what is beneficial to a multitude of people, and what brings happiness to a multitude of people. They are also [motivated by] their compassion for the world and are dedicated to the welfare, benefit, and happiness of gods as well as humans.

117. S: *kleśāvaraṇam,* T: *nyon mongs pa'i sgrib pa.* This type of obscuration is the main obstacle to the attainment of liberation from samsara. Its removal is the goal that is pursued in the Listeners' Vehicle and the person who attains this goal is referred to as an arhat (T: *dgra bcom pa;* see also note 512).

118. S: *jñeyāvaraṇam,* T: *shes bya'i sgrib pa.* This type of obscuration is the main obstacle to the attainment of supreme enlightenment and its removal can only be accomplished by means of the forms of transcendent realization and spiritual practice that are unique to the path of the Great Vehicle.

Regarding this [point], the [bodhisattvas'] superiority that is due to their [superior] skill is the following. Listeners and solitary realizers develop skill in relation to the heaps, the bases, the constituents, dependent origination, proper and improper conditions, and the [four noble] truths.[119] Bodhisattvas do so in relation to these [subjects] as well as all the other branches of learning.[120]

The [bodhisattvas'] superiority that is due to their [superior] result is the following. Listeners attain the result that is the listeners' [form of] enlightenment. Solitary realizers attain the result that is the solitary realizers' [form of] enlightenment. Bodhisattvas attain the result of unsurpassed true and complete enlightenment.

Signs [1.1.4]

There are six [types of] signs of a bodhisattva's spiritual lineage that occur in relation to the perfections. [These are signs] by which others can realize that someone is a bodhisattva. They are the signs of the [Great Vehicle's] spiritual lineage that occur in relation to the perfection of generosity and the signs of the spiritual lineage that occur in relation to the perfections of morality, patience, effort, meditative absorption, and wisdom.

The Signs That Occur in Relation to the Perfection of Generosity [1.1.4.1]

Regarding this [topic], these are signs of the [Great Vehicle's] spiritual lineage that occur in relation to the perfection of generosity: In this case, a bodhisattva naturally takes pleasure in being generous. As long as one continues to have and possess objects that are suitable for giving, one is inclined to share them with others continually and without interruption. One gives with a joyous mind, not with a mind that is distressed. One will share even though one may only have a small amount [of something]. One offers a splendid gift, not one that is inferior.

119. Cf. *ŚBh,* pp. 237–249, for a discussion of the first five of these six topics. The four noble truths are also discussed in several places in *ŚBh*.

120. See *BBh,* Book I, chapter 8, the section entitled "Seeking the Dharma" [I.8.2] for a description of the five branches of learning (S: *vidyāsthānam,* T: *rig pa'i gnas*).

[A bodhisattva] feels shame at having failed to practice generosity.[121] One extols [the virtues of] generosity to others and instills in them a desire to be generous. Upon seeing someone who is being generous, [a bodhisattva] is delighted and feels very happy. He or she rises before those persons worthy of honor,[122] those who are elders, those worthy of being venerated,[123] and those worthy of being shown respect, and offers them a seat.

Whether asked to do so or not, [a bodhisattva] gives suitable instruction concerning the different activities that sentient beings ought to carry out and that will enable them to remain free of misfortune in both this world and the next.[124] One gives protection to those beings who are threatened by such [sources of] fear as the king, robbers, enemies, water, and the like. To the fullest extent of one's powers, one protects those [beings] from those diverse and extensive kinds of serious danger.

If another person's wealth is entrusted into [a bodhisattva's] hand, he or she will not squander it. If one borrows from others, one will not cheat them or default on the loan. One will not cheat or seek to defraud those relatives with whom an inheritance is shared. One truthfully informs an individual who is confused or who has formed a mistaken opinion about various types

121. S: *adānena ca jihreti*. *BBhVy* (f. 8b): "The phrase 'He or she feels shame at having failed to practice generosity' means that [the bodhisattva] feels mental distress because no petitioner has appeared and he or she has not been asked [to give anything]. He or she reflects, 'Because I am of meager fortune my property is worthless. Like the fruit of a tree in a charnel ground, it has not been put to good use.'" The Tibetan translation gives a somewhat different meaning and seems to interpret *adāna* as having two senses: (1) lack of generosity and (2) taking what is not given, i.e., stealing. Hence, the Tibetan reads: "He or she is known for avoiding both lack of generosity and engaging in theft" (T: *sbyin pa mi byed ma byin par len pa la yang 'dzem par byed do zer ro*).

122. S: *guruḥ*, T: *bla ma*. Use of this term is not restricted to a spiritual teacher, as is commonly understood in everyday language. *BBhVy* (f. 9a): "For laypersons, 'those worthy of honor' means one's father and mother; for homeless ascetics [i.e., monks and nuns], it means one's preceptor (S: *upādhyāyaḥ*, T: *mkhan po*) and one's instructor (S: *ācāryaḥ*, T: *slob dpon*)."

123. S: *dakṣiṇīyaḥ*, T: *yon gnas*. *BBhVy* (f. 9a): "For laypersons, 'those worthy of being venerated' means those individuals who are morally upright, those who possess virtuous qualities, spiritual ascetics, and brahmins; for homeless ascetics, it means those wise persons who have attained the Dharma of realization and who are preservers of the scriptural Dharma, as well as those who are esteemed by fellow spiritual practitioners." This term literally also means a person who is "worthy of receiving sacrificial gifts." The Tibetan translation suggests the latter meaning.

124. S: *paralokaḥ*, T: *'jig rten pha rol*. The "next world" is a reference to future lives.

of objects of value, such as gems, pearls, lapis lazuli,[125] conch shells, crystals, coral, gold, silver, emeralds, sapphires, rubies, [conch shells that] turn to the right, and so forth, so that they will not be cheated by others. How, then, could [a bodhisattva] ever directly cheat such a person?

[A bodhisattva] is someone who has a natural propensity for [acquiring] great wealth and gives thought to [how he or she might acquire] all forms of extensive wealth and property. [A bodhisattva] is also someone who has a propensity for wide-ranging business activities, not for those that are minor sources of revenue.

These are [some of] the vices that are pursued in the world: the vice of [pursuing] women, the vice of intoxicating drinks, the vice of gambling, the vice of viewing [public performances by] actors, dancers, jesters, dramatic dancers, and the like. [A bodhisattva] achieves detachment from these kinds of evil pursuits very quickly and easily. He or she exhibits [the moral virtues of] shame and abashment.[126] [A bodhisattva] does not develop great attachment even after acquiring extensive wealth, let alone a small [amount of wealth]. These and other similar qualities should be understood as the signs of a bodhisattva's spiritual lineage that occur in relation to the perfection of generosity.

The Signs That Occur in Relation to the Perfection of Morality [1.1.4.2]

Regarding this [topic], these are signs of the [Great Vehicle's] spiritual lineage that occur in relation to the perfection of morality: In this case, a bodhisattva naturally comes to have [only] weak forms of nonvirtuous deeds of body and speech;[127] he or she does not [come to have] those that are exceedingly violent or that cause great injury to sentient beings. After having committed an evil deed, one feels remorse very quickly. Moreover, one feels shame while carrying out that [misdeed]; one does not feel pleased [as it is being carried out]. [A bodhisattva] is also a type of person who avoids

125. S: *vaiḍūryam*. The Tibetan transliterates the Sanskrit term. We have translated it according to the Tibetan tradition. The exact meaning of Sanskrit names for gems is not always clearly identifiable. MW (p. 1021) identifies this as "cat's-eye gem."

126. These two qualities are included among a group of eleven fundamental virtuous mental factors in the writings of Asaṅga and Vasubandhu. See notes 677 and 678 for definitions. They are both also defined in the opening section of *BBh,* Book I, chapter 17.

127. Sanskrit editions add "mind."

doing injury to other beings with such things as one's hand, a lump of earth, a club, or a weapon.

[A bodhisattva] is naturally affectionate and holds sentient beings dear. One honors those who are worthy of being shown respect at appropriate times with acts of reverential salutation and prostration, by standing up in their presence, making the gesture of joined palms, and engaging in respectful behavior. One is sincere, polite, and willing to comply with the wishes of others. One smiles, extends a pleasant facial expression, does not frown, and speaks in an agreeable manner.[128]

[A bodhisattva] is grateful and appreciative toward those persons who have been helpful [previously]. One behaves in an upright manner toward those who ask for something. One does not mislead them with deceitfulness[129] and guile.[130] One obtains wealth not in an unjust manner but by adhering to what is right and without engaging in cruelty.[131]

[A bodhisattva] is naturally desirous of virtue. One takes an interest[132] in the meritorious activities of others, needless to say in one's own. [A bodhisattva] is greatly upset by the doing of harm to others, such as when he or she has seen or heard that others have been killed, bound, cut, beaten, reviled, threatened, and the like.

128. S: *pūrvābhibhāṣī,* T: *gsong por smra ba.* The Sanskrit literally means "one who speaks first," but it also has a more general sense of "one who speaks politely and agreeably" (cf. MW, p. 644). The Tibetan equivalent suggests "one who speaks sincerely or honestly."

129. S: *māyā,* T: *sgyu. AS* (p. 8): "What is deceitfulness? It is a form of desire and ignorance in which a person who is attached to gain and honor gives the appearance of possessing qualities that he or she does not possess. Its action is to give support to wrong livelihood."

130. S: *śāṭhyam,* T: *g.yo. AS* (pp. 8–9): "What is guile? It is a form of desire and ignorance in which a person who is attached to gain and honor conceals faults that he or she possesses. [Its action] serves to obstruct the obtaining of correct spiritual instruction." *BBhVy* (f. 12a): "[One does not mislead them] 'with deceitfulness and guile' means that one does not agree [to comply with a request] and then allow a long period of time to go by without fulfilling [that pledge]."

131. S: *asāhasena,* T: *bab chol ma yin pa.* The original Sanskrit has several meanings, including "without being reckless" and "without using force, violence, or cruelty." *BBhVy* (f. 12a) indicates the latter sense, giving two readings: "without engaging in evil actions" and "without forcibly summoning those who are subject to the will of others and who are not free and setting them to work."

132. S: *vyāparaṃ gacchati.* This is an idiom that means "to be concerned about" (cf. MW, p. 1038). The Tibetan translation has "praise" (T: *bstod par byed*), but *BBhVy* (f. 12a) paraphrases the overall statement as meaning "to be attentive about helping others in [the performance of] meritorious actions."

[A bodhisattva] is serious about taking up the Dharma and serious about future lives, apprehensive about even a very minor objectionable act,[133] much less one that is great. [A bodhisattva] also assists others in their work and activities. For example, one assists others in [performing the activities of] agriculture, commerce, tending livestock, service to the king, scribal work, counting, record keeping,[134] calculating, and signing;[135] [the activities of] resolving difficulties with an employer/overlord, among family members, between friends and foes, and within a royal palace; [the activities of] accumulating, preserving, storing, making use of, and distributing wealth; [the activities of making] matrimonial arrangements in which a bride is sent out [to another family] or brought into [one's own family]; [the activities of] extensive feasting and communal feasting; as well as other similar types of activities. One does not engage in quarreling, verbal condemnation, contentiousness, disputes, or [any other] activities that are harmful to others, or that bring harm, disadvantage, or suffering both to oneself and others. One stops others from engaging in improper activities, such as the ten evil and nonvirtuous karmic paths.

[A bodhisattva] allows him- or herself to be subject to the will of others and to be put to use by others. As [a form of practice that is] equally patience and morality, one will give up one's own activities and allow oneself to be directed by others in whatever manner they may desire to carry out their activities.

[A bodhisattva] has both a tender and gentle mind. One does not maintain a hostile or angry state of mind for a long period of time; [rather,] one instantly changes that state of mind into one that is pleasant. [A bodhi-

133. S: *avadyam,* T: *kha na ma tho ba. TBh* (p. 76): "An objectionable act is one that is evil, because it is condemned by those who are wise and because it has an undesirable maturation."

134. S: *nyasanam,* T: *shod dgod pa.* Śākyamati's commentary to the *Gayāśīrṣasūtra* (T: *'Phags pa ga ya mgo'i ri mdo dang spel mar bshad pa,* f. 90b): "'Record keeping' is putting down [a record of financial transactions]. A person with this knowledge never makes errors in any [transactions relating to] income and expenditure, thereby increasing his or her wealth." *YBhV* (f. 101b): "'Record keeping' is the recording of numbers on earthen material [clay?]. Others say that 'record keeping' means calculating sums."

135. S: *mudrā,* T: *lag rtsis.* A method of mathematical calculation that is performed using the fingers or hands (T: *lag pa'i tha snad*). Scriptures refer to acts of theft that are carried out by improper use of this method. It is included with several other methods of calculation in a list of thirty-four "practical arts" (S: *śilpakalā,* T: *bzo yi sgyu rtsal*) in *MVy* (no. 4975). See also *BHSD,* p. 435.

sattva] values the truth greatly, does not mislead others with false speech, and does not take pleasure in the estrangement of others from their friends nor cause it to occur.

[A bodhisattva] does not speak in an incoherent manner about things that are useless or meaningless, or without giving due consideration [to his or her words]. One speaks in a pleasant manner and avoids using a sharp tone even with one's own retinue of servants and the like, let alone with anyone else. One has a high regard for virtuous qualities and voices genuine[136] praise of others. These and other similar qualities should be understood as the signs of a bodhisattva's spiritual lineage that occur in relation to the perfection of morality.

The Signs That Occur in Relation to the Perfection of Patience [1.1.4.3]

These are the signs of a bodhisattva's spiritual lineage that occur in relation to the perfection of patience: In this case, when a bodhisattva is harmed by others, he or she naturally avoids displaying a hostile state of mind and also does not undertake to do harm [in return]. Upon being directed to do something, one accepts that directive quickly. One also does not hold on to rancor[137] and does not maintain a hostile attitude that lasts for an extended period of time. These should be understood as the types of signs of a bodhisattva's spiritual lineage that occur in relation to the perfection of patience.

The Signs That Occur in Relation to the Perfection of Effort [1.1.4.4]

These are the signs of a bodhisattva's spiritual lineage that occur in relation to the perfection of effort: In this case, a bodhisattva is naturally energetic.

136. The praise is "genuine" (S: *bhūtam,* T: *yang dag pa*) in that the person truly possesses the qualities that are being attributed to him or her and, thus, the praise is never undeserved or a form of flattery.

137. S: *na khilaṃ dhārayati,* T: *zhe la mi 'dzin pa*. The term *khila* has a metaphorical sense that derives from a noun that means "barren or uncultivated land"; thus, its general sense is that of a form of mental obstruction that represents a "barrenness of mind." Though its meaning is not restricted to anger, it often occurs in combination with "malice" (S: *vyāpadam,* T: *gnod sems*) and "hatred" (S: *dveṣaḥ,* T: *zhe sdang*). Typically, the term is rendered in Tibetan as *tha ba* (cf. MW, p. 340; *BHSD,* p. 205; PTS, online edition).

One rises at daybreak and goes to sleep [only] at the end of the day. One does not indulge excessively in the comfort of sleep, the comfort of lying down, or the comfort of lying on one's side. When an activity is being carried out, one gives careful consideration to [the danger of] being overcome by the disinclination to act and idleness, in order to insure that the activity is brought to completion. One is also firmly resolute with regard to all activities that have been undertaken. As long as [an activity] has not been completed and finished, a bodhisattva will in no way relinquish effort or fall into [a state of] dejection during that time.

One does not become fainthearted about matters that are lofty and important. Nor does one hold a low opinion of oneself. One encourages oneself by thinking, "I am capable and have the strength to accomplish these [goals]." One is confident in a large assembly when presenting arguments [to others] or responding to arguments made by others, or in the face of some other [kind of] difficult activity. One also does not become overly distressed even in the face of matters of consequence that require great exertion, much less those that [only require] minor [exertion]. These should be understood as the types of signs of a bodhisattva's spiritual lineage that occur in relation to the perfection of effort.

The Signs That Occur in Relation to the Perfection of Meditative Absorption [1.1.4.5]

These are the signs of a bodhisattva's spiritual lineage that occur in relation to the perfection of meditative absorption: In this case, a bodhisattva naturally avoids becoming greatly distracted when reflecting upon a Dharma topic. Whenever one sees or hears about remote forest retreats, places for sleeping and sitting that are [located] in outlying regions, that have the quality of being isolated from [other] human beings, and that are free of evil persons and suitable for engaging in inner contemplation, one develops a fervent eagerness for departure [from worldly life] and living in solitude, and thinks to oneself: "Departure [from worldly life] and living in solitude are such states of happiness!"

[A bodhisattva] is a person in whom the mental afflictions are naturally weak, the hindrances[138] [to meditative composure] are [naturally] weak, and

138. S: *nivaraṇam,* T: *sgrib pa.* This term is associated with a group of five obstacles to the attainment of one-pointed concentration. *AS* (p. 48): "There are five hindrances: (1) the

[the states of] indisposition[139] are [naturally] weak. Evil, improper thoughts do not greatly disturb the mind of [a bodhisattva] who has gone into seclusion and who is investigating the subjects that are of concern, nor do [such thoughts] remain [long in one's mind] when they have seized control [of it]. One is able to develop a state of loving-kindness very quickly even toward the class of beings that represent enemies, to say nothing of the class of friends and that of neutral persons.

Whenever one hears about or sees the suffering of sentient beings who are undergoing many different kinds of suffering, one generates an attitude of great compassion and takes action with all one's abilities and with all one's strength to remove the suffering of those beings. One is naturally desirous of benefiting sentient beings and of providing them with happiness. [A bodhisattva] remains steadfast of mind[140] with regard to those who have experienced misfortune, with regard to a relative in difficulty, with regard to someone experiencing distress relating to material wealth, with regard to someone who has undergone corporal [or capital] punishment,

---

hindrance of desire for sense pleasures (S: *kāmacchandam,* T: *'dod pa la 'dun pa*); (2) the hindrance of malice (S: *vyāpādaḥ,* T: *gnod sems*); (3) the hindrance of torpor and drowsiness (S: *styānamiddham,* T: *rmugs pa dang gnyid*); (4) the hindrance of excitation and regret (S: *auddhatyakaukṛtyam,* T: *rgod pa dang 'gyod pa*); and (5) the hindrance of doubt (S: *vicikitsā,* T: *the tshom*). A hindrance should be understood as [an entity that constitutes] a lack of clarity regarding all things that are of a virtuous nature." These are typically referred to in Tibetan as "the five hindrances to meditative composure" (T: *snyoms 'jug gi sgrib pa lnga*). These seven entities are counted as five obstacles because the pairs of (1) torpor and sleep and (2) excitation and regret are each considered as a single hindrance.

139. *A Collection of Determinations* (T: *rNam par gtan la dbab pa bsdu ba*, f. 119b) defines two principal forms of "indisposition" (S: *dauṣṭhulyam,* T: *gnas ngan len*): the indisposition of the outflows (S: *āsravadauṣṭhulyam,* T: *zag pa'i gnas ngan len*) and the indisposition that is related to the outflows (S: *sāsravadauṣṭhulyam,* T: *zag pa dang bcas pa'i gnas ngan len*). (For an explanation of the term "outflow," see note 196 below.) The first of these is an unfitness of body and mind that is caused by the latencies (S: *anuśayaḥ,* T: *bag la nyal*) or seeds of the mental afflictions. It is abandoned when one destroys all the mental afflictions and attains the status of an arhat. The second is defined as the subtle traces or imprints (S: *vāsanā,* T: *bag chags*) of the mental afflictions, which can only be abandoned by attaining the unsurpassed true and complete enlightenment of a buddha.

140. S: *dhṛtimān,* T: *mi dga' ba med pa*. This term literally means to be "possessed of firmness, satisfaction, or contentment." *BBhVy* (f. 15b) explains this statement as describing the sign that a bodhisattva possesses immeasurable equanimity (T: *btang snyoms tshad med kyi rtags*) in that "misfortune does not cause [a bodhisattva's] mind to waver by virtue of the fact that he or she avoids being overcome by sorrow and is able to maintain equanimity through enduring every kind of suffering."

imprisonment, or banishment, as well as with regard to those who have experienced any other similar kinds of misfortune.

[A bodhisattva] is intelligent, able to take up, retain, and comprehend Dharma teachings, and endowed with strong recollection. One is able to recall even something that was done or said long ago. One is also able to cause others to remember [such things]. These should be understood as the types of signs of a bodhisattva's spiritual lineage that occur in relation to the perfection of meditative absorption.

The Signs That Occur in Relation to the Perfection of Wisdom [1.1.4.6]

These are the signs of a bodhisattva's spiritual lineage that occur in relation to the perfection of wisdom: In this case, a bodhisattva is endowed with the innate wisdom [that is able] to take up all the branches of learning and all the objects that need to be realized. He or she is not slow-witted, weak of mind, or a type of person who is [easily] bewildered. He or she possesses the strength [of intellect] to reflect carefully on the various [points] that put a stop to the causes of lack of mindfulness.[141] These should be understood as the types of signs of a bodhisattva's spiritual lineage that occur in relation to the perfection of wisdom.

All of these should be understood as the types of distinct signs through which one can infer [that an individual possesses] the bodhisattva's spiritual lineage. However, with regard to the ascertainment of its actual existence, only the buddhas, the blessed ones, perceive [the presence of the Great Vehicle's spiritual lineage] directly.

Moreover, because the spiritual lineage of bodhisattvas is naturally endowed with good qualities, excellent, virtuous, and possessed of pure spiritual attributes, it serves as a cause for attaining the supreme, eternal, unsurpassed status of a tathāgata that is beyond ordinary thought and so difficult to gain. However, in its absence [the attainment of that goal] is not possible.

141. S: *pramādaḥ,* T: *bag med pa. AS* (p. 9): "What is lack of mindfulness? It is the failure to cultivate virtuous qualities and to guard the mind from impure qualities that occurs on the basis of [forms of] desire, hatred, and ignorance that are accompanied by laziness. Its action is to support the strengthening of nonvirtue and the decrease of virtue."

Four States of Mental Affliction and Four Advantages [1.1.5]

In addition, a bodhisattva naturally will continue to possess these pure spiritual attributes, as long as he or she does not become afflicted by some or all of the four states of mental affliction[142] that oppose those pure spiritual attributes. At those times when he or she does become afflicted [by any of them], those pure spiritual qualities will not be evident and he or she occasionally will be reborn in the lower realms.[143] But even when a bodhisattva is born in [one of] the lower realms, it should be understood that, due to the [Great Vehicle's] spiritual lineage, there is a great difference between him or her and the other sentient beings who have been born in the lower realms.

In this case, a bodhisattva is born in the lower realms only occasionally and once in a great while. Having been born in the lower realms, he or she quickly escapes from there. He or she does not undergo the kind of severe experiences of suffering associated with the lower realms that other beings born there must undergo. When [a bodhisattva] does undergo those lighter forms of suffering, he or she generates great aversion [for the suffering of the lower realms]. Moreover, urged by the spiritual lineage that is the cause for [ultimately developing] a buddha's great compassion, he or she also generates a compassionate attitude toward the suffering beings who have been born there. It should be understood that these are the kinds of characteristics that distinguish a bodhisattva who has been born in the lower realms from the other beings who have been born there.

142. S: *upakleśaḥ,* T: *nye ba'i nyon mongs pa*. This term is usually translated as "secondary mental affliction" in the sense of a nonvirtuous mental factor that is not a root mental affliction. *AS* (p. 47): "Excluding the [root] mental afflictions, all the other afflicted mental factors contained in the formations heap are secondary mental afflictions." *AS* and *PS* identify twenty secondary mental afflictions. *PSV* (p. 275) defines this term as follows: "They are called 'secondary mental afflictions' because they are related to the mental afflictions, they cause the mind to become disturbed, and they closely resemble the mental afflictions." The descriptions of the four states of mental affliction below clearly do not represent that sense of the term. *BBhVy* (f. 17a) describes the usage here as follows: "It is a 'state of mental affliction' because it causes the mind to become defiled."

143. S: *apāyaḥ,* T: *ngan song*. They are generally recognized as being of three kinds: rebirth in the hells, as a tortured spirit, or as an animal. The term is synonymous with "unhappy state" (S: *durgatiḥ,* T: *ngan 'gro*). See also Book III, chapter 6, text accompanying note 1520, where Asaṅga describes this term to mean literally the lower places that one is led to by wicked and crude conduct.

What are the four states of mental affliction that oppose a bodhisattva's pure spiritual qualities?

The first state of mental affliction is the condition of possessing strong mental afflictions and mental afflictions that continue for extended periods of time, due to having previously been a heedless person who repeatedly developed the mental afflictions. The second state of mental affliction is the [activity of] associating with evil companions that is engaged in by a foolish person who is lacking in judgment. The third state of mental affliction is the lack of freedom and the mental trepidation that is experienced by someone who is under the control of a superior, a king, a robber, or an adversary, and the like. The fourth state of mental affliction is the need to obtain a livelihood that is experienced by someone who does not have a means of subsistence.

Four Obstacles to Enlightenment [1.1.6]

There are also four causes that prevent a bodhisattva who possesses the [Great Vehicle's] spiritual lineage from attaining unsurpassed true and complete enlightenment.

What are the four?

In this case, a bodhisattva may not meet initially with a spiritual teacher, a buddha, or a bodhisattva who can reveal the unerring path to enlightenment. This is the first cause. Then again, even though a bodhisattva has met with a spiritual teacher, he or she may wrongly grasp the bodhisattva trainings and wrongly cultivate them. This is the second cause. Furthermore, even though a bodhisattva has met with a spiritual teacher and is cultivating the bodhisattva trainings unerringly, he or she may become lax in carrying out the practice. He or she may become lazy and fail to develop a strong and continuous form of effort. This is the third cause. In addition, even though a bodhisattva has met with a spiritual teacher, is cultivating the bodhisattva trainings unerringly, and has generated effort in relation to the practice, he or she may not possess faculties that are [fully] matured and may not have completed the [two] collections [that bring about] enlightenment, because he or she has not gained mastery of the [spiritual] qualities that are conducive to enlightenment for a [sufficiently] long period of time. This is the fourth cause.

Even if someone possesses the [Great Vehicle's] spiritual lineage, he or she will not attain enlightenment due to the deficiency [brought about] by these causes. On the other hand, if [all the necessary favorable conditions] are present, enlightenment will be attained. However, it should be understood that if someone does not possess the [Great Vehicle's] spiritual lineage, he or she will absolutely never, under any circumstances, attain enlightenment.

Within [Book I of] *The Stage of a Bodhisattva,* [known as] "The Object of Mental Application That Relates to the Support," this completes the first chapter, entitled "The Spiritual Lineage."

2

Generating Enlightenment Mind

Five Characteristics [1.2.1]

A bodhisattva's initial development of [enlightenment] mind is the first correct aspirational prayer[144] among all the correct aspirational prayers of a bodhisattva and the one that causes all the other correct aspirational prayers to be undertaken. Therefore, its essential nature is that of a correct aspirational prayer that occurs at the beginning.

The bodhisattva who is aspiring to [attain] enlightenment formulates the following thought and states the following words: "Oh, how I wish to attain unsurpassed true and complete enlightenment! May I be one who accomplishes the welfare of all sentient beings, and may I establish them in the [form of] nirvana that is an absolute termination[145] and in the knowledge of a tathāgata." In this way, he or she generates [enlightenment] mind by being one who desires both [to achieve] enlightenment and [to accomplish] the welfare of [all] sentient beings. Therefore, the generating of [enlightenment] mind is [a mental state] whose aspect is [a form of] desire. Moreover, the generating of [enlightenment] mind develops its desire by relying upon

144. S: *samyakpraṇidhānam,* T: *yang dag pa'i smon lam.* Book I, chapter 17, the section entitled "Aspirational Prayer" [I.17.13] identifies five types of aspirational prayers, of which correct aspirational prayer is the fourth. It is described there as "the brief or extensive form of aspirational prayer to obtain in the future all the spiritual qualities and all the virtuous qualities of a bodhisattva."

145. S: *atyantaniṣṭhaṃ nirvāṇam,* T: *shin tu mthar thug pa'i mya ngan las 'das pa. BBhVy* (f. 18b): "The welfare of those who possess the spiritual lineage of a listener or of a solitary realizer is accomplished by establishing them in [their respective forms of] nirvana. Therefore, the text states: 'May I establish them in the [form of] nirvana that is an absolute termination.'"

both enlightenment and the welfare of sentient beings as its objects;[146] it does not do so in the absence of [these two] objects. Therefore, the generating of [enlightenment] mind possesses both enlightenment and the welfare of sentient beings as its objects.

Because it is also a necessary antecedent[147] for the collection of all the roots of virtue that are conducive to enlightenment, the act of generating [enlightenment] mind is virtuous[148] and endowed with supremely virtuous qualities; it is excellent[149] and supremely excellent; and it is good[150] and

146. This paragraph addresses both the aspect (S: *ākāraḥ,* T: *rnam pa*) and the objects, or more literally the "mental supports" (S: *ālambanam,* T: *dmigs pa*), of the act of generating enlightenment mind. Its aspect is that it is a form of desire (S: *prārthanam,* T: *sgrub pa*). The Tibetan translation of this term seems to stem from the fact that this is a desire that seeks to *achieve* or *pursue* the goal of buddhahood. This aspect is also identified as a form of the mental factor "aspiration" (S: *chandaḥ,* T: *'dun pa*). *AS* (p. 6): "What is aspiration? It is the state of wanting to do what will enable you to gain possession of this or that desired object. Its action is that it serves as the support for initiating effort." The term translated here as "object" (S: *ālambanam,* T: *dmigs pa*) literally means "that [object] upon which the mind rests" and can refer generally to any object that is grasped by ordinary states of awareness. *AKB* (p. 19): "A mental support (S: *ālambanam,* T: *dmigs pa*) is that [entity] which is grasped by the mind and [its associated] mental factors." This term also refers to an object of spiritual contemplation or meditation. For example, Asaṅga uses the term to explain in great detail four main categories of meditation objects in his *Stage of a Listener* (*ŚBh,* pp. 192–258; see also note 1412 below). In the present context, the sense of the term is meant to indicate that one must reflect properly upon two objects in order to successfully develop a genuine form of enlightenment mind: (1) the duty to be concerned about the welfare of others and (2) the need to achieve supreme enlightenment in order to fulfill that concern.

147. S: *pūrvaṃgamaḥ,* T: *sngon du 'gro ba.* See note 106 above, where the same term is used in relation to the Great Vehicle's spiritual lineage.

148. S: *kuśalaḥ,* T: *dge ba.* There are numerous descriptions of this word, which is the principal term for both the noun "virtue" and the adjective "morally virtuous" (cf. *PSV,* p. 363). As an adjective, the Sanskrit term can mean variously "good," "healthy," "prosperous," "skillful," and even "clever." *PSV* (p. 275) states that "[The eleven virtuous mental factors] are virtues either because they are antidotes to lack of faith, and the like, or because they occur in concomitance with [any of] the [three] roots of virtue. The minds with which [these mental factors] are concomitant are also virtuous." *AKB* (p. 203): "[An entity] that has a favorable [karmic] maturation is said to be 'virtuous.'"

149. S: *bhadraḥ,* T: *bzang po.* This adjective can variously mean "auspicious," "fortunate," "causing prosperity," "excellent," "beautiful," and "good" (in the sense of being skillful at something). *BBhVy* (f. 19a): "[The act of generating enlightenment] is 'excellent' in that it achieves one's own welfare; it is 'supremely excellent' in that it accomplishes the welfare of others."

150. S: *kalyāṇaḥ,* T: *legs pa.* This adjective can mean "beautiful," "virtuous," "good," "benefi-

supremely good. It opposes all the misdeeds of body, speech, and mind that reside within sentient beings. Compared to all other virtuous, correct aspirations that relate to any of the mundane or transcendent aims, the bodhisattva's initial development of [enlightenment] mind is the unsurpassed and most supreme correct aspiration. In this way, the initial development of [enlightenment] mind should be understood in terms of these five characteristics: (1) essential nature, (2) aspect, (3) mental objects, (4) virtuous qualities, and (5) superiority.

Four Points [1.2.2]

As soon as a bodhisattva has generated enlightenment mind, he or she becomes one who has entered into the unsurpassed Great Vehicle [that leads to] enlightenment and also is counted among those who are referred to as bodhisattvas, according to the conventions of everyday usage.[151] Therefore, the act of generating [enlightenment] mind is considered to represent the point of entry. Once a bodhisattva has generated this mind, he or she will eventually attain unsurpassed true and complete enlightenment; this is not the case for anyone who has not generated [enlightenment mind]. Therefore, the act of generating enlightenment mind is the root of unsurpassed true and complete enlightenment.

It is through feeling compassion toward suffering beings and developing the intention to save them that a bodhisattva generates [enlightenment] mind. Therefore, the act of generating [enlightenment] mind is a natural outcome[152] of compassion. Moreover, it is by depending upon and relying upon this [enlightenment] mind that a bodhisattva applies him- or herself

cial," "salutary," and "right." *BBhVy* (f. 19b): "[The act of generating enlightenment] is 'good' in that it accords with and causes the attainment of one's own welfare; it is 'supremely good' in that it accords with the welfare of others and has the same nature [as that of causing one's own welfare to be attained]."

151. *BBhVy* (f. 19b) notes that this represents the conventional sense of who a bodhisattva is and then goes on to point out that the ultimate and pure form of generating the thought to attain unsurpassed true and complete enlightenment occurs when a practitioner attains the first of the ten ārya bodhisattva stages. At that point, one becomes a bodhisattva in the ultimate sense (S: *paramārthabodhisattvaḥ,* T: *don dam pa'i byang chub sems dpa'*).

152. S: *niṣyandaḥ,* T: *rgyu mthun pa*. This term literally means a consequence or result that "flows" naturally from a prior condition. It is also used to describe a specific kind of result, which is translated below as a "corresponding result" (S: *niṣyandaphalam,* T: *rgyu mthun pa'i 'bras bu*). See chapter 8, the section entitled "Five Kinds of Results" [I.8.2.2].

to the bodhisattva training, [which consists of acquiring] the spiritual qualities that are conducive to enlightenment and [carrying out] the activities that are beneficial to sentient beings. Therefore, the act of generating [enlightenment] mind serves as the support[153] for the bodhisattva training. In this way, the initial development of [enlightenment] mind should be understood in terms of (1) the way in which it is considered,[154] as well as in terms of its being (2) a root, (3) a natural outcome, and (4) a support.

Two Types of Enlightenment Mind [1.2.3]

The bodhisattva's initial development of [enlightenment] mind is also briefly of two types: (1) that which leads to emancipation and (2) that which does not lead to emancipation. Regarding them, the [form of enlightenment mind] that leads to emancipation is that which, once developed, perpetually engages [in pursuit of the ultimate goal] and does not turn back [from it at some later time]. The form that does not lead to emancipation is that which, once developed, does not perpetually engage [in pursuit of the ultimate goal] and does turn back [from it].

Moreover, the turning back of the [enlightenment] mind that was [previously] generated is of two types: (1) one that is permanent and (2) one that is not permanent. Regarding them, the one that is permanent is the [form of enlightenment] mind that, once reversed, does not develop again the intention to pursue enlightenment. By contrast, the one that is not permanent is the [form of enlightenment] mind that, after being reversed, does again develop repeatedly the intention to pursue enlightenment.

153. S *saṃniśrayaḥ,* T: *rten.* This term refers to something that is relied upon or resorted to in order to accomplish or pursue a goal. Cf. note 850 below, and associated text, where it is used to identify the four "supports" of a renunciant's spiritual life. The sense of the term here is virtually the same as that of the term *ādharaḥ* (T: *gzhi*), which was applied in the previous chapter not only to the act of generating enlightenment mind but also to the Great Vehicle's spiritual lineage and the spiritual qualities that are conducive to enlightenment. The related term *niśrayaḥ* (T: *rten*), translated as "foundation," is also identified there as a synonym for the same three objects (see note 104).

154. S: *saṃgrahaḥ,* T: *sdud pa.* The Tibetan translation does not easily convey the sense of this term as it is being used here. However, one sense of the verbal root *saṃgrah* is "to understand [something] as." The term here means that the initial act of generating enlightenment is considered the basis for calling someone a bodhisattva in the conventional sense and it is also considered the point of entry (S: *avatāraḥ,* T: *'jug pa*) into the Great Vehicle path.

Four Contributing Factors [1.2.4]

It should be understood that the act of generating [enlightenment] mind [is motivated] by four contributing factors, four causes, and four strengths.

What are the four contributing factors?[155]

In this case, a son of good family or daughter of good family may see an inconceivable and marvelous miraculous act or [an example of] the spiritual power[156] of a tathāgata or a bodhisattva, or may hear about it from a trustworthy person. Upon seeing or hearing this, he or she may have the following thought: "How great is the power of enlightenment! [It is a state] that [enables one] to see or hear about [the performance of] such [an example of] spiritual power or such a miraculous act by [a tathāgata] who resides in it or [a bodhisattva] who has undertaken to attain it." Having developed a strong feeling of devotion toward supreme enlightenment on the strength of having seen or heard about this spiritual power, he or she may then generate the thought to [achieve] supreme enlightenment. This is the first contributing factor for generating [enlightenment] mind.

He or she may neither see nor hear about [some display of] spiritual power but may hear [a discourse on] the true Dharma that relates to [the topic of] unsurpassed enlightenment. Having heard this teaching from the bodhisattva collection [of scriptures], he or she may then develop faith [toward unsurpassed enlightenment]. Having developed this faith and having developed a strong feeling of devotion toward the knowledge of a tathāgata on the strength of [the act of] listening to the true Dharma, he or she may then generate the intention to attain a tathāgata's knowledge. This is the second contributing factor for generating [enlightenment] mind.

He or she may not hear [a discourse on] the Dharma but may observe that the true Bodhisattva Dharma is on the verge of disappearing. Having observed this, he or she may then have the following thought: "Oh, how much the continued existence of the true Bodhisattva Dharma does serve to remove the suffering of immeasurable numbers of beings! Therefore, I must generate [enlightenment] mind in order to preserve the true Bodhisattva Dharma for a long time so that the suffering of those beings might

155. S: *pratyayaḥ,* T: *rkyen*. *BChKG* (f. 7b): "A contributing factor [is a quality that] awakens the efficacy of a cause."

156. S: *prabhāvaḥ,* T: *mthu*. Five forms of spiritual power make up the subject matter of chapter 5.

[continue to] be removed." Having developed a strong feeling of devotion toward the knowledge of a tathāgata on the strength of this very [desire to] preserve the true Dharma, he or she may then generate the intention to attain a tathāgata's knowledge. This is the third contributing factor for generating [enlightenment] mind.

He or she may not observe that the true Dharma is about to disappear but may observe that during a final era and a final age the constitution of beings [who live] in such an age is inferior in that they are afflicted by the following ten secondary mental afflictions: a high degree of ignorance, a high degree of shamelessness and absence of abashment, a high degree of jealousy and stinginess, a high degree of suffering, a high degree of indisposition, a high degree of mental afflictions, a high degree of misdeeds, a high degree of lack of mindfulness, a high degree of laziness, and a high degree of lack of faith. Having observed this, he or she may then have the following thought: "Oh, how great is the degeneracy[157] of the present era! During a time when [beings] are afflicted in this way, it is rare for anyone to generate even the intention to attain the lesser forms of enlightenment [that are pursued by] listeners and solitary realizers, much less for anyone to generate the intention to attain unsurpassed true and complete enlightenment. Therefore, let me generate [enlightenment] mind myself and may this also lead others to emulate me and generate [enlightenment mind] as well." Having developed a strong feeling of devotion toward supreme enlightenment on the strength of [the realization that the act of] generating [enlightenment] mind is so unlikely to occur during a final era, he or she may then generate the intention [to achieve] supreme enlightenment. This is the fourth contributing factor for generating [enlightenment] mind.

Four Causes [I.2.5]

What are the four causes?

Excellence of spiritual lineage is the first cause [that induces] a bodhisattva to generate [enlightenment] mind. Receiving assistance from a buddha, bodhisattva, or spiritual teacher is the second cause [that induces a

157. S: *kaṣāyaḥ,* T: *snyigs ma.* Book I, chapter 17, the section entitled "Knowledge of the World" [I.17.5] addresses the five traditional factors of degeneracy: (1) degeneracy of life span, (2) degeneracy of beings, (3) degeneracy of mental afflictions, (4) degeneracy of views, and (5) degeneracy of a kalpa. *AKB* (p. 183): "The life spans, etc., that are inferior following their decay are called degeneracies because they have become deteriorated."

bodhisattva] to generate [enlightenment] mind. Having compassion for sentient beings is the third cause [that induces] a bodhisattva to generate [enlightenment] mind. Lack of fear regarding the suffering of samsara and the suffering [caused by having to undertake] difficult activities, both of which are long-lasting, have many varieties, are intense, and occur uninterruptedly is the fourth cause [that induces a bodhisattva] to generate [enlightenment] mind.

Regarding these, it should be understood that excellence of spiritual lineage is acquired through the natural order of things.

The excellence of a [spiritual] friend should be understood as being of four types. In this case, for [the person who is] a bodhisattva's [spiritual] friend at the very outset not to be stupid or have a slow intellect, to be learned and discerning [in judgment], and not to be one who has taken on bad views is the first excellence of a [spiritual] friend. For him or her not to direct [a bodhisattva] to engage in lack of mindfulness[158] or provide any opportunity [for a bodhisattva] to engage in lack of mindfulness is the second excellence of a [spiritual] friend. For him or her not to direct [a bodhisattva] to engage in misdeeds or provide any opportunity [for a bodhisattva] to engage in misdeeds is the third excellence of a [spiritual] friend. For [a spiritual friend] not to turn [a bodhisattva] away from those qualities of faith, aspiration, undertaking, effort, or method that relate to a higher purpose and then cause that [bodhisattva] to pursue qualities of faith, aspiration, undertaking, effort, or method that relate to a lesser purpose is the fourth excellence of a [spiritual] friend. Examples [of this latter excellence] are not to turn [a bodhisattva] away from the Great Vehicle and cause him or her to pursue the Listeners' Vehicle or the Solitary Realizers' Vehicle; not to turn [a bodhisattva] away from [qualities] that derive from meditation and cause him or her to pursue those that derive from reflection; not to turn [a bodhisattva] away from [qualities] that derive from reflection and cause him or her to pursue those that derive from [the activity of] listening [to Dharma teachings]; not to turn [a bodhisattva] away from [qualities] that derive from [the activity of] listening [to Dharma teachings] and cause him or her to pursue administrative activities [in support of the spiritual community]; not to turn [a bodhisattva] away from [qualities] that derive from [the practice of] morality and cause him or her to pursue [the practice of] generosity; [as well as other situations] in which [a spiritual friend] does not

158. See above, note 141.

turn [a bodhisattva] away from similar kinds of superior [spiritual] qualities and cause him or her to pursue [other] similar kinds of lesser qualities.

A bodhisattva becomes one who possesses an abundance of compassion toward sentient beings due to four causes. Among the limitless world spheres of the ten directions there are world spheres in which suffering is not found. However, a bodhisattva takes birth in a world sphere where there is suffering and where suffering is found, not one where suffering is absent. He or she observes that others have been affected, stricken, and overcome by some particular form of suffering. He or she is also affected, stricken, and overcome by some particular form of suffering. Moreover, he or she observes that either others, or [oneself], or both [others and oneself] have been affected, stricken, and overcome by many different kinds of long-lasting, intense, and continuous forms of suffering. Therefore, on the basis of his or her spiritual lineage, due to his or her natural goodness, and because of these [four] circumstances that are perceived and these [four] factors, a bodhisattva develops a [form of] compassion that can be small, middling, or great, [and he or she does so] without having engaged in the continuous practice [of spiritual exercises].

Once a bodhisattva has manifested compassion toward sentient beings, there are four causes that keep him or her from become afraid of or alarmed by even samsaric suffering that is long-lasting, of many varieties, intense, and continuous, much less [samsaric suffering] that is small. He or she is naturally courageous, steadfast, and strong. This is the first cause. He or she is learned, disposed to proper reflection, and possesses strong deliberative powers. This is the second cause. He or she possesses strong devotion toward unsurpassed true and complete enlightenment. This is the third cause. He or she possesses strong compassion toward sentient beings. This is the fourth cause.

Four Strengths [1.2.6]

What are the four strengths?

They are (1) the strength that relates to oneself,[159] (2) the strength that

159. S: *adhyātmabalam,* T: *nang gi stobs*. While the Sanskrit adjective *adhyātma* is routinely rendered as "inner" in Tibetan, it literally means "own" or "belonging to self" (MW, p. 23); hence, it is translated here as "that which relates to oneself." In fact, the Derge (T: *sDe dge*) and Choné (T: *Co ne*) Tengyur editions read *nang gi stobs,* but the Peking and Tok Palace editions have *rang gi stobs*.

relates to others, (3) the causal strength, and (4) the strength that derives from practice.

Regarding these, the desire for unsurpassed true and complete enlightenment that is developed through one's own abilities is called the bodhisattva's strength for generating [enlightenment] mind that relates to oneself. By contrast, the desire for unsurpassed true and complete enlightenment that is caused to arise through the influence of another person is called the bodhisattva's strength for generating [enlightenment] mind that relates to others. The previous practice[160] by a bodhisattva of virtuous [spiritual] qualities associated with the Great Vehicle [tradition] that now[161] quickly leads him or her to generate [enlightenment] mind merely by seeing a buddha or bodhisattva or hearing them being praised, let alone by hearing the true Dharma [being taught] or seeing [an example of] spiritual power, is called the causal strength for generating [enlightenment] mind. The long-term cultivation of virtuous activities by a bodhisattva in this life—[activities] such as serving a true spiritual being and listening to and reflecting upon the true Dharma—is called the strength for generating [enlightenment] mind that derives from practice.

Regarding this [topic], whether a bodhisattva relies upon these four contributing factors and four causes either in their entirety or only partially, if he or she develops [enlightenment] mind by means of the strength that relates to oneself and the causal strength in combination or either one individually,[162] then it will be firm, strong, and unwavering. However, the [enlightenment] mind that arises through the strength that relates to others and the strength that derives from practice should be understood as one that will not be firm.

160. That is, the form of practice relating to the path of the Great Vehicle that was carried out in a former life or lives.

161. That is, in the present life.

162. Both Sanskrit editions have only *samastabhyām* (the dual instrumental of the adjective that means "the whole" or "the two [strengths] combined"), for which the Tibetan is *tshogs pa*. This would suggest that the act of generating enlightenment mind will be firm only when both the strength that relates to oneself and the causal strength are present. However, both the Tibetan translation and *BBhVy* (f. 27b) state that it does not matter whether these two strengths are present in combination or only individually, suggesting that the original Sanskrit should read *samastavyastabhyām*.

Four Causes That Turn One Away [1.2.7]

There are four causes that turn a bodhisattva away from [enlightenment] mind.

What are the four?

He or she does not possess the [Great Vehicle's] spiritual lineage. He or she is under the control of an evil companion. He or she has little compassion for sentient beings. He or she is afraid of the suffering of samsara that lasts for a long time, has many varieties, is intense, and occurs uninterruptedly. He or she fears it and is alarmed by it to a very great degree, and falls into a state of terror [about it]. These four causes that turn one away from [enlightenment] mind should be understood as being the opposite of the four causes for developing [enlightenment] mind that were described above at length.

Two Marvelous and Wonderful Qualities [1.2.8]

A bodhisattva who has newly generated a firm [form of enlightenment] mind possesses two marvelous and wonderful qualities that are not shared by the world at large.

What are the two?

He or she embraces all sentient beings in the manner that a spouse[163] [is embraced] and yet is untainted by the fault of embracing a spouse. Regarding this [topic], the fault of embracing a spouse is the following. It is the two qualities of developing afflicted forms of affection and hostility [respectively] in response to favorable or injurious actions [that are carried out] by one's spouse. Neither of these [faults] is found in a bodhisattva.

163. S: *kaḍatra* (also *kalatra*), T: *chung ma*. The principal meaning of the Sanskrit original is "wife," and that is also what the Tibetan translation means. *BHSD* (p. 165) suggests that the meaning could include the broader sense of "family" or "servants." I have chosen to translate it here with the gender-neutral term "spouse." The verbal root "to embrace" (S: *parigrah*, T: *yongs su 'dzin pa*) is meant figuratively and also has the sense of "to assist." *BBhVy* (ff. 28a–28b) states: "The object that the [ordinary] world embraces is the limited and finite object of their own sons, wives, etc. A bodhisattva embraces the entire sphere of sentient beings that reaches to the ends of space in the manner that a spouse [is embraced]. This is a marvelous and wonderful quality." See also Book III, chapter 2, which is entitled "Embracing."

Two Salutary Attitudes [1.2.9]

A bodhisattva who has newly generated a firm [enlightenment] mind exhibits two salutary forms of superior attitude[164] toward sentient beings.

What are they?

They are the beneficial superior attitude and the superior attitude that relates to happiness. Regarding these, the beneficial superior attitude is the desire to cause [sentient beings] to turn away from opportunities [to engage in] nonvirtuous [actions] and become established in opportunities [to engage in] virtuous [actions]. The superior attitude that relates to happiness is the desire to provide those sentient beings who have fallen into misfortune, who have no protector, and who have no shelter with the things that will assist them and free them from their state of affliction.

Two Forms of Application [1.2.10]

A bodhisattva who has newly generated a firm [enlightenment] mind employs two [kinds of] application: (1) the application that relates to [one's] superior attitude and (2) the application that relates to [one's] conduct. The application that relates to [a bodhisattva's] superior attitude is the daily strengthening of the superior attitude that wishes to benefit [sentient beings] and make [them] happy. The application that relates to [a bodhisattva's] conduct is both [one's] daily activities [that seek] to ripen the spiritual qualities of a buddha within oneself and, relying upon the application that relates to [a bodhisattva's] superior attitude, [one's daily] activities [that seek] to provide sentient beings with as much benefit and happiness as [one's] power and strength will allow.

Two Great Doors for Gaining Virtuous Qualities [1.2.11]

There are two great doors by which a bodhisattva who has newly generated a firm [enlightenment] mind gains virtuous qualities: (1) the application that

164. S: *adhyāśayaḥ*, T: *lhag pa'i bsam pa*. Book II, chapter 3, which is devoted entirely to this topic, describes fifteen types of superior attitude. The term is also defined there as follows: "The conviction, understanding, and determination regarding a buddha's qualities, which are preceded by faith and the discernment of entities, are referred to as a 'superior attitude.'"

pursues one's own aim in order to achieve unsurpassed true and complete enlightenment and (2) the application that pursues the aims of others in order to liberate all sentient beings from every form of suffering. As with [the explanation for] the two sources of virtuous qualities, a similar [description should be made with regard to what are referred to as] the two great stores of virtuous qualities and the two immeasurable heaps of virtuous qualities.

Two Forms of Superiority [1.2.12]

From the time that [a bodhisattva] first generates [enlightenment] mind, there are two forms of superiority regarding the acquisition of virtue for the sake of enlightenment by one who has newly generated [enlightenment] mind as compared with the acquisition of virtue by anyone other than that [bodhisattva]. [They are] (1) the superiority that relates to the cause and (2) the superiority that relates to the result. The acquisition of virtue by a bodhisattva is indeed the cause for unsurpassed true and complete enlightenment, and [supreme enlightenment] is the result of that [acquisition of virtue]. This is not the case for the acquisition of virtue by all those other listeners and solitary realizers, much less [for the acquisition of virtue] by any beings other than [the listeners and solitary realizers]. Therefore, the acquisition of virtue by bodhisattvas is abundantly superior to the acquisition of virtue by all others, both in terms of its causal nature and in terms of its result.

Two Benefits of Generating Enlightenment Mind [1.2.13]

These are the two benefits of generating [enlightenment] mind that are gained by a bodhisattva who has newly generated a firm [enlightenment] mind: (1) As soon as [one] has generated [enlightenment] mind, [one] becomes worthy of being venerated[165] by all sentient beings; [one] becomes worthy of honor;[166] [one] becomes a field of merit and is like a father to all beings. (2) One also acquires the merit that will keep one from being harmed.

Regarding this [latter point], the merit that keeps [a bodhisattva] from

165. S: *dakṣiṇīyaḥ,* T: *yon gnas*. See note 123.

166. S: *gurubhūtaḥ,* T: *bla mar gyur pa*. See note 122.

being harmed is such that the bodhisattva who possesses it is safeguarded in a manner that is twice as great as the [form of] protection [experienced] by a wheel ruler.[167] Because it is a form of protection that is always present, neither malicious beings, nor harmful spirits, nor demons, nor local guardian spirits are able to harm [such a bodhisattva], even when he or she is asleep, or in an excited[168] or inattentive state of mind.

Even after a bodhisattva has taken on a different life, he or she meets with little harm and is by nature free of illness through the possession of that merit. He or she also does not experience harm that is long-lasting or intense.

When [a bodhisattva] is striving physically or verbally [to accomplish] the welfare of beings or [to carry out] activities on behalf of sentient beings, or when [a bodhisattva] is teaching the Dharma, [his or her] body does not experience excessive weariness, [his or her] recollection does not become clouded, and [his or her] mind does not become impaired.

A bodhisattva who is established in the [Great Vehicle's] spiritual lineage is a person in whom [the condition of] indisposition[169] is naturally weak. And once he or she has generated [enlightenment] mind, then [that bodhisattva] becomes one in whom [the condition of] indisposition is much more weak, in terms of both indisposition of the body and indisposition of the mind.

The mantra formulas and *vidyā* spells [that are meant] to ward off the disease, misfortune, and contagion of sentient beings but that prove unsuccessful in the hands of someone else do succeed when carried out by that [bodhisattva]. Needless to say, those [mantra formulas and *vidyā* spells] that are successful [in the hands of others will also succeed when carried out by that bodhisattva].

[A bodhisattva who has newly generated a firm form of enlightenment

167. S: *cakravartī,* T: *'khor los sgyur ba*. This expression is the term for a universal emperor. *AKB* (p. 433): "The wheel rulers are those whose nature it is to exercise sovereignty by means of a [magical] wheel." The text further notes that, according to the *Prajñaptiśāstra,* there are four kinds: a wheel ruler who possesses a golden wheel and has dominion over all four continents; one who possesses a silver wheel and governs three continents; one who possesses a copper wheel and governs two continents; and one who possesses an iron wheel and governs only one continent.

168. S: *matta,* T: *myos pa*. This adjective can variously mean "excited by joy," "intoxicated," or "insane."

169. See note 139.

mind] possesses an abundance of patience and gentleness; he or she endures the pain inflicted by others and does not inflict pain upon others. He or she is also greatly distressed upon learning[170] that someone is inflicting pain upon another person. The intensity of his or her secondary mental afflictions such as anger, envy, guile, dissembling,[171] and the like has been blunted. Those weakened forms that occasionally develop quickly disappear.

The kinds of fears, sources of terror, scarcity of provisions, and other faults that can occur in an inhabited region, as well as the misfortunes that are caused by both human beings and [malevolent] spirits, do not occur [when a bodhisattva who has newly generated a firm enlightenment mind] is residing there. Any [such calamities] that have already arisen cease [when a bodhisattva who has newly generated a firm enlightenment mind resides there].

If a bodhisattva who has newly generated [enlightenment] mind should take birth on a particular occasion in the hells that represent a level of the lower realms, he or she will ever so quickly escape from that hell because of possessing the merit that keeps one from being harmed. He or she will also only experience the slightest form of suffering there and will generate both an extremely strong form of aversion [toward the suffering of samsara] and the mental state of compassion toward those [other hell] beings.

These are [some of] the numerous kinds of benefits that a bodhisattva who has newly generated [a firm enlightenment] mind experiences because he or she possesses the merit that keeps one from being harmed.

Within [Book I of] *The Stage of a Bodhisattva,* [known as] "The Object of Mental Application That Relates to the Support," this completes the second chapter, entitled "Generating [Enlightenment] Mind."

170. S: *upalabhya*. The Tibetan translates this as "upon seeing or hearing."

171. S: *mrakṣaḥ,* T: *'chab pa*. *AS* (p. 8): "What is dissembling? It is a form of ignorance that causes an individual who has been properly asked about his or her objectionable acts to conceal them. Its action is to provide support for regret and for remaining in a discontented state."

3

One's Own and Others' Aims

What is the bodhisattva practice [that is undertaken] by those bodhisattvas who have generated [enlightenment] mind in the manner [that was just described]?

In sum, the phrase "bodhisattva practice" refers to the combination of everything that is included [in the following three categories]: (1) [those subjects] in relation to which the bodhisattvas train themselves, (2) the manner in which they train themselves, and (3) those [individuals] who train themselves.

What, then, are [the subjects] in relation to which bodhisattvas train themselves?

They train themselves in relation to seven subjects.[172]

What are the seven subjects?

They are (1) one's own aim, (2) others' aims, (3) the meaning of reality, (4) spiritual power, (5) the ripening of sentient beings, (6) the ripening of a buddha's qualities in oneself, and (7) true and complete enlightenment.

Summary verse:

> One's own and others' aims, the meaning of reality,
> Power, the twofold ripening of beings

172. S: *sthānam,* T: *gnas.* In this context, this term means a "subject matter" or an "object of interest." Sthiramati refers to these seven in *MSAVṛBh* as the five subjects (S: **pañca vastu,* T: *dngos po lnga*) that constitute the "mental supports of the training" (S: **śikṣālambanam,* T: *bslab pa'i dmigs pa*) in the sense of being the aims or concerns that a bodhisattva bears in mind as he or she undertakes to cultivate the trainings. The seven topics mentioned here are counted as five by combining the two aims and the two forms of ripening, respectively, into single subjects.

And of a buddha's qualities in oneself,
And the seventh is supreme enlightenment.

What are one's own and others' aims?

In sum, one's own aim and that of others should be understood as having ten aspects: (1) being exclusive, (2) being related to others, (3) being linked to what is beneficial, (4) being linked to happiness, (5) being included within a cause, (6) being included within a result, (7) being related to this life, (8) being related to a future life, (9) being perpetual, and (10) not being perpetual.

The Qualities of Exclusivity and of Being Related to Others [1.3.1–2]

Regarding these [ten aspects], the quality of being exclusive as it relates both to one's own aim and to the aims of others should be fully understood and then rejected by a bodhisattva, because [this quality] violates and is not in agreement[173] with the bodhisattva's code of conduct. The [nine] remaining [aspects of one's own aim and that of others] should [all] be practiced.

The following are examples of a bodhisattva's [pursuit of] one's own aim that are exclusive and that he or she should fully understand and reject: (1) the seeking after and experiencing of forms of enjoyment by [a bodhisattva] who is desirous of [indulging in] pleasure for him- or herself; (2) the seeking after and retaining of Dharma [instructions] that buddhas and bodhisattvas have taught, by [a bodhisattva] who exercises stinginess regarding the Dharma; (3) the way of life that is engaged in by [a bodhisattva] who is desirous of [being reborn in] a celestial realm[174] in which he or she initiates [the practices of] morality and effort and undertakes [to cultivate] meditative absorption and wisdom in order [to attain rebirth in] a celestial realm; (4) the worshipping of a tathāgata *caitya*[175] by [a bodhisattva] who is desirous of

173. *BBhVy* (f. 33a): "'Not in agreement' (S: *ananurūpam*, T: *'tsham pa ma yin pa*) [here] means to be at odds with the attainment of enlightenment by lacking the qualities [that contribute to] the attainment of enlightenment."

174. S: *svargaḥ*, T: *mtho ris*. In native Tibetan literature this term is usually understood to mean "the status of [being reborn as] a god or a human being." However, the original sense and the way it is meant here is that of rebirth in a divine realm.

175. T: *mchod rten*. A funeral monument in the form of a raised mound that contains the

[gaining] the result of worldly material things[176] and who engages in this act as a means of attaining worldly material things; (5) the meaningless[177] and false utterings made to others by [a bodhisattva] who is desirous of [acquiring] material gain in which [he or she] tries to please [those persons] by telling them that they possess manifold good qualities in order to [obtain] material gain and procure material gain; (6) the attracting of a group [of spiritual followers] in a manner that is contrary to the Dharma and that is not in keeping with the Dharma by [a bodhisattva] who is desirous of obtaining acts of service [from those followers] for him- or herself and [who attracts a following] in order to obtain [such] acts of service; (7) the freeing of beings who were the servants of others from their state of servitude, so that [they may enter into] a state of servitude to you; (8) the freeing of beings who were bound in prison from their imprisonment only to bring them under your control so that they may be made to perform work for you; (9) the freeing of beings who are threatened by others with the dangers of undergoing [judicial] punishment and the like[178] in order to make them subject to the same dangers from you; and (10) the remaining in a state of ease during this life by a bodhisattva, without engaging in careful reflection about the welfare of others. These [descriptions] should be understood as [examples of activities in which] one's own aim is being pursued exclusively. These and other similar kinds of bodhisattva activities that are understood to represent the exclusive pursuit of one's own aim are [circumstances] that a bodhisattva should fully understand and reject.

---

relics of a holy being. See below, the first section of Book I, chapter 16, where this type of devotion is discussed.

176. S: *lokāmiṣam,* T: *'jig rten gyi zang zing.* The original Sanskrit term *āmiṣam* can mean "flesh," "an object of enjoyment," "desire," or a "gift." In the present context, the compound *lokāmiṣam* might be rendered as something like a "desirable worldly object." *BBhVy* (f. 33b) glosses the term as "[material] gain" (S: *lābhaḥ,* T: *rnyed pa*).

177. S: *apārtham* (?), T: *don med pa.* Both Sanskrit manuscripts seem to have the incorrect reading of *mamārtham,* which means "for my benefit." *BBhVy* (f. 34a) also cites the root text as *don med pa* and explains that this adjective indicates that this speech is a form of useless chatter (S: *pralāpaḥ,* T: *bre mo'i gtam*); it then goes on to identify this speech as flattery (S: *lapanā,* T: *kha gsag*), one of five forms of wrong livelihood (S: *mithyājīvaḥ,* T: *log pa'i 'tsho ba*). See note 705 below for a further description of flattery.

178. S: *daṇḍādi,* T: *chad pa la sogs pa.* Literally, the Sanskrit reads "the rod, etc." The rod is a symbol of judicial authority and is understood to include the imposition of such penalties as physical punishment, imprisonment, monetary fines, and the confiscation of property. *BBhVy* (f. 34b) glosses the term "etc." to mean "loss of livelihood."

On the other hand, a bodhisattva's [practice of] generosity and patience, whether they are preceded by compassion, dedicated to enlightenment, or [carried out] for the sake of [attaining rebirth in] a celestial realm, should be understood as always being [instances in which] one's own aim is related to others.[179] Therefore, excluding those types [of activities] that were presented [earlier], all other [forms of the pursuit of] one's own aim that are the opposite of those [examples] should be understood as [instances in which one's own aim] is related to the aims of others.[180]

The following [two cases] are [examples of] a bodhisattva's activities that exclusively carry out the aims of others and that a bodhisattva should fully understand and reject: (1) the generosity of [a bodhisattva] who holds a mistaken view, who does not consider that anything will come [in future lives from acts of generosity], and who does not believe [that the act of generosity will yield any] fruit; and (2) the teaching of Dharma to others by [a bodhisattva] whose morality has been damaged and who does not [him- or herself] cultivate the practice.

The following should also be understood as [examples in which] the aims of others are being pursued exclusively: (1) the carrying out of virtuous qualities that relate to a lower stage by [a bodhisattva] who has transcended such a lower stage,[181] as well as (2) [the carrying out of virtuous qualities that are related to a lower stage] by a bodhisattva who is skilled at turning back[182] the meditative absorptions. In the latter case, even after having remained in the meditative absorptions, such [a bodhisattva] can avert [the natural

179. S: *parasambaddha,* T: *gzhan dang 'brel ba*. This statement is meant to indicate that, unlike morality, effort, meditative absorption, and wisdom, acts of generosity and patience are never exclusively related to one's own aim because, regardless of one's motivation, they always contain some form of benefit to others.

180. And, as such, they represent activities that are proper for a bodhisattva to pursue.

181. *BBhVy* (f. 35b) identifies such a bodhisattva as either one who is a nonreturner or one who is an arhat. Such a person carries out virtues associated with the desire realm solely for the sake of results that will occur in that same life because they will enable him or her to assist others more effectively. In that sense, such virtuous activities are done exclusively for the sake of accomplishing the aims of others.

182. S: *dhyānavyāvartana,* T: *bsam gtan sgyur ba*. The sense of this expression is explained in the very next sentence. Normally, achieving and abiding in any of the meditative absorptions generates a form of "unvarying" karma (S: *aniñjyakarma,* T: *mi g.yo ba'i las*) that will cause one to be reborn in the corresponding level of the form realm. A bodhisattva can attain the power to be reborn in the desire realm despite having cultivated the meditative absorptions.

power of] the meditative absorptions [to bring about rebirth in the higher realms] and, through [the power of] prayer, be born anywhere in the desire realm that he or she may wish [to be born]. [Two more examples are] (3) the performance of beneficial activities for the sake of manifold sentient beings by a bodhisattva who has attained mastery of the controlling powers[183] and [who carries out those activities] by [sending forth] a great variety of emanations into the ten directions; and (4) the performance of immeasurable forms of beneficial activities for the sake of an immeasurable number of sentient beings by a *muni* and a tathāgata who has completed [the perfection of] his own aim and [who carries out those activities] on the basis of the [one hundred and forty] unique qualities of a buddha,[184] which include the [ten] powers, the [four] forms of intrepid confidence, and so forth.

Regarding these [six activities that accomplish the aims of others in an exclusive manner], the first two that were presented are [instances] that should be fully understood by a bodhisattva and rejected. However, [a bodhisattva] should train [him- or herself] with an ever-increasing degree of diligence in relation to the other [four examples that accomplish] the aims of others in an exclusive manner. Therefore, with the exception of those [six] types [of activities], all [other instances in which] bodhisattvas [pursue] the aims of others—including those that are the opposite [of the first two examples[185]]—represent [activities] that are also related to one's own aim. [And, as such,] a bodhisattva should train [him- or herself] in relation to them as well.

183. Ten controlling powers (S: *daśavaśitāḥ,* T: *dbang bcu*) are mentioned in the *Sutra on the Ten Stages* (*DB,* p. 46) among the qualities possessed by a bodhisattva who has reached the eighth ārya stage. Asaṅga briefly describes them in Book II, chapter 4, in the section entitled "The Pleasurable State That Is Free of Signs and Also Free of Effort" [II.4.10].

184. The one hundred and forty unique qualities of a buddha are described in the final two chapters of this work. They are listed below in the opening paragraph of Book III, chapter 5.

185. The two opposite forms are described in *BBhVy* (f. 36a): "The practicing of generosity by [a bodhisattva] who holds excellent [philosophical] views and the teaching of Dharma by [a bodhisattva] whose morality is excellent." When the activities of generosity and teaching the Dharma are characterized in this way, they no longer represent inferior activities that relate exclusively to the aims of others; therefore, they become activities that relate to the aims of others in a manner that also accomplishes one's own aim.

The Quality of Being Linked to What Is Beneficial [1.3.3]

What is a bodhisattva's [pursuit of both] one's own and others' aims that is linked to what is beneficial?

In brief, it should be understood to have five aspects: (1) the characteristic of being irreproachable, (2) the characteristic of being favorable, (3) [the form that] relates to this life, (4) [the form that] relates to future lives, and (5) [the form that] promotes tranquility.

Regarding these, whatever acquisition of virtue or accumulation of virtue, whether small or great, that a bodhisattva carries out, as well as [whatever] acquisition of virtue or accumulation of virtue, whether small or great, that he or she causes others to adopt, leads them [to carry out], introduces them to, and establishes them in, should be understood as the characteristic of being irreproachable as it relates to a bodhisattva's [pursuit of both] one's own and others' aims that is linked to what is beneficial.

Whatever happiness a bodhisattva might provide for him- or herself or for another that is free of affliction, whether it be a state of happiness that arises from the providing of assistance[186] or a state of happiness [that arises from any] of the meditative absorptions, this should be understood as the characteristic of being favorable as it relates to a bodhisattva's [pursuit of both] one's own and others' aims that is linked to what is beneficial.

There are [forms of] a bodhisattva's [pursuit of both] one's own and others' aims that are beneficial to this life but not future lives; [forms that are beneficial] to future lives but not this one; [forms that are beneficial] both to this life and to future lives; and [forms that are] beneficial neither to this life nor to future lives. These four [forms of a bodhisattva's pursuit of both] one's own and others' aims should be recognized, in the same order and in the appropriate manner, as being related to the four ways of taking up what is right.

186. S: *upakaraṇasukham,* T: *yo byad kyi bde ba.* The first word in this compound, *upakaraṇa,* has various meanings, including "the doing of something beneficial for another," an "instrument" or "implement," or a "means of subsistence" (MW, p. 195). The sense of an "instrument" is the basis for the Tibetan rendering of *yo byad;* however, *BBhVy* (f. 36b) glosses the term here as referring to "the arising of a variety of extensive forms of well-being that are experienced in the desire realm." Therefore, in this instance the expression should be understood to mean any substantial act of assistance or the providing of material assistance that brings about physical and/or mental comfort to an individual.

What are the four ways of taking up what is right?[187]

There are ways of taking up what is right that bring happiness in the present but have a ripening in the future that consists of suffering;[188] [ways of taking up what is right] that bring suffering in the present but have a ripening in the future that consists of happiness;[189] [ways of taking up what is right] that bring happiness in the present and also have a ripening in the future that consists of happiness;[190] and [ways of taking up what is right] that bring suffering in the present and also have a ripening in the future that consists of suffering.[191] These categories should be understood in the manner [in which they are presented] in the sutras.

Regarding this [topic], in brief the worldly and transcendent [spiritual] qualities that either constitute nirvana, cause nirvana to be attained, or are conducive to [the attainment of] nirvana constitute [the fifth aspect of] a bodhisattva's [pursuit of both] one's own and others' aims that is linked to what is beneficial—[namely, the one described as the form that] promotes tranquility. [Moreover, this aspect] should be understood as the most outstanding and unsurpassed [of the five].

187. S: *dharmasamādānam,* T: *chos yang dag par blang ba*. *BBhVy* (f. 37a) glosses this term as follows: "'Taking up what is right' is the state of continually engaging in activities in order to develop virtuous qualities and to attain favorable [karmic] ripenings in the future. [In short,] it is [the practice of] virtuous conduct." Given this description, the first and fourth forms that are described here do not represent genuine examples of taking up what is right in a way that is beneficial.

188. *BBhVy* (f. 37a): "The first [way of taking up what is right] is that in which you engage in misdeeds while experiencing [physical] pleasure and mental happiness in the present on the strength of your having repeatedly practiced nonvirtuous activities in the past." Obviously, this is an improper form of conduct that is meant to be avoided.

189. Ibid.: "The second [way of taking up what is right] is that in which you engage in good deeds such as morality and the like [in this life] on the strength of [having] a different existence [from those previous lives in which you commonly practiced misdeeds] even though it requires [physical] pain and mental discomfort to do so, because you possess strong mental afflictions and you have not practiced [virtue] regularly."

190. Ibid.: "The third [way of taking up what is right] is that in which you are able to engage in things of a virtuous nature with [physical] ease and mental happiness, because [of the fact that] your mental afflictions are weak and you previously practiced [virtue] with regularity."

191. Ibid.: "The fourth [way of taking up what is right] is that in which you unwillingly engage in misdeeds through being forced to do so by others, or [you engage in misdeeds for some other reason] in a manner that is physically and mentally painful."

The Quality of Being Linked to Happiness [1.3.4]

What is a bodhisattva's [pursuit of both] one's own and others' aims that is linked to a state of happiness?

In brief, it should be understood as being made up of five types of happiness. The five types of happiness are (1) the causal [aspect of] happiness; (2) the experiential [aspect of] happiness; (3) the [aspect of] happiness that is an antidote to suffering; (4) the [aspect of] happiness that cuts off feelings; and (5) the [aspect of] happiness that is freedom from harm.

Regarding [the first of] these, the two types of faculty and object that are related to pleasant experiences, the contact that is caused by them[192] and that will lead to a pleasant experience, and any form of karma that will have a desirable result either as a seen event[193] or in some future life—all taken together as one—are called "the causal [aspect of] happiness." There are no [causal elements] beyond these [three] and no more than these.

The experience[194] that is favorable to body and mind and is produced by those very three causes included in the causal aspect of happiness, irrespective of the abatement of suffering,[195] is called "the experiential [aspect of] happiness." Moreover, it is of two types: (1) that which is related to the out-

192. That is, the type of contact that is caused by the two preceding forms of faculty and object. Contact (S: *sparśaḥ,* T: *reg pa*) is the mental factor that occurs when there is a convergence of three entities: faculty, object, and consciousness. Thus, faculty and object are two of its principal causes. Cf. *AS* (p. 6): "What is contact? It is the determination of a faculty's modification that occurs upon the convergence of a trio [of entities]. Its action is to provide the basis for feeling."

193. S: *dṛṣṭadharmaḥ,* T: *mthong ba'i chos.* The form of karma that ripens in the same life as the one in which it was committed is known by the phrase "[karma] that will be experienced as a seen event" (S: *dṛṣṭadharmavedanīyam,* T: *mthong ba'i chos la myong bar 'gyur ba*).

194. S: *anubhavaḥ,* T: *myong ba.* This is the essential nature of the entities that make up the feeling heap (S: *vedanāskandhaḥ,* T: *tshor ba'i phung po*), which is the second of the five heaps. *AS* (p. 2): "What is the essential characteristic of feeling? [Feeling is that which has] experience as its essential characteristic. [That is,] experience is the essential quality by which [feelings] experience continually the results that are the maturation of virtuous and nonvirtuous karma."

195. S: *duḥkhapraśamānapekṣam* (D reads *duḥkhapraśamanāpekṣam*), T: *sdug bsngal rab tu zhi ba la ma ltos par.* This phrase may be interpreted as an assertion by Asaṅga that pleasurable forms of experience are distinct in nature from unpleasant ones. Vasubandhu (*AKB,* p. 330) notes with disapproval that certain Buddhist scholars reject such a notion. Nāgārjuna, for example, reveals that he does not believe the two types of experience are distinct when he declares (*RA,* ch. 4, v. 47): "Pleasant feelings of the body are just the abatement of pain; /

flows and (2) that which is free of the outflows.[196] Regarding them, [pleasant experiences] that are free of the outflows can be both a quality of [an ārya] who is still undergoing training[197] and a quality of [an arhat] who is beyond [the need to undergo any further] training.[198]

Further, [pleasant experiences] that are related to the outflows are those of the three realms—[that is to say,] those that are related to the desire, form, and formless realms. All these [feelings] of the three realms can further be distinguished, in the appropriate manner, as being of six types according to the basis[199] [from which they arise], ranging from those that arise from contact with the eye to those that arise from contact with the mind.[200]

Mental [pleasures] consist of conception and are mere creations of thought." See also *Inner Science,* pp. 114–120.

196. "Outflow" (S: *āsravaḥ,* T: *zag pa*) is a synonym for the more common term "mental affliction" (S: *kleśaḥ,* T: *nyon mongs*). *AK* (ch. 1, vv. 4, 5ab): "[All] entities are [made up of] those that are related to the outflows (S: *sāsaravāḥ,* T: *zag pa dang bcas pa rnams*) and those that are free of the outflows (S: *anāsravāḥ,* T: *zag pa med pa rnams*). Conditioned entities, excluding [the truth of] the path, / Are those related to the outflows, because the outflows increase in relation to them. // Those free of the outflows are the truth of the path, as well as the three types of unconditioned entity." In general, all the entities that are included within the noble truth of suffering and the noble truth of the origination of suffering are related to the outflows. Those that form the noble truth of the path are free of the outflows. Asaṅga gives the following description of the term "outflow" (*AS,* p. 49): "There are three types of outflows: the desire outflows (S: *kāmāsravaḥ,* T: *'dod pa'i zag pa*) [i.e., all the mental afflictions of the desire realm with the exception of ignorance]; the existence outflows (S: *bhāvāsravaḥ,* T: *srid pa'i zag pa*) [i.e., all the mental afflictions of the form and formless realms with the exception of ignorance]; and the ignorance outflows (S: *mohāsravaḥ,* T: *ma rig pa'i zag pa*) [i.e., the ignorance that is associated with all three realms]. They are called 'outflows' because they cause the mind to be sent forth in a stream-like manner. How, then, do they do this? The desire outflows cause it to be sent forth in a manner that is directed outwardly; the existence outflows cause it to be sent forth in a manner that is directed inwardly; and the ignorance outflows constitute the basis for causing it to be sent forth in both of these ways."

197. S: *śaikṣaḥ,* T: *slob pa.*

198. S: *aśaikṣaḥ,* T: *mi slob pa.*

199. S: *āyatanam,* T: *skye mched.* Buddhist doctrine formulates twelve bases; six are the inner bases of the eye, ear, nose, tongue, body, and mind; and six are the outer bases of [visible] form, sound, smells, tastes, tangible objects, and entities (i.e., the objects of mind consciousness). These two sets of bases are recognized as the inner and outer causes, respectively, from which the six primary forms of consciousness arise. Here the reference is to the six inner bases. Asaṅga states (*AS,* p. 15): "What is the meaning of 'basis'? The meaning of basis is that of being a source for the arising of consciousness."

200. This formulation is known in Buddhist literature as "the six collections of feelings" (S: *ṣaḍvedanākāyāḥ,* T: *tshor ba'i tshogs drug*).

These six types [of feelings] are also [understood as being subsumed within] two types: corporeal and mental. Regarding [this latter classification], [the feelings] that are related to the five collections of [sense] consciousness are corporeal, and the ones that are related to mind consciousness are mental.[201]

The notion of well-being that arises in relation to the mere quieting of an unpleasant experience, due to the abatement of [any of] the many diverse and varied forms of unpleasant [experiences] that can occur—such as cold, heat, hunger, thirst, and the like—through counteracting that cold, heat, hunger, thirst, and the like, is called "the aspect of happiness that is an antidote to suffering."

The state of composure that causes the cessation of conceptions and feelings[202] is called "the aspect of happiness that cuts off feelings."

In brief, the happiness that is freedom from harm is of four types: (1) the happiness of departure; (2) the happiness of separation; (3) the happiness of tranquility; and (4) the happiness of complete enlightenment.

[The happiness] of a person who has left home properly and entered the homeless state [motivated] by faith, and who has thereby gained freedom

201. Sthiramati explains in his commentary to Vasubandhu's *Summary of the Five Heaps* (*PSV,* pp. 269–270): "[Feelings] can also be combined into two groups, according to whether the basis [i.e., faculty] upon which they depend is corporeal or mental. Because the faculties of the eye, ear, nose, and tongue do not exist apart from the body, because they have resistance, and because they are aggregates [i.e., in the sense of being a composite of atomic particles], they are included within the body and are described as 'corporeal' (S: *kāyika,* T: *lus kyi*). Therefore, the experiences that arise from contact with the eye, ear, nose, tongue, and body are said to be corporeal. Experiences that arise from contact with the mind are described as 'mental' (S: *caitasika,* T: *sems kyi*), because they depend upon a basis that is exclusively mental in nature."

202. This state of composure is usually called simply "the state of composure that is a cessation" (S: *nirodhasamāpattiḥ,* T: *'gog pa'i snyoms par 'jug pa*). *PS* (p. 238): "What is the state of composure that is a cessation? [It is] the cessation of inconstant minds and mental factors, as well as a portion of the constant minds, that is preceded by a form of attention that conceives of abiding [in a state of ease]; and it is achieved by someone who has overcome desire for the Sphere of Nothingness and who has set out to rise above the Peak of Existence." This state of composure can only be entered by a nonreturner ārya who has overcome desire for three of the four levels of the formless realm and an arhat. It is generated because it represents a temporary state of peace in which one can escape from the weariness caused by samsaric feelings and conceptions. It is called a cessation because it is a state of composure in which the six active forms of consciousness and the afflicted mind become inactive and remain suspended until one arises from it. It is a state of one-pointed concentration associated with a specific element of the Peak of Existence, which is the highest of the four levels that make up the formless realm. See also *Inner Science,* pp. 316–318.

from the multiple forms of suffering that arise from attachment to the householder state, is called "the happiness of departure." The joy and ease that is born of separation [from the desire realm and that occurs] in the first meditative absorption through the separation [that comes about] through having abandoned the objects of desire[203] as well as evil and nonvirtuous qualities, is called "the happiness of separation." [The happiness that occurs] in the second meditative absorption and above, through having quelled [both] deliberation and reflection,[204] is called "the happiness of tranquility." The happiness that arises both through having permanently freed oneself from all the mental afflictions and through having attained complete and perfect realization of [all] entities that need to be known as they truly are is called "the happiness of complete enlightenment."

The causal aspect of happiness is identified as [a form of] happiness in that it is the cause of happiness; it does not represent happiness in terms of its essential nature. The experiential aspect of happiness is not [a form of happiness] by virtue of its causal nature; however, [it *does* represent happiness] in terms of its essential nature. The aspect of happiness that is an antidote to suffering is not [a form of happiness] either by virtue of its causal nature or in terms of its essential nature; rather, it is [a form of] happiness only in the sense of quieting [some form of] suffering—[which is to say,] by virtue of the fact that it brings about the removal of [some specific instance of] suffering. The aspect of happiness that cuts off feelings is not [a form of happiness] either by virtue of its causal nature, in terms of its essential nature, or in the sense of bringing about a removal of suffering; however, it is [a form of] happiness in that it is a state [of meditative composure] that one abides in for a limited period of time and that constitutes the cessation of suffering in its highest sense, as [indicated by Buddha] in the phrase:

203. S: *kāmāḥ,* T: *'dod pa rnams;* i.e., the five sense objects.

204. *AS* (p. 10): "What is deliberation (S: *vitarkaḥ,* T: *rtog pa*)? It is a mental discourse that investigates [an object] on the basis of wisdom and/or volition. It is also a coarseness of mind. What is reflection (S: *vicāraḥ,* T: *dpyod pa*)? It is a mental discourse that examines [an object] on the basis of wisdom and/or volition. It is also a fineness of mind." These two mental factors play an essential role in the process of attaining the first meditative absorption. In that context they are referred to as "corrective limbs," because through applying them the practitioner is able to abandon the faults of the desire realm, including desire for sensory pleasures, malice, harmfulness, and [nonvirtuous] deliberative thoughts. However, after the first absorption has been attained, their occurrence is considered an obstacle in that they are no longer needed and they have an unsettling effect on the mind's ability to maintain unbroken one-pointed concentration.

"Whatever feeling [is experienced] here is [a form of] suffering." The final form[205] included in the [category of] happiness that is [described as] freedom from harm—that is, the happiness of complete enlightenment—represents happiness in the sense that it is the permanent cessation in the future[206] of that very same suffering in its highest sense [that was just mentioned] and, as a seen event,[207] the permanent removal of the forms of indisposition present in one's being[208] that are related to the mental afflictions. The remaining [three forms] of [the category of] happiness that is [described as] freedom from harm should be understood as the happiness that is freedom from harm in that they conform to, are supportive of, or are conducive to that very [fourth and] final form.

Regarding this [topic], the bodhisattva should provide for sentient beings [those forms of] happiness that support what is beneficial, not [those forms] that support what is harmful. Moreover, after having fully and accurately realized with his or her wisdom the [forms of] happiness that support what is harmful, [a bodhisattva] should cause beings to give up any desire for them and, to the best of his or her ability, strive to draw them away and divert them from them. Through reliance upon skillful means, a bodhisattva should also provide for sentient beings what is beneficial [for them], even though it may be followed by [some form of] unpleasantness [in the near term] and they might not desire it because it is accompanied by [physical] pain and mental unhappiness. [Similarly,] through reliance upon skillful means, [a bodhisattva] should also draw sentient beings away from and divert them from what is harmful [for them], even though it is followed

205. That is, the fourth and final aspect of the category of happiness referred to as "the happiness that is freedom from harm."

206. This form of happiness will occur in the future in the sense that it will be achieved when the individual who attains enlightenment enters the nirvana without remainder.

207. That is, the happiness of complete enlightenment that occurs while one is still living.

208. S: *āśrayaḥ,* T: *rten.* This term often refers to the physical body. Cf. *AKB* (p. 154): "The basis is the physical body together with the faculties (S: *āśrayo hi sendriyakāyaḥ;* T: *gnas* [also *rten*] *ni dbang po dang bcas pa'i lus*)." In the present context, however, *BBhVy* (f. 39a) glosses the phrase "present in one's being" (S: *āśrayagatasya,* T: *rten la yod pa*) as "that which is present in [one's] consciousness." Similarly, Tibetan literature regularly uses the phrases "physical basis" (T: *lus rten*) and "mental basis" (T: *sems rten*) when it is necessary to distinguish between these two aspects of an individual's being. The condition of "indisposition" (S: *dauṣṭhulyam,* T: *gnas ngan len*) also has both a physical and a mental aspect. See note 139.

by [some form of] pleasantness [in the near term] and they might desire it because it is accompanied by [physical] pleasure and mental satisfaction.

What is the reason for this?

It should be understood with certainty that providing for [sentient beings] what is beneficial [for them even though] it is accompanied by [some form of] unpleasantness and turning them away from what is harmful [for them even though] it is accompanied by [some form of] pleasantness is [done] so that sentient beings [will experience greater forms of] happiness in the future. Therefore, it should be recognized that the bodhisattva who desires what is beneficial for sentient beings also, in fact, desires happiness [for them]. Whoever provides what is beneficial [for beings] should also be recognized as providing [them with] happiness, because what is beneficial represents a cause and what is happiness represents a result. Therefore, anything that possesses [the quality of] being beneficial for sentient beings should be understood as possessing [the quality of] bringing them happiness.

With regard to this [overall topic], a bodhisattva should, unhesitatingly and [with unwavering devotion to this] as one's sole aim, [seek to] provide sentient beings with whatever [forms of] karma both [are recognized as] having a desirable result—either as a seen event or in a future life—and are included in the causal aspect of happiness; with whatever [forms of] happiness are [of the type that is] an antidote to suffering; with whatever [forms of] happiness are [of the type that] cuts off feelings; and with whatever [forms of] happiness are [of the type that] is freedom from harm. [The reason for this is that] these [forms of happiness] are both beneficial and free of reproach. [A bodhisattva] should not, however, provide [sentient beings] with either [those forms of] the experiential aspect of happiness or [those forms of] object, faculty, or contact contained within the causal aspect of happiness that are afflicted [in nature] in [the sense] that they will lead to a state of affliction, and that are, [therefore,] reprehensible,[209] harmful, and unwholesome. On the other hand, a bodhisattva should, to the utmost of [his or her] ability and strength, pursue [for others] whatever [forms of the experiential aspect of happiness and whatever forms of object, faculty, or contact contained within the causal aspect of happiness] are not afflicted [in nature] in [the sense] that they will lead to a state of affliction, [and that are, therefore,] free of reproach, beneficial, and wholesome. Similarly,

209. S: *sāvadyam,* T: *kha na mo tho ba dang bcas pa*. This is a synonym for the more familiar adjective "nonvirtuous" (S: *akusulaḥ,* T: *mi dge ba*).

[a bodhisattva] should also engage in them him- or herself, train him- or herself in them, and experience them for him- or herself. This should be understood as the bodhisattvas' [pursuit of] one's own and others' aims that is linked both to what is beneficial and to what [represents a state of] happiness. There are no [points relating to this topic] beyond these, and there are no [points] other than these.

The Aspects of Being Included within a Cause or a Result [1.3.5–6]

What are [the aspects of] a bodhisattva's [pursuit of] one's own and others' aims that are included within a cause or a result?

In brief, it should be understood that there are three types of causes and three types of results: (1) the causes of the maturations, (2) the results of the maturations, (3) the causes of merit, (4) the results of merit, (5) the causes of wisdom, and (6) the results of wisdom.

The Eight Maturations [1.3.5.1, I.3.6.1]

What are the maturations?

In brief, there are eight kinds of [karmic] maturation: (1) excellence of life span; (2) excellence of physical appearance;[210] (3) excellence of family; (4) excellence of power; (5) the quality of having one's speech accepted; (6) the quality of being regarded as eminent;[211] (7) the quality of being a man; and (8) the eighth is [excellence of] strength.

A bodhisattva's excellence of life span is the quality of possessing a long life span and the condition of remaining [alive] for a long period of time. Excellence of physical appearance is the qualities of having a superior physical form, being very good-looking, and having a pleasing appearance. Excellence of family is the quality of being born into an eminent family. Excellence of power is the quality of possessing much property and the condition of having a large number of supporters as well as that of having a large

210. S: *varṇasaṃpat,* T: *kha dog phun sum tshogs pa.* The Sanskrit noun *varṇaḥ* has many meanings, including "color," "facial complexion," "skin color," "caste," and the like. Here the sense is that of having an attractive physical form.

211. S: *maheśākhyatā,* T: *dbang che bar grags pa.* Literally, "the quality of having the name 'great lord,'" the expression also means to be "highly distinguished or eminent" (MW, p. 802).

retinue.[212] To be trustworthy and credible, to be considered an authoritative arbiter for persons who are involved in every manner of legal dispute, to be someone who does not cause any loss to property that has been entrusted [to him or her] because [he or she] is free of deceit and guile and would not commit fraud by [misrepresenting] brass [as something more valuable than it actually is] or commit theft by [using false] weights, and the like, to be someone who does not break [his or her] word—and for these reasons to be someone whose word is [well] received by others—is called "the quality of having one's speech accepted." For [a bodhisattva] to have great fame and renown, and to be recognized in the world for such things as prowess, strength, steadfastness, skill, proficiency, good conduct, or [for being] the most exceptionally accomplished at [any of] various categories of crafts and occupations—and for these reasons to be esteemed, shown respect, venerated, honored, and revered by a great multitude of persons—is called "the quality of being regarded as eminent." The quality of being a man is the state of being a male [human being] and [the condition of being a person] who possesses the male [sex] faculty. The excellence of strength that occurs naturally [includes] the qualities of [being someone who experiences] few troubles, being a type [of person] who is free of illness, and [being someone who can put forth] great exertion.

The Causes of the Eight Maturations [1.3.5.1.1]

What are the causes of the maturations?

[Practicing] avoidance of harm[213] toward beings and [developing] the attitude of [wanting to] avoid doing harm are causes for [obtaining] excellence of life span. Giving light and [giving] bright[214] clothing are causes for [obtaining] excellence of physical appearance. Overcoming pride toward

212. S: *parivāraḥ,* T: *'khor. BBhVṛ* (f. 52b): "A retinue is made up of children, wife (or wives), male and female servants, workers, and the like."

213. S: *ahiṃsā,* T: *mi 'tshe ba.* This has always been viewed as an essential principle of the Buddhist teaching. Cf. Āryadeva's *Four Hundred Verses,* ch. 12, v. 23ab: "In short, the tathāgatas declared the Dharma to be avoidance of harm." Candrakīrti's commentary (f. 194a) identifies this term with the practice of the ten virtuous karmic paths and adds that it also includes any and all forms of benefit that are provided to others. This is the same term that is often rendered as "nonviolence."

214. S: *śucivastra,* T: *gos sar pa.* The Sanskrit adjective *śuci* can mean "bright" or "clean." *BBhVy* (f. 44b): "Giving clothing makes [a person] attractive by covering up the private

beings is a cause for [obtaining] excellence of family. Giving to beggars and to those who lack material necessities[215] is a cause for [obtaining] excellence of power. Speaking the truth and cultivating the avoidance of divisive speech, harsh speech, and idle talk are causes for [obtaining] the quality of having one's speech accepted. Veneration of the Three Jewels and veneration of those worthy of honor[216] by one who has made prayers of aspiration[217] that he or she might gain a variety of spiritual qualities in the future are causes for [obtaining] the quality of being regarded as eminent. Admiration for male qualities and aversion toward the female state, regarding that [female state] as having disadvantages, and instilling in others the two causes for attaining the male state—[namely,] (1) reversing the desire for the female state that is held by women who delight in female qualities and (2) [causing others], in a proper manner,[218] to set free those men who have been seized and are being led away to have their male faculty destroyed—are causes for [obtaining] the quality of being a man. Physically carrying out yourself on behalf of others whatever duties they may have or assisting them [in their work], with all your strength and ability, in a proper manner, and without being careless; and providing beings with food [such as] boiled grain, porridge, rice gruel, and drink that will strengthen and invigorate them, are causes for [obtaining] excellence of strength. These should be understood as the eight types of causes for [obtaining] the eight types of [karmic] maturation.

regions [of his or her body]. Expressing the [adjective] 'bright' indicates the giving of clothing that possesses color [i.e., dye] and means to give clothing that is unsullied."

215. S: *upakaraṇam,* T: *yo byad.* The original Sanskrit can mean such things as "beneficial act," "implement," and "means of subsistence." The translation "material necessity" is intended to suggest the latter two meanings. Cf. also note 186.

216. S: *guruḥ,* T: *bla ma.* See note 122. *BBhVy* (f. 45b): "To venerate [those worthy of honor] should be understood as meaning to engage in [any of] a wide range of activities, such as conducting oneself in a manner that pleases them and performing [forms of] service."

217. S: *praṇidhānam,* T: *smon lam.*

218. S: *dharmena,* T: *chos dang mthun pas. BBhVy* (f. 46a): "[Causing them to be set free] 'in a proper manner' means to avoid using force and [to purchase their freedom] by paying a ransom or to cause [their captors] to set them free willingly by teaching them the Dharma."

The Conditions That Insure the Effectiveness of the Causes [1.3.5.1.2]

Furthermore, there are, in brief, three conditions that augment these causes so that they will bring about an acquisition of maturations that are complete, abundant, and extensive.

What are the three conditions?

They are (1) purity of mind, (2) purity of application, and (3) purity of field. Regarding these, the purity of attitude, in the sense of dedicating these virtue roots[219] to unsurpassed true and complete enlightenment; the intensity of attitude, in the sense of carrying out [these virtue roots] with deep sincerity and great clarity[220] [of mind]; the joy [that arises] at the sight of one who is an exemplary Dharma follower; and the extensive reflection and deliberation, at every moment of each day, upon just those things that are in accord with these [virtue roots] are what is called purity of mind.

Regarding these [conditions], cultivating [these virtue roots] for a long period of time, performing them continually, performing them diligently, extolling [them] to others in order to cause them to take up those virtuous acts that have not been undertaken, extolling [them to others] in order to encourage [them to continue performing] those [virtuous acts] that have been undertaken, causing those very persons to settle into [the performance of] these virtue roots, and causing them to become firmly established in [their performance] are what is called purity of application.

Regarding [these conditions], in brief it should be understood that the purity of field [comes about] through (1) the correct performance of the

219. That is, the virtue roots that are gained by carrying out the eight types of deeds described in the previous paragraph.

220. S: *prasādaḥ*, T: *dang ba*. This term is used to describe one of three types of faith. *AS* (p. 6): "What is faith? It is firm belief (S: *abhisaṃpratyayaḥ*, T: *mngon par yid ches pa*), clarity [of mind] (S: *prasādaḥ*, T: *rab tu dang ba*), and aspiration (S: *abhilāṣaḥ*, T: *mngon par 'dod pa*) [that is felt] toward [entities] that exist, that possess good qualities, and that are capable of being achieved. "Clarity of mind" in particular is a reverential attitude toward entities that possess virtuous qualities, especially the Three Jewels. *PSV* (p. 284): "The type of faith that is called clarity of mind is a quality that opposes turbidity of mind. Therefore, if the mind is accompanied by it, the turbidity of the [root] mental afflictions and the secondary mental afflictions will not arise. It is called 'clarity of mind' because the presence of faith causes the mind to become clear and bright."

application and (2) the stability of the properly [executed] application in relation to [the generating of] a result.[221]

The Results That Can Be Achieved through the Maturations [1.3.6.1.1]

Regarding this [topic], what are the results of the maturations?

A bodhisattva who is endowed with excellence of life span [is able to] apply him- or herself for a long period of time to [everything] that pertains to virtue[222] and to accumulate a great quantity of the virtue roots that pertain to one's own aim and that of others. This is the result that relates to excellence of life span.

A bodhisattva who is endowed with excellence of physical appearance is liked by a great multitude of persons. Because of this quality of being liked, he or she becomes someone whom others wish to approach. And since the quality of having an attractive physical form causes [others] to come directly into his or her presence, a great multitude of persons will also regard his or her speech as something that ought to be heard. This should be understood as the result that relates to a bodhisattva's excellence of physical appearance.

A bodhisattva who is endowed with excellence of family is thought highly of by a great multitude of persons and is also revered and praised. Because of being thought highly of, revered, and praised, whatever matter [that bodhisattva] urges beings to undertake, they are overwhelmed by his or her majesty and set about doing it quickly; they do not voice [any] opposition or take action to avoid doing it. This should be understood as the result that relates to a bodhisattva's excellence of family.

A bodhisattva who is endowed with excellence of power attracts beings and [spiritually] ripens them through [practicing] generosity. This should be understood as the result that relates to a bodhisattva's excellence of power.

221. *BBhVy* (f. 47b) states that the term "field" (S: *kṣetram,* T: *zhing*) as it is being used here refers to specific qualities of the practitioner's attitude and his or her application and that these are referred to as a field because, like a farmer's field, they "yield abundant and excellent results." It also glosses the phrase "the correct performance of the application" as meaning that the virtuous actions are carried out at the appropriate time, and the phrase "the stability of the properly [executed] application in relation to [the generating of] a result" as meaning that the properly executed application is certain to produce the desired results.

222. S: *kuśalapakṣaḥ,* T: *dge ba'i phyogs.* Literally, "that which is on the side of virtue." See also note 101.

A bodhisattva whose speech is accepted attracts beings and [spiritually] ripens them through [practicing] agreeable speech, beneficial conduct, and sameness of purpose.[223] This should be understood as the result that relates to a bodhisattva's quality of having his or her speech accepted.

A bodhisattva who is regarded as eminent benefits beings by assisting them with a variety of activities that need to be done. Because of this benefit, beings feel a sense of obligation and, out of respect and gratitude toward [that bodhisattva], they very quickly carry out his or her bidding in a courteous and respectful manner. This should be understood as the result that relates to a bodhisattva's quality of being regarded as eminent.

A bodhisattva who is a male and who possesses the male faculty is a [suitable] vessel for [the development of] all [spiritual] qualities, [for carrying out] all [the forms of spiritual] activities [that require] strenuous exertion, and [for generating] all [the forms of] discernment[224] that pertain to [entities] that need to be known. He also is dauntless and his movements are not restricted with regard to traveling, conversing, residing,[225] and sharing

223. Generosity (S: *dānam,* T: *sbyin pa*), agreeable speech (S: *priyavaditā,* T: *snyan par smra ba*), beneficial conduct (S: *arthacaryā,* T: *don spyod pa*), and sameness of purpose (S: *arthasamānatā,* T: *don mthun pa*) constitute the four principles for attracting a following (S: *catvāri saṃgrahavastūni,* T: *bsdu ba'i dngos po bzhi*). See chapter 9 below for a discussion of generosity and chapter 15 for a discussion of the remaining three qualities.

224. S: *pravicayaḥ,* T: *rab tu rnam par 'byed pa*. This noun describes the essential property of the mental factor that is usually translated as "wisdom." *AS* (p. 6): "What is wisdom (S: *prajñā,* T: *shes rab*)? It is the discernment (S: *pravicayaḥ,* T: *rab tu rnam par 'byed pa*) of entities in relation to an object that is being closely examined." While the aim of this mental factor is to discern things correctly, it does not always succeed. *PSV* (p. 280) further explains this mental factor as "an awareness that makes distinctions (S: *vivekāvabodhaḥ,* T: *so sor rtogs pa*), correctly or incorrectly, with regard to entities whose general and specific characteristics have the appearance of being mixed together." This description indicates that the principal quality of "wisdom" is the discerning of discrete qualities that would otherwise remain indistinct or muddled; however, it also points out that this mental factor does not always function accurately. Thus, it is imprecise to always interpret *prajñā* as meaning "wisdom." In fact, Buddhist literature also uses the term "afflicted wisdom" (S: *kliṣṭaprajñā,* T: *shes rab nyon mong can*)—clearly something of an oxymoron in such an English rendering—to describe the types of mental afflictions that are called mistaken views. For example, Vasubandhu describes the erroneous belief in a real, personal self—known technically as "the view of the perishable collection" (S: *satkāyadṛṣṭiḥ,* T: *'jig tshogs la lta ba*)—as "the afflicted wisdom that regards the five grasping heaps as 'I' and 'mine.'" This phrase might be rendered more accurately as "the afflicted form of discernment that [mistakenly] regards the five grasping heaps as 'I' and 'mine.'"

225. S: *samvāsaḥ,* T: *'grogs pa*. The original Sanskrit term includes both the sense of residing

meals with other persons at any time, [as well as] with regard to dwelling alone in secluded places. This should be understood as the result that relates to a bodhisattva's quality of being a male.

A bodhisattva who is endowed with excellence of strength does not become weary from undertaking to acquire virtuous qualities or from undertaking to help sentient beings. He or she is one who has developed effort, one whose effort is strong, and one whose supernatural knowledge[226] takes effect swiftly. This should be understood as the result that relates to a bodhisattva's excellence of strength.

These are the eight results of the eight [karmic] maturations that favor and support bodhisattvas [in their efforts] to benefit sentient beings and to develop the [spiritual] qualities of a buddha. The bodhisattva who has become established in the maturation results is also competent and able to accomplish a great number and variety of aims that pertain to sentient beings. [Other beings] will also become disciples who are willing to be directed to carry out activities according to his or her wishes—that is to say, [to carry out activities] that relate to the accomplishing of their own aims. [On the other hand,] if a bodhisattva is able [to help beings], but his or her disciples are unwilling to act as they have been directed, then the activities that he or she performs on behalf of [other] beings will be neither abundant nor favorable, and he or she will be unable to accomplish the aims of others. [Similarly,] if a bodhisattva is neither competent nor able, then even though other beings become disciples who are willing to be directed [by him or her] to carry out activities that relate to the accomplishing of their own aims, the activities that [such a] bodhisattva performs on behalf of [other] beings will be neither productive nor favorable, and he or she will be unable to accomplish the aims of others. Therefore, it is [only] when both [of these conditions] are present and both [of these conditions] exist that a bodhisattva's activities on behalf of beings will be productive and favorable such that he or she is capable of accomplishing the aims of others. A bodhisattva who finds him- or herself in circumstances [where both of these conditions are present] will quickly ripen the qualities of a buddha in him- or herself, and he or she will quickly ripen [other] beings in relation to the three vehicles.

---

in the same dwelling with others and that of associating with others (MW, p. 1114). The Tibetan translation suggests only the more restricted sense of "associating" with others.

226. See chapter 5 for a discussion of six types of supernatural knowledge (S: *abhijñā,* T: *mngon par shes pa*).

He or she will also attain unsurpassed true and complete enlightenment and liberate those sentient beings who have been [spiritually] ripened.

Because the eight types of maturation results enable bodhisattvas to bring about the benefit and happiness of sentient beings in this way, the samsara that for all [other] sentient beings is barren and meaningless becomes something that for [bodhisattvas] is productive and endowed with great meaning.

Merit and Wisdom [I.3.5.2, I.3.6.2]

What is merit? What is wisdom?

In brief, three of the [six] perfections are called "merit": (1) the perfection of generosity, (2) the perfection of morality, and (3) the perfection of patience. Wisdom, however, is made up of [only] one of the perfections—that is, the perfection of wisdom. The perfection of effort and the perfection of meditative absorption should [both] be understood to have [forms that] promote merit and [forms that] promote wisdom.[227]

The [forms of] effort that are relied upon to practice generosity, to undertake and preserve morality, to cultivate the [four] immeasurable [practices] of loving-kindness and the rest, and [other forms] that are of the same kind [as these] make up the effort that promotes merit. On the other hand, (1) the [form of] effort that is relied upon to apply oneself to the [three types of] wisdom—[namely,] those that derive from learning, reflection, and meditation; (2) [the form of effort that is relied upon] to develop skill regarding the heaps,[228] skill regarding the constituents,[229] skill regarding the bases,[230] skill regarding dependent origination, and skill regarding [what constitute] proper and improper conditions;[231] (3) [the form of effort that is relied upon]

227. The word that is being translated here as "promote" is the adjectival ending *pakṣya* (T: *phyogs*) that was previously rendered as "conducive to." See also note 101.

228. These are the five heaps (S: *skandhaḥ,* T: *phung po*) of form, feeling, conception, formations, and consciousness.

229. This is a reference to the formulation of eighteen constituents (S: *dhātuḥ,* T: *khams*) of the six faculties, the six forms of consciousness, and six objects of those forms of consciousness. See *PSV,* pp. 353–355.

230. These are the six inner and six outer bases (S: *āyatanam,* T: *skye mched*) that represent the two main conditions that govern the arising of consciousness.

231. S: *sthānāsthānam,* T: *gnas dang gnas ma yin pa*. See Book III, chapter 6, the section entitled "The Power of Knowledge regarding Proper and Improper Conditions" [III.6.2.1].

to investigate [the noble truth of] suffering as to the way in which it constitutes suffering, [the noble truth of] origination as to the way in which it constitutes origination, [the noble truth of] cessation as to the way in which it constitutes cessation, and [the noble truth of] the path as to the way in which it constitutes the path; and (4) [the form of effort that is relied upon] to examine and investigate, as they truly are, those entities that are virtuous or nonvirtuous, [as well as] those entities that arise dependently and are [variously] classified as being black or white, blameworthy or beyond reproach, [qualities] to which one ought to devote oneself or to which one ought not to devote oneself, and [qualities] that are inferior or excellent are the ones that are called the effort that promotes wisdom.

The [forms of] meditative absorption that are relied upon to practice generosity, to undertake and preserve morality, to cultivate the [four] immeasurable practices of loving-kindness and the rest, and [other forms of meditative absorption] that are of the same kind [as these] make up the meditative absorption that promotes merit. On the other hand, (1) the [form of] meditative absorption that is relied upon to apply oneself to the [three types of] wisdom—[namely,] those that derive from learning, reflection, and meditation; (2) [the form of meditative absorption that is relied upon] to develop skill regarding the heaps, etc.—[that is, the remainder of] the entire [description] is to be stated in the same manner as was previously done with regard to effort.

This represents a brief [presentation] of the six types of merit and wisdom. However, it should be understood that [the description] would be immeasurably large if an [exhaustive] classification of every one of their individual forms was made.

The Causes of Merit and Wisdom [1.3.5.2.1]

What are the causes of merit and wisdom?

In brief, it should be understood that there are three causes of [both] merit and wisdom: (1) the aspiration to acquire, maintain, and increase merit and wisdom; (2) the conditions that are advantageous and favorable [to the acquisition, etc., of merit and wisdom]; and (3) the prior cultivation of merit and wisdom. With regard to these [causes], the conditions that are favorable [to the acquisition, etc., of merit and wisdom] are the state in which adverse conditions are not present or near at hand as well as the state in which propitious conditions are present or near at hand. Regarding this [point], erring instructions about merit and wisdom that occur through having met with an evil companion or erring notions that come about through erring forms of attention[232] are called "the presence of adverse conditions." [The conditions that are] the opposite of this and that represent the side of [spiritual] purity[233] should be understood to constitute the presence of propitious conditions. In addition, those conditions that remove and prevent the arising of obstacles for someone who has undertaken to acquire, maintain, and increase merit and wisdom are said to be "the favorable conditions" for a bodhisattva's [pursuit of] merit and wisdom. It should be understood that the absence of any of these three causes prevents merit or wisdom from being generated.

The Results of Merit and Wisdom [1.3.6.2.1]

What are the results of merit and wisdom?

On the basis of merit, a bodhisattva remains uninjured[234] as he or she transmigrates in samsara and avoids being afflicted excessively by suffering. He or she is also able to benefit beings and accomplish their aims, in whatever way may be desired.

232. S: *manaskāraḥ,* T: *yid la byed pa*. Asaṅga (*AS,* p. 6) defines this mental factor as follows: "What is attention? It is the bending of the mind (S: *cetasa ābhogaḥ,* T: *sems kyi 'jug pa*). Its action is to cause the mind to keep hold of an object." *PSV* (p. 276): "Bending the mind is the condition by which the mind is directed toward an object." This mental factor is frequently described as being either "proper" (S: *yoniśaḥ,* T: *tshul bzhin du*) or "improper" (S: *ayoniśaḥ,* T: *tshul bzhin ma yin par*). Proper attention occurs when one deliberately and consciously cultivates virtuous states of mind; improper attention occurs when the habitual tendencies of the mental afflictions cause a person to develop and maintain negative or erring thoughts. "Erring forms of attention" (S: *viparītamanaskāraḥ,* T: *phyin ci log gi yid la byed pa*), the expression that is being used here, would seem to be more or less synonymous with "improper attention."

233. S: *śuklapakṣaḥ,* T: *dkar po'i phyogs*. This expression, which literally means "the bright side," can mean the first half of a lunar month during which the light of the moon is increasing. In a metaphorical sense it refers to "the right side" of two contending parties. In connection with this latter sense, the term here means "the side of spiritual purity" as opposed to the "dark side" or the "evil side" (S: *kṛṣṇapakṣaḥ,* T: *nag po'i phyogs*).

234. S: *akṣataḥ,* T: *gnod pa med par*. *BBhVy* (f. 52b) identifies three forms of injury that are avoided by possessing the merit that is represented by the first three perfections: (1) the perfection of generosity overcomes the misfortune of not having sufficient material wealth; (2) the perfection of morality overcomes the misfortune relating to one's own personal well-being; and (3) the perfection of patience overcomes the misfortune due to the absence of a large retinue.

On the basis of wisdom, a bodhisattva collects merit correctly and not in a wrongful manner, and, employing skillful activities of immeasurable variety, [continues to do so] until unsurpassed true and complete enlightenment has been attained.

In brief and in a manner that is appropriate [to each of them], these should be understood as the four types of results that relate to merit and wisdom. However, [the description] would be immeasurably large if an [exhaustive] classification of [all] the types [of results] were made.

Regarding this [topic], all of the maturations, as well as all the causes of the maturations, and all the results of the maturations are based upon merit and arise from merit. For its part, merit is based upon wisdom and arises from wisdom. Therefore, both [wisdom and merit] are essential factors for [the pursuit of] unsurpassed true and complete enlightenment. While merit is an essential factor, wisdom is further [an essential factor] that is unsurpassed. If a bodhisattva lacks either merit or wisdom, he or she cannot attain unsurpassed true and complete enlightenment. This [explanation] should be understood as representing [the aspects of] a bodhisattva's [pursuit of] one's own and others' aims that are contained within a cause or a result.

One's Own and Others' Aims That Relate to This Life and to Future Lives [I.3.7–8]

What are one's own and others' aims that relate to this life? What are [one's own and others' aims] that relate to a future life?

(1) The acquisition of wealth through exercising a proper form of human effort at some type of craft or occupation;[235] (2) the exercise of moderation in the use of those very forms of wealth that one has acquired; (3) the experiencing of results in this life that are the ripening of favorable [forms of] karma [that were carried out] previously; (4) the resorting to states of meditative absorption by a bodhisattva who is skilled at turning them back,[236] so that he or she may abide in a state of ease in this life and so that, by resorting to [those states of composure] in this very life, he or she may accomplish the

235. S: *śilpasthānakarmasthānam*, T: *bzo'i gnas dang las kyi gnas*. See Book I, chapter 8, the opening portion of the section entitled "Seeking the Dharma" [I.8.2] for a description of this topic, which forms one of the five branches of knowledge (S: *vidyāsthānam*, T: *rig pa'i gnas*).

236. See note 182.

aims of others; (5) the entering into nirvana in this life by a person who has become a tathāgata; and (6) the conditioned entities, whether worldly or transcendent, that cause [a buddha's] nirvana to be attained in this life are called "[the elements of] a bodhisattva's own aim that relates to this very life." When other beings who have been spiritually tamed by such a bodhisattva also [achieve] the same qualities that he or she has, this should be understood as [the accomplishing of] others' aims [that relate to this life].

Regarding this [topic], (1) the excellence of material wealth [that is attained] in a future life and the excellence of [a being's] individual existence[237] [that is attained] in a future life, both of which take place in the desire realm; (2) rebirth in the form and formless realms in a future life; and (3) the pursuit, in this life, of the causes of that excellence of material wealth and individual existence that will occur in future rebirths in the form and formless realms, which is [also an exercise that is] accompanied by [physical] pain and mental difficulty and [is sustained by] repeated reflection[238] should be understood to represent a bodhisattva's own and others' aims that relate only to future lives.

By contrast, (1) the pursuit of those causes of excellence of material wealth and [excellence of] individual existence that is carried out in this life in such a manner that it is accompanied by both [physical] pleasure and mental ease; and (2) the meditative absorptions and formless states of composure [that are attained] in this life and [that] do not undergo deterioration should be understood as [a bodhisattva's] own and others' aims that relate both to this life and to future lives.[239]

237. S: *ātmabhāvaḥ*. The Sanskrit term is almost always translated into Tibetan as *lus,* which normally is taken to mean the physical body (in some instances the Sanskrit term is translated as *bdag gi dngos po*). While "body" is often its intended meaning, there are situations where it refers to the totality of one's being (*PSV,* p. 342, glosses the term as "name and form") and sometimes it refers to the "inner heaps" (see note 277). Here the term also refers to an individual's state of being in the formless realm, where there is no physical body. Thus, depending on the context, the term can refer to all five heaps (S: *skandhaḥ,* T: *phung po*) and not just the body, and in certain instances it can refer only to one's mental constituents independently of the physical body.

238. S: *pratisaṃkhyāya,* T: *so sor brtags zhing. BBhVṛ* (f. 156a): "The phrase 'reflection' is meant to indicate that [when one's practice] involves [physical] pain and mental difficulty, it is [nevertheless] pursued because reflection [provides the incentive that comes from recognizing] that [the effort] will yield a favorable result in the future."

239. *BBhVy* (ff. 53b–54a): "When that [bodhisattva] is able to accomplish virtuous activities accompanied by [physical] pleasure and mental ease, that should be understood as [the

One's Own and Others' Aims That Are Perpetual or Not Perpetual [1.3.9–10]

What are one's own and others' aims that are perpetual? What are [one's own and others' aims] that are not perpetual?

The excellence of material wealth and individual existence that occurs in the desire realm, along with both its causes and results, and the mundane purity[240] of ordinary beings, along with both its causes and results, are [forms of] one's own and others' aims that are not perpetual.

(1) The permanent abandonment of all the mental afflictions,[241] (2) the eightfold ārya path, and (3) the worldly virtuous entities that are attained on the basis of that [ārya path] are what are called "one's own and others' aims that are perpetual."

Regarding this point, it should be understood that the qualities of being perpetual and not perpetual are due to three reasons: (1) in terms of essential nature, (2) in terms of being subject to deterioration, and (3) in the sense that the experiencing of a related result [eventually] comes to an end. Regarding these [reasons], nirvana is perpetual in terms of its essential nature. All conditioned entities are not perpetual [in terms of their essential nature]. The eightfold ārya path is perpetual because it is not subject to deterioration and because the experiencing of its result does not come to an end. Those other [conditioned] entities which are virtuous [in nature] but are related

---

pursuit of one's own aim and that of others] that is related both to this life and to future lives." In other words, the fact that such efforts are accompanied by relative comfort and ease in this life means that they are "related to this life" in the sense that one experiences such well-being "as a seen event" (S: *dṛṣṭadharme,* T: *mthong ba'i chos la*). The fact that such efforts will also produce results in a future life for oneself and that one will also be able to benefit others on the basis of those future results is what qualifies them as being related to future lives and the aim or welfare of others.

240. S: *laukikī śuddhiḥ,* T: *'jig rten pa'i dag pa. BBhVy* (f. 54a): "'Mundane purity' [is] the freedom from attachment (S: *vairāgyam,* T: *'dod chags dang bral ba*) that is attained through the mundane path." "Freedom from attachment" here means the overcoming of attachment for the desire realm and lower levels of the form and formless realms that is gained through achieving the various meditative absorptions and formless states of com posure. Because this freedom from attachment is capable of undergoing deterioration it is described here as being "not perpetual." See also note 561.

241. As the next paragraph shows, this "abandonment" (S: *prahāṇam,* T: *spong ba*) of all the mental afflictions should be understood as synonymous with the attainment of nirvana.

to the outflows[242] are not perpetual, both in the sense that they are subject to deterioration and in the sense that the experiencing of their results comes to an end.[243]

This represents both a brief and an extensive [presentation] of the ten aspects of one's own and others' aims. [They are two of the seven subjects] in relation to which the training is undertaken by bodhisattvas with all their ability and with all their strength. There is nothing of greater significance than [these ten aspects] and nothing besides them. All those [bodhisattvas] who have trained themselves in the past and [all] those who will train themselves in the future with regard to one's own and others' aims, have done so and will do so with regard to these very same ten aspects of one's own and others' aims; there is nothing of greater significance than these and nothing besides these.

Within [Book I of] *The Stage of a Bodhisattva,* [known as] "The Object of Mental Application That Relates to the Support," this completes the third chapter, entitled "One's Own and Others' Aims."

242. S: *sāsaravāḥ,* T: *zag pa dang bcas pa*. See note 196 for an explanation of this expression. These virtuous entities are being contrasted with the transcendent ārya path, which represents a group of conditioned entities that are "free of the outflows" (S: *anāsravāḥ,* T: *zag pa med pa*).

243. *BBhVy* (f. 54b): "A virtuous [entity] that is related to the outflows continues to be attached with one's mind continuum until its result is experienced; [but] after [its] result has been generated, [the capacity of that virtuous cause to produce a favorable result] is terminated."

4

The Nature of Reality

What is the nature of reality?[244]

In brief, it is twofold: (1) the true state[245] of entities, which relates to the mode of being that represents their true nature,[246] and (2) the totality of entities, which relates to the mode of being that represents their full range.[247] Thus, reality should be understood in the most comprehensive sense as [referring to] the true state and the totality of entities.

Four Categories of Reality [1.4.1]

Moreover, this reality is fourfold [when considered] in terms of the different types that are to be distinguished: (1) that which is recognized [as true] in the world; (2) that which is recognized [as true] on the basis of reasoning; (3) the object that is perceived[248] by the knowledge that removes the

244. S: *tattvārthaḥ,* T: *de kho na'i don.* This term could be translated more literally as "the meaning of reality" and that is how it is rendered in Tibetan. *BBhVy* (f. 54b) states: "The [compound] *tattvārthaḥ* (T: *de kho na'i don*) can be parsed as 'the meaning of reality' (S: *tattvasyārthaḥ,* T: *de kho na nyid kyi don*). It is the object (S: *gocaraḥ,* T: *spyod yul*) of, and the entity (S: *viṣayaḥ,* T: *yul*) that is perceived by, knowledge." However, idiomatically, the term can also mean simply "truth," or "reality." Because in the present context Asaṅga identifies four types or categories of reality, I have rendered the term as "the nature of reality."

245. S: *bhūtatā,* T: *yang dag pa nyid. BBhVy* (f. 55a) glosses this term as "a state that is free of falsity" (S: **aviparītatā,* T: *phyin ci ma log pa nyid*).

246. S: *yathāvadbhāvikatā,* T: *ji lta ba yod pa nyid.*

247. S: *yāvadbhāvikatā,* T: *ji snyed ba yod pa nyid.*

248. S: *gocaraḥ,* T: *spyod yul.* In this usage, this term literally means the "range," "scope," or "field of action" for a particular type of awareness. Its more straightforward sense is that of an object that is perceived by some form of awareness. Thus, the field of action for eye consciousness is visible objects.

obscurations of the mental afflictions;[249] and (4) the object that is perceived by the knowledge that removes the obscurations to that which needs to be known.[250]

The Objects of Ordinary Experience [1.4.1.1]

Regarding this [fourfold distinction, the first category refers to] that substance[251] toward which all worldly beings[252] share the same view, based on judgments that operate through gaining familiarity with convention and accepted usage, such as when [one says] about the earth [element]: "This is earth; it is not fire." Just as with the earth [element, such shared views also occur] in relation to fire, water, air, [visible] form, sounds, smells, tastes, tangible objects, food, drink, vehicles, clothing, objects that are applied as ornaments, implements and household utensils, incense, garlands, scented oils, [objects that relate to] dance, song, music, [objects that are used to create] light, [objects that relate to] sensual pleasures enjoyed by men and women, and objects that relate to [the cultivation of] fields, [the operation of] commercial shops, and [the maintenance of] private dwellings. [Such shared views also occur] in relation to [the nature of] pleasure and suffering, [such as when worldly beings agree:] "This [experience] is [a form of] suffering; it is not [a form of] pleasure"; or, "This [experience] is [a form of] pleasure; it is

249. See note 117.

250. See note 118.

251. S: *vastu,* T: *dngos po.* The use and meaning of this term is central to the entire discussion of the nature of reality that is developed throughout this chapter. The Sanskrit *vastu* can mean either a "really existing substance or essence," or more loosely, an ordinary "object" or "thing" (MW, p. 932). Asaṅga's usage tends toward the former sense, which he explains as the falsely ascribed essential nature that is posited by a designating assertion (S: *prajñaptivādaḥ,* T: *'dogs pa'i tshig;* see note 262 and accompanying text). On the other hand, he also maintains that there is an ineffable reality that is capable of exerting a causal action. This ultimate nature is to be distinguished from the nominally designated essences that are mentally contrived and unreal. He refers to this ultimate reality with a number of terms, including "bare substance" (S: *vastumātram,* T: *dngos po tsam;* see note 273 and accompanying text). At times, though, he simply calls it a [real] substance (S: *vastu,* T: *dngos po;* see, for instance, notes 269 and 1536, along with accompanying text).

252. S: *laukikaḥ,* T: *'jig rten pa.* This term refers to any person who is not an ārya, that is, to anyone who has not achieved transcendent realization of the pure path. Synonyms of "worldly being" are "immature being" (S: *bālaḥ,* T: *byis pa*) and "ordinary person" (S: *pṛthagjanaḥ,* T: *so so skye bo*).

not [a form of] suffering." In short, it is any thing that is an object of settled and firm belief for all worldly persons, [such that it is held:] "[The nature of] this [object] is this; it is not that"; or, "This [object exists or is used] in this manner; it does not [exist nor is it used] in some other manner." [Likewise, the existence of these objects] is recognized [by such persons] with their own conceptual thought [simply] on the basis of [familiarity with] the traditional usage of terms; it is not [a belief that is] held through having engaged in reflection, contemplation, and investigation. This is called "the [form of] reality that is recognized [as true] in the world."

The Objects That Are Verified through Reasoning [1.4.1.2]

What is the [form of] reality that is recognized [as being true] through reasoning?

[This category of reality pertains to] a knowable substance that has been well perceived and well determined by wise persons who are skilled in what is reasonable, who perceive things clearly, who are logicians, who engage in rational investigation, who are devoted to that which falls within the domain of logic, [a field that] derives from their own ordinary[253] intelligence and that represents the sphere of rational investigation. [Such an object is ascertained] on the basis of [a form of] authoritative knowledge[254] [that is either] direct perception, inference, or the testimony of a reliable person, and it is proven and established through the [form of] application that relates to demonstrating correctness.[255] This is called "the [form of] reality that is recognized [as true] on the basis of reasoning."

253. S: *pārthagjanikī*, T: *so so'i skye bo pa*. This is the adjectival form of the noun that means "ordinary person" (see previous note). *BBhVy* (f. 55a): "[The intelligence of logicians] is called 'ordinary' because they do not possess a [level of] realization that is free of the outflows."

254. S: *pramāṇam*, T: *tshad ma*.

255. S: *upapattisādhanayuktiḥ*, T: *'thad pas grub pa'i rigs pa*. This expression refers to one of four ways of examining Dharma teachings, which I have translated as the "four applications" (S: *catasro yuktayaḥ*, T: *rigs pa bzhi*). This particular application employs the three forms of authoritative knowledge (S: *pramāṇam*, T: *tshad ma*) mentioned here to establish the soundness of such doctrines as impermanence, suffering, and selflessness. Even though I have translated the term *yuktiḥ* in the compound *yuktiprasiddhatattvam* (T: *rigs pas grags pa'i de kho na nyid*) as "reasoning," I render it as "application" (cf. MW, p. 853) when it refers to the four methods of examination because these techniques collectively represent broader forms of reflection that extend beyond logic or inference alone. Moreover, in Asaṅga's most

The Form of Transcendent Awareness That Eradicates the Mental Afflictions [1.4.1.3]

What is the [form of] reality that is the object perceived by the knowledge that removes the obscurations of the mental afflictions?

The objects that are perceived by the uncontaminated[256] knowledge of all the listeners and solitary realizers, as well as by their mundane knowledge that brings forth that uncontaminated knowledge[257] and [their mundane knowledge] that occurs subsequent to that uncontaminated knowledge[258] are called "the [form of] reality that is the object perceived by the knowledge that removes the obscurations of the mental afflictions." Through apprehending those [objects], the awareness [of the listeners and solitary realizers] becomes purified of the obscurations of the mental afflictions and also remains free of those obscurations in the future. Therefore, this is called "the [form of] reality that is the object perceived by the knowledge that removes the obscurations of the mental afflictions."

What, then, is that [form of] reality?

It is the four noble truths—[that is, the noble truths of] suffering, origi-

---

detailed account of the four applications, which appears in *The Stage of a Listener* (*ŚBh,* pp. 140–143), he equates the meaning of *yuktiḥ* (T: *rigs pa*) with a "way" (S: *yogaḥ,* T: *sbyor ba*) or a "means" (S: *upāyaḥ,* T: *thabs*). See note 1199 for a description of the four applications.

256. This is a somewhat loose translation of the technical term that more literally translates as "that which is free of the outflows" (S: *anāsravaḥ,* T: *zag pa med pa*); see note 196 above. This type of knowledge, which is also referred to as "transcendent" (S: *lokottaraḥ,* T: *'jig rten las 'das pa*), in this case refers to an ārya's direct realization of some aspect of the four noble truths.

257. This is a reference to the form of knowledge that is gained on the path of preparation (S: *prayogamārgaḥ,* T: *sbyor ba'i lam*), the second of the five paths that culminate in the attainment of an arhat's status. *BBhVṛ* (f. 157b): "'That [mundane knowledge] which brings forth uncontaminated knowledge' is the [knowledge] that has the essential nature of the path of preparation." The phrase "uncontaminated knowledge" refers to the transcendent awareness that is gained on the third path, which is known as the path of seeing (S: *darśanamārgaḥ,* T: *mthong lam*), and beyond.

258. S: *pṛṣṭalabdhajñānam,* T: *rjes thob ye shes.* This type of awareness is one in which a practitioner recognizes the import of such objects as the selflessness of the person after having arisen from a state of mental composure in which he or she has experienced a direct realization of that object. It is referred to as a "mundane" form of knowledge because it does not directly perceive the true nature of entities; nevertheless, it is considered an element of the truth of the path in that the practitioner's mind is still informed by his or her prior transcendent realization that occurred in a state of meditative composure.

nation, cessation, and the path. Knowledge of these [forms of reality] arises through investigating and attaining a realization of the four noble truths, and [it] also [arises] in relation to [the four noble truths] after a realization of them has been attained. Moreover, this realization of the truths arises for the listeners and solitary realizers when, as a result of their having employed the wisdom that is [cognitively] united with the arising and passing away of dependently arisen conditioned entities to cultivate the view that no person exists apart from the heaps, they perceive [that there is nothing but] the mere heaps [themselves][259] and they do not perceive a self that is a distinct entity and [one that exists] separately from the heaps.

The Form of Transcendent Awareness That Brings Supreme Enlightenment [1.4.1.4]

What is the [form of] reality that is the object perceived by the knowledge that removes the obscurations to that which needs to be known?

[In this context,] the [form of] opposition [that acts as a hindrance] to knowledge regarding that which needs to be known is called "an obscuration." The object that comes within the range of perception of the knowledge that has been freed of the obscuration to that which needs to be known should be understood to constitute the [form of] reality that is the object perceived by the knowledge that removes the obscurations to that which needs to be known.

What, then, is that [form of reality]?

It is the object that bodhisattvas [pursue] in order to attain [a realization of] the insubstantiality of entities and that the buddhas, the blessed ones, have [fully] attained with their extremely pure [transcendent awareness]. [This object,] which represents the ineffable [ultimate] nature of all entities, is perceived by [a form of] knowledge that corresponds exactly to a knowable entity that is free of the conceptual distinctions [that are implicit in] the essential natures [expressed by] designating assertions.[260] This [form of

259. S: *skandhamātram,* T: *phung po tsam.* That is, they recognize that their own existence is limited to the five heaps and that there is no real self that controls or determines the manner and form in which the heaps occur.

260. The essential natures that are expressed by designating assertions (S: *prajñaptivādasvabhāvaḥ,* T: *gdags pa'i tshig gis no bo nyid*) and the eight principal forms of conceptual thought (S: *vikalpaḥ,* T: *rnam par rtog pa*) are both discussed later in this chapter.

reality] is the paramount suchness[261] that is unsurpassed and that reaches to the furthest limit of knowable entities, [and it is that object] for which all correct investigations of entities are carried out and beyond which [such investigations] need not be carried out.

The Concepts of Being and Nonbeing [1.4.2]

Moreover, it should be understood that the [principal] attribute [of this last form of] reality, in the sense of a distinguishing trait, is that it is characterized by the absence of duality. [As it is being used here, the term] "duality" refers to [the concepts of] being and nonbeing.

With regard to these [two concepts], "being" is that which is posited as the essential nature [that is expressed in] a designating assertion.[262] This [notion is one that] has been adhered to by the world in just this manner for a long time. It is the root of all the world's conceptual thoughts[263] and elaborations.[264] These include, for example, [the essential natures that are expressed by such designating assertions as] "form," "feeling," "conception," "formations," and "consciousness"; [those of] "eye," "ear," "nose," "tongue," "body," and "mind"; those of "earth," "water," "fire," and "air"; those of "[visible] form," "sound," "smell," "taste," and "tangible object"; [the qualities of being] "virtuous," "nonvirtuous," and "indeterminate"; [those of] "origination," "disappearance," and [of being] "dependently arisen"; [those of] "past," "future," and "present"; [those of being a] "conditioned [entity]" and [of being] "unconditioned"; [that which is identified as being] "this world" and "the next world"; the pair of "the sun and the moon";[265] [the

261. S: *tathatā,* T: *de bzhin nyid.* This term is a synonym for emptiness (S: *śūnyatā,* T: *stong pa nyid*). *MVBh* (p. 39): "Suchness means not to be otherwise, in the sense of always remaining in just such a manner."

262. S: *prajñaptivādaḥ,* T: *'dogs pa'i tshig. BBhVy* (f. 59b): "A designating assertion means [the same thing as] 'conventional usage' (S: *vyavahāraḥ,* T: *tha snyad*) and 'verbal expression' (S: *abhidhānam,* T: *mngon par brjod pa*)."

263. S: *vikalpaḥ,* T: *rnam par rtog pa.* Asaṅga's description of the eight principal categories of conceptual thought appears below.

264. S: *prapañcaḥ,* T: *spros pa. BBhVy* (f. 60a): "Elaborations are (1) [the objects that are] formed [in the mind] on the basis of such conventional expressions as 'permanent' and the like, and (2) [they are] the conventional expressions that derive from conceptual thought."

265. *BBhVy* (f. 60a): "The phrase 'the pair of the sun and the moon' is meant in the sense of the mental constructs of day and night."

qualities of being] "seen," "heard," "considered," or "perceived"; [those of being] "attained" or "sought"; [those of being something that is] "deliberated upon" or "reflected upon" with the mind; as well as the range of others that end with "nirvana." These and other similar kinds of essential natures that [are thought of as] pertaining to entities and that are conceived of on the basis of designating assertions are what is called the world's[266] [notion of] "being."

Regarding this [topic], nonbeing [is the notion that] the insubstantiality[267] and lack of causal efficacy[268] of those very designating assertions which posit [the series of entities] that begins with "form" and ends with "nirvana" [constitute] the complete and total nonexistence and [the complete and total] absence of [that which is] the underlying support of designating assertions and which designating assertions are dependent upon in order to occur. This is what is called "nonbeing."

Nondual Wisdom Is a Great Means [1.4.3]

By contrast, the [real] substance[269] that is free of both the former [concept of] being and this [latter concept of] nonbeing, and that is included among the defining attributes of entities, is the absence of duality. This absence of duality is the middle way that avoids the two extremes and that is described as being "unsurpassed." It should be understood that the knowledge of this

266. S: *laukasya,* T: *'jig rten gyi. BBhVy* (f. 61b): "The term 'the world's' [notion of being] indicates an essential nature that is artificially fabricated (S: **parikalpita,* T: *yongs su btags pa*) by immature beings."

267. S: *nirvastukatā,* T: *dngos po med pa nyid. BBhVy* (f. 60b): "The refutation of the [real nature] of the first of the five subjects (S: *pañca vastūni,* T: *dngos po lnga*) is [what is meant here by the term] 'insubstantiality.'" The five subjects are (1) names (S: *nāma,* T: *ming*); (2) causality (S: *nimittam,* T: *rgyu mtshan*); (3) conceptual thought (S: *vikalpaḥ,* T: *rnam par rtog pa*); (4) suchness (S: *tathatā,* T: *de bzhin nyid*); and (5) the knowledge that is free of conceptualization (S: *nirvikalpajñānam,* T: *rnam par mi rtog pa'i ye shes*). "Name" refers to the unreal essence that is associated with mentally fabricated objects (S: *parikalpitam,* T: *kun brtags*).

268. S: *nirnimittatā,* T: *mtshan ma med pa nyid. BBhVy* (f. 60b): "The denial that [the mentally fabricated nature] represents, among the three natures, the dependent nature (S: *paratantra,* T: *gzhan dbang*) is indicated by [the expression] 'lack of causal efficacy.'"

269. S: *vastu,* T: *dngos po.* Here Asaṅga is referring to the ultimate reality that he also indicates with such terms as "bare substance" (S: *vastumātram,* T: *dngos po tsam*), "suchness" (S: *tathatā,* T: *de bzhin nyid*), or "emptiness" (S: *śūnyatā,* T: *stong pa nyid*).

[form of] reality that is possessed by the buddhas, the blessed ones, is perfectly pure. On the other hand, the knowledge of it that is possessed by bodhisattvas should be understood to represent [a form of] the path that is being pursued by those who are still undergoing training.

This wisdom is also a bodhisattva's great means for [bringing about] the attainment of unsurpassed true and complete enlightenment.

Why is that?

[This latter point should be understood] as follows. A bodhisattva who applies him- or herself using conviction[270] about [the meaning of] emptiness during various births as he or she continues to be reborn in samsara in order to ripen sentient beings and also to ripen the qualities of a buddha in him- or herself will understand samsara as it truly is. [That bodhisattva] will also not allow his or her mind to become [overly] upset by [the unsatisfactory nature of] samsara through [having contemplated] the aspects of impermanence, etc.[271] [A bodhisattva who] fails to understand samsara as it truly is will be unable to maintain a mind that is [largely] unaffected by all the mental afflictions of desire, hatred, and ignorance, etc. And [a bodhisattva] who cannot maintain a mind that is largely unaffected [by the mental afflic-

270. Conviction (S: *adhimokṣaḥ,* T: *mos pa*) is one of the mental factors that are included in the fourth heap, called formations (S: *saṃskāraskandhaḥ,* T: *'du byed kyi phung po*). *AS* (p. 6): "What is conviction? [It is] the steadfastness [of mind which maintains], in relation to an object about which a determination has been made, that [it does exist] in the manner that has been determined. Its action is [to make an individual] incapable of being led astray." Here the term "conviction" is also meant to suggest that, because the bodhisattva has not yet achieved a direct realization of emptiness, his or her practice is based upon the steadfast conviction that derives from a correct conceptual understanding of emptiness. For example, the path of preparation that leads to the path of seeing (at which time the bodhisattva first attains a direct realization of emptiness) is described as "the stage of conduct that is based upon devotion" (S: *adhimukticaryābhūmiḥ,* T: *mos pas spyod pa'i sa*). The Sanskrit term translated as "devotion" (S: *adhimuktiḥ*) is closely related linguistically to the term translated as "conviction" (S: *adhimokṣaḥ*), and both are rendered in Tibetan by the same term (T: *mos pa*). These two terms literally suggest the sense of the mind being directed with firmness toward an object. See the beginning of chapter 8, where a bodhisattva's devotion is defined as "a [sense of] certainty and eagerness that is preceded by the faith that is a clarity [of mind] toward the eight objects of devotion." One of the eight objects is the topic of this chapter, i.e., the nature of reality.

271. This is a reference to the four aspects of the noble truth of suffering: (1) impermanence, (2) suffering, (3) emptiness, and (4) selflessness. Contemplating the unsatisfactoriness of samsara is meant to engender a sense of apprehension and dissatisfaction (S: *udvegaḥ,* T: *skyo ba*); however, for a follower of the Great Vehicle this can weaken one's resolve to remain in samsara in order to continue the practices that lead to supreme enlightenment.

tions] will become a person who wanders [continuously] in samsara with an agitated mind and [a person] who can neither ripen the qualities of a buddha [in him- or herself] nor ripen [other] sentient beings. Moreover, if a bodhisattva allows his or her mind to become [overly] upset by [the unsatisfactory nature of] samsara through [having contemplated] the aspects of impermanence, etc., then he or she, having developed such [an attitude], will very quickly bring about [the] complete extinction [of samsaric rebirths]. The bodhisattva who very quickly brings about [the] complete extinction [of his or her samsaric rebirths] will, in that way, also fail to ripen the qualities of a buddha in him- or herself and fail to ripen [other] sentient beings, much less attain unsurpassed true and complete enlightenment.

Moreover, the bodhisattva who applies him- or herself using conviction about [the meaning of] emptiness will neither become frightened by nirvana nor desire to attain nirvana [prematurely].[272] If a bodhisattva should become frightened by nirvana, he or she will not, from that point forward, complete the accumulations [that are necessary to attain] nirvana because, through having developed this frightened attitude, he or she will become a bodhisattva who fails to see the benefits of nirvana and who has abandoned [both] the faith and the steadfast devotion toward nirvana that derive from recognizing the good qualities that are gained by its attainment. If a bodhisattva becomes one who abides [too] frequently in [the attitude of] wanting to attain nirvana, he or she will quickly bring about [the] complete extinction [of samsaric rebirths]. And a person who quickly brings about [the] complete extinction [of samsaric rebirths] can neither ripen the qualities of a buddha [in him- or herself] nor ripen [other] sentient beings.

Regarding this [point], (1) the continuous rebirth in samsara by [a person] whose mind is subject to the agitation [of the mental afflictions] because he or she does not understand samsara as it truly is; (2) the swift extinction [of samsaric rebirth] by [a person] whose mind has been upset by [the unsatisfactory nature of] samsara; (3) the failure to complete the accumulations [that are necessary to attain] that [nirvana] by [a person] whose mind has become frightened [by nirvana]; and (4) the swift attainment of the complete extinction [of samsaric rebirth] by [a person] who abides [too] frequently in [the attitude of] wanting to attain nirvana should be understood as [elements of] a bodhisattva's lack of [effective] means with regard

272. That is, seek to attain the termination of samsaric existence before he or she has perfected the two accumulations.

to [the pursuit of] unsurpassed true and complete enlightenment. On the other hand, (1) the continuous rebirth in samsara by [a person] whose mind is not subject to the agitation [of the mental afflictions] because he or she does understand samsara as it truly is; (2) the avoidance of a swift extinction [of rebirth] by [a person] whose mind has not been [overly] upset by [the unsatisfactory nature of] samsara; (3) the [willingness to] complete the accumulations [that are necessary to attain] that [nirvana] by [a person] whose mind has not become frightened [by nirvana]; and (4) the avoidance of a swift extinction [of samsaric rebirth] by [a person] who does recognize the benefits and good qualities of nirvana but does not long for it excessively are [elements of] a bodhisattva's great means for [bringing about] the attainment of unsurpassed true and complete enlightenment.

This [effective] means is one that depends upon a conviction about [the meaning of] supreme emptiness. Therefore, meditation upon a conviction about [the meaning of] supreme emptiness represents [the element] within a bodhisattva's path of training that is called a "great means"—which is to say, [a great means that contributes] to the attainment of a tathāgata's knowledge. Indeed, a bodhisattva who has realized the ineffable nature of all entities as it truly is with [a form of] the knowledge of the insubstantiality of phenomena that has long since penetrated [into its meaning] does not form any type of conceptual thought whatsoever and does not grasp anything other than the bare substance[273] [of entities] and [their] bare suchness. [That bodhisattva] also does not think to him- or herself: "This is the bare substance [of entities]," or "This is the bare suchness [of entities]." Rather, the bodhisattva engages the [true] import.[274] Engaging this ultimate object, he or she perceives, with his or her wisdom, all entities as they truly are—[which is to say,] that they are [all] exactly the same in relation to this suchness.

273. S: *vastumātram,* T: *dngos pa tsam.* As this statement asserts, this term is meant to be synonymous with "suchness" and "ultimate truth."

274. S: *arthe carati,* T: *don ni spyod par byed do.* The use of the term *artham* here is meant to suggest an awareness of ultimate reality rather than a false, conceptualized object.

The Positive Effect of Relying upon Nondual Wisdom [1.4.4]

Seeing this sameness everywhere and having his or her mind [fixed upon] this sameness, [the bodhisattva] attains a supreme equanimity. On the basis of [this equanimity], he or she does not, because of any [type of] fatigue or the occurrence of any [kind of physical] discomfort, give up being continuously devoted to the development of skill in all the branches of learning. With a body and a mind that are exempt from weariness, [the bodhisattva] will quickly perfect these skills. He or she will also achieve a great strengthening of recollection. Yet [that bodhisattva] will not become swollen with pride because of [having attained] these skills. Nor will [that bodhisattva] be one who withholds instruction from others. He or she will not develop a dejected mind toward any of the [requisite] skills but will be energetic and one whose progress is unimpeded. Maintaining a firm, armor-like practice, the more [this bodhisattva] encounters exceptional forms of suffering while undergoing rebirth in samsara, the more he or she will increase exertion toward [the goal of achieving] unsurpassed true and complete enlightenment. The more [this bodhisattva] attains extraordinary positions of eminence, the more he or she will become completely devoid of pride in the presence of [other] sentient beings. The more [this bodhisattva] attains extraordinary [forms of] knowledge, the more he or she will realize to an ever-greater degree [those situations in which] he or she is [about to] criticize or quarrel with another person, engage in rambling conversation,[275] [develop one of] the root or secondary mental afflictions, or engage in mistaken forms of conduct, and [therefore this bodhisattva] will [be able to] keep his or her mind in a heightened state of equanimity. The more [this bodhisattva's] spiritual qualities increase, the more he or she will be inclined to conceal his or her virtuous character. He or she will not seek to be known [by others] as [a person] of high rank or [seek to acquire] gain and honor. These are [some of] the numerous kinds of benefits that are conducive to enlightenment and conform to enlightenment, and that [are acquired] by the bodhisattva who relies upon [nondual] knowledge. Therefore, all those

275. S: *prakīrṇalapitā*, T: *smra ba mang ba*. The Sanskrit adjective *prakīrṇa* literally means "scattered." When used to describe speech, it is usually taken to mean "confused" or "incoherent" speech (MW, p. 654). The Tibetan translation, however, indicates "excessive" conversation, suggesting speech that unnecessarily takes up a wide range of topics.

[bodhisattvas] who have attained enlightenment [in the past], who are [striving to] attain it [now], and who will attain it [in the future] do so by relying upon this very [nondual] knowledge, not [by relying upon] some other lesser [form of knowledge] or one that is more distinguished.

The Bodhisattva Who Is Correctly Established in the Practice [1.4.5]

The bodhisattva who has undertaken the system that is free of elaboration[276] in this way and has gained these numerous benefits becomes one who is correctly established in the practice [that seeks] to ripen the qualities of a buddha in oneself and to ripen the spiritual qualities of the three vehicles in others. Moreover, the way in which he or she becomes one who is correctly established in the practice is [to be understood] as follows.

[That bodhisattva] becomes one who has no craving for possessions or for his or her own individual existence.[277] He or she also trains in relation to this freedom from craving in order [to become able] to give both his or her possessions and self to [other] sentient beings for the exclusive benefit of sentient beings. He or she becomes one who is restrained[278] and one who is extremely well restrained. He or she trains [continually] in body and speech

276. S: *niṣprapañcanayaḥ*, T: *spros pa med pa'i tshul*. That is, the system that represents a correct understanding of emptiness and enables a bodhisattva to practice the trainings of the Great Vehicle effectively.

277. S: *ātmabhāvatṛṣṇā*, T: *lus la sred pa*. See note 237 for general remarks concerning the Sanskrit term *ātmabhavaḥ*. Sthiramati (*PSV*, p. 270) explains *atmabhāvaḥ* as it occurs in this compound to mean attachment toward all of the "inner grasping heaps." The term "inner heaps" means those that are included within one's own continuum. Asaṅga (*AS*, pp. 4, 5) also uses this term to explain "feelings that are accompanied by corporeal desire" (S: *sāmiṣavedanā*, T: *zang zing dang bcas pa'i tshor ba*): "What is a feeling that is accompanied by corporeal desire? It is the feeling that is associated with craving for [one's own] individual existence." Hence, "craving for individual existence" should be understood as meaning attachment to one's own continued samsaric existence.

278. S: *saṃvṛtaḥ*, T: *bsdams pa*. *BBhVy* (f. 64b): "There are three types of bodhisattva morality: (1) the morality of restraint; (2) the morality of collecting virtue; and (3) the morality of accomplishing the welfare of sentient beings [see Book I, chapter 10]. Here, [this term] is stated in the sense of the [bodhisattva] morality that consists of having accepted [one of the forms of] restraint [that pertain to the 'individual liberation' system of discipline; see note 683]."

with regard to the [moral discipline of] restraint,[279] in order to develop a natural aversion to evil and a character that is naturally good and virtuous. He or she is forbearing of every harm and act of hostility that is carried out [against him or her] by others. He or she also trains to develop [even greater] forbearance so that he or she will be slow to anger and will not inflict harm upon others. He or she is either intent upon [mastering] or has [already] become a master of all the branches of learning, [enabling him or her] both to dispel the doubts of sentient beings and to provide them with what is beneficial, as well as [enabling him or her] to obtain the causes of omniscience. He or she also becomes one whose mind remains fixed inwardly and one who is well-established in the states of composure. He or she trains with regard to mental stability,[280] in order to refine the four divine pleasurable states[281] and develop an effortless mastery of the five forms of supernatural knowledge,[282] in order to both accomplish the aims of sentient beings and remove any fatigue that may arise from applying oneself to the topics about

279. S: *saṃvaraḥ,* T: *sdom pa. AKB* (p. 205): "Restraint means the act of putting a stop to, and the complete cessation of, the immorality that has been occurring continuously." The same text continues: "There are three kinds of restraint: (1) the restraint of the 'individual liberation' [system of discipline; see note 683], which is the morality that occurs in the desire realm and pertains to those [human beings] who are of this [world]; (2) the restraint that arises from the meditative absorptions, which is the morality that occurs in the form realm; and (3) the restraint that is pure, which is the morality that is free of the outflows." The restraint that is meant here is the first of these three.

280. S: *cittasthitiḥ,* T: *sems gnas.* This term literally means "a state in which the mind remains stationary or fixed." *ŚBh* (pp. 363–364) describes nine levels of mental stability that culminate in the attainment of the form of one-pointed concentration known as "quiescence" (S: *śamathaḥ,* T: *zhi gnas*).

281. S: *catur brāhmavihārāṇi,* T: *tshangs pa'i gnas bzhi.* These are synonymous with the four immeasurables: (1) loving-kindness, (2) compassion, (3) joy, and (4) equanimity. See Book I, chapter 16, the section entitled "The Immeasurables" [I.16.3].

282. S: *pañcābhijñāḥ,* T: *mngon shes lnga.* These are the first five of the six forms of supernatural knowledge that are described in Book I, chapter 5, namely, (1) the supernatural ability to transform or create objects, (2) the divine ear that can hear sounds beyond the normal range of hearing, (3) the ability to know others' thoughts, (4) the ability to recall the circumstances of one's own and others' previous lives, and (5) the ability to know when and where sentient beings will pass away and subsequently be reborn.

which one should become skilled.[283] He or she is perceptive[284] and knowledgeable about the supreme form of reality. He or she also trains in order to become one who has comprehended fully the ultimate form of reality and so that in the future, within [the path of] the Great Vehicle, he or she can attain complete nirvana.

The bodhisattva who is thus correctly engaged [in the spiritual practice] attends to those beings who are endowed with virtuous qualities by venerating them and bestowing gain and honor upon them. One maintains an attitude of utmost compassion and pity toward those beings who are guilty of wickedness. With all one's ability and strength, one undertakes to eliminate the faults of those [wicked beings]. One maintains an attitude of loving-kindness toward those beings who carry out harmful acts. With all one's ability and strength, and keeping oneself free of both guile and deceitfulness, one provides those harmful beings with happiness and well-being, with the aim of inducing them to abandon the hostile states of mind that are caused by their own wicked thoughts and deeds. With gratitude toward those who carry out beneficial acts, one strives to repay [their kindness] with a [form of] benefit that is equal to or greater [than that shown to oneself]. With all one's ability and strength, one fulfills [one's] virtuous aspirations. And, with regard to those tasks and duties that one may be asked to do but is unable [to complete], one displays a proper regard [for them] and puts forth an effort [to undertake them]; one does not simply abandon them immediately. One [also] ponders, "How can it be made known that [it is because] I am unable [to do such and such a task that I have not completed it], not [because] I am unwilling [to do it]?" It should be understood that these are the kinds of correct practice [that are carried out] by a bodhisattva who has undertaken the system that is free of elaboration and who is relying upon the knowledge of the supreme form of reality.

283. S: *kauśalyam,* T: *mkhas par bya ba. ŚBh* (pp. 192–193) describes five topics about which one should develop skill or knowledge: (1) the five heaps (S: *skandhaḥ,* T: *phung po*); (2) the eighteen constituents (S: *dhātuḥ,* T: *khams*); (3) the twelve bases (S: *āyatanam,* T: *skye mched*); (4) dependent origination; and (5) what is proper and improper [regarding the workings of karma] (S: *sthānāsthānam,* T: *gnas dang gnas ma yin pa*).

284. S: *vicakṣaṇaḥ,* T: *mdzangs pa. BBhVy* (f. 65b) describes this as an innate intelligence that is gained by having cultivated all the branches of knowledge in numerous past lives.

The Form of Application That Establishes the Meaning of Ultimate Reality [1.4.6]

Regarding this [knowledge of ultimate reality], what is the [form of] application[285] by which the ineffable nature of all entities can be understood with precision?

It should be understood that any designation of a unique [essential] characteristic that occurs in relation to those entities that were [described] earlier [with the terms] that range from "form" and "feeling"[286] up to "nirvana" is nothing more than a [nominal] designation. [Such a designation] neither [describes] a [real] essential nature nor something separate from or different from [a real essential nature] that represents a thing to which speech refers or that is an object of speech. That being the case, the essential nature of entities does not exist in the way it is described in words. However, it is also not the case that it is completely and totally nonexistent.

If [an essential nature] does not exist in that manner[287] and it is also not something that is completely and totally nonexistent, how, then, does it exist?

It [exists in a way that] is both the avoidance of a failure of understanding that represents the imputation of something that does not truly exist[288]

285. S: *yuktiḥ,* T: *rigs pa.* While this term can signify "reason" or "reasoning," it also has the sense of an "application," a "means," or an "expedient" (MW, p. 853). *BBhVy* (f. 66b) confirms that the latter sense is the one meant here by making direct reference to the formulation known as the "four applications" (S: *catasro yuktayaḥ,* T: *rigs pa bzhi*) and specifically the form of application that relates to demonstrating correctness (S: *upapattisādhanayuktiḥ,* T: *'thad pas grub pa'i rigs pa*). See also notes 255 and 1199.

286. The Tibetan adds the remaining three heaps of "conception," "formations," and "consciousness."

287. That is, in the way it is described in designating assertions.

288. S: *asadbhūtasamāropāsaṃgrāhavivarjitaḥ,* T: *rang gi mtshan nyid kyis yod pa ma yin pa la sgro btags pa'i legs par ma zung ba spangs pa. BBhVy* (f. 67a) explains this phrase as follows: "'Imputation' (S: *samāropa,* T: *sgro btags pa*) [here means] the perception of the mark of an essence that does not truly exist (S: *asadbhūta,* T: *rang gi mtshan nyid kyis yod pa ma yin pa*); this is also a mistaken form of understanding. 'Avoidance' (S: *vivarjitaḥ,* T: *spangs pa*) means [the act of refraining from believing in] this nonexistent ascription. This very [imputation] is a failure of understanding (S: *asaṃgrāha,* T: *legs par ma zin pa*), since [its object] has the nature of an [imaginary] mental fabrication. Moreover, a mentally fabricated essence is considered to be synonymous with such expressions as 'an erroneously perceived [object]' and the like. [The expression] 'failure of understanding' is meant to indicate that [belief in a nonexistent ascription] is an [erroneous form of] adherence."

and the avoidance of a failure of understanding that represents the denial of something that does truly exist.[289] Moreover, it should be understood that this essential nature of all entities in an ultimate sense is an object that is perceived exclusively by a [form of] knowledge that is free of conceptual thought.[290]

On the other hand, if entities or a substance[291] actually did possess the very nature that is indicated by the verbal expressions that occur in relation to them, then [it would follow absurdly that] a single entity or a single substance must be of many different kinds and possess a multiplicity of essential natures.

Why is that?

[This can be understood] in the following way. Many designations and

289. S: *bhūtāpavādāsaṃgrāhavivarjitaḥ,* T: *yang dag pa la skur ba btab pa'i legs par ma zin pa spangs pa.* Ibid.: "'Denial' (S: *apavādaḥ,* T: *skur ba 'debs pa*) [here means] a distortion that posits the complete nonexistence of substances that do truly exist (S: *bhūta,* T: *yang dag pa*), because they are the basis of words and because they are the causes of [nominal] designations. This very [denial] represents a failure of understanding (S: *asaṃgrāha,* T: *legs par ma zin pa*) in the way that was described previously."

290. S: *nirvikalapasyaiva jñānasya gocaraḥ,* T: *rnam par mi rtog pa'i ye shes kho na'i spyod yul. BBhVy* (f. 67b): "Similarly, [this phrase] indicates that this [ultimate nature of entities] is an object that is [directly] perceived exclusively by āryas."

291. In this phrase, the term translated as "entity" (S: *dharmaḥ,* T: *chos*) appears in the original Sanskrit text in the plural form, and the term translated as "substance" (S: *vastu,* T: *dngos po*) appears in the singular. *BBhVy* and *BBhVṛ* both offer several interpretations of these two terms in the context of this statement, suggesting some uncertainty regarding their precise meaning. Samudramegha offers three explanations. The first one (*BBhVy,* f. 67b) states: "The term 'entity' refers to a dependently arisen essence (S: **pratītyasamutpannasvabhāvaḥ,* T: *rten cing 'brel bar 'byung ba'i ngo bo nyid*) that is considered to be both a real thing (S: *dravyasat,* T: *rdzas su yod pa*) and one that is dependent [on conditions that are distinct from itself] (S: *paratantram,* T: *gzhan dbang*). The term 'substance' refers to the pure state of that very [dependently arisen essence]—that is to say, its ultimate mode of existence and its absolute nature." His second explanation is completely different: "Alternatively, the term 'entity' [is meant] to indicate the absolute essential nature (S: **pariniṣpannasvabhāvaḥ,* T: *yongs su grub pa'i rang bzhin*), because [a *dharma* is an entity that] possesses [literally, "holds"] a unique [essential] attribute (S: *svalakṣaṇadhāraṇāt,* T: *rang gi mtshan nyid 'dzin pa'i phyir*). The term 'substance' refers to, among the five subjects (S: *pañca vastūni,* T: *dngos po lnga*) [see note 267], that of causality (S: *nimittam*), because [this category] constitutes [the element that forms] the basis or occasion for [the application of] terms." The third explanation states: "Or, the term 'entity' is meant to indicate that which has a real mode of existing (S: *dravyasattā,* T: *rdzas su yod pa nyid*), while the term 'substance' is meant to indicate that this very [entity] is based upon names and conceptual thoughts."

figurative expressions of many different kinds can be made using numerous terms in relation to a single entity or substance. Yet among these many and diverse designating assertions, no determination whatsoever can be made which [establishes] that the essential character, composition, or nature of some entity or substance [that is expressed] by one particular designating assertion is correct, and that [the ones that are expressed] by [all] the other remaining designating assertions are not [correct]. Therefore, all entities and substances lack the [forms of] essential character, composition, or nature [that are attributed to them] by all designating assertions, both the ones that [appear] sound and the ones that are flawed.

Moreover, suppose that the entities of form, etc., as they were described previously, did possess the [kind of] essential nature [that is expressed in] a designating assertion. In that case, a substance [would have to arise] first and then, afterward, a designating assertion could be applied to it, according to the wish [of some individual]. [This would mean that,] prior to the application of the designating assertion, [which is to say, at a time] when the designating assertion had not yet been made, such an entity or substance would not possess an essential nature. However, in the absence of an essential nature, it would not be valid for there to be a designating assertion that was not related to a [real] substance. And if no application of a designating assertion is made, then it should not be right for an entity or substance to possess [the kind of] essential nature [that is expressed in] a designating assertion.

On the other hand, suppose that an entity or a substance did possess such a nature[292] prior to the application of a designating assertion when the designating assertion had not yet been made. If that were so, then even without the application of a designating assertion [to the entity called] "form," an awareness of form should occur in relation to the entity that is known as "form" and the substance that is known as "form." But [such an awareness of form] does not occur [in this manner]. For this reason and by means of this [form of] application, it can be understood with precision that all entities possess an essential nature that is ineffable. Just as [has been shown] with regard to form, the same should be understood for the [entire range of] entities as they were described [previously, which is to say, the entire series of entities] from feeling, etc., up to nirvana.

It should be understood that the following two [types of individuals] are

292. That is, the kind of essential nature that is expressed in a designating assertion.

lost to this [spiritual system of] Dharma and Vinaya:[293] (1) [the individual] who, due to having ascribed to the entities of form, etc., or the [underlying] substance of form, etc., a unique [essential] characteristic that does not truly exist and that represents an essence [formulated by] a designating assertion, then [mistakenly] adheres to [the existence of such a unique characteristic]; and (2) [the individual] who, by repudiating the substance that truly exists as ultimate truth in the form of an ineffable essence, and that is also the basis for the signs [by which] designating assertions [are formulated] and the support for the signs [by which] designating assertions [are formulated], repudiates it [by declaring] that it is completely and totally nonexistent.

The errors that occur when there is an imputation of something that does not truly exist have already been investigated, laid open, made evident, and revealed above.[294] Because these are the errors that cause something that does not truly exist to be ascribed to the substance of such [entities] as form, etc., it should be understood that [they are the reason that certain individuals] become lost to this [spiritual system of] Dharma and Vinaya.

Now I shall describe how [the individual] who denies the bare [underlying] substance that pertains to those entities of form, etc., and who [believes in] the complete annihilation of everything becomes lost to this [spiritual system of] Dharma and Vinaya.

For someone who denies the bare [underlying] substance of such entities as form, etc., neither [ultimate] reality nor [verbal] designations exist;

293. S: *dharmavinayaḥ,* T: *chos 'dul ba*. While the most common meanings of the terms *dharma* and *vinaya* are "teaching" and "discipline," respectively, the interpretation that follows indicates that this is not how they should be understood in this Sanskrit compound. For this reason, I have left the terms untranslated. In this context, the term *dharma* represents the means of attaining transcendent knowledge and the term *vinaya* represents the means of bringing about the "removal" or "expulsion" [of the mental afflictions and the obstructions to omniscience] (cf. MW, p. 971). *BBhVy* (f. 68b): "With regard to the phrase '[lost] to this [system of] Dharma and Vinaya,' it should be understood that 'this' means [the spiritual system] 'of the Tathāgata.' Regarding [the compound] *dharmavinaya,* [the term] 'Dharma' means that [this spiritual system] brings about the attainment of right knowledge and [the term] 'Vinaya' means that it brings about the abandonment [of the two types of obstruction]. That is, this phrase is a clear indication that the attainments gained in the Tathāgata's teaching are characterized by knowledge and abandonment, [which is to say] they are characterized by the path and its result." A similar description appears in Asaṅga's *Collection on [Canonical] Topics* (T: *gZhi bsdu ba,* f. 211b): "This [spiritual system of] Dharma and Vinaya is characterized by the Dharma that consists of the eightfold noble path and the results [that are attained by means] of that [Dharma]."

294. This is a reference to the three arguments that were just presented.

they are both invalid. [This can be understood] in the following way: The [nominal] designation of a person is valid only if the heaps of form, etc., [are entities that] exist.[295] It would not be valid if they do not exist, [as then] the [nominal] designation of a person would be one that is not based upon an [underlying] substance. Similarly, as long as the bare [underlying] substance of the entities of form, etc., does exist, then the application of designating assertions to the entities of form, etc., is valid. It would not be [valid] if [the bare underlying substance of form and the rest] did not exist, [because in that case] the application of designating assertions would be [an act] that is not related to a [real] substance.

According to this [interpretation], since no [real] substance exists in association with a [verbal] designation, that [verbal] designation lacks an [underlying] basis and [thus] it, too, does not exist. Therefore, certain individuals[296] who have listened to the profound sutras associated with the Great Vehicle [tradition] that are difficult to understand, that relate to emptiness, and that present a topic expressed with an underlying thought[297] have failed

295. The "heaps of form, etc.," are the five heaps (S: *pañca skandhāḥ,* T: *phung po lnga*) of form, feeling, conceptions, formations, and consciousness. All orthodox Buddhist schools hold that the self or person is a nominally existent entity that is ascribed on the basis of the five heaps (S: *skandhān upādāya prajñaptiḥ,* T: *phung po la brten nas btags pa*). Asaṅga is implying here that such a position is untenable for those who maintain too radical a view of the nature of ultimate reality. It is clear that this is a reference to the position of the Mādhyamika school of Nāgārjuna and his followers.

296. *BBhVy* (f. 69b): "'Certain individuals' means the proponents of the Middle Way school (S: *mādhyamikaḥ,* T: *dbu ma pa*)." Cf. also *PP,* pp. 156–157, where Candrakīrti defends his philosophical position against the charge that it constitutes nihilism.

297. *MSA,* ch. 12, v. 18 states that the sutras of the Great Vehicle tradition can contain four types of "underlying thought" (S: *abhiprāyaḥ,* T: *dgongs pa*). This refers to passages that are expressed with a special purpose. The one that is meant here is called "the underlying thought that has a different meaning [from the one that is explicitly stated]" (S: *arthāntarābhiprāyaḥ,* T: *don gzhan la dgongs pa*). Vasubandhu (*MSAVy,* p. 80) explains that this refers to sutra passages such as those that declare: "'All entities lack any essential nature and do not come into being,' because their meaning is not intended to be taken literally." This is undoubtedly a reference to the Perfection of Wisdom sutras, which the Mind Only school asserts require interpretation in order to be properly understood. Sthiramati provides this further clarification (*MSAVṛBh,* Tg. vol. 125, f. 242b): "The underlying thought that has a different meaning [should be understood as follows]: Those sutras that declare 'All entities lack any essential nature, [they] do not come into being, [they] do not cease to exist, and they are innately liberated' should not be viewed as declaring that [entities] do not exist at all. Rather, they state that all entities lack an essential nature in the sense of the [unreal] nature that is mentally contrived (S: *parikalpitasvabhāvaḥ,* T: *kun brtags kyi rang*

to comprehend in a proper manner the meaning that is being taught [in them]. [Furthermore,] having engaged in improper conjecture, they develop and proclaim the following view that is based upon nothing but wrongly formulated reasoning: "Everything is nothing but a [verbal] designation and this represents [ultimate] reality. Whoever perceives [things] in this way perceives [things] correctly." Because, according to them, the bare [real] substance that is the [underlying] basis of a designation does not exist, [it must also be the case that] the designation itself does not exist at all. How, then, could [the state of being that is] a mere designation represent [ultimate] reality? On the basis of this method [of reasoning], these [individuals] have repudiated both [ultimate] reality and [nominal] designations. And because of this repudiation of both [nominal] designations and [ultimate] reality, it should be understood that this is [the position of] a preeminent nihilist.[298]

Those intelligent persons who are pursuing a pure spiritual life should not converse or associate with such a nihilist. Doing so not only brings ruin upon oneself, misfortune will also befall any region where the views of such a person are looked upon with approval. This was the intent of the Blessed One when he declared: "It would be better here for someone to hold a view that believes in a [real] person than for someone to grasp [the meaning of] emptiness wrongly."

Why is that?

---

bzhin). They state that [entities] do not come into being and do not cease to exist in the sense of their dependent [nature] (S: *paratantrasvabhāvaḥ*, T: *gzhan dbang gi rang bzhin*). And they state that all entities are naturally liberated in the sense of their absolute nature (S: *pariniṣpannasvabhāvaḥ*, T: *yongs grub kyi rang bzhin*)."

298. S: *pradhānanāstikaḥ*, T: *med pa pa gtso bor gyur pa*. Asaṅga is clearly stating here that the main thesis of the Middle Way school represents an egregious form of nihilism. The Middle Way scholar Candrakīrti uses this very expression in his own *Prasannapadā* (Skt. edition, p. 142) to describe how others criticize the position of the Middle Way school: "[Others say:] 'Because you repudiate karma and its results, you are a preeminent nihilist.'" However, Nāgārjuna himself also condemns nihilism (*RA*, ch. 1, v. 57) and refers to his view as that of "[a person] who does not rely upon [either of] two [extremes]" (S: *advayaniśritaḥ*, T: *gnyis la mi brten*): "The nihilist goes to the unhappy migratory states / And the realist goes to the happy migratory states. / One who does not rely on [either of] the two [goes] to liberation / Because he thoroughly realizes things as they truly are." Nevertheless, he also acknowledges the risk of misunderstanding emptiness (*MMK*, ch. 24, v. 11): "An improper view of emptiness / Destroys a person of weak intellect, / Like a serpent wrongly held / Or a spell wrongly performed." Candrakīrti (*PP*, p. 216) describes one possible form of error as follows: "A person might suppose the following: 'Now if all of this is empty, then everything does not exist.' When that happens, he or she has fallen into [a form of] wrong view."

The individual who holds a view that believes in a [real] person is merely confused about [the nature of] objects of knowledge; he or she does not repudiate [the very existence of] all objects of knowledge. That does not cause [such a person] to be reborn in the lower realms.[299] Nor does [such a person] mislead or betray the trust of others who seek the Dharma and who wish to free themselves from suffering. He or she can cause [others] to be led to the Dharma and to the truth. He or she also will not become lax in [observing] the precepts of [moral] training.

On the other hand, by wrongly grasping [the meaning of] emptiness one is both confused about a knowable substance and also discredits all objects of knowledge. In addition, this causes [such a person] to be reborn in the lower realms. He or she brings ruin to those others who are devoted to Dharma and who wish to free themselves from suffering. He or she becomes lax in [observing] the precepts of [moral] training. This is how the person who repudiates a truly existent [real] substance becomes lost to this [spiritual system of] Dharma and Vinaya.

How, then, does emptiness become wrongly grasped?

If an ascetic or brahmin neither assents to that [quality] of which [entities] are empty nor assents to that [state] which constitutes emptiness, this is the way in which emptiness is said to be wrongly grasped.

Why is that?

The validity of emptiness is [defined by] the nonexistence of that [quality] of which [entities] are empty and the existence of that [state] which constitutes emptiness. But if it is [held to be] a [state of] complete nonexistence, what could be [the entity] in relation to which this empty [state] might occur, what could this empty [state] consist of, and what [quality] could [entities] be empty of? It would also not be possible for emptiness [to be a state that] pertains to this [particular entity] or for it to be [a state in which an entity is] empty of this [particular quality]. Therefore, this is how emptiness becomes wrongly grasped.

How, then, does emptiness become correctly grasped?

Because a certain [quality] does not exist in relation to some [entity], one perceives: "This [entity] is empty of that [quality]." Moreover, one truly

299. S: *apāyāḥ*. The usual Tibetan translation of this term is *ngan song,* which in the plural is generally understood to mean all three of the lower realms—that is, the birth state of animals, hungry ghosts, and hell beings. However, the Tibetan translation here is *dmyal ba rnams,* which refers only to the hell regions, suggesting that is how the term is to be taken here.

realizes in relation to what remains there: "This [emptiness] is real and it does exist here." This [latter realization] is called "the true and unerring entry into emptiness." That is to say, [such a person realizes] that there does not exist any entity that possesses the nature [that is expressed by] a designating assertion, such as those of "form," etc., [as they are expressed] in relation to those substances known as form, etc., that were indicated [earlier]. Therefore, the substances that are known as form, etc., are empty of that nature [that is expressed by] designating assertions [that posit entities] such as "form," etc.

What, then, is there that remains in relation to the [real] substance that is [variously] known as form, etc.?

It is just that which constitutes the basis for the designating assertions [that posit entities] such as "form," etc. More specifically, one realizes both of the following things as they truly are: (1) the bare substance and (2) the mere [nominal] designation that exists in relation to that bare substance. Moreover, one does not falsely attribute that which does not truly exist nor does one repudiate that which does truly exist. One does not engage in either [false] augmentation or [unwarranted] diminution. Nothing [valid] is excluded and nothing [invalid] is interpolated. There is a true realization of the genuine suchness [of things] and the ineffable essential nature [of things]. This is called "the emptiness that has been correctly grasped and well penetrated by means of correct wisdom." This favorable form of application that relates to demonstrating correctness is the one by which the ineffable essential nature of all entities can be understood with precision.

Scriptural Evidence [1.4.7]

The ineffable essential nature of all entities can also be understood on the basis of trustworthy scripture. As the Blessed One declared in the *Sutra on [the Manner of] Passing Over to a [New] Existence*,[300] this very meaning is clarified in a verse recitation:

> Verily, by whatever names
> Entities may be expressed,
> That is not to be found there.[301]
> This, indeed, is the true nature of entities.

300. S: *Bhavasaṃkrāntisūtram,* T: *Srid pa 'pho ba'i mdo.*

301. *BBhVy* (f. 71b): "'That' refers to the mentally contrived nature (*S: *parikalpitasvabhāvaḥ,*

How, then, does this verse set forth its meaning?

A name is [a term], such as "form," etc., for the entities that are known as form, etc. [The first two lines of the verse state the following:] By whatever names—such as those of "form," etc.—the entities known as form, etc., are expressed and verbally described—[that is, the entities that are expressed by the names] "form," "feeling," [and so on] at length up to "nirvana" . . . [The third line states:] It is not the case that the entities known as form, etc., themselves, possessing the nature of form, etc., [are to be found] there. It is also not the case that some other entity possessing the nature of form, etc., is to be found in those [entities known as form, etc.]. [The last line of the verse states:] On the other hand, the ineffable mode of existence that pertains to the entities known as form, etc., should be understood to constitute their true essential nature [that exists] in an ultimate sense.

The Blessed One also declared in the [sutras known as] *The Sections on Objects:*[302]

> Whatever things are agreed upon in the world,
> The Muni does not admit to any of them.
> As he does not assent, why would anything be grasped?
> Thus, he generates no desire for what is seen or heard.

How does this verse set forth its meaning?

The designations such as "form," etc., that are made in relation to the substances that are known as form, etc., are what are referred to as "the things

T: *kun tu brtags pa'i ngo bo nyid*). 'There' refers to the dependent nature (*S: *paratantrasvabhāvaḥ,* T: *gzhan gyi dbang gi ngo bo nyid*). [Thus, this line of the verse indicates that] the former is not to be found in the latter."

302. S: *Arthavargiyāḥ,* T: *Chos kyi sde tshan dag. BBhVy* (f. 71b) indicates that this verse is from a text found in the *Saṃyuktāgama* section of the Sanskrit canon of the Listeners' Vehicle.

that are agreed upon."[303] [The Muni] does not admit[304] that the things that are agreed upon [by the world] possess a real substantive essence that is identical in nature with [what is expressed by] those designations.

Why is that?

[The Muni] does not hold a view that [either mistakenly] ascribes [a quality that does not exist] or that [mistakenly] denies [a quality that does exist]. Therefore, he is said to be "one who does not assent,"[305] in the sense that he does not have a view that maintains an error. Being one who does not assent

303. The Sanskrit term *saṃvṛtiḥ* (T: *kun rdzob*) is translated here as "a thing that is agreed upon" not only to distinguish it from the term *vyavahāraḥ* (T: *tha snyad*), which is similar in meaning, but also because it is considered to mean literally "[that which is] generally accepted" or "[that about which there is] common consent" (cf. Pali *sammuti*). It is clear that both Yogācāra and Mādhyamika scholars largely equate the Sanskrit term *saṃvṛtiḥ* (T: *kun rdzob*) with *vyavahāraḥ* (T: *tha snad*), which means a "conventional usage" or "an object of ordinary life." For example, Sthiramati states (*MVṬ,* p. 95): "'a thing that is agreed upon' is a conventional [object]" (S: *saṃvṛtir vyavahāraḥ,* T: *kun rdzob ni tha snad do*). Similarly, Nāgārjuna (*MMK,* ch. 24, vv. 8, 10) recognizes the term usually translated as "conventional truth" or "relative truth" (S: *saṃvṛtisatyam,* T: *kun rdzob bden pa*) to be equivalent with the expression "[object of] conventional usage" (S: *vyavahāraḥ,* T: *tha snyad*). I have not found a literal interpretation (T: *niruktiḥ,* T: *nges tshig*) of the Sanskrit *saṃvṛtiḥ* in Yogācāra literature; however, several occur in Mādhyamika writings, of which perhaps the most well known is this passage from Candrakīrti's *Prasannapadā* (p. 215): "*saṃvṛtiḥ* means 'that which completely obscures,' for ignorance is called *saṃvṛtiḥ* in the sense that it completely conceals the [ultimate] reality of all entities. Or, *saṃvṛtiḥ* means 'mutual arising' in the sense that [things] are dependent on one another. Alternatively, *saṃvṛtiḥ* is an 'agreement'—which is to say, a commonly accepted usage. And that [refers to those things] that have the quality of being an expression, the object of an expression, a [form of] awareness, an object of awareness, etc."

304. S: *upaiti,* T: *zhal gyis bzhes.* The basic meaning of this verb is "to go near to" or "to approach." It can also be understood to mean "to take up" or "to become involved with" something, in the sense of being drawn to it out of desire. As the Tibetan translation suggests, Asaṅga here interprets the verb in a third sense, which is "to admit" or "to agree to" some notion, in this case the mistaken belief that ordinary objects possess real essences. *BBhVy* (f. 71b) identifies two forms of "admission" (T: *khas len pa*) in this verse: "In saying that [the Muni] does not admit [to ordinary conventional entities], the entities of form, etc., are admitted to by a view and by craving. A view grasps at entities in a manner that [mistakenly] adheres to them [in a certain way], while craving grasps at them in a manner that does not want to let go of them. [Both of these forms of grasping represent] the act of making an "admission." Because the Muni is free of both [kinds of admission, the verse states that he] "does not admit to" [ordinary conventional entities]." The second type of admission addressed in the verse is the craving that arises toward objects that are seen or heard.

305. S: *anupagaḥ,* T: *zhal gyis mi bzhes.* This noun is formed from another verb that is virtually identical in meaning with the one addressed in the previous note. It can be rendered

in this way, why would anything be grasped repeatedly? [That is to say,] in the absence such a view, there occurs no repeated grasping at a real substance either in the sense of ascribing [to it a quality that it does not have] or in the sense of denying [of it a quality that it does have] and, [therefore,] he becomes one who sees an object of knowledge correctly. This is what is seen by him. Whatever words are heard regarding an object of knowledge [that is understood] in just this way constitutes what is heard by him. [Therefore,] he neither develops nor strengthens any craving toward that which is seen or heard. There is no other means by which he could abandon [attachment for] an object and remain in a state of equanimity. This is the way in which he avoids generating desire.

The Blessed One again declared to Saṃtha Kātyāyana:

> Here, Saṃtha, a *bhikṣu* does not rely upon earth when he meditates. He does not rely upon water, fire, or air [when he meditates]; [he does not rely upon] the sphere of space, [the sphere of] consciousness, [the sphere of] nothingness, and [the sphere in which there is] neither conception nor absence of conception;[306] [he does not rely upon] this world and the next world; the pair of the sun and moon; that which is seen, heard, considered, or perceived; or that which is attained, sought, deliberated upon, and reflected upon with the mind. He does not rely upon anything when he meditates.
>
> How does he meditate so as not to rely upon earth when he meditates, [and so on, up to how does he meditate] so as not to rely upon anything when he meditates?
>
> Here, Saṃtha, the conception of earth that occurs in relation to earth has been eliminated by the *bhikṣu*. The conception of water that occurs in relation to water, and so on, up to the conceptions that occur in relation to everything have been eliminated [by the *bhikṣu*]. This is how a *bhikṣu* meditates so as not to rely upon earth when he meditates, and so on, up to [this is

literally as "one who does not approach," "one who does not become involved," or, as it is rendered here, "one who does not assent" to mistaken beliefs.

306. These are the names of the four levels of the formless realms and their related forms of meditative composure.

how a *bhikṣu*] meditates so as not to rely on anything when he meditates.

From afar, the gods, together with [their chiefs] Indra, Īśāna, and Prajapati, pay homage to a *bhikṣu* who meditates in this manner, when they declare:

> Homage to you, O noble of men.
> Homage to you, O best of men.
> What is it that we cannot realize about you
> And which you rely upon when meditating?

How, then, does this sutra passage set forth its meaning?

The designation of a conventional name,[307] such as that of "earth," etc., to the substance known as earth, etc., is what is called "the conception of earth," etc. That conception, further, can either be one that [wrongly] ascribes [a quality that does not exist] or it can be one that [incorrectly] denies [a quality that does exist] in relation to the entities known as earth, etc. [The conception which] holds that [an entity] possesses this [or that kind of] substantive essence [is said to be the type] that [wrongly] ascribes [a quality which does not exist]. [The conception which] holds that the bare substance that represents [an entity's] ultimate nature is to be rejected is said to be the [type of] conception that [incorrectly] denies [a quality that does exist]. These [two errors] are what are eliminated [by a *bhikṣu* or *bhikṣuṇī*] from conceptions. Their abandonment and relinquishment are what is called their "elimina-

307. S: *nāmasaṃketaprajñāptiḥ,* T: *ming du brdar brtags pa*. This description of the nature of conception (S: *saṃjñā,* T: *'du shes*)—the mental factor (S: *caittaḥ,* T: *sems byung*) that makes up the third of the five heaps (S: *skandaḥ,* T: *phung po*)—can be compared with the one Asaṅga provides in his *Compendium of Higher Learning* (*AS,* p. 2): "What is the defining attribute of conception? The defining attribute of conception is the act of forming a judgment (S: *saṃjānanam,* T: *'dus te shes par byed pa*). It is that [mental factor] which, through perceiving a variety of qualities and mental images, [enables one to] discuss objects in the manner that they were seen, heard, thought about, or realized." (The published Sanskrit version of this description is somewhat problematic.) Vasubandhu's classic definition (*AK,* ch. 1, v. 14cd) is: "Conception has the nature of grasping a sign" (S: *saṃjñā nimittodgrahanātmikā,* T: *'du shes ni / mtshan mar 'dzin pa'i bdag nyid do*). Sthiramati explains this phrase (*PSV,* p. 271): "'Sign' means that quality of the object which serves as the cause for determining that it is blue or yellow, etc. Thus, to grasp a [particular object's] sign means to make the determination, 'This [object] is blue,' or 'This [object] is yellow,' and the like."

tion." Therefore, it can also be understood on the basis of scripture—[which is to say,] through [relying upon] the Tathāgata's supremely trustworthy word—that all entities have an [ultimate] nature that is ineffable.

If it is true that all entities possess such an ineffable nature, why is it that words are used in relation to them?

Without [the use of] words, it would not be possible for that ineffable true nature to be expressed to others nor [would it be possible for it] to be heard [by others]. Moreover, without speech and the hearing [of speech], it would also not be possible for that ineffable nature to be realized. Therefore, words are used so that [the explanation of the ultimate nature of all entities] might be heard and realized.

The Eight Types of Conceptual Thought [1.4.8]

Because they have not fully realized this very suchness in the manner [that has just been described], immature beings[308] develop the eight types of conceptual thought that give rise to three [kinds of] substance and that bring forth the entire world of sentient beings and their physical environment. [The eight conceptual thoughts] are the following: (1) the conceptual thought [that conceives] of an essential nature, (2) the conceptual thought [that conceives] of a distinguishing characteristic, (3) the conceptual thought that grasps a collection [as a separate entity], (4) the conceptual thought [that conceives] of an "I," (5) the conceptual thought [that conceives] of [entities as being] "mine," (6) the conceptual thought [that conceives] of [entities as being] agreeable, (7) the conceptual thought [that conceives] of [entities as being] disagreeable, and (8) the conceptual thought [that conceives] of [entities as being] the opposite of both of these.[309]

Which of these eight types of conceptual thought give rise to the three substances?

Three conceptual thoughts—that is, the conceptual thought [that conceives] of an essential nature, the conceptual thought [that conceives] of a distinguishing characteristic, and the conceptual thought that grasps a

308. S: *bālaḥ,* T: *byis pa*. *BBhVy* (f. 73a) characterizes them as "the immature beings that lack knowledge of reality." See also note 252.

309. That is, this last type of conceptual thought conceives of entities as neither agreeable nor disagreeable. In other words, it conceives of an entity in a qualitatively neutral manner which, therefore, leads to an attitude of indifference toward it.

collection [as a separate entity]—give rise to the substance that is [variously] known as form, etc., and that serves as [both] the basis for conceptual thought and elaboration[310] and the mental support of conceptual thought and elaboration. While continuously generating elaborations on the basis of [a particular substance], the conceptual thought that is both controlled by and governed by expressions [that derive from] recognition of [an object's] name operates in numerous ways and in many different forms in relation to this very same substance.

With regard to this [point], two conceptual thoughts—that is, the conceptual thought [that conceives] of an "I" and the conceptual thought [that conceives] of [entities as being] "mine"—give rise to the view of the perishable collection,[311] which is the root of all the remaining views,[312] and [also give rise] to egoistic pride,[313] which is the root of [ordinary] pride and the root of all the other forms of pride.[314]

310. S: *vikalpaprapañcaḥ*, T: *rnam par rtog pa'i spros pa*. *BBhVy* (f. 73b) explains this compound as follows: "A conceptual thought itself is an elaboration, because [its object] has an imagined nature (T: *rnam par rtog pa nyid spros pa ste / brtags pa'i ngo bo nyid yin pa'i phyir ro*)." See above, note 264, for further remarks about the term "elaboration."

311. S: *satkāyadṛṣṭiḥ*, T: *'jig tshogs la lta ba*. *AS* (p. 7): "What is the view of the perishable collection? It is the [sense of] acceptance, the [sense of] approval, the [erring] determination, the reflection, and the view in which the five grasping heaps are perceived either as constituting a self or as belonging to a self. Its action is to provide support for all the [mistaken] views that arise." The term "perishable collection" is a reference to the impermanent five heaps. *PSV* (p. 296): "To be 'perishable' means to undergo destruction. To be a 'collection' means to be an assemblage of things."

312. In Buddhist Abhidharma literature, five mistaken views are emphasized. The remaining four are (1) the view that grasps an extreme, (2) wrong view, (3) the consideration that views are supreme, and (4) the consideration that morality and asceticism are supreme. See *PS*, p. 235 and *PSV*, pp. 301–302.

313. S: *asmimānaḥ*, T: *nga'o snyam pa'i nga rgyal*. *AS* (p. 45): "What is egoistic pride? The swelling up of the mind that originates from the mistaken notion that the five grasping heaps either constitute a self or belong to a self."

314. Abhidharma literature identifies seven types of pride. *AS* (p. 45) describes the remaining six as follows: "What is [ordinary] pride (S: *mānaḥ*, T: *nga rgyal*)? The swelling up of the mind in which you think of someone who is inferior to you, 'I am better [than him or her],' or of someone who is your equal, 'I am [his or her] equal.' What is extraordinary pride (S: *atimānaḥ*, T: *che ba'i nga rgyal*)? The swelling up of the mind in which you think of someone who is your equal, 'I am better [than him or her],' or of someone who is superior to you, 'I am [his or her] equal.' What is extreme pride (S: *mānātimānaḥ*, T: *nga rgyal las kyang nga rgyal*)? The swelling up of the mind in which you think of someone who is superior to you, 'I am better [than him or her].' What is exaggerated pride (S: *abhimānaḥ*,

[Continuing] with this point, the conceptual thought [that conceives] of [entities as being] agreeable, the conceptual thought [that conceives] of [entities as being] disagreeable, and the conceptual thought [that conceives] of [entities as being] the opposite of both of these, according to circumstances, give rise to desire, hatred, and ignorance.

This is the manner in which the eight types of conceptual thought operate to bring about the three types of substance—that is, (1) the substance [that engenders] elaboration and is the basis of conceptual thought; (2) [the substance that consists of] the view [of the perishable collection] and egoistic pride; and (3) [the substance that consists of] desire, hatred, and ignorance. Regarding these, the basis for the view of the perishable collection and egoistic pride is the substance [that is the basis of] conceptual thought and [that engenders] elaboration. Desire, hatred, and ignorance are based upon the view of the perishable collection and egoistic pride. The aspect of all the worlds that relates to their progression[315] is explained exhaustively by means of these three [types of] substance.

T: *mngon pa'i nga rgyal*)? The swelling up of the mind in which you think toward higher special attainments that you have not achieved, 'I have achieved them.' What is pride of inferiority (S: *ūnamānaḥ,* T: *cung zad snam pa'i nga rgyal*)? The swelling up of the mind in which you think of someone who is very much superior to you, 'I am only slightly inferior to him.' What is wrong pride (S: *mithyāmānaḥ,* T: *log pa'i nga rgyal*)? The swelling up of the mind in which you think, 'I possess good qualities,' when you are not someone who possesses good qualities."

315. *BBhVy* (f. 73b): "'All the worlds' means the world of sentient beings and their physical environment." The term "progression" (S: *pravṛttiḥ,* T: *'jug pa*) represents one of the twenty-three formations that do not accompany consciousness as described by Asaṅga in *AS* (p. 11): "What is progression? The [nominal] designation 'progression' is [one that is made] in reference to an unbroken succession of causes and effects." In the present usage, "progression" refers to the process by which samsara is repeatedly set in motion and perpetuated until one succeeds in bringing it to an end. *PSV* (p. 338): "'Samsara' refers to the arising of the grasping heaps within the uninterrupted continuum of a class affiliate (S: *nikāyasabhāgaḥ,* T: *rigs mthun pa*) that does not stand still for even an instant. For [samsara] to be 'set in motion' (S: *pravṛttiḥ,* T: *'jug pa*) [this is the same term that is also being translated as "progression"] means [for the grasping heaps] to reenter [a birth state at the conception of] another class affiliate. For samsara to be 'brought to an end' (S: *nivṛttiḥ,* T: *ldog pa*) refers to the states that are called 'the nirvana in which the support of the heaps still remains' and 'the nirvana in which the support of the heaps does not remain.'" The term "class affiliate" refers to the continuum of heaps that occurs within a particular sentient being's single birth (see notes 880 and 1014).

Regarding [the eight types of conceptual thought], what is the conceptual thought [that conceives] of an essential nature?

The conceptual thought [that generates the mental construct] "form," etc., in relation to the [type of] substance that is known as form, etc., is called "the conceptual thought [that conceives] of an essential nature."

What is the conceptual thought [that conceives] of a distinguishing characteristic?

The [form of] conceptual thinking that is based upon the conceptual thought of an essential nature and that forms a mental construct with some distinct meaning in relation to that very substance known as form, etc., such as, "This [object] is material,"[316] "This [object] is immaterial," "This [object] is visible,"[317] or "This [object] is not visible," or that similarly [forms a mental construct with some distinct meaning] in an immeasurable variety of

316. *AS* (p. 17) describes twenty ways in which form should be understood as being material (S: *rupī,* T: *gzugs can*). The first states that form is material because it possesses the nature of form (S: *tadātmataḥ,* T: *de'i bdag nyid kyi phyir*). This response clearly begs the question as to what that nature is. *AS* and *AKB* both identify it with a term that can be translated as "displaying [the quality of] form" (S: *rūpaṇam,* T: *gzugs su yod pa* or *gzugs su rung ba*). A sutra passage that is frequently cited as a source for this term states: "Because [the entities that comprise the form heap] exhibit the nature of form, O monks, that is why it is called the 'grasping heap of form.' What does it mean to exhibit the nature of form? For instance, an object that can be touched with the hand exhibits the nature of form." *AKB* further glosses the quality of exhibiting form to mean that which is "capable of being damaged" (S: *bādhyate,* T: *gnod par bya rung ba*). The damage that form undergoes is further described as meaning that it can be "caused to undergo a transformation" (S: *vipariṇāmotpādanā,* T: *yongs su 'gyur ba bskyed pa*) or to undergo "a deteriorating change" (S: *vikriyā,* T: *rnam par 'gyur ba*). Asaṅga's second explanation regarding the nature of form states that it is "because [form] is based in the [four] elements" (S: *bhūtāśrayataḥ,* T: *'byung ba rten du gyur pa'i phyir*). This description is meant to indicate two things: (1) all derivative form (i.e., the five sense objects and the five sense faculties) is based in the four great elements; and (2) the four elements themselves are mutually dependent in the sense that they always occur in combination.

317. S: *sanidarśanam,* T: *bstan du yod pa*. The meaning of the term *nidarśanam* is clearly stated in *AKV* (vol. 1, p. 78): "That quality which enables an entity to be pointed to is called *nidarśanam*. Alternatively, *nidarśanam* is that quality that enables an eye consciousness to be generated in another person by means of speech." Thus, *sanidarśanam* literally means a quality that makes entities "capable of being pointed out" in the sense that one person can use speech or some other form of communication to cause another person to perceive a particular instance of visible form.

[other] ways including, "This [object] possesses resistance,"[318] "This [object] lacks resistance," "This [object] is related to the outflows,"[319] "This [object] is free of the outflows," "This [object] is conditioned,"[320] "This [object] is unconditioned," "This [object] is virtuous,"[321] "This [object] is nonvirtuous,"

318. S: *sapratighaḥ,* T: *thogs pa dang bcas pa*. *AKB* (p. 19) identifies resistance (S: *pratighaḥ,* T: *thogs pa*) as "opposition" (S: *pratighātaḥ,* T: *rdugs pa*) and describes it as being of three types: (1) obstruction-opposition (S: *āvaraṇapratighātaḥ,* T: *sgrib pa la thogs pa*); (2) the opposition of a [sense] object (S: *viṣayapratighātaḥ,* T: *yul la thogs pa*); and (3) the opposition of a [mental] object (S: *ālambanapratighātaḥ,* T: *dmigs pa la thogs pa*). The principal form of resistance is the first type, which is described as "[one object] preventing another object from arising in the place where it is located, as when [one] hand is struck by [another] hand. Or, [as a hand will not arise] in a place that is occupied by a stone. Or, as a stone [will not arise in a place that is occupied] by either [a stone or a hand]." "The opposition of a [sense] object" is when any of the five sense faculties makes contact with its corresponding object, this being the event that causes the arising of a particular type of sense consciousness. "The opposition of a [mental] object" occurs when any of the different types of consciousness and their attendant mental factors apprehend a specific object. The latter two types of opposition are further described as a case in which the action of an agent—that is, a sense faculty or a form of mind—is limited to some specific object. Thus, the "opposition" consists of the fact that, when this occurs, the agent is not able to act upon some other object.

319. See note 196.

320. S: *saṃskṛtaḥ,* T: *'dus byas*. This Buddhist term refers to any entity that is impermanent and produced by causes. A classic literal explanation of the term appears in *AKB* (p. 4): "[Conditioned entities] are those that are produced by the convergence and combination of conditional factors." Conditioned entities are coextensive with the five heaps and can either be entities that are related to the outflows or entities that are free of the outflows. Those that are of the first type are samsaric in nature and correspond to the first two of the four noble truths. Those that are free of the outflows are represented by the truth of the path. Nirvana, space, emptiness, and the truth of cessation are examples of unconditioned entities (S: *asaṃskṛtaḥ,* T: *'dus ma byas*).

321. Various criteria are presented for identifying an entity as being virtuous. *AKB* (p. 202) states: "[Entities are virtuous] in four ways: (1) in an ultimate sense, (2) by their nature, (3) by association [with entities that are virtuous by their nature], and (4) on the strength of their motivation." *AKB* identifies *nirvāṇa* and *AS* identifies suchness as the entity that is virtuous in an ultimate sense (S: *paramārthataḥ,* T: *don dam pas*). *AS* describes these eleven mental factors as the entities that are virtuous by their nature (S: *svabhāvataḥ,* T: *ngo bo nyid kyis*): faith, shame, abashment, the root virtue that is avoidance of attachment, the root virtue that is avoidance of hatred, the root virtue that is avoidance of ignorance, effort, agility, mindfulness, and equanimity. The entities that are virtuous by association (S: *saṃprayogataḥ,* T: *mtshung par ldan gyis*) are the forms of consciousness and the other mental factors that accompany the eleven virtuous mental factors. The entities that are virtuous on the strength of their motivation (S: *utthānataḥ,* T: *kun nas slong bas*) are the karma of body and speech that is generated by the mental entities that are virtuous by their

"This [object] is determinate,"[322] "This [object] is indeterminate,"[323] "This [object] is of the past," "This [object] is of the future," or "This [object] is of the present," as well as [other mental constructs with some distinct meaning] of the same kind as these, is called "the conceptual thought [that conceives] of a distinguishing characteristic."

What is the conceptual thought that grasps a collection [as a separate entity]?

[The type of conceptual thought] that occurs in relation to that very substance known as form, etc., is accompanied by such conventional names as "self," "sentient being," "living being," or "living creature,"[324] and is caused by grasping a collection that consists of a multiplicity of entities that have been combined into a [single] mass, as well as [the type of conceptual thought that occurs] in relation to such [composite things] as a house, an army, and a forest, etc., or food, drink, a vehicle, and clothing, etc., and is accompanied by the conventional name for those things, is what is called "the conceptual thought that grasps a collection [as a separate entity]."[325]

---

nature and virtuous by association. *AS* describes a number of other categories by which virtuous entities are singled out for their important role in spiritual practice.

322. S: *vyākṛtaḥ,* T: *lung du bstan pa*. Generally, this term refers to those entities about which the Buddha made a declaration or prediction. Virtuous and nonvirtuous entities, in particular, are of this type, because the Buddha declared that they invariably have a favorable and an unfavorable consequence, respectively.

323. S: *avyākṛtaḥ,* T: *lung du ma bstan pa*. Those deeds that the Buddha did not declare as either virtuous or nonvirtuous in nature are described as indeterminate. *AK* (ch. 4, v. 9d) and *AS* (p. 24) both identify two unconditioned entities—space and the nonanalytic cessation (S: *apratisaṃkhyānirodhaḥ,* T: *so sor brtags pa ma yin pas 'gog pa*)—as indeterminate in an absolute sense. Four paradigmatic examples of indeterminate entities are the following: (1) the maturations of virtuous and nonvirtuous deeds; (2) the four types of physical activity—i.e., walking, standing, sitting, and reclining—when carried out in a state of mind that is neither virtuous nor under the influence of any of the mental afflictions; (3) the activity of practicing any of the various physical or manual arts (S: *śilpasthānam,* T: *bzo yi gnas*); and (4) the mind that produces emanations (S: *nirmāṇacittam,* T: *sprul pa'i sems*), i.e., a mental power that can manifest physical objects and that stems from having attained one-pointed concentration.

324. All four of these terms are synonymous in that they are used to designate a living being and occur in relation to the collection of the five heaps.

325. This somewhat complicated statement essentially describes two types of conceptual thoughts that grasp a collection: (1) the conceptual thought that grasps a sentient being other than oneself as a sentient being and (2) the conceptual thought that grasps other composite objects as a single entity. The first of these is described as having three essential elements: (1) It occurs in relation to the five heaps of form, etc. Of these, form is directly

What are the conceptual thoughts [that conceive] of an "I" and [conceive] of [entities as being] "mine"?

The false conceptual thought that arises in dependence upon the substance that is related to the outflows and is related to the act of being grasped, that for a long time has been habitually thought of, [mistakenly] adhered to, and familiarly regarded as [constituting] an "I" or a "mine," and that, because of this habituation to a mistaken understanding, represents the substance that constitutes the object of [an individual's] own [erroneous] views, is called "the conceptual thought [that conceives] of an 'I' and [conceives] of [entities as being] 'mine.'"

What is the conceptual thought [that conceives] of [entities as] agreeable?

It is the [type of] conceptual thought whose mental support[326] is a substance that is beautiful and attractive.

What is the conceptual thought [that conceives] of [entities as] disagreeable?

It is the [type of] conceptual thought whose mental support is a substance that is ugly and unattractive.

What is the conceptual thought [that conceives] of [entities] in a way that is the opposite of both agreeable and disagreeable?

It is the [type of] conceptual thought whose mental support is a substance that is neither beautiful nor ugly, and neither attractive nor unattractive.

In brief, this [explanation] consists of these two [elements]: (1) conceptual thought and (2) the substance that forms the basis of and the mental support for conceptual thought. Both of these should be understood as having existed since beginningless time and as having been each other's reciprocal cause. A previous conceptual thought [serves as the cause] for the appearance of a present substance that constitutes the mental support for [a

perceived; the other four mental heaps are inferred. (2) It is accompanied by any of the various conventional names that is used to refer to a sentient being. (3) It arises after having grasped such a collection of multiple entities as a single living being. The second type of conceptual thought that grasps a collection is described in simpler terms: It is one that grasps a group of entities or a composite entity as a single thing. For example, a collection of trees is conceived of as a forest, a large array of soldiers is thought to constitute an army, threads that have been woven into cloth and fashioned into a garment are regarded as an article of clothing, and a collection of parts that have been assembled in a particular way to construct a wagon or cart are recognized as a vehicle, etc.

326. S: *ālambanam,* T: *dmigs pa.* The literal meaning of this term is "[a thing] that is laid hold of" or "[a thing] that is leaned upon." In Buddhist usage, it refers exclusively to a mental object. See also note 146.

present] conceptual thought. Moreover, a present substance that has been caused to appear and that is the mental support for a conceptual thought [serves as] the cause for the appearance of the present conceptual thought for which it constitutes a mental support.

Regarding this [point], the current lack of thorough knowledge regarding [the nature of] a conceptual thought [serves as the cause] for the appearance of a substance in the future that will become the mental support for [a conceptual thought that exists at] that [time]. Moreover, because of the arising of that [substance], inevitably the appearance of a conceptual thought for which that [substance] serves as the basis and the support will also occur.

The Four Investigations [1.4.9]

How, then, does the thorough knowledge of these conceptual thoughts occur?

[It occurs] by means of the four investigations and the four forms of thorough knowledge of the way things truly are.

What are the four investigations?[327]

[They are] (1) the investigation of names, (2) the investigation of substances, (3) the investigation of [what constitutes] the designation of an essential nature, and (4) the investigation of [what constitutes] the designation of a distinguishing characteristic.

Regarding these, the investigation of names is that [process by] which a bodhisattva perceives, in relation to a name, that it is merely a name. Similarly, [the process that results in] the perception, in relation to a substance, that it is a bare substance constitutes the investigation of substances. The investigation of [what constitutes] the designation of an essential nature is [the process that results in] the perception that the designation of an essential nature is merely the [nominal] designation of an essential nature. The investigation of [what constitutes] the designation of a distinguishing characteristic is [the process that results in] the perception that the designation of a distinguishing characteristic is merely the [nominal] designation of a distinguishing characteristic. [The bodhisattva] perceives both the defining attributes of names and substances that are distinct [from one another], as well as the defining attributes that connect them.[328] He or she also realizes

327. S: *catasraḥ paryeṣanāḥ,* T: *yongs su 'tshol ba bzhi.*

328. S: *anuśliṣṭaṃ lakṣaṇam,* T: *mtshan nyid 'brel ba. BBhVy* (f. 75a): "When [a bodhisattva]

that the designation of an essential nature and the designation of a distinguishing characteristic are [both] based upon the connection [that exists] between a name and a substance.

THE FOUR FORMS OF THOROUGH KNOWLEDGE OF THE WAY THINGS TRULY ARE [1.4.10]

What are the four forms of thorough knowledge of the way things truly are?[329]

They are (1) the thorough knowledge of the way things truly are [that is gained by] having completed the investigation of names, (2) [the thorough knowledge of the way things truly are that is gained by] having completed the investigation of substances, (3) [the thorough knowledge of the way things truly are that is gained by] having completed the investigation of [what constitutes] the designation of an essential nature, and (4) the thorough knowledge of the way things truly are [that is gained by] having completed the investigation of [what constitutes] the designation of a distinguishing characteristic.

What is the thorough knowledge of the way things truly are that has completed the investigation of names?

Having examined, with regard to names, the quality of being a mere name, a bodhisattva gains the following thorough knowledge regarding the true nature of names: This is the extent of the import of a name that is established in relation to [some] substance: its nominal import,[330] its theoretical import,[331] and its suppositional import.[332]

---

investigates [each of these four topics] in this way, he or she perceives that a name and a substance are completely distinct; however, even though they are distinct, the name of a particular substance cannot be applied to any other [substance] and, therefore, he or she also realizes the defining attributes that connect them."

329. S: *catvāri yathābhūtaparijñānāni,* T: *yang dag pa ji lta ba bzhin du yongs su shes pa bzhi.*

330. S: *saṃjñārtham,* T: *'du shes kyi don.* Tibetan editions have *'du byed kyi don,* which seems to be a corruption. *BBhVy* (f. 75b): "Because the defining characteristic of a name is that of causing something to be identified, the sense of the expression 'nominal import' is that of a meaning that is perceived on the basis of a name and a sign."

331. S: *dṛṣṭyartham,* T: *lta ba'i don.* Ibid: "The expression 'theoretical import' indicates the arising of adherence [to a belief] that accords with one's conceptions."

332. S: *upacārārtham,* T: *nye bar 'dogs pa'i don.* Ibid: "The phrase 'suppositional import'

If a name such as "form" is not applied to a substance, such as one that is known as form, etc., then one will not form the conception of any substance whatsoever as being "form," etc. When no conception is made [in relation to a substance], then one will not [mistakenly] adhere to it in the sense of [wrongly] ascribing [to it a quality that it does not possess]. When no [mistaken] adherence is made, then one will not make verbal assertions about it. [When a bodhisattva] truly discerns how this [process] occurs, that is called "the thorough knowledge of the way things truly are [that is gained by] having completed the investigation of names."

What is the thorough knowledge of the way things truly are that has completed the investigation of substances?

Through having investigated, with regard to substances, the nature of being a bare substance, a bodhisattva perceives the substance that is [variously] known as form, etc., as being separate from all expressions and incapable of being described. This is the second form of thorough knowledge of the way things truly are, one that is gained by having completed the investigation of substances.

What is the thorough knowledge of the way things truly are [that is gained by] having completed the investigation of [what constitutes] the designation of an essential nature?

Through having investigated, in relation to the designation of an essential nature that occurs with regard to the substance that is [variously] known as form, etc., the quality of being a mere [nominal] designation, a bodhisattva realizes and understands, as it truly is, that a substance that lacks this [nominally designated] essential nature [only] appears to possess it because of the manner in which the designation of an essential nature occurs. His or her perception that this [nominally designated] essential nature is like a [mentally generated] emanation, a reflection, an echo, a false image, [a reflection of] the moon in water, [an object in] a dream, or a magical illusion, and that this appearance is not [truly] made up of that [nominally designated essential nature], constitutes the third form of thorough knowledge of the way things truly are, one whose field of action is a profound object.

What is the thorough knowledge of the way things truly are [that is gained by] having completed the investigation of [what constitutes] the designation of a distinguishing characteristic?

---

indicates the formulation of verbal assertions that accord with [a doctrinal belief] that is being adhered to."

Through having investigated, in relation to the designation of a distinguishing characteristic, the quality of being a mere [nominal] designation, a bodhisattva perceives, in relation to the substance that is [variously] known as form, etc., the designation of the distinguishing characteristic in a nondual sense—[which is to say,] that a substance is neither a thing that exists nor a thing that does not exist. Because its verbally described nature does not constitute an absolute mode of being,[333] it is not a thing that exists. On the other hand, it is also not a thing that does not exist, because it is characterized by a [real] nature that is ineffable. Similarly, [form] both lacks the quality of being material from the perspective of ultimate truth and does not lack the quality of being material from the perspective of relative truth, since it is described in a provisional sense as constituting form. Just as with [the distinguishing characteristics] of being a thing that exists or a thing that does not exist, and those of being material or immaterial, all the [other] instances of designating a distinguishing characteristic, such as those of being visible or not visible, etc., should be understood according to this method [of explanation]. That which is realized in this way as it truly is—[which is to say,] in this nondual sense—about the designating of a distinguishing characteristic is called "the thorough knowledge of the way things truly are [that is gained by] having completed the investigation of [what constitutes] the designation of a distinguishing characteristic."

333. The "absolute" (S: *parinişpannaḥ,* T: *yongs su grub pa*) is the third of the three natures (S: *svabhāvaḥ,* T: *ngo bo nyid* or *rang bzhin*) described in the Mind Only school. Vasubandhu gives a concise description of them in his *Thirty Verses.* After explaining the mentally contrived nature (S: *parikalpitasvabhāvaḥ,* T: *kun brtags pa'i rang bzhin*) and the dependent nature (S: *paratantrasvabhāvaḥ,* T: *gzhan dbang gi rang bzhin*), he states in verse 21cd: "The absolute, then, is that state in which that [dependent nature] always remains empty of the former [mentally contrived nature]." Sthiramati explains: "It is absolute (S: *parinişpannaḥ,* T: *yongs grub*) in the sense of an unchangeable state of being (S: *avikārapariniṣpattyā paranişpannaḥ,* T: *mi 'gyur bas yongs su grub pa'o*). [The pronoun] 'that' refers to the dependent [nature]; 'the former' means the mentally contrived [nature]. In any particular conceptual thought, the mentally contrived [nature] is that state that constitutes being either a perceived [object] (S: *grāhyam,* T: *gzung ba*) or a perceiving [subject] (S: *grāhakaḥ,* T: *'dzin pa*). That is to say, in a particular conceptual thought, the qualities of being either a perceived [object] or a perceiving [subject], which do not [really] exist, are contrived [by the mind]; thus, they are said to be mentally contrived. The state in which the dependent [nature of an entity] always remains—that is, it is forever—completely empty of [that quality of] being a perceived [object] or a perceiving [subject] constitutes the absolute nature."

Regarding this [topic], the eight types of improper conceptual thought, which cause immature beings to give rise to the three substances[334] and which bring forth the [entire] world [of sentient beings and their physical environment], arise because of [an individual's] lack of competency about and failure to establish the four forms of thorough knowledge of the way things truly are. Furthermore, [the states of] affliction [arise] from the [eight forms of] improper conceptual thought; continuous rebirth in samsara [arises] from [the states of] affliction; and the suffering of birth, old age, illness, death, etc., that follow samsaric existence arises from [the condition of] being reborn continuously in samsara.

When a bodhisattva relies upon the four forms of thorough knowledge of the way things truly are, he or she develops thorough knowledge of the eight types of conceptual thought. Through having developed this true and thorough knowledge in the present life, there will be no appearance [for him or her] in future [lives] of the substance that constitutes the basis and mental support for those [conceptual thoughts] and that bring about the occurrence [of conceptual] elaboration. Because that [substance] does not arise or appear, there will also be no appearance [for him or her] in future [lives] of the conceptual thought for which that [substance would serve as] a mental support. This cessation of conceptual thought together with its [related] substance should be known as the cessation of all [conceptual] elaboration. The cessation of [conceptual] elaboration that occurs in this manner should be known as the bodhisattva's [form of] complete nirvana [that is achieved through] the Great Vehicle.[335]

Through having perfected in one's present life the knowledge that has this supreme form of reality as its field of action,[336] a bodhisattva becomes

334. The three substances are (1) the substance that is the basis for conceptual thought and elaboration, (2) the substance that consists of the view of the perishable collection and egoistic pride, and (3) the substance that consists of desire, hatred, and ignorance.

335. *BBhVy* (f. 76b): "Because the abandonment of conceptual thought brings about a cessation of [conceptual] elaboration, one does not abide in samsara. Also, by having produced [in oneself] the qualities of a buddha that will carry out the activity of ripening sentient beings, one does not abide in [a quiescent form of] nirvana. This is the non-abiding nirvana (S: *apratisthitanirvāṇam,* T: *mi gnas pa'i mya ngan las 'das pa*) [that is achieved through] the Great Vehicle; hence, it is complete nirvana (S: *parinirvāṇam,* T: *yongs su mya ngan las 'das pa*)."

336. *BBhVy* (f. 76b) describes this form of knowledge as the one that removes the obscurations to that which needs to be known (S: *jñeyāvaraṇam,* T: *shes bya'i sgrib pa*) and notes that its perfection is achieved upon reaching the eighth of the ten ārya bodhisattva stages.

one who has attained a mastery of the universal controlling powers,[337] such as [having the ability to generate] a variety of emanation bodies by means of the miraculous power that produces emanations, [having the ability to generate] a variety of supernatural transformations by means of the miraculous power that transforms objects, [having the ability to generate] knowledge regarding all objects of knowledge, [having the ability to] remain [alive] for as long as one wishes, and [having the ability to] pass away without [experiencing] any physical harm, according to one's desires.

Five Beneficial Qualities That Are Most Excellent and Their Respective Actions [1.4.11]

[The bodhisattva] who has attained such powers becomes the most excellent of all sentient beings and one who has no superior. It should be understood that the bodhisattva who has attained this universal mastery gains five most excellent beneficial qualities. (1) He attains a supreme mental peace that is due to the tranquility [that originates from] abiding [in a state of extraordinary ease];[338] it is not due to the tranquility [that originates from having quelled] the mental afflictions. (2) He applies [this] unimpeded, thoroughly purified, and completely accomplished knowledge-vision to all the branches of learning.[339] (3) He does not become weary at having to be reborn successively in samsara in order to [accomplish] the welfare of sentient beings. (4) He is able to understand [the meanings of] all the enigmatic statements[340]

At this point only the most subtle forms of the obscurations to that which needs to be known remain. See Book II, chapter 4, the section entitled "Concluding Remarks" [II.4.13] for a description of three forms of indisposition that relate to the obscurations to that which needs to be known.

337. S: *vaśitā,* T: *dbang.* See Book II, chapter 4, the section entitled "The Pleasurable State That Is Free of Signs and Also Free of Effort" [II.4.10] for a description of the ten controlling powers. Only a few of the ten are alluded to here.

338. S: *vihārapraśāntatayā,* T: *gnas par rab tu zhi bas.* That is, it is a peace associated with the extraordinary ease that results from having attained one-pointed states of mental composure. This phrase is meant to distinguish this state from one that results from practicing the path of the Listeners' Vehicle and is limited to removal of the mental afflictions.

339. See Book I, chapter 8, the section entitled "Seeking the Dharma" [I.8.2] for a description of the five branches of learning.

340. S: *saṃdhāya vacanam,* T: *ldem po'i ngag* (sometimes also *dgongs te gsungs pa*). These are statements that were spoken by the Buddha with a specific purpose in mind. Because the purpose is not evident to everyone, it requires interpretation in terms of explaining the

made by the tathāgatas. (5) He becomes one who cannot be led away from devotion to the Great Vehicle, because he does not have to rely upon others [for spiritual guidance].

It should further be understood that these five forms of benefit have five types of action. (1) [The ability] of a bodhisattva who is thoroughly familiar with the [spiritual] practices that are directed toward enlightenment to abide in a supreme state of ease in the present life so that he may overcome any physical and mental weariness [that might otherwise be] caused by that exertion should be understood as the action that pertains to the beneficial quality of [having attained] a state of mental peace. (2) A bodhisattva's [ability] to ripen all the qualities of a buddha [in himself] should be understood as the action that pertains to the beneficial quality of [having attained] the state in which his knowledge is unimpeded in relation to all the branches of learning. (3) A bodhisattva's [ability] to ripen [other] sentient beings should be understood as the action that pertains to the beneficial quality of [having attained] the state in which he does not become weary [from being reborn repeatedly] in samsara. (4) [A bodhisattva's ability] to eliminate any and all doubt that might arise [in the minds] of those persons who are suitable to be [spiritually] trained [by him], as well as [his ability] to maintain and preserve the Dharma [system of spiritual] guidance for a long time by being thoroughly aware of, exposing, and overcoming those who [promote] a false likeness of the true Dharma and who [contribute to] the disappearance of the [Buddha's] teaching should be understood as the action that pertains to the beneficial quality of understanding [the meanings of] all the enigmatic statements [made by the tathāgatas]. (5) [A bodhisattva's ability] to refute all those who assert verbal challenges, his strong spiritual fortitude, and his ability to avoid falling away from [the commitment to accomplish] the aspirational prayers [that he has made] should be understood as the action

---

Buddha's intent for making such a statement and in terms of what its true import is. *MSA* (ch. 12, v. 16) and *AS* (p. 85) both identify four categories of enigmatic intent (S: *abhisaṃdhiḥ,* T: *ldem por dgongs pa*): (1) the enigmatic intent that is meant to cause entry [into the teaching] (S: *avatāraṇābhisaṃdhiḥ,* T: *zhugs pa la ldem por dgong pa*); (2) the enigmatic intent that relates to essential attributes (S: *lakṣaṇābhisaṃdhiḥ,* T: *mtshan nyid la ldem por dgong pa*); (3) the enigmatic intent that is meant to serve as an antidote (S: *pratipakṣābhisaṃdhiḥ,* T: *gnyen po la ldem por dgong pa*); and (4) the enigmatic intent in which [the ordinary sense of words] has been transformed [into a different meaning] (S: *pariṇāmanābhisaṃdhiḥ,* T: *bsgyur ba la ldem por dgongs pa*). Explanations of these four categories can be found in both *MSAVy* and *MSAVṛBh.*

that pertains to the beneficial quality of being one who cannot be led astray because of not having to rely upon others [for spiritual guidance].

This is the way in which everything whatsoever that pertains to a bodhisattva and represents the things that a bodhisattva ought to accomplish is included within these five beneficial qualities and their related actions.

What, then, are the things that ought to be accomplished?

They are (1) a happiness for oneself that is free of affliction, (2) the ripening of a buddha's qualities [in oneself], (3) the [spiritual] ripening of [other] sentient beings, (4) the preservation of the true Dharma, and (5) the refutation of objections [raised by others] by being one who is unwavering in [the effort to accomplish] his or her aspirational prayers and one in whom intense fortitude has been kindled.

Regarding this [topic], it should be understood that the first two of the four categories of reality are inferior forms, the third is a middling form, and the fourth is the supreme form [of reality].

Within [Book I of] *The Stage of a Bodhisattva*, [known as] "The Object of Mental Application That Relates to the Support," this completes the fourth chapter, entitled "The Nature of Reality."

5
Power

Now then, what is the power[341] of the bodhisattvas?

In brief, [the ability] of [a bodhisattva] who has attained mastery of [one-pointed] concentration [to achieve] complete success in all [one's own] aims through relying on mastery of [one-pointed] concentration and merely by [forming] the desire to do so is called the "noble[342] power of one whose mind is fit for action and one whose mind is very well cultivated." The great results and the highly beneficial nature of the spiritual qualities [that are possessed by bodhisattvas] are also called their "power." The marvelous and wonderful nature of the buddhas and bodhisattvas that they are born with and that derives from the great accumulation of merit that they collected

341. S: *prabhāvaḥ,* T: *mthu*. *MSAVṛBh* (Tg. vol. 215, f. 82a–82b) offers three explanations for why the chapter on power is presented immediately after the chapter on the nature of reality. Here is the first one: "What is the connection [that justifies] explaining the chapter on the characteristics of [a bodhisattva's] power immediately following the explanation of the chapter on [the nature of] reality? There are two aspects to what bodhisattvas seek to accomplish: one's own aim and that of others. One's own aim consists of perfecting the qualities of a buddha. The aim of others consists of ripening sentient beings. Regarding them, the perfection of a buddha's qualities that represents one's own aim takes place through gaining knowledge of reality. After having gained knowledge of reality, [a bodhisattva] seeks to attain the extraordinary qualities of the divine eye, etc., in order [to achieve the ability] to ripen sentient beings. And through [those extraordinary qualities, he or she becomes able] to ripen sentient beings. Moreover, those extraordinary qualities of the divine eye, etc., are achieved by means of both a temporary and an ultimate form of realization. Therefore, this establishes the connection [that justifies] explaining the chapter on power after [the chapter on] the nature of reality."

342. S: *āryaḥ,* T: *'phags pa*. This adjectival form of the word is meant to modify the noun "power." *BBhVy* glosses it in this context as follows: "[This power is] 'noble' because it greatly surpasses all mundane forms."

in the past should also be understood as another natural power that is possessed by them.

In terms of its variety, this [power] of the buddhas and bodhisattvas is of five types: (1) the power of supernatural knowledge, (2) the power of spiritual qualities, (3) natural power, (4) the power that is shared with listeners and solitary realizers, and (5) the power that is not shared with listeners and solitary realizers.

The Six Forms of Supernatural Knowledge [1.5.1]

Regarding this [topic], the six [forms of] supernatural knowledge[343]—that is, (1) miraculous spheres of activity, (2) the divine ear, (3) [knowledge of] diverse states of mind, (4) recollection of former existences, (5) perceiving death and rebirth, and (6) the direct awareness that realizes the outflows have been terminated—are what is called "the power of supernatural knowledge."

Regarding this [topic], the six perfections—that is, generosity, morality, patience, effort, meditative absorption, and wisdom—are called the "spiritual qualities." The potency of these spiritual qualities is called "the power of spiritual qualities."

Miraculous Power [1.5.1.1]

Regarding this [topic], what is miraculous power?[344]

In brief, it is of two types: that which relates to transformation and that which relates to creation. These two types also consist of many kinds when they are distinguished according to their varieties.

343. S: *abhijñā,* T: *mngon par shes pa.*

344. S: *ṛddhiḥ,* T: *rdzu 'phrul.* This noun is derived from a verbal root (S: *ṛdh*) that literally means "to prosper" or "to succeed." In addition to "miraculous power," the term also means such things as spiritual "abundance" and "accomplishment." *AS* (p. 97): "What is the [form of] supernatural knowledge [that consists] of miraculous power (S: *ṛddhyabhijñā,* T: *rdzu 'phrul gyi mngon par shes pa*)? It is the concentration and wisdom, along with the mind and mental factors that accompany them, that is greatly accomplished at performing a variety of forms of miraculous power on the basis of the meditative absorptions."

Transformational Miraculous Power [1.5.1.1.1]

What are the varieties of transformational miraculous power?

They are as follows: shaking, blazing, pervading, revealing, causing a change in condition, going and returning, contracting and expanding, causing all form to enter one's body, approaching a sameness, appearing and disappearing, exercising control, overwhelming the miraculous powers of others, bestowing understanding, bestowing recollection, bestowing ease, and emitting rays of light. These and other similar forms are the type [of miraculous power] that is called "transformational."

Regarding this [topic], shaking is when a tathāgata who has attained mastery of [one-pointed] concentration or a bodhisattva whose mind is fit for action causes a temple building here to shake, or causes a house, or the land near a village or town, or a hell realm, or an animal realm, or a hungry ghost realm, or a human realm, or a god realm, or a world sphere of four continents, or a thousand world spheres, or a double-thousand world spheres, or a great triple-thousand world spheres,[345] or a hundred triple-thousand world spheres, or a thousand triple-thousand world spheres, or a hundred thousand

345. In Buddhist cosmology a single "world sphere" (S: *lokadhātuḥ,* T: *'jig rten gyi khams*) is formed on top of an immense "disk of air" (S: *vāyumaṇḍalam,* T: *rlung gi dkyil 'khor*), which supports a great body of water and a "golden ground" (S: *kāñcanamayī pṛthivīḥ,* T: *gser gyi sa gzhi*). In the center of such a world is Mount Sumeru, the king of mountains, which is ringed by seven golden mountains. Four continents are situated beyond these mountains in the outer ocean, one in each of the cardinal directions. The outer edge of the world is ringed by a circular iron mountain range. The sky above contains a sun, moon, and a complement of stars. This so-called "desire realm" extends down as far as the hell regions and up as high as four celestial god realms. Above the desire realm, in the first of the four levels that make up the form realm, lies Brahmā's world. A thousand such desire realms, along with the corresponding thousand Brahmā worlds, comprise a "lesser thousand" of world spheres (S: *sāhasrikaś cūḍikaḥ,* T: *stong chung ngu*). A thousand of these lesser thousand world spheres is called a "middling double-thousand" (S: *dvisāhasro madhyaḥ,* T: *stong gnyis pa bar ma*), and a thousand of these middling double-thousand world spheres is called a "great triple-thousand" (S: *trisāhasro mahāsāhasraḥ,* T: *stong gsum gyi stong chen po*). Such an entire cluster of a billion worlds is formed and undergoes destruction at the same time, and its existence spans a great kalpa of time. Because such a realm consisting of a billion world spheres is the province of one buddha, it is also known as a single buddha field (S: *buddhakṣetram,* T: *sangs rgyas kyi zhing*). The current realm of a great triple-thousand world spheres is named "Tolerance" (S: *sahālokadhātuḥ,* T: *mi mjed 'jig rten gyi khams;* see note 435). Countless such masses of world spheres lie in each of the ten directions. At any one time, some are being formed while others are undergoing destruction.

triple-thousand world spheres, up to countless, immeasurable numbers of great triple-thousand world spheres to shake.

Regarding this [topic], blazing is when fire blazes forth from the upper part of the body, while jets of cold water stream forth from the lower part of the body. Or it is when fire blazes forth from the lower part of the body, while jets of cold water stream forth from the upper part of the body. It is also when the fire element is meditated upon and then fire blazes forth from the entire body. It is when the entire body is ablaze and light rays of different colors—blue, yellow, red, white, pink, and crystal—are emitted from the body.

Regarding this [topic], pervading is when a house is filled with light, or a temple building, and so forth, up to countless, immeasurable numbers of great triple-thousand world spheres are filled with light, as with the previous description made in relation to shaking.

Regarding this [topic], revealing is when a tathāgata or a bodhisattva reveals the lower realms that lie below to an assembly of ascetics, brahmins, listeners, bodhisattvas, gods, *nāgas, yakṣas, gandharvas, asuras, garuḍas, kinnaras,* and *mahoragas*[346] that have gathered and are seated comfortably; or [when a tathāgata or a bodhisattva] reveals the gods and humans that lie above [to such an assembly]; or [when a tathāgata or a bodhisattva] reveals other buddha fields and buddhas and bodhisattvas that reside in them. [This miraculous power extends] as far as [the ability] to reveal a buddha field that lies beyond [other] buddha fields as numerous as the sands of the River Ganges and the tathāgata who resides there, as well as [the ability] to identify the name by which that buddha field is known and the name of the tathāgata [who resides there]. [This miraculous power includes the ability] to reveal and identify whatever [buddha field he or she] wishes [to reveal and identify], and to do so for as long as [he or she] wishes to [reveal it and identify it], both those [buddha fields] that lie nearer than such [a buddha field] and those that lie farther away.

Regarding this [topic], causing a change in condition is when a firm desiderative intention is developed[347] in which earth is conceived of as water and

346. The seven terms in italics are the names of different kinds of celestial beings or powerful spirits. The Tibetan equivalents are *klu, gnod byin, dri za, lha ma yin, nam mkha' lding, mi'am ci,* and *lto phye chen po,* respectively.

347. S: *adhimucyate,* T: *mos pa.* This is a unique sense of this verb in which the basic meaning of directing the mind strongly in a certain way refers to a magical power in which some object is conceived of in a particular way, causing it to take on that form. See note 270 for

it [magically] takes on that very [watery] nature and not any other, or when it is conceived of as fire or wind, and it also [magically] takes on that very [fiery or windy] nature and not any other. It is when a firm desiderative intention is developed in which water is conceived of as earth or it is conceived of as fire or wind; when fire is conceived of as earth or it is conceived of as water or wind; or when wind is conceived of as earth or it is conceived of as water or fire; and all [three of these elements magically] take on these very natures and not any other.

Just as the act of causing a change in condition can be carried out in the form of reciprocal transformation with regard to the [four] great elements, it should be understood that the same is true for [visible] form, smells, tastes, and tangible objects.[348]

[Causing a change in condition] is also when a firm desiderative intention is developed in which such objects as grass, leaves, cow dung, and [a lump of] earth are conceived of as food, drink, a vehicle, clothing, an ornament, a household article or implement, a fragrant substance, a garland, or fragrant oil; or when a firm desiderative intention is developed in which such objects as a stone, a pebble, or a pottery shard are conceived of as a jewel, a pearl, lapis lazuli, shell, crystal, or coral; or when a firm desiderative intention is developed in which all mountains, beginning with the great snow-filled king of mountains, are conceived of as [being made of] gold; and all [of these objects magically] take on these very natures and not any other.

Similarly, it is when a firm desiderative intention is developed in which beings of an excellent appearance are conceived of as having an inferior appearance, or when those of an inferior appearance are conceived of as having an excellent appearance, or when those who are neither of those two types are conceived of as having either an excellent appearance or an inferior appearance, or as having both types of appearance; and, just as with the qualities of an excellent or inferior appearance, it is also when [a firm desiderative intention is developed in which beings] who are either deficient in their limbs or who have all their limbs intact, or who are thin or stout, etc.,

---

the literal sense of the term *adhimuktiḥ* (T: *mos pa*) and the text accompanying note 1378 for a description of the controlling power over intentions (S: *adhimuktivaśitā,* T: *mos pa la dbang ba*).

348. The two Sanskrit editions do not include "sounds" among the types of derivative form that can be altered; however, the Tibetan translation does include them. Nevertheless, *BBhVy* (f. 80a) states: "The reason that sounds are not said to be transformed is because they do not occur continuously."

are conceived of in some way that is different from their actual nature and is a form that is capable of being conceived of, causing all these [objects and beings to magically] take on the natures that they are conceived of as having.

Regarding this [topic], going and returning is when [a tathāgata or a bodhisattva] passes through a wall, a mountain, or a rampart, etc., without his or her body being obstructed, up to when [a bodhisattva] travels to and returns from as far away as Brahmā's realm, and when he or she travels upward [into the heavens] going as far away as and returning from [the realm called] "Below None."[349] It is also when [a tathāgata or a bodhisattva] travels horizontally, going as far away as and returning from countless, immeasurable numbers of great triple-thousand world spheres with his or her coarse body that is composed of the four great elements. It is also when [a tathāgata or a bodhisattva] travels to and returns from a distant place by making the firm conviction that it lies nearby, or when he or she does so with a swiftness like that of the mind.[350]

349. S: *akaniṣṭhaḥ,* T: *'og min*. This is the name of the highest of the seventeen levels that make up the form realm. It is also the uppermost of the last five, which are called pure abodes (S: *śuddhāvāsaḥ,* T: *gnas gtsang ma*) because only āryas are reborn there. This region should not be identified with the buddha field of the same name. *AKB* (p. 170) explains this term as follows: "Moreover, there is no physical place higher than this one. Therefore, because it is the uppermost region [of the form realm, the deities who reside there] are called "Those Who Are Below None."

350. *AKB* (p. 425) identifies three kinds of supernatural travel (S: *gatiḥ,* T: *'gro ba*): (1) that which carries the body, (2) that which relates to firm conviction, and (3) that which is as swift as thought. The first of these is described as follows: "The [supernatural] travel that carries the body (S: *śarīravāhinī,* T: *lus phyin byed pa*) is also possessed by the listeners and solitary realizers, because they [are able to] carry their bodies [over a great distance] gradually, like a bird." *AKV* (vol. 4, p. 1116) glosses the form of travel that relates to firm conviction (S: *ādhimokṣikī gatiḥ,* T: *mos pa las byung ba'i 'gro ba*) as follows: "It [is a form of supernatural travel] that relates to firm conviction in the sense that it is accomplished by means of firm conviction. Because [it is a form of supernatural travel] in which one quickly reaches [a place] that is far away through developing the firm conviction that it lies nearby, it is called that which relates to firm conviction." Vasubandhu further explains in *AKB* that while the first two forms can be achieved by other disciples, the third form is limited to a buddha. He describes it as follows: "Because its swiftness is like that of the mind, it is [called] the [supernatural] travel that is as swift as thought (S: *manojavā gatiḥ,* T: *yid mgyogs kyi 'gro ba*). This form of travel is possessed only by a buddha and not by any other being, because [a buddha alone is able to] reach even a very distant place at the moment that the thought [to go there] is generated." Because Asaṅga does not seem to restrict this last form of miraculous power in the same way here, it would appear that he believes it can also be possessed by bodhisattvas who have reached an advanced stage of spiritual development.

Regarding this [topic], contracting and expanding is when even the snow-filled king of mountains is compressed to [the size of] a mere atom and when even an atom is increased to [the size of] the snow-filled king of mountains.

Causing all form to enter one's body is when, in the presence of a great and varied gathering [of beings, a bodhisattva] causes a [great] physical mass, one that may include a village, a town, a grassy area, a forest, an earthen region, or a mountain, to enter his or her own body. It is also when that entire gathering realizes that they have entered his or her body.

Regarding this [topic], assuming a sameness[351] is when [a bodhisattva] approaches a group of kṣatriyas[352] and, after having approached [that group], whatever appearance and excellence [the individuals in that group] may have, he or she assumes the same [appearance and excellence]; whatever height and circumference they may have, he or she assumes that same [height and circumference]; whatever style of voice they have, he or she assumes that same style of voice; whatever concerns they discuss, he or she discusses those same concerns; whatever concerns they do not discuss, he or she does not discuss them; and, finally, after having presented a talk to them that accords with the Dharma, after having caused them to take up [the Dharma], after having kindled enthusiasm in them, and after having caused them to rejoice, [that tathāgata or bodhisattva] then disappears. And these [kṣatriyas] are not able to discern who the one that has disappeared was. [They wonder to themselves,] "Who was [this being] that disappeared; was it a god or a human?" As with the group of kṣatriyas, [the tathāgata or bodhisattva] does the same with a group of brahmins, householders, or ascetics; with [the six classes of deities of the desire realm, namely,] the group of the Four Great Kings,[353]

351. S: *sabhāgatopasaṃkrantiḥ,* T: *skal ba mnyam pa'i gan du 'gro ba.*

352. This is the name for individuals who belong to one of the four traditional castes outlined in the Vedic social system. Its members represent the military and ruling elite.

353. S: *cāturmahārājakāyikāḥ,* T: *rgyal chen bzhi'i ris.* The Four Great Kings are the deities Virūḍaka (T: *'phags skye bo*), Virūpākṣa (T: *mig mi bzang*), Dhṛtarāṣṭa (T: *yul 'khor srung*), and Vaiśravaṇa (T: *rnam thos kyi bu*). Their principal domain is the uppermost of four level areas that lie along the side of Mt. Sumeru. The immediate retinue for each of the Four Kings is also found there. In addition, the three levels below that one, and the seven golden mountains that ring Mt. Sumeru are the abodes for the rest of this lowest class of the desire realm's gods.

the Thirty-Three,[354] the Yāma deities,[355] the Tuṣita deities,[356] Those Who Delight in Magical Creations,[357] and Those Who Control Others' Magical Creations;[358] [those deities associated with the first meditative absorption of the form realm, namely,] the Brahma Group,[359] the Brahmapurohitas,[360] and the Mahābrahmāṇas;[361] [those deities associated with the second meditative absorption of the form realm, namely,] Those of Limited Light,[362]

354. S: *trayastriṃśāḥ*, T: *sum cu rtsa gsum*. *AKV* (vol. 2, p. 380): "They are called the [group of] Thirty-Three [deities] because they were born in that place [i.e., Indra's heaven that lies atop Mt. Sumeru] through having done good deeds together. That is to say, [they were born there] through their common merit. According to others, it is the general view of the world that these very deities are called the Thirty-Three because they are [held to be] the foremost ones: the eight Vasu deities (T: *nor lha*), the two Aśvins (T: *tha skar gyi bu gzhon nu*), the eleven Rudras (T: *drag po*), and the twelve Ādityas (T: *nyi ma*). They are also designated with the same names in [Buddhist] scripture to conform to this belief."

355. T: *'thab bral*. *AKV* (vol. 2, p. 380): "They are called Yāma deities because they have escaped suffering and reached [their celestial realm] through merit. Or [they are called Yāma deities] because they have put a stop to suffering."

356. T: *dga' ldan*. *AKV* (vol. 2, p. 380): "They are called Tuṣita deities because they are content and have gone [to their celestial realm] happily. Or [they are called Tuṣita deities] because they experience contentment."

357. S: *nirmāṇaratayaḥ*, T: *'phrul dga'*. *AKV* (vol. 2, p. 380): "These [deities] are called Those Who Delight in Magical Creations because they enjoy the magical creations that they have created themselves."

358. S: *paranirmitavaśavarttinaḥ*, T: *gzhan 'phrul dbang byed*. *AKV* (vol. 2, p. 380): "These [deities] are called Those Who Control Others' Magical Creations because it is their nature to take control of enjoyments that have been magically created by others."

359. S: *brahmakāyikāḥ*, T: *tshangs ris pa rnams*. *AKV* (vol. 2, p. 382): "Brahmā is [the deity] who has come into being through great roots of virtue. Who is he? He is the one called the Great Brahmā. He is great because, through having attained the superior level of the first meditative absorption, he is born before and dies after [all the other deities of his realm] and because he is greater in size and other characteristics. [The deities known as] the Brahma Group are those who form his group in that they are found in his abode [i.e., the first *dhyāna* of the form realm]."

360. T: *tshangs pa'i mdun na 'don*. *AKV* (vol. 2, p. 382): "They are called Brahmapurohitas because they place Brahmā foremost."

361. T: *tshangs chen pa*. *AKV* (vol. 2, p. 382): "They are called Mahābrahmāṇas because Brahmā exceeds them in life span, physical appearance, and other characteristics."

362. S: *parīttābhāḥ*, T: *'od chung*. *AKV* (vol. 2, p. 382): "They are called Those of Limited Light because their light is limited in relation to [the other deities of] their level."

Those of Immeasurable Light,[363] and Those of Brilliant Light;[364] [those deities associated with the third meditative absorption of the form realm, namely,] Those of Limited Good Fortune,[365] Those of Immeasurable Good Fortune,[366] and Those of Complete Good Fortune;[367] [those deities associated with the fourth meditative absorption of the form realm, namely,] the Cloudless Ones,[368] Those Born of Merit,[369] Those of Great Fruit,[370] Those

363. S: *apramāṇābhāḥ,* T: *tshad med 'od. AKV* (vol. 2, p. 382): "They are called Those of Immeasurable Light because it is not possible to measure their light."

364. S: *ābhāsvarāḥ,* T: *'od gsal ba. AKV* (vol. 2, p. 382): "They are called Those of Brilliant Light because they illuminate entirely other [heavenly] regions."

365. S: *parīttaśubhāḥ,* T: *dge chung. AKV* (vol. 2, p. 382): "The well-being that relates to a mental level of existence is called 'good fortune' (S: *śubham,* T: *dge ba*). They are called Those of Limited Good Fortune because their good fortune is limited in relation to [the other deities of] their level."

366. S: *apramāṇaśubhāḥ,* T: *tshad med dge. AKV* (vol. 2, p. 382): "They are called Those of Immeasurable Good Fortune because their good fortune is immeasurable."

367. S: *śubhakṛtsnāḥ,* T: *dge rgyas. AKV* (vol. 2, p. 382): "They are called Those of Complete Good Fortune because their good fortune is complete. The meaning [of the name] is that no more excellent form of ease than this exists anywhere else."

368. S: *anabhrakāḥ,* T: *sprin med. AKV* (vol. 2, p. 382): "They are called the Cloudless Ones because, unlike clouds, they have no connection with any ground. That is to say, the celestial mansions that belong to [each of] these [divine] beings arise and disintegrate at the same time that they do."

369. S: *puṇyaprasavāḥ,* T: *bsod nams skyes. AKV* (vol. 2, p. 382): "They are called Those Born of Merit because they are born of merit in the sense that their [rebirth] is produced by unvarying karma (S: *āniñjyakarma,* T: *mi g.yo ba'i las*)." Unvarying karma is that which is generated by attaining any of the four meditative absorptions of the form realm or the four states of mental composure associated with the formless realm. It is called "unvarying" in the sense that it can only ripen in a manner that causes a being to be reborn in the very same level of the form or formless realms. Thus, the karma that is generated by achieving the fourth meditative absorption of the form realm will only ripen as a rebirth in the fourth level of the form realm.

370. S: *bṛhatphalāḥ,* T: *'bras bu che ba. AKV* (vol. 2, p. 382): "They are called Those of Great Fruit because the fruit that is experienced by these [deities] is much greater than those associated with any other region [inhabited by] ordinary beings." Implicit in this explanation is the understanding that the next five levels of the form realm, which are referred to as the pure abodes, are inhabited exclusively by nonreturner āryas.

Who Are Not More Exalted,[371] Those Free of Torment,[372] Those of Excellent Vision,[373] Those Who Are Extremely Beautiful,[374] and Those Who Are Below None.[375]

Regarding this [topic], appearing and disappearing is when [a bodhisattva] disappears a hundred times, a thousand times, or even more often than that, in the presence of a large assembly. Following that, he or she similarly reappears and makes him- or herself visible again.

Regarding this [topic], exercising control is when [a bodhisattva] causes the beings of a particular realm, whatever its extent may be, to engage in activities such as coming, going, and remaining stationary. If [the bodhisattva] thinks to him- or herself, "He must go," then [that person] does go. [If he or she thinks], "He must stay," then [that person] does stay. [If he or she thinks], "He must come," then [that person] does come. [If he or she thinks], "He must speak," then [that person] does speak.

Regarding this [topic], overwhelming the miraculous powers of others is [the ability of] a tathāgata to overcome the effort of [any and] all [beings] other than [a tathāgata] who possess miraculous powers to perform a miraculous feat, and then to cause everything[376] to arise in whatever manner he wishes. A bodhisattva who has reached perfection[377]—whether [he is] one

371. S: *abṛhāḥ,* T: *mi che ba. AKV* (vol. 2, p. 382): "They are called Those Who Are Not More Exalted because they are not more exalted than those [deities] of the other [four] pure abodes."

372. S: *atapāḥ,* T: *mi gdung ba. AKV* (vol. 2, p. 382): "They are called Those Free of Torment because, through having attained extraordinary one-pointed concentration, the mental afflictions do not torment [anyone] here. Alternatively, [they are called Those Free of Torment] because, due to their virtuous attitudes, they do not torment any other [beings]."

373. S: *sudṛśāḥ,* T: *shin tu mthong ba. AKV* (vol. 2, p. 382): "They are called Those of Excellent Vision because, due to their completely pure vision, they see things in an excellent manner."

374. S: *sudarśanāḥ,* T: *gya nom snang ba. AKV* (vol. 2, p. 382): "They are called Those Who Are Extremely Beautiful because their appearance is very beautiful."

375. S: *akaniṣṭhāḥ,* T: *'og min. AKV* (vol. 2, p. 382): "They are called Those Who Are Below None because they are not situated below [any other beings] in the sense that there is no other more exalted level than the one [inhabited by these deities]." Also see note 349.

376. Dutt's edition of the Sanskrit has *sarvam* ("all" or "everything"); Wogihara's edition has *artham* ("thing," or "concern"). The Tibetan translation has *don,* which accords with the latter Sanskrit edition. *BBhVy* (f. 81a) has *don thams cad,* which incorporates both terms.

377. S: *niṣṭhāgataḥ,* T: *mthar phyin pa. BBhVy* (f. 81a): "A bodhisattva who has reached perfection is [a bodhisattva] of the tenth stage who has received the consecration (S: *abhiṣekaḥ,* T: *dbang bskur ba*) [by all the buddhas of the ten directions]." For a description of this

who is [only] subject to one [more] birth[378] or one who is in his last existence[379]—is [able to] to overcome the effort by all other [beings] who possess miraculous powers to perform a miraculous action, with the exception of a tathāgata and a bodhisattva who is equal in stature [to him]. All other bodhisattvas are [able to] to overcome the effort by all other [beings] who possess miraculous powers to perform a miraculous action with the exception of those bodhisattvas who have entered a higher stage [than their own] and those bodhisattvas who are equal in stature to them.

Regarding this [topic], bestowing eloquence[380] is when [a bodhisattva, through his or her miraculous powers,] provides eloquence to a person whose eloquence has become exhausted.

Regarding this [topic], bestowing recollection is when [a bodhisattva] provides recollection to a person whose recollection has become clouded in relation to entities.[381]

Regarding this [topic], bestowing ease is when [a bodhisattva] who is teaching Dharma provides to persons who are listening [to that teaching] a specific form of ease that consists of agility[382] and is beneficial to the body and mind. [This ease] allows those persons to listen to the Dharma in a

---

consecration, see section ten of the *Sutra on the Ten Stages* (S: *Daśabhūmikasūtram,* T: *Sa bcu pa'i mdo*).

378. S: *ekajātipratibadhaḥ,* T: *skye ba gcig gis thogs pa*. *BBhVy* (f. 81a): "[A bodhisattva] who is subject to one birth is [like a bodhisattva] who has taken birth in Tuṣita with the characteristics that such a being is said to possess."

379. S: *caramabhavikaḥ,* T: *srid pa tha ma pa*. *BBhVy* (f. 81a): "[A bodhisattva] who is in his last existence is one who is characterized by having been born in his final birth, [which is to say that he] will actualize buddhahood in that very existence."

380. S: *pratibhānam,* T: *spobs pa*. This term refers to a form of intelligence that includes such qualities as confidence, clarity of understanding, quick-wittedness, and eloquence. *BBhVy* (f. 81a) states that this inspiration is provided at a time when a person is teaching Dharma or engaging in debate. See also Book I, chapter 17, the section entitled "The Four Forms of Informative Knowledge [I.17.7] and note 1085 for a definition and description of the informative knowledge that confers eloquence, one of four types of informative knowledge (S: *pratisaṃvit,* T: *so so yang dag rig pa*).

381. *BBhVy* (f. 81a): "Bestowing recollection is the act of restoring the recollection of persons whose recollection of scriptures that were previously studied has become clouded, at such times as when [those scriptures] are being recited."

382. S: *praśrabdhiḥ,* T: *shin tu sbyangs pa*. *AS* (p. 6): "What is agility? It is the fitness (S: *karmaṇyam,* T: *las su rung ba*) of body and mind [that occurs] due to the cessation of physical and mental [forms of] indisposition (S: *dauṣṭhulyam,* T: *gnas ngan len*) [see also note 139]. Its action is to eliminate all the obscurations." The term *praśrabdhiḥ* literally suggests

manner that is free of any hindrance. Moreover, it quells [only] in a temporary manner the harms that are caused by an imbalance of the elements, physical injury, or [affliction] unleashed by spirits; [it does] not [quell them] permanently.

Regarding this [topic], emitting rays of light is when a bodhisattva or a tathāgata uses miraculous power to emit the following kinds of light rays from his or her body: Some [light rays extend] into the ten directions and reach countless, immeasurable numbers of world spheres where they quell the hellish suffering [that is experienced by] beings in the hells. Some of them reach the illustrious deities, *nāgas, yakṣas, gandharvas, asuras, garuḍas, kinnaras,* and *mahoragas* that reside in the divine realms, urging them to come to this [world]. Likewise, some of them [extend to the] countless, immeasurable world spheres of the ten directions and urge the bodhisattvas who reside in those other worlds to come to this [world]. In brief, the tathāgatas accomplish countless, immeasurable, and diverse aims of immeasurable beings with countless, immeasurable, and manifold kinds of light rays.

Moreover, it should be understood that if all of these types of transformational miraculous power were classified individually, they would be beyond measure and beyond number. When an object that has one natural condition is caused to take on a form that is different, this is called a "transformation." That is why these are called "transformational [forms of] miraculous power."

Creative Miraculous Power [1.5.1.1.2]

Regarding this [topic], what is creative miraculous power?

In brief, a magical creation[383] is [an object] that is insubstantial.[384] [The type of miraculous power that] produces [magical creations] in whatever shape is desired by a [form of] mind that generates magical creations is

the physical and mental condition in which the corresponding forms of indisposition of body and mind have been "quelled."

383. S: *nirmāṇam,* T: *sprul pa. AKV* (vol. 4, p. 1097): "A magical creation is the act of producing an outer object that did not previously exist." The expression "outer object" here indicates that a magical creation is not the creation of an actual sentient being. See next note.

384. S: *nirvastukam,* T: *dngos po med pa. BBhVy* (f. 81b): "[The phrase] 'a magical creation is [an object] that is insubstantial' means that [magical creations] are not produced by [natural] causes and they are completely unreal."

called "creative miraculous power." This [type of miraculous power] has many forms: the magical creation of a body, the magical creation of speech, and the magical creation of an object.

The Magical Creation of a Body [1.5.1.1.2.1]

The magical creation of a body, furthermore, creates [a body] that may or may not resemble oneself, or [one that] may or may not resemble another being. In addition, the magical creation of a body that either does or does not resemble oneself or some other being creates [a body] that possesses a semblance of faculties and possesses the [physical] seat of faculties, but it does not create [a body that possesses actual] faculties.[385]

[This type of creative miraculous power] also produces magical creations that resemble objects. It creates, in whatever manner is desired, any and all outer objects that are composed of [visible] form, smell, taste, and tangible properties—such as food and drink, etc., as well as jewels, pearls, lapis lazuli, etc. [These objects] resemble [such ordinary objects] but are distinct from them.[386]

Moreover, [the magical creation of a body that is] "like oneself"[387] can be

385. *BBhVy* (f. 82a): "[The magical creation of a body] creates [a body] that possesses the seat of faculties, not [one that possesses actual] faculties. Why is that? It is because faculties are considered to be identical with a sentient being. If [actual] faculties were created, it would incorrectly follow that this [magical power] can create a sentient being that did not previously exist, and there is no such thing as the creation of a sentient being that did not previously exist. [This is established] by the sutra words that declare 'samsara's beginning is unknown.' And then, [if it were possible to magically create actual faculties,] samsara would incorrectly have a beginning. Therefore, it is only the seat [of a faculty] that is magically created." The "seat" of a faculty (S: *indriyādhiṣṭhānam,* T: *dbang po'i rten*) is the region of the body in which a faculty resides. For example, the eyeball is the seat of the eye faculty.

386. *BBhVy* (f. 82b): "The qualifier 'resemble [such ordinary objects]' (S: *tatsadṛśam,* T: *de dang 'dra ba*) means that [these magical creations] function in a way that resembles [ordinary objects] and have attributes that resemble [the attributes of those ordinary objects]. The qualifier 'distinct from them' (S: *tadvinirmuktam,* T: *de ma yin pa*) means that they do not constitute any of the results, such as maturation result." This latter statement seems to indicate that magically created objects are not produced in any of the ordinary ways that occur in the natural universe. "Maturation result" (S: *vipākaphalam,* T: *rnam par smin pa'i 'bras bu*) is the name of one of six types of results that are described in Abhidharma literature.

387. S: *ātmasabhāgam,* T: *bdag dang 'dra ba.* Without the interpretation indicated by the added language that appears in brackets, the initial use of this term in this paragraph is

of many different types—[that is,] it can have the appearance of a god, *nāga, yakṣa, asura, garuḍa, kinnara,* or *mahoraga;* the appearance of a human; the appearance of an animal, hungry ghost, or hell being; the appearance of a listener; the appearance of a solitary realizer; the appearance of a bodhisattva; or the appearance of a tathāgata. If a bodhisattva creates a magical creation that is like him- or herself [in its appearance], then, that [bodhisattva's] magical creation [of a body] is [the type that is] "like oneself." However, if the magical creation is different [in appearance from that bodhisattva], then it is [the type that is] "unlike oneself." If [the bodhisattva] creates [a magical creation of a body] that resembles another being that is a god, then [that] magical creation is [the type that] "resembles another." If [the bodhisattva] creates [a magical creation] that does not resemble another being, then it is [the type that is] "unlike another." It should be understood that the same descriptions that were made in relation to a god can also be made [for all the other beings mentioned] up to a tathāgata.

Regarding this [topic], what is the magical creation of a multitude of bodies?

It is when a tathāgata or a bodhisattva in this world simultaneously accomplishes the aims of countless, immeasurable numbers of sentient beings in immeasurable and countless world spheres that lie in the ten directions, by means of manifold magical emanations that appear in a variety of forms.

In addition, some magical creations are established in such a way that they continue to carry out [their activities] even after the tathāgata or bodhisattva [who created them] has passed away. Some magical creations of buddhas and bodhisattvas are simply intended to reveal illusory objects to sentient beings. On the other hand, some [magical creations] are emanated as actual objects such as food, drink, a vehicle, clothing, etc., or jewels, pearls, lapis lazuli, shell, crystal, coral, etc. [The latter] are exactly the same and no different from [those ordinary objects], such that they are able to serve the same function that [ordinary] riches and useful objects do. This [presentation], then, represents [the description of] magical creations of a body and magical creations of an [inanimate] object.

---

somewhat confusing. The adjective *sabhāgam* (T: *'dra ba*) literally means "having a share"; in the present context it seems to mean simply the quality of being similar in appearance.

THE MAGICAL CREATION OF SPEECH [1.5.1.1.2.2]

Moreover, there are magical creations of speech that possess excellence of voice. There are those [magical creations of speech] that are endowed with a clear voice, those that are connected with oneself, those that are connected with others, those that are not connected [with any sentient being], those that consist of teaching Dharma, and those that consist of admonishing heedless beings.

Regarding this [topic], excellence of voice [refers to] the magically created verbal expressions of buddhas and bodhisattvas that are profound and thunderous, that resemble the pleasing sound of the *kalaviṅka* bird, that touch the heart and give rise to joy. This [type of] magically created speech is also urbane,[388] beautiful, clear, informative, worthy of being heard, free of anything disagreeable, independent [of worldly things], and unlimited.

Regarding this [topic], [the quality of] clarity of voice pertains to a tathāgata or bodhisattva who, if he or she wishes to, can cause him- or herself to be understood in his or her full voice by an entire audience made up of a variety of beings who are assembled and seated, including gods, *nāgas, yakṣas, gandharvas, asuras, garuḍas, kinnaras, mahoragas,* listeners, bodhisattvas, and an assembly whose outer edge extends as far as one league.[389] [He or she is clearly heard equally well by] those who are seated at a distance and those who are seated nearby. If [such a tathāgata or bodhisattva] wishes to, he or she can cause his or her voice to be understood throughout a lesser-thousand[390] of world spheres. He or she can cause his or her voice to be understood throughout a double-thousand world spheres, or a great triple-thousand world spheres, or as far as countless, immeasurable numbers

388. S: *paurī,* T: *grong khyer du 'gro ba*. The adjective literally means "belonging to the city" and suggests such qualities "courteous" and "refined" (*BHSD*, p. 355). *BBhVy* (f. 83b) gives the following description: "[Magically created speech] is 'urbane' in the sense that it possesses the quality of leading one to the city of nirvana, and therefore it contains the most excellent of all meanings."

389. S: *yojanam,* T: *dpag tshad*. The original Indian term is an ancient unit of distance that literally means the distance which animals can travel without having to be unyoked or unharnessed. *AK* (ch. 3, v. 88a) defines a *yojanam* as 8 *krośa* (T: *rgyang grags*), itself a term that literally means the distance that the sound of a shout can carry. A *krośa,* in turn, is defined as 500 lengths of a bow (S: *dhanuḥ,* T: *gzhu 'dom*), each of which is 4 cubits (S: *hastaḥ,* T: *khru*) or the equivalent of the span of a person's two outstretched arms. If a "bow-length" is taken to be five and a half feet, then a *yojanam* is four and one-sixth miles.

390. See note 345.

of world spheres that lie in the ten directions. Dharma teachings that are directed toward sentient beings and that are of many different kinds emanate from this [kind of] voice, and [they are Dharma teachings] that come into being for the sake of sentient beings.

Regarding this [topic], a magical creation of speech that is connected with oneself is one that teaches Dharma or admonishes the heedless with speech that was magically created by oneself. By contrast, [a magical creation of speech] that is connected with others is one that teaches Dharma or admonishes the heedless with speech that was magically created by another being.[391]

Regarding this [topic], a magical creation of speech that is unconnected is when speech magically emanates from [such places as] the sky and is not created from the continuum of a sentient being.

Regarding this [topic], a magical creation of speech that teaches Dharma is one that [is produced] for the purpose of revealing what is proper to those who are confused about a variety of things.[392]

Regarding this [topic], a magical creation [of speech] that admonishes [the heedless] is one that [is generated] for the purpose of engendering shame for the lack of mindfulness that is exhibited by those who are not confused and who have gained reverence [for spiritual matters], but who are behaving heedlessly, and [this type of magical creation of speech] is also generated for the purpose of establishing [such heedless beings] in a state of mindfulness.[393]

391. *BBhVy* (f. 84a): "The teaching of Dharma, etc., up to the admonishing of others that, through the power of buddhas and bodhisattvas, is carried out with speech that has been magically created by the continua of other beings is called 'a magical creation of speech that is connected with the continua of others' because it appears to be dependent upon another person's being." That is, the speech appears to have been magically created by another being when, in fact, it was generated by the power of a particular buddha or bodhisattva.

392. S: *tatra tatra,* T: *de dang der.* Literally, "about this and that"; the double locative of the pronoun "that" indicates a multiplicity of possible subjects. *BBhVy* (f. 84a): "The statement 'Regarding this [topic], a magical creation of speech that teaches Dharma . . . to those who are confused about a variety of things' means that [this type of magical creation] makes accurate and unerring distinctions about the nature of the Three Jewels' virtuous qualities and the essential characteristics of [various] entities and teaches them correctly to those who are ignorant of them, experience doubt about them, or have a mistaken understanding regarding them."

393. S: *apramādaḥ,* T: *bag yod pa. AS* (p. 6): "What is mindfulness? It is the cultivation of virtuous entities and the guarding of the mind from entities that are related to the outflows,

These numerous forms of magical creations should be understood in brief as [consisting of three types]: a magical creation of a body, a magical creation of speech, and a magical creation of an object. This represents [a description of] creative miraculous power. Moreover, it should be understood that if this [type of miraculous power] were distinguished in [all of] its various individual forms, they would be beyond measure and number.

Moreover, in brief, this twofold[394] form of miraculous power of buddhas and bodhisattvas also causes two aims to be achieved: (1) once sentient beings have been won over through the displaying of marvelous abilities,[395] they are caused to take up the Buddha Dharma; and (2) many different kinds and varieties of benefit are provided to sentient beings who are undergoing suffering.

Recollection of Former Existences [1.5.1.2]

Regarding this [topic], what is the buddhas' and bodhisattvas' knowledge of an existence [that took place] in the past?

In this world, a tathāgata or a bodhisattva recalls his or her own former existences.[396] He or she recalls everything [about a particular life], including such things as the group of sentient beings [with whom he or she lived], as [described] at length in the sutras with language that states in part, "The

---

on the basis of avoidance of desire, avoidance of hatred, and avoidance of ignorance that are accompanied by effort. Its action is to develop and perfect all mundane and transcendent [forms of] excellence." *PSV* (p. 289): "Thus, mindfulness is the term that is nominally ascribed to [the three roots of virtue of] avoidance of attachment and the rest, together with effort, because it is on the basis of these [four] mental factors that nonvirtuous entities are abandoned and virtuous ones are cultivated. . . . 'Mundane excellence' means to attain a superior state in samsaric existence and superior forms of those qualities that sustain samsaric existence. 'Transcendent excellence' means to attain the enlightenment of the Listeners' Vehicle or that of any of the other vehicles."

394. That is, transformational and creative miraculous power.

395. Miraculous power is one of three types of marvelous ability (S: *prātihāryam,* T: *cho 'phrul*). The other two are the marvelous ability of revealing others' thoughts (S: *ādeśanāprātihāryam,* T: *kun brjod pa'i cho 'phrul*) and the marvelous ability of giving spiritual instruction (S: *anuśāstiprātihāryam,* T: *rjes su bstan pa'i cho 'phrul*). See also note 444.

396. S: *pūrvanivāsaḥ,* T: *sngon gyi gnas*. The Sanskrit term *nivāsa* here refers to all the circumstances associated with the period of time spent in a particular former life. *BBhVy* (f. 84b): "'Former existence' means [all] the activities of body, speech, and mind [that took place in a former life]."

sentient beings [of the place] where I lived [at that time were known by] such and such a name. I was named thus . . ."

Just as one recalls one's own [former existences], one also causes others to recall their [former existences]. One also recalls [the former existences] of others. One recalls the groups of sentient beings that existed at a previous time and also causes others to recall [such groups of sentient beings], as described at length in the sutras with language that states in part, "The sentient beings [of the place] where I lived [at that time were known by] such and such a name. I was named thus . . ." [One] also recalls those [groups of] sentient beings in all the existences of the past in just the same way that [one] does [the group of sentient beings with whom one lives] in one's own present life.

[A tathāgata or bodhisattva] also remembers minute things [that took place in a former life], [including] whatever infrequent or numerous former actions and former [thoughts] that, once considered, had been lost from memory. In addition, he or she remembers uninterrupted moments—[that is,] the precise order in which something was done continuously and in an uninterrupted manner. He or she remembers as well a measure [of time] that is capable of being counted in terms of a discrete number of kalpas. He or she also remembers an immeasurable and countless [span of time] that is incapable of being counted in terms of a discrete number of kalpas.

In short, this [tathāgata's or bodhisattva's] knowledge of existences [that took place] in the past operates in an unobstructed manner—wherever, in whatever manner, and for however long may be desired. Such is the nature of a bodhisattva's or a tathāgata's power that pertains to existences [that took place] in the past. By means of the knowledge that recalls former existences, he or she reveals to sentient beings the varied and numerous kinds of previous births in which supremely marvelous bodhisattva activities were carried out, in order to cause [those beings] to develop faith and devotion toward the Buddha, the Blessed One, and in order to engender [in them] aversion [toward samsara]. He or she also reveals events from bygone times that relate to the ripening of the karmic fruit of sentient beings. [In this way], he or she can destroy the eternalistic views of those who uphold an eternalistic doctrine—namely, those eternalists who form a speculative doctrine based upon the past that views [the world and the self] as [completely] eternal, and [those who form a speculative doctrine based upon the past] that views a portion of [the world and the self] to be eternal.[397]

397. Asaṅga discusses several forms of eternalism in an early section of the *YBh* (pp. 137–

The Divine Ear [1.5.1.3]

What is the buddhas' and bodhisattvas' knowledge [that is known as] the divine ear?

In this world, a tathāgata or a bodhisattva hears, by means of the divine ear, sounds that are divine and human, noble and vulgar, powerful and minute, distinct[398] and indistinct, [sounds] that are magical creations and [sounds] that are not magical creations, and [sounds that are] distant and near.

Regarding this topic, divine sounds are those [that occur in the regions] above [that are made by] beings who have been born in the celestial realms reaching as far as [the one known as] Below None.[399] This is the case if [a tathāgata or bodhisattva] makes no effort [to hear sounds] beyond that range. If [a tathāgata or bodhisattva] makes such an effort, he or she will also hear sounds from the upper regions that lie beyond there and that occur in other world spheres.

Regarding this topic, human sounds are those that occur horizontally[400] and [that are made by the human] beings who have been born in all of the four continents.

Regarding this topic, noble sounds are those made by buddhas, the buddhas' listeners, bodhisattvas, and solitary realizers. Alternatively, it is [the sounds made by] beings other than these [four groups], who declare [to others] what they have heard directly from [any of] these [four groups]. For example, these are [sounds] that relate both to taking up virtue and to abandoning nonvirtue, and that have the nature of revealing [how this is to be done], that induce others to take up [such a practice], that generate enthusiasm [for such a practice], and that gladden [those who have done so successfully]. Similarly, it includes [the sounds] of those individuals whose

---

142). The two forms that are cited here are also mentioned in *AKB* (p. 281), where Vasubandhu notes that they are addressed in the *Mahākarmavibhāga Sūtra*. As clarified in *AKV*, these two doctrines correspond to the first two categories of mistaken view that are presented in the *Brahmajāla Sūtra*.

398. S: *vyaktam*, T: *gsal ba*. The original Sanskrit adjective has a range of meanings that include "beautiful," "evident," "distinguished," and "learned." *BBhVy* (f. 86b) glosses the term as "having meaning" (S: **sārthakam*, T: *don dang bcas pa*).

399. See note 349.

400. S: *tiryañc*, T: *thad kar*. That is, human sounds are those that occur here parallel to the surface of the earth.

minds are not disturbed [by the mental afflictions] and [who are engaged in acts such as] explaining [doctrine], reciting [scriptures], settling [philosophical meanings], correctly admonishing [others], causing [others] to recall [what is proper], and giving instruction[401] and counsel.[402] It is also any other form of good speech, good conversation, or meaningful [talk]. These are called "noble sounds."

Regarding this topic, vulgar sounds are the sounds of sentient beings that constitute lying, slander, harsh speech, and idle speech, whether they [are made by beings who] have been born below in the lower realms,[403] [beings] who have been born above in the divine realms, or [beings] who have been born horizontally among humans.

Regarding this topic, powerful sounds are the sounds made by a great assembly of beings, the cries of pain made by those who are undergoing various kinds of harm, [the loud cries] of those who are weeping, [the loud sound] of those who are calling out, the sound of thunder, or [such] sounds [as those made by blowing] a conch shell, [or by beating] a *bherī* or *paṭaha* kettledrum.

Faint sounds are the sounds that are as slight as a whisper in the ear.

Distinct sounds are those in which a meaning is understood.

Indistinct sounds are those in which a meaning is not understood—for example, [the sounds] of Dravidian mantras,[404] as well as [the sounds] of the wind, large forest trees, parrots, mynas,[405] cuckoos, pheasants,[406] and the like.

401. S: *avavādaḥ,* T: *gdams ngag.* See Book I, chapter 8, the section entitled "Instruction" [I.8.5].

402. S: *anuśāsanam,* T: *rjes su bstan pa.* See Book I, chapter 8, the section entitled "Counsel" [I.8.6].

403. See note 143 above.

404. S: *drāmiḍānāṃ mantrānāṃ* [*śabdāḥ*]; T: *'gro lding ba'i sngags* [*kyi sgra rnams*]. *BBhVy* (f. 86b): "While all mantras are [speech that is] devoid of [ordinary] meaning, the [text's] exclusive mention of 'Dravidian mantras' is because they are secret spells." The precise sense of this explanation is unclear. One possibility is the notion that, while all mantras are forms of human speech that do not convey ordinary meaning, Dravidian mantras are particularly unintelligible in that they are unrelated to Sanskrit.

405. S: *śārikā,* T: *ri skegs.*

406. S: *jīvaṃjīvakaḥ,* T: *shang shang te'u.* Sometimes described as a mythical two-headed bird; however, Asaṅga appears to be referring to an actual species. The Sanskrit name comes from its cry, which sounds like the words "Live! Live!"

Regarding this topic, sounds that are magical creations are those that are produced by the miraculous power of those who possess miraculous powers and who have attained mastery of their mind.

Distant sounds are those sounds other than the ones that occur in a village, field, or hall, in which a tathāgata or bodhisattva is present, [and they can be heard arising from] as far away as countless, immeasurable world spheres.

Knowledge regarding Death and Rebirth [1.5.1.4]

What is the buddhas' and bodhisattvas' knowledge regarding death and rebirth?

In this world, a tathāgata or a bodhisattva, by means of the pure divine eye that surpasses that of humans, sees beings at the time of their death and also sees the good or bad appearance of those who have died[407] and the inferior or excellent circumstances into which they are reborn in the future. In addition, [a tathāgata or a bodhisattva sees] that [these beings], due to the development and ripening of their faculties and with the variety of their physical exertions, will engage in virtuous, nonvirtuous, and indeterminate [deeds].

Similarly, [he or she] also sees and realizes [gross] appearances,[408] and [he or she] also sees subtle objects, [such as] the form that is a magical creation and the divine form that is clear—reaching as far down as Avīci Hell and as far upward as the celestial realm [known as] Below None. If [a tathāgata or a bodhisattva] makes an effort that relates to seeing the form present in other world spheres that lies in a downward, upward, or horizontal [direction], [he or she] sees all the form that exists, reaching as far away as countless, immeasurable world spheres. [He or she] even sees all the individual

407. *BBhVy* (f. 89a): "To indicate that [a sentient being] also has an outer appearance during the stage of an intermediate-state being [the text] declares: 'the good or bad appearance [of those who have died],' etc. The intermediate-state being who is going to a happy migratory state [i.e., a higher realm rebirth] has the appearance of being enveloped in the light of a waxing moon. The sign of an intermediate-state being who is going to an unhappy migratory state [i.e., a lower realm rebirth] is that of a being who is engulfed in darkness or one who has a very unattractive appearance." See also Book III, chapter 6, the section entitled "The Power of Knowledge regarding Death and Rebirth" [III.6.2.9].

408. *BBhVy* (f. 89a): "The phrase 'Similarly, [he or she] also [sees and realizes gross] appearances' is meant in the sense of indicating inanimate physical form."

tathāgatas in all the different buddha fields who are seated in the midst of a great assembly-circle made up of a great variety [of beings] and teaching the Dharma.

With regard to this [supernatural power], having seen by means of his or her divine eye the good and bad physical acts [that are carried out by sentient beings] in the ten directions, a tathāgata or bodhisattva acts in a fitting manner and in an appropriate manner with regard to those sentient beings. In addition, having heard by means of his or her divine ear the good and bad verbal acts, [a tathāgata or bodhisattva] acts in a fitting manner and in an appropriate manner with regard to those sentient beings. In brief, this is how a bodhisattva or a tathāgata carries out deeds by means of the divine eye and the divine ear.

Knowledge regarding Diverse States of Mind [1.5.1.5]

Regarding this [topic], what is the buddhas' and bodhisattvas' knowledge regarding diverse states of mind?[409]

In this world, a bodhisattva or a tathāgata knows the minds of other beings that have been perturbed by the mental afflictions, [wherever those beings may exist] in countless, immeasurable world spheres that lie in the ten directions. He or she also knows the minds [of other beings] that have been freed of the perturbation caused by the mental afflictions, as well as those [minds] that have a connection with the mental afflictions and are associated with the latencies,[410] those [minds] that have no connection with the mental afflictions and are free of the latencies, as well as those [minds]

409. S: *cetaḥparyāyajñānam,* T: *sems kyi rnam grangs shes pa. AKV* (vol. 4, p. 1108): "[The phrase] 'diverse states of mind' means different ones—that is, an attached, angered, or confused [state of mind]. Or, 'diverse states' means a succession of states of mind—that is, sometimes [the mind] is attached and sometimes it is angered or confused."

410. S: *kleśasānubandham sānuśayam,* T: *nyon mongs pa dang 'brel bar bcas shing bag la nyal ba dang bcas pa. AKB* (p. 278) indicates that the expressions *sānubandham* ("having a connection") and *sānuśayam* ("being associated with the latencies") are to be considered synonymous. *AKV* (vol. 3, p. 762): "'Connection,' further, means the condition that favors the arising of another mental affliction." In the Tibetan translations of *AK, AKB,* and *AKV,* the term *anuśayaḥ* is rendered as *phra rgyas;* here and in *AS* it is translated as *bag la nyal.* It is a technical term that is recognized as a synonym of "mental affliction" (S: *kleśaḥ,* T: *nyon mongs*). The verbal root from which it derives means "to adhere closely" to something. *AS* (p. 46) describes its nature as a specific form of "indisposition" (S: *dauṣṭhulyam,* T: *gnas ngan len*) associated with each of the root mental afflictions. *YBh* (p. 167) further explains

that possess an aspiration that is directed improperly—such as the minds of heretics and any unafflicted minds of individuals whose intentions are driven by corporeal desire.[411] He or she also knows the minds [of those beings] that are the opposite of that—namely, the minds that possess an aspiration that is directed correctly.[412]

[A bodhisattva or a tathāgata] also knows inferior minds—that is to say, those of all sentient beings who have been born in the desire realm, including forest animals and birds. He or she knows middling minds—that is to say, [the minds] of all sentient beings who have been born in the form realm. He or she knows superior minds—that is to say, [the minds] of all sentient beings who have been born in the formless realm. He or she also knows minds that are accompanied by pleasure, minds that are accompanied by pain, and minds that are accompanied by a feeling that is neither pleasurable nor painful.

With a single [moment of] knowledge of other beings' minds, [a bodhisattva or a tathāgata] realizes, immediately and accurately, what manner of mind is present in any given individual, what form it has taken, and how long it will remain in existence. With a single [moment of] knowledge of

---

the meaning of the term as follows: "They are latencies (S: *anuśayāḥ,* T: *bag la nyal rnams*) because they possess the character of seeds that strengthen all things that are worldly."

411. A mind that "possesses an aspiration that is directed improperly" (S: *mithyāpraṇihitam,* T: *smon lam log par btab pa*) should be understood as being one that is at odds with the form of one-pointed concentration called "the door to liberation of wishlessness" (S: *apraṇihitaṃ vimokṣamukham,* T: *rnam par thar pa'i sgo smon pa med pa*), which is one of three "doors to liberation" (S: *trīṇi vimokṣamukhāni,* T: *rnam thar sgo gsum;* see also note 508 and Book I, chapter 17, in the three sections entitled "One-Pointed Concentration on Emptiness," "One-Pointed Concentration on Wishlessness," and "One-Pointed Concentration on Signlessness" [I.17.14–16]). This is a form of awareness in which one does not long for conditioned entities, as a consequence of having perceived their faults and disadvantages. The two examples of an improper aspiration that are indicated here are identified with (1) heretics (S: *tīrthikam,* T: *mu stegs pa*) because they wrongly believe in the existence of a real self and (2) persons who develop attitudes that are free of the mental afflictions but whose intentions are driven by corporeal desire (S: *sāmiṣābhiprāyaḥ,* T: *zang zing dang bcas pa'i bsam pa*). *PSV* (p. 270) defines "corporeal desire" (S: *āmiṣam,* T: *zang zing*) as "craving for one's individual existence" (S: *ātmabhāvatṛṣṇā,* T: *lus la sred pa;* see note 277). This desire for continued samsaric existence can only be overcome by means of the transcendent path.

412. *BBhVy* (f. 90a): "Correct aspiration refers to the minds of those who are followers of this religion (S: **ihadhārmikaḥ,* T: *chos 'di pa*) [i.e., Buddhists] that are directed toward [achieving] nirvana and the unafflicted minds of those beings who possess an attitude that is free of corporeal desire."

other beings' minds, he or she can also realize, immediately and accurately, what manner of mind is present in [each of] those beings, what forms those minds have taken, and how long they will remain in existence.

Moreover, [the aim of] this form of supernatural knowledge that is possessed by a buddha and by bodhisattvas is to gain knowledge regarding the superior and inferior faculties of sentient beings, to gain knowledge regarding their diverse forms of devotion, to gain knowledge regarding their diverse constituent elements and their tendencies to develop unfavorable mental traits, so that he or she might correctly and in whatever manner is appropriate establish [beings] in [any of] the various paths that lead to nirvana.[413] It should be understood that this is the action [that is accomplished] by this [form of supernatural knowledge].

Knowledge regarding Termination of the Outflows [1.5.1.6]

Regarding this [topic], what is the buddhas' and bodhisattvas' knowledge regarding termination of the outflows?

In this world, a tathāgata or a bodhisattva realizes truly the attainment of the termination of the mental afflictions, which is to say that he or she [realizes], "I or others have attained or have not attained the termination [of the mental afflictions]."[414] [A tathāgata or a bodhisattva] also realizes truly, as pertains to him- or herself as well as to others, the means to the attainment of the termination of the outflows. Just as with the means [to such an attainment], he or she also realizes truly what does not constitute a [proper] means [to such an attainment]. [A tathāgata or a bodhisattva] also realizes truly the exaggerated pride[415] of others in relation to the attainment of the termination of the outflows, and he or she also realizes truly the absence of exaggerated pride.

413. These aims correspond directly to the fourth, fifth, sixth, and seventh of a buddha's ten powers. See Book III, chapter 6 for a comprehensive explanation of the ten powers.

414. *BBhVy* (f. 91a): "It is meant in relation to a tathāgata that [the *BBh*] states, 'I or others have attained . . .' Bodhisattvas [only] realize the termination [of the mental afflictions that is attained by] others."

415. S: *abhimānaḥ,* T: *mngon pa'i nga rgyal.* See note 314 for a definition of this and six other forms of pride. In this case, exaggerated pride is a form of pride in which a person believes that he or she has achieved the termination of the mental afflictions when, in fact, he or she has not.

Although a bodhisattva realizes all of this, he or she does not bring about his or her own termination of the outflows. Therefore, a bodhisattva does not generate overt forms of the entities that are related to the outflows and he or she also does not abandon the substantive form of the entities that are related to the outflows together with the outflows.[416] Regarding this [point], [a bodhisattva] investigates the entities that are related to the outflows and he or she also avoids becoming afflicted by them. It should be understood that, among all the [spiritual] powers, this one is [a bodhisattva's] greatest [form of] power. Indeed, it is through this knowledge of the termination of the outflows that buddhas and bodhisattvas prevent themselves from becoming afflicted. It is also [through this knowledge that] they identify others [who have succeeded in terminating the mental afflictions] and destroy the exaggerated pride [of those who mistakenly believe that they have done so]. It should be understood that this is the action [that is accomplished] by this [form of supernatural knowledge].

The Power of Spiritual Qualities [1.5.2]

Regarding this [topic], what is the power of spiritual qualities?

It is the power of generosity, as well as the powers of morality, patience, effort, meditative absorption, and wisdom. Moreover, in brief, this power of the spiritual qualities of generosity, etc., should be understood in terms of four aspects: (1) abandoning the opposing qualities, (2) ripening the accumulations,[417] (3) benefiting oneself and others, and (4) bestowing results in the future.

416. The intent of this statement is to indicate that a bodhisattva both avoids generating overt forms of the mental afflictions (this clause does not appear in the Tibetan) and also deliberately avoids completely eradicating the mental afflictions so that he or she can continue to aid beings and perfect the two accumulations. See note 196 for an explanation of the term "outflow" (S: *āsravaḥ,* T: *zag pa*) as well as the phrase "entities that are related to the outflows."

417. Merit and wisdom make up the two accumulations. See Book I, chapter 3, the section entitled "Merit and Wisdom" [I.3.5.2, I.3.6.2]. Commenting on *MSA,* ch. 18, v. 40, Vasubandhu explains the term "accumulation" (S: *sambhāraḥ,* T: *tshogs*) as follows (*MSAVy,* p. 134): "The syllable *sam* means 'continually.' The syllable *bhā* means 'having attained [proficiency at] meditation.' The syllable *ra* means the 'acquisition [of merit and wisdom] to a greater and greater degree.'" *MSAVṛBh* (Tg. vol. 126, f. 102b) augments this interpretation: "In short, 'accumulation' means [those activities that bring about] the acquisition of a buddha's three bodies through continually meditating upon [the perfections of] generosity and

The Power of Generosity [1.5.2.1]

By practicing generosity, a bodhisattva abandons stinginess, [the fault that] directly opposes generosity. His or her generosity also constitutes an accumulation [of merit that leads to] enlightenment. By means of the generosity that is one of the principles for attracting a following,[418] [a bodhisattva] also brings about the spiritual ripening of sentient beings. Prior to giving, one's mind is favorably disposed; while giving, one gladdens one's heart; after having given, one avoids any sense of regret. By maintaining a joyfulness of mind in relation to the three times,[419] [a bodhisattva] benefits him- or herself. He or she also benefits others by dispelling the suffering that they undergo due to hunger, thirst, cold, heat, illness, unfulfilled desires, and danger. Wherever [a bodhisattva] is reborn in a future existence, he or she becomes wealthy, has many possessions, is endowed with many friends, and has a large following. In addition, he or she takes pleasure in generosity. These are the four aspects that make up the power of generosity. It does not consist of anything superior to this or anything beyond this.

The Power of Morality [1.5.2.2]

A bodhisattva who takes up the morality of restraining oneself in body and speech abandons misconduct, [the fault that] directly opposes morality. The taking up of morality by him or her also constitutes an accumulation [of merit that leads to] enlightenment. By means of [this form of] sameness of purpose[420] that is one of the principles for attracting a following, [a bodhisattva] also brings about the spiritual ripening of sentient beings. Through abandoning the fear, objectionable acts,[421] and enmity that are occasioned by immorality, he or she benefits him- or herself. He or she sleeps contentedly and wakes up contentedly. Similarly, the person who possesses morality benefits him- or herself by [attaining] qualities that range from absence of

---

the rest and by meditating upon the virtues of the six perfections to a greater and greater degree." MW (p. 1179) describes this term as meaning "a collection of things required for any purpose."

418. See note 223.

419. That is, before, during, and after carrying out an act of generosity.

420. See note 223.

421. See note 133.

regret and joyfulness up to one-pointedness of mind. This is how [a bodhisattva] benefits him- or herself. Through avoiding all forms of injury [to others], he or she bestows a sense of safety upon all sentient beings. This is how [a bodhisattva] also benefits others. Because of this, following dissolution of the body he or she is reborn in a happy migratory state[422] among the gods in a celestial realm. In addition, he or she takes pleasure in morality. These are the four aspects that make up the power of morality. It does not consist of anything superior to this or anything beyond this.

The Power of Patience [1.5.2.3]

A forbearing bodhisattva abandons impatience, [the fault that] directly opposes patience. His or her patience also constitutes an accumulation [of merit that leads to] enlightenment. By means of [this form of] sameness of purpose, [a bodhisattva] ripens sentient beings. Protecting both him- or herself and others from great [objects of] fear,[423] [a bodhisattva,] by means of this patience, also benefits him- or herself and others. Because of this, in future [existences], a bodhisattva will be largely free of enmity and alienation [from friends], as well as largely free from [physical] pain and mental suffering. In the present life he or she will also die free of remorse. Following dissolution of the body, he or she will be reborn in a happy migratory state among the gods in a celestial realm. In addition, he or she takes pleasure in patience. These are the four aspects that make up the power of morality. It does not consist of anything superior to this or anything beyond this.

422. *sugatiḥ,* T: *bde 'gro.* Abhidharma literature (cf. *AK,* ch. v. 4) generally recognizes five migratory states (S: *pañca gatayaḥ,* T: *'gro ba lnga*): hell beings, animals, spirits, humans, and gods. Tibetan literature sometimes adds a sixth class of being: demigods (S: *asuraḥ,* T: *lha ma yin*). The happy migratory states are made up of gods and humans. The unhappy migratory states (T: *durgatiḥ,* T: *ngan 'gro*) are represented by hell beings, animals, and spirits. *AKB* (p. 115) gives the following literal explanation of migratory state: "A migratory state is that [state] to which [sentient beings] go."

423. *BBhVy* (f. 94a): "Through quelling [their] enmity, patience leads others to avoid harming you or to cause you to undergo the suffering of being bound and the like. Therefore, it protects [the bodhisattva]. . . . [Patience] also protects [others] from the suffering that would be caused [to them] by the undesirable [karmic] results of their objectionable acts."

The Power of Effort [1.5.2.4]

A bodhisattva who has initiated effort and maintains it abandons laziness, [the fault that] directly opposes effort. This effort constitutes an accumulation [of the merit that leads to] enlightenment; it is also a support [for enlightenment].[424] By means of this [form of] sameness of purpose, [a bodhisattva] also ripens sentient beings. Furthermore, [a bodhisattva] who has initiated effort remains in a state of ease and avoids becoming filled with evil, nonvirtuous qualities. [Over time,] one also sees that one has become more spiritually developed than before. With the joy and delight [that arise in this way], one benefits oneself. Having applied oneself to [everything] that pertains to virtue, one also does not harm others by body or speech. One instills in others a desire to initiate effort. This is how [a bodhisattva] also benefits others. In future lives, [that bodhisattva] becomes one whose [powers of] reasoning are strong[425] and also becomes one who delights in putting forth human effort. These are the four aspects that make up the power of effort. It does not consist of anything superior to this or anything beyond this.

The Power of Meditative Absorption [1.5.2.5]

A bodhisattva who achieves meditative absorption abandons the mental afflictions [in general] and the secondary mental afflictions of discursive thought,[426] joy, ease, and the conceptions of form, etc., which are [the faults that] directly oppose [the various forms of] meditative absorption. His or her meditative absorption also constitutes an accumulation [that leads to] enlightenment and a support[427] [for the attainment] of enlighten-

424. *BBhVy* (f. 94a–94b): "[Effort] is a 'support' (S: *saṃniśrayaḥ,* T: *gzhi*) [for enlightenment] because, when enlightenment [has been achieved], [an enlightened being] initiates [activities] by means of effort."

425. T: *hetubalikaḥ,* T: *rgyu'i stobs can*. *BBhVy* (f. 94b): "[A bodhisattva who has initiated effort] is 'one whose powers of reasoning are strong' [because he or she] has repeatedly cultivated virtuous qualities in the past."

426. S: *vāgvitarkaḥ,* T: *tshig gi rtog pa*. *BBhVy* (f. 94b): "'Discursive thought' means [the secondary mental afflictions of] deliberation (S: *vitarkaḥ,* T *rtog pa*) and reflection (S: *vicāraḥ,* T: *dpyod pa*), which are mental afflictions that relate to the first meditative absorption."

427. *BBhVy* (ff. 94b–95a): "[The phrase 'his or her meditative absorption] also constitutes a support' [for the attainment of enlightenment is made] because the union of quiescence

ment. By means of this very [form of] sameness of purpose, [a bodhisattva] also ripens sentient beings. Through abiding in [the] ease [of meditative absorption] during the present life, [a bodhisattva] benefits him- or herself. Through [gaining the qualities of] a mind that is tranquil, completely pacified, and free of attachment, [a bodhisattva] avoids being harmed or angered in the midst of sentient beings and [thus] is also [able to] benefit others. The results of meditative absorption are [for a bodhisattva to gain] purity of knowledge,[428] [ease in] generating [the various forms of] supernatural knowledge, and rebirth among the pure gods[429] in his or her future existences. These are the four aspects that make up the power of meditative absorption. It does not consist of anything superior to this or anything beyond this.

The Power of Wisdom [1.5.2.6]

A bodhisattva who possesses wisdom abandons ignorance, [the fault that] directly opposes wisdom. His or her wisdom also constitutes an accumulation [that leads to] enlightenment. [A bodhisattva] ripens sentient beings by means of generosity as well as agreeable speech, beneficial conduct, and sameness of purpose.[430] He or she benefits him- or herself by means of the great joy and great delight that is accompanied by accurate and specific knowledge of the objects that need to be realized. Through [giving] instruction that is proper in every way, [a bodhisattva] also benefits sentient beings both in their present and in their future lives [by providing them]

---

and insight are [the essence of] the very path [that leads] to enlightenment." That is, since the nature of quiescence is meditative absorption, it represents a support or foundation in that it is one of the two main elements of the transcendent path that leads to enlightenment.

428. S: *jñānaviśuddhiḥ*, T: *ye shes rnam par dag pa*. *BBhVy* (f. 95a): "'Purity of knowledge' means that, through repeated cultivation of the meditative absorptions, [a bodhisattva] attains powerful knowledge (S: *balajñānam*, T: *stobs kyi ye shes*)." This knowledge is described as giving one the ability to answer questions accurately.

429. The Sanskrit editions have the word "purity," referring to the ability to generate supernatural knowledge; however, *BBhVy* (f. 95a) indicates that it modifies the term "god," as rendered in the Tibetan translation and glosses this expression here to mean rebirth among the gods of the form and formless realms.

430. *BBhVy* (f. 95a): "The totality of the bodhisattva path and the accumulations are mastered through wisdom. Therefore, the text states, '[A bodhisattva ripens sentient beings] by means of generosity, etc.' That is to say, when wisdom has been developed fully, all four [of the principles for attracting a following] also become fully developed."

with assistance and happiness. By means of that [wisdom], he or she also acts correctly to acquire every [form of] the roots of virtue. In future lives, he or she will also [act correctly] to attain separation[431] from the two types of obscurations—that is, separation from the obscurations of the mental afflictions and separation from the obscurations to that which needs to be known. These are the four aspects that make up the power of wisdom. It does not consist of anything superior to this or anything beyond this. This is what is called the power of spiritual qualities.

Natural Power [1.5.3]

What is the natural power that is possessed by buddhas and bodhisattvas?

[One of the natural powers that they possess is] a natural ability to recall [former] births. [Another is] the ability to endure long-lasting, varied, intense, and continuous hardships after having investigated what promotes the welfare of sentient beings. [A third is] a joyful willingness [to take on any] suffering that will bring about the welfare of sentient beings and that is [taken on] exclusively for the sake of sentient beings.

[The natural powers] also include for [a bodhisattva[432]] who has taken birth among [the deities of] the Tuṣita Heaven to remain among [those deities of] the Tuṣita Heaven for the duration of his life. It is the quality by which he surpasses the other deities who have been born in Tuṣita Heaven in three respects: divine life span, divine physical beauty, and divine fame. When [a bodhisattva] is entering the belly of his mother, he also permeates the world sphere with great light. When he enters his mother's belly and remains there, as well as when he emerges [from her belly] and is born, he does so with correct awareness. As soon as he is born, he takes seven steps upon the earth without being held by anyone, and he also utters speech. Once born, he [is honored] with supremely excellent acts of worship by exalted gods, *nāgas, yakṣas, asuras, garuḍas, kinnaras,* and *mahoragas,* who offer him celestial flower garlands, music, incense, garments, parasols, ban-

431. S: *visaṃyogam,* T: *bral ba.* This term is synonymous with the various forms of the noble truth of cessation.

432. *BBhVy* identifies this as the natural power possessed by bodhisattvas who have only one life remaining before they attain supreme enlightenment (S: *ekajātipratibhaddhaḥ,* T: *skye ba gcig gis thogs pa*).

ners, flags, and the like. His body is well marked with the thirty-two unsurpassed marks of a great being.

In his last existence and final birth, he is incapable of being harmed by any hostile beings, followers of Māra,[433] or any [forms of] violence. When seated at the place of enlightenment, he conquers all of Māra's forces by means of his loving-kindness. In all his joints and in [each] single one [individually] he possesses the strength of Narāyaṇa. As a small boy and without having undergone any training,[434] he very quickly and on his own develops an understanding of all the secular arts. Without a spiritual guide and entirely on his own, he achieves the great enlightenment that extends throughout a triple-thousand [world spheres]. Approached by Brahmā himself, lord of the Sahā[435] world sphere, he is beseeched to teach the true Dharma in the world. Without recognizing [even the sound of] great thunder, he does not arise from a state of meditative composure [and remains in] a peaceful state.

Wild beasts, birds, and even small animals regard the bodhisattva with utmost trust, approaching him at all times and remaining next to him for as long as they wish. Even animals honor the Tathāgata. For example, a

433. T: *bdud. ŚBh* (pp. 344–345) describes four forms of Māra. Three are impersonal conditions that exist within a samsaric being's own nature. The fourth is identified as a worldly god of the desire realm who is evil in that he obstructs the efforts of spiritual practitioners to transcend samsaric existence. "Regarding this [topic], there are four forms of Māra—that is, (1) the Māra of the heaps, (2) the Māra of the mental afflictions, (3) the Māra of death, and (4) the Māra that is the son of a [worldly] god. The five grasping heaps are the Māra of the heaps. The mental afflictions that are active in the three realms are the Māra of the mental afflictions. The death and demise of [all] those various sentient beings from [all] those various classes of sentient beings is the Māra of death. That son of a [worldly] god, [a being] who has taken birth in the desire realm, who is fixed in his purpose, and who creates obstacles in order to distract those [individuals] who are devoted to the side of virtue with the aim of transcending [the Māras of] the heaps, the mental afflictions, and death is the one who is called 'the Māra that is the son of a [worldly] god.'" Other texts identify the Māra that is the son of a [worldly] god (S: *devaputramāraḥ,* T: *lha'i bu'i bdud*) as the chief deity of the class of desire realm gods known as Those Who Control Others' Magical Creations (S: *paranirmitavaśavarttinaḥ,* T: *gzhan 'phrul dbang byed*). See note 358, above.

434. The phrase "without having undergone any training" is based on the Tibetan translation (T: *byang bar sbyangs pa ma mdzad bzhin du*), which is supported by *BBhVy* (f. 96b). The two published Sanskrit editions may have improperly deciphered the original term.

435. T: *mi mjed. Karuṇāpuṇḍarīka Sūtra* (vol. 2, p. 195): "Why is [this world] called *Sahā* ('Tolerance')? The sentient beings there are tolerant of desire, they are tolerant of hatred, they are tolerant of ignorance, and they are tolerant of the fetters of the mental afflictions. Therefore, this world sphere is called 'Tolerance.'"

monkey once presented raw[436] honey to the Tathāgata. When the Tathāgata accepted it, the monkey was greatly pleased and withdrew dancing.[437]

When a tathāgata bathes, clouds move toward the blessed one [as if] they deliberately formed the intention to bathe him. When a bodhisattva or tathāgata is seated at the foot of some particular tree, its shadow does not move away from his body even though the shadows of all [other] trees have become inclined toward the east. Even though Māra looks for an opportunity [to harm] the tathāgata for six years after he has attained supreme enlightenment, no opportunity is found. Because [a tathāgata's] recollection is always present, he is constantly and continuously in a state of well-placed [recollection]. [A tathāgata] remains in a state of recollection with regard to the arising, continuous existence, and cessation of each of the feelings, conceptions, and thoughts that he experiences.

Similarly, buddhas possess a [form of] natural power that brings benefit [merely] by being seen, as well as a [form of] natural power that relates to excellence of movement and remaining at rest.[438] Examples in which [buddhas] benefit [beings] by being seen are the following: After seeing a tathāgata, those who are insane or mentally disturbed regain [their soundness of] mind. Women whose wombs are irregular obtain a normal womb. Those who are blind gain their sight. Those who are deaf gain their hearing.

436. S: *aneḍakam,* T: *ma khol ba.* Translation is based on the Tibetan, which literally means "unboiled." *BHSD* (p. 37) states that the adjective means "pure."

437. Cf. *Buddhist Legends,* vol. 1, p. 180.

438. S: *āryacāravihārasaṃgṛhītaḥ,* T: *'phags pa'i spyod pa dang gnas pas bsdus pa. ŚBh* (pp. 294, 296–298) identifies twenty types of mind that constitute the objects of the practice known as "closely placed recollection of the mind" (S: *cittasmṛtyupasthānam,* T: *sems dran par nye bar bzhag pa*), which is one of the four forms of closely placed recollection. These twenty states of mind are divided into two categories: six that occur while one is moving about (S: *cārasahagatam,* T: *rgyu ba dang ldan pa*) and fourteen that occur while one is engaged in meditative practice (S: *vihārasahagatam,* T: *spyod par gtogs pa*). The first category is made up of minds that are either affected by or free of desire, hatred, and ignorance. One of the principal exercises to cultivate in relation to them is restraint of the sense faculties. Of the fourteen states in the second category, eight are described as "contemplative mental states that relate to the stage of purifying oneself of the hindrances" and six are described as "contemplative mental states that relate to purification of the mental afflictions." The first eight states have a correlation with the effort to develop quiescence through overcoming the five hindrances to mental composure, and the last six have a correlation with developing and perfecting the practice of insight through either the worldly or the transcendent paths, in order to bring about the permanent abandonment of the mental afflictions.

Those who are filled with desire become free of the perturbation[439] of desire; those who are hateful [become free of] of the perturbation of hatred; and those who are ignorant [become free of] of the perturbation of ignorance. These kinds of occurrences should be understood as forms of the natural power [by which buddhas] benefit [beings] by being seen.

Regarding the natural power that relates to excellence in moving about and remaining at rest, the following are examples: [A buddha] prepares to sleep by lying on his right side in the manner of a lion. Grass and leaves are spread out for him to lie down upon on one side. This bedding for a tathāgata, arhat, and completely enlightened buddha remains undisturbed. The wind does not blow his monks' robes away from his body. He moves with the gait of a lion. He also moves with the gait of a bull. He raises his right foot first [when walking], followed by his left foot. When he walks, elevated areas [of the ground] descend and lower ones rise up, becoming as even as the palm of the hand and free of stones, pebbles, and shards. He enters a town with a mind that is intent on solitude. When he enters [dwellings], low doors become elevated [to accommodate him]. When he eats food, he does not ingest even a single lump of boiled rice without having separated it [into bite-sized morsels].[440] He does not take a second morsel if there is still some remainder [of the previous one in his mouth]. These kinds of [behavior and physical occurrences] should be understood as [forms of a buddha's] natural power that relates to excellence in moving about and remaining at rest.

At the time of [a buddha's] parinirvana, the great earth shakes, meteors are seen to fall, a fire-like glowing appears on the horizon, the sounds of divine drums are heard in the sky. These phenomena are also instances of the natural power of the tathāgatas; they are not [artificial] creations of supernatural knowledge. This is what is called the natural power of buddhas and bodhisattvas.

439. S: *paryavasthānam*, T: *kun nas kris pa*. This is a synonym for the mental afflictions. Asaṅga glosses the noun several times. *AS* (p. 47): "They are perturbations because they overpower the mind by disturbing it repeatedly." Also, *YBh* (p. 167): "They are perturbations because they occur repeatedly." Although use of this term is not limited to them, Abhidharma literature identifies the following eight secondary mental afflictions as being specifically associated with this term: torpor, sleep, excitation, regret, envy, stinginess, shamelessness, and absence of abashment.

440. *BBhVy* (f. 96b): "[A buddha] does not eat without breaking down a lump of food into smaller [bite-sized pieces]."

The Power That Is Not Shared with Listeners and Solitary Realizers [1.5.4]

What is the power of buddhas and bodhisattvas that is not shared with listeners and solitary realizers and what is [the power of buddhas and bodhisattvas] that is shared with them?

In brief, [the power] that is not shared [with listeners and solitary realizers] should be understood as having three aspects that relate to subtlety, types, and constituents. In this world, a tathāgata or a bodhisattva knows exactly how to do what is beneficial for countless, immeasurable numbers of sentient beings, by employing countless, immeasurable [varieties of] means. This represents [the aspect] that relates to subtlety [of discernment]. [A tathāgata or a bodhisattva] possesses every type of power—the power of supernatural knowledge, the power of spiritual qualities, and natural power. This represents [the aspect] that relates to types [of power]. All the world spheres and all the [types of] constituent elements that are possessed by sentient beings represent the scope of [a taṭhāgata's or a bodhisattva's] powers. This represents [the aspect] that relates to constituents.[441]

By contrast, the scope of the supernatural knowledge that is possessed by listeners is [limited to] a double-thousand world spheres together with the [various] types of sentient beings [that are found there]. The scope of the supernatural knowledge that is possessed by solitary realizer [arhats] is [limited to] the entirety of a triple-thousand [world spheres].

Why is that?

441. Ś: *dhātuḥ,* T: *khams.* The most basic meanings of this term include (MW, p. 513): "layer," "constituent part," "element." In Buddhist literature it is used in a variety of different senses, such as world spheres; the three realms (i.e., the desire realm, the form realm, and the formless realm); the four physical elements of earth, water, fire, and air; the six constituents of a sentient being (i.e., earth, water, fire, air, consciousness, and space); and the eighteen constituents that encompass all entities. Asaṅga gives the following basic definition (*AS,* p. 15): "[A constituent is] that which possesses [literally, "holds"] an essential characteristic (S: *svalakṣaṇadhāraṇārthaḥ,* T: *rang gi mtshan nyid 'dzin pa'i don*)." The two principal meanings intended here are "world sphere" (S: *lokadhātuḥ,* T: *'jig rten gyi khams*) and "constituent element" of sentient beings (S: *sattvadhātuḥ,* T: *sems can gyi khams*), which Asaṅga intends to be taken as encompassing both sentient beings' spiritual lineage (S: *gotram,* T: *rigs;* see note 114) and the multiplicity of unfavorable mental traits (S: *caritam,* T: *spyod pa*) to which sentient beings are susceptible (see Book III, chapter 6, the section entitled "The Power of Knowledge regarding Diverse Constituent Elements" [III.6.2.6]).

It is because each [of the disciples within those two vehicles] is only devoted to bringing about his or her own [spiritual] self-control, not that of all sentient beings. Therefore, the maximum scope of their spiritual power does not extend beyond one [complete] world sphere.

The Power That Is Shared with Listeners and Solitary Realizers [1.5.5]

With the exception of those aspects [that are exclusive], all other [forms of] power that are possessed by buddhas and bodhisattvas should be understood as being shared with the listeners and solitary realizers. Even so, listeners and solitary realizers do not possess supernatural knowledge that is equal in its reach to that of the buddhas and bodhisattvas. This is all the more true for [any powers that are possessed by] all the [worldly] gods, humans, heretics,[442] and ordinary persons.[443]

It should be understood that the bodhisattva's power of marvelous abilities[444]—which encompasses miraculous power, revealing others' thoughts, and giving spiritual instruction—is also included, in the appropriate manner, within the power of supernatural knowledge. [That is, in the same order, they are included] within [these three forms of] the power of supernatural knowledge: (1) miraculous spheres of activity, (2) [knowledge of] diverse states of mind, and (3) knowledge of termination of the outflows.

442. S: *tīrthikaḥ* or *tīrthakaḥ,* T: *mu stegs pa. GB2* (pp. 63–64): "[The word] *tīrthaka* [i.e., 'heretic'] refers to a person who believes in a *tīrthyam* [a sacred bathing place on the bank of a river]. A *tīrthaka* is a person who engages in various forms of spiritual practice, such as asceticism, yoga, and the like, and who adheres to the staircase [or platform] at the edge of a [sacred] river [that is used] to descend into a river [as a sacred place for bathing]. [Literally, the term] means a person who adheres to sacred bathing places [at the edge of certain rivers] as a means of entering the river to nirvana."

443. S: *pṛthagjanaḥ,* T: *so so skye bo.* A Buddhist term that is used to describe any individual who has not yet achieved the status of an ārya (T: *'phags pa*). *AS* (p. 11): "What is the state of an ordinary person (S: *pṛthagjanatvam,* T: *so so skye bo nyid*)? The nominal designation [that is ascribed] to [the condition of] not having achieved the qualities of an ārya is [known as] 'the state of an ordinary person.'" See also note 252.

444. S: *prātihāryam,* T: *cho 'phrul. AKB* (p. 424): "They are [called] 'marvelous abilities' because, at the outset, they greatly captivate the minds of those to be converted. . . . Or, they are [called] 'marvelous abilities' because they capture the minds of [both] those who are hostile and those who are neutral."

Within [Book I of] *The Stage of a Bodhisattva,* [known as] "The Object of Mental Application That Relates to the Support," this completes the fifth chapter, entitled "Power."

6

RIPENING

Regarding this [topic], what is ripening?

In brief, ripening should be understood in terms of six aspects: (1) essential nature, (2) persons who are to be ripened, (3) varieties of ripening, (4) means of ripening, (5) persons who ripen others, and (6) attributes of a ripened person.

THE ESSENTIAL NATURE OF HAVING BECOME SPIRITUALLY RIPE [1.6.1]

Regarding this [topic], the essential nature of having become [spiritually] ripe is a state of fitness[445] and soundness[446] of body and mind that favors the abandonment and complete removal of the obscurations of the mental afflictions and the obscurations to that which needs to be known;[447] and it is the culmination point [of an individual's] right practice[448] that is

445. S: *karmaṇyatā,* T: *las su rung ba*. Fitness of body and mind are identified with the virtuous mental factor known as "agility" (S: *praśrabdhiḥ,* T: *shin tu sbyangs pa;* see note 382). Agility is a quality that is developed in the process of cultivating quiescence. *PSV* (p. 288): "The essential characteristic of agility is fitness of body and mind. Regarding that, fitness of the body is that condition of the body which enables it to engage in activities readily. Fitness of the mind is a distinct mental factor that serves as a cause for bringing delight and facility to a mind that is accompanied by right attention (*S: samyaṅmanasikāraḥ, T: yang dag pa'i yid la byed pa*). It is called 'fitness of the mind' because the mind that possesses this mental factor [i.e., agility] is able to engage an object in an unhindered manner."

446. S: *kalyatā,* T: *nyams bde ba. BBhVy* (f. 99a): "Soundness of the body is the fitness of the body that renders the body capable of abandoning [the obscurations]. Soundness of the mind is the fitness of the mind that renders the mind capable of [engaging in] meditation."

447. See notes 117 and 118 for a description of the two kinds of obscurations.

448. S: *samyakprayoganiṣṭhā,* T: *yang dag pa'i sbyor ba mthar phyin pa. BBhVy* (f. 99a):

due to the presence of the seeds of virtuous qualities and that comes about through having diligently engaged in [the practice of] virtuous qualities. Immediately after this point has been reached, [a practitioner] becomes fit and sufficiently strong to bring about the abandonment of either the obscurations of the mental afflictions or the obscurations to that which needs to be known, irrespective of whether he or she has met with the Master[449] or has not met with the Master.[450] For example, immediately after a boil has reached the ideal state for lancing, it is ready to be lanced and [when it reaches this point] it is said to be ripe. Immediately after a household object made of clay—such as a pitcher, a water jar, or a plate, etc.—has reached the ideal state for being put to use, it is ready to be used and [when it reaches this point] it is said to be ripe.[451] Immediately after fruit such as a mango or a breadfruit, etc., has reached the ideal state for eating, it is ready to be consumed and [when it reaches this point] it is said to be ripe. In just the same way, [the point at which] right practice has reached a state of culmination through [a bodhisattva's] having diligently engaged in [the practice of] virtuous qualities is one that is followed immediately by the purification [of some portion of the obscurations]. This is the essential nature of having become [spiritually] ripe.

The Persons Who Are to Be Ripened [1.6.2]

Regarding this [topic], in brief, there are four [types of] persons who are to be ripened. An individual who possesses the spiritual lineage of a listener is to be ripened by bodhisattvas and the buddhas, the blessed ones, in rela-

"'Culmination of right practice' [means] the final portion of [an individual's] right practice that is included within the accumulation path."

449. S: *śāstaram vāgamya,* T: *ston pa dang phrad kyang rung.* "Master" (S: *śāstā,* T: *ston pa*; literally "teacher" or "instructor") is an epithet of the Buddha. It is the same term that occurs in the phrase translated in chapter 7 as "the Teacher of gods and humans." *BBhVy* (f. 99a): "'Irrespective of whether he or she has met with the Master' refers to the listeners."

450. S: *anāgamya vā śāstaram,* T: *ston pa dang ma phrad kyang rung. BBhVy* (f. 99a): "'Or has not met with the Master' refers to the followers of the solitary realizers and to bodhisattvas."

451. S: *paripakvaḥ,* T: *yongs su smin pa.* The Skt. verbal root *pac* has a range of meanings that include "to cook," "to bake" (i.e., to fire pottery, bricks, etc.) and "to ripen." The same Sanskrit adjective that is derived from this root is used in all three examples that appear here. For the sake of consistency I have translated the term in all three cases as "ripe," even though the sense of the word in this particular example is more properly that of earthenware that has been fully hardened by baking it in a fire.

tion to the Listeners' Vehicle. An individual who possesses the spiritual lineage of a solitary realizer is to be ripened [by bodhisattvas and buddhas] in relation to the Solitary Realizers' Vehicle. An individual who possesses the spiritual lineage of a buddha is to be ripened [by bodhisattvas and buddhas] in relation to the Great Vehicle. An individual who does not abide in any spiritual lineage is to be ripened [by bodhisattvas and buddhas] so that he or she can proceed to a happy migratory state.[452] These are the four persons who are to be ripened in relation to those four worthy objects.[453] This is how the aspect of ripening that relates to persons who are to be ripened should be understood.

The Varieties of Ripening [I.6.3]

Regarding this [topic], what are the varieties of ripening?

In brief, there are six types: (1) the ripening of faculties, (2) the ripening of roots of virtue, (3) the ripening of knowledge, and (4) weak, (5) middling, and (6) great [forms of] ripening.

Regarding this [topic], the ripening of faculties refers to excellence of life span, physical appearance, family, and power, [as well as the qualities of] having one's speech accepted, being regarded as eminent, being human, and having great strength. Through having attained a [physical] basis that possesses these excellent [forms of] maturation results,[454] one becomes fit for [maintaining] fervor[455] in [pursuit of] one's spiritual practice, and one remains free of mental weariness about the constant exertions [that must be made] in order to gain full knowledge of all the branches of learning.

What is the ripening of roots of virtue?

452. Although the person who does not abide in any form of spiritual lineage cannot achieve the enlightenment of one of the three vehicles, he or she is still able to attain a relatively favorable form of samsaric existence.

453. S: *vastu,* T: *dngos po.* Cf. MW, p. 932. In this case the term would seem to be more or less synonymous with "purpose" or "goal."

454. See the section of chapter 3 entitled "The Eight Maturations" [I.3.5.1, I.3.6.1].

455. S: *ātaptaḥ,* T: *brtul ba. BBhVy* (f. 100a): "'Fervor' should be understood as a state of body and mind that is conducive to the abandonment [of obscurations]. It is [an attitude] which causes [a practitioner] to gain a sense toward the three times successively that he or she will feel, is currently feeling, and has felt joy about abandoning [the obscurations]. It is referred to as 'remaining immersed in meditative practice' (S: **yogayuktasthaḥ,* T: *rnal 'byor dang ldan pas gnas pa*)."

It is the quality of having afflictive emotions that are naturally weak. Through having such a quality, one's mind naturally avoids going toward evil, nonvirtuous qualities. In addition, one is [a person whose] hindrances[456] [to meditative composure] are weak, [a person whose] discursive thoughts[457] are weak, and [a person] who is upright and duly observant.[458]

What is the ripening of knowledge?

[It is when] one possesses recollection and learning and is able to perceive, comprehend, retain, and fathom the meaning of teachings that are well explained as well as those that are poorly explained. [Such a person] is endowed with a natural wisdom that, once gained, makes him or her suitable and capable of freeing his or her mind completely and permanently of all the mental afflictions.

Regarding [these varieties of ripening], the ripening of faculties causes one to become free of the maturation obscurations;[459] the ripening of the

456. See note 138.

457. S: *vitarkaḥ,* T: *rtog pa*. I translate this term here as "discursive thought" because in this context it represents an obstacle to the Buddhist training of one-pointed concentration. In *ŚBh* (p. 184), Asaṅga describes one of five personality flaws as possessing a strong tendency to develop discursive thoughts (S: *vitarkacaritaḥ,* T: *rnam par rtog pa spyad pa*). In the context of the fifty-one mental factors, I translate the same term as "deliberation." See note 204 for a general definition. In Asaṅga's presentation it is classified as one of four "variable" mental factors in that it can be virtuous, nonvirtuous, or morally neutral depending upon the circumstances.

458. S: *pradakṣiṇagrāhī,* T: *mthun par 'dzin pa*. This expression is made up of two words that, as the Tibetan translation suggests, could be read "one who grasps favorably." Although the basic sense of the verbal root (*grah*) from which this noun is derived does mean "to seize" or "to grasp," that is not how the word *grāhī* is to be taken here. The relevant secondary meanings of *grah* are to "undertake," "observe," "obey," or "follow" instruction (S: *avavādaḥ,* T: *gdams ngag*) and counsel (S: *anuśāsanam,* T: *rjes su bstan pa*). Also, while the primary sense of the modifier *pradakṣiṇa* (T: *mthun par*) is that of "moving to the right" or "standing or being placed on the right," in this context it means to behave in a "favorable" or "reverential" manner (MW, p. 679). As the following two interpretations clearly indicate, the term refers to a person who is duly observant of the spiritual instruction that he or she has received. *DBV* (f. 186a): "Because someone practices unerringly in relation to the [spiritual] instruction, he or she is 'duly observant.'" *ANṬ* (f. 90b): "'A 'duly observant' [person] is someone who practices in a manner that accords with what he or she has been taught by a preceptor, a teacher, or the like." *MVy* (no. 2365) includes this term in a list of eighty-eight noteworthy virtuous qualities.

459. S: *vipākāvaraṇam,* T: *rnam par smin pa'i sgrib pa*. *BBhVy* (f. 101a): "'Maturation obscuration' refers to [rebirth in any of] the three lower realms, [as a human being of] the northern continent Kurava, or [as a divine] sentient being that lacks conception, because it

roots of virtue causes one to become free of karmic obscurations;[460] and the ripening of knowledge causes one to become free of the obscurations of the mental afflictions.

What is weak ripening?

There are two reasons that [an individual's] spiritual ripening is weak: (1) the causes that ripen the faculties, roots of virtue, and knowledge have not been practiced for a [sufficiently] long period of time; and (2) the causes [of one's spiritual ripening] that are being practiced have not been fully nurtured and are deficient [in strength].

A middling form of [ripening] should be understood as being due to the fact that one of these two conditions is not in effect while the other one is.

A great form of [spiritual] ripening should be understood as [occurring when] neither of these two conditions is in effect.

The Means of Ripening [1.6.4]

What is the means of ripening?

It should be understood as having twenty-seven forms: (1) nurturing the constituent element, (2) implementing present conditions, (3) undertaking, (4) gaining joy, (5) the initial form of setting out, (6) not the initial form of setting out, (7) remote purity, (8) purity that is near, (9) application, (10) mental attitude, (11) providing material objects, (12) providing Dharma, (13) winning over [followers] by means of miraculous powers, (14) guidance, (15) imparting secret Dharma, (16) imparting Dharma that has been disclosed, (17) weak application, (18) middling application, (19) plentiful application, (20) learning, (21) reflection, (22) meditation, (23) supporting, (24) suppressing, (25) personally accomplishing [the ripening of others], (26) requesting

---

is very difficult [i.e., impossible] for the beings who are born in any of these circumstances to acquire the faculties that are represented by the eight maturations." A "being that lacks conception" (S: *asaṃjñisattvaḥ*, T: *'du shes med pa'i sems can*) is a kind of long-lived worldly god who has been born in a particular region of the fourth level of the formless realm. The unique cause for obtaining such a rebirth is the cultivation of a form of one-pointed concentration known as "the state of composure without conception" (S: *asaṃjñīsamāpattiḥ*, T: *'du shes med pa'i snyoms par 'jug pa*). See *PSV*, pp. 314–316.

460. S: *karmāvaraṇam*, T: *las kyi sgrib pa*. This obstacle is identified with the five immediate deeds (S: *pañcānantaryāni*, T: *mtshams med pa lnga*)—that is, (1) killing one's mother, (2) killing one's father, (3) killing an arhat, (4) causing a division in the Sangha wheel, and (5), through malice, doing physical injury to a tathāgata that causes him to bleed. Cf. *AKB*, p. 259.

others, and (27) both [accomplishing something oneself and soliciting help from others].

(1) Regarding this [topic], what is "nurturing the constituent element"?[461]

The generating of a progressively greater development and the maintaining of a supreme development of the seeds of virtuous qualities on the basis of the natural excellence of the seeds of virtuous qualities and through having cultivated virtuous qualities in the past is called "nurturing the constituent element."

(2) Regarding this [topic], what is "implementing present conditions"?

It is the unerring teaching of the Dharma, the unerring form of understanding[462] [that arises] in relation to that [act of teaching the Dharma], and the correct form of practice that accords with Dharma,[463] [all of which occur] during [an individual's] present life. Regarding this, nurturing the constituent element represents the prior cause through which present conditions come into being. Implementing present conditions should be understood as being causes that exist in the present and [that bring about spiritual] ripening in the present.

(3) Regarding this [topic], what is "undertaking"?

For a householder, it is the acceptance of precepts that separate him or her from misdeeds on the strength of having developed faith. Or, for an individual who has gone forth, it is the acceptance of precepts that separate him or her from the sense objects [on the strength of having entered] the homeless state.

(4) What is "gaining joy"?

It is the delight that is felt toward this well-spoken [spiritual system of] Dharma and Vinaya, due to one's having resorted to the path that leads to deliverance from all suffering and the path that is characterized by ease and

461. S: *dhātupuṣṭiḥ,* T: *khams brtas pa*. In this context "constituent element" is a synonym for spiritual lineage (S: *gotram,* T: *rigs*).

462. S: *aviparītagrāhitā,* T: *phyin ci ma log par 'dzin pa*. This term, which translates literally as "the state of unerring grasping," seems to be one that can be understood in two ways (cf. *BBhVy,* f. 190a–190b): (1) the avoidance of mistaken forms of belief and (2) the unerring practice of instruction and counsel that was received from a teacher. Both cases should be understood as activities that result from an unerring form of understanding.

463. S: *dharmānudharmapratipattiḥ,* T: *chos kyi rjes su mthun pa'i chos sgrub pa*. See Book I, chapter 8, the section entitled "The Form of Practice That Accords with the Dharma" [I.8.4], where this expression is explained in terms of five aspects.

the avoidance of the [two] extremes of [overindulging in] sensory pleasures and [engaging in acts of] self-mortification.

(5) Regarding this [topic], what is "the initial form of setting out"?

Having previously developed aversion for those qualities toward which one ought to develop aversion, [the act of] devoting oneself to attainment of the proper aim[464] once the benefits of doing so have been understood is referred to as "the initial form of setting out."

(6) What is "not the initial form of setting out"?

It is the manner in which [spiritual] ripening progresses to an ever-higher degree for a person who has already entered [the path] and who is currently engaged in the process of bringing about his [or her spiritual] ripening, through avoiding disdain toward bodhisattvas and buddhas and through receiving continuous clarification of the [religious] subjects that have already been revealed.

(7, 8) Regarding this [topic], what is "remote purity"?

It is the condition which, due to laziness or the absence of [favorable] conditions, renders [a person] fit to attain complete purification [only] after a very long period time and with the passage of a multitude of lives or the passage of a multitude of kalpas. The opposite of this condition should be understood as "purity that is near."

(9) Regarding this [topic], what is "application"?

It is the continual and respectful safeguarding of the precepts, due to a strong aspiration to achieve one's aims or due to either the fear of falling into a state of downfall[465] in future lives or the fear of being held in low esteem by others in this life.

(10) What is "mental attitude"?

It is the firm belief in the [attainment of] knowledge by others based upon the [conviction] that one becomes incapable of being led away from this [spiritual system of] Dharma and Vinaya through [cultivating] the forbearance that arises from correct reflection[466] upon [a series of] topics,

464. S: *nyāyārthapratipādanam,* T: *rigs pa'i don sgrub pa. BBhVy* (f. 102b): "'Proper aim' and its 'attainment' should be understood as [referring to] the result of the path and the path itself."

465. S: *vinipātaḥ,* T: *rnam par ltung ba.* This term refers to the state of suffering that is experienced in the lower realms. It is described in Book III, chapter 6, in the section entitled "The Power of Knowledge regarding Death and Rebirth" [III.6.2.9].

466. S: *samyaksaṃtīraṇākṣāntiḥ,* T: *yang dag par nges par rtog pa'i bzod pa. BBhVy* (f. 103b) identifies this forbearance as a form of knowledge that is developed by contemplating a

as well as the quality of having unwavering faith in the Three Jewels and in the attainment of one's own aims based upon one's esteem for virtuous qualities.[467]

(11) What is "providing material objects"?

It is the providing of food and drink, etc., to those who are completely lacking in any kind of food and drink, etc., and it is the providing of suitable forms of food and drink, etc., to those who are lacking in suitable forms of food and drink, etc.[468]

(12) Regarding this [topic], what is "providing Dharma"?

It is the bestowing of Dharma [teachings] either by giving explanations of scriptural texts or by giving correct explanations of meanings.

(13) What is "winning over [followers] by means of miraculous powers"?

It is the displaying of the marvelous ability of miraculous powers[469] by [a bodhisattva] who possesses miraculous powers, out of compassion for beings and for the purpose of [causing them to develop] a pure mental attitude or a pure form of practice. In doing so, [that bodhisattva] thinks, "Through seeing or hearing about this marvelous ability, these beings will obtain a pure mental attitude toward the teaching or they will apply themselves properly." In addition, through having had their minds won over by this [display of] marvelous abilities, it is the developing of a pure attitude or the undertaking of a proper form of practice by such [beings].

---

series of objects of devotion. Here the emphasis is on the fact that this reflection will result in unshakable conviction. See the opening section of Book I, chapter 8, entitled "Abundance of Devotion" [I.8.1] for a list of eight objects of devotion. In Book I, chapter 11, it also represents a method for developing "the patience of the devotion that is gained by reflecting upon entities" [I.11.2.3].

467. *BBhVy* (f. 103b) notes that Asaṅga's description of this method of bringing about spiritual ripening makes reference to all of the three types of faith: (1) firm belief (S: *abhisaṃpratyayaḥ,* T: *mngon par yid ches pa*) in entities that exist, such as karma and its results, and the truths of suffering and origination; (2) clarity [of mind] (S: *prasādaḥ,* T: *rab tu dang ba*) toward entities that possess virtuous qualities, such as the Three Jewels; and (3) the aspiration (S: *abhilāṣaḥ,* T: *mngon par 'dod pa*) to attain virtuous qualities that are capable of being achieved, such as the truths of cessation and the path. See also *PSV,* pp. 281–284.

468. *BBhVy* (ff. 103b–104a) explains that this statement is referring to two forms of generosity. The first is an ordinary form that is extended to those who are destitute and in a state of suffering. Providing "suitable forms of food and drink, etc." represents the generosity that is extended to monks and nuns, who are worthy of receiving excellent forms of offerings.

469. S: *ṛddhiprātihāryam,* T: *rdzu 'phrul gyi cho 'phrul.* This is one of three types of marvelous abilities. See note 395.

(14) Regarding this [topic], what is "guidance"?

It is the act of teaching a form of true Dharma to someone who is unable to attain his or her aim by him- or herself that will aid that person in developing a correct form of practice. It is also the act of teaching [a form of true Dharma to] someone who is able [to attain his or her aim by him- or herself] so that he or she will attain a swift realization [of that aim].

(15) Regarding this [topic], what is "imparting secret Dharma"?

It is the act of teaching a Dharma subject that is not revealed to beings whose wisdom is undeveloped due to its extremely wide and deep meaning [by presenting] that subject in a manner that is clear, easily understood, and [provides] an easy means of realization.

(16) What is "imparting Dharma that has been revealed"?

It is the act of providing detailed explanation of an extremely wide and deep subject to beings whose wisdom is great and who already possess a good understanding of the doctrine contained in the Buddha's teaching.

(17) Regarding this [topic], what is "weak application"?

It is one that is both lacking in continual application and lacking in zealous application.

(18) What is "middling application"?

It is one that is characterized by either of these two [deficient] forms of application—namely, that which is lacking in continual application and that which is lacking in zealous application.

(19) What is "plentiful application"?

It is one that is endowed with both [of the positive] forms of application—that is, it is endowed with both continual application and zealous application.

(20) Regarding this [topic], what is "learning"?[470]

It is the diligent effort put forth by [an individual] who is devoted to the Buddha's word to take up, retain, and recite the Dharma teachings that are contained in the sutras, etc.

(21) What is "reflection"?

It is [the activities of] considering, analyzing, and ascertaining[471] the

470. S: *śrutam,* T: *thos pa.* Literally, that which is "listened to" or "heard," this term refers to the sacred teachings that are transmitted orally and are meant to be heard by followers. As a form of practice, "learning" is the first of three stages of spiritual practice; the other two are reflection (S: *cintā,* T: *bsam pa*) and meditation (S: *bhāvanā,* T: *bsgom pa*).

471. *BBhVy* (f. 105a) makes the following remarks about the three forms of investigation identified with the exercise of reflection: "'One who is attentively engaged in contemplation

meaning [of Dharma teachings] in a solitary place by [an individual] who is attentively engaged in contemplation of the Dharma.

(22) What is "meditation"?

It is [the activity of] dedicating [oneself] to the repeated practice of quiescence, insight, and equanimity, which is accompanied by correct attention to the causes that are associated with [the practice of] quiescence, retention,[472] and equanimity.

(23) What is "supporting"?[473]

It is the giving of support[474] [to others] correctly by [an individual] who is free of any desire for material gain and who is acting in the manner of a spiritual teacher or a preceptor. It is [also the activity of carrying out] a

---

of the Dharma' means [an individual] who, by means of the four applications [see notes 255 and 1199], investigates conclusively the meanings of the Dharma teachings that [he or she] has learned. [The activity of] considering (S: *abhyūhanā,* T: *mngon par rtogs pa*) [the meaning of Dharma teachings] represents a lesser form of the wisdom that is derived from reflection; [the activity of] 'analyzing' (S. *saṃlakṣaṇā,* T: *kun tu dpyod pa*) [their meaning] represents a middling form [of the wisdom that is derived from reflection]; and [the activity of] 'ascertaining' (S: *niścayaḥ,* T: *gtan la 'bebs pa*) [their meaning] represents a great form [of the wisdom that is derived from reflection]. Additionally, 'considering' the meaning [of Dharma teachings is recognizing] the lack of contradiction between earlier and later statements; 'analyzing' [their meaning is recognizing that it] is not contradicted by [valid forms of] reasoning; and 'ascertaining' [their meaning is recognizing that] it cannot be disproven by any opposing argument."

472. S: *pragrahaḥ,* T: *rab tu 'dzin pa. ŚBh* (pp. 392–393): "What is retention? It is the gladdening of the mind, [the action of] causing [the mind] to see [its object] well, [the action of] inciting [the mind to maintain its object] through taking hold of any of various [kinds of] objects that have the capacity to cause [the mind] to become clear. Regarding this topic, what is the cause of retention? [Among those objects] which have the capacity to cause [the mind] to become clear, it is that object by which one takes hold of the mind. It is [also] the initiating of effort [by a practitioner] which favors [the purpose of] that [object]. Regarding this topic, what is the time for [undertaking the activity of] retention? The time for retention is when the mind has become languid (S: *līnaṃ cittam,* T: *sems bying bar gyur pa*) or when it is suspected that [the mind is about to become] languid, [and this is an activity that is undertaken] for the sake of [enhancing one's] meditation."

473. S: *saṃgrahaḥ,* T: *sdud pa. BBhVy* (f. 105b): "'Supporting' is the acceptance of [the obligation to carry out] activities that benefit and assist one's following." This word is related in meaning to the four principles for attracting followers to the Dharma (S: *catvāri saṃgrahavastūni,* T: *bsdu ba'i dngos po bzhi*).

474. S: *niśrayadānam,* T: *rten sbyin pa. BBhVy* (f. 105b): "'Giving support' should be regarded [here] as meaning [enabling followers to] go forth [into the state of a religious ascetic] and [enabling them to accept] full ordination [as a *bhikṣu* or *bhikṣuṇī*], etc."

variety of individual forms of service[475] [to others]. For example, it is the service of attending to those who are ill; the service of [providing others with] robes, food, seats, bedding, and medicine for curing the ill in a manner that accords with the Dharma; the service of dispelling sorrow and remorse; and the service of dispelling afflicted states of mind. These and other activities of a similar type should be understood as representing the variety of forms of service.

(24) What is "suppressing"?[476] After fixing [the mind in order to] guard oneself from developing an afflicted state of mind, it is (1) admonishing[477] [a wrongdoer] about the wrongfulness of a minor transgression; (2) censuring[478] [a wrongdoer] in relation to a middling transgression; and (3) banishing [a wrongdoer] in relation to a great transgression.

Regarding this [topic], the acts of admonishing and censuring are done for the benefit and well-being of those [wrongdoers] as well as others. The form of banishing that permits a subsequent return [of the wrongdoer] is also done for the benefit and well-being of those [wrongdoers] as well as others. The form of banishing that does not permit a subsequent return [of the wrongdoer] is done only for the benefit and well-being of others. That is, when others become aware of the transgression that was the cause for [the permanent] banishing of certain individuals, they will decide not to commit such a transgression themselves.

(25) How does one personally accomplish the ripening [of others]?

[A bodhisattva] teaches suitable [forms of] Dharma that cause [others] to turn away from opportunities [to engage in] nonvirtuous [actions] and to become established in opportunities [to engage in] virtuous [actions]. He or she also conducts him- or herself in the [same] manner that he or she tells

475. S: *paricaryā,* T: *bsnyen bskur byed pa.*

476. S: *nigrahaḥ,* T: *tshar gcod pa.* See Book I, chapter 10, the section entitled "Suppressing Those Who Engage in Misconduct" [I.10.2.6.10] for additional descriptions of this activity.

477. S: *codanā,* T: *gleng ba.* The verbal root *cud,* from which this noun is derived, has a range of meanings that can include "incite," "inspire," "ask," and "criticize." An important sense of this noun in a moral context is to describe the act of verbally confronting a wrongdoer with his or her misdeeds. In this sense it can be both an accusation and a form of reproof. The Tibetan translation suggests the somewhat neutral sense of "discuss." In the present context, the intended meaning seems to be for a person of moral authority to confront someone who has committed a lesser offense and counsel him or her with an admonition or a mild form of reproof.

478. S: *avasādanā,* T: *spyo ba.*

[others that they should behave]. An individual who acts in a manner that conforms to his or her own words[479] is a person who is established in a form of practice that accords with Dharma[480] or a person who follows [a form of practice] that resembles that,[481] such that no one would say to him or her: "You yourself are not yet someone who has turned away from opportunities [to engage in] nonvirtuous [actions] and become established in opportunities [to engage in] virtuous [actions]. Why do you think that you can cause others to take up that [behavior], urge them [to do so], and remind them [to do so]? You, in fact, are one who deserves to be urged, reminded, and established by others."

(26) How does one make a request of others?

[A bodhisattva] makes a request of those persons whom sentient beings regard with great affection and esteem and who are knowledgeable and well trained in the methods of teaching Dharma. [To make a request of them means] to persuade them to engage in the activity of ripening [others].

(27) The form of ripening that is both done by oneself and that others are requested [to carry out] should be understood [as occurring] through the combination of these two [previous methods].

It should be understood that the successful attainment of the six varieties of ripening—that is, the ripening of faculties, the ripening of roots of virtue, the ripening of knowledge, and the weak, middling, and great [forms of]

479. This phrase does not occur in either of the two published Sanskrit editions, but it does appear in *BBhVy* (f. 106b).

480. S: *dharmānudharmapratipannaḥ,* T: *chos kyi rjes su mthun pa'i chos la zhugs pa. MSAVṛBh* (Tg. vol. 125, ff. 249b–250a) describes this person as one who is practicing meditation during the stage of conduct that is based upon devotion in order to perfect his or her knowledge of the insubstantiality of the person and the insubstantiality of phenomena so that it will take on the characteristic of becoming a transcendent form of realization.

481. S: *tatsabhāgānuvartī,* T: *de dang mthun par 'jug pa.* That is, a form of practice that resembles that of a person who is established in a form of practice that accords with Dharma. This compound is formed by combining the words *tatsabhāga* (T: *de dang mthun par*) and *anuvartī* (T: *'jug pa*). Both published Sanskrit editions misinterpret the term *tatsabhāga* (Wogihara's edition observes in a footnote that the manuscript reads *tatsabhāga,* but mistakenly amends it to read *svasabhāga*). *Tatsabhāga* is a technical term that indicates resemblance to a particular type of entity without having the same actual nature. Since the former practitioner is one who has attained the stage of conduct that is based upon devotion (see next note), the latter would be an individual who has not yet attained that level but who emulates the conduct of a person who has.

ripening—[is achieved] on the basis of this means of ripening that is made up of twenty-seven types.

The Persons Who Ripen Others [1.6.5]

Regarding this [topic], who are the persons who bring about spiritual ripening [in others]?

In brief, the six [types of] bodhisattvas who are situated on six of the bodhisattva stages[482] are the ones who cause sentient beings to become spiritually ripened. (1) The bodhisattva who is situated on the stage of conduct that is based upon devotion[483] is one who practices devotion. (2) The bodhisattva who is situated on the stage of a pure superior attitude[484] is one whose superior attitude has become pure. (3) The bodhisattva who is situated on the stage of practicing conduct[485] is one who is engaged in practicing conduct. (4) The bodhisattva who is situated on the stage of certainty[486] is one who has reached a state of certainty. (5) The bodhisattva who is situated

482. All of these six stages are addressed in the opening section of Book III, chapter 3, "Seven Stages" [III.3.1].

483. S: *adhimukticaryābhūmiḥ,* T: *mos pas spyod pa'i sa.* This stage is often identified with the preparation path (S: *prayogamārgaḥ,* T: *sbyor lam*), which is the second of the five paths that lead to enlightenment. *AS* (p. 91): "What kind of person is a bodhisattva whose conduct is based upon devotion? He or she is [an individual] who is established on the stage of conduct that is based upon devotion and who possesses the lesser, middling, or great forms of bodhisattva forbearance." These three forms of forbearance are not attained until a practitioner has reached the preparation path (see notes 530 and 995 for discussions of the term "forbearance"). However, Asaṅga also describes this stage in a broader sense later in this work (Book II, chapter 4, in the section entitled "The Essential Nature of the Pleasurable State of Conduct That Is Based Upon Devotion" [II.4.1.2]): "Here, any bodhisattva conduct whatsoever [that is performed] by a bodhisattva from the time of first generating [enlightenment] mind and throughout the period that his or her attitude remains impure is called [that bodhisattva's] 'pleasurable state of conduct that is based upon devotion.'" The terms "stage" (S: *bhūmiḥ,* T: *sa*) and "pleasurable state" (S: *vihāraḥ,* T: *gnas pa*) are interchangeable; see Book II, chapter 4, the last paragraph of the section entitled "The Pleasurable State of Great Joy" [II.4.3], where the literal meaning of the two terms is explained.

484. S: *śuddhādhyāśayabhūmiḥ,* T: *lhag pa'i bsam pa dag pa'i sa.* This name refers to the first of the ten ārya bodhisattva stages, also known as "great joy" (S: *pramuditā,* T: *rab tu dga' ba*).

485. S: *caryāpratipattibhūmiḥ,* T: *spyod pa sgrub pa'i sa.* This stage spans the second through the seventh of the ten ārya bodhisattva stages.

486. S: *niyatabhūmiḥ,* T: *nges pa'i sa.* This stage corresponds to the eighth of the ten ārya bodhisattva stages.

on the stage of certain conduct[487] is one who is engaged in the practice of conduct that is certain. (6) The bodhisattva who is situated on the stage that is the perfect manner of going[488] is one who has reached [or is about to reach] perfection.

Regarding this [topic], the ripening of those persons who abide in a state that lacks [any of the forms of] spiritual lineage—[an effort] which is intended to lead [them] to [rebirth in] a happy migratory state—is repeatedly subject to reversal and [therefore] must be accomplished again and again. By contrast, the ripening of those who abide in [any of the forms of] spiritual lineage is not subject to reversal and [therefore] does not need to be accomplished again and again.

The Characteristics of Persons Who Are Spiritually Ripe [1.6.6]

Regarding this [topic], the characteristics of [persons who are] spiritually ripe are [now] to be described. These are the characteristics, signs, and marks by which persons who have become spiritually ripe can be differentiated and distinguished. Moreover, in brief [these characteristics] are of two types, which are distinguished in terms of whether they represent a cause or a result. The characteristics that represent a cause are also of two types, which are distinguished in terms of attitude and action. They are described as follows.[489]

What are the characteristics of those persons who are spiritually ripe?

When a listener who has practiced virtue in the past abides in a state [that represents] a weak form of ripening, he or she possesses a weak aspiration and a weak [form of] application. He or she also [can] fall into the lower realms and in the present life will neither achieve [any of] the fruits of asceticism nor complete emancipation.[490] When [a listener] abides in a

487. S: *niyatacaryāpratipattibhūmiḥ*, T: *nges pa'i spyod pa sgrub pa'i sa*. This stage corresponds to the ninth of the ten ārya bodhisattva stages.

488. S: *niṣṭhāgamanabhūmiḥ*, T: *mthar thug par 'gyur ba'i sa*. This is the last of seven stages described in the opening section of Book III, chapter 3. It includes both the final or tenth ārya bodhisattva stage and the stage of buddhahood.

489. This paragraph exists only in the Tibetan translation of the text. Nevertheless, *BBhVy* (f. 107b) contains remarks that refer to the distinctions that appear here.

490. S: *parinirvāti*, T: *yongs su mya ngan las 'das pa*. This is a reference to the attain-

state [that represents] a middling form of ripening, he or she possesses a middling aspiration and a middling [form of] application. He or she no longer falls into the lower realms and does achieve [some of] the fruits of asceticism in the present life. However, [a listener who possesses a middling form of ripening] does not achieve complete emancipation in the present life. [A listener] who abides in a great [form of] ripening possesses a great aspiration and a great [form of] application. He or she does not fall into the lower realms, does achieve [all of] the fruits of asceticism in the present life, and also does achieve complete emancipation in the present life.

The solitary realizer should be understood in the same manner as the listener.

Why is that?

It is because his or her path is of the same kind as that of the listeners. However, the following is a difference between a solitary realizer and listeners. In [a solitary realizer's] final existence, when he or she has obtained [the] final physical form, [that practitioner] realizes the status of an arhat through abandoning all the mental afflictions and after having meditated on the thirty-seven spiritual qualities that are conducive to enlightenment,[491] without [having to rely upon] a teacher and on the strength of [his or her] former practice. This is the reason [that such a practitioner] is called a solitary realizer.

A bodhisattva who is situated on the stage of conduct that is based upon devotion should be understood as having [developed] a weak form of ripening. [A bodhisattva] who possesses a pure superior attitude[492] [should be understood] as having [developed] a middling form of ripening. [A bodhisattva] who has achieved certainty and one who has achieved perfection have [developed] a great form of ripening. Regarding this [topic], a bodhisattva who is established in a state of weak ripening possesses a weak aspiration and a weak [form of] application; he or she also [can] go to the lower realms. It should be understood that [such a bodhisattva] is [situated] within the first [of three] periods of countless kalpas. In addition, he or she

ment of Lesser Vehicle nirvāṇa in which the support of the heaps does not remain (S: *nirupadhiśeṣanirvāṇam,* T: *lhag med kyi mya ngan las 'das pa*).

491. See note 101 for a list.

492. Dutt's Sanskrit edition includes the additional phrase "and [who is] on the stage of practicing conduct."

lacks any of the virtues that are conducive to enlightenment in a form that possesses intensity, steadfastness, and complete purity.[493]

A bodhisattva [who has developed] a middling form of ripening possesses a middling aspiration and a middling [form of] application. He does not go to the lower realms and is [situated] within the second [of three] periods of countless kalpas. [A bodhisattva who has developed a middling form of ripening] also is endowed with all of the virtues that are conducive to enlightenment in a form that possesses intensity and steadfastness. However, he lacks them in a form that possesses complete purity.

A bodhisattva who is established in a great form of ripening possesses a great aspiration and a great [form of] application. He does not go to the lower realms and is [situated] within the third [of three] periods of countless kalpas. He is endowed with all the virtues that are conducive to enlightenment in a form that possesses intensity, steadfastness, and complete purity.

Regarding this [topic], [the virtuous qualities of a bodhisattva] are said to be "intense" because they are naturally strong and splendid and because they [yield] exceedingly great fruits and they have many benefits. They are said to be "steadfast" because they are irreversible, they are not subject to being lost, and they become [progressively more] excellent. They are said to be "completely pure" because they [have reached a form] within the [various ārya] bodhisattva stages in which they are unsurpassed.

Regarding this [topic], these five forms of ripening—the ripening that is accomplished on the basis of material things, [the ripening that occurs] through winning over [followers by displaying] miraculous powers, [the ripening that] arises through explaining secret Dharma, [the ripening that is accompanied by] weak application, and the ripening that is accomplished merely on the basis of learning—will be only a weak form [of ripening] even after virtuous qualities have been cultivated for a long period of time, much less when they have been cultivated for a short period of time.

It should be understood that all the other causes of ripening bring about the [spiritual] ripening [of beings] in a threefold manner. A weak form of ripening should be understood [to result] from a weak form of practice, a middling form [of ripening] from a middling form [of practice], and a great form [of ripening] from a great form [of practice]. Each of these three forms

493. The qualities of intensity (S: *uttaptatā,* T: *sbyangs pa*), steadfastness (S: *acalatā,* T: *mi g.yo ba*), and complete purity (S: *suviśuddhatā,* T: *shin tu rnam par dag pa*) are discussed further in Book I, chapter 15, at the end of the section entitled "Sameness of Purpose" [I.15.3].

of ripening—weak, middling, and great—should be understood as occurring in an additional threefold manner. [That is,] the weak form [of ripening] has a weak form of being weak, a middling form of being weak, and a great form of being weak. The middling form [of ripening] has a weak form of being middling, a middling form of being middling, and a great form of being middling. The great form [of ripening] has a weak form of being great, a middling form of being great, and a great form of being great. By a similar process of ever-greater subdivision, it should be understood that the variety of forms in which buddhas and bodhisattvas bring about the ripening of sentient beings is beyond measure.

[What constitutes the essence of spiritual ripening is] the ripening of the causes and effects that relate to a buddha's [spiritual] qualities, [a process that is brought about] by the [twenty-seven] methods [of ripening] that have been described. With the exception of [the method of ripening that consists of] requesting others, [these methods of ripening directly bring about] two forms of well-being[494] in the mind continuum. [This, in turn, promotes the six varieties of ripening that were identified above in terms of the three forms] that range from the ripening of faculties to the ripening of knowledge, and [the three forms that] range from weak to great. [Moreover, the beings] who undergo ripening are made up of three categories: (1) oneself, (2) all other sentient beings, and (3) other persons.[495] Similarly, [the spiritual ripening] that relates to other sentient beings and other persons can also be defined as being obtained through [the ripening of their] faculties, etc.[496]

Regarding this [topic], by means of the [twenty-seven] causes of [spiritual] ripening that have been described, a bodhisattva brings about within him- or herself the ripening of faculties, the ripening of roots of virtue, and the ripening of knowledge, as well as a weak, middling, or great [form

494. T: *bde ba gnyis*. It is not clear what these two forms of well-being are. It may be the fitness and soundness of body and mind that are referred to the opening portion of this chapter.

495. S: **parapudgalāḥ*, T: *gang zag gzhan rnams*. The term "person" here seems to suggest someone who is either capable of achieving or has already achieved a significant form of spiritual development, such as an ārya of one of the three vehicles' paths.

496. This entire paragraph does not appear in either of the two published Sanskrit editions; however, *BBhVy* (f. 109a) does make reference to it. It appears to address the same points that the following paragraph does. The syntax of the Tibetan is problematic and the Derge, Peking, and Tok Palace editions all seem to contain at least one misspelling (*nyes pa smin pa* instead of *shes pa smin pa*).

of] ripening, in order to ripen the qualities of a buddha [in his or her own mind]. He or she also brings about [the same six aspects of ripening] in relation to other beings and other persons in order to [lead them to] the [various forms of] final emancipation [that are attained through] the three vehicles.

Within [Book I of] *The Stage of a Bodhisattva,* [known as] "The Object of Mental Application That Relates to the Support," this completes the sixth chapter, entitled "Ripening."

7

Enlightenment

The Nature of Enlightenment [1.7.1]

Regarding this [topic], what is enlightenment?

In brief, two types of abandonment and two types of knowledge are called "enlightenment."

Regarding this [topic], the two types of abandonment are (1) the abandonment of the obscurations of the mental afflictions and (2) the abandonment of the obscurations to that which needs to be known. The two types of knowledge, on the other hand, are (1) the stainless knowledge that is free from the encumbrance of the mental afflictions through having abandoned the obscurations of the mental afflictions, and (2) the knowledge that is unobstructed in relation to all objects of knowledge through having abandoned the obscurations to that which needs to be known.

Another formulation is that pure knowledge,[497] knowledge of everything,[498] and unimpeded knowledge,[499] together with the complete destruction of all the traces of the mental afflictions and the complete abandonment of the [forms of] ignorance that are unrelated to the mental afflictions, [collectively] are referred to as "unsurpassed true and complete enlightenment."

497. S: *śuddhajñānam,* T: *dag pa'i ye shes.*

498. S: *sarvajñānam,* T: *thams cad mkhyen pa.*

499. S: *asaktajñānam,* T: *chags pa med pa'i ye shes.* The adjective *asakta* (T: *chags pa med pa*) can mean variously "free of attachment" or "unimpeded." As indicated below, the principal meaning in this context is the latter one.

Regarding this [topic], knowledge that is characterized by the complete and permanent abandonment of all the mental afflictions along with their traces is called "pure."

Knowledge that proceeds unobstructedly in relation to all constituents, all entities of every kind, and in relation to all times is called "knowledge of everything."

Regarding this [topic], there are two [types of] constituents: [constituents in the sense of] world spheres and [constituents in the sense of] the constituent elements of sentient beings.[500]

There are two kinds of entities: conditioned and unconditioned. The variety of conditioned and unconditioned entities is immeasurable in terms of the different categories that relate to types of essential characteristics, categories that relate to general characteristics, categories that relate to causes and results, and categories that relate to realm, migratory state, virtuous [entity], nonvirtuous [entity], indeterminate [entity], and the like.

Regarding this [topic], there are three aspects of time: past, present, and future. Thus, the knowledge that relates to all constituents, all entities of every kind, and all times is called "knowledge of everything."

Regarding this [topic], unimpeded knowledge is knowledge that becomes established everywhere as soon as [the attention] has been turned [toward a particular object];[501] it is knowledge that proceeds quickly and without impediment.[502] Without having to be turned [toward an object] repeatedly, this knowledge is only subject to being turned [toward an object] once.[503]

500. See note 441 for a description of these two senses.

501. S: *ābhogamātrād eva sarvatrādhiṣṭhitam;* T: *dgongs pa tsam gyis thams cad du thogs pa med cing.* The noun *ābhogaḥ* on its own is used to describe the essence of the mental factor "attention" (S: *manaskāraḥ,* T: *yid la byed pa*); see note 232. A second meaning of *ābhogaḥ* is "effort"; however, the Tibetan translation *dgongs pa* suggests that this is not the intended meaning here.

502. *BBhVy* (f. 110a): "'Without impediment' means [for this knowledge] to proceed in a manner that is unobstructed."

503. S: *nānyatraikābhogapratibaddham,* T: *lan cig dgongs pa dang 'brel ba.* The negative of the noun *ābhogaḥ* (S: *anābhogaḥ,* T: *lhun gyis grub pa*) is also used to describe a buddha's knowledge as "effortless" or "spontaneous." Thus, *BBhVy* (f. 110a): "Such knowledge is referred to both as 'knowledge that achieves [its object] merely by turning [toward it],' and as 'effortless knowledge.' It is 'knowledge that achieves [its object] merely by turning [toward it]' because it becomes fixed [on any object] by turning [toward it] no more than once. It is 'effortless knowledge' because it does not need to turn [toward an object] repeatedly."

Another formulation is that the one hundred and forty unique qualities of a buddha, together with the tathāgata's avoidance of conflict,[504] knowledge by resolve,[505] and [four] forms of informative knowledge[506] are called "unsurpassed true and complete enlightenment."

Regarding this [topic], these are the one hundred and forty unique and unsurpassed qualities of a buddha: the thirty-two marks of a great person, the eighty secondary signs, the four forms of purity that are complete in every aspect, the ten powers, the four forms of intrepid confidence, the three closely placed recollections, the three forms of having nothing that needs to be concealed, great compassion, the nature of being completely free of confusion, the complete destruction of all the traces [of the mental afflictions], and the knowledge of all aspects and of what is most excellent. A differentiation of these qualities of a buddha will be given in the chapter entitled "Preeminence."

504. *AS* (p. 96): "What is the avoidance of conflict (S: *araṇā,* T: *nyon mongs pa med pa*)? It is the one-pointed concentration, wisdom, and accompanying [forms of] consciousness and mental factors that, on the basis of a meditative absorption, successfully enable one to remain in a state that keeps [others] from developing [any of] the mental afflictions." This concentration is also cultivated by arhats of the Listeners' Vehicle to avoid causing other persons to generate any of the mental afflictions toward them. Such an arhat might do so, for instance, before entering a town to receive alms food. If he realizes that his presence would have such an effect, he can enter the fourth absorption and then, by developing this concentration, avoid becoming a negative influence. However, a buddha can manifest this concentration merely by bringing it to mind, because his mind is always in a state of composure. Moreover, beyond the ability of the listener arhats, he can implant in those persons who see him the inclination to completely eliminate the mental afflictions that might arise relative to a buddha.

505. S: *praṇidhijñānam,* T: *smon nas mkhyen pa. AKB* (p. 418): "Knowledge by resolve is a [form of] knowledge that is preceded by a resolve, [which can be described] thus: Having made the resolve, 'May I come to know such and such [a subject],' one enters the form of the fourth meditative absorption [known as] ultimate eminence (S: *prāntakoṭikam,* T: *rab kyi mthar phyin pa*). [Upon arising from that meditative absorption] one develops genuine knowledge of that [subject] in accord with the manner in which it formed the object of one's one-pointed concentration."

506. S: *catasraḥ pratisaṃvidaḥ,* T: *so so yang dag par rig pa bzhi*. See Book I, chapter 17, the section entitled "The Four Forms of Informative Knowledge" [I.17.7].

Seven Forms of Supremacy [1.7.2]

Regarding this [topic], supreme enlightenment is endowed with seven forms of supremacy, which are the reasons that, of all the forms of enlightenment, it is the one that is said to be supreme.

What are the seven forms of supremacy?

They are (1) supremacy of material basis,[507] (2) supremacy of action, (3) supremacy of accomplishment, (4) supremacy of knowledge, (5) supremacy of power, (6) supremacy of abandonment, and (7) supremacy of pleasurable states.

Regarding these, the physical body of a tathāgata that is well adorned with the thirty-two marks of a great person is what is called "supremacy of material basis."

A tathāgata's dedication to his own benefit, to the benefit of others, to the benefit of a great multitude of beings, to the happiness of a great multitude of beings, his compassion toward the world, and toward the well-being, benefit, and happiness of gods and humans is what is called "supremacy of action."

A tathāgata's quality of being endowed with four unsurpassed and unequaled forms of accomplishment—[that is,] perfection of morality, perfection of [right] view, perfection of conduct, and perfection of livelihood—is what is called "supremacy of accomplishment."

A tathāgata's quality of being endowed with four unsurpassed and unequaled forms of knowledge—[that is,] informative knowledge of Dharma, informative knowledge of meanings, informative knowledge of clear expression, and informative knowledge [that confers] eloquence—is what is called "supremacy of knowledge."

A tathāgata's quality of being endowed with the six unsurpassed and unequaled forms of supernatural knowledge that were described earlier is what is called "supremacy of power."

A tathāgata's quality of being endowed with the abandonment of all the mental afflictions along with their traces, as well as the unsurpassed and unequaled abandonment of the obscurations to that which needs to be known, is what is called "supremacy of abandonment."

The three unsurpassed and unequaled pleasurable states—[that is,] the

507. S: *āśrayaḥ,* T: *rten. AKB* (p. 154): "The material basis is the physical body together with the [sense] faculties."

pleasurable states of the āryas, the pleasurable states of the gods, and the divine pleasurable states—are what a tathāgata abides in to a high degree and they are what is called "supremacy of pleasurable states."

Regarding this [last form of supremacy], [the practice of] abiding in [states of one-pointed concentration upon] emptiness, signlessness, and wishlessness,[508] as well as [the practice of] abiding in the state of composure that is a cessation,[509] are what are called "the pleasurable states of the āryas." The four meditative absorptions and the four formless states of composure are what are called "the pleasurable states of the gods." The four immeasurables are what are called "the divine pleasurable states."

Furthermore, of these three [types of] pleasurable states, four [elements represent the aspects of] the supreme pleasurable states in which the tathāgatas abide to a high degree. [Two are] from the pleasurable states of the āryas—[namely,] abiding in emptiness and abiding in the state of composure that is a cessation; [one is] from the pleasurable states of the gods—[namely,] the fourth meditative absorption, which is known as "immobile";[510] and [one is] from the divine pleasurable states—[namely,] the pleasurable state of abiding in compassion. [These four are the ones] which a tathāgata employs to look upon the world with his buddha eye three times during the night and three times during the day, or six times during the day and night, to determine "Who is growing spiritually? Who is declining spiritually? Whose undeveloped virtue roots can I cause to become firmly established?" . . . and so on, up to "Whom can I establish in the highest fruit of an arhat?"

Regarding this [topic], due to the supremacy of their basis, the tathāgatas are called "great beings." Due to the supremacy of their action, they are

508. This is a reference to the three forms of one-pointed concentration that are called the "three doors to liberation" (S: *trīṇi vimokṣamukhāni,* T: *rnam thar sgo gsum*). Asaṅga provides a Great Vehicle interpretation of them below, Book I, chapter 17, in the three sections entitled "One-Pointed Concentration on Emptiness," "One-Pointed Concentration on Wishlessness," and "One-Pointed Concentration on Signlessness" [I.17.14–16]. He also describes them in a manner that is shared with the Lesser Vehicle tradition in *ŚBh* (pp. 267–268).

509. See note 202.

510. S: *āniñjyam,* T: *mi g.yo ba*. This term is interpreted as indicating the absence of any mental defect. *AKB* (p. 190): "Because the fourth meditative absorption lacks any inner defect, the Blessed One called it 'immobile.' Therefore, no outer defect arises there [either], and thus no [cosmic] destruction occurs there."

called "the ones whose compassion is great." Due to the supremacy of their accomplishment, they are called "the ones whose morality and spiritual qualities are great." Due to the supremacy of their knowledge, they are called "the ones whose wisdom is great." Due to the supremacy of their power, they are called "the ones whose supernatural knowledge is great." Due to the supremacy of their abandonment, they are called "the ones who have attained great liberation." Due to the supremacy of their pleasurable states, they are called "the ones who abide in the great pleasurable states to a high degree."

Recollection of a Tathāgata's Good Qualities [1.7.3]

Moreover, ten aspects make up the verbal description of the good qualities possessed by the tathāgatas; [they] also [form the basis for practicing] recollection of their good qualities.

What are the ten?

[As the sutra passage states:] "So it is that the Bhagavān is the Tathāgata, Arhat, Samyaksaṃbuddha, the One who possesses knowledge and its support, the Sugata, the One who knows the world, the unsurpassed Leader of persons who can be tamed, the Teacher of gods and humans, the Buddha, and the Bhagavān."

(1) Regarding [these expressions], he is the Tathāgata because his speech is unerring.[511]

(2) He is an Arhat because he has attained everything that needs to be attained and because he is worthy of being revered in that he is the unsurpassed field of merit.[512]

(3) He is the Samyaksaṃbuddha because he has become aware of all entities exactly as they are in their ultimate sense.

(4) He is the One who possesses knowledge and its support[513] in that he

511. *AAA* (p. 351): "[Buddha is referred to as] the Tathāgata because he describes entities exactly as they are. This [expression] indicates his nature as a perfect speaker in that he is the one who teaches the Dharma unerringly."

512. Asaṅga also states in his *Commentary on Recollection of the Buddha* (T: *Sangs rgyas rjes su dran pa'i 'grel pa*, f. 12a): "He is an Arhat (T: *dgra bcom pa*) because he has destroyed the [inner] enemy of the mental afflictions."

513. S: *vidyācaraṇasaṃpannaḥ*, T: *rig pa dang zhabs su ldan pa*. The Sanskrit term *caraṇaḥ* (T: *zhabs*) can variously mean "foot," "support," "moving about," and "conduct." *Saṃpannaḥ* can also mean both "possessing" and "perfected." The different meanings associated with

is well endowed with three forms of knowledge[514] and their support, which are described in the sutras as consisting of insight and quiescence as well as those elements that favor both of them.

(5) He is the Sugata because he has attained [the state of] supreme excellence and because he has attained it irreversibly.[515]

(6) He is the One who knows the world[516] because of his knowledge of every way in which the constituent [in the sense] of world spheres and the constituent [in the sense of the constituent elements] of sentient beings undergo affliction and purification.

(7) He is referred to as the unsurpassed Leader of persons who can be tamed[517] because [he possesses] knowledge of the highest methods for taming minds and because he is the sole person [with such knowledge] who has appeared in the world.[518]

---

these terms allow for a number of interpretations. Asaṅga gives several explanations in his *Commentary on Recollection of the Buddha* (f. 12b), including the following: "The expression 'the one who possesses knowledge and its support' indicates the cause [that makes Buddha] the perfect teacher. Regarding [the phrase] 'knowledge and its support,' 'knowledge' is, among the eight limbs of the noble path, [the limb of] right view and the remaining [seven] limbs are 'its support.'"

514. S: *trividyāḥ,* T: *mkhyen pa gsum. BBhVy* (f. 112b): "The three forms of knowledge are (1) the supernatural knowledge that makes recollection of former existences directly evident; (2) the supernatural knowledge that makes knowledge of the termination of the outflows directly evident; and (3) the supernatural knowledge that makes knowledge of death and rebirth directly evident." For descriptions of these three forms of supernatural knowledge, see above, chapter 5, the sections entitled "Recollection of Former Existences" [I.5.1.2], "Knowledge regarding Termination of the Outflows" [I.5.1.6], and "Knowledge regarding Death and Rebirth" [I.5.1.4]. These types of knowledge are also addressed in Book III, chapter 6, among the corresponding forms of a buddha's ten powers.

515. *Commentary on Recollection of the Buddha* (f. 13b): "The term 'sugata' (T: *bde bar gshegs pa*) indicates one who has reached that place which ought to be reached. Thus, the Sugata is one who has fared well, like a fever that has been properly dispelled in the sense that it will not return. The Sugata is [also] one who has attained a realization that is complete. [That is,] he is like a pitcher that is completely full because he has realized everything that needs to be known without remainder."

516. S: *lokavid,* T: *'jig rten mkhyen pa. Commentary on Recollection of the Buddha* (f. 13b): "The phrase 'the One who knows the world' indicates [the act of] observing who is suitable [to be liberated] and who is not suitable."

517. S: *anuttaraḥ puruṣadamyasārathiḥ,* T: *skyes bu 'dul ba'i kha lo sgyur ba bla na med pa.*

518. *AAA* (p. 351): "Observing the worlds [made up of] those who are suitable [to be liberated] and those who are not, the Blessed One trains those suitable persons who can be tamed—that is, those who are worthy of being tamed or who are capable of being tamed—

(8) He is One who is like eyes[519] and also [the source of] knowledge, advantage,[520] and the Dharma, because he renders certain [the meanings of] those entities that are perceptible [to the senses], because he is the object to rely upon for all advantageous meanings, because he is the one who explicates all meanings that have not been explicated, because he is the one who removes all doubt that may arise, because he reveals those subjects that are profound and he causes [others] to become fully accomplished [in their meaning], and because he is the root, the guide, and the object to rely upon for all [aspects of] the Dharma. [For these reasons,] he [is the one who] teaches and properly indicates to gods and humans the remedy that gets rid of all suffering.[521] Therefore, [the Buddha] is called the Teacher of gods and humans.[522]

(9) He is called the Buddha[523] because he has realized in their entirety

---

because he has attained the quality of being their leader. The quality of being a leader [relates to] the act of training, in the sense of leading [beings] away from wrong paths and establishing them in the right path, as well as in the sense of engendering [in beings] extraordinary [spiritual] qualities, like a trainer of horses and the like. The term "unsurpassed" qualifies [the Buddha's unique] nature of being a leader. It indicates that he is one who trains even certain persons who are difficult to tame—that is, those who can be trained [despite] their strong desire, hatred, ignorance, and pride, such as Ārya Sundarānanda, Aṅgulīmāla, Urubilvākāśyapa, and the great King Kapphiṇa." Asaṅga provides a similar description in his *Commentary on Recollection of the Buddha* (f. 14a).

519. S: *cakṣurbhūtaḥ,* T: *mig lta bur gyur pa. BBhVy* (f. 114a) quotes the following verse from Mātṛceṭa's *In Praise of the Praiseworthy* (*Varṇārhavarṇastotram*, ch. 2, v. 56): "No one sees reality without relying upon your teaching. / Homage to you who are like eyes for a world that is blind."

520. S: *arthabhūtaḥ,* T: *don du gyur pa.* The term *arthaḥ* can mean "advantage" as well as "meaning." The former sense is the one that Asaṅga means here. *BBhVy* (f. 114a) again quotes verses from *In Praise of the Praiseworthy* (ch. 2, vv. 61, 62) to describe how Buddha is the source of advantage: "Desiring to forsake that which harms, the fool largely forsakes what is advantageous. / Desiring what is advantageous, he accomplishes what is harmful due to his ignorance. // But after having found you, he accomplishes both [aims] in a proper manner. Because you are the one who reveals that method, homage to you, the one who is [the source of] advantage."

521. S: *sarvadharmasya niḥsaraṇam,* T: *sdug bsngal thams cad kyi byung ba.* The verbal root of the noun *niḥsaraṇam* means "to depart." The term "departure" sometimes is a synonym for nirvana itself; however, it can also mean a "remedy for getting rid of" something, as it is translated here. See also note 1043.

522. S: *śāstā devamanuṣyāṇāṃ* T: *lha dang mi rnams kyi ston pa.*

523. The following interpretations are the basis for the formation of the Tibetan word for a buddha—that is, *sangs rgyas. AKV* (vol. 1, p. 5): "The word *buddhaḥ* is [a noun] formed from

and in every respect the heap of entities that are advantageous, the heap of entities that are disadvantageous, and the heap of entities that are neither advantageous nor disadvantageous.[524]

(10) He is the Bhagavān[525] because he defeated the great assemblage of Māra's army in its entirety.

---

a past participle that signifies an agent. [He is called] a 'buddha' because of the expansion of his mind (S: *buddher vikasanād,* T: *blo rgyas pa'i phyir*). [Thus, 'buddha'] means '[he whose mind has] expanded' (S: *vibuddhaḥ,* T: *rnam par rgyas pa*), like a lotus [blossom] that has expanded [into full bloom]. Alternatively, [he is called] a 'buddha' because he has emerged from the sleep of the two kinds of ignorance (S: *avidyānidrādvayāpagamād,* T: *ma rig pa'i gnyid gnyis dang bral ba'i phyir*). [Thus, 'buddha'] means 'awakened [one]' (S: *prabuddhaḥ,* T: *rab tu sad pa*), like a person that has awakened [from sleep]." Tradition has replaced *sad pa* ("awakened") with *sangs pa* ("dispelled").

524. Regarding the adjectives "advantageous" (S: *arthasaṃhitam,* T: *don dang ldan pa*), "disadvantageous" (S: *anarthasaṃhitam,* T: *don dang mi ldan pa*), and "neither advantageous nor disadvantageous," *BBhVy* (f. 114b) states: "The sutras state that these terms are to be understood as differentiating between that which is right and that which is wrong, or to describe the Buddha as one who has realized the categories of [those entities that are] virtuous, nonvirtuous, and indeterminate." See also Book III, chapter 6, the section entitled "Knowledge of All Aspects and of What Is Most Excellent" [III.6.10] for another reference to these three categories.

525. Elsewhere in the main text I have translated this term as "Blessed One." The explanation here of the word *bhaga* derives from the root *bhañj,* which means "to break," or "to defeat" (T: *bcom pa*). In this sense, *bhagavān* means "one who possesses [the quality of having] defeated [all adversity]." Another interpretation is that the word *bhaga* means "good fortune," "prosperity," and "excellence," in which case *bhagavān* should be taken to mean "one who possesses fortune." A frequently cited verse from the *Saṃpuṭodbhavatantra* describes a buddha's fortune as follows: "Fortune refers to these six: / Complete power, knowledge, / Renown, glory, beauty / And activity [that fulfills] aims (S: *aiśvaryasya samagrasya jñānasya yaśasaḥ śriyaḥ / rūpasyārthaprayatnasya ṣaṇṇāṃ bhaga iti smṛtaḥ;* T: *dbang phyug dang ni gzugs bzang dang / dpal dang grags dang ye shes dang / brtson 'grus phun sum tshogs pa ste / drug po rnams la skal zhes bya*)." Je Tsongkapa explains these qualities in his commentary to Lūyīpāda's *Cakrasaṃvarābhisamaya* (*'Dod pa 'jo ba,* f. 19a): "[A buddha's] 'complete power' [means that he is] not under the control of anyone [or anything] else through having abandoned the two obscurations together with their traces. 'Beauty' [means that he possesses] the unsurpassed major and minor marks. 'Renown' [means that his] fame has spread throughout all the [ten] directions and [three] times. 'Glory' [means that he is] relied upon by all who seek any form of mundane or transcendent prosperity. 'Knowledge' [means that his supreme transcendent awareness] engages all objects of knowledge without [any form of] obstruction or hindrance. 'Activity' [means that he] teaches instruction continually and effortlessly. [The adjective] 'complete' should also be construed with the other five qualities [in addition to power]." According to *GB2,* the final syllable *'das* in the Tibetan equivalent *bcom ldan 'das* was added by the Tibetan translators to indicate that a buddha's qualities are transcendent and superior to all other beings'.

Regarding this [topic], there are many kalpas in which not even a single buddha appears. It is also the case that many buddhas can arise in just a single kalpa. It should be understood that countless, immeasurable numbers of buddhas arise among the countless, immeasurable numbers of world spheres that lie in the ten directions.

Why is that?

[It is because] there are countless, immeasurable numbers of bodhisattvas in the ten directions who have made aspirational prayers at the same time and who have completed equal amounts of the [two] accumulations. In whatever day, half-month, month, or year a single bodhisattva has made the aspirational prayer of enlightenment mind, in that very day, half-month, month, or year all [bodhisattvas have done so as well]. In whatever way a single [bodhisattva] has exerted him- or herself, striven [to practice], and made great effort, all [bodhisattvas have also done so] in the same way. For if even in this very world sphere many hundreds of bodhisattvas are seen to make aspirational prayers at the same time, [if they are seen] to be similar in their generosity, similar in their morality, similar in their patience, similar in their effort, similar in their meditative absorption, and similar in their wisdom, then how much more would this be so throughout the endless and limitless [numbers of] world spheres that lie in the ten directions. The buddha fields that exist throughout the ten directions, [each of which encompasses] a great triple-thousand world spheres, are also measureless and countless [in number].

Now, since it is not possible for two bodhisattvas who have similarly completed their accumulations [of merit and wisdom] to take birth at the same time in the buddha field of one and the same world sphere, how much more would this be so for measureless and countless numbers [of bodhisattvas]. Moreover, it would not be proper for [bodhisattvas whose completion] of accumulations is similar to take birth in succession with one following the other, nor would it be proper for them not to take birth at all. Therefore, it should be understood that those bodhisattvas who have similarly completed their accumulations are born in separate buddha fields throughout the measureless and countless numbers [of world spheres that lie] in the ten directions in regions that are devoid of a buddha and [they are born there] according to [the state of] their purity. In this way, it is entirely proper for there to be a multitude of buddhas in a great number of [separate] world spheres. However, it is not the case that two tathāgatas can take birth simultaneously in a single buddha field.

Why is that?

For a great length of time, bodhisattvas strongly cultivate the following aspirational prayer: "I so wish that I alone may become a leader [of beings] in a world that has no leader, [that I alone may become] one who [spiritually] tames sentient beings, who liberates them from every form of suffering, and who causes them to attain complete nirvana." The correct pursuit of spiritual practice by one who has strongly cultivated such a prayer for a great length of time is sure to bring success. Furthermore, a single tathāgata is able to perform all the deeds of a buddha within a single buddha field that [encompasses] a great triple-thousand [world spheres]. Therefore, it would be meaningless for a second tathāgata to be born [there]. In addition, because of the arising of a single tathāgata in a [particular] world, the successful completion by sentient beings of their own aims occurs in much greater numbers and with much stronger devotion.

Why is that?

The following thoughts occur to [sentient beings]: "Throughout the entire world, there is only this one tathāgata; there is not a second [tathāgata]. If he were to travel to [a different] country or [if he were to] enter nirvana, there would be no second [tathāgata] whatsoever in whose presence we could practice the spiritual life or hear the Dharma." Having made this realization, they make haste with a very firm aspiration and exertion to abide in the spiritual life and hear the true Dharma. However, if they were to encounter a multitude of buddhas, they would not make haste. Thus, through the arising of a single tathāgata, the successful accomplishment by them of their own aims occurs in greater numbers and with stronger devotion.

Regarding this [topic], all buddhas are the same in every respect and free of differences, except for these four things: life span, name, caste, and physical size. The distinction among buddhas is due to a variation in these four qualities and not to anything else whatsoever.

A woman cannot attain unsurpassed true and complete enlightenment.

Why is that?

[This should be understood] as follows: Once a bodhisattva has passed beyond the first [period of a] countless number of kalpas he abandons the state of being a woman, and [from then on] until he sits at the seat of enlightenment,[526] he will never again become a woman. The entirety of

526. S: *bodhimaṇḍaḥ,* T: *byang chub kyi snying po.* In Great Vehicle doctrine, the seat of enlightenment is said to have two forms: (1) the place in a buddha paradise where a

womankind naturally possesses a great many mental afflictions and is subject to inferior wisdom, and it is not possible for [a person with] a mind stream that naturally possesses a great many mental afflictions and is subject to inferior wisdom to attain unsurpassed true and complete enlightenment.

Thus, it should be understood that the essential nature of unsurpassed true and complete enlightenment has been described as it truly is. It should also be understood that the supremacy, the manner of recalling the special description of [a tathāgata's] good qualities, the manner of [a tathāgata's] appearance, and the differences [that exist among tathāgatas] have been described as they truly are. However, unsurpassed true and complete enlightenment is beyond thought, because it transcends all forms of speculative analysis. It cannot be fully grasped, because it possesses spiritual qualities that are immeasurably great. And it is truly unsurpassed in that it produces all the tathāgatas, listener [arhats], and solitary realizer [arhats]. Therefore, this form of enlightenment alone is the foremost, the best, the most eminent, and the most excellent.

Within [Book I of] *The Stage of a Bodhisattva,* [known as] "The Object of Mental Application That Relates to the Support," this completes the seventh chapter, entitled "Enlightenment."

tenth-stage bodhisattva actually achieves enlightenment and (2) the geographical location at Bodhgaya where a buddha's emanation body gives the appearance of attaining enlightenment.

8

The Lineages of the Powers

The presentation of [the seven subjects] in relation to which a bodhisattva should train him- or herself has been completed.[527] Now I shall describe the manner in which [a bodhisattva] should train.

Summary [lines of] verse:

> Abundance of devotion,
> Seeking and teaching Dharma,
> Practice and, likewise,
> Correct instruction and counsel,
> And, lastly, deeds of body, speech, and mind
> That are supported by means.

At the very outset, a bodhisattva who is desirous of training him- or herself here in the bodhisattva trainings must become (1) one whose devotion is abundant. He or she must also become (2) one who seeks the Dharma, (3) one who teaches the Dharma, (4) one who is established in a practice that accords with the Dharma, one who gives correct (5) instruction and (6) counsel, and (7) one who, while abiding in correct instruction and counsel, engages in deeds of body, speech, and mind that are governed by skillful means.

527. See description and summary verse at beginning of Book I, chapter 3. The seven subjects are (1) one's own aim, (2) others' aims, (3) the meaning of reality, (4) spiritual power, (5) the ripening of sentient beings, (6) the ripening of a buddha's qualities in oneself, and (7) true and complete enlightenment.

Abundance of Devotion [1.8.1]

How does a bodhisattva become one whose devotion is abundant?

Here a bodhisattva becomes endowed with a [sense of] certainty and eagerness that is preceded by the faith that is a clarity [of mind] toward the eight objects of devotion, about which he or she thinks: "I am capable of achieving (1) the virtuous qualities of the Three Jewels—that is, the Buddha, Dharma, and Sangha; (2) the powers of a bodhisattva and a buddha that were [previously] described;[528] (3) [knowledge of] the nature of reality that was [previously] described; [knowledge of] the various kinds of (4) causes and (5) results, according to the manner in which they occur; and (6) the unerring aim that is worthy of being achieved." Just as with the aim that is worthy of being achieved, [a bodhisattva regards] (7) the means of achieving [that aim] in the same way, such that he or she thinks: "There exists a means for attaining the aim that is worthy of being achieved." Regarding this [point], the aim that is worthy of being achieved is unsurpassed enlightenment. For its part, the means of achieving [that aim] is all of the paths that make up the bodhisattva training. Just as with them, devotion [should also be developed] toward (8) that which was well expounded, well spoken, and well declared—that is to say, the Dharma teachings [contained in the twelve divisions, which are known as] discourses, songs, declarations, and the rest.[529]

528. See Book I, chapter 5.

529. *AS* (pp. 78–79): "What is the settled opinion about the Dharma? The teaching of the noble ones is the Dharma that consists of twelve divisions (S: *dvādaśaṇgadharmaḥ,* T: *yan lag bcu gnyis kyi chos*). What are the twelve divisions? (1) Discourses (S: *sūtram,* T: *mdo'i sde*); (2) songs (S: *geyam,* T: *dbyangs kyis bsnyad pa'i sde*); (3) declarations (S: *vyākaraṇam,* T: *lung du bstan pa'i sde*); (4) verses (S: *gāthā,* T: *tshigs su bcad pa'i sde*); (5) exalted sayings (S: *udānam,* T: *ched du brjod pa'i sde*); (6) statements of cause (S: *nidānam,* T: *gleng gzhi'i sde*); (7) illustrative narratives (S: *avadānam,* T: *rtogs par brjod pa'i sde*); (8) accounts of past events (S: *itivṛttakam,* T: *de lta bu byung ba'i sde*); (9) birth stories (S: *jātakam,* T: *skyes pa'i rabs kyi sde*); (10) extensive discourses (S: *vaipulyam,* T: *shin tu rgyas pa'i sde*); (11) marvels (S: *adbhūtadharmaḥ,* T: *rmad du byung ba'i chos kyi sde*); and (12) instructions (S: *upadeśaḥ,* T: *gtan la phab pa'i sde*). What are discourses? They are the prose expositions that point out in a succinct manner the meanings that [represent the views that] are approved of [by the Buddha].... What are songs? They are that which is sung in verse in the middle or at the end of discourses. Alternatively, they are [the verses] which explain meanings that were not formulated in the discourses. Therefore, they are called 'songs.' What are declarations? They are the declarations [that identify] the variety of places in which the ārya listeners took birth and from which they expired in the past. It is also the clarification of meanings that were

Regarding this [topic], it should be understood that an abundance of devotion toward the eight objects of devotion is due to two causes: (1) the extensive cultivation of devotion and (2) the development of strong forbearance.[530]

Seeking the Dharma [1.8.2]

Regarding this [topic], when a bodhisattva is seeking Dharma, what does he or she seek? How does he or she seek it? What are his or her motives for seeking it?

In brief, a bodhisattva seeks the bodhisattva collection[531] [of scriptures]

---

formulated in the sutra discourses, by making declarations that expose [the true intent of teachings that have] indirect meanings. What are verses? They are that which is taught in the discourses with a metrical form that employs two, three, four, five, or six lines. What are exalted sayings? They are those pronouncements that a tathāgata occasionally makes in the discourses when his mind is filled with delight. What are statements of cause? They are those statements that are made in response to a question. Alternatively, they are those well-founded statements that prescribe the [precepts to be followed in] spiritual training. They are statements of cause for this reason as well. What are illustrative narratives? They are those statements made in sutras that are accompanied by examples. What are accounts of past events? They are [those scriptures] that indicate the past ordinary events that relate to ārya listeners. What are birth stories? They are [those scriptures] that indicate the [past] events that relate to the Bodhisattva's conduct. What are the extensive discourses? They are those teachings that are contained in the bodhisattva collection. . . . Why are they called "extensive"? It is because they are the source of what benefits and brings happiness to all sentient beings and because they teach the Dharma that is wide ranging and profound. . . . What are marvels? They are those [teachings] in which the supremely marvelous and wonderful qualities of the listeners, bodhisattvas and tathāgatas are revealed. What are instructions? They are the unerring explanations of all the profound and obscure characteristics of entities."

530. S: *kṣāntiḥ,* T: *bzod pa.* This quality is one that arises through developing a deep appreciation of such subjects as the four noble truths. *AKV* (vol. 3, p. 909) describes it as a quality that "accepts the truths in the sense of being favorably disposed toward them" (S: *satyaṃ kṣamate rocate;* T: *bden pa la bzod cing 'dod do*). It occurs in a very strong form on the path of preparation in anticipation of attaining transcendent realization; however, its highest form occurs on the path of seeing. See Book I, chapter 11, in the section entitled "The Patience of the Devotion That Is Gained by Reflecting upon Entities" [I.11.2.3], where Asaṅga describes the latter as arising "through the attainment of perfectly pure knowledge."

531. S: *piṭakam,* T: *sde snod.* Literally, this term means a "basket" or container, such as for grain. It is also used to refer to the collections of Buddhist canonical literature, such as the three "baskets" of Sutra (discourses), Vinaya (code of moral discipline), and Abhidharma (systematic formulations of essential doctrine) literature. Here Asaṅga is using the term to

and also seeks the listener collection [of scriptures], the outer bodies of teachings,[532] and the categories of secular crafts and occupations.

Regarding these [areas of study], among the twelve divisions [of the Buddha's teachings] that were mentioned, the one known as "extensive discourses" represents the bodhisattva collection. The remaining [eleven divisions] should be understood to make up the listener collection.

The outer bodies of teachings, briefly, are of three types: (1) the body of teachings on logic, (2) the body of teachings on grammar, and (3) the body of teachings on the treatment of disease.

Regarding the categories of secular crafts and occupations, they are of numerous types and many diverse forms, including knowledge of the occupations of a goldsmith, ironsmith, jeweler, and the like.

All of these branches of learning are subsumed within the five branches of learning: (1) the inner science, (2) the science of logic, (3) the science of grammar, (4) the science of treating disease, and (5) the science of the categories of crafts and occupations. These five branches of learning are the ones that the bodhisattva seeks. In this way, he or she seeks all the branches of learning.

Regarding this [topic], Buddha's speech is referred to as "the inner body of teachings." In how many forms does [Buddha's speech] occur? The same [question is asked with the other fields] up to: In how many forms do the branches of worldly crafts and occupations occur?

In brief, Buddha's speech occurs in two forms: (1) the form that correctly sets forth causes and results and (2) the form that sets forth [the principles]

---

distinguish the canonical literature of the Great Vehicle from that of the listener traditions. *MSAVy* (p. 55): "What is the reason for referring to these three or two [groups of scriptures] as 'baskets'? [As the *MSA* root text (ch. 11, v. 1a) states,] it is 'because they are collections.' It should be understood [that they are called 'baskets'] because they contain the meanings of everything that needs to be known." Also, *MSAVṛBh* (vol. 125, f. 154b): "For example, just as a container that holds and is able to contain ten measures (T: *'bre*) of grain is called a *piṭakam* (Skt. uncertain, T: *snod*), here these threefold and twofold [collections of canonical literature] are called 'baskets' (S: *piṭakam*, T: *sde snod*) because they contain all the meanings and words that make up the twelve divisions of [Buddhist] scriptures."

532. S: *bāhyakāni śāstrāni*, T: *phyi rol gyi bstan bcos rnams*. The adjective "outer" means that which relates to a tradition that falls outside the realm of what is exclusively Buddhist in nature. While the term *śāstraḥ* (T: *bstan bcos*) is often understood to mean a specific treatise, it can also refer to an entire body of teachings on a particular subject (MW, p. 1069). The latter sense would seem to be the one intended here.

that what has been done will not perish and that what has not been done will not yield any fruition.[533]

The body of teachings on logic also occurs in two forms: (1) the form that sets forth the advantages of responding to criticisms that are raised by others and (2) the form that sets forth the advantages of refuting views that are posited by others.

The body of teachings on grammar also [occurs] in two forms: (1) the form that sets forth how to derive and establish the nature of verbal roots and (2) the form that sets forth the advantages of correct formation [and usage] of words.

The body of teachings on the treatment of disease occurs in four forms: (1) the form that sets forth [how to gain] expertise regarding disease, (2) the form that sets forth [how to gain] expertise regarding all the sources of disease, (3) the form that sets forth [how to gain] expertise about [the methods of] curing diseases that have arisen, and (4) the form that sets forth [how to gain] expertise about preventing diseases that have been cured from arising [again] in the future.

The categories of secular crafts and occupations occur in the form that sets forth how to practice and achieve the goals of each of the various categories of crafts and occupations.

The Ten Causes [1.8.2.1]

How does Buddha's speech unerringly set forth causes and results?

Ten causes make up the unerring presentation of causes and they should be understood as encompassing the complete enumeration of all causes that relate to [the process of] becoming afflicted, [the process of] becoming

533. As Asaṅga explains next, these two aspects of a buddha's speech are directly linked to the attainment of the first two of a buddha's ten powers. The two principles described in the second aspect are axioms that relate to the doctrine of karma. The phrase "what has been done will not perish" (S: *kṛtāvipranāśaḥ,* T: *byas pa chud mi za ba*) indicates that karma does not lose its power to bear fruit, and the phrase "what has not been done will not yield any fruition" (S: *ākṛtānabhyāgamaḥ,* T: *ma byas pa dang mi phrad pa*) means that specific results cannot arise without the prior occurrence of an appropriate cause. *BBhVy* (f. 116b) gives the more specific interpretation that the phrase "what has been done will not perish" means that the spiritual practices of the three vehicles will prove to be effective in achieving their results, and the phrase "what has not been done will not yield any fruition" means that the practices undertaken by followers of other [i.e., non-Buddhist] traditions will prove ineffective in achieving genuine spiritual results.

purified, and the occurrence of the various types of worldly and [morally] indeterminate entities such as agricultural crops.

What are the ten causes?

They are (1) the causes of orderly discourse, (2) requisite causes, (3) propelling causes, (4) supporting causes, (5) originating causes, (6) producing causes, (7) fixed causes, (8) cooperating causes, (9) opposing causes, and (10) compatible causes.

Regarding this [topic], the names that relate to all entities, as well as the conceptions[534] that are preceded by names and the statements that are preceded by conceptions, are called the causes of orderly discourse[535] that relate to those entities.

Regarding this [topic], that entity upon which something is dependent and by which it is caused, and that entity in relation to which something is sought after and acquired are called its requisite cause. For example, the act of grasping is dependent on a hand and is caused by a hand; the acts of going out and coming back[536] are dependent on feet and are caused by feet; the acts of contracting and extending [the limbs] are dependent upon joints and caused by joints; and the pursuit and acquisition of food and drink are dependent upon hunger and thirst and are caused by hunger and thirst. It should be understood that there are an immeasurable number of similar instances of requisite causes that conform to this principle.[537]

Regarding this [topic], a seed is the propelling cause[538] of its own result, which represents the culmination [of its development]. All other condi-

534. S: *saṃjñā,* T: *'du shes.* This term refers to the mental factor that makes up the third of the five heaps. See note 307.

535. *BBhVy* (f. 117a) glosses the term "orderly discourse" (S: *anuvyavahāraḥ,* T: *rjes su tha snyad 'dogs pa*) as follows: "Due to the imprints of repeated conceptual elaboration that occurred in former lives, [human beings engage in] orderly discourse with one another, [that is, they engage in] verbal activity that gives expression to entities."

536. S: *abhikramapratikrame,* T: *'gro ba dang 'ong ba. ŚBh* (p. 112): "Regarding this, going out is when someone here goes to one village or another, to one home or another, or to one monastery or another. Regarding this, coming back is when someone here returns from one village or another, from one home or another, or from one monastery or another."

537. The Tibetan translation for the phrase "that conform to this principle" (S: *nayānugataḥ*) is *yul dang ldan pa.* This is likely a corruption that should be amended to *tshul dang ldan pa.*

538. S: *ākṣepahetuḥ,* T: *'phen pa'i rgyu. BBhVy* (f. 117b): "A seed is a propelling cause because a seed embeds in [all] stages of the series [of entities that follow it], beginning with the sprout and continuing thereafter, a capacity that causes [each of those stages] to arise in a form that resembles [the seed's] own nature."

tions with the exception of the seed constitute supporting causes.[539] The seed is the originating cause[540] of its own [immediate] result. Further, the result that is [immediately] brought into being by the seed is the producing cause[541] of the subsequent results that were propelled by the seed. Fixed causes are the distinct forms of causality that relate to a variety of different classes of things. Requisite causes, propelling causes, supporting causes, originating causes, producing causes, and fixed causes, all taken together as one group, are called "cooperating causes."[542] Causes that obstruct the arising of something are opposing causes. Those that lack any obstructive nature are compatible causes.

Regarding this [topic], briefly there are six kinds of opposition: (1) Opposition relating to speech is, for example, the contradictory statements that are found at different places throughout the treatises of certain brahmins and ascetics. (2) Opposition relating to reasoning is when [a form of] the application that relates to demonstrating correctness does not properly establish the existence of something in relation to a knowable object. (3) Opposition to arising is when, for example, the arising [of something] does not occur because of the absence of those causal factors that promote its arising and the presence of entities that obstruct its arising. (4) Opposition to simultaneous occurrence is [a condition that exists between] such pairs of things as light and darkness, desire and hatred, and pleasure and pain. (5) Opposition of adversaries is [a condition that exists between] species that are adversarial and hostile to one another, such as snakes and mongooses, and cats and mice. (6) Opposition between bad qualities and their antidotes is [a condition that exists between], for example, desire and meditation on

539. S: *parigrahahetuḥ,* T: *yongs su 'dzin pa'i rgyu. BBhVy* (ff. 117b–118a): "The conditions of the field, water, etc., are the supporting causes of a fruit, because they all assist [in the production of] that fruit."

540. S: *nirvṛttihetuḥ,* T: *mngon par 'grub pa'i rgyu. BBhVy* (f. 118a): "That very seed is the originating cause of the sprout that is its own result, because that [sprout] is what arises immediately after [the seed]."

541. S: *āvāhakahetuḥ,* T: *'dren pa'i rgyu. BBhVy* (f. 118a): "The phrase 'result that is brought into being by the seed' refers to the sprout. The phrase 'propelled by the seed' refers to the subsequent results. That is, [the sprout] is the producing cause of those results that arise subsequent to it, because it gradually brings forth those results."

542. S: *sahākārihetuḥ,* T: *lhan cig byed pa'i rgyu. BBhVy* (f. 118a): "All those conditioned entities that are [themselves] governed by causes and conditions, that do not possess an action [that is distinct from themselves], and that carry out an action by their collective presence are called 'cooperating causes.'"

unattractiveness;[543] malice[544] and meditation on loving-kindness; harmfulness[545] and compassion; and between meditation on the limbs of enlightenment[546] and the eightfold noble path on the one hand and all the root and secondary mental afflictions that operate in the three realms on the other. This [last] point is considered to represent [a specific type of] opposition to arising.

All of these causes can be subsumed within two types of causes: (1) generative causes and (2) instrumental causes. Seeds, which are requisite [causes] and originating causes, constitute generative causes. The remaining forms of causes should be understood as instrumental causes.

There are four conditions:[547] (1) causal conditions, (2) homogeneous

543. *ŚBh* (pp. 202–207) describes five kinds of desire (S: *kāmarāgaḥ,* T: *'dod chags*) and six types of unattractiveness that are their antidotes. See *Inner Science,* pp. 157–159 and accompanying note 586.

544. S: *vyāpādaḥ,* T: *gnod sems.* This is the name of the ninth of the ten nonvirtuous karmic paths (S: *daśākuśalakarmapathāḥ,* T: *mi dge ba'i las lam bcu*). *AK,* ch. 4, v. 78a: "Malice is hostility toward beings."

545. S: *vihiṃsā,* T: *rnam par 'tshe ba. AS* (p. 9): "What is harmfulness? It is a form of hatred that is a lack of sympathy, an absence of compassion, and lack of pity [toward others]. Its action is to do injury [to others]."

546. S: *bodhyaṅgāni,* T: *byang chub kyi yan lag.* There are seven limbs of enlightenment: (1) recollection; (2) discernment (S: *pravicayaḥ,* T: *rnam par 'byed pa*); (3) effort; (4) joy; (5) agility (S: *prasrabdhiḥ,* T: *shin tu sbyangs pa*); (6) one-pointed concentration; and (7) equanimity.

547. S: *caturpratyayāḥ,* T: *rkyen bzhi.* Two of the most detailed descriptions of this topic are found in Vasubandhu's *Commentary to the Treasury of Higher Learning* (*AKB,* pp. 98–101) and Jinaputra's *Commentary to the Compendium of Higher Learning* (*ASBh,* pp. 35–42).

Both Candrakīrti and Asaṅga describe the causal condition (S: *hetupratyayaḥ,* T: *rgyu'i rkyen*) as the seed that produces a result. However, while Asaṅga identifies this with the storehouse consciousness (S: *ālayavijñānam,* T: *kun gzhi rnam par shes pa*), Candrakīrti does not. In his *AS,* Asaṅga provides a lengthy series of examples, which are meant to be illustrative in nature rather than providing an exhaustive account. The first of them is the collection of elements including the eye that represent the causal conditions that give rise to eye consciousness. The remaining examples cover a variety of circumstances that relate both to animate beings and to the inanimate world.

Explanations of the homogeneous immediate condition (S: *samanantarapratyayaḥ,* T: *mtshungs pa de ma thag rkyen*) typically limit the meaning of this factor to the way in which each moment of consciousness and its accompanying mental factors, upon their cessation, determine the nature of those mental entities that immediately succeed them. However, Candrakīrti (*PP,* p. 26) extends the meaning of this condition to include entities that are not mental in nature. He states: "The [state of] cessation that occurs immediately following [the moment in which] a cause [existed] is the [homogeneous immediate] condition

immediate conditions, (3) objective conditions, and (4) governing conditions. Regarding this [topic], it should be understood that generative causes are forms of causal conditions, and instrumental causes are forms of governing conditions.

Homogeneous immediate conditions and objective conditions are limited to those entities that are minds and mental factors. That is, those minds and mental factors that are supported by [the minds and mental factors] that arose before them in the sense that [those entities] provide them with the opportunity [to arise] are the ones that come into being. Similarly, those minds and mental factors that are supported by a mental object are the ones that become active. Therefore, it should be understood that homogeneous immediate conditions and objective conditions are subsumed within [the category of] supporting causes.

How Worldly Entities Are Produced [1.8.2.1.1]

Regarding this [topic], how is it that these ten causes produce all worldly entities? How is it that they bring about [the process of] affliction? How is it that they bring about [the process of] purification?

The various kinds of crops that are considered forms of grain in the world and by which the world maintains its livelihood have the following variety of names, conceptions, and forms of verbal usage: barley, rice, wheat, sesame,

---

for the arising of its result. For example, the cessation that occurs immediately following [the moment in which] a seed [existed] is the [homogeneous immediate] condition for the emergence of a sprout."

The objective condition (S: *ālambanapratyayaḥ*, T: *dmigs rkyen*) addresses the kinds of entities that constitute the objects for each of the six types of consciousness and their accompanying mental factors. Asaṅga's list of categories begins with the specific objects that are limited to each of the five types of sense consciousness and ends with the unobstructed object of a person who has eliminated from his mind all the obstacles to omniscience.

The governing condition (S: *adhipatipratyayaḥ*, T: *bdag po'i rkyen*) refers to a type of factor that is both controlling and necessary for the occurrence of some entity. The most commonly cited example is that the eye faculty is the governing condition for the occurrence of eye consciousness, and each of the other sense faculties is the governing condition for its respective form of sense consciousness. Beyond this, samsaric virtuous and nonvirtuous karma are the governing conditions for the various types of result that they generate. Among the mental factors, two examples are that attention (S: *manaskāraḥ*, T: *yid la byed pa*) is the governing condition that determines the type and form of consciousness that will occur, and contact (S: *sparśaḥ*, T: *reg pa*) is the governing condition for the type of feeling (S: *vedanā*, T: *tshor ba*) that will be experienced.

urad beans,[548] mung beans,[549] horse gram beans,[550] etc. "Let the barley be fetched," "Let it be reaped,"[551] "Let it be ground," "Let it be stored," etc., are expressions that provide examples of their causes of orderly discourse. Just as with barley, the same can be understood to apply in relation to the remaining [crops].

In dependence on being hungry, thirsty, physically weak, and the body being at rest, and in dependence on consumption of food that is taken in morsels,[552] there is desire for, as well as pursuit, acquisition, and enjoyment of those [kinds of food]. These are the requisite causes that relate to them.

Whatever individual seeds are the ones from which various individual crops arise, those particular seeds are the propelling causes of those [very crops]. The conditions of earth, rain, etc. that [promote] the arising of sprouts are the supporting causes. The seeds are the originating causes of [their respective] sprouts. The continuous series of sprouts, stems, and leaves, in turn, are the producing causes of that crop's growth and maturation. Barley seeds cause the arising of barley sprouts and, [ultimately, the arising of] a barley crop; they do not [cause the arising] of anything else. The same should be understood for all the remaining [kinds of crops]. This represents [the condition of being] a fixed cause. Beginning with the requisite cause and ending with the fixed cause, all these causes [that contribute to] the arising of a [particular] crop are the cooperating causes. This grain cannot reach maturity if any of these causes is absent. Therefore, the totality of all of them is called the "cooperating cause." Obstacles such as the occurrence of hail and crop diseases are opposing causes. The absence of such obstacles is

548. S: *mudgaḥ,* T: *mon sran sde'u.* Scientific name: *Vigna mungo* or *Phaseolus mungo.* The most common variety is black; however, several varieties are mentioned: *kṛṣṇa* or black, *mahā* or large, *gaura* or pale red, *harita* or green, *pīta* or yellow, *sveta* or white, and *rakta* or red.

549. S: *māṣaḥ,* T: *mon sran gre'u.* Scientific name: *Vigna radiata* or *Phaseolus roxburghii.*

550. S: *kulattaḥ,* T: *rgya sran.* Scientific name: *Dolichos biflorus.*

551. S: *dīyantām,* T: *khyer cig.* The Sanskrit forms for all four of these verbs is the third person passive imperative. This verbal root means "to cut" or "to reap." The Tibetan translation literally means "to carry" or "to bring."

552. S: *kavaḍīkārāharaḥ,* T: *kham gyi zas. AKB* (pp. 152–155) defines food as that which causes the world to continue to exist. This is meant both in the sense of maintaining life and in the sense of perpetuating samsaric existence. There are four types of food: (1) food that is taken in morsels, (2) contact, (3) volition, and (4) consciousness. Food that is taken in morsels is only present in the desire realm and, for those who crave it, it serves as a cause of rebirth there.

the compatible cause. These ten causes should also be understood to occur in relation to other mundane entities just as they do in this summary of [how] grain [is produced], according to the circumstances [of each situation].

The Process of Affliction [1.8.2.1.2]

Regarding this [topic], the names, conceptions, and verbal expressions that relate to all [the elements that make up the doctrine] of dependent origination—ranging from "ignorance," "formations," "consciousness," and "name and form" up to "old age and death," "sorrow," "lamentation," "pain," "mental suffering," and "adversity"—constitute the causes of orderly discourse that pertain to the process of affliction. Regarding [the series of limbs that make up] the orderly discourse that begins with "formations are conditioned by ignorance" and continues up to "old age and death are conditioned by birth," the activities that occur in relation to the limbs of [a sentient being's] existence and that are dependent on the experiencing of objects represent the requisite causes of the process of affliction. The seeds that exist here in this life and that relate to the entities associated with ignorance, etc., are the propelling causes of the birth, old age, and death that will occur in a different life. [Activities] that contribute to the arising of [the limbs of] ignorance, etc.—[such as] associating with evil persons, listening to false teachings, [engaging in] improper attention [of the mind], and [any improper conduct] engendered by one's repeated practice in the past—constitute the supporting causes. Each individual seed of [the limbs of] ignorance, etc., is the originating cause [of that very same element].

Additionally, [the limbs beginning with] ignorance, etc., and ending with existence, which make up a series that functions in such a way that each succeeding member brings into being the next [limb], are the producing causes of [the limbs of] birth and old age and death that will occur in another lifetime. Certain of [these series of limbs that begin with] ignorance, etc., and end with existence, together with each of their individual seeds, function collectively to [bring about] rebirth in the hells. Others do so to [bring about] rebirth as an animal, a hungry ghost, a human being, or a god. This represents [the condition of being] fixed causes in relation to the process of affliction. The [collection of causes] beginning with the requisite causes and ending with the fixed causes are called the "cooperating causes." Additionally, the opposing causes of the process of affliction are [the condition of] possessing a form of spiritual lineage, the appearance of the buddhas, the teaching of the true Dharma, [the activities of] associating with wise persons, listening to the true Dharma, proper attention [of the mind], [engaging in] a form of [spiritual] practice that conforms with Dharma, as well as all the entities that are conducive to enlightenment. The causes that do not oppose [the process of affliction] are a deficiency in or absence of those entities that were just mentioned. This is the manner in which these ten causes should be understood [as bringing about] the entire process of affliction for all sentient beings.

The Process of Purification [1.8.2.1.3]

Regarding this [topic], the names, conceptions, and verbal expressions that relate to all the spiritual qualities that are conducive to purification, as well as the cessation [that occurs in the reversal of the twelve limbs of dependent origination] and nirvana, constitute the causes of orderly discourse that pertain to the process of purification. The kind of entities [that make up this form of the cause] of orderly discourse include [the thirty-seven qualities that are conducive to enlightenment—which begin with] the [four] closely placed recollections,[553] the [four] forms of correct abandonment,[554]

553. S: *smṛtyupasthānāni,* T: *dran pa nye bar gzhag pa*. The four closely placed recollections are a form of practice in which one meditates on four objects—the body, feelings, the mind, and [mental] entities—in order to overcome four erroneous beliefs and develop an understanding of the four noble truths. *ŚBh* (p. 303): "Regarding this [topic], the Blessed One formulated the four closely placed recollections as an antidote for the four errors. Closely placed recollection of the body was formulated as the antidote for the error that regards what is impure as pure. . . . Closely placed recollection of feelings was formulated as an antidote for the error that regards what is unsatisfactory as a state of well-being. . . . Closely placed recollection of the mind was formulated as an antidote for the error that regards what is impermanent as permanent. . . . Closely placed recollection of entities was formulated as an antidote for the error that regards what is not a [real] self as constituting a [real] self." Again, *ŚBh* (p. 303): "What is the meaning of the expression 'closely placed recollection'? Closely placed recollection refers both to that toward which recollection is closely placed and that by which recollection is closely placed. 'That toward which recollection is closely placed' means the meditation object in relation to which closely placed recollection is practiced. 'That by which recollection is closely placed' means the wisdom and recollection that are conducive to one-pointed concentration in relation to that [meditation object]. The latter [description] constitutes the essential form of closely placed recollection. Those other entities that are forms of consciousness and secondary mental factors, and that accompany that [wisdom and recollection], are the concomitants of closely placed recollection." *MSA* (ch. 18, vv. 43–45) identifies fourteen ways in which the Great Vehicle form of this practice is superior that of the listeners.

554. S: *samyakprahāṇāni,* T: *yang dag spong ba*. This fourfold practice is identified as essen-

and continue up to the eightfold noble path,[555] as well as [the elements that make up the reversal of the twelve limbs of dependent origination—which begins with] the cessation of conditioning entities that is brought about by the cessation of ignorance and continues up to the cessation of old age and death that is brought about by the cessation of birth.

Regarding this [topic], [the activities of] seeking purification, accomplishing purification, and completing purification, [all of which] are dependent upon [having become aware of] the disadvantages of the formations, represent the requisite causes of the process of purification.

The [condition of] possessing [a form of] spiritual lineage—[a quality] that relates to those persons who abide in [a state of having] a spiritual lineage and that is a precondition for the attainment of the [form of] nirvana in which the support [of the five heaps] remains and [the form of nirvana] in which the support [of the five heaps] does not remain—represents the propelling cause of the process of purification.

[The activities of] associating with wise persons, listening to the true Dharma, [engaging in] proper attention [of the mind], and the ripening of one's faculties that was accomplished previously [all] constitute the supporting causes.

The seeds of those uncontaminated[556] entities that are conducive to

---

tially a form of effort (S: *vīryam,* T: *brtson 'grus*). Canonical scriptures give this description: "[The practitioner] develops aspiration, strives, initiates effort, takes hold of his or her mind, and places it, in order to keep from developing those evil and nonvirtuous entities that have not arisen [previously], in order to abandon those evil and nonvirtuous entities that have arisen [previously], in order to develop those virtuous entities that have not arisen [previously], and in order to maintain [possession of], avoid indistinctness about, complete meditation on, as well as increase, strengthen, and augment those virtuous entities that have arisen [previously]." *ŚBh* (pp. 307–314) gives a detailed analysis of every expression that appears in this passage.

Buddhist Sanskrit literature also refers to this practice by another term that means "correct placement" (S: *samyakpradhānam,* T: *yang dag par rab tu 'jog pa*). For example, *AKB* (p. 384): "Why is effort called 'correct placement'? [Effort is called that] because it causes the body, speech, and mind to be correctly placed." Yaśomitra's subcommentary (*AKV,* vol. 3, p. 1019) glosses the verb "to be placed" (S: *pradhīyante,* T: *rab tu 'jog pa*) as "to be kept steady" (S: *dhāryante,* T: *'dzin pa*) and "to be controlled" (S: *niyamyante,* T: *nges par byed pa*).

555. S: *āryāṣṭāṅgo mārgaḥ,* T: *'phag pa'i lam yan lag brgyad pa*. This is the last of the seven groups of practices that make up the thirty-seven spiritual qualities that are conducive to enlightenment. Asaṅga's lengthiest discussion of these thirty-seven practices is found in *ŚBh* (pp. 288–330). See also *AS* (pp. 71–75).

556. S: *anāsravaḥ,* T: *zag pa med pa*. This term has been translated more literally as the

enlightenment and that are included within [a person's] spiritual lineage are the originating causes of those entities that are conducive to enlightenment.

Moreover, those very entities conducive to enlightenment that are generated by their respective seeds are the producing causes that gradually [bring about] the realms of the nirvana in which the support [of the five heaps] remains and [the nirvana] in which the support [of the five heaps] does not remain.

Regarding this [topic], the spiritual lineage of a listener is conducive to [the attainment of] parinirvana by means of the Listeners' Vehicle, the spiritual lineage of a solitary realizer is conducive to [the attainment of] parinirvana by means of the Solitary Realizers' Vehicle, and the Great Vehicle's spiritual lineage is conducive to [the attainment of] parinirvana by means of the Great Vehicle. This [distinction] represents the fixed causes that relate to the process of purification.

The [series of causes] that are conducive to purification [and that range from] requisite causes up to fixed causes are called the "cooperating causes" of [the process of purification].

The condition of lacking a spiritual lineage, the absence of the buddhas, an inopportune birth,[557] associating with evil persons, listening to false teachings, [engaging in] improper attention [of the mind], and wrong practice [all] constitute [forms of] opposing causes. The deficiency or absence of those opposing causes is called the compatible causes.

Regarding this [topic], that which is an opposing cause for [the process of] affliction should be regarded as a cause for [the process of] purification. That which is an opposing cause for [the process of] purification should be regarded as a cause for [the process of] affliction.

Such is the manner in which the ten causes [currently] bring about [a state of] affliction [as well as the manner in which] the same ten [types of causes] bring about [a state of] purification. This is also how they have caused affliction and purification in the past and how they will do so in the

---

quality of being "free of the outflows." See note 196. "Uncontaminated" is used here for the sake of brevity.

557. S: *akṣaṇopapattiḥ*, T: *mi khom par skye ba*. *ŚBh* (Tibetan, f. 2b; Skt. missing): "What is an inopportune birth? It is birth in a border region among thieves and foreigners (S: *mlecchaḥ*, T: *kla klo*), where the fourfold following [i.e., fully ordained monks and nuns and laymen and laywomen], the virtuous, those who have undertaken a righteous way of life, and wise persons will not travel. [To be born in such a place] is called an 'inopportune birth.'"

future. There are no other causes of greater significance than these and none besides these.

Five Kinds of Results [1.8.2.2]

Regarding this [topic], what are results?

Briefly, there are five [kinds of] results: (1) maturation results, (2) corresponding results, (3) separation results, (4) results of human effort, and (5) governed results.

The maturation of nonvirtuous entities occurs in the lower realms.[558] That of contaminated virtuous [entities] does so in a happy migratory state.[559] This [type of result] constitutes a maturation result.

The existence of the conditions of delighting in nonvirtuous entities and of being rich in nonvirtuous entities through having [repeatedly] focused one's mind upon nonvirtuous entities,[560] the existence of the conditions of delighting in virtuous entities and of being rich in virtuous entities through having [repeatedly] focused one's mind upon virtuous entities, as well as the condition in which a subsequent result conforms to a previous deed through being similar to it, represent [the nature of] a corresponding result.

The cessation of [any portion of] the mental afflictions through the eightfold noble path constitutes the separation result. By contrast, the cessation of [any portion of] the mental afflictions by ordinary persons through the mundane path[561] is not one that takes effect permanently; therefore, it does not represent a separation result.

558. See note 143 and the text accompanying note 1520.

559. See note 422 and the text accompanying note 1524.

560. *BBhVy* (f. 121a): "Through having [repeatedly] focused one's mind upon nonvirtuous entities in a previous life, [a person] delights in nonvirtuous entities in this life and [his or her] mind becomes fixed upon nonvirtuous entities. Because of this, [he or she] develops the condition of being rich in nonvirtuous entities. This means that one also engages [in nonvirtuous entities] with the body, etc. That is, [one develops] the condition of possessing many nonvirtuous [deeds]."

561. S: *laukikamārgaḥ,* T: *'jig rten pa'i lam.* The mundane path is a form of insight meditation in which seven forms of attention are cultivated in order to accomplish a temporary cessation of the mental afflictions, which Asaṅga describes as their "suppression" (S: *nigrahaḥ,* T: *nyams smad pa*). *AS* (p. 63): "What is cessation in the conventional sense? It is a cessation that is achieved through suppressing the seeds [of the mental afflictions] by means of the mundane paths." Also, *AS* (p. 68): "What is the mundane [form of the meditation] path? It is the worldly forms of the first, second, third, and fourth meditative absorptions, as well as

When any [person], during his or her lifetime, by means of [a form of] human effort associated with some craft or occupation—whether it be cultivation of the soil, [engaging in] commerce, or [such forms of] service to the king as scribal work or [performing the activities of] counting, record keeping,[562] calculating, or signing[563]—causes such results as grain or some other form of profit to be produced, this [result] is called "a result of human effort."

Eye consciousness is a result that is governed by the eye faculty. Likewise, [this description also applies to the other forms of consciousness,] up to: Mind consciousness [is a result that is governed by] the mind faculty. In addition, [the fact that an individual's] vital airs do not become separated [from his or her body is a result that is governed by] the faculty that is [an individual's] life force. Similarly, it should be understood that whatever results come into being through the governing influence of any of the twenty-two faculties,[564]

---

the sphere of unlimited space (S: *ākāśānantyāyatanam,* T: *nam mkha' mtha' yas skye mched*), the sphere of unlimited consciousness (S: *vijñānānantyāyatanam,* T: *rnam shes mtha' yas skye mched*), the sphere of nothingness (S: *ākiṃcanyāyatanam,* T: *ci yang med pa'i skye mched*), and the sphere in which there is neither conception nor absence of conception (S: *naiva saṃjñā nāsaṃjñāyatanam,* T: *'du shes med 'du shes med min skye mched*). Moreover, these meditative absorptions and formless states [of composure] should be understood in terms of their affliction, purification, differentiation, and perfection." A detailed account of this form of practice can be found in *ŚBh,* pp. 436–470.

562. See note 134.

563. See note 135.

564. Abhidharma literature identifies twenty-two faculties: besides the seven mentioned here, the remaining fifteen are (1) the male sex faculty (S: *puruṣendriyam,* T: *pho'i dbang po*); (2) the female sex faculty (S: *strīndriyam,* T: *mo'i dbang po*); the five faculties that are feelings—(3) the faculty of pleasure (S: *sukhendriyam,* T: *bde ba'i dbang po*), (4) the faculty of suffering (S: *duḥkhendriyam,* T: *sdug bsngal gyi dbang po*), (5) the faculty of mental ease (S: *saumanasyendriyam,* T: *yid bde ba'i dbang po*), (6) the faculty of mental discomfort (S: *daurmanasyendriyam,* T: *yid mi bde ba'i dbang po*), and (7) the faculty of equanimity (S: *upekṣendriyam,* T: *btang snyoms kyi dbang po*); the five spiritual faculties—(8) the faculty of faith (S: *śraddhendriyam,* T: *dad pa'i dbang po*), (9) the faculty of effort (S: *vīryendriyam,* T: *brtson 'grus kyi dbang po*), (10) the faculty of recollection (S: *smṛtīndriyam,* T: *dran pa'i dbang po*), (11) the faculty of concentration (S: *samādhīndriyam,* T: *ting nge 'dzin gyi dbang po*), and (12) the faculty of wisdom (S: *prajñendriyam,* T: *shes rab kyi dbang po*); and the three pure faculties—(13) the faculty in which one reflects, 'I shall gain full knowledge of what is not yet fully known' (S: *anājñātamājñāsyāmīndriyam,* T: *kun shes par byed pa'i dbang po*), (14) the faculty of full knowledge (S: *ājñendriyam,* T: *kun shes pa'i dbang po*), and (15) the faculty of possessing full knowledge (S: *ājñātavīndriyam,* T: *kun shes pa dang ldan pa'i dbang po*).

as [described] in the *Collection on [Canonical] Topics*,[565] constitute [examples of] governed results.

Having realized in this manner the form of the Buddha's speech that correctly sets forth causes and results, and as a consequence of continually cultivating [the aspect of] his or her [spiritual] lineage that relates to the power of knowledge regarding proper conditions and improper conditions,[566] a bodhisattva gradually causes [the spiritual lineage of that power] to be refined and further developed.[567]

[A deed that] was not done by one individual or that was done by another will not yield any ripening for that individual. Moreover, those deeds that [an individual] did perform will not perish even after a hundred kalpas with regard to [their ability to] yield a result. Having realized in this manner, as set forth in the Buddha's speech, that what has not been done will not yield any fruition and what has been done will not perish, a bodhisattva gradually causes the [aspect of his or her] spiritual lineage [that relates to] the power of knowledge regarding [the fact that] one's deeds are one's own[568] to be refined and further developed.

565. S: *Vastusaṃgrahaṇī,* T: *gZhi bsdu ba.* This work describes how the subject matter addressed in Asaṅga's Abhidharma works relates to the three divisions of the Buddhist canon—that is, the Sutra, Vinaya, and Abhidharma. The twenty-two faculties are described in folios 323b–324a.

566. S: *sthānāsthānajñānabalam,* T: *gnas dang gnas ma yin pa mkhyen pa'i stobs.* This is the first of a buddha's ten powers (S: *daśabalāni,* T: *stobs bcu*) and it has a connection with the first of the two forms of a buddha's speech (see the opening portion of the section in this chapter entitled "Seeking the Dharma" [I.8.2]). Because a buddha possesses complete understanding of all the intricate workings of karma, he knows what is a "proper condition" (S: *sthānam,* T: *gnas*) in the sense of what can and does occur in the world, and what is an "improper condition" (S: *asthānam,* T: *gnas ma yin pa*) in the sense of what cannot and does not occur in the world. An example of what is "proper" is that virtuous deeds only bring favorable results and never unfavorable ones, and that nonvirtuous deeds only bring unfavorable results and never favorable ones, etc.

567. This statement and the next paragraph clarify the meaning of the expression "lineages of the powers" (S: *balagotram,* T: *stobs kyi rigs*), which forms the title of this chapter. It is that the efforts of a novice bodhisattva to pursue the subjects described in the seven topics that make up this chapter—ranging from an abundance of devotion to the deeds of body, speech, and mind that are governed by skillful means—constitute the lineages or seeds whose cultivation and development ultimately result in the attainment of a buddha's ten powers.

568. S: *karmasvakatājñānabalam,* T: *las bdag gir bya ba shes pa'i stobs.* This is the expression that Asaṅga uses to refer to the second of a buddha's ten powers (see Book III, chapter 6, in the section entitled "The Power of Knowledge regarding [the Fact That] One's Deeds Are

The Correct Manner of Seeking Learning [1.8.2.3]

Regarding this [topic], how does a bodhisattva seek learning?[569]

A bodhisattva seeks the Dharma after he or she has engendered intense respect toward eloquent speech[570] and excellent sayings. Briefly, this is the kind of respect that should be developed toward eloquent speech: It is [a level of respect] in which this bodhisattva would be willing to enter a region consisting of blazing hot iron with utmost delight and respect in order to hear even a single eloquent statement, let alone a great many forms of eloquent speech, if he or she could find no other way of hearing eloquent speech.

Between the fondness and respect that a bodhisattva feels toward the improvement of his or her own physical being,[571] not to mention the entire collection of other objects [that are its means of support], such as food and drink, and the fondness and respect he or she feels toward hearing eloquent speech, having placed the former fondness and respect next to the latter fondness and respect, [the fondness and respect that is felt toward the former] does not reach a hundredth part or even a thousandth part [of that which is felt toward the latter], nor does it reach [any level of] calculation, portioning, reckoning, or factoring.

[A bodhisattva] who has generated such [a sense of] respect toward eloquent speech does not [ever] become weary while listening to eloquent speech, and he or she is insatiable [in the desire to continue hearing it]. He or she is filled with faith and develops an abundance of clarity [of mind].[572] He or she becomes one whose mental continuum possesses the moisture of tender feelings and one who is sincere in outlook. He or she approaches a

One's Own" [III.6.2.2] and accompanying note 1484). Thus, this sentence makes a causal link between learning the second form of a buddha's speech and attaining the second of a buddha's ten powers. The lineages of the remaining eight powers are explicitly referenced at the end of the discussion on the topic of instruction. See below.

569. Literally, "hearing," or "listening to" Dharma teachings. See note 470.

570. S: *subhāṣitam,* T: *legs par gsungs pa*. *BBhVy* (f. 122b): "It is called 'eloquent speech' because it accords with those antidotes [that promote the process of] purification."

571. S: *ātmabhāvaḥ,* T: *lus kyi khog pa*. Here this Sanskrit term does refer specifically to the physical body. See also notes 237 and 277.

572. S: *prasādaḥ,* T: *dang ba*. Clarity of mind represents a particular type of faith (see note 220). This term is also associated with a joyful state of mind. *BBhVy* (f. 124a): "In that way [i.e., through having become filled with faith], one 'develops an abundance of clarity [of mind],' which is to say one attains gladness and great joy."

Dharma teacher [motivated] by a desire for virtuous qualities and a desire for the Dharma, not with the intention of trying to find fault [with the teacher]; with respect, not with the stiffness of pride; seeking [to learn] what is virtuous, not with the aim of promoting him- or herself; and [that bodhisattva] does so thinking, "I shall apply myself and others to roots of virtue," not motivated by [a desire for] gain or honor. Having approached [a Dharma teacher] in this manner, he or she remains unafflicted and undistracted while listening to Dharma.

How does [a bodhisattva] remain unafflicted while listening to Dharma?

He or she does so by becoming free of the affliction of arrogance, free of the affliction of contempt, and free of the affliction of diffidence.[573]

Regarding this [topic], there are six aspects by means of which [a bodhisattva] becomes free of the affliction of arrogance; four aspects by means of which he or she becomes free of the affliction of contempt; and one aspect by means of which he or she becomes free of the affliction of diffidence.

[A bodhisattva] listens [to Dharma] at an appropriate time,[574] acting respectfully, being attentive,[575] remaining free of discontent, aiming to put into practice [what is being heard], and without intending to find fault. By means of these six aspects, one becomes free of the affliction of arrogance.

Having generated respect toward the Dharma and generated respect toward the Dharma teacher, [a bodhisattva] avoids [developing any feeling of] disdain for the Dharma and avoids [developing any feeling of] disdain for a person who is a Dharma teacher. By means of these four aspects, one remains free of the affliction of contempt while listening [to Dharma].

[A bodhisattva] should listen without feeling disdain toward him- or herself. By means of this single aspect, one remains free of the affliction of diffidence while listening [to Dharma]. This is the manner in which a bodhisattva remains unafflicted while listening to Dharma.

573. S: *layaḥ,* T: *zhum pa* (also *bying ba*). Here the sense of this term is that of a lack of confidence in one's own ability. *BBhVy* (f. 125a): "The affliction of diffidence is the belief that one lacks the ability [to accomplish some task or goal]." In the context of meditation, *layaḥ* refers to a mental state characterized by dullness and lack of energy that is brought on by torpor (S: *styānam,* T: *rmugs pa*) and drowsiness (S: *middham,* T: *gnyid*).

574. S: *kālena,* T: *dus su. BBhVy* (f. 124b): "'At an appropriate time' means [a time] that complies with [the wishes of] the Dharma teacher."

575. S: *śuśruṣamāṇaḥ,* T: *sri zhu byed pa.* Literally, "being one who maintains the desire for learning."

Regarding this [topic], how does a bodhisattva remain undistracted while listening to Dharma?

[One remains undistracted] by means of five aspects. One should listen to Dharma with a mind that is fully aware, with a one-pointed mind, with the ears [properly] directed, with the mind [properly] inclined, and having fully focused one's entire mind. This is the manner in which a bodhisattva should seek learning.

The Proper Motives for Seeking Learning [1.8.2.4]

What are a bodhisattva's motives for seeking learning?

A bodhisattva seeks [to learn] the Buddha's speech in order to put it into practice in a manner that accords correctly with the Dharma and in order to [be able to] fully reveal it to others in an extensive manner.

A bodhisattva seeks [to learn] the science of logic in order to [gain] an accurate and complete knowledge of what is badly taught and badly described in that body of teachings, in order to refute the objections that are raised by others, as well as to instill faith toward this [Buddhist] teaching in those who lack it and to further increase the faith of those who have engendered it.

A bodhisattva seeks [to learn] the science of grammar in order to cause those who are devoted to well-composed speech to develop a firm sense of trust toward him or her by virtue of the presentation of well-derived words and syllables[576] and so that he or she might engage in the orderly discourse[577] that [provides] a variety of linguistic interpretations for a single meaning.

A bodhisattva seeks [to learn] the body of teachings on medicine in order to cure the many varieties of illness [that are contracted] by sentient beings and in order to promote the welfare of the greater populace.

576. S: *padavyañjanam,* T: *tshig dang yi ge.* Although the two terms in this compound are translated literally as "words and syllables," I believe that in this construction the term *pada* (T: *tshig*) can be taken to mean a statement that is a complete and meaningful assertion. *AKB* (p. 80) gives two explanations of this sense of the term *padam.* It is (1) "a statement (S: *vākyam,* T: *ngag*) of whatever length [that allows] a meaning to be fully expressed"; and (2) it is "a statement [that enables] a logical connection with [such] properties [as those of] action, quality, and time to be understood." I also believe that the term *vyañjanaḥ* (T: *yi ge*) here can be taken to mean "literal form of expression" as in the statement: "One should rely upon the meaning, not the literal form of expression" (see note 1074).

577. See note 535 above.

A bodhisattva seeks [to learn] the categories of worldly crafts and occupations in order to [be able to] amass wealth so that he or she can benefit sentient beings with little difficulty, in order to generate in sentient beings [an attitude of] high regard [toward him- or herself],[578] and in order to benefit [sentient beings] and attract[579] them [to the Dharma] by providing them with knowledge of a craft.

A bodhisattva seeks all five of these branches of learning in order to perfect the great wisdom accumulation[580] [that leads to the attainment of] unsurpassed true and complete enlightenment. This is because [a bodhisattva] who fails to train in all [of the sciences] will not attain in an orderly manner the knowledge of an omniscient being that is free of [all] obstructions. This completes the presentation of what a bodhisattva seeks, as well as the manner in which it is to be sought and the motives for seeking it.

Teaching the Dharma [1.8.3]

Regarding this [topic], what does a bodhisattva teach others, how does he or she teach [them], and what are his or her motives for teaching [them]?

Regarding this [topic], [a bodhisattva] teaches the very same [subjects] that he or she seeks [to learn]. His or her motives for teaching are also the same as the ones he or she has for seeking [to learn those subjects].

[A bodhisattva] teaches in two ways. He or she explains [using] suitable speech and speech that is pure.

Regarding this [topic], how does [a bodhisattva] explain [using] suitable speech?

He or she teaches those who are seated in a manner that conforms to the [proper] modes of physical behavior,[581] not [those who are seated] in an inappropriate manner. This should be understood to mean that one should

578. *BBhVy* (f. 126a): "Through [gaining knowledge] in the categories of crafts and occupations, [a bodhisattva] will acquire great renown."

579. S: *saṃgrahaḥ,* T: *bsdu ba*. This is a reference to the "four principles of attracting a following" (see Book I, chapter 15). The act of teaching others a worldly craft or occupation would presumably represent both a form of generosity and a form of agreeable speech.

580. S: *jñānasaṃbhāraḥ,* T: *ye shes kyi tshogs*. Wisdom and merit are the two accumulations. See Book I, chapter 3, the section entitled "Merit and Wisdom" [I.3.5.2, I.3.6.2] for a general discussion of these two topics.

581. S: *anurūpeneryāpathena,* T: *spyod lam gyi tshul dang mthun pa'i*. Traditionally, there are four modes of physical behavior: standing, sitting, walking, and reclining. Here the

not [teach] a person seated on a higher seat who is not ill, a person whose head is covered [and who is not ill], a person who is walking in front [of you and who is not ill], etc., as [explained] at length in the sutras.[582]

Why is that?

It is because the Dharma is an object that the buddhas and bodhisattvas venerate. [It is also] because when [it is observed that] the Dharma is being honored, others will develop a high degree of respect for the Dharma. Also, when the Dharma is being heard, others will generate reverence [for it] and they will not develop [an attitude of] disrespect.

[A bodhisattva] also teaches everything to everyone continuously, without being stingy with the Dharma and without exhibiting a preceptor's tightfistedness toward Dharma teachings. He or she teaches words and syllables in a systematic manner. With the systematic teaching of words and syllables, he or she differentiates meanings in a systematic manner. He or she teaches both meaningful Dharma [teachings] and their import but not [subjects] that are empty of meaning.

[A bodhisattva] explains [instruction] to those who are suitable to receive explanations, prompts those who are suitable to be prompted to take up practices [that are appropriate for them], generates enthusiasm in those who are suitable to be encouraged, and pleases those for whom it is suitable to make them feel pleased. He or she teaches [using] speech that is endowed with [the qualities of] direct perception, inference, and trustworthy scripture, not [speech] that is unrelated to valid cognition.[583] [He or she teaches using speech] that promotes reaching the happy migratory states, is free of confusion, and easy to comprehend, not [speech] that is impenetrable. [He or she] also [teaches using speech] that has a connection with the four noble truths. In all assemblies, he or she teaches in whatever manner is appropriate and [using] whatever speech is appropriate to that [particular assembly]. In these fifteen ways, the speech that bodhisattvas use when teaching should be understood as suitable to all the important aims of sentient beings.

---

reference is to the proper physical conduct that is to be observed when spiritual instruction is given.

582. The Mūlasarvāstivāda version of the *Prātimokṣa Sutra* contains twenty-six rules relating to conduct that should be observed when Dharma is being taught. See *Buddhist Monastic Discipline,* p. 105.

583. S: *pramāṇam,* T: *tshad ma*. The first clause identifies three forms of correct cognition: (1) direct perception (S: *pratyakṣam,* T: *mngon sum*); (2) inference (S: *anumānam,* T: *rjes su dpag pa*); and (3) trustworthy scripture (S: *āptāgamaḥ,* T: *yid ches pa'i lung*).

In addition, with regard to sentient beings who commit harm, a bodhisattva establishes [his or her] mind in a state of loving-kindness before speaking [to them]. With regard to sentient beings who engage in misconduct, he or she establishes a beneficial state of mind before speaking [to them]. With regard to beings who have experienced happiness or suffering and who [for that reason] are [in the former case] behaving heedlessly or [in the latter case] feeling dejected, [a bodhisattva] establishes a compassionate state of mind that wishes to benefit and bring happiness [to them] before speaking [to them]. He or she does not, under the influence of the perturbation of jealousy, extol him- or herself; nor does [a bodhisattva] discredit others. With a mind that is free from corporeal desire[584] and avoiding any yearning for gain, honor, or fame, he or she teaches Dharma to others. In these five ways, a bodhisattva explains [using] speech that is pure.

In brief, these [aspects of teaching] can be represented as having twenty forms: [A bodhisattva should teach] (1) at an appropriate time, (2) in a manner that treats [the Dharma] with respect, (3) following a [proper] order, (4) in a [logically] connected manner, (5) in a manner that combines [words and meanings well], (6) in a manner that causes gladness, (7) in a manner that causes eagerness, (8) in a manner that causes satisfaction, (9) in a manner that causes exertion, and (10) in a manner that avoids causing [others] to become discouraged. [He or she should teach a discourse that is] (11) correct,[585] (12) fitting,[586] (13) not jumbled, (14) conforms to the Dharma, and

584. S: *nirāmiṣacittaḥ,* T: *zang zing med pa'i sems.* The adjective "free from corporeal desire" (S: *nirāmiṣa,* T: *zang zing med pa*) is a term that is contrasted with the adjective "associated with corporeal desire" (S: *sāmiṣa,* T: *zang zing dang bcas pa*). In the present context, the expression "corporeal desire" could be taken to mean the desire for some form of material reward. However, *PSV* (p. 270) provides a more technical interpretation: "Corporeal desire (S: *āmiṣam,* T: *zang zing*) is craving for one's individual existence (S: *ātmabhāvatṛṣṇā,* T: *lus la sred pa*). 'Individual existence' refers to the inner grasping heaps [i.e., those included within one's own continuum]. Craving [for one's individual existence] engages [the inner heaps] in a manner that resembles the way in which [a parent] embraces a cherished only child and does not wish to be separated from it. This [form of craving] represents corporeal desire. The expression 'associated with corporeal desire' means to be accompanied by that attitude. The expression 'free from corporeal desire' means not to be accompanied by that craving or to be conducive to a state of separation from it."

585. S: *yuktā,* T: *rigs pa. MSAVy* (p. 78): "[Speech is] correct in that it is not at variance with knowledge."

586. S: *sahitā,* T: *'tsham ba,* also *'brel ba. MSAVy* (p. 78): [Speech is] fitting in that it teaches in a manner that is appropriate to those who are to be spiritually tamed."

(15) is appropriate for the [particular] assembly. [He or she should teach] (16) with an amicable mind, (17) a mind [that seeks to] benefit, (18) a compassionate mind, (19) without consideration for gain, honor, or fame, and (20) without extolling oneself or discrediting others. This is the manner in which a bodhisattva should teach the Dharma to others.[587]

The Form of Practice That Accords with the Dharma [1.8.4]

With regard to this [topic], what is a bodhisattva's form of practice that accords with the Dharma?[588]

In brief, it should be understood as having five aspects: conformity in (1) body, (2) speech, and (3) mind with those very Dharma teachings that have been sought and taken up; (4) correct reflection; and (5) meditation.

Conformity in Body, Speech, and Mind with the Buddha's Admonitions [1.8.4.1]

Regarding those things that the Blessed One forbade being done by body, speech, and mind and those that he approved of being done by body, speech, and mind, the complete avoidance of those deeds of body, speech, and mind in just the manner [that they were forbidden], and the cultivation and accomplishment of those [deeds in just the manner that they were authorized] is called "the practice that accords with the Dharma through conformity in body, speech, and mind."

Correct Reflection [1.8.4.2]

Regarding this [topic], what is correct reflection by a bodhisattva?

A bodhisattva here who has gone alone to an isolated place, who is desirous of reflecting, desirous of pondering, and desirous of examining those Dharma teachings that he or she has heard, initially rejects those subjects that are unsuitable to think about, and then sets about considering those [that are proper to consider]. He or she reflects upon them continuously,

587. This list also appears in *ŚBh* (p. 134). *BBhVy* (f. 128a) suggests that the list of twenty aspects comes from a canonical source.

588. S: *dharmānudharmapratipattiḥ,* T: *chos kyi rjes su mthun pa'i chos sgrub pa.*

with a method of practice that is both constant and attentive, and without becoming lax. Some of the time, a bodhisattva who is engaged in reflection uses the applications[589] to examine [a topic] and penetrate[590] [its meaning]. Some of the time, he or she generates devotion [toward a topic]. [A bodhisattva] relies upon the meaning [of a teaching] as he or she reflects, and does not rely upon the letter.[591] He or she realizes "black" expressions[592] and "great" expressions as they truly are.[593] He or she also enters upon [the practice of] reflection with the initial means of engagement. Having become engaged [in the practice], he or she attains what is of [genuine] value by repeatedly applying [proper] attention.[594]

Rejecting what is unsuitable to think about, a bodhisattva does not develop confusion or distraction. Continuously engaged [with a form of application that is] both constant and attentive, one reflects in a way that comprehends meanings that were not previously understood and gains [a deeper realization] of those that were understood. One does not allow [the understanding of] those meanings that were gained to be lost nor allow [oneself] to become inattentive [with regard to them]. On the one hand, by using the applications at times to examine, investigate, and deliberate, [a bodhisattva] does not have to rely upon others.[595] On the other hand, regarding those subjects that are being examined carefully using the applications, while generating devotion at times toward those profound subjects

589. See notes 255 and 1199 for a description of the four applications.

590. S: *anupraviśati,* T: *rjes su 'jug pa. BBhVy* (f. 128a): "To 'penetrate' [a topic] means to ascertain [its significance] (S: **niścinoti,* T: *nges pa rnyed pa*)."

591. This is a reference to one of the four reliances. See chapter 17, the section entitled "The Four Reliances" [I.17.6].

592. S: *kālāpadeśaḥ,* T: *nag po bstan pa. BBhVy* (f. 128a): "A 'black expression' is one that is not based upon sutras and does not appear in the Vinaya [texts]; [thus,] it is in conflict with the true nature of things. The opposite of that [is an expression that] is on the side of that which is pure (S: *śuklapakṣaḥ,* T: *dkar po'i phyogs*); it is called a 'great expression' (S: *mahāpadeśaḥ,* T: *chen po bstan pa*)."

593. This sentence is also a reference to another of the four reliances—specifically, the one typically described with this formula: "One should rely upon the Dharma, not the person."

594. This paragraph contains the eight aspects of reflection that are referenced at the end of the next paragraph. They correlate closely with nine aspects that are described as defining the essential nature of reflection in the opening portion of the eleventh section of *YBh* (Tg. vol. 127, ff. 200b–201a).

595. S: *na parapratyayo bhavati,* T: *gzhan gyi dring mi 'jog par 'gyur ba.* That is, he or she becomes self-reliant.

that one's mind fails to penetrate, [one] thinks to oneself, "These topics are within a tathāgata's range of understanding; they are not within my mind's range of understanding." In so doing, [a bodhisattva] avoids repudiating those topics and, thus, keeps him- or herself undamaged, uninjured, and free of any objectionable act.[596] Relying upon the meaning and not the letter [of the teachings], a bodhisattva investigates all the enigmatic sayings[597] of the buddhas, the blessed ones. Because he or she possesses skill with regard to "black" expressions and "great" expressions, no one can in any way cause a bodhisattva to waver from or become unsteady about meanings that pertain to ultimate reality. Investigating that which is to be considered first, the bodhisattva obtains a forbearance that had not previously been obtained. Moreover, as he or she attains that forbearance and [also attains] a state of [genuine] value that has been well obtained, a bodhisattva undertakes to engage in meditation. By means of these eight aspects that relate to reflection, a bodhisattva becomes engaged in the form of practice that accords with Dharma that is contained within [the practice of] reflection.

Meditation [1.8.4.3]

What is meditation?

Briefly, it should be understood as being fourfold in nature: (1) quiescence, (2) insight, (3) cultivation of quiescence and insight, and (4) delighting in quiescence and insight.

Regarding this [topic], what is quiescence?[598]

Through having fulfilled the [practice of] reflection with its eight aspects, a bodhisattva then binds [his or her] mind to an object that is beyond expression—one that is a bare substance[599] and a bare import[600]—and

596. S: *anavadyam,* T: *kha na ma tho ba med pa*. *BBhVy* (f. 129a) identifies the misdeed that is being avoided here as that of repudiating the Dharma (S: **dharmapratikṣepakarma,* T: *chos spong gi las*). See also the passage from the *Sarvadharmavaipulyasaṃgrahasūtram* (T: *rNam par 'thag pa thams cad bdus pa'i mdo*) quoted in Śāntideva's *Compendium of Training* (*Śikṣāsamuccayaḥ,* ch. 4, pp. 56–57).

597. See note 340.

598. S: *śamathaḥ,* T: *zhi gnas*.

599. S: *vastumātram,* T: *dngos po tsam*. See notes 251, 269, and 273 for descriptions of how this term is to be understood.

600. S: *arthamātram,* T: *don tsam*. See note 274 for a similar usage of this term. *BBhVy* (f. 129b): "The term 'import' [here] refers to the object of correct knowledge that occurs dur-

then, maintaining zealous devotion toward all [meditation] objects through bringing to mind conceptions[601] that are free of all elaboration and mental unsteadiness, he or she causes the mind to be placed, [continually placed], placed anew, etc., up to causes [the mind] to attain one-pointedness, and causes [the mind] to attain equipoise in relation to the inner signs [that promote] one-pointed concentration.[602] This is what is called [the practice of] quiescence.

What is insight?[603]

[Endowed] with that very form of attention that is pervaded by quiescence, [insight is the series of practices ranging from] the cultivation of [those forms of] attention [that direct the mind to] the signs of those [Dharma topics] that were [previously] reflected upon, the [further] investigation [of them], the intensive investigation [of them], the intensive investigation of

---

ing a pure stage." "Pure stage" (S: **pariśuddhāvasthā,* T: *yongs su dag pa'i gnas skabs*) refers to that level of the path that exists following the attainment of the transcendent path of an ārya.

601. S: *saṃjñā,* T: *'du shes.* The twelfth division of *YBh,* entitled "The Stage That Derives from Meditation" (S: *Bhāvanāmayabhūmiḥ,* T: *bsGom pa las byung ba'i sa,* ff. 265b–268b) makes reference to ten conceptions that are contemplated in order to overcome a variety of obstacles. Among the ten, the conception of unattractiveness (S: *aśubhasaṃjñā,* T: *mi sdug pa'i 'du shes*), the conception of suffering in relation to that which is impermanent (S: *anitye duḥkhasaṃjñā,* T: *mi rtag pa la sdug bsngal gyi 'du shes*), and the conception of light (S: *ālokasaṃjñā,* T: *snang ba'i 'du shes*) are the three that are discussed in greatest detail. The conception of light in particular is identified as the antidote to be applied when the mind of a practitioner who is cultivating quiescence and insight in an isolated place is overcome by the mental darkness that promotes torpor and drowsiness. This conception is further described in the sixth division of the *YBh* (Skt. edition, vol. 1, pp. 139–140), entitled "The Stage of [the States of] Mental Composure" (S: *Samāhitā bhūmiḥ,* T: *mNyam par bzhag pa'i sa*).

602. The term "sign [that promotes] one-pointed concentration" (S: *samādhinimittam,* T: *ting nge 'dzin gyi mtshan ma*) is one of a series of synonyms for the meditation objects that are taken up when cultivating quiescence and insight (see *ŚBh,* p. 195). The last clause of this sentence makes reference to the nine states of mental stability (S: *cittasthitiḥ,* T: *sems gnas pa*) that lead to the attainment of quiescence: (1) placement (S: *sthāpanā,* T: *'jog pa*); (2) continued placement (S: *saṃsthāpanā,* T: *rgyun du 'jog pa*); (3) renewed placement (S: *avasthāpanā,* T: *glan te 'jog pa*); (4) close placement (S: *upasthāpanā,* T: *nye bar 'jog pa*); (5) subduing (S: *damanam,* T: *dul bar byed pa*); (6) pacification (S: *śamanam,* T: *zhi bar byed pa*); (7) heightened pacification (S: *vyupaśamanam,* T: *rnam par zhi bar byed pa*); (8) one-pointedness (S: *ekotīkaraṇam,* T: *rtse gcig tu byed pa*); and (9) equipoise (S: *samādhānam,* T: *mnyam par 'jog pa*).

603. S: *vipaśyanā,* T: *lhag mthong.*

Dharma [teachings], etc., up to [the development of] knowledge [regarding these Dharma topics] and the exercise of wisdom [regarding them]. This is what is called [the practice of] insight.

What is the cultivation of quiescence and insight?

It is a [form of] practice that occurs continuously and a [form of] practice that is attentive in relation to [the development of] quiescence and insight.

What is delighting[604] in quiescence and insight?

It is the stability of the mind in relation to the signs [that are the basis for practicing] quiescence and insight, the condition in which [the mind] moves spontaneously [toward those signs] without [the need for any] application [of effort], [the ability to] maintain control [over the mind in relation to those signs], and [the ability to] keep [the mind] from moving away [from those signs]. This is what is called "delighting in quiescence and insight."

Regarding this [topic], however strongly a bodhisattva cultivates quiescence and insight, [the state of] delighting in quiescence and insight will, to a corresponding degree, be accomplished. However much [a bodhisattva's state of] delighting in quiescence and insight is accomplished, [his or her] quiescence and insight will, to a corresponding degree, become pure.[605] As a result, however much [a bodhisattva's] quiescence becomes pure, [his or her] physical agility and mental agility will reach a state of being abundant, strong, and developed. And however much [a bodhisattva's] insight becomes pure, [his or her] knowledge-vision will reach a state of being abundant, strong, and developed. This is the extent of what is to be accomplished by [the practice of] meditation—that is to say, the indisposition that is present in a [person's] being[606] is what is to be removed and [a bodhisattva's] knowledge-vision in relation to all knowable things is what is to be made pure. All of these actions of meditation are brought about by the four aspects of a bodhisattva's meditation [practice].

604. S: *abhiratiḥ,* T: *mngon par dga' ba.* While the principal meaning of the root from which this noun is derived is "to delight in" something, additional senses are those of being "at rest," "satisfied," and "engaged." Thus, in the present context, this term also suggests the satisfaction and ease that comes with having successfully achieved proficiency in the practice of quiescence and insight.

605. S: *pariśuddhyati,* T: *yong su dag par 'gyur. BBhVy* (f. 129b): "'Will become pure' refers to the point at which the aim [of a practitioner's meditation practice] has been achieved (S: **kāryaniṣpādite,* T: *dgos pa yongs su grub pa nyid na'o*)."

606. S: *āśrayaḥ,* T: *rten.* Literally, a "seat" or "resting place," it is also used to mean a person in the sense of that individual in whom qualities reside or are present. See also note 1460.

INSTRUCTION [1.8.5]

What is instruction?[607]

Briefly, it should be understood as being eightfold in nature. Whether the situation is one in which a bodhisattva is desirous of giving instruction to others, either through relying upon one-pointed concentration or as a consequence of association [with those individuals], or alternatively it is a situation in which another bodhisattva or a tathāgata gives instruction to him or her, at the very outset, that [teacher who intends to give the instruction] examines and realizes [the nature of] the mind [of the person who is to be instructed]. Having examined [that person's] mind, [the teacher] then examines and realizes [the nature of the student's] faculties. Having examined [that person's] faculties, [the teacher] then examines and realizes [the nature of the student's] attitude. Having examined [that person's] attitudes, [the teacher] examines and realizes [the nature of the student's] latent propensities.[608] Having examined [that person's] latent propensities, [the teacher] causes [him or her] to undertake [any of] a variety of means of practice, in whatever manner is suitable and in whatever manner is appropriate [to that person]. Having caused [that person] to undertake [any of] those means of practice that are suitable and appropriate [to him or her]—whether it be through [the practice of] unattractiveness, loving-kindness, dependent origination, the diversity of the elements, or recalling the inhalation

607. S: *avavādaḥ,* T: *gdams ngag. BBhVy* (ff. 130b–131a) gives two interpretations of the term: "Instruction is the enjoyment of spoken discourse because it generates correct understanding (S: **samyag avabodhatvād vādāsvāda ity avavādaḥ;* T: *yang dag par rtogs pa'i phyir smra ba'i tshig gi ro myong ba ni gdams ngag ces bya'o*)." Also: "Instruction is the speaking of suitable words [to someone] after having understood the [nature of his or her] mind (S: **cittam avagamyānukūlavādanam ity avavādaḥ;* T: *sems shes nas mthun pa'i tshig smra ba ni gdams ngag*)."

608. S: *anuśayaḥ,* T: *bag la nyal.* Asaṅga (*AS,* p. 44) describes this term as one of a series of synonyms for the mental afflictions. However, more technically it refers to the dormant or latent state of the mental afflictions as opposed to their overt state. *AS* (p. 46) defines each of seven types of *anuśayaḥ* as the state of indisposition (S: *dauṣṭhulyam,* T: *gnas ngan len*) that relates to a particular kind of mental affliction (see below, note 885). However, in this context the intended sense seems to be that of an individual's latent propensities that are governed by his or her "constituent element." *BBhVy* (f. 131a): "[Examining a person's] 'latent tendencies' means examining [him or her] according to the distinctions that are found in the variety of constituent elements (S: *dhātuḥ,* T: *khams*) [among beings], etc." See also the description of "constituent element" that occurs in Book III, chapter 6, the section entitled "The Power of Knowledge regarding Diverse Constituent Elements" [III.6.2.6].

and exhalation [of the breath]—[the bodhisattva] then teaches [that person] the Middle Way as the antidote to wrongly grasping at the eternalistic extreme. [The bodhisattva also] teaches [that person] the Middle Way as the antidote to wrongly grasping at the nihilistic extreme. [The teacher] causes [that person] to abandon the exaggerated pride [in which he or she mistakenly thinks] that [he or she] has accomplished something that has not been accomplished. [The teacher] causes [that person] to abandon the exaggerated pride [in which he or she mistakenly thinks] that [he or she] has attained [some result] that has not been attained, reached, or realized.

This eightfold form of instruction should be understood as being encompassed more briefly within three categories.

What are the three categories?

They are (1) binding [a person's mind] to a correct mental object, in order to initially bring stability to a mind that has not been stabilized; (2) teaching a path of correct means to a [person whose] mind has been stabilized, in order to cause [him or her] to attain [his or her] own aim; and (3) causing a person who has not completed his or her purpose to give up an intermediate position.[609]

Regarding this [topic], it should be understood that the act of binding [a person's mind] to a correct mental object in order to stabilize it is accomplished by means of the knowledge of [that person's] mind, faculties, attitude, and latent propensities, and by causing [him or her] to undertake a means of practice in whatever way is appropriate.

Regarding this [topic], it should be understood that teaching a path of correct means to a [person whose] mind has been stabilized, in order to cause [that person] to attain [his or her] personal aim, [is accomplished] by [teaching] the Middle Way as an antidote to wrongly grasping at the eternalistic and nihilistic extremes.

Regarding this [topic], it should be understood that causing a person who has not completed his or her purpose to give up an intermediate position [is accomplished] by causing [him or her] to abandon the exaggerated pride [in which he or she mistakenly thinks that he or she has accomplished] something that has not been accomplished, etc., up to causing [him or her] to

609. S: *antarasthānaḥ,* T: *bar ma do'i gnas.* The term is meant to refer to an individual who has not reached the final understanding of right view or the final goal of the path but mistakenly believes that he or she has and therefore no longer continues to seek a true understanding or to strive toward the genuine ultimate goal.

abandon the exaggerated pride [in which he or she mistakenly thinks] that [he or she] has realized something that has not been realized. This is how it should be understood that the eightfold form of instruction is encompassed within these three categories.

A bodhisattva who in this very manner either receives instruction from another person or provides it to others gradually causes the spiritual lineages of eight powers to be refined and further developed, [namely,] (1) that of the power of knowledge regarding the meditative absorptions, the liberations, and entering states of one-pointed concentration; (2) that of the power of knowledge regarding superior and inferior faculties; (3) that of the power of knowledge regarding diverse forms of devotion; (4) that of the power of knowledge regarding diverse constituent elements; (5) that of the power of knowledge regarding the paths that lead everywhere; (6) that of the power of knowledge regarding the recollection of former existences; (7) that of the power of knowledge regarding death and rebirth; and (8) that of the power of knowledge regarding termination of the outflows.

Counsel [1.8.6]

Regarding this [topic], what is counsel?[610]

It should be understood as being fivefold in its nature: (1) forbidding conduct that engages in what is objectionable; (2) approving of conduct that engages in what is free of objection; (3) admonishing[611] a person who has engaged in erroneous conduct that relates to actions that are forbidden and approved; (4) prompting those who continually develop disregard [for proper conduct] and behave erroneously to observe recollection, by censuring them with an attitude that is not impure and that is unaltered[612] and

610. S: *anuśāsanam,* T: *rjes su bstan pa. BBhVy* (f. 132a): "Counsel is a [form of] speech that teaches someone to avoid [improper] actions that are forbidden and to carry out [proper] actions that are recommended, after having realized [the nature of] the mind, [disposition,] etc., [of the person to whom it is addressed]."

611. S: *codanā,* T: *bskul ba. BBhVy* (f. 132b): "'Admonishing' is the [act of] indicating [to someone], 'You did this or that which should not be done, or [you] failed to do this or that which should be done.'" See also note 477.

612. S: *avipariṇatam,* T: *mi mthun pa med pa.* In *ŚBh* (p. 256) Asaṅga describes an 'altered state of mind' as one that has come under the influence of any of a number of perturbations (S: *paryavasthānam,* T: *kun nas dkris pa*). The most relevant of these perturbations in the present context would be malice (S: *vyāpādaḥ,* T: *gnod sems*). Thus, the term "unaltered"

friendly; and (5) giving encouragement to those who are engaged in correct practice regarding those things that are forbidden and approved, by making an agreeable statement about their genuine good qualities. In brief, the five aspects of a bodhisattva's counsel should be understood thus: forbiddance, approval, admonishing, censuring, and encouragement.

Deeds of Body, Speech, and Mind That Are Supported by Means [1.8.7]

What does it mean for bodhisattvas' deeds of body, speech, and mind to be supported by means?

Briefly, the bodhisattvas' four principles for attracting [a following] are what is called "means." As the Blessed One declared, the bodhisattva who possesses the means that are supported by the four principles for attracting a following is [worthy of being] called a bodhisattva.[613]

Why, then, are the four principles for attracting a following called "means"?

Briefly, the means that has as its purpose teaching discipline to sentient beings and attracting them [to the Dharma] is fourfold in nature; there is nothing of greater significance than these [four types of means] and nothing besides these [four types of means]. They are [a type of means] that benefits, [a second type] that brings about comprehension,[614] [a third type] that produces action, and [a fourth type] that has a conforming nature.

Regarding this, generosity[615] is the type of means that benefits. For instance, those beings who are benefited by [receiving] various kinds of gifts having material value will think that they should listen to and act in accordance with the speech [of their benefactors].

Following that, by means of agreeable speech,[616] a bodhisattva causes

---

should be taken to mean a mind that is free of such agitation as that which is caused by malice.

613. This is a reference to one of the qualities in a list of thirty-two mentioned in the *Kaśyapaparivartasūtram* that make one worthy of being called a bodhisattva. Asaṅga's statement is not a direct quote.

614. S: *grāhakaḥ,* T: *'dzin pa.* This noun is formed from the causative of the verb "to grasp" and means the act of causing [someone] to grasp [a meaning] in the mind; therefore, it means to bring about comprehension or understanding.

615. S: *dānam,* T: *sbyin pa.* This is the first of the four principles for attracting a following.

616. S: *priyavāditā,* T: *snyan par smra ba.* This is the second of the four principles. This one,

those who are confused about different subjects to grasp what is correct [about those subjects] and to perceive [what is correct about those subjects] in order to completely remove whatever confusion they might have. This is how agreeable speech is the type of means that brings about comprehension.

Similarly, [a bodhisattva] induces those beings who have been caused to comprehend and perceive by means of correct [instruction] to turn away from opportunities [to engage in] nonvirtuous [actions] and to adopt, be led to, become settled into, and become established in opportunities [to engage in] virtuous [actions]. This is [a bodhisattva's] beneficial conduct,[617] [which represents] a type of means that produces action.

Having caused beings to undertake action in this way, a bodhisattva also complies with [such a practice him- or herself], by [engaging in a form of] conduct that represents a similar lifestyle, such that the students will not be able to reproach him or her and cause him or her to feel regret[618] by saying: "You yourself have not yet become one who possesses faith, one who possesses morality, one who possesses generosity, one who possesses wisdom. Why are you urging others to take up this [form of practice]?" Therefore, sameness of purpose[619] should be understood as a bodhisattva's fourth type of means, one that has a conforming nature.

Those deeds of body, deeds of speech, and deeds of mind that are governed by these four types of means, either collectively or individually, are described as the ones that are "governed by means" for the purpose of correctly attracting beings, teaching them discipline, and ripening them spiritually.

Within [Book I of] *The Stage of a Bodhisattva,* [known as] "The Object of Mental Application That Relates to the Support," this completes the eighth chapter, entitled "The Lineages of the Powers."

---

along with the final two, are the subject matter of Book I, chapter 15.

617. S: *arthacaryā,* T: *don spyod pa*. This is the third of the four principles.

618. S: *smārayati,* T: *dran par byas*. The causative of the root "to remember" can mean to cause someone to regret something by bringing it to his or her attention. That seems to be the intended sense here.

619. S: *samānārthatā,* T: *don mthun pa*.

9

GENEROSITY

Summary verses:

> The essence, all-inclusive,
> Difficult to carry out, directed everywhere,
> Connected with the qualities of a true spiritual person,
> Likewise, all of its forms,
>
> Relating to what is wanted by those in distress,
> What brings happiness here and in the next world,
> And, likewise, that which is pure—
> This, in brief, is the generosity of bodhisattvas.

Having gradually completed the six perfections here, a bodhisattva attains unsurpassed true and complete enlightenment. [The six perfections are] the perfection of generosity, the perfection of morality, the perfection of patience, the perfection of effort, the perfection of meditative absorption, and the perfection of wisdom.

Regarding this [point], what is a bodhisattva's perfection of generosity?

A generosity having nine aspects is what is called a bodhisattva's perfection of generosity. [Those nine aspects are] (1) the essence of generosity, (2) all-inclusive generosity, (3) generosity that is difficult to carry out, (4) generosity that is directed everywhere, (5) the generosity of a true spiritual being, (6) generosity in all of its forms, (7) generosity that relates to what is wanted by those who are in distress, (8) generosity that brings happiness here and in the next world, and (9) generosity that is pure.

The Essence of Generosity [1.9.1]

What is the essence of generosity?

It is the volition[620] of a bodhisattva who is indifferent[621] toward all material objects as well as [his or her] own body, and [a volition] that arises together with [an attitude that is] free of acquisitiveness. It is also the deeds of body and speech that are caused to arise by that [volition] for the purpose of giving up those objects that are suitable to be given, as well as the faultless giving up of all those objects that are suitable to be given. It should be understood that the essential nature of a bodhisattva's generosity is the [act of] providing an entity to that individual by whom it is desired, and [this act is one that is carried out] by an individual who is abiding in the [bodhisattva system of moral] discipline, who sees what is to be gained [by practicing generosity], and who recognizes the results [of practicing generosity].[622]

620. S: *cetanā,* T: *sems pa. AS* (pp. 5–6): "What is volition? It is the shaping of consciousness and the activity of the mind. Its function is to direct the mind toward virtuous, nonvirtuous, and indeterminate [entities]." *PSV* (p. 277) elaborates: "The [phrase] 'shaping of consciousness' (S: *cittābhisaṃskāraḥ,* T: *sems mngon par 'du byed pa*) means [the activity of] setting the mind in motion; it is that entity whose presence causes the mind to flow toward an object, like the movement of iron filings that is caused by a magnet. . . . If volition is described as 'the shaping of consciousness,' why is it also said to be 'activity of the mind' (S: *manaskarma,* T: *yid kyi las*)? Since all the mental factors [help to] shape the mind, volition is described as activity of the mind in order to distinguish it from the other mental factors. Thus, the additional qualification is to suggest that volition alone is the entity that causes the mind to flow outward."

621. "Indifferent" (S: *anapekṣaḥ,* T: *mi ltos pa*) should be taken to mean that a bodhisattva has no selfish motive or desire for personal reward in practicing generosity. *BBhVy* (f. 134b): "The phrase 'indifferent toward all material objects as well as one's own body' means not to have any aspiration for [any of] the three types of results that relate, respectively, to this life, future lives, or even the ultimate stage. This constitutes being indifferent to both [material objects and one's own body]. [The three results are] (1) an [immediate] result that benefits [an individual] in [his or her] present life, (2) a maturation result that occurs in a future life, and (3) the result of liberation that occurs at the time of perfection."

622. These three characteristics of the practitioner provide something of a counterpoint to the quality of being indifferent that was mentioned initially. Thus, while a bodhisattva should not be motivated by any desire for a personal reward in cultivating generosity, he or she nevertheless should properly recognize how this practice relates to other elements of the Great Vehicle path and how it contributes to the ultimate goal. *BBhVy* (f. 135a–135b): "The phrase '[an individual who is] abiding in the [bodhisattva system of moral] discipline' means that [the practitioner] should avoid doing physical harm, etc., to those who are making a request. . . . Bodhisattvas should avoid developing an angry mind toward petitioners, as they should engender toward them the attitude [that they serve a role resembling that]

All-Inclusive Generosity [1.9.2]

What is all-inclusive generosity?

Briefly, what is called "all-inclusive" refers to the two types of object that are suitable to be given: (1) an inner one and (2) an outer one. Regarding this, the giving up by a bodhisattva of [his or her] own body down to the marrow is called "the giving up of what is exclusively an inner object." On the other hand, the food and drink that a bodhisattva continually eats and then vomits for the sake of those [beings] who sustain themselves by consuming vomit[623] is called a bodhisattva's "giving of what is a mixture of an inner and an outer object." The giving up of all remaining forms of objects that are suitable to be given, aside from the ones that were just mentioned, is called "the giving up of what are exclusively outer objects that are suitable to be given."

Regarding this, briefly there are two ways in which a bodhisattva offers [his or her] own body to those individuals who are seeking a body. [One way is that] he or she offers him- or herself to others by placing [him- or herself] under their control and submitting to their will such that [he or she] will do as they wish. It is like an individual agreeing to become a servant for others in order to receive food and clothing. Similarly, with a mind that is free of corporeal desire, a bodhisattva who is desirous of [achieving] supreme enlightenment, who is desirous of [providing] benefit and happiness to others, and who is desirous of completing the perfection of generosity offers him- or herself to others by placing [him- or herself] under their control and submitting to their will such that [he or she] will do as they wish. [The second way is that] to those who request [the bodhisattva's] hands, feet, eyes, head, limbs, or minor appendages, to those who seek [his or her] flesh, blood, or sinews, and to those who seek [his or her] marrow, [the bodhisattva] offers [all of these things,] up to his or her marrow.

---

of a spiritual teacher. The phrase '[an individual who] sees what is to be gained [by practicing generosity]' means to recognize the three types of results that derive from practicing generosity. This meaning is [also] indicated by the phrase '[an individual who] knows the results [of practicing generosity].' The three types of results are maturation results, corresponding results, and the result of attaining enlightenment. . . . [By contrast,] others [i.e., those who are not bodhisattvas] regard [generosity] only as having the result of [bringing about] great wealth."

623. *BBhVy* (f. 135b): "[The phrase] 'those who sustain themselves by consuming vomit' refers to hungry ghosts and certain kinds of animals."

There are two ways[624] in which a bodhisattva gives up outer objects to sentient beings. [One is that] he or she provides a borrowed object[625] so that it may be used however it might please [the petitioner]. [The second is that a bodhisattva] offers [an object] so that [the petitioner] might have dominion over it, and he or she does so with a mind that gives up [ownership of that object] fully and completely. Nevertheless, a bodhisattva does not give all inner and outer objects in every way to sentient beings without exception.

What to Observe and Avoid When Practicing Generosity [1.9.2.1]

Of this twofold distinction concerning inner and outer objects, what [kinds of objects] does a bodhisattva give to sentient beings? What [kinds of objects] does one not give? What is the manner in which one gives [objects to sentient beings]? What is the manner in which one does not give [objects to sentient beings]?

Of those inner and outer objects, [a bodhisattva] does not practice toward others the [kind of] generosity that only brings happiness but is not beneficial, nor [the kind] that neither brings happiness nor is beneficial. On the other hand, [a bodhisattva] does practice toward others the [kind of] generosity that is beneficial even though it may not necessarily bring happiness, as well as [the kind] that both brings happiness and is beneficial. This is a brief description of the [kind of] generosity that is practiced and the [kind of] generosity that is not practiced. What follows below should be understood as a [more] extensive [series of] distinctions.

A bodhisattva who has been called upon here by an improper directive should not give him- or herself up to the control of another and submit to the will of another for the sake of harming someone, [for the sake of killing someone,[626]] or for the sake of deceiving someone. Although a bodhisattva

624. Both Sanskrit editions have two "reasons" (S: *kāraṇam*); however, *BBhVy* (f. 136a) supports two "ways" (S: *ākāraḥ,* T: *rnam pa*), as in the Tibetan translation and as with the description of the bodhisattva's offering of the body in the previous paragraph.

625. S: *yācitakam vastu,* T: *brnyan po.* That is, the object is provided for only a temporary period of time.

626. S: *paravadhāya.* This phrase appears only in Wogihara's Sanskrit edition of the text; it does not appear in Dutt's Sanskrit edition or in any of the Tibetan translations that were consulted. Wogihara notes that it is not found in the Cambridge manuscript, one of the two on which his edition is based.

may have agreed in the presence of others to give up life even a hundred times, a thousand times, or a hundred thousand times, he or she should not, because of [having been given] an order by another or for the sake of pleasing another, harm someone, kill someone, or deceive someone.

Moreover, if a bodhisattva has become one who possesses a pure attitude with regard to [the practice of] generosity, he or she should not offer his or her own body, limbs, or appendages when a great matter relating to sentient beings that ought to be done is near at hand, even though a person may have approached and asked for his or her body, limbs, or appendages.

Why is that?

The bodhisattva who possesses a pure attitude with regard to [the practice of] generosity would not experience any manner of apprehension whatsoever such that he or she might wonder, "Should this be given or should this not be given?" Therefore, while a bodhisattva *should* disregard the presence of matters relating to sentient beings and give[627] [his or her own body] in order to continue purifying his or her attitude, once his or her attitude has become purified, [a bodhisattva] does *not* [need to] disregard the presence of matters relating to sentient beings and give [his or her own body].

[A bodhisattva] also should not give his or her own body, in such a way that involves the separation of the limbs, to those gods who belong to Māra's entourage who have approached him or her with an injurious aim and have asked for [his or her body]. [He or she should refuse to do so] in order to insure that an extremely great injury or loss does not befall those [gods].[628]

627. All Tibetan translations consulted add a negative particle to the verb "should give" in the first clause as well as to the same verb in the second clause, indicating that in both cases the bodhisattva should *not* give body, limbs, or appendages. However, in both Sanskrit editions the verb in the first clause is in the affirmative, suggesting that the situation is one in which the goal of further perfecting one's attitude of generosity takes precedence over that of carrying out some action that directly aids sentient beings. *BBhVy* (ff. 36b–37a) defines an attitude that is pure with regard to generosity as occurring (1) when one is about to achieve the first of the ten ārya bodhisattva levels and (2) when the first level has been achieved. In both of these instances the bodhisattva is no longer subject to the impurity of stinginess (S: **mātsaryamalam,* T: *ser sna'i dri ma*) and so he or she does not need to practice generosity to overcome this fault. Moreover, the second reason for practicing generosity is to benefit sentient beings, but in this instance the mitigating factor is that "a great matter relating to sentient beings that ought to be done is near at hand," meaning that the bodhisattva has the obligation to carry out some greater purpose than whatever might be accomplished by giving his or her own body, limbs, or appendages to a single person.

628. *BBhVy* (f. 137a): "'An [extremely great] injury would befall them' because they would

Just as with the gods who belong to Māra's entourage, the same should be understood with regard to beings who have been directed by those [gods].

Moreover, a bodhisattva should not give his or her own body, in such a way that involves the separation of the limbs, to those who are mad and have deranged minds, for they are neither in their right minds nor petitioners who are seeking [a genuine aim]. [Their requests] are nothing but idle chatter. Therefore, he or she does not give them [what they ask for] because they are not in control of their minds.

With the exception of these situations, a bodhisattva does give up his or her own body to those who ask for it in those situations that are the opposite of those [that were just described], either in the sense of submitting to the will of another or in a way that involves separation of the limbs and appendages. This is how it should be understood that a bodhisattva does and does not practice generosity in relation to inner objects.

On the other hand, with regard to outer objects, a bodhisattva does not offer poison, fire, weapons, or intoxicants to petitioners if they are [to be used] for the purpose of harming sentient beings, regardless of whether they have been asked for by petitioners in order to harm themselves or in order to harm others. However, a bodhisattva does give poison, fire, weapons, and intoxicants to petitioners if they are [to be used] for the purpose of benefiting sentient beings, whether they have been asked for by petitioners in order to benefit themselves or in order to benefit others.[629] In addition, a bodhisattva does not offer movable property[630] to others that belongs to someone else and arouses suspicion. A bodhisattva does not, as a form of procuring, seize someone's wife and offer [her] to others. Nor does [a bodhisattva] offer food or drink that contains sentient beings who are alive.

A bodhisattva also does not give to petitioners and make as the gift of a bodhisattva any object that is associated with pleasure and amusement if it is something that is harmful to sentient beings.

---

accumulate a great amount of nonvirtue. 'An extremely great loss' means to experience an unfavorable result in the future."

629. *BBhVy* (f. 137a) describes poison that benefits as that which also has medicinal properties; fire that benefits as that which is used for such purposes as cooking, etc.; weapons that benefit as being those used for protection or ornamental purposes; and intoxicants that benefit as those that have medicinal properties.

630. S: *draviṇam,* T: *rdzas.* "Movable property" means goods and other tangible property that is not land or buildings (MW, p. 501). *BBhVy* (f. 137b) describes this property as "arousing suspicion" in the sense that it is believed to have been stolen.

Why is that?

Even though [giving] that object might cause those [recipients] to generate some measure of an approving attitude toward that bodhisattva, nevertheless his or her act of generosity might do very great harm [to other sentient beings], by reason of which [the recipients of that gift] would give rise to conceit, lack of mindfulness, and misdeeds, and, following the dissolution of their bodies, they would be reborn in the lower realms. On the other hand, if it were granted that this object of pleasure, amusement, etc., would not cause [the recipients] to go to the lower realms nor cause [them] to accumulate roots of nonvirtue, then a bodhisattva should offer such an object of pleasure, amusement, etc., to petitioners in order to cause [them to generate] an approving attitude [toward him or her], and so that, by means of that object, [those individuals] might also be drawn [to the Dharma] and caused to undergo spiritual ripening.

What sort of object, then, [that is a source of] pleasure and amusement does a bodhisattva not give to petitioners? What sort does he or she give?

For example, a bodhisattva does not provide training in the [methods of] killing wild animals. He or she does not perform either those base forms of sacrifice or those great slaughters at which many living beings are gathered together and deprived of their lives, nor does he or she cause them to be carried out by others. He or she also does not offer the killing of sacrificial animals in temples. If asked to donate geographical areas that are relied upon as a refuge by great numbers of living beings and which are inhabited by beings who are born in water or beings who are born on dry land, so that those living beings might be harmed, he or she does not offer [those areas]. If asked to provide nets, traps, or instruction [in the making of] nets and traps for the purpose of harming living beings, he or she does not provide them. He or she also does not present [his or her own] enemies to [someone who is their] enemy so that they might be reviled, killed, detained, punished, or tortured. In short, a bodhisattva does not give to petitioners any object at all that is a source of pleasure and amusement for sentient beings if its purpose is to inflict pain upon other beings or to injure other beings.

On the other hand, in order to cause petitioners [to generate] an approving attitude [toward him or her], a bodhisattva does offer them the following varieties of objects [that are sources] of pleasure and amusement: elephants, horses, carts, vehicles, and conveyances; clothing and ornaments; excellent food and drink; instruction in dance, song, and music; articles used in dance, song, and music; perfumes, garlands, and ointments; as well as various implements and household utensils; parks, houses, and women for service; and instruction in various fields of crafts and occupations.

However, a bodhisattva does not offer an immoderate amount of food or drink or [food or drink] that is unsuitable to a sick person even if he or she should ask for it. [A bodhisattva] does not offer excellent food and drink to sentient beings of a greedy nature who have already been satisfied. [A bodhisattva] does not give what is desired to those beings who are overcome by grief so that they might hang themselves, beat themselves, ingest poison, or throw themselves over a precipice.

A bodhisattva absolutely never offers his mother or father to petitioners, for a bodhisattva's mother and father represent his or her highest object of veneration. They are the ones who suckled, nourished, and raised [him or her]. A bodhisattva should not tire of carrying them on his or her head[631] for a long time. He or she should also give him- or herself to them as one who is under their control and one who is to be used by them, [as if] he were an object that is being pledged, bartered, deposited [as collateral, etc.], or sold. How could a bodhisattva even consider giving them to others, much less actually do so?

A bodhisattva king and lord who has been anointed does not, within his own domain of sentient beings together with their households, remove the child or wife that belongs to one person from the presence of that individual and offer [either of them] to someone else. Nor does he offer to someone from another [domain] an entire village or part of a village, or an [entire] town or part of a town, as his or her property, thinking, "As [this property] belonged to me, so [now] it belongs to you."

A bodhisattva does not offer his own child or spouse,[632] male or female servants, workers, hired persons, or members of his or her retinue to other petitioners, without having properly informed them, against their will, or if they are disconsolate [at the prospect of being given to someone]. Even if they have been properly informed, if it pleases them, and if they are desirous [of being given to someone else], [a bodhisattva] does not turn them over to

631. *BBhVy* (f. 138b) glosses the expression "to carry [someone] on one's head" (S: *śirodvahanam,* T: *spyi bo la khyer ba*) to mean both to perform arduous activities on someone's behalf and to treat someone with respect. The phrase "for a long time" is interpreted to mean for as long as they live.

632. S: *dāra*, T: *chung ma*. The term literally means "wife"; however, to preserve the aim of gender-neutrality, it is translated as "spouse."

hostile persons, powerful spirits[633] or malignant demons,[634] or those who are violent.[635] Nor does he or she commit into servitude a child or spouse who is of a delicate nature or who is from a distinguished family.

A bodhisattva does not bestow a grant of sovereignty [over some geographical region] to petitioners who are violent and inflict great injury upon others. Moreover, if he or she has the power to do so, [a bodhisattva] causes such persons to have their sovereignty removed.

A bodhisattva does not take away property from his or her mother and father and give it to petitioners. Just as he or she does with father and mother, so too, [he or she does not take away property] from his or her child, spouse, female servants, male servants, and hired persons. He or she does not give up to other petitioners [his or her own] objects to be given in such a way that it would cause harm to his or her mother and father, etc., up to [in such a way that it would cause harm] to his or her workers and hired persons.

A bodhisattva practices generosity after acquiring objects of value in a manner that is just and accompanied by due consideration, not in a manner that is unjust or rash. Nor does he or she do so in a manner that causes pain or injury to others.

A bodhisattva who is established in the teaching of the buddhas, the blessed ones, does not practice generosity in any manner whatsoever that involves violating the system of training. When a bodhisattva is giving a gift, he or she gives it with a mind that views all beings equally, fixing [in mind] the view that [all] are worthy of receiving gifts, [regardless of whether they are] friends, foes, or neutral persons; virtuous individuals or individuals with faults; individuals who are inferior, equal, or superior; or individuals who are happy or suffering.

A bodhisattva does not give a petitioner a lesser gift than the one he or she stated and promised [would be given]; without exception, he or she only gives one that is equal to or greater in value than [what was originally indicated]. Having promised an excellent object, a bodhisattva does not give an inferior one that is of lesser value. Having promised a poor [object] that is

633. S: *yakṣaḥ,* T: *gnod sbyin.*

634. S: *rākṣasaḥ,* T: *srin po.*

635. S: *raudrakarma,* T: *brjed ngas pa.* The Tibetan translation is puzzling, as it is normally understood to mean "one who is forgetful." *BBhVy* (f. 139a): "*brjed ngas pa* (S: *raudrakarmāsu*) means persons who commit acts of extreme violence upon their dependents."

of lesser value, if he should possess one whose quality is excellent, without exception he or she gives the excellent one.

A bodhisattva does not give a gift while feeling disconsolate, angry, or in an agitated state of mind. Nor does he or she, after having made a gift, reproach [a recipient] by repeatedly declaring, "Through generosity, I have aided you in this or that way," or "[Through generosity,] I have fostered you [in this or that way]," or "[Through generosity,] I have lifted you up [in this or that way]."

When giving a gift even to a person of lowly status, a bodhisattva does not offer it in a scornful or disrespectful manner, much less [when giving a gift] to someone who possesses good qualities.

When giving a gift to petitioners who are engaged in various forms of wrongful behavior, who are rowdy[636] and have an unrestrained nature, and who are verbally abusive, irascible, and vituperative, a bodhisattva does not, on account of that wrongful behavior, [allow him- or herself to] become disheartened. Without exception, when giving a gift to such individuals, a bodhisattva realizes that it is their nature to be greatly overcome by mental afflictions and fixes a compassionate attitude [in his or her mind].

He or she does not, influenced by an improper view, give a gift that is [wrongly] considered to be supreme.[637] For example, he or she does not believe that the "gift of harm" that is made during great violent sacrifices represents [a true form of] Dharma. He or she also does not give gifts that are associated with [ineffectual] auspicious ceremonies.[638] Nor does he or she believe that the purity of a mundane or transcendent form of detach-

636. S: *uddhataḥ,* T: *rgod pa*. One of the senses of this adjective is to be agitated. *BBhVy* (f. 140a) supports this interpretation: "'Rowdy' means to have an excitable nature (S: **aśāntātmakaḥ,* T: *ma zhi ba'i bdag nyid can*)." However, MW (p. 188) suggests a broader range of meanings, including "violent," "arrogant," "rude," and "ill-behaved."

637. S: *asaddṛṣṭyā parāmṛṣṭam dānam,* T: *lta ba ngan pa mchog tu 'dzin cing sbyin pa*. This statement is a reference to one of five inferior views that constitute forms of the root mental afflictions—specifically, "the consideration that views are supreme" (S: *dṛṣṭiparāmarśaḥ,* T: *lta ba mchog to 'dzin pa*). *AS* (p. 7): "What is the consideration that views are supreme? It is the acceptance, inclination, notion, opinion, and view that regards an [inferior] view or the five grasping heaps that are the basis of an [inferior] view as foremost, superior, most excellent, and the highest. Its action is to support continued attachment to bad views." The kinds of gifts that are described in this paragraph represent examples of generosity carried out under the influence of this inferior view.

638. S: *kautukamaṅgalam,* T: *dge mtshan dang bkra shis pa*. *BBhVy* (f. 140a): "Although [various auspicious ceremonies] associated with certain classes of [worldly] gods do not lead

ment [can be attained] simply through [making] gifts that are exceedingly pure in every respect. [Rather,] he or she maintains solely that generosity constitutes [a form of] accumulation[639] [that leads to the attainment of] complete purity.

[A bodhisattva] does not practice generosity as one who expects a reward. He or she also dedicates all of [his or her] generosity to unsurpassed true and complete enlightenment. A bodhisattva who, in accordance with the way things truly are,[640] has developed a firm belief[641] with regard to the ripening of every type of result of every type of generosity practices generosity without having to depend on anyone else and without having to be led by anyone else. For example, a person who gives food will become one who is strong, a person who gives clothing will become one who possesses an [excellent] physical appearance, a person who gives vehicles will become one who enjoys physical comfort, and a person who gives lamps will become one who possesses [excellent] eyesight. It should be understood [that this point can be illustrated] at length with additional examples.

A bodhisattva does not become frightened by the risk of poverty when he or she gives a gift. He or she has no other thought but compassion.

A bodhisattva does not give a gift that is unsuitable for the petitioners, such as leftover food and drink to religious ascetics, or [food and drink] that contains excrement, urine, phlegm, mucus, vomit, purging, pus, or blood, or [food and drink] that has become spoiled but was not declared and made known [to be spoiled], or porridge and gruel that ought to be discarded. Similarly, [an unfit gift is the giving of food] that contains onions or has onions mixed in with it to those who do not eat onions. It is also [the giving

---

to good fortune or an auspicious outcome, they are invested with false notions that relate to the sun and other heavenly bodies."

639. See note 417. In particular, of the two forms of accumulation, it constitutes the accumulation of merit. See also Book I, chapter 3, the section entitled "Merit and Wisdom" [I.3.5.2].

640. S: *yathābhūtam,* T: *yang dag pa ji lta ba bzhin du*. *BBhVy* (f. 140b): "The remaining portion of the statement is [a bodhisattva] realizes, on the basis of wisdom, [every type of result that relates to every type of generosity] 'in accordance with the way things truly are.'" In other words, a genuine belief in the karmic results of generosity should be based on knowledge. For a logical justification of the doctrine of karma, see *Inner Science,* pp. 70–89.

641. S: *abhisaṃpratyayaḥ,* T: *mngon par yid ches pa*. This term refers to the type of faith that believes in the doctrine of karma and its results. See note 467. See also *Inner Science,* pp. 281–284.

of food that contains meat or has meat mixed in with it] to those who do not eat meat and the giving of drink that contains alcohol or has alcohol mixed in it to those who do not drink intoxicating beverages. Likewise, a bodhisattva does not engage in any inappropriate action when giving a gift to others. Nor does he or she give any gift that is similar to these in that it is unsuitable [in some way].

A bodhisattva does not give a gift to a petitioner only after [the latter] has become exhausted by having had to make repeated requests, by having had to go away and return again [repeatedly], and by having had to render service [for an extended period of time]. Without exception, [he or she gives a gift] as soon as the request is made.

A bodhisattva does not give a gift that is based on [a desire for] renown, fame, and reputation. He or she does not give [a gift] that is based on [a desire to] receive something in return from another person, nor one that is based on [a desire to attain] the power of Śakra or Māra, or a wheel ruler.

He or she does not give a gift to others in order to [engage in] hypocrisy,[642] by thinking, "I hope that [by this act of generosity] others—[such as] members of the royal family, the king's ministers, [leading] townspersons and countrymen, brahmins, village heads, persons of wealth, leaders of guilds, or merchants—will recognize me as one who is generous and a benefactor, [so that] in the future they will honor, venerate, respect, and revere me."

He or she does not give a gift [that indicates] poverty of spirit.[643] Even if

642. The term translated as "hypocrisy" (S: *kuhanā,* T: *tshul 'chos*) is derived from a verbal root that literally means "to cheat by trickery." It is the name for one of five kinds of wrong livelihood (S: *mithyājīvaḥ,* T: *log par 'tsho ba*) that should be avoided by monks and nuns in particular. *ŚBh* (p. 48) describes the basic form of this type of wrong livelihood as follows: "Further, in a manner that is not proper, this [monk or nun who is greedy, not easily satisfied, difficult to nourish, and difficult to maintain] fabricates an unnatural and altered mode of physical behavior that is [meant to be] an indication that he or she has developed spiritual qualities and presents to others a false show that [he or she possesses] faculties that are free of excitation, faculties that are unwavering, and faculties that are tranquil, in order to [obtain] robes, a begging bowl, bedding, a seat, medicine that is required [to treat] illnesses, and [other permissible forms of] personal belongings. [He or she does this] in such a way that [is designed to make] others think, 'This [monk or nun] is one who has developed spiritual qualities and [therefore, offerings] ought to be given and ought to be made [to him or her]—that is to say, [offerings of] robes, a begging bowl, bedding, a seat, medicine that is required [to treat] illnesses, and [other permissible forms of] personal belongings.'"

643. S: *kārpaṇyam,* T: *bkren pa'i tshul.* This noun is derived from a root that means "to mourn," "to long for," "to lament." Its literal meaning is "poverty," "pitiful circumstances,"

only a small amount [of property is owned], he or she still gives a substantial portion, let alone when large amounts [are owned].

He or she does not give a gift to others in order to deceive them, by thinking, "After enticing and gaining [their] trust with this gift, later I shall cheat them."

He or she does not give a gift to others in order to alienate them from someone else, such as by thinking, "By means of this gift, I shall create discord [between the inhabitants of] a village, a portion of a village, a region, or a portion of a region and their lord. Then, I shall take them away [from that lord] and gain control over them [for myself]."

A bodhisattva is skillful, diligent, and poised for action. Having readied him- or herself with [appropriate] preparations and arranged for the doling out of objects that are to be given, he or she makes gifts and also prompts others to give them out. Without displaying any laziness him- or herself, he or she directs others to make gifts. When he or she further becomes aware that a great multitude and gathering of petitioners has gathered and assembled, including persons of both good and bad moral character, he or she moves back and forth repeatedly presenting all the objects to be given, [proceeding] in an orderly manner from [those situated at] the most senior end [of a row] to [those situated at] the most junior end.

A bodhisattva who possesses abundant, extensive, and vast wealth does not give a meager gift. He or she does not give a gift to others in order to cause injury to someone else, nor does he or she give a gift to verbally abuse, anger, beat, threaten, reproach, kill, bind, amputate, confine, or exile someone.

Before making a gift, a bodhisattva is in a happy state of mind. During the act of giving, he or she remains glad. After having completed the act of giving, he or she does not feel remorse.

He or she does not, [motivated] by deceit, give a gift of fake jewels, pearls, lapis lazuli, conch shell, crystal, or coral, etc., to persons who desire [a genuine form of any of] those [precious objects].

There is no object to be given whatsoever, small or great, that a bodhisattva has not previously given mentally to all sentient beings and that later, [when] a petitioner requests it from the bodhisattva, [he or she does not consider] as [the petitioner's] own wealth that had been borrowed [by the bodhisattva] and [is now being] returned.

---

and "poverty of spirit." It can also mean "stinginess," a sense that is implicit in the present statement.

A bodhisattva makes a gift at a suitable time, not at an unsuitable time. [The gift is one] that is proper both for oneself and others, not one that is improper. [It is given] in a manner that exemplifies good conduct, not in a manner that represents improper conduct. [It is] also [given] with an undistracted mind, not one that is distracted.

A bodhisattva also does not laugh at or show contempt toward a petitioner, nor does he or she cause [a petitioner] to feel embarrassed.

He or she does not frown. He or she exhibits a radiant countenance, greets with a smile, and initiates polite conversation. He or she does not delay in making a gift, nor does he or she do so with great haste. Without being asked to do so, a bodhisattva willingly chooses to extend to others whatever they may seek. He or she personally takes hold of the objects that are granted to them.

Wise Generosity [1.9.2.2]

A bodhisattva also does not practice unwise generosity. When giving, he or she only practices wise generosity.

What is a bodhisattva's wise generosity?

Here a bodhisattva who possesses and has obtained objects that are fit to be given forms [his or her] mind in the following manner, before a petitioner has come forward: "Suppose two petitioners were to approach me, one of whom is comfortable, not miserable, not wretched, has a protector, and has someone to rely upon, while the other is distressed, miserable, wretched, does not have a protector, and does not have someone to rely upon. In that situation, if I should have the wealth to satisfy and fulfill the desires of both, then I should satisfy both; I should fulfill the desires of both. But if I should not have sufficient wealth to satisfy and fulfill the desires of both, then I should turn away the one who is comfortable and make a gift to the one who is distressed. I should turn away the one who is not miserable, not wretched, has a protector, and has someone to rely upon, and make a gift to the one who is miserable, wretched, does not have a protector, and does not have someone to rely upon." Having formed his or her mind in this way, [a bodhisattva] should carry out [this intention] with [his or her] actions, just as it was formed [in the mind]. If [a bodhisattva] is unable to fulfill the wish of the petitioner who is comfortable, after having made that earlier mental determination, he or she should send away that petitioner after assuaging him or her in the following manner: "That donation was committed earlier and promised earlier by me to that person who is in distress. I have [already] presented it to him or her. It is not my desire to deny giving you [a gift]. Therefore, good person,[644] I hope you don't feel any antipathy toward me."

Moreover, a bodhisattva who possesses and has obtained objects that are fit to be given should approach households that are marked by stinginess, that are marked by extreme stinginess, that cling to their possessions, that are avaricious,[645] that have never practiced charity toward ascetics and brahmins and, after having made a friendly greeting and established an air of goodwill, he or she should say the following: "Please, friends, do me a great favor that will not cause you any loss of wealth. In my home, there is an abundance of property and an abundance of objects that are suitable for practicing charity. I am one who seeks petitioners in order to complete the perfection of generosity. If you should encounter any petitioners, please do not abandon them by turning them away. Either take from my wealth and objects for charity and deliver it to them as you wish, or bring those petitioners to me and rejoice at the generosity that I practice."

After hearing this from [the bodhisattva] and being pleased by the fact that their own wealth will not be depleted, those [householders] do as he or she asks, thinking to themselves, "This son or daughter of good family will come to have a favorable attitude toward us." In this way, the bodhisattva plants a seed for them to dispel the impurity of stinginess in the future. Eventually, through engaging in this practice and this form of skillful means that is accompanied by wisdom, [these householders] will also offer small amounts of their own wealth to others. After having relied upon a weak form of avoidance of desire,[646] they will attain one that is middling; after having relied upon a middling form, they will attain one that is great.

Moreover, in a situation where a bodhisattva's teachers, preceptors, the students that he or she lives with, or his or her fellow spiritual practitioners

644. S: *bhadramukhaḥ,* T: *bzhin bzang.* This expression, which literally means "one whose face confers prosperity" (MW, p. 746), is used as a term of address that is the equivalent of "good sir" or "gentle sir"; however, the honorific "sir" does not seem appropriate in the present context.

645. S: *kuṭakuñcakaḥ,* T: *'jungs ba. BBhVy* (f. 140a): "[The term] 'avaricious' means for the mind to be extremely greedy toward possessions."

646. S: *alobhaḥ,* T: *'dod chags med pa.* This mental factor is one of the three roots of virtue (S: *kuśalamulāni,* T: *dge ba'i rtsa ba*). *AS* (p. 6): "What is avoidance of desire? It is the avoidance of attachment toward [samsaric] existence or the things that sustain [samsaric] existence. Its action is to provide support for the avoidance of misdeeds."

are individuals with a nature that is marked by desire, or they are individuals who are prone to attachment, or, though not prone to attachment, they are individuals who have lost the desire [to practice charity] because they lack objects that are suitable for giving, that bodhisattva, being someone who desires to perform substantial forms of meritorious action[647] that derive from generosity and are related either to the Buddha, the Dharma, or the Sangha, gives objects that are suitable for giving to those individuals and does not perform [such acts of generosity] him- or herself but rather causes those individuals to perform them. In this manner, the bodhisattva produces a great quantity of merit for him- or herself, he or she causes some of [his or her] fellow spiritual practitioners to bring their mental affliction under control and others to perfect their desire for Dharma practice, and he or she also both causes sentient beings to be drawn [to the Dharma] and causes sentient beings to attain spiritual ripening.

Moreover, a bodhisattva who possesses and has obtained objects that are fit to be given, having understood [someone to be] a petitioner merely by [recognizing] a sign of his or her intention, presents [that person] with objects that are suitable to be given, according to his or her wishes.

If someone approaches that [bodhisattva] thinking, "I shall cheat him or her with this fraudulent transaction, and [the bodhisattva] realizes this person's intention, he or she conceals that misdeed even from others, let alone from that very individual. [The bodhisattva] also causes the desire of that individual to be fulfilled, in such a way that he or she departs without being embarrassed and feeling highly pleased, confident, and happy, and also in such a way that the bodhisattva [allows him- or herself] to be cheated by that fraudulent act. The [cheater's] deception is not exposed before it occurs nor does [the bodhisattva] expose it afterward. Nor does [the bodhisattva], because of this incident, reproach the cheater or cause him or her to feel regret. [The bodhisattva] acquiesces fully and with a sincere mind to that dishonest act, which constitutes a form of taking what was not given. This and other examples like it should be understood as wise forms of generos-

647. S: *puṇyakriyāvastu,* T: *bsod nams bya ba'i dngos po.* There are various formulations of the principal forms of these activities. One identifies the following three sources: generosity, morality, and meditation. Another recognizes seven actions that are based on material things (S: *aupadhikam,* T: *rdzas la byung ba*) and seven that are not based on material things (S: *niraupadhikam,* T: *rdzas la byung ba ma yin pa*)—that is, they are essentially ways of cultivating virtuous attitudes.

ity [that are performed] by a bodhisattva who possesses and has obtained objects that are fit to be given.

Moreover, a bodhisattva who does not possess and has not obtained objects that are fit to be given but who is skilled in a variety of crafts and occupations takes up one of those crafts or occupations in such a way that, having acquired a great amount of wealth with little difficulty, he or she is able to maintain [him- or herself]. Alternatively, using various forms of discourse, pleasant forms of discourse, and agreeable forms of eloquence, he or she teaches Dharma to others in such a way that even impoverished sentient beings develop a desire to practice generosity, much less those who are wealthy; even stingy persons do so as well, much less those of a charitable disposition. Alternatively, he or she directs those petitioners who appear continuously to the households of individuals who are faithful and where, due to the extensive wealth [of those families], charitable acts are carried out on a daily basis. Having gone to those places where acts of generosity are being practiced and merit is being generated, he or she is skillful, dispels any laziness, and is ready to act. Having gladdened the mind, he or she goes to work physically and verbally, as much as he or she is able and with all his or her strength, and makes sure that the gifts to those petitioners are well presented. In such a manner, the act of generosity is not badly presented due to an absence of attendants, acts of favoritism, the occurrence of improper conduct, or the failure to remain attentive. This is the manner in which a bodhisattva who does not possess and has not obtained wealth becomes a practitioner of wise generosity, for as long as he or she has not attained purity of mental disposition. However, a bodhisattva whose attitude has become pure attains inexhaustible wealth in rebirth after rebirth, just as he or she transcends having to be born in the lower realms.

Moreover, a bodhisattva does not give the Dharma to a heretic who is looking for flaws [in the Buddhist doctrine], either through verbal instruction or in the form of a book. Nor does he or she give a book to a person of an acquisitive nature who desires to sell it or desires [merely] to collect it, but does not seek it for knowledge. On the other hand, if the individual is seeking knowledge and [the bodhisattva] no longer has any need of the book, then he or she may give it to [this person] as he or she sees fit. If [the bodhisattva] has not yet completed the purpose for which the book was acquired, then, after locating another copy or causing one to be copied, he or she should give that one [to the petitioner].

If [the bodhisattva] is unable to locate a copy or have one copied, he or she should first examine his or her [own] mind to determine the following: "I hope that my mind has not been overcome by the impurity of stinginess concerning the Dharma. I hope that I do not have a deeply held desire not to give a written form of the Dharma." If upon making such an examination, he or she realizes, "I have engaged in the impurity of stinginess concerning the Dharma to some extent," then that gift of Dharma should be made, after having formulated his or her mind in the following manner: "Even if this gift of Dharma should cause me to be ignorant in this life, I shall make this gift of Dharma in a manner that refuses to embrace a mental affliction, let alone if it causes me to be deficient in the wisdom accumulation."

On the other hand, if upon making such an examination, he or she realizes, "I have not engaged in the impurity of stinginess concerning the Dharma to the slightest extent," then the bodhisattva should clearly recognize the following: "I ought to make a gift of Dharma either to overcome my own mental afflictions, or to perfect the accumulation of wisdom, or out of affection for sentient beings. I do not see that I have any mental affliction [relating to this act]. Further, I do see that, by not making this gift, [I can attain] an extensive accumulation of wisdom both in this life and in future ones. [However,] by making such a gift, this will not occur and a meager amount [of the wisdom accumulation] in future lives [will have to suffice] for the purpose of obtaining an abundance of Dharma.[648] Moreover, if I do not make this gift, I can accumulate wisdom for the happiness and benefit of all sentient beings and I can also show kindness to this one individual and to all other sentient beings as well. But if I make this gift, I can only show kindness to this single individual." If the bodhisattva refuses to give [the book] after having correctly gained this understanding, he or she remains free of any objectionable act, free of remorse, and does not violate [any portion of] the bodhisattva conduct.

648. This translation is based mainly on the Sanskrit (S: *na pradānāt sāmparāyikam eva pratanukaṃ dharmalābhapracuratāyai*). The Tibetan version suggests a somewhat different reading whose meaning is questionable: "If [the Dharma book] is given, a great understanding will not occur; in future lives an abundance of Dharma will be obtained, not a meager amount."

The Proper Manner in Which to Avoid Making a Gift [1.9.2.3]

How does [a bodhisattva] refuse to make a gift?

Now then, a bodhisattva is incapable of rejecting a petitioner by saying in a harsh manner, "I shall not give you a gift." Rather, using skillful means, he or she should assuage [the petitioner] before sending him or her away.

Regarding this [point], the following represents skillful means. A bodhisattva has from the outset dedicated and entrusted, with a pure attitude, all his or her possessions and objects suitable for practicing charity to the buddhas and bodhisattvas throughout the ten directions, in the same way that a fully ordained monastic dedicates his or her robes to a teacher or preceptor. Because of [having made] this dedication, even though [such an individual] may have obtained an extensive and varied quantity of possessions and objects that are suitable for practicing charity, he or she is referred to as "a bodhisattva who abides in the ārya lineage."[649] He or she becomes one who brings forth an immeasurable amount of merit. Moreover, this merit that is always being brought to mind in a comprehensive manner increases more and more by virtue of its being present at all times.

He or she keeps those objects that are suitable for practicing charity as if they had been entrusted to him or her by the buddhas and bodhisattvas. If [a bodhisattva] sees a petitioner and also sees that the granting of a charitable gift in the manner [that the petitioner] desires is suitable for this [individual], he or she then fulfills the desire of the petitioner, after reflecting, "There is nothing whatsoever that the buddhas and bodhisattvas would not give to sentient beings."

If [a bodhisattva] perceives that [some gift] would be unsuitable, then,

649. S: *āryavaṃśavihārī*, T: *'phags pa'i rigs la gnas pa*. This expression is traditionally associated with an indifference to material prosperity and dedication to a spiritual life. It is being reinterpreted here in the context of Great Vehicle practice, which permits one to have an abundance of wealth as long as it is dedicated to accomplishing the welfare of others. *AKB* (p. 336) presents the conventional explanation: "They are [called] the four ārya lineages because they are [the four qualities] from which āryas originate. Their essential nature is also that of avoidance of desire." The four spiritual qualities are (1) the ārya lineage of being satisfied with any kind of ordinary robes; (2) the ārya lineage of being satisfied with any kind of ordinary alms food; (3) the ārya lineage of being satisfied with any kind of ordinary bed and seat; and (4) the ārya lineage of delighting in abandoning [the mental afflictions] and meditating [on the path].

relying on that very determination,[650] he or she sends away that [petitioner] after having assuaged him or her by declaring in a gentle voice, "Good person, that [object] belongs to another. I am not authorized to give it [to you]." Alternatively, [a bodhisattva] gives [the petitioner] a different object that is two or three times greater in value than the one asked for, and then, after showing him or her respect and honor by making that gift, sends [the petitioner] away in such a way that [the petitioner] realizes, "This bodhisattva was not unwilling to give [me the gift that I wanted] due to his being of an avaricious nature. Rather, the reason that he did not make a gift was certainly because he did not have the authority to do so with regard to this gift of the Dharma in the form of a book." This [example] should also be understood as a bodhisattva's wise form of generosity in relation to a gift of the Dharma.

Moreover, in practicing all forms of generosity—that is, the giving of Dharma, material objects, and protection[651]—a bodhisattva makes him- or herself aware that he or she is doing so in a correct manner, as relates to verbal formulations, [defining] characteristics, clear expression, as well as causes, results, and types [of generosity].[652] This should also be understood as a bodhisattva's wise form of generosity.

Moreover, a bodhisattva maintains an attitude of loving-kindness when practicing generosity toward beings who engage in harmful activities; he or she maintains a compassionate attitude [when practicing generosity] toward beings who are experiencing suffering; he or she maintains a joyful attitude [when practicing generosity] toward beings who possess virtuous qualities;

650. S: *kalpaḥ,* T: *rtog pa.* That is, the determination that, because the bodhisattva has dedicated all his or her possessions to the buddhas and bodhisattvas of the ten directions, they no longer belong to him or her.

651. The Tibetan translation does not include "the giving of protection" (S: *abhayadānam,* T: *mi 'jigs pa'i sbyin pa*).

652. *BBhVy* (f. 144a) interprets this sentence as indicating that a bodhisattva needs to develop the qualities embodied in the four forms of informative knowledge (see Book I, chapter 17, the section entitled "The Four Forms of Informative Knowledge" [I.17.7]) as they relate to the practice of generosity. Thus, knowing "verbal formulations" (S: *paryāyaḥ,* T: *rnam grangs*) refers to the informative knowledge of Dharma; knowing "[defining] characteristics" (S: *lakṣaṇam,* T: *mtshan nyid*) refers to the informative knowledge of meanings; knowing "clear expressions" (S: *nirvacanam,* T: *nges pa'i tshig*) refers to the informative knowledge of clear expression; and knowing "causes, results, and types [of generosity]" (S: *hetuphalaprabhedāni,* T: *rgyu dang 'bras bu dang rab tu dbye ba*) refers to informative knowledge [that confers] eloquence.

he or she maintains an attitude of equanimity [when practicing generosity] toward benefactors, friends, and close associates. This too should be understood as a bodhisattva's wise form of generosity.

Four Obstacles to the Practice of Generosity [1.9.2.4]

Moreover, a bodhisattva correctly understands both the conditions that obstruct generosity and the antidotes to the conditions that obstruct generosity. Regarding this [point], the four conditions that obstruct generosity are (1) not having practiced it in the past, (2) the deficiency of having a limited number of objects suitable for giving, (3) greed for attractive objects of the best quality, and (4) the desire and [high] regard for the result of excellent wealth in the future.

[A bodhisattva] should, by means of wisdom, very quickly make the following observation: "The reason that a bodhisattva's mind does not move toward generosity even though he or she has objects that are suitable for giving and a petitioner is present is that he or she has not cultivated this practice. This is a fault of which I am guilty." He or she should also make the following observation: "It is certain that I did not practice generosity in the past regularly and this is why, even though I currently have objects that are suitable for giving and a petitioner has approached in a proper manner, my mind does not move toward generosity. If, after having made this analysis I should fail to make a gift at this time, then in the future I shall continue to be ill-disposed to [the practice of] generosity." Having made these observations, relied on the antidote to this obstruction to generosity, and completed this analysis, [a bodhisattva] makes a gift. He or she does not continue to adhere to the fault of failing to cultivate the practice and does not remain subject to this [fault].

Moreover, [a bodhisattva] should, by means of wisdom, very quickly make the observation that, if a bodhisattva's mind does not move toward generosity when a petitioner has correctly approached, due to having a limited amount of wealth, this [condition] is a consequence of adversity[653] and a cause that obstructs the practice of generosity. Having accepted and analyzed this suffering that is a consequence of adversity, [a bodhisattva,] motivated by compassion, makes a gift and reflects in the following manner:

653. *vighātakṛtam,* T: *'phongs pa las gyur pa*. "Adversity" here means the absence of wealth.

"Either because of [my] former karmic offenses or because of having been subject to the control of others, I have experienced many great forms of suffering, such as hunger, thirst, and the like, in [samsaric] existence, [yet these have occurred] without my having provided any benefit to others. Even if this generosity were to cause me suffering in this life that leads to my death, it would still be better for me to make a gift rather than turn away this petitioner. This is especially true since an individual can survive by [consuming] leafy vegetables." Accepting in this way the suffering that is a consequence of adversity, a bodhisattva makes a gift.

Moreover, [a bodhisattva] should, by means of wisdom, very quickly make the observation that, if a bodhisattva's mind does not move toward generosity when a petitioner has correctly approached, because of the great attractiveness and excellence of the object to be given, this represents for that bodhisattva a fault that is a consequence of greed. He or she should reflect, "This erroneous conception in which I regard what is suffering as a state of well-being[654] is one that will produce suffering for me in the future." Through realizing that it is an error, [a bodhisattva] abandons [this fault that is a consequence of greed]. Then, after having completed this analysis, he or she gives the object.

Moreover, [a bodhisattva] should, by means of wisdom, very quickly make the observation that if a bodhisattva, after having made a gift, develops the view that the benefit of generosity is the result of [obtaining] great wealth and not [the view] that it is [the result of attaining] unsurpassed true and complete enlightenment, this represents for that bodhisattva a fault that derives from a view that values the wrong result. Then he or she should correctly regard all conditioned entities as having no real value. Regarding all conditioned entities as perishing with each moment and the enjoyments that are their results as both perishable through being lost and perishable through our having to be separated from them,[655] [a bodhisattva] abandons

654. This is a reference to one of the four errors (S: *viparyāsaḥ*, T: *phyin ci log pa*): (1) the error that regards what is impure as pure, (2) the error that regards what is impermanent as permanent, (3) the error that regards what is suffering as a state of well-being, and (4) the error that regards what is not a [real] self as constituting a [real] self. All impure conditioned entities should be understood to constitute suffering. Ordinary sense pleasures, material prosperity, and other forms of well-being in particular represent the suffering of change (S: *vipariṇamaduḥkhatā*, T: *'gyur ba'i sdug bsngal*) in that they are transitory and our attachment to them generates suffering when they come to an end.

655. These observations make reference to two of the four "ends" of conditioned entities

the view that values [the wrong] result and then dedicates everything that he or she may give to great enlightenment.

These [instructions] should be understood as [explanations of] the four types of knowledge that constitute the antidote for the four types of obstacle that obstruct a bodhisattva's practice of generosity. They represent a penetrating observation, an acceptance of suffering, a realization of an erroneous belief, and the perception that conditioned entities have no real value. Regarding this [topic], on the basis of the first three of these corrective forms of knowledge, a bodhisattva practices generosity correctly and with conviction. On the basis of the last form of corrective knowledge, he or she develops a correct understanding of the result of merit. These, too, should be understood as [explanations of] a bodhisattva's wise form of generosity.

Practicing a Form of Generosity That Is Mental in Nature [1.9.2.5]

Moreover, having gone to a secluded place, a bodhisattva fixes [his or her mind] inwardly with a pure attitude and a deeply felt sense of goodwill[656] and, repeatedly visualizing limitless varieties of extensive objects suitable for giving, he or she generates the wish to give and present them to sentient beings. [This practice is one which is done] in such a manner that an immeasurable amount of merit is generated without difficulty. This, too, should be understood as a bodhisattva's wise form of generosity and one which represents a knowledgeable bodhisattva's great form of wise generosity.

In sum, these [explanations] should be understood as [descriptions of] the unique forms of a bodhisattva's wise generosity (1) that relate to the giving of material objects [as performed] both by those who possess objects suitable

---

(T: *'dus byas kyi mtha' bzhi*), namely, that everything that is accumulated ultimately is lost either through being used up or through decay (S: *kṣayam,* T: *zad pa*), and that everything that comes together will ultimately undergo separation (S: *viprayogaḥ,* T: *bral ba*). Cf. *Udānavargaḥ,* ch. 1, v. 22: "All accumulations are lost in the end; / Everything that rises ends up falling; / All coming together ends in separation; / Every living thing in the end must die."

656. S: *prasādaḥ,* T *dang ba*. This term, whose principal meaning is "clarity" or "purity," often is used to indicate a particular kind of faith that views an object, such as the Three Jewels, with joyful reverence (see note 220). However, it can also mean "graciousness," "kindness," "favor," and "aid" (MW, p. 697). Here the term seems to be that of a bodhisattva's favorable disposition toward sentient beings.

for giving and those who do not possess them, as well as [the forms] (2) that relate to the giving of Dharma, (3) that relate to informative knowledge, (4) that relate to the [appropriate type of] superior attitude [that should be employed when practicing] generosity, (5) that relate to the knowledge that corrects obstructions to generosity, and (6) that relate to the generosity [that is cultivated by means] of a superior attitude together with visualizations. Similarly, these [explanations] should also be understood as an extensive presentation of the types of generosity that a bodhisattva practices using all forms of inner and outer objects. [Finally,] it should be understood that from this point forward [the remainder of this chapter will address] all the divisions [relating to the topic of generosity] other than that of all-inclusive generosity, such as the generosity that is difficult to carry out, etc.

The Generosity That Is Difficult to Carry Out [1.9.3]

Regarding this [topic], what is the form of generosity that is difficult for a bodhisattva to carry out?

The first form of generosity that is difficult for a bodhisattva to carry out is that in which one must inflict hardship upon oneself because of possessing only a limited quantity of objects to give and yet one accepts this suffering as one makes an offering to others. The second form of generosity that is difficult for a bodhisattva to carry out is that in which one must overcome one's attachment to a most excellent and choice object that is suitable for giving—an object that is cherished either because of a natural fondness for it, because of a long-term familiarity with it, or because of its great usefulness—as one makes an offering to others. The third form of generosity that is difficult for a bodhisattva to carry out is that in which one must make an offering to others of objects suitable for giving that were acquired with difficulty.

The Generosity That Is Directed Everywhere [1.9.4]

What is the generosity of a bodhisattva that is directed everywhere?

It is that [form of generosity] in which a bodhisattva gives his or her own objects that are suitable for giving, or those that have been acquired from others, to his or her dependents—[including] mother, father, children, spouse, male and female servants, workmen, hired persons, friends, advisers,[657] near relations, and kinsmen—or that [form of generosity] in which [he or she gives either of these two types of objects] to other petitioners. This is known as "the generosity that is directed everywhere." In short, it is a bodhisattva's [generosity] that has four aspects.[658]

The Generosity of a True Spiritual Being [1.9.5]

Regarding this [point], what is the generosity of a true spiritual being that is carried out by a bodhisattva who is a true spiritual being?[659]

The gift that a bodhisattva makes out of faith, respectfully, with his or her own hand, at the appropriate time, and without doing harm to others is [the generosity] of a bodhisattva who is a true spiritual being and it is called "the generosity of a true spiritual being."[660]

Generosity of Every Form [1.9.6]

Regarding this [point], what is a bodhisattva's generosity of every form?

These thirteen forms of generosity that are practiced by a bodhisattva are called "generosity of every form": (1) disinterested generosity,[661] (2) unstinting

657. S: *amātyaḥ,* also *āmātyaḥ;* T: *gros 'grogs pa*. I translate the term here according to the Tibetan equivalent. However, MW (p. 81) has "inmate of the same house," "[person] belonging to the same house or family," "a companion (of a king)," and "minister." This term is also rendered in Tibetan as *blon po* ("minister," *MVy,* no. 3681).

658. *BBhVy* (f. 145b): "Because it is carried out in relation to two types of objects that are suitable to be given and because it is carried out in relation to two types of recipients, it constitutes the generosity that is pursued by every means. It has four aspects because it is carried out with regard to four circumstances." The two types of objects are one's own property and that which is acquired from others; the two types of recipients are those with whom one has a personal relationship and all others who are in need of something.

659. S: *satpuruṣaḥ,* T: *skyes bu dam pa*. Literally a "good person" or a "wise person," I translate the term as "true spiritual being" to indicate a person who is both virtuous and wise. *MSA,* ch. 13, v. 8: "A bodhisattva with extensive learning / Who has perceived the truths, / And who is eloquent, compassionate, and tireless / Should be recognized as a great spiritual being."

660. Cf. *Aṅguttara Nikāya,* V.148.

661. S: *aniśritadānatā,* T: *mi brten par sbyin pa*. The Sanskrit adjective *aniśrita* literally means "not dependent" [on something]. *BBhVṛ* (f. 180a) explains this as generosity "that does not hope for some future reward." *BBhVy* (f. 146b): "'Disinterested generosity' is giving that is done freely (S: **muktatyāgah,* T: *lhug par gtong ba*)—that is, it is done without any desire for fame and the like."

generosity,[662] (3) joyful generosity, (4) constant generosity, (5) generosity toward a worthy person,[663] (6) generosity that is not toward a worthy person,[664] (7) generosity that gives everything,[665] (8) universal generosity,[666] (9) generosity at all times,[667] (10) generosity that is not objectionable, (11) generosity that gives sentient beings,[668] (12) generosity that gives objects consisting of land, and (13) generosity that gives objects consisting of wealth and grain.[669]

Generosity That Relates to the Distressed and What They Want [1.9.7]

What is a bodhisattva's generosity that relates to the distressed and what they want?

A bodhisattva here gives food and drink to those distressed persons who [are in need of and] want food and drink; vehicles to those who want a

662. S: *viśadadānatā,* T: *mi sri bar sbyin pa. BBhVy* (f. 146b): "It is 'unstinting generosity' because the hand is always extended."

663. S: *pātradānatā,* T: *snod la sbyin pa. BBhVy* (f. 146b): "[Generosity] that is excellent is called 'generosity toward a worthy person'; it is generosity toward someone who does not engage in wrong livelihood."

664. S: *apātradānatā,* T: *snod ma yin pa la sbyin pa.* Both *BBhVy* (f. 146b) and *BBhVṛ* (f. 180a) gloss this term as meaning a form of generosity in which one is disposed to share with others. *BBhVy* adds that it is a form in which one is generous with everyone, from religious ascetics to a traveler that one may encounter on a road.

665. S: *sarvadānatā,* T: *thams cad sbyin pa. BBhVy* (f. 146b): "'Generosity that gives everything' is [a form of generosity] that gives every kind of inner object without exception."

666. S: *sarvatra dānam,* T: *kun la sbyin pa. BBhVy* (f. 146b): "'Universal generosity' is generosity that is practiced toward those who harm, those who benefit, those who have good spiritual qualities, and those who are suffering. Alternatively, 'universal generosity' is generosity that is practiced in one's own region as well as elsewhere."

667. S: *sarvakāladadānatā,* T: *dus thams du sbyin pa. BBhVy* (f. 146b): "Giving at all times of the day and night is 'generosity at all times,' that is, [it is a practice] that has no fixed time. Also, 'giving at all times' means giving in all circumstances, that is, when one is wealthy as well as when one is poor."

668. See above where the text indicates that while there are circumstances in which a bodhisattva is willing to give up his or her own child or spouse, male or female servants, workers, hired persons, or members of his or her retinue, he or she is never permitted to give away his or her parents.

669. *BBhVy* (f. 146b) describes the last three types as "generosity [of things that are] a source of income" (S: **āyadvārabhūtadānam,* T: *'du ba'i sgor gyur pa'i sbyin pa*).

vehicle; clothes to those who want clothes; ornaments to those who want ornaments; various household goods and implements to those who want various household goods and implements; fragrances, garlands, and ointments to those who want fragrances, garlands, and ointments; dwellings to those who want dwellings; and lamps to those who want lamps. This should be understood as a bodhisattva's eight forms of generosity that relate to the distressed and what they want.

Generosity That Brings Happiness Here and in the Next World [1.9.8]

What is a bodhisattva's generosity that brings happiness here and in the next world?

In brief, it should be understood that the generosity that brings happiness to sentient beings here and in the next world consists of giving material things,[670] giving the Dharma, and giving protection. Moreover, with the giving of material things [a bodhisattva] dispels the impurity of stinginess and the impurity of hoarding, and gives [a material object] that is excellent, clean, and proper. Regarding this, it should be understood that the impurity of stinginess is dispelled through renouncing [the attitude of] grasping tightly with the mind, and the impurity of hoarding is dispelled through renouncing [the attitude of] grasping tightly to possessions. Giving protection should be understood as that which is accomplished by providing protection from the fear caused by lions, tigers, predatory marine animals,[671] the king, robbers, water, and the like. Giving the Dharma consists of teaching the Dharma unerringly, giving proper instruction,[672] and causing [others] to take up the precepts of spiritual training. All of these nine forms[673]

670. S: *āmiṣadānam,* T: *zang zing gi sbyin pa. BBhVy* (f. 147b): "'Giving material things' is characterized by the giving of [physical] objects that have value (S: *vastu,* T: *dngos po*), because they give support to the [physical] body."

671. S: *grāhaḥ,* T: *chu srin 'dzin khri.* MW (p. 372): "a rapacious animal living in fresh or sea water, any large fish or marine animal (crocodile, shark, serpent, Gangetic alligator, water elephant or hippopotamus)." Thus, any large predatory marine animal that poses a danger even to humans.

672. S: *nyāyopadeśaḥ,* T: *rigs par ston pa. BBhVy* (f. 148a) describes this as "giving instruction in [how to carry out] worldly activities properly and in a manner that avoids anything that is morally objectionable."

673. The commentary to the *Saṃdhinirmocanasūtra* (T: *'Phags pa dgongs pa nges par 'grel*

combined together constitute a bodhisattva's generosity that brings happiness to sentient beings here and in the next world. Regarding that, the varieties [of giving] that constitute giving material things and protection bring happiness here, and the varieties [of giving] that constitute giving the Dharma bring happiness in the next world.

Pure Generosity [1.9.9]

Regarding this [topic], what is a bodhisattva's pure generosity?

It should be understood as having ten forms. [They are] (1) that which is not delayed, (2) that which is not wrongly considered to be supreme, (3) that which does not [consist of] giving things that have been stored up, (4) that which is free of haughtiness, (5) that which is disinterested, (6) that which is free of dejection, (7) that which is not meager, (8) that which is free of aversion, (9) that which doesn't seek anything in return, and (10) that which doesn't seek a [karmic] maturation.

Regarding these, what is generosity that is not delayed?

When a petitioner has appeared, a bodhisattva here makes a gift to him or her quickly and without procrastinating. The petitioner should not feel the [same degree of] urgency about receiving [a gift] that a bodhisattva does in giving it.

What is generosity that is not wrongly considered to be supreme?

A bodhisattva should not consider any of the following views about generosity to be correct: "This act of generosity will not yield a result." "A gift that causes harm constitutes [true] Dharma."[674] "Well-completed generosity by itself will bring about mundane and transcendent purity."

---

pa'i rnam par bshad pa; Tg. vol. 205, ff. 276b–277a) by Jangchub Dzutrul (T: Byang chub rdzu 'phrul) identifies the nine forms as follows: "What are the nine forms of generosity that bring happiness here and in the next world? The three that relate to giving material things are the giving of (1) excellent, (2) clean, and (3) proper [material objects], after having dispelled the impurity of stinginess and the impurity of hoarding. The three that relate to giving protection are the safeguarding of beings from (1) animals, (2) humans, and (3) inanimate things [i.e., water, fire, etc.]. The three that relate to giving the Dharma are (1) teaching the Dharma unerringly, (2) giving proper instruction, and (3) causing [others] to take up the precepts of spiritual training."

674. For example, sacrificing animals to a worldly god should not be considered a form of true Dharma practice.

What is generosity that does not [consist of] giving things that have been stored up?

A bodhisattva does not, after repeatedly collecting things over a long period of time, create a store of objects that are suitable for giving and then later make a gift of them all at once.

Why is that?

A bodhisattva who possesses objects that are suitable for giving is incapable of turning away a petitioner who has appeared in a proper manner. One does not even consider that it would be proper to turn someone away, much less that one should create a store [of objects suitable for giving].

A bodhisattva also does not regard practicing generosity with things that have been stored up to be a greater source of merit, because this is how he or she sees things: "If the quantity of objects that are given is the same and the number of petitioners is identical whether they come separately or in a group, why would someone acquire a different quantity of merit if he or she made gifts to them gradually or all at once?"

A bodhisattva also regards practicing generosity with things that have been stored up to be morally objectionable and practicing generosity with objects of value [by giving them] as they are obtained to be free of any objection.

Why is that?

It is because when the donor who practices generosity with things that have been stored up is asked by petitioners [to make a donation], by initially turning away a hundred petitioners he or she causes them to develop animosity, intolerance, and distrust. Then later, even though not having been asked [to make a donation], he or she makes a gift to some portion of them with things that have been stored up. Therefore, a bodhisattva does not practice generosity with things that have been stored up.

What is generosity that is free of haughtiness?

A bodhisattva makes a gift to a petitioner with a humble mind. He or she does not make a gift out of a sense of rivalry toward others. After having made a gift, he or she also does not, because of that gift, conceitedly think, "I am a donor and great patron; no one else is my equal."

What is generosity that is disinterested?[675]

A bodhisattva does not make a gift that is based upon [a desire for] fame,

675. S: *aniśritadānam,* T: *mi brten pa'i sbyin pa*. See note 661. That is, it is a form of generosity that is not based upon attachment to a worldly aim, such as the desire for fame.

praise, acclaim, or renown. He or she considers fame to be derived from words [generated by] the imagination, bound to nothing more than sound, and as insignificant as dried-up leaves.

What is generosity that is free of dejection?

Before making a gift, a bodhisattva here is happy. During the act of giving, he or she remains glad. After having made a gift, he or she does not feel any remorse. Upon hearing of [other] bodhisattvas' extensive and extremely liberal acts of generosity, he or she does not become timid or disparage him- or herself.

What is generosity that is not meager?

After careful and repeated consideration, a bodhisattva offers, from the objects that [he or she] has to give, the food, drink, vehicles, clothing, etc., that are best and most excellent.

What is generosity that is free of aversion?

When giving a gift, a bodhisattva is even-minded, impartial, and feels the same compassion toward friends, foes, and neutral persons.

What is generosity that doesn't seek anything in return?

A bodhisattva maintains a compassionate mind and a sympathetic mind when making a gift and does not expect to receive anything back from someone else. He or she perceives that [all] humankind desires happiness, is tormented by the fever of craving, is powerless, and is in a natural state of suffering.

What is generosity that doesn't seek a [karmic] maturation?

A bodhisattva who makes a gift does not expect that in the future [that] gift will ripen into the fruit of excellent wealth or an excellent physical form. He or she views all conditioned entities as worthless[676] and supreme enlightenment as what is [truly] beneficial.

It is by means of these ten aspects that the generosity of bodhisattvas becomes pure.

By relying upon the generosity [that was described] in this way as consisting of these nine aspects and after completing the perfection of generosity, bodhisattvas attain unsurpassed and true enlightenment.

676. S: *phalguḥ,* T: *snying po med pa. BBhVy* (f. 149a): "[The bodhisattva] is described as '[one who] views all conditioned entities as worthless' because they are bound by the two forms of impermanence." See above where all conditioned entities are described as being (1) impermanent in that they disappear from moment to moment and (2) perishable either in the sense that they will eventually be lost or in the sense that one will eventually be separated from them.

Within [Book I of] *The Stage of a Bodhisattva,* [known as] "The Object of Mental Application That Relates to the Support," this completes the ninth chapter, entitled "Generosity."

10

Morality

Summary verses:

The essence, all-inclusive,
Difficult to carry out, directed everywhere,
Connected with the qualities of a true spiritual person,
Likewise, all of its forms,

Relating to what is wanted by those in distress,
What brings happiness here and in the next world,
And, likewise, that which is pure—
These, in brief, are the nine aspects of morality.

Regarding this [topic], what is the morality of bodhisattvas?

It should be understood as having nine divisions: (1) the essence of morality, (2) all-inclusive morality, (3) morality that is difficult to carry out, (4) morality that is directed everywhere, (5) the morality of a true spiritual being, (6) morality in all of its forms, (7) morality that relates to what is wanted by those who are in distress, (8) morality that brings happiness here and in the next world, and (9) morality that is pure.

The Essence of Morality [1.10.1]

Regarding this [point], what is the essence of morality?

In brief, it should be understood that the essence of a bodhisattva's morality is possessed of four qualities.

What are the four?

They are (1) to accept [the morality] correctly from another person; (2)

to do so with an extremely pure attitude; (3) to remedy any transgressions; and (4) having developed a respect for remaining free of transgressions, to abide in a state of recollection.

Regarding this [point], through accepting the morality from another person, a bodhisattva develops abashment[677] in relation to others if he or she violates [any precepts of] the training. Through having an extremely pure attitude toward the moral precepts, a bodhisattva develops shame[678] in relation to self if he or she violates [any precepts of] the training. A bodhisattva remains free of regret through these two causes: (1) remedying any transgressions of the training's precepts and (2) developing from the very outset a respect for remaining free of any transgressions. In this way, by relying on acceptance [of the morality] and doing so with a pure attitude, a bodhisattva generates shame and abashment. Through shame and abashment, he or she protects the morality that has been accepted. By protecting it, he or she is free of regret.

Regarding this, the two qualities of accepting [the morality] from another and having a pure attitude [toward the morality] represent the factors that bring forth the two qualities of remedying transgressions and having respect for remaining free of transgressions. Regarding them, the three qualities of (1) accepting [the morality] from another person, (2) having an extremely pure attitude, and (3) taking care to remain free of transgressions should be understood as the ones that prevent a bodhisattva's morality from being ruined. For its part, [the quality of] remedying transgressions should be understood as the countermeasure that restores [a bodhisattva's morality] when it has become marred.

Moreover, the essential morality of bodhisattvas that possesses four qualities should be understood as being good[679] in that it is accepted and

677. *AS* (p. 6): "What is abashment (S: *vyapatrāpyam,* T: *khrel yod pa*)? It is embarrassment about objectionable acts because of [one's relationships with] others. Its action is the very same [as that of shame]." See also description in the opening section of chapter 17.

678. *AS* (p. 6): "What is shame (S: *hrīḥ,* T: *ngo tsha shes pa*)? It is embarrassment about objectionable acts [that is felt] of one's own accord. Its action is to provide the support [that enables you] to restrain yourself from committing misdeeds." See also description in the opening section of chapter 17.

679. S: *kalyāṇam,* T: *dge ba*. This Sanskrit adjective can indicate a wide range of meanings, including "beautiful," "agreeable," "illustrious," "excellent," "virtuous," "good," "beneficial," "salutary," "auspicious," "happy," "prosperous," and "fortunate" (MW, p. 263). The sense of "good" here should be understood to mean "beneficial." *BŚPṬ* (f. 182a): "[A bodhisattva's

cultivated to benefit oneself, to benefit others, to benefit a great number of beings, to provide happiness to a great number of beings, with compassion toward the world, and for the welfare, benefit, and happiness of gods and humans.[680] It should be understood as being immeasurable because it encompasses immeasurable forms of training for a bodhisattva. It should be understood as providing aid to sentient beings, because of its quality of attending to the benefit and happiness of all beings. It should be understood as having a great result and a great benefit because it obtains and bestows the result of unsurpassed true enlightenment.[681]

All-Inclusive Morality [1.10.2]

What is a bodhisattva's all-inclusive morality?

In brief, the morality of a bodhisattva that pertains to the faction[682] that is made up of householders and [the morality of a bodhisattva] that pertains to the faction that is made up of those who have gone forth [into the homeless state] is called "all-inclusive morality."

Moreover, the morality that is observed by the faction that is made up of householders and [the morality] that is observed by the faction that is made up of those who have gone forth [into the homeless state] consists in brief of

---

essential morality is endowed with] the quality of being good because it does not disagree with reality (S: **avisaṃvādanam,* T: *mi slu ba*) [i.e., it is truly effective]. The quality of not disagreeing with reality means that it accomplishes one's own and others' aims (S: **ātmaparārthasaṃpādanam,* T: *bdag dang gzhan gyi don sgrub pa*)." Note: the *BBhVy* commentary on the *BBh* morality chapter simply reproduces *BŚPṬ*, suggesting that Jinaputra's earlier treatise was considered authoritative. The minor differences in language between the two Tibetan versions indicates only that they are the work of different translators. This is why there are no references to *BBhVy* in the footnotes of this chapter.

680. *BŚPBh* (f. 182a–182b) and *BŚPṬ* (ff. 182a–183b) give detailed interpretations of the phrases that indicate why a bodhisattva's morality is characterized as being "good."

681. *BŚPṬ* (f. 183b): "[A bodhisattva's essential morality] 'has a great result' because, while one is on the stage of a bodhisattva, it obtains the great result of unsurpassed true enlightenment [for the practitioner], and it 'has a great benefit' because, when one has reached the stage of a buddha, it bestows that result [upon others]."

682. S: *pakṣaḥ*, T: *phyogs*. This term is meant simply to distinguish between two categories of Great Vehicle practitioners: monastics and householders; no sense of conflict between them is intended. Its use here can be taken to mean simply a "class of beings" (MW, p. 573). Nevertheless, the lifestyle of the "homeless ascetic" or monastic is unambiguously considered to be superior to that of the householder. See the final paragraph of Book II, chapter 2, entitled "Factions," and *MSA*, ch. 20, v. 5.

three types: (1) the morality of restraint, (2) the morality of acquiring virtuous entities, and (3) the morality that acts on behalf of beings.

The Morality of Restraint [1.10.2.1]

Regarding this, the morality of restraint is the acceptance of the discipline of individual liberation,[683] which is made up of seven categories: (1) the morality of a fully ordained monk, (2) the morality of a fully ordained nun, (3) the morality of a probationary nun, (4) the morality of a novice monk, (5) the morality of a novice nun, (6) the morality of a layman, and (7) the morality of a laywoman. These should be understood, in the appropriate manner, as relating either to the faction of beings who are householders or to the faction of beings who have gone forth.

The Morality of Acquiring Virtuous Qualities [1.10.2.2]

Regarding this [topic], the morality of acquiring virtuous qualities is whatever virtue a bodhisattva accumulates by body and speech for the sake of [achieving] enlightenment, following acceptance of the morality discipline.

683. S: *prātimokṣasaṃvaraḥ,* T: *so sor thar pa'i sdom pa.* The term *saṃvaraḥ* (T: *sdom pa*) is often translated as "vow" when it refers to the individual precepts that are accepted as part of one of the forms of Buddhist morality training. I translate it as "restraint" in the phrase "morality of restraint" because the term comes from a verbal root that means "to hold back" or "restrain." See note 279. I also translate it here as "discipline" in the phrase "discipline of individual liberation" to indicate an overall system of ethical practice. The Kadampa Vinaya master Tsonawa Sherab Sangpo (T: mTsho sna ba Shes rab bzang po, fl. late thirteenth–fourteenth century) presents three explanations of the term "individual liberation" (S: *prātimokṣaḥ,* T: *so sor thar pa*) in his commentary *Light Rays of the Sun* (T: *Nyi ma'i 'od zer*). All three are based on different interpretations of the prefix *prāti.* The first takes it to mean "individual" (T: *so sor*) and thus *prātimokṣa* discipline is a "discipline of individual liberation" in the sense that each individual person who observes morality is able to gain his or her own liberation from the lower realms and samsara, but no one can gain liberation through someone else's observance of morality. According to a second interpretation, *prāti* means "first" (T: *dang por*) and, hence, *prātimokṣa* discipline is a "discipline of first liberation" because in the first moment that the *prātimokṣa* discipline is achieved one is liberated from whatever form of negative discipline one may have possessed before. A third interpretation uses Sanskrit grammatical theory to derive the sense of being a "means" (T: *thabs*) and thus *prātimokṣa* discipline is a "discipline that provides a means of [attaining] liberation."

All of that [virtue], in brief, is called "the morality of acquiring virtuous qualities."

What, then, does that consist of?

Here a bodhisattva, relying on morality and being firmly established in morality, exerts [him- or herself] with regard to learning, reflection, and the meditation that consists of quiescence and insight and delights in solitude.

Similarly, [a bodhisattva,] regularly and at appropriate times, makes respectful verbal salutations, makes obeisance, stands up [as a gesture of deference], and greets with joined palms those who are worthy of being venerated. Likewise, one respectfully waits on those very same persons worthy of veneration. One cares for those who are sick and attends to their illnesses with compassion. Likewise, one expresses approval when an eloquent speech is made. One voices genuine praise of persons who possess virtuous qualities. Likewise, after developing a mind that is deeply pleased at all the merit of all sentient beings in the ten directions, one rejoices [at this virtue] and says so in words. Likewise, after pondering all the transgressions [committed by sentient beings], one generates patience toward others. Likewise, [one] dedicates all the virtue that [one] has done and not [yet] done[684] by body, speech, or mind to unsurpassed true enlightenment. Regularly and at appropriate times, one makes a variety of correct aspirational prayers[685] and all manner of extensive forms of worshipping the Three Jewels. One also applies oneself to and initiates effort toward [everything] that pertains to virtue, always and continuously. One abides in [a state of] mindfulness in relation to [one's] body and speech.[686] One keeps watch over the precepts of the training by practicing recollection and vigilance.[687] One keeps the doors

684. T: *byas pa dang ma byas pa*. The Tibetan translation indicates both the virtue that has already been done and that which will be done in the future; the Sanskrit editions only mention that virtue which has been completed.

685. S: *samyakpraṇidhānam*, T: *yang dag pa'i smon lam*. *BŚPṬ* (f. 185a) alludes to the ten great aspirational prayers. Tsongkapa's commentary (*BChZhL*, f. 14a) identifies them as the ones that are mentioned in the *Sutra on the Ten Stages* in connection with a bodhisattva who has attained the first of the ten stages, and also makes reference to the *Aspirational Prayers for Wholly Auspicious Practice* (S: *Samantabhadracaryāpraṇidhānam*, T: *bZang po spyod pa'i smon lam*), a devotional text in verse that appears at the end of the *Gaṇḍavyūhasūtram*. See also note 144.

686. Both Sanskrit editions construe the phrase "in relation to body and speech" with the practice of mindfulness. The Tibetan translation construes it with the aim of keeping watch over the precepts of the training mentioned in the next sentence.

687. Recollection (S: *smṛtiḥ*, T: *dran pa*) and vigilance (S: *samprajanyam*, T: *shes bzhin*) are

of one's faculties guarded, knows moderation with regard to food, strives to remain wakeful during the first and last parts of the night,[688] serves true spiritual beings,[689] and relies upon spiritual teachers.[690] One is aware of one's own mistakes and sees them as faults.[691] Having realized [one's mistakes] and seen [them as faults], one rejects them. Having erred, one also confesses [one's] violations in the presence of the buddhas, bodhisattvas, and followers of the same form of Dharma.[692] The morality [that is cultivated] in order to gain, preserve, and increase these kinds of virtuous entities is called a bodhisattva's "morality of acquiring virtuous qualities."

The Morality That Acts on Behalf of Beings [1.10.2.3]

Regarding this [topic], what is a bodhisattva's morality that acts on behalf of beings?

---

qualities that are essential to Buddhist practice whether one is engaged in ordinary activities or meditating in solitude. Śāntideva states (*BCA,* ch. 5, v. 213): "To those who wish to guard their minds / I make this appeal with palms joined: / You must use every effort to observe / Both recollection and vigilance." Asaṅga describes the generic form of recollection as follows (*AS,* p. 6): "What is recollection? It is the avoidance of inattentiveness toward a familiar object. Its action is to prevent distraction." Śāntideva describes vigilance, which is a form of wisdom, as follows (*BCA,* ch. 5, v. 108): "In short, the essential nature / Of vigilance is simply this: / To examine again and again / The state of your body and mind." The role of vigilance is to observe both one's body in its physical surroundings and one's mind in order to avert potential obstacles and to recognize any improper motivations or mental attitudes that might arise. Moreover, the ability to develop a proper degree of vigilance is dependent on the cultivation of recollection. Again, Śāntideva states (*BCA,* ch. 5, v. 33): "The time at which vigilance arrives / And, once come, does not depart again / Is when recollection, in order to guard / The mind, remains fixed at its door."

688. That is, he or she strives to remain awake and alert throughout the day, sleeping only during the middle third of the night.

689. See note 659.

690. S: *kalyāṇamitraḥ,* T: *dge ba'i bshes gnyen*. See below, Book I, chapter 16, the section entitled "Serving a Spiritual Teacher" [I.16.2]. See also *MSA,* ch. 17, v. 10.

691. S: *doṣadarśī,* T: *nyes par lta ba*. *BŚPṬ* (f. 185b): "Moreover, through seeing that [those mistakes] have bad consequences in this life as well as in future lives, one sees them as faults."

692. S: *sahadhārmikaḥ,* T: *chos mthun pa*. *Bod rgya tshig mdzod chen mo* gives two explanations of this term: (1) "one who adheres to the same philosophical system," and (2) "a person who practices Dharma properly." *BChZhL* (ff. 14b) glosses the term here as meaning those who practice the same form of Dharma. Elsewhere this term is also translated as "exemplary Dharma follower." See notes 732 and note 823.

In brief, it should be understood as having eleven forms.

What are the eleven forms?

They are (1a) assisting sentient beings with a variety of meaningful activities and (1b) assisting sentient beings who are experiencing an illness or any other form of suffering, by helping them deal with their sickness, etc.; (2) similarly, giving proper instruction in the form of teaching Dharma and teaching methods that relate to mundane and transcendent aims; (3) undertaking to return a favor in a suitable manner as a way of showing gratitude toward beings who have helped you; (4) protecting beings from various sources of danger, such as lions, tigers, the king, robbers, water, and fire; (5) dispelling grief caused by misfortune that relates to possessions or family members; (6) providing, in a proper manner, all those objects that are a means of subsistence[693] to beings who are in need of objects that are a means of subsistence; (7) leading a body [of practitioners] by providing [them with] a proper abode, in a manner that accords with Dharma;[694] (8) receiving food, drink, and the like from others by approaching them at appropriate times and conversing with them, chatting with them, and pleasing them; engaging in orderly discourse [with others] regarding worldly affairs;[695] coming and going in response to invitations [from others]—in short, [acting in a way that] complies with the minds [of others], while avoiding all forms of unattractive and wrongful behavior; (9) giving encouragement [to others]

693. S: *upakaraṇam,* T: *yo byad.* The Sanskrit term can mean (MW, p. 195) "instrument" or "implement" (that is used for accomplishing some particular activity) or, more generally, a "means of subsistence" and "anything that supports life." The Tibetan equivalent suggests the narrower sense of "implement." However, as the text clarifies later (see the section entitled "Furnishing the Objects That Are Needed for Subsistence" [I.10.2.6.6]), it would seem that the word is meant in the broader sense of anything that is needed by a person to pursue his or her particular way of life.

694. Both Sanskrit editions present the instrumental case *dharmeṇa,* which means "according to Dharma" or "in a just manner." However, multiple editions of the Tibetan translation render *chos* in the genitive case, which suggests it modifies "body [of practitioners]" and thus should be read "body of Dharma [practitioners]" (T: *chos kyi tshogs*). However, *BŚPṬ* (f. 196a) supports the instrumental form with the following gloss: "leading a body [of practitioners] by providing an abode to those who depend upon [others for] an abode, [and doing so] with a mind that is free of corporeal desire (S: **nirāmiṣacittena,* T: *zang zing med pa'i sems kyis*)."

695. S: *laukikārthānuvyavahārataḥ,* T: *'jig rten pa'i don dang mthun par.* See note 535, where the term *anuvyavahāraḥ* occurs in relation to the first of a group of ten causes. Note also that there the Tibetan equivalent is *rjes su tha snyad 'dogs pa.*

by declaring their genuine good qualities, either in private or openly;[696] (10) carrying out acts of suppression in the form of a reprimand, the imposition of a punishment, or banishment, with a mind that is inwardly affectionate and holds the superior attitude of wanting to benefit [those who are involved, and doing so] for the express purpose of turning them away from opportunities [to engage in] nonvirtuous [actions] and establishing them in opportunities [to engage in] virtuous [actions]; and (11) causing [beings] to recoil from nonvirtue by using miraculous powers to directly reveal the migratory states of the hells, etc., and winning over, pleasing, and astonishing [beings], so that they will dedicate themselves to the Buddha's teaching.

Conduct That Is Well Restrained [1.10.2.4]

How does a bodhisattva who is abiding in the morality of restraint, abiding in the morality of acquiring virtue, and abiding in the morality of acting on behalf of beings become one whose conduct is well restrained, one whose conduct acquires virtue effectively, and one whose conduct addresses every aspect of acting on behalf of sentient beings?

If a bodhisattva who is established here in the discipline of individual liberation were to renounce the kingdom of a wheel ruler to become one who has gone forth [into the homeless state], he or she would have the same lack of interest in that wheel ruler's kingdom as he or she has toward straw or excrement. A person of low social standing who abandons insignificant forms of pleasure and goes forth [into the homeless state] with the aim of [taking up that lifestyle in order to gain] a means of livelihood does not have a lack of interest in those insignificant pleasures that is equal to [the lack of interest] that a bodhisattva who has gone forth motivated by a pure attitude feels toward the most excellent of all human forms of pleasure, [which is to say] the pleasures [that are enjoyed by] a wheel ruler.

696. S: *rahaḥ prakāśaṃ vā*, T: *lkog gam ming* (?) *sngar*. That is, praising the individual directly but without others being present, or doing so before others in a public forum. MW (p. 653) gives one interpretation of *prakāśam* as "before the eyes of all," suggesting that the Tibetan equivalent *ming sngar* ("before the name") may be a corruption of *mig sngar*, which literally means "before the eyes."

A bodhisattva also does not harbor any desire for future pleasures, not even those that are found in Māra's domain,[697] let alone those of any other divine realm. Nor does he or she engage in a pure spiritual life[698] through having resolved to attain [divine pleasures], [since] he or she perceives those [divine] pleasures as they truly are—[which is to say, that they are] like an entrance leading into a dense forest filled with many kinds of great dangers.

With regard to the present, a bodhisattva who has gone forth [into the homeless state] sees by means of his or her right wisdom that even great forms of gain and honor received from exalted beings are like vomited food and does not relish them, much less [does he or she relish] those insignificant forms [of gain and honor] received from beings of low standing.

[A bodhisattva] also dwells alone, delighting in solitude. When in the midst of the Sangha, he or she maintains an isolated mind[699] at all times. He or she is not satisfied just with practicing restraint as a form of morality. Relying on and established in that morality, he or she strives to develop and attain mastery of the bodhisattvas' limitless forms of one-pointed concentration. When associating with others, he or she does not indulge in even the slightest form of wrongful conversation or wrongful speech. When in a place of solitude, he or she does not indulge in even the slightest form of wrongful deliberation.[700]

Regularly and at appropriate times, one generates strong regret at having

697. Māra is identified as the chief deity of the class known as Those Who Control Others' Magical Creations (S: *paranirmitavaśavarttinaḥ,* T: *gzhan 'phrul dbang byed*). See notes 358 and 433.

698. S: *brahmacaryam,* T: *tshangs par spyod pa*. The term *brahmacaryam* (which is not unique to Buddhism) often is meant to indicate the celibate aspect of a Buddhist ordained person's spiritual life. However, its broader meaning encompasses all aspects of that religious lifestyle. *MSA* (ch. 12, v. 15) describes its four main qualities: "The pure spiritual life is regarded as having four qualities: / It is a unique practice that is not shared by others; / It is complete by abandoning the three realms' mental afflictions; / It is naturally pure and it purifies one's stains." Sthiramati's commentary on this verse adds (*MSAVṛBh,* vol. 125, f. 240a): "Purity (S: *brahman,* T: *tshangs pa*) refers to nirvana. . . . The āryas' path that leads to the attainment of nirvana is called 'pure spiritual life.'"

699. S: *vyavakṛṣṭacittavihārī,* T: *sems dben par gnas pa*. *BChZhL* (f. 16a) glosses an "isolated mind" as one that "distances itself from deliberation (S: *vitarkaḥ,* T: *rtog pa*) about sensory pleasures, and the like." See next note.

700. See notes 204 and 457 for descriptions of this mental factor. See also section below entitled "Assisting Those Who Are Experiencing Physical or Mental Suffering" [I.10.2.6.1b], where a variety of topics are identified as improper objects of deliberation.

engaged in [any of] those [forms of wrongful] conduct due to clouded recollection[701] and recognizes the disadvantages [of having done so]. Through having repeatedly generated regret [about such improper behavior] and having [repeatedly] considered its disadvantages, [one's] recollection becomes established very quickly, as soon as any form of wrongful conversation or wrongful deliberation occurs. One also develops the thought that wants to avoid committing [such actions] and [this thought] constitutes the means by which one draws back [from such wrongful thought and speech]. Through cultivating [this impulse of] drawing back [in this way], one gradually comes to abide [in a state that] delights in the avoidance of that conduct and becomes averse to that conduct to the same degree that one previously took pleasure in it.

Upon hearing about all the bodhisattva precepts that are observed by bodhisattvas who have attained the great stages, one does not become frightened, diffident, or timid [about the fact that they are] vast, unlimited, and inconceivable, or that they must be practiced for long periods of time and they are extremely difficult to carry out. One reflects in this very manner: "The ones who have trained themselves gradually in the bodhisattva trainings and who have developed restraint by possessing the physical and verbal discipline that is unlimited and inconceivable did so as human beings. I, too, am a human being and, by gradually training myself, I shall also without doubt attain success in that [very same] physical and verbal discipline."

A bodhisattva also is one who becomes established in the moral discipline by examining his or her own faults and inner failings, not by examining the faults and inner failings of others. He or she does not develop animosity or hatred toward any sentient beings who are violent and engage in wrongful conduct. Relying upon a form of great compassion that is [based upon] entities,[702] he or she develops a bodhisattva's [attitude of] especially strong sympathy toward such beings and a desire to act [on their behalf].

701. S: *muṣitasmṛtitā,* T: *brjed ngas pa*. This mental factor is included in a traditional list of twenty secondary mental afflictions. *AS* (p. 9): "What is clouded recollection? It is recollection that is concomitant with a mental affliction. Its action is to provide support for distraction."

702. S: *dharmamahākaruṇatām upādāya,* T: *chos bzhin gyi snying rje chen po la brten nas*. This expression may be related to the form of compassion that holds entities as the mental object (S: *dharmālambanā karuṇā,* T: *chos la dmigs pa'i snying rje*) by recognizing persons to be a mere collection of entities (see Book I, chapter 16, the section entitled "The Immeasurables" [I.16.3]. *BChZhL* (f. 17a) explains this form of compassion as follows: "How does [a

The bodhisattva who is established in the morality of restraint does not even become angry with others when struck with a hand, a lump of earth, a stick, or a weapon, much less does he or she utter evil speech or return the blow. This is all the more true when he or she experiences the mistreatment of being reprimanded with angry verbal abuse that causes only minor suffering.

The bodhisattva who is established in the morality of restraint also becomes endowed with a mindfulness[703] consisting of five limbs: (1) one that relates to the past, (2) one that relates to the future, (3) one that relates to the present, (4) one that should be cultivated in advance, and (5) one that is practiced concurrently. A bodhisattva who is practicing the bodhisattva trainings and who has incurred an offense in relation to the past remedies that [offense] in accordance with the Dharma.[704] This is mindfulness that relates to the past. Whatever offense may be incurred in the future, he or she also determines to remedy that [offense] in accordance with the Dharma. This is mindfulness that relates to the future. Whatever offense is incurred in the present, he or she remedies that [offense] in accordance with the Dharma. This is mindfulness that relates to the present. A bodhisattva develops an intensely zealous attitude prior to [the occurrence of] an offense [in which he or she resolves], "May I conduct myself and maintain myself in whatever way will insure that I can avoid committing any offense." This is a bodhisattva's mindfulness that should be cultivated in advance. On the basis of that very form of mindfulness that should be cultivated in advance, [a bodhisattva] conducts and maintains him- or herself continuously in whatever way will insure that he or she avoids committing any offense. This is mindfulness that is practiced concurrently.

A bodhisattva who is established in the morality of restraint conceals his or her virtue, exposes his or her evil, has few wants, is satisfied with what he or she has, endures suffering, is indefatigable, does not become excited,

---

bodhisattva] generate compassion [toward such persons]? He or she reflects, 'This [wrongful behavior] is not the fault of this person; it is beyond [his or her] control and occurs through the power of the mental afflictions.'"

703. See note 393.

704. S: *yathā dharmam,* T: *chos bzhin du*. This means to practice confession of the misdeed in the appropriate manner. See below.

is unwavering and calm in his or her physical behavior, and avoids all the qualities that lead to hypocrisy and the other forms of wrong livelihood.[705]

A bodhisattva who is established in the morality of restraint and who is also endowed with [the following] ten qualities becomes one whose conduct is well restrained: (1) indifference to past pleasures, (2) lack of desire for those of the future, (3) lack of attachment to those of the present, (4) delighting in solitude, (5) striving to develop purity in speech and deliberative thoughts, (6) avoiding self-abasement, (7) gentleness, (8) patience, (9) mindfulness, and (10) purity of conduct and means of livelihood.

Acquiring Virtue Effectively [1.10.2.5]

Furthermore, (1) a bodhisattva who is established in the morality that acquires virtuous qualities does not tolerate the occurrence of even a small amount of regard for his or her body and possessions, much less [the occurrence of] a great amount. (2) He or she does not tolerate the occurrence of any of the root or secondary mental afflictions, such as anger, resentment, etc., that constitute the primary cause of all forms of immoral conduct. (3) He or she does not tolerate the occurrence of any feelings of animosity, hatred, or hostility toward others. (4) He or she does not tolerate the occurrence of idleness or laziness. (5) He or she does not tolerate the relishing of [the ease associated with] the states of composure that may occur or [any of] the mental afflictions that [may occur in connection] with the states of composure.

[A bodhisattva] also correctly learns five subjects. He or she correctly learns (1) the benefits[706] that result from virtue. He or she correctly learns

705. See note 642 for a description of hypocrisy (S: *kuhanā*, T: *tshul 'chos*). Five principal forms of wrong livelihood are frequently described in Buddhist literature. The four other than hypocrisy are flattery, intimation, oppression, and acquiring gain through gifts. Flattery (S: *lapanā*, T: *kha gsag*) is when an individual speaks favorably or shows deference to someone as a means of obtaining something of value from him or her. Intimation (S: *naimittikatvam*, T: *gshog slong*) is to obtain material gain by subterfuge or some indirect means. Oppression (S: *naiṣpeṣikatvam*, T: *thob kyis 'jal ba*) is when an individual tries to coerce someone into making a gift. An example of acquiring gain through gifts (S: *labhena lābhaniṣpādanā*, T: *rnyed pas rnyed pa sgrub pa*) is when reference to a previous gift is made as a means of obtaining some object that is desired. *ŚBh* (p. 48) describes all four in one detailed passage.

706. *BChZhL* (f. 18b): "The benefits [of virtue] are [rebirth as] a god or human being, and the three forms of enlightenment [that correspond to each of the three vehicles]."

(2) the causes of virtue, (3) what is erring and (4) unerring about the results of virtuous causes, and (5) the obstacles to acquiring virtue. Recognizing the benefits that result from virtue, a bodhisattva seeks the causes of virtue. Correctly knowing what is erring and unerring about acquiring virtue, a bodhisattva who has attained a result of virtue does not regard what is impermanent as permanent, does not regard what is suffering as a form of well-being, does not regard what is impure as pure, and does not regard what does not constitute a self as constituting a self. Knowing the obstacles to acquiring virtue, he or she abandons them.

With these ten qualities, [a practitioner] who is established in the morality of acquiring virtuous qualities quickly becomes one who acquires virtue, and one who acquires [virtue] of every form. That is to say, [one acquires virtue] by means of the foundation[707] of generosity, by means of the foundation of morality, by means of the foundation of patience, by means of the foundation of effort, by means of the foundation of meditative absorption, and by means of the five forms of wisdom.[708]

Engaging in Every Aspect of Acting on Behalf of Sentient Beings [1.10.2.6]

Moreover, a bodhisattva who is established in all eleven aspects of the morality that acts on behalf of sentient beings possesses each individual aspect in a manner that includes all of the [eleven] forms.

Assisting Those Who Need Help with Various Activities [1.10.2.6.1a]

Here a bodhisattva who assists beings with their activities assists them in considering what ought to be done[709] and in making determinations about

707. S: *upaniṣad,* T: *nyer gnas. BChZhL* (f. 18b): "In this context, the term 'foundation' means those causes that allow you to quickly achieve [the perfections of] generosity, etc." The five foundations that are mentioned here explicitly are the unwillingness to tolerate the obstacles to each of the first five perfections that are described in the first paragraph of this section.

708. The five forms of wisdom are the five forms of knowledge described in the preceding paragraph.

709. S: *kṛtyacintā,* T: *bya ba sems pa. BŚPṬ* (f. 188b): "'Considering what ought to be done'

what ought to be done.[710] He or she also assists [others] with regard to [such activities as] leaving on and returning from journeys, carrying out right occupations,[711] safeguarding possessions, reconciling those who are estranged from one another, religious celebrations,[712] and meritorious deeds.

Assisting Those Who Are Experiencing Physical or Mental Suffering [1.10.2.6.1B]

Alternatively, a bodhisattva who assists [others] with regard to their suffering takes care of those sentient beings who are ill, leads those who are blind and shows them to a road, causes the deaf to understand meanings with a [form of] sign language that represents words through symbols, and transports those whose limbs are deficient by carrying them[713] [bodily] or by means of a vehicle.

He or she dispels the suffering caused by the perturbation of desire for sensory pleasures that is possessed by those who suffer from the perturbation of desire for sensory pleasures. He or she dispels the perturbations of malice, torpor, sleep, excitation, regret, and doubt that are possessed by those who suffer from any of those perturbations.[714] He or she dispels the deliberation about sensory pleasures that is engaged in by those who are suffering from the perturbation of deliberation about sensory pleasures.

---

means to consider an activity in the sense of examining what is gained by carrying it out and what is lost by failing to do so."

710. S: *kṛtyasamarthanam,* T: *bya ba gtan la 'bebs pa. BŚPṬ* (f. 188b): "'Making determinations about what ought to be done' means to make the firm decision that [some activity] should definitely be carried out right away."

711. S: *samyakkarmāntaprayogaḥ,* T: *yang dag pa'i las kyi mtha' la sbyor ba*. The term translated here as "right occupation" is the same as the fourth limb of the eightfold ārya path, which is usually translated as "right action" and refers to the everyday activities of monks and nuns. In this context the term seems to refer more specifically to occupations that are a means of livelihood. *BŚPBh* (f. 184a): "The phrase 'carrying out right occupations' refers to such occupations as shipping (S: **naukarmāntaḥ,* T: *gru'i las kyi mtha'*) [this might include everything from being a sailor to owning and operating merchant vessels] and agriculture (S: **kṛṣikarma,* T: *zhing las*)."

712. S: *utsavaḥ,* T: *dga ston. BŚPṬ* (f. 198b): "occasions in which one participates in particular forms of meritorious activities [that are done] on a fixed date."

713. S: *śirasā,* T: *mgo bo.* Literally, "on one's head."

714. This is a reference to the five hindrances to meditative composure (S: *pañca samāpattinivaraṇāni,* T: *snyoms 'jug gi sgrib pa lnga*). See note 138.

Just as with [the statement regarding] deliberation about sensory pleasures, the same should be understood with regard to deliberation about malice, harmfulness, family relatives, one's homeland, the unlikeliness of one's death, contempt [toward others], and arrogance because of [being from an eminent] family.

He or she dispels the suffering of having been defeated and humiliated by others that is felt by those who are experiencing the suffering of having been defeated and humiliated by others. He or she dispels the suffering of weariness and fatigue that is felt by those who are worn out from travel by providing them with a seat and a place to stay and by massaging their limbs.

Showing What Is Proper [1.10.2.6.2]

Moreover, a bodhisattva who indicates to sentient beings what is proper teaches the Dharma to those beings who engage in wrongful conduct so that they will abandon that wrongful conduct, using words and syllables that are correct, fitting, conformable, appropriate, effective, agreeable, favorable, and that draw together the elements of diligent practice.

Put another way, he or she displays skillful means. Just as he or she [displays skillful means] toward those sentient beings who engage in wrongful conduct so that they will abandon that wrongful conduct, similarly he or she [displays skillful means] toward stingy sentient beings so that they will abandon their stinginess and so that they can acquire and safeguard their wealth in this life, in a correct manner and with little difficulty. He or she [displays skillful means] toward those who are hostile to this teaching so that they will gain faith in it, so that they will develop a [correct philosophical] view,[715] so that with a pure view they will transcend [having to be reborn in] the lower realms, and so that by putting an end to all the fetters[716] they will transcend all suffering.

715. The Tibetan translation of this sentence seems to be corrupted. Instead of the phrase "those who are hostile to this teaching" (S: *śāsane 'smin pratihatānām*), the Tibetan reads "those who have regard for this teaching" (T: *bstan pa 'di la lta ba rnams*); and the phrase "so that they will gain a [correct philosophical] view" (S: *darśanapratilambhāya*) is missing. The Tibetan might be amended to read: *bstan pa 'di la sdang ba rnams dad pa thob par bya ba* and *lta ba thob par bya ba dang*.

716. S: *saṃyojanam*, T: *kun tu sbyor ba*. One of the synonyms for the mental afflictions. *AS* (pp. 44–46) identifies nine fetters—attachment (S: *anunayaḥ*, T: *rjes su chags pa*), hatred, pride, ignorance, views, supreme considerations (S: *parāmarśaḥ*, T: *mchog tu 'dzin pa*),

Showing Gratitude for Benefit Received from Others [1.10.2.6.3]

Moreover, a bodhisattva shows gratitude toward those who have benefited him or her. After seeing them and receiving them hospitably, he or she addresses them, converses with them in a familiar manner, and greets them by saying, "Welcome, please draw near." He or she also receives them by offering a seat and a place to stay. He or she waits upon them by returning an equal or greater form of gain or honor than what was received from them; but [he or she] does not return a lesser form. He or she assists them with their activities even when not asked to do so, much less when asked. Just as [a bodhisattva acts on behalf of his or her benefactors] with regard to assisting them in their activities, a similar description applies with regard to [assisting them] when they are suffering, showing them what is proper, rescuing them from dangers, dispelling the sorrow that arises from being in a state of distress, furnishing the objects that relate to their subsistence, providing a place [in which to reside], complying with their minds, encouraging them by [declaring] their genuine good qualities, suppressing [their wrongful behavior] with an affectionate attitude, and using miraculous powers to frighten them and win them over.

Protecting Beings from Danger [1.10.2.6.4]

Moreover, a bodhisattva protects sentient beings who are frightened from the objects that they fear. He or she protects sentient beings from the fear of vicious wild beasts, as well as the fear of whirlpools and predatory marine animals, the fear of the king, the fear of robbers, the fear of adversaries, the fear of lords[717] and [provincial] rulers,[718] the fear of loss of livelihood, the

---

doubt, jealousy, and stinginess—and describes each of them as having the effect of "binding one to suffering in the sense of producing worldly [i.e., samsaric] suffering in the future."

717. S: *svāmī,* T: *rje bo.* While the Sanskrit term has a range of meanings, such as "owner," "lord," or "master," in the present context it seems to refer to landowners and other owners of property who hold sway over the lives of dependents and those who are obligated to provide some form of service to them. *BŚPṬ* (f. 200a): "lords who own vast amounts of property."

718. S: *adhipatiḥ,* S: *bdag po. BŚPṬ* (f. 200a): "rulers who have the power to impose punishments and exercise authority within their region."

fear of bad reputation, the fear [that stems from] being timid in an assembly, and the fear of spirits and demons [that occupy corpses].[719]

Dispelling Sorrow [1.10.2.6.5]

Moreover, a bodhisattva dispels the sorrow of sentient beings who are in [various] states of distress. Regarding the distress that relates to family relations, he or she dispels the sorrow that arises due to the death of one's mother or father. He or she also dispels the sorrow that arises due to the death of a son or daughter as well as [that which arises] due to the death of a female or male servant, a worker, or a hired person; [that which arises] due to the death of friends, advisers, near relations, and kinsmen; and [that which arises] due to the death of a teacher, a preceptor, or any other venerable person.

Alternatively, with regard to distress that relates to wealth, if the wealth of others has been seized by the king, [a bodhisattva] dispels the sorrow [that occurs] in that situation. [Wealth] may also be stolen by robbers, destroyed by fire, swept away by water, or ruined by having been stored improperly. It may be lost due to having carried out an occupation badly[720] or it may be appropriated by dishonest heirs.[721] Or an irresponsible family member[722] may appear in the family. A bodhisattva correctly dispels the lesser, moderate, or great forms of sorrow that sentient beings experience due to the distress created by any of these types of misfortune.

Furnishing the Objects That Are Needed for Subsistence [1.10.2.6.6]

A bodhisattva who furnishes the objects that are needed for subsistence to those who seek such objects gives food to those who seek food; drinks to those who seek drinks; vehicles to those who seek vehicles; clothing to

719. S: *vetāḍaḥ,* T: *ro langs.* A type of spirit that is induced to enter a corpse by means of spells.

720. That is, one's effort to pursue a business enterprise or some other means of livelihood may prove unsuccessful and end in failure.

721. S: *dāyādaḥ,* T: *bgo skal la spyod pa.* The Sanskrit term refers to those kinsmen and descendants who have common claim to a family fortune. The circumstance being described represents a loss of one's share of that wealth due to the malicious actions of other heirs.

722. S: *kulāṅgāraḥ,* T: *khyim gyi phung khrol.* Literally, a "family firebrand," that is, a family member who causes difficulties in a family and potentially can bring it to ruin.

those who seek clothing; ornaments to those who seek ornaments; implements and utensils to those who seek implements and utensils; fragrances, garlands, and ointments to those who seek fragrances, garlands, and ointments; and dwellings to those who seek a dwelling. He or she gives lamps to those who seek lamps.

Providing a Proper Abode [I.10.2.6.7]

Moreover, employing the morality of embracing,[723] a bodhisattva who is practicing [the act of] embracing [sentient beings] through the act of leading a body of practitioners initially provides a dwelling place, [and does so] with a mind that is free of desire for any material gain and having initially formed a mind that is motivated exclusively by compassion. Following that, in a manner that conforms with the Dharma, one seeks on their behalf robes, food, bedding, seats, medicine for curing the ill, and the other personal belongings from those brahmins and householders who possess faith [in the Dharma]. One also shares one's own robes, food, bedding, seats, medicine for curing the ill, and the other personal belongings that are in keeping with the Dharma and were obtained in a manner that accords with the Dharma; one does not keep them for private use. Regularly and at appropriate times, one also bestows the orderly instruction that has eight aspects and correctly teaches discipline using the counsel that has five aspects. Instruction and counsel should be understood here in the same way that they were explained in the chapter on the spiritual lineages of the powers.[724]

Complying with the Minds of Others [I.10.2.6.8]

Moreover, employing the morality of compliance, a bodhisattva who is complying with the minds of sentient beings at the very outset makes him- or herself aware of the attitude, fundamental nature, and constituent element of sentient beings. Having become aware of their attitude, fundamental nature, and constituent element, one associates with them in whatever man-

723. S: *parigrahaśīlam,* T: *yongs su sdud pa'i tshul khrims.* See note 163 for a discussion of the term "embracing" (S: *parigraha,* T: *yongs su sdud pa*) and also Book III, chapter 2, the section entitled "Embracing by Acceptance" [III.2.3], as it pertains to leading a body of spiritual practitioners.

724. See Book I, chapter 8, the sections entitled "Instruction" [I.8.5] and "Counsel" [I.8.6].

ner one ought to associate with them. One conducts oneself in relation to those sentient beings in whatever manner one ought to conduct oneself.

If a bodhisattva who wishes to comply with the mind of a particular sentient being sees that a certain type of physical or verbal conduct of some significance will cause that [being] to develop suffering or unhappiness of mind and he or she [also sees] that that suffering or unhappiness of mind will not serve to turn [that being] away from opportunities [to engage in] nonvirtuous [actions] and cause [him or her] to become established in opportunities [to engage in] virtuous [actions], then, after consideration, a bodhisattva diligently abandons that significant form of physical or verbal conduct and does not engage in it. On the other hand, if a bodhisattva sees that that suffering or unhappiness of mind [will serve to turn] that [being] away from opportunities [to engage in] nonvirtuous [actions] and cause [him or her] to become established in opportunities [to engage in] virtuous [actions], then, after consideration, [that bodhisattva] generates compassion toward that other [being] and does not comply with [his or her] mind.

If a certain type of physical or verbal conduct of some significance [that might be carried out] in relation to one individual [or group of individuals] should give rise to suffering or unhappiness of mind in a second individual [or group of individuals] and that [conduct] does not serve to turn either of those individuals [or groups of individuals] away from opportunities [to engage in] nonvirtuous [actions] and cause [either of those individuals or groups of individuals] to become established in opportunities [to engage in] virtuous [actions], then, after consideration, a bodhisattva abandons that physical or verbal conduct in order to preserve the opinion of the second individual [or group of individuals]. On the other hand, if he or she sees that either of those individuals [or groups of individuals] or both would be turned away from opportunities [to engage in] nonvirtuous [actions] and caused to become established in opportunities [to engage in] virtuous [actions], after consideration a bodhisattva engages in that physical or verbal conduct. After generating a compassionate attitude, he or she does not comply with the minds of those sentient beings.

If a bodhisattva perceives that his or her particular physical or verbal conduct of some significance would give rise to suffering or unhappiness of mind in others and this physical or verbal conduct is neither included among the precepts of training nor constitutes a form of the merit or wisdom accumulations, and that suffering or unhappiness of mind also does not serve to turn others away from opportunities [to engage in] nonvirtuous actions, etc., as described above, then a bodhisattva avoids that physical or verbal conduct in order to preserve the opinion of others. In the opposite circumstances, [a bodhisattva's] conduct should be understood as described above.[725]

Just as with the suffering or unhappiness of mind [that might be caused to arise in others], a similar explanation should be understood to apply in detail and according to circumstances for the pleasure or happiness of mind [that might be caused to arise in others].[726]

A bodhisattva who complies with the minds of others does not even express praise directly to another [person] who is perturbed by the perturbation of anger, as long as the perturbation of anger has not disappeared, much less does he criticize [such an individual]. [A bodhisattva] also does not offer an apology [to such a person in those circumstances].

Moreover, a bodhisattva who complies with the minds of others addresses and greets another person even if that person does not address him or her. This is all the more true if that person does address and greet him or her.

A bodhisattva who complies with the minds of others does not upset [another person], except in a situation where he or she wishes to reproach someone. Then he or she reproaches those [individuals] with a sense of compassion and with the faculties composed.

A bodhisattva who complies with the minds of others does not ridicule or show contempt toward another [person], or cause him or her to feel embarrassed. [A bodhisattva] also does not cause [another person] to develop regret in order to make [that person] feel unhappy. Nor does he or she ask

725. That is, if a bodhisattva recognizes that his or her conduct is not included among the precepts of training and that it also does not constitute a form of either the merit or wisdom accumulations, but the conduct will serve to turn the individual away from opportunities for engaging in nonvirtuous action, etc., then, after consideration, a bodhisattva should generate compassion toward that individual and refuse to comply with his or her wishes. Also, if a bodhisattva recognizes that his or her physical or verbal conduct is included among the precepts of training and that it does constitute a form of either the merit or wisdom accumulations, then he or she should not comply with the other person's wishes.

726. That is, if a bodhisattva recognizes that his or her conduct will give rise to pleasure or happiness of mind in another, and it also will not cause that person to engage in nonvirtue, then he or she should comply with that person's wishes and continue to engage in the conduct. On the other hand, if a bodhisattva recognizes that his or her conduct may give rise to pleasure or happiness of mind in another person, but that it will also lead that person to engage in nonvirtue, then he or she should not comply with the person's wishes and, after generating compassion toward that individual, he or she should abandon the conduct.

someone who has suffered a defeat and been punished about the particulars relating to that punishment. He or she also does not make known his or her own success to someone who has fallen into low circumstances.

A bodhisattva who complies with the minds of others neither [completely] avoids the company of others nor keeps company with them to an excessive degree. He or she does not keep company with others at inappropriate times. He or she also does not criticize the friends or praise the adversaries of others in their presence. He or she does not confide in those whom he or she does not know well. He or she does not repeatedly solicit [the same person]. He or she shows moderation when accepting gifts. He or she does not refuse an invitation to receive food and drink, etc. Or, as a person who acts in accord with Dharma, he or she offers a proper reason to be excused.

Giving Encouragement to Others [1.10.2.6.9]

Moreover, employing the morality of encouraging [others] based on the good qualities that they genuinely possess, a bodhisattva encourages sentient beings. He or she encourages those who possess the quality of faith by commenting about that quality of faith. [He or she encourages] those who possess the quality of morality by commenting about that quality of morality. [He or she encourages] those who possess the quality of [extensive] learning by commenting about that quality of learning. [He or she encourages] those who possess the quality of generosity by commenting about that quality of generosity. [He or she encourages] those who possess the quality of wisdom by commenting about that quality of wisdom.

Suppressing Those Who Engage in Misconduct [1.10.2.6.10]

Moreover, employing the morality of suppression, a bodhisattva suppresses sentient beings [who have engaged in wrongful conduct]. With an attitude that is inwardly affectionate and free of distress, he or she censures a lesser offense and lesser transgression[727] with a mild reprimand. He or she censures an intermediate offense and intermediate transgression with

727. *BŚPBh* (f. 186a–186b): "An 'offense' (S: *aparādhaḥ,* T: *nyes pa*) is the failure to do what should be done; a 'transgression' (S: *vyatikramaḥ,* T: *'gal ba*) is the doing of what should not be done."

a moderate reprimand, and a great offense and great transgression with a severe reprimand. Just as with reprimands, a similar [description] should be understood for punishments.

For lesser and intermediate offenses and lesser and intermediate transgressions, a bodhisattva expels [the transgressor] as a temporary measure and with the intention of allowing him or her to return. [This expulsion is imposed] for the purpose of correcting those very [transgressors] as well as [serving as instruction for] others, and it is carried out with a compassionate mind and with the intention of benefiting [those involved]. For great offenses and great transgressions, [a bodhisattva] expels [the transgressor] without allowing him or her to associate [with the religious community] or partake of [life in the religious community] again and without allowing him or her to be readmitted [to the religious community] for the remainder of his or her lifetime. [This expulsion is imposed] with compassion toward those very [transgressors] so that they will not continue to acquire any more nonmeritorious karma in relation to the [Buddhist] teaching and with the desire to benefit others as well, by serving as instruction for them.

Displaying Miraculous Powers [1.10.2.6.11]

Moreover, a bodhisattva who is desirous of frightening sentient beings and desirous of winning them over by means of miraculous powers repeatedly brings forth and reveals to those beings who engage in misconduct [visions of] the ripening of that misconduct in the lower realms of the hell regions, [which include] the great [hot] hells, the cold hells, and the partial hells.[728] He or she tells them, "Honorable ones, look at this violent, extremely severe, and undesirable ripening result that is being experienced by human beings who carried out and accumulated misdeeds." Upon seeing this, these beings become frightened, develop apprehension, and refrain from [engaging in any further] misconduct.

Some beings are desirous of causing a bodhisattva's speech not to be

728. The eight hot hells are described in *YBh,* pp. 79–84; the eight cold hells on pp. 86–87. For the partial hells (S: *pratyekanarakaḥ,* T: *nyi tshe ba'i dmyal ba*), Asaṅga (*YBh,* p. 87) only refers to a sutra in which the monk Lakṣmaṇa asks Maudgalyāyana why he smiled at a certain point while they were walking together. For a description of this class of beings, see the *Lakkhaṇasaṃyutta* (Saṃyutta Nikāya, part 2, chapter 8).

accepted[729] through refusing to answer his or her questions[730] when seated in a large gathering. A bodhisattva frightens and terrifies such beings by emanating him- or herself as Vajrapāṇi or some other powerful spirit that is imposing in appearance, has a large body, and [displays] great power. [This is done] so that, because of this [action], he or she can cause those who have been made to develop faith, a high degree of esteem, and respect to answer his or her questions correctly, and so that, by means of those responses, he or she might impose spiritual self-discipline upon that large body of beings.

Alternatively, by means of a variety of magical creations—such as turning [his or her] one [physical body] into many; turning [his or her] many [physical bodies] back into one; traveling with an unobstructed body directly through a wall, directly through a mountain, directly through a rampart, etc.; up to gaining control with his or her body as far as Brahmā's realm; displaying multiple forms of the twin marvelous feats;[731] entering the state of mental absorption in which he or she concentrates on the fire element; or displaying the miraculous powers that are held in common with listeners—he or she wins over [beings] by pleasing and delighting them, and then causes those who lack faith to develop [an abundance of] faith, those who are immoral to develop [an abundance of] morality, those with little learning to develop [an abundance of] learning, those who are stingy to develop [an abundance of] generosity, and those of weak intelligence to develop [an abundance of] wisdom. In this way, a bodhisattva becomes one who possesses, in all its aspects, the morality that acts on behalf of sentient beings.

729. S: *anādeyam vacanam,* T: *tshig mi btsun pa.* This is the opposite of one of the eight "maturation qualities" (see Book I, chapter 3, the section entitled "The Eight Maturations" [I.3.5.1]) that a bodhisattva desires to have in order to deal with others effectively. The point here is that some individuals may seek to discredit a bodhisattva by refusing to answer questions that he or she has posed.

730. S: *praśnasaṃsādanena,* T: *dri bas sma dbab pas.* Cf. *BHSD,* p. 542. Also, *BŚPṬ* (f. 201b): "As for those who refuse to speak to a bodhisattva in a large assembly out of a desire to do him or her harm, [that bodhisattva] frightens such persons by using miraculous powers to reveal a magically created, fearsome image in order to induce them to reply to [his or her] questions."

731. S: *yamakāni prātihāryāni,* T: *cho 'phrul 'phrugs.* Any of a variety of miraculous feats in which pairs of opposites are displayed simultaneously, such as fire from the upper part of the body and water from the lower part. A reference to this appears in Book I, chapter 5, in the section entitled "Transformational Miraculous Power" [I.5.1.1.1], where it is described as "blazing" (S: *jvalanam,* T: *'bar bar byed pa*).

These are a bodhisattva's three heaps of morality that represent immeasurable heaps of merit. They are the heap of morality that consists of the morality of restraint, [the heap of morality] that consists of the morality of acquiring virtuous qualities, and [the heap of morality] that consists of the morality of acting on behalf of sentient beings.

The Ritual for Acceptance of the Bodhisattva Discipline [1.10.2.7]

Regarding this [topic], whether he or she is a householder or one who has gone forth [into the homeless state], a bodhisattva who wishes to train him- or herself in the bodhisattva training that relates to this threefold heap of morality and who has generated the aspiration to achieve unsurpassed true enlightenment should initially throw him- or herself at the feet of a bodhisattva who is an exemplary Dharma follower[732] and who has [also] made the aspiration [to attain enlightenment], is wise, and is able to convey the meaning of the verbal informative form,[733] and make the following entreaty: "O son of good family" [or, "O daughter of good family"],[734] "I wish to receive

732. S: *sahadhārmikaḥ,* T: *chos mthun pa pa. BŚPṬ* (f. 202a): "The expression 'an exemplary Dharma follower' is meant to indicate that, just as one should accept the listener [system of] discipline from one who is beyond reproach, here, too [i.e., in the case of the person from whom you receive the bodhisattva system of moral discipline], it should be the same." *BChZhL* (ff. 31b–32a): "an exemplary Dharma follower, [that is to say,] one who is abiding in the bodhisattva discipline . . ."

733. S: *vāgvijñaptiḥ,* T: *ngag gi rnam par rig byed. AK* (ch. 4, v. 3): "Verbal informative form, however, is the sound of speech." Also, *PSV* (p. 262): "There are two types of informative form: bodily informative form and verbal informative form. Each of these can be of three distinct types: virtuous, nonvirtuous, and indeterminate." These two types of form are called "informative" because they "make known" (S: *vijñapayati,* T: *rnam par rig par byed pa*) something about the state of mind of the individual who is expressing them. For example, in a ritual for accepting the bodhisattva form of discipline, a person's physical demeanor—such as kneeling and holding his or her palms joined together—represents virtuous bodily informative form in that it conveys the individual's devotional state of mind. Similarly, when the words of the ritual are repeated aloud, this represents virtuous verbal informative form in that it conveys the person's resolve to accept and keep the precepts. The entire phrase "able to convey the meaning of the verbal informative form" is meant to indicate that the individual from whom one intends to receive the bodhisattva discipline should have the ability to conduct the formal ritual in a proper manner.

734. The brackets are used here to indicate that one would use the form of address that is appropriate to the actual gender of the preceptor or candidate.

from you the acceptance of the discipline of bodhisattva morality. If it causes no trouble, may it please you, in your compassion, to hear me for a brief moment."

Following this, the bodhisattva who is capable [of conducting the ritual] should describe at length the benefits of the bodhisattva [system of] discipline[735] to the bodhisattva who is desirous of receiving it. He or she should also describe the heavy and light precepts to the individual who is desirous of receiving the discipline and cause him or her to develop enthusiasm by saying the following: "Hear me, O son of good family" [or, "Hear me, O daughter of good family"]. "Do you wish to lead across those who have not crossed over, set free those who have not been set free, comfort those who are in need of comfort, bring to nirvana those who have not reached nirvana,[736] and preserve the lineage of the buddhas? You should generate a firm attitude and a firm determination regarding this." This should be said to those who are recognized to be unaware of these points in order to cause them to develop enthusiasm.[737]

After having properly made the above request, the individual desirous [of accepting the discipline of bodhisattva morality] should place his or her upper garment on his or her shoulder and make salutation to the buddhas, the blessed ones, of the past, present, and future, as well as to those bodhisattvas of the ten directions who have reached the great [ārya bodhisattva] stages and attained great knowledge and powers. He or she should also clearly bring to mind their spiritual qualities and generate a deeply felt reverence, or one that is more limited in form, [but in either case it should be done] to the utmost of one's ability and strength.

735. S: *bodhisattvasaṃvaraḥ*, T: *byang chub sems dpa'i sdom pa*. See note 683 for a discussion of the term *saṃvaraḥ* both as a system of "discipline" and a form of "restraint."

736. According to the traditional interpretation, "those who have not crossed over" (S: *atīrṇāḥ*, T: *ma brgal ba rnams*) refers to Lesser Vehicle arhats who have not abandoned the obscurations to that which needs to be known; "those who have not been set free" (S: *amuktāḥ*, T: *ma grol ba rnams*) refers to beings like the worldly god Brahmā who are bound by both types of obscurations; "those who are in need of comfort" (S: *anāśvastāḥ*, T: *dbugs ma phyin pa rnams*) refers to hell beings and the like who are suffering in the lower realms; and "those who have not reached nirvana" (S: *anirvṛtāḥ*, T: *mya nga las ma 'das pa rnams*) refers to all beings generally who have not yet achieved the "non-abiding nirvana" that is supreme enlightenment. Cf. the Tibetan translation of Abhayākaragupta's *Āmnāyamañjarī* (T: *Man ngag gi snye ma*), f. 109b.

737. This entire paragraph only appears in the Tibetan translation; it is missing from both of the published Sanskrit versions.

Having made reverential salutation before an image of the Tathāgata that had been set up, [the candidate] should place his or her [right] knee on the ground or sit in a squatting position and humbly[738] address the knowledgeable bodhisattva with the following words: "O son of good family [or "O daughter of good family]," [739] or "O long-lived one,"[740] or "O venerable one,"[741] "please bestow upon me the acceptance of the discipline of bodhisattva morality." Having spoken these words, [the candidate] should fix his or her recollection one-pointedly and, with a state of mind that steadily becomes ever more reverential, remain silent while reflecting on the following thought: "Before long now, I shall gain an inexhaustible, immeasurable, and unsurpassed treasure of great merit."

Then, while standing or sitting and with an undistracted mind, the knowledgeable bodhisattva should address the [candidate] bodhisattva who has spoken in this way as follows: "Hear me, O son of good family," or "[Hear me,] O Dharma brother," who is named so-and-so." [Or "Hear me, O daughter of good family," or "Hear me, O Dharma sister, who is named so-and-so."] "Are you a bodhisattva and have you made the aspiration to [attain] enlightenment?"

[The bodhisattva candidate] should then affirm, "Yes, it is so."[742]

Following that, [the officiating bodhisattva] should state the following: "O son of good family who is named so-and-so [or, "O daughter of good family who is named so-and-so], do you accept from me all of the bodhisattva precepts and all of the bodhisattva morality—[namely,] the morality

738. S: *nīccais,* T: *'dud pa'i tshul gyis.* According to MW (p. 565), the principal sense of the Sanskrit term is that of being "below" or "downward," suggesting that the candidate should be situated in a place that is lower than the person who is conferring the discipline. However, additional meanings are "humbly" or "in a soft voice." I follow the Tibetan translation, which indicates literally "in a bowing manner" or "in a respectful manner," emphasizing a deferential physical bearing.

739. S: *kulaputra,* T: *rigs kyi bu,* or S: *kuladuhitar,* T: *rigs kyi bu mo.* This expression should be used if the person from whom the discipline is to be received is a householder.

740. S: *āyuṣmān,* T: *tshe dang ldan pa,* or S: *āyuṣmatī,* T: *tshe dang ldan ma.* Literally, "one who possesses a long life" or "one who possesses vital power." This is a respectful term of address that is generally used to address a younger monk or nun.

741. S: *bhadanta,* T: *btsun pa,* or S: *bhadantī* ?, T: *btsun ma.* A respectful term of address for a Buddhist monk or nun. The Sanskrit verbal root from which the noun derives means "to be greeted with praise," or "to honor" (MW, p. 745).

742. The Sanskrit word of affirmation is *oṃ* (T: *lags so*). MW (p. 235): "[*Oṃ* is] a word of solemn affirmation and respectful assent, sometimes translated by 'yes, verily, so be it.'"

of restraint, the morality of acquiring virtuous qualities, and the morality of acting on behalf of sentient beings—those precepts and that morality which have been observed by all the bodhisattvas of the past, those precepts and that morality which shall be observed by all the bodhisattvas of the future, and those precepts and that morality which currently are being observed by all the bodhisattvas of the present throughout the ten directions, those precepts and that morality with regard to which all the bodhisattvas of the past have trained themselves, with regard to which all the bodhisattvas of the future shall train themselves, and with regard to which all the bodhisattvas of the present are training themselves?"

[The bodhisattva candidate] should then affirm, "I do accept it all."

The knowledgeable bodhisattva should make this statement in the same way a second and a third time.

The bodhisattva who is accepting [the discipline] should also, upon being asked, answer in the affirmative three times.

After the knowledgeable bodhisattva has conferred the acceptance of the discipline of bodhisattva morality upon the recipient bodhisattva three times and its affirmation has also been accepted [by the recipient], and without the recipient bodhisattva rising up [from his or her kneeling or squatting position], [the officiating bodhisattva] should, in front of the very same image of the Tathāgata as before, throw him- or herself at the feet of all the buddhas and bodhisattvas who exist, remain, and live throughout the ten directions and, after performing a respectful salutation, make the following announcement: "The bodhisattva named so-and-so has acknowledged three times that he or she accepts the discipline of bodhisattva morality from me, the bodhisattva named so-and-so. I, the bodhisattva named so-and-so, am a witness to this acceptance of the discipline of bodhisattva morality by this bodhisattva named so-and-so, and I announce it to the supreme āryas in the endless and unlimited world spheres that lie in the ten directions who, though beyond our range of vision, possess an awareness whose range of vision perceives all sentient beings everywhere." [The officiating bodhisattva] should make this declaration in the same way a second and a third time.

It is also a fact of nature that immediately following the rite of accepting the discipline of [bodhisattva] morality, a particular type of sign[743] will

743. *BŚPṬ* (f. 202b): "'A particular type of sign' [refers to] the trembling of [the buddhas' and bodhisattvas'] seats."

become evident to the tathāgatas and the bodhisattvas who have achieved the great [ārya] stages and who exist, remain, and live in the endless and unlimited world spheres that lie in the ten directions. Because of this [sign, those tathāgatas and bodhisattvas] will realize the following: "A bodhisattva has taken up the acceptance of the discipline of bodhisattva morality." And immediately thereafter, their attention will turn toward that bodhisattva. And with that attention, their knowledge-perception[744] will take effect. By means of this knowledge-perception, those [buddhas and great bodhisattvas] become fully aware, in accordance with reality, that a bodhisattva named so-and-so in this particular world sphere has received the acceptance of the discipline of bodhisattva morality from another bodhisattva named so-and-so. And, with favorable minds, they will all react compassionately toward him or her, as one would a son or daughter or a brother or sister. It should be expected that the virtuous qualities of the bodhisattva who is looked upon in this way with a favorable mind and sympathy will increase greatly and they will not decline. It should be understood that [the buddhas and great bodhisattvas thus] recognize this announcement regarding the acceptance of the discipline of [bodhisattva] morality.

Once the rite for accepting the discipline of bodhisattva morality has been completed, both of the bodhisattvas[745] should perform a respectful salutation to, and fall at the feet of, the buddhas and bodhisattvas of the endless and unlimited world spheres that lie in the ten directions. Then the two should rise up.

This acceptance by a bodhisattva of the discipline of [bodhisattva] morality is the most distinguished among all the forms of accepting a [system of] moral discipline. It is unsurpassed, it is accompanied by an immeasurable heap of merit, it is generated by a supreme mental attitude, and it is the antidote to every form of misdeed that relates to all sentient beings. All the acceptances of the discipline of individual liberation[746] do not reach a hundredth part of this acceptance of a [system of] moral discipline, nor do they even reach a thousandth part. In relation to the [amount of] merit that

744. S: *jñānadarśanam,* T: *ye shes gzigs pa*. *BŚPBh* (f. 173b): "Knowledge grasps what is not visible; perception grasps an object that is directly present." *BŚPṬ* (f. 202b): "The perception [that arises] by the knowledge that is preceded by [a buddha's or a great bodhisattva's] attention is 'knowledge-perception.' Alternatively, [a buddha's and a great bodhisattva's] knowledge itself is perception, because it engages [objects] in a direct manner."

745. That is, both the officiant who conferred the discipline and the one who accepted it.

746. See note 683 for an explanation of this term.

is attained, [all the acceptances of the discipline of individual liberation] do not reach [any level of] calculation, portioning, reckoning, or factoring [that can be compared to the merit attained through the acceptance of the discipline of bodhisattva morality].

How to Safeguard the Discipline [1.10.2.8]

Moreover, the bodhisattva who is abiding in the acceptance of the discipline of bodhisattva morality should continually examine [any possible course of action so as to determine] "This is proper for a bodhisattva to do. That is not proper to do." Subsequent to this very [process of reflection, his or her determinations] should be put into action and the training should be carried out. He or she should also diligently study either the collection of bodhisattva sutras or this composition that represents a manual[747] for the collection of bodhisattva sutras in order to carry out a [form of] training that practices in accordance with the many thousands of precepts for bodhisattvas that the Blessed One taught in those scriptures.[748]

In addition, the acceptance of this [system of] moral discipline should not be received from all bodhisattvas, even though they may be knowledgeable. A bodhisattva should not receive it from someone who lacks faith—[which is to say], from someone who, from the outset, feels no devotion toward the acceptance of this form of moral discipline, does not take up its practice, and does not accommodate him- or herself to it in a well-regulated manner. Nor [should he or she receive it] from someone who is greedy, who is overcome by attachment, whose desires are great, or who is not satisfied with what he or she has; nor from someone whose morality is ruined, who has no regard for the trainings, or who is lax; nor from someone who is inclined to anger, who is resentful, who is highly impatient, or who is intolerant of others' transgressions; nor from someone who is slothful, who is lazy, who indulges excessively in the enjoyment of sleep during the day and night, the enjoyment of leaning on one's side, and the enjoyment of lying down, or who spends his or her time socializing with others; nor from someone whose mind is easily distracted and cannot meditate one-pointedly on

747. S: *mātṛkā,* T: *ma mo.* See the introduction for a discussion of this term.

748. The explicit reference to the need to "practice the many thousands of precepts for bodhisattvas that the Blessed One taught in those scriptures" appears only in the Tibetan translation; the two Sanskrit editions present a more abbreviated statement.

a virtuous object even for the length of time it takes to a milk a cow; nor from someone who is dull-witted, who is of a confused nature, whose mind is excessively languid, or who disparages the collection of bodhisattva sutras and the manuals [that present the instructions contained in] the collection of bodhisattva sutras.

A bodhisattva who has taken up and fully understood this ritual for accepting the [bodhisattva] discipline also should not, because of a failure to exercise due caution, declare and make it known to those beings who are hostile toward, and lack faith in, the bodhisattva collection.

Why is that?

It is because upon hearing about it, those who feel no devotion [toward this form of discipline] and who are greatly obscured by the obscurations to that which needs to be known will be led to speak ill of it. Moreover, one who speaks ill of it will remain bound fast to an immeasurable heap of wickedness that is commensurate with the immeasurable heap of merit that is possessed by the bodhisattva who is abiding in the discipline until he or she completely and entirely abandons that evil speech, that evil view, and that evil notion.

Moreover, the precepts of the training and the occasions for [the occurrence of] transgressions that are set forth in this manual for the bodhisattva collection [of scriptures] should be made known beforehand to the bodhisattva who wishes to undertake the acceptance of the [system of] moral discipline. If, he or she is eager [to accept the discipline] after having earnestly examined [the precepts], and after having considered them carefully[749] with his or her wisdom, rather than at the instigation of others or out of rivalry with others,[750] then [such a person] should be known as a resolute bodhisattva. This act of accepting the [system of] moral discipline should be conferred by such a one [who was described above]; it should be given to such a one [who was just described]; and [it should be carried out] by means of the ritual [that was described here].

749. S: *pratisaṃkhyāya,* T: *so sor brtags nas. BŚPṬ* (f. 204a): "'After having considered [the precepts] carefully' means to examine whether one is able to [properly observe them] or not."

750. S: *sphardhayā,* T: *'gran pa'i phyir.* The original Sanskrit term can mean either "out of rivalry" or "out of emulation." I have used the former term to comply with the Tibetan translation; however, the notion of accepting the discipline out of a desire to emulate others or "follow the crowd" may be just as apt.

The Four Acts That Represent an Extreme Form of Defeat [1.10.2.9]

There are four acts that represent an extreme form of defeat[751] for the bodhisattva who is abiding in the [system of] moral discipline in the manner [that has just been described].

What are the four?

Praising oneself and disparaging others by one who is attached to gain and honor is an act that represents an extreme form of defeat for a bodhisattva.

The refusal to give material objects, because of a greedy nature and hard-heartedness, to petitioners who have approached in a correct manner, who are suffering, miserable, and impoverished, and who lack a protector and someone to rely upon, even though one has and possesses wealth, and the refusal to share Dharma teachings with those who seek them and who have approached in a proper manner, because of one's stinginess about the Dharma, are acts that represent an extreme form of defeat for a bodhisattva.

The perturbation of anger can be of a kind that a bodhisattva will cause to become stronger and, therefore, it will not come to an end merely by uttering harsh speech. [A bodhisattva] who has been overcome by [such a form of] anger may strike, harm, or cause injury to sentient beings with [his or her] hand, a clod of earth, a club, or a weapon. Furthermore, by harboring this attitude of anger in a strong form, [a bodhisattva] may not accept and forgive an acknowledgment of wrongdoing made by others, and he or she may fail to let go of that attitude [of anger]. This, too, is an act that represents an extreme form of defeat for a bodhisattva.

751. S: *catvāri pārājayikasthānīyadharmāḥ,* T: *pham pa'i gnas lta bu'i chos bzhi.* While these four acts are not the same as the four expulsory offenses (S: *pārājikaḥ dharmaḥ,* T: *phas pham pa'i chos*) of the Listeners' Vehicle moral code, they are meant to correspond to or resemble them in the sense that they cause the bodhisattva discipline to be destroyed. A principal difference between the two systems is that the discipline of a monk or nun who follows the Listeners' Vehicle cannot be restored, but the bodhisattva [system of] discipline can be restored by accepting it again. Bodhibhadra's *Commentary to the Twenty Verses on the Bodhisattva Discipline* (T: *Byang chub sems dpa'i sdom pa nyi shu pa'i dka' 'grel,* f. 199a): "The term 'extreme defeat' literally means 'having defeated [the practitioner who commits them], they cause [his or her] discipline to be lost.'" The term *sthānīya* (T: *lta bu*), which is only used in the Great Vehicle system of morality, functions as a suffix in a compound and means (MW, p. 1263) "occupying the place of," or "representing." The Tibetan translation suggests the sense of "resembling."

Disparaging the bodhisattva collection [of scriptures] and taking pleasure in, teaching, or establishing counterfeit forms of Dharma by one who is firmly devoted to a counterfeit Dharma [and who behaves in this way] either on his or her own or in imitation of others, is an act that represents an extreme form of defeat for a bodhisattva.

These are the four acts that represent an extreme form of defeat. A bodhisattva who commits any one of these, let alone all of them, will not be able to collect and attain, within that lifetime, an extensive amount of the bodhisattva accumulations. He or she also will not be able to develop the purity of attitude[752] within that lifetime. He or she is a counterfeit bodhisattva, not a genuine one.

Moreover, a bodhisattva does not lose the acceptance of the [bodhisattva system of] moral discipline [by committing any of] these four acts that represent an extreme form of defeat [if they are done] on the basis of a lesser or middling perturbation. However, he or she does lose it [if they are committed] on the basis of a great perturbation. When [the basis for committing any of these acts is such that] a bodhisattva does not develop even a small amount of shame and abashment because he or she has engaged continually in these four acts that represent an extreme form of defeat and, due to that [lack of shame or abashment], he or she is both pleased with and delights in [that conduct], and he or she looks upon that very [conduct] as a good quality, this should be understood as constituting a great perturbation.[753]

752. S: *āśayaviśuddhiḥ,* T: *bsam pa rnam par dag pa*. *BŚPBh* (f. 187b): "'Purity of attitude' is [attained] because of having entered the [ārya bodhisattva] levels."

753. *BChZhL* (ff. 59a–65b) presents a lengthy discussion of the lesser, middling, and great forms of perturbation. Je Tsongkapa interprets Asaṅga's description of a great perturbation (S: *adhimātratā paryavasthānasya,* T: *kun nas dkris pa chen po*) as being made up of these four elements: (1) having the intention to engage in any of the four acts that represent an extreme form of defeat again in the future; (2) not feeling the slightest sense of shame or abashment at having previously engaged in this conduct; (3) being pleased with and delighting in the fact that one has engaged in this conduct; and (4) not regarding this conduct as wrongful. Noting that Asaṅga provides no explicit description of what constitutes a lesser or middling perturbation, Je Tsongkapa concludes that the fourth component—not regarding any of these acts as wrongful—is the pivotal one in that it determines whether any sense of shame or abashment will occur. He asserts that, if after committing any of these four acts, one regards it as wrongful, the act can only constitute a root transgression that was carried out on the basis of a lesser form of perturbation. On the other hand, if one fails to regard it as wrongful, then no matter how many of the other components may be absent the act must be a root transgression that was carried out on the basis of at least a middling perturbation.

However, a bodhisattva does not immediately lose the acceptance of the discipline of bodhisattva morality as soon as he or she has engaged in an act that represents an extreme form of defeat, as, for example, a *bhikṣu* or *bhikṣuṇī* does with the discipline of individual liberation by committing [any of the four] acts that constitute an extreme form of defeat.[754] Moreover, even if a bodhisattva has lost the acceptance [of the system of moral discipline], he or she is still capable of once again receiving the acceptance of the discipline of bodhisattva morality in that same life. He or she is not incapable [of receiving it again], as, for example, a *bhikṣu* or *bhikṣuṇī* who has accepted the discipline of individual liberation is [incapable] when he or she has incurred [any of] the extreme forms of defeat. In short, there are only two causes that can bring about the abandonment of the acceptance of the discipline of bodhisattva morality: (1) giving up the aspiration to attain unsurpassed true and complete enlightenment and (2) committing an act that represents an extreme form of defeat on the basis of a great perturbation.

In addition, a bodhisattva who has neither given up the aspiration [to attain supreme enlightenment] nor committed any of the extreme forms of defeat on the basis of a great perturbation does not abandon the acceptance of the discipline of bodhisattva morality even after having exchanged his or her life and wherever he or she is reborn—whether a higher [rebirth], a lower one, or one that is at the same level.[755] Even though a bodhisattva whose recollection has been clouded due to having exchanged his or her life may accept [the bodhisattva system of discipline] repeatedly [in successive rebirths] after coming in contact with a spiritual teacher, he or she does so for the purpose of awakening his or her recollection; this does not constitute a new acceptance [of the bodhisattva discipline].

Secondary Offenses [1.10.2.10]

Likewise, it should be understood what constitutes an offense and what does not constitute an offense for a bodhisattva who abides in the discipline of bodhisattva morality, as well as what constitutes an afflicted [offense] and

754. The four acts in the Listeners' Vehicle system of morality that require immediate expulsion of a monk or nun from the Sangha are (1) engaging in sexual intercourse, (2) stealing, (3) killing a human being, and (4) falsely claiming to have attained superhuman spiritual qualities.

755. S: *tiryak,* T: *thad kar.* The term literally means "horizontally" in the sense that being reborn in a human rebirth represents the same level of existence.

one that is free of affliction, and what constitutes a lesser, intermediate, or a great [offense].

Not Performing the Three Kinds of Devotion to the Three Jewels [1.10.2.10.1]

A bodhisattva abiding in the discipline of bodhisattva morality who allows a night and day[756] to go by without performing on a daily basis the preeminent form of homage, whether small or extensive, to the Tathāgata in the form of a *caitya*[757] that represents the Tathāgata, to the Dharma in the form of a scripture from the bodhisattva sutra collection or a manual on the bodhisattva sutra collection [either of which] represents the Dharma, or to the Sangha which is made up of [all] the bodhisattvas in the ten directions who have attained the great [ārya] stages—[homage that consists of] at least a single prostration with the body; a recitation by speech of at least one verse of four lines describing the virtuous qualities of the Buddha, Dharma, and Sangha; or at least a single [attitude of] reverence with the mind that is preceded by recollection of the qualities of the Buddha, Dharma, and Sangha—commits an offense and commits a transgression.

If [this misdeed] occurs out of disrespect [for the precepts of moral training], or out of idleness and laziness, [a bodhisattva] acquires an afflicted offense. If it occurs because of a lapse of recollection, he or she acquires an unafflicted offense. There is no offense for [a bodhisattva] who is mentally disturbed.[758] There is no offense for [a bodhisattva] who has attained the stage of a pure [superior] attitude. That is, a bodhisattva who has attained the purity of attitude is like a *bhikṣu* or *bhikṣuṇī* who, after having attained the faith born of insight,[759] naturally and at all times serves and honors the Master, the Dharma, and the Sangha with supreme forms of homage.

756. That is, a period of twenty-four hours.

757. T: *mchod rten*. See Book I, chapter 16, the section entitled "Shrine Worship" [I.16.1.2]. The term *caitya,* which is generally synonymous with *stūpa* (T: also *mchod rten*), typically refers to an object of veneration, either in the form of a large funeral monument or a small reliquary, that symbolizes a buddha's enlightenment. MW, p. 402, suggests that it can also mean an image of a buddha.

758. S: *kṣiptacittaḥ,* T: *sems khrugs pa*. That is, a mentally disturbed person is not responsible for his or her actions.

759. S: *avetyaprasādaḥ,* T: *shes nas dad pa*. This type of faith is of four kinds: (1) faith born of insight regarding Buddha, (2) faith born of insight regarding Dharma, (3) faith born of insight regarding the Sangha, and (4) the morality that is dear to āryas (S: *āryakāntāni*

ALLOWING DESIRE TO REMAIN UNCHECKED [1.10.2.10.2]

A bodhisattva who persists in [the forms of] great desire,[760] lack of satisfaction,[761] and greediness for gain and honor that have [previously] arisen commits an offense and a transgression, and he or she acquires an afflicted offense.[762] There is no offense for [a bodhisattva] who has developed the aspiration to abandon [these forms of desire], and who is making an effort [to abandon them] and is committed to resisting them by adopting their antidote but who still repeatedly generates [them] because he or she is naturally overcome by strong mental afflictions.

FAILING TO RESPECT ONE'S SPIRITUAL ELDERS AND REFUSING TO REPLY VERBALLY [1.10.2.10.3–4]

If a bodhisattva sees an exemplary Dharma follower who is his or her spiritual elder, someone who is endowed with spiritual qualities and deserving of

---

śīlāni, T: *'phags pa dgyes pa'i tshul khrims rnams*). *AKB* (p. 386): "What is the meaning of 'faith born of insight'? Faith born of insight is the firm conviction (S: *saṃpratyayaḥ*, T: *yid ches pa*) that is gained by having realized the [four noble] truths exactly as they are. The traditional order in which they are enumerated conforms to the order in which they occur to a practitioner after he or she has arisen [from the meditative absorption in which the four noble truths were realized directly]. How do they occur to a practitioner who has arisen [from a direct realization of the four noble truths]? He or she thinks: 'How marvelous! Truly, the Blessed One is a fully enlightened buddha! Truly, his system of Dharma is well spoken! Truly, his Sangha of listeners is well established [in a genuine spiritual life]!' The practitioner develops these thoughts because [he or she perceives the Buddha, Dharma, and Sangha] as being like a doctor, medicine, and those who tend the sick, respectively. The fourth quality [i.e., the morality that is dear to āryas] is [also] referred to by this term [i.e., "faith born of insight"] because it is a purity (S: *prasādaḥ*, T: *dang ba*) of morality that is engendered by a purity of mind—which is to say, it is the conduct of one who has developed such purity of thought or because [this purity of morality is perceived] as being a state that is free of affliction. Alternatively, [the four objects of these attitudes] are thought of as representing the guide, the path, traveling companions, and the vehicle." Morality is a "vehicle" in the sense of being the most fundamental of the three trainings by which one traverses the path.

760. S: *mahecchatā*, T: *'dod pa che ba*. *AKB* (p. 335): "To have great desire means to crave things that one does not have, and to want them to be of the best quality or in great quantity."

761. S: *asaṃtuṣṭiḥ*, T: *chog mi shes pa*. *AKB* (p. 335): "To lack satisfaction means to be unhappy because one considers the things that one does have to be inferior in quality or insufficient in quantity."

762. In other words, there is no form of this offense that is unafflicted.

reverence, but he or she fails to rise up and offer [that person] a seat [because of] having been seized by pride or [because] he or she is in a hostile or an angry state of mind, or if [a bodhisattva] who is being addressed, spoken to, or greeted by others, or who has been asked a question [by others] does not reply with a proper form of verbal response [because] he or she has been seized by pride or [because] he or she is in a hostile or an angry state of mind, then he or she commits an offense and a transgression, and acquires an afflicted offense.[763] However, if [a bodhisattva] has not been seized by pride or is not in a hostile or angry state of mind but [behaves in either of these ways] with a mind that is morally indeterminate[764] out of idleness or laziness, or due to a lapse of recollection, then he or she commits an offense and a transgression but does not acquire an afflicted offense.

There is no offense [regarding this behavior] if [a bodhisattva] is gravely ill or mentally disturbed. There is no offense if [a bodhisattva] who was asleep is taken hold of by someone who intended to awaken him or her, and he or she is then spoken to, addressed, greeted, or questioned [by that person]. There is no offense for [a bodhisattva] who is giving a Dharma teaching to others or who is engaged in settling a [Dharma] discussion. There is no offense if [a bodhisattva] is involved in greeting persons other than this individual. There is no offense if [a bodhisattva] is listening intently to someone else who is giving a Dharma teaching or who is settling a [Dharma] discussion. There is no offense if [a bodhisattva does not respond] in order to preserve the opinion[765] of the person who is giving a Dharma discourse, [as conversing with someone during the discourse] would be regarded with

763. Tradition holds that Asaṅga's text presents forty-six lesser offenses. *BSVP* (f. 204b): "Wishing to explain the forty-six misdeeds in the order [that they occur in the root text] . . ." Candragomī's twenty-verse summary of this chapter of *BBh* also contains these two separate lines, "Failing to respect one's elders" and "Not replying when asked a question," which suggests that this sentence in *BBh* is considered to describe two distinct transgressions.

764. S: *avyākṛtacittaḥ,* T: *lung du ma bstan pa'i sems.* That is, the individual's mind is not under the influence of any of the root or secondary mental afflictions and therefore it is in a state that is morally neutral.

765. S: *cittam anurakṣaḥ,* T: *sems srung ba.* This phrase indicates an act that is done in deference to the opinion of another person or persons. In this case the act represents a show of respect toward a Dharma teacher. In the usage below, it suggests a form of the bodhisattva practice of complying with the minds of others (S: *paracittānuvartanam,* T: *gzhan gyi sems dang rjes su 'jug pa*) that was described earlier (see above, the section entitled "Complying with the Minds of Others" [I.10.2.6.8].

disapproval. There is no offense if that [refusal to respond] serves as a means of disciplining or training others [or if it serves as a means] of turning them away from opportunities [to engage in] nonvirtuous [actions] and causes them to become established in opportunities [to engage in] virtuous ones. There is no offense if [a bodhisattva] is observing a rule of the Sangha. There is no offense if [a bodhisattva] is preserving the opinion of a great many other individuals.

Not Accepting an Invitation [1.10.2.10.5]

A bodhisattva who has been invited by others to a home, to another temple, or to another home for food, drink, clothing, or other material objects but who, having been seized by pride or having developed a hostile mind or an angry mind, does not go and does not accept the invitation commits an offense and a transgression, and he or she acquires an afflicted offense. [A bodhisattva] who fails to go out of idleness and laziness acquires an unafflicted offense.

There is no offense if [a bodhisattva] is unable [to go because of being] ill or [because he or she] is mentally disturbed. There is no offense if the place is a long way off or the road is dangerous. There is no offense if, by means of that [refusal of an invitation], [a bodhisattva] wishes to [spiritually] tame or train [the individual who made the invitation], or if [a bodhisattva] wishes to cause him or her to turn away from opportunities [to engage in] nonvirtuous [actions] and become established in opportunities [to engage in] virtuous [actions]. There is no offense if [a bodhisattva] has previously accepted [an invitation] made by someone else. There is no offense if [a bodhisattva] is continually engaged in [activities] that pertain to virtue and he or she refuses to go in order to avoid having to interrupt [activities] that pertain to virtue. There is no offense if [accepting the invitation] would cause [a bodhisattva] to miss hearing an important Dharma teaching that he or she has not previously heard. It should be understood that [this exception] also applies in the case of settling a [Dharma] discussion in the same way that it does for hearing an important Dharma teaching. There is no offense if [a bodhisattva] has been invited by someone who has the intention of causing him or her injury. There is no offense if [a bodhisattva refuses an invitation] in order to prevent a great many other individuals from generating animosity. There is no offense if [a bodhisattva] is observing a rule of the Sangha.

Not Accepting Gold and Other Forms of Wealth [1.10.2.10.6]

A bodhisattva who, having developed a hostile mind or an angry mind, does not accept and refuses varied and abundant amounts of excellent [kinds of wealth] such as gold, silver, jewels, pearls, and lapis lazuli that he or she obtains from others or that are being offered to him or her repeatedly commits an offense and a transgression, and he or she acquires an afflicted offense because [it constitutes an act] of neglecting sentient beings.[766] [A bodhisattva] who does not accept [such wealth] out of idleness and laziness commits an offense and a transgression, but he or she does not acquire an afflicted offense.

There is no offense for [a bodhisattva] who is mentally disturbed. There is no offense if [a bodhisattva] realizes that he or she would develop a desire [for wealth] if he or she were to accept it. There is no offense if [a bodhisattva] believes that [the donor] would develop regret at a later time. There is no offense if [a bodhisattva] believes that the generosity was given in error. There is no offense if [a bodhisattva] believes that the donor is someone who has given up all acquisitiveness, and that, by [accepting] that [wealth, the donor] will become impoverished and fall into a state of [financial] ruin. There is no offense if [a bodhisattva] believes that [the wealth] belongs to the Sangha or has been dedicated to a stupa. There is no offense if [a bodhisattva] believes that [the potential donor] confiscated [the wealth] from someone else, and, because of that, this individual will either be killed, imprisoned, fined, or [be forced to undergo some other form of] harm or reproach.[767]

Refusing to Teach Dharma to Those Who Seek It [1.10.2.10.7]

A bodhisattva who, while in a hostile or angry state of mind, or who, because he or she has been injured by [the wickedness of] envy,[768] does not impart the Dharma to those who seek it commits an offense and a transgression, and he or she acquires an afflicted offense. [A bodhisattva] who does not

766. That is, a bodhisattva should accept such wealth in order to use it to benefit others.

767. Glossing the phrase "harm or reproach," *BChZhL* (f. 72a) states: "such harm as having one's eyes gouged out or the reproach of being banished [from one's native land]."

768. S: *irṣyāviprakṛtaḥ*, T: *rang bzhin gyis phrag dog can yin pa*. The Tibetan translation suggests "[because] he or she is of a jealous nature."

give [Dharma] due to idleness and laziness commits an offense and a transgression, but does not acquire an afflicted offense.

There is no offense if [the person requesting a Dharma teaching] is a heretic[769] who is looking [to find] flaws [in the Buddhist teaching]. There is no offense if [a bodhisattva] is gravely ill or mentally disturbed. There is no offense if, by means of that [refusal to teach], [a bodhisattva] wishes to spiritually tame or train the individual [who made the request], or wishes to cause him or her to turn away from opportunities [to engage in] nonvirtuous [actions] and become established in opportunities [to engage in] virtuous [actions]. There is no offense if [a bodhisattva] is not someone who is engaged in [teaching] the Dharma.[770] There is no offense if [the person requesting Dharma] is someone who would receive it disrespectfully, without showing the proper regard, and would engage in improper physical behavior.[771] There is no offense if [a bodhisattva] believes that the teaching of a lofty Dharma instruction to a person of weak faculties and the acquisition[772] of a Dharma teaching [by such a person] would frighten him or her and cause him or her to develop wrong views and false beliefs and to suffer [spiritual] injury and harm. There is no offense if [a bodhisattva] believes that a Dharma teaching that came into this person's possession[773] would be disseminated to others who are unfit vessels.

Abandoning Those Who Are Immoral [1.10.2.10.8]

A bodhisattva who, while in a hostile or angry state of mind, abandons or neglects immoral and violent persons because of their bad conduct or

769. See note 442.

770. S: *dharme na pravṛttaḥ syāt,* T: *chos mi shes na nyes pa med do.* The Sanskrit seems to indicate that no offense is incurred if a bodhisattva declines to teach because that is not an activity that he or she regularly carries out; however, the Tibetan translation states somewhat differently: "There is no offense if [the bodhisattva] is not knowledgeable about the Dharma."

771. S: *durīryāpathaḥ,* T: *spyod lam ngan pa.* See note 582 for a reference to twenty-six rules of proper physical behavior that should be observed when Dharma is taught.

772. S: *dharmaparyāptyā,* T: *chos thos pas.* It is not clear whether the Tibetan equivalent, which literally means "through the hearing of Dharma," is the intended, if somewhat free, translation of the original Sanskrit or whether it is a corruption of *chos thob pas,* which would be a more literal translation.

773. S: *taddhastagatasya,* T: *de'i lag tu song ba.* Literally, "[Dharma teaching] that came into that [person's] hands."

violence commits an offense and a transgression, and he or she acquires an afflicted offense. If he or she abandons them due to idleness and laziness, or neglects them due to a lapse of recollection, then he or she commits an offense and a transgression, but does not acquire an afflicted offense.

Why is that?

It is because a bodhisattva does not feel the same amount of sympathy toward and does not have the same eagerness to act on behalf of moral individuals and those who are subdued in the performance of their physical, verbal, and mental deeds as he or she does toward those who are violent and immoral, and who are engaged in [conduct that represents] the cause of [their own future] suffering.

There is no offense for [a bodhisattva] who is mentally disturbed [to fail to act on behalf of immoral and violent persons]. There is no offense if, by that means, [a bodhisattva] wishes to spiritually tame [immoral and violent individuals], etc., as [described] before. There is no offense for [a bodhisattva] who is preserving the opinion of a great many other individuals. There is no offense for [a bodhisattva] who is observing a rule of the Sangha.

Not Training Oneself in a Way That Engenders Faith in Others [1.10.2.10.9]

A bodhisattva trains him- or herself in the same way that listeners do and not in any different way with regard to those [transgressions] that the Blessed One established in the moral code of individual liberation as being objectionable by virtue of having been condemned[774] based upon [the principle

774. S: *pratikṣepaṇasāvadyam,* T: *bcas pa'i kha na ma tho ba dang bcas pa*. There are two types of "objectionable act" (see note 133): a misdeed that is "naturally objectionable" (S: *prakṛtisāvadyam,* T: *rang bzhin gyi kha na ma tho ba*) and one that is "objectionable by virtue of having been condemned." An alternate expression for this latter type is an act that is "objectionable by virtue of having been so designated" (S: *prajñaptisāvadyam*). A naturally objectionable misdeed is one that is wrongful regardless of whether one has accepted any system of moral discipline, such as any of the ten nonvirtuous karmic paths. A misdeed that is "objectionable by virtue of having been condemned" is one that is committed by a person who has violated a precept of some Buddhist system of moral discipline. For instance, a person who has accepted a form of Buddhist discipline that includes the precept not to take another being's life commits such a misdeed by taking another being's life. Some transgressions contain aspects of both types of misdeed, such as the act of taking another being's life that is committed by a person who has taken a form of Buddhist discipline containing this precept. These are designated "an offense that contains elements of both types [of misdeed]"

of] preserving the opinion of others in order to engender faith in those who lack it and further increase the faith of those who have already acquired it.

Why is that?

The listeners are indeed chiefly occupied with [achieving] their own aim; yet they train themselves in the moral precepts in such a manner that they do not fail to preserve the opinion of others in order to engender faith in those who lack it and further increase the faith of those who have already acquired it. How much more, then, should bodhisattvas [train themselves in this same way], since they are chiefly occupied with [achieving] the aims of others.

Engaging in Few Activities for the Sake of Sentient Beings [1.10.2.10.10]

On the other hand, [a bodhisattva] does not train him- or herself in the same way that listeners do with regard to those [transgressions] that the Blessed One established for listeners as being objectionable by virtue of having been condemned based upon the principles of having few concerns,[775] engaging in few activities,[776] and abiding with few worries.[777]

Why is that?

It is becoming for a listener who is completely devoted to his or her own aim and who does not take an interest in the aims of others to be one who, as relates to the aims of others, has few concerns, engages in few activities, and abides with few worries. However, it is not becoming for a bodhisattva who is completely devoted to the aims of others to be one who, as relates to the aims of others, has few concerns, engages in few activities, and abides

(T: *gnyis ka'i cha dang ldan pa'i ltung ba*). Others are misdeeds only on the strength of having been so designated by the Buddha, such as the precept not to eat food after midday. This latter type is described as "an offense [that is wrongful] only by virtue of having been condemned [by the Blessed One]" (T: *bcas rkyang gi ltung ba*).

775. S: *alpārthatā*, T: *don nyung ba*. *YBh* (f. 173b): "'Having few concerns' means to avoid striving after and being distracted by [the effort to obtain] monks' robes, food, and beds and seats."

776. S: *alpakṛtyatā*, T: *bya ba nyung ba*. *ANṬ* (f. 226a): "'Having few activities' means to avoid engaging in all worldly activities, such as [those associated with] commerce, agriculture, etc."

777. S: *alpotsukatā*, T: *snying las chung ngu*. *BŚPṬ* (f. 209a): "'Abiding with few worries' means to abide in the [four] ārya lineages." On the latter, see note 649.

with few worries. For example, if a bodhisattva, for the sake of others, has been offered [as many as] a hundred sets of monks' robes or a thousand sets of monks' robes that were sought from brahmins and householders who do not have a close family relation with him or her, he or she should accept from these individuals as many [robes] as are needed after having considered whether [their resources] are sufficiently strong. As with monks' robes, [a bodhisattva] should do the same for food bowls. As with those objects that are sought [from others, a bodhisattva] should also cause [monastic robes] to be woven by weavers who are unrelated to him or her using yarn that [a bodhisattva] him- or herself has solicited [from someone else]. For the sake of others, [a bodhisattva] should also provide [as many as] a hundred silk beds and a hundred sitting mats. He or she should also accept [as much as] a trillion *agra*[778] of gold and silver.

A bodhisattva abiding in the bodhisattva morality who trains him- or herself with regard to these and other similar matters in the same manner as the listeners—for whom [such actions constitute transgressions which] are objectionable by virtue of having been condemned [by the Blessed One] based upon the principles of having few concerns, engaging in few activities, and abiding with few worries—[and who does so] by maintaining few concerns, engaging in few activities, and abiding with few worries as relates to [pursuing] the aims of other beings while in a hostile or angry state of mind commits an offense and commits a transgression, and he or she acquires an afflicted offense. [A bodhisattva] who maintains few concerns, engages in few activities, and abides with few worries due to idleness and laziness commits an offense and a transgression, [but only] acquires an unafflicted offense.

Failing to Act with Sympathy [1.10.2.10.11]

There are also certain naturally objectionable acts[779] such that, when they are performed by a bodhisattva with a particular kind of skillful means, he or she not only remains free of any offense but also generates a great amount of merit. An example would be a situation in which a bodhisattva sees a thief

778. S: *agram,* T: *srang.* According to MW (pp. 6, 259, and 609) an *agra* corresponds to slightly less than one and a half Troy ounces. The Tibetan states "in excess of [a trillion *srang* of gold and silver]."

779. See note 774.

or a robber who is intent upon killing many hundreds of living beings—great persons [such as] listeners, solitary realizers, or bodhisattvas—for the sake of a small amount of material wealth, [making this person] someone who is preparing to commit many instances of an immediate misdeed.[780] Having seen this, [a bodhisattva] then forms the following thought with his or her mind: "Even though I shall have to be reborn in the hells for depriving this living being of his or her life, it is better that I should be reborn in a hell than that this sentient should end up in the hells because of having committed an immediate misdeed." After a bodhisattva who has had such a thought determines that his or her state of mind toward this living being is either virtuous or indeterminate,[781] and after developing a single-minded attitude of sympathy about the future[782] while experiencing [a sense of] abhorrence,[783] he or she then deprives [this living being] of his or her life. [Having done this, a bodhisattva] will not only remain free of any offense but will also generate a great amount of merit.

Another example would be a situation in which a bodhisattva [sees] men of a royal tribe or a king's high officials who are highly prone to violence, lacking in compassion toward sentient beings, and wholly devoted to inflicting harm on others. If he or she has the authority to do so, a bodhisattva, while maintaining a sympathetic mind and an attitude that wishes to benefit and bring happiness [to these individuals], deprives them of their royal power and the position of authority during whose tenure they generated great demerit. Also, [if a bodhisattva sees that] thieves and robbers who steal others' property have stolen the extensive wealth of the Sangha or a

780. S: *ānantaryakarman,* T: *mtshams med pa'i las.* Traditionally, there are five forms: (1) killing one's father, (2) killing one's mother, (3) killing an arhat, (4) shedding the blood of a tathāgata, and (5) creating a division in the Sangha wheel. They are called "immediate" because a person who commits any of them will be reborn in the hells in his or her very next life.

781. *BChZhL* (f. 77b): "At the moment when [a bodhisattva] is taking the life [of such a being], he or she must realize that his or her mind is in a state that is either virtuous or indeterminate, [which is to say,] it cannot be contaminated in any way at all by a [root] mental affliction or any other [secondary mental affliction]."

782. *BŚPṬ* (f. 212a): "'[After developing] a single-minded attitude of sympathy about the future' [means] that if [he or she] develops a single-minded attitude that wishes to benefit this being with regard to the future, no offense [will be incurred] even after such an act [of taking a life] has been committed."

783. *BŚPṬ* (f. 212a): "[The expression] 'while experiencing [a sense of] abhorrence' means that the lack of any other recourse causes [the bodhisattva] distress."

stupa and made it their own because they are desirous of enjoying it, he or she confiscates it from them, thinking to him- or herself, "Indeed, the enjoyment of [this ill-gotten] wealth must not be allowed to bring harm and disadvantage to these [thieves] that would last for a very long time!" After confiscating [the wealth] on the basis of this very conviction, [a bodhisattva] returns that which belongs to the Sangha to the Sangha and also that which belongs to a stupa to the stupa. Further, [when a bodhisattva sees that] administrators and caretakers of [temple] groves, by their bad conduct, are mismanaging the wealth of the Sangha or a stupa and making personal use of [that wealth], he or she considers this [matter] and then thinks to him- or herself, "Indeed, this action and this wrongful enjoyment [of wealth] must not be allowed to bring harm and disadvantage to these [administrators and caretakers] that would last for a very long time!" and then causes them to be removed from their position. Even though, [by proceeding] in this manner in situations such as these, a bodhisattva is carrying out [acts of] taking what was not given, he or she not only remains free of any offense but also generates a great amount of merit.

Another example would be a situation in which a householder bodhisattva engages in sexual intercourse with a woman who is tormented by the desire not to remain chaste, someone whose mind is fixed on that [act] and who is not married to someone else. After having placed his mind [in a state that is characterized] exclusively by sympathy and thinking to himself, "Indeed, [this woman] must not be allowed to generate great demerit through having gained an attitude of hostility. May she become a docile wife[784] [who is devoted] both to the pursuit of whatever roots of virtue she desires and to the abandonment of the roots of nonvirtue," [the householder bodhisattva] who does not remain chaste and engages in the act of sexual intercourse not only remains free of any offense but also generates great merit. On the other hand, it is never acceptable for a bodhisattva who has gone forth [into the state of a celibate ascetic][785] and who is someone who is

784. S: *vaśyā*, T: *dbang du gyur pa*. The adjectival form of this term means such things as "to be subdued," "to be under control," "to be obedient to another's will"; however, the feminine noun specifically refers to "a docile and obedient wife" (MW, p. 929).

785. S: *pravrajitaḥ*, T: *rab tu byung ba*. The term, which literally means "one who has gone forth," refers to a person who has left the householder state and entered that of a homeless ascetic. More specifically, in this instance it also means an individual who has accepted the system of moral discipline of a celibate Buddhist monk or nun.

guarding himself against doing any harm to the [Buddhist] teaching of the listeners to violate the [the vow of] chastity.

Another example would be a situation in which—in order to save the lives of many sentient beings, in order to save [many sentient beings] from bondage, in order to save [many sentient beings] from having their hands, feet, noses, or ears cut off, or in order to rescue [many sentient beings] from being deprived of their eyes—a bodhisattva, after due consideration, utters the false speech that he or she [ordinarily] would not deliberately utter even to save his or her own life. In short, in those situations where a bodhisattva perceives that it would be wholly in the interest of sentient beings [to utter false speech], and he or she perceives that it would not be harmful [to do so], and his or her mind is free of any corporeal desire,[786] and, after having altered his conception [of the facts] motivated exclusively by a desire to benefit beings, he or she deliberately utters speech that is at variance [with the truth], he or she remains free of any offense by speaking [such falsehoods] and also generates great merit.

Another example would be a situation in which a bodhisattva [encounters] sentient beings who have come under the influence of fraudulent spiritual teachers and, with all his or her strength and power, utters speech that separates those beings from those fraudulent spiritual teachers. He or she also takes pleasure in their separation and is pleased by it. Having adopted a completely sympathetic mind, he or she then reflects, "May these beings not have to undergo harm and disadvantage for a very long time because of their association with these evil companions." A bodhisattva who, in this way, causes a division between friends not only remains free of any offense but also generates great merit.

Another example would be a situation in which a bodhisattva, using intensely harsh speech, reproaches beings who are pursuing a wrong path and conducting themselves improperly until, by that means, they have been turned away from opportunities [to engage in] nonvirtuous [actions] so that they can be established in opportunities [to engage in] virtuous [actions]. A bodhisattva who utters harsh speech in such a situation not only remains free of any offense but also generates great merit.

Another example would be a situation in which a bodhisattva who, [motivated] by a sympathetic state of mind, uses various kinds of dance,

786. Here this form of desire can be taken to mean desire for material reward. See note 584 for a more detailed description.

song, and music to satisfy and win over beings who are fond of dance, song, and music and who also employs various forms of conversation that are filled with idle talk [to satisfy and win over] beings who are fond of talk about such topics as the king, thieves, food, drink, prostitutes, and the street and then, after having brought them to a subdued and docile state, causes them to turn away from opportunities [to engage in] nonvirtuous [actions] and establishes them in opportunities [to engage in] virtuous [actions]. In this way, even though he or she has engaged in idle talk, a bodhisattva not only remains free of any offense but also generates great merit.

Persisting in Wrong Forms of Livelihood [1.10.2.10.12]

A bodhisattva who persists in and does not shun those acts of wrong livelihood that he or she previously carried out and had a strong desire to carry out—namely, hypocrisy, flattery, intimation, oppression, and acquiring gain through gifts[787]—commits an offense and a transgression, and he or she acquires an afflicted offense. There is no offense for [a bodhisattva] who has generated the aspiration and initiated the effort to give them up but who still engages in them because his or her mind has been overwhelmed by an abundance of mental afflictions.

Engaging in Mental Excitation and Excessive Merriment [1.10.2.10.13]

A bodhisattva whose mind has not been quieted due to being under the control of excitation,[788] who delights in lack of calmness, who laughs loudly, plays and is boisterous in the company of others, who openly pursues excitation and diversions, and who likes to make others laugh and likes to please others commits an offense and a transgression for these very reasons, and he or she acquires an afflicted offense. [A bodhisattva who behaves this way] because of a lapse of recollection acquires an unafflicted offense.

787. See notes 642 and 705 for a description of these five forms of wrong livelihood.

788. S: *auddhatyam,* T: *rgod pa*. *AS* (p. 9): "What is excitation? It is the lack of calmness in the mind that follows attractive images and is a form of desire. Its action is to obstruct [the attainment of] quiescence." *PSV* (p. 308) describes the cause of excitation to be "recalling previous [experiences] that are consistent with desire, such as [occasions of] laughter, amusement, and the like."

There is no offense for [a bodhisattva] who has generated the aspiration to abandon such behavior, etc., as described before. There is no offense if he or she is desirous of removing, by means of this [behavior], the hostility that has arisen in others. There is no offense if he or she is desirous of dispelling, by means of this [behavior], the grief that has arisen in others. There is no offense if [a bodhisattva behaves this way] in order to comply with [the minds of] those others who are naturally inclined to that [conduct] and who delight in that [conduct], so that [he or she] can draw them [to the Dharma] or preserve their friendship. There is no fault if [a bodhisattva behaves this way] in order to indicate the absence of [any] inner [rancor] by his or her cheerfulness to those others who believe that the bodhisattva is in a bad mood, or who believe that [he or she] has developed [an attitude of] hostility or antipathy.

Regarding Samsara with Complacence [1.10.2.10.14]

Moreover, any bodhisattva who holds the following view or professes it [to others] commits an offense and a transgression, and he or she acquires an afflicted offense: "A bodhisattva should not abide with [an attitude] that delights in nirvana; rather, he or she should abide with [an attitude] that is turned away from nirvana. He or she should not fear the root or secondary mental afflictions, and he or she should not be striving exclusively to separate [his or her] mind from them, for enlightenment must be pursued by a bodhisattva while remaining in samsara for three spans of time that are each made up of a countless number of kalpas."

Why is that?

A bodhisattva should engender delight toward nirvana and aversion for the root and secondary mental afflictions that is a trillion times greater than the delight that a listener cultivates toward nirvana and the aversion that [he or she] develops toward the root and secondary mental afflictions. This is because a listener is dedicated to the pursuit of his or her own welfare, but a bodhisattva is dedicated to the welfare of all sentient beings. Thus, [a bodhisattva] must attain a state of self-discipline in which [his or her] mind remains so free of afflictions that, even though not an arhat, he or she can interact with entities that have the potential to cause the outflows to arise in such a manner that the unafflicted state of mind which he or she possesses is even superior to that of an arhat.

Failing to Dispel a Bad Reputation [1.10.2.10.15]

A bodhisattva who does not protect him- or herself from and dispel the criticism[789] that will cause his or her speech not to be believed and [who does not protect him- or herself from and dispel] the dishonor and infamy that *is* based on something that truly occurred commits an offense and a transgression, and he or she acquires an afflicted offense. [A bodhisattva who] does not dispel [the dishonor and infamy] that is *not* based on something that truly occurred commits an offense and a transgression, and he or she acquires an unafflicted offense.[790]

There is no offense if [the person who makes the criticism] is a heretic who is an adversary or someone else[791] who is irreconcilably attached [to his or her beliefs]. There is no offense if the person criticizes [the bodhisattva] because he or she is a homeless ascetic who begs for food or because he or she is someone who engages in virtuous conduct. There is no offense if the person [who criticizes the bodhisattva] is someone who has been overcome by anger or someone whose thoughts are erroneous.

Failing to Apply a Distressing Measure [1.10.2.10.16]

A bodhisattva who recognizes that some harsh or severe measure would benefit [certain] sentient beings but who does not carry it out because of wishing to avoid making them unhappy commits an offense and a transgression, and he or she acquires an unafflicted offense. There is no offense if [a bodhisattva] recognizes that the benefit [to those beings] in their present life would be small and the unhappiness caused by that [harsh measure] would be great.

789. S: *apaśabdaḥ,* T: *dri ngas*. The Tibetan equivalent means literally, "bad smell." However, this same Sanskrit term is also rendered below in Tibetan as *mi snyan par brjod pa* ("to speak unfavorably").

790. The Tibetan translation of this sentence reads: "[A bodhisattva who] does not dispel [the dishonor and infamy] that is not based on something that truly occurred does not commit an offense and a transgression, and does not acquire an afflicted offense." However, this appears to be a corruption.

791. That is, someone other than a heretic.

Scolding Others in Return for Being Scolded, and the Like [1.10.2.10.17]

A bodhisattva who, having been scolded by others, scolds them in return, or who, having been angered [by others], causes them to become angry in return, or who, having been beaten [by others], beats them in return, or who, having been criticized [by others], criticizes them in return[792] commits an offense and a transgression, and he or she acquires an afflicted offense.

Ignoring Those Who Have Been Angered [1.10.2.10.18]

A bodhisattva who has wronged others or who is believed [by others] to have committed a wrong, and who, having developed a hostile mind or having been seized by pride, does not offer a suitable apology [to those persons] and ignores them commits an offense and a transgression, and he or she acquires an afflicted offense. If [a bodhisattva] fails to offer an apology due to idleness and laziness, or due to lack of mindfulness,[793] he or she commits an offense and a transgression, and acquires an unafflicted offense.

There is no offense if, by that means, [a bodhisattva] wishes to spiritually tame [the aggrieved individuals], or if [a bodhisattva] wishes to train [such individuals] by causing them to turn away from opportunities [to engage in] nonvirtuous [actions] and become established in opportunities [to engage in] virtuous [actions]. There is no offense if [the individual who feels wronged] is a heretic. There is no offense if, [by not apologizing,

792. This misdeed makes direct reference to what are known as the "four principles that make one a spiritual ascetic" (S: *catvāraḥ śramaṇakārakadharmāḥ,* T: *dge sbyong du byed pa'i chos bzhi*); cf. *MVy* no. 8708. They are (1) one who has been scolded should not respond by scolding (S: *ākruṣṭena na pratyākroṣṭavyam,* T: *gshe yang slar mi gshe bar bya*); (2) one who has been angered should not respond by causing others to become angry (S: *roṣitena na pratiroṣitavyam,* T: *khros kyang slar mi khro bar bya*); (3) one who has been criticized should not respond with criticism (S: *bhaṇḍitena na pratibhaṇḍitavyam,* T: *'tshang 'brus kyang slar mi 'bru bar bya*); and (4) one who has been beaten should not respond by beating others in return (S: *tāḍitena na pratitāḍitavyam,* T: *brdeg kyang slar brdeg par mi bya*). Regarding the second of these principles, *BŚPṬ* (f. 213a) states: "'[The act of] angering' (S: *roṣaṇam,* T: *khro ba*) refers to the disagreeable verbal conduct of a person whose intent is to provoke anger [in someone]." Thus, strictly speaking, this principle should be understood to mean that when someone tries to make you angry by speaking to you in an offensive manner, you should not respond to him or her with the same kind of speech.

793. See note 141.

a bodhisattva] desires to receive an apology [from the aggrieved person] for an inappropriate and objectionable act that he or she committed. There is no offense if [the aggrieved person] is naturally contentious and quarrelsome, and offering an apology would only cause him or her to become more agitated and belligerent. There is no offense if the other party is thought to have a forbearing and benign nature and he or she would feel extremely uncomfortable about accepting an apology that relates to his or her having been wronged.

Refusing to Accept an Apology [1.10.2.10.19]

A bodhisattva who has been offered an apology in a manner that accords with Dharma and that is sincere[794] by persons with whom he or she has had an argument concerning some matter but who develops a hostile mind and an injurious intention and does not accept their apology commits an offense and a transgression, and he or she acquires an afflicted offense. If [the bodhisattva] does not have a hostile mind but refuses to accept [the apology] due to an impatient disposition, he or she acquires an unafflicted offense.[795]

There is no offense if, by that means, [a bodhisattva] wishes to spiritually tame [those persons making the apology], etc., as with the rest of the statement that occurs above in its entirety. There is no offense if [the individual] offers an apology in a manner that is contrary to Dharma and that is insincere.

Allowing Anger to Remain Unchecked [1.10.2.10.20]

A bodhisattva who prolongs, maintains, and persists in an attitude of anger that has [previously] arisen toward others commits an offense and a trans-

794. S: *samena,* T: *mthun par.* A possible variant reading is *samayena,* which would mean "at an appropriate time" (T: *dus su*).

795. The two published Sanskrit editions and all the various editions of the Tibetan translation that were consulted state that this second instance also constitutes an afflicted offense. However, both Śāntarakṣita's and Bodhibhadra's Indian commentaries on Candragomī's *Twenty Verses on the Bodhisattva Discipline,* as well as native Tibetan commentaries on Candragomī's work, state that it would constitute an unafflicted offense. Śāntarakṣita's commentary, in particular, explains Candragomī's entire text by citing the relevant passages that appear in the *BBh,* suggesting that variant readings of this passage may have appeared in other Sanskrit editions.

gression, and he or she acquires an afflicted offense. There is no offense for [a bodhisattva] who has developed the aspiration to abandon [this fault], etc., as described previously.[796]

Gathering a Following out of Desire for Gain and Honor [I.10.2.10.21]

A bodhisattva who gathers a following [of disciples] with an attitude that seeks material reward and because he or she desires to be waited on and served [by others] commits an offense and a transgression, and he or she acquires an afflicted offense. There is no offense for [a bodhisattva who] allows him- or herself to be waited on and served [by others] without harboring an attitude that seeks material reward.

Failing to Dispel Laziness, and the Like [I.10.2.10.22]

A bodhisattva who indulges in [any form of] idleness and laziness that may have arisen, and [who indulges in] the ease of sleeping, reclining, and lying on one's side at an inappropriate time or excessively, commits an offense and a transgression, and he or she acquires an afflicted offense.

There is no offense if [a bodhisattva] is gravely ill and unable [to exert him- or herself continuously]. There is no offense for [a bodhisattva] who is exhausted from travel. It should [also] be understood that there is no offense for [a bodhisattva] who has developed the aspiration to abandon [this fault], etc., as described previously.

Engaging in Idle Speech with a Sense of Attachment [I.10.2.10.23]

A bodhisattva who, with an attitude of attachment, spends time socializing with others commits an offense and a transgression, and he or she acquires an afflicted offense. [A bodhisattva] who spends time [in this way] due to clouded recollection acquires an unafflicted offense.

There is no offense if someone else is speaking, and [a bodhisattva] listens for a short time in order to comply with the minds of others and he or she

796. See the misdeed identified earlier as "allowing desire to remain unchecked" [I.10.2.10.2].

does so with a recollection that has been closely placed.[797] There is no offense if the situation is one in which [a bodhisattva] has become astounded by something and is simply making an inquiry about it or if it is one in which [a bodhisattva] is simply replying to a question that has been asked.

Failing to Pursue One-Pointed Concentration [1.10.2.10.24]

A bodhisattva who is desirous of composing his or her mind in relation to [the nine stages of] mental stability but who, having developed a hostile mind or having been seized by pride, does not approach [a teacher] and request instruction commits an offense and a transgression, and he or she acquires an afflicted offense. [If a bodhisattva does not do so] because of idleness and laziness, then he or she acquires an unafflicted offense.

There is no offense if [a bodhisattva] is ill and unable [to seek instruction]. There is no offense if [a bodhisattva] believes the instruction would be erroneous. There is no offense if [a bodhisattva] is already learned [in this subject] and capable of developing mental composure, or if he or she has already completed what needed to be done by means of that instruction.

Failing to Eliminate the Hindrances to Meditative Composure [1.10.2.10.25]

A bodhisattva who persists in and does not dispel the hindrance[798] of desire for sense pleasures that has [previously] arisen commits an offense and a transgression, and he or she acquires an afflicted offense. There is no offense for [a bodhisattva] who has developed the aspiration to abandon [this hindrance] and who is striving [to abandon it] but who still generates it because his or her mind has been overcome by strong mental afflictions. It should be understood that the same [explanation] applies for [the remaining hindrances of] (1) malice, (2) torpor and sleep, (3) excitation and regret, and (4) doubt.

797. See note 687 for general comments relating to recollection (S: *smṛtiḥ,* T: *dran pa*). Closely placed recollection (S: *smṛtyupasthānam,* T: *dran pa nye bar gzhag pa*) is an important spiritual practice that is taught in four forms (see note 563). See also notes 1095, 1096, and 1097 for additional remarks.

798. See note 138.

Regarding Enjoyment of the States of Meditative Absorption as a Good Quality [1.10.2.10.26]

A bodhisattva who relishes [the pleasure and ease of] the mental absorptions or who regards doing so as a good quality[799] commits an offense and a transgression, and he or she acquires an afflicted offense.

There is no offense for [a bodhisattva] who has developed the aspiration to abandon [this fault], etc., as described previously.

Rejecting the Teachings of the Listeners' Vehicle [1.10.2.10.27]

Moreover, any bodhisattva who holds the following view or professes it [to others] commits an offense and a transgression, and he or she acquires an afflicted offense: "A bodhisattva should not listen to, take up,[800] or train him- or herself in any [form of] Dharma that pertains to the Listeners' Vehicle. What does a bodhisattva gain by listening to or taking up the Dharma that pertains to the Listeners' Vehicle? What need is there to train oneself in that [form of Dharma]?" Since a bodhisattva should even strive to learn heretical treatises, how much more so should he or she [study teachings that are] the word of the Buddha.

There is no offense for [a bodhisattva] who has become exclusively devoted to [the teachings of the Listeners' Vehicle to abandon their study] in order to overcome that predilection.

799. S: *guṇadarśī,* T: *yon tan du lta ba. BŚPṬ* (f. 213b): "The expression 'one who regards [relishing the mental absorptions] as a good quality' is meant to indicate that it is a fault for someone who has attained one-pointed concentration to remain satisfied merely with [the attainment of] the mental absorptions."

800. S: *udgrahītavyaḥ,* T: *gzung bar bya ba.* The act of "taking up" Dharma (S: *udgrahaṇam,* T: *len pa*) is included in a list of ten "Dharma activities" (S: *daśadharmacaritāni,* T: *chos spyod bcu;* cf. *MV,* ch. 5, vv. 8c–10). *MVṬ* (p. 159) provides this description: "'Taking up [the Dharma]' is [the act of] employing great reverence to effectively make it one's own." Similarly, *AAA* (p. 293): "[A person who wants to train in the listeners' stage] should also take up [this very Perfection of Wisdom] through bringing it to mind with [a form of practice] that consists of reflection."

Failing to Pursue the Teachings of the Great Vehicle [1.10.2.10.28]

A bodhisattva who possesses [scriptures of] the bodhisattva collection but does not engage in [the study of] the bodhisattva collection and who, having completely ignored the bodhisattva collection, does engage in [the study of] the listener collection commits an offense and a transgression, and he or she acquires an afflicted offense.

Studying Heretical Treatises to the Exclusion of the Buddha's Word [1.10.2.10.29]

A bodhisattva who possesses [scriptures that contain] the word of the Buddha but who does not engage in [the study of] the Buddha's word yet does engage in [the study of] heretical treatises and treatises of outsider traditions commits an offense and a transgression, and he or she also acquires an afflicted offense.

There is no offense for [a bodhisattva] of superior intelligence [to study heretical treatises], [if he or she is] someone who is able to quickly grasp the meaning [of such treatises], who will not forget their meaning for a long period of time, who is able to discern the meaning [of those treatises] that are reflected upon, who possesses a [form of] understanding that has investigated the word of the Buddha by means of the applications and is unshakable [in its devotion to the word of the Buddha], and who engages [in the study of] the word of the Buddha each day with twice as much effort.

Delighting in the Study of Heretical Treatises [1.10.2.10.30]

Moreover, a bodhisattva who has not violated these principles while becoming knowledgeable about heretical treatises and the treatises of outsider traditions but who does so as one who is delighted [by them], and who both enjoys and takes pleasure in them rather than resorting to them as one would bitter medicine, commits an offense and a transgression, and he or she acquires an afflicted offense.

Denigrating the Teachings of the Great Vehicle [1.10.2.10.31]

A bodhisattva who, after hearing the profound subjects [contained] in the bodhisattva collection [of scriptures], fails to develop [proper] devotion toward those supremely profound [subjects] that pertain to the nature of reality or to the powers of the buddhas and bodhisattvas and denigrates them by saying, "These [teachings] do not possess any meaning, they do not possess [any genuine] Dharma, they were not spoken by the Tathāgata, they do not [provide] benefit or happiness to sentient beings," commits an offense and a transgression, and he or she acquires an afflicted offense, [regardless of] whether he or she denigrates them because of his or her own improper manner of thinking or because of his or her [desire] to comply with [the views of] others.

After hearing such profound and supremely profound subjects, a bodhisattva may indeed fail to develop an attitude of devotion [toward them]. Regarding this [point], a faithful and sincere bodhisattva should train him- or herself about this matter [as follows]: "It is not right that I, who am blind and lacking in vision, and who can proceed only by relying on the Tathāgata's vision, should reject the Tathāgata's enigmatic statements."[801] A bodhisattva who considers him- or herself to be lacking in understanding in this way and who regards the Tathāgata as the sole being who is unobscured with regard to a buddha's qualities becomes one who is correctly established [in the practice]. [Thus,] there is no offense for [a bodhisattva] who, though lacking in devotion, does not reject [the teachings on profound subjects].

Praising Oneself and Disparaging Others [1.10.2.10.32]

A bodhisattva whose mind is associated with corporeal desire[802] or who has developed a hateful mind and who then praises him- or herself and disparages others in the presence of other persons commits an offense and a transgression, and he or she acquires an afflicted offense.

801. S: *tathāgatasaṃdhāya bhāṣitam,* T: *de bzhin gshegs pas dgongs te gsungs pa.* See note 340 for comments regarding a similar expression.

802. S: *sāmiṣacittaḥ,* T: *zang zing dang bcas pa'i sems. BSVP* (f. 213b) describes the phrase "one whose mind is associated with corporeal desire" as "a bodhisattva who feels attachment for him- or herself (S: **ātmasnehaḥ,* T: *bdag la chags pa*) due to the vain belief that he or she is naturally virtuous." See also note 584.

There is no offense for [a bodhisattva who speaks this way because] he or she wants to overcome heretics or [because] he or she wants preserve the [Buddhist] teaching. There is no offense if, by that means, [a bodhisattva] wishes to spiritually tame the person [to whom he or she is speaking], etc., as described in detail before. There is no offense if [a bodhisattva's aim is] to engender faith in those who lack it and further increase the faith of those who have already acquired it.

Failing to Pursue Learning [1.10.2.10.33]

A bodhisattva who, having been seized with pride or having developed a hostile or a hateful mind, does not attend a Dharma sermon or a discussion on doctrinal exegesis[803] commits an offense and a transgression, and he or she acquires an afflicted offense. [A bodhisattva] who fails to attend due to idleness and laziness acquires an unafflicted offense.

There is no offense if [a bodhisattva] was not aware [of the event] or if he or she was ill and unable [to attend]. There is no offense if he or she believes that the teaching would be one that is spurious. There is no offense for [a bodhisattva] who [does not attend in order to] preserve the opinion of his or her Dharma teacher. There is no offense for [a bodhisattva] who [does not attend because he or she] recognizes that [the subject of] the talk is one that he or she has heard repeatedly, and [therefore] it has [already] been learned and its meaning has been realized. There is no offense if [a bodhisattva] is very learned and has both retained and stored[804] what he or she has learned. There is no offense for someone who is engaged in the cultivation of a bodhisattva's one-pointed concentration [not to attend], since [that is an exercise for which] the mind must be continually fixed on a meditation object. There is no offense for [a bodhisattva not to attend] if he or she has a very slow intellect and, therefore, would be slow at taking up Dharma, slow at retaining [Dharma], and slow at fixing his or her mind [one-pointedly] on a meditation object.

803. S: *sāṃkathyaviniścayaḥ,* T: *'bel ba'i gtam rnam par gtan la 'bebs pa.*

804. S: *saṃnicayaḥ,* T: *bsags pa.* The principal meaning of this expression is the activity of "accumulating" or "storing up" material goods; however, it would seem that in this context the sense is that of building up knowledge of a large range and number of subjects. *BŚPṬ* (f. 214b): "The condition of having completed [the process of] learning [Dharma] is indicated by the phrase 'he or she is very learned,' etc."

Showing Disrespect toward a Dharma Teacher or the Dharma [1.10.2.10.34]

A bodhisattva who is deliberately contemptuous of, disrespectful toward, laughs at, or ridicules a person who is a Dharma teacher, or who is someone who relies upon the [Dharma's] literal form of expression and not its meaning,[805] commits an offense and a transgression, and he or she commits an afflicted offense.

Failing to Assist Others [1.10.2.10.35]

A bodhisattva who is abiding in the [bodhisattva] discipline and who, while in a hostile or hateful state of mind, does not assist beings with their activities—that is to say, [the activities of] making determinations about what ought to be done, leaving on and returning from journeys, carrying out right activities and occupations, safeguarding possessions, reconciling those who are estranged from one another, religious celebrations, and meritorious deeds—commits an offense and a transgression, and he or she acquires an afflicted offense. [A bodhisattva who] fails to assist beings due to idleness and laziness acquires an unafflicted offense.

There is no offense if [a bodhisattva] is sick and unable [to assist others]. There is no offense if the petitioner is able to do [the activity] him- or herself or if he or she has someone [else] who can be relied upon. There is no offense if the activity is one that is harmful or contrary to Dharma. There is no offense if, by that means, [a bodhisattva] wishes to spiritually tame that very person [who seeks assistance], etc., as described in detail before. There is no offense if [a bodhisattva] has previously agreed [to assist] someone else. There is no offense if [a bodhisattva] asks someone else who is capable [of providing assistance]. There is no offense if [a bodhisattva] is continuously and correctly engaged in [activities] that pertain to virtue.[806] There is no offense if [a bodhisattva] is naturally slow [in intellect] and would

805. "Someone who relies upon the [Dharma's] literal form of expression and not its meaning" is acting in a manner that is contrary to one of the four reliances. See note 1074 and Book I, chapter 17, the section entitled "The Four Reliances" [I.17.6].

806. This statement does not appear in the Tibetan translation; however, it is referred to in *BŚPṬ,* f. 215a.

be [too] slow [in intellect] to give advice, as described previously.[807] There is no offense for [a bodhisattva] who is desirous of preserving the opinion of a great many other individuals [not to assist others]. There is no offense for [a bodhisattva] who is desirous of observing a rule of the Sangha [not to assist others].

Failing to Care for the Sick [1.10.2.10.36]

A bodhisattva who encounters a person who is sick and afflicted by an illness and does not attend to and take care of [that person] because of being in a hostile or hateful state of mind commits an offense and a transgression, and he or she acquires an afflicted offense. [A bodhisattva] who fails to do so because of idleness and laziness acquires an unafflicted offense.

There is no offense if [the bodhisattva] is sick and unable [to take care of anyone]. There is no offense if [the bodhisattva] asks someone else who is both capable and kind [to care for the person who is sick]. There is no offense if the sick person has a benefactor and someone to rely upon. There is no offense if [the sick person] is capable of attending to and taking care of him- or herself. There is no offense if [the sick person] has been cured of a long-standing illness. There is no offense if [a bodhisattva does not care for a sick person] in order to avoid interrupting an ongoing virtuous endeavor that is of great importance. There is no offense for [a bodhisattva not to care for a sick person] if he or she has a very slow intellect and, therefore, would be slow at explaining Dharma, slow at retaining [Dharma], and slow at fixing his or her mind on a meditation object. There is no offense if he or she has previously agreed to do something for another person.

Failing to Assist Those Who Are Suffering [1.10.2.10.37]

It should be understood that [the description of the offense of failing] to assist in dispelling the suffering of those who are afflicted by suffering is similar to [that of failing] to care for those who are sick.

807. That is, just as a slow intellect was a mitigating factor in the misdeed described as "failing to pursue learning."

Not Indicating What Is Proper to Others [1.10.2.10.38]

A bodhisattva who sees beings engaged in wrongful conduct concerning a matter that relates to this life or future ones and who, having developed a hostile or angry mind, does not indicate a proper course of conduct [to them] commits an offense and a transgression, and he or she acquires an afflicted offense. [A bodhisattva] who fails to indicate [a proper course of conduct] due to idleness and laziness acquires an unafflicted offense.

There is no offense if [the bodhisattva] lacks the knowledge [of how to indicate a proper course of conduct] and, [therefore,] is unable [to do so]. There is no offense if he or she requests another person who is capable [of indicating a proper course of conduct to do so]. There is no offense if the person [who is engaged in wrongful conduct] is him- or herself capable [of correcting his or her own behavior]. There is no offense if [the person who is engaged in wrongful conduct] is under the guidance of another spiritual teacher. There is no offense if, by that means, [a bodhisattva] wishes to spiritually tame [the person who is engaged in wrongful conduct], etc., as described in detail before. There is no offense if the person to whom proper instruction should be given has a hostile mind, is difficult to talk to, would take [what is said] the wrong way, is devoid of any affection or respect [for others], or has an unruly nature.

Failing to Return a Benefit Received from Others [1.10.2.10.39]

A bodhisattva who is ungrateful and unappreciative of those persons who have assisted him or her and who, having developed a hostile mind, does not provide a suitable form of assistance in return commits an offense and a transgression, and he or she acquires an afflicted offense. [A bodhisattva] who fails to respond [appropriately] due to idleness and laziness acquires an unafflicted offense.

There is no offense for [a bodhisattva] who makes an effort [to respond appropriately] but lacks the ability or the strength [to do so]. There is no offense if, by that means, [a bodhisattva] wishes to spiritually tame [that person], etc., as described before. There is no offense if that person does not want to receive any form of assistance in return.

Failing to Dispel the Grief That Others Are Experiencing [1.10.2.10.40]

A bodhisattva who, while in a hostile state of mind, refuses to dispel the grief that is being experienced by sentient beings who have undergone a misfortune relating to their family or their wealth commits an offense and a transgression, and he or she acquires an afflicted offense. [A bodhisattva] who fails to dispel [the grief that is being experienced by others] due to idleness and laziness acquires an unafflicted offense. It should be understood that no offense [is incurred for failing to dispel the grief of others] in the same kinds of situations that were described earlier in relation to the failure to assist [others] with their activities.

Failing to Provide Food and the Like to Those Who Seek It [1.10.2.10.41]

A bodhisattva who has been asked in a proper manner and who, while in a hostile state of mind, does not provide food, drinks, and other necessities to those who are seeking food, drinks, and the like commits an offense and a transgression, and he or she acquires an afflicted offense. [A bodhisattva] who fails to provide [such necessities] due to idleness and laziness or due to lack of mindfulness acquires an unafflicted offense.

There is no offense if [a bodhisattva] lacks and does not possess these objects. There is no offense for [a bodhisattva] who has been asked to provide unwholesome or improper substances. There is no offense if, by that means, [a bodhisattva] wishes to spiritually tame or train [those petitioners], etc., as described before. There is no offense if [a bodhisattva] is observing a prohibition imposed by the king. There is no offense if [a bodhisattva] is observing a rule of the Sangha.

Failing to Assist One's Followers [1.10.2.10.42]

After having established a group of followers, a bodhisattva who, while in a hostile state of mind, fails to provide correct instruction and correct counsel, regularly and at the appropriate time, or who fails to seek, in a manner that accords with Dharma, robes, food, bedding, seats, medicine for curing the ill, and [other] personal belongings, on behalf of those [followers] who are in need of them, from those brahmins and householders who possess faith [in the Dharma], commits an offense and a transgression, and he or she acquires an afflicted offense. [A bodhisattva] who fails to provide instruction and counsel [to his or her followers] or who fails to seek [needed personal belongings for them] due to idleness and laziness or due to lack of mindfulness acquires an unafflicted offense.

There is no offense if, by that means, [a bodhisattva] wishes to spiritually tame [his or her followers], etc., as described previously. There is no offense if [a bodhisattva] is observing a rule of the Sangha. There is no offense if he or she is sick and unfit to carry out [these activities]. There is no offense if he or she requests another person [to carry out these activities] who is capable [of doing so]. There is no offense if the group of followers is one that has developed great merit, or [its members] themselves are capable of seeking robes, etc., or the duty of giving instructions and counsel to those [followers] needing instruction and counsel has been completed. There is no offense if [a bodhisattva fails to instruct or provide assistance to] a former heretic that has entered [the group] in order to steal Dharma [teachings] and he or she is someone not suitable to be trained.

Failing to Comply with the Wishes of Others [1.10.2.10.43]

A bodhisattva who, while in a hostile state of mind, does not comply with the minds of others commits an offense and a transgression, and he or she acquires an afflicted offense. [A bodhisattva] who does not comply [with the minds of others] due to idleness and laziness, or due to lack of mindfulness, acquires an unafflicted offense.

There is no offense if [a bodhisattva does not comply with the minds of others] because their intention is [for him or her to do] something that is unwholesome.[808] There is no offense if [a bodhisattva does not comply with the minds of others because] he or she is sick and unfit to carry out [some activity that others would like to have done]. There is no offense if [a bodhisattva does not comply with the minds of others] in observance of a rule

808. S: *apathyaḥ*, T: *mi 'phrod pa*. The principal sense of this term is something that is unwholesome in a medical sense, that is to say, bad for one's health. The Tibetan translation of Bodhibhadra's *BSVP* (f. 215b) renders this adjective as "harmful" (T: *gnod pa dang ldan pa*). *BChZhL* (f. 91b): "[The phrase] 'their intention is [for a bodhisattva to do] something that is unwholesome' means that it would either bring harm to those individuals or it would harm [the bodhisattva] him- or herself."

of the Sangha. There is no offense if [a bodhisattva does not comply with the minds of others] because although [the activity] that one individual would like [a bodhisattva to do] is wholesome for that person it is neither desired nor wholesome for a great many other persons. There is no offense if [a bodhisattva does not comply with the minds of others because] the person [who would like a bodhisattva to do something] is a heretic who deserves to be suppressed.[809] There is no offense if, by that means, [a bodhisattva] wishes to spiritually tame or train [some individual or individuals], as described previously.

Failing to Praise Those Who Deserve to Be Praised [1.10.2.10.44]

A bodhisattva who, having become angry, does not make mention of the genuine good qualities of others, does not express genuine praise [of others], and does not voice his or her approval of an eloquent statement that is made by another commits an offense and a transgression, and he or she acquires an afflicted offense. [A bodhisattva] who fails to make such statements due to idleness or laziness, or due to lack of mindfulness, acquires an unafflicted offense.

There is no offense if [a bodhisattva] believes that [the praiseworthy individual] is someone who naturally has few desires[810] [and, therefore, he or she does not make such statements] because of the desire to preserve that person's opinion. There is no offense if [a bodhisattva] is sick and unable [to make such statements]. There is no offense if, by that means, [a bodhisattva] wishes to spiritually tame or train [the praiseworthy individual], etc., as described previously. There is no offense if [a bodhisattva does not make such statements] in observance of a rule of the Sangha. There is no offense if [a bodhisattva] believes that it would be harmful [to make such a statement] as it would cause [that individual] to develop a mental affliction, [such as]

809. *BŚPṬ* (f. 215a): "Heretics deserve to be suppressed (S: *nigrāhyaḥ,* T: *tshar bcad par bya ba*) because they are enemies of the [Buddhist] teaching."

810. S: *alpecchatā,* T: *'dod pa chung ba*. Typically, this expression is used to indicate lack of acquisitiveness for material things. For example, *AKB* (p. 335) defines this quality as the opposite of, and antidote to, having great desire (see note 760). Here the phrase is meant to suggest a sense of modesty that would cause a person to feel uncomfortable if he or she were to hear him- or herself being praised by someone else. *BŚPṬ* (f. 215a): "'Having few desires' means that [a person] does not even want his or her good qualities to be voiced by others."

conceit[811] or the swelling up[812] [of pride], and so [he or she refrains from making such statements] in order to avoid that [result]. There is no offense if the [person's apparent] good qualities are counterfeit and not genuine; or if the statements [made by that person] only seem to be excellent but they are not truly excellent. There is no offense if the person is a heretic and someone who ought to be suppressed. There is no offense for [a bodhisattva] who is waiting for the conclusion of the discourse.

Failing to Suppress Those Who Engage in Misconduct [1.10.2.10.45]

A bodhisattva who, having developed an afflicted mind, fails to censure those beings who deserve to be censured, or who censures but fails to correct by means of punishment those who deserve to be punished, or who punishes but fails to banish those who deserve to be banished commits an offense and a transgression, and he or she acquires an afflicted offense. [A bodhisattva] who fails to censure, etc., up to fails to banish, due to idleness and laziness, or due to lack of mindfulness, acquires an unafflicted offense.

There is no offense for [a bodhisattva] who ignores a person who is incorrigible, unfit to be spoken to, difficult to talk to, and very hostile. There is no offense for [a bodhisattva] who is waiting for the right time [to act]. There is no offense for [a bodhisattva] who perceives that [taking corrective action] would lead to strife, quarreling, contention, and disputation. There is no offense for [a bodhisattva] who perceives that [such action would lead to] conflict and division in the Sangha. There is no offense if those persons, being free of guile and possessed of a strong [sense of] shame and abashment, will turn away from their wrongdoing [on their own].

811. S: *madaḥ,* T: *rgyags pa*. *AS* (p. 9): "What is conceit? It is a form of desire that is accompanied by joy and gladness, and it arises from [possessing such qualities as] health or youth, or from having perceived an indication [that one will have a] long life or [having perceived oneself as having] some other form of samsaric good fortune. Its action is to give support to all the root and secondary mental afflictions." *ASBh* (p. 7): "[The phrase] 'some other form of samsaric good fortune' should be understood [to mean] an eminent family, strength, beauty, intelligence, knowledge, wealth, power, etc."

812. S: *unnatiḥ,* T: *khengs pa*. This noun represents the essential nature of pride. *AS* (p. 7): "What is pride? It is the swelling up of the mind (S: *cittasyonnatiḥ,* T: *sems kyi khengs pa*) that occurs on the basis of the view of the perishable collection (S: *satkāyadṛṣṭiḥ,* T: *'jig tshogs la lta ba*)." On the latter, see note 311.

Failing to Use One's Miraculous Powers [1.10.2.10.46]

A bodhisattva who possesses a variety of miraculous, supernatural, and spiritual powers but who does not, by means of those miraculous powers, frighten those beings who deserve to be frightened and win over those beings who are suitable to be won over and cause gifts of faith[813] to be given up [by those who are unworthy of them] commits an offense and a transgression, and he or she acquires an unafflicted offense. There is no fault if [a bodhisattva does not use such powers] in a situation that involves beings who are strongly attached [to their beliefs], [such as] heretics who possess the [kinds of] wrong view that lead them to discredit āryas.

Concluding Remarks [1.10.2.11]

It should be understood that no offense ever occurs for an individual whose mind is severely disturbed, or one who is experiencing intense pain or who has not accepted the discipline.

These precepts that pertain to the spiritual training of the bodhisattvas were actually spoken by the Blessed One here and there throughout the sutra scriptures and they were set forth in relation to the morality of restraint, the morality of acquiring virtue, and the morality that acts on behalf of beings. A bodhisattva who has gained respect for the precepts that have been collected and presented in this manual on the bodhisattva collection of scriptures should undertake to practice the training [only] after having generated the utmost reverence [for the bodhisattva system of discipline] and after having accepted the discipline from another person with an attitude that is extremely pure in its desire to practice the training, an attitude that [seeks to attain] enlightenment, an attitude that is dedicated to the welfare of sentient beings, and with a [form of] reverence that [is committed to] not violating [any of the precepts] from the very outset.

813. A "gift of faith" (S: *śraddhādeyam,* T: *dad pas byin pa*) is an offering that is made to a monk or nun by the faithful. *BŚPṬ* (f. 215b): "Because it is morally reprehensible for those who [behave in a way that is] hostile to the teaching to enjoy gifts of faith, [a bodhisattva should use his or her powers] to 'cause [them] to be given up.'" *BChZhL* (f. 92b): "Though a person may abide in the teaching [i.e., live as a monk or nun], if he or she does not [truly] possess the discipline [of a monk or nun], gifts of faith cannot be 'digested' [by such a person; i.e., an impure monk or nun is not fit to accept such offerings], therefore [a bodhisattva should use his or her powers] 'to cause [those gifts of faith] to be given up.'"

CONFESSION [1.10.2.12]

In addition, [a bodhisattva] who does violate [any of these precepts] should restore [the training] by [resorting to] the method of remedy according to the [rules of the] Dharma. It should be understood that all of these offenses are included within [the category of] a bodhisattva's misdeeds and they are to be confessed before any follower of the Listeners' Vehicle or follower of the Great Vehicle who is able to comprehend and accept the [appropriate] verbal informative form.[814]

If a bodhisattva commits an offense that represents an extreme form of defeat on the basis of a great perturbation, his or her moral discipline will be abandoned. [Nevertheless,] it can be received again for a second time.[815] If [a bodhisattva] commits an offense [of the type that represents an extreme form of defeat] on the basis of a middling form of perturbation, he or she should confess this form of wrongdoing before three or more persons. After initially declaring the circumstances [of the offense], [the bodhisattva] should seat him- or herself before [those to whom the confession is to be made] and state the following: "O long-lived ones, please give heed to me. I, who am named so-and-so, in the circumstances that have been declared, have committed an offense that is a form of wrongdoing and [an act] that violates the bodhisattva code of ethics." The remainder [of the statement of confession] should be expressed in the same manner that a *bhikṣu* or *bhikṣuṇī* confesses the forms of wrongdoing [that violate the individual liberation code of ethics].[816] It should be understood that confession of an

814. See note 733. Here this phrase refers to the statement of admission made by the confessor.

815. S: *dvis*, T: *lan gnyis su*. Citing several Indian sources, *BChZhL* (f. 94a–94b) states that the phrase "for a second time" or "twice" does not mean that the bodhisattva discipline can only be accepted again a limited number of times.

816. *BChZhL* (f. 94b): "Regarding that [remainder of the statement], following the word 'offense' state the name of the infraction that was committed. For example, '[I who am named so-and-so] . . . have committed the offense of praising myself and criticizing others, [which is a form of wrongdoing . . . .]' The remainder of the statement, according to the 'old commentary' [i.e., Śāntarakṣita's commentary to *BSV*], is as follows: [The confessor states:] 'I confess and admit these offenses to the Long-Lived Ones and do not conceal them. By confessing and admitting them, I will abide in a contented state. If I fail to confess and admit them, I will not abide in a contented state.' [The hearer of the confession asks:] 'Do you recognize these [acts] to be offenses?' [The confessor responds:] 'I do so recognize them.' [The hearer of the confession then asks:] 'Will you refrain from committing them in the

act that represents an extreme form of defeat [and that was performed] on the basis of a lesser form of perturbation, as well as [confession] of all the other [secondary] offenses, should be done before one person. If there is no suitable person before whom [one] can make confession, one should earnestly generate the conviction not to commit [such forms of wrongdoing] again. In the future, one should also observe such restraint. In this way, [a bodhisattva] is said to be raised up from those offenses.

The Ritual for Accepting the Bodhisattva Discipline If There Is No Qualified Preceptor [1.10.2.13]

Moreover, regarding the acceptance of the bodhisattva discipline, if no individual possessing the [requisite] good qualities is available, the bodhisattva should then, by him- or herself, accept the discipline of bodhisattva morality before an image of the Tathāgata. This should be done in the following manner. After placing the upper garment on the shoulder, he or she should either place the right knee on the ground or sit in a squatting position and say the following: "I, who am named so-and-so, make a declaration to all the Tathāgatas of the ten directions and [all] the bodhisattvas who have attained the great [ārya] stages. Before them, I accept all of the bodhisattva precepts and all aspects of the bodhisattva morality—[namely,] the morality of restraint, the morality of acquiring virtuous qualities, and the morality of acting on behalf of sentient beings—with regard to which all the bodhisattvas of the past have trained themselves, all the bodhisattvas of the future will train themselves, and all the bodhisattvas of the present are now training themselves throughout the ten directions." This should be repeated a second and a third time. After making this recitation, [the bodhisattva] should stand up. It should be understood that the remainder [of the ritual] in its entirety is the same as was described previously.

---

future?' [Confessor:] 'In accord with the Dharma and the Vinaya, I shall keep [the precepts] well and deferentially.' . . . Regarding physical conduct, the 'new commentary' [i.e., *BSVP*] states: 'Gesturing [to the monks and nuns] with joined palms, bow to them and then sit in a lower place and in a squatting position with joined palms.'"

Further Comments about Transgressions [1.10.2.14]

As relates to the bodhisattva's manner of [committing] offenses, there is no offense that is beyond remediation.[817] Moreover, concerning the declaration made by the Blessed One that, "It should be understood that a bodhisattva's offenses are for the most part brought forth by hatred; they are not brought forth by desire," the intent [of this statement] should be understood as follows. Any and all actions that a bodhisattva carries out due to his or her attachment to sentient beings—[which is to say,] one that is due to his or her affection for sentient beings—are proper for a bodhisattva to do; they are not improper for him or her to do. Nor would it be fitting for someone who is doing what is proper to incur an offense. However, a bodhisattva who feels anger toward sentient beings does not act in a way that benefits either him- or herself or others. Nor is that something that is proper for a bodhisattva to do. Thus, it is fitting that someone who is doing what is improper should incur an offense.

The lesser, middling, and great offenses of a bodhisattva should be understood as [they are explained] in the *Collection on [Canonical] Topics*.[818]

Three Forms of Excellence [1.10.2.15]

Moreover, a bodhisattva who is engaged thus in the training that relates to his or her code of ethics[819] comes to have three forms of excellence—[that is,] excellence of practice, excellence of attitude, and excellence of a former cause—and abides in a contented state.

Regarding these, what is excellence of practice?

For example, when a bodhisattva conducts him- or herself in such a manner that he or she does not break the precepts of morality, when his or her behavior of body, speech, and mind is pure, when he or she does not commit offenses repeatedly, and when he or she is someone who reveals his or her evil deeds, this is referred to as "excellence of practice."

817. S: *niravaśeṣaḥ,* T: *lhag ma med pa*. Literally, "without a remainder," or "complete." *BHSD* (p. 299): an offense "that can never under any circumstances be atoned."

818. S: *Vastusaṃgrahaṇī,* T: *gZhi bsdu ba*. *BŚPBh* (ff. 188a–189a) quotes the entire passage. In the Tibetan Tengyur this passage appears in the text identified as *Vinayasaṃgrahaṇī* (T: *'Dul ba bsdu ba,* f. 8a–8b), not the separate work that is titled *gZhi bsdu ba*.

819. I.e., the bodhisattva code of ethics.

What is excellence of attitude?

When [a bodhisattva] is one who has gone forth [into the life of a homeless ascetic] with the aim of pursuing Dharma and not with the aim of gaining an [easy] livelihood, when he or she is one who longs for great enlightenment and not one who fails to long for it, when he or she is one who longs for asceticism[820] and nirvana and not one who fails to long for them, and when [a bodhisattva] who possesses such forms of [spiritual] longing does not abide continuously as one who is lazy, one whose effort is inferior, one who lacks effort, and one who is filled with evil, nonvirtuous qualities that are afflicted, that promote [samsaric] rebirth, that are related to the fevers,[821] that have a painful ripening, and that bring about birth, old age, and death in the future, this is referred to as "excellence of attitude."

What is excellence of a former cause?

For example, when a bodhisattva has previously—[that is,] in former lives—carried out meritorious acts and virtuous acts by reason of which he or she is not currently distressed by [a lack of] robes, food, seats, bedding, medicine for curing the ill, and [other] personal belongings, and he or she is also able to share them with others, this should be known as a bodhisattva's excellence of a former cause.

A bodhisattva who possesses these three forms of excellence and who is engaged in the training that relates to the [Great Vehicle's] code of ethics abides continuously in a contented state. It should be understood that [a bodhisattva] who possesses the three forms of misfortune that are the

820. *AKB* (p. 369): "Asceticism (S: *śrāmaṇyam,* T: *dge sbyong gyi tshul*) refers to the path that is free of the outflows (S: *anāsravo mārgaḥ,* T: *zag pa med pa'i lam*) [i.e., the transcendent path], for it is by means of this [path] that one becomes a [true] ascetic in the sense of having [permanently] quelled [at least a portion of] the mental afflictions. As it is declared in a sutra: 'One is called an ascetic because he or she has quelled many kinds of evil and nonvirtuous entities . . .' and so on up to '[he or she has quelled many kinds of entities] that bring about old age and death.' Because an ordinary person [i.e., a non-ārya] has not completely quelled [any of the mental afflictions], such an individual is not an ascetic in the ultimate sense." *BŚPṬ* (f. 216b): "Bodhisattva asceticism is the path that includes the practice of the three trainings and that occurs on all ten of the [ārya bodhisattva] levels. Nirvana [here] should be understood to mean the complete nirvana of the Great Vehicle's [path]—that is to say, non-abiding nirvana (see note 335)."

821. S: *sajvaraḥ,* T: *rims nad dang bcas pa*. *AS* (p. 50): "There are three fevers: the fever of desire, the fever of hatred, and the fever of ignorance. They are called fevers because, based upon desire, hatred, and ignorance, they burn [beings] with the great fire of desire for that which is contrary to Dharma, they burn [beings] with the great fire of unsuitable forms of eagerness, and they burn [beings] with the great fire of wrongful forms of discipline."

opposite of those [forms of excellence] abides continuously in a discontented state.

This [topic], then, which has been presented in both a succinct and an extensive manner, is referred to as the "all-inclusive morality" of a bodhisattva. It relates both to the faction that is made up of householders and to the faction that is made up of those who have gone forth [into the homeless state]. Furthermore, the remaining [topics—namely,] the morality that is difficult to carry out, etc.—should be understood as subdivisions of this very [category of] all-inclusive morality.

The Morality That Is Difficult to Carry Out [1.10.3]

Regarding [the remaining categories], what is the morality of a bodhisattva that is difficult to carry out?

It should be regarded as being of three types. When a bodhisattva who possesses great wealth and who has great authority and power gives up his or her wealth and gives up his or her great authority and power and accepts the discipline of [bodhisattva] morality, this is called "the morality of a bodhisattva that is difficult to carry out."

Also, when a bodhisattva who has accepted the morality has fallen into distress and is losing his or her life but refuses even to damage the acceptance of morality, much less to cause its destruction, this is a second form of what is called "the morality of a bodhisattva that is difficult to carry out."

When a bodhisattva is so attentive and his or her recollection remains so closely placed with regard to all the forms of attention that pertain both to moving about and meditative practice[822] that during his or her entire lifetime he or she does not acquire even a minor offense and commits no error in relation to the morality, much less a weighty [offense], this is a third form of what is called "the morality of a bodhisattva that is difficult to carry out."

The Morality That Is Directed Everywhere [1.10.4]

What is the morality of a bodhisattva that is directed everywhere?

It should be regarded as being of four types: (1) [the morality] that is accepted, (2) natural morality, (3) [the morality] that has been practiced repeatedly, and (4) [the morality] that is accompanied by means.

822. See note 438 and also *Inner Science,* pp. 184–187.

Regarding these, the morality that is accepted is the threefold acceptance of the discipline of bodhisattva morality—namely, [the acceptance of] the morality of restraint, the morality of acquiring virtue, and the morality of acting on behalf of sentient beings.

Regarding this [topic], natural morality is [the form of morality] that is possessed by a bodhisattva who abides in the [Great Vehicle's] spiritual lineage and who carries out pure deeds of body, speech, and mind due to the natural goodness of his or her mind continuum.

Regarding this [topic], the morality that has been practiced repeatedly is the threefold morality that has already been explained and that a bodhisattva has carried out previously—[that is,] in former lives. Through having generated the strength of this former cause, he or she does not delight in any kind of evil conduct whatsoever, recoils from evil, delights in virtuous conduct, and desires [to engage in] virtuous conduct.

Regarding this [topic], the morality that is accompanied by means is a bodhisattva's [form of morality] that relies upon the four principles for attracting a following to carry out virtuous deeds of body and speech on behalf of sentient beings.

The Morality of a True Spiritual Being [1.10.5]

Regarding this [topic], what is the morality of a true spiritual being?

It should be understood as being of five types: (1) Here a bodhisattva is endowed with morality. (2) He or she causes others to accept morality. (3) He or she praises morality. (4) He or she is pleased at the sight of an exemplary Dharma follower.[823] (5) If an offense is committed, he or she remedies it according to [the rules of] the Dharma.

Morality of Every Form [1.10.6]

Regarding this [topic], what is a bodhisattva's morality of every form?

It should be understood as the thirteen forms [that result from] combining together six forms and seven forms. They are [that a bodhisattva's morality is] (1) abundant because it is dedicated to great enlightenment and because it includes extensive precepts; (2) it is irreproachable and (3) rests in

823. See note 732. *BŚPṬ* (f. 218b): "He or she is pleased at the sight of those who are correctly established [in the Dharma]; he or she does not vie [with them]."

a state of joy because it avoids the two extremes of indulging in sense pleasures and engaging in self-mortification; (4) it is uninterrupted because the training is not given up for as long as one lives; (5) it is firm because it is not capable of being overcome or taken away by any form of gain, honor, false teacher, or the root and secondary mental afflictions; and (6) it possesses the ornament of morality. The ornament of morality should be understood as it is described in *The Stage of a Listener*.[824] [A bodhisattva's morality] is also (1) a morality of cessation [of bad actions], in that it gives up the taking of life, etc.; (2) it is a morality of performance [of good actions], in that it acquires virtue and acts on behalf of sentient beings; (3) it is a morality of preservation, in that it safeguards the morality of cessation and performance; and it is also (4) a morality that brings about the ripening of the marks of a great person,[825] (5) a morality that brings about the ripening of [the training of] superior concentration, (6) a morality that brings about the ripening of a desirable migratory state, and (7) a morality that brings about the ripening of the welfare of sentient beings.

Morality That Relates to the Distressed and What They Want [1.10.7]

What is the morality of a bodhisattva that relates to the distressed and what they want?

It should be understood to be eightfold. Here a bodhisattva him- or herself reflects in the following manner: "I am one who does not want anyone to deprive me of my life, who does not want anyone to take anything of mine that was not given, who does not want anyone to engage in sexual

824. *ŚBh* (pp. 53–54): "Why did [the Bhagavān] refer to morality with the word 'ornament'? All other adornments—such as necklaces, rings, bracelets for the upper arm, seal rings, and strands of gold and silver—make a person look beautiful only as long as they are worn by someone who is young in age and youthful and someone whose hair is black and who is possessed of the bloom of youth. If those adornments are worn by someone who is decrepit, an old person, someone who has reached old age and is eighty years old or ninety years old, and someone whose teeth have fallen out and whose head is grey-haired, he or she will only be called a buffoon. [Those ordinary adornments] also do not make a person who is experiencing poor health, loss of wealth, or loss of relatives look beautiful. On the other hand, morality always makes everyone take on a beautiful appearance. Therefore, [the Bhagavān] referred to it with the word 'ornament.'"

825. That is, the thirty-two marks of a buddha's supreme emanation body. See Book III, chapter 5.

misconduct with me, who does not want anyone to lie to me, engage in divisive speech about me, or express harsh speech or idle speech to me, and who does not want anyone to inflict undesirable and injurious forms of [physical] contact on me—such as the [physical] contact of [being struck by] a hand, a clod of earth, or a whip. If others should carry out against me the opposite of what I want, that would cause me to become distressed and it would be unpleasant for me. Other persons are just like me in that they also do not want anyone to deprive them of their lives, etc., up to they do not want anyone to inflict undesirable and injurious forms of [physical] contact on them. If I were to carry out against them the opposite of what they want, that would cause them to be distressed and it would be unpleasant for them." When [a bodhisattva], after making the determination, "How could I commit against others that which is so unpleasant both for myself and others?" avoids committing against others any of these eight unwanted things, even to save his or her life, this is the [type of] morality that consists of eight aspects and is called "the bodhisattva's morality that relates to the distressed and what they want."

The Morality That Brings Happiness Here and in the Next World [1.10.8]

Regarding this [topic], what is the morality of a bodhisattva that brings happiness here and in the next world?

It should be regarded as being ninefold. (1) Here a bodhisattva forbids [sentient beings from acting in] those situations that are forbidden to sentient beings. (2) He or she urges [sentient beings to act in] those situations that are recommended. (3) He or she draws [to the Dharma] those beings who are worthy of being drawn. (4) He or she suppresses those beings who need to be suppressed. The pure deeds of body and speech that are engaged in by a bodhisattva in relation to [these four situations] constitute the first four forms of this type of morality. In addition, there are five more forms: (5) the morality that accompanies generosity, (6) [the morality] that accompanies patience, (7) [the morality] that accompanies effort, (8) [the morality] that accompanies meditative absorption, and (9) [the morality] that accompanies wisdom. When [all of] these are combined into a single group, they make up a [type of] morality that consists of nine aspects. [This type of morality] is conducive to happiness in this life and in future lives, both for the bodhisattva [who performs it] and for [those] others [in relation to whom it is performed]; therefore, it is called "[the morality that] brings happiness here and in the next world."

Pure Morality [1.10.9]

Regarding this [topic], what is a bodhisattva's pure morality?

It should be understood as being tenfold. (1) At the very outset, [a bodhisattva's morality] is adopted properly—that is, out of a desire [to pursue] asceticism and [achieve] complete enlightenment, not for the purpose of securing a livelihood. (2a) It is not overly slack, because [all forms of] faint regret[826] with regard to [committing] transgressions are absent. (2b) It is not carried too far,[827] because [all forms of] unwarranted regret are absent. (3) It is free of laziness, because the ease of sleep, lying on one's side, and reclining [at inappropriate times] are avoided and strong effort is exerted day and night toward [everything] that pertains to virtue. (4) It is embraced by mindfulness through cultivating the five limbs of mindfulness that were described earlier. (5) It is dedicated correctly, because desire for gain and honor are absent and because [the practitioner] does not agree to abide in a pure spiritual life after having dedicated him- or herself to [the attainment of] a [worldly] god's status. (6) It is embraced by excellence of conduct, because [the four modes of] physical behavior,[828] regular activities,[829] and

826. S: *mandakaukṛtyam,* T: *'gyod pa chung ngu.* An individual who possesses "faint regret" is one who lacks any great concern about cultivating morality and would feel little remorse if he or she committed a misdeed. *ŚBh* (p. 46): "How is [morality] overly slack (S: *atilīnam,* T: *ha cang zhum pa*)? For instance, certain individuals lack shame and have a faint [sense of] regret. They are lax and act in a lax manner toward the moral precepts. This is [what it means to be] overly slack."

827. S: *atisṛtam,* T: *ha cang thal ba. ŚBh* (p. 46): "How is [morality] carried too far? For instance, certain individuals cling to [a form of morality that has been] wrongly grasped and feel [a form of] regret that is unwarranted. Feeling regret toward those objects about which one should feel a sense of having acted properly, he or she develops an inappropriate attitude of contempt toward others or [improperly] proclaims their dishonor."

828. S: *īryāpathāni,* T: *spyod lam.* They are walking, standing, sitting, and reclining. See also note 852.

829. S: *itikaraṇīyam,* T: *'phral gyi bya ba. ŚBh* (p. 38): "'Regular activities' refers to the wearing of monastic robes, defecating and urinating, [drinking] water, [using] a tooth stick, entering a village, receiving and eating alms food, washing and storing the alms bowl, washing the feet, arranging beds and seats and putting them away, activities relating to the alms bowl, activities relating to monastic robes, and a few other similar activities."

practices that pertain to virtue[830] are engaged in with physical and verbal conduct that is most excellent and exemplary. (7) It is embraced by excellence of livelihood, because it has abandoned the fault of carrying out [any of the] wrong forms of livelihood, such as hypocrisy, etc. (8) It has abandoned the two extremes, because it has abandoned the practices of indulging in sense pleasures and engaging in self-mortification. (9) It leads to deliverance because it has abandoned all forms of heretical views. (10) The [pure] morality of bodhisattvas is one whose acceptance has not become ruined, because it has not been damaged or destroyed. This [type of] the bodhisattvas' morality, which is made up of ten aspects, is one that is referred to as "pure."

This [method of practice] represents a bodhisattva's great heap of morality, on the basis of which a bodhisattva, after he or she has fulfilled the perfection of morality, attains unsurpassed true and complete enlightenment. Throughout the period of time during which enlightenment has not yet been attained, [the bodhisattva] who is training him- or herself in this immeasurable heap of morality obtains five benefits: (1) The buddhas hold him or her in their thoughts. (2) He or she passes away while abiding in a state of great joy. (3) Following the dissolution of the body, he or she is reborn in a place where there are [other] bodhisattvas with whom he or she shares the same goal and whose morality is equal or superior to his or hers, and where [those bodhisattvas] are exemplary Dharma followers and spiritual teachers. (4) In this life, he or she will be endowed with an immeasurable heap of merit that brings about the fulfillment of the perfection of morality. (5) In future lives, he or she will also achieve a morality that occurs naturally and a morality that remains fixed in that quality.

It should be understood that all of the morality that has been explained here, with its nine aspects of essential morality, etc., is contained within the three types of morality—that is, the morality of restraint, the moral-

830. S: *kuśalapakṣaprayogaḥ*, T: *dge ba'i phyogs kyi sbyor ba*. *ŚBh* (p. 39): "[Activities] that pertain to virtue include, for example, recitation [of sacred texts], paying homage and attending to venerable ones, likewise taking care of the sick with an attitude of sympathy for one another, giving consent [for some action], giving instruction, undertaking [Dharma], making inquiry [about Dharma], listening to Dharma, performing physical service to those among the spiritual practitioners who are wise and diligent, urging others to engage in activities that pertain to virtue, teaching Dharma, going into seclusion [in order to practice meditation], and sitting in a cross-legged position. These and other similar activities are referred to as 'practices that pertain to virtue.'"

ity of acquiring virtuous qualities, and the morality of acting on behalf of sentient beings. Moreover, this threefold morality accomplishes, in brief, three actions for a bodhisattva. The morality of restraint promotes [the attainment of the levels of] mental stability.[831] [The morality] of acquiring virtuous qualities promotes the ripening of a buddha's qualities in oneself. The morality of acting on behalf of sentient beings promotes the [spiritual] ripening of sentient beings [other than oneself]. [These actions] constitute the full extent of everything that a bodhisattva needs to accomplish. That is to say, mental stability is [needed] for one to abide in a state of ease in this life, and a person whose body and mind are not weary [is able] to ripen a buddha's qualities [in him- or herself] and [is able] to ripen [other] sentient beings. This is the [full] extent of a bodhisattva's morality. This is the [full] extent of the benefits of a bodhisattva's morality. This is the [full] extent of what a bodhisattva's morality needs to accomplish. There is nothing of greater significance than this and nothing besides this. [These are the aims] with regard to which the bodhisattvas of the past, present, and future—those who were, are, and shall be desirous of achieving great enlightenment—have trained themselves, are training themselves, and shall train themselves throughout the limitless world spheres that lie in the ten directions.

Within [Book I of] *The Stage of a Bodhisattva,* [known as] "The Object of Mental Application That Relates to the Support," this completes the tenth chapter, entitled "Morality."

831. See note 280 for an explanation of this expression. This statement indicates that morality is a prerequisite for developing one-pointed concentration.

11

Patience

The summary verses should be understood to be the same [categories] as the ones that were presented in the chapter on morality.

The Essence of Patience [1.11.1]

Regarding this [topic], what is the essence of a bodhisattva's patience?

In brief, the essence of patience should be understood as consisting of the forbearance of harm caused by others, both the forbearance of everyone[832] and the forbearance of everything,[833] by relying upon the strength [that is gained by] careful consideration[834] or [a form of forbearance which occurs]

832. *BBhVy* (f. 179a): "The basis (S: **adhisthānam,* T: *gzhi*) is all sentient beings who cause harm [to you], without distinction. Therefore, the text states 'forbearance' [of everyone]."

833. *BBhVy* (f. 179a): "The object (S: *ālambanam,* T: *dmigs pa*) [of one's forbearance] is every [kind of] harm that has been done you, without distinction. Therefore, the text states 'forbearance of everything.' The two forms of forbearance, depending on whether you are able or unable [to do harm in return], are, respectively, (1) [that which consists of] refraining from doing harm in return and (2) [that which consists of] remaining free of anger."

834. S: *pratisaṃkhyānabalasaṃniśrayena,* T: *so sor brtags pa'i stobs la brten nas. BBhVy* (f. 179a): "The essence of patience is formulated in relation to four elements: (1) the characteristic of the object that is relied upon (S: **āśrayaḥ,* T: *rten*), (2) the characteristic of the basis, (3) the characteristic of the object, and (4) the causal characteristic. Regarding these, the object that is relied upon is the strength of careful consideration [that is carried out] during the stage in which conduct [is based upon] devotion (S: *adhimukticaryāvasthaḥ,* T: *mos pas spyod pa'i gnas skabs*). Therefore, the text states 'by relying upon the strength [that is gained by] careful consideration.' It is called a 'strength' because [the practitioner] is not overwhelmed by the opposing quality (S: *vipakṣaḥ,* T: *mi mthun pa'i phyogs*) [i.e., anger]."

naturally,[835] as well as a forbearance [that is accompanied] by a mind that is free of corporeal desire[836] and by a [form of] compassion that is absolute.[837]

All-Inclusive Patience [1.11.2]

Regarding this [topic], what is a bodhisattva's all-inclusive patience?

It should be regarded as being of two types: (1) [the patience] that relates to the faction that is made up of householders and (2) [the patience] that relates to the faction that is made up of those who have gone forth [into the homeless state]. [The patience] that relates to both factions should be understood as being of three types: (1) the patience that forbears the harm that is inflicted by others,[838] (2) the patience that tolerates suffering,[839] and (3) the patience of the conviction [that is gained by] reflecting upon entities.[840]

835. S: *prakṛtyā,* T: *rang bzhin gyis. BBhVy* (f. 179a): "[The object that is relied upon] by [a bodhisattva] who has entered the [ārya] levels [is attained] by the power of meditation. Therefore, the text states [that it is a form of forbearance that occurs] 'naturally.' Because those who have entered the [ārya bodhisattva] levels have attained a [direct] realization of the two types of insubstantiality (S: *nairātmyam,* T: *bdag med pa*), they are described as 'having become established in [a state of] forbearance regarding the purity of the three spheres,' which is a form of patience [that occurs] naturally."

836. See note 584. *BBhVy* (f. 179a): "[It is called] 'a mind free of corporeal desire' because it does not hope [to receive] a favor in return in this life and because it neither wishes for a desirable migratory state nor fears an undesirable [migratory state] in the future."

837. S: *kevalayā karuṇayā,* T: *snying rje 'ba' zhig gis. BBhVy* (f. 179a): "In order to indicate the causal characteristic, the text states, '[a forbearance that is accompanied] by a [form of] compassion that is absolute.'"

838. *BBhVy* (f. 179b): "The patience of forbearance (S: *marsaṇā kṣantiḥ,* T: *ji mi snyam pa'i bzod pa*) consists of not bringing to mind that you have been harmed and bringing to mind the antidote to animosity. It should be understood that their [respective] essential natures are [the mental states of] avoidance of hatred and avoidance of anger."

839. *BBhVy* (f. 179b): "The patience that tolerates suffering (S: *duḥkhādhivāsanākṣantiḥ,* T: *sdug bsngal dang du len pa'i bzod pa*) is the ability to endure both suffering that has arisen and [suffering] that has not arisen by relying on the physical strength of effort and the strength of proper attention (S: *yoniśo manaskāraḥ,* T: *tshul bzhin yid la byed pa*)."

840. *BBhVy* (f. 179b): "The patience [that arises from] careful consideration of entities (S: **dharmapratisaṃkhyānakṣantiḥ,* T: *chos la so sor rtog pa'i bzod pa*) is a form of great patience [that arises from] an unerring [recognition] of the nature of entities. Moreover, this [form of patience] has the nature of wisdom."

The Patience That Forbears the Harm That Is Inflicted by Others [1.11.2.1]

How does a bodhisattva forbear and endure the harm [that is carried out against him or her] by others?

Four Points [1.11.2.1.1]

Here a bodhisattva rightly learns[841] the following [four points] in relation to intense, continuous, varied, and long-lasting suffering that is being directly experienced and that has arisen from harm inflicted by others. (1) "This [suffering] is the fault of my own karma, because this suffering that I am experiencing is the result of nonvirtuous deeds that I myself carried out." (2) "It is equally true that I do not want suffering[842] and that this impatience represents a cause that will bring me suffering again in the future. If I continue to take up this attitude that is a cause of [future] suffering, by doing so it will certainly be true that I alone am bringing upon myself the very thing that I wish to avoid. Therefore, it will be a case in which I have inflicted harm upon myself and not [one in which the harm was inflicted] by others." (3) "It is also the case that, by their very nature, all formations[843]—both those of my own mental continuum and those of others' [mental continua]—have a basic condition that consists of suffering. Others who create additional suffering for us, whose basic condition is one that consists of suffering, may well do so because they are unaware of this [fact]. However, it would be unseemly for those of us who are aware [of this fact] to create more suffering for others

841. S: *pratisaṃśikṣate,* T: *yang dag par slob pa*. *BBhVy* (f. 179b): "[The phrase] '[a bodhisattva] rightly learns the following [points]' means that he or she develops patience after having reflected using four [forms of] examination (S: **parīkṣā,* T: *brtag pa*)."

842. S: *duḥkhena cāham anarthī.* While the Tibetan translation reads *bdag gi sdug bsngal mi bzod de,* this appears to be a corruption. *BBhVy* (f. 180a) reads *bdag ni sdug bsngal mi 'dod de.*

843. S: *sarvasaṃskārāḥ,* T: *'du byed thams cad. PSV* (p. 273): "All the entities that are included in the [five] heaps of form and the rest are formations in the sense that they are produced by the convergence and combination of conditional factors." This statement is virtually identical with one that occurs in Vasubandhu's *AKB,* p. 4 (S: *sametya sambhūya pratyayaiḥ kṛtā iti saṃskṛtāḥ;* T: *rkyen rnams 'dus phrad nas byas pa dag ni 'dus byas rnams te*) with the exception that it describes "conditioned entities" (S: *saṃskṛtāḥ,* T: *'dus byas rnams*) rather than "formations" (S: *saṃskārāḥ,* T: *'dus byed rnams*), which suggests that, in some instances at least, the two terms can be considered interchangeable.

whose basic condition is also one that consists of suffering." (4) "Moreover, if it is improper for those listeners who are devoted to their own welfare [to develop] the impatience that creates suffering for oneself and others, then how much more should this be true for those of us who are devoted to the welfare of others."

Five Conceptions [1.11.2.1.2]

Having carefully considered these points, a bodhisattva who meditates on a five-part [set of] conceptions endures all forms of harm in relation to those sentient beings who are friends, foes, and neutral persons; those [sentient beings] who are inferior, equal, and superior; those [sentient beings] who are experiencing well-being as well as those who are suffering; and those [sentient beings] who possess good qualities as well as those who possess faults.

What are the five conceptions?

They are (1) the conception of [every other being] having been a person who was well-disposed [toward oneself] in a former life; (2) the conception that conforms to [the condition of others being] a mere [collection of] entities; (3) the conception of [others'] impermanence; (4) the conception of [others'] suffering; and (5) the conception of [regarding others with an attitude of] embracing.[844]

How does a bodhisattva meditate on the conception of [every other being] having been a person who was well-disposed toward him or her, in relation to those beings who have harmed him or her?

Here a bodhisattva rightly learns the following: "This being is not someone who formerly, in other rebirths of the distant past, could not have been my mother, father, brother, sister, teacher, preceptor, a venerable person, or a person worthy of reverence."[845] For [a bodhisattva] who cultivates proper

844. S: *parigrahaḥ*, T: *yongs su bzung ba*. While this noun can cover a broad range of meanings (see MW, p. 593), in the present context it refers to a figurative manner of "embracing" or cherishing all sentient beings in the manner that a husband or wife cares for and cherishes his or her spouse. See also text that accompanies note 163 as well as Book III, chapter 2, which is entitled "Embracing."

845. *BBhVy* (f. 181a) explains that the first four examples pertain to householders who may have harmed you. If the person is an older woman, she should be viewed as one's mother, an older man as one's father, a woman of similar age as one's sister, and a man of similar age as one's brother. The last four examples are suitable for situations in which the person who harmed you was a homeless ascetic.

attention in this way, the notion of being an adversary that is directed toward those beings who have harmed him or her will disappear and the notion of their being a person who is well-disposed [toward him or her] will remain. By relying on this conception of [every other being] being a person who is well-disposed, [a bodhisattva] forbears and endures the harms [that are done to him or her].

How does a bodhisattva meditate on the conception that conforms to [the condition of others being a] mere [collection of] entities, in relation to those beings who have harmed him or her?

Here a bodhisattva rightly learns the following: "This [person] is someone who is subject to causal conditions. He or she is a mere [collection of] formations. He or she is a mere [collection of] entities. There is no self here of any kind, no [real] sentient being, no [real] living being, no [real] person that has taken birth who could scold [someone], who could anger [someone], who could beat [someone], who could speak abusively [to someone], and who could criticize [someone], or who could be scolded, who could be angered, who could be beaten, who could be spoken to abusively, and who could be criticized." For [a bodhisattva] who cultivates proper attention in this way, the notion of [someone] being a [real] sentient being will disappear and the notion of [him or her] being a mere [collection of] entities will remain. By relying on and establishing this conception of mere entities, [a bodhisattva] forbears and endures all the harms that are done [to him or her] by others.

How does a bodhisattva meditate on the conception of impermanence in relation to those beings who have harmed him or her?

Here a bodhisattva rightly learns the following: "Any and all sentient beings who have been born and currently exist are impermanent and subject to death. Moreover, this is the ultimate form of retribution—that is to say, the [individual's] life will come to be extinguished. In addition, it is certainly improper for a knowledgeable person even to develop an agitated[846] state of mind toward those impermanent sentient beings who are naturally subject to death, let alone to strike them with the hand, or with a clod of earth or a club, much less to deprive them completely of their life." For [a

846. S: *kaluṣam,* T: *rnyog pa can.* MW (p. 262): "turbid, foul, muddy, impure, dirty (lit. and fig.)"; but also "troubled" or "agitated." The Tibetan translation follows the primary sense of being "turbid" or "muddy." However, the sense of being agitated by anger seems more accurate in this context. As a noun, it can also mean "sin" and "wrath."

bodhisattva] who cultivates proper attention in this way, the notion of [all beings] being permanent and substantial will disappear and the conception of [their] being impermanent and insubstantial will remain. By relying on this conception of [others] being impermanent and insubstantial, [a bodhisattva] forbears and endures all the harms [that are done to him or her].

How does a bodhisattva meditate on the conception of suffering in relation to those beings who have harmed him or her?

Here a bodhisattva perceives that even those sentient beings who live in a state of great prosperity are closely bound to the three forms of suffering[847]—the suffering of conditioned existence, the suffering of change, and the suffering of suffering—not to mention those [sentient beings] who are abiding in a state of misfortune. Perceiving this, he or she rightly learns the following. "I should be striving to remove the suffering of those beings who are always undergoing suffering in this way; [I should] not [be striving] to cause them suffering." For [a bodhisattva] who cultivates proper attention in this way, the notion [that there is any genuine form] of happiness [in samsara] will be relinquished and the conception of suffering will arise. By relying on this conception of suffering, [a bodhisattva] forbears and endures all the harms that are done [to him or her] by others.

How does a bodhisattva meditate on the conception of embracing those beings who have harmed him or her?

Here a bodhisattva rightly learns the following. "Now in generating the mind [that aspires] to [attain] enlightenment, I have embraced all sentient beings in the manner that a spouse[848] [is embraced] and I have pledged to accomplish what is beneficial for all sentient beings. Therefore, having declared, 'I shall do what is beneficial as relates to all sentient beings,' it would be unseemly for me to do something injurious [to a particular sentient being because] I was unable to endure the harm [inflicted by him or her]." For [a bodhisattva] who cultivates proper attention in this way, the notion of being a foe that is held toward those sentient beings who harm him or her will be relinquished and the conception of embracing them will arise. By relying on this conception of embracing [sentient beings], [a bodhisattva] forbears and endures all the harms that are done [to him or her] by others.

847. S: *tisro duḥkhatāḥ*, T: *sdug bsngal gsum po*. See *Inner Science*, pp. 105–138, for a comprehensive discussion of the three forms of suffering.

848. See note 163.

The Patience That Tolerates Suffering [1.11.2.2]

What is patience? [The mental state] that refrains from becoming angry, [the mental state] that refrains from retaliating for some harm that was done [to you], and [the mental state] that refrains from bearing enmity[849]—these are what is called "patience."

What is a bodhisattva's patience that tolerates suffering?

Here a bodhisattva rightly learns the following: "Formerly, as a person who engaged in the enjoyment of sense pleasures and who pursued those pleasures, I accepted, tolerated, and experienced a multitude of intense forms of suffering as I engaged in [such occupations as] farming, commerce, and service to the king, for the sake of sense pleasures whose [true] nature consists of suffering, knowing full well that [those occupations] would be a cause of suffering [to me]. My willing acceptance of that meaningless great suffering for the sake of what [actually] consists of nothing but suffering was due to the fault of a lack of understanding. However, now, with the recognition that I am pursuing a virtuous activity that will bring about [genuine] happiness, it would be proper for me to willingly tolerate suffering that is a trillion times greater than that [former suffering], let alone some smaller form of suffering."

The Suffering That Occurs in All Situations [1.11.2.2.1]

A bodhisattva who is pursuing enlightenment and who is cultivating proper attention in this way tolerates the suffering that occurs in all situations.

What is the suffering that occurs in all situations?

In brief, it is of eight types: (1) that which is based upon the supports, (2) that which is based upon the worldly conditions, (3) that which is based upon [the four modes of] physical behavior, (4) that which is based upon embracing the Dharma, (5) that which is based upon a mendicant's way of life, (6) that which is based upon the fatigue that arises from striving, (7) that which is based upon acting on behalf of sentient beings, and (8) that which is based upon regular activities.

849. S: *nāpy anuśayaṃ vahati,* T: *sems la khon du mi 'dzin pa. BBhVy* (f. 181a): "'. . . and [the mental state] which refrains from bearing enmity' means to abandon the resentment (S: **upanāhaḥ,* T: *khon 'dzin*) that occurs in the wake of having been harmed by someone."

The Four Supports [1.11.2.2.2]

There are four supports[850] that are relied upon in order to go forth and achieve full ordination into the state of a *bhikṣu* or *bhikṣuṇī* within this well-proclaimed [spiritual system of] Dharma and Vinaya, namely, (1) monastic robes, (2) alms food, (3) beds and seats, and (4) medicine for curing the ill and [other permitted] personal belongings. A bodhisattva does not experience distress[851] or become discouraged when poor forms of these [supports] are acquired, when they are acquired in small quantity, when they are provided in a disrespectful manner, or when they are acquired only after some delay. Nor does he or she, due to any of these causes, relax his or her effort. This is the manner in which [a bodhisattva] tolerates the suffering that is based upon the supports [of a spiritual life].

The Nine Worldly Conditions [1.11.2.2.3]

There are nine worldly conditions: (1) loss [of material things], (2) disrepute, (3) blame, (4) suffering, (5) the perishing of that which is perishable, (6) the disappearance of that which undergoes disappearance, (7) the aging of that which is subject to aging, (8) the sickening of that which is subject to illness, and (9) the death of that which is mortal. The suffering that arises through the occurrence and appearance of these worldly conditions, whether individually or in combination, is called "that which is based on the worldly conditions." Even if a bodhisattva is stricken by any of these [conditions], he or she does not, because of that, relax his or her effort. [Rather,] having carefully considered [the inevitability of that condition], he or she endures it and tolerates it.

The Four Modes of Physical Behavior [1.11.2.2.4]

There are four modes of physical behavior:[852] walking, standing, sitting, and lying down. Regarding these, a bodhisattva purifies his or her mind of

850. S: *saṃniśrayaḥ,* T: *rten*. *BBhVy* (f. 182a): "The four [categories] of monks' robes, etc., which are the articles [needed] for subsistence, are called 'supports' because they are the means by which the body is kept strong."

851. S: *utkaṇṭhyate,* T: *mi 'ga' bar 'gyur ba*. Literally, "to raise the neck," "to open the throat" (MW, p. 175).

852. *BBhVy* (f. 182b): "Both that which causes one to walk, etc., and [the actions of] walking,

those qualities that bring about [mental] obstruction by walking and sitting during the day, and at night tolerates the suffering that arises from the fatigue that is caused by these [two activities]. He or she does not lean on his or her side [to relax] on a couch, a seat, a bed of grass, or a bed of leaves at an inappropriate time.

The Seven Forms of Embracing the Dharma [1.11.2.2.5]

There are seven forms of embracing[853] the Dharma: (1) honoring and serving the Three Jewels; (2) honoring and serving those who are venerable; (3) taking up[854] Dharma [teachings]; (4) teaching others extensively [the Dharma teachings] that one has taken up; (5) reciting [sacred texts] aloud and at length; (6) correctly reflecting upon, pondering, and closely investigating [the meaning of Dharma teachings], alone and having gone to a secluded place; and (7) meditating upon forms of quiescence and insight that are supported by forms of attention that relate to mental application. The suffering that arises for a bodhisattva who is striving in relation to these seven forms of embracing the Dharma is also something that he or she tolerates and that does not cause him or her to relax effort.

Seven Aspects of a Mendicant's Way of Life [1.11.2.2.6]

It should also be understood that there are seven aspects[855] to a mendicant's way of life: (1) acceptance of an unattractive physical appearance, through

etc., are established as [the forms of] physical behavior (S: *īryāpathāni,* T: *spyod lam rnams*). The mind that causes [the actions of] walking, etc., to occur is 'physical behavior' because it is the force that incites them (S: **īraṇam,* T: *skul bar byed pa*). That is, [the mind] sets the [body's four] elements in motion and drives them, and causes them to reach a different place. Its path (S: *pathaḥ,* T: *lam*) is the actions of walking, etc. That is, by means of [the actions of] walking, etc., one arrives at a particular place."

853. S: *parigrahaḥ,* T: *yongs su bzung ba*. While this term literally means "laying hold of on all sides," it also has a range of specific senses, including "homage" and "reverence" (MW, p. 593), which are appropriate for the first two of the seven forms mentioned here. The latter five forms of "embracing" more properly seem to represent ways of "acquiring" or even "mastering" the Dharma, which are also senses of this term.

854. *BBhVy* (f. 183a): "'Taking up Dharma teachings' (S: *dharmānām udgrahaṇam,* T: *chos rnam bzung ba*) means to learn the sutras, etc., that are taught by others." See also note 800.

855. *BBhVy* (f. 183a) states that these are the first seven of twenty-two aspects of a mendicant's way of life that Buddha declared must be reflected upon by homeless ascetics.

having abandoned the marks of a householder by such actions as shaving the head and face; (2) acceptance of unattractive outer appearance,[856] through wearing clothing that is patched and has an unattractive color; (3) undertaking a distinct [form of] behavior, through abiding in a state of restraint as relates to all worldly conduct; (4) relying upon others for one's livelihood, through [adopting] the practice of one who has abandoned all occupations such as agriculture, etc., and who sustains him- or herself with what is received from others; (4) seeking monastic robes, etc., from others for as long as one lives, by [adopting the principle of] not using things that were acquired and then hoarded; (5) abstaining from the human activities of [indulging in] sensory pleasures for as long as one lives, through turning away from a noncelibate life and sexual intercourse; and abstaining from the human activities [of pursuing activities of] pleasure and amusement for as long as one lives, through (6) refraining from attending [performances by] actors, dancers, comedians, and female dancers, etc., as well as through (7) refraining from [behavior that involves] laughing, playing, delighting, and amusing oneself in the company of friends, favorably disposed acquaintances, and lifelong companions. A bodhisattva also tolerates the suffering that arises in relation to a mendicant's way of life that is tightly bound by these kinds of austerities, and he or she does not relax effort because of them.

Bodily Fatigue and Mental Weariness [1.11.2.2.7]

Whatever causes of exhaustion may arise for a bodhisattva who is engaged in activities that pertain to virtue, whether they are [causes] of bodily fatigue or mental weariness, a bodhisattva does not relax his or her effort because of them.

The list of twenty-two items appears in the Tibetan translation of a sutra entitled *Arthavistaranāmadharmaparyāyaḥ* (T: [*'Phags pa*] *Don rgyas pa zhes bya ba'i chos kyi rnam grangs*), ff. 181b–182b.

856. S: *vaivarṇyam*, T: *mdog ngan pa*. While this abstract noun literally translates as "unattractiveness of color," the noun *varṇaḥ* has a broad range of meanings that include "covering" and "cloak." The sense here is clearly meant to refer to the unattractive clothing that a Buddhist monk or nun traditionally wears.

Deeds That Benefit Sentient Beings [I.11.2.2.8]

The deeds that benefit sentient beings should be understood as consisting of the eleven types [of activities] that were described earlier.[857] A bodhisattva also tolerates the suffering that arises due to those [activities] and does not relax his or her effort because of them.

Regular Activities [I.11.2.2.9]

For homeless ascetics, regular activities are those [that relate to] monastic robes, alms bowl, etc.[858] By contrast, for householders, they are those that relate to the correct pursuit of [such occupations as] agriculture, commerce, service to the king, etc. A bodhisattva also accepts the suffering that is caused by these [activities]; however, he or she does not relax effort because of [the suffering that is caused by] them.

No matter what kind of suffering may occur, a bodhisattva [steadfastly] applies him- or herself to [the pursuit of] complete and unsurpassed enlightenment; he or she does not fail to apply him- or herself. And having done so, he or she does not turn away [from that pursuit]. He or she remains unperplexed and maintains a trouble-free mind while applying him- or herself. This is what is called [a bodhisattva's] tolerance of suffering.

The Patience of the Devotion That Is Gained by Reflecting upon Entities [I.11.2.3]

What is a bodhisattva's patience of the devotion [that is gained by] reflecting upon entities?

Here, by means of [a form of] understanding that derives from having thoroughly examined entities using correct discernment,[859] a bodhisattva's devotion becomes well and deeply absorbed in relation to eight objects of devotion: (1) the virtuous qualities of the [Three] Jewels, (2) the nature of

857. See Book I, chapter 10, the section entitled "Engaging in Every Aspect of Acting on Behalf of Sentient Beings" [I.10.2.6].

858. See note 829.

859. "Discernment of entities" is the essential property of the mental factor that is commonly translated as "wisdom" (S: *prajñā,* T: *shes rab*). See note 224.

reality, (3) the great powers of the buddhas and bodhisattvas, (4) causes,[860] (5) results,[861] (6) the goal that is to be achieved for oneself, (7) the means of achieving that goal, and (8) the field of that which needs to be known.[862]

Moreover, this devotion becomes well and deeply absorbed [in those objects] on the basis of two causes: (1) through repeated practice over a long period of time and (2) through the attainment of perfectly pure knowledge.

This [explanation] constitutes the bodhisattvas' all-inclusive patience that relates to the two groups [of individuals, householders and homeless ascetics,] and it should be understood that [this category] forms the basis for [all the other] extensive categories [of patience], such as the patience that is difficult to carry out, etc.

The Patience That Is Difficult to Carry Out [I.11.3]

What is a bodhisattva's patience that is difficult to carry out?

It should be regarded as being of three types. Here a bodhisattva endures harm from beings who are weak. This is the first form of patience that is difficult to carry out. Being a lord, [a bodhisattva] endures [others' harm]. This is the second form of patience that is difficult to carry out. [A bodhisattva] endures extensive and great harm from beings who are of a particularly low birth and lineage. This is the third form of patience that is difficult to carry out.

The Patience That Is Directed Everywhere [I.11.4]

What is a bodhisattva's patience that is directed everywhere?

It should be regarded as being of four types. Here a bodhisattva endures

860. See Book I, chapter 8, the section entitled "The Ten Causes" [I.8.2.1].

861. See Book I, chapter 8, the section entitled "Five Kinds of Results" [I.8.2.2].

862. S: *jñeyagocaraḥ*, T: *shes bya'i spyod yul*. *BBhVy* (f. 184a): "[The phrase] 'field of that which needs to be known' means to gain an accurate determination of the [four noble truths'] aspects of impermanence, etc., [in such a manner that one recognizes:] 'its nature is thus and not otherwise.'" Another list of the eight objects of devotion appears in Book I, chapter 8, the section entitled "Abundance of Devotion" [I.8.1]. Since the eighth object in that list is identified as the twelve categories of the Buddha's word, the "field of that which needs to be known" should be understood to refer to all of the Buddha's teachings, not just the four noble truths.

harm from a friend, a foe, and a stranger, and also endures it from all three of these types who are inferior, equal, or superior to him or her.

The Patience of a True Spiritual Being [1.11.5]

What is a bodhisattva's patience of a true spiritual being?

It should be regarded as being of five types. Here a bodhisattva, from the very outset, regards patience as advantageous. He or she regards it as advantageous in the following ways: (1) in the future, a patient person will not have many enemies; (2) he or she will not frequently experience becoming estranged [from friends]; (3) he or she will experience much comfort and ease of mind; (4) he or she will not pass away in a state of regret; and, (5) following the dissolution of the body, he or she will be reborn in a happy migratory state—[that is,] in the celestial realms among the gods.[863]

[A bodhisattva] is patient and also establishes others in patience. He or she extols patience [to others]. Upon seeing a person who possesses patience, [a bodhisattva] becomes happy and gives rise to joy.

Patience of Every Form [1.11.6]

What is a bodhisattva's patience of every form?

It should be understood as the thirteen forms [that result from] combining together six forms and seven forms. (1) Here a bodhisattva develops patience due to the fear [that arises from] having realized the undesirable

863. As *BBhVy* (f. 184b) notes, Asaṅga makes reference to these five advantages in an earlier section of *YBh* entitled "The Stage That Consists of Learning" (S: *Śrutamayībhūmiḥ,* T: *Thos pa las byung ba'i sa*), Tg. vol. 127, f. 178a–178b. The text explicitly presents the five disadvantages that are experienced by an impatient person who engages in the following five forms of wrongful behavior (S: *vipratipattiḥ,* T: *log par sgrub pa*): (1) causing one's adversaries discomfort and unhappiness due to the rancor and hostility that is felt toward them; (2) destroying the morality that one has accepted; and engaging in misdeeds of (3) body, (4) speech, and (5) mind. The first three disadvantages, which are natural outcomes of this behavior, are (1) to have many enemies, (2) to become estranged from one's friends, and (3) to be subjected to many forms of discomfort and unhappiness by others. The final two disadvantages are (4) to die in a state of regret and (5) to be reborn in the lower states in one's future life. A patient person obtains the five advantages that are described here by carrying out, in relation to his or her adversaries, the five kinds of correct behavior (S: *samyakpratipattiḥ,* T: *yang dag par sgrub pa*) that are the opposite of the five kinds of wrongful behavior just described.

maturations of impatience. (2) [A bodhisattva] who possesses a sympathetic mind and a compassionate mind and an affectionate mind toward sentient beings also develops patience due to affection. (3) [A bodhisattva] who has an intense aspiration to [attain] unsurpassed true and complete enlightenment and who is desirous of completing the perfection of patience also develops patience due to [its being] a productive cause.[864] (4) The Blessed One also referred to those who have gone forth [into the homeless state] as "the ones who possess the strength of patience." Accordingly, because impatience is not a befitting trait for one who has gone forth and who has accepted the [bodhisattva] morality, [a bodhisattva] also develops patience based upon [the principle of] taking up what is right.[865] (5) By abiding in and being firmly established in the excellence of his or her spiritual lineage and his or her prior repeated practice of patience, [a bodhisattva] also develops patience naturally. (6) Having realized that all entities are devoid of a [real] sentient being, [a bodhisattva] who has perceived the ineffable [reality that sentient beings are a] mere [collection of] entities also develops patience through his or her meditation upon entities. (7) [A bodhisattva] develops patience with regard to every kind of harm. (8) [A bodhisattva] also develops patience with regard to everyone.[866] (9) [A bodhisattva] also develops patience everywhere, whether [he or she is] in an isolated place or in the presence of a great number of people. (10) [A bodhisattva] develops patience at all times—[that is,] during the morning, the middle of the day, and the evening; during the day as well as during the night; with regard to the past, present, and future; both when he or she is sick and when he or she is well; and [also does so] both when he or she is in a fallen state and when

864. S: *kāraṇahetuḥ*, T: *byed pa'i rgyu*. This is not one of the ten causes that Asaṅga describes in chapter 8; however, it is the first of the six that are presented in *AK*, ch. 2, v. 49. The term is being used here in the general sense that patience is one of the principal causes that contribute to the arising of enlightenment. *AKV* (vol. 1, p. 278): "Cause (S: *hetuḥ*, T: *rgyu*), factor (S: *pratyayaḥ*, T: *rkyen*), condition (S: *nidānam*, T: *gzhi*), productive element (S: *kāraṇam*, T: *byed rgyu*), reason (S: *nimittam*, T: *rgyu mtshan*), sign (S: *liṅgam*, T: *rtags*), and underlying aspect (S: *upaniṣad*, T: *'bras gnas*) are synonyms." *AKB* (p. 82) gives this more technical definition of the term: "All entities are productive causes of conditioned entities, except for their [own individual] essences, because they abide in a state of nonobstruction with regard to the arising [of all conditioned entities other than themselves]."

865. See note 187.

866. S: *sarvataḥ*, T: *thams cad kyis*. According to MW (p. 1189), this adverb can mean "from all sides," "in every direction," "completely," and "thoroughly," as well as "from all" and "from everyone." I take it here in the latter sense.

he or she is in an elevated state. (11) [A bodhisattva] develops patience with his or her body, by refraining from striking [others]. (12) [A bodhisattva] also develops patience with his or her speech, by refraining from expressing unpleasant speech. (13) And [a bodhisattva] also develops patience with his or her mind, by not becoming angered and by not remaining in an agitated[867] state of mind.

Patience That Relates to the Distressed and What They Want [1.11.7]

Regarding this [topic], what is a bodhisattva's patience that relates to the distressed and what they want?

It should be regarded as being of eight types: (1) the patience [that endures] the inconvenience of being approached by beggars who are suffering; (2) the patience that refrains from developing hostility toward violent persons who commit great evil deeds, by relying upon the Dharma and great compassion; and (3) the patience that refrains from developing hostility toward those homeless ascetics who engage in misconduct, by relying upon the Dharma and great compassion.

[This form of patience] also [consists of] five aspects of patience that constitute the ability to endure [putting forth] strenuous exertion. [They are] the ability to endure [putting forth] strenuous exertion (4) in connection with striving to eliminate the suffering of those beings who are experiencing suffering; (5) in connection with seeking Dharma teachings; (6) [in connection with] being a person who is engaging in the form of practice that accords with Dharma;[868] (7) [in connection with] explaining in detail those very same Dharma teachings to others; and (8) in connection with correctly assisting beings with their activities and the things that need to be done.

This [category] is called "the eightfold patience that relates to the distressed and what they want" because it is the [form of] patience that both removes those [conditions] that cause sentient beings to be distressed and provides [sentient beings] with the things that they want.

867. See note 846.

868. See Book I, chapter 8, the section entitled "The Form of Practice That Accords with the Dharma" [I.8.4].

The Patience That Brings Happiness Here and in the Next World [1.11.8]

What is a bodhisattva's patience that brings happiness here and in the next world?

It should be regarded as being of nine types. Here a bodhisattva is patient (1) as he or she abides in a state of mindfulness with regard to virtuous activities. He or she is patient with regard to (2) cold, (3) heat, (4) hunger and thirst, (5) being bitten by gadflies, (6) being bitten by mosquitoes, (7) the wind and the sun, and (8) being bitten by snakes [and other creeping animals]. He or she is patient with regard to (9) the fatigue and weariness of body and mind that arise from exertion. [All of these forms of patience are] accompanied by sympathy for sentient beings, who are tormented by the suffering of birth, old age, sickness, and death, etc., [as they roam continuously] throughout samsara.

The bodhisattva who is patient in these ways will abide in a state of ease in that same life, and he or she [will do so] without becoming contaminated by evil, nonvirtuous qualities. In future lives, he or she will also be intent on taking up the causes of happiness. He or she will also be one who is dedicated to achieving the happiness of others in both their present lives and their future lives. Therefore, this is referred to as "the patience that brings happiness here and in the next world."

Pure Patience [1.11.9]

What is a bodhisattva's pure patience?

It should be regarded as being of ten types. Here a bodhisattva who is the recipient of harm, distress, or wrongdoing from others (1) does not harm [them] in return, (2) does not develop an angry mind, and (3) does not harbor the attitude of being their adversary. (4) Just as he or she was before [being harmed], [a bodhisattva] remains disposed to providing assistance after [being harmed]; he or she does not abandon doing acts of assistance for the person who harmed [him or her].[869] (5) [A bodhisattva] offers a conciliatory statement to those who committed harmful acts [against him or her]. (6) [A bodhisattva] does not, after having caused [someone] to be disturbed,

869. The translation of the final clause is based on the reading that appears in Wogihara's Sanskrit edition (S: *nopakārakriyāyāpakartāram upekṣate*).

receive an apology from him or her while thinking, "Let [this person] be disturbed." (7) Regarding the impatience [that might occur] under those very conditions, [a bodhisattva] develops strong shame and abashment.[870] (8) Regarding patience, [a bodhisattva] develops strong affection and reverence toward the Master. (9) Regarding the avoidance of harm toward sentient beings, [a bodhisattva] develops a strong feeling of compassion toward sentient beings. (10) Alternatively, [a bodhisattva] becomes free of attachment for the desire realm after having abandoned completely the qualities that support impatience.[871] It should be understood that these ten aspects cause a bodhisattva's patience to be pure and free of stains.

By relying upon the patience that begins with the essential nature of patience and ends with pure patience, [a form of practice that is] extensive and immeasurable and [that] gives rise to the fruit of great enlightenment, a bodhisattva attains unsurpassed true and complete enlightenment.

Within [Book I of] *The Stage of a Bodhisattva,* [known as] "The Object of Mental Application That Relates to the Support," this completes the eleventh chapter, entitled "Patience."

870. See notes 677 and 678, as well as the opening section of Book I, chapter 17, for definitions of these two virtuous mental factors.

871. S: *akṣantidharmasahāyaḥ,* T: *mi bzod pa'i chos kyi grogs. BBhVy* (f. 186a): "[The phrase] 'qualities that support impatience' means the mental afflictions of anger, etc."

12
Effort

The summary verses should be understood in the same manner as before.

The Essence of Effort [1.12.1]

What is the essence of a bodhisattva's effort?

[A bodhisattva's] mental exertion[872] [that is put forth] in order to collect immeasurable virtue and to act on behalf of sentient beings, as well as the energetic, continuous, and unerring movement[873] of body, speech, and mind that is produced by that [mental exertion] is what, in brief, should be known as the essence of a bodhisattva's effort.

All-Inclusive Effort [1.12.2]

Regarding this [topic], what is a bodhisattva's all-inclusive effort?

In brief, it should be understood as being of two types: (1) [the effort] that relates to the faction that is made up of householders and (2) [the effort] that relates to the faction that is made up of those who have gone forth [into the homeless state]. Moreover, that [effort] which relates to both factions

872. S: *cittābhyutsāhaḥ,* T: *sems mngon par spro ba*. This is essentially the same expression as the one that appears in *AS* (p. 7) and *PSV* (p. 387). Other works, such as *BCA* (ch. 6, v. 2), simply state the noun *utsāhaḥ* without the prefix *abhi*. *BBhVy* (f. 186b) makes the following connection between the two terms: "The vigor that is directed toward spiritual action is called 'exertion' (S: **kāryābhimukha utsāho 'bhyutsāho 'bhidīyate;* T: *bya ba la mngon par phyogs pa ni spro ba ste / mngon par spro ba zhes brjod do*)."

873. S: *parispandaḥ,* T: *yongs su g.yo ba*. *BBhVy* (f. 186b) equates this term with the phrase "the shaping of consciousness" (S: *cittābhisaṃskāraḥ,* T: *sems mngon par 'du byed pa*), which is the essential nature of the mental factor "volition" (S: *cetanā,* T: *sems pa*).

should also be understood as being of three types: (1) armor-like effort, (2) [the effort] that collects virtuous qualities, and (3) [the effort] that acts on behalf of sentient beings.

Armor-Like Effort [1.12.2.1]

Regarding this [topic], here is [a description of] a bodhisattva's armor-like effort. By initiating effort beforehand, a bodhisattva here dons the armor that accompanies mental exertion [when he or she reflects] in the following manner: "Even if I had to remain exclusively in the hells and not in any other migratory state for days and nights that last for a thousand great kalpas in order to liberate even a single sentient being from [his or her] suffering, and it took me one trillion times as long to arrive at unsurpassed and complete enlightenment as it does for [other] bodhisattvas[874] to attain unsurpassed true and complete enlightenment, I would still [continue to] exert myself. I would not give up striving for unsurpassed true and complete enlightenment. I would not give up the effort I had undertaken. How much more would this be true [if I only had to strive] for a much shorter period of time and [I only had to endure] a much smaller amount of suffering." This kind [of unwavering determination] is what constitutes a bodhisattva's armor-like effort.

A bodhisattva who even generates mere devotion and mere reverence for such armor-like effort of bodhisattvas is a resolute bodhisattva and he or she nourishes the constituent element[875] of the immeasurable effort that is exerted for the sake of enlightenment. How much more would this be true for a bodhisattva who actually achieves this kind of armor-like effort. Moreover, for such a bodhisattva there is no arduous deed whatsoever that needs to be done for the sake of enlightenment or [that needs to be done] on behalf

874. The length of time required to achieve unsurpassed enlightenment is described as consisting of three separate spans of time, each of which is made up of a "countless" number of great kalpas. See Book II, chapter 4, the section entitled "Concluding Remarks" [II.4.13]. *AKB* (pp. 181–182) describes a "countless" (S: *asaṃkhyeyam,* T: *grangs med*) number of kalpas as 1 times 10 raised to the fifty-ninth power.

875. This term is being used here as a synonym for "spiritual lineage." See notes 114 and 441. This is the same sense as that of the term "spiritual lineage" in Book I, chapter 8, where the latter is used to describe the two aspects of learning the Buddha's teaching and the eight elements of the act of giving instruction as the "spiritual lineages" from which a buddha's ten powers ultimately arise.

of sentient beings with regard to which this bodhisattva would become fainthearted or that he or she would consider too difficult to accomplish.

The Effort That Collects Virtuous Qualities [1.12.2.2]

What is a bodhisattva's effort that collects virtuous qualities?

It is the effort that is applied to the perfection of generosity in order to complete the perfection of generosity, [as well as] that which is applied to the perfections of morality, patience, effort, meditative absorption, and wisdom in order to complete those perfections [that range from morality to] wisdom.

Moreover, this [form of effort], in brief, should be understood as being of seven types: (1) It is unshakable in that it cannot be moved [from its place] by any thought, false notion,[876] [root] mental affliction, secondary mental affliction, verbal challenge from another person, or painful experience. (2) It is strong in that it is applied zealously. (3) It is immeasurable in that it is dedicated to the attainment of complete knowledge regarding all the branches of learning. (4) It is accompanied by [proper] means both in the sense that it follows the unerring path to [any] aim that is worthy of being achieved and in the sense that it has attained a state of equanimity.[877] (5) It is right effort in the sense that it is dedicated to the attainment of aims that are both meaningful and worthy of being achieved. (6) It is prolonged in the sense that it is applied continuously. (7) It is free of pride in the sense that one does not become swollen with pride because of having initiated effort. With these seven aspects, the practice of initiating effort in order to collect virtuous qualities promotes the swift completion of the bodhisattvas' perfections and the [swift] attainment of unsurpassed true and complete enlightenment. In addition, because effort alone is the principal and most excellent cause for attaining all the virtuous qualities that bring about enlightenment and nothing else is comparable to it, the tathāgatas point to

876. *BBhVy* (f. 188a) comments about the terms "thought" (S: *kalpaḥ,* T: *rtog pa*) and "false notion" (S: *vikalpaḥ,* T: *rnam par rtog pa*) that they represent potential obstacles to effort that can occur within a person's own mind. The text states: "Bringing to mind samsara's suffering and the fact that one has been subjected to the wrongful behavior of sentient beings can cause one's effort to be diminished and thus to become unsteady."

877. S: *samatāprativedhāt,* T: *mnyam pa nyid khong du chud pa'i phyir. BBhVy* (f. 188b): "It is also [effort] that is accompanied by [proper] means because it has attained the equanimity that is free of any mental affliction." This quality is described below in connection with the third form of effort that is difficult to carry out.

effort when they are pointing out [what is needed] for [the attainment of] unsurpassed true and complete enlightenment.

The Effort That Acts on Behalf of Sentient Beings [1.12.2.3]

For its part, the bodhisattva's effort that acts on behalf of sentient beings should be understood as being made up of eleven categories, which are the same as the ones that were described in the chapter on morality. What was referred to there as morality should here be called effort.[878] That is the [only] difference.

The Effort That Is Difficult to Carry Out [1.12.3]

What is a bodhisattva's effort that is difficult to carry out?

It should be regarded as being of three types. [The quality by means of] which a bodhisattva remains engaged in meditation upon virtuous qualities uninterruptedly and continually without forming any notion[879] of monastic robes, alms food, a bed and seat, or a self [should be understood as] the first form of a bodhisattva's effort that is difficult to carry out. Moreover, [while exerting him- or herself] with this form of effort, [the quality by means of which] a bodhisattva remains engaged at all times [in the practice of virtuous qualities] until his or her class affiliate has been abandoned[880] [should be understood as] the second form of a bodhisattva's effort that is difficult to carry out. In addition, [the quality by means of which] a bodhisattva gains a [form of] effort that is accompanied by the attribute of having

878. See Book I, chapter 10, the section entitled "Engaging in Every Aspect of Acting on Behalf of Sentient Beings" [I.10.2.6]. Thus, the first of the eleven forms of effort are (1a) the effort of assisting those who need help with a variety of activities and (1b) the effort of assisting those who are experiencing physical or mental suffering. The remaining ten forms should be described in a similar manner.

879. S: *saṃjñām akurvan,* T: *'du shes mi byed par. BBhVy* (f. 188b) describes this first difficulty as the ability to "practice without regard for material possessions, body, or life."

880. S: *ānikāyasabhāganikṣepāt,* T: *ris mthun pa ma dor gyi bar du.* In more straightforward language, this phrase means "for as long as he or she lives." *PSV* (p. 319): "[Thus,] 'class affiliate' (S: *nikāyasabhāgaḥ,* T: *ris mthun pa*) means something that has an affiliation with a class [by virtue of a shared similarity].... [In general,] the term 'class affiliate' refers to the continuum of heaps that occurs within a particular [sentient being's] single birth."

attained equanimity[881] and [therefore] is neither overly listless nor overly energetic, and that it is directed toward an unerring object, should be understood as the third form of a bodhisattva's effort that is difficult to carry out. Now then, it should be understood that compassion toward sentient beings and wisdom are the acquiring causes[882] [by means of which] bodhisattvas [obtain] the strength that relates to the effort that is difficult to carry out.

The Effort That Is Directed Everywhere [I.12.4]

What is a bodhisattva's effort that is directed everywhere?

It should be regarded as being of four types: (1) that which avoids afflicted

881. S: *upekṣā*, T: *btang snyoms*. There are three distinct senses of this term that can be confused: (1) the equanimity that is one of the three types of feeling (i.e., the form of experience that is neither pleasurable nor painful); (2) the equanimity that is one of the four immeasurables (i.e., the attitude that maintains impartiality with regard to all sentient beings and in doing so avoids developing attachment toward friends, animosity toward enemies, and lack of concern toward strangers); and (3) what is sometimes referred to in Tibetan literature as "the equanimity that is a mental formation" (T: *'du byed btang bsnyoms*). This third form of equanimity is the one that is meant here. It is a distinct, virtuous mental factor (*caittaḥ*, T: *sems byung*) that plays a central role in the development of one-pointed concentration. *AS* (p. 6): "What is equanimity? It is [a mental factor] that prevents one from abiding in an afflicted state [of mind] and [one that maintains] an evenness of mind, an inactivity of mind, or a continuous state of effortlessness of mind on the basis of [forms of] avoidance of attachment, avoidance of hatred, or avoidance of ignorance [i.e., the three "roots of virtue"] that are accompanied by effort. Its action is to provide support for preventing the occurrence of [any state of mental] affliction." *PSV* (pp. 289–290): "The three expressions 'evenness of mind . . .' and so on illustrate equanimity in a beginning, middle, and final stage. Languor and excitation are uneven states of mind. The initial stage in which they are absent is called 'evenness of mind.' Following that, there occurs a stage of 'inactivity' in which the mind engaged in meditative absorption is able to function appropriately and evenly without the need to take any action or exert any effort. [However,] during this period there is still some concern that languor or excitation might occur, because the practitioner has not been meditating very long. The period following this is one in which there is no concern that either of those two [faults] might occur, because the practitioner's meditation has reached a degree of excellence and he or she has greatly distanced him- or herself from those obstacles. At this point, the practitioner is able to remain in a state of 'effortlessness' in that he or she does not need to make any exertion in relation to the causes that constitute the antidotes to languor and excitation."

882. S: *saṃgrahahetuḥ*, T: *sdud pa'i rgyu*. *BBhVy* (f. 189a): "'Acquiring cause' means producing cause (S: *āvāhakahetuḥ*, T: *'dren pa'i rgyu*) in the sense of that [factor] which brings something into being—which is to say, the instrumental cause." For Asaṅga's description of a "producing cause," see Book I, chapter 8, in the section entitled "The Ten Causes" [I.8.2.1] and note 541.

qualities; (2) that which gains possession of pure qualities; (3) that which refines deeds; and (4) that which increases knowledge. Concerning this [topic], a bodhisattva's effort that avoids afflicted qualities is [the form of effort that strives] to prevent the arising of those fetters,[883] bonds,[884] latencies,[885] secondary mental afflictions,[886] and perturbations[887] that have not yet arisen and to abandon those that have arisen. Concerning this [topic], a bodhisattva's effort that gains possession of pure qualities is [the form of effort that strives] to generate those virtuous entities that have not yet arisen and to maintain [possession of], avoid indistinctness about, and increase and augment those [virtuous entities] that have arisen. Concerning this [topic], a bodhisattva's effort that refines deeds is [the form of effort that strives] to refine and collect the three types of deeds—that is, the virtuous deeds of body, speech, and mind. Concerning this [topic], the form of a bodhisattva's effort that increases knowledge [is the form of effort that] promotes the attainment and development of the forms of wisdom that derive from learning, reflection, and meditation.

883. S: *saṃyojanam.* See note 716.

884. S: *bandhanam,* T: *'ching ba. AS* (p. 46): "There are three types of bond—the bond of desire, the bond of hatred, and the bond of ignorance. The bond of desire binds beings to the suffering of change. The bond of hatred binds beings to the suffering of suffering. The bond of ignorance binds beings to the suffering of conditioned existence. In addition, based on desire, hatred, and ignorance, one does not gain [the ability to exercise] control in relation to virtuous forms of conduct. Therefore, [each of them] is called a 'bond.'"

885. S: *anuśayaḥ,* T: *bag la nyal. AS* (p. 46): "There are seven latencies: (1) the latency of attachment to sense pleasures; (2) the latency of hatred; (3) the latency of attachment to [samsaric] existence; (4) the latency of pride; (5) the latency of ignorance; (6) the latency of views; and (7) the latency of doubt." Each of these latencies is described as a state of indisposition that favors [the arising of] overt forms of the particular root mental affliction. The text then continues: "Due to the pursuit of sense pleasures, the [two] latencies of attachment to sense pleasures and hatred grow stronger for a person who has not put an end to them. Due to the pursuit of [continued samsaric] existence, the latency of attachment to [samsaric] existence grows stronger for a person who has not put an end to [that form of desire]. Due to the pursuit of a wrongful form of spiritual life (S: *brahmacaryam,* T: *tshangs par spyod pa*) the latencies of pride, ignorance, views, and doubt grow stronger for a person who has not put an end to them." See also notes 139, 410, and 608.

886. See note 142.

887. See note 439.

The Effort of a True Spiritual Being [1.12.5]

What is a bodhisattva's effort of a true spiritual being?

It should be regarded as being of five types: (1) the effort of bodhisattvas that has not been rejected due to the fact that no form of aspiration and practice is ever rejected; (2) [the effort of bodhisattvas] that is not deficient due to the development of a form of effort whose strength is equal to or greater than [what is needed for] the task that is undertaken; (3) [the effort of bodhisattvas] that is not subject to dejection due to having a state of mind that does not become timid or despondent about having to exert strenuous effort continuously and for a long time; (4) [the effort of bodhisattvas] that is unerring due to being governed by a type of means that is directed toward a [genuine] aim; and (5) [the effort of bodhisattvas] whose application is fervent[888] in that it [strives after] unsurpassed true and complete enlightenment with a heightened sense of urgency.

Effort of Every Form [1.12.6]

Regarding this [topic], what is a bodhisattva's effort of every form?

It should be understood as the thirteen forms [of effort that result from] combining together six forms and seven forms. [The first six are] (1) continuous effort, in that it is practiced at all times; (2) zealous effort, in that it is applied earnestly;[889] (3) effort that is a natural consequence, in that it is generated on the strength of being caused by a former effort; (4) effective[890] effort, in that it is applied to [everything] that pertains to virtue after having made careful consideration; (5) imperturbable effort, in that it cannot be disturbed by any painful experience and because it has attained the quality of being unalterable; and (6) insatiable effort, in that it is not satisfied by

888. S: *uttaptaprayogam,* T: *brtun te sbyor ba. BBhVy* (f. 189b): "[An effort] 'whose application is fervent' means a form that is exerted swiftly and in a manner resembling the effort of a person whose head or clothing has caught fire to put out the flames."

889. S: *nipuṇaprayogitayā,* T: *lhur sbyor ba'i phyir.* The Sanskrit adjective *nipuṇa* can vary in meaning according to the context (cf. MW, p. 550). Here it seems to mean "possessing complete devotion." *BBhVy* (f. 189b): "'Zealous effort' (S: *satkṛtyavīryam,* T: *gus pa'i brtson 'grus*) means [a form of effort] that is accompanied by an application possessing strong desire."

890. S: *prāyogikam,* T: *sbyor ba las byung ba. BBhVy* (f. 189b): "'Effective effort' means [a form of effort] that is not overcome by any opposition that may occur or arise."

merely attaining distinctive qualities that are small or insignificant. These six types of the effort of every form cause a bodhisattva who possesses them to be described in relation to virtuous qualities as "one who has taken hold of effort," "one who possesses strength," "one who possesses vigor," "one who is energetic," "one whose courage is firm," and "one whose obligation has not been relinquished."[891]

In addition, [the remaining] seven types [of a bodhisattva's effort of every form are as follows]: (1) A bodhisattva's effort is one that is accompanied by aspiration in that it is strengthened by repeated and fervent aspiration for and dedication to unsurpassed true and complete enlightenment. (2) A bodhisattva's effort that is endowed with equipoise is [the effort] of one who remains unperturbed by keeping his or her mind from becoming afflicted by any of the root or mental afflictions [and] it is a [form of] effort by means of which a bodhisattva becomes one who abides in [a state of] equal suitability toward [all] virtuous qualities. (3) A bodhisattva's exceptional effort is that which, in order to abandon any secondary mental affliction that may have afflicted and perturbed his or her mind, resembles the effort of a person whose head has caught fire to put out the flames. (4) A bodhisattva's effort is one that seeks in that it pursues all the branches of learning. (5) A bodhisattva's effort is one that pertains to the training in that it accomplishes the practice that accords with the Dharma, suitably and appropriately, with regard to those very qualities that are being sought. (6) A bodhisattva's effort that accomplishes the aims of others should be understood as being of eleven types in the manner that was described earlier. (7) A bodhisattva's seventh [form of] effort [strives] to safeguard his or her own correct practice and to counteract his or her errors in a manner that accords with Dharma. These thirteen types of a bodhisattva's effort are called "the effort of every form."

The Effort That Relates to the Distressed and What They Want and the Effort That Brings Happiness Here and in the Next World [1.12.7–8]

[The descriptions of] the effort of bodhisattvas that relates to the distressed and what they want and the effort [of bodhisattvas] that brings happiness here and in the next world should be regarded as being like [the descriptions

891. *BBhVy* (f. 189b) indicates that the six phrases set off by quotation marks are used to describe bodhisattvas in canonical literature.

that were given for the corresponding forms of] patience. The difference between them is this. What was [described as] patience [in the previous chapter] should be described here as effort [and] exertion.

Pure Effort [1.12.9]

What is a bodhisattva's pure effort?

In brief, it should be understood as being of ten types. [They are effort that is] (1) appropriate, (2) experienced, (3) free of laxness, and (4) well informed; (5) [effort in which] the practice is applied according to the occasion; and [effort that is] (6) accompanied by the perception of signs, (7) free of dejection, (8) not deficient, (9) balanced, and (10) dedicated to great enlightenment.

Whichever one of the secondary mental afflictions greatly distresses a bodhisattva here, he or she cultivates the appropriate antidote for that secondary mental affliction in order to abandon it. One meditates on unattractiveness as the antidote for attachment to sense pleasures. [One meditates] on loving-kindness as the antidote for malice. One meditates on the principles of conditionality [taught in the doctrine of] dependent origination as an antidote for ignorance. One meditates on recollection of the breath as an antidote for discursive thoughts. One meditates on the diversity of the constituents[892] as an antidote for pride. This kind [of effort] is called a bodhisattva's "appropriate effort."

892. S: *dhātuprabhedaḥ,* T: *khams gyi rab tu dbye ba*. Buddhist literature contains a number of classifications and meanings that relate to the term "constituent" (S: *dhātuḥ,* T: *khams*; see note 441). The one that is being referred to here describes the individual as comprising these six constituents: (1) the earth element, (2) the water element, (3) the fire element, (4) the air element, (5) space, and (6) consciousness. The four physical elements, in particular, are differentiated in terms of both inner and outer forms. The description of the inner earth and water elements corresponds to the list of thirty-six components that make up the body, beginning with the hair of the head and ending with urine. The constituents of space and consciousness are contemplated as additional elements that make up the practitioner. After listing the range of items that are to be reflected upon for this practice, *ŚBh* (p. 218) declares: "When a person who is highly prone to develop pride contemplates this [explanation pertaining to the] diversity of the constituents, he or she will give up the notion that [his or her] body consists of a [single undifferentiated] mass and gain an awareness of its unattractiveness. This will prevent him or her from becoming swollen up [with a sense of self-importance and superiority] and diminish [his or her] pride. Thus, [meditation on this topic] purifies the mind [of the person] who is prone [to develop] that [mental affliction of pride]."

Here a bodhisattva does not possess the effort of a novice and a beginning practitioner—that is, [when striving] to fix the mind upon the instruction and counsel. He or she [strives] in no other way than as one who has repeatedly practiced the application and one who has become familiar with the application. This [type of effort] is called a bodhisattva's "experienced effort."

A bodhisattva also is not one who has finished repeatedly practicing the application that relates to fixing his or her mind upon the instruction and upon counsel. Rather, the bodhisattva is [one who resembles] a novice whose application is free of laxness with regard to this [form of] application in the sense that one applies oneself continuously and zealously. This [type of effort] is called a bodhisattva's "effort that is free of laxness."

Moreover, [a bodhisattva] initiates effort in order to fix his or her mind by means of an unerring form of understanding, whether it is [gained] from venerable beings or due to the bodhisattva's own kindling of the strength of extensive learning. This [type of effort] is called a bodhisattva's "well-informed effort."

Moreover, the bodhisattva who possesses such an unerring understanding meditates on quiescence at a time [when the goal is to develop] quiescence, takes hold of the mind at a time [when the goal is to develop the quality of] retention,[893] and meditates on equanimity[894] at a time [when the goal is to maintain] equanimity. This [type of effort] is called [a bodhisattva's] "effort that is applied according to the occasion."

Moreover, a bodhisattva exerts him- or herself continually and zealously to observe, to avoid becoming inattentive about, and to achieve the signs of quiescence, retention, and equanimity as well as [to observe, to avoid becoming inattentive about, and to achieve] the signs of developing, maintaining, and arising from one-pointed concentration. This [type of effort] is called a bodhisattva's "effort [that is accompanied by] the perception of signs."

Moreover, having heard the most extensive, most profound, inconceivably great, and immeasurable instructions on the undertaking of effort that

893. This is the form of effort that is applied to overcome languor (S: *layam,* T: *bying ba*). See note 472.

894. See note 881. Although effort is required to dispel either languor or excitation whenever they occur, in their absence it is appropriate for the meditation practitioner to relax his or her effort in order to remain in a state of equanimity. That is what is meant here by the phrase "meditate upon equanimity."

is carried out by bodhisattvas, a bodhisattva does not disparage him- or herself, does not become disheartened, and is not satisfied merely by attaining a small or insignificant distinctive quality. He or she does not strive for something that is not superior. This [type of effort] is called a bodhisattva's "effort that is free of dejection."

Moreover, regularly and at the appropriate time, a bodhisattva takes up and attends to [the practices of] guarding the doors of the senses, observing moderation with regard to food, maintaining wakefulness during the first and last parts of the night, remaining vigilant, and other similar forms of the requisites for one-pointed concentration.[895] He or she also applies him- or herself to them zealously. He or she initiates an unerring exertion that is directed toward a [genuine] aim in all situations. This [type of effort] is called a bodhisattva's "effort that is not deficient."

Moreover, a bodhisattva initiates a form of effort that is neither overly listless nor overly strained. He or she applies a method in a balanced manner. He or she also acts carefully and in a balanced manner with regard to all forms of exertion that need to be carried out. This [type of effort] is referred to as a bodhisattva's "state of balanced effort."

Moreover, a bodhisattva dedicates all forms of effort that are initiated and generated to unsurpassed and complete enlightenment. This [type of effort] is called a bodhisattva's "effort that is correctly dedicated."

This [discussion of] the effort that is practiced by bodhisattvas—beginning with the essence of effort, etc., and ending with pure effort—[describes a spiritual quality] that has great enlightenment as its fruit and [it is a spiritual quality] on the basis of which bodhisattvas, after completing the perfection of effort, have attained, shall attain, and are currently attaining unsurpassed true and complete enlightenment.

Within [Book I of] *The Stage of a Bodhisattva,* [known as] "The Object of Mental Application That Relates to the Support," this completes the twelfth chapter, entitled "Effort."

895. S: *samādhisaṃbhārāni,* T: *ting nge 'dzin gyis tshogs.* These are forms of practice that must be developed in order to be able to cultivate one-pointed concentration effectively.

13

Meditative Absorption

The summary verses should be understood in the same manner as before.

The Essence of Meditative Absorption [1.13.1]

Regarding this [topic], what is the essence of a bodhisattva's meditative absorption?

It is a virtuous one-pointedness of mind that is possessed by bodhisattvas and is preceded by listening to and reflecting upon the collection of bodhisattva scriptures. It can be either mundane[896] or transcendent[897] in nature. [Moreover,] it is a state of mental stability that pertains to quiescence, insight, or both of them in that it constitutes a path in which the two [forms of meditation] are practiced in combination. This should be understood as the essence of the meditative absorption[898] that is practiced by bodhisattvas.

896. S: *laukikam*, T: *'jig rten pa*. *AS* (p. 19): "'Mundane' refers to that which is included in the three [samsaric] realms." The mundane path is a form of insight meditation (S: *vipaśyanā*, T: *lhag mthong*; see Book I, chapter 8, the section entitled "Meditation" [I.8.4.3]) in which a lower level of consciousness is regarded as coarse (S: *audārikam*, T: *rags pa*) and a higher level as tranquil (S: *śāntam*, T: *zhi ba*). This type of practice is described as resulting in "freedom from attachment" (S: *vairāgyam*, T: *'dod chags dang bral ba*) toward eight different levels of samsaric existence. See also note 561.

897. S: *lokottaram*, T: *'jig rten las 'das pa*. *AS* (p. 19): "'Transcendent' refers to the nonconceptual [states of mind] (S: *nirvikalpam*, T: *rnam par mi rtog pa*) that are antidotes for all of the three realms in that they do not conceive of [any of the four] errors (S: *viparyāsaḥ*, T: *phyin ci log*) and they are free of conceptual elaboration (S: *niṣprapañcaḥ*, T: *spros pa*)."

898. S: *dhyānam*, T: *bsam gtan*. *ŚBh* (p. 450): "The term 'meditative absorption' refers to [a state in which the mind] meditates correctly on an object and recollection holds fast [to an object] one-pointedly."

All-Inclusive Meditative Absorption [1.13.2]

Regarding this [topic], what is a bodhisattva's all-inclusive meditative absorption?

It should be regarded as being of two types: mundane and transcendent. In addition, it should be understood, according to circumstances, as being of three types: (1) the meditative absorption [that is cultivated] in order to abide in a state of ease during this life, (2) the meditative absorption [that is cultivated] in order to obtain for a bodhisattva qualities that relate to one-pointed concentration, and (3) the meditative absorption [that is cultivated] in order to act on behalf of sentient beings.

The Meditative Absorption That Enables One to Abide in a State of Ease during This Life [1.13.2.1]

Regarding this [topic], the meditative absorption of bodhisattvas that is free of all conceptual thought,[899] that gives rise to physical and mental agility,[900] that is a state of extreme tranquility,[901] that is free of [mistaken] conjecture,[902] that is not relished,[903] and that is free of all signs[904] should be understood as [the form of meditative absorption that is cultivated by bodhisattvas] in order to abide in a state of ease during their current life.

899. S: *vikalpaḥ,* T: *rnam par rtog pa*. See Book I, chapter 4, the section entitled "The Eight Types of Conceptual Thought" [I.4.8].

900. See note 382.

901. S: *paramapraśāntam,* T: *mchog tu rab tu zhi ba*. *BBhVy* (f. 191b): "[It is] 'a state of extreme tranquility' due to the agility that is generated by its having become extraordinary."

902. S: *manyanā,* T: *rlom sems*. *BBhVy* (f. 191b): "[It is] 'free of [mistaken] conjecture' because [all forms of] mental affliction relating to [mistaken] views have been eliminated."

903. S: *anāsvāditam,* T: *ro myang ba med pa*. *BBhVy* (f. 191b): "[It is] 'not relished' because the mental affliction of craving has been eliminated."

904. S: *sarvanimittāpagatam,* T: *mtshan ma thams cad dang bral ba*. The term "sign" here refers to the objects of the six forms of consciousness. The ordinary person who "grasps at signs" (S: *nimittagrahī,* T: *mtshan mar 'dzin pa*) engages these objects indiscriminately, and subsequently, because of improper attention, develops the mental afflictions. *BBhVy* (f. 191b): "[Meditative absorption is] 'free of all signs' because all the enjoyments of [the sense objects of visible] form, etc., have been abandoned."

The Meditative Absorption That Gains the Spiritual Qualities Related to One-Pointed Concentration [1.13.2.2]

Regarding this [topic], the meditative absorption of bodhisattvas that is conducive to the acquisition of those manifold, inconceivable, and immeasurable forms of one-pointed concentration that are included within the lineages of the ten powers[905]—forms of one-pointed concentration that listeners and solitary realizers do not even know the names of, much less actually attain—as well as [the meditative absorption] that is conducive to the acquisition of those spiritual qualities that are possessed by bodhisattvas in a form that is not common to listeners, such as the [eight] deliverances,[906]

905. S: *balagotram,* T: *stobs kyi rigs.* This term is also used for the title of chapter 8. The ten powers are forms of transcendent knowledge that are exclusive to fully enlightened buddhas. They are discussed extensively in the last chapter of Book III. Their "lineages" are the spiritual qualities that must be cultivated in order to achieve the ten powers. One of these is the form of practice that accords with the Dharma, which includes the practice of quiescence and insight. This would seem to be the reference of the term here.

906. The eight deliverances (S: *aṣṭau vimokṣāḥ,* T: *rnam par thar pa brgyad*) are described in the sixth stage of the *YBh,* which is entitled "The Stage of Mental Composure" (S: *samāhitā bhūmiḥ,* T: *mnyam par bzhag pa'i sa*). *AAA* refers to the first three deliverances as the "emanation path" (S: *nirmāṇamārgaḥ,* T: *sprul pa'i lam*) and the remaining five as the "path in which one abides in a state of ease in one's present life" (S: *dṛṣṭadharmasukhavihāramārgaḥ,* T: *mthong ba'i chos la bde bar gnas pa'i lam*). The first three deliverances are specifically cultivated to overcome the obstacles to attaining mastery over the ability to emanate forms of any kind at will; the latter five are specifically cultivated to overcome the attachment that stems from relishing the ease that occurs in each of these meditative states. All eight are also cultivated in order to achieve extraordinary spiritual attributes, such as the bases of mastery, the universal bases, miraculous powers, the avoidance of conflict, knowledge by resolve, and the forms of informative knowledge. The eight are (1) the deliverance in which one who possesses form perceives forms (S: *rūpī rūpāṇi paśyati,* T: *gzugs can gzugs rnams la lta ba*); (2) the deliverance in which one who conceives of him- or herself internally as lacking form perceives forms externally (S: *adhyātmam arūpasaṃñī bahirdhā rūpāṇi paśyati;* T: *nang gzugs med par 'du shes pas phyi rol gyi gzugs rnams la lta ba*); (3) the deliverance in which one achieves and abides in a deliverance consisting of attractiveness that was manifested with the body (S: *śubhaṃ vimokṣaṃ kāyena sākṣātkṛtvopasaṃpadya viharati;* T: *sdug pa'i rnam par thar pa lus kyis mngon sum du byas te rdzogs par byas nas gnas pa*); (4) the deliverance in which one achieves and abides in the sphere of unlimited space (S: *ākāśānantyāyatanam upasampadya viharati;* T: *nam mkha' mtha' yas skye mched rdzogs par byas te gnas pa*); (5) the deliverance in which one achieves and abides in the sphere of unlimited consciousness (S: *vijñānānantyāyatanam upasampadya viharati;* T: *rnam shes mtha' yas skye mched rdzogs par byas te gnas pa*); (6) the deliverance in which one achieves

the [eight] bases of mastery,[907] the [ten] universal bases,[908] the avoidance

and abides in the sphere of nothingness (S: *ākiṃcanyāyatanam upasampadya viharati;* T: *ci yang med pa'i skye mched rdzogs par byas te gnas pa*); (7) the deliverance in which one achieves and abides in the sphere in which there is neither conception nor absence of conception (S: *nāivsaṃjñānāsaṃjñāyatanam upasampadya viharati;* T: *'du shes med 'du shes med min skye mched rdzogs par byas te gnas pa*); and (8) the deliverance in which one achieves and abides in a cessation of feeling and conception that was manifested with the body (S: *saṃjñāveditanirodhaṃ kāyena sākṣātkṛtvopasampadya viharati;* T: *'du shes dang tshor ba 'gog pa lus kyis mngon sum du byas te rdzogs par byas nas gnas pa*).

907. S: *abhibhvāyatanāni,* T: *zil gyis non pa'i skye mched rnams.* The eight bases of mastery are states of one-pointed concentration in which the practitioner gains the ability to alter the appearance of outer objects. The first basis of mastery is described in canonical scriptures as follows: "Conceiving of him- or herself inwardly as possessing form, [the practitioner] views large outer forms as both beautiful and ugly. Then, overpowering them, he or she both recognizes and perceives them. To view them in this way represents the first basis of mastery." The second basis of mastery is described in exactly the same language, except that the phrase "large outer forms" is replaced with "small outer forms." The third and fourth bases of mastery differ from the first two only in the opening phrase, which becomes "Conceiving of him- or herself inwardly as lacking form." The fifth through the eighth bases of mastery are similar to the third and fourth, differing only in that they specifically view outer forms as blue, yellow, red, and white, respectively.

The first two bases of mastery are attained by means of the first deliverance; the third and fourth bases of mastery are attained by means of the second deliverance; and the fifth through the eighth bases of mastery are attained by means of the third deliverance. The difference between the first three deliverances and the eight bases of mastery is that in the case of the deliverances, the practitioner cultivates the ability to emanate forms in whatever form one might desire, while in the case of the bases of mastery, he or she seeks to attain mastery over them by being able to make them invisible and to transform them at will. For instance, by conceiving of objects as blue, yellow, red, white, and so forth, the practitioner can instantly transform them into those colors. The practitioner "masters" objects in the sense that he or she can transform unattractive ones so that they appear attractive and also because, even as they are transformed, they never cause the practitioner to develop a mind troubled by such mental afflictions as pride.

908. S: *kṛtsnāyatanāni,* T: *zad par gyi skye mched rnams.* There are ten universal bases: those of earth, water, fire, air, blue, yellow, red, white, space, and consciousness. All ten are states of one-pointed concentration, together with the wisdom that accompanies them. The first eight are cultivated within the fourth absorption of the form realm, and the last two within the first two states of composure of the formless realm. They are called "universal bases" because the practitioner who cultivates them achieves the ability both to greatly increase the size of objects and to spread them out to an unlimited degree. When these concentrations have been mastered, the practitioner is able to fill the surrounding space with emanations of earth, water, fire, air, and so forth, at will. He or she can also transform physical objects from one aspect into another, overcome the mental afflictions, and achieve many spiritual qualities. For instance, by mastering the earth universal basis, the practitioner can manifest earth in the sky or on water and walk across them. By means of the water all-pervading

of conflict,[909] knowledge by resolve,[910] etc., should be understood as [the form of meditative absorption that is cultivated by bodhisattvas] in order to obtain a bodhisattva's qualities that relate to one-pointed concentration.

The Meditative Absorption That Relates to Acting on Behalf of Sentient Beings [1.13.2.3]

The meditative absorption that relates to acting on behalf of sentient beings should be understood as being of eleven types, in the manner that they were described earlier. [They are] (1a) the meditative absorption that a bodhisattva relies upon to assist beings with a variety of meaningful activities; (1b) [the meditative absorption that a bodhisattva relies upon] to remove the suffering of those who are experiencing suffering; (2) [the meditative absorption that a bodhisattva relies upon] to give instruction [to others] regarding what is proper; (3) [the meditative absorption that a bodhisattva] who feels a sense of gratitude and appreciation [relies upon] to do something in return for the favors [that he or she has received from others]; (4) [the meditative absorption that a bodhisattva relies upon] to protect [beings] from danger; (5) [the meditative absorption that a bodhisattva relies upon] to dispel the grief of those who are abiding in [a state of] misfortune; (6) [the meditative absorption that a bodhisattva relies upon] to provide objects that are a means of subsistence to those who lack them; (7) [the meditative absorption that a bodhisattva relies upon] to lead an assembly [of practitioners]; (8) [the meditative absorption that a bodhisattva relies upon] to comply with the minds [of others]; (9) [the meditative absorption that a bodhisattva relies upon] to encourage [others] by [declaring] their genuine good qualities; (10) [the meditative absorption that a bodhisattva relies upon] to suppress in a correct manner [those who engage in misconduct]; and (11) [the meditative absorption that a bodhisattva relies upon] to frighten [others in order to turn them away from nonvirtue] and to win them over [to the Buddha's teaching] through [the use of] miraculous powers.

All of these [forms of meditative absorption] combined together into

---

basis, one can transform the earth and mountains into water and oceans. And with the air all-pervading basis, one can manifest space in the middle of a mountain and walk through it, or walk through solid walls.

909. See note 504.

910. See note 505.

one group are called the bodhisattvas' "all-inclusive meditative absorption." There are no [forms of meditative absorption] of greater significance than these and there are none besides these.

The Meditative Absorption That Is Difficult to Carry Out [1.13.3]

Regarding this [topic], what is a bodhisattva's meditative absorption that is difficult to carry out?

It should be regarded as being of three types. Having dwelt in extensive, manifold states of meditative absorption which they have attained and to which they have become well accustomed, bodhisattvas voluntarily turn away from the supreme ease of those meditative absorptions and, [motivated] by sympathy toward [all] sentient beings, carefully consider the [kinds of] extensive actions [that will accomplish] the aims of sentient beings. Then, remaining vigilant about the spiritual ripening of sentient beings, they take birth in the desire realm [in order to fulfill those aims]. This should be understood as the first form of bodhisattvas' meditative absorption that is difficult to carry out. Moreover, a bodhisattva relies upon meditative absorption to attain immeasurable, countless, and inconceivable forms of one-pointed concentration that are achieved by bodhisattvas but that are beyond the grasp of all listeners and solitary realizers. This should be understood as the second form of a bodhisattva's meditative absorption that is difficult to carry out. Further, a bodhisattva relies upon meditative absorption to attain unsurpassed true and complete enlightenment. This should be understood as the third form of a bodhisattva's meditative absorption that is difficult to carry out.

The Meditative Absorption That Is Directed Everywhere [1.13.4]

Regarding this [topic], what is a bodhisattva's meditative absorption that is directed everywhere?

It should be regarded as being of four types: (1) that which is associated with deliberation and reflection,[911] (2) that which is associated with

911. S: *savitarkam savicāram,* T: *rtog pa dang bcas dpyod pa dang bcas.* This is a reference to two of the defining characteristics of the first meditative absorption. Commentarial

joy,[912] (3) that which is accompanied by the ease of pleasure,[913] and (4) that

literature defines each of the four meditative absorptions in terms of their main components or limbs (S: *aṅgam,* T: *yan lag*). The first meditative absorption consists of these five limbs: (1) deliberation, (2) reflection, (3) joy, (4) ease, and (5) one-pointedness of mind. Of these, deliberation and reflection are corrective limbs, in that they enable the practitioner to abandon the faults of the desire realm, including desire for sensory pleasures, malice (S: *vyāpadaḥ,* T: *gnod sems*), harmfulness (S: *vimhiṃsā,* T: *rnam par 'tshe ba*), and [nonvirtuous] deliberative thoughts. Joy and pleasure are beneficial limbs, because the practitioner experiences the joy and ease that arise through having attained separation from the coarseness of the desire realm. One-pointedness of mind is the supporting limb in that the power of concentration enables the other limbs to take effect. The canonical description of the first meditative absorption states: "Separated from the objects of desire, separated from evil and nonvirtuous qualities, [the practitioner] achieves and then remains in the first meditative absorption, which is characterized by the joy and ease that are born of separation and is accompanied by deliberation and reflection."

912. S: *prītisahagatam,* T: *dga' ba dang ldan pa*. The second meditative absorption is made up of these four limbs: (1) inner tranquility (S: *adhyātmasamprasādaḥ,* T: *nang rab tu dang ba*); (2) joy; (3) ease; and (4) one-pointedness of mind. "Inner tranquility" is the corrective limb because it removes the unsettling effect that deliberation and reflection continue to have upon the mind following the attainment of the first meditative absorption. The descriptions of the remaining three limbs are similar to those that were given for the first meditative absorption. The main difference is that here joy, ease, and one-pointed concentration have a greater depth and strength due to the absence of deliberation, reflection, and the mental afflictions that are specific to the first meditative absorption. The canonical description of the second meditative absorption states: "Through having quelled deliberation and reflection, through [having attained] inner tranquility, and through [having reached] a state in which there is uniform attention of the mind, [the practitioner] achieves and then remains in the second meditative absorption, which is characterized by the joy and ease that are born of concentration and is free of deliberation and reflection."

913. S: *sātasukhasahagatam,* T: *sim pa'i bde ba dang ldan pa*. The third meditative absorption is made up of five limbs: (1) recollection, (2) vigilance, (3) equanimity, (4) pleasure, and (5) one-pointedness of mind. The principal obstacles to attainment of the third meditative absorption are joy and the mental afflictions that pertain to the second meditative absorption. Joy, in particular, has an exciting effect upon the mind that prevents the practitioner from maintaining a state of continuous equanimity. This equanimity is an evenness of mind, not the neutral feeling that is neither pleasant nor unpleasant, and it is developed through cultivating recollection and vigilance. Hence, these three mental factors represent the corrective limbs of the third meditative absorption. *ŚBh* (p. 453) describes the fourth limb, called "pleasure" (S: *sukham,* T: *bde ba*), in the following manner: "At that time, [the practitioner] is caused to experience with his physical and his mental body both a pleasant feeling and a pleasurable form of agility. Below the third meditative absorption, there exists neither such a form of pleasure nor uninterrupted equanimity. And while [uninterrupted] equanimity is possessed above the third meditative absorption, no pleasure exists there. Thus, because pleasure and equanimity do not exist together below this [level] and pleasure is not found above it, while this [level]—that is to say, the third meditative absorption—

which is accompanied by equanimity.[914]

The Meditative Absorption of a True Spiritual Being [1.13.5]

Regarding this [topic], what is a bodhisattva's meditative absorption of a true spiritual being?

It should be regarded as being of five types. It is (1) [a meditative absorption] that is not relished, (2) one that is accompanied by [immeasurable] loving-kindness, (3) one that is accompanied by [immeasurable] compassion, (4) one that is accompanied by [immeasurable] joy, and (5) one that is accompanied by [immeasurable] equanimity.

Meditative Absorption of Every Form [1.13.6]

Regarding this [topic], what is a bodhisattva's meditative absorption of every form?

It should be understood as the thirteen types [that result from] combining together six types and seven types. They are (1) the meditative absorp-

---

does support [both of these qualities], the āryas declare in relation to a person who is abiding in such a state of attainment, 'Possessed of recollection and equanimity, [that one] dwells in [a state of] pleasure.'" The canonical description of the third meditative absorption states: "Free of attachment to joy, [the practitioner] abides possessed of equanimity, recollection, and vigilance. He or she is also caused to experience pleasure with the body. [In this way,] he or she achieves and then remains in the third meditative absorption, [a state] in which joy is absent and about which the āryas declare, 'Possessed of recollection and equanimity, [that one] dwells in [a state of] pleasure.'"

914. S: *upekṣāsahagatam*, T: *btang snyoms dang ldan pa*. The fourth meditative absorption is made up of four limbs: (1) purity of equanimity, (2) purity of recollection, (3) a feeling that is neither pleasant nor unpleasant, and (4) one-pointedness of mind. The purity of the first two limbs stems from having overcome any and all movement or instability of the mind that is caused by the principal flaws associated with the first three meditative absorptions—that is, deliberation, reflection, joy, and the inhalation and exhalation of the breath. The third limb—a feeling that is neither pleasant nor unpleasant—refers to the fact that in the fourth meditative absorption there are no pleasant or unpleasant physical or mental feelings. The canonical description of the fourth meditative absorption states: "With the abandonment of pleasure as well as the earlier abandonment of discomfort, and with the disappearance of both happiness and unhappiness of mind, [the practitioner] achieves and then remains in the fourth meditative absorption, which is characterized by the absence of any pleasant or unpleasant feeling, as well as by the purity of equanimity and recollection."

tion that is virtuous; (2) the meditative absorption that is indeterminate and [is cultivated] in order to project emanations; (3) [the meditative absorption] that relates to quiescence and (4) [the meditative absorption] that relates to insight; (5) the meditative absorption [that is cultivated] in order to reflect correctly on one's own and others' aims; (6) the meditative absorption [that is cultivated] in order to achieve the qualities associated with the power of supernatural knowledge; (7) [the meditative absorption] which has names as its object;[915] (8) [the meditative absorption] which has meanings as its object;[916] (9) [the meditative absorption] which has the signs of quiescence as its object; (10) [the meditative absorption] which has the signs of retention as its object; (11) [the meditative absorption] which has the signs of equanimity as its object; (12) [the meditative absorption [that is cultivated] in order to abide in a state of ease in this life; and (13) the meditative absorption [that is cultivated] in order to accomplish the aims of others.

These thirteen forms of meditative absorption [that are cultivated by] bodhisattvas are called "[the meditative absorption] of every form."

The Meditative Absorption That Relates to the Distressed and What They Want [1.13.7]

What is a bodhisattva's meditative absorption that relates to the distressed and what they want?

It should be regarded as being of eight types. [They are] (1) the meditative absorption that governs the effectiveness of spells that quell misfortunes arising from poison, lightning, severe fever, illness, spirits, demons, etc.; (2) the meditative absorption that quells various kinds of illnesses caused by an imbalance of the constituents; (3) the meditative absorption that brings rain when severe famines are occurring; (4) the meditative absorption that saves [beings] from various kinds of human and nonhuman dangers that

915. S: *nāmālambanam,* T: *ming la dmigs pa. BBhVy* (f. 192a): "The [form of] meditative absorption that bodhisattvas rely upon in order to listen to, take up, and uphold what is taught by all the buddhas and by virtue of which they teach Dharma to those beings who have diverse aspirations using a variety of words is called '[the meditative absorption] which has names as its object.'"

916. S: *arthālambanam,* T: *don la dmigs pa. BBhVy* (f. 192b): "[The meditative absorption] which has meanings as its object is the [form of] meditative absorption by virtue of which the meanings of teachings are realized and then taught to others."

can occur in water or on dry land; (5) likewise, the meditative absorption that provides food and drink to those living in a forest wilderness who lack food and drink; (6) the meditative absorption that provides objects of material value to disciples who are in need of them; (7) the meditative absorption that correctly brings about the [spiritual] awakening of careless sentient beings throughout the ten directions; and (8) the meditative absorption that correctly carries out any proper activities relating to sentient beings that may have arisen.

The Meditative Absorption That Brings Happiness Here and in the Next World [1.13.8]

What is a bodhisattva's meditative absorption that brings happiness here and in the next world?

It should be regarded as being of nine types. [They are] (1) the meditative absorption that brings spiritual discipline to sentient beings by means of the marvelous ability of miraculous powers;[917] (2) the meditative absorption that brings spiritual discipline to sentient beings by means of the marvelous ability of revealing others' thoughts;[918] (3) [the meditative absorption that brings spiritual discipline to sentient beings] by means of the marvelous ability of giving instruction;[919] (4) the meditative absorption that reveals the regions of lower realms to those who commit evil deeds; (5) the meditative absorption that bestows eloquence[920] on those sentient beings for whom it has been lost; (6) the meditative absorption that bestows recollection on those sentient beings whose recollection has become clouded; (7) the meditative absorption that enables one to arrange compositions of unerring treatises, poetry, and [instruction] manuals[921] so that the true Dharma will remain in existence for a long time; (8) the meditative absorption that promotes [the learning of] meaningful worldly crafts and occupations that are useful to sentient beings, such as scribal work, counting, record keeping,

917. See notes 344, 395, 444, and 469, together with the accompanying text.

918. See note 395.

919. See note 395.

920. See note 380.

921. *BBhVy* (f. 193a): "A manual (S: *mātṛkā,* T: *ma mo*) is [a work] that presents instructions [that are found in] the sutra collection." See section of the introduction entitled "A Manual for the Entire Bodhisattva Collection of Discourses" for a discussion of the term "manual."

calculating, or signing, etc., as well as [the fabrication of] thrones, seats, parasols, shoes, etc., and various different kinds of vessels and other implements; and (9) the meditative absorption that emits light rays in order to relieve instantly the suffering of beings who have taken birth in the regions of the lower realms.

Pure Meditative Absorption [1.13.9]

What is a bodhisattva's pure meditative absorption?

It should be regarded as being of ten types. [They are] (1) the meditative absorption that is pure by virtue of the mundane purity of not being relished; (2) the meditative absorption that is pure by virtue of the transcendent purity of being unafflicted; (3) the meditative absorption that is pure by virtue of having a pure form of preparation; (4) [the meditative absorption that is] pure by virtue of having a pure main stage; (5) the meditative absorption that is pure by virtue of having [attained] a pure [level] that is higher than and superior to the main stage; (6) the meditative absorption that is pure by virtue of [having attained] the purity of possessing mastery over entering, abiding in, and arising from [states of one-pointed concentration]; (7) the meditative absorption that is pure by virtue of [having attained] the purity that, even after having turned away from states of meditative absorption, still has the power to enter them again [at will]; (8) the meditative absorption that is pure by virtue of [having attained] the purity of mastery over the exercise of supernatural knowledge; (9) the meditative absorption that is pure by virtue of [having attained] the purity in which all forms of [mistaken] views have been eliminated; and (10) the meditative absorption that is pure by virtue of [having attained] the purity of abandoning the obscurations of the mental afflictions and the obscurations to that which needs to be known.

These immeasurable forms of meditative absorption [give rise to] the fruit of great enlightenment and they are [spiritual qualities] on the basis of which bodhisattvas, after having completed the perfection of meditative absorption, have attained, shall attain, and are currently attaining unsurpassed true and complete enlightenment.

Within [Book I of] *The Stage of a Bodhisattva,* [known as] "The Object of Mental Application That Relates to the Support," this completes the thirteenth chapter, entitled "Meditative Absorption."

14

Wisdom

The summary verses should be understood in the same manner as before.

The Essence of Wisdom [1.14.1]

Regarding this [topic], what is the essence of a bodhisattva's wisdom?

The discernment[922] of entities that [seeks] to attain [a realization of] or has attained [a realization of] all objects of knowledge[923] and that operates in relation to the five branches of learning—that is, (1) the inner science, (2) the science of logic, (3) the science of grammar, (4) the science of medicine, (5) and the science of crafts and occupations—should be understood as the essence of a bodhisattva's wisdom.

All-Inclusive Wisdom [1.14.2]

What is a bodhisattva's all-inclusive wisdom?

It should be regarded as being of two types: (1) that which is mundane, and (2) that which is transcendent. It should also be understood, in brief, as being of three types: (1) that which [is cultivated] in order to realize the object of knowledge that is [ultimate] reality; (2) that which [is cultivated] in order to develop expertise in the five branches of learning that were

922. See note 224.

923. *BBhVy* (f. 193b): "The wisdom of bodhisattvas whose conduct is based upon devotion [i.e., the wisdom of those who are on the preparation path] is that which [seeks] to attain [a realization of] objects of knowledge, because it unites [the bodhisattva] with the [direct] realization of the insubstantiality of entities. The wisdom of those [bodhisattvas] who have entered the [ārya] stages is that which has attained [a realization of] objects of knowledge, because it is qualified by [the attainment of transcendent] realization."

previously described as well as [expertise] in the three heaps;[924] and (3) that which [is cultivated] in order to accomplish the aims of sentient beings.

The Wisdom That Is Directed toward Realizing Ultimate Reality [1.14.2.1]

The wisdom of bodhisattvas that [is cultivated] in order to realize the truth that relates to the ineffable insubstantiality of entities, or that is present at the time that this truth is [first] being realized, or that occurs subsequent to that [transcendent] realization of truth [are forms of wisdom] that abide in a state of supreme peace, [forms of wisdom] that are free of conceptualization, [forms of wisdom] in which all [conceptual] elaboration has been eliminated, [forms of wisdom] that have arrived at [a realization of] the sameness of all entities, [forms of wisdom] that have attained [a realization of] the great general characteristic, [forms of wisdom] that have reached the end of objects of knowledge, and [forms of wisdom] that conform to the Middle Way in that they reject the two extremes of [falsely] attributing [a mode of being that does not exist] and [wrongly] discrediting [a mode of being that does exist]. This is what should be understood as the bodhisattva's wisdom that [is cultivated] in order to realize [ultimate] reality.

The Wisdom That Develops Expertise regarding the Five Branches of Learning and the Three Heaps [1.14.2.2]

Expertise in the five branches of learning should be understood in the manner that was explained previously in detail—that is, in the chapter entitled "The Lineages of the Powers." For their part, the three heaps are (1) the heap of entities that are advantageous, (2) the heap of entities that are disadvantageous,[925] and (3) the heap of entities that are neither advantageous nor disadvantageous. Acquiring the expertise that consists of wisdom regarding these eight subjects fulfills the great, unsurpassed accumulation

924. See description below.

925. S: *anarthopasaṃhitānāṃ dharmāṇāṃ rāśiḥ;* T: *don dan mi ldan pa'i chos rnams kyi tshogs*. The word *anartham* can mean "worthless" or "bad." Here it is the latter sense. *BBhVy* (f. 194b): "The second one is the heap of nonvirtuous entities."

of wisdom [that is needed] in order to [attain] unsurpassed true and complete enlightenment.

The Wisdom That Accomplishes the Aims of Sentient Beings [1.14.2.3]

Further, the activities that accomplish the aims of sentient beings should be understood as the eleven types that [pertain to the situations which] were described previously. The wisdom that relates to those very situations should be understood as the wisdom that [is cultivated] in order to accomplish the aims of sentient beings.

The Wisdom That Is Difficult to Carry Out [1.14.3]

Regarding this [topic], what is a bodhisattva's wisdom that is difficult to carry out?

It should be regarded as being of three types: (1) that which is difficult to carry out in order to gain knowledge of the profound insubstantiality of entities; (2) that which is difficult to carry out in order to learn the means [of bringing about] the spiritual discipline of sentient beings; and (3) that which is supremely difficult to carry out in order to gain the knowledge that frees one from the obscurations to that which needs to be known.

The Wisdom That Is Directed Everywhere [1.14.4]

What is a bodhisattva's wisdom that is directed everywhere?

It should be regarded as being of four types: (1) the wisdom that derives from learning both the listener collection [of scriptures] and the bodhisattva collection [of scriptures]; (2) the wisdom that derives from reflection [upon the meanings contained in those two collections of scriptures]; (3) the wisdom that is supported by the strength of careful consideration and that is gained by having made a careful consideration of [what constitute] the proper activities that a bodhisattva should pursue and [what constitute] the improper ones that he or she should refrain from doing; and (4) the immeasurable wisdom that is supported by the strength of meditation and that relates to the stages of mental composure.[926]

926. S: *samāhitabhumikā,* T: *mnyam par gzhag pa'i sa pa*. The sixth stage of *YBh* describes

THE WISDOM OF A TRUE SPIRITUAL BEING [1.14.5]

What is the wisdom of a true spiritual being that is possessed by a bodhisattva who is a true spiritual being?

It should be regarded as being of five types: (1) [the wisdom] that has completed [the activity of] learning the true Dharma; (2) [the wisdom] that is accompanied by proper forms of attention that are directed internally in relation to oneself; (3) [the wisdom] that is accompanied by the means of attaining one's own and others' aims; (4) [the wisdom] that has been properly ascertained with regard to the unerring formulation and the settled nature of entities;[927] and (5) the wisdom that abandons the mental afflictions.

Another [fivefold] formulation [of the wisdom of a true spiritual being] is the following: (1) [wisdom that is] subtle in that it gains an understanding of objects of knowledge in terms of the mode of being that represents their true nature; (2) [wisdom that is] skillful in that it gains an understanding of objects of knowledge in terms of the mode of being that represents their complete extent; (3) [wisdom that is] innate in that it is attained through a prior accumulation of wisdom; (4) [wisdom that is] endowed with [knowl-

---

this topic in terms of four categories: (1) the four meditative absorptions (S: *catvāri dhyānāni,* T: *bsam gtan bzhi*); (2) the eight deliverances (see note 906); (3) various forms of one-pointed concentration (S: *samādhiḥ,* T: *ting nge 'dzin*); and (4) a range of states of composure (S: *samāpattiḥ,* T: *snyoms par 'jug pa*), including the four formless states of composure, the eight bases of mastery (see note 907), the ten universal bases (see note 908), the state of composure that is a cessation (see note 202), and the state of composure without conception (see *PSV,* pp. 314–316).

927. S: *dharmānāṃ dharmasthitidharmavyavasthā aviparītā;* T: *chos rnams kyi chos gnas pa'i chos rnam par gnas pa'i phyin ci ma log pa. BBhVy* (f. 195a) explains this group of five correct forms of wisdom in terms of their opposites—which is to say, five erring forms of discernment that are made by persons who are spiritually corrupt (S: *asatpuruṣaḥ,* T: *skyes bu dam pa ma yin pa*). There is also a natural progression to these five forms of wisdom, with the first three being identified as wisdom derived from learning, reflection, and meditation, respectively, and the final form being wisdom that abandons the mental afflictions. The antithesis of the fourth correct type of wisdom is described as follows: "Through having applied oneself in such a manner [to mistaken forms of discernment that derive from improper learning, reflection, and meditation], one develops an erring understanding about the settled nature of things (S: *dharmasthitiḥ,* T: *chos la gnas pa*) that stems from erring formulations [that are made] regarding the [essential] characteristics of entities." *YBh* (p. 229): "What is the settled nature of things? The settled nature of things is the formulation [that is made] using proper words and letters in a manner that accords with [the natural state of things that is] recognized [as having been true since beginningless time]."

edge of] the scriptural teachings in that it takes up and upholds the meanings of Dharma [teachings] that have been imparted by buddhas and the bodhisattvas who have attained the great [ārya] stages; and (5) [wisdom that is] endowed with spiritual realization in that it has attained the levels ranging from the stage of a pure superior attitude[928] to the stage that is the perfect manner of going.[929]

Wisdom of Every Form [1.14.6]

Regarding this [topic], what is a bodhisattva's wisdom of every form?

It should be understood as being of the thirteen types [that result from] combining together six types and seven types. [The first six are,] with regard to the [four noble] truths, (1) knowledge of [the truth of] suffering; (2) knowledge of [the truth of] origination; (3) knowledge of [the truth of] cessation; (4) knowledge of [the truth of] the path; and, with regard to [the stage of] perfection, (5) the knowledge that [the outflows] have been terminated and (6) the knowledge that [the outflows] cannot arise again. These are the group of six types of wisdom.

Further, the group of seven types [of wisdom] are (1) knowledge of entities; (2) subsequent knowledge; (3) knowledge of relative truth; (4) knowledge of the supernatural forms of knowledge; (5) knowledge of the major marks; (6) knowledge that precedes the ten powers; and (7) knowledge of the applications, which occurs in relation to the four applications.[930]

The Wisdom That Relates to the Distressed and What They Want [1.14.7]

Regarding this [topic], what is a bodhisattva's wisdom that relates to the distressed and what they want?

It should be regarded as being of eight types: (1) a bodhisattva's informative knowledge of the Dharma that relates to an understanding of the formulations of Dharma [teachings]; (2) a bodhisattva's informative

928. S: *śuddhādhyāśayabhūmiḥ*, T: *bsam pa dag pa'i sa*. See Book III, chapter 3, where it is described as the third of seven stages.

929. S: *niṣṭhāgamanabhūmiḥ*, T: *mthar thug par 'gro ba'i sa*. See Book III, chapter 3, where it is described as the last of seven stages.

930. See notes 255 and 1199.

knowledge of meaning that relates to an understanding of the [defining] characteristics [of entities]; (3) a bodhisattva's informative knowledge of clear expression that relates to an understanding of the interpretation of Dharma [terms]; (4) a bodhisattva's informative knowledge [that confers] eloquence and relates to making distinctions about the varieties of points that pertain to Dharma [teachings];[931] (5) a bodhisattva's wisdom that defeats all disputation put forth by opponents; (6) the wisdom that establishes all the formulations of one's own positions; (7) a bodhisattva's wisdom that correctly preserves the propagation of a householder's [family line] and brings prosperity to a family; (8) the wisdom that has ascertained the proper [form of] statecraft [to be followed by] a king and the proper conduct [to be pursued] in secular affairs.

The Wisdom That Brings Happiness Here and in the Next World [1.14.8]

Regarding this [topic], what is a bodhisattva's wisdom that brings happiness here and in the next world?

It should be regarded as being of nine types: (1) the wisdom that has been well refined and well established in relation to the inner science; the wisdom that has been well refined but has not been well established[932] in relation to (2) the science of logic, (3) the science of grammar, (4) the science of medicine, and (5) the science of worldly crafts and occupations; and the bodhisattva's wisdom that, on the basis of these five well-refined sciences, (6) educates, (7) causes to undertake [proper conduct], (8) stirs to action, and (9) gladdens, respectively, those disciples who are confused, heedless, discouraged, and correctly established [in Dharma practice].

Pure Wisdom [1.14.9]

Regarding this [topic], what is a bodhisattva's pure wisdom?

In brief, it should be understood as being of ten types. Two types [of

931. See Book I, chapter 17, the section entitled "The Four Forms of Informative Knowledge" [I.17.7].

932. *BBhVy* (f. 196a): "The phrase 'has not been well established' is made because a person who has developed a practice that is in accord with the Dharma does not become well established in relation to those four branches of knowledge."

pure wisdom] relate to the nature of reality,[933] in that they grasp reality in terms of (1) the mode of being that represents their complete extent and (2) the mode of being that represents their true nature. Two types [of pure wisdom] relate to the subject of progression,[934] in that they correctly grasp (3) causes and (4) effects. Two types [of pure wisdom] relate to the subject of grasping,[935] in that they have a complete understanding of (5) error and (6) absence of error. Two types [of pure wisdom] relate to the subject of [what constitutes a proper] means, in that they have a complete and true understanding of (7) actions that should be carried out and (8) actions that should not be carried out. Two types [of pure wisdom] relate to the subject of perfection,[936] in that they have a complete and true understanding of both (9) the process by which afflicting entities cause affliction[937] and (10) the process by which purifying entities bring about purification.[938] These

933. See note 244.

934. See note 315 for a description of this term.

935. S: *upādānam,* T: *nye bar len pa. AS* (p. 2): "What is grasping? It is aspiration and desire for the heaps. Why are aspiration and desire referred to as 'grasping'? Aspiration and desire are called 'grasping' because [aspiration] brings into being the future heaps by longing for [the existence of the heaps] in the future and [desire] does not want to give up those that exist in the present due to attachment for [those that exist] in the present." The term "grasping" is also the name of the ninth limb in the doctrine of the twelve limbs of dependent origination. Traditional exegesis identifies four types of grasping: (1) grasping at sense objects (S: *kāmopādānam,* T: *'dod pa nye bar len pa*); (2) grasping at views (S: *dṛṣṭyupādānam,* T: *lta ba nye bar len pa*); (3) grasping at morality and austerities (S: *śīlavratopādānam,* T: *tshul khrims dang brtul zhugs nye bar len pa*); and (4) grasping at affirmation of a [real] self (S: *ātmavādopādānam,* T: *bdag tu smra ba nye bar len pa*).

936. S: *niṣṭhā,* T: *mthar thug.* This refers to the supreme enlightenment that marks completion of the Great Vehicle's path.

937. S: *saṃkleśaḥ,* T: *kun nas nyon mongs pa.* The process of "affliction" refers to three aspects of samsaric existence: (1) birth, (2) karma, and (3) the mental afflictions. These three have a correspondence with the twelve limbs of dependent origination. The first, eighth, and ninth limbs of ignorance, craving, and grasping, respectively, represent the mental afflictions; the second and tenth limbs, called "formations" and "existence," represent two phases of karma; and the remaining seven limbs—ranging from the third limb of consciousness through the seventh of feeling, along with the last two limbs of birth, and old age and death—are the result limbs that occur in all samsaric rebirth.

938. S: *vyavadānam,* T: *rnam par byang ba.* This term refers to the process by which the path leads to the ultimate abandonment of the obscurations of the mental afflictions and the obscurations to that which needs to be known.

five aspects and ten types of wisdom [that are attained] by bodhisattvas should be understood as being pure in terms of the highest form of purity.

These immeasurable and well-ascertained [forms of] wisdom give rise to the fruit of great enlightenment and [they are spiritual qualities] on the basis of which bodhisattvas, after having completed the perfection of wisdom, attain unsurpassed true and complete enlightenment.

Now then, this [description] of the six perfections that were taught by the Blessed One intermittently throughout the sutras should be understood as constituting a concise summary [of them]. The [brief] presentations and [detailed] explanations that appear in the sutras that were taught by the Tathāgata—whether they are of generosity or [any of the other perfections] ranging up to wisdom—should be investigated in relation to [the nine categories ranging from] the essence of generosity up to pure generosity. A summary of [generosity] should also be understood in a manner that is appropriate [to that method of description]. Similarly, an investigation [of the canonical teachings on] as well as a summary of the other [five] perfections, ranging from morality to wisdom, should be understood in a manner that is appropriate [to each of those types of presentation].

In addition, all those birth stories of the tathāgatas containing [descriptions of] arduous bodhisattva activities [that were carried out] during immeasurable numbers of lives that deal with generosity should be understood as relating to [the explanation of the perfection of] generosity. Just as with generosity, all those [birth stories] that contain [descriptions] of morality, patience, effort, meditative absorption, and wisdom should be understood as relating to [the explanations that range from the perfection of morality up to the perfection of] wisdom. It should be understood that some [of the birth stories] only have to do with generosity; some only have to do with [each of the remaining perfections up to] wisdom; some have to do with a combination of two [of the perfections]; some have to do with a combination of three; some have to do with a combination of four; some have to do with a combination of five; and some have to do with all six of the perfections.

The bodhisattvas who are seeking to arrive at unsurpassed true and complete enlightenment by means of these six perfections are called "those who are great foaming seas of pure spiritual qualities" and "those who are great oceans of pure spiritual qualities." [They are also] called "those who provide[939] the great jewels that give rise to every kind of good fortune for all sentient beings." Moreover, there is no other fruit of their attainment of the immeasurable accumulations of merit and wisdom that is comparable to that of unsurpassed true and complete enlightenment.

Within [Book I of] *The Stage of a Bodhisattva,* [known as] "The Object of Mental Application That Relates to the Support," this completes the fourteenth chapter, entitled "Wisdom."

939. T: *rin po che chen po sbyin pa*. This reading is based on the Tibetan translation, which is supported by *BBhVy* (f. 197a). This suggests the Sanskrit *pradāḥ,* which Wogihara reports is found in the Kyoto manuscript, one of the two sources that he consulted. Nevertheless, both published Sanskrit editions read *mahāratnahradāḥ,* which means "they who are the lakes [that contain] great jewels."

15

The Principles for Attracting a Following

The summary verses should be understood in the same manner as before.

Agreeable Speech [1.15.1]

The Essence of Agreeable Speech [1.15.1.1]

Regarding this [topic], what is the essence of bodhisattvas' agreeable speech?

Here a bodhisattva utters speech to sentient beings that is appealing, truthful, relates to Dharma, and is meaningful. In brief, this is the essence of bodhisattvas' agreeable speech.

All-Inclusive Agreeable Speech [1.15.1.2]

Regarding this [topic], what is a bodhisattva's all-inclusive agreeable speech?

It should be regarded as being of three types. (1) Here it is the speech of a bodhisattva that is friendly,[940] and it is the speech by which a bodhisattva

940. S: *sammodanī*, T: *yang dag par dga' bar byed pa*. Cf. MW, p. 1180. *BBhVy* (f. 198a): "Speech that is friendly, further, is established as having two aspects: (1) the quality of avoiding physical and verbal faults, and (2) the quality of inquiring about four things." The physical fault is to have a facial expression that indicates an attitude of malice, anger, hostility, or jealousy, etc. The verbal fault is [not to greet a person politely because you] do not feel any sense of deference and to act as though you do not know the person who has come [into your presence], due to pride. The four things to inquire about are whether someone (1) is enjoying good fortune, (2) is in good health, (3) if his or her day or night has gone well, or (4) to express some other form of polite greeting.

who refrains from frowning, who speaks politely,[941] and who shows a welcoming facial expression accompanied by a smile, following social custom and polite behavior, extends a friendly greeting to persons by asking if they are well and enjoying good fortune, if they are in good health, if their day or night has gone well, or expresses some other form of greeting, such as, "Welcome, please draw near." (2) It is also the speech of a bodhisattva that pleases [beings], and the speech by which a bodhisattva, having seen sentient beings' good fortune relating to their children that had not [previously] been known—or their good fortune relating to a wife or husband, their good fortune relating to family relatives, their good fortune relating to wealth, and their good fortune relating to crops—comments on [that good fortune] and [in doing so] pleases them. Alternatively, he or she pleases them [by commenting on] their development of faith, morality, learning, generosity, or wisdom. (3) It is also a bodhisattva's speech that contains Dharma teachings endowed with every type of [spiritual] good quality, that is continuously and uninterruptedly concerned with bringing benefit and happiness to sentient beings, and that is beneficial to them in terms of the highest kind of benefit. These should be understood as the varieties of bodhisattvas' all-inclusive agreeable speech.

Regarding this [topic], what is a concise presentation of bodhisattvas' all-inclusive agreeable speech?

It should be regarded as being of two types: (1) that which corresponds to worldly affairs[942] and (2) that which corresponds to correct Dharma instruction. Regarding this, the speech that is friendly and [the speech] that pleases [sentient beings] should be understood as [the form of agreeable speech] that corresponds to worldly affairs. Regarding this [topic], the speech that is beneficial, that relates to the highest form of benefit, and that is declared [to others in the form of beneficial instruction] should be understood as [the form of agreeable speech] that corresponds to correct Dharma instruction.

941. S: *pūrvābhilāpī*, T: *gsong por smra ba*. Literally, this term means "one who speaks first" as a mark of graciousness or respect (cf. *BHSD*, p. 352). *BBhVy* (f. 198b): "In order to show oneself as being amicably disposed, [a bodhisattva] is the first to speak to those who have arrived [in his or her presence], and addresses them [with such greetings] as 'Welcome.'"

942. S: *lokayātrānugataḥ*, T: *'jig rten pa'i tshul dang ldan pa*. The term *lokayātrā* ("worldly affairs") refers to the ordinary conduct, customs, activities, and concerns that relate to everyday secular life (MW, p. 907).

Agreeable Speech That Is Difficult to Carry Out [1.15.1.3]

Regarding this [topic], what is a bodhisattva's agreeable speech that is difficult to carry out?

It should be regarded as being of three types: (1) When a bodhisattva, after having engaged in careful consideration with a mind that is very pure and free of any defilement, utters friendly, pleasing, or beneficial speech toward murderers, adversaries, and enemies, this should be understood as the first type of agreeable speech that is difficult for a bodhisattva to carry out. (2) Moreover, when a bodhisattva, after having engaged in careful consideration and without becoming discouraged, engages in conversation that pertains to Dharma with beings who are very ignorant and whose faculties are [very] dull, and when he or she, after having [willingly] accepted any trouble [relating to this effort], causes them to take up a [form of] Dharma that is proper and virtuous, this should be understood as the second type of agreeable speech that is difficult for a bodhisattva to carry out. (3) In addition, when a bodhisattva utters friendly, pleasing, or beneficial speech with a mind that is free of animosity and anger to beings who are devious and deceitful, who are established in wrongful forms of practice, and who mislead teachers, preceptors, venerable persons, and persons who are worthy of being honored, this should be understood as the third type of agreeable speech that is difficult for a bodhisattva to carry out.

Agreeable Speech That Is Directed Everywhere [1.15.1.4]

Regarding this [topic] what is a bodhisattva's agreeable speech that is directed everywhere?

It should be regarded as being of four types: (1) the Dharma instruction that is to be given at an early stage[943] in order to abandon obstacles and reach

943. S: *pūrvakālakaraṇīyā*, T: *snga rol du bya ba,* also *dus sngar bya ba*. This expression refers to nine topics that should be taught to new disciples in order to render them fit to hear more advanced teachings. The following passage is quoted in Vasubandhu's *A Hundred Sutra Fragments That Are the Subject of Correct Interpretation* (T: *rNam par bshad pa rigs pa'i mdo sde 'i dum bu brgya,* f. 28a): "The discussions that should be made at an early stage by the buddhas, the blessed ones, are to teach correctly the following topics at length: (1) a discussion of generosity, (2) a discussion of morality, (3) a discussion of the celestial realms

a happy migratory state; (2) the most excellent Dharma instruction pertaining to the four noble truths that is given to one who is free of the obstacles and whose mind is fit; (3) [the Dharma instruction] that correctly admonishes those beings who are inattentive, both householders and homeless ascetics, in order to turn them away from heedless conduct and cause them to become established in a mindful form of conduct; and (4) the Dharma instruction that settles [questions relating to] a [Dharma] discussion and that is meant to remove whatever doubt may have arisen.

The Agreeable Speech of a True Spiritual Being [1.15.1.5]

Regarding this [topic], what is the agreeable speech of a true spiritual being that relates to bodhisattvas who are true spiritual beings?

It should be regarded as being of five types. Here the bodhisattvas who have become true bodhisattvas[944] and [the bodhisattvas] who have become like the tathāgatas[945] teach their disciples (1) a [form of] Dharma that is accompanied by the occasion, (2) [a form of Dharma] that is accompanied by the means of remediation, (3) [a form of Dharma] that is accompanied by the reliances, (4) [a form of Dharma] that is accompanied by strength,[946] and (5) [a form of Dharma] that is accompanied by the marvelous abilities.

[Bodhisattvas] make known the precepts of the spiritual training in an appropriate situation together with the circumstances in which they originated. Therefore, their Dharma is one that is accompanied by the occa-

(S: *svargaḥ,* T: *mtho ris*), (4) the enjoyment of sensory pleasures, (5) the disadvantages [of sensory pleasures], (6) going forth [into the homeless state], (7) living in isolation [from society], (8) the benefits [of going forth and living in isolation], and (9) the qualities that are conducive to spiritual purification."

944. S: *bodhisattvabhūtaḥ,* T: *byang chub sems dpar gyur pa. BBhVy* (f. 200a): "The phrase 'the bodhisattvas who have become true bodhisattvas' means those [bodhisattvas] who have attained the great [ārya] levels and whose nature is evident in their physical form."

945. S: *tathāgatabhūtaḥ,* T: *de bzhin gshegs par gyur pa. BBhVy* (f. 200a): "The phrase '[the bodhisattvas] who have become like the tathāgatas' means those very [bodhisattvas] who have taken on the form of a tathāgata's emanation body."

946. S: *saparākramaḥ,* T: *rtul ba dang bcas pa.* The Sanskrit noun *parākramaḥ* is derived from a verb that means variously (MW, p. 589) "to march forward, advance; to show courage or zeal, excel, distinguish oneself." The noun itself also has a range of meanings, including "bold advance," "attack," "heroism," "courage," "power," "strength," "energy," "exertion," and "enterprise." The Tibetan translation suggests, among these, "strength" and "exertion."

sion. They make known [the means of] recovering from transgressions to those individuals who have undertaken the trainings and incurred violations. Therefore, their Dharma is one that is accompanied by the means of remediation. They make known the unerring practice that relates to this [spiritual system of] Dharma and Vinaya and that is governed by the four reliances.[947] Therefore, their Dharma is one that is accompanied by the reliances. They proclaim the path that irreversibly delivers one from all suffering. Therefore, their Dharma is one that is accompanied by strength. They cause all the instructions to become fruitful by means of the three forms of marvelous ability. Therefore, their Dharma is one that is accompanied by the marvelous abilities.

Agreeable Speech of Every Form [I.15.1.6]

Regarding this [topic], what is the bodhisattvas' agreeable speech of every form?

It should be regarded as being the thirteen types [that result from] combining together six types and seven types: (1) agreeable speech that relates to authorizing the activities that are permitted; (2) [agreeable speech] that relates to forbidding the activities that are forbidden; (3) agreeable speech that sets forth formulations of Dharma teachings in relation to entities; (4) [agreeable speech] that sets forth unerringly the [defining] characteristics [of entities]; (5) [agreeable speech] that sets forth the Dharma unerringly and in clear forms of expression; (6) agreeable speech that sets forth the various kinds of Dharma teachings;[948] (7) agreeable speech that is friendly; (8) agreeable speech that is pleasing; (9) agreeable speech that abundantly fulfills the wishes of others as relates to abiding with few worries about all the implements [that relate to subsistence] as well as abiding with few worries about correctly accomplishing those activities that ought to be carried out; (10) agreeable speech that reassures those who are frightened by a variety of dangers; (11) agreeable speech that is made up of proper instruction; (12) agreeable speech that admonishes and reprimands [others with regard

947. S: *catvāri pratisaraṇāni*, T: *rton pa bzhi*. See Book I, chapter 17, the section entitled "The Four Reliances" [I.17.6] and note 1074.

948. Items three through six in this group represent speech that relates to the four forms of informative knowledge. See Book I, chapter 17, the section entitled "The Four Forms of Informative Knowledge" [I.17.7].

to wrongful conduct] that was correctly seen, heard, or suspected, in order to turn them away from opportunities [to engage in] nonvirtuous [actions] and establish them in opportunities [to engage in] virtuous [actions]; and (13) agreeable speech that accomplishes [tasks] by requesting [that they be carried out by] others who are capable [of doing so]. These should be understood as the thirteen types [of agreeable speech] that make up the bodhisattvas' agreeable speech of every form.

The Agreeable Speech That Relates to the Distressed and What They Want [1.15.1.7]

Regarding this [topic], what is the agreeable speech of bodhisattvas that relates to the distressed and what they want?

It should be regarded as being of eight types. A bodhisattva's speech that relates to the eight noble forms of verbal behavior on the basis of four types of purity of speech is what is called "the agreeable speech of bodhisattvas that relates to the distressed and what they want." Regarding this [topic], these are the four types of purity of speech: (1) the abandonment of false speech; (2) [the abandonment of] divisive speech; (3) [the abandonment of] harsh speech; and (4) the abandonment of meaningless speech. Regarding this [topic], these are the eight noble forms of verbal behavior:[949] (1) saying that you saw what you saw; (2) [saying that you heard] what you heard; (3) [saying that you thought] what you thought; (4) saying that you understood what you understood; (5) saying that you didn't see what you didn't see; (6) [saying that you didn't hear] what you didn't hear; (7) [saying that you didn't think] what you didn't think; and (8) saying that you didn't understand what you didn't understand.

Agreeable Speech That Brings Happiness Here and in the Next World [1.15.1.8]

Regarding this [topic], what is the agreeable speech of bodhisattvas that brings happiness here and in the next world?

949. S: *aṣṭāryavyavahārāḥ*, T: *'phags pa'i tha snyad brgyad*. These are all forms of truthful speech (S: *satyavāditā*, T: *bden par smra ba*). *AKB* (pp. 245–246) records three different interpretations of the terms "seen," "heard," "thought," and "realized." The opposite of these, the eight ignoble forms of verbal behavior, represent the essence of lying (S: *mṛṣāvādaḥ*, T: *rdzun smra ba*).

It should be regarded as being of nine types: (1) the agreeable speech that removes grief [arising from] misfortune relating to family members; (2) [the agreeable speech] that removes grief [arising from] misfortune relating to wealth; (3) the agreeable speech that removes grief [arising from] misfortune relating to health; (4) [the agreeable speech] that removes misfortune relating to morality; (5) the agreeable speech that removes misfortune relating to [mistaken] views; (6) the agreeable speech of Dharma instruction that relates to excellence of morality; (7) [the agreeable speech of Dharma instruction] that relates to excellence of [unerring] views; (8) [the agreeable speech of Dharma instruction] that relates to excellence of conduct; and (9) [the agreeable speech of Dharma instruction] that relates to excellence of livelihood.

Agreeable Speech That Is Pure [1.15.1.9]

What is a bodhisattva's agreeable speech that is pure?

It should be regarded as being of twenty types—that is, the twenty ways of teaching Dharma that were described previously in the chapter entitled "The Lineages of the Powers."[950]

Beneficial Conduct [1.15.2]

Regarding this [topic], beneficial conduct should be understood at length in just the same manner as agreeable speech.[951] I shall also now describe additional forms of beneficial conduct that are distinct from those [that are the same as agreeable speech]. That is to say, a bodhisattva undertakes sentient beings' aims that lead to this or that [result] on the basis of every kind of agreeable speech.

The Essence of Beneficial Conduct [1.15.2.1]

Regarding this [topic], what is the essence of bodhisattvas' beneficial conduct?

950. See Book I, chapter 8, the section entitled "Teaching the Dharma" [I.8.3].

951. *BBhVy* (f. 201b): "Agreeable speech is also beneficial conduct. The agreeable speech that is carried out in this or that situation also accomplishes desired aims; therefore, [in that sense] it is [also] 'beneficial conduct.'"

Having closely placed one's mind in a state of compassion and with an attitude that is free of desire for material reward, [the activities that,] according to circumstances, cause sentient beings who have been taught properly by means of agreeable speech in the manner [that was described above] to adopt,[952] to be led to,[953] to become settled into,[954] or to become established in[955] (1) the trainings,[956] (2) beneficial conduct,[957] or (3) conduct that constitutes the practice that accords with the Dharma is a brief presentation of the essence of beneficial conduct.

All-Inclusive Beneficial Conduct [1.15.2.2]

Regarding this [topic], what is the all-inclusive beneficial conduct of bodhisattvas?

It should be regarded as being of two types: (1) the ripening of sentient

952. S: *samādāpanā,* T: *yang dag par 'dzin du 'jug pa. BBhVy* (f. 36b): "'[Whatever acquisition of virtue . . . that] he or she causes others to adopt' means to induce (*S: *saṃniyojayati,* T: *yang dag par sbyor ba*) them [to act in a certain way] by saying, 'Act in this manner.' The act of causing [someone] to adopt [a certain form of behavior] means to induce them [to undertake it]."

953. S: *vinayanā,* T: *'dul ba. BBhVy* (f. 36b): "'[Whatever acquisition of virtue . . . that] he or she causes others to be led to' means either that he or she causes them to become subject to his or her will (S: **vaśībhūtasaṃpādanam,* T: *dbang du gyur pa sgrub pa*) or that he or she causes their obstacles to be removed (S: **antarayān apanayati,* T: *bar chad sel bar byed pa'o*)." These two interpretations stem from the dual sense of the verbal root *vinī,* which can mean either "to train" someone in the sense of leading him or her to a state of self-discipline, or to "remove" or "expel" an undesirable quality or condition.

954. S: *niveśanā,* T: *'dzud pa. BBhVy* (f. 36b): "'[Whatever acquisition of virtue . . . that] he or she causes others to become settled into' means that he or she causes them to become settled into the practice (S: **pratipattāyām niveśayati,* T: *sgrub pa la 'god pa*)."

955. S: *pratiṣṭhāpanā,* T: *'god pa. BBhVy* (f. 36b): "'[Whatever acquisition of virtue . . . that] he or she causes others to be established in' means that [he or she causes them] to become steadfast (S: **acalabhūtaḥ,* T: *mi g.yo bar gyur pa*) in the sense that no one is able to turn them away [from the true path] (S: **anyena vyāvṛttyaśakyatvāt,* T: *gzhan gyis sgyur du mi nus pa'i phyir te*)."

956. S: *śikṣāḥ,* T: *bslab pa rnams. BBhVy* (f. 202a): "'Trainings' means the three types of training—[that is,] the training of morality, etc."

957. S: *arthacaryā,* T: *don spyod pa. BBhVy* (f. 202b): "Pursuing the aim of the trainings (S: **śikṣārthānucaraḥ,* T: *bslab pa'i don rjes su spyod pa*) is 'beneficial conduct.' It is the performance of [spiritual] activities (S: **prayogakaraṇam,* T: *sbyor ba byed pa*) in accordance with the manner in which the trainings were prescribed, which is to say it is [correct] practice (S: **pratipattiḥ,* T: *sgrub pa*)."

beings who are not yet spiritually mature and (2) the liberation of sentient beings who are spiritually mature. These [two types] should further be understood in terms of three modes: (1) causing [others] to adopt an aim that pertains to this life; (2) causing [others] to adopt an aim that pertains to future lives; and (3) causing [others] to adopt an aim that pertains both to this life and to future lives.

Regarding this [topic], causing [others] to adopt an aim that pertains to this life should be understood in terms of correctly causing [others] to acquire, preserve, and increase their wealth by means of [various] qualities [gained from] actions that are in accord with Dharma.[958] [This is the aim] by means of which an individual acquires praise from others and abides in a state of ease during this life through being benefited by the ease [achieved with] objects [that provide] a means of subsistence.

Regarding this [topic], causing [others] to adopt an aim that pertains to future lives should be understood as [the act of] causing [others] to abandon wealth and adopt the lifestyle of going forth [into the homeless state] in which one's subsistence is dependent upon being a mendicant. [This is an aim] by means of which an individual definitely becomes one who experiences happiness in the future but does not necessarily do so in this life.

Regarding this [topic], causing [others] to adopt an aim that pertains both to this life and to future lives should be understood as [the act of] causing [others], whether they are householders or homeless ascetics, to adopt [the course that] gradually leads to [the state of] freedom from attachment. [This is an aim] by means of which [an individual] abides in a state of happiness in this life through gaining physical and mental agility and, in future lives, is reborn among the pure gods. [Ultimately,] he or she will [also] attain the complete extinction [of all samsaric rebirth] within the realm of the [form of] nirvana in which the support [of the heaps] does not remain.[959]

958. S: *dhārmikaiḥ karmaguṇaiḥ,* T: *chos mthun pa'i las kyi yon tan dag gis. BBhVy* (f. 203a): "'To be in accord with Dharma' means to avoid [any form of] misdeed. 'To possess [good] qualities' means to avoid the guile (S: *śāṭhyam,* T: *g.yo*) and deceitfulness (S: *māyā,* T: *sgyu*) that defrauds, cheats, and falsifies." MW (p. 258): "*karmaguṇaḥ,* a quality or condition resulting from human acts."

959. S: *nirupadhiśeṣanirvānam,* T: *lhag ma med pa'i mya ngan las 'das pa.* This is one of two forms of nirvana. The other is the nirvana in which the support [of the heaps] still remains (S: *sopadhiśeṣanirvāṇam,* T: *lhag bcas kyi mya ngan las 'das pa*). When a practitioner first achieves the status of arhat, he or she attains this latter form of nirvana and continues to possess it for the remainder of that life. Upon death, the realm of [the form of] nirvana in

The Beneficial Conduct That Is Difficult to Carry Out [1.15.2.3]

Regarding this [topic], what is the beneficial conduct of bodhisattvas that is difficult to carry out?

It should be regarded as being of three types. [They are as follows:] (1) The beneficial conduct [that occurs] in relation to beings who have not previously cultivated the causes of the roots of virtue is [a form of] bodhisattvas' [beneficial conduct] that is difficult to carry out, because it is difficult to cause [those persons] to adopt virtue. (2) The beneficial conduct [that occurs] in relation to beings who possess a great abundance of wealth and who have attachment for it is a [form of] bodhisattvas' [beneficial conduct] that is difficult to carry out, because [those persons' minds] are occupied with a great object of heedlessness and a great cause of heedlessness. (3) The beneficial conduct [that occurs] in relation to those heretics who fall outside this [Buddhist tradition] and [that occurs] in relation to those who formerly embraced the views of heretical traditions is [a form of] bodhisattvas' [beneficial conduct] that is difficult to carry out, because [those persons] have caused themselves to be confused about, and they have biased opinions about, this [spiritual system of] Dharma and Vinaya.

The Beneficial Conduct That Is Directed Everywhere [1.15.2.4]

Regarding this [topic], what is the beneficial conduct of bodhisattvas that is directed everywhere?

It should be regarded as being of four types: (1) Here a bodhisattva causes those who lack faith to adopt an excellent form of faith, etc., up to he or she causes them to become established in [an excellent form of faith]. [A bodhisattva also] causes (2) those who are immoral to adopt an excellent form of morality, (3) those whose wisdom is inferior [to adopt] an excellent form of wisdom, and (4) those who are stingy [to adopt] an excellent form of generosity, etc., up to he or she causes them to become established in [an

---

which the support of the heaps does not remain is entered. The "support [of the heaps]" (S: *upadhiḥ*, T: *phung po*) is a reference to the impure physical body that an arhat still possesses after attaining nirvana and continues to possess until the time of death, when the support of that impure body is discarded.

excellent form of morality, an excellent form of wisdom, and an excellent form of generosity].

The Beneficial Conduct of a True Spiritual Being [I.15.2.5]

Regarding this [topic], what is a bodhisattva's beneficial conduct of a true spiritual being?

It should be regarded as being of five types: (1) Here a bodhisattva causes beings to adopt an aim that is genuine. (2) He or she acts in a timely manner to cause them to adopt [such an aim]. (3) He or she causes them to adopt an aim that is meaningful. (4) He or she acts in a gentle manner to cause them to adopt [such an aim]. (5) He or she maintains an attitude of loving-kindness in causing them to adopt [such an aim].

Beneficial Conduct of Every Form [I.15.2.6]

Regarding this [topic], what is the bodhisattvas' beneficial conduct of every form?

It should be regarded as being of thirteen types [that result from] combining together six types and seven types. (1) Here a bodhisattva correctly brings [to the Dharma] those beings who are worthy of being brought to it. (2) He or she correctly suppresses[960] those beings who deserve to be suppressed. (3) He or she dispels the opposition that is felt by those beings who are hostile toward the [Buddhist] teaching. (4) He or she causes those beings who are indifferent toward the teaching to enter it. (5) He or she correctly ripens those beings who have entered [the teaching] in relation to the three vehicles. (6) He or she causes those beings who are [spiritually] ripe to become liberated.

He [or she variously] directs certain individuals (7) to the preservation and collection of the accumulations that relate either to the deliverance of the Lesser Vehicle or to deliverance of the Great Vehicle. As with the preservation and collection of the accumulations, he or she similarly directs

960. S: *nigṛhṇāti,* T: *tshar bcod pa. BBhVy* (204a): "The act of suppressing is of three types—censure, punishment, and banishment—each of which has a lesser, [intermediate, and great] degree." See Book I, chapter 10, the section entitled "Suppressing Those Who Engage in Misconduct" [I.10.2.6.10].

[certain individuals] (8) to [live in] seclusion in order to meditate upon [specific forms of] attention [that lead to] (9) one-pointedness of mind and (10) removal of the obscurations. He or she joins those beings who possess the spiritual lineage of a listener or a solitary realizer (11) to the Listeners' Vehicle or (12) to the Solitary Realizers' Vehicle. He or she joins those who possess the spiritual lineage of the tathāgatas (13) to the vehicle of unsurpassed true and complete enlightenment.

The Beneficial Conduct That Relates to the Distressed and What They Want [1.15.2.7]

Regarding this [topic], what is the bodhisattvas' beneficial conduct that relates to the distressed and what they want?

It should be regarded as being of eight types: [A bodhisattva] causes those beings who are disturbed by the perturbation of shamelessness to dispel and remove (1) the perturbation of shamelessness [that occurs] in relation to those objects toward which one ought to feel shame. Just as with the perturbation of shamelessness, he or she also causes [those beings who are disturbed by the other seven perturbations] to dispel and remove (2) the perturbation of lack of abashment [that occurs] in relation to [those objects] toward which one ought to feel abashment, as well as [causes them to dispel and remove] (3) the perturbation of torpor,[961] (4) the perturbation of sleep, (5) the perturbation of excitation, (6) the perturbation of regret, (7) the perturbation of envy, and (8) the perturbation of stinginess.[962]

961. Abhidharma literature traditionally lists eight perturbations (see note 439). While the Tibetan translation lists all eight here, both published Sanskrit *BBh* editions do not include the perturbation of torpor (S: *styānaparyavasthānam,* T: *rmugs pa'i kun nas dkris pa*) and only mention the other seven. I assume this to be an inadvertent lacuna. *AS* (p. 9): "What is torpor? It is the unfitness of the mind that is a form of ignorance. Its action is to facilitate [the occurrence of] all the root and secondary mental afflictions."

962. Wogihara's Sanskrit edition includes stinginess (S: *mātsaryam,* T: *ser sna*) among this list of perturbations but Dutt's Sanskrit edition does not (it is added in parentheses by the editor, suggesting that it did not appear in the manuscript). *AS* (p. 8): "What is stinginess? It is the acquisitiveness of mind toward personal possessions that is a form of desire possessed by persons who are attached to gain and honor. Its action is to provide support for the avoidance of simplicity." "Simplicity" (S: *saṃlekhaḥ,* T: *yo byad bsnyungs pa*) is the virtuous principle by which an individual seeks to keep desire in check by avoiding the accumulation of possessions that are not necessary for the pursuit of a spiritual life.

The Beneficial Conduct That Brings Happiness Here and in the Next World [1.15.2.8]

Regarding this [topic], what is a bodhisattva's beneficial conduct that brings happiness here and in the next world?

It should be regarded as being of nine types. [They are as follows:] In relation to the purity of physical deeds [that is to be carried out] by other beings, it is (1) the act of causing [others] to adopt every form of abstaining from taking [another being's] life; (2) the act of causing [others] to adopt every form of abstaining from taking what was not given; (3) the act of causing [others] to adopt every form of abstaining from sexual misconduct; and (4) the act of causing [others] to adopt every form of abstaining from [drinking] grain-based[963] or juice-based[964] intoxicating drinks that are a cause of heedlessness. In relation to the purity of verbal deeds, it is (5) the act of causing [others] to adopt every form of abstaining from telling lies; (6) the act of causing [others] to adopt every form of abstaining from divisive speech; (7) the act of causing [others] to adopt every form of abstaining from harsh speech; and (8) the act of causing [others] to adopt every form of abstaining from meaningless speech. In relation to the purity of mental deeds, it is (9) the act of causing [others] to adopt every form of abstaining from covetousness, malice, and wrong view.

Pure Beneficial Conduct [1.15.2.9]

Regarding this [topic], what is a bodhisattva's purity of beneficial conduct?

It should be regarded as being of ten types. Five types occur in relation to an outer purity and five types occur in relation to an inner purity.

963. S: *surā*, T: *'bru'i chang*. *AKB* (p. 219): "*Surā* is spirituous liquor that is made from grain (S: *annāsavaḥ*, T: *zas las sbyar ba'i btung ba*)." The Tibetan translation suggests that the Sanskrit word *āsavaḥ* means any kind of beverage (T: *btung ba*); however, it seems more accurate to interpret it here as a general term for "spirituous liquor" (cf. MW, p. 160).

964. S: *maireyam*, T: *bcos pa'i chang*, also *sbyar ba'i chang*. *AKB* (p. 219): "*Maireyam* is spirituous liquor made from [a mixture of various] 'substances' (S: *dravyāsavaḥ*, T: *rdzas las sbyar ba'i btung ba*)." There is also a variant Sanskrit reading that has *dravāsavaḥ* ("spirituous liquor made from juices [or decoctions]"). The Sanskrit *dravaḥ* means "juice," or "decoction" (cf. MW, p. 500). Apparently, the term *maireyam* originally referred to a fermented drink that was prepared by adding a variety of substances to some form of juice or decoction. *AKV* (vol. 2, p. 634) identifies sugarcane juice as one example of the main ingredient.

What are the bodhisattvas' five types of beneficial conduct toward sentient beings that occur in relation to an outer purity?

They are (1) that which is irreproachable, (2) that which is not misdirected, (3) that which is systematic, (4) that which reaches everywhere, and (5) that which is [carried out] according to the circumstances.

Here a bodhisattva does not direct sentient beings to engage in nonvirtuous deeds that are accompanied by misconduct, that are preceded by misconduct, that are blameworthy, or that are afflicted. This is the form of [a bodhisattva's] beneficial conduct toward sentient beings that is irreproachable.

Moreover, a bodhisattva does not affirm about a state that is not liberation and that is not absolute purity, "This is liberation; this is absolute purity," and then cause beings to take up [its pursuit]. This is the form of [a bodhisattva's] beneficial conduct toward sentient beings that is not misdirected.

Moreover, in order to enable [beings] to attain virtuous qualities in a systematic manner, a bodhisattva initially gives a Dharma teaching that is easily comprehended and imparts instruction and counsel that is easily comprehended to those beings whose wisdom is immature. After realizing that their wisdom has reached a middling level [of understanding], he or she gives them a Dharma teaching of a middling level [of difficulty] and imparts instruction and counsel of a middling level [of difficulty]. After realizing that their wisdom is extensive, he or she gives them a profound Dharma teaching and imparts subtle [forms of] instruction and counsel. This is [a bodhisattva's] beneficial conduct toward sentient beings that is systematic.

Moreover, a bodhisattva applies him- or herself to the aims of [persons] from [all] four castes and all sentient beings, including [both] gods and humans, with all his or her power and strength. He or she seeks [their] benefit and happiness. He or she causes them to adopt those very [goals]. This is the form of [a bodhisattva's] beneficial conduct toward sentient beings that reaches everywhere.

Moreover, whatever beings are capable of being prompted to adopt whatever small, medium, or great virtue is beneficial for them, and whatever means can be used to render them capable of being so prompted, a bodhisattva will, according to the circumstances, cause those beings to adopt those [forms of virtue] in that manner. These, then, are the five outer forms of purity that relate to bodhisattvas' beneficial conduct toward sentient beings.

Regarding this [topic], what are the five inner forms of purity that relate to bodhisattvas' beneficial conduct toward sentient beings?

[They are as follows:] (1) Here a bodhisattva applies him- or herself to the aims [of sentient beings] with a wide-ranging compassionate attitude that is devoted to sentient beings. (2) Moreover, a bodhisattva is one whose mind is not made weary despite all the pain and exertion [that occurs] in [the course of pursuing] the aims of sentient beings and he or she is ever joyful in applying him- or herself to the aims of sentient beings. (3) Further, even though a bodhisattva might be living in a state of foremost and most excellent prosperity, he or she applies him- or herself to the aims of sentient beings like a servant, a slave, an obedient son or daughter, or a young low-caste boy or girl, with a humble mind that has overcome [all] conceit, pride, and haughtiness. (4) Further, a bodhisattva applies him- or herself to the aims of sentient beings with an affection of the highest form that is genuine and free of desire for material reward. (5) In addition, a bodhisattva applies him- or herself to the aims of sentient beings with a mind that possesses a [form of] loving-kindness that is absolutely irreversible. These should be understood as the five inner forms of purity that relate to bodhisattvas' beneficial conduct toward sentient beings.

When the five forms of outer purity and the five forms of inner purity are combined together, this is called the bodhisattvas' "tenfold purity of beneficial conduct."

Sameness of Purpose [1.15.3]

Regarding this [topic], what is a bodhisattva's sameness of purpose?[965]

Whatever purpose and whatever root of virtue a bodhisattva here directs others to adopt, he himself or she herself should be observed[966] to adopt a purpose and a root of virtue that is [at least] equal to that [if not] one that is greater. Therefore, a bodhisattva's purpose that is equal to that of others in this way is what is referred to as "sameness of purpose." Having perceived

965. S: *samānārthatā*, T: *don mthun pa*. *BBhVy* (f. 206a): "[The topic of] sameness of purpose is also [made known] by explaining [that of] beneficial conduct [i.e., the form of practice that disciples are urged to adopt is identical with what the bodhisattva as a teacher should him- or herself carry out]; therefore, [the nine categories of] essence, etc., do not need to be presented, since they have already been established. For this reason, [the topic of] sameness of purpose is presented here in a different manner."

966. S: *svayaṃ saṃdṛśyate*, T: *yang dag par ston pa*. Wogihara's Sanskrit edition reads *svayaṃ saṃśikṣyate* ("train him- or herself"). Dutt's Sanskrit manuscript reads *saṃdṛśyate* but was revised to match Wogihara's edition. *BBhVy* (f. 206a) supports the reading *saṃdṛśyate*.

the bodhisattvas' sameness of purpose, those other disciples become firm in their conviction and irreversible with regard to taking up roots of virtue.

Why is that?

They have the following thought: "The [practice] that this bodhisattva has urged us to adopt is certain to benefit us and bring us happiness, because [this bodhisattva] him- or herself carries out the very [same practice] that he or she has enjoined us to follow and would not carry out [a practice] that he or she knew to be one that did not [bring any] benefit and was not [a source of] happiness." Moreover, those other [disciples] will not say of a bodhisattva who has the same purpose: "You yourself are not living as someone who has adopted virtue. Why do you believe that you should be one who urges others in such an extreme manner to take up virtue, or that you should be one who teaches others and instructs others? Rightfully, you are the one who should be taught, instructed, and corrected by others."

There are bodhisattvas who have the same purpose as others but do not show that sameness of purpose to others. There are those who do not have the same purpose [as others] but who show themselves as having the same purpose. There are those who have the same purpose [as others] and also show their sameness of purpose [to others]. There are those who neither have the same purpose [as others] nor show themselves as having the same purpose.

Regarding this [point], the first alternative is a bodhisattva whose virtuous qualities and [spiritual] power are equal to bodhisattvas of equal virtue and power who have acknowledged themselves to be teachers of the bodhisattva path. By concealing his or her virtuous nature, [this bodhisattva] does not show his virtuous qualities and [spiritual] power [to others].[967]

The second alternative is a bodhisattva who, after having carefully considered [the value of doing so], shows him- or herself to be a follower of the

967. *BBhVy* (f. 206b): "Even though [such a bodhisattva] is equal [in virtue and power] to those [who have acknowledged themselves to be teachers of the bodhisattva path], he or she does not show him- or herself to be the same as them. Why is that? It is because the entire world is respectful of [those bodhisattvas who are teachers], and honors them and venerates them, and the entire world regards them as spiritual teachers. If such a bodhisattva were to show him- or herself to have a sameness of purpose [that is equal to that of those bodhisattva teachers], then those [bodhisattva teachers] might not be held in such high regard, and they might lose the respect and honor that is paid to them. Recognizing this, [such a bodhisattva] does not show him- or herself to have a sameness of purpose [that is equal to that of those bodhisattva teachers]."

same Dharma[968] as those beings of inferior disposition who are frightened of the profound subjects, in order to spiritually tame them by [employing] this [expedient] means. [In addition,] he or she knowingly takes birth in the same station as that of persons of the lowest caste[969] as well as that of dogs, [because] he or she is desirous of accomplishing the aims of [beings] as low as those of the lowest caste and [beings] as low as dogs, [because] he or she is desirous of removing their misfortune, and [because] he or she is desirous of taming them spiritually.

The third alternative is a bodhisattva whose purpose is the same as or superior to [that of his or her disciples] and who shows him- or herself to have a sameness of purpose in order to strengthen the roots of virtue of those disciples who have adopted roots of virtue that are unsteady.[970]

The fourth alternative is [a bodhisattva] who is heedless and who is also indifferent to the aims of others.

Regarding this [topic], among the multiple forms of generosity that have been presented [above], [as well as those of] morality, etc., up to the sameness of purpose, the ripening of the qualities of a buddha within oneself [is accomplished] by means of the [six] perfections, and the [spiritual] ripening of all sentient beings [is accomplished] by means of the [four] principles for attracting a following. In brief, these should be understood as the actions[971] of a bodhisattva's virtuous qualities.

Regarding this [topic], it should be understood that the practice of these multiple and immeasurable forms of virtuous qualities that are favorable to enlightenment—ranging from the multiple forms of generosity up to

968. S: *sahadhārmikaḥ,* T: *chos mthun pa*. In two previous instances (see notes 732 and 823) the term meant "an exemplary Dharma practitioner." Here the term is being used to indicate someone who follows the same form of Dharma practice (see note 692). This distinction is clearly indicated in *BBhVy* (f. 206b), where it is stated that a bodhisattva feigns having the same aims as a listener and others in order to be able to assist them.

969. S: *caṇḍālaḥ,* T: *gdol pa*.

970. S: *calakuśalamūlasamādānānām*. Both Sanskrit editions have the adjective "unsteady" (S: *calaḥ*) qualifying the noun "roots of virtue." The Tibetan translation does not explicitly state this adjective, though it may be understood by implication. *BBhVy* (f. 207a) identifies this type of sameness of purpose, in which a bodhisattva displays a sameness of purpose in order to strengthen others' roots of virtue, as the most widely recognized form of this practice (S: **prasiddhasamānārthatā,* T: *rab tu grags pa'i don mthun pa*).

971. S: *karma,* T: *las*. Here the term means something like "function" or "effect." That is, the purpose of a bodhisattva's virtuous qualities is either to ripen a buddha's spiritual qualities within oneself or to bring others to a state of spiritual maturity.

the sameness of purpose that have been described above—[is carried out] by means of three causes. It should be understood that their excellence [is achieved] by means of two causes. It should be understood that their purity [is accomplished] by means of three causes.

It should be understood that their practice [is carried out] by means of body, speech, and mind.

It should be understood that their excellence, their unsurpassed nature, and their uniqueness [are achieved] by their greatness and their freedom from affliction.

Regarding this, it should be understood that their greatness stems from their absence of limitation regarding sentient beings, their absence of limitation regarding entities, and their absence of limitation regarding time. Regarding this [point], the absence of limitation regarding sentient beings is the quality by which a bodhisattva practices these roots of virtue of generosity, etc., on the basis of all sentient beings and in relation to all sentient beings; he or she does not do so only in relation to his or her own exclusive benefit. Regarding this [point], the absence of limitation regarding entities is the quality by which a bodhisattva abides in these roots of virtue of generosity, etc., after having adopted all of them [and having adopted them] in every form. Regarding this [point], the absence of limitation regarding time is the quality by which a bodhisattva practices these roots of virtue of generosity, etc., during this life, both day and night, continuously and uninterruptedly, with an application in which one's duty is not neglected and one's obligation is not discarded, and, for this very reason, he or she also [practices them] in future lives.

Regarding this [point], freedom from affliction should be understood in terms of four aspects. (1) Here a bodhisattva cultivates these virtuous qualities with a joyful mind; he or she does not do so with a sense of pain or an unhappy disposition. For these reasons, he or she remains free of regret. (2) Moreover, a bodhisattva practices the roots of virtue of generosity, etc., without harming others, without adhering to [mistaken] doctrines, and without allowing [these roots of virtue] to become commingled with [any forms of] misconduct. (3) Further, having undertaken these virtuous qualities with the devotion of his or her entire being, a bodhisattva practices them as one who regards them as advantageous,[972] one who regards them as

972. S: *guṇadarśī*, T: *yon tan du lta ba*. *BBhVy* (f. 208a): "[A bodhisattva is] 'one who regards [virtuous qualities] as advantageous' [because he or she] is intent upon assisting others."

valuable,[973] one who regards them as free from passions,[974] one who is firmly resolved about them, one who does not rely upon others [in order to practice them], and one who does not have to be led by others [in order to practice them]. (4) In addition, a bodhisattva does not long for the ripening of those virtuous qualities of generosity, etc. [in the form of bringing him or her] the status of a wheel ruler or [birth as such deities as] Śakra, Māra, or Brahmā, nor does he or she expect [some form of] recompense from others. He or she is not one who clings to [any of] these [goals]. [He or she is not one who clings] to any form of gain, honor, or fame, nor even one who clings to his or her body or life.

In this manner, the practice of these virtuous qualities, beginning with generosity and ending with sameness of purpose, [that is carried out] in terms of these [four] aspects—namely, (1) that it is accompanied by serene delight,[975] (2) that it is free of adversity, (3) that it is carried out with devotion, and (4) that it is done without attachment [to any personal goal]—is called their "freedom from affliction."

The purity [of the practice] should be understood in terms of the qualities of intensity, steadfastness, and complete purity. Regarding this [point], the virtuous qualities of a bodhisattva who has entered the stage of a pure [superior] attitude are possessed of intensity and steadfastness. Regarding them, the quality of intensity is that in which all the virtuous qualities of a bodhisattva who has attained the purity of attitude are able to be carried out without the need for any close consideration. Regarding them, the quality of steadfastness is that in which a bodhisattva who has attained the purity of attitude does not lose any of the virtuous qualities that he or she has attained and accumulated. Nor is he or she vulnerable to their loss in future [lives]. With the passage of successive days and nights and the passage of a multiplicity of lives, the bodhisattva does nothing other than increase these

973. S: *sāradarśī,* T: *snying por lta ba*. *BBhVy* (f. 208a): "[A bodhisattva is] 'one who regards [virtuous qualities] as valuable' in that he or she recognizes that they bring extraordinarily great results."

974. S: *śāntadarśī,* T: *zhi bar lta ba*. *BBhVy* (f. 208a): "That which represents an antidote for adverse qualities (S: *vipakṣaḥ,* T: *mi mthun pa'i phyogs*) [is what it means to be] 'one who regards [virtuous qualities] as free from passions.'"

975. While the Tibetan translation suggests "supreme delight" (T: *mchog tu dga' ba*), both Sanskrit editions have the compound *prasādaprāmodyam,* which is composed of the nouns "serenity [of disposition]" (S: *prasādaḥ*) and "delight" (S: *prāmodyam,* T: *dga' ba*).

virtuous qualities, like a moon during its waxing phase; he or she does not allow them to diminish.

Moreover, it should be understood that these virtuous qualities reach complete purity for a bodhisattva who has reached the stage that is the perfect manner of going[976]—both one who is [only] subject to one [additional] rebirth[977] and one who is in his final existence.[978] There are none which might attain some greater form of purity on a higher bodhisattva stage.

This is how it should be understood that the practice of the virtuous qualities beginning with generosity and ending with sameness of purpose [is carried out] by means of three causes, their excellence [is accomplished] by means of two causes, and their complete purity [is achieved] by means of three causes.

The Results of the Various Aspects of Practice [1.15.4]

Regarding this [topic], the result of unsurpassed true and complete enlightenment—a state in which the body possesses an adamantine nature and a state in which the true Dharma remains in existence for a long time—comes about through having practiced assiduously, through having developed great purity, and through having attained complete perfection with regard to all-inclusive generosity, all-inclusive morality, etc., up to all-inclusive sameness of purpose.

Regarding this [topic], the result in which a tathāgata possesses unparalleled forms of marvelous and wonderful qualities comes about through having practiced assiduously and through having developed great purity with regard to the generosity that is difficult to carry out, the morality that is difficult to carry out, etc., up to the sameness of purpose that is difficult to carry out.

Regarding this [topic], the result that a tathāgata is worthy of being worshipped from all sides, by preeminent beings, humans as well as gods, comes about through [having practiced assiduously and through having developed

976. S: *niṣṭhāgamanabhūmivyavasthitaḥ,* T: *mthar thug par 'gro ba'i sa la gnas pa. BBhVy* (f. 208b): "'A bodhisattva who has reached the stage that is the perfect manner of going' is one who has received the consecration (S: *abhiṣekaḥ,* T: *dbang bskur ba*) on the tenth stage." This consecration is described in the *Sutra on the Ten Stages*. See also Book III, chapter 3, where a series of seven stages is identified.

977. See note 378.

978. See note 379.

great purity] with regard to the generosity that is directed everywhere, the morality that is directed everywhere, etc., up to the sameness of purpose that is directed everywhere.

Regarding this [topic], the result that a tathāgata is the foremost of all sentient beings—whether they have no feet, are two-footed, four-footed, or have many feet; whether they are of the form realm or the formless realm; and whether they have conceptions, they have no conceptions, or they have reached the sphere in which there is neither conception nor absence of conception—comes about through [having practiced assiduously and through having developed great purity] with regard to the generosity of a true spiritual being, the morality of a true spiritual being, etc., up to the sameness of purpose of a true spiritual being.

Regarding this [topic], the result that a tathāgata possesses a body with thirty-two marks and eighty secondary signs that are produced by an immeasurable variety of virtuous acts comes about through [having practiced assiduously and through having developed great purity] with regard to generosity of every form, morality of every form, etc., up to the sameness of purpose of every form.

Regarding this [topic], the result that when a tathāgata is seated at the seat of enlightenment[979] Māra and all of his hostile forces are unable to disturb, harm, or unsettle him comes about through [having assiduously practiced and through having developed great purity] with regard to the generosity that relates to the distressed and what they want, the morality that relates to the distressed and what they want, etc., up to the sameness of purpose that relates to the distressed and what they want.

Regarding this [topic], the result that a tathāgata attains the ease associated with supreme forms of meditative absorption, [supreme forms of] the liberations, and [supreme forms of] entering one-pointed concentration comes about through [having practiced assiduously and through having developed great purity] with regard to the generosity that brings happiness here and in the next world, the morality that brings happiness here and in the next world, etc., up to the sameness of purpose that brings happiness here and in the next world.

Regarding this [topic], the result that a tathāgata possesses the four forms of purity that are complete in every respect—complete purity regarding the [physical] support, complete purity regarding mental objects, complete purity regarding the mind, and complete purity regarding knowledge—

979. See note 526.

comes about through having practiced assiduously, through having developed great purity, and through having attained complete perfection with regard to pure generosity, pure morality, etc., up to the sameness of purpose that is pure. Similarly, the result of the three qualities of having nothing that needs to be concealed, as well as [the results of] the ten powers, [the four forms of] intrepid confidence, [the three forms of] closely placed recollection, and the purity of all the unique qualities of a buddha, also come about [through having practiced assiduously, through having developed great purity, and through having attained complete perfection with regard to pure generosity, pure morality, etc., up to the sameness of purpose that is pure].

These are the unsurpassed and consummate results of a bodhisattva's virtuous qualities of generosity, etc. It should be understood that [a bodhisattva] also [gains] additional [results] in relation to the bodhisattva activities while [he or she is still being reborn] in samsara that are immeasurable, agreeable, and beyond reproach.

Within [Book I of] *The Stage of a Bodhisattva,* [known as] "The Object of Mental Application That Relates to the Support," this completes the fifteenth chapter, entitled "The Principles for Attracting a Following."

16

Worship, Service, and the Immeasurables

Summary lines [of verse]:

> Worshipping the Jewels, serving a [spiritual] friend,
> And, lastly, the immeasurables.

Worshipping the Three Jewels [1.16.1]

Regarding this [topic], what are [the forms of] worshipping the tathāgatas that a bodhisattva carries out in relation to the tathāgatas?

Briefly, it should be understood as being of ten forms: (1) body worship, (2) shrine worship, (3) face-to-face worship, (4) worship that is not face-to-face, (5) worship that one does oneself, (6) worship that one prompts others to do, (7) worship done with wealth and honor, (8) eminent worship, (9) worship that is free of affliction, and (10) worship that consists of spiritual practice.

Body Worship [1.16.1.1]

Regarding this [topic], the act of worship that a bodhisattva performs directly before the physical body of a tathāgata is called "body worship."

Shrine Worship [1.16.1.2]

Regarding this [topic], the act of worship by a bodhisattva of a *stūpa*[980] monument, a *gaha*[981] shrine, a *kūṭa*[982] shrine, or an ancient or new *caitya*[983] shrine, [all of which are] directed toward the Tathāgata, is called "shrine worship."

Face-to-Face Worship [1.16.1.3]

Regarding this [topic], the act of worship that a bodhisattva performs while standing face-to-face before a tathāgata's body or a tathāgata shrine, and while [either of them] is perceptible to his or her own senses, is called "face-to-face worship."

Regarding this [topic], there is a form of face-to-face worship that is done by a bodhisattva before a tathāgata's body or a tathāgata shrine in which he or she forms the following thoughts that are accompanied by a superior attitude and accompanied by joy: "The nature of one tathāgata is [the same as] the nature of all the tathāgatas of the past, present, and future. The nature of one tathāgata shrine is [the same as] the nature of all tathāgata shrines. Therefore, when I worship the Tathāgata before whom I am standing face-to-face, I also worship all the tathāgatas of the past, present, and future." [Alternatively, he or she thinks:] "When I worship the tathāgata shrine before which I am standing face-to-face, I also worship all the other *stūpa* monuments, *gaha* shrines, *kūṭa* shrines, and the ancient or new *caitya* shrines that exist throughout the limitless world spheres of the ten directions." This should be understood as [a form of] worship of a tathāgata or [a form of] worship of a tathāgata shrine in which [the characteristic of] being face-to-face and [the characteristic of] not being face-to-face both apply.

980. T: *mchod rten*. *BBhVy* (f. 211a): "A *stūpa* is recognized as a [monument] that resembles the shape of a mound of grain [T: *'bru'i phung po'i dbyibs lta bu;* or perhaps 'shaped like a granary,' S: *dhānyakūtaḥ*] that contains relics of the Tathāgata."

981. T: *gtsang khang phyur bu*. *BBhVy* (f. 211a): "A *gaha* is a square structure that contains image(s)."

982. T: *gtsang khang*. *BBhVy* (f. 211a): "A *kūṭa* shrine is a round structure that contains both [images and relics]."

983. S: *caityam,* T: *mchod rten*. Samudramegha suggests that the term *caitya* is meant as a generic term for any of the three types of shrine that are mentioned. *BBhVy* (f. 211a): "These very three types of [structures; i.e., *stūpa, gaha,* and *kūṭa*] are [designated] as being of two types based on their age [or condition]; that is, 'an ancient shrine or a new shrine.'"

Worship That Is Not Face-to-Face [1.16.1.4]

By contrast, when a bodhisattva, after having formed the thought of a tathāgata [in his or her mind], performs an act of worship that is directed toward all buddhas as well as toward all tathāgata shrines while he or she is not standing face-to-face before a tathāgata or a tathāgata shrine, this should be understood as [a bodhisattva's] act of worship that is exclusively [being done in a manner that is] not face-to-face.

Moreover, when a bodhisattva, in relation to a tathāgata who has entered nirvana and in a manner that is directed toward a tathāgata, causes a single [image of a buddha's] body or a *stūpa* monument, *gaha* shrine, or *kūṭa* shrine of a tathāgata to be constructed, or [causes] two [of them], or a great many [of them], up to a trillion [of them to be constructed], according to his or her ability and strength, this constitutes a bodhisattva's extensive [form of] worship of the tathāgatas that is not done face-to-face and it is [an act of worship] that yields the result of an immeasurable amount of merit and one in which the merit of Brahmā[984] is obtained many times. It is such that he or she will not go to a state of downfall[985] for a period of many kalpas and many great kalpas. Also, because of that, he or she will not fail to complete the accumulations of [merit and wisdom that culminate in] unsurpassed enlightenment.

Regarding this [topic], an act of worship by a bodhisattva that is done exclusively in relation to a [single] tathāgata or tathāgata shrine should be regarded as one that is extensive.[986] In comparison to that, an act of worship that is exclusively of the type that is not face-to-face should be regarded as yielding the result of an even more extensive amount of merit. In comparison with this [second case], an act of worship in which [the characteristic

984. *BBhVy* (212a): "The amount of [merit indicated by the expression] 'the merit of Brahmā' is that which causes one to go to the celestial realms (S: *svargaḥ,* T: *mtho ris*) for a kalpa—[thus,] the merit that sets in motion [such a karmic] ripening repeatedly and without interruption [for that length of time] is referred to as 'the merit of Brahmā.' It is recognized as being equal to the merit of the [divine] beings who exist in the first meditative absorption [of the form realm]."

985. The term "state of downfall" (S: *vinipātaḥ,* T: *log par ltung ba*) can refer to the lower realms in general or the hells in particular. See the text associated with note 1522 in Book III, chapter 6, the section entitled "The Power of Knowledge regarding Death and Rebirth" [III.6.2.9].

986. That is, it yields an extensive amount of merit. This statement should be taken to mean an act that is exclusively of the type known as "worship that is face-to-face."

of] being face-to-face and [the characteristic of] not being face-to-face both apply should be regarded as yielding the result of the most extensive amount of merit.

Worship That One Does Oneself [1.16.1.5]

Regarding this [topic], when a bodhisattva who is desirous of performing an act of worship in relation to a tathāgata or a tathāgata shrine carries out that act by his or her own hand and does not cause it to be done by male or female servants, workmen, hired persons, friends, advisers, near relations, or kinsmen due to having become subject to idleness, laziness, or an occurrence of heedlessness, this should be known as a bodhisattva's worship that one does oneself.

Worship That One Prompts Others to Do [1.16.1.6]

Regarding this [topic], when a bodhisattva who is desirous of performing an act of worship in relation to a tathāgata or a tathāgata shrine does not carry out that act exclusively by him- or herself but rather [also] causes his or her mother and father to carry out [such an act], or causes his or her children and spouse, male or female servants, workmen, hired persons, friends, advisers, near relations, and kinsmen to do so, or causes other members of the royal family, high royal officials, brahmins, householders, townspeople, countrymen, persons of wealth, heads of guilds, or leaders of caravans to do so, or [also] even causes [ordinary] men and women, sons and daughters, poor persons, those afflicted by pain, and even those who are outcasts to carry out [such an act], or [also] causes teachers and preceptors, fellow residents of a monastery, fellow spiritual practitioners, homeless ascetics, and even other heretics to perform acts of worship in relation to a tathāgata or a tathāgata shrine, this should be understood as an act of worship in which [the characteristic of] being done by oneself and [the characteristic of] being done by others both apply.

Moreover, when a bodhisattva only possesses a limited quantity of objects to give and [a limited quantity of objects] that are suitable for performing acts of worship, and yet, after having developed a compassionate state of mind, he or she gives those objects to others, thinking, "These beings who are undergoing suffering possess only a small amount of merit and are unable [to practice acts of worship on their own]. [However,] after they have performed acts of worship, they will experience happiness [in the future]," and when those individuals make an offering to a tathāgata or a tathāgata shrine with those objects but the bodhisattva him- or herself does not do so, this should be known as an act of worship that [has been prompted] by a bodhisattva and is carried out exclusively by others.

Regarding this [topic, an act of worship] that is done by oneself exclusively [should be known as] one that yields the result of a great amount of merit. [An act of worship that a bodhisattva] prompts others to do and that is carried out by them exclusively [should be known as] one that yields the result of an even greater amount of merit. Further, [an act of worship in which the characteristics of being done by oneself and being done by others] both apply should be known as one that is unsurpassed and yields the result of the greatest amount of merit.

Worship That Is Carried Out with Wealth and Honor [1.16.1.7]

Regarding this [topic], when a bodhisattva performs an act of worship in relation to a tathāgata or a tathāgata shrine by [offering] robes, alms food, bedding, seats, medicine for curing the ill, and [other] personal belongings [of monastics]; by making respectful verbal salutations, physical gestures of homage, standing up to show respect, and joining the palms together; by [offering] fragrant scents [in the form] of incense, aromatic powder, and unguents, various kinds of flower garlands, various kinds of music, or various kinds of offerings of parasols, banners, pennants, and lamps; by reciting hymns of praise, making prostrations with the five round parts [of the body],[987] or circumambulating in a clockwise manner; likewise, when [a bodhisattva] worships [a tathāgata or a tathāgata shrine] by [offering] inexhaustible gifts,[988] by making offerings of precious objects such as gems, pearls, lapis lazuli, conch shells, crystals, coral, emeralds, sapphires, gold, silver, rubies, and [conch shells] that turn to the right, by making offerings of jewelry encrusted with gems, such as earrings, armlets, and the like, or even by making offerings of bells, the scattering of coins, and [decorations

987. S: *pañcamaṇḍalaḥ,* T: *yan lag lnga*. That is, touching the ground with the two hands, the two knees, and the forehead.

988. S: *akṣayaṇikāpradānaḥ,* T: *zad mi shes pa'i sbyin pa. BBhVy* (f. 213a): "'Inexhaustible gifts' are gifts of objects of value that never become exhausted, such as towns, trees, etc."

made by] wrapping thread, this should be known as a bodhisattva's act of worship in relation to a tathāgata or a tathāgata shrine that is done with wealth and honor.

Eminent Worship [1.16.1.8]

Regarding this [topic], when a bodhisattva performs this very act of worship that is done with wealth and honor in relation to a tathāgata or a tathāgata shrine (1) for a long period of time, (2) using large amounts of objects of value and (3) excellent objects of value, (4) [in a manner that is] both face-to-face and not face-to-face, (5) [in a manner that is] both done by oneself and done by [having prompted] others, (6) with a joy that is felt wholeheartedly and having brought forth an intense form of devotion, and (7) these roots of virtue are dedicated to unsurpassed true and complete enlightenment, this is called a bodhisattva's seven aspects of "eminent worship."

Worship That Is Free of Affliction [1.16.1.9]

Regarding this [topic], (1) when a bodhisattva performs an act of worship in relation to a tathāgata or a tathāgata shrine with his or her own hand and does not have to be caused to do so at the direction of others because of heedlessness or idleness; (2) when he or she performs [an act of worship] with reverence and not in a dismissive manner; when he or she performs [an act of worship] (3) while remaining undistracted and (4) with a mind that is free of affliction; (5) when he or she does not worship [a tathāgata or a tathāgata shrine] with a counterfeit object out of hypocrisy so that [he or she might receive] gain and honor from eminent persons who have strong faith in the Buddha, such as the members of a royal family, etc.; and (6) when he or she does not [perform an act of worship] using [objects] such as ointments containing yellow orpiment,[989] ablutions [made with] ghee, incense made from *guggulu* resin, or *arka* flowers, or with any other unsuitable objects,[990] this should be known as the six aspects of worship that are free of affliction.

Moreover, a bodhisattva performs such an eminent act of worship that is

989. S: *haritālalepanam,* T: *bab las byug pa.* MW (p. 1291): "yellow orpiment or sulphuret of arsenic (described as the seed or seminal energy of Viṣṇu)."

990. S: *akalpika upakaranaḥ,* T: *yo byad mi rung ba. BBhVy* (f. 213b): "'Unsuitable objects' [means] such things as meat and spirituous liquor."

free of affliction and that is accomplished with wealth and honor in relation to a tathāgata or a tathāgata shrine, either with objects of wealth that he or she obtained with the strength of his or her own arms,[991] [objects of wealth] that were solicited from others, or [objects of wealth] that were obtained through the controlling power over implements.[992] Regarding this [point], a bodhisattva who has attained the controlling power over implements emanates one, two, or many bodies, up to many trillions of trillions[993] of bodies, and then makes prostration to the tathāgatas with all of these bodies. Moreover, after emanating a hundred hands, a thousand hands, or even more than that for each of these bodies, he or she, with all of these [hands], scatters over the tathāgatas supremely fragrant and supremely beautiful flowers that surpass those of the gods. All of these exalted bodies that possess the excellent physical qualities of a tathāgata voice hymns of praise. With all of these bodies, he or she offers various kinds of excellent and exceptional armlets, bracelets, and jewel earrings to the tathāgatas and holds up [for them various kinds of excellent and exceptional] parasols, banners, and pennants. These [acts], as well as others of a similar type, are acts of worship that are subject to [the power of] one's mind and are carried out by a bodhisattva who has attained the controlling power over implements.

This [kind of bodhisattva] also does not need to wish for or long for the appearance of a buddha.

Why is that?

[This bodhisattva does not need to wish for the appearance of a buddha] since he or she is able to travel in an unimpeded manner to all the buddha fields, by virtue of having reached the stage of irreversibility.

Worship That Consists of Spiritual Practice [1.16.1.10]

Even though a bodhisattva may not possess objects of wealth that were acquired by the strength of his or her own arms or [objects of wealth] that

991. That is, objects that were obtained through one's own labor.

992. S: *pariṣkāravaśitā*, T: *yo byad la dbang ba*. This is one of the ten controlling powers that are achieved by bodhisattvas who have attained the eighth of the ten ārya stages. They are described in Book II, chapter 4, the section entitled "The Pleasurable State That Is Free of Signs and Also Free of Effort" [II.4.10].

993. S: *koṭīniyutaśatasahasrany anekāni*, T: *bye ba khrag khrig 'bum phrag du ma*. *Koṭī* is ten million, *niyuta* is a trillion, and *śatasahasra* is a hundred thousand. Combining the three figures yields the number indicated.

were acquired through having been solicited from others, and even though he or she may not be a bodhisattva who has attained the controlling power over implements, a bodhisattva who possesses faith can expand his or her mind that is possessed of joy and great devotion [so as to consider] all the lesser, intermediate, and great acts of worship that are being carried out [by others] in this Rose Apple Continent,[994] in this [world that is made up of] four continents, or in the thousand world spheres, the double-thousand world spheres, and the great triple-thousand world spheres, up to the limitless world spheres of the ten directions, and rejoice at them. This, too, is a great and immeasurable form of tathāgata worship that a bodhisattva can perform with little difficulty and that obtains a great accumulation [of merit] for the sake of enlightenment, [and it is one] which a bodhisattva should carry out with a happy mind and an elated mind, continually and without interruption.

Regarding this [topic], when a bodhisattva meditates upon a mind that possesses loving-kindness toward all living beings for a little while, for a moment, even merely for the length of time that it takes to milk a cow, or when he or she meditates upon a mind that is accompanied by compassion, [a mind] that is accompanied by joy, and [a mind] that is accompanied by equanimity; likewise, when he or she meditates upon the concept of impermanence in relation to all conditioned entities, the concept of suffering in relation to impermanence, the concept of selflessness in relation to suffering, and the concept of being advantageous in relation to nirvana; likewise, when he or she meditates upon recollection of the Tathāgata and recollection of the Dharma, the Sangha, and the perfections; likewise, when he or she has generated devotion toward the suchness that is the ineffable [ultimate] nature of all entities with even just a limited [form of] the awareness that possesses a weak amount of forbearance[995] and abides for a little while,

994. S: *jambūdvīpaḥ*, T: *'dzam bu'i gling*. Of the four major continents that make up the world in Buddhist cosmology, this is the name of the southern continent, which corresponds roughly to the area of greater South Asia. It is described in the *AKB* as shaped like a chariot—that is, roughly triangular. In its center lies the Adamantine Seat (S: *vajrāsanaḥ*, T: *rdo rje'i gdan*) where the buddhas attain enlightenment. The name of this continent is said to derive from a great rose apple (*jambu*) tree that lies near Lake Anavatapta at the northern edge of the continent. This lake is sometimes associated with Lake Manasarovar.

995. See note 530 for a discussion of the term "forbearance" (S: *kṣāntiḥ*, T: *bzod pa*). It is a quality that occurs on all four levels of the preparation path (S: *prayogamārgaḥ*, T: *sbyor lam*). On the first two levels, called "heat" (S: *uṣmagatam*, T: *drod*) and "summit" (S:

for a moment, in a [state of] mind that is free of conceptualization and free of signs, much less if [he or she generates and abides in] a [form of awareness] that is higher than this or greater than this; likewise, when he or she preserves the bodhisattva [system of] moral discipline, exerts him- or herself in practicing quiescence and insight, as well as the qualities that are conducive to enlightenment; likewise, when he or she exerts him- or herself correctly in practicing the perfections and the principles for attracting a following, this is a bodhisattva's [form of] tathāgata worship that consists of [spiritual] practice [and it is] the foremost, best, most excellent, and unsurpassed [form of tathāgata worship]. It is the [form of] worship in relation to which all the preceding kinds of worship that are carried out with wealth and honor do not reach even a hundredth part, [in relation to which] they do not even reach a thousandth part, etc., up to [it is the form of worship in relation to which] they do not reach [any level of] factoring.

This [presentation] consisting of ten aspects should be understood as [one that describes] worship of the tathāgatas in all of its forms. Just as with [the description of] worship of the tathāgatas, [the descriptions of] worship of the Dharma and worship of the Sangha should be understood in a similar way, according to the particular circumstances [of those topics].

Regarding this [topic], a bodhisattva who carries out these ten forms of worship of the Three Jewels does so with six types of superior attitude that hold the tathāgatas as their object. [They are] (1) the superior attitude [that regards the tathāgatas] as the unsurpassed field of virtue; (2) the superior attitude [that regards the tathāgatas] as the unsurpassed benefactors; (3) the superior attitude [that regards the tathāgatas] as the foremost of all sentient beings—whether they have no feet or are two-footed, etc.; (4) the superior attitude [that regards the tathāgatas] as extremely rare, like the *udumbara* flower; (5) the superior attitude [that regards the tathāgatas] as unique in that they appear as the sole [enlightened being] within a world system consisting of a great triple-thousand worlds; and (6) the superior attitude [that regards the tathāgatas] as the refuge for all matters relating to mundane and transcendent forms of excellence. Even [a bodhisattva's] minor act of worship of a tathāgata [that is carried out] with these six types of superior attitude, or his or her [minor act of worship] of the Dharma or the Sangha [that is carried out with similar forms of these six types of superior attitude],

mūrdhanaḥ, T: *rtse mo*), this forbearance is of weak and moderate strength, respectively. On the third level it becomes quite strong and, hence, that level is called "forbearance."

yields an immeasurably great result; how much more would it be so for [an act of worship] that is extensive.

Serving a Spiritual Teacher [I.16.2]

Regarding this [topic], what characteristics does a bodhisattva possess in order to be known as a spiritual teacher? What characteristics cause the position of a spiritual teacher to be fruitful? What characteristics should a spiritual teacher possess in order to take on the status of being an object of faith? What are the duties that a bodhisattva who is a spiritual teacher should carry out in relation to his or her disciples? What are the forms of service that a bodhisattva should perform in relation to a spiritual teacher? What kind of conceptions should a bodhisattva maintain when he or she listens to the Dharma in the presence of a spiritual teacher? What circumstances should the bodhisattva who is listening to the Dharma in the presence of a spiritual teacher avoid bringing to mind in relation to that person who is his or her Dharma teacher?

The Attributes of a Spiritual Teacher [I.16.2.1]

Regarding this [topic], a bodhisattva's spiritual teacher who is possessed of eight attributes should be known as one who is complete in every aspect.[996] (1) He or she is one who maintains a virtuous way of life by being one who adheres to [the precepts of] a bodhisattva's morality of restraint and one who keeps them whole and unflawed.[997] (2) He or she is one who possesses extensive learning by not being one who has failed to develop understanding. (3) He or she is also one who is endowed with knowledge by being one who has attained any of the virtuous qualities that derive from meditation and by being one who has attained [any of the virtuous qualities that pertain to] quiescence and insight. (4) He or she is sympathetic [in the sense of being] a compassionate person who has given up any interest in abiding in [a state of] ease in this life and one who is dedicated to the welfare of

996. In a slightly different order and language, these eight qualities are also discussed in *ŚBh*, pp. 127–131. (The descriptions of the first two qualities are lost in the Sanskrit edition; see Tibetan translation, ff. 51a–52b).

997. *BBhVy* (f. 215a): "'One who keeps them unflawed' (S: *acchidrakarī*, T: *skyon med par byed pa*) does so by restoring [the discipline] when an infraction occurs." This restoration is discussed in Book I, chapter 10, the section entitled "Confession" [I.10.2.12].

others. (5) He or she is possessed of self-confidence [in the sense that], when teaching the Dharma to others, his or her recollection and clarity of understanding[998] are not lost due to the fear that arises from shyness. (6) He or she is also one who patiently forbears unwelcome and undesirable remarks from others that are contemptuous, derisive, abusive, and injurious, etc., as well as various kinds of wrongful behavior carried out by beings. (7) He or she is also one who does not become mentally weary [in the sense that] he or she remains strong, exercises much careful consideration, and is tireless when teaching Dharma to the fourfold following.[999] (8) He or she is one whose speech is appealing in that he or she is endowed with the skillful qualities of speech[1000] and one who is naturally articulate and distinct in his or her speech.

Making the Role of a Spiritual Teacher Fruitful [1.16.2.2]

Regarding this [topic], a bodhisattva who is a spiritual teacher and who is endowed with all the virtuous qualities causes the activities of a spiritual teacher to become fruitful in five ways: (1) From the very outset, he or she is desirous of benefiting others and bringing them happiness. (2) He or she also truly knows what is beneficial and will bring happiness and is not erroneous in his or her opinion about these [two aims]. (3) He or she has the ability and the power to spiritually tame any being who is capable [of being tamed] by whatever means and whatever form of Dharma teaching [is most suitable]. (4) He or she avoids becoming mentally weary, and (5) he or she feels compassion equally toward all beings and does not show any partiality toward those who are inferior, average, or superior.

998. S: *pratibhānam,* T: *spobs pa.* Elsewhere this term has been translated as "eloquence." It refers to a form of intelligence that enables one to explain meanings to others clearly and without hesitation. See note 380.

999. S: *catasraḥ pariṣad,* T: *'khor bzhi po.* That is, (1) monks, (2) nuns, (3) laymen, and (4) laywomen.

1000. S: *vākkaraṇenopetaḥ,* T: *tshig gi bya ba dang ldan pa. ŚBh* (p. 131): "How is one endowed with the skillful qualities of speech? He or she possesses speech that is elegant, lovely, distinct, capable of being understood, worthy of being heard, not disagreeable, free of attachment, and not inadequate. [That is,] he or she is one who speaks in an appealing manner."

The Characteristics That Make a Spiritual Teacher Worthy of Being an Object of Faith [1.16.2.3]

Regarding this [topic], a spiritual teacher takes on the status of being an object of faith on the basis of five aspects in such a way that others will feel great reverence toward him or her even when they have [only] heard [about the spiritual teacher from others], let alone when they have seen him or her face-to-face. (1) [A spiritual teacher] possesses [proper] physical behavior, physical behavior that is composed, and excellent physical behavior in which he or she avoids holding all the major and minor parts[1001] of the body in an unbecoming manner. (2) [A spiritual teacher] is one who remains firm in that he or she is unwavering and free of excitation in conducting physical, verbal, and mental activities. (3) [A spiritual teacher] is free of pretense in that he or she does not deliberately affect [a certain type of] physical behavior or [the quality of] steadfastness as an act of hypocrisy.[1002] (4) [A spiritual teacher] is free of envy in that he or she does not become upset in relation to a Dharma discourse that is given by others or the gain and honor that they have received. Instead, when requested by others to give a Dharma discourse or when receiving extensive amounts of gain and honor, he or she directs [that request to teach or that gain and honor] to others with a sincere and gracious mind. Moreover, regarding the Dharma discourses given by others or the gain and honor that they receive, he or she is much more deeply pleased by their gain and honor than by his or her own gain and honor. (5) [A spiritual teacher] is also one who practices simplicity[1003] in the sense of having few possessions and few personal belongings, and giving away all the property that is received.

The Duties of a Spiritual Teacher toward His or Her Disciples [1.16.2.4]

Regarding this [topic], a bodhisattva who is a spiritual teacher carries out five types of activities in relation to those who are his or her disciples. (1) He

1001. S: *aṅgapratyaṅgāni*, T: *yan lag dang nying lag*. According to MW (p. 663), the major elements of the body are the head, torso, arms, and legs; the minor ones include the forehead, nose, ears, chin, fingers, and toes.

1002. That is, he or she does not feign virtuous behavior in order to acquire material gain or honor. See note 642 for a more formal description of this type of wrong livelihood.

1003. See note 962.

or she is one who admonishes, (2) one who reminds, (3) one who instructs, (4) one who counsels, and (5) one who gives Dharma teachings. It should be understood that these terms can be differentiated at length, for example as they are in the *Stage of a Listener*.[1004] The topics of instruction and counsel were also described above, in the chapter entitled "The Lineages of the Powers."

Serving a Spiritual Teacher [1.16.2.5]

Regarding this [topic], it should be understood that the act of serving a spiritual teacher is fully accomplished on the basis of four qualities. [Serving a spiritual teacher is accomplished] (1) by [carrying out] the activities of taking care of [a spiritual teacher] who is sick and waiting upon one who is healthy, regularly and at appropriate times, and [doing so after] having engendered [feelings of] affection, respect, and joy; (2) by [carrying out] the activities of respectful salutation, prostration, standing up [in his or her presence], making the gesture of joined palms, respectful behavior, and honoring, as well as by making offerings of clothing, food, seats, bedding, and medicine for curing the ill in a manner that accords with the Dharma, regularly and at appropriate times; (3) by obeying [a spiritual teacher] who is being relied upon with regard to meaningful spiritual undertakings and endeavors,[1005] by being unwavering [with regard to those activities], and by

1004. *ŚBh*, pp. 131–134. One who admonishes (S: *codakaḥ*, T: *gleng bar byed* or *skul bar byed*) directly asks a disciple who is believed to have violated moral precepts or engaged in misconduct whether, in fact, he or she has committed such wrongdoing. One who reminds (S: *smārakaḥ*, T: *dran par byed*) calls attention to disciples' prior transgressions so that they will not be repeated, reminds disciples about Dharma teachings that have been heard but not yet taken up, and reminds disciples about meanings and forms of practice that have been taught but may have been forgotten. One who instructs (S: *avavādakaḥ*, T: *'dom par byed*) provides instruction relating to practices for cultivating the trainings of one-pointed concentration and wisdom. One who counsels (S: *anuśāsakaḥ*, T: *rjes su rton par byed*) acts in the capacity of a preceptor, instructor, or spiritual teacher to provide instruction in the Buddha's teaching system that relates to conduct, and, when appropriate, admonishes or punishes disciples for any transgressions. One who gives Dharma teachings (S: *dharmadeśakaḥ*, T: *chos ston par byed*) teaches instruction to disciples according to their level of understanding in order to further their spiritual development and to enable the Dharma to remain for as long as possible.

1005. *BBhVy* (f. 216b): "[In the phrase 'with regard to meaningful spiritual undertakings and endeavors'] the term 'spiritual' (S: *dhārmika*, T: *chos dang mthun pa*) means those matters that are not contrary to the Dharma; 'undertakings' (S: *saṃyoga*, *yang dag par*

disclosing [to a spiritual teacher] in a correct manner [how one has behaved with regard to those activities]; and (4) by approaching, waiting on,[1006] asking questions of, and listening to [a spiritual teacher] who has given permission [for one to do so] and who has the desire [that these activities be done], and [by doing so] at appropriate times.

Conceptions to Maintain When Listening to the Dharma [1.16.2.6]

Regarding this [topic], a bodhisattva who is desirous of listening to the Dharma in the presence of a spiritual teacher should listen to the Dharma while maintaining five types of conceptions. [They are] (1) [that one should listen] with the conception that [the Dharma] is a jewel, in the sense that it is difficult to obtain; (2) [that one should listen] with the conception that [the Dharma] is [like one's] eyes, in the sense that it has the nature of being a cause for obtaining an extensive amount of innate wisdom;[1007] (3) [that one should listen] with the conception that [the Dharma] is light, in the sense that, with the eye of innately acquired knowledge, all aspects of objects of knowledge become evident in their true form; (4) [that one should listen] with the conception that [the Dharma yields] a great result and benefit, in the sense that it has the nature of being the cause for attaining the unsurpassed states of nirvana and complete enlightenment; and (5) [that one should listen] with the conception that [the Dharma] is an irreproachable form of pleasure, in the sense that it has the nature of being the cause [for attaining] in this life the irreproachable and great pleasure of quiescence and insight, [which are qualities that enable] one who has not yet attained

gzud pa) are the activities of properly carrying out [meaningful spiritual matters] oneself. 'Endeavors' (S: *viyoga,* T: *rnam par gzud pa*) means the activities of carrying out the words of [advice given by] one's spiritual teacher."

1006. S: *upāsanam,* T: *bsnyen bkur byed pa.* While the term literally means "sitting near," it also carries such connotations as "serving," "waiting on," "homage," and "worship." *BBhVy* (ff. 216b–217a): "'Waiting on' means to attend upon [a spiritual teacher] by engaging in such actions as making prostration [to him or her], etc."

1007. *BBhVy* (f. 217a) explains this conception by interpreting several terms individually: "[The Dharma] is an eye because it is the cause for attaining an ārya's wisdom eye, both in the sense that by hearing Dharma one perceives subtle and extensive meanings and in the sense that, in a future [life], one will acquire a form of wisdom that is attained at birth."

nirvana and complete enlightenment [to develop] genuine discernment of the Dharma.

Circumstances Relating to the Spiritual Teacher That Should Not Be Brought to Mind [1.16.2.7]

Regarding this [topic], a bodhisattva who is listening to the Dharma in the presence of a spiritual teacher should avoid bringing to mind five circumstances that relate to the person who is a Dharma teacher and, having done so, he or she should listen to the Dharma attentively and with a reverential mind. (1) He or she should avoid bringing to mind that [a spiritual teacher's] morality is in [a state of] ruin. [That is,] he or she should not form thoughts like the following: "This is [a person] whose conduct is bad. He or she does not maintain the [system of moral] discipline. I shall not listen [to the Dharma] from him or her." (2) He or she should avoid bringing to mind that [a spiritual teacher's] family is in [a state of] ruin. [That is,] he or she should not form thoughts like the following: "This [person] is from an inferior family. I shall not listen [to the Dharma] from him or her." (3) He or she should avoid bringing to mind that [a spiritual teacher's] appearance is in [a state of] ruin. [That is,] he or she should not form thoughts like the following: "This is a person who is physically unattractive. I shall not listen [to the Dharma] from him or her." (4) He or she should avoid bringing to mind that [a spiritual teacher's] form of expression is in [a state of] ruin. [That is,] he or she should not form thoughts like the following: "This is a person whose speech is unrefined. I shall not listen [to the Dharma] from him or her." One should rely only upon the meaning [of a Dharma teaching], not its literal form of expression. (5) He or she should avoid bringing to mind that [a spiritual teacher's] pleasantness[1008] [of manner] is in a state of ruin. [That is,] he or she should not form thoughts like the following: "This is a person who speaks in a harsh manner. He or she is prone to anger and does not teach a Dharma that is sweet-sounding. I shall not listen [to the Dharma] from him or her."

Having avoided bringing to mind any of these five circumstances, a bodhisattva should embrace the true Dharma respectfully, for the Dharma can never be corrupted by the faults of a person. Regarding this [topic], a

1008. S: *mādhuryam,* T: *snyan pa.* Literally, "sweetness." MW (p. 809) gives additional senses, such as "loveliness," and "charm."

bodhisattva whose wisdom is weak and who, having become upset about a person's faults, does not want to hear the Dharma [from that person] should be understood to be one who has undertaken [a form of behavior] that will only bring harm to him- or herself and [a form of behavior] that will bring a loss of wisdom.

The Immeasurables [1.16.3]

How does a bodhisattva meditate on the four immeasurables—[namely, those of] loving-kindness, compassion, joy, and equanimity?

Here, in brief, a bodhisattva meditates on three forms of the four immeasurables: (1) [the form] in which sentient beings are the mental object, (2) [the form] in which entities are the mental object, and (3) [the form] in which there is no mental object.

After having arranged all sentient beings into three groups—[namely,] those who are experiencing happiness, those who are experiencing suffering, and those who are neither experiencing happiness nor experiencing suffering—when a bodhisattva, in relation to sentient beings who have a desire for happiness, radiates into the ten directions the loving-kindness that consists of the superior attitude [that wishes] to provide them with happiness and he or she abides with a conviction [that believes in the existence of] sentient beings, this should be understood as his or her [form of] loving-kindness in which sentient beings are the mental object.

On the other hand, when [a bodhisattva] who possesses an understanding of [the existence of] mere entities[1009] meditates on that very [form of]

1009. S: *dharmamātram,* T: *chos tsam.* The expression "mere entities" is meant to indicate an awareness that is informed by realization of the insubstantiality of the person (S: *pudgalanairātmyam,* T: *gang zag gi bdag med*). In Book IV of the *ŚBh* (pp. 470–499) Asaṅga describes how a practitioner meditates on the sixteen aspects of the four noble truths. After explaining how a practitioner meditates on the first two aspects of the noble truth of suffering—i.e., those of impermanence and suffering—he describes meditation on the third aspect, known as emptiness, as follows: "[The meditator] has the following thoughts: 'I discern merely a faculty that is fleeting in nature, merely an experience that arises from that [faculty], and merely a mind. The notions of an "I" and a "mine" are mere names, mere impressions, mere figures of speech. There is nothing beyond that, nothing more than that. [The entities] that exist in this way are merely the heaps (S: *skandhaḥ,* T: *phung po*). Among these heaps, no self or sentient being can be found that is permanent, durable, constant, or constitutes an owner [of the heaps]; [there is no self or sentient being] that is born, ages, and dies, or that, having repeatedly performed deeds here and there,

loving-kindness [that was just described] while recognizing with deep conviction that this mere [collection of] entities is designated a sentient being [only] in a figurative sense, this should be understood as his [or her form of] loving-kindness in which entities are the mental object.

Moreover, when [a bodhisattva] meditates on that very [form of] loving-kindness while avoiding even generating a conception of entities, this should be understood as his [or her form of] loving-kindness in which there is no mental object.

It should be understood that [immeasurable] compassion, joy, and equanimity are also [practiced] in the same way as [the three forms of] loving-kindness—[namely,] that in which sentient beings are the mental object, that in which entities are the mental object, and that in which there is no mental object. Regarding those [latter three practices], when a bodhisattva, in relation to sentient beings who are experiencing suffering, meditates upon a mind that is accompanied by compassion [and he or she radiates it] into the ten directions with a [form of] superior attitude [that wishes] to remove [sentient beings'] suffering, this is his or her [immeasurable] compassion. Further, when [a bodhisattva], in relation to sentient beings who are experiencing happiness, meditates upon a mind that is accompanied by joy [and he or she radiates it] into the ten directions with a [form of] superior attitude that rejoices at their happiness, this is his or her [immeasurable] joy. When [a bodhisattva] meditates upon a mind that is accompanied by equanimity [and he or she radiates it] into the ten directions with a [form of] superior attitude [that wishes] to free those very same three types of sentient beings—[namely,] those who are neither experiencing happiness nor experiencing suffering, those who are experiencing suffering, and those who are experiencing happiness—respectively, of their ignorance, hatred, and desire, this is his [or her immeasurable] equanimity.

Regarding these [four practices], it should be understood that [the forms of] a bodhisattva's immeasurable loving-kindness, etc., in which sentient beings are the mental object are [forms of practice] that are shared by others who are followers of non-Buddhist traditions.[1010] Moreover, it should be

experiences the ripening of their fruit. Therefore, these conditioned entities are empty and devoid of a self.' In this way, [the practitioner] arrives at an understanding of the aspect of emptiness (S: *śūnyaḥ,* T: *stong pa*) on the basis of the aspect called 'nondiscernment' (S: *anupalabdhiḥ,* T: *dmigs su med pa*)."

1010. S: *anyatīrthikaḥ,* T: *mu stegs gzhan*. Literally, "others who are heretics"; see note 442 for an explanation of this term. I translate it here as "follower of a non-Buddhist tradition"

understood that those [forms of the four immeasurables] in which entities are the mental object are [forms of practice] that are shared by listeners and solitary realizers, but they are not [forms of practice] that are shared by others who are followers of non-Buddhist traditions. However, it should be understood that [those forms of] a bodhisattva's [practice of] the immeasurables in which there is no mental object are not [forms of practice] that are shared by any listeners, solitary realizers, or followers of non-Buddhist traditions.

Regarding these [four practices], it should be understood that three of the bodhisattvas' immeasurables—namely, loving-kindness, compassion, and joy—consist of [forms of] superior attitude [that wish for] the happiness [of sentient beings]. It should be understood that one of the immeasurables consists of a [form of] superior attitude [that wishes to] benefit [sentient beings]—namely, equanimity. All [four] of the immeasurables are referred to as [forms of] a bodhisattva's "sympathy."[1011] Therefore, those bodhisattvas who possess these [immeasurable attitudes] are described as "the ones who are sympathetic."

Cultivating Compassion by Meditating on One Hundred and Ten Forms of Suffering [1.16.3.1]

Regarding this [topic], bodhisattvas consider one hundred and ten forms of suffering that occur within the domain of sentient beings as they meditate upon compassion toward sentient beings.

What are the one hundred and ten forms of suffering?

Suffering has one form. As relates to "the suffering of [a state of] progression,"[1012] all sentient beings, without exception, are experiencing the suffering that occurs in a continuous manner.

Suffering has two forms. (1) "[The suffering] that is rooted in desire" is

---

to avoid the misconception that "heretic" should be taken to mean a Buddhist whose beliefs are at odds with orthodox doctrine.

1011. S: *anukampā,* T: *snying rtse ba.* The verbal root *kamp* means "to tremble," "to shake"; the root *anukamp* means "to sympathize with."

1012. S: *pravṛttiduḥkham,* T: *'jug pa'i sdug bsngal. BBhVy* (f. 219a): "The general suffering that relates to all conditioned entities without exception is called 'the suffering of [a state of] progression.'" In this usage, the term "progression" (S: *pravṛttiḥ,* T: *'jug pa*) refers to the unmitigated and continuous nature of the suffering that occurs in samsaric existence. See also note 315, where this term is identified as the name for one of the formations that

the suffering that arises when objects that are held dear undergo change and turn into something different. (2) "The suffering that is [caused by] a ripening of ignorance" is those painful physical sensations that cause the individual who experiences them to become bewildered in the sense of [forming the erroneous notions of] an "I" or a "mine" in relation to his or her individual existence[1013] and then to undergo exceedingly great distress. [These two forms of suffering] cause two [types of] painful feelings to be experienced, [one] physical and [the other] mental.

Suffering has three forms: (1) that which is caused by the suffering of suffering, (2) that which is caused by the suffering of conditioned existence, and (3) that which is caused by the suffering of change.

Suffering has four forms. (1) The suffering of separation is that which arises through being separated from those [beings] who are held dear. (2) The suffering of destruction is that which arises because of death, [an event that is characterized by] the casting off of a [particular] class affiliate.[1014] (3) Successive suffering it is that which arises sequentially in [each] rebirth following one's death. (4) Perpetual suffering is the five grasping heaps[1015] of those sentient beings who are not capable of attaining nirvana.

Suffering has five forms: (1) the suffering that is conditioned by the

---

do not accompany consciousness (S: *cittaviprayuktasaṃskāraḥ*, T: *sems dang mtshung par ldan pa ma yin pa'i 'du byed*).

1013. S: *ātmabhāvaḥ*, T: *lus*. See note 237 for comments relating to this term.

1014. S: *nikāyasabhāgaḥ*, T: *ris mthun pa*. I translate the term here as "class affiliate," because in this usage it refers to the continuum of a particular sentient being's heaps (see note 880). However, it is also the name for one of the formations that do not accompany consciousness. In that context, I render the term as "class affiliation" because that usage refers to the similarity that is shared by all sentient beings as a whole, as well as that which is common to members of a particular class of sentient beings. *AS* (p. 11): "What is class affiliation? The term 'class affiliation' is a nominal designation [that is ascribed] to the similarity of individual existence that pertains to the various classes of sentient beings [that exist] among the multiplicity of sentient beings." *PSV* (p. 320) adds: "Thus, [the description of this entity] can be [further] indicated as follows: Among the various sentient beings who are distinguished by type, realm, physical form, etc., there exist [various kinds of] commonality in the makeup or composition of these sentient beings that are distinguished by type, realm, physical form, etc., and it is to this [nominally existent entity] that the term 'class affiliation' is ascribed."

1015. S: *upādānaskandhāḥ*, T: *nye bar len pa'i phung po*. See note 935 for an explanation of the term "grasping" (S: *upādānam*, T: *len pa*). *PSV* (p. 291): "The term 'grasping heaps' is interpreted as meaning either that the impure heaps originate from grasping, or that they are governed by grasping, or that grasping arises from them."

perturbation of desire for sense objects, and [the forms of] suffering that are conditioned by the perturbations of (2) malice, (3) torpor and sleep, (4) excitation and regret, and (5) doubt.

Suffering has six forms. (1) Causal suffering is [that which leads to suffering] by engaging in the causes of [rebirth in] the lower realms. (2) Resultant suffering is [that which occurs] through having been born in the lower realms. [The forms of suffering that occur] in relation to material wealth[1016] are (3) the suffering of pursuing [the acquisition of material wealth], (4) the suffering of having to safeguard [the material wealth that has been acquired], (5) the suffering of not finding satisfaction [by the enjoyment of material wealth], and (6) the suffering [that arises] from the loss [of one's material wealth]. Collectively, these are the six forms of suffering.

Suffering has seven forms. (1) Birth is suffering, (2) old age [is suffering], (3) sickness [is suffering], (4) death [is suffering], (5) meeting with disagreeable things [is suffering], (6) separation from agreeable things [is suffering], and (7) not acquiring what is desired and sought after is also suffering.

Suffering has eight forms: (1) the suffering of cold; (2) the suffering of heat; (3) the suffering of hunger; (4) the suffering of thirst; (5) the suffering of lacking the freedom [to act at one's own discretion]; (6) the suffering of harm done to oneself, such as that of naked ascetics, and the like; (7) the suffering of harm done by others, such as being struck by another person with the hand or a clod of earth, etc., or being stung by gnats and mosquitoes, etc.; and (8) the suffering [that arises from] continually engaging in a single form of physical behavior.

Suffering has nine forms: (1) the suffering of one's own misfortune,[1017] (2) the suffering of others' misfortune, (3) the suffering of misfortune pertaining to family relations, (4) the suffering of misfortune relating to possessions, (5) the suffering of loss of health, (6) the suffering [caused by] a failure of morality, (7) the suffering [caused by] failed views, (8) suffering [experienced] in this life, and (9) suffering [experienced] in future lives.

Suffering has ten forms: (1) the suffering of lacking the food that is a

1016. S: *bhogaḥ,* T: *longs spyod.* Literally, "object of enjoyment," in this usage the term means possessions in the sense of material goods and wealth.

1017. S: *vipattiḥ,* T: *rgud pa.* The first seven of these nine forms of suffering are all qualified by this term, which has meanings that include "adversity," "misfortune," "failure," "disaster," "ruin," "destruction," and "death." The verbal root *vipad* can mean "to go wrong," "to fail," "to come to nothing," "to perish."

material necessity[1018] for the body; the suffering of lacking the material necessities of (2) drink, (3) vehicles, (4) clothing, (5) ornaments, and (6) household utensils; (7) the suffering of lacking the material necessities of scents, garlands, and unguents; (8) the suffering of lacking the material necessities that relate to dance, song, music, etc.; (9) the suffering of lacking the material necessities for [creating] light; and (10) the suffering of lacking the material necessities [used by] women and men [in the pursuit of] sexual pleasure.

It should be understood that there is another [description of] nine forms of suffering: (1) all-encompassing suffering, (2) great suffering, (3) suffering that is directed everywhere, (4) suffering [caused by] wrongful conduct, (5) the suffering of [a state of] progression, (6) the suffering of being unable to fulfill one's desires, (7) the suffering of failure, (8) suffering that follows necessarily, and (9) suffering of every form.

Regarding this [topic], all-encompassing suffering is (1a) that which arises from a former cause, and (1b) that which arises from a condition that exists in the present.

Regarding this [topic], great suffering is that which is (2a) long-lasting, (2b) exceedingly painful, (2c) manifold, and (2d) constant.

Regarding this [topic], suffering that is directed everywhere includes (3a) that which occurs in the hells, (3b) that which occurs in the birth state of animals, (3c) that which occurs in the world of hungry ghosts, and (3d) that which occurs in the happy migratory states.

Regarding this [topic], suffering [caused by] wrongful conduct is (4a) [the suffering] of this life that is experienced due to harm carried out by others and (4b) [the suffering of this life] that is caused to arise by doing harm to others. (4c) It is the suffering that arises from an imbalance of the elements caused by eating unsuitable food. (4d) [It is the suffering] that an individual causes to him- or herself by improperly [engaging in behavior that consists of] doing harm to oneself. (4e) It is the suffering in which one experiences the perturbation [that is caused by] the root and secondary mental afflictions due to continuously engaging in improper forms of attention.[1019] (4f)

1018. S: *pariṣkārah,* T: *yo byad.* The Sanskrit term literally means "that which adorns" or "that which makes ready." Typically, the term refers to "domestic utensils" or "personal belongings."

1019. See note 232.

It is the suffering that one experiences in a future life in the lower realms due to the widespread occurrence of misdeeds of body, speech, and mind.

Regarding this [topic], "the suffering of [a state of] progression"[1020] is that which arises due to six types of uncertainty [that occur] for one who wanders in samsara. (5a) Due to the uncertainty of one's individual existence, a person who was a king becomes a pauper. Due to (5b) the uncertainty relating to one's mother and father, (5c) the uncertainty relating to one's children and spouse, (5d) the uncertainty relating to male and female servants, as well as workers and hired persons, and (5e) the uncertainty relating to friends, advisers,[1021] near relations, and kinsmen, at a different time in one's [samsaric] wandering, those persons who were one's mother or father, etc., up to those persons who were one's friends, advisers, near relations, and kinsmen, will become one's killer or a rival or an enemy. (5f) Due to the uncertainty relating to material possessions, as an individual who previously possessed great wealth continues to wander in samsara, he or she will become, at another time, someone who is extremely poor.

Regarding this [topic], the suffering of being unable to fulfill one's desires is (6a) that which arises for a person who wishes to have a long life but who, contrary to his or her wishes, experiences a short life; (6b) [that which arises for] a person who wishes to be physically attractive but who, contrary to his or her wishes, is physically unattractive; (6c) [that which arises for] a person who wishes to be born in a family of high standing but who, contrary to his or her wishes, is born in a [socially] inferior family; (6d) [that which arises for] a person who wishes to have power[1022] but who, contrary to his or her wishes, has become one who is [living] in a state of poverty; (6e) [that which arises for] a person who wishes to have great strength[1023] but who, contrary

1020. S: *pravṛttiduḥkham,* T: *'jug pa'i sdug bsngal.* This is the same term that was used to describe the first type of suffering in the previous group of fifty-five. Here the term "progression" is meant to suggest that because samsaric existence evolves continuously, all favorable circumstances and personal relations are unstable and will inevitably change into something less favorable. *BBhVy* (f. 220b): "'The suffering of [a state of] progression' means that when someone becomes subject to transformation in the sense of taking on an alternate set of circumstances due to the uncertainty that operates in samsara, he or she gives up the circumstances that existed previously and takes on a different set of circumstances."

1021. See note 657. The term here could also mean "member of the same household."

1022. "Excellence of power" is one of the eight favorable qualities described in Book I, chapter 3, the section entitled "The Eight Maturations" [I.3.5.1].

1023. "Excellence of strength" is another of the eight maturations. See previous note.

to his or her wishes, has become one who is weak; (6f) [that which arises for] a person who wishes to gain knowledge of [many] subjects but who, contrary to his or her wishes, must go through life as one who is bewildered and lacking in knowledge; and (6g) that which arises for a person who wishes to defeat others but who, contrary to his or her wishes, fails to defeat others and is instead forced to experience defeat.

Regarding this [topic], the suffering of failure is, in the case of householders, (7a) [the suffering] that arises from the decline of their children, wife or husband, etc., and, in the case of those who have gone forth [into the homeless state], it is (7b) the suffering that arises from the increase of the mental afflictions of desire, etc. It is also (7c) the suffering that arises from being afflicted by a scarcity of provisions,[1024] (7d) [the suffering that arises] from being defeated by an opposing army, and (7e) [the suffering that arises] from being harmed by the distress and danger [that one encounters upon] entering a forest or a region that is difficult to traverse. It is also (7f) the suffering that arises from having to rely on others for one's subsistence. It is also (7g) [the suffering] that arises from the impediment that is [caused by] lacking limbs or minor appendages. It is also (7h) the suffering that arises from [undergoing] such injuries as being killed, bound, cut, beaten, or banished, etc.

Regarding this [topic], the suffering that follows necessarily[1025] is suffering [that occurs] in relation to eight worldly conditions. [That is, it is suffering that occurs] in relation to (8a) the perishing of that which is perishable, (8b) the disappearance of that which deteriorates, (8c) the aging of that which is subject to aging, (8d) the sickening of that which is subject

1024. S: *durbhikṣam,* T: *mu ge.* This term can also mean "famine," which is the sense of the Tibetan translation.

1025. S: *ānuṣaṅgikam,* T: *rjes su 'brel ba.* The root meaning from which this adjective is derived carries both the sense of "close connection" and that of "attachment." Asaṅga's description of this category of suffering alludes to both meanings. The first five examples suggest suffering that is closely connected with an individual's very existence and, therefore, "follows necessarily" in that it is inevitable. The next three examples—loss, disrepute, and blame—are also conditions that inevitably cause mental suffering for worldly persons. However, the ninth and final example—i.e., "the suffering [that arises because] of longing [for things]"—alludes to the future suffering that "follows necessarily" from worldly forms of desire. The first eight can also be thought of as suffering that ultimately arose from and, therefore, "follows necessarily" from past attachment to samsaric existence. See also Book I, chapter 11, the section entitled "The Nine Worldly Conditions" [I.11.2.2.3]. *BBhVy* (f. 220b): "'The suffering that follows necessarily' is that which is common to all sentient beings."

to illness, and (8e) the death of that which is mortal. It is also the suffering that arises from (8f) loss, (8g) disrepute, and (8h) blame. These eight types of suffering, as well as the suffering [that arises because] of longing [for things], are what is referred to as "suffering that follows necessarily."

Regarding this [topic], suffering of every form [includes] the five types of suffering that are the opposite of what was explained as [the five aspects of] happiness.[1026] They should be understood as (9a) the cause of suffering; (9b) the experience of suffering; (9c) the suffering that is a mere absence of happiness; (9d) the suffering that does not cut off feelings; and (9e) the fifth type is those forms of suffering that oppose the happiness of departure, separation, tranquility, and complete enlightenment—namely, the suffering of living as a householder, [the suffering] that arises from being bound to the desire realm, [the suffering of] deliberation,[1027] and [the suffering of] being an ordinary person.[1028] These make up [one group of this category's] five forms of suffering. [Another five are] (9f) [the suffering] that is due to violence, (9g) [the suffering] that arises from a lack of articles necessary for subsistence, (9h) [the suffering] that arises from an imbalance of the elements, (9i) [the suffering] that arises from a transformation of that which is held dear, and (9j) the fifth is the suffering of the indisposition[1029] that promotes the mental afflictions that operate in the three realms. This group of five combined with the previous [five] make up the ten types of suffering that are called "suffering of every form."

When the previous fifty-five forms [of suffering] are combined together with this [group of] fifty-five, they make up the one hundred and ten forms [of suffering] that are [used as] meditation objects for the [type of] compassion that [is cultivated by] bodhisattvas. [These are] the meditation objects by means of which the compassion of bodhisattvas is developed and increased and their meditation reaches perfection.

1026. See Book I, chapter 3, the section entitled "The Quality of Being Linked to Happiness" [I.3.4].

1027. Deliberation (S: *vitarkaḥ,* T: *rtog pa*) and reflection (S: *vicāraḥ,* T: *dpyod pa*) are two mental factors that are still present when one achieves the first meditative absorption (S: *dhyānam,* T: *bsam gtan*). They represent obstacles to the attainment of the higher stages of the form and formless realms' states of one-pointed concentration.

1028. See note 443.

1029. See note 139.

Great Compassion [1.16.3.2]

Moreover, great compassion arises when nineteen of the types of suffering within this great heap of suffering [are used] as meditation objects.

What are the nineteen types of suffering?

They are (1) the suffering that is [caused by] a ripening of ignorance, (2) the suffering that is included within the suffering of conditioned existence, (3) perpetual suffering, (4) causal suffering, (5) the suffering of birth, (6) the suffering of harm done to oneself, (7) the suffering [caused by] a failure of morality, (8) the suffering [caused by] failed views, (9) the suffering that arises from a former cause, (10) great suffering, (11) the suffering of the hells, (12) the suffering that is included in the happy migratory states, (13) all the [forms of] suffering that arise from wrongful conduct, (14) all the [forms of] suffering of [a state of] progression, (15) the suffering that arises from a lack of knowledge, (16) the suffering that arises from the increase [of the mental afflictions], (17) the suffering that follows necessarily, (18) the experience of suffering, and (19) the suffering of indisposition.

Compassion is called "great compassion" on the basis of four causal factors: (1) [It is a form of compassion] that is developed after one has [mentally] taken hold of the suffering of sentient beings that is profound, subtle, and difficult to realize. (2) [It is a form of compassion] that one has become acquainted with over a long period of time and that one has cultivated for many hundreds of thousands of kalpas. (3) [It is a form of compassion] that has engaged its object with an effort of such intensity that the bodhisattva who is filled with compassion would give up even a hundred lives in order to remove the suffering of beings, let alone a single life or the material possessions [that sustain his or her] physical body. (4) [It is a form of compassion] that is exceedingly pure due to the purity of the [ārya] bodhisattva stage that [has been attained by] those bodhisattvas who have reached the [path's] culmination and [a form of compassion that is exceedingly pure] due to the purity of the stage of a tathāgata that [has been attained by] the tathāgatas.

Now then, those bodhisattvas who meditate upon compassion in relation to sentient beings using these one hundred and ten forms [of suffering] meditate on the complete [form of] bodhisattva compassion. Moreover, they also quickly attain the [form of] compassion that constitutes a purity of attitude—[namely, the compassion] of one who has entered into the [ārya bodhisattva] stage that constitutes a purity of attitude. They also develop a mind that is exceedingly tender toward sentient beings, a mind that is [exceedingly] affectionate [toward sentient beings], a mind that is [exceedingly] desirous of acting [on behalf of sentient beings], a mind that is tireless [in its desire to act on behalf of sentient beings], a mind that is able to endure suffering [as it acts on behalf of sentient beings], and a mind that is both fit and has been brought under control [in order to act on behalf of sentient beings].

Moreover, the mind continuum of a listener ārya who has attained the culmination [of understanding] and possesses a [direct] realization of the truth of suffering, [a mind continuum] that has long since been accompanied by a sense of dissatisfaction [for samsara's suffering], does not engage[1030] [in activities] with the same degree of urgency as [the mind continuum] of a bodhisattva who perceives, with a mind that possesses [great][1031] compassion toward [all] sentient beings, the great mass of one hundred and ten forms of suffering that is being undergone.

There is not any [form of] inner or outer entity that a bodhisattva whose mind is permeated with such compassion would not give up. There is no [form of] moral discipline that he or she would not accept. There is not any [form of] harm inflicted by another that he or she would not endure. There is no application of effort that he or she would not undertake. There is no meditative absorption that he or she would not cultivate. There is no [form of] wisdom that he or she would not develop. Therefore, when the tathāgatas are asked, "Upon what [foundation] does the enlightenment of a bodhisattva rest?" the Ones Who Expound Things Correctly declare: "The enlightenment of a bodhisattva rests upon the foundation of compassion."

Regarding this [topic], each of the immeasurables that have been explained here brings about a bodhisattva's development by means of their immeasurable development. [Each one] acquires immeasurable forms of desirable results.[1032] [Each one] is brought forth by immeasurable forms of virtue that are absolutely irreproachable.

1030. S: *pravartate,* T: *'jug pa*. According to *BBhVy* (f. 222a), "engage" here means that the listener ārya does not pursue the liberation that will bring the elimination of his or her own personal suffering with the same degree of urgency that is possessed by a bodhisattva who seeks to free all sentient beings of their suffering and to establish them in the supreme liberation of buddhahood.

1031. The qualifier "great" appears in the Tibetan translation but not in the two Sanskrit editions.

1032. S: *iṣṭaphalam*. Tibetan translations have *sdud pa'i 'bras bu,* which appears to be a corruption; *BBhVy* (f. 223a) has *'dod pa'i 'bras bu*.

It should be understood that a bodhisattva who is engaged in meditation upon the immeasurables in this manner [obtains] four benefits. (1) From the very outset, [a bodhisattva's] meditation upon the immeasurables promotes his or her abiding in supreme forms of ease during that lifetime. (2) [Meditation upon the immeasurables] promotes the acquisition and collection of immeasurable [forms of] the merit accumulation. (3) It promotes a firmness of attitude in relation to [the pursuit of] true and complete enlightenment. (4) It promotes the ability to endure every [kind of] suffering [while one remains] in samsara for the sake of sentient beings.

Within [Book I of] *The Stage of a Bodhisattva,* [known as] "The Object of Mental Application That Relates to the Support," this completes the sixteenth chapter, entitled "Worship, Service, and the Immeasurables."

17

The Spiritual Qualities That Are Conducive to Enlightenment

Summary verses:

> Shame, firmness, and tirelessness,
> Knowledge of treatises and the world,
> Likewise, the correct forms of reliance
> And the forms of informative knowledge,
>
> The accumulations, the qualities
> Conducive to enlightenment,
> Quiescence, insight, skillful means,
> The retentions, aspirational prayer,
>
> The three concentrations that ought to be known,
> And the four summary statements.

Shame and Abashment [1.17.1]

Regarding this [topic], what are the shame and abashment of bodhisattvas?

In brief, they should be understood in two ways: in terms of (1) their essential nature and (2) their basis.

Shame[1033] is a bodhisattva's [sense of] embarrassment [that is felt] toward objectionable conduct through having realized its impropriety as relates to

1033. S: *hrīḥ,* T: *ngo tsha shes pa*. See also note 678.

oneself. Abashment[1034] is the [sense of] embarrassment [that is felt] toward that very same object out of respect for, or fear[1035] of, others. This [sense of] embarrassment [that is felt] by a bodhisattva is naturally strong, not to mention after it has been developed through repeated practice. This is how a bodhisattva's shame and abashment should be understood in terms of their essential nature.

On the other hand, their basis, in brief, is fourfold. The embarrassment [that is felt] with regard to failing to carry out the practice that a bodhisattva ought to pursue is the first basis. Likewise, the embarrassment [that is felt] with regard to performing activities that a bodhisattva ought to avoid is the second basis. Likewise, a bodhisattva's embarrassment [that is felt] with regard to the concealment of his or her evil deeds is the third basis. Likewise, a bodhisattva's embarrassment [that is felt] with regard to the regret that arises [in response to] his or her own [wrongdoing], along with [the embarrassment that is felt] toward the object that is necessarily relied upon afterward, is the fourth basis.[1036] This is how [shame and abashment] should be understood in terms of their basis.

Firmness [1.17.2]

Regarding this [topic], what is a bodhisattva's development of firmness?

This [quality] also should be regarded in two ways: in terms of (1) its essential nature and (2) its basis.

The quality of restraining one's mind when it has become afflicted, the quality of not allowing oneself to come under the power of the mental afflic-

1034. S: *vyapatrāpyam,* T: *khrel yod pa*. See also note 677.

1035. *BBhVy* (f. 213a): "Fear is the sense of shame that stems from respect, as well as the apprehension about being scorned, both of which can occur either when one is in front of others or when one is not in front of others."

1036. *BBhVy* (f. 223a): "The fourth basis is [the embarrassment that is felt at the prospect of] having committed a transgression and then allowing a long time to go by without confessing it." The "object that is relied upon" (S: *pratisaraṇam,* T: *rton pa*) is an apparent reference to the confession ritual that is a remedy for one's wrongdoing, while the adjective "[which is] necessarily [relied upon] afterward" (S: *ānuṣaṅgikam,* T: *zhar la byung ba*) indicates that one has an obligation to carry out this remedial act subsequent to any misdeeds that one might commit. The Sanskrit *kaukṛtyam* (T: *'gyod pa*), which typically means "regret," appears as *'dod pa* in the Tibetan translations, which is a corruption. This term can also mean "the state of having acted badly." *PSV* (p. 310): "A bad deed is one that is contemptible; [thus,] *kaukṛtyam* means the state of having acted badly."

tions, the quality of having a nature that tolerates suffering, the quality of not wavering from correct practice even in the face of many different and substantial kinds of fear and terror, and the firmness that [arises] either from possessing courage naturally or through careful reflection should be understood as the essential nature of the development of firmness.

In brief, the basis for that development of firmness by bodhisattvas should be understood as being fivefold. [The five aspects are] (1) the occurrence of a variety of samsaric forms of suffering and a variety of mistaken forms of practice that are carried out by disciples; (2) the acceptance of a samsara that is very long-lasting for the sake of sentient beings; (3) teaching the Dharma in a great assembly while one's views are being scrutinized by rivals; (4) the acceptance of all the bodhisattva precepts; and (5) listening to the profound and extensive forms of the Dharma.[1037]

Tirelessness [1.17.3]

Regarding this [topic], the bodhisattvas' quality of remaining mentally tireless in relation to all their correct forms of practice should be understood as being due to five causes. (1) Here a bodhisattva is naturally strong, which keeps him or her from becoming tired. (2) Moreover, that very attribute of remaining mentally tireless is cultivated repeatedly, which keeps him or her from becoming tired. (3) He or she is endowed with [the ability] to initiate a [form of] effort that is supported by skillful means, which, by enabling [the bodhisattva] to perceive different [circumstances] as they occur successively, keeps him or her from becoming tired. (4) [The bodhisattva] possesses a sharp and powerful [form of] discriminating wisdom, which keeps him or her from becoming tired. (5) A bodhisattva's compassionate mind and sympathetic mind remain fixed with great intensity upon sentient beings continually and uninterruptedly, which keeps him or her from becoming tired.

Knowledge of Treatises [1.17.4]

Regarding this [topic], what is a bodhisattva's knowledge of treatises?

Here a bodhisattva is one who has correctly taken up from others the

1037. The identification of these five forms is somewhat problematic. The Tibetan translation suggests that the first basis should be separated into two elements and the final two forms should be combined together to make the fifth aspect.

Dharma that is made up of the collections of names, assertions, and syllables[1038] and that relates to the five branches of learning. He or she also has become well acquainted with [the Dharma] by reciting it aloud. Alternatively, he or she is someone who has become very learned regarding the meaning of that very Dharma [by receiving explanations] from others. Or he or she is someone who on his or her own has reflected well [on those meanings] and reached correct conclusions about them. In addition, the bodhisattva who has gained knowledge of these teachings and their meanings in this manner does not give up this activity, in order to avoid forgetting those teachings and meanings [that have already been learned] and in order to learn additional new and more advanced teachings and meanings. Further, with the perfection of this learning and contemplation, a ripening[1039] [of those activities] created by the passage of time [results in] the attainment of a [form of] clarity[1040] regarding both these teachings and their meanings.

1038. These are three forms of the class of entities known as "formations that do not accompany consciousness." *AS* (p. 11): "What are the collections of names (S: *nāmakāyāḥ,* T: *ming gi tshogs*)? [The phrase] 'collections of names' is a nominal designation [that is ascribed] to the expressions for the essential natures of entities. What are the collections of assertions (S: *pādakāyāḥ,* T: *tshig gi tshogs*)? [The phrase] 'collections of assertions' is a nominal designation [that is ascribed] to the expressions for the distinguishing characteristics of entities. What are the collections of syllables (S: *vyañjanakāyāḥ,* T: *yi ge'i tshogs*)? [The phrase] 'collections of syllables' is a nominal designation [that is ascribed] to the phonemes (S: *akṣaraḥ,* T: *yi ge*) that are the basis for both [the collections of names and the collections of assertions]." *PSV* (pp. 322–333) adds: "Because the essences of dharmas are ineffable, [the word] 'expression' (S: *adhivacanam,* T: *tshig bla dags*) [as it is being used here] means a form of speech that [refers to an essence that] has been [artificially] ascribed. An essence is a unique characteristic (S: *svalakṣaṇam,* T: *rang gi mtshan nyid*). Thus, the term 'name' means a word that indicates the essential nature of an entity, even though [the ultimate nature of] that [essence] is incapable of being expressed. . . . The word 'assertion' (S: *padam,* T: *tshig*) [as it is being used here] means that which causes the meaning of a distinguishing characteristic (S: *viśeṣam,* T: *khyad par*) to be understood. Thus, [the Sanskrit word *padam* as it is being used here] is different from both that of a name and that of the word *padam* [as it is used] in the [everyday] world. . . . Distinguishing characteristics are [attributes] such as impermanence and the like. They [indicate] distinctions that can have the nature of a positive or a negative [meaning], as well as other [propositions] that are inconclusive in nature. Examples include [such statements as] 'All formations are impermanent,' 'All entities are devoid of a self,' and 'Nirvana is peace.' Thus, a name merely states the essence of an entity, while an assertion states the distinguishing characteristics [that pertain to] an entity's essence."

1039. *BBhVy* (f. 224b): "'Ripening' (S: *paripākaḥ,* T: *yongs su smin pa*) means the attainment of [the type of] wisdom that derives from meditation."

1040. *BBhVy* (f. 224b): "The attainment of 'a [form of] clarity' (S: *prasādaḥ,* T: *dang ba*) means a [form of] conviction (S: *adhimokṣaḥ,* T: *lhag par mos pa*), because a realization of

It should be understood that, by means of these elements, a bodhisattva's knowledge of treatises becomes unlimited, complete, and unmistaken.

Knowledge of the World [1.17.5]

Regarding this [topic], what is a bodhisattva's knowledge of the world?

Here a bodhisattva gains, in relation to the world that consists of sentient beings, the following type of true realization. "Alas, this world is in a state of calamity! That is to say, although they take birth, age, die, fall [from a higher state to a lower one][1041] and enter [states of misfortune],[1042] sentient beings still do not correctly discover the deliverance[1043] that lies beyond old age and death."

Moreover, [a bodhisattva] gains a true realization of an era in which the degeneracies[1044] possessed by the world of beings are exceedingly great, as well as an era that is free of the degeneracies and one in which the degeneracies are not exceedingly great. That is to say, he or she does so with regard to the five degeneracies, which are (1) the degeneracy of life spans, (2) the degeneracy of sentient beings, (3) the degeneracy of the mental afflictions, (4) the degeneracy of views, and (5) the degeneracy of a kalpa. For instance, nowadays the life spans of humans are short; an individual who lives a long time lives for [at most around] a hundred years. For instance, nowadays beings to a large extent do not honor their mothers, do not honor their fathers, do not honor spiritual asceticism, do not honor the position of brahmins, do not respect family elders, do not do what is advantageous, do not do what ought to be done, are not fearful of what is objectionable in relation

---

the Dharma and its meaning is gained and because no proponents of opposing views can persuade [the person who has attained this clarity] to give up his or her views."

1041. S: *cyavate 'pi,* T: *'chi pho yang 'chi pho. BBhVy* (f. 225a): "The phrase 'although [the world] falls [from a higher state to a lower one]' means [a loss of life that takes place] in the form and formless realms."

1042. S: *upapadyate 'pi,* T: *skye yang skye mod kyi. BBhVy* (f. 225a): "The phrase 'although [the world] enters [a state of misfortune]' means that one does not attain what has not been attained and that what has been attained does not last—thus, it indicates that one falls into a state of calamity."

1043. S: *niḥsaraṇam,* T: *nges par 'byung ba.* This term is synonymous with nirvana. *AS* (p. 65): "Why does [the truth of cessation] have the characteristic of [being a state of] deliverance? [It has this essential characteristic] because it is a permanent state of well-being."

1044. S: *kaṣāyaḥ,* T: *snyigs ma.* See also note 157.

to this world or the next world, do not practice generosity, do not carry out meritorious acts, do not observe the [one-day] fasting observance,[1045] and do not abide in morality after having accepted it. For instance, nowadays it is evident that [beings] are attached to wickedness[1046] and attached to dishonest ways,[1047] and they become acquainted with many kinds of evil, nonvirtuous activities related to such improper conduct as taking up a weapon, taking up a staff,[1048] strife, quarreling, discord, arguing, guile, deception, dishonesty, and lying. For instance, nowadays many forms of false teachings have appeared that are preceded by the formation of judgments about the meaning of false teachings and that will contribute to the destruction of the true Dharma and the disappearance of the true Dharma. For instance, nowadays frequent famines, which take place when an intermediate kalpa[1049] ends with famine, are being perceived; widespread dis-

1045. S: *upavāsaḥ,* T: *bsnyen gnas.* The Buddhist form of the fasting observance is described in the discipline of individual liberation (see note 683) as a practice for laypersons in which eight forms of abstinence are observed for a twenty-four-hour period: (1) no killing, (2) no stealing, (3) no sexual intercourse, (4) no lying, (5) no drinking of intoxicants, (6) no sitting on high seats, (7) no singing or dancing, or wearing of fragrances or adornments, and (8) no eating food after midday.

1046. S: *adharmarāgaḥ,* T: *chos ma yin pa la 'dod chags pa. BBhVy* (f. 225a–225b): "'One who is attached to wickedness' means one who has engaged in misconduct in relation to the material possessions and sensory pleasures that are the object of improper attention."

1047. S: *viṣamalobhaḥ,* T: *mi mthun pa la chags pa. BBhVy* (f. 225b): "'One who is attached to dishonest ways' means one who seeks wealth in a wrongful manner—such as those who appropriate others' wealth by [engaging in] activities of theft, etc."

1048. S: *śastrādanadaṇḍādānaḥ,* T: *mtshon cha thogs pa dang dbyug pa thogs pa.* As part of the definition of the mental factor anger (S: *krodhaḥ,* T: *khro ba*), *AS* (p. 8) states: "Its action is to give support to such [forms of behavior] as taking up a weapon, taking up a staff, or [some other act of] violence." While the Sanskrit *daṇḍa* (T: *dbyug pa*) does mean "rod," "staff," or "club," the term is also a symbol of judicial authority and punishment, and can stand for all forms of punishment—corporal, verbal, and fiscal; as well as for chastisement, imprisonment, and fines (see MW, p. 466). This same phrase "taking up a staff" is rendered in the Tibetan translation of *AS* as *chad pas gcod pa,* which means "to punish." Butön's commentary to *AS* summarizes the action of anger as initiating all manner of harm to a person's body, life, or wealth.

1049. S: *antarakalpaḥ,* T: *bar gyi bskal pa.* A great kalpa is a span of time measured in terms of four phases: (1) the period during which a region of the universe remains completely empty of any world spheres, (2) the period during which the physical realms of a great triple-thousand world spheres are formed within that region, (3) the period during which those physical realms remain populated by sentient beings, and (4) the period during which those particular triple-thousand world spheres undergo destruction. Each of these phases lasts

eases, which take place when an intermediate kalpa ends with disease, are being perceived; and the widespread taking of life by means of weapons, which takes place when an intermediate kalpa ends with weapons, are being perceived. However, these circumstances did not exist in the past. This is the way in which a bodhisattva is one who knows the world in terms of the world of sentient beings.

In addition, a bodhisattva gains a true realization of the formation and destruction of the external world in that [he or she realizes] the manner in which the external world comes into being and disappears.

A bodhisattva also gains a true realization of the world,[1050] the origination of the world, the cessation of the world, the path that leads to the origination of the world, the path that leads to the cessation of the world, [the manner in which there is] enjoyment[1051] of the world, the disadvantages [of the world], and deliverance[1052] [from the world].

A bodhisattva also realizes in a true manner that the full extent of what is called "the state of being a human"[1053] consists of [the six inner bases] that range from the eye to the mind, the [four] heaps that do not have the nature of form, and a person's body that is made up of the four great elements; that, regarding this [topic], the term "self" or "being" is [nothing more than] a mere appellation; that, regarding this [topic], the assertions "I see forms with the eye," up to "I realize entities with the mind," are mere assertions; and that, regarding this [topic], the expressions [that describe an individual's life, such as,] "He or she was the Long-Lived One who had

---

for a period of twenty intermediate kalpas. The length of an intermediate kalpa is defined by recurring cycles of fluctuating human life spans that take place during the third phase. During the first cycle, human life spans gradually decrease from a maximum number of years to a minimum of ten years. This marks the end of the first intermediate kalpa. This is followed by eighteen cycles during which life spans increase to a maximum and then return to the minimum of ten years. The twentieth and final intermediate kalpa ends when human life spans increase from a minimum of ten years and reach a maximum. Each time human life spans reach the shortest period of ten years, this event is marked variously by outbreaks of widespread murder, pestilence, or famine. Cf. *AK,* ch. 3, vv. 89–93, and v. 99.

1050. *BBhVy* (f. 225b): "[Here the term] 'world' means the five grasping heaps." This paragraph addresses knowledge of the four noble truths.

1051. S: *āsvādam,* T: *ro myang ba. BBhVy* (f. 225b): "'Enjoyment' means the experiencing of [physical] pleasure and mental happiness that is well known in the world."

1052. See note 1043. *BBhVy* (f. 225b): "[The term] 'deliverance' means the abandonment of longing and desire [for the world]."

1053. S: *manuṣyatvam,* T: *mi nyid.*

this name, he or she was from this particular family, he or she was from this particular clan, he or she ate this kind of food, he or she experienced these kinds of happiness and suffering, he or she was long-lived to such an extent, he or she remained alive for such a period, his or her life ended in this way" are [nothing more than] mere expressions.

In this way, a bodhisattva realizes in a true manner (1) the progression of the world of sentient beings,[1054] (2) the progression of the external world,[1055] (3) the eight subjects of investigation that relate to the world,[1056] and (4) the nature of the world in an ultimate sense.[1057] Therefore, he or she is said to be "one who knows the world."

Moreover, after seeing someone who is senior to him- or herself or who has superior spiritual qualities, a bodhisattva addresses [that person] properly and, after standing up, offers a seat to this person and performs acts of salutation, prostration, standing up in his or her presence, making the gesture of joined palms, and respectful behavior.

On the other hand, after seeing someone who is equal to him- or herself in age or spiritual qualities, [a bodhisattva] speaks to [that person] properly

1054. *BBhVy* (f. 226a): "[The phrase] 'progression of the world of sentient beings' means that [beings] are subject to the suffering of [a state of] progression." For a description of the suffering of [a state of] progression see note 1012 and accompanying text.

1055. *BBhVy* (f. 226a): "[The phrase] 'progression of the external world' means its formation and destruction."

1056. *BBhVy* (f. 226a) identifies the eight categories as (1) investigation of the grasping heaps; (2) reliance on the common practices that relate to grasping; (3) the description of the manner in which the world is arranged; (4) the ultimate nature of the world; (5) teaching knowledge of the world in a manner that accords with [correct] knowledge of the world; (6) teaching knowledge of the [external] world in terms of the manner in which it undergoes destruction and formation; (7) practicing correctly, to the best of one's ability, and however is appropriate in relation to the eleven categories of sentient beings; and (8) practicing correctly in relation to oneself. The eleven categories of sentient beings are the ones that are discussed in the following paragraphs. *BBhVy* (f. 226a) identifies the eleven as (1) those who are one's superiors [in age or spiritual qualities]; (2) those who are one's equal; (3) those who are one's inferiors; (4) those lesser persons who seek [something from you]; (5) one's equals who seek [something from you]; (6) one's superiors who seek [something from you]; (7) enemies, friends, and strangers who are experiencing misfortune; (8) those who have no protector; (9) other persons; (10) companions; and (11) those who cause one harm.

1057. This is presumably a reference to knowledge of the insubstantiality of the person (S: *pudgalanairātmyam*, T: *gang zag gi bdag med pa nyid*) and knowledge of the insubstantiality of entities (S: *dharmanairātmyam*, T: *chos kyi bdag med pa nyid*). Asaṅga here makes reference primarily to knowledge of the insubstantiality of the person.

and gives him or her a friendly greeting with gentle and pleasant forms of speech. He or she does not, having resorted to pride, try to raise him- or herself up [in comparison to that person].

In addition, after seeing someone who is his or her lesser either in age or spiritual qualities, [a bodhisattva], according to his or her abilities, encourages [that person] with regard to the enhancement of one's spiritual qualities. He or she makes mention of that person's genuine good qualities, even if they are insignificant. He or she also covers up and does not reveal the genuine faults that would cause that person to become embarrassed. In addition, he or she does not treat that person with contempt.

After realizing that an individual is seeking some matter of a spiritual or material nature, [a bodhisattva] does not turn away or frown. Nor does [a bodhisattva] ridicule that person if he or she should stammer. [A bodhisattva] also does not humiliate a person who has fallen into misfortune. Likewise, [a bodhisattva] speaks in an agreeable manner to all persons—[no matter whether they are] inferior, equal, or superior to him or her. One greets them [all] saying, "Welcome, please draw near," and sets them at ease[1058] in a proper manner. According to one's abilities, one draws them [to the Dharma][1059] in a proper manner, using both spiritual and material methods. [A bodhisattva] does not falsely display toward beings [the appearance] that he or she possesses [a great] depth [of understanding].[1060] One is not haughty because of [possessing] a somewhat elevated status.[1061] One does not fail to attend to beings in whatever manner they are received, whether

1058. S: *pratiśāmakaḥ,* T: *ngal sor 'jug par byed. BBhVy* (f. 226b): "By agreeing to give [petitioners what they are seeking, a bodhisattva] satisfies their wishes, for which [the text] states, '[he or she] sets them at ease.' That is, by allaying their desires, [a bodhisattva] sets them at ease." Note that *BHSD* (p. 369) gives an incorrect explanation of this term.

1059. S: *saṃgrāhakaḥ,* T: *sdud par byed pa.*

1060. S: *kuṭilagāmbhīryopetaḥ,* T: *gya gyus drod mi zin pa dang ldan pa.* Cf. MW (p. 346) entries for the adjectives *gabhīra* and *gambhīra,* as well as (p. 354) for the noun *gāmbhīryam.* The sense of the Tibetan *drod mi zin pa* seems to be that of being "inscrutably wise." *BBhVy* (f. 227a) suggests that one way of conveying a sense of one's gravity is by remaining silent.

1061. S: *na garvitaḥ kena cid evocchrayaviśeṣena;* T: *thos pa'i khyad par 'ga' tsam kyang 'gying bar mi byed do.* Both Sanskrit editions have the noun *ucchrayaḥ,* which means an "elevation," that is, a "high position"; however, the Tibetan translation suggests that the arrogance is due to "learning" (T: *thos pa*). *BBhVy* does not gloss this statement.

they are ill or in good health, using all one's resources[1062] and employing benevolent physical and verbal actions.

Just as with those with whom he or she is acquainted, [a bodhisattva] is also a friend and companion toward all those with whom he or she is not acquainted, and refrains from all antagonism. To the utmost of his or her abilities and with all his or her strength, [a bodhisattva] does what is beneficial for all sentient beings who have no protector and have no refuge. [A bodhisattva] does not, in any manner, cause suffering or mental unhappiness for others but thinks, "I sincerely hope that these [beings] do not remain in a discontented state for even a moment." For this very reason, when he or she laughs with others it is only a proper form of laughter, not one that is improper. He or she also does not use vulgar speech[1063] even when conversing with friends whom there is no risk of offending and in whom he or she has supreme confidence. He or she also does not remain angry with others for a long period of time. Even when angry with others, [a bodhisattva] does not make known sensitive matters relating to them that ought to be kept secret.[1064] When attacked by others, either physically or verbally, after considering the situation carefully, [a bodhisattva] either resorts to the rule of Dharma[1065] or perceives him- or herself alone as being the one who is at fault. He or she is steadfast in mind and avoids being fickle.

1062. S: *sarvopakaraṇaiḥ,* T: *yo byad thams cad kyis.* The Sanskrit noun *upakaraṇaḥ* can mean "act of service" as well as "implement" or "utensil." The Tibetan translation suggests the latter sense, and I have followed that in the English; however, it might also be taken in the sense of "performing every act of service or assistance."

1063. S: *asabhyavacanāni,* T: *tshogs par mi 'byung ba'i tshig.* Literally, "speech that is unfit for an assembly"; both Sanskrit editions wrongly have *asatyavacanāni* ("untrue speech"). *BBhVy* (f. 337a): "The statement 'He or she does not utter vulgar speech' means he or she does not utter disagreeable speech even to a very dear friend." Cf. *MVy* (no. 7193): *asabhyaḥ,* T: *tshogs par mi dbyung ba.*

1064. S: *marmāni,* T: *mtshang.* MW (p. 791): "anything which requires to be kept concealed, secret quality, hidden meaning, any secret or mystery."

1065. S: *dharmatāṃ pratisarati,* T: *chos nyid la rton. BBhVy* (f. 227a): "In order to indicate the principles 'one who has been angered should not respond by causing others to become angry' and 'one who has been beaten should not respond by beating others in return,' the text states, 'When he or she is attacked by others, either physically or verbally,' etc." Thus, Samudramegha seems to take the term "rule of Dharma" (S: *dharmatā,* T: *chos nyid*) here to mean a reference to two of the "four principles that make one a spiritual ascetic" (see note 792).

Steadfast in conduct of body, speech, and mind, [a bodhisattva] turns away from the fourteen impure activities,[1066] covers the six directions,[1067] avoids the four kinds of evil companions,[1068] and is assisted by the four kinds of virtuous friends.[1069] All of these expressions should be understood as they are described in the sutra.[1070]

In relation to the possession of wealth for the purpose of benefiting this life, [a bodhisattva] is energetic, watchful, one who shares the same way of living,[1071] and attains skill in the worldly crafts and occupations. He or she

1066. S: *caturdaśamalakarmāntāpagataḥ,* T: *dri ma'i las kyi mtha' bcu bzhi dang bral ba.* In explaining these fourteen impure activities, *BBhVy* (f. 227b) makes reference to what is undoubtedly the Sanskrit version of the *Sigalovada Sutta:* "Regarding this, the words of the sutra state: 'O son of a householder, there are four afflicted deeds that should be abandoned: killing, stealing, sexual misconduct, and lying. There are four conditions that lead one to commit evil acts: desire, hatred, fear, and ignorance. There are six ways to lose one's wealth: attachment to grain-based or juice-based intoxicating drinks that are a cause of heedlessness, attachment to wandering about at inappropriate times during the night, attachment to shows and social gatherings, attachment to wagering and dice throwing, attachment to evil companions, and attachment to laziness and idleness.' Through abandoning these fourteen impure activities, one attains the quality of having turned away from the fourteen impure activities."

1067. S: *ṣaddigbhāgapraticchanaḥ,* T: *yan phyogs drug gis bkab pa.* This is also a reference to a section of the *Sigalovada Sutta.* The east represents one's parents; the south, one's teachers and preceptors; the west, one's spouse and children; the north, one's friends and associates; the nadir, one's servants; and the zenith, monks and brahmins. These six groups of individuals are to be supported and favored in an appropriate manner.

1068. S: *catuḥpāpamitraparivarjitaḥ,* T: *sdig pa'i grogs po bzhi spangs pa. BBhVy* (ff. 227b–228a): "Regarding the phrase '[a bodhisattva] avoids the four kinds of evil companions,' the four kinds of evil companion are (1) one who appropriates another's wealth, (2) an evil companion who pretends to be a virtuous friend, (3) one who only knows how to flatter using insincere speech, and (4) a companion in misfortune."

1069. S: *catuḥkalyāṇamitraparigṛhītaḥ,* T: *dge ba'i bshes gnyen bzhis yongs su bzung ba. BBhVy* (f. 228a): "The four kinds of virtuous friends are (1) one who is helpful, (2) one who behaves the same toward suffering and happiness, (3) one who reveals what is useful, and (4) one who is sympathetic."

1070. *BBhVy* (f. 228a): "as described in the *Sutra of the Tufted One* (T: *gTsug phud can gyi mdo*)." As mentioned in note 1066, this appears to be a reference to a Sanskrit version of the *Sigalovada Sutta.*

1071. S: *samajīvī,* T: *mthun pas 'tsho ba. BBhVy* (f. 228a): "In relation to [ownership of] property, [the text] states: [A bodhisattva is] 'one who shares the same way of living.' [This quality is] illustrated by the verse that states 'he or she satisfies him- or herself' . . . up to 'he or she trains in the precepts.'" The source of this reference was not identified. This is perhaps a reference to working at a trade or skill in conjunction with others.

does not engage in guile or deceit and is not disposed to cheating others. He or she possesses a sense of shame in relation to blameworthy conduct. He or she is possessed of excellent conduct by being earnest about that [quality] and by being watchful of his or her conduct. He or she avoids doing harm to the property of others that has been entrusted to him or her. He or she does not break his or her word [by defaulting] on a loan that is taken from others. He or she does not defraud a relative with whom he or she shares an inheritance. He or she will not cheat by deception those who are unaware [of the value of something], from a jewel or any object considered precious down to a [single] *kārṣāpaṇa*[1072] coin.

Similarly, [a bodhisattva] is also skilled in the principles of ordinary secular behavior and the acts that are beneficial to the world. When requested by others to provide assistance with regard to various matters that need to be accomplished, [a bodhisattva] does so; he or she does not shrink from [that request] and does not equivocate.[1073] He or she undertakes [to carry out] an activity in an excellent manner, not in an improper manner. When governing, [a bodhisattva] does so in a just manner, not in an unjust manner. He or she also does not take pleasure in [meting out] punishments. After turning the general populace away from immorality, he or she causes them to take up morality. Similarly, [a bodhisattva] is endowed with the eight forms of noble expression—that is, he or she is endowed with the qualities of saying in relation to something that was seen, "I saw it"; in relation to something that was heard, "I heard it"; in relation to something that was thought, "I thought it"; in relation to something that was realized, "I realized it"; in relation to something that was not seen, "I did not see it"; in relation to something that was not heard, "I did not hear it"; in relation to something that was not thought, "I did not think it"; and in relation to something that was not realized, "I did not realize it." A bodhisattva who is endowed with these kinds of qualities knows in a true manner everything as it ought to be understood in relation to the world and [everything] as it relates to [the

1072. The term, which literally means "weighing a *karṣa*," is the name for the ancient minted coinage in the Indian subcontinent. The earliest forms were pieces of silver of any shape but of a specific weight and did not carry any inscription but rather bore a number of symbols that were punched on the coin. The term can also mean "money" or "gold and silver" in a general sense.

1073. S: *nānyenānyaṃ pratisarati*, T: *gtam rlung la mi bskur ba*. *BBhVy* (f. 228b): "'To equivocate' means when you are asked one thing you answer with something else—that is, you do not answer the question that was asked."

conduct] that ought to be observed in the world. Therefore, he or she is said to be "one who knows the world."

The Four Reliances [1.17.6]

Regarding this [topic], how does a bodhisattva apply him- or herself to the four reliances?[1074]

Here a bodhisattva listens to the Dharma from another person as one who is seeking meaning, not as one who is seeking an excellent form of literary expression. As one who seeks meaning when listening to the Dharma and not one who seeks [an excellent form of] literary expression, the bodhisattva who relies on meaning even listens respectfully to Dharma teachings that are given using vernacular speech.

Moreover, a bodhisattva knows both "black" expressions and "great" expressions[1075] as they truly are. Knowing this, he or she relies on correctness;[1076] he or she does not rely on a person, thinking "These teachings were spoken by an elder,[1077] a learned person,[1078] the Tathāgata, or [a member of] the Sangha." Relying on correctness in this way and not relying on the person, he or she does not waver from those meanings that relate to

1074. S: *catvāri pratisaraṇāni,* T: *rton pa bzhi.* They are traditionally described in the following manner: (1) one should rely upon the Dharma, not the person; (2) one should rely upon the meaning, not the literal form of expression; (3) one should rely upon the sutras whose meaning is definitive, not the sutras whose meanings are provisional; and (4) one should rely upon [transcendent] knowledge, not ordinary consciousness. Asaṅga does not discuss them here in the same order.

1075. See note 592 for a description of these two terms.

1076. S: *yuktipratiśaranaḥ,* T: *rigs pa la rton pa.* This reliance is typically expressed as "one should rely upon the Dharma, not the person." *BBhVy* (f. 228b): "Regarding the phrase '[a bodhisattva knows both] black expressions and great expressions,' [it means that he or she understands them] in an unmuddled manner—that is, he or she knows what is correct (S: *yuktijñaḥ,* T: *rigs pa shes pa*) [about them]. Therefore, the text states, 'he or she relies on correctness.'"

1077. S: *sthaviraḥ,* T: *gnas brtan. BBhVy* (f. 228b): "The term 'elder' means one who abides firmly in the true nature of things (S: **dharmatām sthirasthito,* T: *chos nyid la gnas pa brtan pa*); that is to say, it is one who is proficient in his or her practice (S: **pratipattimān,* T: *sgrub pa dang ldan pa*)."

1078. S: *abhijñātaḥ pudgalaḥ,* T: *shes pa'i gang zag. BBhVy* (f. 228b): "A 'learned person' is one who is revered by everyone as a teacher (S: *ācāryaḥ,* T: *slob dpon*); it means a person who has extensive learning (S: *bahuśrutaḥ,* T: *mang du thos pa*)."

the true nature of things and also does not depend upon others as relates to [how to properly understand the meaning of] Dharma teachings.

Moreover, a bodhisattva whose faith and purity of mind toward the Tathāgata are firmly placed, and who is singularly devoted to [the Tathāgata's] speech, relies upon the Tathāgata's sutras that are of definitive meaning; he or she does not rely on [the sutras] that are of provisional meaning. A bodhisattva who relies on the sutras that are of definitive meaning cannot be led away from this [spiritual system of] Dharma and Vinaya. That is to say, the distinctions relating to the subjects that are mentioned in a variety of ways in the sutras of provisional meaning are such that one cannot form definite opinions about them and [therefore] they are a source of uncertainty. Furthermore, if a bodhisattva is uncertain about [how to correctly understand] the sutras of definitive meaning, then he or she can be led away from this [spiritual system of] Dharma and Vinaya.

Moreover, a bodhisattva is one who regards the [transcendent] knowledge that is gained through realization [of the Dharma's meaning] as most important, not the [ordinary] comprehension of the Dharma teachings and their meanings that is gained merely through listening and reflection. Having realized that what one understands with the [transcendent] knowledge that derives from meditation cannot be understood with the [ordinary] comprehension that is gained merely through [the activities of] listening and reflection, he or she does not, after having listened to the most profound Dharma teachings that were explained by the tathāgatas, reject or criticize them.

This is the manner in which a bodhisattva practices the four reliances. Moreover, this is also the manner in which he or she becomes skilled in their practice. Regarding this [topic], in relation to these four reliances there is, in brief, an authoritativeness of the four that is revealed: (1) that which pertains to the meaning that was taught, (2) that which pertains to its correctness, (3) that which pertains to the Teacher, and (4) that which pertains to the knowledge that consists of spiritual realization and that derives from meditation. Moreover, the four reliances jointly elucidate the unerring means of [attaining] deliverance for a bodhisattva who has undertaken the correct form of practice.

The Four Forms of Informative Knowledge [1.17.7]

What are the four [forms of] informative knowledge[1079] that are possessed by bodhisattvas?

The knowledge that derives from meditation and is unimpeded[1080] and unhampered[1081] with regard to all the verbal formulations that pertain to all Dharma teachings, both in terms of the full range [of entities] and in terms of their true nature, is [the bodhisattvas'] informative knowledge of the Dharma.[1082] Further, the knowledge that derives from meditation and is unimpeded and unhampered with regard to all the [defining] characteristics [of the entities mentioned] in all Dharma teachings, both in terms of the full range [of entities] and in terms of their true nature, is [the bodhisattvas'] informative knowledge of meanings.[1083] Moreover, the knowledge that

1079. S: *catasraḥ pratisaṃvidaḥ,* T: *so so yang dag par rig pa bzhi. MSA,* ch. 18, v. 37: "Having realized [the ultimate] sameness [of all entities] / For oneself, that which subsequently imparts knowledge [to others] / In order to eliminate all doubt / Is how informative knowledge is literally explained."

1080. S: *asaktam,* T: *thogs pa med cing. BBhVy* (ff. 229b–230a): "The term 'unimpeded' means that [a bodhisattva] possessing this form of knowledge who has heard all verbal formulations from someone else never experiences any impediment when engaging in practice such that he or she wonders, 'What is the signification of this term?'"

1081. S: *avivartyam,* T: *mi bzlog pa. BBhVy* (f. 230a): "The term 'unhampered' means that [a bodhisattva who possesses this form of knowledge] is not deterred by others when he or she is teaching [verbal formulations that relate to the Dharma]."

1082. S: *dharmapratisaṃvid,* T: *chos so so yang dag par rig pa. AKV* (vol. 4, p. 1102): "With regard to the expression 'informative knowledge of the Dharma,' in this usage [the term 'Dharma'] refers to the Dharma of instruction (S: *deśanādharmaḥ,* T: *bstan pa'i chos*), since the term 'Dharma' has multiple meanings. For example, [when the Buddha declared:] 'O *bhikṣus,* I shall instruct you in the Dharma. I shall reveal [to you the Dharma] that is good in the beginning, middle, and end, that is excellent in meaning, excellent in expression, unique, complete, pure, and relates to a spiritual life,' in this context [the term 'Dharma'] refers to the Dharma of instruction." *MSAVṛBh* (Tg. vol. 126, f. 99a): "Knowledge of the number of synonyms there are for a single entity and knowledge of how many formulations such as being virtuous, nonvirtuous, and the like, apply to entities is called 'informative knowledge of the Dharma.' Knowledge of the synonyms for an entity means, for example, to know all the synonyms that there are for a term such as 'ignorance' (S: *avidyā,* T: *ma rig pa*), which include 'delusion' (S: *mohaḥ,* T: *gti mug*), 'absence of knowledge' (S: *ajñānam,* T: *mi shes pa*), '[mental] darkness' (S: *tamas,* T: *mun pa*), '[mental] blindness' (S: *andhakāra,* T: *mun nag*), and the like. This is the definition of informative knowledge of the Dharma."

1083. S: *arthapratisaṃvid,* T: *don so so yang dag par rig pa. MSAVṛBh* (Tg. vol. 126, ff. 98b–99a): "Unimpeded knowledge of the general and individual characteristics of entities is

derives from meditation and is unimpeded and unhampered with regard to all the [forms of] clear expression that pertain to all Dharma teachings, both in terms of the full range [of entities] and in terms of their true nature, is [the bodhisattvas'] informative knowledge of clear expression.[1084] In addition, the knowledge that derives from meditation and is unimpeded and unhampered with regard to every manner and kind of point relating to all forms of Dharma teachings, both in terms of the full range [of entities] and in terms of their true nature, is [the bodhisattvas'] informative knowledge [that confers] eloquence.[1085]

It should be understood that, on the basis of these four forms of informative knowledge, bodhisattvas attain immeasurably great skill regarding five subjects: (1) skill regarding the heaps,[1086] (2) skill regarding the constituents,[1087]

---

called 'informative knowledge of meanings.' [Regarding] individual characteristics, the individual characteristic of earth is hardness, the individual characteristic of water is fluidity, and so forth. General characteristics are those of impermanence, suffering, emptiness, and selflessness. This is the definition of informative knowledge of meanings."

1084. S: *niruktipratisaṃvid,* T: *nge tshig so so yang dag par rig pa. MSAVṛBh* (Tg. vol. 126, f. 99a–99b): "Unimpeded knowledge of sentient beings' separate and various forms of language and speech is called 'informative knowledge of clear expression.' It is knowledge of all the languages of such sentient beings as gods and *nāgas,* etc. . . . Alternatively, unimpeded knowledge of the statements contained in all grammar treatises is called 'informative knowledge of clear expression.'"

1085. S: *pratibhānapratisaṃvid,* T: *spobs pa so so yang dag par rig pa. MSAVṛBh* (Tg. vol. 126, f. 99b): "[The eloquence] that is able to explain a single entity for a kalpa or until the end of a kalpa, that does not run out of words when giving explanations, and that possesses the knowledge that is able to respond to all arguments, even if all sentient beings were to raise some form of verbal opposition, is called 'informative knowledge [that confers] eloquence.'"

1086. S: *skandhakauśalyam,* T: *phung po la mkhas pa.* This is a reference to proficiency in the topic of the five heaps of form, feelings, conception, formations and consciousness. See *ŚBh,* p. 243, which states in part: "What is skill regarding the heaps? It is [an understanding] which knows the entities as they have been described [i.e., the entities that make up the five heaps] in terms of their distinct natures and their multiple natures, and which does not perceive or conceive of anything beyond them. This, in brief, is what is called 'skill regarding the heaps.'"

1087. S: *dhātukauśalyam,* T: *khams la mkhas pa.* This is a reference to the formulation of eighteen categories into which all entities are classified. Six constituents are faculties, six are outer objects, and six are forms of consciousness. *ŚBh* (p. 245): "Further, [the understanding] that realizes, approves of, and closely reflects upon [the fact] that each of these eighteen [categories of] entities comes into existence, originates, and appears from its own constituent (S: *dhātuḥ,* T: *khams*), its own seed (S: *bījam,* T: *sa bon*), and its own class (S: *gotraḥ,* T: *rigs*) is referred to as 'skill regarding the constituents.'" *AKB* (p. 13): "Just as the

(3) skill regarding the bases,[1088] (4) skill regarding dependent origination,[1089] and (5) skill regarding proper and improper conditions.[1090] By means of

---

many deposits (S: *gotrāṇi,* T: *rigs*) of iron, copper, silver, gold, and the like [that are found] on a single mountain are called 'constituents' (S: *dhātavaḥ,* T: *khams*) [more precisely, this usage is one that means "ore"], the eighteen classes (S: *gotrāṇi,* T: *rigs*) [of entities] that exist within a single support or continuum are called the 'eighteen constituents' (S: *dhātavaḥ,* T: *khams*). In this case, sources (S: *ākarāḥ,* T: *'byung gnas*) are being called 'classes' (S: *gotrāṇi,* T: *rigs*)." Vasubandhu adds that this interpretation of "class" (*gotram*) is meant to indicate that each category of entity is the cause from which its future instances arise. For example, the prior moments of the eye, etc., are the source and "like cause" (S: *sabhāgahetuḥ,* T: *skal ba mnyam pa'i rgyu*) from which their subsequent forms arise.

1088. S: *ayatānakauśalyam,* T: *skye mched la mkhas pa*. The twelve bases are made up of the six faculties (inner bases) and the six objects (outer bases) that are the principal causes for the arising of consciousness. *ŚBh* (pp. 246–247): "What is skill regarding the bases? Regarding this [topic], the eye is the governing condition (S: *adhipatipratyayaḥ,* T: *bdag po'i rkyen*), [visible] forms are the objective condition (S: *ālambanapratyayaḥ,* T: *dmigs pa'i rkyen*), and the mind immediately following its cessation is the homogeneous immediate condition (S: *samanatarapratyayaḥ,* T: *mtshungs pa de ma thag pa'i rkyen*) for the arising of eye consciousness together with its associated [mental factors]. . . . [The description] is the same up to . . . the mind [in the moment immediately following its cessation] is the homogeneous immediate condition, the form of attention that arises from that [mind] is the governing condition, and entities are the objective condition for the arising of the mind consciousness, together with its associated [mental factors]. This is how the appearance of the six groups of consciousness, together with their associated [mental factors], comes about by means of three conditions: the homogeneous immediate condition, the objective condition, and the governing condition. The skill regarding the conditions that pertain in this way to the inner and outer bases is called 'skill regarding the bases.'" See note 547 for a description of the three types of condition (S: *pratyayaḥ,* T: *rkyen*) mentioned here.

1089. S: *pratītyasamutpādakauśalyam,* T: *rten ching 'brel bar 'byung ba la mkhas pa*. *ŚBh* (pp. 248–249): "What is skill regarding dependent origination? Entities alone are what activate entities, entities alone are what generate entities, and formations alone are the factors that bring forth entities. Thus, because [entities] are made to arise by causes and they are made to arise dependently, they come into being without having previously existed and, after having come into being, they disappear once again. Therefore, these formations are impermanent. Moreover, those [formations] that are impermanent have the qualities of undergoing birth, old age, sickness, death, sorrow, lamentation, suffering, misery, despair, and tribulation. Because they have the qualities ranging from birth to tribulation, they have a nature that consists of suffering. Those things that are subject to suffering have no control over their existence; they are powerless and devoid of any self. On the basis of these points, the knowledge of the impermanence, suffering, and selflessness that pertain to the entities that arise dependently is called 'skill regarding dependent origination.'"

1090. S: *sthānāsthānakauśalyam,* T: *gnas dang gnas ma yin pa la mkhas pa*. *ŚBh* (p. 249): "Further, skill regarding proper and improper conditions should be understood as being that very [skill in relation to] dependent origination. Regarding that, this is its special

these four types [of informative knowledge], a bodhisattva becomes highly realized regarding all Dharma teachings and most proficient at revealing [that knowledge] to others. If there is nothing higher than this about which [a bodhisattva] can gain perfect knowledge, how could there be anything [higher] to reveal to others?

The Two Accumulations [I.17.8]

Regarding this [topic], what is a bodhisattva's accumulation that leads to enlightenment?

It should be regarded as being twofold: (1) the accumulation of merit and (2) the accumulation of wisdom. Moreover, it should be understood that this twofold form of accumulation has an extensive classification, for example as was presented in the chapter entitled "One's Own and Others' Aims."[1091]

Furthermore, this accumulation of merit and wisdom should be understood as small during a bodhisattva's first period of countless kalpas,[1092] middling during the second [period of countless kalpas], and great during the third [period of countless kalpas].

---

characteristic. Skill regarding proper and improper conditions realizes the nature of being a compatible cause. There are results that constitute the ripening of virtuous and nonvirtuous deeds. The results that are the ripening of virtuous deeds are favorable. The results that are the ripening of nonvirtuous deeds are unfavorable. The knowledge of the manner in which this is so is called 'skill regarding proper and improper conditions.'" See also Book III, chapter 6, the section entitled "The Power of Knowledge regarding Proper and Improper Conditions" [III.6.2.1].

1091. See Book I, chapter 3, the section entitled "Merit and Wisdom" [I.3.5.2, I.3.6.2]. See also note 417 for a literal interpretation (S: *niruktiḥ,* T: *nges tshig*) of the term "accumulation."

1092. *BBhVy* (f. 230a): "[The first period of countless kalpas, during which] one's practice is based upon conviction, is considered small, because it lacks [the qualities of] fervent effort (S: **uttaptavīryam,* T: *brtson 'grus 'bar ba*), and the like." Note that the verbal root from which the past participle *uttapta* is derived means "to make warm or hot," "to heat thoroughly," "to press hard," "to shine forth," "to give out heat" (MW, p. 177). The past participle also seems to have a meaning of to be "bathed" or "washed." The Tibetan translation that appears in the main text is *sbyangs ba* ("practiced" or "refined"); here in *BBhVy* it is rendered as *'bar ba* ("ablaze"). See also the reference to three periods of countless kalpas in Book I, chapter 6, the section entitled "The Characteristics of Persons Who Are Spiritually Ripe" [I.6.6] and Book II, chapter 4, the section entitled "Concluding Remarks" [II.4.13].

The Thirty-Seven Spiritual Qualities That Are Conducive to Enlightenment [I.17.9]

How does a bodhisattva practice the thirty-seven factors that are conducive to enlightenment?[1093]

Here, relying upon the four forms of informative knowledge and on the basis of the wisdom that is supported by means,[1094] a bodhisattva comes to know the thirty-seven spiritual qualities that are conductive to enlightenment as they truly are; however, he or she does not [fully] actualize them. He or she also comes to know them as they truly are according to the systems of the two vehicles—that is, according to the system of the Listeners' Vehicle and the system of the Great Vehicle. Regarding this [point], [to say that] one comes to know [them] as they truly are according to the system of the Listeners' Vehicle [means] that this entire topic should be understood as it is explained in *The Stage of a Listener*.[1095]

How does a bodhisattva come to know the thirty-seven spiritual qualities that are conducive to enlightenment as they truly are according to the system of the Great Vehicle?

Here a bodhisattva dwells in relation to the body as one who watches the body, but he or she does not conceive of the body as a body that exists. Nor does he or she [conceive of the body] as being completely, and in every way, nonexistent. [That is to say], he or she accurately realizes the ineffable state of being that is the body's true nature. This is his or her ultimate form of closely placed recollection that consists of watching the body in relation

1093. S: *saptatriṃśat bodhipakṣyadharmāḥ*, T: *byang chub kyi phyogs kyi chos sum cu rtsa bdun*. See note 101 for a list of the seven groups that make up these thirty-seven practices.

1094. S: *upāyaparigṛhitena jñānena*, T: *thabs kyis yongs su zing pa'i ye shes kyis*. *BBhVy* (f. 230b): "To be 'supported by means' means to be accompanied by correctness (S: **yuktisamanvāgataḥ*, T: *rigs pa dang yang dag par ldan pa*) and not to be practiced in an improper manner. [Wisdom that is supported by means] is a form of wisdom that understands in a true manner the spiritual qualities that are conducive to enlightenment by means of [the four forms of] informative knowledge. What is that? [It means that they are to be practiced] in such a way that they are not fully actualized (S: **asākṣātkṛtamukhena*, T: *mngon sum du ma byas pa'i sgo nas*)." In other words, they are not practiced in order to achieve nirvana solely to eliminate one's own personal suffering.

1095. *ŚBh*, pp. 288–330. A detailed examination of how the "four closely placed recollections" (S: *catvāri smṛtyupasthānāni*, T: *dran par nye bar bzhag pa bzhi*) are practiced in the Listeners' Vehicle can be found in *Inner Science*, pp. 138–192. A discussion of how the practice differs in the Great Vehicle tradition is also addressed in ibid., pp. 216–223.

to the body. Moreover, it should be understood that, for the conventional method of practice, the closely placed recollection that consists of watching the body in relation to the body corresponds to a bodhisattva's knowledge of an immeasurable number of doctrinal formulations.[1096] The remaining [three] forms of closely placed recollection and the remaining forms of the [thirty-seven] spiritual qualities that are conducive to enlightenment should be understood in a manner that is similar to [this description of] the closely placed recollection that consists of watching the body in relation to the body.

[A bodhisattva] does not conceive of the entities that consist of the body, etc.,[1097] as [constituting a real form of] suffering or [constituting a real form of] origination. He or she also does not conceive of the abandonment that is accomplished by means of this [practice] as a [real form of] cessation and does not conceive of the causes that bring about the attainment of that [abandonment] as a [real] path. Moreover, he or she accurately realizes the true nature of suffering, the true nature of origination, the true nature of cessation, and the true nature of the path, in terms of the ineffable state of being that is their true nature. This represents [a bodhisattva's] meditation on the ultimate nature of the [four noble] truths, in a manner that relies upon meditation upon the [thirty-seven] spiritual qualities that are conducive to enlightenment. By contrast, the bodhisattva's conventional form of meditation upon the object of the [four noble] truths should be regarded as corresponding to [his or her] knowledge of an immeasurable number of doctrinal formulations.

1096. This is a reference to the numerous conventional ways of practicing closely placed recollection of the body. For example, *ŚBh* (pp. 291–292) mentions thirty-five types of physical object, both animate and inanimate, toward which one should develop closely placed recollection. Also, closely placed recollection can be practiced both as a meditation exercise while seated on a cushion and as a method of cultivating vigilance while one is engaged in ordinary activities such as walking, sitting, standing still, or lying down. Other traditional forms of practice include watching the breath, meditating on the body's unattractiveness in terms of both inner and outer impurities, and analyzing the body's four primary elements and their relation with the derivative form of the five sense objects and the five sense faculties. See *Inner Science*, pp. 138–162.

1097. The remaining three objects that form the basis for practicing closely placed recollection are (1) feelings, (2) the mind, and (3) entities (i.e., virtuous and nonvirtuous mental factors and pure and impure mental states). These four categories are coextensive with the five heaps.

QUIESCENCE AND INSIGHT [I.17.10]

Regarding this [topic], a bodhisattva's avoidance of conceptualization in relation to these spiritual qualities[1098] should be regarded as his or her [practice of] quiescence.[1099] In addition, the knowledge of these spiritual qualities that accurately realizes their ultimate nature and the knowledge of the immeasurable doctrinal formulations that are made in relation to them should be regarded as [a bodhisattva's practice of] insight.

Regarding this [topic], in brief a bodhisattva's [practice of] quiescence should be understood as having four aspects: (1) that which is the necessary antecedent of ultimate and conventional forms of knowledge; (2) that which is the result of ultimate and conventional forms of knowledge; (3) that which conveys [the mind to its object] effortlessly in relation to all elaborative conceptions;[1100] and (4) that which, by virtue of [both] the signlessness[1101] [that occurs] in relation to the ineffable bare substance [of entities] and the tranquility of the mind that does not engage in conceptualization, leads to [the experiencing of] the single taste that is the sameness of all entities. By means of these four aspects, the bodhisattvas' path of quiescence is practiced continually until the knowledge-perception of unsurpassed true and complete enlightenment has been perfected and achieved.

Regarding this [topic], in brief the bodhisattvas' [practice of] insight

1098. *BBhVy* (f. 231a) indicates that this is a reference to the fact that quiescence and insight are practiced in relation to the thirty-seven spiritual qualities that are conducive to enlightenment. Regarding the term "avoidance of conceptualization" (S: *nirvikalpanā*, T: *rnam par mi rtog pa*), *BBhVy* makes reference to a form of meditation object that is described in *ŚBh* (pp. 194–195) as a "nonconceptual image" (S: *nirvikalpapratibimbam*, T: *rnam par rtog pa med pa'i gzugs brnyan*). This is the name of the form of meditation object that is used in the cultivation of quiescence. In this type of meditation, the practitioner takes hold of the meditation object but does not examine or investigate it in any way. Instead, he or she stills the mind by holding on to the meditation object using the techniques that relate to the practice of quiescence.

1099. S: *śamathaḥ*, T: *zhi gnas*. Asaṅga presents extensive instruction relating to this topic throughout Books II and III of *ŚBh*.

1100. *BBhVy* (f. 231b): "[This is a form of quiescence] that conveys [the mind to its object] without bringing to mind any conceptions of conventional entities and conveys [the mind to its object] effortlessly. [That is,] because it is an ineffable state in which [the mind] has been isolated from [ordinary forms of] attention."

1101. S: *nirnimittatayā*, T: *mtshan ma med pa'i tshul gyis*. *BBhVy* (f. 231b): "'Signlessness' means the [state of separation] in which [the mind] has been isolated from [forms of attention] that bring to mind [entities] such as form, etc."

should be understood as having four aspects: (1) the [form of] insight for which the four aspects of quiescence are a necessary antecedent; (2) [the form of insight] that avoids the extreme of the wrongful notion that is an [act of] imputation[1102] [made] in relation to all entities; (3) [the form of insight] that avoids the extreme of the wrongful notion that is an [act of] denial[1103] [made in relation to all entities]; and (4) [the form of insight] that corresponds to an immeasurable number of distinct doctrinal formulations. By means of these four aspects, the bodhisattvas' path of insight is practiced continually until the knowledge-perception of unsurpassed true and complete enlightenment has been perfected and achieved. This is a brief description of the bodhisattvas' [practice of] quiescence and insight.

Skillful Means [1.17.11]

Regarding this [topic], what is the skillful means of bodhisattvas?

In brief, there are twelve aspects—six are inner forms that have to do with [one's own] attainment of a buddha's spiritual qualities and six are outer forms that have to do with the spiritual ripening of sentient beings.

Six Inner Forms of Skillful Means [1.17.11.1]

What are the six inner forms of skillful means that have to do with [one's own] attainment of a buddha's spiritual qualities?

They are (1) a bodhisattva's [sympathetic] regard toward all sentient beings that is accompanied by compassion; (2) the knowledge of all conditioned entities as they truly are; (3) the eagerness for the knowledge of unsurpassed true and complete enlightenment; (4) the refusal to abandon samsara based upon one's regard for sentient beings; (5) [a bodhisattva's] continued rebirth in samsara in a manner that avoids becoming afflicted based upon his or her thorough knowledge of conditioned entities as they truly are; and (6) the intensity of effort that is based upon one's eagerness for a buddha's knowledge. These should be understood as the six inner forms

1102. S: *samāropaḥ*, T: *sgro 'dogs pa*. The imputation is of a mode of being that does not exist.

1103. S: *apavādaḥ*, T: *skur ba 'debs pa*. See Book I, chapter 4, the section entitled "The Form of Application That Establishes the Meaning of Ultimate Reality" [I.4.6] for a description of both "the imputation of something that does not truly exist" and "the denial of something that does truly exist."

of skillful means that have to do with [one's own] attainment of a buddha's spiritual qualities.

Six Outer Forms of Skillful Means [1.17.11.2]

What are the six outer forms of skillful means that have to do with the spiritual ripening of sentient beings?

They are (1) the skillful means through which a bodhisattva causes limited roots of virtue to have immeasurable results; (2) likewise, [the skillful means through which a bodhisattva] causes extensive and immeasurable roots of virtue to be developed and collected with little effort; and, likewise, [the skillful means through which a bodhisattva] (3) removes the animosity felt by those beings who have a hostile attitude toward the Buddha's teaching, (4) causes those who have a neutral attitude [toward the Buddha's teaching] to take it up, (5) ripens those who have taken it up, and (6) liberates those who have become ripened.

Causing Limited Roots of Virtue to Have Immeasurable Results [1.17.11.2.1]

Regarding this [topic], how does a bodhisattva cause beings' limited roots of virtue to have immeasurable results?

Here a bodhisattva causes any being whatsoever to give even an insignificant object, including something as small as a handful of barley meal, to an insignificant "field,"[1104] even one as lowly as a sentient being of the animal birth state. Having completed an act of giving, [a bodhisattva] causes [that being] to dedicate [his or her virtue] to unsurpassed true and complete enlightenment. In this manner, by the power of dedication, a root of virtue that is small, both in terms of its object and its field, is caused to have an unlimited result.

Causing Beings to Generate Extensive Roots of Virtue with Little Effort [1.17.11.2.2]

How does a bodhisattva cause beings to generate extensive and immeasurable roots of virtue with little effort?

1104. S: *kṣetram*, T: *zhing*. This term refers to the recipient of a virtuous act. *AK* (ch. 4, v. 117ab): "A field is distinguished by migratory state, suffering, benefit, and virtuous qualities."

Here a bodhisattva points out the noble [one-day] fasting observance[1105] that is made up of eight precepts to beings who are devoted to such forms of wrongful practice as the month-long fast in which food is not eaten, etc. He or she causes them to give up their devotion to the form of fasting that involves hardship and brings about an undesirable result, and causes them to take up this [Buddhist] fasting observance that is easy to undertake and brings a great result. Similarly, he or she points out the Middle Way that is free of the two extremes to beings who are desirous of [achieving] liberation but who engage in practices that consist of self-mortification and who have applied themselves in a wrongful manner, and causes them to take up that [Middle Way]. Similarly, he or she points out correct forms of meditative absorption to beings who are desirous of being reborn in a celestial realm but who have applied themselves in a wrongful manner with such practices as entering fire, falling from a precipice, and abstaining from [eating] food, etc., so that they may abide in a state of ease in their current lives and so that they can effortlessly and with [physical] ease and mental satisfaction be reborn in a celestial realm in the future. In addition, he or she causes those who believe that receiving explanations of Vedic sacred formulas and performing their recitation will lead to a state of purification to take up [instead] the activities of receiving explanations of the Buddha's word, engaging in its recitation, and reflecting on its meaning. Moreover, he or she lays open and clarifies the profound Dharma teachings on emptiness that were spoken by the Tathāgata in such ways that, after hearing them, others are caused to generate intense aversion [for samsaric suffering] and intense faith [in the Three Jewels]. If even a single moment of a mind that possesses [such] aversion and faith is considered[1106] to collect extensive roots of virtue, how much more would this be true for a continuous series [of such a mind].

Moreover, a bodhisattva is devoted to the worship of the Three Jewels of the Buddha, Dharma, and Sangha with a reverential superior attitude and with every kind of excellent and outstanding flower garland and every variety of incense that there is in the world and also causes others throughout the ten directions to develop [the same kind of] devotion. In addition, filling all the directions with that very reverential superior attitude, he or she rejoices at all [forms of] worship of the Three Jewels and causes others

1105. See note 1045.

1106. S: *saṃkhyāṃ gacchati*. The Tibetan translation incorrectly read *grogs su 'gro;* it should read *grangs su 'gro*.

to rejoice at them as well. In addition, he or she practices recollection of the Buddha, recollection of the Dharma, etc., up to recollection of deities, continuously and uninterruptedly, and also causes others to take up [these practices]. Furthermore, he or she uses the time in a productive manner by paying homage to the Three Jewels with forms of mental discourse[1107] and causes [others] to do so as well. Also, he or she rejoices at all the merit of all sentient beings and causes [others] to rejoice as well. Moreover, with a superior attitude that is imbued with extensive compassion toward all sentient beings, [a bodhisattva] wishes to take upon him- or herself all [their] suffering, and he or she prompts others to adopt this very [attitude]. In addition, with a virtuous mind that is desirous of [cultivating] the trainings, he or she confesses before all the buddhas, the blessed ones, [who reside] in all the directions all his or her past and present failings and transgressions, and he or she prompts others to adopt this very [attitude]. Through repeatedly confessing his or her failings in this manner, [a bodhisattva] becomes free of all karmic obscurations with little difficulty.

In addition, a bodhisattva who possesses miraculous powers and has attained mastery of his or her mind acquires limitless merit that is based on the Buddha, Dharma, and Sangha, and that is based upon sentient beings, by emitting abundant and manifold kinds of magical emanations throughout all the directions. Furthermore, a bodhisattva meditates upon loving-kindness, compassion, joy, and equanimity and also causes others to take up [these meditations]. In this way, a bodhisattva produces and causes extensive roots of virtue that have unlimited results to be brought about with little effort.

The Six Methods That Accomplish Four Aims [1.17.11.2.3]

How does a bodhisattva remove the animosity that is felt by those beings who have a hostile attitude [toward the Buddha's teaching]? [How does he or she] cause those who have a neutral attitude [toward the Buddha's teaching] to take it up? [How does he or she] ripen those who have taken up [the Buddha's teaching] and liberate those who have become ripened?

1107. S: *manojalpaiḥ*, T: *yid la brjod pa dag gis*. *BBhVy* (f. 232b) refers to this form of practice as "worshipping with ideas formed in the mind" (S: **saṃkalpapūjaḥ*, T: *kun tu rtog pa'i mchod pa*). As it is being used here, this term suggests a form of reflection on the spiritual qualities of the Three Jewels as a devotional exercise.

Here, too, it should be understood that, in brief, there are six types of method that a bodhisattva uses to accomplish these four aims that relate to sentient beings: (1) the benevolent [method], (2) [the method] of standing as an obstacle, (3) [the method] that has a dissimilar attitude, (4) [the method] that derives from suppression, (5) [the method] that relates to returning a favor, and (6) the pure method.

Benevolent Skillful Means [1.17.11.2.3.1]

Regarding this [topic], a bodhisattva's benevolent method is as follows. Here, at the very outset, a bodhisattva uses gentle and pleasant physical and verbal conduct and conduct that is magnanimous and compliant to remove the animosity within those beings to whom he or she is desirous of teaching the Dharma. Having removed their animosity, he or she engenders in them [feelings of] affection and respect. Having engendered affection and respect, he or she engenders in them an aspiration for the Dharma. Following that, he or she teaches them the Dharma.

Moreover, the Dharma that he or she teaches is one that is appropriate and easily undertaken, [one that] generates an understanding, is meaningful, and [one that is revealed] at a suitable time, in an orderly manner, and correctly. He or she is forbearing of hostility and possesses a sympathetic mind that has the utmost desire to bring spiritual self-discipline to beings. He or she brings spiritual self-discipline to beings by means of miraculous powers, reading [others'] minds, and teaching a form of Dharma that is efficacious, by requesting others [to instruct them], or by emitting abundant and manifold kinds of magical emanations.

[A bodhisattva] benefits beings and carries out their aims by explaining in detail those treatises that are filled with meaning [but are composed] in an abbreviated form and by giving a condensed explanation of those that are [composed] in an extremely extensive form. Likewise, [he or she benefits beings and carries out their aims] by correctly revealing the meanings of Dharma teachings that have been memorized through giving explanations of them and [exposing the meanings of teachings] that have been taken up through causing them to be recited and answering questions about them. [He or she] also [benefits beings and carries out their aims] by teaching systematic instructions that relate to all the meditation objects associated with the various methods of pursuing one-pointed concentration.

There are persons who have not understood the intended meaning of the tathāgatas [as presented] in the profound sutras that were spoken by the tathāgatas with regard to [the topic of] emptiness. These are the sutras that declare that entities lack an essential nature, that they are insubstantial, that they do not arise, that they do not cease to exist, that they are identical with space, and that they resemble illusions and dreams. Having failed to understand the meaning of these [sutras], these persons who are frightened by them reject them completely and totally, declaring, "These were not spoken by the Tathāgata." Using the benevolent form of skillful means, a bodhisattva properly explains in an orderly manner the intended meaning of these sutras and causes these beings to comprehend them.

Moreover, this is how he or she gives that orderly explanation. These entities are not completely and totally nonexistent. However, they do not possess an essential nature that can be expressed in words. Therefore, they are described as "lacking an essential nature." Even though a real substance[1108] that is capable of being described is considered to exist and verbal expressions occur in relation to that [perceived substance], nevertheless the essential nature that is described by means of verbal expressions does not have such a mode of being in an ultimate sense. Therefore, [entities] are said to be "insubstantial."[1109] And, because this is so, the essential natures of entities that are expressed in words have, from the very beginning, been completely and totally incapable of being found. So how could it be that they arise or cease to exist? Therefore, it is said that they "do not arise" and they "do not cease to exist."

Consider the following analogy. A great variety and profusion of physical objects as well as their actions are observed [to exist] in space. It is also the case that space makes room for those physical objects and their actions, such as those of going, coming, remaining still, rising, falling, retracting [a limb], or extending [a limb], and the like. Moreover, when those physical objects and their actions are removed, the pure space whose nature is a mere absence of physical objects becomes evident. In a similar way, the conceptions and false notions that resemble physical objects and their actions and that are both created by a variety of expressions and accompanied by attachment to [verbal] elaborations arise in the ineffable reality that resembles space. In addition, the ineffable reality that resembles space makes room for all those conceptions and false notions that resemble the variety of physical objects and their actions and that are both created by a variety of expressions and accompanied by attachment to [verbal] elaborations. Moreover, when

1108. S: *vastu,* T: *dngos po.* See note 251.

1109. S: *nirvastukaḥ,* T: *dngos po med pa.*

bodhisattvas, by means of an excellent knowledge, have completely and totally removed those false conceptions and notions that are caused to arise by expressions and that are accompanied by attachment to [verbal] elaborations, the ārya knowledge of those supremely excellent bodhisattvas causes the ineffable reality that is a mere absence of all the essential natures that are expressed in words and that is a space-like purity to become evident. [Bodhisattvas] do not seek [a realization of] any other essential nature which is superior to that. Therefore, entities are said to be "identical with space."

For example, an illusion is something that does not truly exist in the way that it appears. Nor is an object that is created by a magical illusion something that is completely and totally nonexistent. Similarly, entities do not truly exist in the way that they appear to immature beings by the power of their habituation to expressions. Nor are they completely and totally nonexistent, by virtue of their ultimate, ineffable nature. Through the application of this method, [entities] are [determined to be] beyond duality—that is, neither existent nor nonexistent—like illusions. Therefore, they are said to "resemble illusions." In this way, a bodhisattva does not put forward anything, does not reject anything, does not subtract anything, does not add anything, and does not cause anything to disappear in relation to this entire "entity-source."[1110] He or she perceives reality as it is and makes it known in just that manner. This should be known as a bodhisattva's benevolent method.

The Method of Standing as an Obstacle [1.17.11.2.3.2]

What is a bodhisattva's method of standing as an obstacle?

Here a bodhisattva stands as an obstacle to beings who are seeking the ten personal articles for the body,[1111] such things as food and drink, etc., by

1110. S: *dharmadhātuḥ*, T: *chos kyi dbyings*. *MV* (ch. 1, vv. 15, 16) identifies this term as one of a number of synonyms for ultimate truth. *MVBh* (p. 39) interprets it as follows: "[Emptiness] is called the 'entity-source' because it is the cause of an ārya's spiritual qualities in the sense that the spiritual qualities of an ārya arise from [the mind] that holds that [emptiness] as its object. Here the meaning of the word 'source' (S: *dhātuḥ*, T: *dbyings*) is that of a cause." Sthiramati's commentary adds (*MVṬ*, p. 39): "Here the word 'entity' (S: *dharmaḥ*, T: *chos*) means [all] the spiritual qualities of an ārya, such as [the eight of] right view, etc., and [the remaining ones] that end with right knowledge of [the attainment of] liberation (S: *samyagvimuktijñānam*, T: *yang dag pa'i grol ba'i ye shes*)."

1111. S: *daśa kāyādipariṣkārāḥ*, T: *lus kyi yo byad bcu*. They are (1) food; (2) drink; (3) vehicles;

saying, "If you honor your mother, honor your father, honor spiritual asceticism, honor the position of brahmins," and so on as described earlier,[1112] up to "If you in abide in morality after having accepted it, I shall give you as much of the personal articles for the body, food and drink, etc., as you desire. Otherwise, I shall not give them to you." Similarly, he or she stands as an obstacle to beings who seek a matter relating to land, a house, a marketplace, sovereignty, a country, wealth, or grain; to beings who seek knowledge regarding the subjects of crafts and occupations; to beings who seek his or her friendship; to beings who seek to find a bride or who seek to marry off a daughter; to beings who seek to engage in extensive feasting and communal feasting; and to beings who seek assistance [in carrying out] their activities, saying in each case up to the last one, "I shall come and assist you with your activities, if you honor your mother," etc., as before.

Moreover, a bodhisattva who is capable and has the power [to help] stands as an obstacle to beings who are guilty of offenses, who have become corrupted, who have committed harmful acts, who have been seized by others for the purpose of being killed, bound, cut, beaten, reviled, threatened, or exiled, or who have been seized for the purpose of being pledged, bartered, or sold [into servitude], by saying, "If you honor your mother, honor your father," etc., at length as before, "I shall free you from this predicament."

Moreover, a bodhisattva stands as an obstacle to beings who are imperiled by the king, robbers, water, fire, humans, spirits, loss of livelihood, or a bad reputation, by saying, "If you honor your mother," etc., at length as before, "I shall save you from this danger."

Moreover, a bodhisattva stands as an obstacle to beings who wish to meet with something agreeable or beings who wish to be separated from something disagreeable, by saying, "If you honor your mother," etc., at length as before, "I shall bring it about that you meet with something agreeable," or "[I shall bring it about that you are] separated from something that is disagreeable."

Moreover, a bodhisattva stands as an obstacle to beings who have been stricken by illness and are in bad health, by saying, "If you honor your

(4) clothing; (5) ornaments; (6) household utensils; (7) incense, garlands, and scented oils; (8) dance, song, and music; (9) [methods of creating] light; and (10) personal possessions used by men and women for the enjoyment of sensual pleasures.

1112. See the activities listed above in the section entitled "Knowledge of the World" [I.17.5] that are said to be illustrative of the degeneracy of sentient beings.

mother," etc., at length as before, "I shall free you from the suffering caused by this illness." These beings for whom a bodhisattva has stood as an obstacle in these ways will be caused ever so quickly to take up virtue and abandon evil deeds in the manner that is desired. This is what is referred to as a bodhisattva's "method of standing as an obstacle."

The Method That Has a Dissimilar Attitude [1.17.11.2.3.3]

On the other hand, when those beings for whom a bodhisattva has stood as an obstacle to [the attainment of] the objects that were just described do not ever so quickly behave in the manner that is desired, he or she refuses to give the objects that were described to the beings who seek them, out of a desire to benefit them. However, he or she should not do so with an attitude that [genuinely] wishes to withhold [those objects]. Rather, out of a desire to benefit those beings who are experiencing misfortune, those who are in a state of danger, those who are desirous of meeting with something agreeable or being separated from something disagreeable, and those who are afflicted by the suffering of an illness, he or she should remain indifferent to them for a certain period of time. However, he or she should not do so with an attitude that is [genuinely] indifferent to them or an attitude that genuinely refuses to protect them. These beings toward whom a bodhisattva is behaving in this way with harsh actions but not with a [genuine] attitude [of harshness] will at a later time be caused to abandon evil deeds and take up virtuous ones in the manner that is desired.

In addition, a bodhisattva should cause those beings who are not seeking something from him or her, those beings who are not experiencing misfortune, and so on, up to those beings who have not been stricken by an illness, but who are his or her acquaintances and friends, to take up these very same forms of virtue—namely, that of honoring one's mother, and so on, up to that of observing the morality that has been undertaken. If those beings who have been urged by a bodhisattva to take up virtue in this manner should fail to practice it due to an inconstant temperament, a bodhisattva should, out of a desire to benefit them, give the appearance of having become angered. However, he or she should not genuinely be angry. Out of a desire to benefit [such persons], he or she should give the appearance of being in opposition to their interests; however, he should not genuinely be opposed to them. Out of a desire to benefit, he or she should even bring about some worldly[1113] [form of] harm; however, he or she should not genuinely have a desire to inflict harm.

The attitude that is possessed by a bodhisattva toward these beings is one that is at variance with his or her conduct. It is by this [means] that he or she causes them to abandon evil deeds and take up virtuous ones. Therefore, this method that brings sentient beings to a state of spiritual self-discipline is called a bodhisattva's "[method] that has a dissimilar attitude."

The Method That Derives from Suppression [1.17.11.2.3.4]

Regarding this [topic], what is a bodhisattva's method that derives from suppression?[1114]

Here a bodhisattva who is a lord[1115] or a king or who has attained [some form of regional] authority should correctly govern his own retinue or his own subjects [by saying] the following: "I shall discontinue or revoke [any] privilege bestowed by me or [any right of] food or clothing to anyone among my retinue or my subjects who does not honor his or her mother," and so on, up to "[I shall discontinue or revoke . . . to anyone who] adopts and abides in [a state of] immorality," or, [he should correctly govern by saying,] "I shall cause him or her to be beaten," or "I shall cause all his or her wealth to be confiscated," or "I shall cause him or her to be banished completely and totally from this country." He should also entrust this action to his skilled and intelligent subordinates. The beings who are frightened by these great forms of punishment will then abandon evil deeds and, having adopted virtuous deeds, abide in them. On the basis of this method, which constitutes a form of forceful suppression, even those beings who do not wish to engage in virtuous deeds will do so. Therefore, it is called "the method that derives from suppression."

1113. S: *laukikam,* T: *'jig rten gyi. BBhVy* (f. 235b): "[Some] 'worldly' [form of harm means that he or she] should cause a [form of] suffering or mental distress that is of a temporary duration and is [limited to] this world [i.e., this life]."

1114. S: *avaṣṭhambaja upayaḥ,* T: *nan tur las byung ba'i thabs.* The *Tibetan-Sanskrit Dictionary* gives *daṇḍanītiḥ* ("application of the rod," "administration of justice") as another synonym for *nan tur.* The term is also used in the Vinaya to refer to several forceful methods of imposing the rules of the Sangha on those who are unwilling to observe them.

1115. S: *svāmī,* T: *rje bo.* See note 717.

The Method That Relates to Returning a Favor [1.17.11.2.3.5]

Regarding this [topic], what is a bodhisattva's method that relates to returning a favor?

Here a bodhisattva who has done something that was of benefit to beings in the past, whether small or great, either in the form of generosity or rescuing them from some misfortune or danger, or helping them to meet with something agreeable or be separated from something disagreeable, or helping them to be cured of an illness, requests and accepts as an [act of] recompense from those who are grateful for and appreciative of the help they have received, and from those who are desirous of doing something favorable in return, only that they take up virtuous deeds; he or she does not [request] the slightest form of worldly material gift. And he or she should express the wish that they return the favor by taking up virtue by saying the following: "If you would honor your mother, honor your father," and so on, up to "[If you would] abide in morality after having accepted it, this alone would be the greatest way for you to repay my assistance." Using this means, he or she causes others to take up these forms of virtue. Therefore, this is called "the method that relates to returning a favor."

The Pure Method [1.17.11.2.3.6]

Regarding this topic, what is a bodhisattva's pure method?

Here a bodhisattva who is abiding on the bodhisattva [stage called] the stage that is the perfect manner of going[1116] and who has completed the perfection of the bodhisattva path takes birth among the assembly of deities in Tuṣita Heaven so that immeasurable numbers of beings might correctly develop the following aspiration and generate it frequently: "A certain bodhisattva who has taken birth among the assembly of deities in Tuṣita Heaven before long shall attain unsurpassed complete and true enlightenment in the Rose Apple Continent. We should gratify and not displease him. May we be reborn in the presence of this bodhisattva."

1116. Here, this term refers to the tenth ārya bodhisattva stage, called "Dharma cloud" (S: *dharmameghaḥ*, T: *chos kyi sprin*) in the *Sutra on the Ten Stages*. See Book III, chapter 3, the section entitled "Seven Stages" [III.3.1] for a description of this stage.

Then, after having passed away from Tuṣita Heaven and its assembly of deities, he is reborn in an exalted or a highly regarded family—that is, in a royal family or the family of a [brahmin] priest. Likewise, he gives up [a life filled with] great pleasures and departs [the worldly life] in order to cause beings to develop great regard [for him]. After that, he takes up the practice of austerities in order to cause those beings who are devoted to austerities to give up that desire. Then, he attains unsurpassed true and complete enlightenment in order to cause beings other than himself to long for the shared form of enlightenment and liberation.[1117] Then, after having attained unsurpassed true and complete enlightenment, he reflects to himself, "So that the declaration of Dharma does not become something of little consequence, now Brahmā himself should request that the Blessed One teach the Dharma," and waits for Brahmā to make this request before he teaches the Dharma to beings, in order to engender in beings respect for the Dharma. Then, with the eye of a buddha, he gazes upon the world[1118] in order to dispel the following wrong belief among certain beings, "Upon receiving a request from Brahmā, he has taught the Dharma out of respect for Brahmā. [Thus, he has taught] because he was prompted by someone else, not because of his own compassion for sentient beings and not because he realized that it was fitting for him alone to do so." Following that, he sets in motion in the world the wheel of the Dharma that has not been set in motion before. In this manner, he teaches the Dharma and declares the precepts that relate to the training. This is called a bodhisattva's "pure method," compared to which there is no other method that is higher, more superior, or more excellent.

This represents the abbreviated and detailed presentation of the bodhisattva's six types of skillful means that remove the animosity felt by those beings who have a hostile attitude, that cause those who are neutral [toward the Buddha's teaching] to take it up, that ripen those who have taken up [the Buddha's teaching], and that liberate those who have become ripened. There are no [methods] of greater significance than these and none besides these. This completes [the topic of] the skillful means of bodhisattvas.

1117. S: *bodhivimuktisāmānyam,* T: *byang chub dang rnam par grol ba thun mongs du 'gyur pa*. *BBhVy* (f. 236a): "The phrase 'shared form of enlightenment and liberation' means the form of enlightenment and liberation that is common both to listeners and himself."

1118. The act of gazing upon the world is to determine the persons to whom the Dharma might be taught. See *Lalita Vistara Sutra,* the opening passage of chapter 26.

Mental Retention [1.17.12]

Regarding this [topic], what are the bodhisattvas' forms of [mental] retention?[1119]

In brief, they should be regarded as being of four types: (1) retention of the Dharma, (2) retention of meaning, (3) retention by means of spells, and (4) the retention that is directed toward attainment of a bodhisattva's forbearance.

Regarding this [topic], what is retention of the Dharma?

Here a bodhisattva attains a development of power[1120] consisting of wisdom and recollection such that by means of it he or she can retain [in the mind] for an immeasurable period of time[1121] immeasurable numbers of scriptures containing collections of words, assertions, and syllables that were not committed to memory and were not recited aloud, in the order that they were created and in the order that they were arranged, merely by having listened to them.

Regarding this [topic], what is retention of meaning?

[The description] is the same as before, but in this case there is this difference. [A bodhisattva] retains [in the mind] for an immeasurable period of time immeasurable numbers of meanings relating to the very same Dharma teachings [contained in those scriptures], without having committed them to memory and without having reviewed them in the mind.

Regarding this [topic], what is retention by means of spells?

Here a bodhisattva attains a power of one-pointed concentration such that by means of it those mantra spells that [have the potential to] spiritually influence beings and cure their infectious diseases are rendered effective, supremely effective, and unfailing [in their ability] to cure many different kinds of infectious diseases. This [quality] is called a bodhisattva's "retention by means of spells."

Regarding this [topic], what is a bodhisattva's [form of mental] retention that is directed toward attainment of a bodhisattva's forbearance?

1119. S: *dhāraṇī,* T: *gzungs. BBhVy* (f. 236a): "It is called '[mental] retention' because it retains [in the mind] what all the buddhas and all the bodhisattvas were heard to say."

1120. S: *balādhānatā,* T: *stobs bskyed pa. BBhVy* (f. 236a): "'[A bodhisattva] attains a 'development of power' in the sense that he or she cannot be overcome by the obstacles to [wisdom and recollection]."

1121. *BBhVy* (f. 236a): "'For an immeasurable period of time' means until the attainment of unsurpassed true and complete enlightenment."

Here a bodhisattva who has him- or herself practiced the causes fully,[1122] who is possessed of wisdom, lives in solitude, who neither utters speech nor comes within the sight of anyone else, who likewise eats in moderation, does not eat in a haphazard manner,[1123] and eats only one kind of food,[1124] who is dedicated to meditation, sleeps only a little at night, and maintains a high degree of alertness contemplates, ponders, and examines the meaning of those mantra spells that the Tathāgata uttered for the sake of attaining forbearance, such as [the one which states]: *iṭi miṭi kiṭi bhikṣānti padāni svā hā*.[1125] Having correctly undertaken [the practice of] these mantra spells and without having heard their meaning from anyone else, he or she realizes it in the following manner: "There is no realization of the meaning of these mantra spells. They do not contain any meaning. Their meaning is that they have no meaning." Following that, he or she does not seek any further meaning. In this way, he or she gains a correct realization of the meanings of these mantra spells.

Having gained a correct realization of the meanings of these mantra spells, he or she then gains a correct realization of the meanings of all entities that conforms with that very [understanding of the mantra spells]. Without having heard [the meaning of all entities] from anyone else, he or she realizes it in the following manner: "No meaning that pertains to a [real] essence can be established by means of any expressions in relation to any entity. This ineffable essential nature is the meaning that represents their essential nature." After he or she has correctly realized the meaning that represents the essential nature of all entities in this way, [a bodhisattva] does not seek any other meaning. Through having gained a realization of that meaning, he or she attains a joyful rapture. What a bodhisattva attains on the strength of these mantra spells is called a "forbearance." Through having gained that [forbearance], a bodhisattva will before long attain the purity of his or her

1122. *BBhVy* (f. 236b): "The phrase '[a bodhisattva who has] practiced the causes fully' means that he or she has properly acquired the accumulations of wisdom and merit during the stage in which practice is based upon devotion." That is to say, the practitioner has become proficient in the practices of the preparation path (S: *prayogamārgaḥ,* T: *sbyor lam*).

1123. *BBhVy* (f. 236b): "Because [a bodhisattva] eats at a fixed time, 'he or she does not eat in a haphazard manner.'"

1124. *BBhVy* (f. 236b): "Because [a bodhisattva] does not eat [food] that is mixed with anything that is detrimental, 'he or she eats only one kind of food.'"

1125. Dutt's edition renders the mantra as *iṭi miṭi kiṭi bhiḥ kṣāntipadāni svā hā*. Both versions appear in different Tibetan translations.

superior attitude. He or she has advanced to the great form of forbearance that occurs on the stage in which conduct is based upon devotion. This should be understood as the [form of mental] retention that is directed toward the attainment of a bodhisattva's forbearance.

Regarding this [topic], after having gone beyond the first span of time that is made up of countless kalpas,[1126] a bodhisattva who has entered the stage of a pure superior attitude[1127] attains forms of the retention of the Dharma and the retention of meanings that are sure, firm, and exalted. Prior to that time, they are attained on the strength of aspirational prayers or on the basis of meditative absorptions, but they are not sure, firm, or exalted. As with the retentions of the Dharma and meanings, the same should be understood as being true for the retention by means of spells. However, the retention that is directed toward the attainment of a bodhisattva's forbearance is only attained in the manner that was just described.

Furthermore, a bodhisattva will attain all of these [forms of] retention if he or she possesses four qualities; he or she will not do so if any one of them is missing.

What are the four qualities?

(1) He or she does not have attachment for sensory pleasures. (2) He or she does not develop envy toward those who have attained an elevated status and he or she remains free of envy. (3) He or she is one who gives everything that is requested of him or her and is not a giver who regrets [acts of generosity] afterward. (4) He or she takes pleasure in the Dharma and is devoted to the Dharma that relates to the bodhisattva collection [of scriptures] or to the manuals for that collection.

Aspirational Prayer [1.17.13]

What is a bodhisattva's aspirational prayer?[1128]

In brief, it should be regarded as being of five types: (1) the aspirational prayer of generating [enlightenment] mind, (2) the aspirational prayer that

1126. See note 874.

1127. S: *adhyāśayaviśuddhibhūmiḥ*, T: *lhag pa'i bsam pa dag pa'i sa*. See note 484.

1128. S: *praṇidhānam*, T: *smon lam*. *MSA* (ch. 17, v. 74) describes aspirational prayer as "a [form of] volition that is accompanied by aspiration." See note 620 for a description of volition and note 146 for a description of aspiration.

relates to birth, (3) the aspirational prayer that relates to the field of action, (4) the correct aspirational prayer, and (5) the great aspirational prayer.

Regarding this [topic], a bodhisattva's initial development of the mind [that wishes to attain] unsurpassed true and complete enlightenment is called "the aspirational prayer of generating [enlightenment] mind."

A bodhisattva's aspirational prayer to be reborn in the future in happy migratory states that are favorable to the aims of sentient beings is called "the aspirational prayer that relates to birth."

The aspirational prayer to [attain] the correct discernment of entities,[1129] as well as the aspirational prayer to [develop] the objects of those meditations that relate to such spiritual qualities as the [four] immeasurables is called a bodhisattva's "aspirational prayer that relates to the field of action."

The brief or extensive form of aspirational prayer to obtain in the future all the spiritual qualities and all the virtuous qualities of a bodhisattva is called a bodhisattva's "correct aspirational prayer."

The great aspirational prayer of a bodhisattva should be understood on the basis of that very correct aspirational prayer. Moreover, it is of ten types: (1) The first aspirational prayer that is called a "great aspirational prayer" is [the wish] to carry out every manner of immeasurable worship and honor of the tathāgatas in the future. [The remaining nine are] (2) the great aspirational prayer to follow and protect the true Dharma of the buddhas, the blessed ones, and to preserve the way of the Dharma; (3) the great aspirational prayer to [carry out the activities] that range from [approaching the buddhas who are] abiding in Tuṣita Heaven, and so on, [and worshipping and honoring them, as well as following and protecting the true Dharma] as described previously, up to [the activity of approaching the buddhas who are] entering complete nirvana [and worshipping and honoring them]; (4) the great aspirational prayer to correctly practice every form of bodhisattva activity; (5) the great aspirational prayer to spiritually ripen all sentient beings; (6) the great aspirational prayer to fully perceive all world spheres; (7) the great aspirational prayer to purify a buddha field; (8) the great aspirational prayer to enter the Great Vehicle by having the same thoughts and deeds as all bodhisattvas; (9) the great aspirational prayer that all one's

1129. S: *samyagdharmapravicayapraṇidhānam*, T: *chos yang dag par rab tu rnam par 'byed pa'i smon lam*. *BBhVy* (f. 238a): "'The aspirational prayer to [attain] the discernment of entities' [takes] the form of [aspiring] to become skilled at discerning the [nature of] profound and extensive spiritual qualities."

correct activities should be fruitful; and (10) the great aspirational prayer to attain unsurpassed true and complete enlightenment.[1130]

One-Pointed Concentration on Emptiness [I.17.14]

Regarding this [topic], what is a bodhisattva's one-pointed concentration on emptiness?

The stability of mind[1131] in which [a bodhisattva] perceives the reality that is an ineffable essential nature that is free of all forms of essential nature that can be described with verbal expressions is called his or her "one-pointed concentration on emptiness."

One-Pointed Concentration on Wishlessness [I.17.15]

What is one-pointed concentration on wishlessness?

Having perceived here how that very reality that is an ineffable essential nature becomes defiled by numerous faults through one's having been overpowered by the mental afflictions and suffering that are generated by [forming] wrongful concepts [about the nature of reality], a bodhisattva's state of mental stability that is preceded by the avoidance of any future aspiration for those [faults] is called "one-pointed concentration on wishlessness."

One-Pointed Concentration on Signlessness [I.17.16]

What is one-pointed concentration on signlessness?

Having cleared away from that very reality that is an ineffable essential nature all the signs that consist of mistaken notions and verbal elaborations [about it], a bodhisattva's state of mental stability [that remains fixed upon it] as it truly is, in a tranquil manner, and in a manner that brings it to mind [properly] is called "one-pointed concentration on signlessness."

1130. This paragraph is an abbreviated description of the ten great aspirational prayers that are generated by a bodhisattva after he or she has attained the first ārya bodhisattva stage (see *DB*, pp. 9–11). They are also mentioned in Book II, chapter 4, the section entitled "The Pleasurable State of Great Joy" [II.4.3].

1131. S: *cittasya sthitiḥ,* T: *sems gnas pa*. This term literally means "a state in which the mind remains stationary or fixed." It is a reference to the mental stability that is achieved through practicing one-pointed concentration. Quiescence (S: *śamathaḥ,* T: *zhi gnas*), in particular, is described as the culmination of an exercise that progressively develops nine levels of mental stability. See note 602.

What, then, is the reason for setting forth these three forms of one-pointed concentration?

It is because there are none that are more significant or greater than these.

The two [principal logical categories] are existence and nonexistence. Regarding them, conditioned and unconditioned [entities] are what exist, and the self and [the quality of] belonging to a self are what do not exist. Regarding this, the formulation of the one-pointed concentration on wishlessness is based on the fact that one should not have any aspiration for the conditioned entities that do exist, meaning that one should [view them] as disagreeable.[1132]

In addition, the formulation of the one-pointed concentration on signlessness is based on the fact that one should have an aspiration for the unconditioned entity of nirvana, meaning that one should apprehend it with a correct attitude of delight.

On the other hand, a bodhisattva should neither develop an aspiration for, nor avoid developing an aspiration for, the reality that relates to what does not exist.[1133] Rather, that [reality] should be regarded accurately as

1132. S: *saṃskṛte saty apraṇidhānataḥ prātikūlyataḥ;* T: *'dus byas la mi mthun par bden par smon pa las*. The sense of the Tibetan translation of the first adverbial construction (*bden par smon pa las*) is somewhat unclear. It seems to read the first adverbial construction as *satya* + *praṇidhānataḥ,* meaning "in the sense of having the aspiration [that conditioned entities] are true." My interpretation is that *saty* is an adjective in the locative case that modifies *saṃskṛte* and means "conditioned entities that do exist." Similarly the adverbial term should be read as *apraṇidhānataḥ* with negative prefix, meaning "in the sense that one should not have any aspiration [for conditioned entities that exist]." In this case, the second adverbial term, *prātikūlyataḥ* ("meaning that they are disagreeable"), is meant to clarify the manner in which one should not have any aspiration for conditioned entities—which is to say, one should view them as disagreeable because their nature is one that consists of suffering.

1133. S: *asad vastu,* T: *med pa'i dngos po*. The description of the one-pointed concentration on emptiness that Asaṅga presents here is meant to be consistent with the one that he gives in *ŚBh* (p. 268). There he states: "One does not develop longing for that which is unreal and nonexistent. Thus, the door to liberation of emptiness is established through knowing and perceiving exactly how that which does not exist is nonexistent." However, in that context, "emptiness" is understood to mean the nonexistence or insubstantiality of a real personal self (S: *pudgalanairātmyam,* T: *gang zag gi bdag med*). Here Asaṅga describes the object of the one-pointed concentration on emptiness as "the reality that is an ineffable essential nature" (S: *nirabhilāpyasvabhāvaṃ vastu,* T: *brjod du med pa'i ngo bo nyid kyi dngos po*). This reality, which pertains to the fact that entities do not exist in the way that they are described in words, is also known as the insubstantiality of entities (S: *dharmanairātmyam,* T: *chos kyi bdag med*). This twofold object is also how the object of this form of one-pointed concentration is described in *MSA,* ch. 18, v. 77.

relates to what is nonexistent. And it should be understood that the formulation of the one-pointed concentration on emptiness [is made] on the basis of this perception.

This is how a bodhisattva practices in relation to these three [forms of] one-pointed concentration and it is also how he or she accurately understands their formulations. In addition, by taking up the accurate doctrinal formulations of the alternate versions[1134] of these three [forms of] one-pointed concentration and by taking up the [corresponding] methods of meditating upon them, he or she will also accurately understand [those alternate versions] in relation to which the listeners train themselves and attain realization.

The Four Summary Statements of the Dharma [1.17.17]

There are four summary Dharma statements which the buddhas and bodhisattvas teach in order to bring about the spiritual purification of sentient beings.

What are the four?

They are (1) the summary Dharma statement that "all formations[1135] are impermanent"; (2) the summary Dharma statement that "all formations are [a form of] suffering"; (3) the summary Dharma statement that "all entities lack a self"; and (4) the summary Dharma statement that "nirvana is a state of peace." The Dharma teachings that the buddhas and bodhisattvas express to beings with great frequency are ones that relate to the meanings of these [statements]. Therefore, they are called summary Dharma statements. They are also called summary statements because [they are utterances] that were constantly repeated by the ancient *muni*s, [those beings] who possess tranquil minds. In addition, they are called summary statements because they constitute a path that leads to great fortune[1136] and [a path] that leads to [a place that is] higher than the peak of existence.

1134. S: *tadanyākārāḥ*, T: *de las gzhan pa'i rnam pa dag*. These alternate versions are the Lesser Vehicle forms that are described in *ŚBh*, pp. 267–268. There Asaṅga refers to the three forms of one-pointed concentration as the three "doors to liberation" (S: *trīṇi vimokṣamukhāni*, T: *rnam thar sgo gsum*).

1135. See note 843.

1136. S: *mahodayaḥ*, T: *'byor pa chen pa*. *BBhVy* (f. 239b): "Regarding [the expression] 'great fortune,' the term 'fortune' (S: *udayaḥ*, T: *'byor pa*) means the arising of a great multitude, for example when one says that a great fortune arose from just a small amount." Here "great

All Formations Are Impermanent [I.17.17.1]

How does a bodhisattva perceive all formations as impermanent?

Here a bodhisattva recognizes all formations as impermanent through having ascertained that the essential nature of all formations that is expressed in words is one that has never existed.[1137] Moreover, through ascertaining that the arising and perishing [of formations] is caused by the failure to realize correctly their ineffable reality,[1138] he or she perceives all formations, which are [entities] whose essential nature is ineffable, as impermanent.

[A bodhisattva] considers past formations that have already arisen and passed away, and does not ascertain either a cause or an essential nature that relates to them. Therefore, he or she perceives that they do not have any mode of existence that relates either to a cause or an essential nature. He or she considers the [formations] of the present that have arisen but not yet passed away, and does not ascertain a cause in relation to them, because they are results that have been produced.[1139] On the other hand, he or she does ascertain[1140] an essential nature in relation to them, because they have not yet ceased to exist. Therefore, he or she perceives that they have a mode of existence that relates to an essential nature, but not one that relates to a cause. He or she considers the future formations that have neither arisen nor passed away, and ascertains a cause [in relation to them], because they are not results that have been produced. However, he or she does not [ascertain]

---

fortune" clearly is to be understood in the sense of spiritual prosperity. MW (p. 802) also gives "final emancipation" as one of the meanings of this term.

1137. This interpretation of impermanence as a form of "nonexistence" (S: *asadarthaḥ,* T: *med pa'i don*) is one that is mentioned both in *MSA,* ch. 17, v. 81, and *MV,* ch. 3, v. 5. It is identified as referring to the fact that mentally fabricated entities (S: *parikalpitam,* T: *kun brtags*) do not exist in the manner that they are mistakenly believed to exist.

1138. *BBhVy* (f. 240a): "[The phrase] 'caused by the failure to realize' means that the failure to realize [the ineffable nature] of entities causes them to come into being on the basis of conceptual thought. Thus, their arising and perishing is occasioned by the power of conceptual thought."

1139. S: *phaladattvatvāt,* T: *'bras bu skyed zin pa'i phyir. BBhVy* (f. 240a): "A cause is not ascertained in relation to formations of the present because they have already arisen, which means that a cause disappears after it has produced its result."

1140. All the Tibetan translations that were consulted state: "He or she does *not* perceive an essential nature in relation to them" (T: *ngo bo nyid ni mi dmigs te*); however, in light of the very next statement, the negative clearly does not conform to the line of thought being presented here.

an essential nature, because they have not yet come into being. Therefore, a bodhisattva perceives that they have a mode of existence that relates to a cause but not one that relates to an essential nature.

Having examined the ongoing and unbroken continuum of formations in relation to the three times, he or she perceives the three attributes of conditioned entities [that are present] in every single moment of a formation. He or she [also] recognizes a fourth attribute of conditioned entities in the moment subsequent [to their existence]. Regarding [these four attributes], immediately following the destruction of the essential nature of the formation that existed in the preceding moment, he or she perceives the appearance of the essential nature of a momentary formation that had not existed before. This is its "arising." He or she perceives that [a formation] which has arisen does not perish during that moment [of its existence]. This is its "duration." He or she perceives the otherness or the differentness of that [formation] which has come into being in comparison to the essential nature of the formation [that existed in] the previous moment and has now ceased. This is its "aging." Subsequent to its arising, he or she perceives the destruction of the essential nature of that very momentary formation that had arisen. This is its "disappearance."

He or she recognizes that what constitutes the essential nature [of a formation] is limited to the moment during which a formation has arisen. [He or she also recognizes] that the arising, duration, and aging [of a formation] form part of its essential nature as well. However, he or she does not perceive anything else as forming part of its essential nature. He or she also perceives accurately that the passing away of the essential nature of momentary formations in the moment following [their existence] also applies to their [three attributes of] arising, etc.

Taken altogether, these four attributes of conditioned entities, in brief, can also be characterized in relation to two states: those that are characterized as being existent and those that are characterized as being nonexistent. Regarding this [point], [the quality of being] existent is one attribute of conditioned entities that was formulated by the Blessed One. [The quality of being] nonexistent[1141] is a second attribute that was formulated. More-

1141. Both Sanskrit editions read: *yas tv abhāvaḥ,* which translates as "[the quality of] being nonexistent." While this phrase does correspond with the previous statement that identifies the two states of being "existent" and being "nonexistent," the Tibetan translation has *ngo bo nyid gang yin pa,* which translates as "[the quality of] being an essential nature." (This can be reconstructed *yaḥ svabhāvaḥ*). *BBhVy* (f. 241a) conforms to the reading of the Tibetan

over, the existence of formations that is characterized as the "modification of [a conditioned entity's] duration"[1142] is a third attribute that was formulated.[1143] Regarding this [topic], except for a formation's bare reality, a bodhisattva perceives that [the attributes of] its arising, duration, aging, and impermanence never achieve [the quality of having] a substantive essence.[1144]

Why is that?

[A bodhisattva] does ascertain a formation's bare reality that arises, but he or she does not [ascertain] an arising, a duration, an aging, or an impermanence that are separate from that [bare reality]. He or she also ascertains a formation's bare reality that endures [for an instant], that [undergoes] aging, and that [undergoes] destruction but does not [ascertain] a duration, an aging, or an impermanence [that are separate] from that.

By means of reasoning too, a bodhisattva examines these [attributes of] arising, etc., and fails to ascertain that they exist as real substances. Moreover, he or she fails to ascertain [any substantive reality] by examining [those attributes] in the following manner. If [the attribute of] arising were an entity that existed separately from the formations of form and the rest, it would be something that arises [on its own], just as the formations of form, etc., arise on their own. If that were so, there would be two births, the birth of the formation and the birth of its arising. Regarding this, the birth of the

---

translation by saying: "The phrase '[the quality of] being an essential nature' refers to cessation, which means the nonexistence of [a formation's] essential nature (T: *ngo bo nyid gang yin pa zhes bya ba ni 'gag pa ste, de'i ngo bo med pa nyid do*)." It is difficult to sort out this discrepancy and I am inclined to believe that the Tibetan translation represents a corruption.

1142. S: *sthityanyathātvam,* T: *gnas pa gzhan du 'gyur ba nyid. AKB* (p. 75) records that the Vaibhāṣikas consider this term to be a synonym for the attribute of "aging." The Sautrāntikas, however, define "duration" as the continued existence of a series of momentary entities (S: *sa eva pravāho anuvartamānaḥ,* T: *rgyun de nyid rjes su 'jug pa*) and describe the modification of [a conditioned entity's] duration as "the difference between the earlier and later [stages] of that [series' duration] (S: *tasyāḥ [sthityāḥ] pūrvāparaviśeṣaḥ,* T: *de'i snga phyi'i bye brag*)." Given Asaṅga's earlier description of "aging," his interpretation is probably more in line with that of the Vaibhāṣikas except, of course, that he does not regard these attributes as real.

1143. This appears to be a reference to the *Saṃskṛtalakṣaṇasūtram* (cf. *Aṅguttara Nikāya,* I.152), which declares: "O *bhikṣus,* there are three attributes of a conditioned entity. What are the three? An arising is perceived, a disappearance is perceived, and the modification of its duration is perceived."

1144. S: *dravyasvabhāvaniṣpattitaḥ,* T: *rdzas kyi ngo bo nyid yongs su grub pa.*

arising would have to be either something that is identical with the birth of the formation or something that is distinct from it. If it were identical with it, then the notion that [the attribute of] arising is a real substance would be incoherent, because it would be logically untenable to maintain that a distinct [attribute of] arising exists as a real substance. On the other hand, [if the birth of the arising] were distinct [from the birth of the formation], then [the attribute of arising] would not be an arising that brings a formation into being. In that case, [the notion that the attribute of arising is] an arising that brings a formation into being would not be one that is logically sound.

Just as with [the attribute of] arising, it should be understood that the same [kind of] detailed [explanation can be made] for [the attributes of] duration, aging, and destruction. If that which is called "destruction" were an entity that existed absolutely in the sense of having its own essential nature, then that [entity] would also be something that both comes into being and ceases to exist. And when that destruction came into being, then it would bring about the cessation of all formations. If this were so, then just as with one who has entered the state of composure that is a cessation,[1145] the suspension of the mind and mental factors would occur with little difficulty.[1146] In addition, with the [subsequent] cessation of that destruction, those formations that had previously been made to cease would once again come into being, because the destruction of those [formations] no longer existed. Therefore, it is unreasonable that [the attribute of] destruction could [be a real entity] that comes into being and ceases.

It is also unreasonable that a son of good family or a daughter of good family who believes that a substantively real form of existence is one that remains in existence at all times[1147] or [who believes] that a nominal form of existence is one that exists absolutely in that it possesses a [real] essential

1145. See note 202.

1146. *BBhVy* (f. 241b) describes the force of this statement to be the following: The state of composure that is a cessation is not one that can be entered easily; in fact, it can only be entered by nonreturner āryas and arhats. Yet, if the attribute of destruction were a separate real entity that caused all formations to cease, then everyone, including all ordinary beings, would be able to enter it with ease.

1147. This a reference to adherents of the doctrine of the Buddhist Sarvāstivāda school, which maintains that all conditioned entities of the three times (i.e., the past, present, and future) exist in a real sense.

nature,[1148] could [develop] dissatisfaction[1149] and detachment, and [attain] liberation. However, it is reasonable for one who perceives the opposite of these [positions] to do so.[1150]

These are the ways in which a bodhisattva accurately realizes that all formations are impermanent.

All Formations Are a Form of Suffering [1.17.17.2]

Moreover, because the formations that are impermanent in this way exist as an [uninterrupted] series, a bodhisattva perceives that they serve as the basis for the three types of suffering—that is, the suffering of conditioned existence, the suffering of change, and the suffering of suffering.[1151] In this way, a bodhisattva accurately realizes that "all formations are [a form of] suffering."

All Entities Lack a Self [1.17.17.3]

Furthermore, a bodhisattva accurately realizes the two types of insubstantiality that relate to conditioned and unconditioned entities—[that is,] the insubstantiality of the person and the insubstantiality of entities. Regarding them, this is [what is meant by] the insubstantiality of the person: None of these existing entities constitutes a person, nor is there anything else, separate from these existing entities, that constitutes a person. This is [what is meant by] the insubstantiality of entities: There is no entity whose essential nature is capable of being described in words that exists in relation to all the

1148. S: *svabhāvapariniṣpattiḥ,* T: *ngo bo nyid kyis yongs su grub pa.* This may be a further reference to the followers of the Buddhist Sautrāntika school, who adhere to a realist doctrine that accepts the existence of the external world.

1149. S: *nirvid,* T: *skyo ba.* That is, a dissatisfaction with or an aversion toward samsaric existence.

1150. *MSAVṛBh* (Tg. vol. 126, f. 137b): "Because a yogī [or yoginī] who is meditating upon the four noble truths and practicing [the various forms of] attention that relate to them brings to mind [the understanding] that formations possess the attributes of arising and passing away, he or she will perceive that formations arise and pass away with each moment. Perceiving them in this way, he or she will develop dissatisfaction [with samsara]. Having developed dissatisfaction, he or she will then become detached. Having become detached, he or she will then attain liberation and nirvana."

1151. Asaṅga's most detailed explanation of the three kinds of suffering can be found in *ŚBh,* pp. 254–257. His views are discussed in *Inner Science,* pp. 105–138.

objects that are described in words. In this way, a bodhisattva accurately realizes that "all entities lack a self."[1152]

Nirvana Is a State of Peace [1.17.17.4]

The subsequent complete cessation of those very formations whose causes were previously eradicated and the absolute inability for any others to be produced or appear again is called "nirvana." Further, it should be understood as a state of peace because it is one in which the mental afflictions and suffering have been brought to an end. Moreover, a bodhisattva who has not yet attained a pure superior attitude or a follower of the Listeners' Vehicle who has not [directly] perceived truth develops a firm conviction[1153] about such a nirvana and declares, "Nirvana is a state of peace." However, he or she does not have an accurate understanding of this nirvana and does not engage it with a correct [form of] knowledge-perception.

Nevertheless, there is this[1154] proper [form of] attention[1155] [about the topic of nirvana]. For example, consider the son of a king, or the son of an eminent householder, who has been raised within the inner apartments [of a home] by a king or an eminent householder. Suppose that the king or the eminent householder provides a toy deer-cart, an ox-and-horse cart, or elephant-cart for that tender youth. As the young son of the king or the young son of the eminent householder plays with, enjoys, and amuses himself with those [toy carts], he thinks of the toy deer as [real] deer, the toy oxen and horses as [real] oxen and horses, and the toy elephants as [real] elephants.

Then, one day, after the son has grown up and his faculties have matured, the king or the eminent householder describes real deer, and so on, up to [the king or the householder] describes real elephants. After hearing those descriptions, the son of the king or the son of the eminent householder has the following thought: "The king is describing [the deer of] my deer-cart,"

1152. This use of the term "self" (S: *ātman,* T: *bdag*) does not refer to a personal self; rather, it is meant in the sense of a real essential nature that is capable of being described in words.

1153. S: *adhimukto bhavati,* T: *mos par 'gyur te.*

1154. While the following parable bears obvious similarities to the one that appears in chapter 3 of the *Lotus Sutra,* the point that is being explained here differs from the one expressed in the sutra.

1155. See note 232.

or "The eminent householder [is describing the deer of my deer-cart]," and so on, up to "[The king] is describing [the elephants of] my elephant-cart," or "[The eminent householder is describing the elephants of my elephant-cart]."

Then, on a different occasion, the king or the eminent householder takes his son outside the home and shows him real deer, and so on, up to [the king or the eminent householder] shows [him] real elephants. After seeing those [animals], this time [the son] gains for himself a genuine understanding. Then he becomes embarrassed by his previous conviction and reflects to himself, "These are the real deer-carts that my father had been describing to me for such a long time," and so on, up to "[These are] the real elephant-carts [that my father had been describing to me]. However, I had [mistakenly] developed the firm conviction [that he was talking] about those unreal objects, which are mere imitations, mere representations and semblances [of real carts]."

In the same way, the father-like buddhas, as well as the bodhisattvas who have attained the great [ārya] stages and perceived nirvana directly, describe nirvana exactly as they have seen it to those son-like bodhisattvas who have been raised inside the home of samsara and who do not yet possess the pure superior attitude, and they also [describe it] to those listeners who have not yet seen truth. On the basis of an understanding that relies merely upon the sound [of words], those [disciples] also maintain a strong conviction regarding the excellent qualities of nirvana for a long time.

When those bodhisattvas who have gained a pure superior attitude[1156] through the ripening and growth of their virtuous accumulations and those listeners who have perceived truth develop a direct [form of] knowledge[1157] in relation to nirvana, they also develop a [form of] realization that accords with reality [in which they reflect to themselves,] "This is the nirvana that pertains to all the listeners and solitary realizers and [the one] that the buddhas and bodhisattvas describe. Previously, due to our immature understanding, we did not develop an accurate conviction about it. It

1156. Both Sanskrit editions have *śraddhāśayānām*, which translates as "[those bodhisattvas] who possess attitudes of faith." However, this should be amended to *śuddhāśayānām* as indicated by the Tibetan translation (T: *bsam pa dag pa*), which means that they have achieved the stage of an ārya of the Great Vehicle tradition.

1157. Wogihara's edition has *pratyakṣajñānam* ("a direct form of realization"); while Dutt's edition has *pratyakṣajñānadarśanam* ("a direct form of knowledge-perception"); see note 744. The Tibetan translation and *BBhVy* (ff. 242b–243a) both agree with the text of Wogihara's edition.

was a counterfeit [form of conviction] about this [nirvana]; it was a mere semblance of it." Based upon this subsequent accurate conviction, they are embarrassed by the former one.

For example, suppose that a certain great physician were to treat some person who was afflicted by an illness with suitable medicines in order to cure the illness that that [individual] was experiencing. Suppose that because he or she had been taking those medicines for a long time, this afflicted person also maintained a firm conviction about them, took pleasure in them, and valued them highly. Then suppose that this very same afflicted person were to become cured of that first illness through having taken those medicines, and that he or she were to then develop a different illness, one that he or she had never experienced before and that needed to be treated by different kinds of medicine.

Suppose that the great physician, having realized that the previous illness had been cured and that the illness that had arisen subsequently needed to be treated by different kinds of medicine, were to stop the previous treatment of medicine and were to prescribe a different medicine that was suitable [for the new illness]. An immature afflicted person who had developed a firm conviction about the previous medicines and who thought that they alone were beneficial would not believe the great physician who prescribed [different] medicines at earlier and later times and who said directly, "Those former medicines will not be beneficial for your subsequent illness." [That afflicted person] would not have faith in [the great physician's] words.

In just this way, it should be understood that immature bodhisattvas and listeners resemble [the afflicted person in this parable]. Like the afflicted person, they have been seized by the mental afflictions and they do not take up and do not feel devotion toward the Dharma teachings, the correct statements, the instructions, and the counsel of the Tathāgata who is the great physician—[the one whose teachings, etc.,] are higher than the high and the highest of all, clearer than the clear, more profound than the profound and the most profound of all, more exalted than inferior ones, much more exalted than them, and the most exalted of all. [Immature bodhisattvas and listeners also] do not undertake the practices that accord with the Dharma.

The bodhisattva or listener who has faith in these [teachings, etc.,] does not generate the slightest doubt or uncertainty about anything that the Tathāgata has asserted. Moreover, he or she climbs onto the Dharma chariot of the Tathāgata's assertions that resembles a chariot drawn by well-bred horses and possesses all the excellent components and equipment and, like a skillful driver, continues traveling ever so quickly and without delay, until he or she has reached and attained the [ārya] stages.

Within [Book I of] *The Stage of a Bodhisattva,* [known as] "The Object of Mental Application That Relates to the Support," this completes the seventeenth chapter, entitled "The Spiritual Qualities That Are Conducive to Enlightenment."

18

The Qualities of a Bodhisattva

Summary verse:

> Marvels and also what are not marvels,
> Even-mindedness, assistance,
> Acts of requital; likewise, aspirations
> And fruitful methods of practice.

Five Marvelous Qualities [1.18.1]

Five [qualities] should be understood as the marvelous and wonderful qualities of a bodhisattva who is training in the vehicle [that leads to] unsurpassed true and complete enlightenment.

What are the five?

They are (1) [to have a form of] affection toward all sentient beings that is not prompted by any motive;[1158] (2) [to have] the ability to bear immeasurable [forms of] suffering in samsara for the sake of sentient beings; (3) [to have] knowledge of the means for engendering self-discipline in sentient beings whose mental afflictions are strong and who are difficult to train; (4) [to have] gained entry into the reality that is extremely difficult to realize; and (5) [to have] inconceivable power. These five marvelous and wonderful qualities of bodhisattvas are not held in common with any sentient beings other than themselves.

1158. S: *niṣkāraṇavatsalatā,* T: *rgyu med par mnyes bshin pa. BBhVy* (f. 243b): "Bodhisattvas have [a form of] affection for all sentient beings that is not prompted by any motive, because they have no expectation [that this attitude will bring them some favorable form] of [karmic] ripening."

Five Qualities That Bodhisattvas Do Not Regard as Marvelous [1.18.2]

There are five [qualities] that do not constitute marvels[1159] for a bodhisattva but whose possession causes a bodhisattva to be called "one who possesses marvelous and wonderful qualities."

What are the five?

When it is a bodhisattva's nature to be pleased by the suffering that is caused [to him or her] by benefiting others and he or she accepts in its entirety the suffering that is caused by benefiting others, this is the first [quality] that does not constitute a marvel for a bodhisattva but whose possession causes a bodhisattva to be called "one who possesses marvelous and wonderful qualities."

Moreover, when a bodhisattva, knowing the faults of samsara and also knowing the good qualities of nirvana, desires to bring about the spiritual purification of sentient beings and it is his or her nature to be pleased by that very [aim], and he or she accepts [being reborn in] samsara solely for the purpose of bringing about the spiritual purification of sentient beings, this is the second [quality] that does not constitute a marvel for a bodhisattva, [and so on,] as before.

Moreover, when a bodhisattva, while aware of the pleasurable experience that comes from observing silence,[1160] desires to bring about the spiritual purification of sentient beings and it is his or her nature to be pleased by that very [aim], and he or she undertakes to teach the Dharma to sentient beings solely for the purpose of bringing about the spiritual purification of

1159. S: *anāścaryam,* T: *ngo mtshar ma yin pa*. This term literally means "[something that is] not a marvel." The sense is that a bodhisattva regards these qualities as something that is natural for him or her, but others consider them as marvelous. *BBhVy* (f. 243b): "[These qualities] do not constitute a marvel from the perspective of [the bodhisattva] him- or herself."

1160. S: *tūṣṇīṃbhāvaḥ,* T: *mi smra ba*. This term does not mean simply to refrain from speaking to others. Silence refers to a quality that is maintained while one engages in reflection and meditation. *ŚBh* (pp. 119–120): "For instance, here a certain [monk or nun] who has gone alone into seclusion reflects upon, examines, and investigates the meaning of those Dharma teachings that he or she has heard, understood, and recited aloud. Or he or she retires [in order to practice meditation] and places his or her mind inwardly, subdues, pacifies, and pacifies it intensely, causes it to become one-pointed, and attains equipoise. Alternatively, he or she engages in the practice of insight. This is called 'observing silence.'"

sentient beings, this is the third [quality] that does not constitute a marvel for a bodhisattva, [and so on,] as before.

Moreover, when a bodhisattva desires to bring about the spiritual purification of sentient beings and it is his or her nature to be pleased by that very [aim], and he or she sincerely delivers over to all sentient beings roots of virtue that consist of [forms of] the six perfections he or she has collected solely for the purpose of bringing about the spiritual purification of sentient beings, and he or she does not seek any [favorable karmic] maturation for having delivered that [virtue], this is the fourth quality that does not constitute a marvel for a bodhisattva, [and so on,] as before.

Moreover, when a bodhisattva makes the concerns of others his or her very own concern and is observed to be engaging in every kind of action that accomplishes the aims of others, this is the fifth quality that does not constitute a marvel for a bodhisattva but whose possession causes a bodhisattva to be called "one who possesses marvelous and wonderful qualities."

Even-Mindedness [1.18.3]

A bodhisattva should be understood as being even-minded toward all sentient beings in five ways.

What are the five?

(1) [A bodhisattva is even-minded] by virtue of the initial aspiration in which he or she generates the intention to achieve enlightenment, for a bodhisattva generates that mind equally on behalf of all sentient beings. (2) He or she is even-minded by virtue of his or her sympathetic mind. (3) A bodhisattva is even-minded by virtue of his or her affectionate mind, in that he or she [views] all sentient beings in the same way as [the parent] of an only child [views that child]. (4) Having realized [the meaning of] the term *sattva*[1161] both in relation to all sentient beings and in relation to dependently arisen formations, a bodhisattva maintains an even mind toward all sentient

1161. The Sanskrit term *sattva* (T: *sems can*) is commonly understood to mean "sentient being"; however, it can also mean "being," "existence," and "reality" (MW, p. 1135). Asaṅga here seems to intend the term to be taken in both senses. That is, in relation to sentient beings, the term *sattva* (i.e., "sentient being") should be understood to mean the nominal designation of a person that is made with respect to the five heaps and, in relation to dependently arisen formations, the term *sattva* (i.e., "existence") should be understood to mean their ultimate nature of emptiness. This clause, then, describes a bodhisattva who has realized both the insubstantiality of the person and the insubstantiality of entities.

beings by virtue of having a mind that [understands] the sameness of [all] entities, which is to say, "The true nature of any single sentient being is [the true nature] of all [sentient beings]." (5) A bodhisattva maintains an even mind toward all sentient beings by virtue of having a mind that pursues the welfare [of others] in such a way that he or she acts on behalf of all [sentient beings] in the same way that he or she does on behalf of a single sentient being. These are the five ways in which a bodhisattva is even-minded toward sentient beings.

Assistance [1.18.4]

All the acts of assistance that bodhisattvas [carry out] in relation to sentient beings should be understood as being of five types.

What are the five?

They are (1) providing advice about correct livelihood; (2) providing proper instruction about meaningful activities that are being pursued in a contrary manner; (3) giving protection to those who lack a protector, who are suffering, who are wretched, and who have no one to rely upon; (4) providing instruction about the path that leads to a happy migratory state; and (5) providing instruction in [the teachings of] the three vehicles.

Acts of Requital [1.18.5]

There are five ways in which sentient beings exert themselves to carry out acts of requital toward a bodhisattva who has benefited them.

What are the five?

(1) They obtain good qualities for themselves. (2) They induce others to obtain good qualities. (3) They give protection to those who lack a protector, who are suffering, who are wretched, and who have no one to rely upon. (4) They worship the tathāgatas. (5) They take up and worship the Dharma that was spoken by the Tathāgata, by reciting it aloud or by making a written copy.

Aspirations [1.18.6]

There are five conditions that are always wished for[1162] by a bodhisattva.

What are the five?

1162. *BBhVy* (f. 244b): "The phrase [these five conditions] 'are always wished for' means that

They are [the wish] (1) to propitiate[1163] the buddhas when they appear; (2) to hear the six perfections and the collection of bodhisattva scriptures directly from those very buddhas; (3) [to gain] the ability to ripen sentient beings in every way; (4) to attain unsurpassed true and complete enlightenment; and (5) that there exist concord among the listeners[1164] following the attainment of enlightenment.

Fruitful Methods of Practice [1.18.7]

Five conditions render fruitful the methods of practice that a bodhisattva undertakes in order to carry out beneficial activities on behalf of sentient beings.

What are the five?

From the very outset, a bodhisattva here desires to (1) benefit and (2) bring happiness to sentient beings. He or she truly knows what will (3) benefit and (4) bring happiness [to them]. (5) He or she is one whose mind is free of error. This entire [topic] should be understood as it was described previously in the chapter entitled "Worship, Service, and the Immeasurables."[1165]

---

a bodhisattva makes aspirational prayers about them many times even during a single day, because he or she values them highly."

1163. S: *ārāgaṇatā*, T: *mnyes par bya ba*. *BHSD* (p. 103) gives two principal meanings to this term: "attainment" and "propitiation." The Tibetan translation seems to follow the latter sense and I have rendered the English accordingly. However, *BBhVy* (ff. 244b–245a) gives this description: "[The expression] *buddhotpādārāgaṇatā* (T: *sangs rgyas 'byung ba mnyes par bya ba*) means to make the aspirational prayer to be reborn at the time and place where a buddha appears." Thus, the phrase could be paraphrased as the aspiration to gain the opportunity of honoring a buddha through being reborn at a time when one is able to meet with him directly.

1164. S: *śrāvakasāmagrī*, T: *nyan thos mthun par 'gyur ba*. The term *sāmagrī* can mean "totality" or "completeness" (cf. MW, p. 1204), as well as "concord" (cf. *BHSD*, p. 591). The Tibetan translation suggests that the latter meaning is intended here. Consider *Udānavargaḥ*, ch. 30, v. 22cd: "Happiness is accord within the Sangha / Happiness is the austerities of those in accord." However, *BBhVy* (f. 246a) glosses this condition as "praying that the assembly of listeners become complete for those who have attained enlightenment." One might also regard concord among the listeners to be accomplished by their remaining together as one complete community.

1165. See Book I, chapter 16, the section entitled "Making the Role of a Spiritual Teacher Fruitful" [I.16.2.2].

Summary verse:

> Correct methods of practice,
> Decline and, likewise, improvement;
> Counterfeit and genuine qualities;
> Likewise, providing guidance.

Correct Methods of Practice [1.18.8]

It should be understood that all of the correct methods of practice undertaken by a bodhisattva are contained within five methods of practice.

What are the five?

[They are] (1) the method of practice that safeguards; (2) the irreproachable method of practice; (3) the method of practice [that is accompanied by] the power of analysis; (4) the method of practice [that is accompanied by] a pure superior attitude; and (5) the method of practice in which certainty has occurred.

The Method of Practice That Safeguards [1.18.8.1]

Regarding this [topic], using the method of practice that safeguards, a bodhisattva preserves his or her intelligence by means of an innate [form of] understanding that takes up spiritual qualities very quickly. He or she preserves recollection by means of a [form of] recollection that retains those spiritual qualities that have been taken up. He or she preserves knowledge by means of a [form of] understanding that examines the meanings of those spiritual qualities that have been retained. He or she achieves penetrating insight[1166] by means of a [form of] right wisdom that both avoids the causes that contribute to the diminishing of one's intelligence, recollection, and understanding and cultivates the causes that contribute to their retention and development. He or she watches over his or her own mind by guarding the doors of the faculties. He or she watches over the minds of others by correctly complying with their minds.[1167]

1166. S: *pratividhyati,* T: *so sor rtogs par 'gyur ro. BBhVy* (f. 245a): "The phrase 'he or she achieves penetrating insight' refers to [the wisdom] that derives from meditation."

1167. S: *paracittānuvartaṇam,* T: *gzhan gyi sems rjes su 'jug pa*. This is a reference to one of

The Irreproachable Method of Practice [1.18.8.2]

Regarding this [topic], a bodhisattva's irreproachable method of practice is one that is unerring, fervent, immeasurable, and constant in relation to [the pursuit of] virtuous qualities, and it is one that dedicates [those virtuous qualities] to [the attainment of] enlightenment.

The Method of Practice That Is Accompanied by the Power of Analysis [1.18.8.3]

For its part, the method of practice [that is accompanied by] the power of analysis should be understood as the one [that a bodhisattva undertakes] throughout the entire stage of conduct that is based upon devotion.[1168]

The Method of Practice That Is Accompanied by a Pure Superior Attitude [1.18.8.4]

The method of practice [that is accompanied by] a pure superior attitude should be regarded as the one [that a bodhisattva undertakes] on both the stage of a pure superior attitude and the stage of practicing conduct.[1169]

The Method of Practice in Which Certainty Has Been Reached [1.18.8.5]

The method of practice in which certainty has been reached should be regarded as the one [that a bodhisattva undertakes] on the stage of certainty, the stage of certain conduct, and the stage that is the perfect manner of going.[1170]

---

the eleven ways of acting on behalf of beings. See Book I, chapter 10, the section entitled "The Morality That Acts on Behalf of Beings" [I.10.2.3].

1168. This stage corresponds to the pleasurable state of the same name (see Book II, chapter 4, the section entitled "The Pleasurable State of Conduct That Is Based upon Devotion" [II.4.2]). See also note 483.

1169. These two stages span the first seven of the ten ārya bodhisattva stages (see notes 484 and 485).

1170. These three stages correspond to the final three of the ten ārya bodhisattva stages (see notes 486, 487, and 488).

This is how all of the correct methods of practice that are undertaken by a bodhisattva are contained within these five methods of practice.

Qualities That Contribute to a Bodhisattva's Decline [1.18.9]

It should be understood that five qualities contribute to a bodhisattva's decline.

What are the five?

[They are] (1) disrespect toward the Dharma and Dharma teachers; (2) heedlessness and laziness; (3) developing and tolerating the mental afflictions; (4) engaging in and tolerating misdeeds; and (5) comparing oneself with and [developing] exaggerated pride[1171] toward other bodhisattvas and [developing] an erring attitude and exaggerated pride toward the Dharma.

Qualities That Contribute to a Bodhisattva's Improvement [1.18.10]

It should be understood that five qualities contribute to a bodhisattva's improvement.

What are the five?

By contrast, it should be understood that they are, respectively, the opposite of those very five bad qualities.

Counterfeit Qualities [1.18.11]

It should be understood that, for a bodhisattva, there are five faults that constitute the counterfeit qualities of bodhisattvas.

What are the five?

[They are] (1) to do harm to violent and ill-behaved beings because [they possess] those [base qualities]; (2) for a hypocrite[1172] to feign excellent physical behavior; (3) to become someone who is considered learned by acquiring a reputation as one who possesses [knowledge of] the Materialist[1173] texts

1171. See note 314.

1172. S: *kuhakaḥ,* T: *tshul 'chos pa*. That is, a person who commits the wrong form of livelihood known as "hypocrisy" (see note 642).

1173. S: *lokāyataḥ,* T: *'jig rten rgyang 'phen pa*. This is the name for followers of the Indian

and the heretical treatises; (4) to engage in conduct that [while seemingly] virtuous actually consists of objectionable forms of generosity, etc.; and (5) to take pleasure in, teach, or establish [beliefs that are] counterfeit forms of the true Dharma.

Genuine Qualities [1.18.12]

It should be understood that, for a bodhisattva, there are five genuine spiritual qualities that pertain to bodhisattvas.

What are the five?

[They are] (1) to have especially strong compassion for beings who are violent and ill-behaved; (2) to have excellent physical behavior naturally; (3) to become someone who is considered learned by acquiring a reputation as one who is knowledgeable about the canonical scriptures taught by the Tathāgata; (4) to engage in irreproachable forms of virtuous conduct such as generosity, etc.; and (5) to teach the true Dharma and reject [beliefs that are] counterfeit forms of the true Dharma.

Providing Guidance [1.18.13]

In brief, bodhisattvas correctly instruct disciples in relation to ten subjects.

What are the ten?

[They are] (1) to remain free of misconduct; (2) to separate oneself from sensory pleasures; (3) to strive to avoid committing transgressions; (4) to guard the doors of the faculties; (5) to observe vigilance;[1174] (6) to separate

---

Materialist tradition, also known as the Cārvaka school (T: *mdzes pa pa*). They are considered nihilists because they do not accept the existence of past and future lives, or the doctrine of karma.

1174. S: *saṃprajānadvihāritā*, T: *shes bzhin du spyod pa nyid*. This topic is explained in considerable detail in *ŚBh* (pp. 111–127; although the final portion of the discussion is missing in the Sanskrit edition, it is preserved in the Tibetan translation). The initial summary description (pp. 11–12) states: "[The monk or nun who] has thus applied him- or herself to [maintaining] a state of wakefulness observes vigilance when going out [from his or her residence] or returning, when gazing without forethought or gazing intentionally, when drawing back or extending [a foot, arm, hand, or other appendage], and when taking hold of his or her cloak, robe, or alms bowl; [he or she observes vigilance] in relation to that which is eaten, chewed, drunk, or savored; and he or she observes vigilance when dispelling drowsiness, when going, standing, sitting, or reclining, and when remaining wakeful, speaking, or remaining silent."

oneself from [improper] social contact;[1175] (7) for a person living in solitude, to remain free of improper [forms of] deliberation;[1176] (8) to remain free of the obstacles; (9) to remain free of the perturbation that is caused by the mental afflictions; and (10) to remain free of the indisposition [brought on by] qualities that relate to the mental afflictions.

Summary verse:

> Prophecy, the occurrence of certainty,
> What is to be done out of necessity,
> What is to be done continually,
> And the final one is what is preeminent.

Prophecy [1.18.14]

In brief, there are six ways in which the tathāgatas prophesy that a bodhisattva will attain unsurpassed true and complete enlightenment.

What are the six?

[The tathāgatas make prophecies about] (1) individuals who possess the [Great Vehicle's] spiritual lineage but who have not yet generated [enlightenment] mind,[1177] and, likewise, (2) individuals who have generated [enlight-

1175. S: *saṃsargaḥ,* T: *'du 'dzi.* Asaṅga (*YBh,* p. 164) counts [improper] social contact as one of six causes of the mental afflictions and describes it as the situation in which the mental afflictions arise in an individual who emulates [the behavior of] bad persons.

1176. S: *asadvitarkaḥ,* T: *rtog pa ngan pa.* See note 204 for a general definition of deliberation; see Book I, chapter 10, the section entitled "Assisting Those Who Are Experiencing Physical or Mental Suffering" [I.10.2.6.1b] for a variety of topics that represent improper objects of deliberation (cf. *RA,* ch. 5, vv. 25–27).

1177. *BBhVy* (f. 246b): "Prophecy regarding an individual who possesses the [Great Vehicle's] spiritual lineage means to prophesy the enlightenment of a sentient being who possesses extraordinarily good fortune and who is endowed with all the signs of the [Great Vehicle's] spiritual lineage that occur in relation to the [six] perfections, by declaring that he or she will achieve enlightenment [at some time] in the future. This does not mean that [buddhas] make such a prophecy about all persons who possess the [Great Vehicle's] spiritual lineage, but rather that they make this prophecy only in relation to certain sentient beings who possess extraordinary [spiritual] attitudes and [forms of] practice." Regarding the signs of the Great Vehicle's spiritual lineage, see Book I, chapter 1, the section entitled "Signs" [I.1.4].

enment] mind,[1178] (3) individuals who are dwelling in their presence, and (4) individuals who are dwelling far from their presence. [They also make prophecies that someone's enlightenment will occur] (5) at a definite time, saying, "At such a time, he or she will attain unsurpassed true and complete enlightenment," or [that it will occur] (6) at an indefinite time—that is, they do not declare that it will occur at a specific time.

The Occurrence of Certainty [1.18.15]

There are three occurrences of certainty.

What are the three?

A bodhisattva who will always abide in [his or her] spiritual lineage is said to be "one in whom certainty has occurred."

Why is that?

He or she is possessed of fortune[1179] [in the sense that], as the [necessary] conditions are met with, unsurpassed true and complete enlightenment is certain to be attained.

Furthermore, one type of bodhisattva is certain to generate the mind that seeks unsurpassed true and complete enlightenment and will not turn back from that [goal] until he or she has attained unsurpassed true and complete enlightenment.

In addition, a bodhisattva who has attained the controlling powers[1180] is able to cause all the activities that [he or she carries out] on behalf of sentient beings to become fruitful in just the manner that he or she desires and in just the manner that he or she undertakes them.

These three are the occurrences of certainty: (1) the occurrence of certainty that relates to abiding in the [Great Vehicle's] spiritual lineage; (2) the occurrence of certainty that relates to having generated the mind [that seeks

1178. *BBhVy* (f. 246b): "Prophecy regarding an individual who has generated [enlightenment] mind refers to certain persons who possess singularly strong and pure faith and who, after having acquired extensive merit, generate the mind that seeks to attain complete enlightenment in the presence of a tathāgata. [The enlightenment] of such persons is prophesied in order to encourage them."

1179. S: *bhavyaḥ,* T: *skal ba can.* While this term has a range of meanings (see MW, p. 750), in the present context it refers to a person who is "suitable" or "fit" in the sense of having the ability to attain enlightenment. *BHSD* (p. 407) translates it as "able" or "capable."

1180. The ten controlling powers are described in Book II, chapter 4, in the section entitled "The Pleasurable State That Is Free of Signs and Also Free of Effort" [II.4.10].

enlightenment]; and (3) the occurrence of certainty that relates to fruitful activities. Regarding these, it is in relation to the last of these occurrences of certainty that the tathāgatas prophesy a bodhisattva as having become one in whom certainty has occurred.

What Is to Be Done out of Necessity [1.18.16]

There are five things that are to be done by a bodhisattva out of necessity. They are such that, if a bodhisattva fails to do them, he or she will lack the fortune [that will enable him or her] to attain unsurpassed true and complete enlightenment.

What are the five?

They are (1) the initial development of [enlightenment] mind; (2) sympathy toward sentient beings; (3) a [form of] effort that is fervent; (4) competence in all the branches of learning; and (5) indefatigability.

What Is to Be Done Continually [1.18.17]

There are five things that are to be done by a bodhisattva continually.[1181]

What are the five?

(1) Mindfulness is [a form of practice that is] to be done by a bodhisattva continually. [So too are] (2) giving protection to those sentient beings who lack a protector, who are suffering, and who have no one to rely upon; (3) worshipping the tathāgatas; and (4) being aware of [one's] mistaken actions. (5) Insuring that all one's actions, conduct, pleasurable states, and forms of attention are accompanied by enlightenment mind is the fifth thing that is to be done by a bodhisattva continually.

Ten Preeminent Things [1.18.18]

There are ten things that are regarded as preeminent by bodhisattvas and that bodhisattvas hold to be foremost and that they declare to be the foremost topics of instruction.

What are the ten?

(1) The bodhisattva spiritual lineage is preeminent among all the [forms of] spiritual lineage. (2) The initial development of [enlightenment] mind

1181. *BBhVy* (f. 247a): "The phrase 'what is to be done continually' means that which must be done both in all one's births and also every day."

is preeminent among all correct forms of aspirational prayer. (3) Effort and wisdom are preeminent among all the perfections. (4) Agreeable speech is preeminent among all the principles for attracting a following. (5) A tathāgata is preeminent among all sentient beings. (6) Compassion is preeminent among the immeasurables. (7) The fourth meditative absorption[1182] is preeminent among all the states of meditative absorption. (8) Among the three forms of one-pointed concentration,[1183] one-pointed concentration on emptiness is preeminent. (9) Among all the states of composure, the state of composure that is a cessation[1184] is preeminent. (10) Among all the forms of skillful means, the pure skillful means[1185] that was described [earlier] is preeminent.

Summary verses:

> The formulations of teachings;
> Likewise, the subjects of investigation,
> Knowledge of the way things truly are,
> And, similarly, the immeasurables.
>
> The fruits of instruction, greatness,
> The summary of the vehicle,
> The ten bodhisattvas that are to be known,
> And, likewise, descriptive appellations.

The Four Formulations of Teachings [I.18.19]

There are four formulations of teachings that are made by bodhisattvas and that tathāgatas and bodhisattvas alone correctly make known and establish. No one else can make them—not a god, a human, an ascetic, or a brahmin—unless they have heard them from those [tathāgatas and bodhisattvas].

What are the four?

1182. S: *caturthaṃ dhyānam*, T: *bsam gtan bzhi pa*. See note 914.

1183. The three forms of one-pointed concentration are described in Book I, chapter 17, in the sections entitled "One-Pointed Concentration on Emptiness" [I.17.14], "One-Pointed Concentration on Wishlessness" [I.17.15], and "One-Pointed Concentration on Signlessness" [I.17.16].

1184. See note 202.

1185. See Book I, chapter 17, the section entitled "The Pure Method" [I.17.11.2.3.6].

They are (1) the formulation of teachings on the Dharma, (2) the formulation of teachings on truth, (3) the formulation of teachings on the applications, and (4) the formulation of teachings on the vehicles.

The Formulation of Teachings on the Dharma [1.18.19.1]

Regarding this [topic], the orderly expression and the arrangement of orderly formulations of the twelve divisions of the sutras, etc.,[1186] that consist of speech is called "the formulation of teachings on the Dharma."

The Formulation of Teachings on Truth [1.18.19.2]

For its part, the formulation of teachings on truth is made up of numerous classifications. In the sense of not being false, there is only one truth;[1187] it has no second form. Truth is twofold [in the sense of] relative truth and ultimate truth. Truth is threefold [in the sense of] the truth that relates to attributes,[1188] the truth that relates to speech,[1189] and the truth that relates to actions.[1190] Truth is fourfold [in the sense of] the truth of suffering, etc., up to the truth of the path. Truth is fivefold [in the sense of] the truth that relates to causes, the truth that relates to results, the truth that relates to knowledge, the truth that relates to objects of knowledge, and the foremost truth.[1191]

1186. See note 529.

1187. S: *satyam,* T: *bden pa*. The verbal root of the Sanskrit term for "truth" is *as,* which means "to be" or "to exist." Thus, in addition to "truth," the noun *satyam* also indicates the idea of "reality" or "that which actually exists."

1188. *BBhVy* (f. 248a): "Truth that relates to attributes (S: *lakṣaṇasatyam,* T: *mtshan nyid kyi bden pa*) refers to the necessary connection (S: **avinābhāvaḥ,* T: *med na mi byung ba*) that exists between entities and their specific and general attributes."

1189. *BBhVy* (f. 248a): "Truth that relates to speech (S: *vāgsatyam,* T: *ngag gi bden pa*) is truthful speech—[that is,] the quality of not violating one's word."

1190. *BBhVy* (f. 248a): "Truth that relates to actions (S: *kriyāsatyam,* T: *bya ba'i bden pa*) is to act in a manner that accords with what one has said."

1191. *BBhVy* (f. 248b) gives two interpretations of this fivefold formulation. The first one equates the truth that relates to causes with the truth of origination; the truth that relates to results with the truth of suffering; the truth that relates to knowledge with the truth of the path; the truth that relates to objects of knowledge with the four truths collectively; and the foremost truth with nirvana. The second interpretation equates the unerring formula-

Truth is sixfold [in the sense of] the truth regarding what is true,[1192] the truth regarding what is false,[1193] the truth regarding what should be thoroughly known,[1194] the truth regarding what should be abandoned, the truth regarding what should be made evident, and the truth regarding what should be meditated upon.

Truth is sevenfold [in the sense of] the truth regarding [the act of] enjoying,[1195] the truth regarding disadvantages, the truth regarding deliverance, the truth regarding the ultimate nature of things, the truth regarding devotion, the truth for āryas, and the truth for those who are not āryas.

Truth is eightfold [in the sense of] the truth regarding the suffering of conditioned existence, the truth regarding the suffering of change, the truth regarding the suffering of suffering, the truth regarding progression,[1196] the truth regarding the termination [of samsara],[1197] the truth regarding the

---

tion of all causes with the first category, a similar formulation of all results with the second category, the various forms of successive knowledge that relate to all four of the noble truths with the third category, correct knowledge and suchness with the fourth category, and nirvana with the fifth category.

1192. S: *satyasatyam,* T: *bden pa'i bden pa.* The noun *satyam* can also mean what is "pure," "virtuous," "good," and "valid" (MW, p. 1135). *BBhVy* (f. 248b) indicates that this phrase is variously interpreted as meaning (1) truthful speech, (2) ineffable reality, and (3) the noble truths of cessation and the path. Samudramegha seems to prefer the first two interpretations and to attribute the third description to other scholars.

1193. S: *mṛṣāsatyam,* T: *brdzun pa'i bden pa. BBhVy* (f. 248a): "[The phrase] 'truth regarding what is false' refers to the closely grasping heaps that are active throughout the three realms, as indicated by the sutra phrase that describes them as being 'like illusions' (S: *māyopamāḥ,* T: *sgyu ma lta bu*)."

1194. S: *parijñeyasatyam,* T: *yongs su shes par bya ba'i bden pa. BBhVy* (f. 249a): "The truth regarding what should be thoroughly known refers to the four noble truths." The next three forms of truth also refer to the noble truth of origination, the noble truth of cessation, and the noble truth of the path, respectively.

1195. S: *āsvādasatyam,* T: *ro myang ba'i bden pa. BBhVy* (f. 249a): "The truth regarding the act of enjoying is the unerring physical and mental enjoyment of pleasurable feelings that relate to the conditional factors or the sense objects."

1196. See note 315 for a description of the term "progression." Here Samudramegha (*BBhVy,* f. 249a) equates it with relative truth (S: *saṃvṛtisatyam,* T: *kun rdzob bden pa*), perhaps in the sense that belief in and attachment to relative truth as represented by the five grasping heaps are the main factors that perpetuate samsaric existence.

1197. S: *nivṛttiḥ,* T: *ldog pa.* This term refers to the process by which samsaric existence is brought to an end and is usually associated with the manner in which the realization of selflessness destroys the seeds of the mental afflictions. *BBhVy* (f. 249a) equates it with ultimate truth.

process of affliction, the truth regarding the process of purification, and the truth regarding correct methods of practice.

Truth is ninefold [in the sense of] the truth regarding impermanence, the truth regarding suffering, the truth regarding emptiness, the truth regarding selflessness, the truth regarding craving for existence, the truth regarding craving for extinction, the truth regarding the means of abandoning those [two forms of craving], the truth regarding the nirvana in which the support [of the heaps] remains, and the truth regarding the nirvana in which the support [of the heaps] does not remain.

Truth is tenfold[1198] [in the sense of] the truth regarding the suffering that arises from violence, the truth regarding the suffering that arises from a lack of possessions, the truth regarding the suffering that is due to an imbalance of the [body's four] elements, the truth regarding the suffering that is due to a transformation of what is dear, the truth regarding the suffering of indisposition, the truth regarding deeds, the truth regarding the mental afflictions, likewise, the truth regarding [the act of] listening [to Dharma teachings] and [engaging in] proper forms of attention, the truth regarding right view, and the truth regarding the result [that is attained by means] of right view.

This [collection of topics] is called "the formulation of teachings on truth." Further, it should be understood that [a detailed description of] the individual varieties [of truth] would be immeasurably large.

The Formulation of Teachings on the Applications [1.18.19.3]

The four applications are called "the formulation of the teachings on the applications." Moreover, they should be understood as they were differentiated previously.[1199]

1198. The first five in this group of ten are described as the last five forms of suffering in the last category of the one hundred and ten forms of suffering that serve as objects for meditating upon compassion. See Book I, chapter 16, the section entitled "Cultivating Compassion by Meditating on One Hundred and Ten Forms of Suffering" [I.16.3.1].

1199. Although one or more of the four applications (S: *catasro yuktayaḥ,* T: *rigs pa bzhi*) are referred to several times in the *BBh,* they are not described substantively in this text. They are, however, discussed in considerable detail several times in the *ŚBh,* an earlier section of the *YBh.* Those discussions are presumably what the text is referring to here. The four

The Formulation of Teachings on the Vehicles [1.18.19.4]

The seven ways in which a formulation of teachings is made for each of the three vehicles is called "the formulation of teachings on the vehicles"—[that is to say,] the Listeners' Vehicle, the Solitary Realizers' Vehicle, and the Great Vehicle.

It should be understood that the formulation of teachings on the Listeners' Vehicle in its entirety is made up of these seven elements: (1) the wisdom that relates to the four noble truths, (2) the basis of that very wisdom, as well

---

applications are meant to be practiced within the context of the activity known as reflection upon the Dharma (S: *cintā,* T: *bsam pa*).

Here is an abbreviated description of them that appears in *AS* (p. 81), with additional comments from *ASBh* (p. 99). *AS:* "What is the application that relates to dependence (S: *apekṣāyuktiḥ,* T: *ltos pa'i rigs pa*)? It is that [application] which [examines how] the arising of formations (S: *saṃskārāḥ,* T: *'du byed rnams*) is dependent upon causal factors." *ASBh:* "For example, [it examines how] the arising of a sprout depends upon a seed, water, and a field; [the arising of a particular form] of consciousness [depends upon] a faculty, an object, and [the mental factor of] attention, etc."

AS: What is the application that relates to the performance of actions (S: *kāryakāraṇayuktiḥ,* T: *bya ba byed pa'i rigs pa*)? It is that [application] which [examines how] entities that possess distinct unique attributes perform their own individual actions." *ASBh:* "For example, [it examines how the faculties of] the eye, etc., have the nature of [serving as] the basis (S: *āśrayaḥ,* T: *rten*) for [the arising of] eye consciousness, etc.; [the objects of] visible form, etc., have the nature of [serving as] the mental support (S: *ālambanam,* T: *dmigs pa*) [for those forms of consciousness]; and [those forms of] eye consciousness, etc. [perform the actions of] repeatedly generating an awareness (S: *prativijñāpanam,* T: *so sor rnam par rig pa*) of visible form, etc. Likewise, craftsmen such as goldsmiths, etc., also [perform the actions of] processing gold, etc."

AS: "What is the application that demonstrates the correctness of things (S: *upapattisādhanayuktiḥ,* T: *'thad pas grub pa'i rigs pa*)? It is that [application] which [examines the act of] showing that an object to be proven is consistent with valid forms of knowledge." *ASBh* specifies that the act of "showing" (S: *upadeśaḥ,* T: *ston pa*) refers to the elements of a philosophical argument—which is to say, its thesis, etc.

AS: "What is the application that relates to the nature of things (S: *dharmatāyuktiḥ,* T: *chos nyid kyi rigs pa*)? [It is that application which reflects upon] the well-established natures of entities, [which is to say that their] general and specific attributes have remained constant since beginningless time." *ASBh:* "For example, [among] the well-established natures of entities are [the facts that] fire burns and water moistens, etc. [The well-established nature of entities is also indicated in the statement which] declares that 'the fully developed eye is empty of [the quality of] permanence, [etc.,] up to [it is empty of the quality of] pertaining to a [real] self. Why? Because that is its natural condition.'" See also note 255.

as (3) the object, (4) the concomitants, (5) the action, (6) the requisites, and (7) the fruit of that very wisdom.

The formulation of teachings on the Solitary Realizers' Vehicle is similar to the formulation of teachings on the Listeners' Vehicle.

It should be understood that the formulation of teachings on the Great Vehicle is made up of these seven elements: (1) the wisdom that, having taken hold of the ineffable reality, has developed an awareness of the suchness that pertains to all entities and the sameness that does not engage in conceptualization about them, (2) the basis of that very wisdom, as well as (3) the object, (4) the concomitants, (5) the action, (6) the requisites, and (7) the fruit of that very wisdom.

Any bodhisattvas of the past, future, or present who have made, shall make, or are making correct formulations of teachings, all do so by means of these four subjects. There are none of greater significance than these and there are none besides these.

The Four Subjects of Investigation [1.18.20]

These are the four subjects that bodhisattvas investigate in order to gain thorough knowledge of the way things truly are: (1) the investigation of names, (2) the investigation of substances, (3) the investigation of [what constitutes] the designation of an essential nature, and (4) the investigation of [what constitutes] the designation of a distinguishing characteristic. The [explanation of] distinctions relating to these [topics] should be understood as it was presented in the chapter entitled "The Nature of Reality."[1200]

Thorough Knowledge of the Way Things Truly Are [1.18.21]

There are four forms of thorough knowledge of the way things truly are[1201] that bodhisattvas gain with regard to all entities.

What are the four?

They are (1) the thorough knowledge of the way things truly are that has completed the investigation of names, (2) the thorough knowledge of the way things truly are that has completed the investigation of substances, (3)

1200. See Book I, chapter 4, the section entitled "The Four Investigations" [I.4.9].

1201. S: *yathābhūtaparijñānam*, T: *yang dag pa ji lta ba bzhin du yongs su shes pa*.

the thorough knowledge of the way things truly are that has completed the investigation of [what constitutes] the designation of an essential nature, and (4) the thorough knowledge of the way things truly are that has completed the investigation of [what constitutes] the designation of a distinguishing characteristic. The [explanation of] distinctions relating to these [topics] should also be understood as it was presented in the chapter entitled "The Nature of Reality.[1202]

The Five Immeasurables [I.18.22]

There are five immeasurables that are conducive to making bodhisattvas skillful in all their activities.

What are the five?

They are (1) the immeasurable constituent of sentient beings; (2) the immeasurable constituent of world spheres; (3) the immeasurable constituent of entities;[1203] (4) the immeasurable constituent of beings who are to be trained; and (5) the immeasurable methods of training [others].

The constituent of sentient beings consists of the sixty-four classes of sentient beings, as they are listed in the *Stage of the Mind*.[1204] In terms of separate mental continua, [the constituent of sentient beings] is immeasurable.

1202. See Book I, chapter 4, the section entitled "The Four Forms of Thorough Knowledge of the Way Things Truly Are" [I.4.10].

1203. S: *dharmadhātur aprameyaḥ,* T: *chos kyi khams dpag tu med pa*. Earlier this term was translated as "entity-source" (see note 1110). As Asaṅga's remarks below suggest, he does not use the term *dharmadhātuḥ* here as a synonym for emptiness. Instead, he describes it as referring to the totality of entities that either cause sentient beings to continue to generate mental afflictions or enable them to pursue their spiritual purification.

1204. S: *manobhūmiḥ,* T: *yid ki sa*. This is the second of the seventeen stages that make up the *YBh*. The sixty-four classes of sentient beings that are mentioned there (*YBh,* pp. 48–49) are (1) hell beings; (2) animals; (3) tormented spirits; (4) gods; (5) humans; (6) humans of the ruling class (S: *kṣatriyaḥ,* T: *rgyal rigs*); (7) brahmins; (8) humans of the working class (S: *vaiśyaḥ,* T: *rje'u rigs*); (9) humans of the servile class (S: *śūdraḥ,* T: *dmangs rigs*); (10) women; (11) men; (12) sexually deficient persons (S: *paṇḍakaḥ,* T: *ma ning*) [that is, a man or woman who possesses a sexual faculty, but one that is deficient]; (13) inferior persons; (14) middling persons; (15) excellent persons; (16) householders; (17) homeless ascetics (S: *pravrajitaḥ,* T: *rab tu byung ba*); (18) extreme ascetics; (19) moderate ascetics; (20) holders of [a form of moral] discipline (S: *saṃvārikaḥ,* T: *sdom pa can*); (21) holders of negative discipline (S: *asaṃvaraḥ,* T: *sdom pa ma yin pa*) [negative discipline is acquired by adopting a form of livelihood that harms other beings, such as that of a person who slaughter animals for a living, as well as fishermen, hunters, thieves, and the like]; (22) those who hold neither [a form

Throughout the ten directions there are world spheres [of] immeasurable [vastness] with immeasurable [numbers of] names. For example, this world sphere is named Sahā,[1205] and it is because of this name that Brahmā is called the Lord of the Sahā [world sphere].

The [totality of] entities that are virtuous, nonvirtuous, and indeterminate should be understood as immeasurable in terms of their variety.

Those who are to be trained can be considered as being of one type in the sense that all sentient beings are beings who need to be trained. They can be considered as being of two types: (1) those who are entirely bound and (2) those who are not entirely bound. They can be considered as being of three types: (1) those of weak faculties, (2) those of middling faculties, and (3) those of sharp faculties. They can be considered as being of four types: (1) those of the ruling class, (2) brahmins, (3) those of the working class, and (4) those of the servile class. They can be considered as being of five types: (1) those with a strong tendency to develop desire, (2) those with a strong tendency to develop hatred, (3) those with a strong tendency to develop ignorance, (4) those with a strong tendency to develop pride, and (5) those with a strong tendency to develop discursive thoughts. They can be considered as being of six types: (1) householders, (2) homeless ascetics, (3) those who are not

---

of moral] discipline nor negative discipline; (23) those who are free of desire (S: *vītarāgaḥ,* T: *'dod chags dang bral ba*); (24) those who are not free of desire; (25) the group [of beings] who are firmly devoted to wrongfulness; (26) the group [of beings] who are firmly devoted to correctness; (27) the group [of beings] who are firmly devoted to not being restricted; (28) fully ordained monks (S: *bhikṣuḥ,* T: *dge slong*); (29) fully ordained nuns (S: *bhikṣuṇiḥ,* T: *dge slong ma*); (30) probationary nuns (S: *śikṣamāṇaḥ,* T: *dge slob ma*); (31) novice monks; (32) novice nuns; (33) holders of the layman's [system of] discipline; (34) holders of the laywoman's [system of] discipline; (35) those who are pursuing abandonment [of the mental afflictions]; (36) those who practice scripture recitation; (37) those who engage in service to the Sangha; (38) elders; (39) those of middling seniority; (40) the newly ordained; (41) spiritual teachers; (42) preceptors; (43) those who dwell with [a teacher]; (44) those [pupils] who dwell near [their teacher]; (45) guests who have arrived unexpectedly; (46) those who carry out work related to the Sangha; (47) those who desire material gain; (48) those who desire honor; (49) those who have few possessions; (50) those who possess wide learning; (51) those who possess knowledge and have acquired great merit; (52) those who are established in a practice that accords with Dharma [see note 480]; (53) those who are masters of the sutra scriptures; (54) those who are masters of the Vinaya code of morality; (55) those who are masters of the commentarial manuals; (56) those who are ordinary beings; (57) those who have seen the truths; (58) those who are training themselves [in the path]; (59) those who have completed the training; (60) listeners; (61) solitary realizers; (62) bodhisattvas; (63) tathāgatas; and (64) wheel rulers [see note 167].

1205. See note 435 for an explanation of this name.

spiritually mature, (4) those who are spiritually mature, (5) those who are not liberated, (6) those who are liberated. They can be considered as being of seven types: (1) those who have a hostile attitude [toward the Dharma], (2) those who have a neutral attitude [toward the Dharma], (3) those who learn by means of extensive explanation, (4) those who learn by means of a brief indication, (5) those who become spiritually tamed right away, (6) those who become spiritually tamed after an extended period, and (7) those who are spiritually tamed through being influenced by conditions, which is to say that they are transformed according to the particular conditions that they encounter. They can be considered as being of eight types, which is to say the eight assemblies,[1206] ranging from the assembly of kṣatriyas to the assembly of the gods of Brahmā's realm. They can be considered as being of nine types: (1) those who are trained by a tathāgata, (2) those who are trained by a listener or a solitary realizer, (3) those who are trained by a bodhisattva, (4) those who are difficult to train, (5) those who are not difficult to train, (6) those who are trained in a gentle manner, (7) those who are trained by being censured, (8) those who are trained from a distance, and (9) those who are trained while being nearby. They can be considered as being of ten types: (1) hell beings, (2) animals, (3) those [spirits] that abide in Yāma's world, (4) gods and humans whose range of activity is the desire realm, (5) those beings of the intermediate state, (6) those beings of the form realm, (7) those beings of the formless realm, (8) those beings who have conceptions, (9) those beings who lack conceptions, and (10) those beings who neither have nor lack conceptions. In terms of separate categories, this [constituent of beings to be trained] consists of fifty-five types. However, in terms of separate mental continua, it should be understood as being immeasurable.

Regarding this [topic], what distinguishes the constituent of those to be trained from the constituent of sentient beings?

The constituent of sentient beings is made up of all sentient beings without making any distinction—which is to say, both those who abide in a spiritual lineage and those who do not abide in a spiritual lineage. By contrast, [the category of sentient beings] that is limited to those who abide

1206. S: *aṣṭau parṣadaḥ,* T: *'khor brgyad.* They are (*YBh,* p. 72): (1) the assembly of kṣatriyas (members of the ruling class); (2) the assembly of brahmins; (3) the assembly of householders; (4) the assembly of spiritual ascetics (S: *śramanaḥ,* T: *dge sbyong*); (5) the assembly of the class of gods related to the four great kings; (6) the assembly of the gods of the Heaven of Thirty-Three; (7) the assembly of [the followers of] Māra (see note 433); and (8) the assembly of the gods of Brahmā's realm.

in a spiritual lineage and who have reached this or that stage [of spiritual development] is called "the constituent of those to be trained."

The means of training [those beings who are to be trained] should be understood as indicated previously.[1207] This [topic] is also immeasurable in terms of the variety of its individual forms.

These topics taken together make up the five immeasurables.

Why is that?

Here those sentient beings on whose behalf a bodhisattva undertakes activities make up the first immeasurable. Furthermore, the [world spheres] in which those sentient beings find a place to live make up the second immeasurable. Moreover, the entities by means of which those beings who live in those various world spheres undergo both the process of affliction and the process of purification make up the third immeasurable. In addition, among those sentient beings, the ones who are suitable for and capable of being permanently freed of their suffering make up the fourth immeasurable. The methods by which those very sentient beings are liberated make up the fifth immeasurable. Therefore, these [categories] make up the five immeasurables that are conducive to making bodhisattvas skillful in all their activities.

The Extensive Fruits and Benefits of Teaching Dharma [1.18.23]

It should be understood that five extensive fruits and benefits occur when the buddhas and bodhisattvas teach the Dharma to sentient beings.

What are the five?

(1) At the very time that the true Dharma is being taught, certain beings develop the Dharma eye that is free of dust and free of impurities toward all entities. (2) Certain beings attain the termination of the outflows while the true Dharma is being taught. (3) Certain beings develop the mind that aspires [to attain] unsurpassed complete and true enlightenment. (4) Certain beings attain the supreme bodhisattva forbearance immediately after hearing the true Dharma. (5) Furthermore, the teaching of the true Dharma by buddhas and bodhisattvas is conducive to the longstanding existence of

1207. *BBhVy* (f. 251b): "The phrase 'as indicated previously' means as indicated in the chapter entitled 'The Lineages of the Powers.'" The last section of that chapter describes the four principles for attracting a following as "deeds of body, speech, and mind that are governed by skillful means." The four principles themselves are addressed at length in Book I, chapters 9 and 15.

the eye of the Dharma that guides [beings], [a result] that occurs through its being successively taught, recited, and correctly practiced. These five should be understood as the extensive fruits and benefits of teaching [the true Dharma].

The Greatness of the Bodhisattva Vehicle [1.18.24]

Because the vehicle of the bodhisattvas possesses seven forms of greatness, it is called the "Great Vehicle."

What are the seven?

They are (1) the greatness of the Dharma, that is, the bodhisattva collection of extensive discourses that is included among the twelve divisions of the [Buddha's] speech;[1208] (2) the greatness of mental development, that is, certain individuals develop the mind that aspires to attain unsurpassed true and complete enlightenment; (3) the greatness of devotion, that is, certain individuals are devoted to that very greatness of the Dharma; (4) the greatness of superior attitude, that is, certain individuals enter the stage of a pure superior attitude once they have transcended the stage of conduct that is based upon devotion; (5) the greatness of the accumulations, [that is,] the accumulation of merit and the accumulation of wisdom, whose perfection brings about the attainment of unsurpassed true and complete enlightenment; (6) the greatness of time, [that is,] the three spans of "countless" kalpas that represent the length of time it takes to attain unsurpassed true and complete enlightenment; and (7) the greatness of attainment, [that is, the attainment of] unsurpassed true and complete enlightenment itself, [an attainment] whose nature is such that no other attainment has a nature that is its equal, much less one that is higher or greater.

Regarding this [topic], it should be understood that six of these [forms of] greatness—that is, the greatness of the Dharma, the greatness of mental development, the greatness of devotion, the greatness of superior attitude, the greatness of the accumulations, and the greatness of time—make up the causes of the greatness of attainment, while that single greatness of attainment is [the form of greatness] that represents the result of those six.

1208. Extensive discourses (S: *vaipulyam,* T: *shin tu rgyas pa'i sde*) make up the tenth category in the twelve divisions of the Buddha's speech. See note 529.

The Summary of the Great Vehicle [1.18.25]

These eight qualities serve as a summary of the entire Great Vehicle: (1) teaching the bodhisattva collection of scriptures; (2) elucidating the true nature[1209] of all the entities [that are presented] in that very bodhisattva collection of scriptures; (3) elucidating the inconceivable and supremely vast powers of the buddhas and bodhisattvas [that are mentioned] in that very bodhisattva collection of scriptures; (4) properly listening to those [topics]; (5) attaining the superior attitude[1210] that is preceded by proper reflection upon those [topics]; (6) devoting oneself to the forms of meditation[1211] that are preceded by attainment of the superior attitude; (7) perfecting the results of meditation[1212] that are preceded by devotion to the [various] forms of meditation; and (8) the state of permanent deliverance[1213] that is achieved by having perfected those very results of meditation. This is the manner in which the bodhisattvas who train themselves achieve unsurpassed true and complete enlightenment.

The Ten Bodhisattvas [1.18.26]

Who, then, are the bodhisattvas who attain supreme true and complete enlightenment by training themselves in this manner?

In brief, it should be understood that there are ten types [of bodhisattvas]: (1) the one who abides in the spiritual lineage, (2) the one who has entered [the path], (3) the one whose attitude is not pure, (4) the one whose attitude is pure, (5) the one who is not spiritually ripe, (6) the one who is spiritually ripe, (7) the one for whom certainty has not occurred, (8) the

1209. S: *tattvārthaḥ*, T: *de kho na'i don*. This term is the subject matter of chapter 4, where it is translated as "the nature of reality."

1210. S: *adhyāśayopagamanam*, T: *lhag pa'i bsam pa nyams su blang ba*. *BBhVy* (f. 252b) interprets this phrase as referring to attainment of the Great Vehicle's path of seeing (S: *darśanamārgaḥ*, T: *mthong ba'i lam*).

1211. S: *bhāvanākārapraveśaḥ*, T: *bsgom pa'i rnam pas 'jug pa*. *BBhVy* (f. 252b) identifies this phrase as encompassing the spiritual practices that are cultivated from the second through the ninth of the ten ārya bodhisattva stages.

1212. S: *bhāvanāphalaniṣpattiḥ*, T: *bsgom pa'i 'bras bus yongs su grub pa*. *BBhVy* (f. 252b) identifies this phrase as a reference to the last of the ten ārya bodhisattva stages.

1213. S: *atyantanairyāṇikatā*, T: *gtan du nges par 'byin pa*. *BBhVy* (f. 252b) identifies this expression with the result of the Great Vehicle path—that is, supreme enlightenment.

one for whom certainty has occurred, (9) the one who is hindered by one rebirth,[1214] and (10) the one who is in his final existence.

Regarding this [topic], a bodhisattva who abides in the spiritual lineage, is practicing the trainings, and has developed [enlightenment] mind is called "the one who has entered [the path]." As long as that very [bodhisattva] who has entered [the path] has not yet achieved the stage of a pure attitude, he or she is called "the one whose attitude is not pure." However, once he or she has entered [that stage], he or she becomes "the one whose attitude is pure." Moreover, as long as that very [bodhisattva] whose attitude is pure has not yet achieved the stage that is the perfect manner of going, he is called "the one who is not spiritually ripe." However, once he has entered [that stage], he becomes "the one who is spiritually ripe." As long as [a bodhisattva] who is not spiritually ripe has not yet attained the stage of certainty or the stage of certain conduct, he is called "the one for whom certainty has not occurred." However, once he has attained [either of those stages], he becomes "the one for whom certainty has occurred." Moreover, there are two types of [bodhisattvas] who are spiritually ripe: (1) [a bodhisattva] hindered by one rebirth who will attain unsurpassed true and complete enlightenment in his next rebirth, and (2) [a bodhisattva] in his final existence who will attain unsurpassed true and complete enlightenment within that very lifetime.

These ten bodhisattvas who have been described from the [point at which they are abiding in their] spiritual lineage up to [the point at which they are on the verge of attaining] unsurpassed true and complete enlightenment are the ones who train themselves in the bodhisattva trainings. There are no higher forms of training for them than these, [which include the seven subjects] in relation to which they should train themselves[1215] and [the manner] in which they should train themselves.[1216] Nor is there any bodhisattva who surpasses the bodhisattvas described [here] and who is someone who should train in the bodhisattva trainings.

1214. S: *ekajātipratibhaddhaḥ*, T: *skye ba gcig gis thogs pa*. *BBhVy* (f. 209a): "'A bodhisattva who is hindered by one rebirth' is one who has taken rebirth in Tuṣita Heaven."

1215. S: *yatra śikṣeran*, T: *gang la slob pa*. This is a reference to the subject matter contained in chapters 3 through 7. See the opening section of Book I, chapter 3, where these seven subjects (S: *sthānam*, T: *gnas*) are first mentioned.

1216. S: *yathā śikṣeran*, T: *ji ltar slob pa*. The discussion of the manner in which bodhisattvas train themselves begins with Book I, chapter 8 and continues with all the chapters that describe the actual forms of training.

Descriptive Appellations [1.18.27]

Moreover, all of these bodhisattvas, without distinction, are known by such names as the following ones that make reference to their spiritual qualities: enlightenment being,[1217] great being,[1218] wise one,[1219] one who possesses supreme brilliance,[1220] child of the victorious ones,[1221] one who supports the victorious ones,[1222] conqueror,[1223] sprout of a victorious one,[1224] valiant one,[1225] supremely worthy one,[1226] leader of a company of travelers,[1227] one

1217. *BBhVy* (f. 253b): "He or she is called an 'enlightenment being' (S: *bodhisattvaḥ,* T: *byang chub sems dpa'*) because he or she takes hold of [the two mental objects of] enlightenment and [the welfare of] sentient beings."

1218. Ibid.: "He or she is called a 'great being' (S: *mahāsattvaḥ,* T: *sems dpa' chen po*) because he or she possesses the seven forms of greatness."

1219. Ibid.: "He or she is called 'wise one' (S: *dhīmān,* T: *blo dang ldan pa*) because he or she possesses very deep and extensive wisdom and because he or she has the ability to explain the intent of the most profound object [i.e., emptiness]."

1220. Ibid.: "He or she is called 'one who possesses supreme brilliance' (S: *uttamadyutiḥ,* T: *mchog tu gsal ba*) because he or she has attained the quality that is the splendor of wisdom."

1221. Ibid.: "He or she is called 'child of the victorious ones' (S: *jinaputraḥ,* T: *rgyal ba'i sras*) because he or she has taken birth in the lineage of the tathāgatas."

1222. Ibid.: "He or she is called 'one who supports the victorious ones' (S: *jinādhāraḥ,* T: *rgyal ba'i gzhi*) because he or she strives to keep the lineage of the buddhas from becoming extinct."

1223. Ibid.: "He or she is called 'conqueror' (S: *vijetā,* T: *rgyal byed*) because he or she conquers both the mental afflictions within his or her own continuum and [the mental afflictions] within others' [continua]."

1224. Ibid.: "He or she is called 'sprout of a victorious one' (S: *jinānkuraḥ,* T: *rgyal ba'i myu gu*) because he or she possesses the causes that will develop into the Buddha's qualities of the [ten] powers, the [four] forms of intrepid confidence, etc., that are like the leaves, etc., [that develop from a sprout]."

1225. Ibid.: "He or she is called 'valiant one' (S: *vikrāntaḥ,* T: *rtsal dang ldan pa*) because he or she is a preeminent hero."

1226. Ibid.: "He or she is called 'supremely worthy one' (S: *paramāryaḥ,* T: *'phags pa'i mchog*) because he or she pursues the supreme aim in its entirety."

1227. Ibid.: "He or she is called 'leader of a company of travelers' (S: *sārthavāhaḥ,* T: *ded dpon*) because he or she leads the great company of sentient beings who are wandering in samsara to the city of nirvana."

who possesses great renown,[1228] compassionate one,[1229] one who possesses great merit,[1230] mighty lord,[1231] and righteous one.[1232]

Moreover, it should be understood that there are immeasurable numbers of individual names that have been received by [each of] the limitless numbers of bodhisattvas who are found throughout the endless and limitless world spheres that lie in the ten directions.

Regarding this [topic], it should be understood that those bodhisattvas who declare themselves to be bodhisattvas but who do not correctly practice the bodhisattva trainings are counterfeit bodhisattvas; they are not genuine [bodhisattvas]. On the other hand, it should be understood that those [bodhisattvas] who declare themselves to be bodhisattvas and who also correctly practice the bodhisattva trainings are genuine bodhisattvas.

Within [Book I of] *The Stage of a Bodhisattva,* [known as] "The Object of Mental Application That Relates to the Support," this completes the eighteenth chapter, entitled "The Qualities of a Bodhisattva." This also completes "The Object of Mental Application That Relates to the Support."

1228. *BBhVy* (ff. 253b–254a): "He or she is called 'one who possesses great renown' (S: *mahāyaśaḥ,* T: *grags pa chen po*) because the fragrance of his or her virtuous qualities spreads in all the directions."

1229. *BBhVy* (f. 254a): "He or she is called 'compassionate one' (S: *kṛpāluḥ,* T: *snying rje can*) because he or she possesses great compassion."

1230. Ibid.: "He or she is called 'one who possesses great merit' (S: *mahāpuṇyaḥ,* T: *bsod nams chen po*) because he or she possesses the great merit of generosity and the rest."

1231. Ibid.: "He or she is called 'mighty lord' (S: *īśvaraḥ,* T: *dbang phyug*) because he or she is one who possesses the authority that comes with having great power, etc."

1232. Ibid.: "He or she is called 'righteous one' (S: *dhārmikaḥ,* T: *chos dang ldan pa*) because his or her conduct of body, etc., is beyond reproach." These sixteen epithets are the same ones that are cited in *MSA,* ch. 19, vv. 73, 74. While Asaṅga's Sanskrit text simply lists the terms consecutively, the Tibetan text cites them in verse form.

BOOK II

The Qualities That Accord with the Support

I

The Marks of a Bodhisattva

Summary lines [of verse]:

> Essential nature, basis, fruits and benefits,
> Successive order, and inclusion.

These five are the bodhisattva-marks of a genuine bodhisattva. [They are such that] one who possesses them is counted among those who are referred to as bodhisattvas.

What are the five?

[They are] (1) sympathy, (2) agreeable speech, (3) fortitude,[1233] (4) open-handedness, and (5) [the ability to] explain profound meanings and intents.

Furthermore, [each of] these five spiritual qualities should be understood according to five ways of being considered: (1) essential nature, (2) basis, (3) fruits and benefits, (4) successive order, and (5) manner of inclusion.

The Essential Natures of the Marks [II.1.1]

Regarding this [topic], there are two aspects to the essential nature of [a bodhisattva's] sympathy: (1) that which relates to his or her attitude and (2) that which relates to his or her activities. Regarding this, [the essential nature] that relates to [a bodhisattva's] attitude is the attitude of wanting to benefit [sentient beings] and the attitude of wanting to bring [them] happiness. This is called a bodhisattva's "sympathy toward sentient beings." The essential nature of [a bodhisattva's] sympathy that relates to his or her activities is a

1233. S: *vairyam,* T: *brtan pa. BBhVy* (f. 254b): "'Fortitude' means that because [one's mind] is [strongly] directed to the practice of virtuous entities, one cannot be shaken by nonvirtuous ones."

bodhisattva's use of his or her body and speech to provide sentient beings with [the aims of] that very attitude, as much as he or she is able and with all his or her strength.

Regarding this [topic], the essential nature of agreeable speech should be understood as those forms of speech that were described previously in the chapter entitled "The Principles for Attracting a Following" as [speech that is] pleasing, friendly, and provides assistance.[1234]

Regarding this [topic], the strength of a bodhisattva that consists of courage,[1235] firmness,[1236] and absence of dejection[1237] is called "the essential nature of a bodhisattva's fortitude."

Regarding this [topic], a bodhisattva's extensive generosity as well as his or her generosity that is free of affliction should be understood as the essential nature of his or her openhandedness.

The four forms of informative knowledge, as well as the understanding that arises from correctly applying oneself to develop those [forms of informative knowledge], should be understood as the essential nature of the bodhisattvas' [ability to] explain profound meanings and intents.

1234. See the opening section of Book I, chapter 15, where these three qualities are collectively identified as representing "all-inclusive agreeable speech." Both Sanskrit editions here mention "pleasing speech" (S: *āmodanī vāc,* T: *kun tu dga' bar byed pa*) as the first of the three qualities. Although this is not precisely the same term as the second quality described in chapter 15—namely, "speech that pleases (S: *ānandanī,* T: *so sor yang dag par dga' bar byed pa*) sentient beings"—it is apparently meant to be taken as synonymous with it. The Tibetan translation reverses the order of the first two qualities here, perhaps to correspond to the original order of the three types of all-inclusive agreeable speech that are described in chapter 15.

1235. S: *sattvam,* T: *snying stobs.* T: *BBhVy* (f. 255a): "'Courage' is the combined application of three qualities—wisdom, compassion, and effort—to the aims of sentient beings. . . . Also, courage is absence of fear."

1236. S: *dhṛtiḥ,* T: *sran thub pa. BBhVy* (f. 255a): "Firmness is [the quality of] being indomitable in the face of adversity. . . . [Also,] firmness is to be unwavering in the face of suffering."

1237. S: *alīnatvam,* T: *zhum pa med pa. BBhVy* (f. 255a): "Absence of dejection is the quality of remaining mentally undaunted with regard to the profound and extensive spiritual qualities. . . . [Also,] absence of dejection means to remain free of fear even when one hears about something formidable."

The Bases of the Marks [II.1.2]

The Bases of Sympathy [II.1.2.1]

Regarding this [topic], there are five bases[1238] of sympathy.

What are the five?

They are (1) sentient beings who are suffering, (2) [sentient beings] who engage in misconduct, (3) [sentient beings] who are heedless, (4) [sentient beings] who have undertaken a wrongful [form of] practice, and (5) [sentient beings] who are closely attached to the mental afflictions.[1239]

Any sentient beings, including those in the hells, who have entered a state in which they uninterruptedly and continuously experience feelings[1240] characterized by suffering are called "those who are suffering." Moreover, those beings who are not unavoidably experiencing suffering but who are engaging in physical misconduct and are engaging in verbal and mental misconduct to a great degree, and who have a nature that delights in those [forms of misconduct], are called "those who engage in misconduct." Examples [of this type of being] are individuals who slaughter sheep, hogs, poultry, and the like. Moreover, those beings who are not unavoidably experiencing suffering and not engaging in misconduct but who are highly attached to sensory pleasures and repeatedly enjoy them; who are chiefly devoted to spending time watching actors, dancers, jesters, and those who perform expressive dance; and who are chiefly concerned with amusing themselves are called "those who are heedless." An example of a portion [of this overall group] is those individuals who are fond of sensory pleasures. Moreover, those beings who are not unavoidably experiencing suffering, who are not engaging in misconduct, and who are not heedless but who have undertaken to free themselves from suffering by relying upon views that

1238. S: *adhiṣṭhānam,* T: *gnas.* The noun *adhiṣṭhānam* means literally "that thing upon which something stands," and hence "basis." *BBhVy* (f. 254b): "The term 'basis' indicates the object (S: *viṣayaḥ,* T: *yul*) [of sympathy, etc.]."

1239. S: *kleśānuśayitāḥ sattvāḥ,* T: *nyon mongs pa'i bag la nyal dang ldan pa'i sems can.* The Sanskrit adjective *anuśayita* is formed from the same root (S: *anuśī*) as the noun that means "latency" (S: *anuśayaḥ,* T: *bag la nyal*), which is synonymous with the "seeds" (S: *bījam,* T: *sa bon*) or "traces" (S: *vasanā,* T: *bag chags*) of the mental afflictions (see note 608). The Tibetan alludes to this sense in its rendering, even though here it literally means one who is "closely attached" to the mental afflictions.

1240. S: *vedanā,* T: *tshor ba.* This term is the name for the second of the five heaps (S: *skandhaḥ,* T: *phung po*). See note 194 for a definition of its essential nature.

are ruinous are called "those who have undertaken a wrongful [form of] practice." An example is those who have abandoned sensory pleasures and gone forth into a badly taught system of spiritual discipline. Moreover, those beings who are not necessarily experiencing suffering, etc., up to those who have not undertaken a wrongful [form of] practice but who are completely bound or partially bound by the mental afflictions are called "those who are closely attached to the mental afflictions." Examples are those virtuous ordinary persons who have applied themselves [to the Dharma] correctly, as well as those [āryas] who are still undergoing spiritual training. This represents the full extent of the [beings who constitute] bases for the sympathy of bodhisattvas. They are the bases and the [mental] objects by means of which sympathy is generated. There are none of greater significance than these and there are none besides these.

The Bases of Agreeable Speech [II.1.2.2]

There are five bases of bodhisattvas' agreeable speech.

What are the five?

They are [the activities of] (1) correctly conversing,[1241] (2) correctly pleasing,[1242] (3) correctly providing reassurance,[1243] (4) correctly fulfilling

1241. S: *samyag ālapanā,* T: *legs par smra bar bya ba*. *BBhVy* (f. 255b) identifies this as a form of speech that is directed toward "those who are in a normal state" (S: **prakṛtisthaḥ,* T: *rang bzhin du gnas pa*)—that is, a state that is unimpaired or healthy. This seems to correspond to the first of the three types of all-inclusive agreeable speech, namely, that which is "friendly" (S: *sammodanī,* T: *dga' bar byed pa*), etc.

1242. S: *samyag ānandanā,* T: *legs par kun tu dga' bar bya pa*. *BBhVy* (f. 255b) identifies this as a form of speech that is directed toward "those who are enjoying good fortune" (S: **vṛddhika,* T: *'phel ba thob pa*). This corresponds to the second of the three types of all-inclusive agreeable speech, namely, agreeable speech that is "pleasing" (S: *ānandanī,* T: *dga' bar byed pa*), etc.

1243. S: *samyag āśvāsanā,* T: *legs par dbugs dbyung ba*. *BBhVy* (f. 255b) identifies this as a form of speech that is directed toward those who are "frightened" (S: **sabhayaḥ,* T: *'jigs pa dang ldan pa*). This corresponds to the tenth type of agreeable speech of every form that "reassures those who are frightened by a variety of dangers" (see Book I, chapter 15).

wishes,[1244] and (5) giving proper instruction.[1245] Their classifications should be understood as they were explained in the chapter entitled "The Principles for Attracting a Following." These are the five bases and [mental] objects by means of which the agreeable speech of bodhisattvas comes into being. There are none of greater significance than these and there are none besides these.

The Bases of Fortitude [II.1.2.3]

It should be understood that there are five bases of a bodhisattva's fortitude.

What are the five?

It should be understood that the bases of a bodhisattva's fortitude are the very same five aspects that were mentioned in the chapter entitled "The Spiritual Qualities That Are Conducive to Enlightenment" as being the ones by means of which bodhisattvas [accomplish] the development of firmness."[1246] These are the bases and [mental] objects by means of which a bodhisattva's fortitude comes into being. There are none of greater significance than these and there are none besides these.

The Bases of Openhandedness [II.1.2.4]

There are five bases of a bodhisattva's openhandedness.

What are the five?

They are (1) constant generosity, (2) joyful generosity, (3) respectful generosity, (4) generosity that is free of affliction, and (5) disinterested

1244. S: *samyak pravāraṇā*, T: *legs par bstabs pa*. *BBhVy* (f. 255b) identifies this as a form of speech that is directed toward those who are "rightly established [in the spiritual practice]" (S: **samyakpratipannaḥ*, T: *yang dag par zhugs pa*). This corresponds to the ninth type of agreeable speech of every form that "abundantly fulfills the wishes (S: *viśadapravāraṇī*, T: *rgya cher stobs pa*) of others as relates to abiding with few worries about all the implements [that relate to subsistence] as well as abiding with few worries about correctly accomplishing those activities that ought to be carried out." See Book I, chapter 15.

1245. S: *nyāyopadeśaḥ*, T: *rigs pas bstan pa*. *BBhVy* (f. 255b) identifies this form of speech as being directed toward those who are "confused about what is proper" (S: **nyāyamūḍhaḥ*, T: *rigs pa la rmongs pa*). This corresponds to the eleventh type of agreeable speech of every form that "is made up of proper instruction" (S: *nyāyopadeśasaṃgṛhītā*, T: *rigs pa bstan pas bsdus pa*). See Book I, chapter 15.

1246. See Book I, chapter 17, the section entitled "Firmness" [I.17.2].

generosity.[1247] Moreover, their distinctions should be understood in detail as they were described in the chapter entitled "Generosity." These are the bases and [mental] objects by means of which a bodhisattva's openhandedness comes into being. There are none of greater significance than these and there are none besides these.

The Bases of Explaining Profound Meanings and Intents [II.1.2.5]

There are five bases of explaining profound meanings and intents.

What are the five?

Those profound sutra scriptures that the Tathāgata taught in which the profound is illuminated, those that contain [discussions of] emptiness, and those that conform to the [doctrine of] dependent origination [in which] the nature of the particular causes [by which entities are conditioned is revealed] represent the first basis. Further, the skillfulness that relates to [understanding the nature of] transgressions and the skillfulness that relates to turning away from transgressions [as revealed] in the Vinaya scriptures represent the second basis. Moreover, the unerring formulations of the attributes of entities [that are found] in the [Abhidharma] summary listings[1248] represent the third basis. The clear ascertainment of terms and meanings that are associated with obscure Dharma teachings that possess an underlying meaning represents the fourth basis. The differentiation of the entities, meanings, interpretations, and distinct classifications associated with all Dharma teachings represents the fifth basis. [Each of these] is a basis and a [mental] object by means of which the explaining of profound meanings and intents comes into being. There are none of greater significance than these and there are none besides these.

1247. S: *aniśritadānatā,* T: *mi gnas par sbyin pa*. See note 661. The earlier Tibetan translation of this same Sanskrit term is slightly different.

1248. S: *mātṛkā,* T: *ma mo*. This use of the term refers to the summary listings of essential Abhidharma topics. See the introduction for a discussion of this term.

The Fruits and Benefits of the Marks [II.1.3]

The Fruits and Benefits of Sympathy [II.1.3.1]

At the very outset, a bodhisattva's sympathy serves to abandon animosity toward sentient beings. A bodhisattva who is sympathetic in this way applies him- or herself to all the activities that are beneficial to sentient beings without having a dispirited mind. He or she does not become weary of these undertakings. The sympathy that remains dedicated to this [aim] to a high degree is conducive to abiding in a state of irreproachable happiness in this life and also to receiving benefits in future lives. In addition, it should be understood that all the benefits that the Blessed One declared in relation to loving-kindness—that neither poison nor weapons have any [harmful] effect upon [the bodhisattva's] body, etc.[1249]—are also [acquired] by a bodhisattva who is sympathetic. These should be regarded as the fruits and benefits of the sympathy that is possessed by bodhisattvas.

The Fruits and Benefits of Agreeable Speech [II.1.3.2]

A bodhisattva who engages in agreeable speech abandons four types of verbal faults in the present life. [The four are] (1) lying, (2) divisive speech, (3) harsh speech, and (4) idle talk. His or her speech is intent upon bringing benefit to self and bringing benefit to others. Both in this life and in future lives, a bodhisattva who engages in agreeable speech becomes one whose speech is accepted and one whose speech is adhered to. It should be understood that these are the fruits and benefits of a bodhisattva's agreeable speech.

1249. Sutta 15 of the Book of Elevens in the *Aṅguttara Nikāya* collection lists eleven benefits of loving-kindness: (1) you sleep comfortably; (2) you awaken comfortably; (3) you do not have wicked dreams; (4) you are dear to human beings; (5) you are dear to nonhuman beings (i.e., gods and spirits); (6) the gods will protect you; (7) neither fire, nor poison, nor weapons have any harmful effect upon you; (8) you can concentrate your mind quickly; (9) you have a serene countenance; (10) you pass away without being confused in mind; and (11) should you fail to reach a higher state, you will be reborn in Brahmā's realm. Sutta 1 in the Book of Eights also lists eight of these eleven benefits. See also *RA,* ch. 3, vv. 84–85, which describes eight benefits of loving-kindness.

The Fruits and Benefits of Fortitude [II.1.3.3]

A resolute bodhisattva is one who is completely and entirely free of idleness and laziness in this life. He or she also accepts the discipline of bodhisattva morality with a joyful mind.[1250] Having done so, he or she does not become despondent. He or she patiently benefits self and others. In future [lives], he or she becomes one whose enterprising nature is firm with regard to taking up every form of a bodhisattva's duties. He or she does not turn away from [duties] without having completed them. These should be understood as the fruits and benefits of the fortitude that is possessed by bodhisattvas.

The Fruits and Benefits of Openhandedness and of Explaining Profound Meanings and Intents [II.1.3.4–5]

The fruits and benefits of openhandedness and of explaining profound meanings and intents should be understood in the manner that the power of generosity and the power of wisdom were explained in the chapter entitled "Power."[1251]

This constitutes [the description of] the fruits and benefits of the marks that are possessed by bodhisattvas.

The Successive Order of the Marks [II.1.4]

What is the successive order of these [marks]?

First of all, a bodhisattva assists sentient beings on the basis of sympathy. [On the basis of this quality], he or she is also attentive toward them and desirous of acting on their behalf. As a consequence of that, he or she tells them what is proper, causes them to learn [what is proper], and points out to them [what is proper], in order to turn them away from opportunities [to engage in] nonvirtuous [actions] and establish them in opportunities [to engage in] virtuous [actions]. Because of refusing to abandon either beings

1250. Both Sanskrit editions indicate that the quality of having a joyful mind should be read with the first sentence: "A resolute bodhisattva is one who is completely and entirely free of idleness and laziness in this life and is one who possesses a joyful mind." I have followed the Tibetan translation, which identifies it with the act of taking up the bodhisattva morality.

1251. See Book I, chapter 5, the sections entitled "The Power of Generosity" [I.5.2.1] and "The Power of Wisdom" [I.5.2.6].

who are [properly] engaged in practice or beings who are engaged in erroneous practice, [a bodhisattva] is willing to endure hostile encounters with those individuals who have undertaken [to conduct themselves] in the manner [that has been suggested] but who are behaving badly toward [other] beings and who are oppressed in manifold ways by the mental afflictions. [The bodhisattva] who is resolute in this way ripens some beings by attracting them [to the Dharma] using material objects; [he or she ripens] some by attracting them on the basis of the Dharma; and [he or she ripens] some by attracting them using both material objects and the Dharma. It should be understood that this is the order in which the five marks of a bodhisattva [become evident].

The Manner of Their Inclusion [II.1.5]

These five marks of a bodhisattva are [forms of] the six perfections.

Among the six perfections, which mark is included within which perfection?

Sympathy is included with the perfection of meditative absorption. Agreeable speech is included within both the perfection of morality and the perfection of wisdom. Fortitude is included within the perfection of effort, the perfection of patience, and the perfection of wisdom. Openhandedness is only included within the perfection of generosity. The quality of explaining profound meanings and intents is included within both the perfection of meditative absorption and the perfection of wisdom.

This is how the five marks of a bodhisattva should be understood according to five ways of being considered—that is, according to their essential natures, their bases, their fruits and benefits, their order, and their [manner of] inclusion.

Within [Book II of] *The Stage of a Bodhisattva*, [known as] "The Object of Mental Application That Relates to the Qualities That Accord with the Support," this completes the first chapter, entitled "The Marks of a Bodhisattva."

2

FACTIONS

Summary lines [of verse]:

> Having completed one's spiritual activities well;
> Skillfulness; assisting others; and, lastly, dedication.

It should be understood that, in brief, there are four qualities that pertain to a bodhisattva who belongs either to the householder faction or to the faction of homeless ascetics. They are such that the householder or homeless ascetic who trains in relation to them will quickly attain unsurpassed true and complete enlightenment.

What are the four?

[They are] (1) the quality of having completed one's spiritual activities well, (2) skillfulness, (3) providing assistance to others, and (4) dedication.

THE QUALITY OF HAVING COMPLETED ONE'S SPIRITUAL ACTIVITIES WELL [II.2.1]

Regarding this [topic], what is a bodhisattva's quality of having completed the spiritual activities well?

It is (1) the quality of carrying out activities in relation to the perfections in a definite manner, (2) the quality of carrying out activities [in relation to the perfections] in a proficient manner,[1252] (3) the quality of carrying out

1252. S: *nipuṇakāritā,* T: *byang bar byed pa*. While the adjective *nipuṇa* typically means "clever," "adroit," or "skillful," it can also mean "perfect," "complete," or "absolute" (MW, p. 550). *BBhVy* (f. 257b): "Because [a bodhisattva] acts respectfully (S: **satkṛtyakāri,* T: *gus par byed pa*) when he or she is giving up everything, it is therefore called 'the quality of carrying out activities in a proficient manner.'"

activities [in relation to the perfections] continually, and (4) the quality of carrying out activities [in relation to the perfections] in an irreproachable manner.

How does a bodhisattva become one who carries out activities in a definite manner, specifically in relation to generosity?

Here a bodhisattva who possesses entities that are suitable to be given will surely give them to a petitioner who has approached him or her in a correct manner, [regardless of] whether [that petitioner] is someone who has harmed or benefited him or her, and [regardless of] whether [that petitioner] is someone who possesses good qualities or someone who possesses faults. No one is capable of altering [that bodhisattva's] intention to practice generosity—whether a human being, nonhuman being, ascetic, brahmin, or anyone else in the world [who is acting] in a way that accords with the Dharma.

How does a bodhisattva become one who carries out activities in a proficient manner, specifically in relation to generosity?

Here a bodhisattva who possesses entities that are suitable to be given will give them all to a petitioner who has approached him or her in a correct manner. There is nothing that he or she would fail to give up for the sake of sentient beings—not even an entity that is an inner one, much less an outer one.

How does a bodhisattva become one who carries out activities continually, specifically in relation to generosity?

Here a bodhisattva is one who does not tire of [practicing] generosity; he or she engages in acts of generosity whenever the opportunity arises, and does so continually, uninterruptedly, and at all times.

How does a bodhisattva become one who carries out activities in an irreproachable manner, for instance in relation to generosity?

Here a bodhisattva avoids those afflicted forms of generosity that were described in the chapter entitled "Generosity" and practices acts of generosity that are free of affliction.[1253]

This is how a bodhisattva completes the spiritual activities well in relation to generosity. As with generosity, this topic should be understood in a manner that accords with the circumstances for the perfections of morality, patience, effort, meditative absorption, and wisdom in terms of these

1253. See Book I, chapter 9, the section entitled "What to Observe and Avoid When Practicing Generosity" [I.9.2.1].

very same four aspects of (1) carrying out activities in a definite manner, (2) carrying out activities in a proficient manner, (3) carrying out activities continually, and (4) carrying out activities in an irreproachable manner.

Skillfulness [II.2.2]

Regarding this [topic], what is a bodhisattva's skillfulness?

In brief, it should be understood as being of ten types: (1) the skillful means that removes the enmity of those beings who have hostile intentions; (2) [the skillful means] that causes those beings who are indifferent [toward the teaching] to enter it; (3) [the skillful means] that spiritually ripens those beings who have entered [the teaching]; (4) the skillful means that liberates those beings who have become spiritually ripe; (5) skillfulness in all worldly treatises; (6) skillfulness gained through carefully considering the errors [that can occur] in relation to adoption of the discipline associated with bodhisattva morality; (7) skillfulness regarding [how to perform] correct aspirational prayers; (8) skillfulness regarding the Listeners' Vehicle; (9) skillfulness regarding the Solitary Realizers' Vehicle; and (10) skillfulness regarding the Great Vehicle. The particulars that relate to all these forms of skillfulness should be understood according to the previous descriptions that were made here and there in this very *Stage of a Bodhisattva*.

These ten forms of a bodhisattva's skillfulness accomplish five actions: (1) By means of the first four forms of skillfulness, a bodhisattva unites sentient beings with their individual aims. (2) By means of skillfulness in all worldly treatises, a bodhisattva refutes all the verbal challenges made by adversaries. (3) By means of skillfulness gained through carefully considering the errors [that can occur] in relation to adoption of the discipline associated with bodhisattva morality, a bodhisattva avoids committing transgressions. If [a transgression] should be incurred, he or she remedies it in accordance with the Dharma. He or she reflects constantly on [how to keep] exceedingly pure the morality whose discipline has been adopted. (4) By means of skillfulness regarding [how to perform] correct aspirational prayers, a bodhisattva attains success in the future with regard to all his or her desired aims. (5) By means of skillfulness in the three vehicles, a bodhisattva teaches a form of Dharma that corresponds to the [particular] spiritual lineages, faculties, and forms of devotion that are possessed by beings and points out a suitable method of practice. This is how a bodhisattva carries out five actions by means of the ten forms of skillfulness. It is by means of these five actions that all of the duties relating to the aims of both this life and future lives are fully achieved.

Providing Assistance to Others [II.2.3]

Regarding this [topic], what is the assistance that a bodhisattva provides to others?

Here a bodhisattva, by relying upon the four principles for attracting a following—[namely,] generosity, agreeable speech, beneficial conduct, and sameness of purpose—provides benefit to certain sentient beings, provides happiness [to others], and provides both benefit and happiness [to still others]. This is a brief statement of the assistance that bodhisattvas provide to others. In addition to this, the extensive explanation should be understood as described earlier in the chapter entitled "One's Own and Others' Aims."

Dedication [II.2.4]

Regarding this [topic], what is a bodhisattva's dedication?

Here, with deep-felt faith, a bodhisattva dedicates to unsurpassed true and complete enlightenment any and all roots of virtue of the past, present, or future that he or she has ever collected by these three methods, [namely,] the quality of having completed spiritual activities well, skillfulness, and providing assistance to others. He or she does not wish for the ripening of those roots of virtue in the form of any fruit other than unsurpassed true and complete enlightenment.

It should be understood that whatever elements of spiritual training the Blessed One taught to householder [bodhisattvas][1254] and homeless bodhisattvas, they are all included within these four categories: (1) the quality of having completed spiritual activities well, (2) skillfulness, (3) providing assistance to others, and (4) dedication. Therefore, it should be understood that for a bodhisattva who has completed the spiritual activities well, who is skillful, who provides assistance to others, and who engages in [the act

1254. *BBhVy* (f. 258b): "The path of training that pertains to bodhisattvas who are householders is taught in the *Sutra of Questions Posed by [the Householder] Ugra*" (S: [*Ārya*] *Gṛhapatyugraparipṛcchāmahāyānasūtram*, T: [*'Phags pa*] *Khyim bdag drag shul can gyis zhus pa zhes bya ba theg pa chen po'i mdo*).

of] dedication, the enlightenment that is difficult to reach and difficult to attain becomes [a state that] is nearby and in close proximity.

Any and all bodhisattvas of the three times who train themselves in [the elements of spiritual practice that relate to] the factions of householder [bodhisattvas] and homeless bodhisattvas have attained, are attaining, and shall attain unsurpassed true and complete enlightenment on the basis of these very four spiritual qualities. There are none of greater significance than these and there are none besides these.

Moreover, [the above explanations describe] the manner in which a householder [bodhisattva] and a homeless bodhisattva become correctly applied to these four spiritual qualities. Nevertheless, it should be understood that, compared to [that of] a householder bodhisattva, [the lifestyle of] a bodhisattva who has gone forth into the homeless state is greatly superior and also has qualities that distinguish it greatly. For example, a bodhisattva who is a homeless ascetic is from the very outset free of the faults [associated with] a household that consists of such [family members] as a mother, father, children, and a spouse.[1255] However, it should be understood that a householder [bodhisattva] is not free [of these responsibilities]. Moreover, a bodhisattva who is a homeless ascetic is also free of the suffering associated with [activities] like agriculture, commerce, and service to the king [that are pursued] for the sake of [supporting] one's household. However, it should be understood that a householder [bodhisattva] is not free [of these difficulties]. Moreover, a bodhisattva who is a homeless ascetic is able to engage in a form of pure spiritual conduct in which he or she adheres to it completely; however, a householder bodhisattva is not able to do so. Moreover, a bodhisattva who is a homeless ascetic quickly becomes knowledgeable about all the spiritual qualities that are conducive to enlightenment, and he or she is able to perfect very easily whatever form of virtue is undertaken. However, a householder bodhisattva cannot accomplish these things in the same way. Moreover, because a bodhisattva who has gone forth [into the homeless state] is observing religious austerities, he or she is one whose speech is accepted by others. However, a householder bodhisattva is not regarded in the same way. Because of such qualities as these, it should

1255. S: *mātāpitṛputradārādikalatraparigrahaḥ*, T: *pha ma dang / bu dang chung ma la sogs pa bu smad yongs su 'dzin pa*. I have translated in a gender-neutral way a phrase that is written from a male perspective. Despite the masculine form of the word, *dāraḥ* (T: *chung ma*) means a "wife," and cannot be understood as a spouse who is a husband.

be understood that [the lifestyle of] a bodhisattva who is a homeless ascetic is very different from that of a householder bodhisattva.

Within [Book II of] *The Stage of a Bodhisattva*, [known as] "The Object of Mental Application That Relates to the Qualities That Accord with the Support," this completes the second chapter, entitled "Factions."

3
Superior Attitudes

Summary verse:

> The affection of the intelligent ones
> Toward all beings has seven aspects.
> Their fifteen attitudes are regarded
> As accomplishing ten actions.

The Seven Aspects of Affection [II.3.1]

The affection[1256] that bodhisattvas develop toward sentient beings has seven aspects. [This affection is such that] by virtue of possessing it, bodhisattvas are described as "the ones who have a virtuous attitude" and "the ones who have a supremely virtuous attitude."

What are the seven aspects of affection?

[They are an affection that is] (1) free of fear, (2) proper, (3) tireless, (4) unsolicited, (5) free of desire for material reward, (6) extensive, and (7) impartial.

(1) A bodhisattva is not affectionate due to fear of anyone. He or she acts with favorable deeds of body, speech, and mind that are attractive and that [bring about] both benefit and happiness. (2) Moreover, the affection that a bodhisattva develops toward beings is not one that is lacking in propriety. For example, [it does not occur] in order to induce [others] to take up any

1256. S: *vātsalyam,* T: *mnyes bzhin pa*. This noun is derived from an adjective that means "child-loving" or "affectionate toward offspring." *BBhVy* (f. 259a): "'Affection' is a quality that fulfills the wishes of sentient beings."

form of wickedness,[1257] immodesty,[1258] vulgar conduct,[1259] or conduct that is inappropriate for the occasion. (3) Similarly, a bodhisattva is affectionate toward beings in such a way that he or she never feels weary from all the exertions that are made on their behalf. (4) A bodhisattva also is affectionate toward beings in a manner that is unsolicited; [that is,] he or she has not been asked by anyone [to act favorably]. (5) [A bodhisattva] also possesses an affectionate mind that is free of any desire for material reward; [that is,] he or she does not expect to receive something in return from others nor does he or she hope for a desirable [karmic] maturation in the future. Therefore, he or she is a bodhisattva whose affection toward beings is not prompted by any motive. (6) The affection of such a bodhisattva toward beings is also great; it is not limited. It is so great that even though every kind of harm is done to him or her by other beings, [the bodhisattva] would not reject them. He or she lets them do whatever unkind things they may wish to do to him or her and does not desire [to do] any kind of evil deed to them. (7) Moreover, the affection of bodhisattvas that has such characteristics and that is endowed with these good qualities is felt equally toward all sentient beings in their entirety; it is not limited to a portion of the realm of sentient beings. Those bodhisattvas who are endowed with an affection having these seven aspects are described as "the ones who have a virtuous attitude"[1260] and "the ones who have a supremely virtuous attitude."[1261]

1257. S: *adharmaḥ*, T: *chos ma yin pa*. This noun literally means something that is "contrary to the *dharma*," but it should be taken in the general sense of anything that is wicked or unrighteous; in this usage it does not mean something that is contrary to the Buddhist doctrine (see MW, p. 20).

1258. S: *avinayaḥ*, T: *'dul ba ma yin pa*. Similar to the previous term, this literally means "contrary to the *vinaya*," but it should be taken in the sense of ill-mannered, immodest, or rude behavior, rather than an action that specifically violates the Buddhist code of moral discipline also known as the Vinaya (T: *'dul ba*); see MW, p. 109.

1259. T: *tshogs par kun tu spyod par mi 'ongs pa*. The two Sanskrit editions have *asatyasamudācara*, but the Tibetan suggests the reading should be *asabhyasamudācara*. See also note 1063 for a similar instance in which the adjective *asabhya* occurs (MW, p. 119: "unfit for an assembly," "vulgar," "low").

1260. S: *kalyāṇāśayaḥ*, T: *dge ba'i bsam pa can*. *BBhVy* (f. 260a): "Because they possess an attitude that desires to benefit beings and bring them happiness, [bodhisattvas] are said to be 'the ones who have a virtuous attitude.'"

1261. S: *paramakalyāṇāśayaḥ*, T: *mchog tu dge ba'i bsam pa can*. *BBhVy* (f. 260a): "Because they carry out a practice that benefits [beings], [bodhisattvas] are said to be 'the ones who have a supremely virtuous attitude.'"

The Fifteen Superior Attitudes [ii.3.2]

Regarding this [topic], the conviction,[1262] understanding, and determination regarding a buddha's qualities, which are preceded by faith and the discernment of entities, are referred to as a "superior attitude." Moreover, it should be understood that, in brief, there are fifteen superior attitudes that pertain to a bodhisattva.

What are the fifteen?

[They are] (1) the attitude that relates to the foremost objects, (2) the attitude that relates to virtuous conduct, (3) the attitude that relates to the perfections, (4) the attitude that relates to the nature of reality, (5) the attitude that relates to [spiritual] power, (6) the attitude that seeks to benefit [others], (7) the attitude that seeks to bring happiness [to others], (8) the detached attitude, (9) the firm attitude, (10) the attitude that does not disagree with reality, (11) the impure attitude, (12) the pure attitude, (13) the exceedingly pure attitude, (14) the attitude in which the mind needs to be curbed, and (15) the natural attitude.

Regarding this [topic], the superior attitude of a bodhisattva that is directed toward the [Three] Jewels of the Buddha, Dharma, and Sangha is called "the attitude that relates to the foremost objects." The superior attitude that is directed toward the acceptance of the discipline associated with bodhisattva morality is called "the attitude that relates to virtuous conduct." The superior attitude that seeks to attain full knowledge of generosity, morality, patience, effort, meditative absorption, and wisdom is called "the attitude that relates to the perfections." The superior attitude that is directed toward the insubstantiality of entities and of the person, [and, in particular,] the highest truth—which is to say, the profound suchness [that is the true nature] of entities—is called "the attitude that relates to the nature of reality." The superior attitude that is directed toward the inconceivable powers of supernatural knowledge that are possessed by buddhas and bodhisattvas, as well as [the superior attitude] that is directed toward their [inconceivable] natural powers, is called "the attitude that relates to [spiritual] power." The desire to provide beings with virtue is called "the attitude that seeks to benefit others." The desire to provide assistance to beings is called "the attitude that seeks to bring happiness [to others]." The state of mind in which [a bodhisattva] has no desire to receive any material reward

1262. See note 270 for an explanation of this term.

from sentient beings and the state of mind that is unhindered by [any longing] for a desirable karmic maturation are called "the detached attitude." The single-minded dedication to [the attainment of] unsurpassed true and supreme enlightenment is called "the firm attitude." The devotion that is accompanied by unerring knowledge regarding the means of [accomplishing] the aims of beings and the means of [attaining] enlightenment is called "the attitude that does not disagree with reality." The superior attitude of bodhisattvas that is present throughout the entire stage of conduct that is based upon devotion is called "the impure attitude." The superior attitude of bodhisattvas that is present from the stage of a pure attitude up to the stage of certain conduct is called "the pure attitude." The superior attitude of bodhisattvas on the stage that is the perfect manner of going is called "the exceedingly pure attitude." Regarding this [topic], the impure attitude is also called "the attitude in which the mind needs to be curbed," because systematic analysis must still be cultivated. Moreover, the [two] forms of superior attitude that are called "pure" and "exceedingly pure" are also called "the natural attitude," because they possess that [purity] naturally and because [on those stages] the practitioner's mind has become thoroughly absorbed [in that purity].

The Ten Actions of the Superior Attitudes [II.3.3]

In brief, bodhisattvas accomplish ten actions by means of these fifteen forms of virtuous superior attitude that are present on all of the stages [of the Great Vehicle's path].

What are the ten?

(1) By means of the attitude that relates to the foremost objects, [bodhisattvas] undertake every aspect of worshipping the [Three] Jewels, which constitutes the foremost among all the accumulations [that are necessary] for enlightenment. (2) By means of the attitude that relates to virtuous conduct, they do not incur any deliberate transgressions in relation to the acceptance of the bodhisattvas' moral discipline, even to save their lives, and, if they should incur [a transgression], they confess it very quickly. (3) By means of the attitude that relates to the perfections, they abide in a state of mindfulness and they abide in a state of supreme mindfulness through engaging in the continual practice of virtuous qualities. (4) By means of the attitude that relates to the nature of reality, they maintain a mind that is free of the afflictions as they continue to be reborn in samsara for the sake

of sentient beings, and they also refrain from giving up the superior attitude [that seeks to attain] nirvana. (5) By means of the attitude that relates to [spiritual] power, they impart [to others] a deeply felt reverence toward the teaching. They also value meditation highly and maintain a great eagerness [to practice it, that is,] they are not satisfied with learning and reflection alone. (6) By means of the attitude that seeks to benefit [others], the attitude that seeks to bring happiness [to others], and the detached attitude, they undertake every form of activity that accomplishes the aims of others and, having undertaken them, they do not become weary [as they continue to pursue them]. (7) By means of the firm attitude, they initiate and maintain a fervent effort and an extensive effort; they refrain from becoming lax in their practice and they do not develop a defective practice. (8) By means of the attitude that does not disagree with reality, they gain forms of supernatural knowledge that quickly accomplish various kinds of virtuous qualities. They also do not become satisfied merely by attaining lesser forms [of supernatural knowledge] that are smaller and ordinary. (9) By means of the attitude in which the mind needs to be curbed, they bring forth the natural superior attitude. (10) Finally, by means of the natural attitude, they quickly attain unsurpassed true and complete enlightenment for the welfare, benefit, and happiness of gods and human beings.

Regarding this [topic], it should be understood that whatever forms of superior attitude the Buddha, the Blessed One, declared, prescribed, and revealed to bodhisattvas in relation to a variety of different subjects, they can all be included within these very fifteen forms of superior attitude. Therefore, all bodhisattvas of the three times who have attained, are attaining, and shall attain unsurpassed true and complete enlightenment on the basis of virtuous superior attitudes do so on the basis of these very fifteen forms of superior attitude. There are none of greater significance than these and there are none besides these. This is the manner in which these fifteen forms of superior attitude are possessed of the fruit and benefit of great enlightenment.[1263] Therefore, a bodhisattva should attain unsurpassed and supreme enlightenment by relying upon them.

1263. The Dutt manuscript reads *mahābodhiphalānuśaṃsāḥ* but was amended to *mahāphalānuśaṃsāḥ,* presumably to mirror the Wogihara edition. However, the Tibetan translation (T: *byang chub chen po'i 'bras bu'i phan yon can yin*) supports the unamended form, and I have translated it accordingly.

Within [Book II of] *The Stage of a Bodhisattva*, [known as] "The Object of Mental Application That Relates to the Qualities That Accord with the Support," this completes the third chapter, entitled "Superior Attitudes."

4
The Pleasurable States

Summary verses:

> Spiritual lineage; likewise, devotion, joy,
> Superior morality, superior mind training,
> The three forms of wisdom, the two forms of signlessness—
> That which requires effort and that which is effortless—
>
> The [four] forms of informative knowledge, and the supreme.
> The highest pleasurable state is that of a tathāgata.

There are, in brief, twelve pleasurable states[1264] that pertain to bodhisattvas, beginning with the excellence of the [Great Vehicle's] spiritual lineage and [including the pleasurable states of those bodhisattvas] who are training themselves in the bodhisattva trainings that were described, who are displaying the marks of bodhisattvas that were described, who are correctly engaged in the practices that relate to the bodhisattvas, and who are refining the bodhisattva superior attitudes that were described. It should be understood that these pleasurable states of bodhisattvas are such that all [forms of] bodhisattva conduct are included within them. The thirteenth pleasurable state is that of a tathāgata and it is the unsurpassed pleasurable state of true and complete enlightenment.

1264. S: *vihāraḥ,* T: *gnas pa*. This term has a wide range of meanings. The principal sense in this context is that of a period of time that is spent in a pleasurable manner. Later in this chapter Asaṅga interprets the term as meaning the condition or position of "remaining in a state of enjoyment" (see note 1305). *MSA* (ch. 21, v. 39) also gives the following literal interpretation: "The bodhisattvas' stages are known as pleasurable states / Because one abides in them pleasurably / At all times and everywhere / To accumulate virtue in a variety of ways."

Regarding this [topic], what are the twelve bodhisattva pleasurable states? [Five are] (1) the pleasurable state of the spiritual lineage; (2) the pleasurable state in which conduct is based upon devotion; (3) the pleasurable state of great joy; (4) the pleasurable state of superior morality; and (5) the pleasurable state of superior mind training.

There are three pleasurable states of superior wisdom: (6) [the pleasurable state of superior wisdom] that relates to the spiritual qualities that are conducive to enlightenment; (7) [the pleasurable state of superior wisdom] that relates to the [four noble] truths; and (8) [the pleasurable state of superior wisdom] that relates to the forward and reverse forms of [the process of] dependent origination. [Of these three, the first represents the pleasurable state] by means of which a bodhisattva perceives reality, [the second represents the pleasurable state] that perceives reality, and [the third represents the pleasurable state which perceives] the manner in which the suffering of sentient beings arises because reality has not been realized as well as [the manner in which their suffering] does not arise because [reality] has been realized. These are the three pleasurable states of superior wisdom in which a bodhisattva employs wisdom to deliberate in three separate ways.

[The last four are] (9) the pleasurable state that is free of signs and is accompanied by both mental preparation and effort, [a pleasurable state] in which one proceeds by a path that is free of interruptions; (10) the pleasurable state that is free of signs and free of any mental preparation, [a pleasurable state] in which one proceeds by a path that is effortless; (11) the pleasurable state of informative knowledge; and (12) the bodhisattva's supreme and fully developed pleasurable state. These are the twelve types of pleasurable states that pertain to bodhisattvas. They include all of their pleasurable states and they include all forms of bodhisattva conduct.

In addition, the pleasurable state of a tathāgata is the pleasurable state that transcends all the bodhisattva pleasurable states and pertains to the enlightenment of a complete buddha. Regarding this [topic], the final pleasurable state—that is, the one that pertains to a tathāgata—will be presented in its entirety in the final object of mental application, [that is,] the one that relates to the state of preeminence.[1265]

Now I shall describe the manner in which the twelve pleasurable states that pertain to bodhisattvas are formulated.

1265. This is a reference to the final two chapters of Book III, which together present the one hundred and forty unique qualities of a buddha.

A Brief Description of the Twelve Bodhisattva Pleasurable States [II.4.1]

The Essential Nature of the Pleasurable State of the Spiritual Lineage [II.4.1.1]

What is the bodhisattva's pleasurable state of the [Great Vehicle's] spiritual lineage? How does a bodhisattva who is established in the [Great Vehicle's] spiritual lineage abide?

Here a bodhisattva who is abiding in the [Great Vehicle's] spiritual lineage naturally possesses the qualities of a bodhisattva and the virtuous qualities that are appropriate to a bodhisattva because his or her mental continuum is one that is naturally excellent. He or she is also observed to engage in such forms of proper conduct. He or she engages in those virtues on the basis of natural excellence, not in a forced manner. Nevertheless, he or she is one who maintains restraint on the basis of careful consideration.[1266] The bodhisattva who is abiding in the [Great Vehicle's] spiritual lineage is also one who holds the seeds of all the spiritual qualities possessed by a buddha. All the seeds of the totality of a buddha's spiritual qualities are present within his or her being and within his or her substratum.

A bodhisattva who is abiding in the [Great Vehicle's] spiritual lineage is also one in whom the coarse impurities are not present. He or she is not one who is capable of exhibiting the type of perturbation of the mental afflictions such that, having become upset by that perturbation, he or she would

1266. There is some uncertainty surrounding this sentence. The various editions of the Tibetan translation of Asaṅga's text cast it as a negative statement (T: *so sor brtags te gags dang bcas par gyur pa ni ma yin no*), which can be rendered: "[The bodhisattva] does not [have to] apply any obstruction [to his or her actions] through engaging in careful consideration." However, *BBhVy* reproduces this sentence with a double negative (T: *so sor brtags te gags dang bcas par ma gyur pa ni ma yin no*), suggesting a different interpretation: "[However, the bodhisattva] does not fail to apply restraint [to his or her actions when necessary], through engaging in careful consideration." While the two published Sanskrit editions are in agreement and seem to support Samudramegha's version, both also have amended the text that appears in the available manuscripts.

commit any of the [evil] deeds that have an immediate consequence[1267] or completely sever his or her roots of virtue.[1268]

The comportment of an individual who is established in the [Great Vehicle's] spiritual lineage that was presented in the chapter entitled "The Spiritual Lineage" should be understood as a detailed account of [the conduct of] a bodhisattva who is abiding in the [Great Vehicle's] spiritual lineage. This [mode of behavior] is called "a bodhisattva's pleasurable state of the spiritual lineage."

The Essential Nature of the Pleasurable State of Conduct That Is Based upon Devotion [II.4.1.2]

Regarding this [topic], what is a bodhisattva's pleasurable state of conduct that is based upon devotion?

Here, any bodhisattva conduct whatsoever [that is performed] by a bodhisattva from the time that he or she first generates [enlightenment] mind and throughout the period that his or her attitude remains impure is called his or her "pleasurable state of conduct that is based upon devotion."[1269]

1267. S: *ānantaryakarma,* T: *mtshams med pa'i las. AKB* (p. 259): "The five [deeds] that have an immediate consequence are [forms of] a karmic obstacle. They are, specifically, (1) killing one's mother; (2) killing one's father; (3) killing an arhat; (4) causing a division in the Sangha; and (5) [motivated by] a malicious intent, causing the Tathāgata's body to shed blood. . . . What is the meaning of the term 'that which has an immediate consequence'? They are [deeds] that have an immediate consequence in the sense that, with regard to their ripening, no other deed whose fruit is [to be reborn in] a different birth is capable of intervening. That is to say, [their consequence] cannot be averted. Or, [the term 'that which has an immediate consequence' is derived from the noun] 'that which has no interval,' in the sense that, for a person who commits [any of] these [deeds], there is no interval before being reborn in one of the hells after he or she has passed away from this life. This condition is the state of having an immediate consequence. It is that quality whose possession makes someone an individual for whom there is no interval, in the same way that [a person] who possesses [the quality of] asceticism [becomes an ascetic]."

1268. S: *kuśalamūlasamucchedaḥ,* T: *dge ba rtsa ba kun tu gcod pa. AKB* (p. 248): "However, the severing of the roots of virtue is caused by a fully manifested great form of the wrong view." *AKB* (p. 248) also notes that the roots of virtue that are completely severed are those of the desire realm that are innate. The term "roots of virtue" (S: *kuśalamūlāni,* T: *dge ba'i rtsa ba*) is often associated with these three virtuous mental factors: (1) avoidance of desire (S: *alobhaḥ,* T: *'dod chags med pa*); (2) avoidance of hatred (S: *adveśaḥ,* T: *zhe sdang med pa*); and (3) avoidance of ignorance (S: *amohaḥ,* T: *gti mug med pa*).

1269. This description seems to include both the accumulation path (S: *sambhāramārgaḥ,* T: *tshogs lam*) and the preparation path (S: *prayogamārgaḥ,* T: *sbyor lam*).

Regarding this [topic], a bodhisattva who is abiding in the spiritual lineage is only occupied with the causes of all the other eleven pleasurable states of a bodhisattva, as well as [the causes of] the pleasurable state of a tathāgata, in the sense of [attempting to] gain mastery of those causes. However, he or she has not commenced any bodhisattva pleasurable state other than [the pleasurable state of the spiritual lineage], nor has he or she attained or perfected [any other bodhisattva pleasurable state], much less has he or she done so with regard to the pleasurable state of a tathāgata.

By contrast, the bodhisattva who is abiding in the [pleasurable state of] conduct that is based upon devotion has commenced [the practices that lead to] all of the [other] bodhisattva pleasurable states as well as the pleasurable state of a tathāgata; however, he or she has not attained [any of them] nor perfected [any of them]. The only [pleasurable state] that he or she has attained is the pleasurable state of conduct that is based upon devotion. In addition, this is the only [pleasurable state] that he or she has set out to perfect.

When the pleasurable state of conduct that is based upon devotion has been perfected, [a bodhisattva] attains the initial onset of the pleasurable state of great joy and also becomes one who has set out to perfect that very [pleasurable state]. When the pleasurable state of great joy has been perfected, [a bodhisattva] attains the initial onset of the pleasurable state of superior morality and also becomes one who has set out to perfect that very [pleasurable state]. It should be understood that this process continues in the same way until [one reaches] the bodhisattva's supreme and fully developed pleasurable state. It should also be understood that immediately after the bodhisattva's supreme and fully developed pleasurable state has been perfected, the attainment of the initial onset of the pleasurable state of a tathāgata and the perfection [of the pleasurable state of a tathāgata] occur simultaneously. This [final point] should be understood as the characteristic that distinguishes the pleasurable state of a tathāgata from that of [all] the pleasurable states that pertain to bodhisattvas.

The Essential Natures of the Remaining Bodhisattva Pleasurable States [II.4.1.3]

Regarding this [topic], what is a bodhisattva's pleasurable state of great joy?

It is the pleasurable state of a bodhisattva whose superior attitude has become pure.

Regarding this [topic], what is a bodhisattva's pleasurable state of superior morality?

It is the pleasurable state of [a bodhisattva] who possesses a form of morality that occurs naturally, based upon the purity of his or her superior attitude.

Regarding this [topic], what is a bodhisattva's pleasurable state of superior mind training?

It is the pleasurable state in which [a bodhisattva abides] in the worldly forms of meditative absorption, one-pointed concentration, and states of composure, on the basis of the purity of the pleasurable state of superior morality.

Regarding this [topic], what is a bodhisattva's pleasurable state of superior wisdom that relates to the spiritual qualities that are conducive to enlightenment?

It is the pleasurable state in which, through reliance upon the worldly forms of one-pointed concentration that represent the basis for [attaining] purity of spiritual realization, [a bodhisattva abides in a state that] correctly investigates the thirty-seven spiritual qualities of closely placed recollection, etc., that are conducive to enlightenment, in order to gain a deep awareness of the [four noble] truths.

Regarding this [topic], what is a bodhisattva's pleasurable state of superior wisdom that relates to the [four noble] truths?

It is the pleasurable state in which, through reliance upon the investigation of [those spiritual qualities] that are conducive to enlightenment, [a bodhisattva abides in a state of] deep awareness regarding the exact nature of the [four noble] truths.

Regarding this [topic], what is a bodhisattva's pleasurable state of superior wisdom that relates to the forward and reverse forms of dependent origination?

It is the pleasurable state that, on the strength of that deep awareness of the truths, is distinguished by the investigation of how suffering, together with its causes, arises because those [truths] have not been realized and is also distinguished by the investigation of how suffering, together with its causes, ceases when [those truths] have been realized.

Regarding this [topic], what is a bodhisattva's pleasurable state that is free of signs and is accompanied by both mental preparation and effort?

It is the pleasurable state that, on the strength of those three [forms of] the pleasurable state of superior wisdom, is accompanied by a [form of] meditation that employs mental preparation and effort [to cultivate] continuously and uninterruptedly the nonconceptual wisdom [that perceives] the suchness that pertains to all entities.

Regarding this [topic], what is a bodhisattva's pleasurable state that is free of signs and is also free of both mental preparation and effort?

It is the pleasurable state in which, through having practiced extensively the [form of] meditation of that very previous pleasurable state that is free of signs, [the bodhisattva] arrives at a path that conveys [the mind to its object] continuously and uninterruptedly, through its own [natural] inclination.

Regarding this [topic], what is the bodhisattvas' pleasurable state of informative knowledge?

It is a pleasurable state in which, through relying upon those highly refined forms of unwavering wisdom and concentration, [a bodhisattva] who has attained an abundance of great intelligence [abides in a state that] examines the verbal formulations, meanings, [forms of] clear expression, and the different points that relate to the Dharma, in connection with [the aim of] teaching the Dharma in an unsurpassed manner to other beings.

Regarding this [topic], what is the bodhisattva's supreme pleasurable state?

The bodhisattva who is established in this [pleasurable state] is one who has perfected the bodhisattva path and has received the great Dharma consecration that relates to unsurpassed true and complete enlightenment, and he is either one who is [only] subject to one [additional] rebirth or one who is in his final existence. It is the pleasurable state immediately following which and just after which [a bodhisattva] attains unsurpassed true and complete enlightenment and performs all the activities of a buddha.

The Essential Nature of Meditation Practice during the Bodhisattva Pleasurable States [II.4.1.4]

During the pleasurable state of conduct that is based upon devotion, a bodhisattva practices the bodhisattva [forms of] meditation in a limited way. He or she practices in an intermittent and uncertain manner; that is, he or she repeatedly loses [whatever form of practice] has been gained. During the pleasurable state of great joy, a bodhisattva is able to practice the very same bodhisattva [forms of] meditation extensively. He practices in an unbroken and certain manner and does not lose whatever [form of practice] has been gained. Just as it is during the pleasurable state of great joy, [the manner of practice] is the same up through the three pleasurable states that relate to [the training of] superior wisdom. From the first pleasurable state that is free of signs up to the bodhisattva's supreme pleasurable state, a bodhisattva practices the bodhisattva [forms of] meditation in an unbroken and certain manner, and in a way that is beyond measure.[1270]

Regarding this [topic], it should be understood that, during the pleasurable state of conduct that is based upon devotion, there is a commencement of [the process that leads to the gaining of] the bodhisattva [form of] meditation that is free of signs. It should be understood that, during the pleasurable state of great joy, as well as during the pleasurable states that relate to [the trainings of] superior morality, superior mind training, and superior wisdom, there is a gaining of the bodhisattva [form of] meditation that is free of signs. It should be understood that, during the first pleasurable state that is free of signs, there is a full realization of the bodhisattva [form of] meditation that is free of signs, and on the second pleasurable state that is free of signs, there is a complete refinement [of the bodhisattva form of meditation that is free of signs]. It should be understood that, during the pleasurable state of informative knowledge and the supreme pleasurable state, there is a recurrent experiencing of the fruit of the bodhisattva [form of] meditation that is free of signs.

The Pleasurable State of Conduct That Is Based upon Devotion [II.4.2]

What are the aspects, marks, and signs[1271] of a bodhisattva who is abiding in the pleasurable state of conduct that is based upon devotion?

A bodhisattva who is abiding in the pleasurable state of conduct that is based upon devotion is one who possesses the ability to engage in repeated analysis in a powerful manner. Having carefully considered the proper

1270. S: *apramāṇakārī,* T: *tshad med par byed pa. BBhVy* (f. 265b): "[The bodhisattva] is said to 'practice in a way that is beyond measure' because the amount of virtue that he or she generates in a single moment is beyond measure."

1271. *BBhVy* (ff. 265b–266a): "The various aspects, etc., that relate to each of the pleasurable states are presented in order to cause those who are abiding in them to be recognized. The three terms 'aspect,' etc., are synonyms. It is an aspect (S: *ākāraḥ,* T: *rnam pa*) because it appears in such and such a manner. It is a mark (S: *lingaḥ,* T: *rtags*) because it causes [an object] to be indicated or understood. It is a sign (S: *nimittam,* T: *mtshan ma*) because it serves as an indication [of something]."

forms of bodhisattva practice, he or she employs wisdom to apply him- or herself to them. However, he or she has not attained [the ability] to practice the bodhisattva [forms of] meditation in that manner naturally, firmly, and irreversibly. As is the case with meditation, the same is true for the various types of informative knowledge, supernatural knowledge, liberations, one-pointed concentration, and states of composure that are the fruit of that meditation. In addition, he or she has not transcended the five fears: (1) the fear of having no livelihood, (2) the fear of gaining a bad reputation, (3) the fear of dying, (4) the fear of [being reborn in] the unhappy migratory states, and (5) the fear of being timid in a group.

Moreover, while he or she does pursue the welfare of sentient beings after having engaged in careful consideration, [a bodhisattva who is abiding in the pleasurable state of conduct that is based upon devotion] does not do so on the basis of an affection [for beings] that stems from a natural [form of] sympathy. Sometimes, he or she even carries out a mistaken form of physical, verbal, or mental practice as relates to sentient beings.[1272] Sometimes, he or she even develops attachment[1273] toward an object. Sometimes, he or she even exhibits the quality of acquisitiveness toward personal possessions.[1274]

[A bodhisattva who is abiding in the pleasurable state of conduct that is based upon devotion] is one who proceeds on the basis of faith[1275] in others, [namely,] buddhas and bodhisattvas. He or she has not attained a realization of the truth, that is to say, [the truth] as relates to the Tathāgata, the Dharma, the Sangha, the meaning of reality, the powers of the buddhas and bodhisattvas, causes, results, the aims that are to be achieved, the means of

1272. *BBhVy* (f. 266a): "This means that he or she may do something that is detrimental [to sentient beings] or that causes [them] suffering."

1273. The term "one who has developed attachment" (S: *adhyavasitaḥ,* T: *lhag par chags pa*) here is meant in the sense of a form of the root mental affliction of desire. *TBh* (p. 84): "Regarding this, desire is attachment toward (S: *adhyavasānam,* T: *lhag par chags pa*) and longing for (S: *prārthanā,* T: *smon pa*) [samsaric] existence and objects of enjoyment."

1274. The term "the quality of being one who has developed acquisitiveness toward personal possessions" (S: *āgṛhitapraiṣkāratā,* T: *yo byad rnams la kun tu 'dzin pa nyid*) should be understood as a manifestation of stinginess (S: *mātsaryam,* T: *ser sna*); see note 962.

1275. S: *śraddhāgamī,* T: *dad pas 'gro ba*. *BBhVy* (f. 266a): "The statement 'He or she is one who proceeds on the basis of faith' means that he or she is one who is led [along the spiritual path] by means of dependence upon others." The expression "by means of dependence upon others" (S: *parapratyayena,* T: *gzhan gyi rkyen gyis,* also *gzhan gyi dring gis*) means that a practitioner must rely upon instruction received from others, and that he or she is not completely self-reliant.

attaining them, or the field [of that which needs to be known].[1276] He or she possesses limited forms of the knowledge that is derived from listening and reflection; [he or she] does not [possess them] in a form that is beyond measure. Moreover, this [knowledge] sometimes becomes clouded. He or she is subject to inattention.[1277] He or she possesses [a form of] the bodhisattva path in which supernatural knowledge is slow and acquired with difficulty. His or her aspiration for enlightenment is not intense. He or she does not possess an effort that is fervent or an exceedingly deep-seated sense of joy[1278] toward the profound.

[A bodhisattva who is abiding in the pleasurable state of conduct that is based upon devotion] develops clouded recollection[1279] in connection with three circumstances. (1) On certain occasions, [it occurs] in relation to attractive and unattractive objects that consist of [visible] forms, sounds, smells, tastes, and tangible entities, due to [the occurrence] of an erroneous state of mind.[1280] (2) [It occurs] for one who has been reborn repeatedly in rebirths within a variety of different states of existence, due to having forgotten [his or her] former states of existence. (3) On certain occasions, [clouded recollection] also [occurs] due to the failure to recall—among [all] the Dharma teachings that were explained to him or her and that he or she

1276. *BBhVy* (f. 266a): "The statement [that includes the phrase] 'powers of the buddhas and bodhisattvas,' [etc.,] means that [the practitioner] is one who becomes established in the eight subjects that were indicated earlier, by the power of others." The "eight subjects" are the topics toward which one cultivates devotion. See Book I, chapter 8, the section entitled "Abundance of Devotion" [I.8.1].

1277. S: *sampramoṣaḥ,* T: *brjed ngas pa*. Both Asaṅga and Vasubandhu define recollection (S: *smṛtiḥ,* T: *dran pa*) as the antithesis of this quality (see note 687). Sthiramati (*PSV,* p. 279) describes avoidance of inattention as "the quality that enables you to keep from losing hold of a mental object." Thus, inattention is the mental quality that causes one's hold of a mental object to be lost (S: *ālambanagrahaṇavipraṇāśaḥ,* T: *dmigs pa la 'dzin pa chud za ba*). As such, it is more or less synonymous with the secondary mental affliction known as "clouded recollection" (S: *muṣitā smṛtiḥ,* T: *brjed ngas pa*).

1278. S: *prasādaḥ,* T: *dga' ba*. This is another sense of the Sanskrit word *prasādaḥ* (see also notes 220, 467, 572, and 656) that, as indicated by the Tibetan translation, indicates a feeling of joy and delight that stems from the awareness that the topic of emptiness is crucially important. In this case, the point is that at this stage of the path a bodhisattva does not always exhibit this quality, which does arise strongly in the next stage.

1279. See note 701.

1280. *BBhVy* (f. 266b): "Clouded recollection toward objects means the erroneous state of mind that arises due to having developed attachment toward attractive [objects] and aversion toward unattractive ones."

took up—the ones that were given a long time ago and that were taught a long time ago. This is the way that clouded recollection occurs in relation to these three circumstances.

Sometimes he or she is astute and able to take up, retain, and understand the meaning of Dharma teachings; sometimes he or she is not able to do so. Sometimes he or she is possessed of [strong] recollection; sometimes his or her nature is that of one whose recollection is clouded.

[A bodhisattva who is abiding in the pleasurable state of conduct that is based upon devotion] does not know in an exact manner the means by which sentient beings can be spiritually tamed; nor does he or she know [in an exact manner] the means by which he or she can develop a buddha's spiritual qualities. He or she teaches Dharma to others, or sets forth instruction and counsel, [only] when pressed to do so.[1281] Furthermore, [the instruction and counsel] that he or she has been pressed to set forth [is taught] without having exact knowledge of how to do so. Sometimes [this effort] is fruitless and sometimes it is fruitful. As such, its success is accidental, like arrows that have been shot in the night.

Sometimes, he or she will even abandon the mind that has been generated to [seek] great enlightenment. Sometimes, he or she will stop observing the acceptance of the bodhisattva [system of] moral discipline, or he or she will not strive [to observe it continually]. Sometimes, even though having dedicated him- or herself to acting on behalf of sentient beings, he or she may become weary during the course of doing so and, therefore, turn away from that practice of acting on behalf of sentient beings. He or she desires his or her own happiness with heartfelt sincerity [but] desires the happiness of others [only] after having engaged in repeated reflection.

He or she possesses extensive knowledge regarding the erroneous actions of bodhisattvas. However, despite repeatedly becoming aware of them, he or she fails to abandon them in their entirety in that these errors are committed again and again.

Sometimes, he or she is led away from the [spiritual system of] Dharma and Vinaya that is contained in this bodhisattva collection [of scriptures]. Sometimes, he or she becomes frightened after hearing a Dharma teaching

1281. S: *haṭhena,* T: *nan gyis.* The Sanskrit adverb has a range of meanings that include "forcibly," "obstinately," and "necessarily" (MW, p. 1287). However, in the present context, *BBhVy* (f. 266b) explains: "'When pressed to do so' means on the strength of having been requested by others."

on the profound [topic of emptiness] and extensive [nature of the bodhisattva practices]. Mental wavering, uncertainty, and doubt also arise. He or she may also abandon, completely and totally, exercising great compassion toward sentient beings. He or she also [only] serves sentient beings by providing small forms of benefit and happiness; he or she does not do so by providing extensive and immeasurable forms [of benefit and happiness].

He or she does not train fully in all the bodhisattva trainings as they have been presented. He or she is not endowed fully with all of the marks of a bodhisattva as they have been presented. He or she does not fully exhibit all of the practices that pertain to bodhisattvas as they have been presented. Even though it has been a long time since he or she agreed [to strive toward] unsurpassed true and complete enlightenment, he or she has not developed a superior attitude toward nirvana that is anything like [the attitude] that he or she continues to have toward his or her ongoing transmigration in samsara. He or she does not possess ardent and unwavering forms of the virtuous spiritual qualities that are conducive to enlightenment.

These marks, signs, and aspects, and others like them, should be understood as the ones that are possessed by a bodhisattva who is abiding in the pleasurable state of conduct that is based upon devotion.

It should be understood that a bodhisattva who has reached the lesser level of forbearance[1282] on the pleasurable state of conduct that is based upon devotion possesses these [unfavorable] aspects, marks, and signs in a great form. It should be understood that [a bodhisattva] who has reached the middling level of forbearance possesses them in a moderate form. And it should be understood that a bodhisattva who has reached the great level of forbearance possesses these aspects, marks, and signs in a lesser and weakened form. Moreover, it should also be understood that immediately after a bodhisattva who is abiding in the great level of forbearance has completely abandoned these aspects, marks, and signs, he or she enters the pleasurable state of great joy, by virtue of having attained it.

For that [bodhisattva] who is abiding in the pleasurable state of great joy, all of those [unfavorable] qualities are completely and totally gone. Moreover, all those qualities that belong to the side of purity and that are the opposite of the ones that were said to be possessed by [a bodhisattva] who is abiding in the pleasurable state of conduct that is based upon devotion are now present there. By being endowed with these qualities, this bodhisattva is said to be "one who has a pure superior attitude."

1282. See note 995 for a description of these three levels of forbearance.

Moreover, for a bodhisattva who is abiding in the pleasurable state of conduct that is based upon devotion, no matter how much the purity of his or her conviction[1283] increases through lesser, middling, and great stages of development, it can never be called "a purity of superior attitude."

Why is that?

It is because that conviction is one that is afflicted by those multiple forms of secondary mental afflictions [that were described above]. However, because all of the secondary mental afflictions [that could agitate] his or her conviction have been abandoned, the conviction of the bodhisattva who is established in the pleasurable state of great joy is one that is free of those mental afflictions and it is one that is pure.

The Pleasurable State of Great Joy [II.4.3]

Regarding this [topic], what aspects, what marks, and what signs should a bodhisattva who is abiding in the pleasurable state of great joy be understood to possess?

Here a bodhisattva who enters the pleasurable state of great joy after [having completed] the pleasurable state of conduct that is based upon devotion abandons the former [types of] bodhisattva aspirational prayers [that were dedicated] to [the attainment of] unsurpassed true and complete enlightenment—which did not properly fathom enlightenment and did not properly fathom the means of [attaining] enlightenment, and which were made, for the most part, through relying upon others and [were such that their unerring form] had not yet been fully ascertained—and gives rise to different and new forms of bodhisattva aspirational prayers which, on the basis of [the following] six aspects, are extremely well ascertained and the product of meditation that has been generated by oneself. (1) [These aspirational prayers] completely surpass all other [forms of] virtuous aspirational prayers, they are unequaled, and they have unique results. (2) They are both [an object] that relates to the world and one that completely surpasses all [other] objects that are found throughout all the worlds. (3) Because they have the effect of delivering all sentient beings from suffering, they are distinct from anything that pertains to all the listeners and the solitary realizers. (4) Even if this [type of] aspirational prayer is generated for only a single instant, its Dharma nature is such that it brings the result of immeasurable spiritual

1283. See note 270 for a discussion of the terms "conviction" and "devotion." This seems to be a case where the two terms are synonymous.

qualities that are desired by bodhisattvas. (5) Moreover, these aspirational prayers are not subject to change and they are inexhaustible. Once attained, they are not perceived to undergo any manner of diminution or alteration. (6) Their character is to become ever more excellent, they continue to be effective until the furthest end [of time], and they are conducive to great enlightenment.[1284]

Moreover, this bodhisattva aspirational prayer that has been extremely well ascertained is referred to as "the development of [enlightenment] mind."[1285] Also, this development of [enlightenment] mind by a bodhisattva should be understood in brief as having four aspects.

What are the four aspects?

(1) What kind of bodhisattvas initially develop this [form of enlightenment] mind? (2) What [objects] have been taken hold of when it is developed? (3) What type of [of mind], [possessing] what attributes and having what nature, is developed? (4) When this [enlightenment] mind has arisen, what are its benefits? It should be understood that these are the four aspects that relate to this development of [enlightenment] mind.[1286]

1284. It seems reasonable to assume that the latter portion of this paragraph provides a description of the six aspects of a bodhisattva's transcendent aspirational prayers that are alluded to by Asaṅga. There is no corresponding passage in the *Sutra on the Ten Stages* that contains this exact language and can be recognized as the source for this point. My identification of the six aspects is based on the structure of the Tibetan translation of this passage. *BBhVy* (ff. 267b–268b) gives a different and somewhat more complex explanation of the six aspects: (1) the quality of surpassing all other [non-transcendent forms of] virtuous aspirational prayers, (2) the quality of being unequaled, (3) the quality of having unique results, (4) the quality of surpassing all [other] objects that are found throughout all the worlds, (5) the quality of not being subject to change, and (6) the quality of being cultivated in ever more excellent forms. The text goes on to list eight aspects that make up the pleasurable state of great joy as a whole and then relates everything that is mentioned in this paragraph, including the six aspects of the aspirational prayers, to those eight aspects.

1285. S: *cittotpādaḥ,* T: *sems bskyed pa.* This expression is most often associated with the act of generating the conventional form of enlightenment mind (S: *sāṃvṛtaś cittotpādaḥ,* T: *kun rdzob pa'i byang chub kyi sems*), which is the main topic of Book I, chapter 2. Here the expression represents the development of the ultimate form of enlightenment mind (S: *pāramārthikaś cittotpādaḥ*), which is first gained when a bodhisattva achieves this pleasurable state of great joy. See also *MSA,* ch. 4, vv. 8–14, which addresses this form of enlightenment mind.

1286. As *BBhVy* (f. 268b) notes, this section is based on a passage from the *Sutra on the Ten Stages* (see *Flower Ornament Scripture,* pp. 702–703) that describes what type of bodhisattva attains the first of the ten bodhisattva stages. *BBhVy* also refers to the analysis of the passage that appears in *DBV* (ff. 128a–131b), which describes the passage as consisting

Regarding this [topic], this [enlightenment] mind is developed by bodhisattvas who are abiding in the pleasurable state of conduct that is based upon devotion, who have fully collected every form of virtue roots, and who, in brief, have familiarized themselves completely with the correct forms of bodhisattva conduct.

This [enlightenment] mind is developed by bodhisattvas after they have mentally taken hold of [the following objects as things] to be swiftly and correctly accomplished in the future: the perfection of all the accumulations [that are necessary to achieve] enlightenment, the perfection of all the ways that a bodhisattva acts on behalf of sentient beings, [the attainment of] unsurpassed true and complete enlightenment, the perfection of every aspect of the spiritual qualities possessed by a buddha, and the perfection of the activities that are performed by a buddha.

This [enlightenment] mind is also developed [in a form] that swiftly and correctly accords with all the forms of all the accumulations [that are necessary to achieve] enlightenment, [in a form] that [swiftly and correctly] accords with all the kinds of bodhisattva activities that should be carried out in relation to sentient beings, [in a form] that [swiftly and correctly] accords with attaining the self-originated knowledge of unsurpassed true and complete enlightenment, and [in a form] that [swiftly and correctly] accords with carrying out every kind of a buddha's activities.

In addition, through having developed this [enlightenment] mind, a bodhisattva has gone beyond the stage of an immature bodhisattva who is an ordinary person.[1287] He has entered into the bodhisattva's state of certainty.[1288] He has been born into the family of the tathāgatas. He is a

---

of four sets of ten terms each. Each of the four sets corresponds to one of the four aspects that Asaṅga mentions here.

1287. See note 443.

1288. S: *bodhisattvaniyāmaḥ.* Both Sanskrit editions have this spelling. The Tibetan translation (T: *byang chub sems dpa'i skyon med pa*) suggests a slightly different spelling, *bodhisattvanyāmaḥ,* which can be rendered as "the bodhisattva state of flawlessness." Both spellings refer to attainment of the transcendent path of seeing for the first time. *MVṬ* (pp. 198–199): "Because it is the very first arising of the ārya path that has not existed before this time, it is 'entry into flawlessness.' A fault or a disease is called a 'flaw' (S: *āmaḥ,* T: *skyon*). A state where that is absent is called 'flawlessness' (S: *nyāmaḥ,* T: *skyon med pa*), like a place that is free of wind, that is to say, it is a stage that is free of the outflows.... Further, according to the reading that states 'entry into the state of certainty,' *niyama* means a state of certainty. That is to say, one who has given rise to the path of seeing is certain [to be reborn] in the happy states of migration and [to attain] nirvana."

spiritual son born from the Tathāgata's breast.[1289] He is one who with certainty is destined to reach complete enlightenment and one who is established in the lineage of the tathāgatas. Being of such a nature, he attains the faith that is born of insight[1290] and experiences great elation.

He greatly avoids being contentious, wanting to do harm, or developing anger toward others. With a pure superior attitude, [this bodhisattva] holds in mind every way in which bodhisattvas act on behalf of sentient beings and every way in which to perfect all the accumulations [that are necessary for] enlightenment, as well as every aspect of enlightenment, of a buddha's spiritual qualities, and of the manner in which a buddha's activities are carried out. He maintains strong devotion [toward these aims] and undertakes [to achieve] them. Seeing and realizing himself to be in accord with the swift attainment of these [goals], he feels great elation.

[He has the following thoughts:] "I am endowed with extensive virtue that relates to departure [from the world], is free of desire, and is unequaled; I am endowed with an elation that benefits both body and mind; and I am endowed with intense forms of virtuous qualities. I am also near to unsurpassed true and complete enlightenment. My superior attitude toward great enlightenment is completely pure. All my fears are gone." For these reasons, too, he feels great elation.

The five fears that have ceased for a bodhisattva who has developed the extremely well-ascertained form of [enlightenment] mind are as follows. (1) Since belief in a self no longer arises for [the bodhisattva] who has cultivated well the knowledge of selflessness, how then could he develop attachment toward a self or attachment for those things that are a means of subsistence? Therefore, he has no fear of being without a livelihood. (2) He also does not hope to receive anything from others. This is what [such a bodhisattva] desires: "May I be able to provide these beings with every [kind of] object." Therefore, he has no fear of gaining a bad reputation. (3) Because the view that believes in a self is gone, he no longer develops the belief that the self will

1289. S: *tathāgatasyaurasaḥ putraḥ*, T: *de bzhin gshegs pa'i thugs kyi sras*. In a secular context, the term "a son or daughter born from one's breast" means a "legitimate son or daughter," i.e., one born by a wife of the same caste married according to the rules (MW, p. 239). In the following passage from the sutra entitled *The Lion's Roar of Śrīmaladevī* (T: *['Phags pa] lHa mo dpal phreng gi seng ge'i sgra*, f. 274a), this term is used to refer to an ārya bodhisattva: "Whatever [beings] see correctly, they are the sons or daughters of the Blessed One who are born from his breast."

1290. See note 759.

cease to exist. Therefore, he has no fear of dying. (4) He forms the following certain conviction: "In the future [lives] following my death, I am sure to meet with buddhas and bodhisattvas." Therefore, he has no fear of [being reborn in] the unhappy migratory states. (5) He thinks, "Throughout the entire world, no one[1291] is seen to have a [spiritual] attitude that is the equal of mine, much less one that is higher." Therefore, he has no fear of becoming timid in a group. In these ways, he is one in whom all fears are gone, one in whom all trepidation about instructions regarding the profound is gone, one in whom all arrogance and pride due to having an elevated status[1292] are gone, one in whom all hatred toward those who commit acts of harm and wrongful behavior is gone, and one in whom all excitement about worldly [forms of] enjoyment is gone.

With a [spiritual] attitude that is unimpaired because it is free of mental afflictions and that is extraordinary because of its fervor, he generates every form of bodhisattva effort in this life in order to attain every form of virtuous quality, and he does so governed by and preceded by faith. While on this pleasurable state of great joy, with regard to the future he also carries out, based upon the purity of his attitude, the ten great aspirational prayers that were described previously in the chapter entitled "The Spiritual Qualities That Are Conducive to Enlightenment."[1293] Having carried out the [first] great aspirational prayer to honor the masters and lords of Dharma, the foremost beings who are worthy of being venerated, he carries out the second [great aspirational prayer] to maintain the true Dharma that they teach, the third [great aspirational prayer] to advance the true Dharma in a regular manner, the fourth [great aspirational prayer] to practice the bodhisattva conduct in a manner that accords with that [aim of advancing the Dharma], the fifth [great aspirational prayer] to ripen those beings who are [suitable] vessels for that [true Dharma], the sixth [great aspirational prayer] to travel to buddha fields, see the tathāgatas who are present there, honor them, and hear the true Dharma [from them], the seventh [great aspirational prayer]

1291. *BBhVy* (f. 273a): "Except for the bodhisattvas who have attained the stages, all other [beings] lack a [spiritual] attitude that is the equal of this [bodhisattva]."

1292. S: *ucchrayamānastambhaḥ*, T: *thos pa'i nga rgyal gyis khengs pa*. The Tibetan suggests that the elevated status is gained through being someone who is learned. See note 1061 for a similar occurrence.

1293. See Book I, chapter 17, the section entitled "Aspirational Prayer" [I.17.13]. These aspirational prayers are found in the first section of the *Sutra on the Ten Stages* (see English translation of *DB*, pp. 704–706).

to purify one's own buddha field, the eighth [great aspirational prayer] never to be separated from buddhas and bodhisattvas in all one's rebirths and to have the same thoughts and actions as those of other bodhisattvas, the ninth [great aspirational prayer] that all one's activities that are done to benefit sentient beings should be fruitful, and the tenth great aspirational prayer to attain unsurpassed true and complete enlightenment and perform the deeds of a buddha.

[That bodhisattva] also fixes [his aspirational mind] correctly in the following manner: "In an uninterrupted manner that resembles both the limitlessness of the realm of sentient beings and the limitlessness of worldly qualities, may these great aspirational prayers of mine never fail to come to pass, never be lost [from my mind], and never become disconnected [from their intended aims], in rebirth after rebirth until I reach the ultimate goal of enlightenment."

It should be understood that the former[1294] [descriptions identify] the aspirational prayers in terms of the goals toward which the mind is being fixed, while the latter[1295] [description identifies the prayers] in terms of the manner in which the mind is being fixed [upon those goals]. Moreover, after having carried out these initial great aspirational prayers, the bodhisattva generates countless hundreds of thousands of groups of ten aspirational prayers as correct forms of aspirational prayers.

In order to perfect the pleasurable state of great joy, ten spiritual qualities are developed by the [bodhisattva] who, in this manner, has carried out aspirational prayers that relate to the future and has generated effort in this life. He develops intense faith toward all the spiritual qualities of a buddha. Through perceiving how the entire mass of suffering that sentient beings experience comes about through the process of dependent origination, compassion [arises]. Through reflecting, "I must be the one who liberates sentient beings from this entire mass of suffering," loving-kindness [arises]. Through having the intention to save [sentient beings] from their suffering, [there arises] a lack of concern for oneself. The renunciation [that gives away] inner and outer objects to sentient beings [is developed] by one who possesses such a lack of concern [for himself]. The tirelessness that seeks

1294. That is, the ten great aspirational prayers described in the paragraph prior to the previous one.

1295. This refers to the preceding paragraph, where the limitless form in which the great aspirational prayers are carried out is described.

mundane and transcendent qualities from others for the sake of those very sentient beings also [is developed]. Knowledge of the teachings [is developed] by one who is tireless about perfecting the attainment of knowledge of the entire [body of] teachings. Knowledge of the world [is developed] by one who has knowledge of the teachings, in the sense of [knowing how] to engage in practices that accord with lesser, intermediate, and superior sentient beings in a manner that befits their circumstances. Shame and abashment concerning the observance of a [proper] time, opportunity, and measure in relation to those very activities also [is developed]. The power of firmness [is developed] in the sense that one never turns back from those very activities. In addition, the qualities of worshipping and serving the tathāgatas [are developed] through [cultivating] the practices of [offering] both [material] gain and honor. These ten spiritual qualities are the ones that are developed in order to perfect this state of abiding, that is to say, (1) faith, (2) compassion, (3) loving-kindness, (4) the willingness to give away [inner and outer objects], (5) tirelessness, (6) knowledge of the teachings, (7) knowledge of the world, (8) shame and abashment, (9) developing the power of firmness, and (10) worshipping and serving the tathāgatas.

Having taken up these ten qualities, the bodhisattva observes them and practices them extensively. In addition, he seeks [to learn] from the buddhas and bodhisattvas every aspect of the path's virtuous qualities and faults that pertain to the remaining nine pleasurable states of superior morality, etc. Having become knowledgeable regarding these [subjects], it is easy for him to avoid losing the way on the path and he becomes one who has properly taken up the signs that relate to the aspects, the attainments, and their successive effects. After having proceeded through all the pleasurable states, he reaches great enlightenment. He also conveys a great company of sentient beings along the path that leads them out of samsara's wilderness. It should be understood that these aspects are the ones by means of which [a bodhisattva] enters [the various pleasurable states]; entry [into the pleasurable states] is their attainment; and the arising and realization of those great results and benefits [that are achieved] by [a bodhisattva] who has entered [any of the pleasurable states] are their successive effects.

On the basis of two causes, many buddhas appear to the vision of [the bodhisattva] who is established in this pleasurable state. These [buddhas] are both the ones that he has learned about in the bodhisattva collection of scriptures and the ones toward whom he has developed devotion. They are tathāgatas who have many different names [and who exist] in world spheres having many different names that lie throughout the ten directions. With a mind possessed of great faith, he implores them to let themselves be seen. This entreaty of [the bodhisattva] who has such a nature continues to grow ever stronger. This is one of the causes. He also generates the following aspirational prayer: "May I take birth in that [world] where a buddha has appeared." This aspirational prayer of [the bodhisattva] who has such a nature continues to grow ever stronger. Having seen these tathāgatas on the basis of a vision that is gained through sincere faith and by means of the strength of his aspirational prayers, he provides them with every form of worship and means of comfort. With all his ability and strength, he also honors the Sangha. He also listens to the Dharma from those tathāgatas, and then both takes up [the Dharma] and maintains it. He successfully implements [those Dharma teachings] by means of a [form of] practice that accords with the Dharma.[1296] He dedicates these roots of virtue to great enlightenment. He ripens sentient beings by means of the four principles for attracting a following.

By means of these three purifying causes—worshipping and paying homage to the tathāgatas, the Dharma, and the Sangha; ripening beings with the principles for attracting a following; and dedicating roots of virtue to enlightenment—[the bodhisattva's] roots of virtue are purified to an ever-greater degree over a period lasting many trillions of trillions of kalpas. For example, gold that is in its natural state becomes ever more pure as it is repeatedly placed into fire by an expert smith. In the same way, the virtue roots of a bodhisattva who possesses a pure attitude become ever more refined by means of these purifying causes.

Moreover, as a form of birth, the [bodhisattva] who is established on this [pleasurable state] mostly becomes a wheel ruler who is lord of the Rose Apple Continent in rebirth after rebirth. Having become free of all forms of the stain of stinginess, he is a master at removing the stinginess that is possessed by [other] sentient beings. Whatever action he undertakes on the basis of [any of] the four principles for attracting a following never fails to be accompanied by thoughts that are directed toward the [Three] Jewels and the attainment of every aspect of enlightenment. He reflects, "How much I

1296. S: *dharmānudharmapratipattiḥ*, T: *chos kyi rjes su mthun pa'i chos*. Here the term refers to the meditative practices that are regularly and continuously cultivated at this level. See also the description that appears in Book I, chapter 8.

wish to become the foremost among all sentient beings and the one who is relied upon for every need."

If he wishes to, he can initiate the kind of effort that is willing to give up home, spouse, and all his wealth, and go forth into the Tathāgata's teaching. Having done so, he can enter a hundred bodhisattva concentrations within a single instant, moment, or brief period;[1297] see a hundred tathāgatas in their separate buddha fields with his divine eye; and perceive the magical emanations and supernatural power of those [buddhas] as well as the supernatural power of bodhisattvas. He can cause a hundred world spheres to shake[1298] and, similarly, can travel to them with his body. Having filled [those worlds] with light, he can reveal them to others. By [generating] a hundred magical emanations, he can ripen a hundred sentient beings who are suitable to be disciplined. If he wishes to, he can also empower himself to remain alive for a hundred kalpas. His knowledge-perception can reach a hundred kalpas into the past or the future.[1299] He can examine a hundred Dharma doors,[1300] which are Dharma doors for such topics as the heaps, the constituents, and the bases.[1301] He can magically create a hundred physical forms [of himself] and also manifest a hundred bodhisattvas as a retinue for each of those physical forms.

1297. S: *ekakṣaṇalavamuhūrtena;* T: *skad cig thang cig yud tsam chig gis.* A *kṣanaḥ* is the term for the smallest unit of time. A traditional Buddhist description is that a healthy person's finger snap is made up of sixty-five instants. A *lavaḥ* is defined as consisting of sixty instants, and a *muhūrtam* is one-thirtieth of a day or forty-eight minutes.

1298. *BBhVy* (f. 277a–277b): "'He or she can cause a hundred world spheres to shake' is [an act that is carried out] for the purpose of drawing beings [to the Dharma]."

1299. *BBhVy* (f. 277b): "[The phrase] 'His or her knowledge-perception can reach a hundred kalpas' means that distinct births can be grasped [over that range of time]. 'Into the past and future' is meant in relation to the purpose of causing [other] sentient beings to abandon [committing] evil deeds, because by revealing [past] karma and states of existence, [sentient beings] will learn their past accumulation of causes and they will undertake to develop virtuous deeds that pertain to the future."

1300. S: *dharmamukhaśatam vicinoti,* T: *chos kyi sgo brgya rnam par 'byed pa. DBV* (f. 154a) glosses this phrase as "In order to ripen the mind, he or she can contemplate the meanings of [a hundred different] Dharma formulations" and (f. 110a) equates the term "Dharma door" with the term "Dharma formulation" (S: *dharmaparyāyaḥ,* T: *chos kyi rnam grangs*). *APMK* (f. 81a) identifies a "Dharma formulation" as any specific instance of a Dharma teaching (S: *dharmaprabhedaḥ,* T: *chos kyi rab tu dbye ba*).

1301. That is, the five heaps (S: *skandhaḥ,* T: *phung po*), eighteen constituents (S: *dhātuḥ,* T: *khams*), and twelve bases (S: *āyatanam,* T: *skye mched*). See *PS* and *PSV* for a discussion of all three of these topics.

Beyond these qualities, it should be understood that bodhisattvas who are established in this pleasurable state of great joy are able to produce immeasurable numbers of supernatural magical creations on the strength of aspirational prayers, for they are beings who possess the power of aspirational prayers and, by means of special kinds of aspirational prayers, they generate [magical creations].[1302] It would not be easy to count the number of these correct aspirational prayers, even if one spent up to a trillion trillion kalpas trying to do so.

It should be understood that this represents a brief description of the bodhisattvas' pleasurable state of great joy, in terms of [the aspirational prayers] that are extremely well ascertained, in terms of the four aspects of the [enlightenment] mind that is developed, in terms of the correct aspirational prayers that are carried out and the effort that is generated, in terms of the manner in which this pleasurable state is perfected, in terms of the manner in which the subsequent pleasurable states are caused to arise, in

1302. *DB* (p. 14) mentions the following series of magical creations (S: *vikurvaṇaḥ,* T: *rnam par sprul pa*) that bodhisattvas on this pleasurable state can generate: (1) physical bodies, (2) light, (3) miraculous powers, (4) the [divine] eye, (5) [its] spheres of action, (6) voices, (7) going about, (8) arrays, (9) supernatural power, (10) intentions, and (11) formative actions. *DBV* (f. 154b): "Regarding this [topic], 'physical bodies' are the basis for all the bodhisattva activities. From these [physical bodies] arise light and miraculous powers (S: *ṛddhiḥ,* T: *rdzu 'phrul;* see Book I, chapter 5, the section entitled "Miraculous Power" [I.5.1.1], including its several subsections). On the basis of these [bodies] arise the divine eye and its spheres of action, which should be understood to mean all of the five eyes [see below]. On the basis of miraculous powers arise voices, going about, arrays, and supernatural power. 'Voices' means the speech uttered by magically created bodies. 'Going about' means the act of [magically] traveling [great distances]. 'Arrays' means generating magical displays. 'Supernatural power' (S: *adhiṣṭhānam,* T: *byin gyi rlabs*) means that by which one empowers others [thereby enabling them to acquire extraordinary knowledge and abilities]. 'Intentions' (S: *adhimuktiḥ,* T: *mos pa*) means accomplishing powerful activities in accordance with one's desiderative intentions and on the basis of various types of one-pointed concentration (see also note 347). 'Formative actions' (S: *abhisaṃkārāḥ,* T: *'du byed rnams*) means teaching the Dharma on the basis of different forms of [the power of] retention that are subsumed within the wisdom eye." The five eyes are the corporeal eye, the divine eye, the Dharma eye, the wisdom eye, and the Buddha eye. The corporeal eye is able to see all manner of physical objects, large and small, that are situated at vast distances. The divine eye correctly sees where beings die and are reborn. The wisdom eye directly perceives the ultimate nature of all entities. The Dharma eye perceives the nature of the faculties of other āryas. The buddha eye is able to perceive every aspect of all entities that exist. While the true form of the buddha eye is possessed only by fully enlightened buddhas, bodhisattvas can possess a semblance of this knowledge, which enables them to realize how to further develop their practice correctly without having to rely upon others.

terms of the manner in which roots of virtue are refined, in terms of [the forms of] rebirth [that occur], and in terms of the spiritual powers [that are possessed].

In addition, a more extensive description can be found in the sutra itself, within the section of the *Sutra on the Ten Stages* that addresses the stage of great joy.[1303] It should also be understood that the ten bodhisattva stages [that are described] in the *Sutra on the Ten Stages* are the [very same] ten pleasurable states that are presented here in this manual on the bodhisattva collection [of scriptures], beginning with the pleasurable state of great joy and continuing in the same order up to the supreme pleasurable state. Regarding this [point], it is called a "stage" in the sense of being [a position] that bodhisattvas take possession of[1304] and it is called a "pleasurable state" in the sense of being [a position] in which they remain in a state of enjoyment.[1305]

1303. S: *pramuditā*, T: *rab tu dga' ba*.

1304. S: *parigrahārthena*, T: *yongs su gzung ba'i don gyis*. *BBhVy* (ff. 277b–278a): "[The statement] 'it is called a stage in the sense of being a state that [bodhisattvas] take possession of' means that just as with the ordinary sense [of the term *bhūmi*—that is, an area of ground or territory that can be taken possession of—in this context, a stage is a state in which] a bodhisattva has taken possession of a certain group of spiritual qualities. That is to say, it means he [has taken possession] of an excellent stage [of spiritual development] (S: **avasthāviśeṣena*, T: *gnas skabs kyi khyad par gyis*)." Also, *MSA* (ch. 21, v. 40): "Those very [states] are regarded as stages, / Because one ascends ever higher / On those immeasurable [states] / In order to free immeasurable beings from fear." This description represents an example of the literary form in which the explanation of a word or expression contains the syllables of the word that is being explained. Thus, "ever higher" (*bhūyo bhūyo*) contains the syllable *bhū* and "on those immeasurable states" (*amitāsu*) contains the syllable *mi*. Similarly, the compound "in order to free immeasurable beings from fear" (*bhūtāmitābhayārthāya*) also incorporates the same two syllables.

1305. S: *upabhogavāsārthena*, T: *nye bar longs spyod pa'i gnas kyi don gyis*. *BBhVy* (f. 278a): "[Asaṅga indicates that] a stage is called a 'pleasurable state' in the sense of [a position in which bodhisattvas] remain in a state of enjoyment. Likewise, a state in which one remains at ease by abiding in a variety of spiritual qualities is called a 'pleasurable state' (S: **tasmin tasmin dharme vāsena yo sukhavihāraḥ sa vihāra iti;* T: *chos de dang de la gnas pas bde bar gnas pa gang yin pa de ni gnas pa zhes bya'o*). Alternatively, [it is called a pleasurable state] in the sense that one abides in a state of ease, as [in the phrase] to abide in a state of ease in one's present life (S: *dṛṣṭadharmasukhavihāraḥ*, T: *mthong ba'i chos la bde bar gnas pa*). Or, [the term *vihāraḥ*] should be regarded as meaning an abode, as in the expression an 'abode for austerity' (S: **tapovāsaḥ,* T: *dka' thub kyi gnas*)."

The Pleasurable State of Superior Morality [II.4.4]

Regarding this [topic], what aspects, what marks, and what signs should the bodhisattvas [who are abiding] in the pleasurable state of superior morality be understood to possess?

In this case, a bodhisattva first attains a purity of attitude that is characterized by ten types of mental attitude while he is still [abiding] in the pleasurable state of great joy. They are (1) the superior attitude that never violates a promise made to any spiritual teacher, anyone worthy of respect, or anyone worthy of being venerated; (2) the attitude that is genial toward those bodhisattvas who are exemplary Dharma practitioners and dwells happily with them; (3) the attitude that exercises control over one's own mind and overcomes all the root and secondary mental afflictions and deeds of Māra;[1306] (4) the attitude that all [conditioning] formations[1307] are flawed; (5) the attitude that nirvana is advantageous; (6) the attitude that the virtuous entities that are conducive to enlightenment are to be cultivated continually; (7) the attitude of [wanting to live in] solitude because it is conducive to meditation upon those [spiritual qualities]; (8) the attitude that is indifferent to worldly objects of desire and positions of eminence, as well as gain and honor; (9) the attitude that rejects the Lesser Vehicle and [seeks to] master the Great Vehicle; and (10) the attitude that [wants to] accomplish all the aims of all sentient beings. It is due to the arising of these ten correct attitudes in the mind that [a bodhisattva's] attitude is said to be purified. Moreover, through having developed these same ten attitudes to a level of greatness and having brought them to a state of fullness, a bodhisattva enters into and advances along the second [of the ten ārya bodhisattva pleasurable states], which is the pleasurable state of superior morality.

1306. S: *mārakarma,* T: *bdud kyi las.* Sutras describe all manner of evil actions that are performed by an individual who has come under the influence of an evil worldly deity known as Devaputra Māra. See notes 433 and 697.

1307. S: *saṃskārāḥ,* T: *'du byed rnams.* This is the active form of a noun that is sometimes used to refer only to the fourth of the five heaps, which I usually translate as "the formations heap" (S: *saṃskāraskandhaḥ,* T: *'du byed kyi phung po*). In that form, the term is meant to suggest that impermanent entities exert a causal efficacy, hence the term might also be translated "conditioning entities." A similar term, "conditioned entities" (S: *saṃskṛtāḥ,* T: *'dus byas rnams*), that is formed from the past participle of the same verb (S: *saṃskṛ,* T: *'du byed pa*) is meant to indicate that all impermanent entities are the products of causes. However, as mentioned earlier in note 843, in some instances the two terms are interchangeable.

While on the pleasurable state of superior morality, [a bodhisattva] becomes one who observes morality naturally. He does not engage in even very minor forms of immorality that are included among the wrongful action-paths,[1308] much less any of the middling or great forms. He also naturally displays complete forms of the ten virtuous action-paths. [The bodhisattva] who observes morality naturally in this way uses [wisdom] to discern correctly the process by which deeds that are afflicted or unafflicted action-paths constitute causes that give rise to the results of [being reborn in either] the unhappy or the happy migratory states, [as well as to discern correctly the process by which virtuous deeds constitute causes that give rise to the various respective results] within the three vehicles. He also correctly discerns [the nature of] deeds in terms of their maturation results and corresponding results.[1309]

1308. S: *karmapathaḥ*, T: *las kyi lam*. This term, which appears in the sutras, is closely associated with the ten most prominent forms of virtuous and nonvirtuous karma. *AK* (ch. 4, v. 66): "Having grouped together their greatest forms, / Ten were declared to be action-paths / That are virtuous or nonvirtuous, as appropriate." The ten nonvirtuous action-paths are (1) killing, (2) stealing, (3) sexual misconduct, (4) lying, (5) divisive speech, (6) harsh speech, (7) idle speech, (8) coveting, (9) malice, and (10) wrong view. The ten virtuous action-paths are their opposites—that is, the avoidance of killing, etc. Buddhist philosophical schools held different positions regarding the precise nature of physical and verbal karma. The Yogācāra school holds that physical and verbal karma are not the body's movement or the sound of the voice, respectively, but rather the specific forms of volition (S: *cetanā*, T: *sems pa;* see note 620) that generate that physical movement and verbal sound. The term "path" in the expression "action-path" is also explained several ways. One is that physical movement and verbal sound are paths in that they provide the means by which volition is set in motion. Another is that these virtuous and nonvirtuous actions are paths in that they lead to happy or unhappy migratory states, respectively.

1309. *BBhVy* (f. 280a): "Regarding this, a maturation result (S: *vipākaphalam*, T: *rnam par smin pa'i 'bras bu*) means to be reborn in the hells due to a great [nonvirtuous karmic] cause, as an animal due a moderate one, and as a hungry ghost due to a lesser one. A corresponding result (S: *niṣyandaphalam*, T: *rgyu mthun gyi 'bras bu*) is when, after passing away from [an unhappy migratory state] and having been reborn as a human being, one experiences a short life span [due to having previously killed] as well as [a range of other consequences] that end with deceit and guile [due to having generated wrong view]." Virtuous deeds also have their own respective forms of maturation and corresponding results. The *Sutra on Ten Stages* cites two forms of corresponding result for each of the ten nonvirtuous action paths: (1) killing results in a short life and having to undergo many illnesses; (2) stealing results in having little wealth and having to possess wealth jointly; (3) sexual misconduct results in having an untrustworthy following and a hostile spouse; (4) lying results in being the frequent object of calumny and having the promises that are made to you by others violated; (5) divisive speech results in a divided following and an inferior following; (6) harsh speech

[Such a bodhisattva] can be seen to abandon nonvirtuous deeds and take up virtuous deeds. He also wants to cause others to take up this same behavior and [in fact] causes them to do so. Through feeling sympathetic toward the entire realm of sentient beings who are defiled by the fault of having engaged in wicked deeds, who without exception are suffering in an ultimate sense whether they are in prosperous or unfortunate circumstances, and who live in a state of adversity that subjects them to multiple forms of calamity, [the bodhisattva] develops [toward all those sentient beings] a [form of] sympathy that is extensive and repeatedly considers [their condition].

It should be understood that, as in the previous [pleasurable state], [the bodhisattva] who is established in this pleasurable state of superior morality sees [many] buddhas and purifies his roots of virtue. In this case there is the following difference. For example, just as that same gold that is being placed into fire by an expert smith becomes even more pure when it is also dipped in vitriol, it should be understood that this bodhisattva's roots of virtue similarly [achieve an even greater form of] purity.

Because the purity of [a bodhisattva's] mental attitude in this pleasurable state has reached a point of culmination, he is mostly reborn as a wheel ruler with dominion over all four continents, and to a great degree causes beings to turn away from immorality and the nonvirtuous action-paths and to take up the virtuous action-paths. It should be understood that his powers are ten times greater than they were during the previous [pleasurable state].

It should be understood that this represents a brief description of the bodhisattvas' pleasurable state of superior morality, in terms of the natural observance of morality, in terms of the elimination of every aspect of the impurity of immorality, in terms of the knowledge that fathoms every aspect of the causes and results that pertain to every [form of] action-path, in terms of the desire to cause others to take up virtuous deeds, in terms of the development of extensive sympathy [toward sentient beings], in terms of reflection upon the suffering and misfortune that [those in] the realm of sentient beings create by their deeds, in terms of the purification of roots of

---

results in having to hear unpleasant speech and being argumentative; (7) idle speech results in being one whose speech is not believed and being unable to express oneself decisively; (8) covetousness results in never being satisfied and having great desire; (9) malice results in having the desire to do harm and in being subjected to injury by others; and (10) wrong view results in being one who develops inferior views and one who is both devious and deceitful.

virtue, in terms of [the forms of] rebirth [that occur], and in terms of the spiritual powers [that are possessed].

In addition, a more extensive description can be found in the sutra itself, within the section of the *Sutra on the Ten Stages* that addresses the stainless stage. It is called the "stainless stage"[1310] because the stain of immorality is gone. It is called the "pleasurable state of superior morality" for the very same reason that the stain of immorality is gone. It should be understood that what is [referred to] there as the stainless stage is [referred to] here as the pleasurable state of superior morality.

The Pleasurable State of Superior Mind Training [II.4.5]

Regarding this [topic], what aspects, what marks, and what signs are possessed by bodhisattvas [who are abiding] in the pleasurable state of superior mind training?

In this case, a bodhisattva previously brought to mind, delighted in, and thoroughly comprehended ten [forms of] pure attitude while he was still [abiding] in the pleasurable state of superior morality. By employing ten further ways of bringing to mind these pure attitudes in order to develop them to a level of greatness and bring them to fullness, he rises above the pleasurable state of superior morality and enters the pleasurable state of superior mind training. He enters [this pleasurable state] by bringing to mind the following ten mental attitudes: (1) the form of attention [in which he reflects], "My mental attitude is pure in ten ways"; (2) the form of attention [in which he reflects], "It is improper for me to lose [any of] these ten kinds of virtuous attitude"; (3) the form of attention [in which he reflects], "My mind does not rush toward [any of] the outflows or [any of] the entities that are related to the outflows; it remains in a state of opposition to them"; (4) the form of attention [in which he reflects], "My consciousness remains fixed in meditation upon their antidotes"; (5) the form of attention [in which he reflects], "It is improper for me to subsequently lose [any of] these antidotes"; (6) the form of attention [in which he reflects], "It is improper that I, who adhere firmly in this way to the antidotes, should be overcome by any of the outflows, by any of the entities that are related to the outflows, or by any [influence of] Māra"; (7) the form of attention [in which he reflects],

1310. S: *vimalā,* T: *dri ma med pa.*

"My mind remains free of any despondency with regard to [pursuing] all the spiritual qualities of a buddha"; (8) the form of attention [in which he reflects], "There is no uneasiness in my mind with regard to any of the forms of conduct that are difficult to carry out"; (9) the form of attention [in which he reflects], "My mind is devoted exclusively to the Great Vehicle; it does not [feel drawn] toward any of the other [forms of practice] that pertain to the Lesser Vehicle"; and (10) the form of attention [in which he reflects], "My mind delights in accomplishing the aims of all sentient beings."

The bodhisattva who is established in the pleasurable state of superior mind training discredits[1311] conditioning formations on the basis of their manifold disadvantages. He also deliberately develops aversion[1312] toward them. He regards a buddha's knowledge favorably on the basis of its manifold benefits, and develops a longing for it with an aspiration that is deeply felt.[1313] He observes that the realm of sentient beings is afflicted by manifold forms of suffering and develops a mind that has concern for sentient beings and a mind that resorts to what will benefit them. He remains mindful with regard to all conditioning formations and possesses a form of effort that pur-

1311. S: *vidūṣayati,* T: *sun 'byin par byed.* This verb refers to the process of reflection by which a practitioner comes to recognize pleasurable forms of samsaric existence as having the unsatisfactory nature that is characterized by the suffering of change (S: *pariṇamaduḥkatā,* T: *'gyur ba'i sdug bsngal nyid*). *AKB* (pp. 330–331): "Whatever feeling [i.e., pleasant feeling] has an essential characteristic that is agreeable in nature can never also take on one that is disagreeable in nature. It is through some other aspect of those [pleasant feelings] that the āryas discredit them, so that they will take on a disagreeable quality. For example, they will regard them as the abode of heedlessness (S: *pramādapadam,* T: *bag med pa'i gnas*), as requiring great exertion to acquire, as undergoing change, and as being impermanent." *DB* (p. 19) describes two sets of ten qualities that represent why "everything that constitutes a [conditioning] formation" (S: *sarvasaṃskāragatam,* T: *'du byed du gyur pa thams cad*) should be recognized as flawed and therefore something toward which one should abandon all forms of attachment. *Inner Science* (pp. 111–120) presents a range of views on the topic of the suffering of change.

1312. S: *udvegaḥ,* T: *skyo ba.* This term refers to a state of mind that is central to the process of developing renunciation. The Tibetan equivalent, *skyo ba,* can be somewhat misleading, as its meaning in ordinary usage is that of "sadness," which is too passive for this particular context. The original Sanskrit, *udvegaḥ,* suggests more a sense of intense agitation, distress, anxiety, and fear (MW, p. 192). Thus, properly understood, it represents the antithesis of desire for and attachment to samsaric existence. It also acts as the antidote for complacency and lack of concern about our everyday condition.

1313. The Tibetan translation and *BBhVy* both construe the adverbial phrase "with an aspiration that is deeply felt" with the sentence that follows; however, it seems more logical to read it as translated here, which accords with the two Sanskrit editions.

sues enlightenment ardently. He possesses an attitude that feels abundant compassion toward sentient beings.

He recognizes that the sole means of liberating sentient beings from suffering permanently is the knowledge that is completely free of the obstruction caused by the mental afflictions. He also recognizes that, for the purpose of bringing about that liberation, wisdom regarding the "entity-source"[1314] is the antidote for all occurrences of conceptual thought and for the arising of afflicted existence.[1315] He further recognizes that true one-pointed concentration [is necessary] to perfect that light of knowledge. He recognizes as well that attainment of the meditative absorptions, the deliverances,[1316] [the forms of] one-pointed concentration, and the states of composure must be preceded by learning the bodhisattva collection of scriptures and that such learning constitutes their cause.

Having understood [these things], he undertakes to seek such learning by putting forth great effort. There is no [form of] property, possession, or inner or outer object that he would not give up for the sake of learning the true Dharma. There is no form of service to a venerable teacher that he would not accept. There is no act of humility[1317] that he would not accept. There is no physical pain that he would not accept. He is more pleased at hearing a single verse [of Dharma that consists] of four lines than if he [were to obtain] a great heap of jewels so large that it would fill the triple-thousand [world spheres]. He is more pleased at hearing a single Dharma saying on the purification of bodhisattva activities that was taught by a true and complete buddha than if he were to obtain birth in all such positions as those of Śakra, Māra, Brahmā, a Lokapāla, or a wheel ruler.

If someone were to say to him: "I will enable you to hear a Dharma statement on the purification of bodhisattva activities that was taught by a true

1314. S: *dharmadhātuḥ,* T: *chos kyi dbyings.* Here this term is a synonym for ultimate truth; see note 1110.

1315. See note 1110.

1316. S: *vimokṣaḥ,* T: *rnam par thar pa.* See note 906. This term does not appear in the two published Sanskrit editions.

1317. S: *saṃnatiḥ,* T: *'dud pa.* This statement is missing from the Wogihara Sanskrit edition and is rendered incorrectly in the Dutt edition. It is also rendered incorrectly as *'dun pa* in the Tibetan Derge edition. It corresponds to the expression in the *DB* (p. 20) that states: "[form of] humble conduct that casts off pride and haughtiness" (S: *mānābhimānotsarga-nirmāṇopacāratā,* T: *nga rgyal dang lhag pa'i nga rgyal yongs su gtang bas nga rgyal med pa la sbyang ba*).

and complete buddha if you will throw yourself into a great pit of fire and agree to undergo that great suffering," upon hearing this, he would think, "For the sake of that Dharma statement . . . I would endure throwing myself from Brahmā's domain into a pit of fire equal in size to the great triple-thousand [world spheres], let alone into an ordinary [pit of fire]. We should seek the Buddha's Dharma teachings even if it means having to endure the suffering of the hells multiple times, not to mention having to undergo ordinary [forms of] suffering."

Having sought Dharma teachings while putting forth this kind of effort, he properly brings to mind the following thought: "The Buddha's Dharma teachings should be pursued in accordance with the form of practice that accords with Dharma, not merely by perfecting [one's knowledge of] the form of expression and sound [with which the teachings are conveyed]." After having gained such an understanding and relying upon that very learning, by correctly taking up the signs of entities[1318] as meditation objects, [the bodhisattva successively] achieves and abides in the first, second, third, and fourth mundane meditative absorptions, the four mundane states of composure of the formless realm, the four immeasurables, and the five forms of supernatural knowledge,[1319] which are described in the scriptural passages that declare "separated from the objects of desire,"[1320] etc.

1318. S: *dharmanimittāni,* T: *chos kyi mtshan ma. BBhVy* (f. 282b): "[The expression] 'signs of entities' means that [the bodhisattva] fixes his or her mind upon the sign that is an image (S: *pratibimbanimittam,* T: *gzugs brnyan gyi mtshan ma*) of some particular entity." The phrase "by correctly taking up the signs of entities as meditation objects" is a reference to the overall process of cultivating the two forms of meditation practice known as "quiescence" (S: *śamathaḥ,* T: *zhi gnas*) and "insight" (S: *vipaśyanā,* T: *lhag mthong*) within the context of the worldly path. *ŚBh* summarizes this method on pp. 249–251 as one of two forms of the meditation object that eliminates the mental afflictions (S: *kleśaviśodhanālaṃbanam,* T: *nyong mongs rnam par sbyong ba'i dmigs pa*). The other form of this meditation object is the sixteen aspects of the four noble truths that are practiced within the context of the transcendent path.

1319. *DB* (pp. 21–22) describes the first five of the six forms of supernatural knowledge (S: *abhijñāḥ,* T: *mngon par shes pa*) that Asaṅga presents in Book I, chapter 5. It is likely that only these five are mentioned here because the sixth form of supernatural knowledge is called "termination of the outflows" and it would be contrary to the pursuit of the ultimate goal of buddhahood for bodhisattvas to bring about the permanent termination of their mental afflictions prematurely.

1320. "Separated from the objects of desire" (S: *viviktaṃ kāmair,* T: *'dod pa rnams kyis dben pa*) is the initial phrase in the canonical description of how a meditation practitioner achieves the first meditative absorption. See note 911 for the complete passage. This descrip-

After having stayed in these [meditative states] extensively, [the bodhisattva] turns away from the meditative absorptions, one-pointed concentrations, and states of composure, and by the strength of aspirational prayers is reborn in the desire realm in places where he perceives that the welfare of beings [can be accomplished] and the spiritual qualities that are conducive to enlightenment can be perfected. It is not the case that he takes birth by the power of those [meditative states].[1321]

Through having overcome desire for the desire realm, [a bodhisattva's] bonds of desire are abandoned.[1322] Through having turned away from the meditative absorptions, one-pointed concentrations, and states of composure, [a bodhisattva] abandons the bonds of existence.[1323] The bonds that were generated by [erring] views were previously abandoned while [that bodhisattva] was still on the stage in which practice is based upon devotion, on the strength of his conviction about the suchness [that is the ultimate nature] of [all] entities. His wrongful [emotions of] desire, anger, and ignorance have become completely inactive.

The manner in which he sees [many] buddhas and purifies his roots of virtue should be understood as it was described at length previously.[1324] In this instance there is the following difference. For example, just as the gold from which impurities and contaminants have been removed retains the same weight and measure in the hands of a skillful smith, it should be understood that this [bodhisattva's] roots of virtue also become purified in the same way.[1325] In terms of rebirth, for the most part he becomes Śakra,

---

tion, along with those of the other three meditative absorptions and the four formless states of composure, also appears in *DB* (pp. 20–21).

1321. The point of this sentence is that despite cultivating these meditative states, this bodhisattva counteracts their karmic force by the power of aspirational prayers in order to avoid being reborn in the form and formless realms. See also note 182.

1322. S: *prahīṇaḥ,* T: *spangs pa*. The use of this term here should not be understood in the sense of attaining a truth of cessation in relation to these mental afflictions. Rather, it should be understood in terms of having suppressed their power to become active on the strength of one-pointed concentration (see note 561). *DB* describes the bonds of desire as well as the bonds of existence as having become "thin" or "weak" (S: *tanu,* T: *bsrabs pa*).

1323. S: *bhavabandhanāni,* T: *srid pa'i 'ching ba rnams*. The term "existence" here is understood in the sense of samsaric existence in the form and formless realms.

1324. That is, in the previous pleasurable state.

1325. That is, just as a skillful smith does not lose any of the gold in the process of refining it, a bodhisattva on this state of abiding possesses the skill to eliminate mental imperfections while purifying his or her roots of virtue.

the lord of gods, and one who is skilled at turning sentient beings away from desire for sensory pleasures. It should be understood that the spiritual powers described in the previous pleasurable state in a magnitude of a thousand are possessed here in a magnitude of a hundred thousand.

It should be understood that this represents a brief description of the bodhisattvas' pleasurable state of superior mind training, in terms of its being entered by perfecting [forms of] attention in which [a range of] mental states are reflected upon, in terms of having correctly understood conditioning formations, the body of sentient beings, and great enlightenment, in terms of correctly seeking the means of liberating sentient beings from their suffering, in terms of seeking the Dharma with an attitude of great respect, in terms of [developing] a form of practice that accords with the Dharma and [enables the practitioner] to achieve and abide in the mundane states of meditative absorption, one-pointed concentration, states of composure, and supernatural knowledge, in terms of generating the aspirational prayers that turn back [the karmic power of] those [meditative states] and taking birth wherever one desires, in terms of the purification of roots of virtue, in terms of [the forms of] rebirth [that occur], and in terms of the spiritual powers [that are possessed].

In addition, a more extensive description can be found in the sutra itself, within the section of the *Sutra on the Ten Stages* that addresses the stage that produces light. Because this stage is characterized by the appearance of the light of the Dharma in the form of learning and the appearance of the light that consists of one-pointed concentration, it is called "[the stage that] produces light."[1326] This light comes into being due to the inner purity of the mind. Therefore, this pleasurable state is called [the pleasurable state of] "superior mind training." [As such,] it should be understood that the very same reason [for calling this] the stage that produces light is also the reason [for calling it] the pleasurable state of superior mind training.

1326. S: *prabhākarī*, T: *'od byed pa*.

The Pleasurable State of Superior Wisdom That Relates to the Spiritual Qualities That Are Conducive to Enlightenment [II.4.6]

Regarding this [topic], what is a bodhisattva's pleasurable state of superior wisdom that relates to the spiritual qualities that are conducive to enlightenment?

In this case, a bodhisattva previously attained ten [forms of] entry into the light of the Dharma[1327] on the strength of his having pursued learning, while he was still in the pleasurable state of superior mind training. Through developing those to a level of greatness and bringing them to fullness, he goes beyond the pleasurable state of superior mind training and enters the first pleasurable state of superior wisdom. Furthermore, the wording for the ten forms of entry into the light of the Dharma should be understood just as it appears in the sutra. The essential import of what is indicated by these [ten forms of entry] into the light of the Dharma should be understood as follows: (1) the beings who are nominally designated; (2) the place where it is nominally designated that they exist; (3) the reason that they are nominally designated entities;[1328] (4) what those [nominally designated sentient beings] resemble in an ultimate sense; (5) the entity whose affliction and purification causes [nominally designated sentient beings] to become afflicted and undergo purification; (6) the state of affliction their relation to which causes them to become afflicted; and (7) the unsurpassed form of purity which causes them to be purified.[1329]

1327. S: *daśa dharmālokapraveśāḥ,* T: *chos la snang ba 'jug pa bcu*. In the Tibetan translation of *DB* this Sanskrit compound is rendered as *chos snang ba la 'jug pa* ("entry into the Dharma light"), while in *DBV* it is rendered as *chos la snang bas 'jug pa* ("entry into the Dharma by means of light"). *DBV* (f. 180b) glosses the expression as follows: "'Light' means the knowledge that is gained through realization (S: **adhigamajñānam,* T: *rtogs pa'i ye shes*). When such a realization occurs, one gains entry into the Tathāgata's Dharma teachings by means of this knowledge; therefore, it is [called] 'entry into the Dharma by means of light.'"

1328. S: *yena prajñapyante*. This phrase does not appear in any of the Tibetan editions that were consulted.

1329. The correspondence between these seven categories and the ten forms of entry into the light of the Dharma should be understood as follows (*DBV,* f. 181a): (1) "The beings who are nominally designated" refers to entry into the light through contemplating the realm of sentient beings. (2) "The place where it is nominally designated that they exist" refers to entry into the light through contemplating the realm of [all the ten directions'] worlds. (3) "The reason that they are [merely] nominally designated entities" refers to entry

The bodhisattva who is established in this pleasurable state possesses [a series of] spiritual qualities, beginning with an adamantine attitude, that bring about the ripening of his knowledge. They are described in the sutra as causing one's knowledge to be ripened in ten ways. Through acquiring the [ten] qualities that possess this nature, he becomes one who has joined the family of the tathāgatas.

As described in the sutra, [these bodhisattvas] meditate upon the thirty-seven spiritual qualities that are conducive to enlightenment, beginning with the [four] closely placed recollections, [and they do so] on the basis of every aspect of the bodhisattva perspective.[1330] Through cultivating those spiritual qualities in a manner that is supported by skillful means, even subtle forms of the perishable collection view, as well as all the impulses to believe that the heaps, bases, and constituents are real, are abandoned in the sense that they become completely inactive. Through their abandonment, [the bodhisattva] completely and entirely refrains from engaging in those acts that the Tathāgata disapproves of. In addition, he also pursues in a proper manner all those acts that the Tathāgata approves of. Having

into the light through contemplating the "entity-source" (S: *dharmadhātuḥ,* T: *chos kyi dbyings*). (4) "What those [nominally designated entities] resemble in an ultimate sense" refers to entry into the light through contemplating the realm of space. (5) "The entity whose affliction and purification causes [nominally designated sentient beings] to become afflicted and undergo purification" refers to entry into the light through contemplating the realm of consciousness. (6) "The state of affliction their relation to which causes them to become afflicted" refers to three forms of entry into the light of the Dharma: that which arises through contemplating the desire realm, that which arises through contemplating the form realm, and that which arises through contemplating the formless realm. (7) "The unsurpassed form of purity that causes sentient beings to become purified" refers to two forms of entry into the light of the Dharma: that which arises through contemplating the realm that consists of having conviction about the Great Vehicle's extensive attitude and that which arises through contemplating the realm that consists of having conviction about the high-minded attitude that accomplishes the welfare of sentient beings.

1330. *DB* (pp. 24–25) follows the description of these thirty-seven spiritual qualities with a statement of the following ten motivations that inform their spiritual practice at this level: (1) out of concern for all sentient beings; (2) supported by the former prayers that one has undertaken to accomplish; (3) having been preceded by great compassion; (4) accompanied by great loving-kindness; (5) with the mind firmly focused on omniscient knowledge; (6) intending to create a buddha field and generate its adornments; (7) intending to achieve a tathāgata's powers, [forms of] intrepid confidence, unique buddha qualities, major and minor marks, and perfect voice; (8) seeking ever-higher forms of excellent spiritual qualities; (9) following what one has learned about liberation from the Buddha's profound Dharma teachings; and (10) reflecting on the power of great skillful means.

developed such a nature, he becomes one whose mind is increasingly more agreeable, gentle, and endowed with fitness.[1331] Likewise, he becomes one whose mind is extremely pure in a variety of ways. He becomes one who possesses a range of virtuous qualities that are in keeping with those attitudes, including gratitude and appreciation [for past benefits], etc. Seeking [to cultivate] the acts that purify the higher stages, he achieves and maintains the ability to put forth great effort. Because of that, the constituent elements of his attitude, superior attitude, and [form of] devotion[1332] become fully developed. Because of that, he also becomes incapable of being led astray or shaken [in resolve] by any heretics, [influence of] Māra, or persons who are hostile to the teaching.

The manner in which [a bodhisattva] sees [many] buddhas and purifies his roots of virtue should be understood as it was described at length previously. In this instance there is the following difference. For example, just as that same gold that a skillful smith has fashioned into decorative objects cannot be outshone by gold that has not been made into ornaments, this bodhisattva's roots of virtue cannot be outshone by the virtue roots of bodhisattvas who are established on other less developed pleasurable states. For example, the light that is emitted by the [wheel ruler's] precious jewel[1333] cannot be outshone by that of any other jewels and its splendor cannot be destroyed by any form of wind, water, or rain. Similarly, this bodhisattva

1331. S: *karmaṇyam,* T: *las su rung ba.* This quality is acquired through developing proficiency in one-pointed concentration. It is the essential characteristic of the mental factor called "agility" (S: *praśrabdhiḥ,* T: *shin tu sbyangs pa;* see note 382).

1332. *DBV* (f. 186b) glosses "attitude" as the intention to attain enlightenment, "superior attitude" as the intention to cultivate the path, and "devotion" as the highly developed resolve to attain extraordinary spiritual states. The term "constituent element" (S: *dhātuḥ,* T: *khams*) here seems to be a synonym for "lineage" (S: *gotram,* T: *rigs*), as this term was used in Book I, chapter 8.

1333. S: *maṇiratnam,* T: *nor bu rin po che.* One of the seven symbols of a wheel ruler's authority. Traditional accounts describe it as having these eight qualities: (1) it has the brilliance of the full moon in the autumn night; (2) it makes one cool by dispelling heat during the day; (3) it provides water having eight excellent qualities that dispels thirst when one is tormented by lack of water while traveling; (4) it grants the king's every wish; (5) it emits five-colored light rays from each of its eight facets; (6) no one within a radius of one hundred leagues (see note 389) becomes ill and it enables one to become mentally composed and achieve one's aims; (7) it prevents hostile *nāgas* from causing harmful rains and it causes trees and forests to grow in barren places; and (8) it prevents anyone from having an untimely death and wards off the effects of snakes and other harmful animals.

cannot be outshone by all the listeners and solitary realizers nor can the light of his wisdom be destroyed by any form of Māra or other adversary.

In terms of rebirth, he becomes a king of the class of gods known as Suyāma[1334] and one who is skilled at removing the perishable collection view that is possessed by sentient beings. With regard to the spiritual powers that were declared to have a magnitude of a hundred thousand on the previous pleasurable state, it should be understood that here they are declared to have a magnitude of ten million.

It should be understood that this represents a brief description of the bodhisattvas' pleasurable state of superior wisdom that relates to the spiritual qualities that are conducive to enlightenment, in terms of perfecting [the forms of] entry into the light of the Dharma; in terms of ripening their knowledge; in terms of cultivating the spiritual qualities that are conducive to enlightenment; in terms of abandoning all the impulses to generate erring beliefs, such as the perishable collection view, etc.; in terms of avoiding those acts that are forbidden and observing those that are approved of; in terms of how that [quality] causes the mind to become more gentle; in terms of increasing those spiritual qualities that accord with that [preceding characteristic]; in terms of putting forth the great effort that relates to seeking [to cultivate] the acts that purify the stages; in terms of how that purifies one's attitude, superior attitude, and [form of] devotion; in terms of how that prevents one from being led astray by any persons who are hostile to the teaching; in terms of the purification of roots of virtue; in terms of [the forms of] rebirth [that occur]; and in terms of the spiritual powers [that are possessed]. A more extensive description can be found in the section of the *Sutra on the Ten Stages* that addresses the stage of blazing light.

On this stage the spiritual qualities that are conducive to enlightenment are light rays of [transcendent] knowledge that correctly teach the Dharma and generate the light of wisdom throughout the worlds. Therefore, this stage is called "blazing light."[1335] That very [stage] is referred to here as "the pleasurable state of superior wisdom that relates to the spiritual qualities that are conducive to enlightenment."

1334. T: *rab 'thab bral.* See Book I, chapter 5, the section entitled "Transformational Miraculous Power" [I.5.1.1.1], where this class of worldly gods is simply called Yāma (T: *'thab bral*).

1335. S: *arciṣmatī,* T: *'od 'phro can,* also *'od 'phro ba.*

The Pleasurable State of Superior Wisdom That Relates to the Truths [II.4.7]

Regarding this [topic], what is the bodhisattvas' second pleasurable state of superior wisdom—that is, the one that relates to the truths?

Here a bodhisattva enters the second pleasurable state of superior wisdom by developing to a level of greatness and bringing to fullness the ten [forms of] sameness of purified attitude[1336] that were attained on the previous pleasurable state of superior wisdom. The wording for the ten [forms of] sameness of purified attitude should be understood as it appears in the sutra. The essential import of [the forms of] sameness of purified attitude should be understood as follows: The buddhas are the same in the sense that they are the enlightened ones who are unequaled and because they have gone completely beyond the sphere of [unenlightened] sentient beings from whom they are distinct. They are also the same in terms of the spiritual qualities that they possess and in terms of the manner in which they possess them.

[The bodhisattva] who is established in this pleasurable state and who is desirous of [achieving] a more excellent form of knowledge perceives the four noble truths as they truly are on the basis of ten aspects. The wording for all of them should be understood as it appears in the sutra. The essential import of the ten aspects of knowledge regarding the four noble truths should be understood as follows: (1) [the aspect] that is taught in relation to [the aim of] informing others, (2) [the aspect that is taught in relation to] the knowledge that must be gained for oneself, and (3) [the aspect that is taught in relation to] both of these subjects; (4) [the aspect] that represents the means by which [the four noble truths] are taught in relation to the Sutra [collection], (5) [the aspect that represents the means by which the

1336. S: *viśuddhāśāyasamatā*, T: *rnam par dag pa la bsam pa mnyam pa nyid*. The wording of this term as it appears in the *DB* is slightly different: "sameness in the purity of mental attitude" (S: *cittāśāyaviśuddhisamatā*, T: *rnam par dag pa la sems kyi bsam pa mnyam pa nyid*). *DBV* (f. 187b): "The antidote for distinct forms of pride (S: **mānaviśeṣapratipakṣaḥ*, T: *nga rgyal gyi khyad par gyi gnyen po*) is the ten forms of sameness regarding the purity of mental attitude, along with the forms of attention that bring them to mind in an irreversible manner. Previously they were taught as an antidote for the pride that arises from having attained a realization of the Dharma. On this [fifth] stage they are taught as the antidote for the form of exaggerated pride (S: *abhimānaḥ*, T: *mngon pa'i nga rgyal*) [that believes] the purity of [one's own] mind continuum is exceptional." For a general definition of "exaggerated pride," see note 314.

four noble truths are taught in relation to] the Vinaya [collection], and (6) [the aspect that represents the means by which the four noble truths are taught in relation to] to the summary listings;[1337] and (7) [the aspect] that represents the manner in which [the four noble truths] are taught in relation to that which has the nature of suffering in the present, (8) [the aspect that represents the manner in which the four noble truths are taught in relation to] the cause that gives rise to suffering in the future, (9) [the aspect that represents the manner in which the four noble truths are taught in relation to] the inability for that [suffering] to arise again once it has been terminated through having its cause terminated, and (10) [the aspect that represents the manner in which the four noble truths are taught in relation to] the pursuit of the means by which that [cause of suffering] is abandoned.[1338]

[The bodhisattva] who in this manner has developed skill regarding [the ten forms of] truth uses his wisdom to correctly discredit all conditioning formations. He strengthens a compassionate attitude toward the realm of sentient beings. He correctly discerns the wrong forms of practice that immature sentient beings carry out in relation to both the past and the future. He firmly fixes his [mind] upon [the aim of] acquiring a great quantity of the merit and wisdom accumulations in order to liberate those [beings] and also develops an attitude that is directed toward that [aim]. He

1337. See note 1248.

1338. Asaṅga's description corresponds to forms of knowledge that represent skillfulness regarding these ten forms of truth (*DB*, p. 27): (1) relative truth (S: *saṃvṛtisatyam*, T: *kun rdzob kyi bden pa*); (2) ultimate truth (S: *paramārthasatyam*, T: *don dam pa'i bden pa*); (3) truth regarding the attributes (S: *lakṣaṇasatyam*, T: *mtshan nyid kyi bden pa*) that are possessed by entities; (4) truth regarding the distinctions (S: *vibhāgasatyam*, T: *rnam par dbye ba'i bden pa*) that are made about entities; (5) truth regarding meticulous judgments (S: *nistīraṇasatyam*, T: *phye ste rtogs pa'i bden pa*) that are made about the heaps, constituents, and bases; (6) truth regarding the actual nature of things (S: *vastusatyam*, T: *dngos po'i bden pa*) in the sense of the harm that befalls physical and mental entities; (7) truth regarding the source of renewed suffering (S: *prabhavasatyam*, T: *rab tu skye ba'i bden pa*) in the sense of having to take rebirth in a samsaric migratory state; (8) truth regarding the termination of suffering and the inability for it to arise again (S: *kṣayānutpādasatyam*, T: *zad pa mi skye ba shes pa'i bden pa*); and (9) truth regarding entry into knowledge of the path (S: *mārgajñānāvatārasatyam*, T: *lam shes pa la 'jug pa'i bden pa*) and (10) truth regarding how a tathāgata's knowledge ultimately arises by completing the series of all the levels of the bodhisattva stages (S: *sarvabodhisattvabhūmikramānusaṃdhiniṣpādanatayāyāvat-tathāgatajñānasamudayasatyam*, T: *byang chub sems dpa'i sa'i go rims thams cad kyis mtshams sbyar ba sgrub pa nas / bde bzhin gshegs pa'i ye shes yang dag par 'byung ba'i bar gyi bden pa*).

becomes abundantly endowed with a multitude of different kinds of virtuous qualities, beginning with recollection, understanding, and realization. Having abandoned [all] other forms of thought, he ripens sentient beings using a variety of methods that cause them to become spiritually mature.

Out of compassion for sentient beings and with the aim of ultimately establishing them in enlightenment, [this bodhisattva] engages in every kind of secular occupation and craft that is beneficial to sentient beings, such as scribal work, treatises, signing, counting, keeping security deposits, etc.,[1339] as mentioned in the sutra. The summary import of the occupations and crafts that are beneficial to sentient beings should be understood as follows: With the aim of [benefiting sentient beings] progressively until they have been brought to enlightenment, [the bodhisattva engages in these occupations] in a manner that conforms with the affairs of secular life, using methods for overcoming poverty; by removing imbalances of the [body's four] elements and the harm that is inflicted by humans and nonhuman [spirits]; by turning [sentient beings] away from wicked forms of pleasure through providing them with objects [that can be used to engage in] irreproachable forms of entertainment and enjoyment; by enabling those who desire the [structural and environmental] elements that are needed for communal living to obtain those elements with little difficulty; by providing protection from the harm that is inflicted by the king, robbers, and the like; by approving of proper activities and forbidding improper ones; by causing beings to take up auspicious subjects and abandon inauspicious ones; and by teaching beings not to injure one another in this life and [to pursue] the correct paths [that will lead] to a high status in future lives.

[The descriptions regarding] everything else [about this pleasurable state] are the same as the ones that were given previously. Regarding this [pleasurable state], there is the following difference. For example, just as that same

1339. *DBV* (ff. 194b–195a) describes "scribal work" (S: *lipiḥ,* T: *yi ge*) as the antidote for the defect of failing to remain aware of matters relating to wealth and activities. The term "treatise" (S: *śāstram,* T: *bstan bcos*) is identified as referring particularly to works on logic and grammar, because they are what remove the defects of having inferior views and an undeveloped mind. [The skill of] "signing" (S: *mudrā,* T: *rgya*) is described as an antidote for the failure to preserve wealth that has been collected (see also note 135, where the Tibetan translation is *lag rtsis*). "Counting" (S: *gaṇanā,* T: *rtsis*) and "keeping security deposits" (S: *nikṣepaḥ,* T: *shod thabs*) are antidotes for ignorance regarding revenue and disbursements. "Counting" refers to arithmetic computations and "accepting security deposits" is the holding of collateral that has been pledged (see MW, p. 545). The last occupation is included in the Tibetan translation of *BBh* but does not appear in the two Sanskrit editions of the text.

gold which a skillful smith has embellished with sapphires and adorned in an incomparable manner cannot be outshone by any other kinds of gold, this bodhisattva cannot be outshone by any of the listeners and solitary realizers or by the bodhisattvas who are established in any of the other [lesser] stages. For example, just as the light of the moon, the sun, and the stars remains undiverted by all the whirlwinds even as [these sources of light] all share the quality of being conveyed by the wind,[1340] the wisdom of this bodhisattva cannot be diverted by any of the listeners and solitary realizers even as it also operates in concert with worldly activities.[1341]

In terms of rebirth, he becomes a king among the Tuṣita class of gods and one who is skilled at turning [beings] away from all heretical teachers. It should also be understood that [his] spiritual powers are described as being possessed in a magnitude of a billion.

It should be understood that this represents a brief description of the bodhisattvas' pleasurable state of superior wisdom that relates to the truths, in terms of its being entered by perfecting [forms of] a sameness of pure attitude; in terms of strengthening the manner in which [skillful] means and the truths are investigated; in terms of discrediting all [forms of] conditioning formations; in terms of the strengthening of one's compassionate attitude toward sentient beings; in terms of generating aspirational prayers to collect the merit and wisdom accumulations for the sake of those [sentient

1340. S: *vātavāhasādharaṇā,* T: *rlung dang 'gro bar ni 'dra'o.* Asaṅga's interpretation of the example in this analogy is that the light from these celestial objects is not harmed by the wind even as the wind is the vehicle that causes them to move through the sky. This reading seems to be based on a phrase in the sutra which states that the light from all these celestial objects "rests on the same support of the wind" (S: *marutā sādharaṇā*). However, the Tibetan translation of this phrase states that "[their light] does not occur in a manner that has anything in common with the wind" (S: *rlung dang thun mong du mi spyod pa yin*). See also next note.

1341. S: *laukikakriyāsādharaṇā,* T: *'jig rten pa'i bya ba byed par 'dra ba.* Both *BBh* and *BBhVy* read the adjective in this compound as *sādharaṇā* (the Tibetan equivalent is rendered here as *'dra ba*) and take it to mean that the bodhisattvas of this level deliberately engage in worldly activities as a way of benefiting beings. While this description does accord with the earlier passage that refers to a range of secular occupations that the bodhisattva pursues on behalf of sentient beings, the corresponding phrase in *DB* states that the virtue roots of the bodhisattva on this fifth stage "have nothing in common with those that are worldly" (S: *laukikāsādharaṇāni,* T: *'jig rten pa dang thun mong du mi spyod pa yin*), which seems to indicate that the bodhisattvas' roots of virtue are not adversely influenced by worldly activities. While the meanings expressed by these two versions are not mutually exclusive, I cannot with certainty explain the apparent verbal inconsistency.

beings]; in terms of strengthening such virtuous qualities as recollection, understanding, and realization; in terms of having no other thought except applying oneself to the ripening of sentient beings in every manner; in terms of their engaging in secular occupations; in terms of the purification of roots of virtue; in terms of [the forms of] rebirth [that occur]; and in terms of the spiritual powers [that are possessed]. A more extensive description can be found in the sutra itself, in the section of the *Sutra on the Ten Stages* that addresses the stage on which it is very difficult to be overcome. [This is a stage where] it is very difficult for the knowledge [of a bodhisattva] that possesses certainty about the truths to be overcome. This is also what has been elucidated here. That is why this stage is called [the stage on which it is] "very difficult to be overcome."[1342] For the very same reason, [this stage] should also be regarded as the pleasurable state of superior wisdom that relates to the truths.

The Pleasurable State of Superior Wisdom That Relates to Dependent Origination [II.4.8]

Regarding this [topic], what is the bodhisattva's pleasurable state of superior wisdom that relates to dependent origination?

In this case, a bodhisattva attains ten [forms of] sameness that apply to all entities while still on the pleasurable state of superior wisdom that relates to the truths. The wording [that describes] them should be understood as it appears in the sutra. Through developing these [ten forms of sameness] to a level of greatness and bringing them to fullness, he gains entry to this pleasurable state. The individual meanings of these ten forms of sameness that apply to [all] entities should be understood as follows:[1343] [The bodhisattva enters this pleasurable state] by means of (1) the sameness in which all entities [are perceived to] lack any sign of an essence that exists in an ultimate sense, (2) the sameness in which [all entities are perceived to] lack any attribute [that is possessed] by the appearances that are described with words and that carry out actions, (3) the sameness in which [all entities are perceived] not to have been born [in such a way that they exist] on their own due to the nonexistence of that very attribute, (4) the sameness in which [all

1342. S: *sudurjayā*, T: *shin tu sbyang dka' ba*.

1343. Asaṅga does not describe these ten forms of sameness in the same order that they appear in *DB*.

entities are perceived] not to have arisen from a cause, (5) the sameness in which [all entities are perceived to] have always been completely tranquil[1344] because they have not arisen [in such a way that they exist] on their own and [they have not arisen] from causes, (6) the sameness in which [all entities are perceived to be] free of elaboration[1345] when the [transcendent] awareness that apprehends reality is present, (7) the sameness in which [all entities are perceived to] abstain from the activities of taking on and giving up,[1346] (8) the sameness in which [all entities] are [perceived to be] isolated[1347] in the sense that those very [entities that do not engage in the activities of taking on and giving up] are separated from the state of affliction [that is represented by] the mental afflictions and suffering, (9) the sameness in which [all] entities that possess conceptually fabricated essences [are perceived to] resemble illusions and magical creations,[1348] and (10) the sameness in which [all entities are perceived to be] beyond the duality of existence and nonexistence,[1349] this being their [true] essence and the one that is discerned by nonconceptual awareness.

[The bodhisattva] who is established in this pleasurable state is one whose compassion toward sentient beings has increased greatly and one who has generated an intense aspiration and desire for enlightenment. He exam-

1344. S: *atyantam ādiśāntasamatā,* T: *gzod ma nas shin tu zhi ba'i mnyam pa nyid. BBhVy* (f. 288b) glosses this quality as referring to the fact that ordinary entities neither arise nor perish in a real sense. This apparently corresponds to the quality that is listed sixth in *DB* as "the sameness in which all entities [are perceived to] have always been pure" (S: *sarvadharmādiviśuddhisamatā,* T: *chos thams cad snga nas rnam par dag pa mnyam pa nyid*). *DBV* (f. 196b) explains this as referring to the fact that ordinary entities do not undergo a process of purification (S: *vyavadānam,* T: *rnam par byang ba*) in a real sense.

1345. S: *niṣprapañcasamatā,* T: *spros pa med pa'i mnyam pa nyid.* See note 264 for a description of the term "elaboration." This sameness is listed seventh in *DB*.

1346. S: *ādānatyāgābhisaṃskāravigamasamatā,* T: *blang ba dang dor ba mngon par 'du byed pa dang bral ba'i mnyam pa nyid. BBhVy* (f. 288b) identifies "giving up" as meaning the act of discarding the heaps of one migratory state when a sentient being passes away and "taking on" as meaning that of adopting the heaps of another migratory state when a sentient being is reborn. This sameness corresponds to the one that is listed eighth in *DB*.

1347. S: *viviktasamatā,* T: *rnam par dben pa'i mnyam pa nyid.* This sameness is listed fifth in *DB*.

1348. S: *māyānirmitasamatā,* T: *sgyu ma dang sprul pa lta bu'i mnyam pa nyid.* These two similes are the first and last among the seven that are mentioned in the corresponding sameness in *DB*.

1349. S: *bhāvābhāvādvayasamatā,* T: *dngos po dang dngos po med pa'i gnyis su med pa'i mnyam pa nyid.*

ines and discerns the origin and disintegration of the worlds by correctly scrutinizing [the doctrine of] dependent origination in every way. He also develops [an understanding of] the three doors to liberation that is based upon this knowledge of dependent origination—namely, [the door to liberation] of emptiness, [the door to liberation] of signlessness, and [the door to liberation] of wishlessness.[1350] Because of that, he does not give rise to the conceptions of self and other, an agent [that performs actions] and a being that experiences[1351] [the results of those actions], or existence and nonexistence.

[The bodhisattva] who in this manner has developed skill regarding ultimate truth and who possesses concern for sentient beings correctly comprehends the following: "Conditioned entities—which are naturally weak, which neither constitute a self nor belong to a self, and which are marred by a multitude of faults—come into being through a connection with the mental afflictions and through the convergence of causal conditions. They will not [come into being] in the absence of a connection with the mental afflictions and when those causal conditions have not converged. Therefore, I should disrupt the connection with the mental afflictions and the convergence of the causal conditions in order to safeguard myself, but I should not completely and totally put an end to conditioned entities so that I may continue to benefit sentient beings."

[The bodhisattva] who possesses such a form of knowledge and compassion on this pleasurable state is one who is facing toward a pleasurable state [in which one abides in a form] of the perfection of wisdom that is called "facing unobstructed knowledge." [This pleasurable state is one] by means of which he remains free of attachment while engaging in every [kind of] mundane conduct. It should be understood that this pleasurable state also includes a [type of] forbearance that conforms to the intense [form of] bodhisattva forbearance [that occurs] on the seventh stage and marks the culmination of conduct that derives from the application [of effort].

Through being one whose face is turned toward the pleasurable state [in which one abides in the form of] the perfection of wisdom that is called "facing unobstructed knowledge," [the bodhisattva] collects the causal factors that bring forth enlightenment but does not remain in a state of continuous association with worldly conditioned entities. He perceives the

1350. See the three concentrations of the same name that are described in Book I, chapter 17.

1351. S: *vedakaḥ,* T: *tshor ba po.*

quietude[1352] [represented by their emptiness] to be a state of peace but does not settle down in it. A hundred thousand sets of ten doors to one-pointed concentration [on emptiness], beginning with the [set of ten in which the first] one-pointed concentration [is the one named] "the emptiness that enters," become manifest to [the bodhisattva] who has attained this knowledge that includes [both] means and wisdom. It should be understood that, just as with the [hundred thousand sets of] one-pointed concentration on emptiness, the same also occurs for one-pointed concentration on wishlessness and [one-pointed concentration] on signlessness.

Through the appearance of these [forms of one-pointed concentration, the bodhisattva] becomes one who possesses an adamantine attitude. He also becomes one who is incapable of being led away from any aspect of the [Buddha's] teaching by any form of Māra or heretics or persons who are hostile to the teaching.

The remaining [descriptions regarding this pleasurable state] are the same as the ones that were given previously. With regard to this [pleasurable state], there is the following difference. For example, just as that same gold which a skillful smith has embellished and adorned with gems of lapis lazuli cannot be outshone by any other kinds of gold, similarly the roots of virtue of this bodhisattva have been purified to a much higher extent and cannot be outshone. [The rest of this analogy is] as was described previously. For example, just as the light of the moon refreshes the bodies of sentient beings and is a light that cannot be destroyed by any of the four spheres of wind, similarly the light of wisdom possessed by this bodhisattva extinguishes the burning fires of all sentient beings' mental afflictions and it cannot be destroyed by any [of the forms of] Māra or by any hostile persons.

He becomes a king of the Sunirmita[1353] class of gods and one who is skilled at turning [beings] away from all forms of exaggerated pride. It should also be recognized that [his] spiritual powers are described [as being possessed] in a magnitude of a trillion.

1352. S: *praśamaḥ,* T: *rab tu zhi ba.* This is a reference to the ultimate nature of all conditioned entities. It is a form of quietude in the sense that meditation on it puts a stop to the mental afflictions. The bodhisattva deliberately avoids meditating continuously on this ultimate nature because doing so would put an end to his or her samsaric existence and, in the words of the sutra, at this stage of the path "the limbs of enlightenment have not yet been fulfilled."

1353. This is an alternate name for the class of deities known as Those Who Delight in Magical Creations (S: *nirmāṇaratayaḥ,* T: *'phrul dga'*). See note 357.

It should be understood that this represents a brief description of the pleasurable state of superior wisdom that relates to dependent origination, in terms of its being entered by perfecting the [ten] forms of sameness that apply to all entities, in terms of how dependent origination is realized and the doors to liberation arise, in terms of how all forms of wrong conception are no longer developed, in terms of the means by which samsara is embraced, in terms of being one who is facing toward a pleasurable state [in which one abides in the form] of the perfection of wisdom that is called "facing unobstructed knowledge," in terms of [the bodhisattva's] attaining immeasurable forms of one-pointed concentration, in terms of [the bodhisattva's] attaining an adamantine attitude, in terms of [the bodhisattva's] being incapable of being led away from the teaching, in terms of the purification of roots of virtue, in terms of [the forms of] rebirth [that occur], and in terms of the spiritual powers [that are possessed]. A more extensive description can be found in [the section of the sutra that discusses] the stage of facing toward. [That stage] is called "facing toward"[1354] because one is facing toward the pleasurable state [in which one abides in a form] of the perfection of wisdom that is called "facing unobstructed knowledge." It should be understood that this very reason also [explains the name of] this pleasurable state.

The Pleasurable State That Is Free of Signs and Is Accompanied by Both Mental Preparation and Effort [II.4.9]

Regarding this [topic], what is the bodhisattvas' pleasurable state that is free of signs and is accompanied by both mental preparation and effort?

In this case, immediately following the [third] pleasurable state of superior wisdom, a bodhisattva attains ten extraordinary ways of undertaking a distinct path[1355] which are accomplished by both means and wisdom, and

1354. S: *abhimukhī,* T: *mngon du gyur pa.*

1355. S: *antaramārgārambhaviśeṣaḥ,* T: *lam gzhan rtsom pa'i khyad par. DBV* (f. 208b): "'Extraordinary way of undertaking a distinct path' means [a way of undertaking] a path [that leads] to an elevated state [of existence] and that is controlled by an antidote. It is a distinct form of transcendent path [i.e., one that is distinct from that of the listeners and solitary realizers] and it is distinct from the mundane form of the path that leads to an elevated state [of existence]." *MSAVṛBh* (Tg. vol. 126, f. 5a): "An elevated state [of existence] (S: *abhyudayaḥ,* T: *mngon par mtho ba,* sometimes *mngon par 'byung ba*) means a samsaric

which, though mundane in nature, have nothing in common with all [ordinary] sentient beings and all [samsaric] worlds. Through developing them to a level of greatness and bringing them to fullness, he enters the seventh pleasurable state. The extensive wording [that describes] them should be understood as it appears in the sutra. In brief, the principal concerns of these ten extraordinary ways of undertaking a distinct path, which are qualities that are produced by both means and wisdom, should be understood as follows. They relate to (1) the acquisition of the merit that produces mundane forms of excellence; (2) the attitude that wishes to benefit and bring happiness to sentient beings; (3) increasing to a higher level the merit accumulation and the spiritual qualities that are conducive to enlightenment, in order to [achieve] enlightenment; (4) being separate from the listeners; (5) being separate from the solitary realizers; (6) the entity-source of sentient beings; (7) the entity-source of the worlds; and knowledge of a tathāgata's (8) body, (9) speech, and (10) mind.

Endowed with these [qualities, the bodhisattva] comprehends the immeasurable and innumerable objects that constitute a tathāgata's sphere of action. Perceiving as well that a tathāgata's immeasurable sphere of action arises by means of [the attributes of] effortlessness, signlessness, and becoming free of concepts and conceptual thoughts,[1356] he applies himself continuously and without interruption, in all physical behavior, conduct, pleasurable states of abiding, and forms of attention, to the aim of generating that [ability]. In every situation that [the bodhisattva] is in, he never strays from the path. In each moment of thought, all the spiritual qualities that are conducive to enlightenment, headed by the ten perfections, are being developed to an extraordinary degree.

This [activity] is not, however, accomplished in the same way in other

---

[existence] that is possessed of wealth and happiness." This term is generally understood to mean rebirth as a human being or a worldly god. The "antidote" that controls this path is the fact that the practitioner has cultivated the perfection of wisdom to a very high level.

1356. S: *akalpāvikalpanatayā,* T: *rtog pa med pa dang rnam par rtog pa med pas. MSAVy* (p. 173): "It should be understood that a concept (S: *kalpaḥ,* T: *rtog pa*) is the mental construct of an essence, and a conceptual thought (S: *vikalpaḥ,* T: *rnam par rtog pa*) is the mental construct of a distinguishing characteristic." Sthiramati (*MSAVṛBh,* Tg. vol. 125, f. 265a) gives as examples of concepts such notions as "the essence of the earth element is hardness" and "the essence of the water element is fluidity," and, as examples of conceptual thoughts, such notions as "the earth element undergoes destruction, it is impermanent, and it has the nature of suffering."

pleasurable states. In the first pleasurable state of great joy, [all the spiritual qualities that are conducive to enlightenment are developed] by strongly taking hold of aspirational prayers. In the second, [they are developed] by removing the stains of immorality from the mind; in the third, by strengthening aspirational prayers and attaining the light of the Dharma; in the fourth, by entering the path; in the fifth, by engaging in worldly activities; and in the sixth, by becoming absorbed in the profound. By contrast, in this seventh pleasurable state, the limbs of enlightenment are developed in a way that creates all the spiritual qualities of a buddha, because the culmination of the bodhisattva conduct that derives from the application of effort occurs within this pleasurable state and also because [this pleasurable state] brings entry into the eighth state of abiding in which transcendent awareness, supernatural knowledge, and conduct have become pure. That is to say, immediately following this pleasurable state, a bodhisattva enters the eighth pleasurable state, and that pleasurable state is one that is absolutely pure. These [first] seven pleasurable states, however, have a [form of purity that is] mixed. They are unafflicted in that they are the precursors of the [eighth] pleasurable state that is completely pure; however, because they have not yet attained that [complete purity], they are said to be [pleasurable states] where afflicted conduct has occurred.

All of the [bodhisattva's] mental afflictions—beginning with desire, etc.—are abandoned on this [seventh] state of abiding. He should be understood as one who is neither subject to mental affliction nor completely free of affliction, because he no longer generates [the mental afflictions] and because he desires [to attain] a buddha's knowledge. [The bodhisattva] who possesses such a nature gives rise to unlimited acts of body, speech, and mind that are endowed with a pure superior attitude. He [becomes one who has transcended] those acts that were condemned by the Tathāgata, [and so on,] as [was described] previously. The knowledge of the worldly crafts that was pursued by him during the fifth pleasurable state is perfected here. He is esteemed as a teacher throughout the great triple-thousand [world spheres by everyone] except for the tathāgatas and those bodhisattvas who are established in higher pleasurable states. No one is his equal in thought or action. All the [forms of] meditative absorption, etc., that are spiritual qualities conducive to enlightenment become manifest [in him] through his being turned toward the [various] kinds of meditation. They do not, however, [become manifest in him] through being a condition that is a ripening [of earlier practice], as they do on the eighth pleasurable state. Having applied himself in this way, he achieves, among the bodhisattva forms of one-pointed concentration, a hundred thousand sets of ten forms of one-pointed concentration, beginning with the [ten in which the first] one-pointed concentration [is the one named] "well-examined examination."[1357] Through having attained these [forms of one-pointed concentration, the bodhisattva] goes completely beyond the range of the [forms of] one-pointed concentration that are possessed by listeners and solitary realizers.

In this way, [the bodhisattva] abides in a state that is difficult to comprehend, one in which his actions of body, speech, and mind are isolated from all the mental afflictions, and in which all occurrences of conceptual thought have disappeared. With a sympathetic regard for sentient beings, he does not relax the effort to seek higher forms of excellence. In order to bring about enlightenment, he gives rise to acts of body, speech, and mind that are limitless, free of all signs, and extremely purified, and that will cause the appearance of the forbearance of the nonarising of entities.[1358]

On this pleasurable state, [bodhisattvas] completely surpass all the listeners and solitary realizers on the basis of the range of their intellect. However, on the other six [pleasurable states, bodhisattvas surpass all the listeners and solitary realizers] on the basis of [the manner in which] they strongly take hold of [the intention to attain] the qualities of a buddha. Also, while a bodhisattva [is able to] enter the state of composure that is a cessation on the sixth pleasurable state, on this [pleasurable state] he [can] enter it in each instant [of thought]. It is also a marvelous and inconceivable quality of [the bodhisattva's] actions that, although he abides in the summit of reality,[1359] he does not manifest that [state of] cessation.[1360]

1357. S: *suvicitavicayaḥ*, T: *rnam par 'byed pa shin tu rnam par phye ba*. Both Sanskrit editions of *BBh* give corrupt versions of the name of this one-pointed concentration. The correct Sanskrit expression is taken from the Sanskrit edition of *DB*.

1358. S: *anutpattikadharmakṣāntiḥ*, T: *me skye ba'i chos la bzod pa*. This form of forbearance is achieved upon reaching the eighth ārya bodhisattva stage. Asaṅga's description of it appears below at the beginning of his discussion of the next pleasurable state.

1359. S: *bhūtakoṭiḥ*, T: *yang dag pa'i mtha'*. *MV* (ch. 1, v. 15) indicates that this term is one of a number of synonyms for emptiness. *MVṬ* (p. 39): "'Reality' is [that which is] true and unerring. A 'summit' is a limit. Therefore, the summit of reality can be called 'the limit of reality' in the sense that no other knowable object exists beyond it."

1360. *BBhVy* (f. 295a): "[The phrase] 'he or she does not manifest that [state of] cessation' means that [this seventh-stage bodhisattva] does not manifest [the state of composure that is a cessation] in the way that nonreturners and arhats do." In other words, even though this bodhisattva can enter this state of composure in an instant, he or she forgoes doing

On the strength of practicing this very [combination of] skill and knowledge, he carries out a [form of] bodhisattva conduct that is distinct from that of all sentient beings [in the sense that], while it has the appearance of being worldly [conduct], it does not have such a nature. [This can be understood] as [it is described] in the sutra.[1361] Nevertheless, an abbreviated [statement of the] meaning of this [passage] is as follows. [This conduct] has to do with (1) [carrying out] activities that generate merit, as well as (2) taking care of a spouse and a following, (3) undertaking the desire [to achieve] a specific result,[1362] (4) abiding in the three doors to liberation, (5) exercising the skill that enables one to lead beings away from their devotion to the Lesser Vehicle, (6) enjoyment of sensory pleasures, (7) seeking specific forms of sensory pleasures, (8) turning [beings] away from heretical teachers, (9) complying with the minds of others, and (10) complying with a great multitude of people.

The remaining [descriptions regarding this pleasurable state] are the same as the ones that were given previously. With regard to this [pleasurable state], there is the following difference. For example, just as the same gold which a skillful smith has embellished and adorned all over with [wheel rulers'] precious jewels, and that glitters so strikingly, cannot be outshone by any other of the Rose Apple Continent's ornaments, similarly the roots of virtue of [this bodhisattva] that have been purified to such a high extent cannot be outshone by the roots of virtue that are possessed by any of the listeners and solitary realizers or the roots of virtue that are possessed by any other bodhisattvas who are established in much lower pleasurable states. For example, just as the light of the sun causes the great majority of whatever wet things there are in the Rose Apple Continent to become completely dry and it also cannot be outshone by the light of any other [luminous bodies], similarly the light of wisdom that is possessed by this bodhisattva destroys all the poison of the mental afflictions that is possessed by sentient beings

so despite the fact that it represents a state of ease that provides respite from the travails of samsaric existence, because abiding in that state does not contribute to the attainment of enlightenment.

1361. See *DB*, p. 40.

1362. S: *abhinirvṛttiviśeṣaprārthanāsamārambhaḥ*, T: *mngon par grub pa'i khyad par 'dod pa yang dag par brtsams pa*. This expression refers to the act of generating the kind of aspirational prayers that will insure being reborn in a form that allows one to benefit sentient beings effectively.

and it cannot be outshone by the light of the knowledge possessed by all the listeners, etc., as described before.

[The bodhisattva] becomes a king of the Vaśavartī[1363] class of gods and one who is skilled at causing listeners and solitary realizers to attain spiritual realizations. It should be understood that [his] spiritual powers are described [as being possessed] in a magnitude of one trillion trillion.[1364]

It should be understood that this represents a brief description of the pleasurable state that is free of signs and is accompanied by both mental preparation and effort, in terms of its being entered by perfecting the [ten] extraordinary ways of undertaking a distinct path that are accomplished by both means and wisdom, in terms of how [the means of] generating a tathāgata's sphere of action is comprehended and [the activities that generate that quality] are carried out uninterruptedly, in terms of how all the spiritual qualities that are conducive to enlightenment are developed each moment, in terms of how it is formulated that [the first seven pleasurable states] are both afflicted and unafflicted, in terms of how the culmination of the bodhisattva conduct that derives from the application of effort occurs within this pleasurable state, in terms of how every kind of mundane occupation and craft, etc., becomes perfected on the strength of actions that are brought forth with a pure attitude, in terms of how immeasurable forms of one-pointed concentration that are distinct from those possessed by listeners and solitary realizers are attained, in terms of being able to enter the state of composure that is a cessation in each instant [of thought], in terms of how worldly conduct that is distinct from that of all sentient beings is carried out, in terms of the purification of roots of virtue, in terms of [the forms of] rebirth [that occur], and in terms of the spiritual powers [that are possessed]. As stated previously, a more extensive description can be found in [the section of the sutra that discusses] the stage that goes a long way. It is called [the "stage that] goes a long way"[1365] because the culmination of the form of bodhisattva conduct that derives from the application of effort occurs within it. It should be understood that this very reason also [explains the name of] this pleasurable state.

1363. This is another name for the class of deities known as Those Who Control Others' Magical Creations (S: *paranirmitavaśavarttinaḥ,* T: *gzhan 'phrul dbang byed*); see note 358.

1364. See note 993.

1365. S: *dūraṃgamā,* T: *ring du song ba.*

The Pleasurable State That Is Free of Signs and Also Free of Effort [II.4.10]

Regarding this [topic], what is a bodhisattva's pleasurable state that is free of signs and also free of effort?

In this case, on the immediately prior pleasurable state a bodhisattva attains ten[1366] forms of knowledge that penetrate into the highest truth as it relates to all entities. With regard to the three times and according to the particular circumstances, [these forms of knowledge] have to do with the fact that [all entities] are primordially without origination, that [all entities] do not undergo birth, and that [all entities] lack any attributes; they have to do with the fact that [all entities] are neither produced nor destroyed by some other entity that has a causal nature; they have to do with the fact that the very same essence which appears to be capable of verbal description and [appears] to carry out an action, but which, in relation to the reality that is ineffable in an ultimate sense, does not exist by way of an attribute or a causal nature, also is not something by which the [samsaric] process of affliction is set in motion or terminated; they have to do with the fact that, in relation to the ineffable reality that does exist, [the process of] affliction—which is caused by ignorance of that [ultimate reality] or a belief that apprehends it wrongly—is characterized by a sameness that applies at all times [as indicated by the terms] beginning, middle, and end; and they have to do with [the fact that] the process of affliction is eliminated by means of the sameness that does not conceptualize and that correctly enters into suchness. Through developing these ten forms of knowledge to a level of greatness and bringing them to fullness, [the bodhisattva] enters into this eighth pleasurable state that is totally pure. [The one who is] established here attains the supreme and exceedingly pure form of a bodhisattva's forbearance of the nonarising of entities.

1366. The manner in which the ten forms of knowledge are to be identified is somewhat problematic as they are described in the sutra with eleven terms. Both *DBV* and *BBhVy* suggest that the seventh form of knowledge is indicated by two expressions: (1) that "no [samsaric process] is set motion" (S: *apravṛttitām,* T: *mi 'jug pa* or *mi rgyu ba*) and (2) that "no [samsaric process] is terminated" (S: *anabhinivṛttitām,* T: *mi ldog pa*) by the essences that appear to be capable of being described verbally. Similarly, they identify the eighth form of knowledge as pertaining to "the nature of insubstantiality" (S: *abhāvasvabhāvatām,* T: *dngos po med pa'i ngo bo nyid*). *BBhVy* (f. 296a) indicates that Asaṅga refers to this form knowledge with the phrase "[the process of affliction] is caused by ignorance of that [ultimate reality] or a belief that apprehends it wrongly."

What is that [forbearance] like?

Having investigated all entities by means of the four investigations,[1367] when a bodhisattva fully comprehends them on the basis of the four kinds of thorough knowledge of the way things truly are, and after all forms of adherence to mistaken concepts have been dispelled, he perceives, in that life, a condition that is favorable to the nonarising of any afflictive states in relation to all entities.[1368] Moreover, he [will] perceive, in a future life, the complete and total nonarising without remainder [of those afflictive states] in relation to those very entities that previously arose because of adherence to mistaken conceptual thoughts. The four investigations [should be understood] as they were previously described in the chapter entitled "The Nature of Reality."

Moreover, from the pleasurable state of conduct that is based upon devotion until the pleasurable state that is free of signs and is accompanied by effort, the four kinds of thorough knowledge of the way things truly are do not possess the characteristic of being completely pure. However, on this pleasurable state, they do become totally pure. Therefore, the bodhisattva [who has reached this state of abiding] is said to be "one who has attained the forbearance that relates to the nonarising of entities."[1369] Through having attained this forbearance, he becomes one who has achieved the bodhisattva's pleasurable state that has a profound nature.

[The bodhisattva's] four defects that occur on the previous pleasurable state that is free of signs are abandoned: (1) the form of preparation that is accompanied by effort is abandoned; (2) the concern about [needing to attain] the higher, pure forms of pleasurable states is abandoned; (3) the concern about [needing to gain] the power to act on behalf of sentient beings in every manner is abandoned; and (4) the activity of generating subtle conceptions is abandoned.[1370] Therefore, this pleasurable state is one that is said to be "perfectly pure."

1367. See Book I, chapter 4, the section entitled "The Four Investigations" [I.4.9].

1368. *BBhVy* (f. 296b): "'All entities' [means all those entities that are] contained with one's being (S: **ātmabhāvasaṃgṛhītānāṃ sarvadharmāṇām,* T: *bdag gi dngos pos bsdus pa'i chos thams cad kyi*)."

1369. S: *anutpattikeṣu dharmeṣu kṣāntipratilabdhaḥ;* T: *mi skye ba'i chos rnams la bzod pa thob pa*. Although this phrase is not identical to the expression that appears in *DB* (p. 42)—S: *anutpattikadharmakṣāntiprāptaḥ,* T: *mi skye ba'i chos la bzod pa thob pa*—it is undoubtedly a reference to it.

1370. *BBhVy* (ff. 296b–297a) identifies the passages in *DB* that correspond to the absence of these four faults.

In addition, [the bodhisattva] who is reposing in this profound pleasurable state is urged and prompted by the tathāgatas to collect, within this stream that is a [form of] entry into the Dharma, unlimited ways of attaining transcendent knowledge, supernatural knowledge, and deeds. The way in which [the bodhisattva] who has been urged in this manner develops knowledge using immeasurable varieties of bodies and his attainment of the ten controlling powers[1371] should be understood as they are described at length in the sutra.

[The bodhisattva] who has attained the [ten] controlling powers is able to live for as long as he wishes.[1372] He is able to remain in such mental states as the meditative absorptions and the deliverances for as long as he wishes.[1373] He can obtain an abundance of every kind of implement, such as food, etc., merely by forming the determination [to acquire it].[1374] He is able to perform any artistic craft or occupation that he wishes to. He can also take birth however may be desired in relation to deeds that are conducive to every [kind of] rebirth and in relation to every place that one can be reborn.[1375] He can perform every feat of miraculous power according to his wishes.[1376]

1371. S: *daśa vaśitāḥ,* T: *dbang bcu.*

1372. This is known as "controlling power over one's life span" (S: *āyurvaśitā,* T: *tshe la dbang ba*).

1373. This is known as "controlling power over one's mind" (S: *cittavaśitā,* T: *sems la dbang ba*).

1374. This is known as "controlling power over implements" (S: *pariṣkāravaśitā,* T: *yo byad la dbang ba*).

1375. *BBhVy* (f. 297b) states that this sentence together with the previous one make reference to both the "controlling power over deeds" (S: *karmavaśitā,* T: *las las dbang ba*) and the "controlling power over rebirth" (S: *upapattivaśitā,* T: *skye ba la dbang ba*): "Controlling power over deeds is indicated by [the portion of the text] ranging from '[He or she is able to perform] any artistic craft or occupation . . . up to [He or she can also take birth however may be desired] . . . in relation to every place where one can be reborn,' because [this bodhisattva] can manifest whatever karmic deeds and whatever state of [karmic] maturation he or she may desire. Controlling power over rebirth [is indicated by the fact that this bodhisattva can] perform every kind of deed that [will allow] him or her to take birth however may be desired in relation to every place that one can be reborn." *DB* (p. 46): "[This bodhisattva] attains the controlling power over deeds by displaying [the ability to] control the ripening of karma in a way that accords with the proper time. He or she [attains] the controlling power over rebirth by displaying [the ability to] take birth throughout all the world spheres."

1376. This is known as "controlling power over miraculous powers" (S: *ṛddhivaśitā,* T: *rdzu 'phrul la dbang ba*), whose purpose is to instill faith in others.

All his aspirational prayers are achieved just as they were intended.[1377] However [the bodhisattva] may form a desiderative intention toward some particular substance, that [substance] comes into being in exactly that form and not in any other.[1378] Whatever object he is desirous of knowing, he realizes it exactly as it is.[1379] He is able to obtain whatever is wished for in relation to the collections of names, assertions, and syllables. He is skilled at presenting a correct formulation for every form of Dharma teaching.[1380] These are the controlling powers that are attained by this bodhisattva. In addition to this, the benefits that derive from having attained the controlling powers should be understood as they are described at length in the sutra.

Having abandoned the ordinary way of seeing buddhas, he is never without a constant and continuous vision of [endless numbers of] buddhas. The remaining [descriptions of the way in which] his roots of virtue are purified, together with the analogies of gold and light, should be understood as they appear in the sutra. The type of rebirth that is taken by the bodhisattva who is [established] in this pleasurable state, as well as the particular form of his spiritual powers, should also be understood as [they are described] in the sutra.

It should be understood that this represents a brief description of the pleasurable state that is free of signs and is also free of effort, in terms of how it is entered by perfecting the ten forms of knowledge that penetrate into the highest truth; in terms of the forbearance that is attained in relation to the nonarising of entities; in terms of the attainment of the profound form of a bodhisattva's pleasurable state in which all faults are gone; in terms of how [the bodhisattva of this pleasurable state is urged] by the buddhas to collect,

1377. This is known as "controlling power over aspirational prayers" (S: *praṇidhānavaśitā,* T: *smon lam la dbang ba*).

1378. This is known as "controlling power over intentions" (S: *adhimuktivaśitā,* T: *mos pa la dbang ba*). *DB* (p. 26) describes it as the ability "to display all the world realms as filled with Buddhas" *MSAVṛBh* (Tg. vol. 216, f. 114a) describes it as the ability to transform earth into water, etc., through the strength of one's intention.

1379. This is known as "controlling power over transcendent awareness" (S: *jñānavaśitā,* T: *ye shes la dbang ba*). *DB* (p. 26) describes it as the ability "of a tathāgata to display his [ten] powers of knowledge, [four] forms of intrepid confidence, [eighteen] unique qualities, as well as his [thirty-two] major and [eighty] minor marks, and supreme enlightenment."

1380. *BBhVy* (f. 297b) indicates that this sentence and the previous one taken together describe the "controlling power over the Dharma" (S: *dharmavaśitā,* T: *chos la dbang ba*). *DB* (p.26) describes it as a power that "manifests the light of the Dharma door(s) that is/are free of [both] extremes and a [self-existent] middle [way]."

within the stream that is a [form of] entry into the Dharma, unlimited ways of attaining transcendent knowledge, supernatural knowledge, and deeds; in terms of how knowledge is developed using immeasurable varieties of bodies; in terms of the controlling powers that are attained; in terms of the benefits of the controlling powers that are experienced; in terms of the purification of roots of virtue; in terms of [the forms of] rebirth [that occur]; and in terms of the spiritual powers [that are possessed]. A more extensive description can be found in [the section of] the sutra that discusses] the stage of immovability. This stage is called [the "stage of] immovability"[1381] because the mental preparation that occurred previously is gone and because on this stage the [bodhisattva's] mind has entered a path where no effort is required and where it can proceed in an unwavering manner. This very reason should also be regarded as [explaining the name of] this pleasurable state.

The Pleasurable State of Informative Knowledge [II.4.11]

Regarding this [topic], what is the bodhisattvas' pleasurable state of informative knowledge?

In this case, the bodhisattva, being unsatisfied even with the profound pleasurable state, pursues ever higher and more excellent forms of knowledge. In doing so, he realizes everything as it truly is about the formative actions of entities[1382] and [the formative action of] the knowledge [regarding those entities]—which enable a bodhisattva to teach every aspect of the Dharma to others—and also [realizes everything as it truly is] about what ought to be done in relation to [the activity of] proclaiming the Dharma. Regarding

1381. S: *acalā,* T: *mi g.yo ba.*

1382. *DB* (p. 49) identifies ten categories of formative actions that relate to entities (S: *dharmābhisaṃskāraḥ,* T: *chos mngon par 'du byed pa*): (1) the formative actions of virtuous, nonvirtuous, and indeterminate entities; (2) the formative actions of entities that are related to the outflows and entities that are free of the outflows; (3) the formative actions of mundane and transcendent entities; (4) the formative actions of conceivable and inconceivable entities; (5) the formative actions of definite and indefinite entities; (6) the formative actions of entities that relate to the listener and solitary realizer disciples; (7) the formative actions of entities that relate to bodhisattva conduct; (8) the formative actions of entities that relate to the stage of a buddha; (9) the formative actions of conditioned entities; and (10) the formative actions of unconditioned entities.

this, what ought to be done in relation to [the activity of] proclaiming the Dharma is [to gain] true knowledge of the following subjects that relate to the [ten] impenetrable processes:[1383] (1) the things that undergo affliction and purification, (2) the things that bring about affliction and purification, (3) the things that constitute affliction and purification, (4) the thing that constitutes a state of uncertainty regarding those [conditions of affliction and purification], (5) the thing that constitutes a state of certainty regarding those [conditions of affliction and purification], and (6) the thing that constitutes both a state of certainty and a state of uncertainty regarding those [conditions of affliction and purification].[1384]

[The bodhisattva] who is both skilled with regard to teaching the Dharma and skilled with regard to what is to be done in relation to [the activity of] teaching [is described in a number of ways]: (1) the way in which he develops the quality of being a great teacher for every aspect of the Dharma who has attained immeasurable forms of mental retention,[1385] who is skilled in all the diverse qualities of voice, and who possesses inexhaustible eloquence; (2) the kind of power for retaining and taking up the Dharma that he comes to possess; (3) the kinds of speech that he develops [by means of the various] bodhisattva [forms of] informative knowledge;[1386] (4) the kind of Dharma seat upon which he sits; (5) the extent of the doors [to the Dharma] by which he teaches the Dharma in various places to various kinds of beings; and (6)

1383. S: *gahanopavicāram,* T: *'thibs po rgyu ba. DBV* (f. 233a) explains the adjective "impenetrable" to mean both a multiplicity [of things] and an activity that is incapable of being understood [by ordinary persons]. *DB* (p. 49) presents the ten impenetrable processes as those of (1) the minds of sentient beings, (2) mental afflictions, (3) deeds, (4) faculties, (5) forms of devotion, (6) constituent elements, (7) attitudes and latent propensities, (8) births, (9) the condition of being continuously connected with the traces [of the mental afflictions], and (10) the nature of the three groups [of sentient beings]. *DBV* (f. 237a) defines the three groups as those who are incapable of attaining nirvana; those who will attain the nirvana of one of the three vehicles, though which one it will be is uncertain; and those who will attain the nirvana of one of the three vehicles and which one it will be is certain. The sutra elaborates on each of these ten topics and *DBV* (ff. 232b–237b) provides an analysis of the discussion.

1384. *BBhVy* (f. 298a–298b) identifies how these categories relate to the ten impenetrable processes.

1385. For a description of this spiritual quality, see the section of the same name in Book I, chapter 17 [I.17.12].

1386. See the section of the same name in Book I, chapter 17 [I.17.7]. *DB* (pp. 51–52) gives ten separate interpretations of the four forms of informative knowledge.

the kind of power he possesses for carrying out the activities of informing and satisfying sentient beings. These are all points that should be understood as they are described at length in the sutra.

The particular way in which [the bodhisattva's] roots of virtue are purified, the particular type of rebirth that is taken, and the particular qualities of his spiritual powers should also be understood as [they are described] in the sutra.

It should be understood that this represents a brief description of the bodhisattvas' pleasurable state of informative knowledge, in terms of how it is entered by his not being satisfied with a state of tranquil liberation, in terms of knowledge of the formative actions and its relation to [the activity of] proclaiming the Dharma, in terms of knowledge of what ought to be done in relation to that [activity of proclaiming the Dharma], in terms of [the bodhisattva's] attaining the quality of being an inconceivably great Dharma teacher, in terms of the purification of roots of virtue, in terms of [the forms of] rebirth [that occur], and in terms of the spiritual powers [that are possessed]. A more extensive description can be found in [the section of] the sutra [that discusses] the stage of excellent understanding. This stage is called "excellent understanding"[1387] because it is a position of spiritual authority in which the Dharma is correctly explained on the strength of a form of understanding that consists of the bodhisattva forms of informative knowledge and that is thoroughly pure in its intention to benefit and bring happiness to all sentient beings. This very reason should also be regarded as [explaining the name of] this pleasurable state.

The Supreme Pleasurable State [II.4.12]

Regarding this [topic], what is the bodhisattvas' supreme pleasurable state?

A brief description of the supreme pleasurable state should be understood in terms of [the following points]. When every aspect of the pleasurable state of informative knowledge has been purified, the bodhisattva who here has become worthy of the rank of a Dharma king and has reached the point where he is about to undergo the Dharma consecration attains immeasurable numbers of one-pointed concentrations, beginning with the one named "stainless," and completes their aims. After coming face-to-face with the final concentration, [which is named] "consecration into the excellence

1387. S: *sādhumatī*, T: *legs pa'i blo gros.*

of omniscient knowledge," [the bodhisattva] who has attained a seat, bodily form, and retinue that are suitable for this [event], through emanating and drawing back light rays, receives from all the buddhas the consecration of the knowledge that is omniscient in every way. After having been consecrated, [the bodhisattva] realizes [how to] assemble all those beings who are to be converted as well as the means of liberating them, and [realizes all] the buddha activities. [The bodhisattva] attains immeasurable numbers of deliverances, forms of mental retention, and supernatural knowledge. The great [form of] recollection and knowledge that is developed by the influence of those [qualities] is [the basis for] establishing the literal explanation [of the name of this stage]. Great forms of supernatural knowledge are developed. There are also [descriptions of] the extraordinary purity of the roots of virtue, the [extraordinary] manner of rebirth, and the [extraordinary] spiritual powers. A more extensive description can be found in [the section of] the sutra [that discusses] the Dharma cloud stage.

The bodhisattva who has completed the bodhisattva path and who has fully completed the accumulations [that are necessary] for enlightenment receives from the tathāgatas an extremely vast shower of the true Dharma, one that resembles a [massive] cloud of Dharma and that cannot be borne by all other sentient beings. [That bodhisattva] resembles a great cloud—[manifesting both forms that] do not represent the enlightenment of a complete buddha and [forms that] do represent the enlightenment of a complete buddha—and causes the dust of innumerable sentient beings' mental afflictions to be settled by an incomparably great rain of true Dharma. While established in this stage, he also causes manifold roots of virtue to sprout, grow, and ripen. Therefore, this stage is called "the Dharma cloud."[1388] This very reason should also be regarded as [explaining the name of] this pleasurable state.

Concluding Remarks [ii.4.13]

It is not the case that the elements that were described [as being present] in the higher pleasurable states are completely absent in the preceding pleasurable states. However, due to their weakness, they are not counted [as being present there]. It should be understood that they are formulated as having either been achieved or perfected on those other higher stages because they have been developed to a moderate or great degree.

1388. S: *dharmameghā*, T: *chos kyi sprin*.

Moreover, concerning this [topic], each pleasurable state is achieved and then perfected over [a period lasting] many trillions of great kalpas, or over [a period lasting] even a much larger number [of great kalpas]. All of these pleasurable states [collectively] are completed during three spans of time that are each made up of a countless number of kalpas. The [first] interval of countless great kalpas is [the period during which] one goes beyond the pleasurable state of conduct that is based upon devotion and attains the pleasurable state of great joy. Moreover, [only the practitioner] who strives with [unwavering] firmness [will reach] that [pleasurable state within that period of time], not one who fails to strive [continuously]. During the second interval of countless great kalpas, [a bodhisattva] goes beyond [the seven pleasurable states that range from] the pleasurable state of great joy up to the pleasurable state that is free of signs and is accompanied by effort and attains the [pleasurable state that is] free of signs and also free of effort. This [process of spiritual development] is also one that occurs within a definite period of time, since a bodhisattva whose attitude has become pure strives constantly. During the third interval of countless great kalpas, [a bodhisattva] goes beyond the pleasurable state that is free of signs and also free of effort as well as the [pleasurable state of] informative knowledge, and attains the bodhisattva's supreme pleasurable state.

Regarding this [topic], it should be understood that [the expression] "countless kalpas" has two senses. A great kalpa itself is said to be "countless" because it is a [period of] time that cannot be measured by an enumeration of days, nights, months, and half-months. "Countless" also means that the number of those great kalpas is something that is beyond all forms of reckoning.[1389] According to the former sense of countless kalpas, enlightenment is attained over a period lasting a great many countless kalpas. In addition, according to the latter sense, [it is attained] over a period of three [intervals of] countless kalpas, and a greater number [than three such intervals] is

1389. S: *sarvagaṇanāsamatikrāntā*, T: *grangs ba thams cad las 'das pa'i*. *BBhVy* (f. 300b): "The phrase 'beyond all forms of reckoning' [should be taken to mean] beyond all ordinary forms of reckoning, because that is what is established by that term [i.e., the term 'countless']. [The term 'countless'] is also used to indicate a number that represents a particular place value." *BBhVy* then essentially repeats the explanation of the term "countless" that occurs in *AKB* (p. 181), which is that a certain "isolated sutra" (S: *muktakasūtram*, T: *mdo sil bu*) gives a list of the names of sixty place values (Vasubandhu also notes that eight of the sixty names were already lost by his time). In any case, the sixtieth place is referred to by the term "countless." Thus, the term "countless" is interpreted to mean the number one followed by fifty-nine zeros.

not required. Nevertheless, some of those individuals who exert themselves with the greatest of the great forms of effort can reduce [the three intervals of innumerable great kalpas] by a great many intermediate kalpas.[1390] Others can reduce [the time it takes to reach enlightenment] by as much as [a large number of] great kalpas. However, it should be understood that no one reduces [the overall amount of time] by an [entire interval of] countless [great kalpas].

In addition, over the course of these twelve bodhisattva pleasurable states and three [intervals of] countless [great kalpas], both the [form of] indisposition that is associated with the obscurations of the mental afflictions and [the form of indisposition] that is associated with the obscurations to that which needs to be known are abandoned. Regarding this, it should be understood that the abandonment of the form of indisposition that is associated with the obscurations of the mental afflictions occurs during three pleasurable states. On the pleasurable state of great joy, [the form of indisposition associated with] the portion of the mental afflictions that lead to [rebirth in] the lower realms has been completely and totally abandoned. However, in terms of the active arising [of the mental afflictions], [only] that of the great and middling portions of all the [innate] mental afflictions [has been abandoned].[1391]

1390. See note 1049 for a description of this term.

1391. See note 139 for additional remarks about the two types of "indisposition" (S: *dauṣṭhulyam,* T: *gnas ngan len*). *BBhVy* (f. 301a) describes indisposition as "the seed that strengthens [the mental afflictions]" (S: **paripoṣaṇabījam,* T: *yongs su rgyas par byed pa'i sa bon*) and further distinguishes the dormant state (S: *anuśayaḥ,* T: *bag la nyal*) of the mental afflictions as a "subtle seed" (S: **sūkṣmabījam,* T: *sa bon phra mo*). Regarding the forms of indisposition that are associated with the obscurations of the mental afflictions (S: *kleśāvaraṇam,* T: *nyong mongs pa'i sgrib pa*), Abhidharma literature distinguishes between two classes of mental afflictions: (1) contrived (S: *parikalpitam,* T: *kun brtags*) and (2) innate (S: *sahājam,* T: *lhan skyes*). The former are abandoned by the seeing path (S: *darśanaheyam,* T: *mthong bas spang bar bya ba*), which in the Great Vehicle corresponds with attainment of the pleasurable state of great joy. This is what is meant by the phrase "the complete and total [removal] of the indisposition that is associated with the mental afflictions that lead to the lower realms." The innate forms of the mental afflictions are abandoned by the meditation path (S: *bhāvanāheyam,* T: *sgom pas spang bar bya ba*), which is identified primarily with the remaining nine ārya bodhisattva stages. The innate forms of the mental afflictions are distinguished into three main categories: great, middling, and small. Each of these three has three subdivisions—for example, the great of the great, the middling of the great, and the small of the great, etc.—making a total of nine forms. The three great forms are the most coarse and thus are the first ones to be removed, followed by the three middling and three

It should be understood that, on the pleasurable state that is free of signs and also free of effort, the [form of] indisposition associated with the portion of the mental afflictions that obstruct [the attainment of] the purity [represented by] the forbearance of the nonarising of entities has been completely and totally abandoned. However, in terms of the active arising [of the mental afflictions], that of all [portions of] the mental afflictions [has been abandoned].[1392] By contrast, it should be understood that, on the supreme pleasurable state, all of the mental afflictions, together with the obscurations that relate to their traces and latencies, are abandoned. Moreover, this takes place at the time of entering the tathāgata's pleasurable state.

It should also be understood that the [form of] indisposition that relates to the obscurations to that which needs to be known is of three types: (1) that which constitutes the outer covering;[1393] (2) that which constitutes the underlying layer;[1394] and (3) that which constitutes the innermost core.[1395] Regarding these, the form [of indisposition] that constitutes the outer covering is abandoned upon [attainment of] the pleasurable state of great joy; the form [of indisposition] that constitutes the underlying layer is abandoned upon [attainment of] the pleasurable state that is free of signs and also free of effort; and the form [of indisposition] that constitutes the innermost core is abandoned upon [attainment of] the tathāgatas' pleasurable state. This [last event] also [constitutes the attainment of] the state of knowledge in which all the obscurations have been purified. The other [eight] pleasurable states, in due succession, represent the stages for collecting the accumulations

---

small forms. Although none of the seeds of the innate mental afflictions are abandoned on the pleasurable state of great joy, Asaṅga notes here that the type of indisposition that causes the great and middling forms of the innate mental afflictions to arise in their active or overt forms is overcome. This statement implies that the three small forms of the innate mental afflictions still arise in an active form on the pleasurable state of great joy.

1392. This statement should be understood to mean that although none of the mental afflictions ever arise in an active form once the eighth bodhisattva stage has been attained, this does not mean that the seeds of all the mental afflictions have been completely and totally abandoned.

1393. S: *tvaggatam,* T: *lpags pa la yod pa*. Literally, "that which constitutes the skin."

1394. S: *phalguḥ,* T: *bri*. This term refers to the layer of wood that is next to the core and so, not being the essence, it often means figuratively "that which is insubstantial or worthless." However, *BBhVy* explains that the three terms "[outer] covering," "underlying layer," and "[innermost] core" here refer to the forms of indisposition which are, respectively, relatively easy, moderately difficult, and very difficult to eliminate.

1395. S: *sāragatam,* T: *snying po la yod pa*.

that are needed to abandon the obscurations of the mental afflictions and [the obscurations] to that which needs to be known on those three pleasurable states.

It should be understood that, in brief, there are eleven types of purity that relate to these thirteen pleasurable states: (1) The purity of the [bodhisattva's] spiritual lineage [is present] in the first [pleasurable state]. (2) The purity of faith and devotion [is present] in the second [pleasurable state]. (3) The purity of superior attitude [is present] in the third [pleasurable state]. (4) The purity of morality [is present] in the fourth [pleasurable state]. (5) The purity of mind training [is present] in the fifth [pleasurable state]. (6) The purity of developing correct knowledge [is present] in the sixth, seventh, and eighth [pleasurable states]. (7) The purity that completes the [form of] conduct that derives from application [of effort is present] in the ninth [pleasurable state]. (8) The purity that generates knowledge of reality [is present] in the tenth [pleasurable state]. (9) The purity of the informative knowledge that correctly explains the meaning of that [reality] to others [is present] in the eleventh [pleasurable state]. (10) The purity of the knowledge that realizes every aspect of all objects of knowledge [is present] in the twelfth [pleasurable state]. (11) The purity of [having eliminated] all the obscurations of the mental afflictions and [all the obscurations] to that which needs to be known, together with their traces, [is present] in the thirteenth [pleasurable state, which is the] pleasurable state of the tathāgatas.

It should also be understood that these thirteen pleasurable states are included within the eight qualities that constitute a summary of the Great Vehicle and that were presented earlier.[1396] It should be understood that [the acts of] listening to and reflecting upon the bodhisattva collection of scriptures [occur] on the first and second pleasurable states [and they are carried out] by [a bodhisattva who] has generated faith and developed firm devotion; [the act of] practicing a superior attitude that is preceded by the attainment of various forms of meditation [occurs] on the third pleasurable state; [the act of practicing] an abundance of meditation [occurs] on all the other pleasurable states up to [and including] the pleasurable state that is free of signs and is accompanied by effort; [the act of] perfecting the fruits of meditation [occurs] on the three pleasurable states that lie above those [preceding ones] and that contain conduct that is completely pure; and the

1396. See the section of the same name in Book I, chapter 18 [I.18.25]. The eight activities that represent these qualities are alluded to in the next sentence.

state of [having attained] absolute deliverance [is present] on the pleasurable state of the tathāgatas.

It should be understood that the succession of the twelve bodhisattva pleasurable states is comparable to that of the listeners' pleasurable states. [A bodhisattva's] first [pleasurable state] should be understood to resemble a listener disciple's pleasurable state of abiding in his or her own spiritual lineage. [A bodhisattva's] second [pleasurable state] resembles [a listener's] pleasurable state that prepares him or her for entry into the flawlessness [that leads to] ultimate correctness.[1397] [A bodhisattva's] third [pleasurable state] resembles [a listener's] pleasurable state of entry into flawlessness. [A bodhisattva's] fourth [pleasurable state] resembles [a listener's] pleasurable state of the superior morality that is dear to the āryas, which [is attained] by one who has achieved the faith that is born of insight[1398] in order to terminate additional forms of the outflows. [A bodhisattva's] fifth [pleasurable state] resembles [a listener's] pleasurable state in which the superior form of mind training is completed on the basis of that superior morality. It should be understood that [a bodhisattva's] sixth, seventh, and eighth [pleasurable states] resemble [a listener's] pleasurable state in which the training of superior wisdom [is cultivated] in accord with the knowledge of the [four noble truths] that was [previously] achieved. [A bodhisattva's] ninth [pleasurable state] resembles the pleasurable state in which [a listener] who has closely examined objects of knowledge prepares him- or herself to enter the [form of] one-pointed concentration that is free of signs. [A bodhisattva's] tenth [pleasurable state] resembles [a listener's] perfected pleasurable state that is free of signs. [A bodhisattva's] eleventh [pleasurable state] resembles [a listener's] pleasurable state of [abiding in] the seat of liberation, which is attained by one who has arisen from [those signless forms of one-pointed concentration]. It should be understood that [a bodhisattva's] twelfth [pleasurable state] resembles [a listener's] pleasurable state of abiding in every aspect of the status of an arhat.

1397. S: *samyaktvanyāmāvakrāntiprayogavihāraḥ,* T: *yang dag par skyon med pa la 'jug pa'i sbyor ba'i gnas pa. AKB* (pp. 157, 350) states that "ultimate correctness" (S: *samyaktvam,* T: *yang dag pa nyid*) refers to nirvana, noting that a sutra declares: "The complete abandonment of desire, the complete abandonment of hatred, the complete abandonment of ignorance, and the complete abandonment of all the mental afflictions is called 'ultimate correctness.'" See also note 1288.

1398. See note 759 for a description of this type of faith.

Within [Book II of] *The Stage of a Bodhisattva,* [known as] "The Object of Mental Application That Relates to the Qualities That Accord with the Support," this completes the fourth chapter, entitled "The Pleasurable States." This also completes the second object of mental application.

BOOK III

The Perfection of the Support

1

Births

In brief, the births of bodhisattvas are of five types. [They represent] all [the births] of all bodhisattvas in all the pleasurable states, and they are [births that are] irreproachable and dedicated to the benefit and happiness of all sentient beings. [The five types are] (1) [a birth] that puts an end to calamities, (2) [a birth] that conforms by taking on a semblance of shared qualities, (3) birth in a state of greatness, (4) birth as a lord, and (5) the final birth.

A Birth That Puts an End to Calamities [III.1.1]

Regarding this topic, what is a birth that puts an end to calamities?

In this case, during times of famine, distress, and great catastrophe, after having made aspirational prayers [to achieve that result],[1399] a bodhisattva is born in such birth states as that of a large fish, etc., in order to become a means of sustenance for sentient beings that only requires little effort. Possessing a large body wherever he or she has taken birth, [the bodhisattva] satiates an entire populace with his or her own flesh. After having made aspirational prayers [to do so], he or she assumes the physical form of a great physician who has attained mastery of magic spells in the midst of sentient beings who are afflicted by many illnesses, in order to cure those afflicted beings. With regard to sentient beings who are being attacked by a powerful and hostile army, he or she becomes a strong monarch in order to quell the attack made by a hostile army in a just manner, peacefully, and using skillful

1399. *BBhVy* (f. 303a): "The phrase 'after having made aspirational prayers [to achieve that result]' (S: *praṇidhāya,* T: *smon lam btab nas*) [means that,] at an earlier time, the bodhisattva makes an aspirational prayer by forming a thought such as this: 'In order to bring happiness to these types of sentient beings, may I become [born as] such and such a sentient being.'"

means. With regard to sentient beings who are at odds with one another, he or she becomes a person whose speech is accepted [by others], for the purpose of bringing about their reconciliation and causing them to abandon their hostile attitudes. With regard to kings who engage in all manner of harmful actions toward their subjects, [such as] punishing and imprisoning them, he or she takes birth in the royal families of such kings, in order to put an end to the misfortune that is being experienced by such beings. He or she also becomes a just monarch who is compassionate toward beings. Out of compassion for sentient beings who hold wrong views and commit evil deeds, and who also have devotion toward some particular deity's abode, he or she takes birth in that deity's abode, in order to cause those [beings] to give up their wrong views and evil conduct.[1400] It should also be understood that this [type of] birth—which is generated on the strength of aspirational prayers and through the controlling power [over rebirth], and which is preceded by compassion—can occur in immeasurable ways. An extensive presentation would include [examples of bodhisattvas who] were reborn in a variety of [different] birth states and among many different kinds of sentient beings. This [description] represents [only] a brief presentation of this [type of birth].

A Birth That Conforms by Taking on a Semblance of Shared Qualities [iii.1.2]

What are births that conform by taking on a semblance of shared qualities?[1401]

In this case, after having made [appropriate] aspirational prayers or through having achieved the controlling power [over rebirth], a bodhisattva takes birth among a variety of sentient beings who have been reborn in the animal birth state, as well as among deities, *yakṣas*, *nāgas*, *asuras*, and the like, and among beings who are at odds with one another and trying to harm one another. Likewise, [he or she takes birth] among brahmins who hold wrong views, as well as among sentient beings who engage in misconduct, [among beings] who pursue a form of livelihood [that involves engaging in misconduct], or [among beings] who take pleasure [in engaging in

1400. Cf. ch. 29 of Āryaśūra's *Jātakamālā* (T: *sKyes pa'i rabs kyi rgyud*), entitled "The Birth Story of Brahma."

1401. S: *tatsabhāgaḥ*, T: *skal ba mnyam par mthun pa*.

misconduct]. Likewise, [he or she takes birth] among sentient beings who have a strong attachment or devotion to sensory pleasures. [A bodhisattva takes birth] in a form that is the same as these sentient beings [and he or she does so] as their chief, in order to turn them away from those faults. Having become their chief, he or she abstains from carrying out the [kinds of wrongful] conduct that those beings carry out, and he or she actively pursues the [kinds of] virtuous deeds that they do not carry out. In addition, he or she teaches them the Dharma so that they will carry out virtuous deeds. By these [actions of] teaching the Dharma and engaging in dissimilar conduct, he or she exercises the skillful means that turns [these sentient beings] back from those faults. As with the previous [type of birth], it should be understood that this [type of] birth is also one that can occur in immeasurable ways.

Birth in a State of Greatness [III.1.3]

Regarding this [topic], what is birth in a state of greatness?

In this case, a bodhisattva who is taking birth naturally generates a [karmic] maturation that is superior to everyone in the world as relates to such qualities as life span, physical appearance, family, power, etc. He then carries out deeds on the basis of the maturations that were mentioned in the chapter entitled "One's Own and Others' Aims."[1402] It should be understood that this [type of] bodhisattva's birth is also one that can occur in immeasurable ways in a variety of different birth states.

Birth as a Lord [III.1.4]

Regarding this [topic], what is a bodhisattva's birth as a lord?

The [types of] bodhisattva's birth that were described [as occurring in the ārya pleasurable states that range] from the first one, the pleasurable state of great joy, and continue up through the tenth [ārya pleasurable state] are referred to as his "birth as a lord." These range from [birth as] a lord of the Rose Apple Continent and continue up through [birth as the deity known as] the Great Supreme Lord.[1403] This most distinguished of all the states of birth lies beyond that of the deities [called] Those Who Are Below

1402. See Book I, chapter 3, the section entitled "The Eight Maturations" [I.3.5.1, I.3.6.1].

1403. S: *maheśvaraḥ,* T: *dbang phyug chen po.* While this name is also associated with several

None,[1404] and it is one in which only the bodhisattvas who have attained the supreme pleasurable state take birth. It is [a state of birth] that those [bodhisattvas of the supreme pleasurable state] create through the power of their own deeds.

The Final Birth [III.1.5]

Regarding this [topic], what is a bodhisattva's final birth?

It is the birth that is taken into the family of a religious priest or the family of a king[1405] by a bodhisattva who has completed the accumulations for enlightenment, and the one in which true and complete enlightenment is attained. [It is] also [the one in which a bodhisattva] carries out all the activities of a buddha. This birth is called the "final [birth]" and the "last [birth]."

Whatever bodhisattvas have been reborn, are being reborn, or shall be reborn in splendid, auspicious, and excellent births of the past, present, or future, all [of those bodhisattvas] do so within these very five [types of birth]. Excluding the births that take place [while a bodhisattva is still] on the stage of an immature being, there are none that are higher than these and none that are greater than these, for these five [types of] birth are the ones that have been approved of by wise bodhisattvas. Indeed, these are the births that yield the fruit of great enlightenment and they are the ones on the basis of which bodhisattvas quickly attain unsurpassed true and complete enlightenment.

Within [Book III of] *The Stage of a Bodhisattva*, [known as] "The Object of Mental Application That Relates to the Perfection of the Support," this completes the first chapter, entitled "Births."

---

non-Buddhist deities, here it refers to the ārya bodhisattva of the tenth stage who is consecrated by all the buddhas.

1404. See note 375.

1405. S: *rājakule,* T: *rgyal po'i pho brang.* The original Sanskrit term can mean both "the family of a king" and "the palace of a king." The Tibetan translation follows the latter sense.

2

Embracing

It should be understood that, in brief, bodhisattvas carry out six forms of correct embracing[1406] in relation to all the bodhisattva activities that occur during the pleasurable states: (1) embracing all sentient beings at once, (2) embracing through authority, (3) embracing by acceptance, (4) long-term [embracing], (5) short-term [embracing], and (6) the final form of embracing.

Embracing All Sentient Beings at Once [III.2.1]

When enlightenment mind is developed for the very first time, a bodhisattva embraces the entire sphere of sentient beings in the manner that a spouse [is embraced].[1407] [Reflecting], "I must use all my abilities and all my strength to provide every form of benefit and happiness to [all sentient beings]," he or she also acts in just this way. This constitutes a bodhisattva's embracing of all sentient beings at once.

Embracing through Authority [III.2.2]

A bodhisattva who is the head [of a household] maintains the conception of embracing through authority toward the household that is made up of his or her mother, father, children, spouse, male and female servants, workmen,

1406. Both printed Sanskrit editions read *samyaktvaparigrahaḥ*. The Derge and Tok editions of the Tibetan translation read *sems can thams cad la yang dag par yongs su 'dzin pa* or "correct forms of embracing all sentient beings." *BBhVy* (f. 304a) seems to support the former reading.

1407. See note 163 and accompanying text.

and hired persons; and [a bodhisattva] who is a sovereign ruler [maintains the conception of embracing through authority] toward his or her subjects.

[The bodhisattva who is the head of a household] maintains [this attitude] by [carrying out] activities that are appropriate to that household and by [acting] in a manner that accords with [being] a bodhisattva. Using a variety of methods, he or she causes his or her mother and father to take up virtue. At appropriate times, he or she honors and serves them. He or she shows gratitude and appreciation [toward them]. He or she complies with the wishes of mother and father. He or she submits to their will in matters that relate to duty. He or she provides food and clothing properly and at appropriate times to children, spouse, and male and female servants, etc. He or she does not overburden them with work. He or she is tolerant of their errant behavior. He or she takes care of them properly when they are sick. He or she causes them to take up virtue. At appropriate times, he or she shows them affection in the form of a reward of considerable value and expressions of kind speech. He or she does not think of them as male and female servants [who are inferior], and takes care of them just as one does oneself, or [even] in a manner superior to that.

The bodhisattva who is a sovereign rules his or her subjects without [resorting to] punishments and weapons.[1408] He or she collects revenue in a just manner. He or she enjoys the kingdom that he or she has inherited and does not forcefully and without warning invade a foreign country. Using all his or her abilities and powers, he or she causes beings to turn away from evil. He or she acts as a parent to his or her subjects. He or she is naturally disposed to share [wealth] even with strangers, needless to say with those who are his or her own dependents. He or she avoids doing injury [to others] and speaks truthfully. [He or she is one who has] given up doing such forms of harm to sentient beings as killing, imprisoning, punishing, cutting off [limbs], and beating, etc.

Embracing by Acceptance [III.2.3]

Regarding this topic, the act of correctly leading a body of followers is called "embracing by acceptance."[1409] [A bodhisattva] correctly embraces a follow-

1408. *BBhVy* (f. 305): "The phrase 'without [resorting to] punishments,' etc., means without confiscating property and putting [subjects] to death."

1409. S: *upādānaparigrahaḥ,* T: *'dzin pas yongs su 'dzin pa*. This is an uncommon use of the

ing on the basis of two causes: (1) He or she embraces [a following] with a mind that does not seek any selfish gain and (2) he or she directs each individual to his or her own aim. [A bodhisattva] does not employ a wrongful means to deceive them. In all forms of embracing [a following], he or she maintains an impartial mind and does not fall into [the error of showing] favoritism. He or she is not stingy with the Dharma in relation to them and also is not a teacher who withholds instructions [from them].[1410] He or she does not expect them to engage in the service of waiting on him or her. However, he or she does not turn back those who do so of their own accord from a desire to be virtuous, in order that they may build up an accumulation of merit. When the circumstances are appropriate, [that bodhisattva] also carries out the service of waiting on them.

He or she causes them to develop [an understanding of] meanings that they have not yet attained, to perfect those that they have attained, and to overcome all forms of doubt that may arise. He or she dispels [their] regret. Having fathomed statements of profound meaning with his or her wisdom, he or she reveals them [to others] at appropriate times. He or she shares in their suffering and happiness. He or she will make an exceptional exertion for the sake of objects of material value so that [followers] might [be able to obtain them] from him or her. At appropriate times, he or she is one who correctly admonishes them for their transgressions. At appropriate times, he or she is also one who censures them in the proper manner. He or she does not fail to pursue in every possible way the aim of curing the illness of those who are afflicted by disease or eliminating the sadness of those who are mentally distraught.

He or she does not humiliate those who have an inferior physical appearance [or inferior powers of] recollection, effort, or knowledge, etc. Having comprehended [the nature of] their distress,[1411] he or she gives them a suitable

---

Sanskrit term *upādānam* (T: *nye bar len pa*), which the Abhidharma tradition identifies as one of a series of terms that refer to different aspects of the mental afflictions (see *AS,* pp. 48–49, and *AKB,* p. 306). Since the general meaning of the noun is "the act of taking for oneself" (MW, p. 213), I translate it here as "acceptance" in the sense of taking on followers. Cf. Vasubandhu's comment on *MSA,* ch. 21, v. 7.

1410. S: *ācāryamuṣṭiḥ,* T: *slob dpon gyi dpe mkhyud.* This is a free rendering of the idiom that literally translates as the "closefistedness of a teacher."

1411. S: *teṣāṃ khedam anupraviśya,* T: *de dag gi skyo ba dang du blangs te.* Although forms of this Sanskrit verb typically mean to penetrate into the meaning of something with the mind, the Tibetan equivalent here indicates "having accepted their distress."

form of Dharma teaching at appropriate times. He or she also gives them correct instruction about meditation objects[1412] at appropriate times.

He or she is forbearing of conflict and does not become agitated. He or she engages in conduct that is similar or superior to [that of his or her following], not [conduct that is of] a lower form. He or she has no desire for gain or honor. He or she is compassionate. He or she does not become excited, [has a nature that] is unwavering, and possesses excellent [forms of] morality, views, conduct, and means of livelihood. He or she is one who shows a welcoming facial expression and is one who refrains from frowning. He or she is amiable, speaks in a kindly manner, and speaks politely and accompanied by a smile. He or she is always and continually intent upon that which relates to virtue. He or she is free of heedlessness and laziness. He or she [maintains] such [qualities] as these in order to serve as an example for his or her following and so that he or she can reach a state of excellence.

A bodhisattva does not always acquire a following, nor does he or she [always] avoid acquiring a following. He or she also does not act in a contrary manner.[1413]

Long-Term Embracing [III.2.4]

Regarding this [topic], those sentient beings whose state of [spiritual] ripening is slight are said to be a bodhisattva's long-term acceptance, because their suitability for [attaining] purification is such that it will take a long period of time.

1412. S: *ālambanam,* T: *dmigs pa*. Asaṅga explains in great detail four categories of meditation objects (*ŚBh,* pp. 192–258): (1) the comprehensive meditation object (S: *vyāpyālambanam,* T: *khyab pa'i dmigs pa*); (2) the meditation object that eliminates unfavorable mental traits (S: *caritaviśodhanam ālambanam,* T: *spyad pa rnam par sbyong ba'i dmigs pa*); (3) the meditation object that develops skillfulness (S: *kauśalyālambanam,* T: *mkhas pa'i dmigs pa*); and (4) the meditation object that eliminates the mental afflictions (S: *kleśaviśodhanam ālambanam,* T: *nyon mongs pa rnam par sbyong ba'i dmigs pa*).

1413. *BBhVy* (f. 306b): "When followers are [too] difficult to discipline or when [a bodhisattva] is unable to discipline them, then he or she does not gather a following and [acts like] a solitary realizer in order to avoid becoming agitated by the mental afflictions. ... [The statement] 'He or she also does not act in a contrary manner' (S: *na cānyathā karoti,* T: *gzhan du yang mi byed do*) means that [a bodhisattva] does not [gather a following] in an improper manner."

Short-Term Embracing [iii.2.5]

On the other hand, those [sentient beings] whose state of [spiritual] ripening is moderate are said to be a bodhisattva's short-term acceptance, because their suitability for [attaining] purification is such that it will not take a long period of time.

The Final Form of Embracing [iii.2.6]

For their part, those [sentient beings] whose state of [spiritual] ripening is great are said to be a bodhisattva's final acceptance, because their suitability for [attaining] purification is such that it will occur in that very birth.

These are the bodhisattvas' six forms of correctly embracing sentient beings, and they are ones by means of which the bodhisattvas of the past, present, and future have embraced, are embracing, and shall embrace sentient beings. Moreover, there are none of greater significance than these and there are none besides these.

Twelve Difficult Situations That Are Stressful [iii.2.7]

It should also be understood that there are twelve encounters with stressful and difficult situations that can be experienced by bodhisattvas who are engaging in correct forms of embracing sentient beings. Moreover, a bodhisattva should exercise sagacity in dealing with them. (1) [To decide] whether to oppose or ignore sentient beings who are committing transgressions is an encounter with a difficult situation that is stressful. (2) To protect one's own mind from mental afflictions while carrying out a harsh procedure in relation to a sentient being is an encounter with a difficult situation that is stressful. (3) To have only a few Dharma teachings to give when one has been approached by a large number of petitioners for the purpose of requesting [teachings] is an encounter with a difficult situation that is stressful. (4) To be asked by many persons to assist them with a multitude of activities that have arisen when one is by oneself is an encounter with a difficult situation that is stressful. (5) For one who does not possess fitness of mind, [to develop] an agreeable mundane state of composure that represents a [potential] source of lack of mindfulness which will result in rebirth in a divine realm is an encounter with a difficult situation that is stressful.[1414] (6) For someone who desires to benefit sentient beings, to be unable to accomplish that aim is an encounter with a difficult situation that is stressful. (7) [To decide] whether to teach the Dharma to sentient beings who are dull-witted, deceitful, and unruly or to ignore them is an encounter with a difficult situation that is stressful. (8) To regard samsara as defective at all times while [at the same time] not allowing oneself to escape from samsara is an encounter with a difficult situation that is stressful. (9) To die in a state of clouded recollection without having attained a pure form of superior attitude is an encounter with a difficult situation that is stressful. (10) To be requested by others to give them the object of foremost importance that is held to be extremely precious when one has not yet attained a pure form of superior attitude is an encounter with a difficult situation that is stressful. (11) [To decide] whether to provide instruction to sentient beings who have a variety of different opinions and diverse aspirations or to ignore them is an encounter with a difficult situation that is stressful. (12) To maintain a very great form of mindfulness while [at the same time] refraining from completely abandoning all of the mental afflictions is an encounter with a difficult situation that is stressful.

A bodhisattva who encounters any of these stressful and difficult situations should take action only after having considered its relative importance. In some cases, he or she should investigate the persons who are involved. In some cases, he or she should maintain composure and, after having adopted a [particular] motive, carry it out. He or she should also make correct aspirational prayers. In some cases, he or she should not allow the mind to engage [the matter]. In some cases, after having given [the matter] intense consideration, he or she should maintain tireless patience. In some cases, he or she should remain indifferent. In some cases, he or she should generate effort and act with fervor. In some cases, he or she should employ skillful

1414. *BBhVy* (f. 307a–307b) interprets this dilemma in the following manner: "If [a bodhisattva] fails to develop an agreeable state of composure, he or she will lack the power to further ripen a buddha's spiritual qualities. On the other hand, if he or she does generate a particular state of composure it represents a [potential] source of lack of mindfulness for him or her. By relishing [the ease associated with] that [state of composure], those who have not attained mastery [of the states of one-pointed concentration] will be reborn in divine realms. . . . Therefore, in this situation one should rely on [the following]. Either abandon the relishing [of that ease] by means of the causes that represent its antidote or resort to a means that will cause one to pass away from that [rebirth in a divine] state quickly."

means. In this way, a bodhisattva who is skilled at [applying] the correct remedy does not become despondent no matter what kind of encounter with a stressful and difficult situation he or she may be faced with, and he or she also protects him- or herself correctly.

Within [Book III of] *The Stage of a Bodhisattva*, [known as] "The Object of Mental Application That Relates to the Perfection of the Support," this completes the second chapter, entitled "Embracing."

3
The Stages

Seven Stages [III.3.1]

It should be understood that seven stages correspond to the thirteen pleasurable states that were already described. Six [of the seven] are stages that pertain to a bodhisattva and one is a stage that is a mixture of a bodhisattva's stage and a tathāgata's stage. The seven bodhisattva stages are (1) the stage of the spiritual lineage, (2) the stage of conduct that is based upon devotion, (3) the stage of a pure superior attitude, (4) the stage of practicing conduct, (5) the stage of certainty, (6) the stage of certain conduct, and (7) the stage that is the perfect manner of going. The last of these is a mixed [stage].

Regarding this [topic], the pleasurable state of the spiritual lineage and the pleasurable state of conduct that is based upon devotion correspond to [the first] two [of these] stages. The pleasurable state of great joy corresponds to the stage of a pure superior attitude. The [two] pleasurable states that relate to superior morality and superior mind training, the three pleasurable states that relate to superior wisdom, and the pleasurable state that is free of signs and is accompanied by effort [collectively] correspond to the stage of practicing conduct. The pleasurable state that is free of signs and free of effort corresponds to the stage of certainty. In this [latter] stage, a bodhisattva enters the third occurrence of a certainty.[1415] The pleasurable state of informative knowledge corresponds to the stage of certain conduct. The supreme pleasurable state and the pleasurable state of a tathāgata [together]

1415. See Book I, chapter 18, the section entitled "The Occurrence of Certainty" [I.18.15], for a description of three types of certainty. The third of these is called "the occurrence of certainty that relates to fruitful activities."

correspond to the stage that is the perfect manner of going. The pleasurable state of a tathāgata and the stage of a tathāgata will be described later in the chapter [entitled "Preeminence,"] which addresses the preeminence of a buddha's qualities.

Transcending Rebirth in the Lower Realms [III.3.2]

Regarding this [topic], how does a bodhisattva who is entering the stage of a pure superior attitude following the stage of conduct that is based upon devotion transcend [having to be reborn in] the lower realms?

In this case, relying on a purified mundane meditative absorption, the bodhisattva who is on the stage of conduct that is based upon devotion and who has accumulated extremely well the accumulations [that are necessary] for enlightenment meditates with attention focused exclusively on compassion toward sentient beings, using the one hundred and ten aspects that were described previously.[1416] As a consequence of this meditation, he or she attains a sympathetic and compassionate attitude toward sentient beings having the form [that corresponds to those one hundred and ten aspects]. [This attitude is one] on the strength of which [a bodhisattva] would [be willing to] remain in the lower realms for the sake of sentient beings in a manner that resembles inhabiting [one's own] dwelling.[1417] In order to dispel the suffering of sentient beings, he or she reflects, "If I could attain unsurpassed true and complete enlightenment while residing in those very [lower realms], I would be able to endure that." On the strength of that pure attitude, he or she is also desirous that all sentient beings' deeds [that would cause rebirth in] the lower realms might ripen on him- or herself. He or she also generates the wish that [sentient beings] never commit any form of nonvirtuous deed. The purified mundane meditative absorption that is being cultivated by him or her in this way removes from [that bodhisattva's] being the [type of] indisposition that relates to the mental afflictions that

1416. See Book I, chapter 16, the section entitled "Cultivating Compassion by Meditating on One Hundred and Ten Forms of Suffering" [I.16.3.1].

1417. S: *agārāvāsayogena*, T: *khyim gyi gnas pa'i tshul du*. *BBhVy* (f. 308b): "Just as those householders who are attached to sensory pleasures take delight in inhabiting their homes, the bodhisattvas who are dedicated to the welfare of sentient beings take delight in residing in the lower realms and develop the aspiration: 'May I experience the [karmic] maturations of any and all deeds that all sentient beings have done to cause themselves to be reborn in the lower realms.'"

bring rebirth in the lower realms. Not long after that [indisposition] has been abandoned, the individual nature of that bodhisattva is transformed in such a manner that he or she never again commits the type of evil deed that causes rebirth in lower realms and he or she [never again] has to go to the lower realms. This is how a bodhisattva transcends all forms of the lower realms and also how he or she transcends the stage of conduct that is based upon devotion and enters the stage of a pure superior attitude.

Several Points regarding the Ten Spiritual Qualities [III.3.3]

The ten spiritual qualities of faith, etc.,[1418] that were described in the chapter entitled "The Pleasurable States" as bringing about the purification of the pleasurable states should also be understood in this case as bringing about the purification of the stages. Their formulation should be understood in terms of [how they serve] as antidotes for specific negative qualities. It should also be understood that they have an essential purpose and a successive order.

With regard to this [topic], there are ten qualities that oppose the ten qualities that bring about the purification of the stages and for the sake of which those [ten positive qualities] were formulated as antidotes.

What are the ten?

The condition of having never, at any time, generated enlightenment mind or accepted the precepts of the bodhisattva training is the quality that opposes faith and [the quality] for which faith serves as an antidote. The mind that wishes to harm sentient beings is the quality that opposes compassion and [the quality] for which compassion serves as an antidote. Malice toward sentient beings is the quality that opposes loving-kindness and [the quality] for which loving-kindness serves as an antidote. The concern for possessions and for remaining alive is the quality that opposes generosity and [the quality] for which the willingness to give up [inner and outer objects] serves as an antidote. Developing a wrong form of practice that harms sentient beings and the quality of [thinking] that one has too much to do are the qualities that oppose tirelessness and [the qualities] for which tirelessness serves as an antidote. The undertaking of ineffective activities

1418. See Book II, chapter 4, the section entitled "The Pleasurable State of Great Joy" [II.4.3].

is the quality that opposes knowledge of the teaching and [the quality] for which knowledge of the teaching serves as an antidote. Unfriendliness and the unwillingness to comply with others' minds are the qualities that oppose knowledge of the world and [the qualities] for which knowledge of the world serves as an antidote. Heedlessness and laziness with regard to the cultivation of virtuous qualities are the qualities that oppose shame and abashment and [the qualities] for which shame and abashment serve as an antidote. Being afraid of the manifold, continuous, intense, and long-lasting forms of suffering in samsara is the quality that opposes developing the power of firmness and [the quality] for which developing the power of firmness serves as an antidote. Uncertainty, ambivalence, and doubt toward the Master are the qualities that oppose worshipping and serving the tathāgatas and [the qualities] for which worshipping and serving the tathāgatas serve as an antidote. This is the formulation of those [ten spiritual qualities] in terms of how they serve as antidotes.

What, then, is their essential purpose?

In brief, these ten qualities kindle purity of attitude and purity of activities.

Regarding this, it should be understood that the first three qualities [kindle] purity of attitude and the remaining ones [kindle] purity of activities.

A bodhisattva who has intense faith in enlightenment feels compassion for sentient beings who are afflicted by suffering. [A bodhisattva] who feels compassion reflects, "I must save these [sentient beings]," and develops loving-kindness. Similarly, [a bodhisattva] who has [developed] loving-kindness in his or her mind is willing to give up everything and is indifferent to possessions and remaining alive. [A bodhisattva] who is indifferent [to those two aims] will apply him- or herself on behalf of [sentient beings] and not become tired. [A bodhisattva] who is tireless will develop knowledge of the teaching. [A bodhisattva] who possesses knowledge of the teaching will know the proper way to apply him- or herself in the world and thus will develop knowledge of the world. He or she will feel shame and abashment if he or she should develop any of the mental afflictions. [A bodhisattva] who feels shame and abashment will not let him- or herself be controlled by the mental afflictions and will attain the power of firmness. Through engaging in correct practice, [a bodhisattva] who has attained the power of firmness will not become deficient, will strengthen the virtuous qualities, and will worship and serve the tathāgatas, by means of the form of worship that consists of spiritual practice and by means of the form of worship that is carried out with wealth and honor. It should be understood that this represents the successive order in which these ten qualities are attained. The purification of all the stages is accomplished by means of these ten qualities.

Within [Book III of] *The Stage of a Bodhisattva,* [known as] the Object of Mental Application That Relates to the Perfection of the Support, this completes the third chapter, entitled "The Stages."

4
Conduct

Four Types of Conduct [iii.4.1]

It should be understood that in all the bodhisattva stages, beginning with the stage of conduct that is based upon devotion, the conduct of bodhisattvas is, in brief, of four types.[1419]

What are the four?

They are (1) conduct relating to the perfections, (2) conduct that is conducive to enlightenment, (3) conduct relating to supernatural knowledge, and (4) conduct relating to the ripening of sentient beings.

Conduct Relating to the Perfections [iii.4.1.1]

Regarding this [topic], the combination of these ten perfections is called "conduct relating to the perfections": the six perfections that were presented earlier, the perfection of skillful means, the perfection of aspirational prayer, the perfection of power, and the perfection of knowledge.

Regarding this, the twelve types of skillful means that were described earlier[1420] constitute the perfection of skillful means. The five types of aspirational prayer that were described earlier[1421] constitute the perfection of aspirational prayer. The purification of the practice [that leads to] the ten

1419. Cf. *MSA,* ch. 21, v. 42. See also the Tibetan translation of *Ratnacūḍaparipṛcchā Sūtra* in the *dKon brtsegs* section of Kg., vol. 6 (*Cha*), *gTsug na rin po ches zhus pa'i mdo.*

1420. See Book I, chapter 17, the section entitled "Skillful Means" [I.17.11].

1421. See Book I, chapter 17, the section entitled "Aspirational Prayer" [I.17.13].

powers[1422] constitutes the perfection of power. The knowledge of [how to present] a systematic formulation of all entities as they truly are constitutes the perfection of knowledge.

Regarding this, the wisdom that is occupied with grasping ultimate truth is the perfection of wisdom. By contrast, [the wisdom] that is occupied with grasping conventional truth is the perfection of knowledge. This represents the difference between these two [perfections].

Another formulation [is the following]: (1) Immeasurable knowledge is the perfection of skillful means. (2) The aspiration [to achieve] higher and higher forms of excellent knowledge is the perfection of aspirational prayers. (3) The quality that makes one incapable of being cut off from the path by any of Māra's forces is the perfection of power. (4) The proper realization of that which needs to be known is the perfection of knowledge.

Conduct That Is Conducive to Enlightenment [III.4.1.2]

The combination of all thirty-seven of the spiritual qualities that are conducive to enlightenment, which begin with closely placed recollection, as well as the four investigations[1423] and the four forms of thorough knowledge of the way things are,[1424] as they were described earlier, is called the bodhisattvas' "conduct that is conducive to enlightenment."

Conduct Relating to Supernatural Knowledge [III.4.1.3]

The six forms of supernatural knowledge, as they were explained in the chapter entitled "Power," are called the bodhisattvas' "conduct relating to supernatural knowledge."

1422. These practices form the subject matter of Book I, chapter 8, "The Lineages of the Powers."

1423. See the section of the same name in Book I, chapter 4 [I.4.9].

1424. See the section of the same name in Book I, chapter 4 [I.4.10].

Conduct Relating to the Ripening of Sentient Beings [III.4.1.4]

Two topics that are beyond measure were presented earlier—the immeasurable forms of beings to be trained and the immeasurable means of accomplishing their training. The combination of all these forms of ripening sentient beings, which were presented in the chapter entitled "Ripening," is called a bodhisattva's "conduct relating to the ripening of sentient beings." It should be understood that all the forms of bodhisattva conduct are included within these four categories of bodhisattva conduct.

The Meaning of the Term "Perfection" [III.4.2]

Regarding this [topic], because they are developed over three [extremely] long periods of time that are [each made up of] countless [great kalpas], because they have an innate purity that is superior to that of all other roots of virtue—[namely,] those that are mundane and those that are possessed by listeners and solitary realizers—and because they bring attainment of the result of supreme enlightenment, these ten spiritual qualities of generosity and the rest—which are developed over a period of time of supreme [length], which are purified by a supreme form of innate purity, and which bestow a supreme result—are called "perfections."[1425]

Three Reasons for the Order of the Perfections [III.4.3]

It should be understood that there are three reasons for the order in which the perfections are arranged.

What are the three?

They are (1) [the reason] that relates to their being an antidote, (2) [the

1425. This is Asaṅga's literal interpretation (S: *niruktiḥ,* T: *nges tshig*) of the term "perfection" (S: *pāramitā,* T: *pha rol tu phyin pa*), which turns on the three uses of the adjective translated here as "supreme" (S: *parama,* T: *mchog*). *BBhVy* (f. 310b) includes the following comment: "The literal interpretation of the term 'perfection' is as follows: They are called 'perfections' in the sense of [being qualities that] reach a state of preeminence (S: **prakarṣaparyantagamanārthena,* T: *rab kyi mthar thug par 'gro ba'i don gyis na*)."

reason] that relates to their arising, and (3) [the reason] that relates to their maturation results.[1426]

Regarding this [topic], the six qualities of (1) stinginess, (2) bad conduct, (3) hostility and harmfulness toward sentient beings, (4) laziness, (5) distraction, and (6) dull-wittedness and extreme bewilderment represent obstructions to enlightenment. In the same order, the six perfections should be understood as the antidotes for these six qualities. The other [four] perfections are also included within these [six]. This is the how [the order of] their formulation relates to the manner in which they serve as antidotes.

How does [their order] relate to the manner in which they arise?

In this case, at the very outset a bodhisattva who is indifferent to possessions adopts morality after having given up the sensory pleasures that relate to the householder's state. Out of respect for morality, he or she bears patiently the harm that is carried out [against him or her] by others and does not carry out harm against others. [A bodhisattva] whose morality is pure both through having adopted it and through [having developed] patience undertakes activities that relate to virtue in an unwavering and continuous manner. Having become free of heedlessness in this way through effort, he or she attains a one-pointedness of mind that is virtuous in nature. Having become one whose mind is composed in this way, he or she realizes those objects that need to be known and perceives those objects that need to be seen, as they truly are. It should be understood that this is how their formulation corresponds to the successive manner in which they arise.

An Abundance of Possessions and the Fivefold Inner Excellence [III.4.4]

How does [their order] relate to the ripening of results?

In this case, a bodhisattva who has taken up and observes the [six] virtuous qualities of generosity and the rest in the present life, will, because of that, become one who in future [lives] attains the external quality of having an abundance of possessions, through having practiced generosity. He or

1426. S: *vipākaphalam,* T: *rnam par smin pa'i 'bras bu.* This term is usually understood to mean the type of karmic result that ripens in the form of a particular kind of rebirth. The maturation result of nonvirtuous deeds is to be reborn in one of the unhappy migratory states and the maturation result of virtuous deeds is to be reborn in a happy migratory state. Here the term seems to be meant in the more general sense of the specific type of karmic ripening that corresponds to each of the six perfections.

she will also become one who attains a fivefold inner excellence of his or her individual existence, through having practiced the five remaining perfections of morality and the rest.

What is the fivefold excellence of one's individual existence?

The first excellence is [that of being born] in a happy migratory state as a god or a human being who possesses [qualities such as] a life span, etc., that are superior to those of other beings. The second excellence is [the qualities of] being naturally tireless about carrying out virtuous activities, [naturally] tolerant of the wrongs committed [against one] by others, and [naturally] averse to harming others. The third excellence is the quality of being naturally firm in one's efforts [to pursue] all activities that are undertaken. The fourth excellence is the fact that a person who [only] possesses weak forms of the mental afflictions possesses a natural ability to control the mind and a natural fitness of mind, both of which lead to the swift [attainment of] supernatural knowledge regarding all matters. The fifth excellence is to possess a vast intellect from birth and to achieve erudition and sagacity with regard to all matters. These are [the qualities] that are produced through the ripening of results. It should be understood that this represents another [reason] for the order in which the six perfections are arranged.

Regarding this [topic], it should be understood that the bodhisattvas' training of superior morality is completed by means of four of the [six] perfections—which constitute its requisite, essential nature, attendant factor, and [method of] preservation; the training of superior mind practice [is completed] by means of the perfection of meditative absorption; and the training of superior wisdom [is completed] by means of the perfection of wisdom. Moreover, there is no higher course of training for a bodhisattva to attain [than these]. Therefore, because the entire course of training for bodhisattvas is included within these three [trainings], it is established that there are just six perfections. Moreover, there are none of greater significance than these and there are none besides these.

Four Acts That Must Be Accomplished [III.4.5]

In brief, there are four acts that bodhisattvas must accomplish, which are inclusive of all their acts: (1) cultivating virtue for the sake of [attaining] enlightenment, (2) the perception of the nature of reality that is preceded by that [cultivation of virtue], (3) attainment of the powers, and (4) ripening sentient beings. Bodhisattvas carry out and practice these four acts in this order, by means of the four types of conduct. Therefore, there are also no higher forms of conduct than these to be formulated.

Within [Book III of] *The Stage of a Bodhisattva,* [known as] "The Object of Mental Application That Relates to the Perfection of the Support," this completes the fourth chapter, entitled "Conduct."

5

The Marks and the Secondary Signs

Regarding this [topic], in relation to the pleasurable state of a tathāgata and the tathāgatas' aspect of the stage that is the perfect manner of going, the blessed ones possess one hundred and forty unique buddha qualities. They are (1) the thirty-two marks of a great person, (2) the eighty secondary signs, (3) the four forms of purity that are complete in every respect, (4) the ten powers of a tathāgata, (5) the four forms of intrepid confidence, (6) the three closely placed recollections, (7) the three forms of having nothing that needs to be concealed, (8) great compassion, (9) the nature of being completely free of confusion, (10) complete destruction of the [mental afflictions'] traces, and (11) the knowledge of all aspects and of what is most excellent.

The Thirty-Two Marks of a Great Person [III.5.1]

What are the thirty-two marks of a great person?

(1) A great person is one whose feet are placed down well—that is, he treads evenly upon the earth. This is a great person's mark [that is indicative] of [being] a great person. (2) On the undersides of the [hands and] feet,[1427] on both [palms and] soles, a wheel with a thousand spokes that is fully formed in every respect, including a hub and a rim, is apparent. (3) A great person is one whose fingers [and toes] are long. (4) His feet have prominent[1428] heels. (5) His hands and feet are soft and youthful. (6) His

1427. The Tibetan translation indicates that the wheel marks are also apparent on the palms of the hands (T: *phyag dang zhabs gnyis kyi mthil nas*); however, the Sanskrit editions only refer to the soles of the feet.

1428. S: *āyata,* T: *yangs pa*. The Sanskrit adjective means literally "extended" and also is used to describe shapes as "oblong." Some scholars have taken this term to mean that the heels are "wide"; my sense is that the term should be understood to mean that the heels extend

hands and feet have a weblike membrane [between the fingers and toes]. (7) His feet [have ankles that] do not protrude.[1429] (8) His calves are like those of the *eṇeya* deer. (9) His body is not bent over.[1430] (10) His sexual organ is concealed in a sheath. (11) His [body] is symmetrical, like the *nyagrodha* tree. (12) His [body] emits light that extends [a distance of] one fathom.[1431] (13) His body hairs point upward. (14) His body hairs grow singly and [each] hair that grows singly on his body[1432] is soft,[1433] dark blue, and curls to the right. (15) His skin is golden colored. (16) His skin is smooth and, because of its smoothness, dust and impurities do not remain on his body. (17) His body has seven elevated areas, [that is,] there are seven areas on his body [where the flesh] is well filled out: two are on [the backs of] the hands, two are on [the tops of] the feet, two are on the shoulders, and one is on [the nape of] the neck. (18) The upper part of his body is like that of a lion. (19) His shoulders are well developed.[1434] (20) The area between his shoulders is well filled out.[1435] (21) His body is large and straight. (22) He possesses forty even

---

or project in a posterior direction and do so in such a way as to make them prominent. To describe them as "extended" seems awkward and unclear in meaning.

1429. S: *utsaṅgacaraṇaḥ,* T: *zhabs 'bar 'bur med pa*. The exact sense of the Sanskrit adjective *utsaṅga* is unclear. The English translation is based on the Tibetan equivalent, which literally states "feet that are not knobby." The principal meaning seems to be that the ankle bones do not protrude greatly, since an alternate Tibetan rendering in *MVy* (no. 260) clearly means "feet with ankle [bones] that are not prominent" (T: *zhabs kyi long bu mi mngon pa*).

1430. S: *anavanatakāyaḥ,* T: *sku ma btud pa*. This statement seems to correspond to the quality that is often expressed in language that describes arms that reach to the knees without the body bending over.

1431. S: *vyāmaprabhaḥ,* T: *'od 'dom gang dang ldan pa*. The Sanskrit texts present this quality here in the listing of the marks and seem to indicate that it represents a separate mark, as with the listing of the marks in the *Mahāprajñāpāramitāśāstra* (*Le Traité de la Grand Vertu de Sagesse*, vol. 2, p. 277 and vol. 3, p. 1912). However, in the Tibetan translation this quality is moved down in the order of presentation, where it appears to be combined with the quality of having "golden-colored skin" (mark no. 15). See also note 1436.

1432. S: *ekaikam asya roma kāye jātam* (Wogihara edition), T: *de'i sku'i spu re re nas skye la*. Dutt's Sanskrit edition reads *ekaikam asya romakūpe jātam,* which translates as "[each hair] that grows singly in [each] *pore* . . ."

1433. S: *mṛdu,* T: *'jam*. The adjective "soft" only appears in the Tibetan translation; it is missing from both Sanskrit editions. However, this adjective does appear in the *Eighteen Thousand Line Perfection of Wisdom Sutra*.

1434. S: *susaṃvṛttaskandhaḥ,* T: *dpung mgo legs par grub pa*. The Sanskrit translates literally as "well-rounded shoulders"; however, the sense seems to be that the shoulders are large and fully developed.

1435. S: *citāntarāṃsaḥ,* T: *thal gong rgyas pa*. That is, his chest is broad and massive.

teeth.[1436] (23) His teeth have no gaps. (24) His teeth are extremely white. (25) His jaws are like those of a lion. (26) His tongue is large and slender and, because of its length, if the tongue is extended from the mouth it can cover the entire face up to the hairline. (27) He has attained [the ability to experience all] tastes as a supreme taste.[1437] (28) He possesses divine speech, [that is,] his speech is as appealing as [the sound of] the *kalaviṅka* bird and the sound of his voice has a drumlike resonance. (29) His eyes are an intensely dark shade of blue. (30) His eyelashes are [long and well-developed] like those of an ox. (31) [The top of] his head has a crown protrusion. (32) A circle of hair that is as white as a conch shell and turns to the right grows between his eyebrows. This [also] is a great person's mark [that is indicative] of [being] a great person.

The Eighty Secondary Signs [III.5.2]

What are the eighty secondary signs?

The twenty fingers and toes of the hands and feet, together with the joints and nails make up twenty secondary signs. The hands and feet have eight surfaces; four are those of the two hands and four are those of the two feet. These make up eight secondary signs. The sixfold collection that is associated with the ankles, knees, and thighs[1438] makes up six secondary signs. The sixfold collection that is associated with the arms makes up six secondary signs. The hips[1439] and the perineal raphe[1440] [each make up a single secondary

1436. S: *catvāriṃśatsamadantaḥ*. The two Sanskrit editions seem to present "forty even teeth" as a single mark. However, the Tibetan translation separates this phrase into two qualities—one being that he has forty teeth and the other that the teeth are even—as in the listing that appears in the Perfection of Wisdom sutras. For example, the *Eighteen Thousand Line Perfection of Wisdom Sutra* states: "The quality of having even teeth means that none of his teeth are higher or lower [than the others]." If these are considered as two separate marks, then it would appear the nimbus of light extending a distance of one fathom (mark no. 12) should not be counted as a separate mark.

1437. *BBhVy* (f. 315b): "Through possessing the quality that [experiences all] tastes as a supreme taste, whatever rubs against the tongue becomes a supremely excellent taste."

1438. S: *ūruḥ,* T: *brla*. The various editions of the Tibetan translation all seem to have misspelled this term. Some have just the syllable *ba;* the Derge edition has *bar*.

1439. S: *jaghanam,* T: *sta zur*.

1440. S: *sīvanī,* T: *rked pa*. The exact meaning of this term is uncertain. The basic sense appears to be that of a "seamlike" attribute. Several Sanskrit references on physiology identify this term with "perineal raphe." MW (p. 1218) gives "frenum of the prepuce" as another

sign]. The testicles make up two secondary signs. The generative organ [is a single secondary sign]. The buttocks make up two secondary signs. The pelvic region,[1441] the abdomen,[1442] and the navel [make up three secondary signs]. The two lateral rib areas, the two armpits, and the two breasts taken together make up six secondary signs. The chest, the heart,[1443] the throat, and the back [make up four secondary signs]. These are the sixty secondary signs that are situated in the lower part of the body, and they are exclusive of those that appear above the neck.

The two rows of teeth make up two secondary signs. The palate [is a secondary sign]. The two lips that cover [the mouth] make up two secondary signs. The well-developed cheeks[1444] [make up a single secondary sign]. The two well-formed sides of the face[1445] make up two secondary signs. The two eyes and the surrounding areas make up two secondary signs. The two eyebrows make up two secondary signs. The two nostrils make up two secondary signs. The forehead [is a secondary sign]. The two temporal bones[1446] and the two ears form a set of four secondary signs. The head, together with the hair, makes up a single secondary sign. These are the twenty secondary signs that are found on the body in the area above the neck.

The sixty previous [secondary signs] combined with these latter twenty make up the eighty secondary signs. These are the excellent marks and signs that a bodhisattva who has entered the stage of a pure [superior] attitude attains through a [karmic] maturation. It should be understood that beyond that [stage], their purity becomes ever greater until [the bodhisattva] becomes seated at the seat of enlightenment. [At that time,] he also attains the unique and thoroughly excellent [buddha qualities] of the [four] purities, etc., that are most pure and perfectly complete in every respect.

---

possible meaning, though this seems unlikely. The Tibetan translation usually means such things as "waist," or "base of spine," which also do not seem to be the intended meaning.

1441. S: *trikā,* T: *dku do*. MW (p. 461): "the loins, regio sacra, hips."

1442. S: *udaram,* T: *phyal*. That is, the belly.

1443. S: *hṛdayam,* T: *thugs ka*. Presumably the region in the center of the chest.

1444. S: *kapolam,* T: *mkhur ba*. Given the two terms that are often identified with "cheek" (i.e., *kapolam* and *gaṇḍaḥ*), it is unclear how to differentiate the two. The *Pali Critical Dictionary* gives one sense of this word as "the mucous membranes on the side-walls of the mouth-cavity." The Tibetan suggests "cheeks."

1445. S: *gaṇḍe,* T: *'gram pa*. In addition to "cheek," MW (p. 344) indicates "entire side of the face." The Tibetan can also mean "jaw."

1446. S: *śaṃkhau,* T: *spyan gyi gra gnyis*.

However, prior to that time, he or she also possesses [the marks and secondary signs] in an incomplete form while still a bodhisattva, beginning with the stage of a pure superior attitude.

Without distinction, the accumulation [of the requisites] for enlightenment, in its entirety, [is the factor that] brings about all of the marks and secondary signs. Moreover, the accumulation [of the requisites] for enlightenment is of two types: that which is distant from enlightenment and that which is near to it. Regarding this [topic], the type [of accumulation] that is distant [from enlightenment] is the one that occurs during the time that the marks and secondary signs have not yet been attained in the form of a [karmic] maturation. The type [of accumulation] that is near [to enlightenment] is the one that occurs after the marks and secondary signs have been attained initially in the form of a maturation, as well as following that point, during the time that they are becoming more excellent as their purity increases to an ever-greater degree.

The Virtuous Deeds That Produce the Marks [III.5.3]

However, these marks and secondary signs are results that are formed by a variety of deeds, which the Blessed One taught for the sake of those disciples who are desirous [of attaining them].

Why is that?

Sentient beings delight in carrying out many different kinds of evil deeds. On the other hand, upon hearing about the variety of virtuous deeds that are antidotes for those manifold evil deeds that are inimical to [spiritual development], and that also [are the factors that] bring about the marks and secondary signs, as well as that [those virtuous deeds] have a variety of beneficial results, they develop a strong aspiration [to gain] those great beneficial results and they turn away from those evil deeds. They also aspire to take up those virtuous deeds and abide in them. [These virtuous deeds and their beneficial results should be understood] as they are described in the *Lakṣaṇa Sūtra*.[1447]

By having been firmly established in [the acts of] morality, austerities, patience, and liberality [in giving], one attains the quality of having feet that are placed down well.

1447. The Sanskrit version of this sutra is not extant, nor does it exist in Tibetan translation. Cf. the Pali version, *Dīgha Nikāya*, Sutta 30.

Through traveling about here and there, etc., in order to serve one's father and mother in manifold ways, and in order to protect beings from many kinds of calamities, one attains the quality of [hands[1448] and] feet that are marked with a wheel.

By abandoning doing harm to others and taking what was not given, by making verbal salutations, honoring, standing up [as a gesture of deference], and greeting with joined palms and performing acts of homage to those worthy of being venerated, by pleasing others, by not diminishing their cherished wealth, and by overcoming one's own pride, one attains the quality of having long fingers [and toes] that is a mark of a great person.

By [carrying out] a combination of all three [types of] deeds that were taught [as producing] those three marks of a great being, one attains the quality of having feet with heels that are prominent. Moreover, regarding this [mark, it is one that is achieved this way,] because it depends upon those three marks as its support.

By bringing together venerable persons[1449] on the basis of the four principles for attracting a following, one attains the quality of hands and feet that have a weblike membrane.

By massaging the limbs of venerable beings with fragrant unguents, bathing them, and presenting them with clothing, one attains the quality of having hands and feet that are soft and youthful.

By being insatiable about [acquiring] virtuous qualities, and by developing virtuous qualities to an ever-higher degree, one attains the quality of having feet [with ankles that] do not protrude.

By having taken up and mastered the Dharma teachings properly and then taught them to others, as well as by having served properly as an emissary for others, one attains the quality of having calves like those of the *eṇeya* deer.

By being a leader who teaches the Dharma in an orderly manner, by becoming a person who has restrained him- or herself [from committing] evil deeds of body, speech, and mind and one who is not inclined to commit them, by taking care of those who are sick and giving them medicine, by raising up those who are bent over from illness, and by being a person who is moderate in his or her food and is not inclined [to indulge excessively] in

1448. Reference to the wheel mark on the hands only occurs in the Tibetan translation.

1449. *BBhVy* (f. 314a): "through bringing together the field of venerable beings and [ordinary] sentient beings . . ."

sensory pleasures, one attains the quality of having a body that is not bent over.

A person who, in a just and suitable manner, takes in those sentient beings who have been expelled by others and who, possessing [the qualities of] shame and abashment, gives them clothing attains the quality of having a sexual organ that is concealed in a sheath.

Through avoiding the pursuit of wicked acts or improper[1450] gifts and forms of enjoyment and through properly treating an imbalance of the [body's] elements, a person who is restrained in body, speech, and mind, who knows moderation regarding the acceptance of gifts and [the consuming of] food, and who gives medicine to the sick attains [a body that is] symmetrical, like the *nyagrodha* tree.

By means of the very same acts that enable one to attain the quality of having feet [with ankles that] do not protrude, one also attains the quality of having body hairs that point upward.

Through dwelling alone, through relying upon singularly excellent [spiritual] friends, through gaining an understanding of subtle meanings, through clearing away rubbish, such as grass, leaves, etc., and through clearing away dirt that occurs occasionally,[1451] a person who investigates virtue for him- or herself, who frequents those who are learned and wise, who reflects on [topics that have] subtle meanings, and who cleans the dwellings of those who are venerable, gives them massages, and bathes them attains the quality of having body hairs that grow singly.

Through having given beautiful and pleasing articles for the body, such as food, drink, vehicles, clothing, and ornaments, a person who is free of anger attains both the quality of having skin that is golden colored and [a body] that emits light a distance of one fathom.

It should be understood that the very same acts that were said [to produce] the quality of having body hairs that grow singly cause one to attain the quality of skin that is fine and smooth.

By satisfying a large multitude of people with large amounts of many different kinds of excellent food and drink, one attains the quality of [a body that has] seven elevated areas.

1450. S: *vaiṣamya*. Tibetan translations have *ma 'ongs pa,* which is undoubtedly a corruption. Perhaps the correct reading should be *ma 'os pa*.

1451. S: *āgaṃtukamalāpakarṣaḥ,* T: *blo bur gyi dri ma sel ba*. *BBhVy* (f. 315a) explains this last phrase as meaning "through sweeping places that are naturally pure, such as a *stūpa*."

A person who continually acts as a chief[1452] with regard to whatever spiritual activities need to be done for sentient beings, without being proud or cruel, and who turns sentient beings away from what is harmful and joins them to [a proper understanding of] good and evil[1453] attains the quality of having a body whose upper part is like that of a lion. This is because [such a person's behavior] resembles that of a lion in that [he or she] acts courageously in relation to the concerns of sentient beings.

It should be understood that [one] also [attains] both the quality of having well developed shoulders and the quality of having the area between the shoulders well filled out by means of these very same deeds.

The very same deeds that cause one to attain the quality of having long fingers also cause one to attain the quality of having a large and straight body.

Through abandoning slanderous speech that separates friends and reconciling those persons who are estranged, one attains the quality of having forty teeth as well as the qualities of having teeth that are even and that have no gaps.

By meditating on the form of loving-kindness that relates to the desire realm, a person who reflects upon subjects that relate to the Dharma attains the quality of having teeth that are extremely white.

One attains the quality of having jaws that resemble those of a lion by correctly giving wealth to those sentient beings who are petitioners in accordance with their wishes.

A person who is faithful and compassionate, who provides medicine and is kind[1454] attains the quality of [experiencing all] tastes as a supreme taste through protecting sentient beings as one would one's own children. [This mark is] also [attained] through having given [others] the taste of the

1452. S: *pramukhenāvasthitaḥ*, T: *gtso bor gnas pa*. *BBhVy* (f. 315a): "'A person who continually acts as a chief' means [one who is a chief] for those [persons] who are of his or her lineage (S: *vaṃśaḥ*, T: *rigs brgyud*), etc." Thus, the term "etc." (S: *ādi*, T: *la sogs pa*) indicates that the term "chief" is meant in the broadest sense of an individual who is regarded with respect as the leader of any group of individuals.

1453. S: *hitāhite*. The Tibetan drops the word "evil" (S: *ahita*) that appears in this compound and states simply: "joins them to what is beneficial" (T: *phan pa la ni btsud*).

1454. S: *prasannaḥ*, T: *dang ba dang phan pa*. This adjective has many shades of meaning, including "pure," "tranquil," "kind," and "gracious." The Tibetan translation for this term is either a corruption of *dang ba dang ldan pa* or it is rendered with two descriptive terms to reflect this breadth of meaning, which would be somewhat unusual.

Dharma, through having experienced [oneself] the taste of the Dharma, and through having restored the taste [of the Dharma] that was lost.[1455]

By taking up oneself and safeguarding the five precepts of training that consist of refraining from taking lives, etc.,[1456] by prompting others to take them up, and by being a person who, on the basis of a compassionate mind, practices taking up the Dharma to a high degree, one attains the quality of having a crown protrusion on the head and the quality of having a tongue that is large and slender.

By speaking truthfully, by speaking agreeably, and by speaking the Dharma at suitable times, one attains the quality of divine speech.

By viewing the entire world sympathetically with an attitude of loving-kindness, as a mother and father do [toward their offspring], one obtains the quality of eyes that are an intensely dark shade of blue and the quality of eyelashes that are like those of an ox.

A person who expresses genuine approval and praise for those who possess virtuous qualities attains the circle of hair between the eyebrows that is as white as a conch shell and turns to the right.

It should be understood that, without distinction, morality is the cause for attaining all of the thirty-two marks of a great person.

Why is that?

A bodhisattva whose morality is ruined will indeed not even attain the status of a human being, let alone the marks of a great person.

Regarding this [topic], it should be understood that the quality of having a crown protrusion on the head is one and the same mark of a great person as the quality of [others] not being able to see the top of [a tathāgata's] head, because [the latter] is not considered to be distinct from [the former].

This constitutes a detailed formulation of the various kinds of deeds that accord with the creation of the marks [of a great person].

1455. S: *pranaṣṭarasapariśodhanāt,* T: *nyams pa'i ro bcos pa*. The Tibetan translation does not clearly associate this sentence with the acts that generate the quality of experiencing all tastes as a supreme taste; however, there seems to be little reason to doubt that they should be associated with this mark. The sense of the phrase "through having restored the taste [of the Dharma] that was lost" is somewhat obscure; it seems to indicate the restoration of a spiritual sentiment that had been lost. *BBhVy* (f. 315b) contains the phrase "revealing clearly a meaning that was not understood," which appears to gloss this phrase.

1456. These are the layperson's five precepts of (1) not killing, (2) not stealing, (3) not engaging in sexual misconduct, (4) not lying, and (5) not drinking intoxicants.

The Four Aspects of Well-Done Spiritual Activities That Relate to the Two Factions [III.5.4]

It should be understood that the creation of all the marks is accomplished by means of the four aspects of the quality of having completed one's spiritual activities well,[1457] which pertains to the two factions.[1458] Regarding this [topic], the quality of having feet that are placed down well is produced by having carried out [spiritual] activities in a definite manner. The qualities of having [the design of] a wheel on the [hands and] feet, having feet [with ankles] that do not protrude, having hands and feet with a weblike membrane, having fine[1459] skin, having seven elevated areas, having the area between the shoulders well filled out, having shoulders that are well developed, having a body that is large and straight, and having a tongue that is large and slender are produced by having carried out [spiritual] activities in a complete manner. The qualities of having long fingers [and toes], having feet with prominent heels, having an erect body, having [a body that is] symmetrical, like the *nyagrodha* tree, and having teeth without gaps are produced by having carried out [spiritual] activities continually. The remaining marks are produced by having carried out [spiritual] activities in an irreproachable manner.

Regarding this [topic], the quality of having hands and feet that are soft and youthful and the quality of having skin that is smooth and fine are produced by employing a method of practice that does not harm sentient beings. The quality of having calves like those of the *eṇeya* deer is produced by employing a method of practice that is both orderly and timely. The qualities of emitting light that extends a distance of one fathom, having golden-colored skin, white teeth, and a white circle of hair [between the eyebrows] are produced by practicing virtue with a clear mind that is joyful and glad. The quality of having a sexual organ that is concealed in a sheath is produced by not being devoted to fame, renown, and praise, and by concealing one's good qualities. The qualities of having body hairs that point upward, hav-

1457. S: *sukṛtakarmāntatā*, T: *las kyi mtha' legs par byas pa*. See the section of the same name in Book II, chapter 2 [II.2.1], where these four aspects are addressed.

1458. The two factions are those of householders and homeless ascetics.

1459. S: *sūkṣmatvacatā*, T: *lpags pa srab pa*. The Sanskrit adjective that was used previously in relation to the sixteenth mark describes the skin as "smooth" (S: *ślakṣṇa*). Presumably, the two are meant to be understood as interchangeable. The Tibetan translation in both instances is the same—that is, "thin" or "fine."

ing forty even teeth, [experiencing all] tastes as a supreme taste, and having a crown protrusion on [the top of] the head are produced by dedicating one's virtue roots to enlightenment. The qualities of having a body whose upper part resembles that of a lion and jaws that resemble those of a lion are produced by employing a method of practice [that pursues] virtue insatiably and [with a mind that is] free of dejection. The qualities of having even teeth, eyes that are intensely dark blue, and eyelashes that are like those of an ox are produced by regarding all sentient beings equally and with a mind that seeks to benefit them. The quality of divine speech is produced by employing a method of practice that is not satisfied with anything that is deficient.

This is the manner in which the thirty-two marks of a great person are attained and perfected by means of the four aspects that relate to the quality of having completed one's spiritual activities well.

Regarding this [topic], it should be understood that these marks exist for bodhisattvas merely in a seedlike condition during the stage of the spiritual lineage. It should be understood that the course of action that is devoted to the means of attaining them [occurs] during the stage of conduct that is based upon devotion. It should be understood that [the initial form of] their attainment occurs during the stage of a pure superior attitude. It should be understood that their refinement occurs during the remaining bodhisattva stages that lie above these [first three stages]. It should be understood that their complete perfection and the state in which they have become unsurpassed occurs on the tathāgatas' aspect of the stage that is the perfect manner of going.

Regarding this [topic], because among all the spiritual qualities that are possessed by a buddha and that represent distinguishing characteristics of a great person, these marks [in particular] can be easily observed by lesser, middling, and superior beings due to their physical nature, they alone are the ones that are designated as "the marks of a great person." Moreover, [the eighty secondary attributes] are called "secondary signs" because they support the thirty-two marks of a great person by serving as their seat,[1460] and [because] they enhance the physical beauty of [a tathāgata] by their agreeable form.

1460. S: *āśrayaḥ,* T: *rten.* Literally, "that [entity] on which [the marks] rest."

The Amount of Merit That Is Required to Produce the Marks and Secondary Signs [III.5.5]

Regarding this [topic], in brief, each individual body pore of a tathāgata is produced by a heap of merit that is equal to the merit that is possessed by all sentient beings. Each individual secondary sign is produced by the same amount of merit as that which is contained in the heap of merit [necessary to create] all the body pores [of a tathāgata]. A single mark of a tathāgata is produced by a heap of merit that is a hundred times greater than that which is contained in the heap of merit [necessary to create] all the secondary signs. The circle of hair [between the eyebrows] is produced by a heap of merit that is a thousand times greater than that which is contained in the heap of merit [necessary to create] all the marks excluding the circle of hair [between the eyebrows] and the crown protrusion. The crown protrusion on top of the head, [which is also described as] the quality of not being able to see the crown of [a tathāgata's] head, is produced by a heap of merit that is a hundred thousand times greater than that which is contained in the heap of merit [necessary to create] the circle of hair [between the eyebrows]. Another quality of a tathāgata, called "the Dharma conch shell,"[1461] which is not included among the marks and secondary signs, is produced by a heap of merit that is a trillion times greater than that which is contained in the heap of merit [necessary to create] the crown protrusion. [This quality is one] by which a tathāgata, if he wishes to, can cause his voice to be understood throughout [all] the endless and limitless world systems. This is the manner in which the inconceivable and unsurpassed physical body of the tathāgatas is produced, [a body] that is attained by an immeasurable collection of merit and [a body] that encompasses every aspect of excellence.[1462]

Moreover, in brief, it should be understood that the characteristic of being immeasurable that pertains to the virtuous qualities that produce the marks and secondary signs is due to three reasons. Since [the marks and secondary signs] are attained by practicing [virtuous activities] for three [periods of] countless kalpas, there is an immeasurability of time. Since [the virtuous activities that produce the marks and secondary signs] are governed by an attitude that seeks to bring benefit and happiness to an immea-

1461. S: *dharmaśaṃkhaḥ*, T: *chos kyi dung*.

1462. In *ANS*, see the section of the topic on the inexhaustibility of effort (S: *vīryākṣayatā*, T: *brtson 'grus mi zad pa*) that addresses the merit accumulation. See also *RA*, ch. 3, vv. 1–8.

surable number of sentient beings, there is an immeasurability of attitude. Since [the marks and secondary signs] are produced by an immeasurable variety of virtuous deeds, there is an immeasurability of the types [of deeds]. Therefore, the attainment of an immeasurable collection of merit is called "the creation of the marks and secondary signs" that are possessed by the tathāgatas.

Within [Book III of] *The Stage of a Bodhisattva*, [known as] "The Object of Mental Application That Relates to the Perfection of the Support," this completes the fifth chapter, entitled "The Marks and the Secondary Signs."

6

Preeminence

The Four Forms of Complete Purity [iii.6.1]

What are the four forms of purity that are complete in every respect?

They are (1) complete purity regarding the support, (2) complete purity regarding mental objects, (3) complete purity regarding the mind, and (4) complete purity regarding knowledge.

Regarding this [topic], what is complete purity regarding the support?

The absolute termination without remainder from one's being of all forms of indisposition [brought on by entities] that relate to the mental afflictions, including their traces, along with the quality of having control over [the activities of] taking on,[1463] maintaining,[1464] and discarding[1465] one's body in whatever manner is desired is called "the purity that is complete in every respect regarding the support."

Regarding this [topic], what is complete purity regarding mental objects?

The quality of having control over all mental objects with regard to [the

1463. S: *ādānam*, T: *len pa*. *BBhVy* (f. 317b): "'Taking on' means such actions as revealing the presence of an emanation body in Tuṣita Paradise, etc. Such acts as the revealing of a buddha's body to a buddha's disciples should be learned by examining the *Sūtra on the Mysteries of the Tathāgata*." This may be a reference to the *Tathāgatācintyaguhyanirdeśa-sūtra,* which is the third work in the Ratnakūṭa collection.

1464. S: *sthānam*, T: *gnas pa*. *BBhVy* (ff. 317b–318a): "'Maintaining' means to remain for as long as samsara exists for the sake of sentient beings or to have the power to remain [alive] by empowering one's life force."

1465. S: *cyutiḥ*, T: *'chi pho ba*. *BBhVy* (f. 318a): "'Discarding' means to display the appearance of [entering] the great nirvana or to have the power to give up one's life."

activities of] emanating,[1466] transforming,[1467] and manifesting[1468] is called "the purity that is complete in every respect regarding mental objects."

Regarding this [topic], what is complete purity regarding the mind?

As [described] before,[1469] the removal of all forms of indisposition that relate to the mind as well as the accumulation of every form of the roots of virtue in the mind is called "the purity that is complete in every respect regarding the mind."[1470]

Regarding this [topic], what is complete purity regarding knowledge?

As [described] before, the quality of having control over knowledge because all forms of indisposition [brought on by entities] that relate to ignorance have been removed and because one's knowledge is not obscured anywhere with regard to objects that need to be known is called "the purity that is complete in every respect regarding knowledge."

The Ten Powers [III.6.2]

Regarding this [topic], what are the ten powers of a tathāgata?

They are (1) the power of knowledge regarding proper and improper conditions; (2) the power of knowledge regarding [the fact that] one's deeds are one's own; (3) the power of knowledge regarding the absorptions, the liberations, and entering states of one-pointed concentration; (4) the power of knowledge regarding superior and inferior faculties; (5) the power of knowledge regarding diverse forms of devotion; (6) the power of knowledge regarding diverse constituent elements; (7) the power of knowledge regarding the paths that lead everywhere; (8) the power of knowledge regarding recollection of former existences; (9) the power of knowledge regarding death and rebirth; and (10) the power of knowledge regarding termina-

1466. S: *nirmāṇam,* T: *sprul pa. BBhVy* (f. 318a): "'Emanating' means the act of creating a form that did not exist before and that has the appearance of a sentient being."

1467. S: *pariṇāmaḥ,* T: *bsgyur ba. BBhVy* (f. 318a): "'Transforming' means the act of causing an object to become a different object."

1468. S: *saṃprakhyānam,* T: *bstan pa. BBhVy* (f. 318a): "'Manifesting' means the act of causing an object to appear that did not exist before and that is considered to be a sentient being."

1469. *BBhVy* (f. 318a): "'As [described] before' means as was indicated [previously] by the phrase 'including the traces.'"

1470. *MSAVy,* p. 177: "Complete purity regarding the mind is [defined] in terms of the quality of having control over every aspect of one-pointed concentration."

tion of the outflows. These ten powers should be understood as they are described at length in the *Sutra on the Ten Powers.*[1471]

The Power of Knowledge regarding Proper and Improper Conditions [III.6.2.1]

Regarding this [topic], he is called "the Tathāgata" because everything whatsoever that he utters, speaks, or declares is unerring and exists in the manner [that he declares it to be].[1472]

Regarding this [topic], a cause that is not at variance with both pleasant and unpleasant results and that will truly lead to their occurrence is called their "proper condition,"[1473] their "base,"[1474] their "foundation,"[1475] and their "originating factor."[1476] A cause that is incompatible with those very pleasant and unpleasant results is called their "improper condition" by virtue of its being the opposite of [a proper condition].

Knowledge that is free of exaggerated pride[1477] [is the kind that] is said to be "in accordance with reality." It should be understood that knowledge

1471. S: *Daśabalasūtram,* T: *sTobs bcu'i mdo.* Significant portions of the text also appear in *AKV,* vol. 4, pp. 1083–1085.

1472. See Book I, chapter 7, for a similar explanation of the literal meaning of the epithet "Tathāgata." Asaṅga addresses here all the significant terms and phrases that appear in the canonical descriptions of each of the ten powers. They are presented in the translation in quotation marks. The complete passage that relates to this power declares: "O Long-Lived Ones, here the Tathāgata knows, in accordance with reality, how proper conditions are proper and improper conditions are improper. O Long-Lived Ones, that which the Tathāgata knows, in accordance with reality, regarding how proper conditions are proper and improper conditions are improper is the first of the Tathāgata's [ten] powers. By having gained possession of this power, the Tathāgata, the Arhat, the true and complete Buddha affirms [that he has attained] the exalted and most excellent state, he turns the divine wheel, and he utters the true roar of a lion in an assembly."

1473. S: *sthānam,* T: *gnas.* Other translations generally render this term as meaning what is "possible." MW (p. 1263) gives a wide range of meanings. The relevant ones are "proper place," "case," "occurrence," "occasion," "opportunity," and "cause."

1474. S: *pratiṣṭhā,* T: *gzhi. BBhVy* (f. 318b): "It is a base because a result is based upon it."

1475. S: *niśrayaḥ,* T: *rten. BBhVy* (f. 318b): "It is a foundation because [a result] arises in dependence upon it."

1476. S: *abhinirvartakaḥ* (W: *nirvartakaḥ*), T: *mngon par 'grub par byed pa. BBhVy* (f. 318b): "It is an originating factor because it is the means by which [a result] is produced."

1477. S: *nirabhimānam,* T: *mngon pa'i nga rgyal med pa.* "Exaggerated pride" (see note 314) is a form of pride that stems from mistakenly believing oneself to know something, when,

of everything, unimpeded knowledge, and pure [knowledge are the types that here] are [described as being] free of exaggerated pride. The explanation of such terms as "knowledge of everything," etc., should be understood as [explained] previously in the chapter on supreme enlightenment.[1478]

In accordance with the regular order of enumeration, [the power of knowledge regarding proper and improper conditions] is the first [of the ten powers].

Because it is [a quality that is] unsurpassed, because it possesses the ability to act on behalf of all sentient beings in every manner, and because it defeats absolutely[1479] all the forces of Māra, it is called a "power."

The quality of having control over the use [of this power] in whatever way is desired, through having correctly acquired the causes [that bring about its] attainment, is called its "possession."

Because it is unsurpassed, nirvana is called an "exalted" [state]. Because it is attained by means of the eightfold ārya path and because it [is a state] in which all misfortune and fear have been eliminated, [nirvana] is called the "most excellent"[1480] [state].

Because of the [Buddha's] assertion regarding his own attainment [of this state, the sutra] states that he "affirms" [this].

Because, following his own attainment [of this state], he also taught it to others extensively out of compassion, [the sutra] states that he "turns the divine wheel."

Why is [his act of teaching described in] that [way]?

The following are epithets of the Tathāgata: "Divine One,"[1481] "Tran-

---

in fact, one does not. A form of knowledge that is free of this attitude represents knowledge that is unmistaken.

1478. See Book I, chapter 7, for a description of these three characteristics.

1479. S: *atyantam*, T: *gtan du*. This adverbial element can mean variously "absolutely," "perfectly," "completely," and "perpetually" (MW, p. 16).

1480. S: *ārṣabham*, T: *khyu mchog*. This adjective is derived from the noun *ṛshabhaḥ* (T: *khyu mchog*), which literally means "a bull" or "any male in general," and metaphorically "the best or most excellent of any kind or race" (MW, p. 226). Asaṅga illustrates here the tradition of presenting a literal interpretation (S: *nirvacanam*, T: *nges tshig*) of a term by incorporating each of its syllables in the explanation—that is, the two syllables *ārṣa* are represented by the phrase "by the eightfold ārya path" (S: *āryāṣṭāṅgeṇa mārgeṇa*) and the final syllable *bham* is represented by the word "fear" (S: *bhayam*) that occurs in the phrase "all misfortune and fear have been eliminated."

1481. S: *brahmaḥ*, T: *tshangs pa*. This term derives from a verbal root that means "to expand" or "to increase." The masculine form of the noun generally means the "one divine essence

quil One,"[1482] and "Emancipated One."[1483] He is the one who turned [the wheel of the Dharma] and the one who did so for the first time; [then] other persons [turned] it again for [still] others. In this way, through an uninterrupted series [of teachers], [the wheel] that was set in motion by the Divine One reached the entire collection of sentient beings. Therefore, it is called "the divine wheel."

Because he proclaimed himself to be the one whose instruction is supreme and the one who attained the perfection of [being] the unsurpassed teacher, because he defeats all false doctrines by teaching the [true] path, because he remains completely undaunted in the presence of those who voice opposition to his path, and because he raises his exalted and unsurpassed voice to defeat all opponents, [the sutra] states "he utters the true roar of a lion in an assembly."

In short, [this passage] lays open, reveals, points out, and expresses the perfection of knowledge regarding what is beneficial to oneself, the perfection of knowledge regarding what is beneficial to others, and the unique nature of the perfection of knowledge regarding what is beneficial both to oneself and to others.

Another formulation of the summary meaning [of this passage is that it indicates the following.] "There is [a goal] to be attained, a method of attaining it, and the protection [provided] to all beings by that method. Any and all human beings or gods who wish to can obtain that method from me."

Regarding this [topic], the exalted and most excellent state [of nirvana] should be regarded as resembling [a state in which] an illness has been cured. The turning of the divine wheel should be regarded as resembling the means of curing that illness. The utterance of the true roar of a lion in an assembly should be regarded as resembling the refutation of all the assertions made by inferior physicians as well as the [the Buddha's] affirmation that he is the one who will surely cure the illness.

---

from which all things emanate" (MW, p. 738). In the Buddhist context, it is used to indicate that Buddha is the supremely divine being. The neuter form of the noun is also used to refer to the state of nirvana or supreme enlightenment.

1482. S: *śāntaḥ,* T: *zhi ba*. Literally, the term means "the one who has pacified him- or herself" in the sense of having become free of the passions or mental afflictions.

1483. S: *śītībhūtaḥ,* T: *bsil bar gyur pa*. The adjective *śīta* (T: *bsil ba*) means "cold" or "cool," and in this context alludes to the cooling of the mental afflictions. The term *śītībhūtaḥ* ("one who has become cool") indicates one who has attained emancipation.

The Power of Knowledge regarding [the Fact That] One's Deeds Are One's Own[1484] [III.6.2.2]

Those deeds that have been performed and accumulated,[1485] and that have since ceased, are said to be [deeds] of the "past." Those that have not yet been performed, have not yet ceased, and are not [currently] being performed but will be performed in the future are said to be those of the "future." Those deeds whose performance has not yet been completed and has not yet ceased but which have been resolved [to be done] and are in the course of being carried out are said to be those of the "present." Moreover, these [deeds] are classified as being of three kinds: physical deeds, verbal deeds, and mental deeds.

1484. S: *karmasvakajñānabalam,* T: *las bdag gir bya ba mkhyen pa'i stobs.* The term *svaka* in this phrase literally means that which is "one's own." In this case, it refers specifically to the fact that each sentient being is subject to the consequences of the deeds that he or she carries out personally. This aspect of the doctrine of karma is also described as a condition for which each individual must accept responsibility (S: *svīkaraṇam,* T: *bdag gir byed pa*). Another name for this power is "the power of knowledge regarding deeds and their ripening" (S: *karmavipākajñānabalam,* T: *las dang rnam par smin pa mkhyen pa'i stobs*). The introductory statement from the sutras that addresses this power declares: "Furthermore, O Long-Lived Ones, the Tathāgata knows, in accordance with reality, the past, present, and future deeds that relate to taking up what is right in terms of their place, their cause, their basis, and their ripening. O Long-Lived Ones, that which the Tathāgata knows, in accordance with reality, regarding the past, present, and future deeds that relate to taking up what is right in terms of their place, their cause, their basis, and their ripening, is the second of the Tathāgata's [ten] powers."

1485. *YBh* (p. 190): "What is a deed that has been performed (S: *kṛtaṃ karma,* T: *las byas pa*)? It is one that has been considered and then fixed in the mind, after which it is further carried out physically or verbally. A deed that has not been performed is one that was not considered and was not fixed in the mind, and [therefore] was not carried out either physically or verbally. What is a deed that has been accumulated? It is any [performed] deed other than the following ten kinds: (1) one that was performed in a dream; (2) one that was performed unknowingly; (3) one that was not performed intentionally; (4) one that was neither performed with intensity nor continually; (5) one that was performed erroneously; (6) one that was performed because of a lapse of recollection; (7) one that was performed unwillingly; (8) one that has an indeterminate nature; (9) one that has been weakened through regret; and (10) one that has been weakened by an antidote. A deed that has not been accumulated is [any of] those ten types that were just described. An intentional deed is one that was either performed or accumulated intentionally. An unintentional deed is one that was performed unintentionally. A deed that is certain to be experienced is an intentional [deed] that was both performed and accumulated. A deed that is not certain to be experienced is an intentional [deed] that was performed but was not accumulated."

As was described earlier,[1486] there are four ways of taking up what is right—that is to say, "there is a way of taking up what is right that is pleasant in the present but has a ripening that consists of suffering,"[1487] and so forth. These [four ways of taking up what is right] should be understood, in the appropriate manner, in terms of how they are beneficial or harmful in the present life and in future lives.

The region in which [deeds] are carried out is called their "place." The animate or inanimate entities in relation to which [deeds] are carried out is called their "basis." The particular root of nonvirtue or root of virtue that is the motivating factor which causes [deeds] to be carried out is called their "cause." The desirable results that have beneficial qualities and the undesirable [results] that have adverse qualities are called the "ripening" [of deeds].

Combining all of these [elements] together, [the meaning of this power is that] the tathāgatas possess knowledge of deeds in all their aspects—[including those of] all the [three] times, in all their varieties, in all the circumstances in which they are carried out, in all the regions [where they are carried out], as well as all the bases [in relation to which deeds are carried out], all their motivating factors, and all their disadvantages and benefits. There is no [knowledge of deeds] that is superior to this and none that exceeds it.

The Power of Knowledge regarding the Meditative Absorptions, the Liberations, and Entering States of One-Pointed Concentration[1488] [III.6.2.3]

There are four "meditative absorptions" and eight "liberations." The way in

1486. See Book I, chapter 3, in the section entitled "The Quality of Being Linked to What Is Beneficial" [I.3.3].

1487. This statement describes the first of the four ways of taking up what is right (S: *dharmasamādānam,* T: *chos yang dang par len pa*), which in fact represents an improper form of conduct.

1488. S: *dhyānavimokṣasamādhisamāpattijñānabalam,* T: *bsam gtan dang rnam par thar pa* and *ting nge 'dzin la snyoms par 'jug pa mkhyen pa'i stobs.* The sutra passage that relates to this power declares: "Furthermore, O Long-Lived Ones, the Tathāgata knows, in accordance with reality, [the ways of] becoming afflicted and becoming more refined and what the formulations and [methods of] purification are that pertain to the meditative absorptions, the liberations, and the entering of states of one-pointed concentration. O Long-Lived Ones, that which the Tathāgata knows, in accordance with reality, regarding [the ways of] becoming afflicted and becoming more refined and what the formulations and

which those who have gained fitness of mind[1489] and control of the mind by means of the meditative absorptions and liberations are able to enter various forms of one-pointed concentration that conform to those [absorptions and liberations] in order to achieve any aim that is desired is called "entering a state of one-pointed concentration."[1490] As a portion [of a sutra passage] declares, "The Blessed One entered a state of one-pointed concentration that conformed to that [aim]. In accordance with the way his mind was composed, the entire Brahmā realm became filled with extraordinary light. The sound of his speech was also heard, but no one could see him." In just this way, whatever common worldly aim or unique [transcendent aim] a tathāgata desires to accomplish, he does so with great ease by entering a state of one-pointed concentration that conforms to that [aim].

Regarding this [topic], the successful attainment of all the desired aims that depend on the mind [comes about] by means of the meditative absorptions and the liberations and through gaining power over the mind. That is the full extent of what all practitioners of meditative absorption need to accomplish. There is nothing superior to this and nothing beyond this. And the tathāgatas have attained every aspect of what practitioners of meditative absorption need to accomplish. This is the reason for the phrase: "the meditative absorptions, the liberations, and entering states of one-pointed concentration."

Moreover, in brief there are two [ways of] "becoming afflicted" that pertain to the meditative absorptions, etc. [One is] the [form of] affliction [that acts as] an obstruction to the attainment of those [meditative absorptions, etc.,] that have not yet been attained, such as making use of an ineffective means [of attaining them] or engaging in any of the [five] hindrances.[1491]

[methods of] purification are that pertain to the meditative absorptions, the liberations, and the entering of states of one-pointed concentration, is the third of the Tathāgata's [ten] powers."

1489. S: *karmaṇyacetasaḥ,* T: *sems las su rung ba*. This quality, which is associated with the mental factor "agility," is gained with the development of one-pointed concentration. See note 382.

1490. S: *samādhisamāpattiḥ,* T: *ting nge 'dzin la snyoms par 'jug pa*. The term *samāpattiḥ* (T: *snyoms par 'jug pa*) can be understood either as the abstract noun "state of composure" or as the action of "entering" a meditative state. Here Asaṅga interprets it in the latter sense and that is how it is translated into Tibetan. However, the four terms that are referenced in connection with this power might also be rendered as a simple series: "the absorptions, the liberations, the one-pointed concentrations, and the states of composure."

1491. See note 138.

[The second is to be overcome by] the perturbing action of an [overt] mental affliction that occurs on the particular level [of a meditative absorption, etc.,] that has been attained or [to be adversely affected by] the latency[1492] [of such a mental affliction]. By contrast, there are two [ways of] "becoming more refined." They should be understood as being the opposites of those [two ways of becoming afflicted].

The [verbal act of] formulating, in an appropriate manner and using suitable words and expressions, those various states of meditative absorption, etc., that have been achieved is called their "formulation."[1493]

The further development of those very states of meditative absorption, etc., that have been attained, by means of [continued] meditative practice, as well as the attainment [of a level of development] in the manner desired and the attainment of a state of excellence [and the ability to do so] without difficulty is called [the method of] their "purification."[1494]

Regarding this [topic], a tathāgata knows everything about how these [meditative absorptions, etc.,] fail to be achieved, how they are achieved, what is inferior about them, what is excellent about them, the terms [to use in explaining] them, as well as the culmination of their development. Therefore, this unsurpassed [power] of the tathāgatas is called "the power of knowledge regarding the absorptions, the liberations, and entering states of one-pointed concentration."

The Power of Knowledge regarding Superior and Inferior Faculties[1495] [III.6.2.4]

The condition of being weak, middling, or great that pertains to the five

1492. See notes 608 and 885.

1493. S: *vyavasthānam*, T: *rnam par gzhag pa*. This term refers to a precise and accurate presentation or verbal description of the range of essential points relevant to a particular topic.

1494. S: *viśuddhiḥ*, T: *rnam par dag pa*. Literally, the term means "complete purification"; it includes both the process of refinement that removes imperfections and the state that marks the completion of that process.

1495. S: *indriyaparāparajñānabalam*, T: *dbang po mchog dang mchog ma yin pa mkhyen pa'i stobs*. The sutra passage that relates to this power declares: "Furthermore, O Long-Lived Ones, the Tathāgata knows, in accordance with reality, the superior and inferior state of the faculties of other beings and other persons. O Long-Lived Ones, that which the Tathāgata knows, in accordance with reality, regarding the superior and inferior state of the faculties of other beings and other persons, is the fourth of the Tathāgata's powers."

faculties[1496] of faith, etc., according to the [level of] development that their ripening has reached, is called "the superior and inferior state of the faculties."

The Power of Knowledge regarding Diverse Forms of Devotion[1497] [III.6.2.5]

The lesser, moderate, and great forms of admiration[1498] that are preceded by faith toward others[1499] and the precise understanding[1500] that is preceded by reflection upon the Dharma[1501] are called "the nature of diverse forms of devotion."

1496. S: *pañcendriyāṇi,* T: *dbang po lnga*. As Asaṅga notes, the term "faculty" here refers to the five spiritual faculties of faith, recollection, effort, one-pointed concentration, and wisdom. See note 564 and accompanying text for a comprehensive list of the twenty-two kinds of faculties that are addressed in Buddhist literature.

1497. S: *nānādhimuktijñānabalam,* T: *mos pa sna tshogs mkhyen pa'i stobs*. The sutra passage that relates to this power declares: "Furthermore, O Long-Lived Ones, the Tathāgata knows, in accordance with reality, the state of diverse forms of devotion that are possessed by other beings and other persons. O Long-Lived Ones, that which the Tathāgata knows, in accordance with reality, regarding the state of diverse forms of devotion that are possessed by other beings and other persons, is the fifth of the Tathāgata's powers."

1498. S: *ruciḥ,* T: *'dod pa*. While this term generally refers to the mental attitude of "liking," "taking pleasure in," or "longing for" something (MW, p. 882), here it is being used in connection with the feeling of faith toward a spiritual teacher. Therefore, it is translated here as "admiration."

1499. S: *paraśraddhāpūrvā,* T: *gzhan las dad pa sngon du 'gro ba*. *BBhVy* (f. 322a) identifies this form of devotion with the type of person who pursues the Dharma by relying upon faith (S: *śraddhānusarī,* T: *dad pas rjes su 'brang ba*) in the instruction that is received from those teachers who are looked upon with admiration.

1500. S: *pratyavagamaḥ,* T: *rtogs pa*. This "precise understanding" is one that is gained by an individual who pursues the Dharma after having personally verified its meaning.

1501. S: *dharmavicāraṇapūrvā,* T: *chos kyi spyod pa sngon du 'gro ba*. *BBhVy* (f. 322a) identifies this form of devotion with the type of person who pursues the Dharma by relying upon knowledge gained by carefully investigating the meaning of instruction for him- or herself (S: *dharmānusarī,* T: *chos kyi rjes su 'brang ba*).

The Power of Knowledge regarding Diverse Constituent Elements[1502] [III.6.2.6]

The formulations of the different kinds of spiritual lineage include the spiritual lineages of the listener disciple, the solitary realizer, and [the bodhisattvas who belong to the lineage of] the tathāgatas. In addition, according to the doctrine that classifies [persons as having] a strong tendency to develop desire, etc.,[1503] there are also up to eighty thousand kinds of unfavorable mental traits[1504] [that can be exhibited by] sentient beings. [These distinctions] are called "the nature of diverse constituent elements."[1505]

1502. S: *nānādhātujñānabalam,* T: *khams sna tshogs mkhyen pa'i stobs.* The sutra passage that relates to this power declares: "Furthermore, O Long-Lived Ones, the Tathāgata knows, in accordance with reality, the world with its diverse and multiple constituent elements. O Long-Lived Ones, that which the Tathāgata knows, in accordance with reality, regarding the world with its diverse and multiple constituent elements, is the sixth of the Tathāgata's powers."

1503. Asaṅga describes several classifications of personality types in his *ŚBh.* One classification identifies seven types of person based on the degree to which one may be especially susceptible to any of five mental afflictions. The seven are described as (1) one who has a strong tendency to develop desire; (2) one who has a strong tendency to develop hatred; (3) one who has a strong tendency to develop ignorance; (4) one who has a strong tendency to develop pride; (5) one who has a strong tendency to develop discursive thoughts; (6) one who is equally [but only moderately] disposed [to all the mental afflictions]; and (7) one whose mental afflictions are weak.

1504. S: *caritam,* T: *spyod pa.* Although this term literally means "conduct" or "behavior," in this context, it refers to the tendency for an individual to be under the influence of a particular form of the mental afflictions, of which there are eighty thousand possible permutations; hence I translate it as "unfavorable mental trait." Five principal forms are the strong tendency to develop desire, hatred, ignorance, pride, or discursive thoughts. See previous note.

1505. S: *nānādhātukatā,* T: *khams sna tshogs pa nyid.* Asaṅga here interprets the term *dhātuḥ* (T: *khams*) as being synonymous with "spiritual lineage" (S: *gotram,* T: *rigs*) and also as referring to various classifications of types of persons. See note 114, where "constituent element" is a synonym for the term "spiritual lineage."

The Power of Knowledge regarding the Paths That Lead Everywhere[1506] [III.6.2.7]

The forms of spiritual practice that are the appropriate starting points for [each of] those very [individuals][1507]—for example, unattractiveness is [the meditation topic that is meant] for those who have a strong tendency to develop desire, [etc., as explained] at length in *The Stage of a Listener*—are called "the paths that lead everywhere." An alternate interpretation is that all of those [forms of conduct] that lead to the five migratory states[1508] are called "the paths that lead everywhere." Yet another interpretation is that the forms of conduct that allow us to proceed in an irreproachable manner in all ways, both in this world and in future lives, are called "[the paths] that lead everywhere," as opposed to [what is urged by] those ascetics and brahmins who fall outside of this [Buddhist] tradition, who are in opposition with one another, who rely on a variety of [biased] philosophical positions, and who profess views and predilections that are regarded with mutual hostility. For example, [these forms of conduct are described] in the *Kālāma Sūtra*[1509] and others.

1506. S: *sarvatragāminīpratipajjñānabalam,* T: *thams cad du 'gro ba'i lam mkhyen pa'i stobs*. The sutra passage that relates to this power declares: "Furthermore, O Long-Lived Ones, the Tathāgata knows, in accordance with reality, the paths that lead everywhere. That which the Tathāgata knows, in accordance with reality, regarding the paths that lead everywhere, is the seventh of the Tathāgata's powers."

1507. That is, the ones referred to in the previous power as having "a strong tendency to develop desire, etc." The appropriate meditation topics for the other four types of person are loving-kindness for those who have a strong tendency to develop hatred; dependent origination for those who have a strong tendency to develop ignorance; the diversity of the elements for those who have a strong tendency to develop pride; and recollection of one's breath for those who have a strong tendency to develop discursive thoughts.

1508. S: *pañca gatāni,* T: *'gro ba lnga*. They are hell beings, hungry ghosts, animals, humans, and gods.

1509. T: *sGyu stsal shes kyi bu'i mdo*. Both published Sanskrit editions incorrectly read "in the *Kāma Sūtra* and others." While there are in fact Buddhist sutras with this title, both in verse and prose, the Tibetan translation seems to be the correct reading. Though no Sanskrit example of the *Kālāma Sūtra* seems to be extant, in the Pali version (see *Aṅguttara Nikāya,* The Book of Threes, Sutta 65) the Buddha tells the Kālāmas, a people from the town of Keśaputra, how to conduct themselves in an environment where ascetics and brahmins are propounding a variety of competing views and contentiously reviling those who disagree with them. The Buddha teaches irreproachable moral principles to live by and advises that these will enable an individual to obtain four kinds of "solace" or "relief" (S:

The Power of Knowledge regarding the Recollection of Former Existences[1510] [III.6.2.8]

As [the Tathāgata] recalls his diverse former existences, he remembers, in brief, six circumstances[1511] about his previous, bygone existences that correlate with the eight basic elements of life[1512] that consist of having distinct names, [observing distinct] customs, and [experiencing distinct] occurrences [due to having been born in] a variety of classes of sentient being—such as those that lie in the east, south, west, and north.

What are the eight basic elements of life?

They are (1) having a certain name, (2) being of a certain family, (3) being of a certain clan, (4) eating certain kinds of food, (5) experiencing certain kinds of happiness and suffering, (6) being one who has a certain [potential] longevity, (7) being one who [actually] remains alive for a certain period of time, and (8) being one whose life ends in a certain way.

---

catvāryāśvāsāḥ, T: *dbugs dbyung ba bzhi*) that will be beneficial both in this life and in future lives. The main forms of irreproachable conduct that are mentioned in this sutra are to cultivate (1) the three roots of virtue—that is, avoidance of desire, avoidance of hatred, and avoidance of ignorance; (2) avoidance of the ten nonvirtuous karmic paths; and (3) the four immeasurables of loving-kindness, compassion, joy, and equanimity.

1510. S: *pūrvanivāsānusmṛtijñānabalam,* T: *sngon gyi gnas rjes su dran pa mkhyen pa'i stobs.* The sutra passage that relates to this power declares: "Furthermore, O Long-Lived Ones, the Tathāgata recalls multiple former existences, such as a single birth, two, three, four, five, six, seven, eight, nine, ten, twenty, thirty, forty, fifty, a hundred births, a thousand births, a hundred thousand births, as well as many hundreds of births, many thousands of births, and many hundreds of thousands of births, a kalpa of dissolution, a kalpa of formation, as well as a kalpa of dissolution and formation, many kalpas of dissolution, many kalpas of formation, and many kalpas of dissolution and formation. He recalls, 'The beings [of the place] where I existed [at that time were known by] such and such a name. I had this name, was of this family and of this clan. [I ate] this food, experienced this happiness and suffering, had this longevity, this life span, and this end of life. Having passed away from that place, I was born in this other place. Having passed away from that place as well, I was born here.' In this way, the Tathāgata recalls multiple former existences together with their aspects, particulars, and features. That which the Tathāgata knows, with regard to recalling multiple former existences, . . . is the eighth of the Tathāgata's powers."

1511. S: *ṣaḍvidhaṃ caritam,* T: *spyod pa rnam pa drug.* While *caritam* usually means "conduct," "behavior," "acts," "deeds" (MW, p. 389), the description of its six types in the present usage led to the rendering "circumstance."

1512. S: *aṣṭau vyavahārapadāni,* T: *tha snad kyi gzhi brgyad.* (MW, p. 1034): The term *vyavahāra* here means "a matter that relates to ordinary life" and *pada* means some "basis" or "element" of those affairs; hence I have rendered the compound as "basic element of life."

What are the six circumstances that relate to the basic elements of life?

They are (1) the name by which one is addressed; (2) the caste, such as the ruling class,[1513] etc., to which one belongs; (3) one's mother and father; (4) the type of food and drink that one consumes; (5) one's good and bad fortune; and (6) the diversity of one's life span.

Thus, when individuals describe themselves or others in the world, they make reference to these six circumstances that are based on the eight basic elements of life. [For example,] one says, (1) "This is my name," or "That is his or her name." (2) "I belong to the ruling class," or "He or she belongs to the ruling class," or "I belong to the priestly class," or the working class, or the servile class; or, "He or she belongs to the priestly class," or the working class, or the servile class. (3) "This is my father," or "This is his or her father." Just as with someone's father, the same applies to that [person's] mother. (4) "I eat this type of food," whether it is mixed beverages,[1514] cakes, or different kinds of porridge and sour gruel; or, "Others [eat them]." (5) Similarly, "I experienced such a misfortune or good fortune," or "This person [experienced them]." (6) "I have reached such a stage of life," whether a youth, a middle-aged person, or an elderly person; or, "This person [has reached some stage of life]." These are the six circumstances that correlate with the [eight] basic elements of life. There are no circumstances or basic elements of life beyond these. Therefore, this is the full range of what [a tathāgata] recalls. There is nothing more than this.

Regarding this [topic], the circumstances that constitute the affairs of [a person's] life are its "aspects." The basic elements of [a person's] life are its "features." Because [a tathāgata] recalls them, [the sutra] declares that "[the Tathāgata] recalls [multiple former existences] together with their aspects and features."

1513. The four traditional castes are (1) the priestly class (S: *brāhmaṇaḥ,* T: *bram ze*); (2) the ruling class (S: *kṣatriyaḥ,* T: *rgyal rigs*); (3) the working class (S: *vaiśya,* T: *rje'u rigs*), traditionally those who engage in agriculture, raising cattle, or commerce; and (4) the servile class (S: *śūdraḥ,* T: *dmangs rigs*).

1514. S: *manthaḥ,* T: *de khu*. A beverage in which other ingredients are mixed by stirring; a typical example is parched barley-meal mixed with milk.

The Power of Knowledge regarding Death and Rebirth[1515] [III.6.2.9]

Regarding this [topic], the divine abodes [of the gods] are said to be those that are related to the [four] meditative absorptions. Because [the Tathāgata's] eye is based upon those [meditative absorptions], because it is the fruit of those [meditative absorptions], and because it is taken hold of by those [meditative absorptions], it is called the "divine eye." Because [the Tathāgata's] eye is the fruit of the meditative absorptions that have been most highly accomplished and fully perfected, it is called [the divine eye that is] "perfectly pure." Because [the Tathāgata's eye] is distinct even in name from that of humans, it called [the divine eye] "which surpasses that of humans." There is also a divine eye that the gods who live in the desire realm obtain at birth and that resembles [the Tathāgata's eye] only to the extent that it has the same name. By contrast, [the ordinary eye] of humans does not even have the quality [that would allow it to be referred to by that name].

Sentient beings who are dying are described by the expression "[those] who are passing away." Those who are in the intermediate state are described by the expression "those who are being reborn." Those two types [of sentient

1515. S: *cyutyupapattijñānabalam,* T: *'chi 'pho ba dang skye ba mkhyen pa'i stobs.* The sutra passage that relates to this power declares: "Furthermore, O Long-Lived Ones, the Tathāgata, by means of his pure, divine eye, which surpasses that of humans, sees those sentient beings who are passing away as well as those who are being reborn. He knows, in accordance with reality, those sentient beings of good appearance as well as those of bad appearance, those who are inferior as well as those who are excellent, and those who are proceeding according to their deeds by going either to a happy migratory state or going to an unhappy migratory state. He recognizes that those sentient beings who possess physical misdeeds and who possess verbal and mental misdeeds, who discredit the āryas, who hold wrong views, and who, on account of their deeds that relate to taking up what is right in the form of wrong views, due to that cause, due to that condition, following the dissolution of their bodies and their death, will [descend into] the lower realms, the unhappy migratory states, and the states of downfall, and be reborn in the hells. He also recognizes that those sentient beings who possess good physical deeds and who possess good verbal and mental deeds, who do not discredit the āryas, who hold the right view, and who, on account of their deeds that relate to taking up what is right in the form of right view, due to that cause, due to that condition, following the dissolution of their bodies and their death, will be reborn among the gods in a happy migratory state and in a celestial world. O Long-Lived Ones, that which the Tathāgata, by means of his pure, divine eye, which surpasses that of humans, sees . . . is the eighth of the Tathāgata's powers."

beings] who are traveling into darkness[1516] are proceeding to their next existence as intermediate state beings whose [subtle] mental body resembles either a [piece of] black felt cloth or a night that is enveloped in thick darkness. Therefore, they are called "those [sentient beings] of bad appearance." On the other hand, those two types [of sentient beings] who are traveling into light[1517] are proceeding to their next existence as intermediate state beings whose [subtle] mental body resembles either a moonlit night or a fine [piece of] Varanasi cloth. Therefore, they are called "those [sentient beings] of good appearance." Regarding this [topic], those of bad appearance are "inferior"; those of good appearance are "excellent." Those who are inferior are the ones who are proceeding to the unhappy migratory states. Those who are excellent are the ones who are proceeding to the happy migratory states.

Due to their errant conduct, along with [the errant thoughts] that gave rise to [their conduct], they are described as "those who possess physical, verbal, and mental misdeeds." Those who hold the two types of wrong understanding and errant views—[namely,] the discrediting of everything[1518] and the discrediting of those āryas who abide in the opposite of that opinion[1519]— are called "those who hold wrong views" and "those who discredit the āryas."

Due to these wrong views, [sentient beings] develop wrong beliefs about causes and results. For that reason and due to that condition, they carry out wrongful deeds. Those who carry out wrongful deeds adopt either the way of taking up what is right that is pleasurable in the present but has a painful ripening in the future or the way of taking up what is right that is both painful in the present and also has a painful ripening in the future. Therefore,

1516. T: *tamaḥparāyaṇaḥ,* T: *mun khrod du 'gro ba*. The scriptures describe four kinds of sentient beings: (1) those who travel from darkness to light, (2) those who travel from darkness to darkness, (3) those who travel from light to light, and (4) those who travel from light to darkness. The ones being referred to here are those sentient beings who are going to be reborn in the "darkness" of one of the unhappy migratory states.

1517. S: *jyotiṣparāyaṇaḥ,* T: *snang bar 'gro ba*. That is, those who are going to be reborn in one of the happy migratory states.

1518. S: *sarvāpavādaḥ,* T: *thams cad la skur pa 'debs pa*. That is, the discrediting of cause and effect, the doctrines of karma and of past and future lives.

1519. "That opinion" is the opinion of those who discredit cause and effect. "Those āryas" are buddhas, bodhisattva āryas, solitary realizer āryas, and listener āryas.

[the sutra] states: "on account of their deeds that relate to taking up what is right in the form of wrong views."

Because they will proceed to the lower realms on the basis of those very [wrong views and wrongful deeds], even though they may possess many other virtuous qualities, [the sutra] states: "due to that cause, due to that condition."

Because name and form become separated from one another, [the sutra] states: "[following] the dissolution of their bodies."

Because this is the very lowest of all deaths, [the sutra] states: "following death."

In order to present an expression that refers to the hells, [the sutra] refers to them as "the lower realms, the unhappy migratory states, and the states of downfall."

In order to describe the nature [of those realms], the bodies [of the beings who are born there], and the conditions [that the beings who are born there must experience, the sutra] refers to [those realms] as "the hells."

Regarding this [topic], wicked and crude conduct is called "a downward path," because it leads to a [lower] place. Therefore, [the places that one is led to by such conduct] are called "the lower realms."[1520] They are called "unhappy migratory states"[1521] because one encounters suffering there and because many kinds of intense suffering are experienced there continually and for a long time. They are called "states of downfall"[1522] because [beings who are born there] abide in a lower region, because those [regions] resemble a great abyss, and because [the beings who are born there] wail [in the form of] anguished, pitiful, wretched, and loud cries of woe. They are called "hells"[1523] because they generate extreme [forms of] distress.

On the basis of these terms, this [presentation] has clarified what causes [beings] to be born [in the hells], what [the beings] who are born there experience, and, due to those experiences, what other [forms of] suffering [those beings] create for themselves.

In the appropriate manner, the opposite of the above explanations should be understood as constituting the virtuous side of this topic. With regard to that, the following [two comments] are of a distinct nature. A migratory

1520. S: *apāyaḥ,* T: *ngan song.*

1521. S: *durgatayaḥ,* T: *ngan 'gro rnams.*

1522. S: *vinipātaḥ,* T: *log par ltung ba.* This term can also be rendered as "calamitous state."

1523. S: *narakāḥ,* T: *sems can dmyal ba rnams.*

state that is preceded by good conduct is called a "happy migratory state."[1524] Because it is a place where the highest forms of happiness are experienced, it is called a "celestial world."[1525]

The Power of Knowledge regarding Termination of the Outflows[1526] [III.6.2.10]

The mind that is free of the outflows and is their antidote in that it abandons in their entirety the latent forms of all the outflows, as well as the wisdom that is free of the outflows—which together constitute the supreme forms of superior mind [training] and superior wisdom [training]—are referred to as "the liberation of mind and the liberation of wisdom" [that are manifested] "through having terminated the outflows."

Moreover, after having attained that liberation of mind and that liberation of wisdom in their final existence on the basis of the path of seeing and on the basis of the path of meditation, [the tathāgatas] realize for themselves, by means of the sixth [form of] supernatural knowledge,[1527] their own attainment as it truly is, and they announce [their attainment] to those others who are desirous of knowing it. Therefore, [the sutra passages] declare [in part,] "and after having manifested and attained by means of his own supernatural knowledge and within his very lifetime [the liberation of mind and the liberation of wisdom that are free of the outflows], the

1524. S: *sugatayaḥ,* T: *bde 'gro rnams.*

1525. S: *svargalokaḥ,* T: *mtho ris kyi 'jig rten.*

1526. S: *āsravakṣayajñānabalam,* T: *zag pa zad pa mkhyen pa'i stobs.* The sutra passage that relates to this power declares: "Furthermore, O Long-Lived Ones, through having terminated the outflows, and after having manifested and attained by means of his own supernatural knowledge within his very lifetime the liberation of mind and the liberation of wisdom that are free of the outflows, a tathāgata proclaims, 'My rebirths have been brought to an end. I have carried out the spiritual life. I have completed that which needs to be done. I shall not know another existence after this one.' That quality by means of which, through having terminated the outflows, and after having manifested and attained through his own supernatural knowledge and within his very lifetime the liberation of mind and the liberation of wisdom that are free of the outflows, a tathāgata proclaims, 'Birth has come to an end for me. The spiritual life has been carried out. That which needed to be done has been done. I shall not know another existence after this one,' is the tenth of the Tathāgata's powers."

1527. This form of supernatural knowledge is called "knowledge regarding termination of the outflows" (S: *āsravakṣayajñānam,* T: *zag pa zad pa mkhyen pa*). See the section of the same name in Book I, chapter 5 [I.5.1.6].

tathāgatas proclaim[1528] . . ." The statement "Birth has come to an end for me," along with the various other statements [that occur in this passage] should be understood as [they are explained] in the *Collection of Canonical Expressions*.[1529]

Seven Aspects of a Tathāgata's Ten Powers [III.6.3]

Summary verse:

> Essential nature; category; exclusivity;
> And, likewise, sameness;
> Performance of action; successive order;
> And, lastly, differences.

The essential nature of the tathāgatas' ten powers should be understood; their categories should be understood; their exclusivity should be understood; their sameness should be understood; the action that [a tathāgata] performs [with each of them] should be understood; their successive order should be understood; and their differences should be understood. In short,

1528. Although Asaṅga casts this sentence in the plural, the sutra versions typically express this statement in the singular—that is, "A tathāgata proclaims."

1529. *rNam grangs bsdu ba* (Tibetan translation of *Paryāyasaṃgrahaṇī,* ff. 31b–32a): "'Birth has come to an end for me' means an eighth existence and those beyond it [will not occur]. [This is a reference to the doctrine that, after attaining the transcendent seeing path, a practitioner will have at most seven more rebirths.] 'The spiritual life has been carried out' means that nothing about it was deficient because the path was practiced in a most excellent manner. 'That which needed to be done has been done' means that all the fetters have been terminated and all the paths have been attained. 'I shall not know another existence after this one' means that even a [possible] seventh existence has been terminated. 'Birth has come to an end for me,' [can] also [be interpreted as follows.] There are two kinds of birth, the birth that is [the] rebirth [of an individual] and the birth [that is the arising] of the mental afflictions. The birth that is [the] rebirth [of an individual should be understood] as previously indicated. [The meaning of this statement is that] both of these forms [of birth] have been diminished, that is to say, weakened. This refers to the first two fruits [i.e., those of a stream-enterer and a once-returner]. 'The spiritual life has been carried out' [can also mean that] the nonreturner has abandoned the desire to violate the chastity [of a pure spiritual life]. [Similarly, the statements] 'That which needed to be done has been done' [and] 'I shall not know another existence after this one' [can also be interpreted as referring] to an arhat. These [expressions] are declarations of having attained [various] aspects of full [transcendent] realization."

a tathāgata's ten powers should be understood on the basis of these seven aspects.

Essential Nature [III.6.3.1]

Regarding this [topic], what is the essential nature [of the ten powers]?

Their essential nature is the five [spiritual] faculties;[1530] however, they are described as having the essential nature of wisdom, because of wisdom's predominance. For example, [the first power is described] as "the power of knowledge regarding proper and improper conditions"; it is not described as the power of faith nor is it described as the power of any of the other [faculties]. As is the case with the power of knowledge regarding proper and improper conditions, the same [explanation] should be regarded [as applying to] the remaining powers.

Category [III.6.3.2]

Regarding this [topic], what are the categories [of the ten powers]?

In brief, it should be understood that they possess three types of immeasurability. This is because, in relation to the category of time, they engage all the entities that exist in the past, present, and future; in relation to the category of kinds of entities, they engage every form of individual and general characteristic that relates to each and every conditioned entity; and, in relation to the category of mind continuum,[1531] they engage all the needs of every individual mind stream that exists within the sphere of all sentient beings that extends throughout the ten directions. In this way, it should be understood, on the basis of these categories, a tathāgata's ten powers possess the quality of being immeasurable.

1530. S: *pañcendriyāni*, T: *dbang po lnga*. *AKB* (p. 38): "[All of the twenty-two faculties (see note 564 and accompanying text)] are faculties because they have power over some particular thing." *AKB* (p. 39): "The power of the five [faculties] of faith, etc., occurs in relation to purification, that is, they block the mental afflictions and they bring forth the path." *AKB* (p. 385): "In reliance upon one-pointed concentration, the faculties of faith, etc., exert a controlling influence over the transcendent qualities."

1531. S: *saṃtānaḥ*, T: *rgyud*. This term refers to the moment-to-moment "continuum" of a sentient being's consciousness.

Exclusivity [III.6.3.3]

Regarding this [topic], what is the exclusivity [of the ten powers]?

These ten powers are qualities that are possessed exclusively and solely by a tathāgata. They are not possessed by any of the listeners or solitary realizers.

Sameness [III.6.3.4]

These powers are the same for all tathāgatas and there are no variations [in the degree of excellence that pertains to them]. This represents their quality of sameness. However, there is a difference regarding the manner in which the tathāgatas resort to [the powers]. One particular tathāgata may rely to a great degree on one particular power; another [tathāgata] may do so with a different one.

Performance of Action [III.6.3.5]

Regarding a tathāgata's ten powers, what [specific] action does he perform with each one?

By means of the power of knowledge regarding proper and improper conditions, a tathāgata knows, in accordance with reality, the manner in which causes are causes and results are results. He also repudiates those ascetics and brahmins who [wrongly] profess what is not a cause [to be a cause] and what is an incompatible cause [to be a cause].

By means of the power of knowledge regarding [the fact that] one's deeds are one's own, a tathāgata knows, in accordance with reality, the nature of the deeds that an individual performs him- or herself and the results [of those deeds] that he or she experiences. He also repudiates those ascetics and brahmins who [wrongly] profess that [the benefits of acts of] generosity and [other forms of] merit can be transferred.[1532]

By means of the power of knowledge regarding the absorptions, the liberations, and entering states of one-pointed concentration, a tathāgata

1532. S: *dānapuṇyakriyāsaṃkrāntivādaḥ,* T: *sbyin pa dang bsod nams 'pho bar smra ba. BBhVy* (f. 327b): "The thesis that virtue and nonvirtue can be transferred [from one person to another either] through the method of giving it [to someone else] or taking it [upon oneself] constitutes a doctrine which claims that [the results of] virtue or nonvirtue that are performed by one person can be experienced by another."

correctly instructs his followers on the basis of the three marvelous abilities[1533] and also repudiates those ascetics and brahmins who maintain doctrines that are hostile, contentious, and adversarial.

By means of the power of knowledge regarding superior and inferior faculties, a tathāgata distinguishes and knows, in accordance with reality, the lesser, middling, and great faculties of sentient beings. He also gives them Dharma teachings in a manner that is befitting and appropriate.

By means of the power of knowledge regarding diverse forms of devotion, a tathāgata knows, in accordance with reality, the virtuous and nonvirtuous forms of devotion [of sentient beings] that are lesser, middling, and great. He causes those [forms of devotion] that are virtuous to become strengthened and those that are nonvirtuous ones to be given up.

By means of the power of knowledge regarding diverse constituent elements, a tathāgata distinguishes and knows, in accordance with reality, the inferior, intermediate, and excellent forms of constituent element [that each sentient being possesses].

In accordance with their faculties, attitudes, and latent propensities, [a tathāgata] correctly and in an appropriate manner joins sentient beings to this or that starting point for engaging in [spiritual practice], through the action of [giving] instruction. Regarding this [point], the manner in which the tathāgatas give instruction to listeners about the various starting points for engaging in [spiritual practice] has been promulgated, laid out, disclosed, prescribed, and made clear in its entirety and without leaving any gaps in *The Stage of a Listener.*

How, then, do the tathāgatas present instructions for [cultivating] mental stability to a bodhisattva who is a novice and a beginning practitioner, and who is both engaged in the effort to acquire the requisites for [achieving] one-pointed concentration and desirous of [achieving] mental stability?

In this case, a tathāgata initially instructs a sincere bodhisattva, one who is a novice and a beginning practitioner, and who is serious about [pursuing] the requisites for [achieving] one-pointed concentration, in the following manner:

> Draw near, O child of good family. Having gone alone and unaccompanied to an isolated dwelling place, direct your attention inwardly to that very name given to you by your mother and

1533. See notes 395 and 444.

father, or [that very name given to you] by your teacher and preceptor. Also direct your attention further in the following manner: "Is there any inherently established entity apart from my six [inner] bases[1534] that exists internally, externally, or [in some way] other than those two, and [that constitutes the object] in relation to which this name, this appellation, this designation, and this figure of speech occur?" As you direct your attention properly in this way, you will not perceive any such entity. You will have no thought other than the following: "This adventitious appellation only occurs in relation to these adventitious entities."

O child of good family, when this conception of being adventitious has arisen in you and been understood [by you] in relation to your name, then also direct your attention inwardly in a proper manner to the name "eye," the appellation "eye," and the designation "eye" [that occur] in relation to your eye. Also direct your attention further in the following manner: Two things are perceived in relation to the eye. [One is,] "This is the name, the appellation, and the designation 'eye,'" and [the other is,] "That is the bare substance[1535] in relation to which this name, appellation, and designation [occur]." There is nothing beyond that and nothing more than that.

Regarding this [point], not only are the name, appellation, and designation [that occur] in relation to the eye not the eye, that substance in relation to which the appellation "eye" [occurs] is also not an eye that exists inherently.

Why is that?

Concerning this [point], without the name "eye," the appellation "eye," and the designation "eye," no one could develop the awareness of an eye. [However,] if that substance were truly established in the sense of possessing an essence that could be described by a name, then the awareness of [that which is called] an "eye" would no longer come into being in such a way that

1534. S: *ṣaḍāyatanāni,* T: *skye mched drug.* See note 111. *BBhVy* (f. 328b): "The substantive basis of a sentient being is [his or her] six bases. Since there is no defining attribute [of a sentient being] that exists apart from them, the text states, 'apart from my six [inner] bases . . .'"

1535. This term is synonymous with suchness (S: *tathatā,* T: *de bzhin nyid*) or ultimate reality as explained by Asaṅga in Book I, chapter 4. See notes 251, 269, and 273 and accompanying text.

is dependent [upon the name "eye"]; [instead,] the awareness of [that which is called] an "eye" would simply occur naturally in relation to that substance, even without [one's] ever having heard or conceived of any names. Nevertheless, its [continuous] occurrence is not [so] perceived. Therefore, this name "eye" and [this] appellation "eye" are also adventitious [phenomena that occur] in relation to an adventitious entity. Through directing your attention to the eye in this way, inwardly and in a proper manner, the conception of being adventitious will also arise and be understood in relation to the appellation "eye."

As is the case with respect to the eye, the same is true with respect to the ear, the nose, the tongue, the body, and so on at length up to those [entities] that are seen, heard, thought about, and realized, those that have been attained, those that are sought after, as well as those that are deliberated about and reflected upon with the mind. In short, the conception of being adventitious will also arise and be understood in relation to all the appellations that occur in relation to entities.

In this way, you will correctly take hold of the path of preparation whose aim is to remove the settled conception that you have regarding your personal self. [This point is repeated] at length [for all other entities] up to: You will correctly take hold of the path of preparation whose aim is to remove the settled conception that you have regarding all entities. In this way, having repeatedly cleared away all the elaborative conceptions that occur in relation to all entities by means of an awareness that effectively examines all objects of knowledge and by means of the conception that all the appellations regarding entities are adventitious, abide at length in the [real] substance[1536] with a nonconceptualizing mind that is free of signs and is engaged in apprehending merely the true mode of being. In this way, through the lineage of one-pointed concentration that pertains to a tathāgata's pure knowledge, you will attain one-pointedness of mind. If you direct your attention to [the meditation object of] unattractiveness, you should not relinquish this form of attention [that

1536. S: *vastu,* T: *dngos po.* This term refers to the absence of duality that is ultimate truth. See notes 251 and 269.

> apprehends ultimate reality]. If you direct your attention to [any other meditation object, such as those of] loving-kindness, the mere conditionality of dependent origination, the diversity of the elements, recollection of one's breath, the first meditative absorption, and so on up to the sphere in which there is neither conception nor absence of conception, or [any of] the immeasurable bodhisattva forms of meditative absorption, supernatural knowledge, one-pointed concentration, and states of composure, you should not relinquish this very form of attention. In this way, this bodhisattva form of attention [that is being practiced] by you will eventually arrive at unsurpassed true and complete enlightenment.

It should be understood that this is [the form of] the path that leads everywhere [that is practiced] by bodhisattvas. This is the way that the tathāgatas have instructed novice bodhisattvas in the past, the way that they shall instruct them in the future, and the way that they are currently instructing them. A listener who applies him- or herself using this form of attention will also become one who attains supernatural knowledge very swiftly for the purpose of realizing the Dharma, if he or she is capable of understanding it properly.

By means of the power of knowledge regarding the paths that lead everywhere, a tathāgata knows, in accordance with reality, the paths that [lead to] deliverance from all suffering as well as the paths that do not lead to deliverance. Rejecting the paths that do not lead to deliverance, he sets forth the path that leads to deliverance.

By means of the power of knowledge regarding recollection of former existences, a tathāgata recalls both past events [relating to other beings' lives] and the experiences of [his own] past births and reveals them to his followers in order to engender in their minds aversion [for the samsaric condition] and faith [toward a bodhisattva's deeds]. He also repudiates those ascetics and brahmins who profess an eternalistic doctrine.

By means of the power of knowledge regarding death and rebirth, a tathāgata declares where listeners who died at some time in the past were reborn. He also repudiates those ascetics and brahmins who profess a nihilistic doctrine.

By means of the power of knowledge regarding the termination of the outflows, a tathāgata becomes free of doubt and uncertainty regarding his own liberation. He also repudiates the exaggerated pride of those ascetics and brahmins [who wrongly believe they have attained] the status of an arhat. This, then, should be understood [to constitute a description of] the actions of the ten powers.

Three Formulations of the Successive Order of a Tathāgata's Ten Powers [III.6.3.6]

Regarding this [topic], what is the successive order of a tathāgata's ten powers?

A tathāgata acquires all of the ten powers at the same time that he attains unsurpassed true and complete enlightenment. Though acquired simultaneously, they become evident in a successive manner. As soon as a tathāgata has attained enlightenment, he correctly observes the systematic arrangement of causes and effects that relate to entities by means of the power of knowledge regarding proper and improper conditions. Having observed that, by means of the power of knowledge regarding [the fact that] one's deeds are one's own, he correctly reveals to those in the desire realm who wish to attain certain kinds of favorable results that correspond to that realm [the need to] avoid nonvirtuous karma and undertake virtuous karma. Moreover, by means of the power of knowledge regarding the absorptions, the liberations, and entering states of one-pointed concentration, he provides instruction in a correct manner for achieving the paths that will bring about attainment of the worldly form of detachment to those beings who are desirous of gaining the worldly form of detachment. In addition, by means of a tathāgata's remaining seven powers, he reveals the path for attaining the transcendent form of detachment to those [beings] who are desirous of gaining the transcendent form of detachment.

Regarding this [latter point], by means of the power of knowledge regarding inferior and superior faculties, [a tathāgata] first examines the faculties of those who desire the transcendent form of detachment. Then, by means of the power of knowledge regarding diverse forms of devotion, he examines the attitudes that accompany those faculties. Following that, by means of the power of knowledge regarding diverse constituent elements, he examines the latent propensities that accompany those attitudes. Having realized the faculties, attitudes, and latent propensities [of such beings] in this way, he introduces them in an appropriate manner to the [meditation] objects that represent the starting points [for their spiritual practice] by means of the power of knowledge regarding the paths that lead everywhere. Following that, once they have been caused to take hold of mental stability by practicing the appropriate meditation object that represents the starting point for engaging in [spiritual practice] and after they have purified themselves of their unfavorable mental traits,[1537] he reveals, by means of the power of knowledge regarding recollection of former lives and the power of knowledge regarding death and rebirth, the middle way that rejects grasping at the eternalistic and nihilistic extremes that are rooted in the perishable collection view, so that they will abandon all the mental afflictions. After that, by means of the power of knowledge regarding the termination of the outflows, he likewise causes those who have applied themselves to the practice correctly and who are established in quiescence to abandon the form of exaggerated pride that, as a consequence of no longer exhibiting overt forms of the mental afflictions even though they have not been abandoned, wrongly leads them to believe they have completed [the practice] when they have not done so. This, then, constitutes one formulation of the order of the powers.

Here is another formulation [of the successive order of a tathāgata's ten powers]. In this case, after having attained unsurpassed true and complete enlightenment, a tathāgata first manifests the power of knowledge regarding proper and improper conditions and ponders well the supreme knowledge of the settled nature of entities[1538] in relation to all entities that arise dependently. Relying upon the knowledge [that perceives] the settled nature of entities, he observes the faction of [beings that is made up of] householders with the power of knowledge regarding [the fact that] one's deeds are one's own. [By doing so, he perceives] all the various kinds of deeds that have brought about, will bring about, and are currently bringing about the [temporary] attainments of those who rely upon the householder state of existence. After observing the faction of [beings that is made up of] householders, he observes the faction of [beings that is made up of] those who have gone forth [into the homeless state] with the power of knowledge regarding the absorptions, the liberations, and entering states of one-pointed concentration, and reflects, "Is there or is there not anyone in the faction of [beings

1537. See note 1504.

1538. S: *dharmasthitijñānam,* T: *chos gnas pa'i ye shes. BBhVy* (f. 330a): "[The nature of] this [doctrine of] dependent origination is such that, by failing to realize it, one [is forced to] remain in samsara for a long time. This is also something that the knowledge of the settled nature of entities realizes." See also note 927.

that is made up of] those who have gone forth who has attained deliverance from suffering and who teaches [others] the path [that leads] to deliverance from suffering?" Realizing that there is not [any such person] and gazing upon the entire world that has no [source of] protection and has no [source of] refuge, he surveys it using the buddha eye and motivated by great compassion. As he surveys [the world], he manifests the knowledge of inferior and superior faculties and realizes, "There are sentient beings who have been born in the world and who have become full-grown in the world whose faculties are weak, [there are sentient beings] whose faculties are moderately developed, and [there are sentient beings] whose faculties are sharp." Having realized this, his mind moves toward [the act of] teaching the Dharma. Following that, it should be understood that the succession of the remaining powers of knowledge regarding diverse forms of devotion, etc., takes place in the manner [that was described] previously. This is a second formulation of the successive order of the [ten] powers.

Here is yet another formulation. At the very outset, as soon as a tathāgata has attained enlightenment, he examines the sphere of dependently arisen entities with the power of knowledge regarding proper and improper conditions. Following that, he examines the sphere of sentient beings—[which is to say, that sphere] among the dependently arisen entities that is universally recognized as [being made up of] sentient beings—and [recognizes,] "These sentient beings are experiencing this type of result of this type of deed that each one has carried out him- or herself." Having closely examined in accordance with reality the sphere of entities and the sphere of sentient beings by means of the power of knowledge regarding the absorptions, the liberations, and entering states of one-pointed concentration, he correctly instructs those very sentient beings on the basis of the three marvelous abilities in order to free them from their suffering. [A tathāgata] who instructs [those sentient beings] after having realized their faculties, etc., and who then causes them to enter the path, [finally] liberates them from their suffering by means of the remaining powers in the successive manner that [was described] previously. This is the third formulation of the successive order of the [ten] powers.

Differences [III.6.3.7]

Regarding this [topic], what is the difference between the power of knowledge regarding proper and improper conditions and the power of knowledge regarding [the fact that] one's deeds are one's own?

The way in which [a tathāgata realizes that] virtuous and nonvirtuous deeds bring about desirable and undesirable results is through the power of knowledge regarding proper and improper conditions. On the other hand, the way in which [a tathāgata realizes that] only that very individual who performs a particular virtuous or nonvirtuous deed will experience its [corresponding] desirable or undesirable result is through the power of knowledge regarding [the fact that] one's deeds are one's own.

The way in which [a tathāgata realizes that] only that very individual who enters a particular meditative absorption, liberation, etc., will possess it and not anyone else is through the power of knowledge regarding [the fact that] one's deeds are one's own. By contrast, the way in which [a tathāgata] relies upon those very same meditative absorptions, etc., to instruct his followers using the three marvelous abilities is through the power of knowledge regarding the absorptions, the liberations, and entering states of one-pointed concentration.

The way in which [a tathāgata] perceives minds that are naturally accompanied by [the faculties of] faith, etc., is through the power of knowledge regarding the absorptions, the liberations, and entering states of one-pointed concentration. By contrast, the way in which [a tathāgata] distinguishes the different types of lesser, middling, and great faculties is through the power of knowledge regarding inferior and superior faculties.

The way in which [a tathāgata] perceives [sentient beings'] attitudes, which are accompanied by the [spiritual] faculties and [are directed] toward a variety of different objects, is through the power of knowledge regarding inferior and superior faculties. By contrast, the way in which [a tathāgata] distinguishes the diversity of those very attitudes is through the power of knowledge regarding diverse forms of devotion.

Six Types of Attitude [III.6.3.7.1]

Moreover, in brief, it should be understood that there are six different types of attitude: (1) the attitude that does not lead to deliverance—such as that of beings who aspire to [be reborn in] such worlds as those of [the worldly gods] Maheśvara, Narāyana, and Brahmā; (2) the attitude that does lead to deliverance—such as that of beings who aspire to [pursue any of] the three vehicles; (3) the attitude that is far from purity—such as that of beings who are established in a [form of spiritual] ripening that is small or middling; (4) the attitude that is near to purity—such as that of beings who are established in a [form of spiritual] ripening that is great; (5) the attitude that can bring attainment of nirvana within the same lifetime—such as that of beings who aspire to attain nirvana by means of the Listeners' Vehicle; (6) the attitude that will bring attainment of nirvana in the future—such as that of beings who aspire to attain nirvana by means of the Great Vehicle.

The way in which [a tathāgata] perceives the seeds that correspond to and are awakened by those [particular] forms of devotion is through the power of knowledge regarding diverse forms of devotion. By contrast, the way in which [a tathāgata] distinguishes and perceives the different forms of those very seeds is through the power of knowledge regarding diverse constituent elements.

Four Types of Constituent Element [III.6.3.7.2]

Moreover, in brief, it should be understood that there are four different types of constituent element: (1) the seed that exists naturally;[1539] (2) the seed that has been awakened by former practice;[1540] (3) the seed that is capable of being purified, that is to say, [the seed that is possessed by] those who have the capacity to attain nirvana; and (4) the seed that is incapable of being purified, that is to say, [the seed that is possessed by] those who do not have the capacity to attain nirvana.

The way in which [a tathāgata] knows [the means of] entering the path that accords with a particular constituent element is through the power of knowledge regarding diverse constituent elements. By contrast, the way in which [a tathāgata] distinguishes all the individual aspects of these very paths—that is to say, [the recognition that] this path leads to [continued] affliction, this path leads to purification, this path leads to ultimate purification, this path does not lead to ultimate purification—is through the power of knowledge regarding the paths that lead everywhere.

The way in which [a tathāgata] who is remembering the past knows, in accord with reality, all the causes of the migratory states that occurred in the past is through the power of knowledge regarding the paths that lead everywhere. By contrast, the way in which [a tathāgata] distinguishes and

1539. S: *prakṛtisthaṃ bījam,* T: *rang bzhin du gnas pa'i sa bon.* This corresponds to the innate form of a sentient being's spiritual lineage. See note 109 and accompanying text.

1540. S: *pūrvābhyāsasamutthitam,* T: *sngon goms pa las byung ba.* This corresponds to the form of a sentient being's spiritual lineage that has been awakened and actualized. Such a form is referred to as the lineage that has been "developed" (S: *samudānītaṃ,* T: *yang dag par blangs pa;* see note 110 and accompanying text).

knows the six circumstances that correlate with the [eight] basic elements of life as [described] earlier is through the power of knowledge regarding the recollection of former existences.

The way in which [a tathāgata] knows the passing away and rebirth of sentient beings in relation to the past is through the power of knowledge regarding the recollection of former existences. By contrast, the way in which [a tathāgata] sees the passing away and rebirth of sentient beings that will occur in the future is through the power of knowledge regarding death and rebirth.

The way in which [a tathāgata] knows the conception[1541] and future rebirth of those sentient beings who have not completed their [ultimate] aim is through the power of knowledge regarding death and rebirth. By contrast, the way in which [a tathāgata] knows those beings who have completed their [ultimate] aim and achieved a fully liberated mind by attaining nirvana within their lifetime is through the power of knowledge regarding termination of the outflows. This [presentation] should be understood to constitute [a description of] both the differences and similarities that exist among a tathāgata's ten powers.

The Four Forms of Intrepid Confidence [iii.6.4]

The scriptural description of the four forms of intrepid confidence should be understood as it appears in the sutras.[1542]

1541. S: *pratisaṃdhiḥ,* T: *nying mtshams sbyor ba*. Literally "reentry," this is the moment at which an intermediate-state being becomes conceived and is reborn in one of the five or six migratory states of samsaric existence.

1542. S: *catvāri vaiśāradyāni,* T: *mi 'jigs pa bzhi*. *PVPP* (Tib. edition, vol. 1, ff. 342a–343b; Skt. edition, vol. 1, pp. 352–353) states: "Moreover, O Subhūti, the Great Vehicle of the Bodhisattva, of the Great Being, includes, specifically, four forms of intrepid confidence. What are the four? Having affirmed, indeed, that I attained true and complete enlightenment, I see no reason why any ascetic or brahmin or god or Māra or Brahmā or anyone else in this world might criticize me justly about this [by saying], 'These are entities that [you] have not fully realized.' Seeing no reason for this, I abide as one who has attained a state of ease, as one who has attained freedom from fear, as one who has attained intrepid confidence, and I affirm that I have attained the exalted and most excellent state, I utter the true roar of a lion in an assembly, and I turn the divine wheel that has never been turned properly in the world by any ascetic or brahmin or god or Māra or Brahmā.

"Having affirmed, indeed, that I have terminated the outflows, I see no reason why any ascetic or brahmin or god or Māra or Brahmā or anyone else in this world might criticize me justly about this [by saying], 'These are outflows that [you] have not terminated.' Seeing

Regarding this topic, these four states are ones that the tathāgatas affirm in an assembly. [They affirm that they have attained a state] that is *not* shared with the listeners, [that is to say,] the supremely perfect understanding [that realizes] all aspects of all entities through having become liberated from the obscurations to that which needs to be known. This is the first state. [They affirm having attained a state] that *is* shared with the listeners, [that is to say,] liberation from the obstructions of the mental afflictions. This is the second state. [They affirm that] the path [which they teach] is one whose purpose is to transcend [all] suffering and it is one that will lead those beings who are desirous of attaining liberation to deliverance [from samsara]. This is the third state. [They affirm that] the qualities that [they have declared] to be obstacles and that are obstructions to the attainment of that very path are, [in fact, qualities] that ought to be abandoned. This is the fourth state.

A tathāgata is also one who makes affirmations that accord with reality about these four states. Therefore, not seeing [any] actions of body, speech, or mind that are at variance with the affirmations made in relation to the prior two states, [not seeing any] internal contradictions or occurrences of unreasonableness that are at variance with the affirmations made in relation to the latter two states, and [not seeing anything] that constitutes a reason which those who possess divine vision as well as those who lack divine vision and those who are able to discern others' thoughts as well as those who are not able to discern others' thoughts could use to argue [justifiably] against the states [being set forth] in the affirmations, he affirms these states with

---

no reason for this, I abide as one who has attained a state of ease, as one who has attained freedom from fear, as one who has attained intrepid confidence. . . .

"[Regarding] those qualities that I have declared to be obstructive [in nature], I see no reason why any ascetic or brahmin or god or Māra or Brahmā or anyone else in this world might have an occasion to criticize me justly about this [by saying], 'These [qualities] are not obstructive [in nature] for one who engages in them.' Seeing no reason for this, I abide as one who has attained a state of ease, as one who has attained freedom from fear, as one who has attained intrepid confidence. . . .

"[Regarding] the path that I have declared to be the one that pertains to the noble ones, the one that leads to deliverance, and the one that correctly delivers the person who practices it to the termination of suffering, I see no reason why any ascetic or brahmin or god or Māra or Brahmā or anyone else in this world might have an occasion to criticize me justly about this [by saying], '[The person who practices it] will not attain deliverance.' Seeing no reason for this, I abide as one who has attained a state of ease, as one who has attained freedom from fear, as one who has attained intrepid confidence." See also *AKV,* vol. 4, pp. 1090–1091.

intrepid confidence, with a mind that is undaunted, free of any apprehension, and free of any fear.

This also constitutes the extent of what the Master has affirmed—namely, that the [form of] practice [that accomplishes] what is beneficial to oneself and the [form of] practice [that accomplishes] what is beneficial to others have been fulfilled. Regarding this [point], fulfillment of the [form of] practice [that accomplishes] what is beneficial to oneself is affirmed by the former two states and fulfillment of the [form of] practice [that accomplishes] what is beneficial to others is affirmed by the latter two states.

Regarding this [topic], through his own [attainment of] the supremely perfect understanding [that realizes] all entities, a tathāgata affirms true and complete buddhahood to those bodhisattvas who are firmly established in the Great Vehicle. In addition, he affirms the termination of all the outflows to those who are firmly established in the Listeners' and Solitary Realizers' vehicles. He affirms the path that leads to deliverance [from samsara] and the qualities that are obstructive to [those who are firmly established in] both of those [types of vehicles].

This is how the tathāgata taught this sutra statement: "The path that leads to deliverance which I taught to bodhisattvas and listeners . . . ," and so on. The compilers of the listener collection of scriptures have taken out the word "bodhisattva" from that section [of the canon]. By contrast, in the bodhisattva collection of scriptures, the word "bodhisattva" alone is mentioned.

The Three Closely Placed Recollections [iii.6.5]

The scriptural description of the three closely placed recollections should be understood as it appears in the sutras.[1543] The Tathāgata has long held

1543. S: *trīṇi smṛtyupasthānāni*. Ratnākaraśānti's *Sāratamā* (p. 177): "As the three closely placed recollections are described [in the sutras]: 'When the Tathāgata teaches the Dharma, some persons listen attentively. Their ears are turned [toward the Dharma]. They fix their minds closely on the [Buddha's] directives. They develop a practice that accords with the Dharma teaching. However, this does not cause the Tathāgata to become overjoyed or elated, or cause his mind to jump [with excitement]. Others do not listen attentively. Their ears are not turned [toward the Dharma] . . . , etc. This does not cause the Tathāgata to become angry, impatient, dissatisfied, or displeased. [There are also occasions when] some listen attentively while others do not listen attentively. This causes the Tathāgata neither to rejoice nor to become angry. In all of these instances the Tathāgata is [both] mindful and vigilant and remains in [a state of] equanimity.'"

the following aspiration: "Having taught the Dharma well to my disciples, I hope that they will become properly established in the practice." In brief, [the ability of] the Master of the Dharma and the leader of a group of followers who has long held this aspiration to remain free of mental affliction in response to both the fulfillment of that prayer and its lack of fulfillment [is a quality that] derives its strength from the three closely placed recollections.

Three Types of Assembly [III.6.5.1]

Moreover these three [closely placed recollections] are established on the basis of three types of assembly.

What are the three assemblies?

One is an assembly in which everyone without exception practices correctly. A second is an assembly in which everyone without exception practices incorrectly. In addition, a third assembly is one in which some practice correctly while others practice incorrectly.

The Three Forms of Having Nothing That Needs to Be Concealed [III.6.6]

The scriptural description of the three forms of having nothing that needs to be concealed should be understood as it appears in the sutras.[1544] In brief, the condition of having abandoned any form of misdeed that needs to be covered up is what is indicated by a tathāgata's three forms of having nothing that needs to be concealed. A tathāgata also never at any time incurs any form of those slight indeterminate misdeeds that even arhats sometimes, occasionally, commit due to a lapse of recollection. Therefore, a tathāgata's nature is exactly as he has affirmed it to be.

1544. S: *trīṇy arakṣyāṇi*, T: *bsrung ba med pa gsum. PVPP* (based on Tibetan translation, vol. 3, f. 333b): "O Subhūti, what are a tathāgata's three forms of having nothing that needs to be concealed? A tathāgata is one whose physical conduct is completely pure. A tathāgata has no physical conduct that is not completely pure and that he believes needs to be covered up, [causing him to reflect,] 'I hope no one will become aware [of this].' This is the first form of having nothing that needs to be concealed. A tathāgata is one whose verbal conduct is completely pure. A tathāgata has no verbal conduct that is not completely pure and that he believes needs to be covered up, [causing him to reflect,] 'I hope no one will become aware [of this].' This is the second form of having nothing that needs to be concealed. A tathāgata is one whose mental conduct is completely pure. A tathāgata has no mental conduct that is not completely pure and that he believes needs to be covered up, [causing him to reflect,] 'I hope no one will become aware [of this].' This is the third form of having nothing that needs to be concealed."

He proclaims [this nature] to listeners as a way of suppressing[1545] them repeatedly. He censures some of them as a way of continually subduing them. He banishes some of them and even treats them harshly. [Since he has no faults,] it does not occur to him to preserve their goodwill [by thinking:] "I do not want the listeners to become aware of my impure physical, verbal, and mental conduct through their close association with me and, because they have become displeased and upset by that, to admonish me. Nor do I want them to report it to others."

Great Compassion [III.6.7]

Regarding this [topic], all the aspects of the tathāgatas' great compassion should be understood as they were explained in the chapter entitled "Worship, Service, and the Immeasurables." Moreover, it should be understood that the [form of compassion] possessed by the tathāgatas is immeasurable and unsurpassed.

The Nature of Being Completely Free of Confusion [III.6.8]

Regarding this [topic], because a tathāgata correctly carries out that which he intends to carry out, in relation to the intended object, in the intended manner, and at the intended time, this [quality] is called a tathāgata's "nature of being completely free of confusion."[1546] Thus, regarding this [topic], the condition by which a tathāgata's recollection avoids inattentiveness and his recollection remains ever fixed at all times, in relation to all things that ought to be done, in relation to all places, and in relation to all means [for accomplishing] those actions, should be regarded here as the nature of being completely free of confusion.

The Complete Destruction of the Traces [III.6.9]

Regarding this [topic], a tathāgata's quality of not displaying any physical actions pertaining to bodily movement, gaze, speech, or comportment that correspond to the existence of a mental affliction is called a tathāgata's

1545. See Book I, chapter 10, the section entitled "Suppressing Those Who Engage in Misconduct" [I.10.2.6.10].

1546. S: *asammoṣadharmatā*, T: *bsnyel ba mi mnga' ba'i chos nyid*.

"complete destruction of the traces."[1547] By contrast, even though arhats have terminated the mental afflictions, they still display actions that correspond to the existence of mental afflictions in their bodily movements, manner of gazing, speech, or comportment.[1548]

Knowledge of All Aspects and of What Is Most Excellent [III.6.10]

In brief, a tathāgata attains supreme enlightenment with regard to three groups of entities.

What are the three?

[They are] (1) entities that are advantageous,[1549] (2) entities that are disadvantageous,[1550] and (3) entities that are neither advantageous nor disadvantageous. Regarding this [topic], a tathāgata's knowledge of all those entities that are disadvantageous and [all those entities] that are neither advantageous nor disadvantageous is called a tathāgata's "knowledge of all aspects."[1551] Regarding this [topic], a tathāgata's knowledge of all those entities that are advantageous is called a tathāgata's "knowledge of what is most excellent."[1552] Regarding this [topic], the combination of a tathāgata's knowledge of all aspects and his knowledge of what is most excellent is called a tathāgata's "knowledge of all aspects and of what is most excellent."[1553]

1547. S: *vāsanāsamudghātaḥ,* T: *bag chags yang dag par bcom pa.*

1548. Various commentaries give as examples of an arhat's behavior that is caused by the traces of the mental afflictions that he or she may at times still jump like a monkey because of having previously been born as monkey, or may refer to a woman as a "female servant" (S: *dāsī,* T: *dmangs mo*). The latter example represents use of a derogatory term that relates to the caste system because of having previously been born as a brahmin, even though the Buddha condemned the use of such terms.

1549. S: *arthopasaṃhitā dharmāḥ,* T: *don dang ldan pa'i chos rnams. BBhVy* (f. 334a): "'Advantageous [entities]' means those that are conducive to purification (S: *vyavadānapakṣyāḥ,* T: *rnam par byang ba'i phyogs*), [that is,] they are the qualities that are most beneficial and bring about happiness."

1550. S: *anarthopasaṃhitā dharmāḥ,* T: *don dang mi ldan pa'i chos rnams. BBhVy* (f. 334a): "'Disadvantageous [entities]' means those that are conducive to [the state of] being afflicted (S: *saṃkleśapakṣyāḥ,* T: *kun nas nyon mongs ba'i phyogs*), [that is,] they are the qualities that bring about what is harmful."

1551. S: *sarvākārajñānam,* T: *rnam pa thams cad mkhyen pa.*

1552. S: *varajñānam,* T: *mchog mkhyen pa.*

1553. S: *sarvākāravarajñānam,* T: *rnam pa thams cad dang mchog mkhyen pa.*

All of these [attributes] combined together constitute a buddha's one hundred and forty unique qualities. Among them, the marks and secondary signs are attained in their most perfect form by a bodhisattva in his final existence. When a bodhisattva who is in his last existence and who has fully completed the path of the [two] accumulations [that are needed] for enlightenment sits down at the seat of enlightenment, and as he is meditating on the thirty-seven qualities that are conducive to enlightenment without [the aid of] a teacher, he attains a [form of] one-pointed concentration called [the one-pointed concentration] "that bestows in an instant the knowledge that is free from any obstructions." [This concentration is] included in the diamond-like one-pointed concentration that is possessed by a bodhisattva who is still pursuing the spiritual training. In the moment immediately following that, he attains the unsurpassed state of perfect purity in which all the remaining qualities ranging from the ten powers up to the knowledge of all aspects and what is most excellent arise simultaneously. By virtue of their attainment, the perfectly pure and immaculate [transcendent] awareness that engages the totality of objects of knowledge is free of any resistance or obstruction and is subject to nothing more than the turning [of the mind].[1554] He becomes one who has fulfilled all his aims. Having become one who in this manner has fulfilled his desired object, he has transcended the conduct of a bodhisattva and the stage of a bodhisattva, and has entered upon the conduct of a buddha and the stage of a buddha.

Through having abandoned without remainder the innermost core[1555] of the [type of] indisposition that relates to the obstructions to that which needs to be known, [the former bodhisattva's] being[1556] becomes transformed.

1554. S: *ābhogamātrapratibaddham,* T: *brtsal ba tsam la thogs pa med pa.* The noun *ābhogaḥ* can mean "effort"; likewise, the adjective *anābhoga* and adverb *anābhogam* which are formed from it mean "effortless" and "effortlessly," respectively. However, *ābhogaḥ* can also mean the "bending" or "turning" [of the mind] (S: *cetasa ābhogaḥ,* T: *sems kyi 'jug pa;* see note 232), as in the definition of the mental factor "attention" (S: *manaskāraḥ,* T: *yid la byed pa*). While the latter meaning seems to be its sense in the present context, the phrase "subject to nothing more than the turning [of the mind]" in fact indicates that the Buddha's mind engages objects "effortlessly." See also note 501.

1555. This is the last of the three types of this form of indisposition and it represents the most subtle form of the obscurations to that which needs to be known (see Book II, chapter 4, in the section entitled "Concluding Remarks" [II.4.13].

1556. S: *āśrayaḥ,* T: *rten. AKB* (p. 63) states: "For the [individual] being of āryas has been transformed by the power of the paths of seeing and meditation in such a way that the mental afflictions that are abandoned by those [two paths] are not capable of arising again."

This is the unsurpassed [form of] transformation [that is undergone] by his being. It should be understood that all the other transformations [that were previously gained] by bodhisattvas up to the supreme pleasurable state have a form that is superior to them.

Concluding Remarks [III.6.11]

The Differences between the Transcendent Awareness of a Tathāgata and That of a Tenth-Stage Bodhisattva [III.6.11.1]

Regarding this [topic], how should the distinguishing characteristics of the transcendent awareness possessed by a bodhisattva who is established in the stage that is the perfect manner of going and those of [the transcendent awareness] possessed by a tathāgata be understood? [How should it be understood that the two represent] distinct [forms of] transcendent awareness?

In this instance, the transcendent awareness of a bodhisattva who is established in the stage that is the perfect manner of going should be understood [to perceive] all objects of knowledge in a manner that resembles the way a sighted person perceives visible objects that are covered by a thin cloth. By contrast, the transcendent awareness of a tathāgata should be regarded [as perceiving all objects of knowledge] in a manner [that resembles the way a sighted person perceives visible objects] that are not covered by anything.

For example, the transcendent awareness of the bodhisattva [of this stage] should be regarded as being like a painting that has been filled in with every type of color but has not yet been completed by [applying] the last, perfected paint strokes. A tathāgata's transcendent awareness should be regarded as being like a perfectly completed [painting].

For example, the transcendent awareness of the bodhisattva [of this stage should be understood to perceive all objects of knowledge] in a manner that resembles the way a sighted person perceives visible objects under slightly darkened conditions. The transcendent awareness of a tathāgata should be regarded [as perceiving all objects of knowledge] in a manner [that resem-

---

AKV (vol. 1, p. 215) glosses the term "being" (S: *āśrayaḥ*) here as "individual existence" (S: *ātmabhāvaḥ*, T: *lus*). See also note 237.

bles the way a sighted person perceives visible objects] when there are no elements of darkness at all.

For example, [the transcendent awareness] of the bodhisattva [of this stage should be understood to perceive all objects of knowledge] in a manner that resembles the way a sighted person [perceives] visible objects from a distance. [The transcendent awareness] of a tathāgata [should be regarded as perceiving all objects of knowledge] in a manner that resembles [the way a sighted person perceives visible objects] that are near.

For example, [the transcendent awareness] of the bodhisattva [of this stage should be understood to perceive all objects of knowledge] in a manner that resembles the way a person with slightly diminished eyesight perceives visible objects. [The transcendent awareness] of a tathāgata [should be regarded as perceiving all objects of knowledge] in a manner that resembles the way a person with extremely clear eyesight [perceives visible objects].

A bodhisattva who is established in the stage that is the perfect manner of going should be regarded as resembling the body [of a being] who is still in the womb. A tathāgata should be regarded as resembling the body of a being who has been born into a [particular] birth existence.[1557]

The mental activity of a bodhisattva who is situated on the stage that is the perfect manner of going should be regarded as resembling that of an arhat while he or she is in the dream state.[1558] A tathāgata's [mental activity] should be regarded as resembling that of the very same [arhat] when he or she is awake.

The nature of the transcendent awareness of a bodhisattva who is established in the stage that is the perfect manner of going should be regarded as resembling that of a lamp that is not bright. The nature of a tathāgata's transcendent awareness should be regarded as resembling that of a lamp that is extremely bright.

Therefore, it should be understood that there are great differences between the transcendent awareness, body, and thought of a tathāgata and [the transcendent awareness, body, and thought] of a bodhisattva who is established in the stage that is the perfect manner of going.

1557. S: *upapattibhavaḥ,* T: *skye ba'i srid pa.* This term is found in Buddhist canonical literature and has various interpretations depending on the context. Here it seems to mean a sentient being who has come forth from the womb.

1558. S: *svapnāntaragataḥ,* T: *rmi lam.* The original Sanskrit term (*svapnaḥ*) can refer either to sleep or dream. I follow the Tibetan translation, which specifies the dream state.

A Buddha's Ten Deeds [III.6.11.2]

A tathāgata who possesses the understanding associated with such a [form of] supreme enlightenment carries out all the activities of a fully enlightened being throughout the entire buddha realm that extends in the ten directions.

Regarding this [topic], what are a buddha's activities?

In brief, the following ten are the deeds of a tathāgata that ought to be done and the activities of a tathāgata that ought to be carried out. Each of the deeds carried out by a tathāgata accomplishes the aims of immeasurable sentient beings. There are none that are higher than these and none that are greater than these.

What are the ten?

The first deed of a tathāgata is to engender, at the very outset, a clarity of mind[1559] [in others] toward his own nature as a great being and to generate [in them] a firm conviction[1560] about the state of a great person. He accomplishes this by means of the marks and secondary signs.

Providing every kind of instruction to all sentient beings is the deed of a tathāgata that he accomplishes by means of the four forms of complete purity. This is the second deed of a tathāgata.

The ability to accomplish all sentient beings' aims combined with the ability to remove all their doubts represents the third deed of a tathāgata and it is one that he accomplishes by means of a tathāgata's ten powers. That is to say, a tathāgata is able to accomplish all the aims of all sentient beings by means of the ten powers that were described earlier. And, whatever persons ask questions of a tathāgata relating to his [ten] powers, he answers their questions by expounding those things that are known, seen, understood, and realized by a tathāgata, in exactly the manner that they are known, seen, understood, and realized by him.

The refutation of all the verbal challenges made by opponents combined with the formulation of his own doctrine represents the fourth deed of a

1559. S: *cittaprasādaḥ,* T: *sems kyi dang ba.* This represents a particular type of faith toward the Buddha in particular and the Three Jewels in general. *PSV* (pp. 282–283): "Faith in the Lord Buddha is the clarity of mind that is demonstrated by a bristling of the body hair or the flowing of tears and is felt toward that object which has perfected all virtuous qualities and completely removed all faults." See also note 220.

1560. S: *saṃpratyayaḥ,* T: *yid ches pa.* This term represents a type of faith that believes firmly in entities that do in fact exist.

tathāgata and it is one that a tathāgata accomplishes by means of the four forms of intrepid confidence.

The condition of remaining free of mental affliction toward both those followers who abide by his directives and those who do not abide by them is the fifth deed of a tathāgata and it is one that a tathāgata accomplishes by means of the [three] closely placed recollections.

The quality of acting in a manner that accords with what he asserts is the sixth deed of a tathāgata and it is one that a tathāgata accomplishes by means of the [three] forms of having nothing that needs to be concealed.

The quality of watching over the entire world both day and night with the eye of a buddha is the seventh deed of a tathāgata and one that a tathāgata accomplishes by means of his great compassion.

The quality of never failing to do everything that needs to be done for all sentient beings is the eighth deed of a tathāgata and it is one that a tathāgata accomplishes by possessing a nature that is completely free of confusion.

A tathāgata's quality of carrying out and practicing proper behavior is the ninth deed of a tathāgata and it is one that a tathāgata accomplishes by means of the condition of having completely destroyed all the traces [of the mental afflictions].

The rejection of [both] those entities that are disadvantageous and those entities that are neither advantageous nor disadvantageous, followed by the naming, explaining, and revealing of those entities that are advantageous, is the tenth deed of a tathāgata and it is one that a tathāgata accomplishes by means of his knowledge of all aspects and what is most excellent.

This is the manner in which a tathāgata, by carrying out the ten deeds of a tathāgata, accomplishes all the activities of a buddha by means of a buddha's one hundred and forty unique qualities. Furthermore, it would not be easy to give a detailed enumeration of the different forms of a buddha's activities even [if one described them] for up to a trillion trillion kalpas.

Buddhahood Is Called a State of Preeminence [III.6.11.3]

The pleasurable state of a tathāgata and the stage of a tathāgata are called "preeminence."

Why is that?

It is that [state] which zealous bodhisattvas are desirous of achieving and which they rely upon and depend upon as they train themselves in the bodhisattva [forms of] training. After it has been attained, it is also the high position that is relied upon and depended upon in order to accomplish all the aims of all sentient beings. Therefore, it is called "preeminence."

The Qualities of a Buddha Are Unique [III.6.11.4]

All of these buddha qualities that the tathāgatas possess are conducive to accomplishing others' aims to an exceedingly great degree and they are distinguished by [the characteristic of] accomplishing others' aims, unlike [the qualities] that the listeners and solitary realizers possess. Therefore, those [qualities of a tathāgata] are said to be "unique."[1561] There are certain qualities of a buddha that are not seen in any form at all among the listeners and solitary realizers. These include, for example, great compassion, the nature of being completely free of confusion, the complete destruction of the traces, and the knowledge of all aspects and what is most excellent. There are others that are perceived [among the listeners and solitary realizers] but not in a form that is complete in every respect. However, all of those that are possessed by a tathāgata are perceived in a form that is complete in every respect, that have greatly surpassed [others], and that are most excellent. Therefore,

1561. S: *āveṇikaḥ,* T: *ma 'dres pa*. This term is typically glossed as meaning that which is "uncommon" or "unshared" (S: *asādharaṇam,* T: *thun mong ma yin pa*) with anyone else. MW (p. 111) explains that the adjective is derived from another adjective that means "not commingled (as the waters of a river)." Here Asaṅga uses it to refer to the entire collection of one hundred forty qualities of a tathāgata. *AS* (p. 99) and *ASBh* (p. 131) also use it to describe the following group of eighteen qualities: (1) a buddha is without error in bodily activities; (2) he does not cry out excitedly, as persons do when they have lost their way; (3) he never has a lapse of recollection regarding the appropriate time for a particular action; (4) his mind is always absorbed in a state of composure; (5) he does not have diverse conceptions, such as "samsara is misery and nirvana is peace"; (6) he does not neglect beings through failing to engage in proper consideration; (7) he is unfaltering in his aspiration to act on behalf of sentient beings; (8) he is unfaltering in generating fortitude; (9) he is unfaltering in his recollection that is ever committed to the goal of aiding all sentient beings; (10) he is unfaltering in his one-pointed concentration that focuses on the ultimate nature of all things; (11) he is unfaltering in the wisdom that knows beings' minds and knows what Dharma to teach them; (12) he never wavers from the desire to deliver all beings from suffering; (13) all his bodily acts are preceded by and in agreement with transcendent knowledge; (14) all his verbal acts are preceded by and in agreement with transcendent knowledge; (15) all his mental acts are preceded by and in agreement with transcendent knowledge; (16) his transcendent knowledge perceives the past without obstruction or impediment; (17) his transcendent knowledge perceives the future without obstruction or impediment; and (18) his transcendent knowledge perceives the present without obstruction or impediment.

they are called "unique." It should be understood that the meaning of the term "unique" is that of being exclusive.

Alternate Names for This Work and the Benefits of Supporting Its Dissemination [III.6.11.5]

This [presentation] has revealed the bodhisattvas' complete path of training as well as the result of that training. It constitutes a foundation for describing the entire path of training for bodhisattvas and all the aspects of the results of that path of training. Indeed, this [work, which is entitled] *The Stage of a Bodhisattva,* can also be referred to as "A Manual[1562] for the Bodhisattva Collection," "A Summary of the Great Vehicle," "An Explanation of the Path That Leads to Destruction and the Path That Avoids Destruction," and "The Foundation for Developing the Purity of Unobstructed Knowledge."

Within the world of gods, humans, and demigods, whatever divine being, human being, ascetic, or brahmin generates a strong [sense of] devotion toward this *Stage of a Bodhisattva*, and then listens to it, takes it up, retains it, and practices it in the form of meditation, reveals it at length to others, or at least preserves it through causing it to be copied, and then worships and honors it should, in brief, expect [to generate] a heap of merit that is as great in size as the heap of merit that the Lord promulgated, laid out, disclosed, prescribed, and made clear [would be gained] by [carrying out] the act of listening to, etc., [all] the sutras that are contained in the bodhisattva collection [of scriptures].

Why is that?

1562. S: *mātṛkā,* T: *ma mo.* See note 62 and accompanying text in the introduction that examines how Asaṅga intends this term to be understood. *BBhVy* (f. 336a): "This *Stage of a Bodhisattva* is described as a manual for the extensive bodhisattva collection of scriptures—which is to say, it includes [the subjects that are contained in] all of the sutra scriptures, just as an alphabet [includes all the basic characters that are necessary for writing]." MW (p. 807): "a mother (also, fig. = source, origin)"; "a nurse"; "a grandmother"; "any alphabet." *Oxford Dictionary of Buddhism:* "A rubric or tabulated summary of contents used in the philosophical sections of the books of the Abhidharma Piṭaka. Originally a Vinaya term, used in the singular (Pāli, *mātikā*), it meant a keyword. Used in the plural (also *mātikā*), it means the keywords for a topic, and hence a list." The first hypothesis emphasizes the practice of formulating matrices or taxonomic lists (*mātṛkā*) of all topics found in the traditional teaching, which are then arranged according to both numeric and qualitative criteria. *BHSD* (p. 428): "a summary or condensed statement of contents."

It is because all the most important brief and extensive explanations [found throughout] the entire bodhisattva collection [of scriptures] have been included and set forth in this *Stage of a Bodhisattva*. Moreover, as long as the [Buddha's spiritual system of] Dharma and Vinaya that has been revealed at length in this *Stage of a Bodhisattva* shall endure, develop widely, and achieve greatness through being frequently explained, recited, and practiced in a manner that accords with the Dharma, for that length of time the counterfeit forms of the true Dharma that bring about the disappearance of the true Dharma will not abound. On the other hand, as soon as the counterfeit forms of the true Dharma abound, that will bring about the disappearance of the true Dharma that is connected with what really exists.

Within [Book III of] *The Stage of a Bodhisattva*, [known as] "The Object of Mental Application That Relates to the Perfection of the Support," this completes the sixth chapter, entitled "Preeminence." This concludes *The Stage of a Bodhisattva*.

The Successive Order of the Topics

The following represents the successive order [of the topics that are presented] in *The Stage of a Bodhisattva.*

A bodhisattva who abides in the [Great Vehicle's] spiritual lineage generates the thought to [achieve] unsurpassed true and complete enlightenment. [The bodhisattva] who has generated that thought applies him- or herself to [the attainment of] one's own aim and that of others. The person who is applying him- or herself to [the attainment of] one's own aim and that of others finds the means by which to avoid becoming afflicted. The person who remains unafflicted finds the means by which to remain free of weariness. The person who is unwearied finds the means by which to increase [his or her] roots of virtue. The person who increases his or her roots of virtue [ultimately] achieves unsurpassed true and complete enlightenment.

The person who is pursuing the practices [that will accomplish] one's own aim and that of others, [pursuing] the means by which one can avoid becoming afflicted, the means by which one will remain free of weariness, the means by which one will increase [one's] roots of virtue, and [ultimately pursuing] the attainment of enlightenment, at the very outset fixes his or her devotion upon the profound and extensive subjects. The person who has fixed his or her devotion upon those subjects will seek them. Having sought them, one will both teach them to others and [strive to] achieve them by one's own practice.

As one [strives to] achieve them, one practices in whatever way, in relation to whatever object, and for the sake of whatever purpose one ought to practice. While proceeding in that way, in relation to that object, and for that purpose, one practices in whatever way will bring about the accumulation of merit and the accumulation of wisdom. The person who has accumulated merit and wisdom practices the means by which to avoid abandoning samsara. While practicing in that way, one undertakes to avoid developing the mental afflictions [while remaining] in samsara. While practicing in that way, one undertakes to avoid becoming attached to one's own happiness. While practicing in that way, one undertakes to avoid being made weary by the suffering of samsara.

While avoiding being made weary by that [suffering], [a bodhisattva] relies upon the [inner and outer] bodies of teachings and becomes one who is proficient in all the bodies of teachings. Having become a person who knows the [various] bodies of teachings, [one] learns what should be taught to whom and how to go about doing so, thereby becoming one who knows the world. The person who knows the bodies of teachings and who knows the world in this way seeks the Dharma in a proper manner.

The person who is seeking [the Dharma] in this way develops the ability to remove all doubts possessed by all sentient beings. As the person who possesses this ability increases his or her merit through removing the doubts of others, he or she will complete the accumulation of merit. By increasing one's knowledge, one will also complete the accumulation of wisdom. While completing [the two accumulations], one will apply oneself in a genuine manner to [the practice of] meditating upon the [spiritual] qualities that are conducive to enlightenment. One will also know the [proper] method of [engaging in] meditation. The person who has applied him- or herself in this manner will dedicate his or her meditation [practice] to [the attainment of] the Great Vehicle's form of complete nirvana, not to [the attainment of] the form of complete nirvana [that is pursued in] the vehicles of the listeners or the solitary realizers.

The person who possesses this kind of skillful means will retain [in his or her mind those teachings that were] uttered by all the buddhas and bodhisattvas and that were [previously] heard. Through the power of meditation, every aspect of the Dharma [teachings] that one has not previously heard will also become clear. The person who possesses this power of retention and this clarity of understanding will practice the three doors to liberation with the aim of abandoning all the obscurations.[1563] The person who practices in this way will become one who is established in the aim of

1563. S: *āvaraṇaprahaṇāya*. This translation is based on the Sanskrit reading, which seems more straightforward in meaning than the Tibetan. The Tibetan translation reads "in order to abandon all [erring] mental objects" (T: *dmigs pa thams cad spangs pa'i phyir*). This may be a corruption that should read *sgrib pa thams cad spangs pa'i phyir*.

abandoning one's own [forms of] erring belief and exaggerated pride as well as those of others. This constitutes [a bodhisattva's] form of practice that is excellent in every respect.

Bodhisattvas Are the Most Distinguished of Spiritual Practitioners

The person who is established [in the practice] in this way will become more distinguished than all sentient beings, including the listeners and solitary realizers, as relates both to the differences in the qualities of their spiritual practice and the differences in their favorable qualities.

Differences in the Qualities of Spiritual Practice

Regarding this [point], the differences in the qualities of their spiritual practice [are as follows]. A bodhisattva is established [in the spiritual practice] in order to benefit [both] oneself and others, and he or she is also one who considers one's duty to be the pursuit of others' aims. A listener and a solitary realizer do not consider their duty to be the pursuit of others' aims in the same way. [A bodhisattva] is one who has the same attitude toward all sentient beings as one does toward oneself. With this mind that views [everyone] equally, he or she is always intent upon aiding [everyone], and does not wish for anything in return. As one [whose mind] is directed in this way, [a bodhisattva] always desires to benefit others and bring them happiness. Having such an intention to benefit and bring happiness [to others], he or she puts forth fruitful efforts on their behalf. This constitutes the distinguishing characteristic that relates to the qualities of [bodhisattvas'] spiritual practice, one that [over time] is accomplished to an ever-increasing degree.

Differences in Their Favorable Qualities

Regarding this [point], the differences in their favorable qualities[1564] [are as follows]. A bodhisattva receives a prophecy [regarding his or her enlightenment] from the buddhas. A listener and a solitary realizer disciple do not.

1564. S: *anuśaṃsaguṇaḥ*, T: *phan yon gyi yon tan*. The term *anuśamsaḥ* (T: *phan yon*) is often understood to mean a "benefit" or an "advantage," and it is typically used to describe attributes of a goal or spiritual quality that make it worthy of pursuing, such as the "benefits

[A bodhisattva] who has received a prophecy is one who resides on the stage of irreversibility. [A bodhisattva] who abides there obtains the nature of being completely free of confusion with regard to what is to be done out of necessity and what is to be done continually. A declaration about the quality of being completely free of confusion in this way is made by buddhas and bodhisattvas when they are making pronouncements about those who are the best among all sentient beings. [A bodhisattva who resides on the stage of irreversibility] also does not fail to carry out all those activities that ought to be done. Nor does one leave unfinished those [goals] that are unattained and still incomplete.

By not leaving anything unfinished, [a bodhisattva] is always increasing his or her virtuous qualities. Because [that bodhisattva] increases his or her virtuous qualities like [the moon] during the waxing half [of the month], he or she is a genuine bodhisattva, not a counterfeit one. By being a genuine bodhisattva, one knows every aspect of every method for [attaining spiritual] self-discipline. By knowing this, one becomes skilled about all the circumstances that relate to why something should be investigated, what subjects should be investigated, and the means by which they should be investigated. Through engaging in these investigations, one causes these matters to be ascertained.

By becoming skilled regarding these circumstances, [a bodhisattva] will become skilled about giving instruction. By becoming skilled about giving instruction, he or she attains the king of one-pointed concentrations, one whose objects are immeasurable. Having attained this concentration, [a bodhisattva] becomes one who teaches the Dharma in a fruitful manner. He or she becomes a teacher [whose efforts are] productive in a variety of ways. He or she becomes one who is completely familiar with [the doctrine of] the Great Vehicle. Having become familiar with that [doctrine] to a high degree, one becomes a supporter of the Great Vehicle. On any of a variety of occasions when one has become completely familiar with [the doctrine of] the Great Vehicle, one receives any of a variety of names, and the buddhas and bodhisattvas refer to and praise one with a name that is

---

of one-pointed concentration." The term is often contrasted with *ādīnavaḥ* (T: *nyes dmigs*), which means "fault" or "disadvantage," such as the "disadvantages of samsara." Here the beneficial or favorable qualities of a bodhisattva are being contrasted with those of listeners and solitary realizers.

common to all bodhisattvas. These should be understood to be distinguishing characteristics that relate to the [bodhisattvas'] favorable qualities.

The ones who have such names[1565] should be understood to [have been given them because] they are a mark of being a bodhisattva. By possessing these marks, one can be successful in every aspect of the practice both within the householder faction and within the faction of those who have gone forth [into the homeless state]. [The bodhisattva] who can be successful within either of these two factions becomes one whose practice is meaningful and one whose superior attitude is solely devoted to the side of virtue. Whether adopting the householder faction or the faction of those who have gone forth, the person who has such an attitude will remain on the side of virtue for as long as he or she lives.

Following that [life], one will knowingly take birth where one can meet with buddhas and bodhisattvas and be of benefit to sentient beings. One will experience circumstances in which buddhas and bodhisattvas continually and uninterruptedly provide the support of their instruction and [will experience circumstances] in which one will [continually and uninterruptedly have the opportunity to] attain superior qualities that relate to the side of virtue. Seizing the benefits of that experience, one enters into that situation in which superior qualities can be attained in a manner [that resembles entering one's own] abode.[1566] With a mind that is established in that situation, one advances in every way to ever-higher extraordinary states, without being satisfied until the state of perfection has been reached. Advancing in this way, one will obtain the state of perfection beyond which one no longer seeks anything higher or greater and where the unsurpassed state has been attained. This concludes the successive order of [the topics that are presented in] *The Stage of a Bodhisattva*.

This treatise was translated into Tibetan, edited, and finalized by the senior Indian teacher Prajñāvarma and the great translator and editor, the Venerable [Tibetan] teacher Ye shes sDe, and others. It is made up of six thousand seven hundred and fifty ślokas.

1565. S: *evaṃ nāmnaḥ*, T: *de lta bu'i ming can*. This is presumably a reference to the sixteen epithets that appear at the end of Book I, chapter 18, in the section entitled "Descriptive Appellations" [I.18.27].

1566. See note 1417 above for a similar example of this simile. The sense is that a bodhisattva takes on this activity as readily as one would enter one's own home.

ये धर्मा हेतुप्रभवा हेतुं तेषां तथागतो ह्यवदत् ।
तेषां च यो निरोध एवंवादी महाश्रमणः ॥

ye dharma hetuprabhava hetuṃ teṣaṃ tathagato hy avadat |
teṣāṃ ca yo nirodha evaṃ vādī mahāśramaṇaḥ ||

ཆོས་རྣམས་ཐམས་ཅད་རྒྱུ་ལས་བྱུང་། །དེ་རྒྱུ་དེ་བཞིན་གཤེགས་པས་གསུངས། །
རྒྱུ་ལ་འགོག་པ་གང་ཡིན་པ། །དགེ་སྦྱོང་ཆེན་པོས་འདི་སྐད་གསུངས། །

The Tathāgata has declared the causes
Of those entities that are causally produced,
As well as what constitutes their cessation.
The Great Ascetic is one who teaches thus.

Outline and Summary Verses

BOOK I. The Support

1. The Spiritual Lineage 3

Support, marks, factions,
Superior attitudes, pleasurable states,
Births, embracing, stages,
Conduct, and, lastly, preeminence.

Support [1.1.1] 3
The Two Types of Spiritual Lineage [1.1.2] 5
The Superiority of Bodhisattvas [1.1.3] 7
Signs [1.1.4] 8
The Signs That Occur in Relation to the Perfection of Generosity [1.1.4.1] 8
The Signs That Occur in Relation to the Perfection of Morality [1.1.4.2] 10
The Signs That Occur in Relation to the Perfection of Patience [1.1.4.3] 13
The Signs That Occur in Relation to the Perfection of Effort [1.1.4.4] 13
The Signs That Occur in Relation to the Perfection of Meditative Absorption [1.1.4.5] 14
The Signs That Occur in Relation to the Perfection of Wisdom [1.1.4.6] 16
Four States of Mental Affliction and Four Advantages [1.1.5] 17
Four Obstacles to Enlightenment [1.1.6] 18

2. Generating Enlightenment Mind 21

Five Characteristics [1.2.1] 21
Four Points [1.2.2] 23
Two Types of Enlightenment Mind [1.2.3] 24
Four Contributing Factors [1.2.4] 25
Four Causes [1.2.5] 26
Four Strengths [1.2.6] 28
Four Causes That Turn One Away [1.2.7] 30
Two Marvelous and Wonderful Qualities [1.2.8] 30
Two Salutary Attitudes [1.2.9] 31
Two Forms of Application [1.2.10] 31
Two Great Doors for Gaining Virtuous Qualities [1.2.11] 31
Two Forms of Superiority [1.2.12] 32
Two Benefits of Generating Enlightenment Mind [1.2.13] 32

3. One's Own and Others' Aims 35

One's own and others' aims, the meaning of reality,
Power, the twofold ripening of beings
And of a buddha's qualities in oneself,
And the seventh is supreme enlightenment.

The Qualities of Exclusivity and of Being Related to Others [1.3.1–2] 36
The Quality of Being Linked to What Is Beneficial [1.3.3] 40
The Quality of Being Linked to Happiness [1.3.4] 42
The Aspects of Being Included within a Cause or a Result [1.3.5–6] 48
  The Eight Maturations [1.3.5.1, 1.3.6.1] 48
    The Causes of the Eight Maturations [1.3.5.1.1] 49
    The Conditions That Insure the Effectiveness of the Causes [1.3.5.1.2] 51
    The Results That Can Be Achieved through the Maturations [1.3.6.1.1] 52
  Merit and Wisdom [1.3.5.2, 1.3.6.2] 55
    The Causes of Merit and Wisdom [1.3.5.2.1] 56
    The Results of Merit and Wisdom [1.3.6.2.1] 57
One's Own and Others' Aims That Relate to This Life and to Future Lives [1.3.7–8] 58

One's Own and Others' Aims That Are Perpetual or Not Perpetual [1.3.9–10] 60

4. The Nature of Reality 63

Four Categories of Reality [1.4.1] 63
The Objects of Ordinary Experience [1.4.1.1] 64
The Objects That Are Verified through Reasoning [1.4.1.2] 65
The Form of Transcendent Awareness That Eradicates the Mental Afflictions [1.4.1.3] 66
The Form of Transcendent Awareness That Brings Supreme Enlightenment [1.4.1.4] 67
The Concepts of Being and Nonbeing [1.4.2] 68
Nondual Wisdom Is a Great Means [1.4.3] 69
The Positive Effect of Relying upon Nondual Wisdom [1.4.4] 73
The Bodhisattva Who Is Correctly Established in the Practice [1.4.5] 74
The Form of Application That Establishes the Meaning of Ultimate Reality [1.4.6] 77
Scriptural Evidence [1.4.7] 84
The Eight Types of Conceptual Thought [1.4.8] 89
The Four Investigations [1.4.9] 96
The Four Forms of Thorough Knowledge of the Way Things Truly Are [1.4.10] 97
Five Beneficial Qualities That Are Most Excellent and Their Respective Actions [1.4.11] 101

5. Power 105

The Six Forms of Supernatural Knowledge [1.5.1] 106
Miraculous Power [1.5.1.1] 106
Transformational Miraculous Power [1.5.1.1.1] 107
Creative Miraculous Power [1.5.1.1.2] 116
The Magical Creation of a Body [1.5.1.1.2.1] 117
The Magical Creation of Speech [1.5.1.1.2.2] 119
Recollection of Former Existences [1.5.1.2] 121
The Divine Ear [1.5.1.3] 123
Knowledge regarding Death and Rebirth [1.5.1.4] 125
Knowledge regarding Diverse States of Mind [1.5.1.5] 126

Knowledge regarding Termination of the Outflows [1.5.1.6] 128
The Power of Spiritual Qualities [1.5.2] 129
The Power of Generosity [1.5.2.1] 130
The Power of Morality [1.5.2.2] 130
The Power of Patience [1.5.2.3] 131
The Power of Effort [1.5.2.4] 132
The Power of Meditative Absorption [1.5.2.5] 132
The Power of Wisdom [1.5.2.6] 133
Natural Power [1.5.3] 134
The Power That Is Not Shared with Listeners and Solitary Realizers [1.5.4] 135
The Power That Is Shared with Listeners and Solitary Realizers [1.5.5] 139

6. Ripening 141

The Essential Nature of Having Become Spiritually Ripe [1.6.1] 141
The Persons Who Are to Be Ripened [1.6.2] 142
The Varieties of Ripening [1.6.3] 143
The Means of Ripening [1.6.4] 145
The Persons Who Ripen Others [1.6.5] 153
The Characteristics of Persons Who Are Spiritually Ripe [1.6.6] 154

7. Enlightenment 159

The Nature of Enlightenment [1.7.1] 159
Seven Forms of Supremacy [1.7.2] 162
Recollection of a Tathāgata's Good Qualities [1.7.3] 164

8. The Lineages of the Powers 171

Abundance of devotion,
Seeking and teaching Dharma,
Practice and, likewise,
Correct instruction and counsel,
And, lastly, deeds of body, speech, and mind
That are supported by means.

Abundance of Devotion [1.8.1] 172

Seeking the Dharma [1.8.2] 173
The Ten Causes [1.8.2.1] 175
How Worldly Entities Are Produced [1.8.2.1.1] 179
The Process of Affliction [1.8.2.1.2] 181
The Process of Purification [1.8.2.1.3] 182
Five Kinds of Results [1.8.2.2] 185
The Correct Manner of Seeking Learning [1.8.2.3] 188
The Proper Motives for Seeking Learning [1.8.2.4] 190
Teaching the Dharma [1.8.3] 191
The Form of Practice That Accords with the Dharma [1.8.4] 194
Conformity in Body, Speech, and Mind with the Buddha's Admonitions [1.8.4.1] 194
Correct Reflection [1.8.4.2] 194
Meditation [1.8.4.3] 196
Instruction [1.8.5] 199
Counsel [1.8.6] 201
Deeds of Body, Speech, and Mind That Are Supported by Means [1.8.7] 202

9. Generosity 205

The essence, all-inclusive,
Difficult to carry out, directed everywhere,
Connected with the qualities of a true spiritual person,
Likewise, all of its forms,

Relating to what is wanted by those in distress,
What brings happiness here and in the next world,
And, likewise, that which is pure—
This, in brief, is the generosity of bodhisattvas.

The Essence of Generosity [1.9.1] 206
All-Inclusive Generosity [1.9.2] 207
What to Observe and Avoid When Practicing Generosity [1.9.2.1] 208
Wise Generosity [1.9.2.2] 218
The Proper Manner in Which to Avoid Making a Gift [1.9.2.3] 223
Four Obstacles to the Practice of Generosity [1.9.2.4] 225
Practicing a Form of Generosity That Is Mental in Nature [1.9.2.5] 227

The Generosity That Is Difficult to Carry Out [1.9.3] 228
The Generosity That Is Directed Everywhere [1.9.4] 228
The Generosity of a True Spiritual Being [1.9.5] 229
Generosity of Every Form [1.9.6] 229
Generosity That Relates to the Distressed and What They Want [1.9.7] 230
Generosity That Brings Happiness Here and in the Next World [1.9.8] 231
Pure Generosity [1.9.9] 232

10. **Morality** 237

The essence, all-inclusive,
Difficult to carry out, directed everywhere,
Connected with the qualities of a true spiritual person,
Likewise, all of its forms,

Relating to what is wanted by those in distress,
What brings happiness here and in the next world,
And, likewise, that which is pure—
These, in brief, are the nine aspects of morality.

The Essence of Morality [1.10.1] 237
All-Inclusive Morality [1.10.2] 239
The Morality of Restraint [1.10.2.1] 240
The Morality of Acquiring Virtuous Qualities [1.10.2.2] 240
The Morality That Acts on Behalf of Beings [1.10.2.3] 243
Conduct That Is Well Restrained [1.10.2.4] 244
Acquiring Virtue Effectively [1.10.2.5] 248
Engaging in Every Aspect of Acting on Behalf of Sentient Beings [1.10.2.6] 249
Assisting Those Who Need Help with Various Activities [1.10.2.6.1a] 249
Assisting Those Who Are Experiencing Physical or Mental Suffering [1.10.2.6.1b] 250
Showing What Is Proper [1.10.2.6.2] 251
Showing Gratitude for Benefit Received from Others [1.10.2.6.3] 252

Protecting Beings from Danger [1.10.2.6.4] 252
Dispelling Sorrow [1.10.2.6.5] 253
Furnishing the Objects That Are Needed for Subsistence [1.10.2.6.6] 253
Providing a Proper Abode [1.10.2.6.7] 254
Complying with the Minds of Others [1.10.2.6.8] 254
Giving Encouragement to Others [1.10.2.6.9] 257
Suppressing Those Who Engage in Misconduct [1.10.2.6.10] 257
Displaying Miraculous Powers [1.10.2.6.11] 258
The Ritual for Acceptance of the Bodhisattva Discipline [1.10.2.7] 260
How to Safeguard the Discipline [1.10.2.8] 265
The Four Acts That Represent an Extreme Form of Defeat [1.10.2.9] 267
Secondary Offenses [1.10.2.10] 269
Not Performing the Three Kinds of Devotion to the Three Jewels [1.10.2.10.1] 270
Allowing Desire to Remain Unchecked [1.10.2.10.2] 271
Failing to Respect One's Spiritual Elders and Refusing to Reply Verbally [1.10.2.10.3–4] 271
Not Accepting an Invitation [1.10.2.10.5] 273
Not Accepting Gold and Other Forms of Wealth [1.10.2.10.6] 274
Refusing to Teach Dharma to Those Who Seek It [1.10.2.10.7] 274
Abandoning Those Who Are Immoral [1.10.2.10.8] 275
Not Training Oneself in a Way That Engenders Faith in Others [1.10.2.10.9] 276
Engaging in Few Activities for the Sake of Sentient Beings [1.10.2.10.10] 277
Failing to Act with Sympathy [1.10.2.10.11] 278
Persisting in Wrong Forms of Livelihood [1.10.2.10.12] 282
Engaging in Mental Excitation and Excessive Merriment [1.10.2.10.13] 282
Regarding Samsara with Complacence [1.10.2.10.14] 283
Failing to Dispel a Bad Reputation [1.10.2.10.15] 284
Failing to Apply a Distressing Measure [1.10.2.10.16] 284
Scolding Others in Return for Being Scolded, and the Like [1.10.2.10.17] 285
Ignoring Those Who Have Been Angered [1.10.2.10.18] 285
Refusing to Accept an Apology [1.10.2.10.19] 286

Allowing Anger to Remain Unchecked [1.10.2.10.20] 286
Gathering a Following out of Desire for Gain and Honor [1.10.2.10.21] 287
Failing to Dispel Laziness, and the Like [1.10.2.10.22] 287
Engaging in Idle Speech with a Sense of Attachment [1.10.2.10.23] 287
Failing to Pursue One-Pointed Concentration [1.10.2.10.24] 288
Failing to Eliminate the Hindrances to Meditative Composure [1.10.2.10.25] 288
Regarding Enjoyment of the States of Meditative Absorption as a Good Quality [1.10.2.10.26] 289
Rejecting the Teachings of the Listeners' Vehicle [1.10.2.10.27] 289
Failing to Pursue the Teachings of the Great Vehicle [1.10.2.10.28] 290
Studying Heretical Treatises to the Exclusion of the Buddha's Word [1.10.2.10.29] 290
Delighting in the Study of Heretical Treatises [1.10.2.10.30] 290
Denigrating the Teachings of the Great Vehicle [1.10.2.10.31] 291
Praising Oneself and Disparaging Others [1.10.2.10.32] 291
Failing to Pursue Learning [1.10.2.10.33] 292
Showing Disrespect toward a Dharma Teacher or the Dharma [1.10.2.10.34] 293
Failing to Assist Others [1.10.2.10.35] 293
Failing to Care for the Sick [1.10.2.10.36] 294
Failing to Assist Those Who Are Suffering [1.10.2.10.37] 294
Not Indicating What Is Proper to Others [1.10.2.10.38] 295
Failing to Return a Benefit Received from Others [1.10.2.10.39] 295
Failing to Dispel the Grief That Others Are Experiencing [1.10.2.10.40] 296
Failing to Provide Food and the Like to Those Who Seek It [1.10.2.10.41] 296
Failing to Assist One's Followers [1.10.2.10.42] 296
Failing to Comply with the Wishes of Others [1.10.2.10.43] 297
Failing to Praise Those Who Deserve to Be Praised [1.10.2.10.44] 298
Failing to Suppress Those Who Engage in Misconduct [1.10.2.10.45] 299
Failing to Use One's Miraculous Powers [1.10.2.10.46] 300

Concluding Remarks [1.10.2.11] 300
Confession [1.10.2.12] 301
The Ritual for Accepting the Bodhisattva Discipline If There Is No Qualified Preceptor [1.10.2.13] 302
Further Comments about Transgressions [1.10.2.14] 303
Three Forms of Excellence [1.10.2.15] 303
The Morality That Is Difficult to Carry Out [1.10.3] 305
The Morality That Is Directed Everywhere [1.10.4] 305
The Morality of a True Spiritual Being [1.10.5] 306
Morality of Every Form [1.10.6] 306
Morality That Relates to the Distressed and What They Want [1.10.7] 307
The Morality That Brings Happiness Here and in the Next World [1.10.8] 308
Pure Morality [1.10.9] 309

11. Patience 313

The Essence of Patience [1.11.1] 313
All-Inclusive Patience [1.11.2] 314
The Patience That Forbears the Harm Inflicted by Others [1.11.2.1] 315
Four Points [1.11.2.1.1] 315
Five Conceptions [1.11.2.1.2] 316
The Patience That Tolerates Suffering [1.11.2.2] 319
The Suffering That Occurs in All Situations [1.11.2.2.1] 319
The Four Supports [1.11.2.2.2] 320
The Nine Worldly Conditions [1.11.2.2.3] 320
The Four Modes of Physical Behavior [1.11.2.2.4] 320
The Seven Forms of Embracing the Dharma [1.11.2.2.5] 321
Seven Aspects of a Mendicant's Way of Life [1.11.2.2.6] 321
Bodily Fatigue and Mental Weariness [1.11.2.2.7] 322
Deeds That Benefit Sentient Beings [1.11.2.2.8] 323
Regular Activities [1.11.2.2.9] 323
The Patience of the Devotion That Is Gained by Reflecting upon Entities [1.11.2.3] 323
The Patience That Is Difficult to Carry Out [1.11.3] 324
The Patience That Is Directed Everywhere [1.11.4] 324
The Patience of a True Spiritual Being [1.11.5] 325

Patience of Every Form [1.11.6] 325
Patience That Relates to the Distressed and What They Want [1.11.7] 327
The Patience That Brings Happiness Here and in the Next World [1.11.8] 328
Pure Patience [1.11.9] 328

12. Effort 331

The Essence of Effort [1.12.1] 331
All-Inclusive Effort [1.12.2] 331
Armor-Like Effort [1.12.2.1] 332
The Effort That Collects Virtuous Qualities [1.12.2.2] 333
The Effort That Acts on Behalf of Sentient Beings [1.12.2.3] 334
The Effort That Is Difficult to Carry Out [1.12.3] 334
The Effort That Is Directed Everywhere [1.12.4] 335
The Effort of a True Spiritual Being [1.12.5] 337
Effort of Every Form [1.12.6] 337
The Effort That Relates to the Distressed and What They Want and the Effort That Brings Happiness Here and in the Next World [1.12.7–8] 338
Pure Effort [1.12.9] 339

13. Meditative Absorption 343

The Essence of Meditative Absorption [1.13.1] 343
All-Inclusive Meditative Absorption [1.13.2] 344
The Meditative Absorption That Enables One to Abide in a State of Ease during This Life [1.13.2.1] 344
The Meditative Absorption That Gains the Spiritual Qualities Related to One-Pointed Concentration [1.13.2.2] 345
The Meditative Absorption That Relates to Acting on Behalf of Sentient Beings [1.13.2.3] 347
The Meditative Absorption That Is Difficult to Carry Out [1.13.3] 348
The Meditative Absorption That Is Directed Everywhere [1.13.4] 348
The Meditative Absorption of a True Spiritual Being [1.13.5] 350
Meditative Absorption of Every Form [1.13.6] 350
The Meditative Absorption That Relates to the Distressed and What They Want [1.13.7] 351

The Meditative Absorption That Brings Happiness Here and in the Next World [1.13.8] 352
Pure Meditative Absorption [1.13.9] 353

14. Wisdom 355

The Essence of Wisdom [1.14.1] 355
All-Inclusive Wisdom [1.14.2] 355
The Wisdom That Is Directed toward Realizing Ultimate Reality [1.14.2.1] 356
The Wisdom That Develops Expertise regarding the Five Branches of Learning and the Three Heaps [1.14.2.2] 356
The Wisdom That Accomplishes the Aims of Sentient Beings [1.14.2.3] 357
The Wisdom That Is Difficult to Carry Out [1.14.3] 357
The Wisdom That Is Directed Everywhere [1.14.4] 357
The Wisdom of a True Spiritual Being [1.14.5] 358
Wisdom of Every Form [1.14.6] 359
The Wisdom That Relates to the Distressed and What They Want [1.14.7] 359
The Wisdom That Brings Happiness Here and in the Next World [1.14.8] 360
Pure Wisdom [1.14.9] 360

15. The Principles for Attracting a Following 365

Agreeable Speech [1.15.1] 365
The Essence of Agreeable Speech [1.15.1.1] 365
All-Inclusive Agreeable Speech [1.15.1.2] 365
Agreeable Speech That Is Difficult to Carry Out [1.15.1.3] 367
Agreeable Speech That Is Directed Everywhere [1.15.1.4] 367
The Agreeable Speech of a True Spiritual Being [1.15.1.5] 368
Agreeable Speech of Every Form [1.15.1.6] 369
The Agreeable Speech That Relates to the Distressed and What They Want [1.15.1.7] 370
Agreeable Speech That Brings Happiness Here and in the Next World [1.15.1.8] 370
Agreeable Speech That Is Pure [1.15.1.9] 371

Beneficial Conduct [1.15.2] 371
The Essence of Beneficial Conduct [1.15.2.1] 371
All-Inclusive Beneficial Conduct [1.15.2.2] 372
The Beneficial Conduct That Is Difficult to Carry Out [1.15.2.3] 374
The Beneficial Conduct That Is Directed Everywhere [1.15.2.4] 374
The Beneficial Conduct of a True Spiritual Being [1.15.2.5] 375
Beneficial Conduct of Every Form [1.15.2.6] 375
The Beneficial Conduct That Relates to the Distressed and What They Want [1.15.2.7] 376
The Beneficial Conduct That Brings Happiness Here and in the Next World [1.15.2.8] 377
Pure Beneficial Conduct [1.15.2.9] 377
Sameness of Purpose [1.15.3] 379
The Results of the Various Aspects of Practice [1.15.4] 384

16. Worship, Service, and the Immeasurables 387

Worshipping the Jewels, serving a [spiritual] friend,
And, lastly, the immeasurables.

Worshipping the Three Jewels [1.16.1] 387
Body Worship [1.16.1.1] 387
Shrine Worship [1.16.1.2] 388
Face-to-Face Worship [1.16.1.3] 388
Worship That Is Not Face-to-Face [1.16.1.4] 389
Worship That One Does Oneself [1.16.1.5] 390
Worship That One Prompts Others to Do [1.16.1.6] 390
Worship That Is Carried Out with Wealth and Honor [1.16.1.7] 391
Eminent Worship [1.16.1.8] 392
Worship That Is Free of Affliction [1.16.1.9] 392
Worship That Consists of Spiritual Practice [1.16.1.10] 393
Serving a Spiritual Teacher [1.16.2] 396
The Attributes of a Spiritual Teacher [1.16.2.1] 396
Making the Role of a Spiritual Teacher Fruitful [1.16.2.2] 397
The Characteristics That Make a Spiritual Teacher Worthy of Being an Object of Faith [1.16.2.3] 398
The Duties of a Spiritual Teacher toward His or Her Disciples [1.16.2.4] 398

Serving a Spiritual Teacher [1.16.2.5] 399
Conceptions to Maintain When Listening to the Dharma [1.16.2.6] 400
Circumstances Relating to the Spiritual Teacher That Should Not Be Brought to Mind [1.16.2.7] 401
The Immeasurables [1.16.3] 402
Cultivating Compassion by Meditating on One Hundred and Ten Forms of Suffering [1.16.3.1] 404
Great Compassion [1.16.3.2] 411

17. The Spiritual Qualities That Are Conducive to Enlightenment 415

Shame, firmness, and tirelessness,
Knowledge of treatises and the world,
Likewise, the correct forms of reliance
And the forms of informative knowledge,

The accumulations, the qualities
Conducive to enlightenment,
Quiescence, insight, skillful means,
The retentions, aspirational prayer,

The three concentrations that ought to be known,
And the four summary statements.

Shame and Abashment [1.17.1] 415
Firmness [1.17.2] 416
Tirelessness [1.17.3] 417
Knowledge of Treatises [1.17.4] 417
Knowledge of the World [1.17.5] 419
The Four Reliances [1.17.6] 427
The Four Forms of Informative Knowledge [1.17.7] 429
The Two Accumulations [1.17.8] 432
The Thirty-Seven Spiritual Qualities That Are Conducive to Enlightenment [1.17.9] 433
Quiescence and Insight [1.17.10] 435
Skillful Means [1.17.11] 436
Six Inner Forms of Skillful Means [1.17.11.1] 436

Six Outer Forms of Skillful Means [1.17.11.2] 437
Causing Limited Roots of Virtue to Have Immeasurable Results [1.17.11.2.1] 437
Causing Beings to Generate Extensive Roots of Virtue with Little Effort [1.17.11.2.2] 437
The Six Methods That Accomplish Four Aims [1.17.11.2.3] 439
Benevolent Skillful Means [1.17.11.2.3.1] 440
The Method of Standing as an Obstacle [1.17.11.2.3.2] 442
The Method That Has a Dissimilar Attitude [1.17.11.2.3.3] 444
The Method That Derives from Suppression [1.17.11.2.3.4] 445
The Method That Relates to Returning a Favor [1.17.11.2.3.5] 446
The Pure Method [1.17.11.2.3.6] 446
Mental Retention [1.17.12] 448
Aspirational Prayer [1.17.13] 450
One-Pointed Concentration on Emptiness [1.17.14] 452
One-Pointed Concentration on Wishlessness [1.17.15] 452
One-Pointed Concentration on Signlessness [1.17.16] 452
The Four Summary Statements of the Dharma [1.17.17] 454
All Formations Are Impermanent [1.17.17.1] 455
All Formations Are a Form of Suffering [1.17.17.2] 459
All Entities Lack a Self [1.17.17.3] 459
Nirvana Is a State of Peace [1.17.17.4] 460

18. The Qualities of a Bodhisattva 465

Marvels and also what are not marvels,
Even-mindedness, assistance,
Acts of requital; likewise, aspirations
And fruitful methods of practice.

Five Marvelous Qualities [1.18.1] 465
Five Qualities That Bodhisattvas Do Not Regard as Marvelous [1.18.2] 466
Even-Mindedness [1.18.3] 467
Assistance [1.18.4] 468
Acts of Requital [1.18.5] 468
Aspirations [1.18.6] 468
Fruitful Methods of Practice [1.18.7] 469

Correct methods of practice,
Decline and, likewise, improvement;
Counterfeit and genuine qualities;
Likewise, providing guidance.

Correct Methods of Practice [1.18.8] 470
The Method of Practice That Safeguards [1.18.8.1] 470
The Irreproachable Method of Practice [1.18.8.2] 471
The Method of Practice That Is Accompanied by the Power of Analysis [1.18.8.3] 471
The Method of Practice That Is Accompanied by a Pure Superior Attitude [1.18.8.4] 471
The Method of Practice in Which Certainty Has Been Reached [1.18.8.5] 471
Qualities That Contribute to a Bodhisattva's Decline [1.18.9] 472
Qualities That Contribute to a Bodhisattva's Improvement [1.18.10] 472
Counterfeit Qualities [1.18.11] 472
Genuine Qualities [1.18.12] 473
Providing Guidance [1.18.13] 473

Prophecy, the occurrence of certainty,
What is to be done out of necessity,
What is to be done continually,
And the final one is what is preeminent.

Prophecy [1.18.14] 474
The Occurrence of Certainty [1.18.15] 475
What Is to Be Done out of Necessity [1.18.16] 476
What Is to Be Done Continually [1.18.17] 476
Ten Preeminent Things [1.18.18] 476

The formulations of teachings;
Likewise, the subjects of investigation,
Knowledge of the way things truly are,
And, similarly, the immeasurables.

The fruits of instruction, greatness,
The summary of the vehicle,

The ten bodhisattvas that are to be known,
And, likewise, descriptive appellations.

The Four Formulations of Teachings [I.18.19] 477
The Formulation of Teachings on the Dharma [I.18.19.1] 478
The Formulation of Teachings on Truth [I.18.19.2] 478
The Formulation of Teachings on the Applications [I.18.19.3] 480
The Formulation of Teachings on the Vehicles [I.18.19.4] 481
The Four Subjects of Investigation [I.18.20] 482
Thorough Knowledge of the Way Things Truly Are [I.18.21] 482
The Five Immeasurables [I.18.22] 483
The Extensive Fruits and Benefits of Teaching Dharma [I.18.23] 486
The Greatness of the Bodhisattva Vehicle [I.18.24] 487
The Summary of the Great Vehicle [I.18.25] 488
The Ten Bodhisattvas [I.18.26] 488
Descriptive Appellations [I.18.27] 490

BOOK II. THE QUALITIES THAT ACCORD WITH THE SUPPORT

1. The Marks of a Bodhisattva 495

Essential nature, basis, fruits and benefits,
Successive order, and inclusion.

The Essential Natures of the Marks [II.1.1] 495
The Bases of the Marks [II.1.2] 497
The Bases of Sympathy [II.1.2.1] 497
The Bases of Agreeable Speech [II.1.2.2] 499
The Bases of Fortitude [II.1.2.3] 499
The Bases of Openhandedness [II.1.2.4] 499
The Bases of Explaining Profound Meanings and Intents [II.1.2.5] 500
The Fruits and Benefits of the Marks [II.1.3] 500
The Fruits and Benefits of Sympathy [II.1.3.1] 500
The Fruits and Benefits of Agreeable Speech [II.1.3.2] 501
The Fruits and Benefits of Fortitude [II.1.3.3] 501
The Fruits and Benefits of Openhandedness and of Explaining Profound Meanings and Intents [II.1.3.4–5] 502

The Successive Order of the Marks [II.1.4] 502
The Manner of Their Inclusion [II.1.5] 503

2. Factions 505

Having completed one's spiritual activities well;
Skillfulness; assisting others; and, lastly, dedication.

The Quality of Having Completed One's Spiritual Activities Well [II.2.1] 505
Skillfulness [II.2.2] 507
Providing Assistance to Others [II.2.3] 508
Dedication [II.2.4] 508

3. Superior Attitudes 511

The affection of the intelligent ones
Toward all beings has seven aspects.
Their fifteen attitudes are regarded
As accomplishing ten actions.

The Seven Aspects of Affection [II.3.1] 511
The Fifteen Superior Attitudes [II.3.2] 513
The Ten Actions of the Superior Attitudes [II.3.3] 514

4. The Pleasurable States 517

Spiritual lineage; likewise, devotion, joy,
Superior morality, superior mind training,
The three forms of wisdom, the two forms of signlessness—
That which requires effort and that which is effortless—

The [four] forms of informative knowledge, and the supreme.
The highest pleasurable state is that of a tathāgata.

A Brief Description of the Twelve Bodhisattva Pleasurable States [II.4.1] 519

The Essential Nature of the Pleasurable State of the Spiritual Lineage [II.4.1.1] 519
The Essential Nature of the Pleasurable State of Conduct That Is Based upon Devotion [II.4.1.2] 520
The Essential Natures of the Remaining Bodhisattva Pleasurable States [II.4.1.3] 521
The Essential Nature of Meditation Practice during the Bodhisattva Pleasurable States [II.4.1.4] 523
The Pleasurable State of Conduct That Is Based upon Devotion [II.4.2] 524
The Pleasurable State of Great Joy [II.4.3] 529
The Pleasurable State of Superior Morality [II.4.4] 540
The Pleasurable State of Superior Mind Training [II.4.5] 543
The Pleasurable State of Superior Wisdom That Relates to the Spiritual Qualities That Are Conducive to Enlightenment [II.4.6] 549
The Pleasurable State of Superior Wisdom That Relates to the Truths [II.4.7] 553
The Pleasurable State of Superior Wisdom That Relates to Dependent Origination [II.4.8] 557
The Pleasurable State That Is Free of Signs and Is Accompanied by Both Mental Preparation and Effort [II.4.9] 561
The Pleasurable State That Is Free of Signs and Also Free of Effort [II.4.10] 567
The Pleasurable State of Informative Knowledge [II.4.11] 571
The Supreme Pleasurable State [II.4.12] 573
Concluding Remarks [II.4.13] 574

BOOK III. The Perfection of the Support

1. Births 583

A Birth That Puts an End to Calamities [III.1.1] 583
A Birth That Conforms by Taking on a Semblance of Shared Qualities [III.1.2] 584
Birth in a State of Greatness [III.1.3] 585
Birth as a Lord [III.1.4] 585
The Final Birth [III.1.5] 586

2. Embracing 587

Embracing All Sentient Beings at Once [III.2.1] 587
Embracing through Authority [III.2.2] 587
Embracing by Acceptance [III.2.3] 588
Long-Term Embracing [III.2.4] 590
Short-Term Embracing [III.2.5] 591
The Final Form of Embracing [III.2.6] 591
Twelve Difficult Situations That Are Stressful [III.2.7] 591

3. The Stages 595

Seven Stages [III.3.1] 595
Transcending Rebirth in the Lower Realms [III.3.2] 596
Several Points regarding the Ten Spiritual Qualities [III.3.3] 597

4. Conduct 601

Four Types of Conduct [III.4.1] 601
  Conduct Relating to the Perfections [III.4.1.1] 601
  Conduct That Is Conducive to Enlightenment [III.4.1.2] 602
  Conduct Relating to Supernatural Knowledge [III.4.1.3] 602
  Conduct Relating to the Ripening of Sentient Beings [III.4.1.4] 603
The Meaning of the Term "Perfection" [III.4.2] 603
Three Reasons for the Order of the Perfections [III.4.3] 603
An Abundance of Possessions and the Fivefold Inner Excellence [III.4.4] 604
Four Acts That Must Be Accomplished [III.4.5] 605

5. The Marks and the Secondary Signs 607

The Thirty-Two Marks of a Great Person [III.5.1] 607
The Eighty Secondary Signs [III.5.2] 609
The Virtuous Deeds That Produce the Marks [III.5.3] 611
The Four Aspects of Well-Done Spiritual Activities That Relate to the Two Factions [III.5.4] 616
The Amount of Merit That Is Required to Produce the Marks and Secondary Signs [III.5.5] 618

6. Preeminence 621

The Four Forms of Complete Purity [III.6.1] 621
The Ten Powers [III.6.2] 622
The Power of Knowledge regarding Proper and Improper Conditions [III.6.2.1] 623
The Power of Knowledge regarding [the Fact That] One's Deeds Are One's Own [III.6.2.2] 626
The Power of Knowledge regarding the Meditative Absorptions, the Liberations, and Entering States of One-Pointed Concentration [III.6.2.3] 627
The Power of Knowledge regarding Superior and Inferior Faculties [III.6.2.4] 629
The Power of Knowledge regarding Diverse Forms of Devotion [III.6.2.5] 630
The Power of Knowledge regarding Diverse Constituent Elements [III.6.2.6] 631
The Power of Knowledge regarding the Paths That Lead Everywhere [III.6.2.7] 632
The Power of Knowledge regarding the Recollection of Former Existences [III.6.2.8] 633
The Power of Knowledge regarding Death and Rebirth [III.6.2.9] 635
The Power of Knowledge regarding Termination of the Outflows [III.6.2.10] 638
Seven Aspects of a Tathāgata's Ten Powers [III.6.3] 639

Essential nature; category; exclusivity;
And, likewise, sameness;
Performance of action; successive order;
And, lastly, differences.

Essential Nature [III.6.3.1] 640
Category [III.6.3.2] 640
Exclusivity [III.6.3.3] 641
Sameness [III.6.3.4] 641
Performance of Action [III.6.3.5] 641
Three Formulations of the Successive Order of a Tathāgata's Ten Powers [III.6.3.6] 646

Differences [III.6.3.7] 648

Six Types of Attitude [III.6.3.7.1] 649

Four Types of Constituent Element [III.6.3.7.2] 650

The Four Forms of Intrepid Confidence [III.6.4] 651

The Three Closely Placed Recollections [III.6.5] 653

Three Types of Assembly [III.6.5.1] 654

The Three Forms of Having Nothing That Needs to Be Concealed [III.6.6] 654

Great Compassion [III.6.7] 655

The Nature of Being Completely Free of Confusion [III.6.8] 655

The Complete Destruction of the Traces [III.6.9] 655

Knowledge of All Aspects and of What Is Most Excellent [III.6.10] 656

Concluding Remarks [III.6.11] 658

The Differences between the Transcendent Awareness of a Tathāgata and That of a Tenth-Stage Bodhisattva [III.6.11.1] 658

A Buddha's Ten Deeds [III.6.11.2] 660

Buddhahood Is Called a State of Preeminence [III.6.11.3] 661

The Qualities of a Buddha Are Unique [III.6.11.4] 662

Alternate Names for This Work and the Benefits of Supporting Its Dissemination [III.6.11.5] 663

The Successive Order of the Topics 665

Bodhisattvas Are the Most Distinguished of Spiritual Practitioners 667

Differences in the Qualities of Spiritual Practice 667

Differences in Their Favorable Qualities 667

Bibliography

The bibliography is divided into four sections, of which only the first, Canonical Works, lists the entries by title. The other three sections—Indian Treatises, Tibetan Works, and Reference Materials—with a few exceptions are arranged by author or translator. The order follows the roman alphabet, with both Tibetan authors and titles presented according to the capitalized "main" letter of the first word.

Wherever a Sanskrit text is known to have survived and a published edition is available, I have listed that first. Footnote references are to the page number(s) of the published Sanskrit edition. To accommodate readers with little or no facility in either Tibetan or Sanskrit, I have also tried to include information for any English translations that may be available. Therefore, as many as three editions may appear for a number of entries: first the original Sanskrit, followed by Tibetan and English translations.

For works in the Kangyur (Kg.) and Tengyur (Tg.), folio numbers (abbreviated "f." or "ff." as appropriate) refer to the Derge edition. The volume numbers of the Tengyur works follow the system used in the digital edition of these collections that is distributed by the Tibetan Buddhist Resource Center. The volume numbers for the Kangyur works follow the order of the particular section in which they are found. I have also provided the reference numbers for those works that are given in the well-known catalogues published by Tohoku University (Toh.), which are listed in the last section below.

Canonical Works

Bhavasaṃkrāntisūtram. Skt. reconstruction by N. A. Śastri. In *Journal of Oriental Research, Madras,* vol. 5, 1931. Tibetan translation: *'Phags pa srid pa 'pho ba zhes bya ba theg pa chen po'i mdo*. In *mDo sde* section of Kg., vol. 19 (*Dza*), ff. 175a–177a (Toh. 226).

Blo gros mi zad pas bstan pa zhes bya ba'i theg pa chen po'i mdo (Tibetan translation of *Akṣayamatinirdeśasūtram*). In *mDo sde* section of Kg., vol. 16 (*Ma*), ff. 79a–174b (Toh. 175). English translation: *Akṣayamatinirdeśasūtra*. 2 vols. Tr. Jens Braarvig. Oslo: Solum Forlag, 1993.

Daśabalasūtram. In "Ein zweites Daśabalasūtra," *Mitteilungen des Instituts für Orientforschung* 6 (1958), pp. 382–387, 397–403. Ed. Ernst Waldschmidt. Partial Tibetan translation in *Chos mngon pa'i mdzod kyi 'grel bshad,* in *mNgon pa* section of Tg., vol. 143 (*Ngu*), ff. 265b–267a. English translation in *The Middle Length Discourses of the Buddha*. Tr. Bikkhu Ñāṇamoli and Bikkhu Bodhi. Boston: Wisdom Publications, 1995, pp. 165–167.

Daśabhūmikasūtram. Buddhist Sanskrit Texts, no. 7. Darbhanga, India: Mithila Institute, 1958. Tibetan translation: *Sa bcu pa'i mdo* (ch. 30 of *Sangs rgyas phal po che zhes bya ba shin tu rgyas pa chen po'i mdo*). In *Phal chen* section of Kg., vol. 3 (*Ga*), ff. 67a–234b (Toh. 44). English translation in *Flower Ornament Scripture*. Tr. Thomas Cleary. Boston: Shambhala Publications, 1984. Ch. 26, pp. 695–811.

[*'Phags pa*] *Don rgyas pa zhes bya ba'i chos kyi rnam grangs* (Tibetan translation of *Arthavistaranāmadharmaprayayaḥ*). In *mDo sde* section of Kg., vol. 28 (*Sa*), ff. 188a–193b (Toh. 318).

Gaṇḍavyūhasūtram. Buddhist Sanskrit Texts, no. 5. Darbhanga, India: Mithila Institute, 1960. Tibetan translation: *sDong po bkod pa'i mdo* (also *sDong po brgyan pa'i mdo*). In *Phal chen* section of Kg.; final chapter of sutra, vol. 5 (*Ca*), ff. 24a–vol. 6 (*Cha*) (Toh. 44). English translation: *Entry into the Realm of Reality*. Tr. Thomas Cleary. Boston: Shambhala Publications, 1989.

[*'Phags pa*] *dGongs pa nges par 'grel pa zhes bya ba theg pa chen po'i mdo* (Tibetan translation of *Āryasaṃdhinirmocananāmamahāyānasūtram*). In *mDo sde* section of Kg., vol. 5 (*Ca*), ff. 1b–55b (Toh. 106). English translation: *Wisdom of Buddha: The Saṁdhinirmocana Mahāyāna Sūtra*. Tr. John Powers. Berkeley: Dharma Publishing, 1995.

[*'Phags pa*] *lHa mo dpal phreng gi seng ge'i sgra zhes bya ba'i theg pa chen po'i mdo* (Tibetan translation of *Śrīmālādevīsiṃhanādasūtram*). In *dKon brtsegs* section of Kg., vol. 6 (*Cha*), ff. 255a–277b (Toh. 92). English translation in *The Lion's Roar of Queen Śrīmālā*. Tr. Alex and Hikedo Weyman. Reprint, Delhi: Motilal Banarsidass, 2007. Pp. 57–113.

Kālāma Sutta. In *Aṅguttara Nikāya,* Book of Threes, Sutta 65. No Tibetan translation available. English translation in *The Numerical Discourses of the Buddha*. Tr. Bhikkhu Bodhi. Boston: Wisdom Publications, 2012. Pp. 279–283.

Karuṇāpuṇḍarīka. In *The White Lotus of Compassion*. 2 vols. Ed. by I. Yamada. Reprint, New Delhi: Heritage Publishers, 1989. Tibetan translation: *sNying rje chen po'i padma dkar po zhes bya ba theg pa chen po'i mdo*. In *mDo sde* section of Kg., vol. 6 (*Cha*), ff. 56a–128b (Toh. 111).

Kāśyapaparivartasūtram. Ed. A. von Staël-Holstein. Shanghai: Commercial Press, 1926. Tibetan translation: *'Od srung gi le'u shes bya ba theg pa chen po'i mdo*. In *dKon brtsegs* section of Kg., vol. 6 (*Cha*), ff. 119b–151b (Toh. 87). English translation in *A Treasury of Mahāyāna Sūtras*, ch. 20, "The Sūtra of Assembled Treasures." Translated from the Chinese by the Buddhist Association of the United States. University Park: The Pennsylvania State University Press, 1983. Pp. 387–414.

['Phags pa] *Khyim bdag drag shul can gyis zhus pa zhes bya ba'i theg pa chen po'i mdo* (Tibetan translation of *Gṛhapatyugraparipṛcchānāmamahāyānasūtram*). In *dKon brtsegs* section of Kg., vol. 4 (*Nga*), ff. 257a–288a (Toh. 63). English translation in *A Few Good Men*. Tr. Jan Nattier. Honolulu: University of Hawai'i Press, 2005 (paperback edition). Pp. 207–321.

Lakkhaṇasaṃyutta. In *Saṃyutta Nikāya*, part 2, chapter 8. No Tibetan translation available. English translation in *The Connected Discourses of the Buddha*. Tr. Bhikkhu Bodhi. Boston: Wisdom Publications, 2000. Pp. 700–705.

Lalitavistaraḥ. Buddhist Sanskrit Texts No. 1. Darbanga, India: Mithila Institute, 1958. Tibetan translation: ['Phags pa] *rGya cher rol pa zhes bya ba theg pa chen po'i mdo*. In *mDo sde* section of Kg., vol. 2 (*Kha*), ff. 1–216b (Toh. 95). English translation: *The Voice of the Buddha* (2 vols.). Berkeley: Dharma Publishing, 1983.

Mañjuśrīmūlakalpaḥ. Buddhist Sanskrit Texts, no. 18. Darbhanga, India: Mithila Institute, 1964. Tibetan translation: *'Jam dpal gyi rtsa ba'i rgyud*. In *rGyud* section of Kg., vol 12 (*Na*), ff. 105a–351a (Toh. 543).

Pañcaviṃśatisāhasrikāprajñāpāramitāsūtram. (Recast version of the original sutra that conforms to the sections of the *Abhisamayālaṃkāraḥ*.) 3 vols. Bibliotheca Indo-Tibetica Series 61. Ed. Dr. Vijay Raj Vajracharya. Sarnath, India: Central Institute of Higher Tibetan Studies, 2006–2008. Tibetan translation: *Shes rab kyi pha rol tu phyin pa stong phrag nyi shu lnga pa*. In *Sher phyin stong phrag nyi shu lnga pa* section of Kg., vols. 1–3 (*Ka–Ga*) (Toh. 9). English translation: *The Large Sutra on Perfect Wisdom*. Tr. Edward Conze. Berkeley: University of California Press, 1975.

Sigalovada Sutta. In *Dīgha Nikāya*, Sutta 31. No Tibetan translation available. English translation in *The Long Discourses of the Buddha*. Tr. Maurice Walsh. Reprint edition, Boston: Wisdom Publications, 1995. Pp. 461–469.

gTsug na rin po ches zhus pa zhes bya ba theg pa chen po'i mdo. (Tibetan translation of *Ratnacūḍaparipṛcchānāmamahāyānasūtram*). In *dKon brtsegs* section of Kg., vol. 6 (*Cha*), ff. 210a–254b (Toh. 91).

Indian Treatises

Abhayākaragupta. *dPal yang dag par sbyor ba'i rgyud kyi rgyal po'i rgya cher 'grel pa Man ngag gi snye ma* (Tibetan translation of *Śrīsaṃpuṭatantrarājaṭīkā Āmnāyamañjarī*). In *rGyud* section of Tg., vol. 7 (*Cha*), 316 ff. (Toh. 1198).

———. *Shes rab kyi pha rol tu phyin pa brgyad stong pa'i 'grel pa gnad kyi zla ba'i 'od* (Tibetan translation of *Aṣṭasāhasrikāprajñāpāramitāmarmakaumudī*). In *Shes phyin* section of Tg., vol. 90 (*Da*), 228ff. (Toh. 3805).

Āryadeva. *bsTan bcos bzhi brgya pa zhes bya ba'i tsig le'ur byas pa* (Tibetan translation of *Catuḥśatakaśāstrakārikā*). In *dBu ma* section of Tg., vol. 97 (*Tsha*), ff. 1b–21b (Toh. 3846).

Āryaśūra. *Jātakamālā*. Sanskrit and English in *Garland of the Buddha's Past Lives*. 2 vols. New York: New York University Press & JJC Foundation, 2009. Tibetan translation: *sKyes pa'i rabs kyi rgyud*. In *sKyes rabs* section of Tg., vol. 168 (*Hu*), ff. 1–135a (Toh. 4150).

Asaṅga. *Abhidharmasamuccayaḥ*. Ed. Prahlad Pradhan. Shantiniketan, India: Visva-Bharati, 1950. Tibetan translation: *Chos mngon pa kun las btus pa*. In *Sems tsam* section of Tg., vol. 134 (*Ri*), ff. 44a–120a (Toh. 4049). English translation: *Abhidharmasamuccaya: The Compendium of the Higher Teaching*. Tr. Sara Boin-Webb (from Walpola Rahula's French translation). Berkeley: Asian Humanities Press, 2001.

———. *Bodhisattvabhūmiḥ*. Ed. Nalinaksha Dutt. Patna: K. P. Jayaswal Research Institute, 1978. Also ed. Unrai Wogihara. Reprint edition, Tokyo: Sankibo Buddhist Book Store, 1978. Tibetan translation: *(rNal 'byor spyod pa'i sa las) Byang chub sems dpa'i sa*. In *Sems tsam* section of Tg., vol. 129 (*Wi*), 213 ff. (Toh. 4037).

———. *'Dul ba bsdu ba* (Tibetan translation of the second of the three sections of *Vastusaṃgrahaṇī*). In *Sems tsam* section of Tg., vol. 132 (*'I*), ff. 1b–22a (Toh. 4040).

———. *rNam grangs bsdu ba* (Tibetan translation of *Paryāyasaṃgrahaṇī*). In *Sems tsam* section of Tg., vol. 132 (*'I*), ff. 22b–47b (Toh. 4041).

———. *rNam par bshad pa bsdu ba* (Tibetan translation of *Vyākhyāsaṃgrahaṇī*). In *Sems tsam* section of Tg., vol. 132 (*'I*), ff. 47b–68b (Toh. 4042).

———. *rNam par gtan la dbab pa bsdu ba* (Tibetan translation of *Viniścayasaṃgrahaṇī*). In *Sems tsam* section of Tg., vols. 130 (*Zhi*) and 131 (*Zi*), ff. 1b–127a (Toh. 4038).

———. *Sangs rgyas rjes su dran pa'i 'grel pa* (Tibetan translation of *Buddhānusmṛtivṛttiḥ*). In *mDo 'grel* section of Tg., vol. 113 (*Ngi*), ff. 11b–15a (Toh. 3982).

———. *Śrāvakabhūmiḥ*. Tibetan Sanskrit Works Series, vol. 14. Ed. Karunesha Shukla. Patna: K. P. Jayaswal Research Institute, 1973. Tibetan translation: *(rNal 'byor spyod pa'i sa las) Nyan thos kyi sa*. In *Sems tsam* section of Tg., vol. 128 (*Dzi*), 195 ff. (Toh. 4036).

———. *Theg pa chen po bsdus pa* (Tibetan translation of *Mahāyānasaṃgrahaḥ*). In *Sems tsam* section of Tg., vol. 134 (*Ri*), ff. 1b–43a (Toh. 4048).

———. *Yogācārabhūmiḥ* (incomplete). Parts 1–5 in *The Yogācāra-bhūmi of Ācārya Asaṅga*. Ed. Vidhushekhara Bhattacharya. Calcutta: University of Calcutta, 1957. Pp. 1–232. Part 6 in *Samāhitā Bhūmiḥ*. 2 vols. Vienna: Arbeitskreis für Tibetische und Buddhistische Studien Universität Wien, 2009. Parts 8, 9, 11, and 14 in *Buddhist Insight*. Ed. Alex Wayman. Reprint Delhi: Motilal Banarsidass, 1984. Pp. 327–331 and 333–352. See separate listings for *Śrāvakabhūmiḥ* (part 13) and *Bodhisattvabhūmiḥ* (part 15). Tibetan translation: Parts 1–12, 14, 16, and 17, referred to as *Sa mang po pa*, in *Sems tsam* section of Tg., vol. 127 (*Tshi*), ff. 1–283a (Toh. 4035).

———. *gZhi bsdu ba* (Tibetan translation of the first of the three sections of the *Vastusaṃgrahaṇī*). In *Sems tsam* section of Tg., vol. 131 (*Zi*), ff. 127a–335a (Toh. 4039).

Bodhibhadra. *Byang chub sems dpa'i sdom pa nyi shu pa'i dka' 'grel* (Tibetan translation of *Bodhisattvasaṃvaraviṃśikāpañjikā*). In *Sems tsam* section of Tg., vol. 138 (*Hi*), ff. 184b–217b (Toh. 4083).

Candragomī. *Byang chub sems dpa' i sdom pa nyi shu pa* (Tibetan translation of *Bodhisattvasaṃvaraviṃśikā*). In *Sems tsam* section of Tg., vol. 138 (*Hi*), ff. 166b–167a (Toh. 4081).

Candrakīrti. *Byang chub sems dpa' i rnal 'byor spyod pa bzhi brgya pa' i rgya cher 'grel pa*. (Tibetan translation of *Bodhisattvayogācāracatuḥśatakaṭikā*). In *dBu ma* section of Tg., vol. 103 (*Ya*), ff. 29a–264b (Toh. 3865).

———. *Prasannapadā*. In *Madhyamakaśāstra of Nāgārjuna*. Buddhist Sanskrit Texts, no. 10. Darbhanga, India: Mithila Institute, 1960. Pp. 1–259. Tibetan translation: *dBu ma rtsa ba' i 'grel pa tshig gsal ba zhes bya ba*. In *dBu ma* section of Tg., vol. 102 (*'A*), ff. 1a–200a (Toh. 3860).

Guṇaprabha. *Byang chub sems dpa' i sa' i 'grel pa* (Tibetan translation of *Bodhisattvabhūmivṛttiḥ*). In *Sems tsam* section of Tg., vol. 132 (*'I*), ff. 141a–182a (Toh. 4044).

———. *Byang chub sems dpa' i tshul khrims kyi le'u' i bshad pa* (Tibetan translation of *Bodhisattvaśīlaparivartabhāṣyam*). In *Sems tsam* section of Tg., vol. 132 (*'I*), ff. 182a–191a (Toh. 4045).

Haribhadra. (*Āryāṣṭasāhasrikāprajñāpāramitāvyākhyā*) *Abhisamayālaṃkārālokaḥ*. In *Aṣṭasahasrikā Prajñāpāramitā*. Buddhist Sanskrit Texts, no. 4. Darbhanga, India: Mithila Institute, 1960. Pp. 267–558. Tibetan translation: (*'Phags pa shes rab kyi pha rol tu phyin pa brgyad stong pa' i bshad pa*) *mNgon par rtogs pa' i rgyan gyi snang ba*. In *Shes phyin* section of Tg., vol. 85 (*Cha*), 341 ff. (Toh. 3791).

Jinamitra (attribution uncertain). *rNal 'byor spyod pa' i sa rnam par bshad pa* (Tibetan translation of *Yogācārabhūmivyākhyā*). In *Sems tsam* section of Tg., vol. 132 (*'I*), ff. 69a–140b (Toh. 4043).

Jinaputra. *Abhidharmasamuccayabhāṣyam*. Ed. Nathmal Tatia. Patna, India: K.P. Jayaswal Research Institute, 1976. Tibetan translation: *mNgon pa chos kun las btus pa' i rnam par bshad pa*. In *Sems tsam* section of Tg., vol. 135 (*Li*), ff. 119a–296a (Toh. 4054).

———. *Byang chub sems dpa' i tshul khrims kyi le'u' i rgya cher 'grel pa* (Tibetan translation of *Bodhisattvaśīlaparivartaṭīkā*). In *Sems tsam* section of Tg., vol. 132 (*'I*), ff. 191a–221a (Toh. 4046).

Maitreya Nātha. *Abhisamayālaṃkāraḥ* (Sanskrit and Tibetan texts). Ed. T. Stcherbatsky and E.E. Obermiller. Leningrad: Bibliotheca Buddhica, 1929. Tibetan translation: (*Shes rab kyi pha rol tu phyin pa' i man ngag gi bstan bcos*) *mNgon par rtogs pa' i rgyan zhes bya ba' i tshig le'ur byas pa*. In *Shes phyin* section of Tg., vol. 80 (*Ka*), ff. 1b–13a (Toh. 3786). English translation: *Abhisamaya Alaṃkāra*. Tr. Edward Conze. Rome: Serie Orientale Roma, 1954.

———. *Madhyāntavibhāgakārikā*. Contained in *Madhyānta Vibhāga Śāstra*. Ed. by Ramchandra Pandeya. Delhi: Motilal Banarsidass, 1971. Tibetan translation: *dBus dang mtha' rnam par 'byed pa' i tshig le'ur byas pa*. In *Sems tsam* section of Tg., vol. 123 (*Phi*), ff. 40b–45a (Toh. 4021).

———. *Mahāyānasūtrālaṃkāraḥ*. In Buddhist Sanskrit Texts, no. 13. Darbhanga, India: Mithila Institute, 1970. Tibetan translation: *Theg pa chen po mdo sde'i rgyan zhes bya ba'i tshig le'ur byas pa*. In *Sems tsam* section of Tg., vol. 123 (*Phi*), ff. 1–39a (Toh. 4020).

Mātṛceṭa. *Varṇārhavarṇastotram*. Ed. D.R. Shackleton Bailey. Sanskrit not complete, includes English translation and Tibetan (chs. 5–12 only). *Bulletin of the School of Oriental Studies*, 1950. Part I (chs. 1–4), pp. 671–701; Part II (chs. 5–12), pp. 947–1003. Tibetan translation: *Sangs rgyas bcom ldan 'das la bstod pa bsngags par 'os pa bsngags pa las bstod par mi nus par bstod pa* (*bsngags 'os bsngags bstod*). In *bsTod pa* section of Tg., vol. 1 (*Ka*), ff. 84a–100b (Toh. 1138).

Nāgārjuna. *Mūlamadhyamakakārikā*. In *Mūlamadhyamakaśāstra of Nāgārjuna*. Buddhist Sanskrit Texts, no. 10. Darbhanga, India: Mithila Institute, 1960. Tibetan translation: *dBu ma rtsa ba'i tshig le'ur byas pa shes rab ces bya ba*. In *dBu ma* section of Tg., vol. 96 (*Tsa*), ff. 1b–19a (Toh. 3824). English translation: *The Fundamental Wisdom of the Middle Way: Nagarjuna's Mulamadhyamakakarika*. Tr. Jay L. Garfield. New York: Oxford University Press, 1995.

———. *Ratnāvalī* (incomplete text). In *Nāgārjuna's Ratnāvalī*, ed. Michael Hahn. Bonn: Indica et Tibetica Verlag, 1982. Tibetan translation: *rGyal po la gtam bya ba rin po che'i phreng ba*. In *sPring yig* section of Tg., vol. 172 (*Ge*), ff. 107a–126a (Toh. 4158). English translation in *The Precious Garland and the Precious Song of the Four Mindfulnesses*. Tr. Jeffrey Hopkins and Lati Rinpoche with Anne Klein. New York: Harper and Row, 1975.

———. *bShes pa'i spring yig* (Tibetan translation of *Suhṛllekhaḥ*). In *sPring yig* section of Tg., vol. 173 (*Nge*), ff. 40b–46b (Toh. 4182). English translation with commentary in *Nāgārjuna's Letter*. Tr. Geshe Lobsang Tharchin and Artemus B. Engle. Dharamsala, India: Library of Tibetan Works and Archives, 1979.

Ratnākaraśānti. *Sāratamā. A Pañjikā on the Aṣṭasāhasrikā Prajñāpāramitā Sūtra by Ratnākaraśānti* (Tibetan Sanskrit Works Series, 18). Ed. P. S. Jaini. Patna: Kashi Prasad Jayaswal Research Institute, 1979. Tibetan translation: (*'Phags pa*) *Shes rab kyi pha rol tu phyin pa brgyad stong pa'i dka' 'grel snying po mchog*. In *Shes phyin* section of Tg., vol. 89 (*Tha*), 230 ff. (Toh. 3803).

Śākyamati. *'Phags pa ga ya mgo'i ri mdo dang spel mar bshad pa* (Tibetan translation of *Gayāśīrṣasūtramiśrakavyākhyā*). *In mDo 'grel* section of Tg., vol. 113 (*Ngi*), ff. 76b–103a (Toh. 3992).

*Samudramegha (original Sanskrit name not certain; Tibetan translation of name is *rGya mtsho sprin*). *rNal 'byor spyod pa'i sa las byang chub sems dpa'i sa'i rnam par bshad pa* (Tibetan translation of *Yogācārabhūmau bodhisattvabhūmivyākhyā*). In *Sems tsam* section of Tg., vol. 133 (*Yi*), 338 ff. (Toh. 4047).

Śāntarakṣita. *sDom pa nyi shu pa'i 'grel pa* (Tibetan translation of *Saṃvaraviṃśikāvṛttiḥ*). In *Sems tsam* section of Tg., vol. 138 (*Hi*), ff. 167a–184b (Toh. 4082).

Śāntideva. *Bodhicaryāvatāra*. (Sanskrit and Tibetan texts.) Ed. Vidushekhara Bhattacharya. Calcutta: The Asiatic Society, 1960. Tibetan translation: *Byang chub sems dpa'i spyod pa la 'jug pa*. In *dBu ma* section of Tg., vol. 105 (*La*), ff. 1–40a (Toh. 3871). English translation: *A Guide to the Bodhisattva Way of Life*. Tr. Vesna A. Wallace and B. Alan Wallace. Ithaca, N.Y.: Snow Lion Publications, 1997.

———. *Śikṣāsamuccayaḥ*. Buddhist Sanskrit Texts, no. 11. Darbhanga, India: Mithila Institute, 1960. Tibetan translation: *bSlab pa kun las btus pa*. In *dBu ma* section of Tg., vol. 111 (*Khi*), ff. 3a–194b (Toh. 3940). English translation: *Śikṣā Samuccaya, A Compendium of Buddhist Doctrine*. Tr. Cecil Bendall and W.H.D. Rouse. Reprint, Delhi: Motilal Banarsidass, 1971.

Sthiramati. *mDo sde rgyan gyi 'grel bshad* (Tibetan translation of *Sūtrālaṃkāravṛttibhāṣyam*). In *Sems tsam* section of Tg., vols. 125 (*Mi*) and 126 (*Tsi*) (Toh. 4034).

———. *Madhyāntavibhāgaṭīkā*. In *Madhyānta-Vibhāga-Śāstra*. Ed. Ramchandra Pandeya. Delhi: Motilal Banarsidass, 1971. Tibetan translation: *dBus dang mtha' rnam par 'byed pa'i 'grel bshad*. In *Sems tsam* section of Tg., vol. 124 (*Bi*), ff. 189b–318a (Toh. 4032).

———. *Pañcaskandhakavibhāṣā* (Parts I and II). Ed. Jowita Kramer. Published jointly by the China Tibetology Publishing House and the Austrian Academy of Sciences Press. Beijing-Vienna, 2013. Tibetan translation: *Phung po lnga'i rab tu byed pa bye brag tu bshad pa*. In *Sems tsam* section of Tg., vol. 136 (*Shi*), ff. 195b–250a (Toh. 4066). English translation in *The Inner Science of Buddhist Practice*, pp. 245–369.

———. *Triṃśikābhāṣyam*. In *Sthiramati's Triṃśikāvijñaptibhāṣya*. Ed. Hartmut Buescher. Vienna: Verlag der Österreichischen Akademie der Wissenschaften, 2007. Tibetan translation: *Sum cu pa'i bshad pa*. In *Sems tsam* section of Tg., vol. 136 (*Shi*), ff. 146b–171b (Toh. 4064).

Vasubandhu. *Abhidharmakośabhāṣyam*. Ed. Prahlad Pradhan. Patna: K. P. Jayaswal Research Institute, 1975. Tibetan translation: *Chos mngon pa'i mdzod kyi bshad pa*. In *mNgon pa* section of Tg., vol. 140 (*Ku*), f. 25a–vol. 141 (*Khu*), f. 97b. (Toh. 4090). English translation: *Abhidharmakośabhāṣyam*. 4 vols. Tr. Leo M. Pruden (from Louis de La Vallée Poussin's French translation). Berkeley: Asian Humanities Press, 1988.

———. *Abhidharmakośakārikā*. Ed. G.V. Gokhale. *Journal of the Royal Asiatic Society*, vol. 22. Bombay: Royal Asiatic Society, 1946. Tibetan translation: *Chos mngon pa'i mdzod kyi tshig le'ur byas pa*. In *mNgon pa* section of Tg., vol. 140 (*Ku*), ff. 1–25a (Toh. 4089). English translation in *Abhidharmakośabhāṣyam*. 4 vols. Tr. Leo M. Pruden. Berkeley: Asian Humanities Press, 1988.

———. [*'Phags pa*] *Blo gros mi zad pas bstan pa rgya cher 'grel pa* (Tibetan translation of *Āryākṣayamatinirdeśaṭīkā*). In *mDo 'grel* section of Tg., vol. 114 (*Ci*), 269 ff. (Toh. 3994).

———. *Madhyāntavibhāgabhāṣyam*. In *Madhyānta-Vibhāga-Śāstra*. Ed. Ramchandra Pandeya. Delhi: Motilal Banarsidass, 1971. Tibetan translation: *dBus dang mtha' rnam par 'byed pa'i 'grel pa*. In *Sems tsam* section of Tg., vol. 124 (*Bi*), ff.

1b–27a (Toh. 4027). English translation in *Seven Works of Vasubandhu*. Tr. Stefan Anacker. Delhi: Motilal Banarsidass, 1998 (corrected edition). Pp. 191–286.

———. *rNam par bshad pa rigs pa'i mdo sde'i dum bu brgya* (Tibetan translation of *Vyākhyāyuktisūtrakhaṇḍaśatam*). In *Sems tsam* section of Tg., vol. 136 (*Shi*), ff. 17b–29a (Toh. 4060).

———. *Pañcaskandhaprakaraṇam*. In *Vasubandhu's Pañcaskandhaka*. Ed. Li Xuezhu and Ernst Steinkellner. Published jointly by the China Tibetology Publishing House and the Austrian Academy of Sciences Press. Beijing & Vienna, 2008. Pp. 1–23. Tibetan translation: *Phung po lnga'i rab tu byed pa*. In *Sems tsam* section of Tg., vol. 136 (*Shi*), ff. 11b–17a (Toh. 4059). English translation in *The Inner Science of Buddhist Practice*, pp. 229–244.

———. [*'Phags pa*] *Sa bcu pa'i rnam par bshad pa* (Tibetan translation of *Āryadaśabhūmivyākhyānam*). In *mDo 'grel* section of Tg., vol. 113 (*Ngi*), ff. 103b–266a (Toh. 3993).

———. *Sūtrālaṃkāravyākhyā*. Buddhist Sanskrit Texts, no. 13. Darbhanga, India: Mithila Institute, 1960. Tibetan translation: *mDo sde'i rgyan gyi bshad pa*. In *Sems tsam* section of Tg., vol. 123 (*Phi*), ff. 129b–260a (Toh. 4026). English Translation: *The Universal Vehicle Discourse Literature*. Tr. L. Jamspal et al. New York: American Institute of Buddhist Studies, 2004.

Yaśomitra. *Sphuṭārthābhidharmakośavyākhyā*. 4 vols. Ed. Swami Dwarikadas Shastri. Varanasi: Bauddha Bharati, 1970. Tibetan translation: *Chos mngon pa'i mdzod kyi 'grel bshad*. In *mNgon pa* section of Tg., vols. 142–143 (*Gu–Ngu*) (Toh. 4092).

Tibetan Works

'Brom ston pa rGyal ba'i 'byung gnas. *Jo bo rin po che rje dpal ldan A ti sha'i rnam thar rgyas pa yongs grags*. In *bKa' gdams glegs bam*, vol. 1, item 2 (*Kha*), 125 ff. Gangtok: Sikkim Research Institute of Tibetology, 1977.

Bu ston Rin chen grub. *Chos mngon pa kun las btus pa'i rnam bshad nyi ma'i 'od zer*. In vol. 20 (*Wa*) of *The Collected Works of Bu-ston* (28 vols.), 335 ff. New Delhi: International Academy of Indian Culture, 1966. (Toh. 5183).

Byang chub rdzu 'phrul. *'Phags pa dgongs pa nges par 'grel pa'i rnam par bshad pa*. In *sNa tshogs* section of Tg., vol. 205 (*Cho*)–206 (*Jo*), f. 183b (Toh. 4358).

Bye brag tu rtogs pa chen po (aka *Mahāvyutpattiḥ*). In *sNa tshogs* section of Tg., vol. 204 (*Co*), ff. 1b–131a (Toh. 4346). References to this text are based on the numbering system used in the 2-vol. reprint edition with Sanskrit and Tibetan indices. Tokyo: Suzuki Gakujutsu Zaidan, 1962.

sGra sbyor bam po gnyis pa. In *sNa tshogs* section of Tg., vol. 204 (*Co*), ff. 131b–160a (Toh. 4347).

[rJe btsun] Grags pa rgyal mtshan. *Byang chub sems dpa'i sdom pa gsal bar ston pa shloka nyi shu pa'i rnam par bshad pa*. In vol. 9 (*Ta*) of *Sa skya bka' 'bum* (15 vols., photographic reproduction of the 1736 *sDe dge* edition), item 31, 77 ff. Dehra Dun,

India: Sakya Center, 1992–1993. English translation: *Candragomin's Twenty Verses on the Bodhisattva Vow and Its Commentary by Sakya Drakpa Gyeltsen* (2nd edition). Tr. Mark Tatz. Dharamsala, India: Library of Tibetan Works and Archives, 1997.

mKhas grub bsTan pa dar rgyas. *bsTan bcos mngon par rtogs pa'i rgyan rtsa 'grel gyi spyi don rnam bshad snying po rgyan gyi snang ba* (*Phar phyin spyi don*). New Delhi: Geshe Lobsang Tharchin, 1980.

Phur bu lcog Ngag dbang byams pa. *rTogs brjod rin po che 'dun legs ma'i 'grel pa mkhas pa'i gzhung lam*. In vol. 1 of *The Collected Works* (*gsuṅ 'bum*) *of Phur-bu-lcog Ṅag-dbang-byams-pa* (4 vols.), 71 ff. New Delhi: Ngawang Sopa, 1973–1974.

Thu'u bkwan Blo bzang chos kyi nyi ma (aka Dharma Ba dzra). *Theg pa chen po mdo sde'i rgyan dang byang chub sems dpa'i sa'i don gcig tu sbyar nas rgyal ba'i sras kyi lam nyams su len tshul mdo tsam bshad pa theg chen lam bzang gsal ba'i nyi ma*. In vol. 3 of *The Collected Works of Thu'u bkwan blo bzang chos kyi nyi ma*. 31 ff. New Delhi: Ngag dbang dge legs sde mo, 1969–1971.

mTsho sna ba Shes rab bzang po. *'Dul ba mdo rtsa'i 'grel pa legs bshad nyi ma'i 'od zer*. Beijing: Krung go'i bod kyi shes rig dpe skrun khang, 1993. (Toh. 6850A).

[rJe] Tsong kha pa [Blo bzang grags pa'i dpal]. *Bla ma dBu ma pa la mdo khams su phul ba*. In *The Collected Works of the Incomparable Lord Tsongkhapa blo bzang grags pa* (18 vols.). In vol. 2 (*Kha*), *bKa' 'bum thor bu* (item no. 65), ff. 68b–70a. New Delhi: Mongolian Lama Guru Deva, 1978–1983. (Toh. 5275).

———. *Byang chub lam gyi rim pa chen mo* (aka *Lam rim chen mo*). Vol. 13 (*Pa*) of *Collected Works* (Toh. 5392). English translation: *The Great Treatise on the Stages of the Path to Enlightenment.* 3 vols. Ithaca, N.Y.: Snow Lion Publications, 2000–2004.

———. *Byang chub sems dpa'i tshul khrims kyi rnam bshad byang chub gzhung lam*. In *Collected Works*, vol. 1 (*Ka*), 109 ff. (Toh. 5271).

———. *rNal 'byor gyi dbang phyug lū i pas mdzad pa'i bcom ldan 'das dpal 'khor lo bde mchog gi mngon par rtogs pa'i rgya cher bshad pa 'dod pa 'jo ba* (aka *'Dod pa 'jo ba*). In *Collected Works*, vol. 9 (*Ta*), 184ff. (Toh. 5320).

———. *Rang gi rtogs pa brjod pa mdo tsam du bshad pa* (aka *'Dun legs ma*). In *Collected Works*, vol. 2 (*Kha*), *bKa' 'bum thor bu* (item no. 58), ff. 52b–55b (Toh. 5275). English translation in *Life & Teachings of Tsong Khapa*. Ed. Robert A. F. Thurman. Dharamsala, India: Library of Tibetan Works and Archives, 1982. Pp. 40–46.

———. *Shes rab kyi pha rol tu phyin pa'i man ngag gi bstan bcos mngon par rtogs pa'i rgyan 'grel pa dang bcas pa'i rgya cher bshad pa legs bshad gser gyi phreng ba*. In *Collected Works*, vol. 17 (*Tsa*)–vol. 18 (*Tsha*). (Toh. 5412).

(gTsang nag pa) brTson 'grus seng ge. *Byang chub sems dpa'i sa'i dka' 'grel*. In vol. 13 of *Bka' gdams gsung 'bum phyogs sgrig thengs dang po'i dkar chag*. Chengdu: Si khron mi rigs dpe skrun khang, 2006. 48 ff.

Reference Materials

L'Abhidharmakośa de Vasubandhu. 6 vols. Traduction et annotations par Louis de la Vallée Poussin. Nouvelle édition par Étienne Lamotte. Brussels: Institut belge des hautes études chinoise, 1971–1980.

Asanga's Chapter on Ethics with the Commentary of Tsong-Kha-Pa, The Basic Path to Awakening, The Complete Bodhisattva. Tr. Mark Tatz. Lewiston/Queenston: The Edwin Mellen Press, 1987.

The Aṣṭādhyāyī of Pāṇini. 2 vols. Ed. Śrīśa Chandra Vasu. 1891. Reprint, Delhi: Motilal Banarsidass, 1962.

Bod rgya tshig mdzod chen mo. Beijing: Mi rigs dpe skrun khang, 1985.

Buddhist Hybrid Sanskrit Dictionary. 2 vols. Ed. Franklin Edgerton. New Haven: Yale University Press, 1953. Reprint, Delhi: Motilal Banarsidass, 1970.

Buddhist Legends. 3 vols. Tr. E. W. Burlingame. Cambridge, Mass.: Harvard University Press, 1921.

Buddhist Monastic Discipline: The Sanskrit Prātimokṣa Sūtras of the Mahāsaṃghikas and Mūlasarvāstivādins. Charles S. Prebish. Delhi: Motilal Banarsidass, 1996.

A Catalogue of the Tohoku University Collection of Tibetan Works on Buddhism. Ed. Y. Kanakura, et al. Sendai, Japan: Tohoku Imperial University, 1953.

A Complete Catalogue of the Tibetan Buddhist Canons. Ed. Hakuju Ui, et al. Sendai, Japan: Tohoku Imperial University, 1934.

Critical Pali Dictionary Online. Department of Cross-Cultural and Regional Studies (ToRS) at The University of Copenhagen. URL: http://pali.hum.ku.dk/cpd/.

Encyclopedia of Hinduism. Ed. N.K. Singh. New Delhi: Anmol Publications, 2001.

Encyclopedia of Indian Philosophies. 17 vols. Ed. Karl Potter, et al. Delhi: Motilal Banarsidass, 1970–2014.

The Inner Science of Buddhist Practice. Artemus B. Engle. Ithaca, N.Y.: Snow Lion Publications, 2009.

On Knowing Reality: The Tattvārtha Chapter of Asaṅga's Bodhisattvabhūmi. Tr. Janice Dean Willis. Delhi: Motilal Banarsidass, 1982.

Oxford Dictionary of Buddhism. New York: Oxford University Press, 2004.

The Pali Text Society's Pali-English Dictionary. Ed. T. W. Rhys Davids and William Stede. Chipstead: The Pali Text Society, 1921–25.

A Sanskrit-English Dictionary. Sir Monier Monier-Williams. London: Oxford University Press, 1899. Reprint, Delhi: Motilal Banarsidass, 1963.

Sanskrit Grammar. William Dwight Whitney. London: Oxford University Press, 1879. Reprint, Cambridge, Mass.: Harvard University Press, 1973 (thirteenth issue).

La Théorie du Tathāgatagarbha et du Gotra. David S. Ruegg. Paris: École française d'Extrême-Orient, 1969.

Tibetan-Sanskrit Dictionary. 16 vols. Ed. J. S. Negi. Sarnath, Varanasi: Central Institute of Higher Tibetan Studies, 1993–2005.

Le Traité de la Grand Vertu de Sagesse. 4 vols. Tr. Étienne Lamotte. Louvain: Institut Orientaliste, 1949; reprint, 1966.

Index

abandonment, 159, 160, 162, 164, 182
abashment, 10
  in acts of extreme defeat, 268
  as antidote, 598
  essence and basis of, 415–416
  marks produced by, 613
  morality that generates, 238
  in pleasurable state of great joy, 535
  pure patience and, 329
  purity of activities and, 598
Abhidharma, xx
  in *Bodhisattvabhūmiḥ*, xxxi–xxxiv, xlii
  consciousness in, 5n111
  explaining meanings and intents of, 500
  five migratory states in, 131n422
  Indian traditions of, xxiii–xxvi
  mental afflictions, two classes in, 576n1391
  perturbation, meaning of in, 137n439
  pride in, 90n314
  in Tengyur, xviii
  twenty-two faculties in, 186n564
Abhidharmakośabhāṣyam (Vasubandhu), 92n316, 122–123n397
  on asceticism, 304n820
  on "Below None," 110n349
  on conditioned entities, 315n843
  on constituents, 430n1087
  on "countless," meaning of, 575n1389
  on effort, 182–183n554
  on faith born of insight, 270–271n759
  on five spiritual faculties, 640n1530
  on four ārya lineages, 223n649
  on four conditions, 178n547
  on four types of food, 180n552
  on fourth meditative absorption, 163n510
  on immediate consequence, meaning of, 520n1267
  on knowledge by resolve, 161n505
  on marvelous abilities, 139n444
  on nonarising of mental afflictions, 657n1556
  on *padam*, meaning of term, 190n576
  on pleasant and unpleasant experiences, 42n195
  on pleasant feelings, 544n1311
  on productive causes, 326n864
  on roots of virtue, 520n1268
  on supernatural travel, 110n350
  on ultimate correctness, 579n1397
Abhidharmakośakārikā (Vasubandhu), xx, xxiii, xixn27
  on action-paths, 541n1308
  on conception, 88n307
  on fields, 437n1104
  on indeterminate entities, 94n323
  on malice, 178n544
  on migratory states, 131n422
  on outflows, 43n196
  on verbal informative form, 260n733
Abhidharmasamuccayabhāṣyam (Jinaputra), 178n547, 480–481n1199, 662n1561
Abhidharmasamuccayaḥ (Asaṅga), xixn23, xxiii, xxiv, xxxii, 88n307
  on abashment and shame, 238nn677–678
  on anger, 420n1048
  on avoidance of conflict, 161n504
  on avoidance of desire, 219
  on bonds, three types, 336n884
  on class affiliation, 405n1014
  on collections of names, assertions, syllables, 418n1038

Abhidharmasamuccayaḥ (*continued*)
on conceit, 299n811
on conception, 88n307
on deliverance, 419n1043
on equanimity as mental factor, 335n881
on excitation, 282n788
on form as material, 92n316
on four applications, 480–481n1199
on four conditions, 178n547
on grasping, 361n935
on inferior view in generosity practice, 214n637
on latencies, 199n608, 336n885
on meditative absorption, transcendent and mundane, 343nn896–897
on miraculous power, 106n344
on mundane paths, 185n561
on ordinary persons, state of, 139n443
on pride, 299n812
on recollection, 241–242n687, 246n701
on stinginess, 376n962
on torpor, 376n961
on twelve divisions of Dharma, 172n529
on unique buddha qualities, 662n1561
on virtuous entities, 93n321
on volition, 206n620
Abhisamayālaṃkāraḥ (Maitreya Nātha), xviin9, xxiv
Abhisamayālaṃkārālokaḥ (Haribhadra), 164n511, 165n518, 289n800, 345n905
abstinence, eight forms of, 420n1045
acceptance, ritual of
description of, 261–263
preceptors, qualities of, 265
prerequisites for, 266
requesting, 260–261
signs of, 263–264
without preceptor, 302
accumulation path, 141–142n448, 520n1269
accumulations, two, 129n417, 432
beneficial conduct and, 375–376
bodhisattvas' rebirths and, xxvii
completion of, 657, 666
inability to collect, 268
in pleasurable state of superior wisdom that relates to the truths, 554, 555
spiritual practice and, 665–666
worship and, 389–390
action-paths, 541–542
activities
assisting with others', 243, 249–250
fourteen impure, 425
of magical creations, 118
meditative absorption and, 347
in pure morality, 309–310
regular, 323
adamantine attitude, 550, 560
Adamantine Seat, 394n994. *See also* enlightenment, seat of
admission, meaning of, 86n303
adventitious, conception of being, 643–644
affection, 30, 326, 329, 511–512, 525
afflictions
avoiding, 665
as cause for purification, 184–185
causes of, 175, 181–182
four aspects of freedom from, 382–383
impenetrable processes concerning, 572
in meditative absorption, 628–629
naturally weak quality of, 144
nonarising of, 568
worship free from, 392–393
agility, 115–116, 141n445, 198, 344, 373, 551n1331, 628n1489
agreeable speech, 202–203
all-inclusive, 365–366, 496n1234
bases of, 498–499
essence of, 365
fruits and benefits of, 501
preeminence of, 477
thirteen types, 369–370
toward afflicted beings, 367
of true spiritual being, 368–369
as truthful and pure, 370, 371
aims, one's own and others'
accomplishment of, 653, 660
conditions for, 54
in current and future lives, 58–59, 373
delighting in, 544
exclusively pursuing one's own, 36–37, 39
linked to what is beneficial, 40–48
meditative absorption and, 348, 351
perpetual and not perpetual, 60–61
reality and power, connection in, 105n341
ten aspects, 36, 61
wisdom and, 358
as worthy of being achieved, 172

Ajita. *See* Maitreya
Akṣayamatinirdeśasūtram, xixn25
Akṣayamatinirdeśaṭīkā (Vasubandhu), 144n458, 277n776
analysis, xxxi, 170, 225–226, 471, 514, 524–525. *See also* investigation
anger, 420n1048
  absence of in morality, 247
  allowing unchecked, 286–287
  dissimilar attitude of, 444–445
  marks produced by freedom from, 613
  of others, ignoring, 285
  pure patience and, 328
  transgression of, 267, 303
Aṅguttara Nikāya, 501n1249, 632n1509
animal sacrifice, 211
Annotated Explanation of the Ornament of Discourses. See *Sūtrālaṃkāravṛttibhāṣyam* (Sthiramati)
antidotes, 339, 597–599, 603, 604
appearance, physical
  desiderative intentions and, 109–110
  divine beauty, 134
  excellence of, 48, 49, 52
  of mendicants, 321–322
  ripening and, 143
application
  purity of, 51
  in superior attitude and conduct, 31
  in three vehicles, differences in, 154–156
applications, four, 65n255, 77n285, 195, 359, 480n1199
arhats, xxvii, 38n181, 43, 261n736, 656
arrogance, 189, 251, 423n1061, 533
Arthavargiyāḥ, 85n302, 87–88
Āryadeva, *Catuḥśatakaśāstrakārikā*, xxn29, 49n213
āryas
  discrediting, 300, 635n1515, 636
  four lineages of, 223n649
  as free of outflows, 43
  as nonreturners, 113n370, 458n1146
  perception of, 78n290
  pleasurable states of, 163
  rebirth of, 110n349
Asaṅga, xv–xviii
  Commentary on Recollection of the Buddha, 164–165nn512–513, 165nn515–516
  lineage of, xxi
  Mahāyānasaṃgrahaḥ, xviiin22, xix
  Main Treatise on the Stages, The, xvii, xviii, xlii
  Paryāyasaṃgrahaṇī, xviiin20, 639
  role in Buddhist tradition, xx
  Vinścayasaṃgrahaṇī, xviiin17
  **Vyākhyāsaṃgrahaṇi*, xviiin21, xxxii, xxxiii
  See also *Abhidharmasamuccayaḥ*; *Bodhisattvabhūmiḥ*; *Śravakabhūmiḥ*; *Vastusaṃgrahaṇī*; *Yogācārabhūmiḥ*
ascetics, homeless, xxxvii
  effort related to, 331
  four principles of, 285n792, 424n1065
  four qualities pertaining to, 505, 508–510
  leading through beneficial conduct, 373
  longing of, 304, 309
  morality related to, 239–240
  patience related to, 314, 326
  regular activities of, 323
  tathāgatas' perceptions of, 647–648
aspirational prayers
  beneficial actions of, 102–103
  correct, 21
  in developing morality, 241
  five types, 450–452, 601
  as form of retention, 450
  perfection of, 601, 602
  in pleasurable state of great joy, 529–530, 538
  in pleasurable state of superior wisdom that relates to the truths, 556
  for rebirth, 583n1399, 584
  in resolving difficulties, 592
  skillfulness in, 507
  ten great, 451–452, 533–534
  transcendent, 530n1284
aspirations
  of bodhisattvas, 155–156
  correct, 127n412
  even-mindedness of, 467
  as faith, 51n220
  fervent, 338
  for five conditions, 468–469
  giving up, 269
  improper, 127n411
  of listeners, 154–155
  as mental factor, 22n146

aspirations (*continued*)
  for nirvana, 453
  in pleasurable state of conduct based on devotion, 526
  for rebirth near buddhas and bodhisattvas, 446, 536
  spiritual friend, role in developing, 27
assembly, three types, 654
assertions, 418. *See also* designating assertions
assistance, five types, 468
Atīśa, xx–xxii, xxv
attachment
  difficult beneficial conduct and, 374
  freedom from, 60n240, 329, 343n896, 559
  to idle speech, 287–288
  in morality, absence of, 245, 248
  overcoming in generosity practice, 228
  in pleasurable state of conduct based on devotion, 525
  proper, 303
attention
  bodhisattva form of, 645
  on compassion, 596
  definitions of, 57n232, 160n501, 657n1554
  as governing condition, 178–179n547, 431n1088
  improper, 181, 184, 344n904, 407, 420n1046
  insight and, 185n561, 197, 321
  nirvana and, 460–463
  proper, 182, 183, 195, 314n839, 317–318, 319, 358
  right, 141n445
  ten attitudes of, 543–544
  wisdom and, 358
  See also one-pointed concentration
attitude
  excellence of, 304
  six types, 648–650
  See also superior attitudes
attracting a following, 37, 53n223, 508
  embracing in, 588–590
  four principles of, 202–203
  generosity in, 130, 202
  marks produced by, 612
  for material gain, 287
  sameness of purpose in, 379–384
  by teaching worldly crafts, 191
  when to avoid, 590n1413
  wisdom in, 133n430
  See also agreeable speech; beneficial conduct
Avīci Hell, 125
Ayodhya, xvi

bare reality, 457
bare substance, 72, 80–83, 84, 88–89, 196–197, 643
bases
  six inner, 5–6, 43n199, 421, 643
  ten universal, 346n908
  twelve, 5n111, 43n199, 55n230, 431
behavior, correct and wrongful forms of, 325n863
behavior, physical
  in developing morality, 248
  four modes of, 309, 320–321
  proper for listening to Dharma, 191–192
  of spiritual teachers, 398
being and nonbeing, 68–69
Below None, 110, 123, 125, 585–586
beneficial conduct, 203
  difficult, 374
  eight perturbations and, 376
  essence of, 371–372
  tenfold purity of, 377–379
  thirteen types, 375–376
  of true spiritual being, 375
benefiting beings, 323, 667
  immeasurables and, 404
  by meditation on suffering, 411–412
  methods of, 469
  natural desire for, 15
  one and all, 468
  in pleasurable state of conduct based on devotion, 525, 527, 528
  superior attitudes and, 513, 515
  through happiness, 46–48, 208
  through morality, 239, 243–244, 249–260
  See also embracing
Bhavasaṃkrāntisūtram, 84n300
births
  among sentient beings, 584–585
  aspirational prayer for, 451
  deliberate, of bodhisattvas, xxvii–xxix, 28, 33, 34, 101, 102, 466, 560n1352, 669

final, of bodhisattvas, 115, 115n379, 135–136, 384, 489, 586, 657–658
human, ripening and, 143
inopportune, 184
as a lord, 585–586
as male, 49, 50, 53–54
one additional, of bodhisattvas, 115, 134n432, 384, 489
in pleasurable state of great joy, 536
sameness of purpose and, 381
in state of greatness, 585
of tathāgatas, perfections in stories of, 362
that end calamities, 583–584
that take on semblance of shared qualities, 584–585
in Tuṣita Heaven, 134, 446–447
See also rebirth

blazing light stage, 552. *See also* pleasurable state of superior wisdom that relates to qualities conducive to enlightenment

Blessed One, translation of term, 167n525

Bodhibhadra, *Commentary to the Twenty Verses on the Bodhisattva Discipline*, 267n751

Bodhicaryāvatāraḥ (Śāntideva), xxin36, 241–242n687

bodhicitta, xxiin41

bodhisattva collection, 173, 174, 268, 488, 545, 653, 663, 664

bodhisattva discipline
differentiated from listener, 267n751, 283
losing and regaining, 268–269, 301n815
reverence for, 300
ritual for acceptance of, 260–265, 302
safeguarding, 265–266
See also morality

bodhisattva qualities
beneficial and related actions, 101–103
counterfeit and genuine, 472–473, 491
marvelous, 465
natural, 466n1159, 467
summary verses on, 465, 470, 474, 477
ten preeminent, 476–477

Bodhisattvabhūmiḥ (Asaṅga)
alternate names for, 663
benefits of studying, xxvi–xxxi, 663–664
Mahāyānasūtrālaṃkāraḥ and, xxxix–xlvii
order of topics, 665–669
place in Great Vehicle tradition, xxxi–xxxiv
structure of, xxxiv–xxxix
Thüken Losang Chökyi Nyima on, xliii–xlvii
translations of, xviiin16, xx, xlvii–xlviii

Bodhisattvabhūmivṛttiḥ (Guṇaprabha), 49n212, 59n238, 66n257, 78n291, 229n661, 230n664

Bodhisattvabhūmivyākhyā (*Samudramegha)
on acquiring cause, 335n882
on admonishing, 201n611
on advantageous and disadvantageous entities, 656nn1549–1550
on agreeable speech, 366n941, 371n951, 498–499nn1241–1245
on arising and perishing of entities, 455n1138
on aspect, mark, sign, 524n1271
on aspiration for rebirth, 469n1163, 583n1399
on beneficial conduct, 372nn952–957, 379n965
on birth in lower realms to benefit beings, 596n1417
on bodhisattvas and listeners, compared, 412n1030
on bodhisattvas' lack of ulterior motives, 465n1158
on buddhas' knowledge, 160n503
on clarity, 418n1040
on clouded recollection, 526n1280
on composure, 564n1360, 592n1414
on concealing virtuous qualities, 380n967
on conditioned entities, worthlessness of, 234n676
on controlling powers over deeds and rebirth, 569n1375
on correct aspiration, 127n412
on counsel, 201n610
on destruction, attribute of, 458n1146
on development of power, 448n1120
on Dharma as eye, 400n1007
on diffidence, 189n573
on efficacy of spiritual practices, 175n533

Bodhisattvabhūmivyākhyā (*continued*)
on effort, 333n877, 337nn888–890
on eloquent speech, 188n570
on enlightenment mind, 530n1284
on entities and substance, 78n291
on erring forms of discernment, 358n927
on evil companions, 425n1068
on faith, 148n467, 525n1275
on fervor, 143n455
on fortitude, 495n1233, 496nn1235–1237
on four reliances, 427nn1076–1078
on friendly speech, 365n940
on generosity, 209n627, 215n640, 229n658
on giving instruction, 231n672
on great joy state, 537nn1298–1299
on impatience, 325n863
on impermanence of causes, 455n1139
on impure activities, 425n1066
on indifference, 206nn621–622
on ineffectual ceremonies, 214n638
on informative knowledge, 429nn1080–1081
on instructions, two interpretations of term, 199n607
on investigation, 149n471
on knowledge, 165n514
on latent tendencies, 199n608
on maturation, 185n560, 541n1309
on meditative absorption, 351nn915–916
on mental retention, 448n1119
on merit of Brahmā, 389n984
on names for bodhisattvas, 490–491nn1217–1232
on not attracting a following, 590n1413
on orderly discourse, 176n535
on patience, 131n423, 313–314nn832–835, 314n840
on physical behavior, 320n852
on practice beyond measure, 524n1270
on practicing causes fully, 449n1122
on proper aim and attainment, 147n464
on prophecy, 474–475nn1177–1178
on providing material objects, 148n468
on purity of mental objects, 622nn1466–1468
on purity of support, 621nn1463–1465
on quiescence, 435n1100
on sameness of purpose, 381n970
on settled nature of entities, 647n1538
on shrine worship, 388nn980–983
on signlessness, 435n1101
on signs of entities, 546n1318
on six bases, 643n1534
on stage, use of term, 539nn1304–1305
on suffering of progression, 408n1020
on support, 150nn473–474
on supports for subsistence, 320n850
on suppression, 375n960
on ten causes, 176–177nn538–542
on term "perfection," 603
on thought and false notion, 333n876
on transfer of merit, 641n1532
on true spiritual beings, 368nn944–945
on truth, 478–479nn1188–1197
on universal generosity, 230n666
on virtuous attitudes, 512nn1260–1261
on virtuous friends, 425n1069
on virtuous qualities, 382–383nn972–974
on vulgar speech, 424n1063
on wisdom, 355n923
on wisdom supported by means, 433n1094
on worldly knowledge, 422n1056
bodhisattvas
accomplishments of, 103
activities to be rejected, 36–37, 38, 39
appellations for, 362–363, 490–491, 668–669
benefits received by, 295
and buddhas, differentiated, 70, 659
characteristics of ripened, 155–156
counterfeit, 268, 472–473, 491, 668
decline of, 472
distinctions of, 667
faculties of, 7, 18
formulations exclusive to, 477–482
four acts that must be accomplished, 605–606
gender-neutral sense of term, xlviii–xlix
homeless ascetic and householder, distinguishing, 509–510
immature, 462, 531
immeasurable numbers of, 168
lack of ulterior motives, 465n1158, 467, 512
length of life, 537
marks of, 497–503

natural excellence of, 519
noble sounds of, 123–124
occurrence of certainty in, 475–476
perfection of, 114n377
point of entry, 23, 24n154
state of mind of, 12–13
superiority of, 7–8, 32
ten types, 488–489
true, 368
unsurpassed transformation of, 657–658
wonderful nature of, 105–106
Bodhisattvasaṃvaraviṃśikā (Candragomī), 272n763, 286n795
Bodhisattvaśīlaparivartabhāṣyam (Guṇaprabha), 250n711, 257n727, 264n744, 268n752
Bodhisattvaśīlaparivartaṭīkā (Jinaputra)
on bodhisattva asceticism, 304n820
on enjoying absorption, 289n799
on exemplary Dharma follower, meaning of, 260n732
on gifts of faith, 300n813
on knowledge-perception, 264n744
on morality, 239n681
on using miraculous powers, 259n730
body, 59n237
of bodhisattvas, 33, 73
of buddhas, xxxv, 162, 384
fitness and soundness of, 141
generosity of, 207, 209, 210
indisposition of, 46n208
magical creation of, 117–118, 121
of tathāgatas and tenth-stage bodhisattvas, differentiated, 659
ten personal articles for, 442–443
body worship, 387–390
bonds, three types, 336n884
Brahmā, 107n345, 112n359, 261n736, 389, 484
Brief Account of My Spiritual Life (Tsongkapa), xlii
buddha eye, 163, 538n1302, 661
buddha fields, 107n345, 108, 168–169
buddha qualities
one hundred and forty unique, 161, 386, 607, 657–658, 661
ten aspects of, 164–170
as unique, meaning of, 662–663
Buddha Śākyamuni, xv, xxi, 86–87, 135–136, 164–167
buddhahood, xxxv, 653, 661–662. *See also* enlightenment
buddhas
appearance of, 168
avoidance of conflict, 161
and bodhisattvas, differences between, 70
etymology of, 166n523
formulations exclusive to, 477–482
four distinctions among, 169
natural powers of, 135–137
noble sounds of, 123–124
perception of spiritual lineage by, 16
sameness of, 553
ten deeds of, 660–661
visions of in pleasurable states, 535–536, 542, 551–552, 570
wonderful nature of, 105–106
See also tathāgatas
Buddha's speech
motivation from, 190
ten causes and, 175–185, 187
two forms, 174–175
See also scriptures
Butön Rinchen Drup, xviii
Byang chub sems dpa'i tshul khrims kyi rnam bshad byang chub gzhung lam (Tsongkapa)
on aspirational prayers, 241n685
on benefits of virtue, 248n706
on bodhisattva discipline, 301n815
on confession, 301n816
on exemplary Dharma follower, meanings of, 242n692, 260n732
on five foundations, 249n707
on gifts of faith, 300n813
on great compassion, 246n702
on "harm or reproach," meaning of, 274n767
on "isolated mind," meaning of, 245n699
on perturbation, 268n753
on taking life, 279n781
on unwholesome acts, 297n808

caityas, 36–37, 388
Candragomī, *Bodhisattvasaṃvaraviṃśikā*, 272n763, 286n795
Candrakīrti, *Prasannapadā*, 82n298, 86n303, 178n547

Cārvaka school, 472–473n1173
castes, four traditional, 634n1513
Catuḥśatakaśāstrakārikā (Āryadeva), xxn29, 49n213
causal conditions, convergence of, 559
causal efficacy, lack of, 69
causes, 48
  acquiring, 335n882
  practicing fully, 449
  producing, 176, 177, 326
  proper and improper conditions and, 623
  purifying, 536
  ten, 175–185
celestial beings, 108n346
celestial realms, 36, 38
certain conduct, stage of, 154, 471, 489, 595
certainty, 172, 475–476, 531
certainty, stage of, 153, 471, 489, 595
Chökyab Zangpo, Khenchen, xxivn52
class affiliate, meanings of term, 91n315, 405n1014
cognition, three forms of correct, 192n583
Collection of Canonical Expressions. See *Paryāyasaṃgrahaṇī* (Asaṅga)
Collection of Determinations, A. See *Vinścayasaṃgrahaṇī* (Asaṅga)
Collection on [Canonical] Topics. See *Vastusaṃgrahaṇī* (Asaṅga)
Collection on Exegesis, A. See **Vyākhyāsaṃgrahaṇī* (Asaṅga)
Collection on the Vinaya. See *Vastusaṃgrahaṇī* (Asaṅga)
Commentary on Recollection of the Buddha (Asaṅga), 164–165nn512–513, 165nn515–516
Commentary to the Treasury of Higher Learning (Jinaputra). See *Abhidharmasamuccayabhāṣyam* (Jinaputra)
Commentary to the Twenty Verses on the Bodhisattva Discipline (Bodhibhadra), 267n751
compassion
  abiding in pleasurable state of, 163
  absolute in forbearance, 314
  as acquiring cause, 335
  as antidote, 597
  based on entities, 246
  beneficial conduct as, 379
  cultivation through meditating on suffering, 404–410
  four causes of, 26–28
  generating enlightenment mind and, 23–24
  in generosity practice, 224, 225–226, 227, 234
  in pleasurable states, 55, 534, 545, 554, 558, 559
  preeminence of, 477
  pure patience and, 329
  purity of attitude and, 598
  as skillful means, 436
  of spiritual teachers, 396–397
  tirelessness and, 417
  toward hell beings, 34
  in transcending rebirth in lower realms, 596–597
  See also great compassion
Compendium of Higher Learning. See *Abhidharmasamuccayaḥ* (Asaṅga)
Compendium of Training, The. See *Śikṣāsamuccayaḥ* (Śāntideva)
compliance, 272n765
  failing in, 297–298
  meditative absorption and, 347
  morality of, 254–257, 287–288
  safeguarding, 470
composure
  as cessation, 44n202, 45–46, 163, 458, 477, 564
  with conception, 144–145n459
  difficulties due to, 591–592
  establishment in, 75
  four formless states of, 163
  in pleasurable state of superior mind training, 522, 545, 546, 547
  result in current and future lives, 59
consecration, 573–574
conceptions, 88n307, 144–145n459, 176, 400–402, 559, 561
conceptual elaborations, 68–69, 90, 100, 176n535, 356
conceptual thoughts, 68–69
  avoidance of, 435
  and concepts, distinguished, 562n1356
  eight types, 89–96, 100
  four investigations of, 96–97
  impermanence of, 455n1138

meditative absorption free from, 344
in pleasurable state free of signs with preparation and effort, 562, 564
conditions, 108–110, 178–179, 431n1088
conduct
application relating to, 31
conducive to enlightenment, 602
(*See also* enlightenment, thirty-seven factors; knowledge, of the way things are)
four types, xxxviii, 601–603
improper, 181, 218, 221, 420
(*See also* misconduct)
in pleasurable states, 517, 559, 565
showing an attitude at variance with, 445
that need not be concealed, 654n1544
well restrained, 244–248
See also beneficial conduct; certain conduct, stage of; practicing conduct, stage of; state of conduct based on devotion
confession, 242, 247n704, 301–302, 416n1036, 439, 514
confidence, four forms of intrepid, 161, 386, 651–653, 661
confusion, freedom from, 161, 655, 661, 668
consciousness
Abhidharma formulation of, 5n111
arising of, 43n199, 431n1088
objects of, freedom from, 344n904
shaping of, 206n620
constituents, 138, 199n608
distinctions of those to be trained, 485–486
eighteen, 55n229
immeasurable, 483, 484
meanings of, 339n892
nurturing the element, 146
skill regarding, 430
as spiritual lineage, 332–333
two types, 160, 165
See also under sentient beings
contact, definition of, 42n192
conventional truth. *See* relative truth
conventional usage, 68n262, 86n303
conviction, 70n270, 460–461, 660
corporeal desire
as craving for individual existence, 74n277
freedom from in forbearance, 314
generosity free from, 207
interpretations of, 193n584
in the minds of afflicted beings, 127
correct means, path of, 200
correct placement, 182–183n554
cosmology, Buddhist, 107n345, 110n349
counsel, five aspects, 171, 201–202
courage, 337, 368n946, 417, 496
coveting, 541n1308
crops, example of ten causes, 179–181
crown protrusion, 609, 615, 617, 618

Daśabalasūtram, 623
Daśabhūmikasūtram, xixn26, xxxvii, 39n183, 530n1284
on action-paths, 541n1309
on conditioning formation, 544n1311
on controlling powers over deeds and rebirth, 569n1375
on magical creations in pleasurable state of great joy, 538n1302
on motivations related to thirty-seven spiritual qualities, 550n1330
on supernatural knowledge, 546n1318
ten stages in, 539, 543, 548, 552, 557
Daśabhūmivyākhyānam (Vasubandhu)
on antidote for exaggerated pride, 553n1336
on entry into Dharma by light, 549n1327, 549n1329
on miraculous powers in pleasurable state of great joy, 538n1302
on undertaking distinct path, 561n1355
death
knowledge regarding, 125–126, 635–638
suffering from, 405
deceitfulness, 11n129, 208–209, 217
dedication, 341, 437, 508, 617
deeds
of body, speech, mind, 171, 194, 202–203
effort that refines, 336
five immediate, 145n460, 520
immeasurable types of, 619
knowledge of all aspects, 627
in pleasurable state free of signs and effort, 571, 596
ten, of buddhas, 660–661
definitive meaning, xv, xvi, xxxiii, 428

degeneracies, 26n157, 419–421
deities, 111–114
dejection, absence of, 231, 234, 341, 496
deliberation, 45, 410, 474
delight
  in Dharma, 146–147, 172–173n529, 188
  from fitness of mind, 141n445
  in perfections, 132, 133
  in quiescence and insight, 198
  serene, 383
  toward nirvana, 283, 453
  See also joy
deliverance
  affirming path that leads to, 653
  attitudes toward, 648–650
  eight types, 345, 346n907
  in Great Vehicle, 488
  knowledge of, 419, 421
dependent origination
  as causes of afflictions, 181–182
  reversal of, 182–184
  samsara and, 361n937
  settled nature of entities and, 647n1538
  skill regarding, 431nn1089–1090
  tathāgatas' power to examine, 648
  See also pleasurable state of superior wisdom that relates to dependent origination
desiderative intention, 108–109
designating assertions
  of arising, 79
  basis for, 84
  essential nature and, 67n260, 68
  of multiplicity, 78–79
  of unique characteristics, 77–78
desire
  abandoning bond of, 547
  allowing, offense of, 271
  avoiding, 85, 87, 219–220
  conceit as, 299n811
  conceptual thoughts and, 91
  in generating enlightenment, 21–22
  in morality, absence of, 245, 248
  in pleasurable state of conduct based on devotion, 525n1273
  separation from objects of, 546n1320
  suffering of, 404–405, 406, 408
  See also corporeal desire; sensory pleasures
desire realm, 38n182, 39, 107n345, 111–112, 127, 547
detachment, 514, 515, 646
determinate objects, 94
devotion
  to armor-like effort, 332–333
  eight objects of, 172–173, 323–324
  to enlightenment, 28
  failing to develop, 291
  to meditation objects, 197
  from seeing or hearing spiritual powers, 25
  skillful means of, 438n1107, 439n1108
  that does not disagree with reality, 514
  wisdom and, 355n923
  worship and, 394
  See also pleasurable state of conduct based on devotion; Three Jewels
Dharma
  branches of learning, inclusive of, xxix
  desire to preserve, 26
  disrespecting, 293
  exemplary follower of, 260
  formulations, 477–482, 537n1300
  four summary statements of, 394, 454–463
  four ways of examining, 65n255 (*See also* applications, four)
  fourfold following, 397
  generosity of, 221–222, 224, 228, 231–232
  hostility toward, 375
  of instruction, 429n1082
  listening to, 25, 188–191, 400–402
  magical creation of speech regarding, 120
  marks produced by mastering and teaching, 612–613, 614–615
  as means of ripening, 146, 148, 149, 156
  pleasure in, 450, 545–546
  practice that accords with, 171, 194–198
  preservation of, 103
  repudiating, 196n596
  retention of, 448, 450
  seeking, 171, 173–191
  seven forms of embracing, 321
  six methods regarding sentient beings, 439–447
  specific usage of, 80n293
  twelve divisions of, 172n529, 174
  wisdom of learning, 358, 359

Dharma cloud stage, 446n1116, 573–574
Dharma conch shell, 618
Dharma doors, 537
Dharma eye, 486, 487, 538n1302
Dharma king, 573–574
Dharma teaching, 39n185, 171, 191–194
  in accordance with faculties of beings, 642
  agreeable speech in, 366, 367–368
  difficult situations in, 591, 592
  eight aspect of providing, xxx–xxxi
  embracing in, 589, 590
  explaining meanings and intents of, 500
  fruitful manner of, 668
  fruits and benefits of, 486–487
  immeasurable methods of, 483, 486
  morality and, 243, 250–251
  for new disciples, 367n943
  in pleasurable state of conduct based on devotion, 527–528
  from pleasurable state of informative knowledge, 571–573
  stinginess regarding, 36, 267
  systematic manner of, 378
  ten powers and, 646–647, 648
  three closely placed recollections and, 653n1543
  through birth with semblance of shared qualities, 585
  twenty forms of, 193–194
Dharma Wheel, turnings of, xv. *See also* divine wheel, turning
Dharmadharmatāvibhāgaḥ (Maitreya Nātha), xviin8, xix, xxiii
Dharmakīrti (Lama Serlingpa), xxii
Diamond-Cutter. See *Vajracchedikā*
diamond-like one-pointed concentration, 657
Differentiating Phenomena from Ultimate Reality. See *Dharmadharmatāvibhāgaḥ* (Maitreya Nātha)
Differentiating the Middle Way from Extremes. See *Madhyāntavibhāgaḥ* (Maitreya Nātha)
diffidence, freedom from, 189
Dīpaṃkara Śrījñāna. *See* Atīśa
discernment, 53
  devotion due to, 323–324
  as essence of wisdom, 355
  five erring forms of, 358n927
  genuine, 400–401
  subtlety of, 138
disciples. *See* spiritual followers
discipline, 75, 173n531, 206. *See also* bodhisattva discipline
Discourse in Response to Questions Posed by Ratnacūḍa. See *Ratnacūḍaparipṛcchā Sūtra*
Discourse That Clarifies the Intent, The. See *Saṃdhinirmocana Sūtra*
discriminating wisdom, 417
disease, treatment of, 174, 175. *See also* illness
disparaging others, 291–292
dissembling, 34
distinguishing characteristic, 89, 90, 92–94, 96–97, 98–99
divine abodes, 635
divine ear, 123–125, 126
divine eye, 125–126, 537, 635
divine speech, 609, 615, 617
divine vision, 652
divine wheel, turning, xv, 624–625
doubt, 14–15n138, 288, 368, 528, 645–646, 666
downfall, state of, 147, 389
Dravidian mantras, 124
Dromton Gyalwe Jungne, *Extensive Biography of the Precious Lord, the Glorious Master Atisha*, xxi, xxii
duality, 68–70
duly observant, quality of being, 144
Dutt, Nalinaksha, xlvii

ease, bestowing, 115
effort, 13–14
  armor-like, 332–333
  difficult, 334–335, 384
  directed everywhere, 335–336
  for distressed beings, 338–339
  essence of, 331
  four aspects of power of, 132
  fourfold correct abandonment and, 182–183n554
  pertaining to virtue, 241
  in pleasurable state of great joy, 537
  in pleasurable state of superior mind training, 545–546
  preeminence of, 477

effort (*continued*)
in promoting merit and wisdom, 55–56
pure, 339–341
as skillful means, 436
spiritual friend, role in developing, 27
superior attitude toward, 515
thirteen forms of, 337–338
tirelessness and, 417
of true spiritual being, 337
virtuous qualities collected by, 332, 333–334
when unable to complete action, 76
eight assemblies, 485
eightfold ārya path, 60, 185
eloquence, 397n998
bestowing, 115
in developing morality, 241
in generosity of Dharma, 221
informative knowledge conferring, 360, 430, 572
meditative absorption and, 352
respect for, 188
emanations
controlling power over implements and, 393
manifold magical, 118
meditative absorption and, 346nn907–908, 351
power of, 39
as purity of support, 621n1463
emancipation. *See* enlightenment
embracing
by acquisition, 588–591
all sentient beings at once, 587
beings who have caused harm, 318
Dharma, 321
in difficult situations, 591–593
final form, 591
meaning of term, xxxviii, 30n163
morality of, 254
through authority, 587–588
eminence, 49, 50, 53, 73, 143, 392–393
emptiness
abiding in, 163
conviction in, xxviii, 70–72
correct understanding of, 83–84
joy in, 526n1278
misunderstanding, 82n298
one-pointed concentration on, 452, 453–454, 477
scriptural evidence for, 84–89
as skillful means, 438, 441–442
synonyms for, 68n261, 564n1359
encouragement, 243, 257, 347
enigmatic statements, 101, 102, 196, 291
enjoyment, understanding and rejecting, 36
enlightenment, xxxviii–xxxix
acquisition of ten powers at, 646
attaining by meditative absorption, 348, 353
benefits conducive to, 73–74
causes of, 16
in degenerate times, 26
desire for, 558
effort, importance of in, 132, 333–334, 339
four obstacles to, 18–19
generating enlightenment mind as root of, 23
great compassion and, 412–413
in Great Vehicle, steps toward, 665–669
happiness of complete, 44
length of time required for, 332n874
limbs of, 563
marks and signs, accumulations needed for, 611
meditative absorption as support for, 132–133
merit and wisdom as essential to, 58
morality, importance of in, 309, 310
nature of, 159–161
nondual wisdom as means to, 70–72
patience as productive cause of, 326
practices that lead to, 384–386
prophecies on, 474–475, 476
seat of, 169, 385, 394n994, 610, 657
seven limbs of, 178
spiritual lineage, role in attaining, xlv–xlvii
states immediately prior to, 523
superior attitude toward, 514
supremacy, seven forms of, 162–164
supreme of Great Vehicle, 361n936, 362
thirty-seven factors of, 433–434, 602, 657
of women, 169–170
See also tathāgatas, pleasurable state of
enlightenment mind
causes of, 26–28

continuous, 476
embracing and, 587
five characteristics, 23
four aspects, 530–532
as support, xxxvi
turning away from, 24, 30
See also generating enlightenment mind
entities
adventitious, 643
collection of, 316, 317
conditioned, 60, 93n320, 160, 226–227, 234, 436, 455–459, 540n1307, 559, 560n1352
defining attributes of, 69, 360
essential nature of, 84, 85
forms of knowledge penetrating, 567
immeasurability, 483, 484, 640
indeterminate, 176
informative knowledge of meanings and, 429–430
insubstantiality of, 67–68, 441
knowable, 67–68
knowledge of, 359
mere, 402–403
mode of existence of, 77–79, 85
patience from reflection on, 314, 323–324, 326
reality of, 63
sameness of, 468
settled nature of, 358, 647
signs of, 546
superior attitudes toward, 513
tathāgatas' knowledge of, 656
unconditioned, 93n320, 160
virtuous, 60, 61n243, 93n320
wisdom of insubstantiality of, 357
worldly, xxviii, 179–181
entity-source, 442
Entry into the Conduct That Leads to Enlightenment. See *Bodhicaryāvatāraḥ* (Śāntideva)
envy, freedom from, 398, 450
equanimity, xxviii, 15n140
appropriate effort in, 340
effort and, 333, 335
in generosity practice, 213, 214, 225
immeasurable, 403
in means of ripening, 150
meditative absorption and, 351
from nondual wisdom, 73–74
three closely placed recollections and, 653n1543
errors, four, 182n553, 226n654
even-mindedness, 467–468
evil companions, four kinds, 425
examination, four forms of, 315–316
excellence
fivefold inner, 605
mundane and transcendent, 120–121n393
three forms of, from ethics, 303–305
excellent understanding, stage of, 573. *See also* pleasurable state of informative knowledge
exertion, 73, 327, 328, 331
exhaustion, forbearing, 322. *See also* tirelessness
existence
abandoning bond of, 547
desire for, 127n411
impermanence of, 456–459
mistaken adherence to, 80
one-pointed concentration on, 453
Exposition of the Ornament of Discourses. See *Sūtrālaṃkāravyākhyā* (Vasubandhu)
expressions, black and great, 195, 196, 427
Extensive Biography of the Precious Lord, the Glorious Master Atisha (Dromton Gyalwe Jungne), xxi, xxii
extremes, two, 69–70, 310, 356, 436, 647

facing toward, stage of, 561. *See also* pleasurable state of superior wisdom that relates to dependent origination
factions, 239n682, 505–510, 616–617, 669. *See also* ascetics, homeless; householders
faculties, 186n564
five spiritual, 186n564, 630n1496, 640
governing results and, 186
guarding, 242, 470
ripening of, 143, 144, 157
faith
as antidote, 597
beneficial conduct and, 374–375
born of insight, 270, 532, 579
in dedication, 508
in generating enlightenment mind, 25
gifts of, 229, 300

faith (*continued*)
in karma and results, 215n641
as means of ripening, 146
morality, helping others to gain through, 251, 257
nirvana and, 462–463
in pleasurable state of conduct based on devotion, 525–526
in pleasurable state of great joy, 534
purity of attitude and, 598
from respect for eloquence, 188
spiritual friend, role in developing, 27
three types of, 51n220, 148n467
worship through, 394
fame, 134, 216, 233–234
family, 48, 50, 52, 143, 212, 213
fasting observance, 420, 438
faults
counterfeit qualities of, 472–473
of desire realm, 45n204, 348–349n911
examining, 246
of speech/verbal, 365n940, 501
See also transgressions
fear
abashment and, 416
affection and, 511
five types, 525, 532–533
of impatience, 325–326
protection from, 131
fearlessness, 27
feelings, 42n194, 43n200, 44, 544n1311
fervor, 143, 337n888, 338, 471, 476
fetters, 251, 336, 639n1529
fevers, three, 304n821
fields, 51–52, 52n221, 164
firmness, 416–417, 496, 499, 535, 598
five heaps, 55n228
as class affiliates, 334n880
closely placed recollections and, 434n1097
conditioned entities and, 93n320
contemplating, 317
error of nonexistence of, 81
form as material, 92n316
as formations, 315n843
grasping, 74n277, 405, 421n1050
in Listeners' and Solitary Realizers' vehicles, 67
living beings and, 94n324
as perishable collection, 90n311
selflessness of, 402n1009
skill regarding, 430
five immeasurables, 483–486
Five Sections on the Stages, xvii–xix
Five Teachings of Maitreya, xvi–xvii, xix
food
in developing morality, 242
failing to provide, 296
four types of, 180n552
generosity of, 207, 215
retention and, 449
forbearance, 147–148
development of, 173
from hearing the Dharma, 486
of nonarising of entities, 564, 567–568, 577
in pleasurable states, 528, 559
on preparation path, 153n483
regarding three spheres, 314n835
retention of, 448–450
of spiritual teachers, 397
that accords with Dharma, 196
two forms of, 313n832
in worship, 394–395
form realm, 38n182, 107n345, 110n349, 112–114, 389n984
formations
conditioning, 540, 544, 545, 554
continuum of, 455–456
suffering as basis of, 315–316
that do not accompany consciousness, 418n1038
formative actions, 538n1302, 571–572, 573
formless realm, 44n202, 87n306, 113n369, 127, 144–145n459
fortitude, 495, 496, 499, 501. *See also* firmness
Four Great Kings, 111
Four Hundred Verses. See *Catuḥśatakaśāstrakārikā* (Āryadeva)
four immeasurables, 75n281
benefits of meditation on, 413
as divine pleasurable states, 163
in generosity practice, 224–225
meditation on three forms of, 402–404
meditative absorption in, 350
in pleasurable state of superior mind training, 546
for self and others, 439
as worship, 394–395

four noble truths, 324n862, 478, 546n1318
  agreeable speech in teaching, 368
  bodhisattvas' understanding of, 434
  conditioned and unconditioned, 93n320
  forbearance and, 173n530
  four closely placed recollections and, 182n553
  knowledge of, 66–67, 421n1050
  in Listeners' Vehicle, 481
  outflows and, 43n196
  speech and, 192
  wisdom of, 359
  See also pleasurable state of superior wisdom that relates to the truths
four reliances, 195n591, 195n593, 368, 369, 427–428, 666
fraudulent transactions, 220–221
friendliness, 365–366, 367, 369, 498n1241

gaha shrine, 388
Gelukpa school, xvii, xxiv
gender, translation issues of, xlviii–xlix
general characteristics, great, 356
generating enlightenment mind, 4
  abandoning, 527
  aspirational prayer of, 450, 451
  benefits of, 32–34
  four causes and contributing factors, 25–28, 29
  four strengths in, 28–29
  four ways of understanding, 23–24
  in Great Vehicle lineage, 665
  intentions in, 23–24
  as preeminent aspiration, 476–477
generosity, 148n468, 223
  in accomplishing two aims, 39n185
  as antidote, 597
  benefiting others by, 38
  of body, 207, 209, 210
  completing well, 506–507
  dedicating, 215, 223–224
  difficulties in, 228, 384
  disinterested, 232, 233–234
  for distressed beings, 230–231
  equality and fairness in, 213–216
  essence of, 206
  four aspects of power of, 130
  happiness based in, 208, 231–232
  harm, avoiding in, 208–209, 210, 211
  inferior views, avoiding, 214–215
  involving parents and spouses, 210, 212–213
  marks produced by, 611, 613, 614
  mental, 227–228
  of objects of pleasure, 210–212
  obstacles to, 225–227
  as openhandedness, 496
  of outer and inner objects, 207–208
  proper refusal of, 223–225
  as quality for retention, 450
  response time, 216
  signs of, 8–10
  skillful means of, 217–218, 221
  of sovereignty, 213
  state of mind for, 214, 217–218, 234
  suitability of recipient, 208, 210, 213, 218–220
  summary verse on nine aspects, 205
  ten pure forms, 232–234
  thirteen forms of, 229–230
  toward afflicted beings, 212, 214, 225
  of true spiritual being, 229
  See also under attracting a following; Dharma
gentleness, 246, 248
gifts, 278, 391
goes a long way, stage that, 566. *See also* pleasurable state free of signs with preparation and effort
gold analogy, 536, 542, 547, 551, 556, 560, 565
governed results, 185, 186–187
grammar, 174, 175, 190
grasping
  renouncing, 231
  a sign, 88n307
  and view, relationship of, 87
  wisdom that understands, 361
gratitude, 243, 252, 347
great compassion, xxxvii, xxxix, 411–413
  abandoning, 528
  based on entities, 246
  of buddhas, 161, 655, 661
  patience and, 327
  as sign of mental absorption, 15–16
  spiritual lineage and, 17
  See also compassion
Great Supreme Lord, 585
Great Treatise on the Stages of the Path (Tsongkapa), xliii

Great Vehicle, xv, xx
  Abhidharma in, xx, xxiii–xxvi, xxxi–xxxiv
  appreciating, xxvi
  beneficial conduct and, 375–376
  canonical literature of, 173–174n531
  denigrating, 290, 291
  devotion to, 544
  enlightenment factors in, 433–434
  pleasurable state of spiritual lineage in, 519–520
  qualities constituting summary of, 488, 578–579
  seven forms of greatness of, 487
  spiritual lineage of, xliv–xlv, 5–7, 184
  wealth permitted in, 223n649
greed, 212, 225, 226, 267. *See also* stinginess
grief, 212, 243, 296, 347, 371
guile, 11n130
Guṇaprabha
  Bodhisattvabhūmivṛttiḥ, 49n212, 59n238, 66n257, 78n291, 229n661, 230n664
  Bodhisattvaśīlaparivartabhāṣyam, 250n711, 257n727, 264n744, 268n752

happiness
  agreeable speech and, 370–371
  avoiding attachment to, 666
  based on generosity, 208, 231–232
  based on morality, 239, 256, 308–309
  beneficial conduct regarding, 373, 377, 667
  five types, 42–48
  free from affliction, 103
  linked to what is beneficial, 40
  from meditative absorption, 352–353
  in pleasurable state of conduct based on devotion, 527
  as samsaric suffering, 318
  superior attitudes and, 31, 513, 515
  wisdom that brings, 360
hardships, enduring, 134, 228
Haribhadra, xxiv
  Abhisamayālaṃkārālokaḥ, 164n511, 165n518, 289n800, 345n905
harm
  avoiding, 49, 131, 208–209, 210, 214, 217
  forbearing, 75, 315–316, 324–325, 326, 328, 329
  freedom from, 44–46
  patience toward, 313, 314, 315–318
hatred, 91, 303. *See also* anger
haughtiness, 231, 233
heaps, three, 356–357
Heart Sutra, xlix
heedlessness, 544n1311
  abode of, 544n1311
  antidote for, 598
  of bodhisattvas, 390, 392, 472
  in developing mental afflictions, 18
  freedom from, 590, 604
  magical speech to admonish, 119, 120
  in sameness of purpose, 381
  turning others away from, 368, 374, 377
hells, 34, 83n299, 125
  beings of, 261n736
  birth in due to causes and conditions, 637
  deliberate birth in, 279
  displaying visions of, 258, 347
  suffering of, 407, 411
heretics, 139, 221, 285, 290, 292, 298, 374
Higher Doctrine of the Great Vehicle. See *Mahāyānottaratantraḥ* (Maitreya Nātha)
hindrances, five, 14–15, 144, 250n714, 288
householders, xxxviii
  effort related to, 331
  embracing and, 587–588
  four qualities pertaining to, 505, 508–510
  leading through beneficial conduct, 373
  morality related to, 239–240
  patience related to, 314, 316n845
  regular activities of, 323
  suffering particular to, 409, 410
  tathāgatas' perceptions of, 647
humans, 185, 186, 421–422
Hundred Sutra Fragments That Are the Subject of Correct Interpretation (Vasubandhu), 367n943
hypocrisy, 216, 248, 398

ignorance, 34n171, 91, 133, 405, 411
illness, 212, 241, 243, 250–251, 294, 351, 443–444
illusion, 98, 441, 442, 479n1193, 558

immovability, stage of, 571. *See also* pleasurable state free of signs with preparation and effort
impenetrable processes, ten, 572
impermanence
as conditioned, 93n320
in developing patience, 316, 317–318
summary statement of, 454, 455–459
two forms, 234n676
import
bare, 196–197
suppositional and theoretical, 97
true, 72
imputation, 77n288, 436
In Praise of the Praiseworthy. See *Varṇāhavarṇastotram* (Mātṛceṭa)
inattention, 526
indefatigability, 476
indeterminate
meditative absorption, 351
objects, examples of, 94n323
Indian Buddhist tradition, xx–xxiv
indifference, 206, 244, 248
indisposition, 15, 33, 46, 198, 199n608
absolute termination of, 621, 622
innermost core of, 657
in pleasurable states, 576–578
suffering of, 410, 411
in transcending rebirth in lower realms, 596–597
individual existence, 59, 60, 74, 405, 409n1025, 411
individual liberation
and bodhisattva discipline, compared, 264–265, 269, 276–278
fasting observance in, 420n1045
morality of restraint and, 240
inference, 192
informative form, 260n733, 301
informative knowledge, four forms, 161, 164, 369n948, 429–432
in explaining meaning and intents, 496
generosity practice and, 224n652, 228
wisdom and, 359–360, 433
See also pleasurable state of informative knowledge
injury, avoided through merit, 57n234
inner science, xxviii, 174
Inner Science of Buddhist Practice, The (Engle), xxvi
insight (*vipaśyanā*), xxii, 197–198
closely placed recollection and, 136n438
delight in cultivating, 198
in means of ripening, 150
meditative absorption and, 343, 351
morality and, 241
on mundane path, 185n561
signs in, 546n1318
thirty-seven enlightenment factors and, 435, 436
instruction
Asaṅga's definition of, xxxiii
eightfold classification of, 171, 199–200
threefold classification of, 200–201
See also Dharma teaching
insubstantiality
nature of, 567n1366
nonbeing and, 69
of persons, 402n1009, 422n1057
of phenomena, xxvii, 67–68, 72, 355n923, 356, 357
two types, xxiii, 152n480, 314n835, 453n1133, 459–460, 467n1161, 513
intelligence
of eloquence, 115n380, 397n998, 523
innate, 76n284
ordinary, 65
safeguarding, 470
as sign of perfection of wisdom, 16
intermediate position, 200–201
intermediate state, 125n407, 635, 636
intoxicants, 210, 377
investigation, 668
eight worldly subjects of, 422
four subjects of, 96–97, 482, 568
and shared views, differentiated, 65
irreproachability, 40, 471, 632, 632–633n1509
irreversibility, stage of, 668

Jangchub Dzutrul, *'Phags pa dgongs pa nges par 'grel pa'i rnam par bshad pa*, 231–232n673
Jewel Garland. See *Ratnāvalī* (Nāgārjuna)
Jinaputra
Abhidharmasamuccayabhāṣyam, 178n547, 480–481n1199, 662n1561
See also *Bodhisattvaśīlaparivartaṭīkā*
joy
in face-to-face worship, 388

joy (*continued*)
  gaining as means of ripening, 146–147
  in generosity practice, 224
  in pleasurable states, 526
  worship through, 394

Kālāma Sūtra. See *Aṅguttara Nikāya*
kalpas
  "countless," meanings of, 575–576
  length of, 420n1049
  merit accumulated in, 432
Kangyur, xxxviii
karma
  Buddha's speech and, 175n533
  buddhas' understanding of, 187n566
  and confession, effect on, 439
  in current life, 58
  discrediting doctrine of, 636n1518
  forms of virtuous and nonvirtuous, 541n1308
  individual consequences of, 626n1484
  knowledge of results of, 215n640
  obscurations of, 145
  as seen event, 42, 46
  suffering and, 315–316
  in taking up what is right, 41n187, 627
  turning back, 548
  unvarying, 113n369
  See also maturations, eight
Karuṇāpuṇḍarīka Sūtra, 135n435
killing, 211, 279n781, 377, 541n1308
king of one-pointed concentration, 668
kings and sovereigns, bodhisattvas as, 212–213, 583–584, 586, 588
knowledge
  of all aspects and of what is most excellent, 656, 661
  authoritative, 65
  complete purity regarding, 622
  corrective, 227
  effort that increases, 336
  free of conceptual thoughts, 78
  having supreme reality as field of action, 100–101
  mundane, 66
  perfection of, 602, 625
  in pleasurable state of conduct based on devotion, 526
  in pleasurable state of great joy, 535
  purity of, 133
  ripening of, 144, 145, 158
  safeguarding, 470
  subsequent, 359
  suffering from lack of, 411
  supremacy of, 162, 164
  of teaching, 598
  types related to enlightenment, 159–161
  uncontaminated, 66
  unobstructed, 559–560, 561
  of the way things are, 97–101, 482–483, 568, 602
  worldly, 419–427, 598
  See also informative knowledge; supernatural knowledges; ten powers of tathāgatas; transcendent knowledge
knowledge-perception, 264, 435, 436, 460–463, 537
knowledge-vision, 198
kūṭa shrine, 388

Lakṣaṇa Sūtra, 611
Lama Serlingpa. *See* Dharmakīrti
Lamrim (Stages of the Path), xx–xxiii, xxiv, xxvi, xliiin90
latencies, 126, 199, 199n608, 336, 629, 646
laziness, 18, 132, 147, 287, 309, 502
learning, 144, 149, 156, 188–191, 292
learning, five branches of, xxix
  bodhisattva superiority due to, 8
  competence in, necessity of, 476
  effort and, 333, 338
  knowledge of, 418
  mastery of, 101, 102
  proper motives for, 190–191
  in seeking Dharma, 174–175
  wisdom and, 355, 356–357, 360
Lesser Vehicle, xvii, xlvi, 154–155n490, 261n736, 375–376, 454n1134, 540, 544, 565. *See also* Listeners' Vehicle; Solitary Realizers' Vehicle
Letter Sent to Lama Umapa (Tsongkapa), xxiv–xxvi
liberation
  of mature sentient beings, 373, 375
  of mind and wisdom, 638–639
  purification of, 629
  in tathāgata powers, 627–628
  three doors to, 127n411, 163n508, 559, 666
  See also enlightenment

life span, 48, 49, 52, 134, 143
light
  of celestial objects analogy, 556, 560
  emitting rays of, 116, 353
  in one-pointed concentration state, 628
light, stage that produces, 548, 549. *See also* pleasurable state of superior mind training
Light Rays of the Sun (Tsonawa Sherab Sangpo), 240n683
limitation, absence of, 382
lineages, transmission, xx–xxiii
lion's roar, 625
Lion's Roar of Śrīmālādevī. See *Śrīmālādevīsiṃhanādasūtram*
Listeners' Vehicle, xxviin54
  attainments in, 645
  attitude toward nirvana in, 650
  avoidance of conflict in, 161n504
  and bodhisattva vehicle, distinctions between, 529, 561n1355, 562, 564, 667–668
  characteristics of, 154–155
  closely placed recollections in, 433
  compassion of, 412
  concord in, 469
  expulsory offenses of, 267n751, 269n754
  immeasurables in, 404
  intrepid confidence and, 652
  knowledges of, 66–67
  nirvana of, 460, 461–462
  noble sounds in, 123–124
  patience in, 316
  pleasurable states of, 579–580
  powers of, 138–139
  rejecting, 289
  ripening of, 142–143
  and Solitary Realizers' Vehicle, differentiated, 155
  spiritual lineage of, xliii, 6–8, 184
  supernatural travel of, 110n350
  suppression of, 655
  teachings on, 481–482
  ten powers and, 641
  termination in, 653
livelihood
  of bodhisattvas, 221
  excellence of, 310
  need for, 18
  of others, assisting with, 249–250, 468
  purity of, 248
  relying upon others for, 322
  wrong, 216n642, 282
logic, 175, 190
loving-kindness
  as antidote, 597
  benefits of, 501
  in generosity practice, 224
  irreversible, 379
  marks produced by, 615
  in pleasurable state of great joy, 534
  purity of attitude and, 598
  as sign of mental absorption, 15
  in teaching Dharma, 193
  of true spiritual being, 375
lying, 370n949, 541n1308

Mādhyamika. *See* Middle Way
Madhyāntavibhāgabhāṣyam (Vasubandhu), 68n261, 442n1110
Madhyāntavibhāgaḥ (Maitreya Nātha), xviin7, xix
Madhyāntavibhāgakārikā (Maitreya Nātha), 289n800, 442n1110, 455n1137, 564n1359
Madhyāntavibhāgaṭīkā (Sthiramati), 74n277, 86n303, 88n307, 442n1110, 531n1288, 564n1359
magical creation
  of body, 117–118, 121
  definition of, 116–117
  of objects, 117, 118
  in pleasurable state of great joy, 537, 538
  skillful means of, 439
  of sounds, 125
  of speech, 119–120, 121
Mahāvyutpattiḥ, 12n135, 144n458, 285n792, 608n1429
Mahāyānasaṃgrahaḥ (Asaṅga), xviiin22, xix, xli
Mahāyānasūtrālaṃkāraḥ (Maitreya Nātha), xvin6, xix, xxiii, xxxix–xlvii
Mahāyānasūtrālaṃkārakārikā (Maitreya Nātha)
  on aspirational prayers, 450n1128
  on "collections," 173–174n531
  on enigmatic intent, 101–102n340
  on equivalency between pleasurable states and stages, 539n1304
  on informative knowledge, 429n1079

Mahāyānasūtrālaṃkārakārikā (*continued*)
  on pleasurable states, 517n1264
  on pure spiritual life, 245n698
  on true spiritual beings, 229n659
  on underlying thought, 81n297
Mahāyānottaratantraḥ (Maitreya Nātha), xviin10
Main Treatise on the Stages, The (Asaṅga), xvii, xviii, xlii
Maitreya, xvi, xxi
Maitreya Nātha
  Abhisamayālaṃkāraḥ, xviin9, xxiv
  Dharmadharmatāvibhāgaḥ, xix, xxiii, xviin8
  Madhyāntavibhāgaḥ, xviin7, xix
  Madhyāntavibhāgakārikā, 289n800, 442n1110, 455n1137, 564n1359
  Mahāyānasūtrālaṃkāraḥ, xvin6, xix, xxiii, xxxix–xlvii
  Mahāyānottaratantraḥ, xviin10
  See also *Mahāyānasūtrālaṃkārakārikā*
male, birth as, 49, 50, 53–54
malice, 13n137, 14–15n138, 45n204, 145n460, 178, 201n612, 288, 339, 377, 514nn1308–1309, 541n1308, 597. *See also* perturbations
Mañjuśrī, xxi
Mañjuśrīmūlakalpaḥ, xvin4
Mañjuśrī's Fundamental Sacred Precepts. See *Mañjuśrīmūlakalpaḥ*
mantra spells, 33, 448, 449, 450
Māra, 135n433, 136, 209–210, 624
marks, thirty-two major, 135, 161, 607–609, 657, 660
  aspects of well-done spiritual activities and, 616–617
  deeds that produce, 611–615
  knowledge of, 359
  as material basis, 162
  as result, 385
marvelous abilities, 121n395, 139, 148, 369, 642, 648
marvelous feats, twin, 259
mastery, eight bases of, 346
Materialists, 472–473
Mātṛceṭa, *Varṇābhavarṇastotram*, 166nn519–520
mātṛkā, meanings of, xviii, xxxii–xxxiv, 663n1562
maturation obscurations, 144
maturations, eight, 408nn1022–1023
  bodhisattva birth and, 585
  causes of and conditions for, 49–52
  description of, 48–49
  generosity not seeking, 231, 234
  merit as basis of, 58
  results of, 52–55, 117n386, 143, 185, 206–207n622, 541, 604
meanings and intents, explaining, 496, 500, 502
meditation, 666
  appropriate for specific afflictive tendencies, 632n1507
  effort in, 334
  on emptiness, 72, 452, 453–454, 477
  four aspects of, 196–198
  knowledge derived from (*See* informative knowledge, four forms)
  literature associated with, xxii
  as means of ripening, 150
  mental support for, 22n146
  not relying on conceptions in, 87–88
  objects, 197n602, 435n1098, 590n1412, 644–647
  during pleasurable states, 523–524
  on suffering, 411–412
  superior attitude toward, 515
  wisdom from, 357
  See also meditative absorptions; one-pointed concentration
meditation, path of, 576n1391, 638–639, 657n1556
meditative absorptions
  deities of, 112–114
  difficult, 348, 384
  for distressed beings, 351–352
  divine abodes and, 635
  enjoyment of, 289
  first, 410n1027, 546–547n1320
  as form of retention, 450
  four aspects of power of, 132–133
  happiness in, 40, 45, 352–353
  karma and, 113n369
  limbs of, 348–350
  miraculous power from, 106n344
  mundane and transcendent, 343, 344
  as pleasurable state of gods, 163
  in pleasurable state of superior mind training, 522, 546, 547, 605
  preeminence of fourth, 477

purification of, 629
restraint from, 75n279
results of, 59, 385
signs of, 14–16
as skillful means, 438
spiritual qualities gained from, 345–347
of tathāgatas, 201, 345, 627–629
that promote merit and wisdom, 56
thirteen types, 350–351
for transcending rebirth in lower realms, 596–597
of true spiritual being, 350
turning back, 38–39, 58
on worldly path, xxiin45, 185n561

meditative composure, 14–15, 45–46, 66n258, 87n306, 135, 144, 250n714, 288

mendicants, 321–322, 373. *See also* ascetics, homeless

mental afflictions
abandonment of, 60, 162
aversion for, 283
of bodhisattvas, 14–15, 34, 70–71
clarity of mind and, 51n220
complete destruction of, 655–656, 661
conceit as supporting, 299n811
destruction of all traces of, 161, 621
in developing morality, 248, 272n764, 283, 307
effort that avoids, 333, 336, 338, 666
four states of, 17–18
improper attention and, 407–408
from improper conceptual thoughts, 100
improper social contact and, 474n1175
keeping others from developing, 161n504
meditative absorption, abandoning through, 132
in nirvana, 460
opposition to, 178
in pleasurable state free of signs with preparation and effort, 563, 564
in pleasurable state of superior morality, 540
in pleasurable state of superior wisdom that relates to dependent origination, 559
suffering of, 411
sympathy for, 498
synonyms for, 137n439, 199n608, 251n716
torpor as supporting, 376n961
in transcending rebirth in lower realms, 596–597
types of persons and, 631n1503
when embracing sentient beings, difficulties in, 591
wisdom and, 73, 358, 361
of women, 170
See also mental afflictions, secondary; obscurations, two; outflows

mental afflictions, secondary, 17n142, 246n701, 336
antidotes for, 339
blunted by generating enlightenment mind, 34
eight associated with perturbations, 137n439
in first meditative absorption, 132n426
ten in degenerate era, 26

mental stability, 75n280, 197n602, 288, 311, 343, 647. *See also* one-pointed concentration

mental support, 22n146, 95n326, 96, 100

mental traits, unfavorable, 631n1504

"merging of three rivers," xxi

merit
accumulation from generosity, 214–215, 220, 223, 233
bodhisattvas' deliberate rebirth and, xxvii
causes of, 56–57
from generating enlightenment mind, 32–34
limitless, 439
from meditation on immeasurables, 413
perfection of morality and, 310
to produce marks and signs, 618–619
rebirth and, 113n369
results of, 57–58, 227
six types, 55–56
of studying *Bodhisattvabhūmiḥ*, 663–664
transferring, 641
wisdom as basis of, 58
from worship, 389–390

Middle Way (Mādhyamika), 81nn295–296, 82
Abhidharma in, xxiv

Middle Way (*continued*)
  Asaṅga's view of, xv–xvi, xx, 81n295, 82n298
  Atīśa and, xxii
  instruction in, 200
  saṃvṛtiḥ, understanding of in, 86n303
  skillful means that points out, 438
  wisdom and, 356
migratory states
  causes of rebirth in, 636–637
  five, 131n422, 632
  giving up and taking on, 558n1346
  suffering of, 407, 411
mind
  of bodhisattvas, 33, 73
  clarity of, 51, 188, 660
  continuum of, 640
  fitness of, 141, 628
  four conditions and, 179
  knowledge regarding diverse states of, 126–128, 139
  liberation of, 638–639
  purity regarding, 622
  turning of, 657
Mind Only school, xxi, 81n296, 99n333
mindfulness
  continuous, 476
  in developing morality, 241, 248
  difficulties due to, 592
  five limbs of, 247, 248
  lack of, 16, 27
  magical creation of speech for, 120
  in pure morality, 309
miraculous powers, 106, 139
  creative, 116–121
  failing to use, 300
  as means of ripening, 148, 156
  meditative absorption and, 347, 352
  merit of, 439
  morality and, 244
  skillful means of, 439
  for teaching Dharma, 440
  transformational, 107–116
misconduct, 130, 193
  abandoning all forms of, 654
  continuous awareness of, 476
  immediate, 279
  of others, 246, 257–258, 295, 299, 497–498
  in pleasurable state of conduct based on devotion, 527
  suffering caused by, 407–408, 411
  See also offenses
morality, 300
  of acquiring virtue, 240–242, 244, 248–249, 260, 300, 306, 311
  agreeable speech and, 371
  on behalf of beings, 242–244, 249–260, 300
  beneficial conduct and, 374–375
  benefits of, 310, 311
  difficult, 305, 384
  directed everywhere, 305–306
  for distressed beings, 307–308
  of embracing, 254
  essence of, 237–239
  joy in, 502
  marks produced by, 611, 615
  natural, 306, 541
  nine divisions, list of, 237
  power of, 130–131
  pure, 309–310
  of restraint, 74–75nn278–279, 244–248, 260, 300, 306, 310–311, 396
  signs of, 10–13
  skillfulness in, 507
  suffering from failure of, 411
  summary verses on, 237
  superior attitudes and, 513, 514
  thirteen forms of, 306–307
  of true spiritual beings, 306
  See also bodhisattva discipline; pleasurable state of superior morality; transgressions
Mūlamadhyamakakārikā (Nāgārjuna), xixn28, 82n298, 86n303
mundane path, 60n240, 185, 343n896

Nāgārjuna, xv–xvi, xvii, xix, xxi, 81n295, 82n298, 86n303
  Mūlamadhyamakakārikā, xixn28, 82n298, 86n303
  Ratnāvalī, xxiiin49, 42n195, 82n298
  Sixfold Collection on Correct Reasoning, xix
name and form, 5–6n111
names
  causes of, 176
  collection of, 418
  conceptual thoughts derived from, 90
  designation of, 88

function of, 85
investigation of, 96–98
as object of meditation, 351
Namkha Gyeltsen, xxivn52
nihilism, 81n296, 82. *See also* extremes, two
nirvana
as abandonment, 60n241
as absolute termination, 21
aspiration for, 453
attitudes toward, 648–650
bodhisattvas' understanding of, 71
delighting in, 283
display of entering, 621n1465
as exalted state, 624, 625
of Great Vehicle, 666
linked to what is beneficial, 41
longing for, 304
non-abiding, 100n335
as perpetual, 60
purification and, 182–184
summary statement of, 454, 460–463
superior attitude toward, 515
synonyms of, 419n1043
with and without remainder, 91n315, 373n959
nominal designations, 77–78, 81–82, 84, 96–97, 98–99, 139n443, 405n1014, 418n1038, 467n1161
nonbeing, xv, 68–69
nonexistence, 69, 78n289, 80–83, 453, 455n1137, 456–459, 558–559
nonreturners/nonreturner āryas, 38n181, 113n370
nonviolence, 49n213. *See also* harm, avoiding
nonvirtuous deeds. *See* misconduct

objectionable acts, 12, 34n171, 130, 131n423, 222, 276n774, 278–282
objects
in generosity practice, 207–208, 210–218, 225–226, 227–229, 231, 233
of knowledge, 83, 355
magical creation of, 117, 118
material, 148, 156, 231–232
mental, 200, 402–404, 621–622
unimpeded knowledge and, 160
unsuitable, 392
of worship, 390–391
obscurations, two, xxvii, 7
abandoning, 159, 666
fervor and, 143n455
indisposition related to, 576–578
meditative absorption and, 353
ripening and, 141–142
subtle, 657n1555
transcendent awareness and, 66–68
wisdom and, 134
offenses, four expulsory, 267n751, 269n754
offenses, secondary, 269–270
failing to assist others, 293–300
faith, engendering lack of in others, 276–277
idle speech, 287–288
immoral beings, abandoning, 275–276
invitations, not accepting, 273
laziness, 287
learning, failing to pursue, 292
mental excitation and excessive merriment, 282–283
not applying distressing measures, 284
not dispelling bad reputation, 284
not honoring the Three Jewels, 270
of praising and disparaging, 291–292
regarding apologies, 285–286
regarding Dharma, 274–275, 293
regarding heretical teachings, 290
regarding meditation, 288–289
rejecting Great Vehicle, 290, 291
rejecting Listeners' Vehicle, 289
samsara, complacency toward, 283
scolding, 285
seeking material rewards, 287
spiritual elders, lacking respect for, 271–272
sympathy, lack of, 278–282
unchecked anger, 286–287
unchecked desire, 271
verbal reply, refusing, 271, 272–273
wealth, not accepting, 274
wrong livelihood, 282
offerings. *See* worship
omniscience, 75, 574
one-pointed concentration
appropriate effort in, 340, 341
in bodhisattvas' final existence, 657
developing through morality, 245, 311
entering state of, 628

one-pointed concentration (*continued*)
 failing to pursue, 288
 instructions for novice, 642–645
 mantra spells and, 448
 in pleasurable states, 522, 545, 547, 560, 564, 573–574
 purification of, 629
 pursuing learning and, 292
 in quiescence, 197
 of three doors to liberation, 163n508, 559, 560
 three forms of, 452–454, 477
openhandedness, xxxvii, 496, 499–500, 502, 503. *See also* generosity
orderly discourse, 176, 180, 181, 182, 190, 243
ordinary persons, 64n252, 65n253, 139, 185, 304n820, 344n904, 410, 498, 531
Ornament of Realizations, The. See *Abhisamayālaṃkāraḥ* (Maitreya Nātha)
Ornament of the Great Vehicle's Discourses. See *Mahāyānasūtrālaṃkāraḥ* (Maitreya Nātha)
outflows
 conditioned entities and, 93n320
 description of, 43n196
 indisposition and, 15n139
 knowledge regarding termination of, 128–129, 139, 359, 638n1527
 as not perpetual, 61
 termination of, 201, 486, 638–639, 653

Pañcaskandhaprakaraṇam (Vasubandhu), 44n202
Pañcaskandhavibhāṣā (Sthiramati)
 on afflicted wisdom, 53n224
 on agility, 141n445
 on clarity of mind, 660n1559
 on class affiliation, 405n1014
 on collections of names, assertions, syllables, 418n1038
 on corporeal desire, 193n584
 on equanimity, 335n881
 on excitation, 282n788
 on feelings, 44n201
 on formations, 315n843
 on grasping heaps, 74n277, 405n1015
 on inattention, 526n1277
 on informative forms, 260n733
 on sign, meaning of, 88n307
 on volition, 206n620
Pañcaviṃśatisāhasrikāprajñāpāramitā-sūtram, 651n1542, 654n1544
parables
 of great physician, 462–463
 of king and son, 460–461
parents, offering of, 212, 213
parinirvana, 100n335, 137, 184
Paryāyasaṃgrahaṇī (Asaṅga), xviiin20, 639
path systems, xviii, xx, xxiv, xxvn54. *See also* vehicles
patience
 all-inclusive categories of, 314, 324
 benefiting others by, 38
 of body, speech, mind, 327
 difficult, 324, 384
 enduring and forbearing, 315–318
 essence of, 313–314
 four aspects of power of, 131
 happiness from, 328
 morality and, 12, 247, 248
 pure, 328–329
 from reflecting on entities, 314, 323–324
 signs of, 13
 that tolerates suffering, 319–323
 thirteen forms of, 325–327
 of true spiritual being, 324
Pawo Dorje, Lama Umapa, xxiv
Peak of Existence, 44n202
penetrating insight, 470
perception, 63–67, 96–97, 98
 direct, 65, 192
 See also knowledge-perception
perfect manner of going, stage of, 154, 359, 471
 pleasurable states corresponding with, 596
 pure method and, 446–447
 transcendent awareness in, 658–659
 unique buddha qualities in, 607
 virtuous qualities at, 384
Perfection of Wisdom, xxiv, 81n296
perfections, six, xxxv, xlv
 beneficial conduct and, 374–375
 bodhisattva marks and, 503
 completing well, 505–507
 effort applied to all, 333
 merit and wisdom in, 55–56, 57n234

morality in all, 308–309
morality that accompanies all, 308–309
proper understanding of, 362
sameness of purpose of, 381–384
signs of, 8–16
supernatural knowledges and, 106, 129–134
See also individual perfections
perfections, ten, 562, 601–604
perishable collection, 90, 91, 94, 550, 647
perturbations, 137
assisting those with, 250–251
confession of, 301–302
effort that avoids, 336
eight, 376
exhibiting lack of, 519–520
lesser, middling, great, 268n753, 269
suffering from, 405–406
See also mental afflictions, secondary
'Phags pa dgongs pa nges par 'grel pa'i rnam par bshad pa (Jangchub Dzutrul), 231–232n673
phenomena. *See under* insubstantiality
pleasurable state free of signs and effort, 523, 567, 571
forbearance of, 567–568
forms of knowledge on, 567
ten controlling powers in, 39n183, 101, 393, 475, 569–570, 584
pleasurable state free of signs with preparation and effort, 522–523, 566
conduct in, 565
four defects of, 568
meditative states in, 564
qualities of, 562–563
ten ways of undertaking distinct path in, 561–562
pleasurable state of conduct based on devotion, 520–523, 547
analysis and, 471, 524–525
based upon devotion, 152nn480–481, 153, 155
enlightenment mind in, 531
faith in, 525–526
meditation in, 523, 524
teaching Dharma from, 527–528
pleasurable state of great joy, 521, 539
aspiration prayers in, 529–530
enlightenment mind in, 530–532
entering, 528
meditation in, 523, 524
mental afflictions on, 576
miraculous powers of, 537–538
pure superior attitude in, 532–533
seeing path and, 576n1391
ten spiritual qualities in, 534–535, 597–599
ten types of mental attitude, 540
vision of buddhas in, 535–536
See also pure superior attitude, stage of
pleasurable state of informative knowledge, 523, 524, 571–573
pleasurable state of superior mind training, 522, 605, 638–639
ten forms of entry, 543–544, 549n1329
pleasurable state of superior morality, 522, 540–543, 605
pleasurable state of superior wisdom that relates to dependent origination, 522, 557–561
pleasurable state of superior wisdom that relates to qualities conducive to enlightenment, 522, 549–552
pleasurable state of superior wisdom that relates to the truths, 522, 553–554, 557–558
pleasurable state of the spiritual lineage, 519–520
pleasurable states, 471n1168, 574
of bodhisattvas and listeners, compared, 579–580
eight qualities of Great Vehicle in, 578–579
indisposition in, 576–578
meditation practice during, 523–524
order of perfecting, 521
purity and, 563, 578
range of meanings of, 517n1264
and seven stages, correspondences, 595–596
spiritual development in, 563
summary verses on, 517
supreme, 523, 524, 573–574, 577
thirty-two marks in, 617
three unsurpassed, 162–163, 164
time required to perfect, 575–576
twelve, 518, 519–523
types of birth in, 585–586
use of term, 539
poverty, 215, 216–217, 408, 555

practicing conduct, stage of, 471, 595
praising
  deserving beings, neglect of, 298–299
  morality and, 241
  transgression of, 267, 291–292
Prajñāvarma, 669
Prasannapadā (Candrakīrti), 82n298, 86n303, 178n547
precepts
  beneficial conduct of, 377
  in developing morality, 241
  lack of fear of, 246
  marks produced by, 615
  as means of ripening, 146, 147
  restoring, 301–302
  See also bodhisattva discipline
preparation, path of
  aims of, 644
  conduct based on devotion and, 153n483, 520n1269
  forbearance on, 173n530
  knowledges on, 66n257
  proficiency in, 449n1122
  wisdom of, 355n923
pride
  effort free from, 333
  egoistic, 90, 91
  exaggerated, 128, 129, 200–201, 553n1336, 560, 623–624, 646, 647, 667
  of others, not engendering, 299
  seven types, 90n314
progression, 91, 361, 404, 407, 408, 411, 422
prophecies, xvi, 474–475, 476, 667–668
protection, 9, 33, 34, 468
  continuous, 476
  generosity and, 231–232
  marks produced by, 612
  meditative absorption and, 347
  morality and, 243, 252–253
  patience and, 131
provisional meaning, xvi, 428
punishment and reprimand, 244, 257–258, 299, 369–370, 420n1048, 426. *See also* suppression
Purbuchok Ngawang Jampa, xlii–xliii
pure abodes, 110n349, 113n370
pure attitude
  in generosity practice, 209, 221, 223, 227
  marvelous abilities and, 148
  in pleasurable states, 536, 543, 556, 566
  toward morality, 238, 244
  See also superior attitudes, fifteen
pure stage, 196–197n600
pure superior attitude, stage of, xxxviii, 359, 470, 489
  appearance of marks and signs in, 610–611, 617
  compassion of, 411
  entering, 596–597
  method of practice on, 471
  nirvana of, 461–462
  virtuous qualities of, 383–384
purity/purification
  of attitude and activities, 598–599
  complete, 156
  four forms of, 161, 385–386, 621–622, 660
  of great compassion, 411
  impenetrable processes concerning, 572
  inner, 377, 379
  of meditative absorption, 353
  morality and, 245, 248, 309–310
  mundane, 60
  outer, 377–378
  of physical deeds, 377
  of pleasurable states, 567, 578
  remote, 147
  space-like, 442
  spiritual, 57
  ten causes and, 176, 182–185
  three conditions of, 51–52
  of two obscurations, 6–7
  unsurpassed perfect, 657
  of virtuous qualities, 383–384
  of wisdom, 360–362
Purushapura, xvi

quiescence (*śamathaḥ*), xxii, 75n280, 196–197
  agility, developing in, 141n445
  appropriate effort in, 340
  closely placed recollection and, 136n438
  delight in cultivating, 198
  in means of ripening, 150
  meditative absorption and, 343, 351
  mental stability in, 452n1131
  morality and, 241
  signs in, 546n1318

thirty-seven enlightenment factors and, 435
quietude, 560

Ratnacūḍaparipṛcchā Sūtra, xxxviii
Ratnākaraśānti, xxi
Sāratamā, 653n1543
Ratnāvalī (Nāgārjuna), xxiiin49, 42n195, 82n298
realist traditions, xv, xx. *See also* Sarvāstivāda school
reality, nature of
devotion to, 172
fourfold, 63–68, 103
importance of perceiving, 605
and power, connection between, 105n341
pure wisdom of, 361
superior attitudes and, 513, 514–515
twofold, 63
realization
declarations of, 639n1529
of Dharma, 428, 553n1336
of four truths, direct, 66n256, 67, 270–271n759, 412, 522
as light, 549n1327
of nirvana, 461–462
power and, 105n341
of suchness, 84
(*See also* emptiness)
of sugatas, 165n515
transcendent, xxiii, 64n252, 66n258, 152n480, 173n530, 355n923, 356, 639n1529
unique to Great Vehicle, xxvii, 7n118
wisdom and, 355–356, 359
worldly knowledge and, 419–421
See also transcendent awareness
reasoning, 65, 82, 132, 177, 457–458
rebirth
of bodhisattvas, deliberate, xxvii–xxix, 28, 33, 34, 101, 102, 466, 560n1352, 669
conducive and not conducive to enlightenment, 71–72, 306
continuance of bodhisattva discipline through successive, 269
due to perfection of morality, 310
due to spiritual qualities, 130, 131, 132, 133
in hells, deliberate, 279
from improper conceptual thoughts, 100
knowledge regarding, 125–126, 635–638, 651
in lower realms, 17, 83
as maturation obscuration, 144n459
from pleasurable states, 536, 542, 547–548, 552, 556, 560
recollection of, 121–122, 134
of sentient beings, causing, 438
successive suffering in, 405, 406, 408
that avoids affliction, 436
transcending lower realms of, 596–597
of virtuous qualities throughout, 383–384
where Buddha appears, 469n1163
recollection
abiding in, 238
bestowing, 115
of bodhisattvas, 33
closely placed, four, 136n438, 182, 288, 305, 433, 434nn1096–1097, 550
closely placed, three, 161, 386, 607, 653–654, 661
clouded, 246, 352, 526–527, 592
continuous, 136
in developing morality, 241
of former existences, 121–122
ripening of knowledge and, 144
safeguarding, 470
as skillful means, 439
strengthening, 73
of tathāgatas, 655
of tathāgatas' good qualities, 164–170
of Three Jewels, 394–395
reflection, 410n1027
eight aspects, 194–196
as means of ripening, 149–150
in second meditative absorption, 45
and shared views, differentiated, 65
regret
basis of, 416
dissembling and, 34n171
freedom from, 382
generosity and, 130, 450
hindrance of, 14–15n138, 288
morality and, 131, 238, 245–246, 309
not causing in others, 203, 220, 256, 274, 589
as secondary mental affliction/perturbation, 137n439, 250, 376, 406

regret (*continued*)
  at time of death, 325
relative truth, 86n303, 99, 359, 478, 479n1196, 554n1338, 602
remediation, 303, 368, 369
renunciation, 534, 544n1312
resistance, three types, 93n318
resolve, knowledge by, 161, 345n906, 347
restraint
  marks produced by, 613
  of mendicants, 322
  of sense faculties, 136n438
  See also under morality
results
  of bodhisattva practices, 384–386
  corresponding, 185, 541
  five kinds, 185–187
  of morality, 239
  separation results, 185
  spiritual lineage and, 6n116
  three types, 48, 206–207n622
  See also under maturations, eight
retention, mental, 666
  appropriate effort in, 340
  four types, 448–450
  immeasurable forms of, 572
  in means of ripening, 150
  meditative absorption and, 351
  safeguarding, 470
retinues, offering against their will, 212–213
right action, 250n711
right practice, 141–142n448
ripening
  causes of, 156–157
  characteristics of the ripe, 154–155
  conduct relating to, 603
  essential nature of, 141–142, 157
  four types of persons for, 142–143
  generosity in, 130
  importance of, 605
  by outer forms of skillful means, 437–439
  personally accomplishing, 151–152
  power of spiritual qualities in, 130, 131, 132
  sameness of purpose of, 381–384
  spiritual lineage, effect of in, 154
  through beneficial conduct, 372–373, 375
  through morality, 311
  twenty-seven means of, 145–153
  types who ripen others, 153–154
  varieties of, 143–145, 152–153, 157–158
Rose Apple Continent, 394, 536, 565, 585

sacrifices, 211, 214, 232n674
Sahā world sphere, 484
Śakra, 547–548
Saṃdhinirmocana Sūtra, xvn1
sameness
  assuming, 111–114
  perception of, 73
  of purified attitude, 553, 557–558
  of purpose, 130, 132, 133, 203, 379–384
  in quiescence, 435
  wisdom and, 356
Saṃpuṭodbhavatantra, 167n525
samsara
  bodhisattvas' understanding of, xxvii–xxix, 70–71
  difficulties in remaining in, 592
  four causes not to fear, 28
  not abandoning, 436, 665–666
  progression of, 91n315
  regarding with complacence, 283
  three aspects of, 361n937
Saṃskṛtalakṣaṇasūtram, 457n1143
*Samudramegha, xlviii. See also *Bodhisattvabhūmivyākhyā*
Saṃvaraviṃśikāvṛttiḥ (Śāntarakṣita), 286n795, 301n816
Śāntarakṣita, xxiv
  Saṃvaraviṃśikāvṛttiḥ, 286n795, 301n816
Śāntideva, xxi
  Bodhicaryāvatāraḥ, xxin36, 241–242n687
  Śikṣāsamuccayaḥ, xxin37
Sāratamā (Ratnākaraśānti), 653n1543
Sarvāstivāda school, xx, 458n1147
sattva, meaning of, 467–468
Sautrantikas, 457n1142, 459n1148
scriptures, xviii, xxv
  explaining meanings and intents of, 496, 500
  listener collection, 174, 653
  twelve divisions of, xxxii, xxxiii, 172n529, 174
  wisdom derived from, 357
  See also bodhisattva collection

seat of enlightenment, 169, 385, 394n994, 610, 657
Sections on Objects, The. See *Arthavargiyāḥ*
secular behavior, 426, 555, 556n1341
seeing, path of, 488n1210, 531n1288
  forbearance on, 173n530
  knowledges on, 66n257
  liberation of mind and wisdom on, 638–639
  mental afflictions and, 576n1391, 657n1556
  transcendent, 639n1529
self
  conceptual thoughts and, 90, 91, 94–95
  as five heaps, 81n295
  lack of, summary statement of, 454, 459–460
  in Listeners' and Solitary Realizers' vehicles, 67
  See also under insubstantiality
self-abasement, 245–248
sense faculties, 92n316, 93n318, 136n438, 162n507, 178–179n547, 434n1096
sensory pleasures
  abstaining from, 322
  antidote for desiring, 339
  assisting those who desire, 250–251
  desire for, 14–15n138, 45n204, 348–349n911
  lack of attachment to, 450
  sympathy for attachment to, 497–498
sentient beings
  acts of requital by, 468
  agreeable speech in aiding, 368
  aims of, 357, 507
  as base of sympathy, 497–498
  beneficial conduct toward all, 378–379
  benefits of single buddha for, 169
  careless, awakening of, 352
  conceptual thoughts and, 94
  constituent elements of, 138n441, 160, 165, 339n892, 483, 631, 650–651
  creation of, 117n385
  death and rebirth of, 635–638
  with deranged minds, acts to avoid, 210
  effect of bodhisattvas' virtuous deeds on, 611
  effort on behalf of, 334
  eleven categories of, 422n1056
  equal affection for all, 512, 667
  failing to assist, 293–300
  forbearance of, 313n832
  immeasurable number of, 619
  knowing minds of, 128
  knowledge of world of, 419–421
  liberation of, from pleasurable state of superior mind training, 545
  meditating on connections in former lives, 316–317
  recalling former existence of, 122
  spiritual lineage as quality of, 5–6n111
  superior attitude toward, 31
  tathāgatas' power to examine, 648
  that need to be trained, 483, 484–486
  types and classes of, 193, 402–404, 425, 483n1204
  virtuous and wicked, attitude toward, 76
  welfare of as object of enlightenment mind, 22
  See also benefiting beings
sexual intercourse, 280–281
sexual misconduct, 377, 541n1308
sGra sbyor bam po gnyis pa, 139n442, 167n525
shame, 9, 10
  in acts of extreme defeat, 268
  as antidote, 598
  essence and basis of, 415–416
  marks produced by, 613
  morality that generates, 238
  in pleasurable state of great joy, 535
  pure patience and, 329
  purity of activities and, 598
shrine worship, 388, 389–390
Sigalovada Sutta, 425nn1066–1067
signlessness, 163, 435, 452–453, 559–560, 562
signs, eighty secondary, 609–611, 617, 657, 660
Śikṣāsamuccayaḥ (Śāntideva), xxin37
silence, observing, 466–467
simplicity, 376n962, 398
single taste, 435
Sixfold Collection on Correct Reasoning (Nāgārjuna), xix
skillful means, 666
  benevolent, 440–442
  of certain objectionable acts, 278–282
  of dissimilar attitude, 444–445

skillful means (*continued*)
five immeasurables in, 483–486
happiness and, 46–48
inner and outer forms of, 436–439
perfection of, 601, 602
pure method, 446–447, 477
of returning a favor, 445
of standing as obstacle, 442–444
supported by, 202–203
ten types, 507–508
toward misconduct of others, 251
social contact, improper, 474
Solitary Realizers' Vehicle, xxviin54
characteristics of, 155
formulation of teachings on, 481, 482
and Great Vehicle, distinctions between, 529, 561n1355, 562, 564, 641, 667–668
immeasurables in, 404
knowledges of, 66–67
in *Main Treatise on the Stages*, xviii
nirvana of, 461–462
noble sounds of, 123–124
powers of, 110n350, 138–139
ripening of, 143
spiritual lineage of, 6–8, 184
termination in, 653
solitude, 14, 241, 245, 248
space
as analogy for emptiness, 441–442
as constituent of sentient beings, 138n441, 339n892
meditation on, 87, 185–186n561, 345n906, 549–550n1329
as unconditioned entity, 93n320, 94n323
as universal base, 346n908
speech
acceptance of, 49, 50, 53, 143, 259
based on worldly knowledge, 422–424
eight noble forms of, 370, 426
in embracing, 590
false, harsh, 50, 267, 370, 377
idle, 287–288
magical creation of, 119–120, 121
marks produced by proper, 614, 615
nonvirtuous, 541nn1308–1309
objects of, 77
in one-pointed concentration state, 628
opposing cause to, 177
purpose of, 89
refusing to reply, 271, 272–273
as sign of morality, 11, 13
skillful means of objectionable, 281
of spiritual teachers, 397
suitable for teaching Dharma, 191–192
as verbal informative form, 260n733
vulgar, 124, 424
words, purpose of, 89
See also agreeable speech
Sphere of Nothingness, 44n202
Sphuṭārthābhidharmakośavyākhyā (Yaśomitra)
on *buddhaḥ*, etymology of, 166n523
on forbearance, 173n530
on informative knowledge, 429n1082
on supernatural travel, 110n350
Spiritual Aims Fulfilled. See *Brief Account of My Spiritual Life* (Tsongkapa)
spiritual followers
failing to assist, 296–297
instruction of, 473–474
morality and, 306
relying on meditative absorption to lead, 347
suitability of, 192
supporting, 150n473
See also attracting a following
spiritual friends, 27–28, 613
spiritual lineages
of bodhisattva, superiority/preeminence of, 6–7, 476
certainty in, 475
conduct appropriate to each, 376
as constituent element, 146n461, 332n875
developing patience through, 326
excellence of, 26, 27
formulations of, 631
natural and developed, 5–7, 650nn1539–1540
obstacles to enlightenment in, 18–19
pleasurable states and, 521
of powers, meaning of, xxix–xxx, 187n567, 201
purification process and, 182–185
rebirth and, 17
ripening in, 142–143
signs of, 8–16
as support, xxxvi, xliv, 4, 5
synonyms for, 5, 6
teaching in accordance with, 507

of three vehicles, 184
Thüken Rinpoche on, xlii–xlvii
See also pleasurable state of the spiritual lineage
spiritual powers, xxxvi, 25n156, 35, 652–653
attitude that relates to, 513, 515
displaying to develop morality, 258–259
and enlightenment mind, as contributing factor, 25, 29
exclusive to bodhisattvas, 138–139
five types, 25n156, 106
natural, 106, 134–137
noble, 105
sameness of purpose of, 380
shared, 139
See also miraculous powers; spiritual qualities; supernatural knowledges; ten powers of tathāgatas
spiritual practice
aspirational prayers, effect on, 169
benefits in present life, 102
of bodhisattvas, distinctions in, 35, 667–668
canonical scripture and, xxv–xxvi
correct establishment in, 74–76
excellence of, 303
factions and, 509
five methods of, 470–472
in *Mahāyānasūtrālaṃkāraḥ* and *Bodhisattvabhūmiḥ*, differentiated, xlii–xliii
for sentient beings, appropriateness of, 642, 646–647
and study, relationship between, xxvi–xxxi
thirty-seven forms of, 3n101
three stages of, 149n470, 150
unique to Great Vehicle, xx–xxi, xxvii, 7n118
worship as, 393–395, 598–599
spiritual qualities
of buddhas, 519
conducive to enlightenment, 3–5, 18, 433–434, 666
(*See also* pleasurable state of superior wisdom that relates to qualities conducive to enlightenment)
power of, 105–106, 129–134
summary verses on, 415
as support, xxxvi
ten that purify pleasurable states and stages, 534–535, 540, 597–599
See also bodhisattvas, marks of; individual qualities
spiritual teachers
affection toward, 329
attributes of, 396–397
as cause of generating enlightenment mind, 26–27
correct approach to, 189
in developing morality, 242
disciples and, 398–399
disrespecting, 293
faults of, attitude toward, 401–402
fraudulent, separating beings from, 281
as objects of faith, 398
role of, 18, 397
serving, four qualities of, 399–400
spouses, 210, 212–213
Śravakabhūmiḥ (Asaṅga), xviin15, xxiii
on activities pertaining to virtue, 310n830
on altered states of mind, 201n612
on closely placed recollection, 434
on constituents, 339n892, 430–431n1087
on dependent origination, skill regarding, 431nn1088–1090
on discursive thoughts, 144n457
four categories of meditation objects, 590n1412
on four closely placed recollections, 182n553
guidance in Dharma instruction, 642
on hypocrisy, 216n642
on inopportune birth, 184n557
on meditation on emptiness, 402n1009
on meditative absorption, 343n898
on observing silence, 466–467
on one-pointed concentration on emptiness, 453n1133
on ornament, use of term, 307n824
on pure morality, 309nn826–827
on regular activities, 309n829, 310
on retention, 150n472
on skill regarding bases, 431n1088
on skill regarding heaps, 430n1086
on skillful speech, 397n1000
on teacher-disciple relationship, 399n1004

Śravakabhūmiḥ (*continued*)
  on types of persons based on afflictions, 631n1503
  on vigilance, 473n1174
Śrīmālādevīsiṃhanādasūtram, 532n1289
Stage of a Bodhisattva, The. See *Bodhisattvabhūmiḥ* (Asaṅga)
Stage of a Listener, The. See *Śravakabhūmiḥ* (Asaṅga)
stages, seven, xxxviii, 539, 595–596
Stages of Spiritual Practice. See *Yogācārabhūmiḥ* (Asaṅga)
Stages of the Path. *See* Lamrim
stainless stage, 543. *See also* pleasurable state of superior morality
steadfastness, 15
  as cause of eminence, 49
  as conviction, 70n270
  in generating enlightenment mind, 28
  as hypocrisy, 398
  on pure superior attitude stage, 383–384
  as sign of ripening, 157
  in worldly matters, 424–425
stealing, 9n121, 220–221, 269n754, 280, 377, 420n1045, 425n1066, 541nn1308–1309, 615n1456
Sthiramati, xix, xxiii
  on absolute nature, 99n333
  Madhyāntavibhāgaṭīkā, 74n277, 86n303, 88n307, 442n1110, 531n1288, 564n1359
  Triṃśikābhāṣyam, 12n133, 525n1273
  See also *Pañcaskandhavibhāṣā*; *Sūtrālaṃkāravṛttibhāṣyam*
stinginess
  abandoning, 130, 209n627
  in degenerate era, 26
  generosity, dispelling through, 219, 231
  morality, dispelling through, 251
  in pleasurable state of conduct based on devotion, 525n1274
  as poverty of spirit, 216–217n643
  regarding Dharma, 36, 222
storehouse consciousness, 178n547
stream entry, 569, 571, 639
strength
  in bodhisattvas' last birth, 135
  excellence of, 49, 50, 54
  four types of, 28–29
  gained by careful consideration, 313
  ripening and, 143
  through wisdom and compassion, 335
stūpa, 270n757, 388
subsistence
  beneficial conduct regarding, 373
  meditative absorption and, 347, 352
  providing, 243, 253–254
  suffering relating to, 406–407, 410
substance
  agreed upon, 85–86
  conceptual thoughts and, 89–91
  investigation of, 96–97, 98–99
  knowable, 65, 83
  meanings of, 64n251, 69n269
  mode of existence of, 77–79
  real, 64n251, 79, 81–82, 83, 84, 87, 458, 644
  three, 100n334
substantive essence, 86, 88, 457
suchness, 69n267, 93n321
  bare, 72
  devotion toward, 394
  in Great Vehicle, 482
  paramount, 68
  on pleasurable states, 523, 547, 567
  realization of, 84
  synonyms of, 69n269, 643n1535
  as truth, 478–479n1191, 513
suffering
  ability to endure, 413, 666
  accepting, 466
  antidote to, 44, 45–46
  compassion for, 28, 403
  as consequence of adversity, 225–226, 227, 228
  from embracing Dharma, 321
  failing to assist others, 294
  four aspects of truth of, 70n271
  generosity in dispelling, 130
  from harm inflicted by others, 315–316, 318
  from improper conceptual thoughts, 100
  of lower realms, 147n465
  as meditation objects, 411
  meditative absorption and, 347, 353
  morality and, 250–251, 255
  in nirvana, 460
  one hundred and ten forms of, 404–410, 596
  patience toward, 314, 319–323

protection from, 34
shared views of, 64–65
summary statement of, 454, 459
sympathy for, 497–498
taking on others', 134
in taking up what is right, 41, 627
three forms of, 318
from worldly conditions, 320
Sumeru, Mount, 107n345, 111n353
Summary of the Five Heaps. See *Pañcaskandhaprakaraṇam* (Vasubandhu)
Summary of the Great Vehicle, The. See *Mahāyānasaṃgrahaḥ* (Asaṅga)
summit of reality, 564
Sun That Illuminates the Excellent Path of the Great Vehicle, The (Thüken Losang Chökyi Nyima), xliii–xlvii
Sunirmita gods, 560
superior attitudes, 31, 153, 228, 488
attaining, 450
definition of, 513
in face-to-face worship, 388
fifteen, 513–514
immeasurables and, 404
lack of offense with, 270
in pleasurable state of conduct based on devotion, 528
in pleasurable state of great joy, 521, 522
pure, 592
summary verse on, 511
with tathāgatas as object, 395–396
ten actions of, 514–515
supernatural knowledges, 165n514
of death and rebirth, 125–126
of diverse states of mind, 126–128, 139
divine ear, 123–125, 126
of listeners and solitary realizers, 138–139
meditative absorption and, 353
miraculous spheres of activity (*See* miraculous powers)
of outflows, termination of, 128–129, 139, 638n1527
in pleasurable state of conduct based on devotion, 526
in pleasurable state free of signs and effort, 571, 596
in pleasurable state of superior mind training, 546
recollection of former existences, 121–122
as result of excellence of strength, 54
six forms, 75n282, 106, 602
superior attitudes and, 513, 515
as supremacy of power, 162, 164
wisdom of, 359
support
four for developing patience, 320
meaning of term, xxxvi, 3–4, 24n153
as means of ripening, 150–151
purity regarding, 621
of qualities conducive to enlightenment, xxxvi
suppression, 151, 257–258, 347, 375, 445, 655
Sutra on [the Manner of] Passing Over to a [New] Existence. See *Bhavasaṃkrāntisūtram*
Sutra on the Ten Stages, The. See *Daśabhūmikasūtram*
Sūtrālaṃkāravṛttibhāṣyam (Sthiramati), xix, xxiii, xlin85, 35n172
on accumulation, meaning of, 129n417
on concepts and conceptual thoughts, 562n1356
on elevated state of existence, 561n1355
on impermanence and enlightenment, 459n1150
on informative knowledge, 429–430nn1083–1085
on person established in practice that accords with Dharma, 152n480
on pure spiritual life, 245n698
on three baskets, 173–174n531
on underlying thoughts, 81n297
Sūtrālaṃkāravyākhyā (Vasubandhu), xln81, xlin84, xliiin93
on accumulation, meaning of, 129n417
distinguishing concept and conceptual thought in, 562n1356
on purity regarding the mind, 622n1470
on three baskets, 173–174n531
on underlying thought, 81n297
syllables, collection of, 418
sympathy
bases of, 497–500
even-mindedness of, 467
fruits and benefits of, 501
immeasurables and, 404
nature of, 495–496

sympathy (*continued*)
  necessity of, 476
  patience and, 328
  successive order of developing, 502–503
  in pleasurable state of superior morality, 542
  tirelessness and, 417

taking what was not given. *See* stealing
Tathāgata, epithets and meanings of, 164–167, 623, 624–625
tathāgatas
  bodhisattvas emanating as, 368
  epithets for, 164–167, 623, 624–625
  as foremost of all beings, 385, 477
  pleasurable state of, 517, 518, 521, 577, 595–596, 607, 657, 661–662
  sons or daughters of, 531–532
  sphere of action, 562
  and tenth-stage bodhisattvas, differentiated, 659
  transcendent awareness of, 658–659
  worship of physical body of, 387, 388
Teachings of Akṣayamati, The. See *Akṣayamatinirdeśasūtram*
ten ārya bodhisattva stages, xl, 100n336, 153–154nn484–488, 355n923, 359, 471nn1169–1170, 488nn1211–1212. *See also* pleasurable states
ten powers of tathāgatas, xxx–xxxi, xxxix, 128n413, 161, 660
  actions that accompany, 641–646
  buddha speech and, 175n533, 187n566
  constituent elements, diverse, 201, 631
  death and rebirth, 201, 635–638
  devotion, diverse forms of, 201, 630
  differences and similarities among, 648–651
  essential nature of, 640
  exclusivity and sameness of, 641
  immeasurability of, 640
  importance of attaining, 605
  knowledge that precedes, 359
  list of, 622–623
  meditative absorption, liberation, one-pointed concentration, 201, 345, 627–629
  one's deed are one's own, 626–627
  paths that lead everywhere, 201, 632
  perfection of, 601–602
  proper and improper conditions, 623–625
  recollection of former existences, 201, 633–634
  results of, 386
  seven aspects, list of, 639–640
  successive order of, 646–648
  summary verse on, 639
  superior and inferior faculties, 201, 629–630
  termination of outflows, 201, 638–639
Tengyur, xvii–xix
that which needs to be known
  field of, devotion to, 324
  removing obscurations to, 100n336, 357
  transcendent awareness of, 67–68, 657
  See also obscurations, two
Thirty Verses (Vasubandhu), 99n333
three "baskets," xviii, 173n531
Three Jewels
  devotion to, 172
  faith in, 148
  not honoring, 270
  superior attitudes and, 513, 514
  worshipping, 387–396, 438–439, 536–537
three natures, 69n268, 81–82n296, 99n333
Thüken Losang Chökyi Nyima, *Sun That Illuminates the Excellent Path of the Great Vehicle, The*, xliii–xlvii
Tibetan Buddhism, xix–xxiii, xxiv
time, 160, 537n1297, 618–619, 640
tirelessness, 417, 534–535, 597, 598, 665
"Tolerance" world sphere, 107n345, 135n435
torpor and drowsiness, 14–15n138, 189n573, 288, 376
training, xxix–xxx, xxxvi
  aim of, 172
  generating enlightenment mind in, 24
  generosity practice according with, 213
  in pleasurable state of conduct based on devotion, 528
  seven subjects of, 35–36, 171n527, 187n567
tranquility
  from abiding in ease, 101, 102
  happiness of, 45, 410
  in meditative absorption, 344, 349n912
  promoting, 41
  in quiescence, 435

transcendent awareness, 657
mental afflictions, eradicating, 66–67
obscurations, two and, 66–68
of tathāgatas and tenth-stage bodhisattvas, differentiated, 659
transcendent knowledge
attaining, specialized term for, 80n293
as light rays, 552
in pleasurable state free of signs and effort, 571, 596
relying upon, 427n1074, 428
in unique qualities of a buddha, 662n1561
See also ten powers of tathāgatas
transgressions
action of superior attitude toward, 514
four of extreme defeat, 267–269, 301–302
morality as remedy, 238
of others, patience toward, 241
remediation of, 303
See also offenses, four expulsory; offenses, secondary; remediation
Treasury of Higher Learning. See *Abhidharmakośakārikā* (Vasubandhu)
Treatise of Multiple Stages, The, xvii
treatises, 174n532, 417–419, 624n1480
Triṃśikābhāṣyam (Sthiramati), 12n133, 525n1273
true spiritual beings
agreeable speech of, 368–369
beneficial conduct of, 375
effort of, 337
meditative absorption of, 350
morality of, 306
patience of, 325
results of, 385
wisdom of, 358–359
truth
formulation on, 478–480
relative, 86n303, 99, 359, 478, 479n1196, 554n1338, 602
ten forms of, 554n1338
ultimate, 72n273, 442n1110, 545n1314, 559, 602, 644
See also four noble truths
Tsonawa Sherab Sangpo, *Light Rays of the Sun*, 240n683
Tsongkapa, Je, xxiv–xxvii, 167n525
Brief Account of My Spiritual Life, xlii
Great Treatise on the Stages of the Path, xliii
Letter Sent to Lama Umapa in Dokham, xxiv–xxvi
See also *Byang chub sems dpa'i tshul khrims kyi rnam bshad byang chub gzhung lam*
Tuṣita deities, 112, 556
Tuṣita Heaven, 115n378, 134, 446–447
Twenty Verses on the Bodhisattva Discipline. See *Bodhisattvasaṃvaraviṃśikā* (Candragomī)

ultimate correctness, 579
ultimate reality, xxvi–xxix, 64n251, 77–85, 196, 356, 643n1535
ultimate truth, 72n273, 442n1110, 545n1314, 559, 602, 644
uncertainty, six types, 408

Vaibhāṣikas, 457n1142
Vajracchedikā, xixn24
valid cognition, 192
Varṇāhavarṇastotram (Mātṛceṭa), 166nn519–520
Vaśavartī class of gods, 566
vastu, meanings of, 64n251, 69n269, 78n291, 143n453, 664n1536
Vastusaṃgrahaṇī (Asaṅga)
Collection on [Canonical] Topics in, xviii, 80n293, 187, 303
Collection on the Vinaya in, xviii
Vasubandhu, xix, xxiii, xxxix–xl
Akṣayamatinirdeśaṭīkā, 144n458, 277n776
Hundred Sutra Fragments That Are the Subject of Correct Interpretation, 367n943
Madhyāntavibhāgabhāṣyam, 68n261, 442n1110
Pañcaskandhaprakaraṇam, 44n202
Thirty Verses, 99n333
See also *Abhidharmakośabhāṣyam*; *Abhidharmakośakārikā*; *Daśabhūmivyākhyānam*; *Sūtrālaṃkāravyākhyā*
Vehicle of Defining Attributes, xxvn54
vehicles, xviii, xx, 653. *See also* individual vehicles

veneration
  description of, 50n216
  of Dharma, 192
  marks produced by, 612
  objects of, 270n757
  of parents, 212
  relying on morality, 241
  of spiritual elders, 271–272
  worthiness of, 32, 384–385
verbal designations, 80–82
very difficult to be overcome, stage on which it is, 557. *See also* pleasurable state of superior wisdom that relates to the truths
vidyā spells, 33
views, shared, 64–65
views, wrong, 82n298, 541n1308
  abandoning bond of, 547
  on causes and results, 636–637
  causing others to abstain from, 377
  eliminating through meditative absorption, 353
  five types, 90n312
  on generosity, 214, 226–227, 232
  suffering from, 411
  sympathy for, 497–498
vigilance, 241, 349n913, 434n1096, 473
Vinaya
  as base of meanings and intents, 500
  Kadampa, 240n683
  specific usage of, 80n293
Viniścayasaṃgrahaṇī (Asaṅga), xviiin17
virtue
  acquiring through morality, 248–249
  activities of, 310
  concealing, 247–248
  descriptions of, 22n146
  four kind of friends with, 425
  importance of cultivating, 605
  linked to what is beneficial, 40
  maintaining, 73–74
  of meditative absorption, 351
  perfections and, 249
  remaining on the side of, 669
  as sign of morality, 11
virtue roots
  accumulation of every form of, 622
  avoidance of desire, 219
  beneficial conduct and, 374, 379–380, 381
  dedication of, 508
  in developing spiritual lineage, 6
  equanimity and, 335n881
  gaining, 51
  generating extensive, 437–439
  limited, 437
  mindfulness and, 120–121n393
  in pleasurable states, 536, 542, 547, 551–552, 565
  ripening of, 143–144, 145, 157
  role in enlightenment, 665
  wisdom and, 134
virtuous activities/conduct
  four ways of taking up what is right, 40–41, 627
  for others' sake, 38n181
  with pleasure and ease, 59n239
  that produce marks and signs, 611–615
virtuous qualities
  attaining, 31–32, 378
  concealing, 380
  effort and, 332, 333–334, 336, 338
  esteem for, 148
  generating, 5–6n111
  immeasurability of, 618–619
  as intense, 156
  morality of acquiring, 240–242
  in pleasurable states of superior wisdom, 551, 555
  purpose of, 381n971
  right practice and, 142
  ripening, 146
  of spiritual teachers, 396
**Vyākhyāsaṃgrahaṇī* (Asaṅga), xviiin21, xxxii, xxxiii

wealth
  aims of, 58, 59, 60
  in attracting a following, 191
  beneficial conduct regarding, 373
  to benefit current life, 425–426
  confiscating stolen, 280
  difficult beneficial conduct and, 374
  dispelling sorrow and, 253
  generosity and, 9–10, 217, 219, 221, 225–226
  giving up, 305
  in Great Vehicle, view of, 223n649
  as sign of morality, 11
  suffering from, 406
  worship and, 391, 393

wheel rulers, 33, 536, 542
precious jewel of, 551, 565
wisdom, 55–56
accumulating through generosity, 222
as acquiring cause, 335
beneficial conduct and, 374–375
causes of, 56–57
difficult and directed everywhere, 357, 384
of discernment, 323n859
essential nature of, 640
four aspects of power of, 133–134
issues in translating terms for, 53n224
liberation of, 638–639
mundane and transcendent, 355–357
nonconceptual, 523
nondual, 69–74
patience as, 314n840
perfection of, 602, 605
preeminence of, 477
pure, 360–362
relating to distressed beings, 359–360
results of, 57–58
signs of, 16
supported by means, 433
thirteen types, 359
of true spiritual being, 358–359
unobstructed knowledge and, 559
wishlessness, 125n411, 163, 452, 453, 559, 560
Wogihara, Unrai, xlvii
women, enlightenment of, 169–170
world spheres, 107n345
causing to shake, 537
constituents of, 138n441, 160, 165, 483, 484
magical speech in, 119–120
Tolerance, 135n435
worldly beings, 64–65. *See also* sentient beings
worldly conditions, 320, 409–410, 411
worldly crafts and occupations, 174, 191, 352–353, 425, 555, 563
worldly life, 366, 633–634
worldly path, xxii
worship
as antidote, 598
at birth of bodhisattvas, 134–135
by bodhisattvas themselves, 390
body and shrine, 387–388
causing others to, 390–391
continuous, 476
in developing morality, 241
face-to-face, 388, 389n986
not face-to-face, 389–390
objects of, 391–393
in pleasurable state of great joy, 535, 536
purity of activities and, 598–599
skillful means of, 438–439
spiritual practice as, 393–395
summary verse on, 387
See also spiritual teachers

Xuanzang, xvi

Yāma deities, 112, 552n1334
Yaśomitra. See *Sphuṭārthābhidharmakośavyākhyā*
Ye shes sDe, 669
Yogācāra
Indian tradition of, xvii–xix, xxii
karma in, 541n1308
literature of, xvii–xx, xxii–xxiii, xliii
samvṛtiḥ, understanding of in, 86n303
Tibetan tradition of, xix
Yogācārabhūmiḥ (Asaṅga), xviiin11
on classes of sentient beings, 483n1204
on conceptions to overcome obstacles, 197n601
on deeds performed and accumulated, 626n1485
on improper social contact, 474n1175
on settled nature of things, 358n927
Yogācāra-Svatantrika, xxiv

Six-Armed Mahākāla